NINTH CANADIAN EDITION

Understanding
Canadian
Business

William G. Nickels
University of Maryland

James M. McHugh
St. Louis Community College at Forest Park

Susan M. McHugh
Applied Learning System

Rita Cossa
DeGroote School of Business, McMaster University

Julie Stevens
Brock University

Bob Sproule
University of Waterloo

Mc
Graw
Hill
Education

Understanding Canadian Business
Ninth Canadian Edition

ISBN-13: 978-1-25-908737-0
ISBN-10: 1-25-908737-9

1 2 3 4 5 6 7 8 9 0 TCP 1 9 8 7 6

Printed and bound in Canada.

Director of Product Management: Rhondda McNabb
Group Product Manager: Kim Brewster
Marketing Manager: Cathie Lefebvre
Product Developer: Amy Rydzanicz
Senior Product Team Associate: Stephanie Giles
Supervising Editor: Janie Deneau
Photo/Permissions Editor: Monika Schurmann
Copy Editor: Skyline Media (Cat Haggert)
Plant Production Coordinator: Michelle Saddler
Manufacturing Production Coordinator: Emily Hickey
Cover Design: Jodie Bernard
Cover Image: Wood: Tortoon / Getty Images Royalty Free
Interior Design: Jodie Bernard
Page Layout: SPi Global
Printer: Transcontinental Printing Group

Dedication

To my husband, Stephen, and our children, Mattia and Leila, for their support during the creation of this edition. And to my students whose questions and discussions have contributed to a textbook with their learning in mind.

Rita Cossa

To Ron, my husband, and our children, Nolan and Turner, for their support, encouragement, and patience. For my past and present students whose dreams for the future inspired much of my writing.

Julie Stevens

To my wife for her ongoing support and encouragement of me as a teacher. To my children for keeping me connected to today's students. To my students, who provide me with the opportunity to support their learning.

Bob Sproule

To our families – Marsha, Joel, Carrie, Claire, Casey, Dan, Molly, Michael, Patrick, and Quinn. Thank you for making everything worth doing and giving us the support to do it well!

Bill Nickels, Jim McHugh, Susan McHugh

About the Authors

Bill Nickels is emeritus professor of business at the University of Maryland, College Park. He has over 30 years' experience teaching graduate and undergraduate business courses, including introduction to business, marketing, and promotion. He has won the Outstanding Teacher on Campus Award four times and was nominated for the award many other times. He received his MBA degree from Western Reserve University and his PhD from The Ohio State University. He has written a marketing communications text and two marketing principles texts in addition to many articles in business publications. He has taught many seminars to business people on subjects such as power communications, marketing, non-business marketing, and stress and life management.

Jim McHugh holds an MBA degree from Lindenwood University and has had broad experience in education, business, and government. As chairman of the Business and Economics Department of St. Louis Community College–Forest Park, Jim coordinated and directed the development of the business curriculum. In addition to teaching several sections of Introduction to Business each semester for nearly 30 years, Jim taught in the marketing and management areas at both the undergraduate and graduate levels. Jim enjoys conducting business seminars and consulting with small and large businesses. He is actively involved in the public service sector and served as chief of staff to the St. Louis County Executive.

Susan McHugh is a learning specialist with extensive training and experience in adult learning and curriculum development. She holds an MEd degree from the University of Missouri and completed her coursework for a PhD in education administration with a specialty in adult learning theory. As a professional curriculum developer, she has directed numerous curriculum projects and educator training programs. She has worked in the public and private sectors as a consultant in training and employee development.

Rita Cossa is an Assistant Professor at the DeGroote School of Business, McMaster University. This textbook marks her sixth edition as an author for *Understanding Canadian Business*. For over fifteen years she has taught introduction to business courses to undergraduate students. Rita has also taught Business Policy & Strategic Management, and Introduction to Marketing courses at both the undergraduate and master's levels, as well as Marketing in the Non-Profit Sector. Teaching highlights include a nomination to *TV Ontario's Best Lecturer Competition*, multiple nominations for a McMaster Student Union Teaching Award, and notations in the *Maclean's Guide to Canadian Universities* as a Popular Prof for Marketing. Prior to her teaching career, Rita held management-level positions in the financial services industry.

Julie Stevens is an Associate Professor in the Department of Sport Management at Brock University. During the past fifteen years she has taught several graduate and undergraduate management courses related to organization theory, policy, change and innovation, governance, and professionalism within commercial, non-profit, and public sectors. She holds Instructional Skills Workshop training and has served on various teaching and learning committees. Her teaching philosophy, which emphasizes critical commentary and active learner engagement, is enacted through a diverse range of practices within classroom and online forums. Drawing upon her background as a Research Fellow with the North American Society for Sport Management, she integrates current affairs and scholarship to provide relevant, problem-based learning opportunities for students.

Bob Sproule is a faculty member in the School of Accounting and Finance at the University of Waterloo. Teaching in some capacity for over 30 years, Bob has been challenged by and enjoyed being part of the learning journey of thousands of students. Most recently he received two international teaching awards recognizing his innovation in teaching, one from the Society for Teaching and Learning in Higher Education and the other from Desire to Learn. He has been the Associate Director of Teaching and Learning and a member of the Teaching Excellence Council at the University of Waterloo. He is a trained facilitator for the Instructional Skills Workshop and has leadership roles both nationally and internationally in a number of organizations supporting teaching and learning.

Brief Contents

Contents

Contents

Contents

APPENDIX A
Working Within the Legal Environment of Business *162*

CHAPTER 10
Producing World-Class Goods and Services *378*

Contents

PART 4
MANAGEMENT OF HUMAN RESOURCES   *426*

CHAPTER 11
Motivating Employees   *426*

CHAPTER 12
Human Resource Management: Finding and Keeping the Best Employees *466*

Contents

CHAPTER 13
Dealing with Employee–Management Issues and Relations *512*

Contents

CHAPTER 15
Managing the Marketing Mix: Product, Price, Place, and Promotion *602*

PART 6
ACCOUNTING INFORMATION AND FINANCIAL ACTIVITIES *654*

CHAPTER 16
Understanding Accounting and Financial Information *654*

CHAPTER 17
Financial Management *696*

APPENDIX C
Managing Risk   *736*

Preface

Understanding Canadian Business has been created with you and your students in mind. We've listened and that's helped us offer you:

Resources that were developed based directly on your feedback—all geared to make the most of your time and to help students succeed in this course. The supplemental resources have been reviewed to ensure cohesion with the text.

Technology that leads the way and is consistently updated to keep pace with you and your students. Connect offers students a truly interactive and adaptive study arena. Interactive applications, SmartBook, and Connect Insight are designed to engage students and have been proven to increase grades by a full letter.

Support that is always available to help you plan your course, work with technology, and meet the needs of you and your students.

Keeping up with What's New

Users of *Understanding Canadian Business* have always appreciated the currency of the material and the large number of examples from for-profit and non-profit companies of *all* sizes and industries in Canada and around the world. Accordingly, this edition features the latest business practices and other developments affecting business including:

- Sustainability
- B corporations
- Social enterprise
- Crowdfunding vs. crowdsourcing
- Motivation myths
- Generation Z
- Types of social media
- Positioning
- Green marketing vs. greenwashing
- Ethnic marketing
- Mobile marketing
- Global freelancing and virtual professionals
- Chartered Professional Accountant (CPA) designation
- The Canadian financial system
- P3s (private-public partnerships)
- Green procurement
- Bitcoin and other cryptocurrencies
- Exchange-traded funds (ETFs)
- And much more

We remain dedicated to listening vigilantly to what you tell us you need in this course. We have made changes and enhancements in this revision that are all based on what we heard from you. As you look through the next few pages, you'll find what you need to navigate your way most effectively through this book and its supplements.

Integration of Important Concepts Throughout the Text

Understanding Canadian Business, Ninth Canadian Edition, is revised, updated, and filled with new examples of business in Canada and around the world.

Learning Objectives

Tied directly to the summaries at the end of the chapter and to the test bank questions, the learning objectives help students preview what they should know after reading the chapter, and then test that knowledge by answering the questions in the summary. These learning objectives are also incorporated in the margins throughout the chapter, at the start of the discussion that pertains to the learning objective. This way, students can quickly see where the content aligns with each objective.

LEARNING OBJECTIVES

After you have read and studied this chapter, you should be able to:

LO1	Describe basic economics.
LO2	Explain what capitalism is and how free markets work.
LO3	Compare the benefits and negative consequences of socialism and communism.
LO4	Describe the mixed economy of Canada.
LO5	Illustrate the significance of key economic indicators and the business cycle.

Getting to Know Business Professionals

Each chapter begins with a profile of a business person whose career relates closely to the material covered in that chapter. Not all of the personalities are famous, since some of them work in small businesses and non-profit organizations. Take some time to consider their career choices and how they spend their time applying the business principles discussed in the textbook.

Source: Courtesy of Fox 40 International Inc. Used with permission.

URLs Within the Chapter Content

At the first mention of a relevant company we have included the company's URL for your reference—these are be hotlinked in your eBook so you can quickly jump to the company's website for additional information.

Few issues have captured the attention of the international business community more than climate change.[59] **Climate change** is the movement of the temperature of the planet up or down over time. The issue now is global warming. Some of the world's largest firms—including General Electric <*http://www.ge.com/ca*>, Coca-Cola <*http://www.cocacola.ca*>, Shell <*http://www.shell.ca*>, Nestlé <*http://www.nestle.ca*>, DuPont <*http://www2.dupont.com/inclusive-innovations/en-us/gss/sustainability.html*>, Johnson & Johnson <*http://www.jnjcanada.com*>, British Airways <*http://www.britishairways.com*>, and Shanghai Electric <*http://www.shanghai-electric.com/en*>—say the evidence for climate change is overwhelming. Saving energy and producing products that cause less harm to the environment is a trend called **greening**. Greening has become such a pervasive issue that impacts every type

Photo and Illustration Essays

More and more students have expressed that they are visually oriented learners; therefore, increased emphasis on the pedagogical value of illustrations is essential. Some photos and illustrations are accompanied by a short caption that highlights the relevance of the visuals to the material in the text.

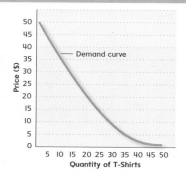

A free-market system is evident at a farmer's market. As a buyer, what can you do to ensure that you pay the best price for produce?

■ **FIGURE 2.2**

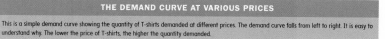

THE DEMAND CURVE AT VARIOUS PRICES

This is a simple demand curve showing the quantity of T-shirts demanded at different prices. The demand curve falls from left to right. It is easy to understand why. The lower price of T-shirts, the higher the quantity demanded.

Boxed Features

Important business concepts and themes are incorporated throughout the text. Certain topics deserve special emphasis and are highlighted in feature boxes titled "Spotlight on Small Business," "Making Ethical Decisions," "Seeking Sustainability," "Reaching Beyond Our Borders," and "Adapting to Change" appearing throughout the chapters.

Spotlight *On* SMALL BUSINESS

The Key to Capitalism Is Capital

Making ETHICAL DECISIONS

Smokers Need Not Apply

Seeking SUSTAINABILITY

2015 Pan Am and Parapan Am Is LEEDing the Way

Reaching *Beyond* OUR BORDERS

Economic Expansion in Africa

Adapting *to* CHANGE

Challenges of Family Businesses

Progress Assessments

To ensure that students understand and retain the material, Progress Assessments stop them and show them what they need to review before proceeding. The Progress Assessment is a proven learning tool that helps students comprehend and retain material.

Progress Assessment

- What is the difference between revenue and profit?
- What is risk, and how is it related to profit?
- What is the difference between standard of living and quality of life?
- What do the terms stakeholders, offshoring, outsourcing, and insourcing mean?

Interactive Summaries

The end-of-chapter summaries are directly tied to the Learning Objectives and are written in a question-and-answer format—great for chapter review and studying.

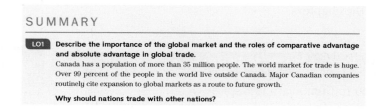

SUMMARY

LO1 **Describe the importance of the global market and the roles of comparative advantage and absolute advantage in global trade.**
Canada has a population of more than 35 million people. The world market for trade is huge. Over 99 percent of the people in the world live outside Canada. Major Canadian companies routinely cite expansion to global markets as a route to future growth.

Why should nations trade with other nations?

Key Terms

Important terms, highlighted throughout the text with an accompanying definition, are listed in alphabetical order at the end of the chapter and in the glossary.

KEY TERMS

Crown corporation	fiscal policy	National Policy
deficit	industrial policy	privatization
deregulation	marketing boards	surplus
equalization	monetary policy	transfer payments
federal budget	national debt (federal debt)	

Critical Thinking Questions

Found in each chapter, Critical Thinking Questions ask students to pause and think about how the material they are reading applies to their own lives.

CRITICAL THINKING

Many say that business people do not do enough for society. Some students choose to work for non-profit organizations instead of for-profit organizations because they want to help others. However, business people say that they do more to help others than non-profit groups because they provide jobs for people rather than giving them charity, which often precludes them from searching for work. Furthermore, they believe that businesses create all the wealth that non-profit groups distribute. Can you find some middle ground in this debate that demonstrates how both business people and those who work for non-profit

Developing Workplace Skills

The Developing Workplace Skills section has activities designed to increase student involvement in the learning process. The exercises develop analytical communication, technological, and team-based skills. Some of these mini-projects require library or online searches, while others can be used as team activities either in or out of the classroom.

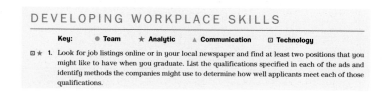

DEVELOPING WORKPLACE SKILLS

Key: ● **Team**   ★ **Analytic**   ▲ **Communication**   ☑ **Technology**

☑ ★ 1. Look for job listings online or in your local newspaper and find at least two positions that you might like to have when you graduate. List the qualifications specified in each of the ads and identify methods the companies might use to determine how well applicants meet each of those qualifications.

Analyzing Management Decisions

Each chapter concludes with a case that allows students to analyze management decision making. These cases are intentionally brief and are meant to initiate discussion rather than take up the entire class period.

ANALYZING MANAGEMENT DECISIONS

The Rule of 72

No formula is more useful for understanding inflation than the rule of 72. Basically, the rule allows you to quickly compute how long it takes the cost of goods and services to double at various compounded rates of growth. For example, if houses were increasing in cost at 9 percent a year, how long would it take for the price of a home to double? The answer is easy to calculate. Simply divide 72 by the annual increase (9 percent) and you get the approximate number of years it takes to double the price (eight years). Of course, the same calculation can be used to predict how high food prices or auto prices will be 10 years

Video Cases

Video cases from CBC programs and custom segments from the McGraw-Hill Management Library filmed specifically for the Nickels text are provided for each chapter. They feature companies, processes, practices, and managers that highlight and bring to life the key concepts, and especially the themes, of the ninth edition. These videos are available through Connect and on DVD for in-class viewing.

VIDEO CASE 5

Protect the World You Play In: Ten Tree Apparel

How do you combine a love for nature with a desire to change lives? The answer—create Ten Tree Apparel <http://www.tentree.com/ca>. While hiking in Hawaii, Dave Luba and Kalen Emsley reached the top of a mountain looking out over the beautiful forest. The view inspired them to take action—immediately. The pair wanted to create something where consumers could sustain the environment.

Ten Tree Apparel is both a lifestyle apparel company and an environmental advocate. The early phase of the small business was high tempo and soon after being formed on January 1, 2012, the two founders, along with Kalen's brother Derek Emsley, appeared on CBC's Dragons' Den. Their pitch was

End-of-Part Running Case

The chapters in this edition are divided in six parts. A six-part running case has been created based on Fox 40 International Inc., a proudly Canadian company that dominates the global whistle industry. For successful Canadian entrepreneur and inventor Ron Foxcroft, it all started with a dream for a pealess whistle. Read the case at the end of each part to learn how Ron, his son Dave, and their management team apply the business principles introduced in the chapters for each part. The discussion questions encourage students to further evaluate these business concepts.

RUNNING CASE

Ron Foxcroft: The Dream for a Pealess Whistle

For successful Canadian entrepreneur and inventor Ron Foxcroft, it all started in 1982 when he purchased Fluke Transport, a Southern Ontario trucking business. The company slogan—If It's On Time . . . It's A "FLUKE"—was soon recognized throughout North America. Over the years, Foxcroft diversified into new ventures and the Foxcroft Group of Companies now includes Fluke Transportation Group, Fluke Warehousing Inc., Foxcroft Capital Corp., Fox 40 International Inc., and Fox 40 USA Inc.

The formation of Fox 40 International Inc. (Fox 40) is the result of a dream for a pealess whistle.

Market Leading Technology

connect®

Learn Without Limits

McGraw-Hill Connect® is an award-winning digital teaching and learning platform that gives students the means to better connect with their coursework, with their instructors, and with the important concepts that they will need to know for success now and in the future. With Connect, instructors can take advantage of McGraw-Hill's trusted content to seamlessly deliver assignments, quizzes and tests online. McGraw-Hill Connect is a learning platform that continually adapts to each student, delivering precisely what they need, when they need it, so class time is more engaging and effective. Connect makes teaching and learning personal, easy, and proven.

Connect Key Features:

SmartBook®

As the first and only adaptive reading experience, SmartBook is changing the way students read and learn. SmartBook creates a personalized reading experience by highlighting the most important concepts a student needs to learn at that moment in time. As a student engages with SmartBook, the reading experience continuously adapts by highlighting content based on what each student knows and doesn't know. This ensures that he or she is focused on the content needed to close specific knowledge gaps, while it simultaneously promotes long-term learning.

Connect Insight®

Connect Insight is Connect's new one-of-a-kind visual analytics dashboard—now available for instructors—that provides at-a-glance information regarding student performance, which is immediately actionable. By presenting assignment, assessment, and topical performance results together with a time metric that is easily visible for aggregate or individual results, Connect Insight gives instructors the ability to take a just-in-time approach to teaching and learning, which was never before available. Connect Insight presents data that empowers instructors improve class performance in a way that is efficient and effective.

Simple Assignment Management

With Connect, creating assignments is easier than ever, so instructors can spend more time teaching and less time managing.

- Assign SmartBook learning modules.
- Edit existing questions and create their own questions.

- Draw from a variety of text specific questions, resources, and test bank material to assign online.
- Streamline lesson planning, student progress reporting, and assignment grading to make classroom management more efficient than ever.

Smart Grading

When it comes to studying, time is precious. Connect helps students learn more effectively by providing feedback and practice material when they need it and where they need it. This is done in several ways.

- Automatically score assignments, giving students immediate feedback on their work and comparisons with correct answers.
- Access and review each response; manually change grades or leave comments for students to review.
- Track individual student performance—by question, assignment or in relation to the class overall—with detailed grade reports.
- Reinforce classroom concepts with practice tests and instant quizzes.
- Integrate grade reports easily with Learning Management Systems including Blackboard, D2L, and Moodle.

Instructor Library

The Connect Instructor Library is a repository for additional resources to improve student engagement in and out of the class. It provides all the critical resources instructors need to build their course.

- Access Instructor resources.
- View assignments and resources created for past sections.
- Post your own resources for students to use.

Instructors' Resources

Understanding Canadian Business, Ninth Edition, offers a complete, integrated supplements package for instructors to address all of their needs.

Instructor's Manual: The instructor's manual, prepared by Thomas McKaig, University of Guelph-Humber, accurately represents the text's content and supports instructors' needs. Each chapter includes the learning objectives, the glossary of key terms, a chapter synopsis, a lecture outline, and solutions to the end-of-chapter discussion questions and videos.

Computerized Test Bank: This flexible and easy-to-use electronic testing program allows instructors to create tests from book-specific items. Created by Thomas McKaig, University of Guelph-Humber, the test bank has undergone a rigorous auditing and revision process for the ninth edition. It contains a broad selection of multiple choice, true/false, and essay questions. Instructors may add their own questions as well. Each question identifies the relevant page reference and difficulty level. Multiple versions of the test can be created and printed.

PowerPoint Presentations: These robust presentations offer high-quality visuals from the text and highlight key concepts from each chapter to bring key business concepts to life. Two different presentations offer instructors choice on how they like to present the material to their classes.

The basic set was authored by Valerie Miceli, Seneca College, and the advanced set was authored by Tim Richardson, Seneca College and the University of Toronto.

Videos for All Chapters: Complementary videos from CBC programs and customized business segments from the McGraw-Hill Management Library filmed specifically for the Nickels text are available on DVD and also can be accessed on the password-protected area of Connect. Detailed teaching notes written by the text authors are available in the instructor's manual and on the instructor area of Connect.

Manager's Hotseat

The **Manager's HotSeat** is a resource that allows students to watch over 14 real managers apply their years of experience when dealing with daily issues such as ethics, diversity, teamwork, and the virtual workplace. Students are prompted for their feedback throughout each scenario and can then submit a report evaluating the manager's choices, while defending their own. The Manager's HotSeat is ideal for group or classroom discussions.

Business Plan Pro

Business Plan Pro is available as a bundled option that includes more than 250 sample business plans and 400 case studies to give you a wide variety of examples as you create your own business plan. It helps you set up your business by answering questions that help the software customize your plan. Then you enter your financial data to generate financial worksheets and statements.

Superior Learning Solutions and Support

The McGraw-Hill Education team is ready to help you assess and integrate any of our products, technology, and services into your course for optimal teaching and learning performance. Whether it's helping your students improve their grades, or putting your entire course online, the McGraw-Hill Education team is here to help you do it. Contact your Learning Solutions Consultant today to discover how to maximize all of the resources!

For more information on the latest technology and Learning Solutions offered by McGraw-Hill Education and its partners, please visit us online: **http://www.mheducation.ca/he/solutions**.

Acknowledgements

Development of the Text and Supplements Package

To ensure continuous improvement of our product, we have used an extensive review and development process for each of our editions. Building on that history, the development process for this Ninth edition included evaluation by a broad panel of instructors where new ideas were exchanged. The Ninth edition continues to be the market's gold standard due to involvement of these committed instructors. We thank them all for their help, support, and friendship—your suggestions to improve the quality, coverage, and the supplements package were invaluable.

Reviewers who were vital in helping us develop the Ninth edition include:

Shawna DePlonty, *Sault College*
David Fleming, *George Brown College*
Jai Goolsarran, *Centennial College*
Steve Janisse, *St. Clair College*
Carolan McLarney, *Dalhousie University*
Kayrod Niamir, *Dawson College*
Grace O'Farrell, *University of Winnipeg*
Morden Shapiro, *University of Ontario Institute of Technology*
Kenneth Wong, *Langara College*
Leo Wong, *Grant MacEwan University*

Many thanks are also due to the following people who worked hard to make this book a reality: Kim Brewster, Group Product Manager; Amy Rydzanicz, Product Developer; Janie Deneau, Supervising Editor; Michelle Saddler, Production Coordinator; Cat Haggert, Copy Editor; Monika Schurmann, Permissions and Photo Researcher; and Jodie Bernard, Designer.

The authors would also like to extend their appreciation to Ron Foxcroft for allowing them to highlight Fox40 International Inc. as this edition's running case. Started over twenty-five years ago, this privately held, family-run organization exemplifies many of the business principles introduced in this edition.

PART 1

The Dynamic Business Environment

LEARNING OBJECTIVES

After you have read and studied this chapter, you should be able to:

LO1 Illustrate the importance of key business fundamentals to wealth generation.

LO2 Identify business stakeholders and their importance to non-profit organizations and business activities.

LO3 Explain how entrepreneurship is critical to the wealth of an economy, and list the five factors of production that contribute to wealth.

LO4 State the six elements that make up the business environment and explain why the business environment is important to organizations.

LO5 Give examples of how the service sector has replaced manufacturing as the principal provider of jobs, but why manufacturing remains vital for Canada.

PROFILE

GETTING TO KNOW RON FOXCROFT OF FOX 40 INTERNATIONAL INC.

For successful Canadian entrepreneur and inventor Ron Foxcroft, it all started in 1982 when he purchased Fluke Transport, a Southern Ontario trucking business. The company slogan—If It's On Time . . . It's A "FLUKE"—was soon recognized throughout North America. Over the years, Foxcroft diversified into new ventures and the Foxcroft Group of Companies now includes Fluke Transportation Group <http://www.fluke.ca>, Fluke Warehousing Inc., Foxcroft Capital Corp., Fox 40 International Inc. <http://www.fox40world.com>, and Fox 40 USA Inc.

The formation of Fox 40 International Inc. is the result of a dream for a pealess whistle. When Foxcroft began developing the whistle, he was motivated by his knowledge and experience as an international basketball referee. Frustrated with faulty pea whistles, he spent three years of development with design consultant Chuck Shepherd, resulting in the creation of the Fox 40 Classic Whistle. (The whistle was named for Foxcroft, who was 40 when his invention was being developed). Introduced in 1987, this finely tuned precision instrument does not use a pea to generate sound. In fact, there are no moving parts whatsoever. There is nothing to obstruct sound, nothing to stick, freeze, or fail. The patented design moves the air blast through three tuned chambers. Fox 40 whistles are constructed entirely of high-impact ABS plastic so they are impervious to moisture. A quick rinse in disinfectant eliminates bacteria. Every time, they deliver on faultless performance (e.g., loudness), and they never fail.

In 1987, Shepherd said to Foxcroft, "Ron, we have just developed the 'best whistle in the world.' You must pledge to me that you will dedicate your life to making the Fox 40 whistle better." To this day, Foxcroft and the company employees continue to honour this pledge.

Fox 40 International Inc., a proudly Canadian company, dominates the global whistle industry. Tens of thousands of Fox 40 whistles are produced monthly for shipment to 140 countries. They are sold to referees, coaches, water safety, search and rescue teams, personal security, animal trainers, all sport enthusiasts, as well as the outdoor and premium incentive markets. The complete line of Fox 40 products has grown substantially with over 900 active stock-keeping units (SKUs) that include the following: nineteen Fox 40 Whistles styles; lanyards & attachments; Fox 40 gear; SmartCoach coaching boards; the SICK Self Impression Custom Kit and Heat Alert mouthguards; marine & outdoor products; pink products; and logo imprinted products.

An avid sportsman, Ron Foxcroft's philosophy of "be the best at what you do" has contributed to his success both on and off the basketball court. He has been named one of the 52 most influential persons in North American Officiating of all time. In 2010, the National Association of Sports Officials named him—the only Canadian—to a group of 30 who have made a difference in the world of sports officials. He continues to work as a game observer for the National Basketball League (NBA). Off the court, PROFIT magazine voted him to be one of the top ten Canadian businessmen of the decade. He has been honoured as Entrepreneur of the Year by the Burlington Economic Development Corporation. More recently, he received the Queen

Elizabeth II Diamond Jubilee Medal to mark his contributions to the Hamilton–Burlington community. He was also gratified to receive an Honourary Graduation Diploma from Mohawk College. Today, Foxcroft continues his active role as Founder and Chief Executive Officer (CEO) of Fox 40 International Inc. and Chairman and CEO of Fluke Transportation.

Foxcroft credits his customers and employees for the improvements to the original whistle. In his words, "When you are the best, you need to be better." This all starts with watching people to understand their needs. It involves developing products and services that customers might want. Making decisions along the way is challenging, but if you are successful, you can make a lot of customers very happy. Throughout this process, you need to have a vision, be focused, adapt to change, and never give up. His advice for future entrepreneurs, in the words of Walt Disney, is to "Get a good idea and stay with it. Dog it, and work it until it's done and done right."

The purpose of this text is to introduce you to the exciting and challenging world of business. Each chapter will begin with a story similar to this one. You will meet more successful entrepreneurs who have started a business. You will also learn about people who work for companies and have succeeded far beyond their original expectations. You will learn about all aspects of business: management, human resource management, marketing, accounting, finance, and more. You will also learn about businesses of all sizes. We begin by looking at some key terms and exploring the rapidly changing business environment so that you can prepare to meet tomorrow's challenges today.

Sources: Ron Foxcroft, CEO of Fox 40 International Inc. and Chairman and CEO of Fluke Transportation, and Juliana Child, VP Promotional Sales & Events, Fox 40 International Inc., 11 March 2015; "The Story of Fox 40," Fox 40 International Inc., 21 February 2014, http://www.fox40world.com/index.cfm?id=55884; "Ron Foxcroft presented with prestigious Queen Elizabeth II Diamond Jubilee Medal," Fox 40 International Inc., 15 August, 2012, http://www.fox40world.com/index.cfm?returnid=56106&newsid=3393&pagepath=KEEPING_IN_TOUCH/News_Releases&id=57428; Ron Foxcroft, Founder and CEO, Fox 40 International Inc., in-person interview, 19 December 2011; "BEDC Inducts Mr. Ron Foxcroft into the Entrepreneur Hall of Fame," Burlington Economic Development Corporation, 10 June 2011, www.bedc.ca/sites/default/files/PDF/businessnews/MediaRelease—BEDCInductsMr. RonFoxcroftintotheEntrepreneurHallofFame.pdf; John Kernaghan, "Fox 40 founder Foxcroft feted," *The Hamilton Spectator*, 18 October 2010, www.thespec.com/sports/local/article/268488—fox-40-founder-foxcroft-feted; REFEREE Staff, "Not An Inadvertent Whistle," *REFEREE Magazine*, July 2007, 45–47; and Global TV, "Ron Foxcroft," Summit of Life, Summer 2005.

Using this Course to Prepare for Your Career

Since you have signed up for this course, we are guessing you already know the value of higher education. When averaged across gender and fields of study, the holders of a post-secondary education make a cumulated average of about $1,000,000 over 20 years compared to a cumulated average of about $670,000 for high school graduates.[1] That is nearly 60 percent more for post-secondary graduates compared to those with just a high school diploma. Thus, what you invest in a post-secondary education is likely to pay you back many times.

See Figure 1.1 for more of an idea of the earnings of a business post-secondary education after 20 years compared to an overall post-secondary and high school education. That does not mean there are not good careers available to non–post-secondary graduates. It just means those with an education are more likely to have higher earnings over their lifetime. In addition, for both men and women a degree is associated with more years of coverage in an employer-sponsored pension plan and fewer layoffs than a person with a high school diploma.[2]

The value of a post-secondary education is more than just a larger paycheque. Other benefits include increasing your ability to think critically and communicate your ideas to others, improving your ability to use technology, and preparing yourself to live in a diverse and competitive world. Knowing you have met your goals and earned a degree also gives you the self-confidence to work toward future goals.

The rewards of post-secondary education are well worth the effort for graduates, who can expect to earn nearly 60 percent more than high school graduates over the 20 years. Businesses like graduates too, because the growing needs of a global workplace require knowledgeable workers to fill the jobs of the future. What other benefits do you see from earning a degree?

■ **FIGURE 1.1**

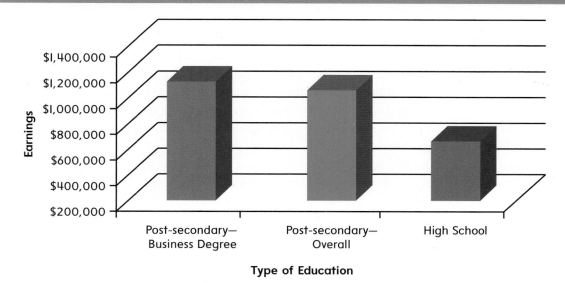

EARNINGS COMPARISON OF POST-SECONDARY AND HIGH SCHOOL GRADUATES OVER 20 YEARS

Note: Earnings are averaged across men and women; Post-secondary-Overall earnings is averaged across nine areas of study.

Source: Yuri Ostrovsky and Marc Frenette, "The Cumulative Earnings of Postsecondary Graduate Over 20 Years: Results by Field of Study," Statistics Canada, October 2014, Catalogue no. 11-626-X, accessed March 15, 2015, http://www.statcan.gc.ca/pub/11-626-x/11-626-x2014040-eng.htm.

Experts say today's post-secondary graduates will likely hold seven or eight different jobs (often in several different careers) in their lifetime.[3] You too may want to change careers someday. It can be the path to long-term happiness and success. That means you will have to be flexible and adjust your strengths and talents to new opportunities. Learning has become a lifelong job. You will need to constantly update your skills to achieve high competence and remain competitive.

If you are typical of many post-secondary students, you may not have any idea what career you would like to pursue. That is not necessarily a big disadvantage in today's fast-changing job market. After all, many of the best jobs of the future do not even exist today. Figure 1.2 lists 10 careers that did not exist 10 years ago. There are no perfect or certain ways to prepare for the most interesting and challenging jobs of tomorrow. Rather, you should continue your education, develop strong technology and Internet skills, improve your verbal and written communication skills, and remain flexible and forward thinking while you explore the job market. But without a doubt, business knowledge will be valuable in the future.

■ FIGURE 1.2

NEW CAREERS
These careers did not exist 10 years ago:
• IOS Developer • Android Developer • Zumba Instructor • Social Media Intern • Data Scientist • UI/UX Designer • Big Data Architect • Beachbody Coach • Cloud Services Specialist • Digital Marketing Specialist

Source: LinkedIn, www.linkedin.com, accessed May 2014.

One of the objectives of this class, and this book, is to help you choose an area in which you might enjoy working and have a strong chance to succeed. You will learn about economics, global business, ethics, entrepreneurship, management, marketing, accounting, finance, and more. At the end of the course, you should have a much better idea which careers would be best for you and which you would not enjoy. But you do not have to be in business to use business principles. You can use marketing principles to get a job and to sell your ideas to others. You can use your knowledge of investments to make money in the stock market. You will use your management skills and general business knowledge wherever you go and in whatever career you pursue including government agencies, charities, and social causes.

Post-secondary courses are best at teaching you concepts and ways of thinking about business. However, to learn first-hand how to apply those ideas to real business situations, you need to explore and interact with other resources. You can extend your understanding and awareness of the business world through contact with others who have business experience. For example, many college students have had experience working in business or non-profit organizations. Hearing and talking about those experiences exposes you to many real-life examples that are invaluable for understanding business. Outside contact also offers a wealth of information. Who can tell you more about what it is like to start a career in accounting than someone who is doing it now? One of the best ways to learn about different businesses is to visit them in person. The world can be your classroom.

LO1 Illustrate the importance of key business fundamentals to wealth generation.

Business Fundamentals

One thing that you can learn from the chapter-opening Profile is that success in business if often based on the strategy of finding a need and filling it. Ron Foxcroft saw the need for a pealess whistle and he filled it. This strategy lets you help the community in several ways. You provide needed goods, jobs, and services to people in the area. **Goods** are tangible products such as computers, food, clothing, cars, and appliances. **Services** are intangible products (i.e., items that cannot be held in your hand) such as education, health care, insurance, recreation, and travel and tourism.

goods
Tangible products such as computers, food, clothing, cars, and appliances.

services
Intangible products (i.e., products that can't be held in your hand) such as education, health care, insurance, recreation, and travel and tourism.

Although you do not need to have wealth as a primary goal, one result of successfully filling a market need is that you can make money for yourself, sometimes a great deal, by giving customers what they want. A **business** is any activity that seeks to provide goods and services to others while operating at a profit. An **entrepreneur** is a person who risks time and money to start and manage a business. You will read more about successful entrepreneurs throughout this text.

business
Any activity that seeks to provide goods and services to others while operating at a profit.

entrepreneur
A person who risks time and money to start and manage a business.

An entrepreneur learns early that a business needs a reliable accountant, a good lawyer, and strong managers. Entrepreneurs may have to go to financial institutions (e.g., banks) or to venture capital firms to borrow money. In today's economy, borrowing from a financial institution is harder than usual.[4] Therefore, later on in the text, we will talk about ways to get closer to financial institutions so that they will be more inclined to give you a loan. Entrepreneurs will also need to learn more about business, including how to deal with unions, what kind of insurance to buy, and how to find the right people to hire. Usually that means studying business at a post-secondary institution.[5] Access to a college or university education is much easier today now that so many courses are available online.[6]

Revenues, Profits, and Losses

Revenue is the total amount of money received during a given period for goods sold and services rendered and from other financial sources. **Profit** is the amount of money a business earns above and beyond what it spends for salaries and other expenses. Since not all businesses make a profit, starting a business can be risky. A **loss** occurs when a business's expenses are more than its revenues. If a business loses money over time, it will likely have to close, putting its employees out of work. It should be no surprise, therefore, that thousands of businesses enter and exit the marketplace throughout the year.[7] Some owners close down one business to start another one or to retire. Even though such closings are not failures, they are reported as exits by Industry Canada. Only a small proportion of firms that exit the marketplace end up filing for *bankruptcy*, which refers to the liquidation of the business debtor's assets and the end of the commercial entity's operations.[8] As discussed later in this textbook, most business failures are due to poor management or problems associated with cash flow.

revenue
The total amount of money received during a given period for goods sold and services rendered, and from other financial sources.

profit
The amount a business earns above and beyond what it spends for salaries and other expenses.

loss
When a business's expenses are more than its revenues.

The business environment is constantly changing. What seems like a great opportunity one day—for example, online grocery shopping—may become a failure when the economy changes. Starting a business may come with huge risks. But huge risks can result in huge profits. We'll explore that concept next.

Matching Risk with Profit

Starting a business involves risk. Generally speaking, **risk** refers to the chance of loss, the degree of probability of loss, and the amount of possible loss. Risk is the chance an entrepreneur takes of losing time and money on a business that may not prove profitable. Profit, remember, is the amount of money a business earns *above and beyond* what it pays out for salaries and other expenses. For example, if you were to start a business selling hot dogs in the summer, you would have to pay for the cart rental, for the hot dogs and other materials, and for someone to run the cart while you were away. After you paid your employee and yourself, paid for the food and materials you used, paid the rent on the cart, and paid your taxes, any money left over would be profit.

> **risk**
> The chance of loss, the degree of probability of loss, and the amount of possible loss (i.e., time and money).

Keep in mind that profit is over and above the money you pay yourself in salary. You could use any profit you make to rent or buy a second cart and hire other employees. After a few summers, you might have a dozen carts employing dozens of workers.

Even among companies that do make a profit, not all make the same amount. Those companies that take the most risk may make the most profit. There is high risk, for example, in making a new kind of automobile.[9] Elon Musk, CEO of Tesla Motors <*http://www.teslamotors.com*>, has experienced both success and failure as the company tries to move the automotive industry toward electric cars. Tesla planned to boost production to 500,000 cars in 2020 but disappointing sales in 2014 have placed this target at risk.[10]

As a potential business owner, you need to do research (e.g., talk to other business people and read business publications) to find the right balance between risk and profit for you. Different people have different tolerances for risk. To decide which is the best choice for you, you have to calculate the risks and the potential rewards of each decision. The more risks you take, the higher the rewards may be. In Chapter 7, you will learn more about the risks and rewards that come with starting a business.

Standard of Living and Quality of Life

Entrepreneurs such as Elon Musk, the founder of Tesla Motors and SpaceX, not only became wealthy themselves, they also provide employment for many other people. Businesses and their employees pay taxes to the different levels of government (federal, provincial, and municipal). This money is used to build hospitals, schools, libraries, playgrounds, roads, and other public facilities. Taxes also help to keep the environment clean, support people in need, and provide police and fire protection. Thus, the wealth businesses generate and the taxes they pay help everyone in their communities. A country's businesses are part of an economic system that contributes to the standard of living and quality of life for everyone in the country (and, potentially, the world). How has the most recent economic slowdown affected the standard of living and quality of life in Canada?

The term **standard of living** refers to the amount of goods and services people can buy with the money they have. For example, Canada has one of the highest standards of living in the world, even though workers in some other countries may on average make more money per hour. How can that be? Prices for goods and services might be higher than in Canada, so a person in that country can buy less than what a person in Canada can buy with the same amount of money. For example, a pound of local cheese may cost $8.43 in Japan and $5.25 in Canada.[11]

> **standard of living**
> The amount of goods and services people can buy with the money they have.

Often, goods cost more in one country than another because of higher taxes and stricter government regulations. Finding the right level of taxes and regulation is important in making a country or city prosperous. We'll explore that issue more deeply in Chapter 2. At this point, it is enough to understand that Canada enjoys a high standard of living partly because of the wealth created by its businesses.

When Nick Woodman wanted to show off videos of his stunts to other surfers, he used rubber bands and a surfboard leash to attach cameras to his wrist. His early attempts did not work, but after a lot of work and a $235,000 investment, his GoPro cameras are now the gold standard for self-documenting extreme sports. Today Woodman's company brings in $526 million in annual revenue. What risks and rewards did Woodward face when starting his business?

The term **quality of life** refers to the general well-being of a society in terms of its political freedom, natural environment, education, health care, safety, amount of leisure, and rewards that add to the satisfaction and joy that other goods and services provide. Maintaining a high quality of life requires the combined efforts of businesses, non-profit organizations (to be discussed soon), and government agencies. The more money businesses create, the more is potentially available to improve the quality of life for everyone. It's important to be careful, however. Working to build a higher standard of living may lower the quality of life if it means less time with family or more stress.[12]

quality of life
The general well-being of a society in terms of its political freedom, natural environment, education, health care, safety, amount of leisure, and rewards that add to the satisfaction and joy that other goods and services provide.

LO2   Identify business stakeholders and their importance to non-profit organizations to business activities.

Responding to the Various Business Stakeholders

Stakeholders are all of the people who stand to gain or lose by the policies and activities of a business and whose concerns the business needs to address. As noted in Figure 1.3, stakeholders include many different groups such as customers, employees, financial institutions (e.g., banks and credit unions), investors (e.g., shareholders), environmentalists, and government. Stakeholders may also have direct and indirect impact upon a business or organization. Each of the stakeholder types shown in Figure 1.3 can be considered either primary, those who without whom whose participation the business would not exist, or secondary, whose influence is not essential to the survival of a business. Don't forget that businesses can also influence government policies through the activities and efforts of their associations, lobbyists, and trade unions.

stakeholders
All the people who stand to gain or lose by the policies and activities of a business.

■ **FIGURE 1.3**

A BUSINESS AND ITS STAKEHOLDER

Often the needs of a firm's various stakeholders will conflict. For example, paying employees more may cut into shareholders' profits. Balancing such demands is a major role of business managers.

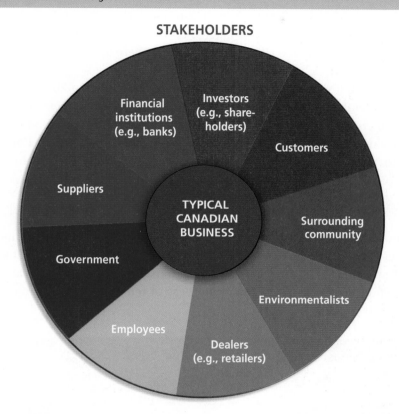

STAKEHOLDERS

The challenge of the twenty-first century will be for organizations to balance, as much as possible, the needs of all stakeholders. For example, the need for the business to make profits must be balanced against the needs of employees for sufficient income. The need to stay competitive may call for offshoring jobs to other countries, recognizing that this sound business strategy might do harm to the community because jobs would be lost.[13] **Offshoring** entails sourcing part of the purchased inputs outside of the country.[14] **Outsourcing** means contracting with other companies to do some or all of the functions of a firm, such as production or accounting.[15]

offshoring
Sourcing part of the purchased inputs outside of the country.

outsourcing
Assigning various functions, such as accounting, production, security, maintenance, and legal work to outside organizations.

You may be wondering, how are the terms insourcing, outsourcing, and offshoring different? A Statistics Canada *<http://www.statcan.gc.ca>* report highlights the distinction. As stated, "Outsourcing decisions affect the boundaries of the firm—what production takes place within the firm and what is purchased from outside the firm. Changes in offshoring may be, but are not necessarily, related to changes in outsourcing. They involve decisions both to purchase outside of the firm and to do so from abroad. Considerations to do the latter are at the heart of the study of international trade. Interest in outsourcing arises because it may foretell changes in industrial structure. Interest in offshoring arises because it may signify changes in international trading patterns."[16]

Companies have gone from outsourcing production jobs to offshoring research and development and design functions. Such decisions may prove disastrous to these firms doing the offshoring if the overseas companies use the information to produce their own competitive products.[17] In Canada, most of the offshoring that occurs is with the United States, though there has been some increase over the last decade with developing countries.[18]

A recent study indicated outsourcing will continue to grow at 12 to 26 percent across functions such as information technology, legal services, and human resource management.[19] It is also expected that governments will create legislation to reduce offshoring. **Insourcing** initiatives to return jobs to companies exist in various industries, such as the automotive sector, where Ford Motor Company advanced workers to higher pay scales and as a result, hired more entry level employees.[20]

---

insourcing
Assigning various functions that could go to an outside organization to employees in the company.

It is legal to outsource and offshore, but is that best for all stakeholders, including workers? Business leaders must make decisions based on all factors, including the need to make a profit. As you can see, pleasing all stakeholders is not easy and it calls for trade-offs that are not always acceptable to one or another stakeholder. Keep in mind that regardless of temptations, company officials do have a responsibility to their stakeholders.

Media have also become an important stakeholder in the business environment. Two telecommunications conglomerates, Bell <http://www.bell.ca> and Rogers <http://www.rogers.com>, paid Can$1.32 billion to acquire a 75 percent share of Maple Leaf Sports and Entertainment <http://www.mlse.com>. The purchase gave them a majority share of the corporation that owns and manages the Toronto Maples Leafs, Marlies, Raptors, Toronto FC, real estate such as the Air Canada Centre, and television properties. What media stakeholders impact business in other industries? How do they impact the business? Are they primary or secondary stakeholders?[21]

Such trade-offs are also apparent in the political arena. As will be discussed in Chapter 4, governments make policies that affect many stakeholders. However, budget limitations force governments to make difficult choices, and these decisions are often not popular. Consequently, after years of insufficient funding, any changes in the areas of the environment, health care, and education generate a great deal of attention. As you will learn, balancing the demands of stakeholders is not limited to for-profit businesses.

Using Business Principles in Non-Profit Organizations

Despite their efforts to satisfy all of their stakeholders, businesses cannot do everything that is needed to make a community all it can be. Non-profit organizations—such as schools, hospitals, and charities—also make a major contribution to the welfare of society as well as economic activity and jobs. A **non-profit organization** is an organization whose goals do not include making a personal profit for its owners or organizers. Non-profit organizations strive for financial gains because revenue is needed to operate but such gains are used to meet their social or educational goals rather than for personal or shareholder profit.

non-profit organization
An organization whose goals do not include making a personal profit for its owners or organizers.

Non-profit organizations also include the different levels of government in our country. They are increasingly involved in business decisions and operations even though the primary purpose is not to generate a profit. We will consider the role of government in business in Chapter 4.

Non-profit organizations use for-profit business principles to achieve results. Canadian Blood Services <http://www.blood.ca> is a national not-for-profit charitable organization whose mission is to manage the blood and blood products supply for Canadians. The organization employs approximately 2,800 full-time employees and generates over Can$1 million in revenue?[22] Did you know that approximately every minute of every day, someone in Canada needs blood? The good news is that one blood donation—in just one hour—can save up to three lives. This is a poster that has been used in schools across Canada with the purpose of encouraging people to donate blood.

Social entrepreneurs are people who use business principles to start and manage non-profit organizations and help address social issues. Muhammad Yunus won the Nobel Prize for starting the Grameen Bank <*http://www.grameen.com*>, a microlending organization that provides small loans to entrepreneurs too poor to qualify for traditional loans. Yunus has started 30 of what he calls social businesses that do not have profit as their goal. One, for example, provides cataract operations for a fraction of the usual cost.[23] The Spotlight on Small Business box features the Canadian Social Entrepreneurship Foundation. Would you consider becoming a social entrepreneur?

Your interests may lead you to work for a non-profit organization. Two million people, including professionals and staffers, work for Canada's approximately 170,000 charities and non-profit organizations.[24] This does not mean, however, that you should not study business. If you want to start or work in a non-profit organization, you will need to learn business skills such as information management, leadership, marketing, and financial management. Therefore, the knowledge and skills you acquire in this and other business courses will be useful for careers in any organization, including non-profits. We shall explore entrepreneurship right after the Progress Assessment.

Spotlight *On* SMALL BUSINESS

Social Entrepreneurship

The Canadian Social Entrepreneurship Foundation (CSEF) site <*http://www.csef.ca*> was created by Jason Carvalho to spur innovation and "bridge the gap" that was developing between the non-profit, business, and government sectors. The motto of the CSEF is taken from a famous quote paraphrased by Robert Kennedy which is as follows: "Some men and women see things as they are and say, 'Why?' I dream things that never were and say, 'Why not?'"

To begin to bridge this gap, CSEF looks for social entrepreneurs who are under the age of 40 and who want to develop and take a new service or product to market. Although social entrepreneurs share some characteristics and techniques with traditional business entrepreneurs—for example, an emphasis on innovation and the utilization of time-tested business theories and practices—their work and impact span the sectors noted earlier.

CSEF, which is 60 percent a virtual organization, provides access to funding, media resources, mentorship and support, and an online community. It invests in Canadian social enterprises that produce revenue and focus on specific areas such as (social) inventors, children and youth (e.g., employing at-risk youth), the environment (e.g., clean technologies and energy efficiency), and civic engagement.

Can you see yourself as a social entrepreneur? You could become a small business owner in Canada, but you could also use the business skills you learn in this course to be a social entrepreneur in Canada and other countries. Think of the possibilities.

Source: The Canadian Social Entrepreneurship Foundation. Copyright 2010, www.csef.ca. Used with permission.

Progress Assessment

- What is the difference between revenue and profit?

- What is risk, and how is it related to profit?

- What is the difference between standard of living and quality of life?

- What do the terms stakeholders, offshoring, outsourcing, and insourcing mean?

LO3 Explain how entrepreneurship is critical to the wealth of an economy, and list the five factors of production that contribute to wealth.

Entrepreneurship Versus Working for Others

There are two ways to succeed in business. One is to rise up through the ranks of large companies such as Royal Bank of Canada <*http://www.rbcroyalbank.com*> or Manulife Financial <*http://www.manulife .ca*>. The advantage of working for others is that somebody else assumes the entrepreneurial risk and provides you with benefits such as paid vacation time and health insurance. It's a good option and many people choose it.

The other, riskier, path is to start your own business and become an entrepreneur. While you may hear about success stories, keep in mind that many small businesses fail each year; thus, it takes a brave person to start a small business or to turn a business around. Furthermore, as an entrepreneur you do not receive any benefits such as paid vacation time and health insurance. You have to provide them for yourself!

How well do you know yourself? Are you more excited at the prospect of starting your own small business or would you prefer to work for a large- or medium-sized business? The answer to this question may start with understanding your personal risk tolerance.

Before you take on the challenge of entrepreneurship it makes sense to study the experiences of those who have succeeded to learn the process. Consider the example of Ron Joyce, who in 1963 purchased a Dairy Queen outlet *<http://www.dairyqueen.com/ca-en>*. Two years later, he invested $10,000 to become a franchisee in the first Tim Hortons *<http://www.timhortons.com>* (we will discuss franchising in Chapter 6). By 1967, he became a full partner in the company with Tim Horton. In the early years, both partners worked on expanding the business. When Horton died in 1974, Joyce became the sole owner of the chain. In the following years, he continued to develop the business, spending hundreds of hours piloting his plane in search of new franchise opportunities and doing everything from training new store owners to baking donuts. When Joyce sold the chain to Wendy's for US$450 million in 1995, there were more than 1,000 Tim Hortons restaurants. Tim Hortons became Canada's largest quick-service restaurant chain, with 5,515 systemwide restaurants, including 4,590 in Canada, 869 in the United States, and 56 in the Gulf Cooperation Council, an alliance of six Middle Eastern countries.[25] In 2014, the company merged with Burger King to form a new Canadian-based parent company, called Restaurant Brands International, and become the third-largest fast-food chain in the world.[26]

What you can learn from successful entrepreneurs like Ron Joyce is that you need to find something that you love to do. Before he became an entrepreneur, Joyce was a police officer. He started to get experience in business with his Dairy Queen outlet, and from there went on to great success with his Tim Hortons restaurants. While there were many challenges along the way, he was willing to put in the long hours needed to be successful. In addition to the original coffee and donut offerings, he continuously added new products to the restaurants to meet his customers' needs.

This is also the case for Ron Foxcroft, the focus of the chapter-opening Profile. Nearly 30 years after introducing the Fox 40 Classic Whistle, Fox 40 International Inc. sells an expanded whistle product line, pro coaching boards, mouthguards, and Fox 40 marine products (e.g., first aid and safety kits).

Small businesses and entrepreneurs contribute enormously to the Canadian economy. While these terms have been briefly mentioned in this chapter, be aware that more time will be spent discussing their significance in Chapters 6 and 7. After all, without the initial ideas and risks taken by entrepreneurs, we would not have successful businesses today.

The Importance of Entrepreneurs to the Creation of Wealth

Have you ever wondered why some countries are relatively wealthy and others are poor? Economists have been studying the issue of wealth creation for many years. They began the process by studying potential sources of wealth to determine which are the most important. Over time, they came up with five factors that seemed to contribute to wealth, which they called **factors of production**. Figure 1.4 describes those five factors, which are:

> **factors of production**
> The resources used to create wealth: land, labour, capital goods, entrepreneurship, and knowledge.

1. *Land (or natural resources).* Land and other natural resources are used to make homes, cars, and other products.

2. *Labour (workers).* People have always been an important resource in producing goods and services, but many people are now being replaced by technology.

3. *Capital Goods.* This includes machines, tools, buildings, or whatever else is used in the production of goods. It does not include money. Money is used to buy factors of production but is not always considered to be a factor by itself.

4. *Entrepreneurship.* All the resources in the world have little value unless entrepreneurs are willing to take the risk of starting businesses to use those resources.

5. *Knowledge.* Information technology has revolutionized business, making it possible to quickly determine wants and needs and to respond with desired goods and services.

■ **FIGURE 1.4**

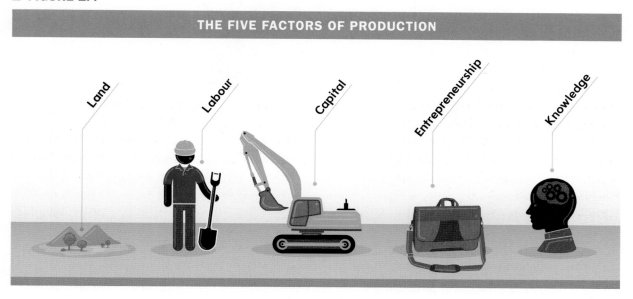

THE FIVE FACTORS OF PRODUCTION

Traditionally, business and economics textbooks have emphasized only four factors of production: land, labour, capital, and entrepreneurship. But management expert and business consultant Peter Drucker said that the most important factor of production in our economy is and always will be *knowledge.*

What do we find when we compare the factors of production in rich and poor countries? Some poor countries often have plenty of land and natural resources. Russia, for example, has vast areas of land with many resources such as timber and oil, but it is not considered a rich country (yet). In contrast, Japan is a relatively rich country but is poor in land and other natural resources. Therefore, land is not the critical element for wealth creation.

Most poor countries such as Mexico have many labourers, so labour is not the primary source of wealth today. Labourers need to find work to make a contribution; that is, they need entrepreneurs to provide jobs for them. Furthermore, capital—machinery and tools—is now easy for firms to find in world markets, so capital is not the missing ingredient. Capital is not productive without entrepreneurs to put it to use.

What makes countries rich today is a combination of *entrepreneurship* and the effective use of *knowledge.* Entrepreneurs use what they have learned (knowledge) to grow their businesses and increase wealth. Economic and political freedom also matter.

The business environment either encourages or discourages entrepreneurship. That helps explain why some provinces and cities in Canada grow rich while others remain relatively poor. In the following section, we'll explore what makes up the business environment and how to build an environment that encourages growth and job creation.

To create wealth for its citizens, a country requires more than natural resources like timber. No matter how vast its forests or other inputs like labour, fuel, and waterways, a country needs the efforts of entrepreneurs and the skill and knowledge to produce goods and services. How can the government support entrepreneurship and the spread of knowledge?

Progress Assessment

- What are some of the advantages of working for others?

- What benefits do you lose by being an entrepreneur, and what do you gain?

- What are the five factors of production? Which ones seem to be the most important for creating wealth?

The Business Environment

The **business environment** consists of the surrounding factors that either help or hinder the development of businesses. Figure 1.5, which summarizes some of the points discussed in this chapter, shows the six elements in the business environment:

1. The legal environment

2. The economic environment

3. The technological environment

4. The competitive environment

5. The social environment

6. The global environment

> **business environment**
> The surrounding factors that either help or hinder the development of businesses.

Businesses that create wealth and jobs grow and prosper in a healthy environment. Thus, creating the right business environment is the foundation for social benefits of all kinds, including good schools, clear air and water, good health care, and low rates of crime. Businesses normally cannot control their environment, but they need to monitor it carefully and do what they can to adapt as it changes.

■ **FIGURE 1.5**

TODAY'S DYNAMIC BUSINESS ENVIRONMENT

GLOBAL BUSINESS ENVIRONMENT

GLOBAL COMPETITION

FREE TRADE

THE QUALITY IMPERATIVE

The Legal Environment
1. Tax laws
2. Contract laws
3. Elimination of corruption

The Economic Environment
1. Income and expenditures
2. Currency shifts
3. Economic systems

The Competitive Environment
1. Components of competition
2. Customer-driven
3. Organization structure

BUSINESS GROWTH AND JOB CREATION

The Technological Environment
1. Information and technology
2. Databases
3. The Internet

The Social Environment
1. Diversity
2. Demographic changes
3. Family changes

LO4 State the six elements that make up the business environment and explain why the business environment is important to organizations.

The Legal Environment

People are willing to start new businesses if they believe that the risk of losing their money is not too great. Part of that decision is affected by how governments work with businesses. Governments can do a lot to lessen the risk of starting and running a business through the laws (also known as Acts) that are passed by its elected officials. The Constitution Act defines the powers that can be exercised by the different levels of government. In Chapter 4, we will review some of the responsibilities of these different levels.

Each piece of legislation authorizes an agency (such as Industry Canada) to write regulations that interpret the law in more detail and indicate how it will be implemented and enforced. Consequently, **regulations** consist of restrictions that provincial and federal laws place on businesses with respect to the conduct of their activities.[27] Regulations exist to protect consumers as well as businesses.[28] In Chapter 4, you will be introduced to some government departments that deal with businesses.

regulations
Restrictions that provincial and federal laws place on businesses with respect to the conduct of their activities.

LAWS AFFECT BUSINESS

Businesses need to be aware of the laws that are in place (or that may be passed) that will affect their operations. For example, government can keep taxes and regulations to a minimum, thereby encouraging entrepreneurship and increasing wealth. Entrepreneurs are looking for a high return on investment (ROI), including the investment of their time. If the government takes away much of what the business earns through high taxes, the ROI may no longer be worth the risk. Provinces and territories that have high taxes and restrictive regulations tend to drive entrepreneurs out, while areas with low taxes and less restrictive regulations can attract entrepreneurs.

The government can also lessen the risks of entrepreneurship by passing laws that enable business people to write contracts that are enforceable in court. You can read more about the importance of business law in Canada in Appendix A.

There are many laws in Canada that are intended to minimize corruption, and businesses can flourish when these laws are followed. Nonetheless, corrupt and illegal activities at some companies do negatively affect the business community and the economy as a whole. The news media widely reports these scandals.[29] Ethics is so important to the success of businesses and the economy as a whole that we feature Making Ethical Decisions boxes in each chapter and devote Chapter 5 to the subject.

The capitalist system relies heavily on honesty, integrity, and high ethical standards. Failure of those fundamentals can weaken the whole system as was the case with the subprime mortgage scandal in the United States.[30] The faltering economy of 2008–09 was due in large part to such failure. Some mortgage lenders, for instance, failed to do the research necessary to ensure their borrowers' creditworthiness. Many subprime borrowers forfeited their loans. The ripple effects of these unpaid debts not only cost many people their homes but also reduced the value of housing across the country and made it difficult for even business borrowers to get new loans. Part of the blame for this economic disaster can be placed on the borrowers who did not tell the truth about their income or who otherwise deceived the lenders. Financiers also assume blame for irresponsible lending decisions that exposed their bank or financial institution to significant risk.[31] This subprime mortgage crisis will be discussed in Chapter 4.

Starting a business is more difficult in some countries than in others. In India, for example, it is a time-consuming and bureaucratic process to obtain government permission. Nonetheless, new businesses can become a major source of wealth and employment. This sari shop is one small example. What do you think would be the effect of a little more freedom to create business opportunities in this country of over a billion people?

It is easy to see the damage caused by the poor moral and ethical behaviour of some business people. What is not so obvious is the damage caused by the moral and ethical lapses of the everyday consumer—that is, you and me. The Making Ethical Decisions box discusses that issue in more depth.

Making ETHICAL DECISIONS

How Ethical Are You?

It is easy to criticize the ethics of people whose names appear in the headlines. It is more difficult to see the moral and ethical misbehaviour of your own social group. Do you find some of the behaviours of your friends morally or ethically questionable?

A survey found that the number of employees calling in sick had reached a five-year high, and three-fifths were not sick at all. Other employees have been caught conducting personal business at work, such as paying their bills or going on Facebook. And others play video games on their work computers. We are sure you can add many more examples.

Several companies today are creating ethics codes to guide their employees' behaviour. We believe the trend toward improving ethical behaviour is so important that we have made it a major theme of this book. Throughout the text you will see boxes like this one, called Making Ethical Decisions, that pose ethical dilemmas and ask what you would do to resolve them. The idea is for you to think about the moral and ethical dimensions of every decision you make.

Here is your ethical dilemma. You have become addicted to your electronic gadgets. Some days at work you spend most of the time playing games, watching TV, texting, sending e-mails to friends, or reading a book or magazine on your devices. What is the problem in this situation? What are your alternatives? What are the consequences of each alternative? Which alternative will you choose? Is your choice ethical?

The Economic Environment

The economic environment affects both businesses and consumers. For our discussion, the focus will be on businesses. The economic environment looks at income, expenditures, and resources that affect the cost of running a business. Businesses review the results of major economic indicators such as consumer spending, employment levels, and productivity. This analysis will give them a sense of what is happening in the marketplace and what actions they may need to take. Since Chapter 2 is dedicated to how economic issues affect businesses, the discussion here will be very brief.

The movement of a country's currency relative to other currencies also pertains to this environment. Currency movements are especially critical for countries that generate a great deal of business activity from exports, such as Canada. For instance, in the late 2000s the Ontario economy was negatively impacted as a result of the strong Canadian dollar, which surpassed parity with the U.S. dollar in the fall of 2007. The province lost tens of thousands of manufacturing jobs in just a few years as manufacturers shifted operations overseas. Some of the province's flagship employers, like General Motors, closed factories and trimmed production at other manufacturing facilities.[32] The opposite is also true. For example, a lower Canadian dollar value relative to the U.S. dollar makes our exports cheaper and more attractive to the U.S. market, as consumers can buy more products with their higher-valued currency. What is the value of the Canadian dollar compared to other currencies today? How does it compare to the value of the U.S. dollar? What is the impact of the currency difference upon the Canadian economy?

Another aspect of the economic environment is the degree of entrepreneurship that is present. One way for governments to actively promote entrepreneurship is to allow private ownership of businesses. In some countries, the government owns most businesses and there is little incentive for people to work hard or create a profit. Around the world today, however, some governments are selling those businesses to private individuals to create more wealth. In Chapter 2, we will discuss the different economic systems around the world.

You should soon realize, as we continue with our brief introduction to the other business environments, that the activities occurring in one environment have an impact on the others. In short, all of the environments are linked. For example, if a new government regulation decreases business taxes, then the impact will be seen in the economic environment when one considers expenditures. As a business person you need to scan all of the environments to make good business decisions.

The Technological Environment

Since prehistoric times, humans have felt the need to create tools that make work easier. Few technological changes have had a more comprehensive and lasting impact on businesses, however, than the emergence of information technology (IT): computers, networks, smartphones, and the Internet. Read the nearby Reaching Beyond Our Borders box to learn more about how technology makes it possible for freelance employees to find good, lucrative work even though they do not even live in the same country as their employers.

Smartphones and other mobile devices, as well as social media like Facebook and Twitter, have completely changed the way people communicate with one another. Advertisers and other business people have created ways of using these tools to reach their suppliers and customers. Even politicians have harnessed the power of the Internet to advance their causes.[33]

IT is such a major force in business today that we discuss its impact on businesses throughout the entire text. New technologies are dramatically changing business practices and the way businesses and customers buy and sell.[34]

HOW TECHNOLOGY BENEFITS WORKERS AND YOU

One of the advantages of working for others is that the company often provides the tools and technology to make your job more productive. **Technology** means everything from phones and copiers to computers, mobile devices, medical imaging machines, and the various software programs and apps that make business processes more effective, efficient, and productive. Applied science or engineering research often leads to new technology. *Effectiveness* means producing the desired result. *Efficiency* means producing goods and services using the least amount of resources. Effectiveness is usually more important than efficiency.

technology
Everything from phones and copiers to computers, mobile devices, medical imaging machines, and the various software programs and apps that make business processes more effective, efficient, and productive.

Productivity is the amount of output you generate given the amount of input, such as the number of hours you work. The more you can produce in any given period, the more money you are worth to companies. Today, the high rate of productivity means employers need fewer workers, which in turn, contributes to the high unemployment rate we are now experiencing.[35]

productivity
The amount of output that is generated given the amount of input (e.g., hours worked).

Vivametrica <*http://www.vivametrica.com*>, a Calgary-based data analytics platform company, is a new entrant in the wearable intelligence industry. The Canadian firm is taking advantage of the emerging wearable technology market which is expected to reach US$2 billion by 2018. While its services target consumers, healthcare providers, and researchers, the company's immediate appeal is to corporate wellness programs for various enterprises that seek to improve employee productivity. Companies in the manufacturing, financial, oil and gas, insurance, education, and health industries see the value data analytics can serve to improve their return on investment for employee wellness initiatives.[36]

Technology affects people in all industries. For example, Don Glenn, a farmer, uses his personal computer to compare data from the previous year's harvest with infrared satellite photos of his farm that show which crops are flourishing. He has a desktop terminal called a DTN that allows him to check the latest grain prices, and he uses AgTalk, a web-based bulletin board, to converse with other farmers from all over the world. He also bids for bulk fertilizer on FarmTrade <*http://www.farmtrade.com*>, an online agricultural exchange. High-tech equipment tells Glenn how and where to spread fertilizer and seed, tracks yields yard by yard, and allows him to maintain high profit margins. Companies look to technology to allow them to be more efficient, effective, and productive. More tech often means fewer workers. Is that a good or bad thing for farmers?

THE GROWTH OF ELECTRONIC COMMERCE (E-COMMERCE)

E-commerce is the buying and selling of goods and services online. There are two major types of e-commerce transactions: business-to-consumer (B2C) and business-to-business (B2B). In 2013, Canadian enterprises sold $136 billion in goods and services over the Internet. Approximately 61 percent of the sales involved wholesale trade, manufacturing, and retail trade.[37] The increase resulted from more online shoppers (B2C) as well as a higher volume of Internet B2B orders.

e-commerce
The buying and selling of goods and services over the Internet.

Reaching *Beyond* OUR BORDERS

Connecting Companies with Global Freelancers

www.elance.com

In the years since the recession of 2007–09, freelancers have become more important to the business world than ever before. Rather than spend money on recruiting and retaining full-time employees, many companies prefer to hire temporary workers to cut costs. In fact, thanks to the Internet, freelance employees do not even need to live in the same country as their employers to do good, lucrative work. The company Elance acts as an online marketplace that connects freelancers with companies looking for contractors. For instance, if a Silicon Valley start-up is looking for an affordable engineer, Elance can introduce the company to a qualified candidate from Eastern Europe or India. Elance then collects an 8.75 percent transaction fee from the company. With more than 8 million registered individuals, in 2013 Elance saw its revenues grow to $300 million. Following a merger with its former rival ODesk, Elance expects billings to increase by more than $1 billion annually as businesses become more dependent on freelance labour, and workers adapt to its flexible structure. "Millennials want to work independently and control their careers," says Elance founder Fabio Rosati. "If I had to give advice to anybody about their careers, I would say your number one priority should be to remain employable as opposed to remaining employed."

Sources: Laura Weber, "Elance Taps Growing Demand for Freelancers," *The Wall Street Journal,* 4 February 2014; Ari Levy, "Elance Merges with ODesk to Enlarge Service for Freelancers," *Bloomberg Businessweek,* 18 December 2013; and Patrick Clark, "What Elance-ODesk Merger Means for Freelancers," *Bloomberg Businessweek,* 19 December 2013.

As important as the Internet has been in the consumer market to retailers like Amazon, it has become even more important in the B2B market, which consists of selling goods and services from one business to another, such as IBM *<http://www.ibm.com>* selling consulting services to a local bank. Websites have become the new stores.

Traditional businesses have been learning how to deal with the competition from B2B and B2C firms, and vice versa. People would just as soon sell used items posted on Kijiji *<http://www.kijiji.ca>* and Craigslist *<http://www.craigslist.org>* than throw away unwanted household items.[38] Many entrepreneurs use e-commerce to start a business and are recognized by eBay through its Entrepreneur of the Year awards.[39] Just consider one country: over 215 million Chinese citizens are using the Internet.[40] And what did people do before they could Google? E-commerce has become so important that we will discuss it throughout the text.

Do not confuse e-commerce with electronic business (e-business). Mostly done with web technologies, the term **e-business** refers to any information system or application (e.g., business software) that empowers business processes.[41] While e-commerce is frequently mixed up with the term e-business, e-commerce only covers one aspect of e-business (i.e., the use of an electronic support for the commercial relationship between a company and individuals).[42]

e-business
Any information system or application that empowers business processes.

USING TECHNOLOGY TO BE RESPONSIVE TO CUSTOMERS

A major theme of this text is that those businesses most responsive to customer wants and needs will succeed.[43] That realization points to one way in which even traditional retailers can use Internet technology. For example, businesses use bar codes to identify products that customers buy and their size, quantity, and colour. The scanner at the checkout counter can read that information and put it into a **database**, an electronic storage file in which information is kept.

database
An electronic storage file for information.

Databases enable stores to carry only the merchandise their local population wants. But because companies routinely trade database information, many retailers know what you buy and from whom you buy it. Thus they can send you catalogues and other direct mail advertising offering the kind of products you might want, as indicated by your past purchases.[44] We discuss other ways businesses use technology to be responsive to consumers throughout the text and in more detail in Appendix A.

Unfortunately, the legitimate collection of personal customer information also opens the door to identity theft. **Identity theft** is the act of obtaining personal information about a person, such as social insurance number and/or credit card number, and using that information for illegal purposes, such as making purchases. Just before Christmas 2013, hackers stole more than 110 million credit card numbers from Target's computer system, requiring all customers to monitor activity on these accounts or to get new credit cards. The company's profits fell nearly 50 percent for the quarter.[45]

identity theft
Obtaining an individuals' personal information, such as Social Insurance Number and credit card numbers, for illegal purposes.

In response to consumer complaints, federal privacy laws have been created. The Personal Information Protection and Electronic Documents Act (PIPEDA) sets out ground rules for how private sector organizations may collect, use, or disclose personal information in the course of commercial activities.[46] If you think an organization covered by the Act is not living up to its responsibilities under the law, you have the right to lodge an official complaint. The Office of the Privacy Commissioner of Canada advocates privacy rights for Canadians.

What you should learn from this example is to limit those to whom you give personal information.[47] You also need antivirus software on your computer as well as a firewall and antispyware software. You may also want to monitor your credit report. It is important for you to understand identity theft, security, privacy, stability, and other important IT issues (please refer to the discussion in Appendix A for more detail).

SOCIAL MEDIA MARKETING[48]

In Chapter 14 you will read how some Canadian companies are in the midst of the emergence of the social media marketing era. The most common tools or platforms used by both consumers and organizations are social networking sites (e.g., Twitter and Facebook), blogs, wikis, podcasts, and other shared media sites (e.g., YouTube). To survive in this social media world, organizations must understand, navigate, and adapt to this new landscape. Some organizations are heeding this advice. A recent report found 57 percent of small business owners use social media, and Facebook and LinkedIn are the most common tools.[49] In particular, small businesses and entrepreneurs are leveraging social media as a way to connect and communicate with current and potential customers.

Social media is also used for **crowdsourcing**, which helps a business find solutions to challenges. It is a valuable tool to better understand the dynamics of a business market.[50] The future may also utilize crowdsourcing to build better collaboration between government and citizens, students and universities, patients and hospitals.[51]

crowdsourcing
Using the expertise of a large group of people to solve a business problem.

Progress Assessment

- List the six elements of the business environment.
- What are four ways in which the government can foster entrepreneurship?
- How does technology benefit workers and customers?

The Competitive Environment

Competition among businesses has never been greater than it is today. Some companies have found a competitive edge by focusing on quality. The goal for many companies is zero defects—no mistakes in making the product. However, simply making a high-quality product is not enough to allow a company to stay competitive in world markets. Companies now have to offer both high-quality products and good value—that is, outstanding services and products at competitive prices. Figure 1.6 shows how competition has evolved to a new, world-class model.

■ FIGURE 1.6

HOW COMPETITION HAS CHANGED BUSINESS	
Traditional Businesses	Modern Businesses
Customer satisfaction	Delighting the customer[1]
Customer orientation	Customer and stakeholder orientation[2]
Profit orientation	Profit and social orientation[3]
Reactive ethics	Proactive ethics[4]
Product orientation	Quality and service orientation
Managerial focus	Customer focus

[1] *Delight* is a term from total quality management. *Bewitch* and *fascinate* are alternative terms.
[2] Stakeholders include customers, employees, investors, suppliers, dealers (e.g., retailers), and the community; the goal is to please *all* stakeholders.
[3] A social orientation goes beyond profit to do what is right and good for others.
[4] *Proactive* means doing the right thing before anyone tells you to do it. *Reactive* means responding to criticism after it happens.

COMPONENTS OF COMPETITION[52]

When developing their strategies, companies must consider the factors that drive competition: entry, bargaining power of buyers and suppliers, existing rivalries, and substitution possibilities. Scanning the competitive environment requires a look at all of these factors.

Entry In considering the competition, a firm must assess the likelihood of new entrants. Additional producers increase industry capacity and tend to lower prices. *Barriers to entry* are business practices or conditions that make it difficult for new firms to enter the market. Barriers to entry can be in the form of capital requirements, product identity, distribution access, or switching costs. The higher the expense of the barrier, the more likely it will deter new entrants, and vice versa (e.g., barriers to exit).

Power of Buyers and Suppliers Powerful buyers exist when they are few in number, there are low switching costs, or the product represents a significant share of the buyer's total costs. This last factor leads the buyer to exert significant pressure for price competition. A supplier gains power when the product is critical to the buyer and when it has built up switching costs.

Existing Competitors and Substitutes   Competitive pressure among existing firms depends on the rate of industry growth. In slow-growth settings, competition is more heated for any possible gains in market share. High fixed costs also create competitive pressures for firms to fill production capacity. (We will discuss production in Chapter 10.) For example, airlines offer discounts for making early reservations and charge penalties for changes or cancellations in an effort to fill seats, which represent a high fixed cost.

COMPETING BY EXCEEDING CUSTOMER EXPECTATIONS

Manufacturers and service organizations throughout the world have learned that today's customers are very demanding. Companies have to offer both high-quality products and outstanding service at competitive prices (value). Business is becoming customer-driven, not management-driven as in the past. This means that customers' wants and needs must come first.

Customer-driven organizations include Disney amusement parks *<http://disney.com>*, where the parks are kept clean and appeal to all ages, and Moto Photo *<http://www.motophoto.com>*, which does its best to please customers with fast, friendly service. Such companies can successfully compete against Internet firms if they continue to offer better and friendlier service. Successful organizations must now listen more closely to customers to determine their wants and needs, then adjust the firm's products, policies, and practices to meet those demands. We will explore these concepts in more depth in Chapter 14.

COMPETING BY RESTRUCTURING AND EMPOWERMENT

To meet the needs of customers, firms must give their front-line workers (e.g., office clerks, front-desk people at hotels, and salespeople) the responsibility, authority, freedom, training, and equipment they need to respond quickly to customer requests. They must allow workers to make other decisions essential to producing high-quality goods and services. The process is called **empowerment**, and we'll be talking about it throughout this book. To implement a policy of empowerment, managers must train front-line people to make decisions within certain limits, without the need to consult managers.

> **empowerment**
> Giving front-line workers the responsibility, authority, and freedom to respond quickly to customer requests.

As many companies have discovered, it sometimes takes years to restructure an organization so that managers are willing to give up some of their authority and employees are willing to assume more responsibility. We'll discuss such organizational changes and models in Chapter 9.

The Social Environment

Demography is the statistical study of the human population with regard to its size, density, and other characteristics such as age, race, gender, and income. In this book, we are particularly interested in the demographic trends that most affect businesses and career choices. The Canadian population is going through major changes that are dramatically affecting how people live, where they live, what they buy, and how they spend their time. Furthermore, tremendous population shifts are leading to new opportunities for some firms and to declining opportunities for others. For example, there are many more retired workers than in the past, creating new markets for all kinds of goods and services.

> **demography**
> The statistical study of the human population with regard to its size, density, and other characteristics such as age, race, gender, and income.

Adapting *to* CHANGE

Gourmet Airport Eateries Take Flight

Although the poor quality of airline food has been an easy punch line for decades, often the food served inside the airport itself isn't much better. Airport diners are more than just cranky people in a hurry: they also tend to be more affluent than average consumers. As a result, more gourmet restaurants are setting up shop in airports in order cash in on vacationing eaters. However, airport restaurants are especially difficult to operate on account of a number of security regulations.

The Greater Toronto Airports Authority is changing that perception by partnering with internationally renowned chefs to change the face of the airport restaurant scene. For instance, Massimo Capra, Italian chef and Food Network celebrity, opened two locations at Pearson International Airport in 2012.

Most recently, Canadian chef Roger Mooking, also of Food Network fame, partnered with HMSHost Corporation to open Twist. He noticed that the most popular food choice of airport travellers is a hamburger, but he tweaked his menu to include items such as a lamb burger with a fennel-mint relish—no ketchup or mustard in sight. Mooking brings one important secret ingredient to his airport venture–"Food has to be tasty and well-made and beautiful, but it has to be fun as well." Bon voyage!

Sources: Richard Ouzounian, "Many Ingredients in Roger Mooking's Success," *Toronto Star*, 15 January 2015; Michelle Henry, "Haute-cuisine checks in at Toronto's Pearson Airport," *Toronto Star*, 17 January 2013; Jan Chris Nuttell-Smith, "Chef Massimo Capra Flies into Pearson," *The Globe and Mail*, 7 July 2012.

THE AGING POPULATION

The Canadian population has been aging for several decades. More people are living longer due to better medical knowledge and technology and better health habits, more exercise, and a reduction in the number of people who smoke. The portion of the population that is very young continues to decrease because of birth rates that have declined since the mid-1960s. **Generation Y**, also known as Millennials (those born in the period from 1977 to 1994) represents the children of the large number of **Baby Boomers** (those born in the period from 1946 to 1964). Some students are part of Generation Y while others may be part of **Generation Z**, who include those born from 1995 onward.

Generation Y (Millennials)
A demographic group of Canadians that were born in the period from 1977 to 1994; the children of the Baby Boomers.

Baby Boomers
A demographic group of Canadians that were born in the period from 1946 to 1964.

Generation Z
A demographic group of Canadians that were born in the period from 1995 onward.

Figure 1.7 shows the population projections for Canada. You will notice that the 20–34 years and 35–64 years age groups are declining, while the 65 years and over age group is increasing steadily. Based on these projections, it is expected that seniors will become more numerous than children sometime around 2021. According to Statistics Canada, by 2036 nearly one quarter of the population will be Generation Z.[53]

■ **FIGURE 1.7**

POPULATION DISTRIBUTION BY AGE GROUP					
YEAR	0–4	5–19	20–34	35–64	65 AND ABOVE
2016	5.7%	16.3%	20.5%	41.2%	16.3%
2021	5.6%	16.5%	19.3%	40.1%	18.5%
2026	5.5%	16.9%	18%	38.8%	20.8%
2031	5.2%	16.8%	17.5%	37.7%	22.8%
2036	5%	16.5%	17.7%	37.1%	23.7%

Source: Adapted from "Population Projections for Canada, Provinces and Territories 2009–2036," Cat. No. 91-520-X, June 2010. Retrieved from http://www.statcan.gc.ca/pub/91-520-x/2010001/t370-eng.htm.

WORKFORCE TRENDS

What do such demographics mean for you and for businesses in the future? In his book *Boom Bust & Echo: Profiting from the Demographic Shift in the 21st Century,* economist and demographer David Foot writes that demographics play a pivotal role in the economic and social life of our country. According to Foot, demographics explain about two-thirds of everything—including which products will be in demand in five years.[54] According to Statistics Canada, by 2031 seniors will account for nearly 25 percent of the Canadian population. This amount will grow to nearly 30 percent by 2056.[55] Immigration and the projected birth rates are not expected to balance the workforce losses created by the aging population, both in Canada and globally.[56] We will discuss some of the human resource management issues related to an aging population in Chapter 12.

Think of the products and services that middle-aged and elderly people will need—anything from travel and recreation to medicine, nursing homes, assisted-living facilities, adult day care, home health care, and the like—and you will see opportunities for successful businesses of the twenty-first century. Don't rule out computer games and online services, even Wii. Don't forget the impact of aging baby boomers; more grandparents with extra money in their pockets will buy extra gifts for their grandchildren. Businesses that cater to older consumers will have the opportunity for exceptional growth in the near future. The market is huge.

Canada boasts enormous ethnic and racial diversity. Its workforce is also widely diverse in terms of age, which means that managers must adapt to the generational demographics of the workplace. In addition to changes in the demand of goods and services the demographic shift also impacts labour supply. What are some challenges of working with someone much younger or much older than you?

MANAGING DIVERSITY[57]

Canada has a strong multicultural population. In the last ten years, it has welcomed close to 2.7 million permanent residents. The high level of annual admission of immigrants and the relatively slow rate of natural growth of the population explain why the proportion of the foreign-born in the Canadian population has been increasing since the 1990s.

Citizenship and Immigration Canada's plan is to admit approximately 250,000 immigrants each year.[58] In order to meet this target, the government manages a number of immigration programs to enable people from other countries to become Canadian citizens. Approximately 62 percent of immigrants come to Canada through economic categories, such as the skilled worker, skilled trade, and business immigrant. The remaining 38 percent gain citizenship through family and humanitarian categories.

While this information is not exhaustive, it should give you an idea of some of the demographic trends that business people track as they develop their products and services. Can you think of some opportunities that are not currently being met as a result of some of these trends?

Progress Assessment

- Describe the components of competition.
- What is empowerment?
- What social trends are evident in Canada?

The Global Environment

The global environment of business is so important that we show it as surrounding all other environmental influences in Figure 1.5. Two important environmental changes in recent years have been the growth of global competition and the increase of free trade among nations.

World trade, or *globalization*, has grown thanks to the development of efficient distribution systems (we'll talk about these later in the text) and communication advances such as the Internet. Globalization has greatly improved living standards around the world. China and India have become major competitors. For example, Lenovo *<http://www.lenovo.com>*, a Chinese firm, bought IBM's PC unit. Shop at Walmart *<http://www.walmart.ca>* and most other retail stores, and you cannot help but notice the number of "Made in China" stickers you see. Call for computer help, and you are as likely to be talking with someone in India as someone in Canada.

World trade has its benefits and costs. You will read much more about its importance in Chapter 3 and in the Reaching Beyond Our Borders boxes in each chapter.

Seeking SUSTAINABILITY

Getting Involved Personally

There are an increasing number of terms that recognize today's preoccupation with how individual and business actions impact us nationally and internationally. Some examples include *carbon footprint* (defined as the impact of human activity measured in terms of the amount of carbon dioxide it causes to be emitted into the atmosphere), *food miles* (the distance travelled from the place where food is produced to the place where it is eaten, considered in terms of the environmental damage that transporting it entails), *green tax* (a tax imposed with the intention of discouraging activities that may damage the environment), and *eco-village* (a small-scale, environmentally friendly settlement designed for sustainable living). There is little doubt humans can take action to protect the environment. What can we do now to start?

It's not necessary to change your lifestyle radically to make a difference. Simply heating or cooling your apartment or house more efficiently is a good start. Why not buy a reusable grocery bag? It is also a good idea to change your light bulbs. A 25-watt compact fluorescent bulb produces about as much light as a 100-watt conventional bulb but uses one-quarter of the energy. You can recycle paper and containers. You can walk or ride a bike instead of driving. You can reduce your use of electrical equipment and of water (pumping water takes a lot of electricity). Buy locally grown produce to save the energy used in shipping food from faraway places. If you are in the market for a car, you could "go green" by buying a hybrid or a small, fuel-efficient car.

In addition to ecological awareness, what else can you do to help keep sustainability on the agenda for business? The environmental movement in Canada relies on citizen action and needs people, such as you, to get involved. Government and foundations will support environmental non-governmental organizations but they do not always make decisions with future generations in mind. Everyone benefits when the environment is protected. That is part of what the green movement is all about.

Sources: Dru Oja Jay, "Where's the democracy in the Environmental Movement?" Kira Vermond, "Is the Environmental Movement Dying?" *Canadian Dimension*, 12 September 2013; *The Globe and Mail*, 30 August, 2011; Mya Frazier, "Who's in Charge of Green?" *Advertising Age*, 9 June 2008; Anne Underwood, "10 Fixes for the Planet," *Newsweek*, 14 April 2008; Rebecca Smith, "A Little Knowledge . . .," *The Wall Street Journal*, 30 June 2008; Arden Dale, "Green Products Gain from New Price Equation," *The Wall Street Journal*, 24 June 2008; and Associated Press, "Wardrobe Malfunction Joins the Credit Crunch," *Toronto Star*, 16 August 2008, www.thestar.com/article/478662.

HOW GLOBAL CHANGES AFFECT YOU

As businesses expand to serve global markets, new jobs will be created in both manufacturing and service industries. Global trade also means global competition. The students who will prosper will be those prepared for the markets of tomorrow. Rapid changes create a need for continuous learning, so be prepared to pursue your education throughout your career. You will have every reason to be optimistic about job opportunities in the future if you prepare yourself well.

THE ECOLOGICAL ENVIRONMENT

Few issues have captured the attention of the international business community more than climate change.[59] **Climate change** is the movement of the temperature of the planet up or down over time. The issue now is global warming. Some of the world's largest firms—including General Electric *<http://www.ge.com/ca>*, Coca-Cola *<http://www.cocacola.ca>*, Shell *<http://www.shell.ca>*, Nestlé *<http://www.nestle.ca>*, DuPont *<http://www2.dupont.com/inclusive-innovations/en-us/gss/sustainability.html>*, Johnson & Johnson *<http://www.jnjcanada.com>*, British Airways *<http://www.britishairways.com>*, and Shanghai Electric *<http://www.shanghai-electric.com/en>*—say the evidence for climate change is overwhelming. Saving energy and producing products that cause less harm to the environment is a trend called **greening**. Greening has become such a pervasive issue that impacts every type of business decisions.

climate change
The movement of the temperature of the planet up or down over time.

greening
The trend toward saving energy and producing products that cause less harm to the environment.

The term **sustainability** has different meanings depending upon the context in which it is used. Social perspectives of sustainability focus upon the quality of human life over time while economic views of sustainability emphasize a steady-state economy.[60] We shall discuss business and sustainability issues in the Seeking Sustainability boxes throughout the text and in Chapter 5.

sustainability
Development that meets the needs of present and future generations.

LO5 Give examples of how the service sector has replaced manufacturing as the principal provider of jobs, but why manufacturing remains vital for Canada.

The Evolution of Canadian Business

Many managers and workers are losing their jobs in major manufacturing firms. Businesses in Canada have become so productive that, compared to the past, fewer workers are needed in industries that produce goods. If global competition and improved technology are putting skilled people out of work, should we be concerned about the prospect of high unemployment rates and low incomes? Where will the jobs be when you graduate? These important questions prompt us to look briefly at the manufacturing and service sectors.

Progress in the Agricultural and Manufacturing Industries

Canada has seen strong economic development since the nineteenth century. The agricultural industry led the way, providing food for Canadians and people in other parts of the world. Inventions such as the harvester and cotton gin did much to make farming successful, as did ongoing improvements to such equipment. The modern farming industry has become so efficient through the use of technology that the number of farms has dropped. Due to increased competition, many of the farms that existed even 50 years ago have been replaced by some huge farms, some merely large farms, and some small but highly specialized farms. The loss of farm workers over the past century is not a negative sign. It is instead an indication that Canadian agricultural workers are more productive.

Most farmers who lost their jobs went to work in factories. The manufacturing industry, much like agriculture, used technology to become more productive. The consequence, as in farming, was the elimination of many jobs. Again, the loss to society is minimal if the wealth created by increased productivity and efficiency creates new jobs elsewhere. This is exactly what has happened over the past 50 years. Many workers in the industrial sector found jobs in the service sector. Most of those who cannot find work today are people who need retraining and education to become qualified for jobs that now exist.

CANADA'S MANUFACTURING INDUSTRY

The goods-producing sector includes the manufacturing, construction, utilities, agriculture, forestry, fishing, mining, quarrying, and the oil and gas industries. Of this sector, manufacturing employs just under ten percent of Canada's working population, as noted in Figure 1.8. Manufacturing is diverse in Canada and it includes food, beverage, clothing, chemical, machinery, wood, and petroleum and coal products manufacturing.[61]

Tens of thousands of Canadian jobs were lost in the late 2000s. The rising Canadian dollar and increasing global competition were two of the reasons for these losses. Despite such losses, manufacturing still remains an important contributor to the Canadian economy.

The Canadian Manufacturers & Exporters highlights some of the reasons why this sector is important to Canada:

- Employs 1.8 million Canadian and represented 10.5 percent of the workforce in 2012;[62]
- Generates $3.15 in economic spin-off of every for every $1.00 in manufacturing output;[63]
- 45 percent of manufacturers and exporters foresee a 1 to 10 percent rise in their workforce;[64] and
- 59 percent of manufacturers and exporters plan to increase research and development investments.[65]

■ **FIGURE 1.8**

THE IMPORTANCE OF THE SERVICES-PRODUCING AND GOODS-PRODUCING SECTORS IN CANADA		
Canada is a service economy, where the majority of jobs are generated in the services-providing sector. This table highlights the importance of each sector, as well as the three largest-employer industries in each.		
	Number of Employed (thousands)	Total Workforce (percent)
Total Employed in Canada	17,802.2	100.0
Services-Producing Sector	13,905.1	78
Trade	2,729.3	15.3
Health Care and Social Assistance	2,219.7	12.5
Professional, Scientific & Technical Services	1,333.3	7.5
Goods-Producing Sector	3,897.1	22
Manufacturing	1,711	9.6
Construction	1,371.5	7.7
Forestry, Fishing, Mining, Quarrying, Oil & Gas	372.6	2

Source: Statistics Canada. Table 282-0008 - Labour force survey estimates (LFS), by North American Industry Classification System (NAICS), sex and age group, annual (persons unless otherwise noted), CANSIM Accessed on March 4, 2015 from http://www5.statcan.gc.ca/cansim /pick-choisir?lang=eng&p2=33&id=2820008.

While the manufacturing sector is much smaller today than it was 25 years ago, it is still clearly an integral part of our business economy. We will discuss the manufacturing sector and production in more detail in Chapter 10.

The entire process of growing food and getting it to our tables is so smooth that it's easy to take the agriculture industry for granted. But behind those well-stocked supermarkets is an army of farmers and distributors who supply our needs. The use of technology has led to increased productivity and made farmers more efficient, resulting in larger farms. This trend has meant less expensive food for us, but a continual reduction in the number of small, family-run farms. Is it still possible for small farms to be successful, and if so, how?

Progress in Service Industries

In the past, the dominant industries in Canada produced goods such as steel, railroads, and machine tools. The shift in Canada's employment profile began slowly in the early twentieth century, and has accelerated rapidly since the 1950s. Today, the leading firms are in services (such as legal, health, telecommunications, entertainment, financial services, etc.). As noted in Figure 1.8, the services-producing sector employs 78 percent of the working population.

There are several reasons why there has been growth in this sector. First, technological improvements have enabled businesses to reduce their payrolls while increasing their output. Since staffing has been downsized by many companies, business has become more complex and specialized companies have relied more heavily on outside services firms. Secondly, as large manufacturing companies seek to become more efficient, they contract out an increasing number of services, creating more opportunities for business people. Other service firms have risen or expanded rapidly to provide traditional services that used to be performed by women at home. Since many women have entered the workforce, there is increased demand for food preparation, child care, and household maintenance, to name just a few services.

Chances are very high that you will work in a service job at some point in your career. Another bit of good news is that there are *more* high-paying jobs in the services-producing sector than in the goods-producing sector. High-paying service-sector jobs abound in health care, accounting, finance, entertainment, telecommunications, architecture, law, software engineering, and more. Projections are that some areas of the service sector will grow rapidly, while others may have much slower growth. Figure 1.9 lists many service-sector jobs; look it over to see where the careers of the future are likely to be. Retailers like SportChek <*http://www.sportchek.ca*> are part of the service sector. Each new retail store can create managerial jobs for post-secondary graduates.

■ **FIGURE 1.9**

WHAT IS THE SERVICE SECTOR?

There's much talk about the service sector, but few discussions actually list what it includes. Here is a representative list of services as classified by the government:

Lodging Services

Hotels, rooming houses, and other lodging places
Sporting and recreation camps
Trailer parks and campsites for transients

Personal Services

Laundries	Child care
Linen supply	Shoe repair
Diaper service	Funeral homes
Carpet cleaning	Tax preparation
Photographic studios	Beauty shops
Health clubs	

Business Services

Accounting	Exterminating
Ad agencies	Employment agencies
Collection agencies	Computer programming
Commercial photography	Research & development labs
Commercial art	Management services
Stenographic services	Public relations
Window cleaning	Detective agencies
Consulting	Interior design
Equipment rental	Web design
Tax preparation	Trash collection

Automotive Repair Services and Garages

Auto rental	Tire retreading
Truck rental	Exhaust system shops
Parking lots	Car washes
Paint shops	Transmission repair

Miscellaneous Repair Services

Radio and television	Welding
Watch	Sharpening
Reupholstery	Septic tank cleaning

Motion Picture Industry

Production	Theatres
Distribution	Drive-ins

Amusement and Recreation Services

Restaurants	Racetracks
Symphony orchestras	Golf courses
Pool halls	Amusement parks
Bowling alleys	Carnivals
Fairs	Ice skating rinks
Botanical gardens	Circuses
Video rentals	Infotainment

Health Services

Physicians	Nursery care
Dentists	Medical labs
Chiropractors	Dental labs

Legal Services

Educational Services

Libraries	Computer schools
Schools	Online schools

Social Services

Child care	Family services
Job training	Elder care

Noncommercial Museums, Art Galleries, and Botanical and Zoological Gardens

Selected Membership Organizations

Business associations	Civic associations

Financial Services

Banking	Real estate agencies
Insurance	Investment firms (brokers)

Miscellaneous Services

Architectural	Surveying
Engineering	Utilities
Telecommunications	Lawn care
Vending	Delivery

The strategy for graduates is to remain flexible, find out where jobs are being created, and move when appropriate. Such was the case for Edmonton-based FourQuest Energy <*http://www.fourquest .com*>, which was singled out by PROFIT 200 as Canada's Fastest-Growing Company. The company provides mechanical precommissioning, shutdown, and maintenance services for oil-and-gas facilities. "I just felt the business had such a great probability of success. I couldn't see any potential for failure if we could just get it started." says Nik Grgic, President. He and fellow entrepreneur, Karl Gannon, Executive Vice President, decided it was worth abandoning a steady paycheque with a multinational energy firm to start this company.[66]

Your Future in Business

Despite the growth in the service sector, the service era now seems to be coming to a close as a new era is beginning. We are now in the midst of an information-based global revolution that will alter all sectors of the economy. It's exciting to think about the role you will play in that revolution. You may be a leader; that is, you may be one of the people who will implement the changes and accept the challenges of world competition based on world quality standards. This book will introduce you to some of the concepts that will make such leadership possible, not just in business but also in government agencies and non-profit organizations. Business cannot prosper in the future without the co-operation of government and social leaders throughout the world.

Progress Assessment

- What changes have affected the global environment?
- Give examples of how the service sector has replaced manufacturing as the principal provider of jobs, but why manufacturing remains vital for Canada.
- Why is the services-producing sector important to the economy?

SUMMARY

LO1 **Illustrate the importance of key business fundamentals to wealth generation.**
A business is any activity that seeks to provide goods and services to others while operating at a profit.

What are the relationships between risk, profit, and loss?
Profit is money a business earns above and beyond the money that it spends for salaries and other expenses. Business people make profits by taking risks. *Risk* is the chance an entrepreneur takes of losing time and money on a business that may not prove profitable. A loss occurs when a business's costs and expenses are higher than its revenues.

LO2 **Illustrate the importance of stakeholders and non-profit organizations to business activities.**

Stakeholders include customers, employees, stockholders, suppliers, dealers, bankers, the media, people in the local community, environmentalists, and elected government leaders. The goal of business leaders is to try to recognize and respond to the needs of these stakeholders and still make a profit.

How do non-profit organizations differ from profit-seeking organizations?

A non-profit organization is an organization whose goals do not include making a personal profit for its owners or organizers.

Which stakeholders are most important to a business?

The goal of business leaders is to try to balance the needs of all stakeholders and still make a profit. Some businesses put the needs of shareholders above the other interests, but most businesses today seek a balance among the needs of the various stakeholders.

LO3 **Explain how entrepreneurship is critical to the wealth of an economy, and list the five factors of production that contribute to wealth.**

Working for others means getting benefits like paid vacations and health insurance. Entrepreneurs are people who risk time and money to start and manage a business. They gain the freedom to make their own decisions, more opportunity, and possible wealth.

What are the five factors of production?

Businesses use five factors of production: land (natural resources), labour (workers), capital goods (buildings and machinery), entrepreneurship, and knowledge. Of these, the most important are entrepreneurship and knowledge, because without them land, labour, and capital are not of much use. What makes rich countries rich today is a combination of *entrepreneurship* and the effective use of *knowledge*.

LO4 **State the six elements that make up the business environment and explain why the business environment is important to organizations.**

The business environment consists of the surrounding factors that either help or hinder the development of businesses. The six elements are the legal environment, the economic environment, the technological environment, the competitive environment, the social environment, and the global environment.

The legal environment in influenced by government who may allow private ownership of businesses, pass laws that enable business people to write contracts that are enforceable in court, establish a currency that is tradable in world markets, help to lessen corruption in business and government, and keep taxes and regulations to a minimum. From a business perspective, lower taxes mean lower risks, more growth, and thus more money for workers and the government.

Technology enables workers to be more effective, efficient, and productive. *Effectiveness* means doing the right thing in the right way. *Efficiency* means producing items using the least amount of resources. *Productivity* is the amount of output you generate given the amount of input (e.g., hours worked).

Within the social environment, diversity has come to mean much more than recruiting and keeping minority and female employees. Diversity efforts now include seniors, disabled people, people with different sexual orientations, atheists, extroverts, introverts, married people, singles, and the devout. Managing diversity means dealing sensitively with workers and cultures around the world.

Explain why the business environment is important to organizations.

Scanning the business environment on a continual basis is important to organizations so that they can take advantage of trends. These trends could affect the organization's ability to achieve its objectives, steer clear of threats, or take advantage of new opportunities.

LO5 **Give examples of how the service sector has replaced manufacturing as the principal provider of jobs, but why manufacturing remains vital for Canada.**

Canada has evolved from an economy based on manufacturing to one based on services.

Why is manufacturing still a vital industry for Canada?

While the services-producing sector employs almost 78 percent of the working population, the manufacturing industry employs approximately 9.6 percent of workers. Every $1 of manufacturing in Canada generates $3.15 in total economic activity. Forty-five percent of manufacturers foresee a growth in their workforce and nearly 60 percent plan to increase research and development investment.

KEY TERMS

baby boomers	factors of production	productivity
business	Generation Y	profit
business environment	Generation Z	quality of life
climate change	goods	regulations
crowdsourcing	greening	revenue
database	identity theft	risk
demography	insourcing	services
e-business	loss	stakeholders
e-commerce	non-profit organization	standard of living
empowerment	offshoring	sustainability
entrepreneur	outsourcing	technology

CRITICAL THINKING

Imagine that you are thinking of starting a restaurant in your community. Answer the following questions.

1. Who will be the various stakeholders of your business?

2. You need to consider whether you will purchase locally grown produce versus foreign-grown produce. What are the advantages and disadvantages of using either, especially if the foreign-grown produce is cheaper or of better quality?

3. What are some of the things you could do to benefit your community other than provide jobs and generate tax revenue?

4. You are considering paying your employees the minimum wage. Do you think that you would attract better employees if your wages were higher?

5. How might you be affected by the six environmental factors outlined in this chapter? Which factor(s) might have the biggest impact on your business?

DEVELOPING WORKPLACE SKILLS

Key: ● **Team**   ★ **Analytic**   ▲ **Communication**   ▣ **Technology**

● ★
▣ ▲ **1.** Make a list of non-profit organizations in your community that might offer you a chance to learn some of the skills you will need in the job you hope to have when you graduate. How could you make time in your schedule to volunteer or work at one or more of those organizations? Write a letter to a non-profit organization to inquire about such opportunities. Hint: You can identify organizations and events in your city by going to 411 Local Search *<http://www.411.ca>* and inputting "non-profit organizations and events *your city name*" in the cell under Business, near the top. A less targeted source is the Charity Village website *<http://www.charityvillage.com>*. Charity Village supports Canada's charities and non-profit organizations as well as the stakeholders who support them.

● ★ **2.** Form into teams of four or five and discuss creating an entirely new product or service. What value does this new product or service create? Who are the stakeholders for this new product or service? Could an entrepreneur readily produce it or would its chance of success be higher if it was produced by a large company? Explain.

▣ ★ **3.** Imagine that you are a local business person who has to deal with the various issues involved with outsourcing. You want to begin with the facts. How many jobs have been lost to outsourcing in your area, if any? Are there any foreign firms in your area that are creating jobs (insourcing)? You will need to use the Internet to find the data you need.

● ▣
▲ **4.** Form into teams of four or five and discuss the technological and e-commerce revolutions. How many students now shop for goods and services online? What have been their experiences? What other high-tech equipment do they use to make purchases (smartphones, tablets, laptops, etc.)? What products do they plan on buying in the next year?

ANALYZING MANAGEMENT DECISIONS

Canada's Fastest-Growing Companies

Every year, *PROFIT* magazine publishes a list of Canada's fastest-growing companies. The importance of many of the points we discussed in this chapter is evident in a recent issue, especially when one considers the breakdown among the types of companies. Services providers dominate the marketplace, which reinforces that Canada is a service economy. Here is a breakdown of the Top 100:

Focus	Number of Firms
Information Technology	17
Manufacturing	17
Construction	8
Marketing and media	7
Industrial Services	7
Retail	7
Consumer services	6

(continued)

(continued)

Focus	Number of Firms
Human Resources Services	6
Software development	6
Financial Services	4
Professional Services	4
Telecommunications	4
Transportation and Logistics	3
Wholesale/distribution	3
Agriculture	1

While the companies were located across Canada, Ontario continued to support the largest share of these companies:

Province/Territory	Number of Firms
Ontario	55
Alberta	16
British Columbia	12
Quebec	12
Saskatchewan	2
Manitoba	1
Nova Scotia	1
Northwest Territories	1

What makes these companies leaders is that they grew rapidly, with a minimum revenue growth of 663 percent over the past five years. It does not matter whether they are high-tech or old-economy companies, manufacturing or service companies, they all are exceptional. A remarkable assortment of products and services are offered by these companies. Examples include oil and gas services, gummy-based vitamins, English-as-a-second-language schools, experiential marketing, mobile applications and analytics, biopharmaceuticals, hospitality and travel services, and residential roofing and siding.

Source: Deborah Aarts, "A Look Inside Canada's Fastest-Growing Companies," *PROFIT*, 12 June 12 2014, http://www.profitguide.com/microsite /profit500/2014; *Canadian Business*, 87 no. 7, July 2014, 83–103.

Discussion Questions

1. Which of these data support the information discussed in the chapter? Explain your answer.
2. Why do certain provinces or regions have so many (e.g., Ontario) or few (e.g., Atlantic Canada) companies?
3. Review the most recent edition of PROFIT 200 for information on the companies that have made the list. Are there any surprises? How much has changed since these results were posted?

VIDEO CASE 1

No Clowning Around—Cirque du Soleil

Several themes were introduced in this first chapter, including the importance of entrepreneurship to the success of the overall economy, the need for entrepreneurs to take risks (and the greater the risk, the higher the profit may be), and the dynamic business environment and the challenges it presents. Few organizations in today's society are more indicative of the new challenges than Cirque du Soleil <*https://www.cirquedusoleil.com*>.

First, Guy Laliberté took a huge risk by challenging the established circus tradition. The elaborate shows are expensive to start, and the talent must be the best in the world. But the risk pays off big time with sales of almost a billion dollars per year. Cirque du Soleil creates thousands of new jobs and contributes greatly to the communities it serves. It does this not only through the taxes it pays, but also through community outreach programs. Because of its entertainment value, Cirque contributes to both standard of living (through the taxes it pays) and the quality of life (the fun it provides for citizens of all ages).

Like all organizations, Cirque du Soleil has many stakeholders. They include the owners, the employees, and the local community. The organization is especially focused on the stakeholder group called customers. It wants to put on the best show possible, and that means providing the best talent in the best locations. To reach as many people as possible, many of the shows go on the road. You can even watch some of the shows on TV.

The business environment presents many challenges for Cirque du Soleil, as it does for all businesses. The economic and legal environment of Canada greatly supports entrepreneurs like Laliberté. The technological environment in Canada and the United States is also supportive of new business ventures. No circus in the past came close to the elaborate technological devices used by Cirque du Soleil. The stage for one of the Cirque productions in Las Vegas, for example, is a huge pool that delights the audience with its ability to change from a place where the actors can seem to walk on water to one where they can dive from many feet above it.

The social environment is also conducive to new businesses. The variety of the Canadian population has contributed greatly to the ability of the circus to find diverse acts and to recruit acts from around the world. The ability of the organization to adapt to many cultures is shown by its success in various cities throughout the world.

Of course, success is likely to breed much competition, and Cirque has its share. Even traditional circuses are tending to offer more exciting programs that reflect what Cirque has been doing for years. Competition is good for business, as it prompts all businesses to offer the best products possible.

One of the best things about this video is that it allows you to see part of Cirque du Soleil in action. If you have never seen a Cirque show, search one out—if only on TV. It is exciting and fun, and it shows that entrepreneurship is alive and well and providing wonderful new services. The result is profits for the owners and a better quality of life for us.

Discussion Questions

1. Guy Laliberté is an example of an entrepreneur that found an opportunity within a changing business environment. What are other lessons that you can take from this video that might result in an entrepreneur's success?

2. What are some of the challenges and opportunities you can identify for Cirque du Soleil in the six elements of today's dynamic business environment?

3. How would you compare the excitement and fun of working for a new entrepreneurial venture like Cirque du Soleil with working for a large, traditional business? What are the risks? The rewards? The challenges?

How Economic Issues Affect Business

LEARNING OBJECTIVES

After you have read and studied this chapter, you should be able to:

LO1   Describe basic economics.

LO2   Explain what capitalism is and how free markets work.

LO3   Compare the benefits and negative consequences of socialism and communism.

LO4   Describe the mixed economy of Canada.

LO5   Illustrate the significance of key economic indicators and the business cycle.

PROFILE

GETTING TO KNOW: MATT FLANNERY

People talk about the state of "the economy" so much that it can seem as if economics only deals with big, world-shaking financial issues. In reality, though, economics can be found all around us in daily life. From a family saving money for the future to a major corporation measuring its revenue, the world is full of economies both large and small.

It's these small economies that are the major concern of Matt Flannery, co-founder and CEO of the microlending company Kiva <*http://www.kiva.org*>. His company offers small loans to entrepreneurs working in developing countries in Africa, Asia, and South America, as well as to borrowers in more established nations in North America and Europe. Unlike business people operating in the United States, these entrepreneurs don't need thousands upon thousands of dollars to see their dreams become reality. Instead, many loans issued by Kiva are little more than a few hundred dollars.

But it's not the size of the loans that makes Flannery's work notable. In fact, microlending has been a common source of financing for the developing world since the early 1980s. What sets Kiva apart from the rest is the company's approach. Kiva operates in a similar way to crowdfunding sites like Kickstarter <*http://www.kickstarter.com*> or Indiegogo <*http://www.indiegogo.com*>. These companies rely on small

Source: Photos by @jibees for LeWeb11 Conference @ Les Docks-Paris /https://www.flickr.com/photos/leweb3/6491865213/07/23/14

donations from many people in order to fund a larger goal. At Kiva, users first go to the site to select the person or family they'd like to fund. Next, they lend $25 to the entrepreneur of their choice. If the funding goal is reached, then Kiva covers the loan arranged by field partners who work with the entrepreneurs. The borrowers gradually make repayments to the field partners who transfers them back to Kiva so it may distribute the money back to the lenders. Although lenders don't earn any interest, the satisfaction of helping another human being thousands of miles away is enough to ensure that 70 percent of all lenders make another loan.

Flannery took a winding road to reach this point in his career. Interestingly enough, other than Kiva, he doesn't have any previous background in either financing or the non-profit sector. After getting a degree from Stanford University, Flannery got a job developing software at TiVo <http://www.tivo.com>, but he really wanted a business of his own. "I tried to start maybe ten companies," says Flannery. "It was like I had a midlife crisis at 22." For example, Flannery attempted to start a DVD-rental machine business years before Redbox existed. He also tried his hand at starting an online luxury clothes rental company. "A lot of those other ideas for me were a little empty . . . they weren't proactive movements towards something I loved. This idea is different. The actual content of the idea I enjoy every day . . . this is my dream job."

The inspiration for Kiva didn't hit him until he spent a few months working in rural communities throughout Africa. The impact of small businesses on the communities Flannery visited made a profound impression on him. Kiva launched in 2005, after he spent a year researching the aid industry and talking with experts. Today Kiva has distributed more than $500 million in loans to entrepreneurs throughout the world. "Small loans used for business growth encourage self-respect, accountability, and hope among loan recipients," says Flannery. "Primarily, the challenges they [entrepreneurs in Africa] face are very similar to the challenges we face . . . a story about a woman selling fish on the side of the street in Uganda, you can get into profit margins, inventory management, the same things that businesses here think about. There's a commonality that can unify people. Which is exciting."

Many people don't realize the importance of the economic environment to the success of business. That is what this chapter is all about. You will learn to compare different economic systems to see the benefits and the drawbacks of each. You will learn how the free-market system of Canada works. And you will learn more about what makes some countries rich and other countries poor. By the end of the chapter, you should understand the direct effect economic systems have on the wealth and happiness of communities throughout the world.

Sources: Mohana Ravindranath, "Microfinance Nonprofit Kiva Launches in D.C.," The *Washington Post*, 8 January 2013; Interview, "Why Purpose Matters For Matt Flannery of Kiva.org," Yscouts, 11 September 2013; Charles Blass, "Matt Flannery: Co-Founder and CEO, Kiva Microfunds," Thefuturemakers. net, 2 May 2013; and www.kiva.org.

How Economic Conditions Affect Business

If you want to understand the underlying situation and conditions in which Canadian businesses operate, it is essential that you (1) have some grasp of economics, (2) be aware of the impact of the global environment, and (3) understand the role of the federal and provincial governments in Canada.

The Canadian economy is an integral part of the world economy. Business firms use labour from other countries, export to and import from other countries, buy land in other countries for their facilities, and receive money from foreign investors. To understand events in the Canadian economy, therefore, one has to understand the world economy.

Why is South Korea comparatively wealthy and North Korea suffering economically, with many of its people starving? Why is China's income per person lower than Taiwan's? Such questions are part of the subject of economics. In this chapter, we explore the various economic systems of the world and how they either promote or hinder business growth, the creation of wealth, and a higher quality of life for all.

A major part of business success is due to an economic and social climate that allows businesses to operate freely. Foreign investors like Canada because we have a stable economic and political environment. Investing is risky enough without having to worry about unpredictable governments, massive corruption, and weak laws. Therefore, any change in our economic or political system can have a major influence on businesses.

Global economics and global politics also have a major influence on businesses in Canada. For example, there is even some talk today about rewriting international tax rules.[1] For example, a one-time global wealth tax was proposed by the International Monetary Fund (IMF).[2] The idea is to tax the wealth of individuals around the world by 10 percent to bring the debt of nations closer to the pre-recession levels. Think of how such a tax would affect businesses and workers in Canada. Clearly, to understand business, you must also understand basic economics and politics. This is especially true of new post-secondary graduates looking for jobs.

LO1   Describe basic economics.

What Is Economics?

Economics is the study of how society chooses to employ resources to produce goods and services and distribute them for consumption among various competing groups and individuals. Remember from Chapter 1 that these resources (land, labour, capital goods, entrepreneurship, and knowledge) are called *factors of production.*

> **economics**
> The study of how society chooses to employ resources to produce goods and services and distribute them for consumption among various competing groups and individuals.

The economic contrast is remarkable. Business is booming in Seoul, South Korea (as shown in the top photo). But North Korea, a communist country, is not doing well, as the picture on the bottom shows. What do you think accounts for the dramatic differences in the economies of these two neighbouring countries?

Businesses may contribute to an economic system by inventing products that greatly increase available resources. For example, businesses may discover new energy sources, new ways of growing food, and new ways of creating needed goods and services.[3] Ballard Power Systems <*http://www.ballard .com*>, a global leader in the design, development, and manufacture of hydrogen fuel cells, is doing just this. Among other initiatives, Ballard is working with auto manufacturers to develop the next generation of efficient and clean engines for buses, automobiles, and trucks.[4]

Your buying behaviour falls under the study of microeconomics. How does understanding spending patterns benefit a country's economy?

There are two major branches of economics: **macroeconomics** looks at the operation of a nation's economy as a whole, and **microeconomics** looks at the behaviour of people and organizations in particular markets.[5] For example, while macroeconomics looks at how many jobs exist in the whole economy, microeconomics examines how many people will be hired in a particular industry or a particular region of the country. Topics discussed in this chapter that are part of macroeconomics include gross domestic product, unemployment rate, and price indexes. Chapter topics that deal with microeconomic issues include pricing and supply and demand.

> **macroeconomics**
> The part of economic study that looks at the operation of a nation's economy as a whole.
>
> **microeconomics**
> The part of economic study that looks at the behaviour of people and organizations in particular markets.

Some economists define economics as the allocation of "scarce" resources. They believe that resources are scarce and that they need to be carefully divided among people, usually by the government. There's no way to maintain peace and prosperity in the world by merely dividing the resources we have today among the existing nations. There are not enough known resources available to do that. **Resource development** is the study of how to increase resources (say by getting oil from shale and oil sands) and to create the conditions that will make better use of them (like recycling and oil conservation).[6]

> **resource development**
> The study of how to increase resources and the creation of the conditions that will make better use of those resources (e.g., recycling).

Businesses can contribute to an economic system by inventing products that greatly increase available resources. For example, they can discover new energy sources (natural gas for autos), new ways of growing food (hydroponics), and new ways of creating needed goods and services such as nano-technology and 4D technology (moving 3D, with time as the fourth dimension). Aquaculture, or raising fish in pens out in the ocean, could lead to more food for everyone and more employment. It is believed that Canada could become one of the world's top three aquaculture producers with an industry value of approximately $6.6 billion annually.[7]

New ways of producing goods and services add resources to the economy and create more employment. Fish farms, for instance, create both food and jobs. Can you think of other innovations that can help increase economic development?

The Secret to Creating a Wealthy Economy

Imagine the world when kings and queens and other rich landowners had most of the wealth, and the majority of the people were peasants. The peasants had many children, and it may have seemed a natural conclusion that if the situation continued as usual there would soon be too many people and not enough food and other resources. Economist Thomas Malthus made this argument in the late 1700s and early 1800s, leading the writer Thomas Carlyle to call economics "the dismal science."

Followers of Malthus today (who are called neo-Malthusians) still believe there are too many people in the world and that the solution to poverty is radical birth control, including forced abortions and sterilization.[8] The latest world statistics, however, show population increasing more slowly than expected. In some industrial countries—like Japan, Germany, Italy, and Russia—population growth may be so slow that eventually there will be too many old people and too few young people to care for them.[9] In the developing world, on the other hand, population will climb relatively quickly and may lead to greater poverty and more unrest. Studies about the effects of population growth on the economy are part of macroeconomics.

Some macroeconomists believe that a large population, especially an educated one, can be a valuable resource. You've probably heard the saying "Give a man a fish and you feed him for a day, but teach a man to fish and you feed him for a lifetime." You can add to that: "Teach a person to start a fish farm, and he or she will be able to feed a village for a lifetime." *The secret to economic development is contained in this last statement.* Business owners provide jobs and economic growth for their employees and communities as well as for themselves.[10]

The challenge for macroeconomists is to determine what makes some countries relatively wealthy and other countries relatively poor, and then to implement policies and programs that lead to increased prosperity for everyone in all countries. One way to begin understanding this challenge is to consider the theories of Adam Smith.

Seeking SUSTAINABILITY

2015 Pan Am and Parapan Am Is LEEDing the Way

The 2015 Pan Am and Parapan Am Games in Toronto represent an important legacy for each of the 16 southwestern Ontario communities hosting the event. Ten new, world-class facilities were built including an athletics stadium, aquatics centre and field house, velodrome, and soccer stadium. A key part of the host committee mission is to leave a Games legacy of sustainable excellence. To meet this goal, Games organizers wanted each venue to be environmentally friendly. The $674 million Pan Am/Parapan Am Games infrastructure budget included building requirements that ensured environmental factors. Each building is Leadership in Energy and Environmental Design (LEED) certified, which means the buildings focus on healthy indoor environments, reduce greenhouse gas emissions, and efficiently use energy, water, and other resources. Since 2004, the Canada Green Building Council has certified over 1,800 LEED buildings and registered over 5,000 in Canada.

Bouygues Building Canada <http://www.bouyguesbuildingcanada.com> built three venues: the Milton velodrome, the Hamilton soccer stadium, and the York University rugby stadium, in a joint venture with Kenaidan Contracting <http://www.kenaidan.com> and Infrastructure Ontario <http://www.infrastructureontario.ca>. Each venue has LEED certification, reflecting Canada's goal for the Games to be completely "green" and carbon neutral. The projects include the use of materials with low volatile organic compound emissions, indoor air quality controls, and waste sorting and recycling. The Markham PanAm Centre complies with FLAP (Fatal Light Awareness Program) guidelines for Bird-Friendly buildings.

"It's important when you design venues for international games to create a legacy use," says Bob Fatovic, Vice President of Cannon Design <http://www.cannondesign.com>, the architect of record on all three projects. "The re-use of all of these venues after the games was the impetus to fund these projects." The athlete's village, which housed 10,000 athletes, coaches, and team officials during the competition, is earmarked as a mixed-use neighbourhood with affordable housing, new condominiums, a YMCA and college dormitory. The massive scale of major international sport events means governments and communities must pay greater attention to the "triple bottom line": "people, planet and profits" of hosting an event of this kind.

Are new facilities, such as arenas, pools, recreation centres, and libraries being built in your community? Does sustainability pay a role in the decisions and plans made by your city council?

Sources: 2015 PanAm/ParapanAm Games; http://www.toronto2015.org/; Canada Green Building Council, http://www.cagbc .org; Backgrounder: PanAmerican Aquatics Centre, Field House and Canadian Sport Institute Project, 1 June 2011, http://www .infrastructureontario.ca/uploadedFiles/PAAC%20-%20Pre-Qualified%20Bidder%20-%20Backgrounder%20-%20Final%20%28Revised%29 .pdf; Bouygues Building Canada-PanAm Games Facilities, http://www.buildingandconstruction-canada.com/index.php/sections /community/586-bouygues-building-canada-panam-games-facilities.

Growth Economics and Adam Smith

Rather than believing that fixed resources had to be divided among competing groups and individuals, Scottish economist Adam Smith envisioned creating more resources so that everyone could become wealthier. The year was 1776. Adam Smith's book, *An Inquiry into the Nations and Causes of the Wealth of Nations* (simply called *The Wealth of Nations*), was later considered the foundation of the study and understanding of the newly developing capitalist industrial society.

Smith believed that *freedom* was vital to the survival of any economy, especially the freedom to own land or property and the freedom to keep profits from working the land or owning a business.[11] He believed that people will work hard if they have incentives for doing so—that is, if they know that they will be rewarded. According to Smith, as long as farmers, labourers, and business people (entrepreneurs) could see economic rewards for their efforts (i.e., receive enough money in the form of profits to support their families), they would work long hours and work hard. As a result of these efforts, the economy would prosper—with plenty of food and all kinds of products available to everyone. Smith's ideas were later challenged by Malthus and others who believed economic conditions would only get worse, but Smith is considered the *father of modern economics*.

How Businesses Benefit the Community

In Adam Smith's view, business people do not necessarily deliberately set out to help others. They work primarily for their own prosperity and growth. Yet as people try to improve their own situation in life, Smith said, their efforts serve as an "invisible hand" that helps the economy grow and prosper through the production of needed goods, services, and ideas. Thus, the **invisible hand** turns self-directed gain into social and economic benefits for *all*.

> **invisible hand**
> A phrase coined by Adam Smith to describe the process that turns self-directed gain into social and economic benefits for all.

How is it that people working in their own self-interest produce goods, services, and wealth for others? The only way farmers in a given area can become wealthy is to sell some of their crops to others. To become even wealthier, farmers would have to hire workers to produce more food. As a consequence, people in that area would have plenty of food available and some would have jobs on the farms. So the farmers' self-centred efforts to become wealthy lead to jobs for some and food for almost all. Stop and think about that process for a minute because it is critical to your understanding of economic growth in Canada and other countries in the world. The same principle applies to other products as well—everything from clothing to houses to iPhones.

Smith assumed that as people became wealthier, they would naturally reach out to help the less fortunate in the community. That has not always happened. In fact today there is a great disparity between the amount of money the wealthy have and the amount of money poor people have.[12] This is called "inequality" and is the central concern of many political, religious, and social leaders today.[13] Many business people are becoming more concerned about social issues and their obligation to return to society some of what they have earned.[14] The economic question is: What can and should we do about poverty and unemployment in Canada and around the world?

As we mentioned in Chapter 1, it is important for businesses to be ethical as well as generous. Unethical practices undermine the whole economic system. The Making Ethical Decisions box explores the tensions that may arise between business and society in a free market economy.

According to Adam Smith's theory, business owners are motivated to work hard because they know they will earn, and keep, the rewards of their labour. When they prosper, as the owner of this restaurant has, they are able to add employees and grow, indirectly helping the community and the larger economy grow in the process. What might motivate you to start your own business?

Making ETHICAL DECISIONS

Smokers Need Not Apply

Companies set numerous rules that guide employee conduct in the workplace. But a new trend has emerged—one that tells people how they should behave even before they work for a company. It's called a "smokers need not apply" hiring policy and many businesses are using it as a way to promote a healthy working environment and reduce group insurance premiums.

What might be the ramifications of an applicant being turned away from prospective work on the grounds of being a smoker? Is smoking a right that should be protected? Is the policy discriminatory? Should business tell society how to behave in a free market economy?

Progress Assessment

- What is the difference between macroeconomics and microeconomics?
- What does Adam Smith's term *invisible hand* mean? How does the invisible hand create wealth for a country?

LO2   Explain what capitalism is and how free markets work.

Understanding Free-Market Capitalism

Basing their ideas on free-market principles, such as those of Adam Smith, business people began to create more wealth than had ever been created before. They hired others to work on their farms and in their factories and nations began to prosper as a result. Business people soon became the wealthiest people in society. While there were great disparities between the wealthy and the poor, there was always the promise of opportunities to become wealthy.

The economic system that has led to wealth creation in much of the world is known as capitalism. Under **capitalism**, all or most of the factors of production and distribution—such as land, factories, railroads, and stores—are owned by individuals (i.e., not owned by the government). They are operated for profit, and business people, not government officials, decide what to produce and how much, what to charge, and how much to pay workers. They also decide whether to produce goods in their own countries or have them made in other countries. Capitalism is the popular term used to describe free-market economies.

> **capitalism**
> An economic system in which all or most of the factors of production and distribution are privately owned and operated for profit.

No country is purely capitalist, however. Often the government gets involved in issues such as determining minimum wages and subsidizing certain sectors, as the federal government does in Canada for the agriculture sector. Today, capitalism is the foundation for the economies of Canada, England, Australia, the United States, and most other developed nations. We will discuss Canada's mixed economy in some detail later in this book.

Capitalism, like all economic systems, has its faults, and income inequality is a major issue that concerns many today. However, John Mackey, CEO of Whole Foods, believes that "conscious capitalism," that is, capitalism based on businesses that serve all major stakeholders, is the best system in the world.[15] Here is what he says about capitalism: "In the long arc of history, no human creation has had a greater positive impact on more people more rapidly than free-enterprise capitalism. . . . This system has afforded billions of us the opportunity to join in the great enterprise of earning our sustenance and finding meaning by creating value for each other."[16]

The root word of *capitalism* is "capital." The Chapter Profile and Spotlight on Small Business box show how a little capital can help small businesses grow in the poorest countries of the world.

A free-market system is evident at a farmer's market. As a buyer, what can you do to ensure that you pay the best price for produce?

How Free Markets Work

The free market is one in which decisions about what to produce and in what quantities are made by the market—that is, by buyers and sellers negotiating prices for goods and services. Consumers (such as you and me) send signals to tell producers what to make, how many, in what colours, and so on. We do that by choosing to buy (or not to buy) certain goods and services. Note that just as no country is purely capitalist, no market is truly free. "Free" markets work not just from the interaction of buyers and sellers, but also from government signals (e.g., laws and regulations, taxes, warnings, advice, etc.).

The economic concept of demand measures the quantities of goods and services that people are willing to buy at a given price. All else equal, the lower the price, the higher the demand will be. Do you think there would be this many customers rushing to shop on Boxing Day if it wasn't for those low price/low quantity deals?

How Prices Are Determined

In a free market, prices are not determined by sellers; they are determined by buyers and sellers negotiating in the marketplace. A seller may want to receive $50 for a T-shirt, but the quantity demanded at that price may be quite low. If the seller lowers the price, the quantity demanded is likely to increase. How is a price that is acceptable to both buyers and sellers determined? The answer is found in the microeconomic concepts of supply and demand.

Spotlight *On* SMALL BUSINESS

The Key to Capitalism Is Capital

FINCA (the Foundation for International Community Assistance) <http://www.FINCACanada.org> is a non-profit organization whose mission is to alleviate poverty through lasting solutions that help people build assets, create jobs, and raise their standard of living. Their vision is to build a global network of sustainable and scalable social enterprises that improve lives worldwide.

FINCA offers small loans, savings, and other financial services to those often turned down by traditional banks. With microloans, families can invest in and build their own small businesses and increase their income-earning capacity. FINCA currently serves nearly two million clients across 23 countries on five continents. Worldwide, their borrowers have on-time repayment rates of over 98 percent.

The story of one hardworking FINCA small entrepreneur will help you understand the process. Yvrose St. Louis lives in Haiti, where the poverty rate is a staggering 80 percent. She had a little grocery store in town, but—like many Haitians—she lost everything in the earthquake that struck in 2010. She heard about FINCA from a neighbour and decided to apply for a loan in order to rebuild her family's business and make a better life for her children.

Yvrose obtained a small loan from FINCA, and with help from her FINCA credit agent, got her store going again and she was soon earning enough from it that she could afford to better feed her family and repay her loan on time. Today, Yvrose's store is not only back on its feet, but her business is growing steadily. Her children are in school and the family can put aside money for savings, helping them plan for and build a brighter future.

The Economic Concept of Supply

Supply refers to the quantity of products that manufacturers or owners are willing to sell at different prices at a specific time. Generally speaking, the amount supplied will increase as the price increases because sellers can make more money with a higher price.

supply
The quantity of products that manufacturers or owners are willing to sell at different prices at a specific time.

With 75,000 hotel rooms and an estimated 300,000 visitors, some Vancouverites rented out their homes during the 2010 Vancouver Olympics. Would you have paid $36,000 for a two-bedroom condo for one month? Do you think people were willing to pay the same price for accommodation in Sochi, Russia, during the 2014 Olympic Winter Games? What about during the 2015 Pan Am/Parapan Am Games in Toronto?

Economists show this relationship between quantity supplied and price on a graph. Figure 2.1 shows a simple supply curve for T-shirts. The price of the T-shirts in dollars is shown vertically on the left of the graph. The quantity of T-shirts that sellers are willing to supply is shown horizontally at the bottom of the graph. The various points on the curve indicate how many T-shirts sellers would provide at different prices. For example, at a price of $5 a T-shirt, a vendor would provide only five T-shirts, but at $50 a T-shirt the vendor would supply 50 shirts. The supply curve indicates the relationship between the price and the quantity supplied. All things being equal, the higher the price, the more the vendor will be willing to supply.

■ **FIGURE 2.1**

THE SUPPLY CURVE AT VARIOUS PRICES

The supply curve rises from left to right. Think it through. The higher the price of T-shirts goes (the vertical axis), the more sellers will be willing to supply.

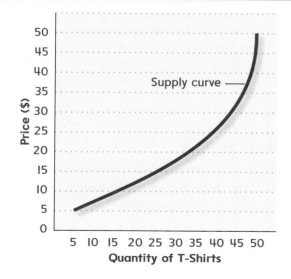

The Economic Concept of Demand

Demand refers to the quantity of products that people are willing to buy at different prices at a specific time. Generally speaking, the quantity demanded will increase as the price decreases. Again, the relationship between price and quantity demanded can be shown in a graph. Figure 2.2 shows a simple demand curve for T-shirts. The various points on the graph indicate the quantity demanded at various prices. For example, at a price of $45, the quantity demanded is just five T-shirts, but if the price were $5, the quantity demanded would increase to 35 T-shirts. The line connecting the dots is called a demand curve. It shows the relationship between quantity demanded and price.

> **demand**
> The quantity of products that people are willing to buy at different prices at a specific time.

■ **FIGURE 2.2**

THE DEMAND CURVE AT VARIOUS PRICES

This is a simple demand curve showing the quantity of T-shirts demanded at different prices. The demand curve falls from left to right. It is easy to understand why. The lower the price of T-shirts, the higher the quantity demanded.

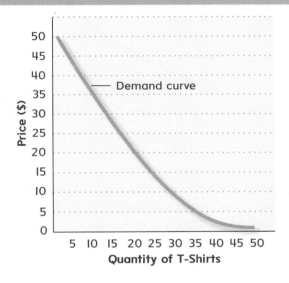

The Equilibrium Point and the Market Price

It should be clear to you after reviewing Figures 2.1 and 2.2 that the key factor in determining the quantity supplied and the quantity demanded is *price*. Sellers prefer a high price, and buyers prefer a low price. If you were to lay one of the two graphs on top of the other, the supply curve and the demand curve would cross. At that crossing point, the quantity demanded and the quantity supplied are equal. Figure 2.3 illustrates that point. At a price of $15, the quantity of T-shirts demanded and the quantity supplied are equal (25 shirts). That crossing point is known as the *equilibrium point* or the *equilibrium price*. In the long run, that price will become the market price. **Market price**, then, is determined by supply and demand.

> **market price**
> The price determined by supply and demand.

Supporters of a free market would argue that because supply and demand interactions determine prices, there is no need for government involvement or government planning. If surpluses develop (i.e., if quantity supplied exceeds quantity demanded), a signal is sent to sellers to lower the price. If shortages develop (i.e., if quantity supplied is less than quantity demanded), a signal is sent to sellers to increase the price. Eventually, supply will again equal demand if nothing interferes with market forces.

■ **FIGURE 2.3**

THE EQUILIBRIUM POINT

The place where quantity demanded and supplied meet is called the equilibrium point. When we put both the supply and demand curves on the same graph, we find that they intersect at a price where the quantity supplied and the quantity demanded are equal. In the long run, the market price will trend toward the equilibrium point.

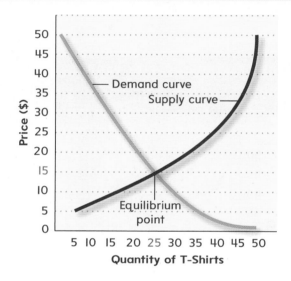

Such price swings were evident when the oil supply was cut because of Hurricane Katrina. When supplies were low because of the hurricane, the price of gasoline went up (dramatically). When supplies were again plentiful, the price of gas fell a little. Then it rose again as demand increased globally, especially in China and India. Food prices went up when more corn was being used for ethanol fuel and less for food.[17]

In countries without a free market, there is no such mechanism to reveal to businesses (via price) what to produce and in what amounts, so there are often shortages (not enough products) or surpluses (too many products). In such countries, the government decides what to produce and in what quantity, but the government has no way of knowing what the proper quantities are. Furthermore, when the government interferes in otherwise free markets, such as when it subsidizes farm goods, surpluses and shortages may also develop.

Competition Within Free Markets

Economists generally agree that four different degrees of competition exist: (1) perfect competition, (2) monopolistic competition, (3) oligopoly, and (4) monopoly.

Perfect competition exists when there are many sellers in a market and no seller is large enough to dictate the price of a product. Under perfect competition, sellers' products appear to be identical. Agricultural products (e.g., apples, corn, potatoes) are often considered to be the closest examples of such products. You should know, however, that there are no true examples of perfect competition. Today, government price supports and drastic reductions in the number of farms make it hard to argue that even farming is an example of perfect competition.

perfect competition
The market situation in which there are many sellers in a market and no seller is large enough to dictate the price of a product.

Monopolistic competition exists when a large number of sellers produce goods that are very similar but are perceived by buyers as different (e.g., hot dogs, candy, and T-shirts). Under monopolistic competition, *product differentiation* (the creation of real or perceived product differences) is a key to success. Through advertising and packaging, sellers try to convince buyers that their products are different from competitors', though they may be very similar or even interchangeable. The fast-food industry, in which there are often promotional battles between hamburger restaurants, offers a good example of monopolistic competition.

monopolistic competition
The market situation in which a large number of sellers produce very similar products that buyers nevertheless perceived as different.

An **oligopoly** occurs when a few sellers dominate a market. Oligopolies exist in industries that produce goods in the areas of oil and gas, tobacco, automobiles, aluminum, and aircraft. One reason some industries remain in the hands of a few sellers is that the initial investment required to enter the business is tremendous. In an oligopoly, prices for products from different companies tend to be close to the same. The reason for this is simple. Intense price competition would lower profits for all competitors, since a price cut on the part of one producer would most likely be matched by the others. As in monopolistic competition, product differentiation, rather than price, is usually the major factor in market success.

oligopoly
A form of competition in which just a few sellers dominate the market.

A **monopoly** occurs when there is only one seller for a good or service, and that one seller controls the total supply of a product and the price. Traditionally, monopolies were common in areas such as water, electricity, and telephone services that were considered essential to a community. Legislation has ended the monopoly status of utilities in some areas, letting consumers choose among providers. The intention of such deregulation is to increase competition among utility companies and, ultimately, lower prices for consumers. Figure 2.4 highlights where these forms of free-market competition fall when one considers the number of sellers (i.e., competitors) in the marketplace.

monopoly
A market in which there is only one seller for a product or service.

Although WestJet Airlines Ltd. <*http://www.westjet.com*> operates within an oligopoly in Canada, it still has to listen to the needs of its customers and try to be innovative. As a result, customers can choose to check in at the counter, on the Web, on mobile devices, at kiosks, and they can tag their bags themselves.

■ **FIGURE 2.4**

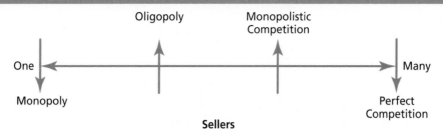

One of the benefits of the free market

Benefits and Limitations of Free Markets

One benefit of the free market is that it allows open competition among companies. Businesses must provide customers with quality products at fair prices with good service. If they do not, they lose customers to businesses that do. Do government services have the same incentives?

The free market—with its competition and incentives—was a major factor in creating the wealth that industrialized countries now enjoy. Some people even talk of the free market as an economic miracle. Free-market capitalism, more than any other economic system, provides opportunities for poor people to work their way out of poverty. Capitalism also encourages businesses to be more efficient so they can successfully compete on price and quality.

Yet even as free-market capitalism has brought prosperity, it has brought inequality as well. Business owners and managers make more money and have more wealth than workers. There is much poverty, unemployment, and homelessness. People who are old, disabled, or sick may not be able to support themselves. What should society do about such inequality?[18]

Smith assumed that as people became wealthier, they would naturally reach out and help the less fortunate in the community. As was discussed earlier, while this has not always happened, business people are becoming more concerned about social issues and their obligation to return to society some of what they have earned. For example, Warren Buffet, Chairman and Chief Executive Officer of Berkshire Hathaway *<http://www.berkshirehathaway.com>* and ranked as one of the world's wealthiest people, has pledged to give away most of his money to the Bill and Melinda Gates Foundation.[19] In another example, every year an amount equivalent to 1 percent of Cirque du Soleil's earnings is dedicated to environmental policies for sustainable development managed by Cirque, as well as to the ONE DROP Foundation.[20]

One of the dangers of free markets is that some people let greed dictate how they act. Criminal charges brought against some big businesses in banking, oil, accounting, telecommunications, insurance, and pharmaceuticals indicate the scope of the potential problem. Some business people have deceived the public about their products; others have deceived shareholders about the value of their stock, all in order to increase executives' personal assets. Clearly, some government rules and regulations are necessary to make sure that all of a business's stakeholders are protected and that people who are unable to work get the basic care they need. To overcome the limitations of capitalism, some countries have adopted an economic system called socialism. It, too, has its good and bad points. We explore the advantages and disadvantages of socialism after the Progress Assessment questions.

Progress Assessment

- How do business people know what to produce and in what quantity?
- How are prices determined?

- Describe the four degrees of competition.

- What are some of the limitations of free markets?

LO3 Compare the benefits and negative consequence of socialism and communism.

Understanding Socialism

Socialism is an economic system based on the premise that some, if not most, basic businesses—such as steel mills, coal mines, and utilities—should be owned by the government so that profits can be evenly distributed among the people. Entrepreneurs often own and run the smaller businesses, and individuals are often taxed relatively steeply to pay for social programs.

> **socialism**
> An economic system based on the premise that some, if not most, basic businesses should be owned by the government so that profits can be evenly distributed among the people.

Socialists acknowledge the major benefit of capitalism—wealth creation—but believe that wealth should be more evenly distributed than occurs in free-market capitalism. They believe that the government should be the agency that carries out the distribution and be much more involved in protecting the environment and providing for the poor.[21]

Socialism has been more successful in some countries than in others. This photo shows Denmark's clean and modern public transportation system. In Greece, overspending caused a debt crisis that forced the government to impose austerity measures that many Greeks oppose. What other factors might lead to slower growth in socialist countries?

The Benefits of Socialism

The major benefit of socialism is supposed to be social equality. Ideally, it comes about because the government takes income from wealthier people, in the form of taxes, and redistributes it to poorer people through various government programs. Free education, free health care, and free child care are some of the benefits socialist governments, using the money from taxes, may provide to their people. Workers in socialist countries usually get longer vacations, work fewer hours per week, and have more employee benefits (e.g., generous sick leave) than those in countries where free-market capitalism prevails.

The Negative Consequences of Socialism

Socialism may create more equality than capitalism, but it takes away some of business people's incentives to work hard, as their profits will be heavily taxed. For example, tax rates in some nations once reached 85 percent.

Today, doctors, lawyers, business owners, and others who earn a lot of money pay very high tax rates. As a consequence, some of them leave socialist countries for capitalistic countries with lower taxes, such as the United States. This loss of these educated people to other countries is called a **brain drain**.

> **brain drain**
> The loss of educated people to other countries.

Imagine an experiment in socialism in your own class. Imagine that after the first exam, those with grades of 90 and above have to give some of their points to those who make 70 and below so that everyone ends up with grades in the 80s. Would those who got 90s study as hard for the second exam? What about those who got 70s? Can you see why workers may not work as hard or as well if they all get the same benefits regardless of how hard they work?

Socialism also results in fewer inventions and less innovation because those who come up with new ideas usually do not receive as much reward as they would in a capitalist system. Generally speaking, over the past decade or so, most socialist countries have simply not kept up with more capitalist countries in new inventions, job creation, or wealth creation.[22]

Communism may be considered a more intensive version of socialism. We shall explore that system next.

Understanding Communism

Communism is an economic and political system in which the state (the government) makes almost all economic decisions and owns almost all of the major factors of production. Communism affects personal choices more than socialism does. For example, some communist countries have not allowed their citizens to practice certain religions, change jobs, or move to the town of their choice.

> **communism**
> An economic and political system in which the state (the government) makes all economic decisions and owns almost all of the major factors of production.

One problem with communism is that the government has no way of knowing what to produce because prices do not reflect supply and demand as they do in free markets. As a result, shortages of many items may develop, including shortages of food and basic clothing. Another problem with communism is that it does not inspire business people to work hard, because the government takes most of their earnings. Therefore, although communists once held power in many nations around the world, communism is slowly disappearing as an economic form.

Most communist countries today are suffering severe economic depression. In North Korea, many people are starving. In Cuba, people suffer from a lack of goods and services readily available in most other countries, and some fear the government. While some parts of the former Soviet Union remain under communist ideals, Russia itself now has a flat tax of 13 percent. Even this low tax rate increased the government's tax revenues by nearly 30 percent, because more people were willing to pay.

The Trend Toward Mixed Economies

The nations of the world have largely been divided between those that followed the concepts of capitalism and those that adopted the concepts of communism or socialism. Thus, to sum up the preceding discussion, the two major economic systems vying for dominance in the world today can be defined as follows:

1. A **free-market economy** exists when the market largely determines what goods and services are produced, who gets them, and how the economy grows. *Capitalism* is the popular term used to describe this economic system.

2. A **command economy** exists when the government largely decides what goods and services are produced, who gets them, and how the economy will grow. *Socialism* and *communism* are the popular terms used to describe variations of this economic system.

> **free-market economy**
> An economy in which the market largely determines what goods and services are produced, who gets them, and how the economy grows.
>
> **command economy**
> An economy in which the government largely decides what goods and services are produced, who gets them, and how the economy will grow.

Experience has shown that neither of these systems has resulted in optimum economic conditions. Free-market mechanisms have not been responsive enough to the needs of the poor, the old, or the disabled. Some people also believe that businesses in free-market economies have not done enough to protect the environment. Over time, voters in free-market countries, such as Canada, have therefore elected officials who have adopted social and environmental programs such as medicare, unemployment compensation, and various clean air and water acts. What new or enhanced social policies do you know of that have been enacted or are being considered today?

Russia has been moving away from communism toward a viable market economy. As poverty begins to decline, a middle class is emerging, but many of the country's vast natural resources are difficult to tap. Laws that promote business are few, and an active black market for goods exists. Many observers are optimistic that Russia can prosper. What do you think?

Socialism and communism, for their part, have not always created enough jobs or wealth to keep economies growing fast enough. As a consequence, communist governments are disappearing and socialist governments have been cutting back on social programs and lowering taxes for businesses and workers. The idea is to generate more business growth and thus generate more revenue.[23]

The trend, then, has been for so-called capitalist countries to move toward socialism and so-called socialist countries to move toward more capitalism. We say "so-called" because no country in the world is purely capitalist or purely socialist. All countries have some mix of the two systems. Thus, the long-term global trend is toward a blend of capitalism and socialism. This trend likely will increase with the opening of global markets as a result of the Internet. The net effect of capitalist systems moving toward socialism and socialist systems moving toward capitalism is the emergence throughout the world of mixed economies (see the Reaching Beyond our Borders box for an example of a changing economy).

Mixed economies exist where some allocation of resources is made by the market and some is made by the government. Most countries do not have a name for such a system. If the dominant way of allocating resources is by free-market mechanisms, then the leaders of such countries still call their system capitalism. If the dominant way of allocating resources is by the government, then the leaders call their system socialism. Figure 2.5 compares the various economic systems.

mixed economies
Economic systems in which some allocation of resources is made by the market and some by the government.

Reaching *Beyond* OUR BORDERS

Economic Expansion in Africa

For much of the twentieth century, stories about Africa's economy inevitably focused on the continent's rampant poverty. The end of colonial rule in Africa brought military dictatorships and other oppressive forces to power in many countries. Coupled with disease and an almost nonexistent infrastructure, Africa's economy and its people suffered horribly.

Thankfully, so far the twenty-first century has been brighter for many Africans. A booming commodities market along with expanding manufacturing and service economies are leading to unprecedented growth. Over the last decade, six of the world's ten fastest-growing countries have been African. In eight of those years, Africa has even outpaced the growth of East Asia, including Japan. Looking to the future, experts expect the continent's GDP to grow 6 percent annually over the next 10 years.

Many Africans have seen their lives change radically as economies on the continent have expanded. Income per person has shot up 30 percent over the last decade, while life expectancy has increased by 10 percent. Even small, formerly war-torn nations are seeing improvements. For instance, in the 1990s. Rwanda suffered a horrific civil war and genocide that claimed the lives of hundreds of thousands of citizens. Subsequent years of peace and a relatively stable government have since turned the country around significantly.

Although many on the continent still experience major hardships, improving economic conditions are allowing more and more people to enter the middle class. Goods and services that used to be scarce are now becoming commonplace. There are now three mobile phones for every four people in Africa, and by 2017 nearly 30 percent of households are expected to own a television. School enrolment has also skyrocketed in the last few years. Experts hope that this younger generation will take advantage of improving educational opportunities and ensure Africa's place on the global economic stage.

Sources: "A Hopeful Continent," *The Economist,* 2 March 2013; "Business in Rwanda: Africa's Singapore?" *The Economist,* 25 February 2012; and John O'Sullivan, "Middle East and Africa: Digging Deeper," *The Economist,* 18 November 2013.

■ FIGURE 2.5

COMPARISONS OF KEY ECONOMIC SYSTEMS			
	Capitalism (United States)	Socialism (Sweden)	Communism (North Korea)	Mixed Economy (Canada)
Social and economic goals	Private ownership of land and business. Freedom and the pursuit of happiness. Free trade. Emphasis on freedom and the profit motive for economic growth.	Public ownership of major businesses. Some private ownership of smaller businesses and shops. Government control of education, health care, utilities, mining, transportation, and media. Very high taxation. Emphasis on equality.	Public ownership of all businesses. Government-run education and health care. Emphasis on equality. Many limitations on freedom, including freedom to own businesses, change jobs, buy and sell homes, and assemble to protest government actions.	Private ownership of land and business with government regulation. Government control of some institutions (e.g., mail). High taxation for the common welfare. Emphasis on a balance between freedom and equality.
Motivation of workers	Much incentive to work efficiently and hard, because profits are retained by owners. Workers are rewarded for high productivity.	Capitalist incentives exist in private businesses. Government control of wages in public institutions limits incentives.	Very little incentive to work hard or to produce quality products.	Incentives are similar to capitalism except in government-owned enterprises, which have few incentives.
Control over markets	Complete freedom of trade within and among nations. No government control of markets.	Some markets are controlled by the government and some are free. Trade restrictions among nations vary and include some free trade agreements.	Total government control over markets except for illegal transactions.	Some government control of trade within and among nations (trade protectionism).
Choices in the market	A wide variety of products is available. Almost no scarcity or oversupply exists for long because supply and demand control the market.	Variety in the marketplace varies considerably from country to country. Choice is directly related to government involvement in markets.	Very little choice among competing products.	Similar to capitalism, but scarcity and oversupply may be caused by government involvement in the market (e.g., subsidies for farms).
Social freedoms	Freedom of speech, press, assembly, religion, job choice, movement, and elections	Similar to mixed economy. Government may restrict job choice, movement among countries, and who may attend upper-level schools (i.e., post-secondary institution).	Very limited freedom to protest the government, practice religion, or change houses or jobs.	Some restriction on freedoms of assembly and speech. Separation of church and state may limit religious practice in schools.

Progress Assessment

- What led to the emergence of socialism?
- What are the benefits and drawbacks of socialism?
- What are the characteristics of a mixed economy?

LO4 Describe the mixed economy of Canada.

Canada's Mixed Economy

Like most other nations of the world, Canada has a mixed economy. The degree of government involvement in the economy today—in areas such as health care, education, and business regulation, just to name a few—is a matter of some debate. (In Chapter 4, we will discuss the role of government in more detail.) The government's perceived goal is to grow the economy while maintaining some measure of social equality. The goal is very hard to attain. Nonetheless, the basic principles of freedom and opportunity should lead to economic growth that is sustainable.

Several features have played a major role in Canada becoming an independent economic entity with high government involvement in the economy. First, we are one of the largest countries in the world geographically, but we have a small population (over 34.8 million).[24] We have one of the lowest population densities in the world.

Most important, our neighbour to the south has ten times the population and an economy even greater than that proportion, speaks our language, is very aggressive economically, and is the most powerful country in the world. The United States exerts a very powerful influence on Canada as our largest trading partner. (We will discuss details in Chapter 3.) To control our destiny, Canadian governments have passed many laws and regulations to ensure that significant economic and cultural institutions, such as banks, insurance companies, and radio and TV stations, remain under Canadian control. (Even powerful countries like the United States and Japan have similar regulations.)

All of these factors led to the Canadian capitalist system taking on many characteristics of a mixed economy. Massive government support was necessary to build our first national rail line, the CPR, in the 1880s. When air transport was beginning in the 1930s no company wanted to risk investing heavily in such a large country with only 10 million people spread thinly across the land. So the government set up Air Canada (then called Trans Canada Airlines) to transport mail, people, and freight. There are many such examples of government action to protect the national interest.

In the 1980s, many countries, including Canada, began to reduce government involvement in, and regulation of, the economy. This trend toward deregulation was widespread. In Canada, airlines, banks, and the trucking industry have all seen a marked reduction in regulatory control.

This trend continues today as groups lobby the government to relax regulations to allow them to be more competitive. For example, to encourage competitiveness, the Competition Policy Review Panel *<http://www.competitionreview.ca>* recommends lowering barriers to foreign investment in a number of industries, including telecommunications and air transportation.[25] The Conference Board of Canada *<http://www.conferenceboard.ca>* has released a report that warns that Canadian industries need to do a better job competing for global investment dollars, attracting foreign investors, and establishing new investments overseas.[26]

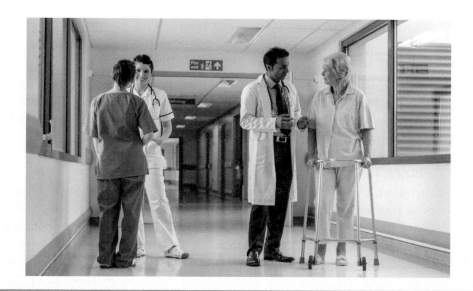

Governed by the Canada Health Act, public care is designed to make sure that all eligible people in the country have reasonable access to insured health services on a prepaid basis, without direct charges at the point of service. Private care covers anything beyond what the public system will pay for. Who would benefit from private health coverage? What happens if someone is not eligible for private coverage?

There are also many new players entering the Canadian marketplace that are competing with publicly funded (i.e., government-funded) institutions. One such industry is health care, where private health care supporters continue to lobby for a greater presence in Canada.

In the years to come, we can expect to see more examples of our mixed economy moving toward a more capitalist system, as the private sector will play a greater role in delivering some goods and services (e.g., health care) that have historically been managed by public institutions. Keep in mind that during tough economic times, voters demand more government involvement. Thus, it is a traditional and desirable role of government to increase expenditures (e.g., provide financial aid to industries, increase spending on infrastructure, etc.) to support and stabilize the economy. The question is how much involvement, debt, etc. is appropriate.

Understanding Canada's Economic System

The strength of the economy has a tremendous effect on business. When the economy is strong and growing, most businesses prosper and almost everyone benefits through plentiful jobs, reasonably good wages, and sufficient revenues for the government to provide needed goods and services. When the economy is weak, however, businesses are weakened, employment and wages fall, and government revenues decline as a result.

Because business and the economy are so closely linked, business literature is full of economic concepts. It is virtually impossible to read business reports with much understanding unless you are familiar with the economic terms being used. One purpose of this chapter is to help you learn additional economic concepts, terms, and issues—the kinds that you will be seeing daily if you read the business press, as we encourage you to do.

LO5   Illustrate the significance of key economic indicators and the business cycle.

Key Economic Indicators

Three major indicators of economic conditions are (1) the gross domestic product (GDP), (2) the unemployment rate, and (3) the price indexes. Another important statistic is the increase or decrease in productivity. When you read business literature, you will see these terms used again and again. It will greatly increase your understanding if you learn the terms now.

GROSS DOMESTIC PRODUCT

Gross domestic product (GDP) is the total value of final goods and services produced in a country in a given year. Either a domestic company or a foreign-owned company may produce the goods and services included in the GDP as long as the companies are located within the country's boundaries. For example, production values from Japanese automaker Toyota's factory <*http://www.toyota.ca*> in Cambridge, Ontario, would be included in the Canadian GDP. Likewise, revenue generated by Magna International's manufacturing and assembly plants in Brazil would be included in Brazil's GDP, even though Magna <*http://www.magna.com*> is a Canadian company.

> **gross domestic product (GDP)**
> The total value of goods and services produced in a country in a given year.

REPORT CARD						
	Economy	Innovation	Environment	Education and Skills	Health	Society
Australia	B	D	D	B	B	C
Austria	C	D	C	C	B	B
Belgium	B	C	C	B	n.a.	B
Canada	B	D	C	B	B	B
Denmark	B	C	C	C	D	A
Finland	B	C	A	A	B	B
France	D	C	B	C	B	B
Germany	D	B	C	B	B	B
Ireland	A	A	C	C	C	C
Italy	D	D	B	D	B	C
Japan	C	B	C	B	A	D
Netherlands	A	B	C	B	C	A
Norway	A	D	A	C	B	A
Sweden	A	B	A	B	B	A
Switzerland	A	A	A	B	A	B
U.K.	B	B	B	C	D	C
U.S.	B	A	D	C	D	D

Note: Data for the most recent year available used.
Source: Used with permission of the Conference Board of Canada, 2009.

According to the Conference Board of Canada, businesses need to work smarter to improve productivity. This includes producing higher-value-added products and services that are worth more in the marketplace. This report card summarizes country ratings in a variety of areas.

If GDP growth slows or declines, there are often many negative effects on business. What can account for increases in GDP? A major influence on the growth of GDP is how productive the workforce is—that is, how much output workers create with a given amount of input. This is linked to the combination of creating jobs, working longer hours, or working smarter. Working smarter means being more productive through the use of better technology and processes and employing a more educated and efficient workforce. In the past, GDP growth has been affected by rising employment (to be discussed soon), low inflation, and low interest rates.[27]

The more you produce, the higher the GDP and vice versa. The economy benefits from a strong GDP. Money that is earned from producing goods and services goes to the employees that produce them in the form of wages. People who own the business generate a return on their investment, and government benefits from tax collection.

A strong economy usually leads to a high standard of living for Canadians. In your opinion, have too many people in Canada sacrificed their quality of life to have a higher standard of living by working more? Since productivity is central to a country's GDP, we will look at this next.

PRODUCTIVITY IN CANADA

An increase in productivity means a worker can produce more goods and services than before in the same time period, usually thanks to machinery or other equipment. Productivity in Canada has risen because computers and other technology have made production faster and easier. Improved productivity can decrease production costs which can then result in lower prices. Therefore, business people are eager to increase productivity.

The Canadian economy is a service economy. Productivity is an issue because service firms are very labour-intensive. Spurred by foreign competition, productivity in the goods-producing sector is rising rapidly. In the service sector, however, productivity is growing more slowly because service workers—like teachers, clerks, lawyers, and barbers—have fewer new technologies available than there are for factory workers.

PRODUCTIVITY IN THE SERVICES-PRODUCING SECTOR

One problem with the services-producing sector is that an influx of machinery may add to the *quality* of the service provided but not to the *output per worker*. For example, you have probably noticed how many computers there are on campus. They add to the quality of education but they do not necessarily boost professors' productivity. The same is true of some equipment in hospitals, such as CAT scanners, PET scanners (more modern versions of the X-ray machine), and MRI scanners. They improve patient care but they do not necessarily increase the number of patients doctors can see. In other words, today's productivity measures in the services-producing sector fail to capture the improvement in quality caused by new technology.

Clearly Canada and other countries need to develop new measures of productivity for the service economy, measures that include quality as well as quantity of output. Productivity is extremely important to a country, as it is a measure of its economic prosperity. Canadian businesses are criticized for not spending enough on research and development, relative to other advanced countries. By not doing so, these businesses will fall behind in the fierce global competitive battle. We will discuss the importance of research and development in Chapter 10.

Of course, technological advances usually lead to people being replaced by machines, often contributing to unemployment. We will now examine this important issue.

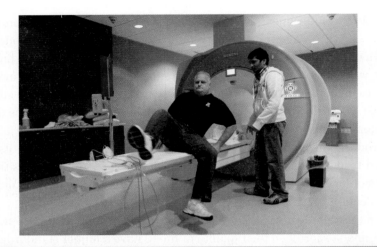

It can be difficult to accurately measure productivity in service industries because new technologies, like high-tech medical scanning, can greatly improve the quality of services provided without necessarily increasing the number of people served. A doctor can make much more accurate diagnoses with better scans, for instance, but can still see only so many patients in a day. How can productivity measures try to capture improvements in service quality?

THE UNEMPLOYMENT RATE

The **unemployment rate** refers to the percentage of the labour force (15 years and over) that actively seeks work but is unable to find work at a given time.[28] Figure 2.6 describes different types of unemployment. Figure 2.7 highlights Canada's unemployment rate over 25 years. The real rate is higher because Statistics Canada does not include people who have given up looking for jobs, those who were unable to work, those who stay in or return to school because they cannot find full-time work, and various other categories of people. The unemployment rate is a key indicator of the health of the economy and of society more generally. That is, when economic growth is strong, the unemployment rate tends to be low and a person who wants a job is likely to experience little trouble finding one. On the other hand, when the economy is stagnating or in recession (to be discussed soon), unemployment tends to be higher.[29]

> **unemployment rate**
> The percentage of the labour force that actively seeks work but is unable to find work at a given time.

People are unemployed in Canada for various reasons. Perhaps their employer goes out of business or their company cuts staff. Young persons enter the job market looking for their first job and other employees quit their jobs but have trouble finding new ones. Companies merge and jobs are consolidated or trimmed. Companies transfer their operations to another country, or a branch of a foreign company is closed down. When a job is lost, not only is it a loss to society and the economy, but the loss of income can also create hardship for individuals and families.

According to Statistics Canada, the unemployed include persons who (during the reference period) were as follows: (1) were on temporary layoff during the reference week with an expectation of recall and were available for work; (2) were without work, had looked for work in the past four weeks, and were available for work; or (3) had a new job to start within four weeks from reference week, and were available for work.[30] Unemployment insurance only goes so far to relieve such unemployment.

■ **FIGURE 2.6**

FOUR TYPES OF UNEMPLOYMENT

The types of unemployment are:

Frictional unemployment

Frictional unemployment refers to those people who have quit work because they didn't like the job, the boss, or the working conditions and who haven't yet found a new job. It also refers to those people who are entering the labour force for the first time (e.g., new graduates) or are returning to the labour force after significant time away (e.g., parents who reared children). There will always be some frictional unemployment because it takes some time to find a first job or a new job.

Structural unemployment

Structural unemployment refers to unemployment caused by the restructuring of firms or by a mismatch between the skills (or location) of job seekers and the requirements (or location) of available jobs (e.g., coal miners in an area where mines have been closed).

Cyclical unemployment

Cyclical unemployment occurs because of a recession or a similar downturn in the business cycle (the ups and downs of business growth and decline over time). This type of unemployment is the most serious.

Seasonal unemployment

Seasonal unemployment occurs where demand for labour varies over the year, as with the harvesting of crops.

■ **FIGURE 2.7**

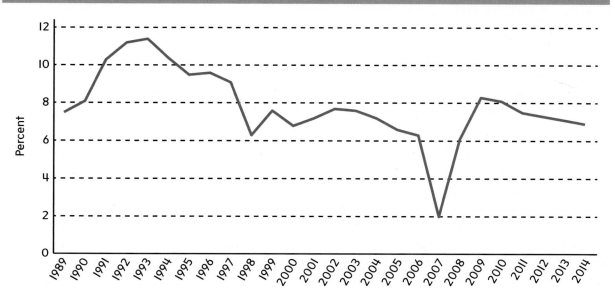

THE UNEMPLOYMENT RATE IN CANADA 1989–2014

Source: Statistics Canada. Table 282-0002 - Labour force survey estimates (LFS), by sex and detailed age group, annual (persons unless otherwise noted), CANSIM (database). (accessed: 2015-03-04); Statistics Canada, Labour Force Survey, http://www.stats.gov.nl.ca/statistics/Labour/PDF/UnempRate.pdf.

The overall unemployment rate in Canada fluctuates. Over the last decade, it has been as low as 6 percent and as high as 8 percent. Unemployment insurance goes only so far to relieve the loss of income caused by losing your job. How high is the unemployment rate in your area today?

THE PRICE INDEXES

The price indexes indicate the health of the economy by measuring the levels of inflation, disinflation, deflation, and stagflation. **Inflation** refers to a general rise in the prices of goods and services over time. Rapid inflation is scary. If the cost of goods and services goes up by just 7 percent a year, everything will double in cost in just ten years or so. Inflation increases the cost of doing business. When a company borrows money, interest costs are higher, employees demand increases to keep up with the rise in the cost of living, suppliers raise their prices, and as a result the company is forced to raise its prices. If other countries succeed in keeping their inflation rates down, then Canadian companies will become less competitive in the world market.

> **inflation**
> A general rise in the prices of goods and services over time.

Disinflation describes a condition where price increases are slowing (the inflation rate is declining). **Deflation** means that prices are actually declining.[31] It occurs when countries produce so many goods that people cannot afford to buy them all. That is, too few dollars are chasing too many goods. **Stagflation** occurs when the economy is slowing but prices are going up regardless.[32]

> **disinflation**
> A situation in which price increases are slowing (the inflation rate is declining).
>
> **deflation**
> A situation in which prices are declining.
>
> **stagflation**
> A situation in which the economy is slowing but prices are going up regardless.

The **consumer price index (CPI)** is a monthly statistic that measures the pace of inflation or deflation. To determine the CPI, costs of a "basket" of goods and services for an average family—including food, shelter, transportation, and clothing and footwear—are calculated to see if they are going up or down. For example, Canadian consumers paid, on average, 1 percent more for such a basket in February, 2015, than twelve months earlier; this was led by increases alcoholic beverages and tobacco products (5.2 percent) and food prices (3.9 percent) but offset by a drop in transportation costs, such as gasoline for cars (5.0 percent).[33] The CPI is an important figure because it affects nearly all Canadians, either directly or indirectly. For example, government benefits (such as Old Age Security and Canada Pension Plan), rental agreements, some labour contracts, and interest rates are based on the CPI.

consumer price index (CPI)
A monthly statistic that measures the pace of inflation or deflation.

Other indicators of the economy's condition include housing starts, retail sales, motor vehicle sales, consumer confidence, and changes in personal income. You can learn more about such indicators by reading business periodicals, contacting government agencies, listening to business broadcasts, and exploring the Internet.

The United Nations suggests the development of a country cannot be based only upon economic measures. Some indexes measure social factors that are considered along with economic information. One example is the **human development index (HDI)**, which examines the wealth, health, and education of a country according to incomes, life expectancy, and years of schooling. A recent United Nations report identifies the HDI for many countries throughout the world is slowing down.[34]

human development index
A measure of a country's progress that includes wealth, health, and education.

The Business Cycle

Business cycles (also known as **economic cycles**) are the periodic rises and falls that occur in economies over time.[35] These fluctuations are often measured using the real GDP.[36] Economists look at a number of types of cycles, from seasonal cycles that occur within a year to cycles that occur every 48 to 60 years. Economist Joseph Schumpeter identified the four phases of long-term business cycles as boom, recession, depression, recovery, as illustrated in Figure 2.8.

business cycles (economic cycles)
The periodic rises and falls that occur in economies over time.

1. An economic **boom** is just what it sounds like—business is booming. Periods of economic boom bring jobs, growth, and economic prosperity.

2. Two or more consecutive quarters of decline in the GDP result in a **recession**. In a recession, prices fall, people purchase fewer products, and businesses fail. A recession has many negative consequences for an economy: high unemployment, increased business failures, and an overall drop in living standards. The 2009 recession is an example.

3. A **depression** is a severe recession usually accompanied by deflation. Business cycles rarely go through a depression phase. In fact, while there were many business cycles during the twentieth century, there was only one severe depression (in the 1930s).

4. A **recovery** occurs when the economy stabilizes and starts to grow. This eventually leads to an economic boom, starting the cycle all over again.

■ **FIGURE 2.8**

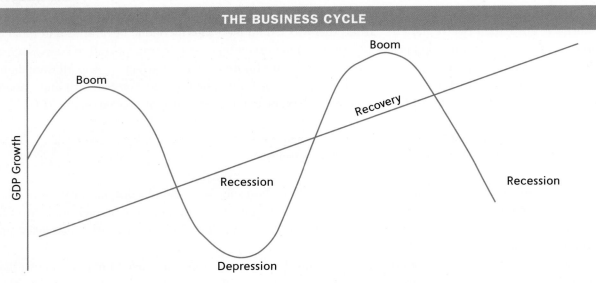

THE BUSINESS CYCLE

boom
A period that brings jobs, growth, and economic prosperity.

recession
Two or more consecutive quarters of decline in the GDP.

depression
A severe recession.

recovery
When the economy stabilizes and starts to grow.

One goal of some economists is to predict such ups and downs. That is very difficult to do. Business cycles are identified according to facts, but we can explain those facts only by using theories. Therefore, one cannot predict with certainty. But one thing is certain: over time, the economy will rise and fall as it has done in recent years.

Since dramatic swings up and down in the economy cause all kinds of disruptions to businesses, the government tries to minimize such changes. The government uses fiscal policy and monetary policy to try to keep the economy from slowing too much or growing too rapidly. We will discuss both of these policies in Chapter 4.

Progress Assessment

- What factors have contributed to the decision to have a mixed economy in Canada?
- Name three economic indicators and describe how well Canada is doing using each one.
- What is the difference between a recession and a depression?

SUMMARY

LO1 **Describe basic economics.**

Economics is the study of how society chooses to employ resources to produce goods and services and distribute them for consumption among various competing groups and individuals.

What are the two branches of economics?

There are two major branches of economics: macroeconomics studies the operation of a nation's economy as a whole, and microeconomics studies the behaviour of people and organizations in particular markets (e.g., why people buy smaller cars when gas prices go up).

LO2 **Explain what capitalism is and how free markets work.**

Capitalism is an economic system in which all or most of the means of production and distribution (e.g., land, factories, railroads, and stores) are privately owned and operated for profit.

Who decides what to produce under capitalism?

In capitalist countries, business people decide what to produce; how much to pay workers; how much to charge for goods and services; whether to produce certain goods in their own countries, import those goods, or have them made in other countries; and so on.

How does the free market work?

The free market is one in which decisions about what to produce and in what quantities are made by the market—that is, by buyers and sellers negotiating prices for goods and services. Buyers' decisions in the marketplace tell sellers what to produce and in what quantity. When buyers demand more goods, the price goes up, signalling suppliers to produce more. The higher the price, the more goods and services suppliers are willing to produce. Price, then, is the mechanism that allows free markets to work.

What is supply and demand?

Supply refers to the quantity of products that manufacturers or owners are willing to sell at different prices at a specific time. Demand refers to the quantity of products that people are willing to buy at different prices at a specific time. The key factor in determining the quantity supplied and the quantity demanded is price.

What is the relevance of the equilibrium point?

The equilibrium point, also referred to as the equilibrium price, is the point where the quantity demanded is the same as the quantity supplied. In the long run, that price becomes the market price.

LO3 **Compare the benefits and negative consequences of socialism and communism.**

Socialism is an economic system based on the premise that some businesses should be owned by the government. Socialism creates more social equality. Compared to workers in capitalist countries, workers in socialist countries not only receive more education and health care benefits but also work fewer hours, have longer vacations, and receive more benefits in general, such as child care. The major disadvantage of socialism is that it lowers the profits of owners, thus cutting the incentive to start a business or to work hard. Socialist economies tend to have a higher unemployment rate and a slower growth rate than capitalist economies.

Under communism, the government owns almost all major production facilities and dictates what gets produced and by whom. Communism is more restrictive when it comes to personal freedoms, such as religious freedom. With communism, one can see shortages in items such as food and clothing, and business people may not work as hard as the government takes most of their earnings. While many countries practice socialism, only a few (e.g., North Korea) still practice communism.

LO4 Describe the mixed economy of Canada.

A mixed economy is one that is part capitalist and part socialist. That is, some businesses are privately owned, but taxes tend to be high to distribute income more evenly among the population.

What countries have mixed economies?

Canada has a mixed economy, as do most other countries of the world.

What does it mean to have a mixed economy?

A mixed economy has most of the benefits of wealth creation that free markets bring plus the benefits of greater social equality and concern for the environment that socialism offers.

LO5 Illustrate the significance of key economic indicators and the business cycle.

Three major indicators of economic conditions are (1) the gross domestic product (GDP), (2) the unemployment rate, and (3) the price indexes.

What are the key terms used to describe the Canadian economic system?

Gross domestic product (GDP) is the total value of goods and services produced in a country in a given year. The unemployment rate represents the number of unemployed persons expressed as a percentage of the labour force. The consumer price index (CPI) measures changes in the prices of a basket of goods and services that consumers buy. It is a monthly statistic that measures the pace of inflation (consumer prices going up) or deflation (consumer prices going down). Productivity is the total volume of goods and services one worker can produce in a given period. Productivity in Canada has increased over the years due to the use of computers and other technologies.

What are the four phases of business cycles?

In an economic boom, businesses do well. A recession occurs when two or more quarters show declines in the GDP, prices fall, people purchase fewer products, and businesses fail. A depression is a severe recession. Finally, recovery is when the economy stabilizes and starts to grow.

KEY TERMS

brain drain	demand	invisible hand
business cycles (economic cycles)	depression	macroeconomics
	disinflation	market price
capitalism	economics	microeconomics
command economy	free-market economy	mixed economies
communism	gross domestic product (GDP)	monopolistic competition
consumer price index (CPI)	human development index	monopoly
deflation	inflation	oligopoly

perfect competition   socialism   unemployment rate
recession   stagflation
resource development   supply

CRITICAL THINKING

Many say that business people do not do enough for society. Some students choose to work for non-profit organizations instead of for-profit organizations because they want to help others. However, business people say that they do more to help others than non-profit groups because they provide jobs for people rather than giving them charity, which often precludes them from searching for work. Furthermore, they believe that businesses create all the wealth that non-profit groups distribute. Can you find some middle ground in this debate that demonstrates how both business people and those who work for non-profit organizations contribute to society and need to work together more closely to help people? Could you use the concepts of Adam Smith to help illustrate your position?

DEVELOPING WORKPLACE SKILLS

Key: ● **Team**   ★ **Analytic**   ▲ **Communication**   ☐ **Technology**

● ★ 1.   In teams, develop a list of the advantages of living in a capitalist society. Then develop lists
▲   headed "What are the disadvantages?" and "How could such disadvantages be minimized?"
         Describe why a person in a socialist country might reject capitalism and prefer a socialist state.

☐ ★ 2.   Show your understanding of the principles of supply and demand by looking at the oil mar-
         ket today. Go online and search for a chart of oil prices for the last few years. Why does the
         price of oil fluctuate so greatly? What will happen as more and more people in China and India
         decide to buy automobiles? What would happen if most Canadian consumers decided to drive
         electric cars?

● ★ 3.   This exercise will help you understand socialism from different perspectives. Form three
▲   groups. Each group should adopt a different role in a socialist economy: one group will be the
         business owners, another group will be workers, and another will be government leaders. Within
         your group discuss and list the advantages and disadvantages to you of lowering taxes on busi-
         nesses. Then have each group choose a representative to go to the front of the class and debate
         the tax issue with the representatives from the other groups.

▲ ★ 4.   Draw a line and mark one end "capitalism" and the other end "socialism." Mark where Can-
         ada is now on that line. Explain why you marked the spot you did. Students from other
         countries may want to do this exercise for their own countries and explain the differences
         to the class.

● ★ 5.   Break into small groups. In your group, discuss how the following have affected people's pur-
▲   chasing behaviours and attitudes toward Canada and its economy: development of the Alberta
         oil sands; the Atlantic seal hunt; mad cow disease; and the growth of the Internet. Have a group
         member prepare a short summary for the class.

ANALYZING MANAGEMENT DECISIONS

The Rule of 72

No formula is more useful for understanding inflation than the rule of 72. Basically, the rule allows you to quickly compute how long it takes the cost of goods and services to double at various compounded rates of growth. For example, if houses were increasing in cost at 9 percent a year, how long would it take for the price of a home to double? The answer is easy to calculate. Simply divide 72 by the annual increase (9 percent) and you get the approximate number of years it takes to double the price (eight years). Of course, the same calculation can be used to predict how high food prices or auto prices will be 10 years from now.

Here is an example of how you can use the rule of 72. If the cost of attending a post-secondary institution increases by 6 percent a year, how much might you have to pay to send your child to a post-secondary institution in 24 years (this assumes you will have a child six years from now) if costs are now $10,000 a year? To find the answer, you divide 72 by 6, which shows that the cost of an education would double in 12 years. It would double twice in 24 years. Your son or daughter can expect to pay $40,000 per year to attend college.

Discussion Questions

1. If the cost of a post-secondary institution education is about $20,000 per year now, what will it cost your children per year if costs go up 9 percent a year and your children go to a post-secondary institution 16 years from now?

2. If the value of a home doubles in 12 years, what is the annual rate of return? (Hint: Use the rule of 72 in reverse.)

3. If you put $1,000 into a savings account and earned 6 percent per year, how much money would you have in the account after 48 years?

VIDEO CASE 2

The Bank of Canada: Count on Us

The Bank of Canada <*http://www.bankofcanada.ca*> contributes to the well-being of the Canadian economy through the implementation of monetary policy, its role in the Canadian financial system, and its management of Canada's bank notes. Located in Ottawa, Ontario, the Bank of Canada is our country's central bank. It is not a commercial bank and it does not offer banking services to the public. Its principal role, as defined in the Bank of Canada Act, is "to promote the economic and financial welfare of Canada." The Bank was founded in 1934 as a privately owned corporation. In 1938, it became a Crown corporation belonging to the federal government. (Crown corporations are discussed in Chapter 4.)

Take a second and think of your bank balance. What makes that money valuable? According to the Bank of Canada's former Governor, Mark Carney, you do not have to worry about your money or the financial system in Canada due to the work of the Bank of Canada.

The Bank of Canada's main job is to direct monetary policy, which involves setting the interest rates that people and businesses pay when they borrow money. The Bank's objective is to influence interest rates so that the economy can remain healthy and create jobs. A healthy and stable economy helps families and businesses adapt to the changing conditions in the world economy.

As long as inflation is low, stable, and predictable we can remain confident in the future value of our money. The Bank of Canada and the Government of Canada aim for an annual inflation rate of 2 percent. This is known as the inflation target. The Bank of Canada sets the policy interest rate, which influences commercial interest rates. For consumers, low interest rates mean that it costs less to borrow money. For businesses, low-cost loans help them buy new equipment and expand their operations. All of this economic activity helps to push rates up. On the reverse, when everyone spends less due to higher interest rates, inflation tends to come down.

From buyers to sellers, from sellers to banks, and from banks back to businesses and consumers, it is easy to take all of these millions of transfers for granted. Money moves through a financial system. The Bank of Canada oversees these large complex systems that are used to make these daily financial transfers.

Since Canada is an open economy (i.e., we depend more on international trade and capital flows than many other countries), it is important to understand the global economic environment. To this end, the Bank of Canada works to ensure that the financial system stays strong and secure by working with the G20 (the 20 largest countries in the world) <*https://g20.org*>, the IMF (International Monetary Fund) <*http://www.imf.org*>, and the BIS (Bank of International Settlements) <*https://www.bis.org*> to raise the standard of regulation and also ensure that other countries are applying these regulations and supervision through their banks, insurance companies, and financial systems so that Canada is not impacted by shocks from abroad.

When the Bank of Canada was established, it was given the sole authority to issue bank notes in Canada and to preserve the value of money. Bank notes are designed to be attractive, easy to use, durable, and difficult to counterfeit. If it was hard to tell a real Canadian bank note from a fake, confidence in our currency would disappear. All of our bank notes have security features that are easy to check.

Discussion Questions

1. The Bank of Canada has the mandate to contribute and enhance the well-being of Canadians. What three areas are targeted by the Bank of Canada as a way to do this?

2. How does the Bank of Canada try to keep inflation in check?

3. What is the impact of high interest rates for consumers and businesses? How about low interest rates?

Competing in Global Markets

LEARNING OBJECTIVES

After you have read and studied this chapter, you should be able to:

LO1 Describe the importance of the global market and the roles of comparative advantage and absolute advantage in global trade.

LO2 Explain the importance of importing and exporting and define key terms used in global business.

LO3 Illustrate the strategies used in reaching global markets and explain the role of multinational corporations in global markets.

LO4 Evaluate the forces that affect trading in global markets.

LO5 Debate the advantages and disadvantages of trade protectionism, define tariff and non-tariff barriers, and give examples of common markets.

LO6 Discuss the changing landscape of the global market.

PROFILE

GETTING TO KNOW LEILA JANAH

For decades Canadian companies have outsourced work overseas to countries known for providing cheap labour. The practice is controversial. While it saves businesses money, that is often the only benefit. Not only may it hurt job creation domestically, outsourcing can also overload foreign job markets with underpaid work that often offers little chance for advancement. Leila Janah saw this problem firsthand when she befriended a call centre employee working in India. The young man took a long commute to his job from one of Mumbai's worst slums, which was the only place he could afford. "I knew there were more people like him capable of doing quality work," says Janah. She then came up with the idea for Samasource

<http://www.samasource.org>, a non-profit "microwork" company that helps young men and women in developing countries earn extra income in order to rise out of poverty.

The bulk of the work provided by Samasource involves simple, computer-related tasks—such as tagging images, moderating comments on websites, and transcribing interviews. These jobs normally end up in countries like India and the Philippines through large outsourcing corporations. Unlike these companies, however, Samasource carefully selects potential employees based on the skills they lack, not the ones they have already. "The criteria for selecting agents is that they must be between the ages of 18 and 30, have no formal work experience, and are currently earning less than a living wage," says Janah. "Agents are then provided free, specialized technology training, soft skills training, and project-specific training before beginning work." Samasource's contracts with companies like Google, Microsoft, and eBay have helped more than 4,000 people and their families rise above the poverty line. In fact, a recent study projected that by 2020 more than 2.9 million people will be employed through "impact sourcing" companies like Samasource.

Janah's commitment to combating world poverty has been her driving force since her teenage years. She earned a $10,000 scholarship, which funded a trip to Ghana to teach English. Janah continued to travel the world while also studying at Harvard University. After graduating with a degree in economic development, she took a job with the World Bank that made her question traditional methods of providing aid. "The more time I spent in developing countries, and the more time I spent talking to poor people, I realized what they want more than anything is a good job," says Janah. "We spend billions on international aid annually, but we don't find ways to connect people to dignified work."

Janah hopes that Samasource will change that. The non-profit currently operates 16 centres in nine countries and is always expanding. One of Samasource's clients is 360incentives <http://www.360incentives .com>, a global incentives and rebate company in Whitby, Ontario. In an effort to modernize and better integrate technology into its services, 360incentives partnered with Samasource to meet its needs, which included bilingual customer service representatives, during exponential growth. In the end, though, much of the non-profit's future success depends on outside companies choosing to work with Samasource instead of other outsourcing services. "We tell [clients], 'You're going to spend this money on an outsourcing company anyway—why not end poverty and save the world without spending more money than you already spend?'" says Janah.

Leila Janah is an example of an emerging global business person. She has learned to speak other languages, understands cultural and economic differences, and knows how to adapt to changes successfully. This chapter explains the opportunities and challenges businesspeople like Janah face every day in dealing with the dynamic environment of global business.

Sources: Jason Ankeny, "The 7 Most Powerful Women to Watch in 2014: The Humanitarian," *Entrepreneur*, January 3, 2014; Catherine Dunn, "40 Under 40: Leila Janah," *Forbes*, September 19, 2013; Visi R. Talik, "'Rising Star' Leila Janah on Fighting Poverty," *The Wall Street Journal*, November 29, 2012; and "A Letter from Leila Janah, Founder and CEO," www.samasource.org, accessed February 2014; 360incentives: Customer Case Study, Copyright 2014, Accessed March 25, 2015 from http://www.samasource.org/customers/case-study-360incentives/.

LO1   Describe the importance of the global market and the roles of comparative advantage and absolute advantage in global trade.

The Dynamic Global Market

Have you ever dreamed of travelling to exotic cities such as Paris, Tokyo, Rio de Janeiro, or Cairo? Today, over 90 percent of the companies doing business globally believe it is important for their employees to have experience working in other countries.[1] The reason is not surprising. Although Canada is a market of more than 35.7 million people, there are over 7 billion potential customers in the 194 independent countries that make up the global market.[2] (See Figure 3.1 for a map of the world and important statistics about the world's population.[3]) That is too many people to ignore.

■ **FIGURE 3.1**

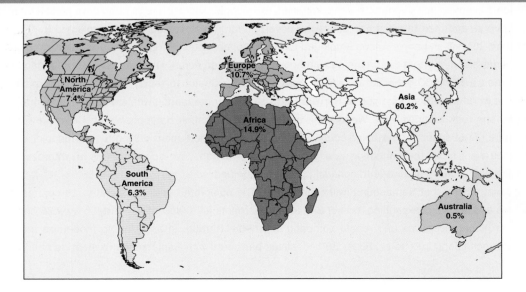

WORLD POPULATION BY CONTINENT

In 2013, Canadian consumers bought $52.7 billion in merchandise from China.[4] Canadian companies, both large and small, continuously look for opportunities to grow their businesses. For example, Rogers Communication signed a 12-year, $5.2 billion deal with the National Hockey League (NHL) for the league's broadcast and media rights.[5] TSN and Sportsnet paid an undisclosed amount to share the multimedia rights for 380 Barclays Premiere League football matches.[6]

The inclusion of National Hockey League (NHL) players in the Olympics builds the league's global appeal. Between 2007 and 2011, the NHL held a Premiere Series of preseason exhibition games versus European clubs. Some season-opening NHL games were also held abroad. Do you think the NHL will ever stage regular season games in Europe? Is the global market strong enough for NHL expansion beyond North America?[7]

Bombardier Inc. <http://www.bombardier.com> is a world-leading manufacturer of innovative transportation solutions in the areas of aerospace and rail transportation.[8] Headquartered in Montreal, the company has 80 production and engineering sites in 28 countries, and a worldwide network of service centres.[9]

Companies also continuously review their global operations to ensure that they are operating at a profit. One Canadian industry that has been particularly hard hit as a result of global trends is the auto industry. Factors such as the increasing price of gas and weakening demand for trucks and sport utility vehicles (SUVs) have forced companies to consider restructuring plans. As a result, thousands of Canadian jobs have been eliminated. Layoffs have occurred at General Motors Canada <http://www.gm.ca>, Fiat Chrysler Automobiles <http://www.fcacanada.ca>, Ford Motor Company of Canada <http://www.ford.ca>, and many parts suppliers.[10] Canada's share of North American auto production fell to a record low of 14 percent in 2013.[11] The global market is truly dynamic, and progressive companies continuously scan the business environment to ensure that they take advantage of the opportunities and minimize the impact of threats.

Because the global market is so large, it is important to understand the language of international trade. Canada is a large exporting nation. **Exporting** is selling products (i.e., goods and services) to another country. **Importing** is buying products from another country. Competition in exporting is very intense and Canadian companies face aggressive rivalry from exporters around the world who also have the same objectives of growing their businesses.

exporting
Selling products to another country.

importing
Buying products from another country.

This chapter will familiarize you with global business and its many challenges. As competition in global markets increases, the demand for students with training in global business is almost certain to grow. If you choose such a career, prepare yourself to work hard and always be ready for new challenges.

Why Trade with Other Nations?

No country, not even a technologically advanced one, can produce all of the goods that its people want and need. Even if a country did become self-sufficient, other nations would seek to trade with that country to meet the needs of their citizens. Some nations, like Venezuela and Russia, have an abundance of natural resources but have limited technological know-how. Other countries, such as Japan and Switzerland, have sophisticated technology but few natural resources. Global trade enables a nation to produce what it is most capable of producing and to buy what it needs from others in a mutually beneficial exchange relationship. This happens through the process of free trade.

Free trade is the movement of goods and services among nations without political or economic barriers. It is often a hotly debated concept.[12] Figure 3.2 offers some of the pros and cons of free trade.

free trade
The movement of goods and services among nations without political or economic barriers.

■ **FIGURE 3.2**

THE PROS AND CONS OF FREE TRADE

PROS

- The global market contains more than 7 billion potential customers for goods and services.

- Productivity improves when countries produce goods and services in which they have a comparative advantage.

- Global competition and less-costly imports keep prices down, so inflation does not curtail economic growth.

- Free trade inspires innovation for new products and keeps firms competitively challenged.

- The uninterrupted flow of capital gives countries access to foreign investments, which helps keep interest rates low.

CONS

- Domestic workers (particularly in manufacturing-based jobs) can lose their jobs due to increased imports or production shifts to low-wage global markets.

- Workers may be forced to accept pay cuts from employers who can threaten to move their jobs to lower-cost global markets.

- Moving operations overseas because of intense competitive pressure often means the loss of service jobs and white-collar jobs.

- Domestic companies can lose their comparative advantage when competitors build advanced production operations in low-wage countries.

The Theories of Comparative and Absolute Advantage

Global trade is the exchange of goods and services across national borders. Exchanges between and among countries involve more than goods and services, however. Countries also exchange art, sports, cultural events, medical advances, space exploration, and labour. Comparative advantage theory, suggested in the early nineteenth century by English economist David Ricardo, was the guiding principle that supported this idea of free economic exchange.[13]

Comparative advantage theory states that a country should sell to other countries those products that it produces most effectively and efficiently, and buy from other countries those products it cannot produce as effectively or efficiently. Japan has shown this ability with cars and electronic items. Canada has such an advantage with certain forestry and agricultural products, and various minerals. In contrast, Canada lacks a comparative advantage in growing coffee; thus, we import most of the coffee we consumer. By specializing and trading, Canada and its trading partners can realize mutually beneficial exchanges.[14]

> **comparative advantage theory**
> A theory that states that a country should sell to other countries those products that it produces most effectively and efficiently, and buy from other countries those products that it cannot produce as effectively or efficiently trade.

Canada became a diamond producer in 1998 when the Ekati diamond mine opened about 300 kilometres northeast of Yellowknife. Here you see the Diavik Diamond Mine, located on a 20-square-kilometre island in the same area. With the opening of new mines, Canada's global diamond market share is expected to grow to a world-leading 25.2 percent in 2018.[15]

In practice, the comparative advantage theory does not work so neatly. For various reasons, many countries decide to produce certain agricultural, industrial, or consumer products despite a lack of comparative advantage. To facilitate this plan, they restrict imports of competing products from countries that can produce them at lower costs. The net result is that the free movement of goods and services is restricted. We will return to the topic of trade protectionism later in the chapter.

A country has an **absolute advantage** if it has a monopoly on producing a specific product or is able to produce it more efficiently than all other countries. However, an absolute advantage in natural resources does not last forever. For instance, South Africa once had an absolute advantage in diamond production but this is no longer the case. Global competition also causes other absolute advantages to fade. Today there are very few instances of absolute advantage in global markets.

> **absolute advantage**
> The advantage that exists when a country has a monopoly on producing a specific product or is able to produce it more efficiently than all other countries.

LO2 Explain the importance of importing and exporting and define key terms used in global business.

Getting Involved in Global Trade

People interested in finding a job in global business often think of firms like Bombardier, Magna International, and Sony *<http://www.sony.ca>*, which have large multinational accounts. The real job potential, however, may be with small businesses. Small businesses contribute between 25 and 41 percent to Canada's gross domestic product and employ approximately seven million individuals (or 69.7 percent of the total labour force in the private sector). As well, small businesses account for about 90 percent of Canadian exporters.[16] With the help of government agencies, such as Foreign Affairs and International Trade Canada *<http://www.international.gc.ca>* and Export Development Canada *<http://www.edc.ca>*, many small businesses are becoming more involved in global markets.

China produces and exports 80 percent of the toys manufactured in the world. What products do you use that are imported from China?

Getting started globally is often a matter of observation, determination, and risk. What does that mean? First, it is important to observe and study global markets. Your library, the Internet, and your fellow classmates are good starting points for doing your research. Second, if you have the opportunity, travelling to different countries is a great way to observe foreign cultures and lifestyles and see if doing business globally appeals to you.

Importing Goods and Services[17]

The Canada Border Services Agency *<http://www.cbsa-asfc.gc.ca>* deals with importers across the whole range of goods and services that enter our country. These products (also referred to as items) are subject to compliance with certain conditions imposed by the federal and, sometimes, provincial government(s). Some of the conditions may include the following:

- Is the article prohibited entry into Canada (e.g., baby walkers are prohibited due to Canadian safety standards)?

- Is the article allowed to be imported only under the authority of an import permit? Examples include textiles and clothing, steel, wheat, barley and their products, certain farm products (e.g., dairy, chicken, eggs, and turkey), and firearms.

- Is the article subject to some other federally-imposed condition? For example, goods for retail sale have to comply with labelling laws; motor vehicles have to meet emission control standards; and food and agricultural products have to pass the necessary health and sanitary checks.

- Is the article subject to some privately-certified standard? For example, all electrical appliances and equipment must be certified by a recognized certification body before they can be sold in Canada.

- Is there a provincial rule to comply with? For example, imports of liquor, wine, and beer require prior authorization from the appropriate liquor commission.

Review Figure 3.3 for categories and examples of goods and services that are imported as well as exported.

Nickelback began as a cover band in Hanna, Alberta, and to date has sold millions of records worldwide. Other Canadian-born entertainers that have global appeal include Justin Bieber, Celine Dion, Drake, and Nelly Furtado. Do you prefer to support Canadian talent?

Exporting Goods and Services[18]

You may be surprised at what you can sell in other countries. The fact is, you can sell just about any good or service that is used in Canada to other countries—and often the competition is not nearly as intense for producers in global markets as it is at home. You can, for example, sell snowplows to Saudi Arabians who use them to clear sand off their driveways. Don't forget that services can be exported as well.

While Canada has a small population, it produces vast quantities of goods. Based on the most recent data, Canadian exports represented 2.4 percent (US$458 billion) of world merchandise trade and 1.7 percent (US$78 billion) of world services trade.[19] Why is trade so important? Trade with other countries enhances the quality of life for Canadians and contributes to our country's economic well-being. Exports alone account for one in three Canadian jobs.

■ **FIGURE 3.3**

CATEGORIES AND EXAMPLES OF CANADA'S MERCHANDISE AND SERVICE TRADE	
Categories	**Examples**
Merchandise Trade	
Industrial Goods and Materials	Metals and metal ores, chemicals and plastics, and other industrial goods and materials
Machinery and Equipment	Industrial and agricultural machinery, aircraft and other transportation equipment, and other machinery and equipment
Energy Products	Crude petroleum and other energy products such as natural gas, petroleum, and coal products
Automotive Products	Passenger autos and chassis, trucks and other motor vehicles, and motor vehicle parts
Agricultural and Fishing Products	Wheat, fruits and vegetables, and other agricultural and fishing products such as live animals, feed, beverages, and tobacco
Forestry Products	Lumber and sawmill products, wood pulp and other wood products, and newsprint and other paper products
Other Consumer Goods	Apparel and footwear, and miscellaneous consumer goods such as watches, sporting goods and toys, and television and radio sets
Service Trade Categories	
Travel Services	Business travel and personal travel
Transport Services	Air transport, water transport, land, and other transport
Commercial Services	Communication, construction, insurance, computer and information, architectural, engineering, research and development, and other financial services
Government Services	Military activities and business support

Sources: "Canada's International Trade in Services, 2013," Statistics Canada, 1 October 2014, http://www.statcan.gc.ca/daily-quotidien/141001/dq141001b-eng.pdf; Canadian International Merchandise Trade, Statistics Canada, January 2015, Catalogue no. 65-001-X.

Canadian goods and services can be sold abroad directly as an export from a Canadian company or they can be sold indirectly via a foreign-located subsidiary of a Canadian company. Sales by majority-owned foreign affiliates of Canadian businesses are an important means by which Canadian companies engage in international commerce, and they are equivalent to slightly over 90 percent of the value of goods and services exports.

Spend some time reviewing Figure 3.4. By understanding this information, you will realize why you hear so much about imports and exports in the news. After all, such activities are vital to our economy. What questions might you ask about Canada's trade performance? It is also important for businesses to be aware of these great opportunities. But don't be misled. Selling in global markets is not by any means easy. (Review the Spotlight on Small Business box for an example of a one export area where Canadian businesses thrive.) Adapting goods and services to specific global markets is potentially profitable but can be very difficult. We shall discuss a number of forces that affect global trading later in this chapter.

Measuring Global Trade

In measuring the effectiveness of global trade, nations carefully follow two key indicators: balance of trade and balance of payments. The **balance of trade** is a nation's ratio of exports to imports.

■ FIGURE 3.4

CANADA'S GOODS AND SERVICES IMPORT/EXPORT PERFORMANCE, 2013				
	SERVICES		GOODS	
	Exports	Imports	Exports	Imports
Value (billions)	$86,760	$111,309	$478,975	$486,308
Annual Growth (%)	3.2%	2.8%	3.6%	2.5%

Source: "Canada's State of Trade: Trade and Investment Update—2014," Office of the Chief Economist, Foreign Affairs, Trade and Development Canada, accessed 24 March 2015, http://www.international.gc.ca/economist-economiste/performance/state-point/state_2014_point/index .aspx?lang=eng#3.0.

A *favourable* balance of trade, or **trade surplus,** occurs when the value of the country's exports exceeds that of its imports. An unfavourable balance of trade, or **trade deficit,** occurs when the value of the country's imports exceeds that of its exports. In 2009, Canada registered its first trade deficit in 15 years and this continued to be the case in 2014.[20] It is easy to understand why countries prefer to export more than they import. If I sell you $200 worth of goods and buy only $100 worth, I have an extra $100 available to buy other things. However, I'm in an unfavourable position if I buy $200 worth of goods from you and sell you only $100.

balance of trade
A nation's ratio of exports to imports.

trade surplus
A favourable balance of trade; occurs when the value of a country's exports exceeds that of its imports.

trade deficit
An unfavourable balance of trade; occurs when the value of a country's imports exceeds that of its exports.

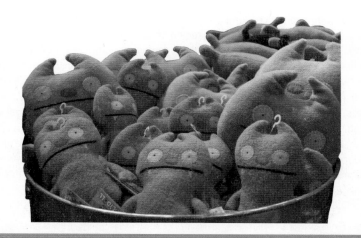

Things may not have started off "pretty" for Ugly Dolls, a venture founded almost by accident, but the two-person company has grown into a global business selling its products in over 1,000 stores around the world. The original dolls have been joined by accessories, books, calendars, action figures, and T-shirts. Does a career in exporting or importing sound appealing to you?

Spotlight *On* SMALL BUSINESS

Let the Games Begin

Members of Generation Z, a demographic group born between 1995 and the present, love to play video games. Statistics show they multitask across five screens daily and spend 41 percent of their time outside of school with computers or mobile devices. While many of the video gaming platforms have big business names, such as Sony, Apple, and Nintendo, much of the work to design the games comes from small businesses. In 2013, Canada's video gaming industry ranked third in the world and contributed $2.3 billion in GDP to the Canadian economy.

The Canadian companies are primarily small and micro-sized businesses based in urban centres. But there are exceptions: Other Ocean Interactive <*http://www.otherocean.com*>, which operates offices in Charlottetown, Prince Edward Island, and St. John's, Newfoundland, is best known for the development of Konami's award-winning Xbox LIVE™ Arcade download, *Castlevania*™; *Symphony of the Night*™, Midway's Nintendo DS release of the popular franchise *Ultimate*™ *Mortal Kombat*®; and the highly popular *Sega's Super.* While a location away from the California gaming hub may seem a challenge, studio head Deidre Ayre sees the choice a different way, "I am proud to say we have created 75 jobs in the Atlantic region so far and that number is still growing."

Bight Games, also in PEI, built success on "freemium" games (apps that are free with fees for virtual goods) *Trade Nation,* a perennial top-grossing game in the App Store, and *The Simpsons:Tapped,* a popular mobile video game. The business was so successful Electronic Arts (EA) acquired the indie mobile games developer. "Video games are not IT in the traditional sense. We're in the entertainment business," says Stuart Duncan, founder of Bight Games. "We employ as many artists as programmers, and deal with original intellectual property, as well as patents. And, we make more money than Hollywood."

With these products, both companies gain an edge in the competitive environment of the global gaming industry that has an estimated value of $30 billion. According to the Entertainment Software Association of Canada, 65 percent of Canadians believe the video gaming industry has a positive effect on the Canadian economy. Thanks to small businesses like these, it's true.

Source: Matthew Bambach, "Canada's video-game industry ranks No.3 worldwide," *The Globe and Mail,* 18 March 2013, http://www .theglobeandmail.com/report-on-business/small-business/sb-digital/biz-categories-technology/canadas-video-game-industry-ranks-no -3-worldwide/article9875545/; Entertainment Software Association of Canada, "Facts and Figures," 2012, http://theesa.ca/facts -research/; Hayley Peterson, "Millennials are old news – Here's everything you should know about Generation Z," Business Insider-Retail, 25 June 2014, http://www.businessinsider.com/generation-z-spending-habits-2014-6; "Prince Edward Island's Video gaming industry showing signs of making serious noise," *The Guardian,* 8 January 2008, http://www.gameplan.ca/documents/guardianstory1.pdf; Dean Takahashi, "EA acquires mobile game developer Bight Games," VB, 15 August 2011, http://venturebeat.com/2011/08/15 /ea-acquires-mobile-game-developer-bight-games/.

The **balance of payments** is the difference between money coming into a country (from exports) and money leaving the country (for imports) plus money flows coming into or leaving a country from other factors such as tourism, foreign aid, military expenditures, and foreign investment. The goal is always to have more money flowing into the country than flowing out of the country; in other words, a *favourable* balance of payments. Conversely, an *unfavourable* balance of payments is when more money is flowing out of a country than coming in.

balance of payments
The difference between money coming into a country (from exports) and money leaving the country (for imports) plus money flows from other factors such as tourism, foreign aid, military expenditures, and foreign investment.

Trading in Global Markets: The Canadian Experience

At first glance, Canada's foreign trade statistics are impressive. As a country, we rank eleventh in the world as leading exporter and thirteenth the world as leading importer in world merchandise trade.[21] While our abundant natural resources are a major area for exports, developing countries continue to give Canada stiff competition in these areas. When we look carefully at the numbers in Figure 3.5, we see that we are dependent on one country, the United States. Over the long-term, Derek Burleton, Deputy Chief Economist with Toronto-Dominion Bank (TD) *<http://www.td.com>*, expects that Canada's economic prosperity will be increasingly driven by trade with economies other than the United States'. He predicts that by 2020, the United States will account for only two-thirds of Canada's exports, down from a peak of 85 percent in 2002.[22] Read the next section to learn about these priority markets.

■ **FIGURE 3.5**

CANADA'S GOODS AND SERVICES TRADE BY REGION, 2014		
	Exports %	Imports %
United States	74.5	67.8
European Union	8.2	8.8
China	3.8	7.3
Japan	2.2	1.7
Mexico	1.4	3.4
Rest of World	9.9	11

Source: "Monthly Report on Canada's International Merchandise Trade Performance, January 2015," Foreign Affairs, Trade and Development Canada, accessed on 24 March 2015, http://www.international.gc.ca/economist-economiste/performance/monthly-mensuel.aspx?lang=eng.

Canada's Priority Markets[23]

Technological advances in most fields, primarily in the area of transmission and storage of information, have shattered the archaic notions of how things ought to function, from production and trade to war and politics. The new ways of communicating, organizing, and working are inviting the most remote corners of the world to be actors on the global economic stage. These *emerging economies* are enjoying high growth rates, rapid increases in their living standards, and a rising global prominence.

Tapping into these markets is crucial. For example, in 30 years a gain of just .1 percent in the Canadian share of the import markets of Brazil, Russia, India, and China (BRIC countries) would mean an export gain of $29 billion.

Based on extensive consultation with government, academic, and Canadian business and industry representatives, the federal government developed its Global Markets Action Plan. The plan identifies three priority market types: emerging markets with broad Canadian interests, emerging markets with specific opportunities for Canadian businesses, and established markets with broad Canadian interests. These emerging market types include 21 countries and focus upon Asia Pacific (ten countries), Latin America and Caribbean (four countries), North America (one country), Middle East and Africa (four countries), and Europe (two countries).[24]

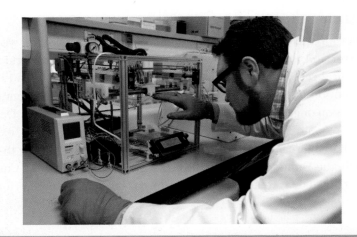

One objective of the federal government's Science and Technology program is to identify and incorporate world-leading research into the development of innovative processes, goods, and services in Canada. What are some other benefits of such initiatives?

China and India are of particular interest as they are growing and emerging markets due to their size and economic transformation. A Conference Board of Canada report notes that by 2050, India will be the world's third-largest economy, with a GDP approaching US$30 trillion, behind only the United States and China, which will top the list. Steps already taken to encourage a stronger Canadian presence in the global marketplace include tax cuts, increased support for research and development, and critical investments in infrastructure at Canada–U.S. border crossings and Canada's Asia-Pacific Gateway.

Progress Assessment

- How do world population and market statistics support the expansion of Canadian businesses into global markets?
- What is comparative advantage? How does this differ from absolute advantage?
- How are a country's balance of trade and balance of payments determined?

LO3 Illustrate the strategies used in reaching global markets and explain the role of multinational corporations in global markets.

Strategies for Reaching Global Markets

Businesses use many different strategies to compete in global markets. The key strategies include licensing, exporting, franchising, contract manufacturing, creating international joint ventures and strategic alliances, and engaging in foreign direct investment. Each of these strategies provides opportunities for becoming involved in global markets, along with specific commitments and risks. Figure 3.6. places the strategies discussed on a continuum showing the amount of commitment, control, risk, and profit potential associated with each one. Take a few minutes to look it over before you continue.

■ **FIGURE 3.6**

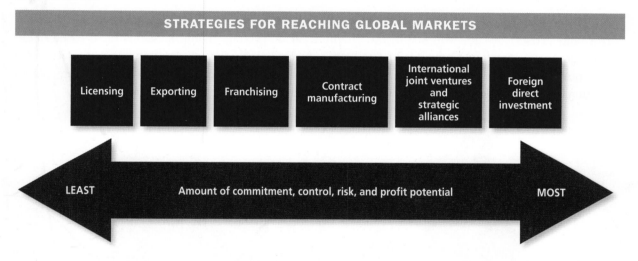

Licensing

A firm (the licensor) may decide to compete in a global market by **licensing** the right to manufacture its product or use its trademark to a foreign company (the licensee) for a fee (a royalty). A company with an interest in licensing generally needs to send company representatives to the foreign producer to help set up the production process. The licensor may also assist or work with a licensee in such areas as distribution, promotion, and consulting.

> **licensing**
> A global strategy in which a firm (the licensor) allows a foreign company (the licensee) to produce its product in exchange for a fee (a royalty).

A licensing agreement can benefit a firm in several ways. First, the firm can gain revenues it would not otherwise have generated in its home market. Also, foreign licensees must often purchase start-up supplies, component materials, and consulting services from the licensing firm. Coca-Cola has entered into global licensing agreements with over 300 licensees that have extended into long-term service contracts that sell over $1 billion of the company's products each year.[25] Service-based companies are also active in licensing. For example, retailer Frederick's of Hollywood *<http://www.fredericks.com>*

entered into a licensing agreement with Emirates Associated Business Group to build and operate Frederick's of Hollywood stores in the Middle East.

A final advantage of licensing is that licensors spend little or no money to produce and market their products. These costs come from the licensee's pocket. Therefore, licensees generally work hard to succeed. However, licensors may also experience some problems. Often, a firm must grant licensing rights to its product for an extended period, 20 years or longer. If a product experiences remarkable growth in the foreign market, the bulk of the revenues earned belong to the licensee. Perhaps even more threatening is that a licensing firm is actually selling its expertise. If a foreign licensee learns the company's technology or product secrets, it may break the agreement and begin to produce a similar product on its own. If legal remedies are not available, the licensing firm may lose its trade secrets, not to mention promised royalties.

Exporting

Canadian companies export goods and services (e.g., call centres, IT consultants, and cultural and performing artists). As you will see in the chapters on marketing, many decisions have to be made when a company markets a new product or goes into new markets with existing products. Often the first export sales occur as a result of unsolicited orders received. Regardless of how a company starts exporting, it must develop some goals and some strategies for achieving those goals.

Warner Bros. <http://www.warnerbros.com> has licenses with hundreds of companies to make products related successful film franchises like *The Hobbit*. Do you think Hobbit-licensed products will maintain their global popularity with new generations of viewers?

Canadian firms that are still hesitant can engage in indirect exporting through specialists called export-trading companies (or export-management companies) that assist in negotiating and establishing trading relationships. An export-trading company not only matches buyers and sellers from different countries but also deals with foreign customs offices, documentation, and even weights and measures conversions to ease the process of entering global markets. It also helps exporters get paid. If you are considering a career in global business, export-trading companies often provide internships or part-time opportunities for students.

Franchising

Franchising is a contractual agreement whereby someone with a good idea for a business sells the rights to use the business name and sell a product or service in a given territory in a specified manner.

Franchising is popular domestically and internationally. (We will discuss it in depth in Chapter 6.) Canadian franchisors such as Molly Maid *<http://www.mollymaid.ca>* and Tim Hortons have global units operated by foreign franchisees.

In 1986, brothers Michael and Aaron Serruya, then aged 19 and 20, wanted to buy a franchise, but no one would take a chance on them. So, they started their own frozen yogourt shop, Yogen Früz *<http://www.yogenfruz.com>*. Today, Yogen Früz has grown to be a world leader in the frozen yogourt category, with over 1,300 locations worldwide and a 20-year Top 500 Global Franchise rating.[26] Another Canadian business, BeaverTails Pastry *<http://www.beavertailsinc.com>*, was started in 1978. The company produces whole-wheat pastries that are stretched by hand to resemble the tail of a beaver, one of Canada's best-known national symbols. The pastries are then float cooked on high quality canola oil and served piping hot, topped with butter and a choice of delectable flavours. The company operates over 80 franchised and licensed outlets across Canada, together with two locations in Saudi Arabia and two stores in Colorado's ski country.[27]

Tired of studying and want a quick snack? How about a piping hot Domino's pizza with potatoes and corn topped with mayo? Domino's serves pizzas around the globe that appeal to different tastes (the mayo pizza is a hit in Japan). How can franchisors ensure their products are appropriate for global markets?

Franchisors have to be careful to adapt their product or service to the countries they serve. Yum! Brands' has 40,000 of its KFC, Taco Bell, and Pizza Hut restaurants in 130 countries around the world.[28] They learned quickly that preferences in pizza toppings differ globally. Japanese customers, for example, enjoy squid and sweet mayonnaise pizza. In the company's KFC restaurants in China, the menu is chicken with Sichuan spicy sauce and rice, egg soup, and a "dragon twister" (KFC's version of a traditional Beijing duck wrap).[29] Read the nearby Reaching Beyond Our Borders box that highlights another global franchise champion, McDonald's.

Contract Manufacturing

Contract manufacturing involves a foreign company's production of private-label goods to which a domestic company then attaches its own brand name or trademark. (This practice falls under the broad category of *outsourcing*, which we introduced in Chapter 1 and which will be discussed in more depth later in this chapter.) For example, Dell Computer *<http://www.dell.com>* contracts with Quanta Computer of Taiwan *<http://www.quantatw.com>* to make notebook PCs, on which it then puts the Dell brand name, while Nike *<http://www.nike.com>* has almost 700 contract factories around the world that manufacture its footwear and apparel. The worldwide contract manufacturing business is estimated to be a $250 billion industry that is expected to grow to $325 billion soon.[30]

> **contract manufacturing**
> A foreign country's production of private-label goods to which a domestic company then attaches its brand name or trademark; also called outsourcing.

Contract manufacturing enables a company to experiment in a new market without incurring heavy start-up costs such as building a manufacturing plant. If the brand name becomes a success, the company has penetrated a new market with relatively low risk. A firm can also use contract manufacturing temporarily to meet an unexpected increase in orders and, of course, labour costs are often very low.

One company, featured in *PROFIT* magazine's ranking of Canada's emerging growth companies, has used contract manufacturing successfully. FouFou Dog *<http://www.foufoudog.com>* is a dog apparel company whose collection includes canine track suits, hoodies, jewelled collars and leashes, as well as chew toys. At the age of 24, Cheryl Ng, owner of a Maltese dog named Ernie, started the company because she liked how Paris Hilton dressed her dog. Today, the company exports 95 percent of its products. According to Ng, "All our stuff is made in Argentina. In China, quality control can be hit-and-miss or downright sloppy—you could have a disaster on your hands—but it's been consistently good from my suppliers." And she has other reasons for heading south instead of east: "My suppliers will make me a small quantity if I want to try something out. You can't get that from China anymore, and I don't want to be stuck with a colour or style nobody wants; besides, they let me check out the textiles before I buy and they always have good stuff." She also likes the shorter flights and the fact that she only has to cross two time zones.[31]

Reaching *Beyond* OUR BORDERS

McDonald's Over 100 Cultures Served

www.mcdonalds.com

For decades McDonald's has been the undisputed king of global food franchising. With more than 34,000 restaurants in over 118 countries, Mickey D's serves more than 69 million customers every day.

So how did McDonald's become such a global powerhouse? It certainly didn't get there through hamburgers alone. Since it first began expanding overseas, McDonald's has been careful to include regional tastes on its menus along with the usual Big Mac and french fries. For instance, in Thailand patrons can order the Samurai Burger, a pork-patty sandwich marinated in teriyaki sauce and topped with mayonnaise and a pickle. If fish is more your taste, try the Ebi Filet-o-Shrimp sandwich from Japan.

McDonald's is also careful to adapt its menus to local customs and culture. In Israel, all meat served in the chain's restaurants is 100 percent kosher beef. The company also closes many of its restaurants on the Sabbath and religious holidays. McDonald's pays respect to religious sentiments in India as well by not including any beef or pork on its menu. For more examples, go to www.mcdonalds.com and explore the various McDonald's international franchises' websites. Notice how the company blends the culture of each country into the restaurant's image.

McDonald's main global market concern as of late has been Asia. So far McDonald's strategy seems to be working. In Shanghai the company's Hamburger University attracts top-level college graduates to be trained for management positions. Only about eight out of every 1,000 applicants make it into the program, an acceptance rate even lower than Harvard's! McDonald's is reaching out further in Asia and in 2014 opened its first store in Vietnam. The Vietnamese location in Ho Chi Minh City is the country's very first drive-thru restaurant. Bringing McDonald's to Vietnam is a dream come true for Henry Nguyen, founder of Good Day Hospitality, who has been wanting to introduce the brand to Vietnam for over a decade. Nguyen brought in 20 top McDonald's employees from Australia to help with the opening while also sending prospective Vietnamese employees to Queensland to learn the ropes in a real-life restaurant setting. In the end, one can only hope that McDonald's remains dedicated to quality as it continues adapting and expanding into the global market.

Sources: Erin Smith, "Some McSkills to Share," *The Warwick Daily News*, 4 February 2014; Kate Taylor, "New Year, New Expansion: McDonald's to Open First Restaurant in Vietnam," *Entrepreneur*, 23 December 2013; Vivian Giang, "McDonald's Hamburger University: Step inside The Most Exclusive School in the World," *Business Insider*, 7 April 2012; and McDonald's, www.mcdonalds.com, accessed February 2014.

International Joint Ventures and Strategic Alliances

A **joint venture** is a partnership in which two or more companies (often from different countries) join to undertake a major project. Joint ventures are often mandated by governments as a condition of doing business in their country, as often occurs in China. For example, Disney and state-owned Shanghai Shendi Group entered a joint venture to create a Disneyland theme park in Shanghai that is expected to open in 2015.[32]

joint venture
A partnership in which two or more companies (often from different countries) join to undertake a major project.

The Bank of Nova Scotia <http://www.scotiabank.com> formed a joint venture with the Bank of Beijing <http://www.bankofbeijing.com.cn/en2011/index.html>. The Bank of Beijing Scotiabank Asset Management Co. Ltd. markets mutual funds to retail and institutional customers through the Chinese bank's national branch network.

Joint ventures are developed for many different reasons. Marriott International *<https://www.marriott.com/>* and AC Hotels in Spain entered a joint venture to create AC Hotels by Marriott *<http://achotels.marriott.com>* in order to increase their global footprint and future growth.[33] PepsiCo *<http://pepsico.ca>*, as part of its Performance with Purpose global vision, agreed to joint ventures with Tata Global Beverages of India *<http://www.tataglobalbeverages.com>* to develop packaged health and wellness beverages for the mass consumer market in India and the Strauss Group *<http://www.strauss-group.com>* in Mexico to provide fresh dips and spreads.[34]

The benefits of international joint ventures are clear:

1. Shared technology and risk.

2. Shared marketing and management expertise.

3. Entry into markets where foreign companies are often not allowed unless goods are produced locally.

The drawbacks are not so obvious but are important. One partner can learn the other's technology and practices, and then use what it learned to its own advantage. Also, a shared technology may become obsolete or the joint venture may become too large to be as flexible as needed.

The global market is also fuelling the growth of strategic alliances. A **strategic alliance** is a long-term partnership between two or more companies established to help each company build competitive market advantages. Unlike joint ventures, strategic alliances do not share costs, risks, management, or even profits. Thanks to their flexibility, strategic alliances can effectively link firms from different countries and firms of vastly different sizes. Hewlett-Packard *<http://www.hp.com>* has strategic alliances with Hitachi *<http://www.hitachi.ca>* and Samsung *<http://www.samsung.com>*, and Chevron *<http://www.chevron.com>* has alliances with the Western Australian Energy Research Alliance *<http://www.waera.com.au>*.

---

strategic alliance
A long-term partnership between two or more companies established to help each company build competitive market advantages.

Foreign Direct Investment

Foreign direct investment (FDI) is buying permanent property and businesses in foreign nations. As the size of a foreign market expands, many firms increase FDI and establish a foreign subsidiary. A **foreign subsidiary** is a company owned in a foreign country by another company (called the *parent company*). The subsidiary operates like a domestic firm, with production, distribution, promotion, pricing, and other business functions under the control of the subsidiary's management. The subsidiary must observe the legal requirements of both the country where the parent firm is located (called the *home country*) and the foreign country where the subsidiary is located (called the *host country*).

---

foreign direct investment (FDI)
The buying of permanent property and businesses in foreign nations.

foreign subsidiary
A company owned in a foreign country by the parent company.

The primary advantage of a subsidiary is that the company maintains complete control over any technology or expertise it may possess. The major shortcoming is the need to commit funds and technology within foreign boundaries. Should relationships with a host country falter, the firm's assets could be *expropriated* (taken over by the foreign government). Swiss-based Nestlé has many foreign subsidiaries. The consumer-products giant spent billions of dollars acquiring foreign companies such as Jenny Craig (weight management) <*http://www.jennycraig.com*>, Ralston Purina <*http://www.purina .com*>, Chef America (maker of Hot Pockets), and Dreyer's Ice Cream <*http://www.dreyers.com*>, as well as Perrier <*http://www.perrier.com*> in France. It employs over 328,000 people in factories and operations in almost every country in the world.[35]

Canada has been and remains a popular global spot for foreign direct investment. Global automobile manufacturers like Toyota and Honda have spent millions of dollars building facilities in Canada, like the Toyota plant in Cambridge, Ontario, pictured here. Do you consider a Toyota made in Ontario to be a Canadian car or a Japanese car?

Nestlé is a **multinational corporation,** one that manufactures and markets products in many different countries and has multinational stock ownership and management. Multinational corporations are typically extremely large corporations like Nestlé, but not all large global businesses are multinationals. A business could export everything it produces, deriving 100 percent of its sales and profits globally, and still not be a multinational corporation. Only firms that have *manufacturing capacity* or some other physical presence in different nations, such as Magna International, can truly be called multinational. Figure 3.7 lists the ten largest multinational corporations in the world.

multinational corporation
An organization that manufactures and markets products in many different countries and has multinational stock ownership and multinational management.

Canadian subsidiaries of foreign-based companies have played a major role in developing the Canadian economy. There are, however, several disadvantages to foreign investment. One is that Canada has been criticized for having a "branch plant economy." This occurs when many subsidiaries are owned by foreign companies and profits are returned to the home country rather than reinvested in Canada. There are concerns that decisions made by the parent company are not primarily based on the needs of Canadians. For example, if a U.S. company decides to reduce its workforce or close a plant, it may more readily do that to a Canadian subsidiary rather than in its home country.

■ FIGURE 3.7

THE LARGEST MULTINATIONAL CORPORATIONS IN THE WORLD		
Company	Country	Website
I Walmart Stores	United States	walmart.com
2 Sinopec Group	China	sinopecgroup.com
3 Royal Dutch Shell	Netherlands	shell.com
4 China National Petroleum	China	cnpc.com.cn
5 ExxonMobil	United States	exxonmobil.com
6 BP	Britain	bp.com
7 State Grid	China	sgcc.com.cn
8 Volkswagen	Germany	volkswagen.com
9 Toyota Motor	Japan	toyota.co.jp
I0 Glencore	Switzerland	glencore.com

Source: *Fortune*, 23 July 2015.

In the early 1990s, Michael Porter, the competition guru from Harvard University Business School, released a report titled *The Competitive Advantage of Nations* that was commissioned by the Canadian government. While this report is now 25 years old, some of his points still ring true today:

> *One of Canada's competitive problems is the high concentration of foreign-owned firms that perform little sophisticated production or R&D. It matters a lot where a multinational calls home, because a company's home base is where the best jobs exist, where core R&D is undertaken, and where strategic control rests... Home bases are important to an economy because they support high productivity and productivity growth.*

Regardless of these concerns, more countries are welcoming subsidiaries as a way to develop their economies.

Getting involved in global business requires selecting an entry strategy that best fits your business goals. The different strategies discussed reflect different levels of ownership, financial commitment, and risk. However, this is just the beginning. You should also be aware of market forces that affect a business's ability to trade in global markets. After the Progress Assessment, we will discuss them.

Progress Assessment

- What are the advantages to a firm of using licensing as a method of entry in global markets? What are the disadvantages?
- What is the key difference between a joint venture and a strategic alliance?
- What makes a company a multinational corporation?

Bombardier Transportation was awarded a contract to supply Bombardier Flexity Swift high-floor light rail vehicles to the Bursa Metropolitan Municipality, Turkey. The vehicles will be built at Bombardier's manufacturing facility in Bautzen, Germany. Train cars will come from the Siegen site, while the electrical equipment will be supplied by the Mannheim plant.

LO4 Evaluate the forces that affect trading in global markets.

Forces Affecting Trading in Global Markets

The hurdles to success are higher and more complex in global markets than in domestic markets. Such hurdles include dealing with differences in sociocultural forces, economic and financial forces, legal forces, and physical and environmental forces. Let's take a look at each of these global market forces to see how they challenge even the most established and experienced global businesses.

Sociocultural Forces

The word **culture** refers to the set of values, beliefs, rules, and institutions held by a specific group of people.[36] Culture can also include social structures, religion, manners and customs, values and attitudes, language, and personal communication. An attitude that one's own culture is superior to all others is known as **ethnocentricity.** If you hope to get involved in global trade, it is critical to be aware of the cultural differences among nations.

> **culture**
> The set of values, beliefs, rules, and institutions held by a specific group of people.
>
> **ethnocentricity**
> An attitude that one's own culture is superior to all others.

Different nations have very different ways of conducting business. Canadian businesses that wish to compete globally must adapt to those ways. In North America, we like to do things quickly. We tend to call each other by our first names and try to get friendly even on the first encounter. In Japan, China, and other countries these actions would be considered surprising and even rude. Canadian negotiators will say no if they mean no, but Japanese negotiators usually say maybe when they mean no.

Religion is an important part of any society's culture and can have a significant impact on business operations. Consider the violent clashes between religious communities in India, Pakistan, Northern Ireland,

and the Middle East—clashes that have wounded these areas' economies. Companies sometimes ignore religious implications in business decisions. Both McDonald's and Coca-Cola offended Muslims in Saudi Arabia by putting the Saudi Arabian flag on their packaging. The flag's design contains a passage from the Quran (Islam's sacred scripture), and Muslims feel that their holy writ should never be wadded up and thrown away.

Successful companies are those that can understand these differences and develop goods and services accordingly. Regardless of whether the focus is a large or small global market, understanding sociocultural differences is important when managing employees. In Latin American countries, workers believe that managers are placed in positions of authority to make decisions and be responsible for the well-being of their workers. Consider what happened to one North American manager in Peru who was unaware of this characteristic and believed that workers should participate in managerial functions. This manager was convinced that he could motivate his workers to higher levels of productivity by instituting a more democratic decision-making style than the one already in place. Soon workers began quitting their jobs in droves. When asked why, the workers said the new manager did not know his job and was asking the workers what to do. All stated that they wanted to find new jobs, since obviously this company was doomed due to incompetent managers.

Many companies still fail to think globally. A sound philosophy is: *Never assume that what works in one country will work in another.* Companies such as Roots <*http://www.roots.com*>, Nike, and Toyota have developed brand names with widespread global appeal and recognition. However, even these successful global marketers often face difficulties.[37] To get an idea of the problems companies have faced with advertising translations, take a look at Figure 3.8.

■ FIGURE 3.8

OOPS, DID WE SAY THAT?

A global marketing strategy can be very difficult to implement. Look at the problems these well-known companies encountered in global markets.

PepsiCo attempted a Chinese translation of "Come Alive, You're in the Pepsi Generation" that read to Chinese customers as "Pepsi Brings Your Ancestors Back from the Dead."

Coors Brewing Company put its slogan "Turn It Loose" into Spanish and found it translated as "Suffer from Diarrhea."

KFC's patented slogan "Finger-Lickin' Good" was understood in Japanese as "Bite Your Fingers Off."

On the other side of the translation glitch, Electrolux, a Scandinavian vacuum manufacturer, tried to sell its products in the North American market with the slogan "Nothing Sucks Like an Electrolux."

Economic and Financial Forces

Economic differences can also make entering global markets more challenging. It is hard for us to imagine buying chewing gum by the stick instead of by the package. Yet this buying behaviour is commonplace in economically depressed nations like Haiti, where customers can afford only small quantities. You might suspect that with more than 1 billion people, India would be a dream market for companies like PepsiCo and Hershey's <*http://www.hersheys.com*>. However, Indians consume an average of only three soft drinks per person a year, and most cannot afford chocolate due to India's low per-capita income.[38]

Global financial markets unfortunately do not have a worldwide currency. Mexicans shop with pesos, South Koreans with won, Japanese with yen, and Canadians with dollars. Globally, the U.S. dollar is considered a dominant and stable currency.[39] However, it does not always retain the same market value.[40] In an international transaction today, one dollar may be exchanged for eight pesos; tomorrow, you may only get seven. The **exchange rate** is the value of one nation's currency relative to the currencies of other countries.

---

exchange rate
The value of one nation's currency relative to the currencies of other countries.

Changes in a nation's exchange rates can have important implications in global markets. A *high value of the dollar* means that a dollar would be traded for more foreign currency than normal. The products of foreign producers would be cheaper because it takes fewer dollars to buy them, but the cost of Canadian-produced goods would become more expensive to foreign purchasers because of the dollar's high value. Conversely, a *low value of the dollar* means that a dollar is traded for less foreign currency than normal. Therefore, foreign goods become more expensive because it takes more dollars to buy them, but Canadian goods become cheaper to foreign buyers because it takes less foreign currency to buy Canadian goods.

Global financial markets operate under a system called *floating exchange rates,* in which currencies "float" according to the supply and demand for them in the global market for the currency. This supply and demand is created by global currency traders, who develop a market for a nation's currency based on the perceived trade and investment potential of the country.

Changes in currency values cause many problems globally.[41] For instance, labour costs for multinational corporations like Bombardier, Nestlé, General Electric, and Sony can vary considerably as currency values shift, causing them to juggle production from one country to another.

Currency valuation problems can be especially harsh on developing economies. At certain times a nation's government will intervene and adjust the value of its currency, often to increase the export potential of its products. **Devaluation** is lowering the value of a nation's currency relative to other currencies. Argentina and Venezuela both devalued their currencies in 2014 to try to alleviate severe economic problems in each country.[42] Sometimes, due to a nation's weak currency, the only way to trade is *bartering,* which is the exchange of merchandise for other merchandise, or service for other service, with no money involved.[43]

---

devaluation
Lowering the value of a nation's currency relative to other currencies.

Countertrading is a complex form of bartering in which several countries may be involved, each trading goods for goods or services for services. Let's say that a developing country such as Jamaica wants to buy vehicles from Ford Motor Company in exchange for bauxite, a mineral compound that is a source of aluminum ore. Ford does not need Jamaican bauxite, but does need compressors. In a counter-trade agreement, Ford may trade vehicles to Jamaica, which then trades bauxite to another country—say, India—which then exchanges compressors with Ford. All three parties benefit in the process, and avoid some of the financial problems and currency constraints in global markets. Estimates are that countertrading accounts for over 20 percent of all global exchanges, especially with developing countries.[44]

> **countertrading**
> A complex form of bartering in which several countries may be involved, each trading goods for goods or services for services.

When the dollar is "up," foreign goods and travel are a bargain for Canadian consumers. When the dollar trades for less foreign currency, however, foreign tourists (like these viewing Niagara Falls) often flock to Canadian cities to enjoy relatively cheaper vacations and shopping trips. Do Canadian exporters profit more when the dollar is up or when it is down?

Legal Forces

In any economy, the conduct and the direction of business are firmly tied to the legal environment. In Canada, federal and provincial laws heavily affect business practices. In global markets, the absence of a central system of law means many different systems of laws may apply. This makes conducting global business difficult as business people navigate a sea of laws that are often inconsistent. Antitrust rules, labour relations, patents, copyrights, trade practices, taxes, child labour, product liability, and other issues are governed differently country by country.

Canadian businesses must follow Canadian laws in conducting business globally. For example, bribery is not considered legal in Canada. The problem is that this runs contrary to beliefs and practices in many countries where corporate or government bribery not only is acceptable, but also may be the only way to secure a lucrative contract. The Organisation for Economic Co-operation and Development (OECD) <*http://www.oecd.org*> and Transparency International <*http://www.transparency.org*> have led a global effort to fight corruption and bribery in foreign markets, with limited success.[45] Figure 3.9 shows a partial list of countries where bribery or other unethical business practices are most common.

■ **FIGURE 3.9**

COUNTRIES RATED HIGHEST ON CORRUPT BUSINESS
The corruption perceptions index ranks countries and territories according to their perceived level of public sector (government) corruption. This list starts with the most corrupt countries.
1. Somalia
2. North Korea
3. Sudan
4. Afghanistan
5. South Sudan
6. Iraq
7. Turkmenistan
8 Uzbekistan
9. Libya
10. Eritrea
165. Canada (10th least corrupt country in the world)
174. Denmark (least corrupt country in the world)

Source: Corruptions Perceptions Index 2014:Results, Transparency International, Accessed March 2015.

The co-operation and sponsorship of local business people can help a company penetrate the market and deal with laws and bureaucratic barriers in their country.

Physical and Environmental Forces

Certain technological forces can also have an important impact on a company's ability to conduct business in global markets. In fact, technological constraints may make it difficult given the nature of exportable products. For example, houses in most developing countries do not have electrical systems that match those of Canadian homes, in kind or in capacity. How would the differences in electricity available (110 versus 220 volts) affect a Canadian appliance manufacturer wishing to export?

Also, computer and Internet usage in many developing countries is rare or non-existent. You can see how this would make for a challenging business environment in general and would make e-commerce difficult, especially as this is becoming a critical element of business. After the Progress Assessment, we will explore how trade protectionism affects global business.

Progress Assessment

- What are the major hurdles to successful global trade?
- What does ethnocentricity mean, and how can it affect global success?
- How would the low value of the dollar affect Canadian exports?

Debate the advantages and disadvantages of trade protectionism, define tariff and non-tariff barriers, and give examples of common markets.

Trade Protectionism

As we discussed in the previous section, sociocultural, economic and financial, legal, and physical and environmental forces are all challenges to global trade. What is often a much greater barrier to global trade, however, is trade protectionism. **Trade protectionism** is the use of government regulations to limit the import of goods and services. Supporters of trade protectionism believe that it allows domestic producers to survive and grow, producing more jobs. Those against trade protectionism argue that it not only impedes global trade, but that it also adds millions of dollars to the price of products, costing consumers billions of dollars.

> **trade protectionism**
> The use of government regulations to limit the import of goods and services.

Countries often use protectionist measures to guard against practices such as dumping. **Dumping** is selling products in a foreign country at lower prices than those charged in the producing country. This tactic is sometimes used to reduce surplus products in foreign markets or to gain a foothold in a new market. Some governments may offer financial incentives to certain industries to sell goods in global markets for less than they sell them at home. China and Taiwan for example, were found guilty of dumping solar panels in the United States.[46] To understand how trade protectionism affects global business, let's briefly review some global economic history.

> **dumping**
> Selling products in a foreign country at lower prices than those charged in the producing country.

Business, economics, and politics have always been closely linked. What we now call economics was once referred to as the *political* economy, indicating the close ties between politics (government) and economics. In the seventeenth and eighteenth centuries, business people and governments advocated an economic policy called *mercantilism*. The overriding idea of mercantilism was for a nation to sell more goods to other nations than it bought from them; that is, to have a favourable balance of trade. According to the mercantilists, this resulted in a flow of money to the country that sold the most globally. This philosophy led governments to implement **tariffs,** which are taxes on imports, thus making imported goods more expensive to buy.

> **tariff**
> A tax imposed on imports.

There are two kinds of tariffs: protective and revenue. *Protective tariffs* (import taxes) are designed to raise the retail price of imported products so that domestic products will have a more competitive price. These tariffs are meant to save jobs for domestic workers and to keep industries—especially infant industries that have companies in the early stages of growth—from closing down entirely because of foreign competition. Such tariffs are usually met with resistance. Sometimes a tariff affects products and services indirectly. For example, in a dispute over labelling laws the World Trade Organization has ruled that American beef producers have an unfair advantage over Canadian producers. It is believed the U.S. protective tariff policy, which raises the price of Canadian-made beef sold in the United States,

Business leaders believe that too many sales have been lost due to the growing number of imported products. This is the case in the renewable energy industry where Canada placed a tariff on cheap Chinese-made solar panels.[47] While the change protects Canadian companies, will it slow the development of solar projects in Canada?

reduces sales and costs Canada's beef and pork industries more than $1 billion a year.[48] If the U.S. does not comply with the World Trade Organization regulation, Canada may impose retaliatory tariffs on a long list of American-made goods, some of which have nothing to do with beef. *Revenue tariffs*, the second kind of tariff, are designed to raise money for the government.

Believing that the annual seal hunt off the East Coast is inhumane, the European Union has imposed an import ban (or trade embargo) on all products from Canada's seal hunt. The Canadian government believes that it is a trade law violation and has appealed this decision to the World Trade Organization. Which perspective do you support?

An **import quota** limits the number of products in certain categories that a nation can import. Canada has import quotas on a number of products including textiles and clothing, agricultural products, steel, and softwood lumber.[49] The goal is to protect Canadian companies and to preserve jobs. Products subject to export controls include softwood lumber, firearms, sugar and sugar-containing products, peanut butter, and B.C. logs.[50] The Canadian Export and Import Control Bureau sets various regulations regarding import controls (goods and services entering Canada) and export controls (goods and services exiting Canada) in accordance with the Export and Import Permits Act (EIPA).

> **import quota**
> A limit on the number of products in certain categories that a nation can import.

An **embargo** is a complete ban on the import or export of a certain product or the stopping of all trade with a particular country. Political disagreements have caused many countries to establish embargoes, such as Canada's embargo against North Korea, reflecting its condemnation of the North Korean regime's complete disregard for human rights and ongoing repression of the democratic movement.[51]

> **embargo**
> A complete ban on the import or export of a certain product or the stopping of all trade with a particular country.

Non-tariff barriers are not as specific or formal as tariffs, import quotas, and embargoes but can be as detrimental to free trade.[52] Such barriers include restrictive standards that detail exactly how a product must be sold in a country. For example, India imposes a number of restrictive standards like import licensing, burdensome product testing requirements, and lengthy customs procedures that inhibit the sale of imported products. The discovery of mad cow disease resulted in a temporary import ban of Canadian beef by Taiwan, Peru, Belarus, China, and other countries.[53]

Would-be exporters might view trade barriers as good reasons to avoid global trade, but overcoming trade constraints creates business opportunities. Next, we'll look at organizations and agreements that attempt to eliminate barriers.

The GATT and the WTO

In 1948, government leaders from 23 nations formed the **General Agreement on Tariffs and Trade (GATT),** a global forum for reducing trade restrictions on goods, services, ideas, and cultural programs. In 1986, the Uruguay Round of the GATT convened to renegotiate trade agreements. After eight years of meetings, 124 nations voted to lower tariffs an average of 38 percent worldwide, and expand new trade rules to areas such as agriculture, services, and the protection of patents.

> **General Agreement on Tariffs and Trade (GATT)**
> A 1948 agreement that established an international forum for negotiating mutual reductions in trade restrictions.

The Uruguay Round also established the **World Trade Organization (WTO)** *<http://www.wto.org>* to mediate trade disputes among nations. The WTO, headquartered in Geneva, Switzerland, is an independent entity of 161 member nations, and its purpose is to oversee cross-border trade issues and global business practices among those nations.[54] Trade disputes are presented by member nations with decisions made within a year, rather than languishing for years, as in the past.

> **World Trade Organization (WTO)**
> The international organization that replaced the General Agreement on Tariffs and Trade, and was assigned the duty to mediate trade disputes among nations.

The WTO has not solved all global trade problems. Legal differences (discussed earlier) often impede trade expansion. And a wide gap separates developing nations (80 percent of the WTO membership) and industrialized nations like Canada. The WTO meetings in Doha, Qatar, began in 2001 to address dismantling protection of manufactured goods, eliminating subsidies on agricultural products, and overturning temporary protectionist measures. Unfortunately, the Doha Round ended in 2008 with no significant agreements.[55]

Canada's long dispute with the United States over softwood lumber cost the economy billions of dollars and thousands of jobs. In 2002, the United States imposed duties of 27 percent on Canadian softwood lumber, arguing that Canada unfairly subsidized producers of spruce, pine, and fir lumber. While international trade tribunals sided with Canada, it was not until 2006 that an agreement between both countries was signed. The United States agreed to return over $4.5 billion in duties it had collected and remove tariffs on lumber. The current softwood lumber agreement will expire in 2015 and hopes are that both countries will extend the trade arrangement until 2022.

In the past, this Indian family used to use bullocks to pull their plow, but had to sell them because the cost to maintain the animals is now too high. Do you think a Doha resolution regarding tariff protection would help families like these?

The IMF and the World Bank

The **International Monetary Fund (IMF)** *<http://www.imf.org>* was created in 1944. The IMF is an international bank supported by its members that usually makes short-term loans to countries experiencing problems with their balance of trade. The IMF's basic objectives are to promote exchange stability, maintain orderly exchange arrangements, avoid competitive currency depreciation, establish a multilateral system of payments, eliminate exchange restrictions, and create standby reserves. The IMF makes long-term loans at low interest rates to the world's most destitute nations to help them strengthen their economies. The function of the IMF is very similar to that of the World Bank.

International Monetary Fund (IMF)
An international bank that makes short-term loans to countries experiencing problems with their balance of trade.

The **World Bank** <*http://www.worldbank.org*>, an autonomous United Nations agency, is concerned with developing infrastructure (e.g., roads, schools, hospitals, power plants, etc.) in less-developed countries. The World Bank borrows from more prosperous countries and lends at favourable rates to less-developed countries. (In recent years, the IMF and the World Bank have forgiven some loans to highly indebted countries, such as Guinea.) To qualify for the program, numerous macroeconomic policies (such as inflation and poverty reduction) have to be implemented. These new requirements allow the lending organizations to continue to fulfill their objectives.

> **World Bank**
> An autonomous United Nations agency that borrows money from the more prosperous countries and lends it to less-developed countries to develop their infrastructure.

Some countries believe that their economies will be strengthened if they establish formal trade agreements with other countries. Some of these agreements, involving forming producers' cartels and common markets, are discussed next.

Producers' Cartels

Producers' cartels are organizations of commodity-producing countries. They are formed to stabilize or increase prices, in order to optimize profits over the long term. The most obvious example today is the Organization of the Petroleum Exporting Countries (OPEC). Similar attempts have been made to manage prices for copper, iron ore, bauxite, bananas, tungsten, rubber, and other important commodities. These cartels are all contradictions to unrestricted free trade and letting the market set prices.

> **producers' cartels**
> Organizations of commodity-producing countries that are formed to stabilize or increase prices to optimize overall profits in the long run.

Common Markets

An issue not resolved by the GATT or the WTO is whether common markets create regional alliances at the expense of global expansion. A **common market** (also called a **trading bloc**) is a regional group of countries that have a common external tariff, no internal tariffs, and the coordination of laws to facilitate exchange among member countries. Two examples are the North American Free Trade Agreement and the European Union. Let's look briefly at both.

> **common market (trading bloc)**
> A regional group of countries that have a common external tariff, no internal tariffs, and a coordination of laws to facilitate exchange; also called a trading bloc. An example is the European Union.

THE NORTH AMERICAN FREE TRADE AGREEMENT (NAFTA)

A widely debated issue of the early 1990s was the ratification of the **North American Free Trade Agreement (NAFTA),** which created a free-trade area among Canada, the United States, and Mexico. In January 1993 NAFTA came into effect, replacing the previous Free Trade Agreement between Canada and the United States. The objectives of NAFTA were to (1) eliminate trade barriers and facilitate cross-border movement of goods and services among the three countries; (2) promote conditions of fair competition in this free-trade area; (3) increase investment opportunities in the territories of the three nations; (4) provide effective protection and enforcement of intellectual property rights (e.g., patents, copyrights, etc.) in each nation's territory; (5) establish a framework for further regional trade co-operation; and (6) improve working conditions in North America.

North American Free Trade Agreement (NAFTA)
An agreement that created a free-trade area among Canada, the United States, and Mexico.

Officially, almost all trade in the NAFTA region now flows tariff-free. Leaders from Canada, the United States, and Mexico meet to discuss several major areas of dispute. Many areas have yet to be resolved including trucking, immigration, the environment, and agricultural tariffs.

NAFTA was driven by the desire of Mexico to have greater access to the U.S. market. Improved access would spur growth, provide more employment for Mexicans, and raise the low standard of living in Mexico. The U.S. government was hoping to create jobs in Mexico and stop the flow of illegal immigrants who were crossing its border. Canada was really a minor player in this deal; the Canadian government was concerned that it would be left out or penalized indirectly unless it joined the bloc. Canadians do have something to gain by having freer access to the growing Mexican market, but the country is still a minor customer for Canada.

Today, the three NAFTA countries have a combined population of over 460 million and a gross domestic product of more than US$19.2 trillion.[56] The agreement permits all three countries to reduce trade barriers with one another while maintaining independent trade agreements with other countries.

There is continuing concern by some groups (e.g., unions) in Canada and the United States that NAFTA has contributed to employment losses and that economic benefits were not realized. Some Canadian business people remain opposed because they did not like many of the details in NAFTA. In addition, Mexico has a weak policy on environmental problems, poor working conditions, and a questionable record on human rights and political freedom. The country has repeatedly been condemned by many organizations in North America and abroad for serious flaws on all these counts. Others believe that NAFTA will force Mexico to gradually improve these conditions. This has been happening, but at a very slow pace.

THE EUROPEAN UNION

The European Union (EU) began in the late 1950s as an alliance of six trading partners (then known as the Common Market and later the European Economic Community). Today the EU is a group of

87 member nations (see Figure 3.10), with a population of over 508 million citizens and a GDP of almost US$18.5 trillion.[57] Though the EU is represented as a unified body in the WTO, the economies of six members (Germany, France, United Kingdom, Italy, Spain, and the Netherlands) account for over three-fourths of the EU's GDP.

■ FIGURE 3.10

MEMBERS OF THE EUROPEAN UNION

Current EU members are highlighted in yellow. Countries that have applied for membership are in orange. Iceland (not shown) is also an EU candidate.

European unification was not easy, but in 1999 the EU took a significant step by adopting the euro as a common currency. The euro has helped EU businesses save billions by eliminating currency conversions and has challenged the U.S. dollar's dominance in global markets. Eighteen member nations now use the euro as their common currency. In 2013, the EU faced debt, deficit, and growth problems due to financial difficulties in member nations Greece, Italy, Portugal, and Spain that required bailout assistance.[58] EU officials moved forward with broad economic policies to ensure the financial stability of the union.

The EU sees continued economic integration as the major way to compete for global business. Canada negotiated the Canada–European Union Comprehensive Economic Trade Agreement (CETA) in order to provide preferential treatment for Canadian goods and services to enter the EU market[59] For example, Canadian shrimp faced up to a 20 percent duty, making it more expensive for consumers and, therefore, less competitive compared to shrimp products from other countries. CETA eliminates this duty, making Canadian-produced shrimp more affordable in the EU and giving these businesses a 20 percent boost in competitiveness.[60]

Seeking SUSTAINABILITY

The Politics of Oil

The tar-like bitumen has to be melted out of the ground and processed in a highly energy-intensive manner before it can be refined like regular oil. The U.S. Environmental Protection Agency says that "GHG emissions from the Canadian oil sands crude would be approximately 82 percent greater than the average crude refined in the U.S. on a well-to-tank basis." And in confidential briefing notes, the Canadian government has acknowledged that the emissions-per-barrel will likely increase as the industry is forced to pursue harder-to-access reserves deeper underground. Further expansion of the oil sands—which are the fastest growing source of greenhouse gas emissions in Canada, and the biggest energy project in the world—would lock Canada into a high-carbon economy for decades to come.

Canada has the second-largest oil sands reserve on the planet, estimated at 170 billion barrels. The oil sands are the largest proven reserve of oil outside of Saudi Arabia, and the world's largest reserve of "unconventional" oil, which requires much more energy and water to extract and process than conventional oil.

The EU has adopted a "Fuel Quality Directive" aimed at making those who sell and supply fuel reduce the carbon footprint of their products by 6 percent over the next decade. The EU is ranking fuels to help sellers and buyers identify those fuels with the largest carbon footprint. In line with that position, some members of the EU are pushing to rate oil sands fuel as more environmentally damaging than fuel from conventional crude oil.

The federal government and the government of Alberta lobbied the EU, at a cost of $30 million, to prevent the EU rating from happening. A "dirty oil" classification would amount to a European ban on oil sands crude. It would impose financial disincentives to discourage refiners and marketers from using fuel derived from oil sands bitumen in favour of lower-carbon sources of fuel.

In Fall 2014, the Canadian government's effort paid off. The EU voted not to impose a veto on Alberta bitumen (also called tar sands) oil. The decision was a setback in Europe and North America for supporters of low-carbon fuel regulations that are aimed at reducing greenhouse gas emissions in the transportation sector.

Although Canadian oil companies gained better access to the EU market, the ability to move Alberta bitumen deposits to other global markets is on hold. U.S. President Barack Obama vetoed the pipeline and a U.S. Senate vote in March 2015 failed to overturn his decision. The future of the pipeline and Alberta bitumen is uncertain. The debate of the merits of a pipeline down the middle of the continent creates opposing views. On one hand, government leaders could capitalize on the situation and create higher standards that ensure regulations are in place to keep oil companies honest. On the other hand, environmental lobbyists believe the decision not to permit the pipeline will delay further oil sands investment and generate momentum toward a clean energy future.

(continued)

(*continued*)

How have the Canadian government and environmentalists reacted to both the EU and United States decisions? What are the economic and environmental implications of each decision?

Sources: Jonathan Waldman, "Don't kill Keystone XL. Regulate It," *The New York Times,* 6 March 2015, http://www.nytimes .com/2015/03/06/opinion/dont-kill-keystone-xl-regulate-it.html?ref=topics; Coral Davenport, "Senate fails to override Obama's Keystone Pipeline veto," *The New York Times,* 4 March 2015, http://www.nytimes.com/2015/03/05/us/senate-fails-to-override-obamas -keystone-pipeline-veto.html?ref=topics&_r=0; Mark Downie, "Keystone and the Riddle if the Tar Sands," *Newsweek,* 25 February 2015, http://www.newsweek.com/keystone-and-riddle-tar-sands-309522; Barbara Lewis, "EU lawmakers fail to approve tar sands oil veto," Reuters, 17 December 2014, http://www.reuters.com/article/2014/12/17/eu-energy-canada-idUSL6N0U12Q820141217; Natural Resources Defense Council, "Stopping the Keystone XL," accessed 27 March 2105, http://www.nrdc.org/; Lorne Gunter, "A European reprieve for Canada's oil sands," *The Globe and Mail,* 24 February 2012, A14.

OTHER TRADE AGREEMENTS[61]

According to Foreign Affairs, Trade and Development Canada, Canada is involved in 11 free-trade agreements (FTA) including the Canada–Korea FTA effective in 2015 and the Canada–Honduras FTA brought into effect in 2014. Negotiations for new FTAs are ongoing with many countries. For example, a Canada–Caribbean Community (CARICOM) agreement seeks to create new opportunities for Canadian business in sectors including manufacturing, agriculture and financial services. A Canada–India FTA presents estimated GDP gains from US$6–$15 billion for Canada and US$6–$12 billion for India with potential exports gains ranging between 36 to 60 percent for each country.

Progress Assessment

- What are the advantages and disadvantages of trade protectionism?

- What is the difference between protective tariffs and revenue tariffs?

- What is the primary purpose of the WTO?

- State four objectives of NAFTA.

- What is the primary objective of a common market like the EU?

LO6   Discuss the changing landscape of the global market.

Globalization and Your Future

Not long ago, FDI in China was considered to be not worth the risk, but the value of Chinese trade has roughly doubled every four years over the last three decades.[62] In 2013, China attracted US$117 billion in FDI.[63] Today, over 400 of the Fortune 500 companies (the world's largest companies) have invested in China. According to Goldman Sachs Group and the London Center for Economic and Business Research, China could overtake the United States as the world's largest economy by 2028.[64]

Since 2009, China has been the largest motor vehicle market in the world with sales and production topping nearly 22 million vehicles in 2013.[65] It is estimated that by 2030, there could be more cars on the road in China than all the cars in the world today. Walmart began operations in China in 1996 and now has over 390 stores with plans to open more. Even newcomers like IMAX Corporation <*https://www .imax.com*> are expanding in this fast-growing market. IMAX currently has 229 movie theatres in China, with plans to add 219 theatres by 2021.[66]

Many view China as a free trader's dream, where global investment and entrepreneurship will lead to wealth. However, concerns remain about China's one-party political system, human rights abuses, currency issues, and increasing urban population growth. China's underground economy also generates significant product piracy and counterfeiting, although the country has been more responsive to these problems since its admission to the WTO. With the global economy continuing to grow, China will be a key driver of the world economy along with the United States, the EU, and Japan.

Bombardier Inc. is the world's largest manufacturer of planes and trains. Its 2012–2033 market forecast shows a strategy to expand in markets including China, the Middle East, and Africa.[67] What challenges will the company have to address in order to enter these markets?

While China attracts most of the attention in Asia, India's population of 1.2 billion presents a tremendous opportunity. With nearly 575 million of its population under 25, India's working-age population will continue to grow while Canada expects a decline in the 2020s. Already India has seen huge growth in information technology and biotechnology, and its pharmaceutical business is expected to grow to $30 billion, a jump of over 150 percent by 2020. Still, it remains a nation with difficult trade laws and an inflexible bureaucracy.[68]

Russia is an industrialized nation with large reserves of oil, gas, and gold that became a member of the WTO in 2012. Multinationals like Chevron, ExxonMobil *<http://corporate.exxonmobil.com>*, and BP *<https://www.bp.com>* have invested heavily in developing Russia's oil reserves. However, Russia's economy slowed when world oil prices declined and the government admitted that growth prospects for the economy were not strong for the next two decades.[69] Unfortunately, Russia is plagued by political, currency, and social problems.

Brazil is an emerging nation that, along with China, India, and Russia, was projected to be one of the wealthier global economies by 2030. In fact, the term *BRIC* has been used as an acronym for the economies of Brazil, Russia, India, and China. Today, Brazil is the largest economy in South America and the seventh-largest economy in the world with well-developed agriculture, mining, manufacturing, and service sectors. Along with Russia, Brazil was expected to dominate the global market as a supplier of raw materials. China and India were predicted to be leading global suppliers of manufactured goods and services. Unfortunately, the past few years have been difficult for Brazil's economy with increasing inflation and slow growth. Still, its expanding consumer market of over 200 million people is a target for major exporters like the United States and China.

The BRIC economies are certainly not the only areas of opportunity in the global market. The developing nations of Asia, including Indonesia, Thailand, Singapore, the Philippines, Korea, Malaysia, and Vietnam, also offer great potential for Canadian businesses. Africa, especially South Africa, has only begun to emerge as a centre for global economic growth. Business today is truly global and your role in it is up to you.

China's economy is booming, and a highly educated middle class with money to spend is emerging, especially in the cities. Many observers believe China will continue its rapid growth and play a major role in the global economy. Are Canadian firms prepared to compete?

As you learned in Chapter 1, outsourcing means contracting with other companies to do some or all of the functions of a firm, rather than providing them within the company. In Canada, companies have outsourced payroll functions, accounting, and some manufacturing operations for many years. However, the shift in outsourcing manufacturing and services from domestic businesses to primarily low-wage markets outside of Canada is getting more attention. This shift is referred to as offshoring. Take a look at the pros and cons of offshore outsourcing in Figure 3.11. The Making Ethical Decisions box describes one issue related to this practice.

To remain competitive, Canada must focus on innovation and entrepreneurship. It is increasingly important for Canadian workers to obtain the proper education and training needed to stay ahead in the future. Whether you aspire to be an entrepreneur, a manager, or some other type of business leader, think globally in planning your career. By studying foreign languages, learning about foreign cultures, and taking business courses (including a global business course), you can develop a global perspective on your future. As you progress through this text, keep two things in mind: globalization is real, and economic competition promises to intensify.

Also keep in mind that global market potential does not belong only to large, multinational corporations. Small and medium-sized businesses have a world of opportunity in front of them. In fact, these firms are often better prepared to leap into global markets and react quickly to opportunities than are large firms. Finally, don't forget the potential of franchising, which we will examine in more detail in Chapter 6.

■ **FIGURE 3.11**

THE PROS AND CONS OF OFFSHORE OUTSOURCING

PROS

- Less strategic tasks can be outsourced globally so companies can focus on where they can excel and grow.
- Outsource work allows companies to create efficiencies that in fact let them hire more workers
- Consumers benefit from lower prices generated by effective use of global resources and developing nations grow, thus fuelling global economic growth.

CONS

- Jobs are lost permanently and wages fall due to low-cost competition offshore.
- Offshoring may reduce product quality, which can cause permanent damage to a company's reputation.
- Communication within the company, with its suppliers, and with its customers becomes much more difficult.

Progress Assessment

- How has the Internet affected doing business in global markets?

- What are the economic risks of doing business in countries like China?

- What might be some important factors that will have an impact on global trading?

- What can you do in the next few years to ready yourself for a career in global business?

Making ETHICAL DECISIONS

How Much Information Is Necessary?

Imagine that you're having a problem with your computer. Not able to fix the problem yourself, you take out the operator's manual and dial customer service. Your call is answered by a service technician who identifies himself

(continued)

(continued)

as Jeff. You explain to Jeff the problem you are having and wait for his reply. Unfortunately, Jeff cannot solve your problem and transfers your call to his colleague Jennifer. Jennifer analyzes the situation and promptly provides a suggestion that fixes your computer. Impressed, you ask Jennifer for her direct line so you can call her if you have additional questions. She says she is unable to give you her direct number, according to company policy. Upset, you call customer relations and inquire why a service technician cannot give her direct number to a customer. The company representative says, "Because the service centre is overseas. You were talking to people trained to identify themselves as Jeff and Jennifer." Should a company let customers know if its service facilities are being outsourced or as in this case, offshored? Should service people be required to give their real names when dealing with customers? What are the consequences of each alternative?

SUMMARY

LO1 **Describe the importance of the global market and the roles of comparative advantage and absolute advantage in global trade.**

Canada has a population of more than 35 million people. The world market for trade is huge. Over 99 percent of the people in the world live outside Canada. Major Canadian companies routinely cite expansion to global markets as a route to future growth.

Why should nations trade with other nations?

Nations should trade globally as (1) no country is self-sufficient, (2) other countries need products that prosperous countries produce, and (3) natural resources and technological skills are not distributed evenly around the world.

What is the theory of comparative advantage?

The theory of comparative advantage contends that a country should make and then sell those products it produces most efficiently but buy those it cannot produce as efficiently.

What is absolute advantage?

Absolute advantage means that a country has a monopoly on a certain product or can produce the product more efficiently than any other country. There are few examples of absolute advantage.

LO2 **Explain the importance of importing and exporting and define key terms used in global business.**

Anyone can get involved in world trade through importing and exporting. Business people do not have to work for big multinational corporations.

What kinds of products can be imported and exported?

Just about any kind of product can be imported and exported. Companies can sometimes find surprising ways to succeed in either activity. Selling in global markets is not necessarily easy, though.

What terms are important in understanding world trade?

Exporting is selling goods and services to other countries. Importing is buying goods and services from other countries. The balance of trade is the relationship of exports to imports.

The balance of payments is the balance of trade plus other money flows such as tourism and foreign aid. Dumping is selling products for less in a foreign country than in your own country. See the Key Terms list after this Summary to be sure you know the other important terms.

LO3 **Illustrate the strategies used in reaching global markets and explain the role of multinational corporations in global markets.**

A company can participate in world trade in a number of ways.

What are some ways in which a company can get involved in global business?

Ways of entering world trade include licensing, exporting, franchising, contract manufacturing, joint ventures and strategic alliances, and foreign direct investment.

How do multinational corporations differ from other companies that participate in global business?

Unlike other companies that are involved in exporting or importing, multinational corporations also have manufacturing facilities or some other type of physical presence in different nations.

LO4 **Evaluate the forces that affect trading in global markets.**

The forces include sociocultural, economic and financial, and legal. Each can be examined in detail to determine their impact in various global markets.

What are some of the forces that can discourage participation in global business?

Potential stumbling blocks to global trade include sociocultural forces (e.g., religion), economic and financial forces (e.g., disposable income), legal forces (e.g., laws on bribery), and physical and environmental forces (e.g., Internet usage).

LO5 **Debate the advantages and disadvantages of trade protectionism, define tariff and non-tariff barriers, and give examples of common markets.**

Political differences are often the most difficult hurdles to international trade.

What is trade protectionism?

Trade protectionism is the use of government regulations to limit the import of goods and services. Supporters believe that it allows domestic producers to survive and grow, producing more jobs. The key tools of protectionism are tariffs, import quotas, and embargoes.

What are tariff and non-tariff barriers?

Tariffs are taxes on foreign products. There are two kinds of tariffs: (1) protective tariffs, which are used to raise the price of foreign products, and (2) revenue tariffs, which are used to raise money for the government. Non-tariff barriers include safety, health, and labelling standards.

What are some examples of trade organizations that try to eliminate trade barriers and facilitate trade among nations?

The World Trade Organization (WTO) replaced the General Agreement on Tariffs and Trade (GATT). The purpose of the WTO is to mediate trade disputes among nations. The International Monetary Fund (IMF) is an international bank that makes short-term loans to countries experiencing problems with their balance of trade. The World Bank is a United Nations agency that borrows money from the more prosperous countries and lends it to less-developed countries to develop their infrastructures.

What is a common market? State some examples.

A common market is a regional group of countries that have a common external tariff, no internal tariff, and a coordination of laws to facilitate exchange. The idea behind a common market is the elimination of trade barriers that existed prior to the creation of this bloc. Examples include NAFTA, the EU.

LO6 **Discuss the changing landscape of the global market.**

The landscape of global business is changing and it is important for graduates to learn about global market trends in order to consider possible career options..

How is business changing?

New and expanding markets present great potential for trade and development. For example, changes in technology, especially through the Internet, allow access to global customers.

What countries offer opportunities for Canadian businesses?

Expanding markets such as China, India, Brazil, and Russia present great potential for trade and development.

KEY TERMS

absolute advantage	exporting	North American Free Trade
balance of payments	foreign direct investment (FDI)	Agreement (NAFTA)
balance of trade	foreign subsidiary	producers' cartels
common market (trading bloc)	free trade	strategic alliance
comparative advantage theory	General Agreement on Tariffs	tariff
contract manufacturing	and Trade (GATT)	trade deficit
countertrading	import quota	trade protectionism
culture	importing	trade surplus
devaluation	International Monetary Fund	World Bank
dumping	(IMF)	World Trade Organization
embargo	joint venture	(WTO)
ethnocentricity	licensing	
exchange rate	multinational corporation	

CRITICAL THINKING

1. About 99 percent of the world's population lives outside Canada, but many Canadian companies, especially small businesses, still do not engage in global trade. Why not? Do you think more small businesses will participate in global markets in the future? Why or why not?

2. What can businesses do to prevent unexpected problems in dealing with sociocultural, economic and financial, legal, and physical and environmental forces in global markets?

3. Countries like Canada that have a high standard of living are referred to as industrialized nations. Countries with a low standard of living and quality of life are called developing countries. (Terms formerly used were *underdeveloped* or *less-developed countries*.) What factors prevent developing nations from becoming industrialized nations?

4. How would you justify the use of revenue or protective tariffs in today's global market?

DEVELOPING WORKPLACE SKILLS

Key:　● **Team**　★ **Analytic**　▲ **Communication**　▢ **Technology**

▲　**1.** Find out firsthand the impact of global trade on your life. How many different countries' names appear on the labels in your clothes? How many languages do your classmates speak? List the ethnic restaurants in your community. Are they family-owned or corporate chains?

★▲　**2.** Prepare a short list of the advantages and disadvantages of trade protectionism. Share your ideas with others in the class and debate the following statement: Canada should increase trade protectionism to save Canadian jobs and companies.

●★　**3.** The economies of Ontario and British Columbia depend heavily on exports. Ontario relies
▢▲　primarily on trade to the United States and Europe, while British Columbia relies heavily on trade with Asia. In a group of four, research these statements. Use Excel to develop two graphs that break down the exporting countries that trade with each of these provinces. Present your findings to the class.

●★　**4.** In a group of four, list the top five Canadian-based multinationals. When researching,
▢▲　create a table that will include the following pieces of information: the company names, the year each was created, the number of global employees, the industry or industries in which they operate, annual revenues, and number of countries in which they have offices. Present your findings to the class.

ANALYZING MANAGEMENT DECISIONS

The Challenge of Offshoring

Outsourcing, as noted in Chapter 1, is the process of assigning various functions, such as accounting, production, security, maintenance, and legal work to outside organizations. In Canada, companies have outsourced payroll functions, accounting, and some manufacturing operations for many years. However, the shift to primarily low-wage global markets, called offshoring (or offshore outsourcing), has become a major issue. Export Development Canada believes that there are about 4,000 Canadian companies with some sort of overseas presence, an increase from 10 years ago.

Canadian companies such as Bombardier Inc. (manufactures state-of-the-art planes and trains) and Gildan Activewear Inc. *<http://gildan.com>* (one of the world's largest T-shirt makers) have outsourced manufacturing offshore for years. Fundamentally, as lower-level manufacturing became more simplified, Canadian companies shifted focus from assembling products to design and architecture. Today, economists agree that we are moving into the "second wave" of offshoring that involves sizable numbers of skilled, well-educated middle-income workers in service-sector jobs such as accounting, law, financial and risk management, health care, and information technology that were thought to be safe from foreign market competition. For example, the financial sector, including the Royal Bank of Canada, has been criticized for making its employees train the foreign workers hired to replace them. This shift is potentially more disruptive to the Canadian job market than was the first, which primarily involved manufacturing jobs. The pros and cons of offshoring were identified earlier in this chapter (see Figure 3.11). China and India are oftentimes named as country providers of offshoring. Currently, China is primarily involved with manufacturing at the low end of the technology scale, and India focuses on call centres, telemarketing, data entry, billing, and low-end software development. However, China is intent on developing advanced manufacturing technology and India has a deep pool of scientists, software engineers, chemists, accountants, lawyers, and physicians. The technology talent in these nations also keeps growing: China graduates 250,000 engineers each year and India about 150,000.

When you consider the impact of offshoring on Canada, research supports that more than two-thirds of imported services are from the United States, not China and India. A Statistics Canada paper finds that globalization and technology are the two key factors driving offshoring by Canadian companies. Services offshoring does not seem to affect productivity or employment. It does seem to reduce wages in the services-producing sector, though not in the goods-producing sector. Finally, on an industry-by-industry basis, rising offshoring of services seems to be associated with rising value-added activities. In the financial sector, for instance, low value-added activities such as general accounting are outsourced while high value-added activities such as strategizing are kept in-house and in-country.

Sources: "RBC Foreign Workers Controversy: No more replacing Canadians, bank vows," *Huffington Post Canada*, 24 May 2013, http://www .huffingtonpost.ca/2013/05/24/rbc-foreign-workers-hire-canadians_n_3332240.html; John Baldwin and Wulong Gu, "Offshoring and Outsourcing in Canada," Economic Analysis Research Paper Series, 11F0027M No. 055, Statistics Canada, http://www.statcan.gc.ca/pub/11f0027m/2008055/s7-eng .htm; Christine Dobby, "Offshore opportunities 'too good to pass up'," *The Financial* Post, 22 November 2011, FP16; William Watson, "Myth-Busting Offshoring," *National Post,* 30 May 2008, http://network.nationalpost.com/np/blogs/fpcomment/archive/2008/5/30/myth-busting-offshoring.aspx; Pete Engardio, "The Future of Outsourcing," *BusinessWeek*, 30 January 2006, 50–58; and Richard Ernsberger, "The Big Squeeze: A 'Second Wave' of Offshoring Could Threaten Middle-Income, White-Collar and Skilled Blue-Collar Jobs," *Newsweek International*, 30 May 2005.

Discussion Questions

1. Why are more Canadian companies investigating offshoring as a possible business strategy?

2. Do you think that offshoring is detrimental to the Canadian economy? Explain.

3. In your opinion, what are some business activities that should not be offshored? Explain.

VIDEO CASE 3

Electra Bicycle Company

Doing business in global markets can be tricky, but the benefits that come from overseas success justify much of the risk. That's what Electra Bicycle Company's founders discovered after their business's growth suddenly halted. Throughout the early 2000s, many bicycle manufacturers concentrated on producing mountain and speed bikes while discontinuing casual models. Benno Baziger and Jeano Erforth of Electra didn't follow the fad, though, choosing instead to stick with cool, upright bikes perfect for cruising city streets.

The company thrived for years thanks to its unique "comfort bikes." However, major competitors like Schwinn eventually took notice and began making their own sleek street bikes. Electra's explosive growth halted, and the company's two founders searched for a solution. To grow further, the pair knew they would have to enter the global marketplace. They went on a search for places where their vintage sense of style and up-to-date technology would give them a comparative advantage against their bigger competitors.

Electra eventually settled on Taiwan as the site for its overseas manufacturing site. From Taiwan, the California-based company can simply export bikes to neighbouring Asian countries like China where bikes are most popular. They can in turn feed their domestic demand by importing bikes into the United States, a practice that is actually cheaper for Electra than producing bikes on their home soil.

This outsourcing of production to a foreign manufacturing plant helps Electra keep its costs down. If labour costs increase or instability flares up between Taiwan and China, Electra could move its production to a less turbulent location.

Such unexpected problems represent just a few of the hurdles companies can face when they go global. For example, laws against motorized bikes forced Electra to tweak the design for its Townie Go model in order to make the bike acceptable in some foreign markets. Despite these issues, global commerce puts companies on the radar of millions of new customers. This immense access can make all the additional effort needed for going global worth it. In fact, Electra now sells more than 100,000 bikes each year.

Electra's success eventually brought it to the attention of Trek, a multinational corporation with offices in Wisconsin, the United Kingdom, and Germany. The conglomerate bought Electra, which can now use Trek's established distribution network to reach new markets more quickly and effectively. Letting their parent company worry about matters like capitalization and manufacturing infrastructure allows Electra to focus on other things, such as designing stylish bikes that are easy to ride and fun to own by people all over the world.

Thinking It Over

1. What major advantages did Electra gain by using a contract manufacturer in Taiwan to produce bikes?

2. When Electra produced its bikes in Taiwan, did the company have to follow the laws of Taiwan or the laws of the United States?

3. What major forces impact Electra (or any global producer) in trading in global markets?

The Role of Government in Business

LEARNING OBJECTIVES

After you have read and studied this chapter, you should be able to:

LO1 List the six categories of government activities that can affect business.

LO2 Trace the historical role of government in the Canadian economy and explain why Crown corporations were created.

LO3 Demonstrate why understanding laws and regulations at all levels of government is critical to business success.

LO4 Explain how taxation and financial policies affect the Canadian economy.

LO5 Describe how government expenditures benefit consumers and businesses alike.

LO6 Illustrate how purchasing policies and services assist Canadian businesses.

PROFILE

GETTING TO KNOW LISA VON STURMER OF GROWING CITY

In this chapter, you will learn how government activities can assist businesses of all sizes. To this end, there are many government agencies mandated to provide support for entrepreneurs. One example is Futurpreneur Canada (<*http://futurpreneur.ca*>) where Lisa von Sturmer obtained a start-up loan of $15,000 for her company, Growing City.

Based in Vancouver, Growing City is the first company in North America to offer a corporate organics composting program. Like many entrepreneurs, Lisa got the idea from personal experience. While vacationing on Savary Island in British Columbia, where recycling and composting are mandatory, she realized

Source: © National Post/BEN NELMS

the opportunity of social enterprise. Social enterprise is a small but growing segment of the Canadian economy. Social enterprises are organizations that make money and deliver social or environmental benefits. They may be not-for-profits organizations or profit-making companies.

The company provides office composting, recycling, and event services. It also puts sustainability into its own business practices through supportable uniforms, ethically-made bins, and soil donation programs to non-profit organizations.

In 2012, Growing City won the National Best Green Business Award from the Canadian Youth Business Foundation followed by an appearance on CBC's *Dragon's Den* in 2013. At the time, von Sturmer serviced 82 offices in Vancouver, but the television exposure generated so much interest that Growing City considered a franchise model to meet global demand. As of 2014, the company was expanding its 10-person workforce and already had 200 clients in Metro Vancouver. Corporate customers are the target and current clients include BC Hydro and the South Terminal of the Vancouver International Airport.

Von Sturmer was an official Canadian Delegate for the 2014 G20 Young Entrepreneurs Alliance Summit in Sydney, Australia. She, along with other young Canadians, have found a niche in social enterprise. "I wanted to create a business where I knew I was making a tangible, positive impact," von Sturmer said. What's the key to success? "I think the thing that makes Growing City so special and different is that we really look at the problem of waste production from a service standpoint."

Five years ago, reports indicated Canada was lagging behind in social enterprise activity. With small businesses like Growing City, the gap is closing.

Sources: Rhea Seymour, "The Rise of Social Enterprise," Women of Influence, 3 November 2014, http://www.womenofinfluence.ca/2014/11/03/rise-social-enterprise/; Brian Morten, "Turning garbage into gold - Vancouver organics recycling program growing like a weed," *The Vancouver Sun*, 18 July 2014, http://www.vancouversun.com/technology/Turning+garbage+into+gold/10043546/story.html; Mary Teresa Bitti, "Growing City composting company put the brakes on franchising after dragon's Den appearance," *Financial Post*, 28 January 2013, http://business.financialpost.com/2013/01/28/growing-city-composting-company-puts-the-brakes-on-franchising-after-dragons-den-appearance/; Growing City - About Us, 2015, http://www.growingcity.com/; Simon Avery, "Canada playing catch-up in social enterprise," *The Globe and Mail*, 19 October 2010, http://www.theglobeandmail.com/report-on-business/small-business/sb-growth/sustainability/canada-playing-catch-up-in-social-enterprise/article1316055/.

LO1 List the six categories of government activities that can affect business

Government Affects Business

Government activities that affect business may be divided into six categories: Crown corporations, laws and regulations, taxation and financial policies, government expenditures, purchasing policies, and services. Because all of these activities are scattered among different levels of government and many departments, agencies, and corporations, it is not possible to present this information in such neatly divided categories. However, as you make your way through the rest of the chapter you will be able to see how elements of these different aspects of government actions affect business.

Since the focus of this chapter is on the role of government in business, there will be limited discussion on how business affects government. It should become obvious as you read that governments are trying to respond to businesses' needs. This includes anything from creating laws that create a level playing field to providing services that support business initiatives. Figure 4.1 provides an overview of the six categories of government activity discussed in this chapter.

■ **FIGURE 4.1**

GOVERNMENT INVOLVEMENT WITH BUSINESS
Government activities that affect business can be divided into six categories. (LOI)
1. **Crown Corporations.** There are hundreds of such companies, and they play an important role in the economy. Crown corporations sometimes compete with for-profit businesses. (LO2)
2. **Laws and Regulations.** These cover a wide range, from taxation and consumer protection to environmental controls, working conditions, and labour–management relations. Review Appendix A for some examples. (LO3)
3. **Taxation and Financial Policies.** All levels of government collect taxes—income taxes, the GST or HST, provincial sales taxes, and property taxes. Taxation is also fine-tuned by government to achieve certain goals or to give effect to certain policies. This is called fiscal policy. (LO4)
4. **Government Expenditures.** Governments pay out billions of dollars to Canadians. When these recipients spend this money, businesses benefit. All levels of government provide a host of direct and indirect aid packages as incentives to achieve certain goals. These packages consist of tax reductions, grants, loans, and loan guarantees. (LO5)
5. **Purchasing Policies.** Governments are very large purchasers of ordinary supplies, services, and materials to operate the country. Because the federal government is the single largest purchaser in Canada, its policies regarding where to purchase have a major effect on particular businesses and the economy. (LO6)
6. **Services.** These include a vast array of direct and indirect activities, among them helping companies go international, bringing companies to Canada, and training and retraining the workforce. (LO6)

LO2 Trace the historical role of government in the Canadian economy and explain why Crown corporations were created.

Government Involvement in the Economy

As noted in Chapter 2, the Canadian economic system is described as a mixed economy—that is, an economic system in which some allocation of resources is made by the market and some is made by the government. Every country's government is involved in its economy, but the specific ways in which the governments participate vary a great deal. There are particular historical reasons why Canada developed into a nation in which governments play very important roles.

I WANT
TO GAIN EXPERIENCE

FEDERAL STUDENT WORK EXPERIENCE PROGRAM

Various government programs support student employment opportunities. For example, the Federal Student Work Experience Program provides thousands of full-time students with work experience. With only one application, you can be considered for temporary jobs in various federal organizations across the country.

When Canada was formed as a country in 1867, the federal government was given the power to "regulate trade and commerce." When the western provinces later joined this Confederation, it became clear that it would take special efforts to build a unified Canada. The very small population was scattered across a huge country, and there was no railway to connect it. Trading patterns were in a north to south configuration because, like today, most people lived near the U.S. border. The United States developed much faster and with a larger population and a bigger economy—which provided products not available in the provinces, either because they were not made in Canada or because there was no transportation to distribute them.

This led the Canadian governments, starting with our first prime minister, Sir John A. Macdonald, to develop what was called a **National Policy**. The policy placed high tariffs on imports from the United States to protect Canadian manufacturing, which had higher costs. In addition, the federal government began to grapple with the difficult question of building a costly rail line from the east coast to the west coast.

National Policy
Government directive that placed high tariffs on imports from the United States to protect Canadian manufacturing, which had higher costs.

These two issues set the tone for the continuous and substantial involvement of Canadian governments in developing and maintaining the Canadian economy. As you make your way through this chapter and read about these complex activities, you should not be surprised to learn that the different levels of government are large employers in the country. The federal government and the provinces with the largest populations and levels of economic activity—namely, Ontario, Quebec, British Columbia, and Alberta—have been excellent sources of employment for graduates in the past.

As you will see in this chapter, we also have an interventionist government that through its activities (e.g., regulatory and fiscal policy) tries to create a stable economy for businesses. In Chapter 3, you learned that trade agreements, such as the North American Free Trade Agreement (NAFTA) and the European Union (EU) have focused on eliminating tariffs between countries. But the work has not stopped, and the federal government is in the midst of negotiating 14 international free trade agreements.[1]

Before we go into more detail, let us briefly review how government affects business. You never know, one day you may have a job in one of these areas.

✴ *Crown Corporations*

In Canada, an important aspect of the role of government is expressed through **Crown corporations**, which are companies that are owned by the federal or provincial governments. Review Figure 4.2 for a brief list of the top federal and provincial Crown corporations in Canada. The federal government has Crown corporations related to 13 portfolios[2]. These include the Canadian Broadcasting Corporation (CBC) in Canadian Heritage, the Royal Canadian Mint in Finance, Canadian Tourism Commission in Industry, and VIA Rail Canada Inc. in Transport.

Crown corporations
Companies that are owned by the federal or provincial government.

■ **FIGURE 4.2**

CANADA'S LARGEST FEDERAL AND PROVINCIAL CROWN CORPORATIONS BY REVENUE		
Rank	Federal Crown corporation	2012 Revenue ($ billions)
1	Canada Mortgage and Housing Corp.	13.9
2	Canada Post Corp.	7.5
3	Atomic Energy of Canada	1.6
4	Canadian Commercial	1.6
5	Export Development Canada	1.5
Rank	Provincial Crown corporation	
1	Hydro-Québec	12.4
2	Caisse de Dépôt et Placement du Québec	8.4
3	Ontario Power Generation	5.6
4	Hydro One	5.5
5	Insurance Corporation of British Columbia	4.2

Source: Material reprinted with the express permission of the *National Post*, a division of Postmedia Network Inc.

Crown corporations are set up for several reasons. They provided services that were not being provided by businesses, which is how Air Canada *<http://www.aircanada.com>* came into being in the 1930s. Crown corporations were also created to bail out a major industry in trouble, which is how the Canadian National Railway (CNR) *<http://www.cn.ca>* was formed in 1919. Lastly, they provided some special services that could not otherwise be made available, as in the case of the Bank of Canada.

Set up in 1977, VIA Rail Canada <*http://www.viarail.ca*> operates 420 trains weekly and serves some 450 Canadian communities throughout the country. Have you ever taken advantage of the student savings offered by VIA Rail?

Each province also owns a variety of Crown corporations. Typically, a Crown corporation owns the province's electric power company. Some examples are NB Power <*http://www.nbpower.com*> in New Brunswick and Hydro-Québec <*http://www.hydroquebec.com*> in Quebec. Alberta owns a bank called ATB Financial <*http://www.atb.com*>. It was originally set up to help farmers in difficult times. The province of Saskatchewan owns all the liquor stores, the power company that supplies the entire province, the provincial telecom, all auto and home insurance, as well as a TV station and different corporations that assist farmers.[3] Two other examples are discussed next.

The Financial Role of Two Special Provincial Crown Corporations

The Alberta Heritage Savings Trust Fund <*http://www.finance.alberta.ca/business/ahstf*> was established in the 1970s, when the Alberta economy was prospering as a result of the oil boom. The government set aside a part of its oil royalty revenue to start the fund. In 2015 the Fund's assets were valued at $17.2 billion.[4] It must operate on a sound financial basis, but, as much as possible, it makes investment decisions that will benefit Alberta.

Quebec has the Caisse de dépôt et placement du Québec <*http://www.lacaisse.com*> (which means Quebec Deposit and Investment Fund), a giant fund that was established to handle the monies collected by the Quebec Pension Plan. With $214 billion in total net assets under management, it is one of the largest pools of funds in North America.[5] This plan was set up parallel to the Canada Pension Plan in 1966. The fund also handles other Quebec government funds, and it is a very powerful investment vehicle that is used to guide economic development in Quebec. Although it, too, must operate on a sound financial basis, it has a broad scope to make decisions that will benefit the Quebec economy.

The Role for Government

Since the 1990s, federal and provincial governments have embarked upon a series of measures designed to reduce the role of government in the economy. Over the years, large corporations like Teleglobe Canada, Air Canada, and CNR were sold. The national system of air traffic control, the management of airports, hundreds of ports and ferries, and other Maritime installations were also sold. The whole process of selling publicly-owned corporations is called **privatization**.

privatization
The process of governments selling Crown corporations.

This disposal of government assets and companies signalled a minor revolution in Canadian history. Also during this time, industries that had been regulated, such as airlines, oil and gas, and trucking, were partially or completely deregulated. **Deregulation** means that the government withdraws certain laws and regulations that seem to hinder competition. Review Appendix A for a discussion on deregulation.

deregulation
Government withdrawal of certain laws and regulations that seem to hinder competition

The federal government sold its remaining stake in Petro-Canada *<http://www.petro-canada.ca>*, an oil and gas company, in 2005. Analysts claim the decision has made the company more efficient and profitable.

Similar activities were undertaken by provincial governments. Alberta privatized its liquor board. Saskatchewan reduced its interest in giant uranium producer Cameco Corporation *<http://www.cameco .com>* and the British Columbia provincial government sold the British Columbia Railway Co. *<http:// www.bcrco.com>*. The Ontario provincial government has considered selling Crown corporations such as Hydro One Inc. *<http://www.hydroone.com>*, the Ontario Lottery and Gaming Corp. *<http://www.olg.ca>*, and the Liquor Control Board of Ontario *<http://www.lcbo.com>* to decrease the province's deficit.[6] Deficits will be discussed later in this chapter.

Municipal governments are also looking to privatize services such as water systems, garbage collection, and cleaning. Everywhere you look, government agencies, like for-profit organizations, are looking at ways to lower costs and improve efficiencies.

It may seem odd that this introduction on the role of government includes a discussion on how the different levels of government are selling some of their Crown corporations and getting out of these services. What is important to note is that Crown corporations exist and that they provide important services to both businesses and consumers.

Progress Assessment

- What are the six categories of government involvement with business?
- What are Crown corporations? Why were they created?
- What does privatization refer to? Can you cite any examples?

LO3 Demonstrate why understanding laws and regulations at all levels of government is critical to business success.

Laws and Regulations

In Chapter 1 you were introduced to the importance of the legal environment. These laws (and resulting regulations) are created by elected politicians. Consequently, the political parties in power can greatly affect the business environment. This is why it is important to be aware of the beliefs of the different political parties. Some think the government should have more say in business, while others think that less government intervention is best. Regardless of the political party, public perception and changing opinion can affect government policy making. This is why all stakeholders should be considered when laws and regulations are created, modified, approved, and implemented.

The Supreme Court of Canada has the final decision on constitutional questions and on important cases of civil and criminal law. It also deals with appeals from decisions of the provincial courts of appeal. It is comprised of nine Supreme Court Justices (seen here in February 2015) who are recommended by the prime minister and appointed by the governor general.

The power to make laws is based on the British North America Act, 1867 (BNA Act). The BNA Act was passed by the British Parliament in 1867. It is the law that created the Canadian Confederation and it sets the legal ground rules for Canada. In 1982, the BNA Act became part of the new Constitution and was renamed the Constitution Act, 1867.

How Canadians
Govern Themselves

8th Edition

How Canadians Govern Themselves is a publication that describes Canada's Constitution, the judicial system, and government powers. It is an excellent resource tool if you wish to learn more about Canada's system of government.

Laws are derived from four sources: the Constitution, precedents established by judges, provincial and federal statutes, and federal and provincial administrative agencies.[7] As a business person, you will be affected by current (and potential) laws and regulations. Appendix A considers the importance of working within the legal environment of business.

Canada has a legislature in each province and territory to deal with local matters. The Parliament in Ottawa makes laws for all Canadians. The Constitution defines the powers that can be exercised by the federal and provincial governments. In the event of a conflict, federal powers prevail.

Federal Government Responsibilities[8]

The federal government is responsible for issues that affect citizens across Canada. Its primary responsibility is to ensure and support the country's economic performance. This includes overseeing such industries as aeronautics, shipping, railways, telecommunications, and atomic energy. Some other responsibilities that have an impact on business operations are listed below:

- trade regulations (interprovincial and international)
- incorporation of federal companies
- taxation (both direct and indirect)
- the banking and monetary system
- hospital insurance and medicare
- the public debt and property
- national defence

- unemployment
- immigration
- criminal law
- fisheries

Let us consider hospital insurance and medicare, as here we see some overlap with federal, provincial, and territorial government responsibilities. The national Parliament, in effect, established nationwide systems of hospital insurance and medical care by making grants to the provinces and territories on condition that their plans reach certain standards of service. This has been largely successful, despite some differences in modes of financing and program coverage.

The Canada Health Transfer (CHT) is the largest major funds transfer to provinces and territories. It provides long-term predictable funding for health care and supports the principles of the federally regulated Canada Health Act, which are universality, comprehensiveness, portability, accessibility, and public administration. The CHT cash transfer was $34 billion in 2015–16 and is expected to reach 42 percent of provincial and territorial expenditure by 2020.[9] In summary, while the federal government is responsible for health care, it is still up to the provinces and territories to implement these policies, and their co-operation is critical for success.

Industry Canada is the federal agency that administers a variety of laws affecting businesses and consumers. One of the most relevant pieces of legislation is the Competition Act, which aims to ensure that mergers of large corporations will not restrict competition and that fair competition exists among businesses. (Some of the major consumer protection laws are shown in Figure 4.3.) The Act covers many areas, including discriminatory pricing, price fixing, misleading advertising, and the refusal to deal with certain companies.

■ **FIGURE 4.3**

SOME MAJOR FEDERAL CONSUMER PROTECTION LAWS
These laws all provide consumers with information and protection in various ways. There are also provincial consumer protection laws.
Personal Information Protection and Electronics Document Act: sets rules for how private-sector organizations collect, use, and disclose personal information for commercial activities.
Canadian Agricultural Products Standards Act: covers a wide range of farm products such as organic, meat, poultry, eggs, maple syrup, honey, and dairy products.
Consumer Packaging and Labelling Act: applies to all products not specifically included in other Acts.
Food and Drugs Act: covers a whole range of regulations pertaining to quality, testing approval, packaging, and labelling.
Hazardous Products Act: covers all hazardous products.
Textile Labelling Act: includes apparel sizing and many other special areas.
Weights and Measures Act: applies to all equipment that measures quantities such as scales, gas pumps, and so forth.

Consider the clothes you wear. They are required to have a label showing the country of origin, size, type of fabric, and washing instructions. When you buy 25 litres of gasoline, you can feel confident that you have received a true measure because of the sticker on the equipment showing when it was last inspected. There are laws that give consumers the right to cancel contracts or return goods within a certain period of time. It is not possible to go through a day and not find an instance where laws have helped you in some way.

As noted in Chapter 1, competition has never been greater than it is today, both internationally and domestically. For example, despite trade agreements, new government policies (e.g., the "Agreement on Internal Trade," discussed later in this chapter), limit the movement of products such as gasoline, and chicken, dairy, and egg product among provinces and territories and can create barriers to trade.[10] The federal government lobbies the governments of other countries to decrease such trade barriers in an attempt to create business opportunities for Canadian firms. The flip side to this is that these countries may request the same of Canada.

THE COMPETITION BUREAU: CHOCOLATE CONSPIRACY[11]

The Competition Bureau probed whether competitors were colluding to control the prices of chocolate bars in Canada. The investigation involved Canada's largest candy bar makers and provided the basis for a class-action lawsuit based upon the claim consumers paid inflated prices for products such as Twix, Mars, Oh Henry, Dairy Milk, Crispy Crunch, Aero and Smarties between 2001 and 2008. In 2013, four companies, Cadbury Adams Canada Inc., Nestlé Canada Inc., Mars Canada Inc., and Hershey Canada Inc. paid $23.2 million to settle a class-action lawsuit regarding the matter.

The candy bar example demonstrates how the Competition Bureau helps protect Canadian consumers from artificially high prices for goods and services. However, critics claim the Competition Bureau is anti-consumer because it is just as likely to force companies to raise the price of a good or service as lower the price. For example, the bureau recently initiated legal action against Sears Canada *<http://www.sears.ca>* and Hudson's Bay Co. *<http://www.hbc.com>* for offering low prices for an excessive period of time in its mattress businesses. The bureau stated that the companies "failed to offer certain sleep sets at the regular price or higher for a substantial period of time [and]. . .did not sell a substantial volume of some sleep sets at the regular price or higher for a substantial period of time." In 2005, Sears was fined $500,000 for a similar low-price practice for its automotive tire business. According to competition law, a store must offer regular pricing for a substantial period of time, normally 50% of the time.

What do you think? Does the Competition Bureau protect shoppers or harass stores that have low prices?

Do you eat Cadbury, Hershey, Nestlé, or Mars chocolate products? Maybe the chocolate bar prices aren't as low as they should be.

MARKETING BOARDS

In Canada, we have a special system of **marketing boards** that control the supply or pricing of certain agricultural products. Consequently, they often control trade. This supply management is designed to give some stability to an important area of the economy that is normally very volatile. Farmers are subject to unique conditions and that have a great effect on their business and on our food supply. Weather and disease are major factors in the operation of farms and are beyond the control of the individual farmer. The same is true for unstable prices, changes in supply resulting from uncoordinated decision making by millions of farmers around the world, and the exercise of market power by concentrated business organizations.

marketing boards
Organizations that control the supply or pricing of certain agricultural products in Canada.

In the past farmers have experienced periods of severe drought, flooding, severe cold, and diseases that affected crops, livestock, and poultry. The situation regarding international markets and supply has a serious impact on Canada's grain farmers, since Canada exports much more wheat than it consumes domestically. This market fluctuates greatly depending on the supply in other major grain-exporting countries such as the United States, Argentina, and Australia. The market also depends on demand from major importers such as China and Russia, whose abilities to meet their own requirements are subject to wide variation. Often the Canadian government (like other governments) grants substantial loans with favourable conditions to enable these countries to pay for their imports of our wheat and other agricultural products.

Because we export billions of dollars of agricultural products annually, the ability to hold our own in international markets has a major impact on the state of the Canadian economy. When farmers are flourishing, they buy new equipment and consumer goods and their communities feel the effects of ample cash flow. So does the transportation industry. Conversely, when farmers are suffering, all of these sectors hurt as well.

To smooth out the effects of these unusual conditions on this sector of our economy, and to ensure a steady supply of food to consumers at reasonable prices, some government agencies were set up to control dairy products and poultry. The Canadian Dairy Commission <*http://www.cdc-ccl.gc.ca*> controls the output and pricing of milk and other dairy products. The Egg Farmers of Canada <*http://www.eggs.ca*>, Chicken Farmers of Canada <*http://chicken.ca*>, the Turkey Farmers of Canada <*http://www.turkeyfarmersofcanada.ca*>, and the Canadian Hatching Egg Producers <*http://www.chep-poic.ca*> consist of representatives from the provinces that produce these items. These organizations control the amount of production for all of the goods under their supervision by allocating quotas to each province that produces them. Provincial agencies administer these quotas and set prices for their province. Each agency controls products that are sold only in its province.

The Canadian system of marketing boards has been under attack by various organizations because it does not permit normal competitive conditions to operate in this field. It is argued that this distorts the whole industry and raises prices for Canadian consumers. Defenders of the system argue that other countries have different systems that create the same effect as our marketing boards but are just less visible. The EU spends billions of dollars on subsidies for their farmers. The United States, which often complains about other countries' unreasonable trade barriers, has its own restrictions, such as on sugar imports.

In Chapter 3, we referred to the World Trade Organization, whose main purpose is to reduce barriers to trade among countries. If the organization is successful, we may see a very different picture emerging worldwide over the next decade: limited protection for domestic markets, reduced tariffs and other restrictions, and the market having a much greater impact on prices and production. For example, the EU–Canada Comprehensive Economic and Trade Agreement (CETA) will allow 92 percent of EU agriculture and food products to be exported to Canada duty free.[12] The effect on Canadian farmers and on the agricultural industry in general is enormous, as everyone would be trying to cope with the necessary adjustments to such new conditions.

The Canadian Wheat Board[13]   There is a perception that Canadian farmers are more subsidized than farmers in other countries. According to information gathered by the Organisation for Economic Co-operation and Development (OECD), Canadian farmers received 17 percent of their income from subsidies. American wheat producers received 49 percent of their income from subsidies, while EU wheat farmers received 43 percent of their income from subsidies.

A privatized Canadian Wheat Board was supposed to add a strong Canadian competitor to the market. Who might purchase the board? What changes will result for farmers? The Canadian Wheat Board <http://www.cwb.ca>, a farmer-controlled organization that marketed wheat and barley grown by western Canadian producers, was one of the world's largest grain-trading companies. In 2012, a law was implemented to stop the Canadian Wheat Board's monopoly over the sale of all wheat and barley grown in Western Canada. The federal government backed the Wheat Board financially for five years but farmers were free to sell their grain to the Wheat Board or to private companies.[14] Currently, the federal government is reviewing a proposed $250-million deal by foreign buyers to purchase 50.1% of the CWB.[15]

✷ Provincial Government Responsibilities[16]

Each province and territory has its own government. Issues that affect provincial residents but do not necessarily affect all Canadians are governed at the provincial level. Provincial government responsibilities include the following areas:

- regulation of provincial trade and commerce
- natural resources within their boundaries
- incorporation of provincial companies
- direct taxation for provincial purposes
- licensing for revenue purposes
- the administration of justice
- health and social services

- municipal affairs
- property law
- labour law
- education

The retention of a high degree of provincial autonomy in the provision of elementary and secondary school education and the accommodation of religious and linguistic preferences has resulted in a variation in school systems. Both government levels also fund programs for post-secondary education.

One trend that we are seeing today is the merging of public and private philosophies in public–private partnerships (P3s or PPPs). P3s represent a method of privatizing public services or public infrastructure. Figure 4.4 indicates the extent and estimated value of public–private partnerships in Canada. In a Nanos Research Poll, 62 percent of Canadians were open to the private sector delivering services in partnership with the government in areas such as roads, hospitals, transit systems, and public housing. Recent statistics indicate Canada has over 220 P3 projects valued at $70 billion. Let us consider health-care facilities (e.g., hospitals). In a typical P3 deal, the government allows for-profit private corporations to finance, design, build, and operate health facilities. The government commits to lease the facility and use certain services for a period of as much as 30 years or more. Some provinces enter into P3 arrangements to build needed hospitals, promising that the P3s will save money and be more efficient. P3 opponents say that some P3s cost more to build and operate, take private profits from the public health budget, hide their costs, and erode the quality of services. With more than 80 P3 hospitals in operation or development, governments, health-care leaders, and communities are clearly P3 supporters.

■ **FIGURE 4.4**

NUMBER AND CAPITAL VALUE OF P3 PROJECTS IN CANADA, 2015		
	Number	Capital value (C$ million)
Transportation	50	31,761
Hospitals & Health care	84	24,196
Justice/Corrections	19	5,458
Energy	6	4,458
Education	11	1,936
Recreation & Culture	18	1,380
Environmental	23	1,229
Real Estate	5	944
Defence	2	867
Government Services	4	482
IT Infrastructure	2	1
Total	224	72,712

Source: Canadian PPP Project database, Canadian Council for Public-Private Partnerships, http://projects.pppcouncil.ca/ccppp/src/public/search-project?pageid=3d067bedfe2f4677470dd6ccf64d05ed, downloaded 11 May 2015.

FREE TRADE BETWEEN PROVINCES[17]

While interprovincial trade is a $300-billion industry in Canada, many Canadian companies and individuals face obstacles when trying to do business outside of their home province or territory. Some trade barriers exist because governments created them to protect their economies from outside competition. Governments also put policies in place to protect the environment, establish workforce standards, or achieve other regulatory purposes. Such regulations limit the movement of workers from one province or territory to another in areas such as health care, financial and legal services, engineering, and teaching. Estimates on the costs of these interprovincial barriers in Canada are $14 billion per year. Interprovincial trade barriers are damaging to the economy and to Canadians' standards of living. A recent report indicated that policy makers and economists recognize the economic loss of such interprovincial and territorial trade barriers yet lack a vision on how to deal with internal trade issues. While it is clear why they were created (i.e., to protect provincial jobs), these protectionist barriers discourage competition, distort market forces, and reduce efficiency.

The federal government works with participating provinces and territories to implement the Canada Student Grants Program and the Canada Student Loans Program. Quebec, the Northwest Territories, and Nunavut offer their own student financial aid programs and do not participate in the Canada Student Loans Program. Even though this support is offered, recent student protests across Canada advocate for lower tuition costs. Which approach do you believe is better for students—affordable student loans or tuition reductions?

The Agreement on Internal Trade (AIT) is an intergovernmental trade agreement signed by Canadian First Ministers. Its purpose is to reduce and eliminate barriers to the free movement of persons, goods, services, and investment within Canada. The objective is to reduce extra costs to Canadian businesses by making internal trade more efficient, increasing market access for Canadian companies, and facilitating work mobility for tradespeople and professionals. For example, the Certified General Accountants of New Brunswick <*http://www.cga-nb.org*> successfully appealed to the Internal Trade Secretariat to have the government of Quebec stop restricting access to those who were recognized as qualified to practice accounting in that province.

AIT amendments have removed barriers that have made it difficult, and sometimes impossible, for workers from one province or territory to work in another. While it is not expected that such amendments will address all barriers, it is a step in the right direction. Amendments to the AIT will lead to full labour mobility for workers and professionals, except where protection of public health or safety justifies barriers. (They will also provide for an effective dispute resolution mechanism, including monetary penalties for ignoring a trade panel ruling.) It is estimated that Alberta will create 400,000 jobs over the next decade and labour mobility is seen as key to filling these jobs.

Municipal Government Responsibilities[18]

Municipal governments—cities, towns, villages, counties, districts, and metropolitan regions—are set up by the provincial legislatures. Their authority is defined by the specific province in which they operate. There are roughly 4,000 municipal governments in Canada that provide a variety of services. Municipalities provide services such as water supply, sewage and garbage disposal, roads, sidewalks, street lighting, building codes, parks, playgrounds, libraries, and so forth. Schools are generally looked after by school boards or commissions elected under provincial education acts.

Municipalities also play a role in consumer protection. For example, they have regulations and laws regarding any establishment that serves food. Inspectors regularly examine the premises of all restaurants for cleanliness. Local newspapers often publish lists of restaurants fined for failing to maintain required standards. There are similar laws (called zoning laws) about noise, odours, signs, and other activities that may affect a neighbourhood. Certain zones are restricted to residences, and others permit only certain quiet businesses to operate.

Zoning requirements also limit the height of buildings and define how far they must be set back from the road. Most Canadian cities require that all high-rise buildings have a certain ratio of garage space so that cars have off-street parking spots. Parking problems in residential areas due to overflow of vehicles from adjacent businesses have led to parking being limited to residential permit holders on certain streets, so that stores and other places of business must offer commercial parking lots for their customers. And, of course, there are speed limits set by municipal or provincial authorities.

All businesses usually must obtain a municipal licence to operate so the appropriate department can track them to ensure they are following regulations. Many municipalities also have a business tax and a charge for water consumption.

In summary, each level of government has its own roles and responsibilities. Sometimes there is overlap and in other instances there is downloading of responsibilities. Such is the case with some municipal services. An understanding of these responsibilities will contribute to a better understanding of who is responsible for developing, implementing, and overseeing policies that are important to business.

LO4 Explain how taxation and financial policies affect the Canadian economy.

Taxation and Financial Policies

Mention the word taxes and most people frown. That's because taxes affect almost every individual and business in the country. Taxes are how all levels of government redistribute wealth. The revenue that is collected allows governments to discharge their legal obligations. This revenue is used to pay for public services (e.g., fire, police, and libraries), pay down debt, and fund government operations and programs. Taxes have also been used as a method of encouraging or discouraging taxpayers. For example, if the government wishes to reduce the use of certain classes of products (e.g., cigarettes and alcohol), it passes what is referred to as a *sin tax*. It is hoped that the additional cost of the product from increased taxes discourages additional consumption.

In other situations the government may encourage business to hire new employees or to purchase new equipment by offering a tax credit. A tax credit is an amount that can be deducted from a tax bill. For example, a recent report indicated that between 1961 and 2013, the federal department of industry provided $22.4 billion to businesses.[19] Pratt & Whitney Canada, a private business that manufactures jet engines, has received $3.3 billion in subsidies since 1970.[20]

Pratt & Whitney Canada recently announced it will invest $1 billion in research and development by 2019. Some of the funds will involve projects with Canadian universities. The new technology will include designs for environmentally-friendly and fuel-efficient aircraft. Should government support companies such as Pratt & Whitney Canada? Why or why not?

Taxes are levied from a variety of sources. Income (personal and business), sales, and property are the major bases of tax revenue. The federal government receives its largest share of taxes from personal income. "Taxes from all levels of government make up the single largest expenditure facing Canadian families," says Charles Lammam, the Fraser Institute's Associate Director of Tax and Budget Policy Research.[21] In a recent study (some results from the report are summarized in Figure 4.5), the total tax bill of the typical Canadian family was calculated by adding up the various taxes that a family pays to federal, provincial, and local governments.[22] This includes income taxes, sales taxes, Employment Insurance and Canadian Pension Plan contributions, and "hidden" taxes such as import duties, excise taxes on tobacco and alcohol, amusement taxes, and gas taxes.

■ **FIGURE 4.5**

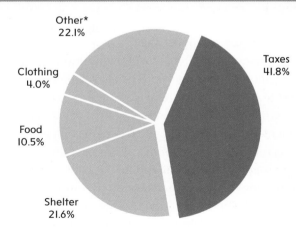

THE AVERAGE CANADIAN FAMILY'S TOTAL EXPENDITURES AS A PERCENTAGE OF CASH INCOME, 2013

Other*
22.1%

Taxes
41.8%

Clothing
4.0%

*"Other expenditures" include household operations (communications, child care expenses, pet expenses), transportation, health care, recreation, education, tobacco products, and alcoholic beverages.

Food
10.5%

Shelter
21.6%

Source: Milagros Palacios and Charles Lammam, "Taxes versus the Necessities of Life: The Canadian Consumer Tax Index 2014 Edition," The Fraser Institute, August 2014, https://www.fraserinstitute.org/uploadedFiles/fraser-ca/Content/research-news/research/publications/canadian-consumer-tax-index-2014.pdf, 8.

Queen's University Faculty of Law Professor Kathleen Lahey believes that information from reports such as the one mentioned above is limited and that it looks at only one component of the tax system.[23] Public outcry at personal income tax rates (as a possible outcome of this report's perspective) could make it easier for the government to cut these rates. However, the result would shift more of the tax burden to taxes such as sales taxes, employment insurance premiums, and Canada Pension Plan (CPP) contributions. Those forms of taxation weigh most heavily on low-income families, couples and individuals, disabled people, and those with unequal access to well-paying jobs, such as women and Aboriginal and immigrant workers, says Lahey. She believes that the impact that corporate tax cuts had on tax revenue is frequently ignored.

Can you see how it is important to consider all aspects when information is released? Start by asking yourself some questions. What is the purpose of this information? From what perspective is this report written? What is the call to action? As you can read from the above, there are always different perspectives that should be explored before making business decisions that will impact many stakeholders.

Progress Assessment

- What are responsibilities of the federal government?
- What are responsibilities of the provincial governments?
- Why are there interprovincial trade barriers?
- What are responsibilities of the municipal governments?

⚡ Stabilizing the Economy Through Fiscal Policy

Fiscal policy refers to the federal government's effort to keep the economy stable by increasing or decreasing taxes or government spending. The first half of fiscal policy involves taxation. Theoretically, high personal income and corporate tax rates tend to slow the economy because they draw money away from the private sector and are remitted to the government. High corporate tax rates may discourage small business ownership because they decrease the profits businesses can make, and this can make the effort less rewarding. It follows then that, theoretically, low tax rates would tend to give the economy a boost.[24] The government can use taxation to help move the economy in a desired direction. For example, taxes may be lowered to stimulate the economy when it is weak. Similarly, taxes may be raised when the economy is booming to cool it off and slow down inflation.

> **fiscal policy**
> The federal government's effort to keep the economy stable by increasing or decreasing taxes or government spending.

Federal and provincial governments constantly use the lever of fiscal policy to stimulate specific geographic and industrial areas. They offer special tax credits to companies that open plants in areas of chronically high unemployment, such as Cape Breton or Newfoundland and Labrador. All companies that invest in specific activities considered desirable by the government (such as the technology sector) may be eligible to receive a tax credit that reduces the income tax they have to pay. Unfortunately, some of these programs have been scaled back or eliminated due to budget constraints.

The second half of fiscal policy involves government spending. The government spends money in many areas, including social programs, highways, the environment, and so on. If the government spends over and above the amount it gathers in taxes for a specific period of time (namely, a fiscal year), then it has a **deficit**.

> **deficit**
> Occurs when a government spends over and above the amount it gathers in taxes for a specific period of time (namely, a fiscal year).

One way to lessen annual deficits is to cut government spending. This is difficult to do. Every year, there is demand by the provinces and territories for increased transfer payments (to be discussed soon), the need for funds due to unexpected situations (such as the massive flooding in Calgary and southern Alberta in 2013), more pressure from international bodies to increase peacekeeping support, and so on. Some people believe that spending by the government helps the economy grow. Others believe that the money the government spends comes out of the pockets of consumers and business people—especially when taxes have been increased—and that this slows growth. What do you think? Let us look at government actions that have been taken over the past decade.

THE NATIONAL DEBT (FEDERAL DEBT)

For many years, the Canadian government spent more than it received in revenues, and it had to borrow heavily. However, it did not reduce spending when times were good to pay back these loans. The **national debt** (also known as the **federal debt**) is the accumulation of government surpluses and deficits over time. At the time this chapter was updated, the national debt was approximately $615 billion. When all three level of government are considered—federal, provincial, and municipal— the debt level was $1.2 trillion.[25] You may research the current national and provincial debt levels as calculated by the Canadian Taxpayers Federation (go to <http://www.debtclock.ca>).

> **national debt (federal debt)**
> The accumulation of government surpluses and deficits over time.

Increased government borrowing and spending stimulates an economy. Such was the case when the federal government tried to stimulate the economy through its 2009–2012 Economic Action Plan.[26] A total of $5.53 billion was spent on initiatives such as increased spending (e.g., infrastructure) and decreased taxes. This was in response to some economic challenges during that time: a falling world GDP, a continuing U.S. recession, and a drop in commodities prices.[27] (You can see how an understanding of economics and global business is critical when reviewing the federal budget.) The changes to spending and taxes contributed to the first deficit in over ten years.

Cuts in spending have the opposite effect as they slow down the economy. Such decisions influence many stakeholders. The Making Ethical Decisions box highlights how cuts in government spending can negatively impact individuals.

Why is it important to control the debt? Financial security is critical to a country's investment in its people and businesses. A lower debt means that less money will need to go toward paying down the national debt and any outstanding interest. Reducing government spending on interest charges will allow the government to spend more money on social programs or to lower taxes. Lower taxes will stimulate the economy, as companies will have higher net profits and individuals will have more disposable income.

Making ETHICAL DECISIONS

Tackling the Deficit

In the late 1990s the federal government was under strong pressure from the business community to reduce or wipe out the annual deficit in the annual budget. Business was convinced that these constant deficits and the resulting accumulated debt were dragging the Canadian economy down and making Canada less competitive with other major countries. As a result, the federal government drastically cut its expenditures.

There were significant reductions in funding to the provinces for health care, post-secondary education, and other important activities. Combined with other budget-cutting measures (e.g., lower and fewer payments to the unemployed and laying off employees), the result was an increase in poverty levels, especially among children and women.

These facts lead to some ethical questions. How could such severe budget cuts have been avoided? Does the business community bear some responsibility for the increase in poverty in Canada? In other words, was it ethical for businesses to allow our national debt to grow so large and not challenge the government's annual deficits much earlier? What do you think?

With a lower debt and commitment to social programs, Canada could be considered a more attractive country for investment. A country with stable and well-funded government social programs encourages business development, including hiring, because there is less risk that the business will be asked to increase employee benefits. A lower debt load also means that in times of economic slowdown or when unexpected events occur (such as the global financial crisis) the government may have funds available to alleviate the ensuing pressures. Of course, if the debt is high, there is less money that can be dedicated to social programs and initiatives to assist businesses in becoming more competitive.

Reductions in the national debt have been the result of surpluses—a **surplus** is an excess of revenues over expenditures. As the debt comes down the annual interest costs are also reduced. This reduction in the national debt translates into a savings of billions of dollars each year on debt interest payments.

surplus
An excess of revenues over expenditures.

THE FEDERAL BUDGET

On an annual basis (around springtime), the federal finance minister releases a blueprint for how the government wants to set the country's annual economic agenda. This document, called the **federal budget**, is a comprehensive report that reveals government financial policies and priorities for the coming year. This political document shows how much revenue the government expects to collect, any changes in income and other taxes, and whether a deficit or a surplus is expected. The federal budget answers questions that affect businesses and Canadians, such as: How much money will go to pay down the debt? How much money will go to social programs such as health care? Will there be more money for research and development? Will taxes go up or down?

federal budget
A comprehensive report that reveals government financial policies for the coming year.

Each year (normally in February or March), Finance Ministers for the federal and provincial/territorial governments present their budgets. Budgets identify where the government plans to spend money, the amount of expected revenues, and the expected economic forecast for the upcoming year. What were some of the most important aspects of the last federal government budget? What aspects of the budget impact you? How?

The budget is reviewed carefully by businesses, consumers, and other countries because the information it contains affects all of these stakeholders. It reflects revenues (from taxation) and expenditures (e.g., Canada Pension Plan payments) for the past year. In addition, the government will communicate program changes for the future, as well as forecasted growth projections. From this document stakeholders can get an idea of what issues are important to the government. For example, in the 2012 federal budget, Finance Minister Jim Flaherty expected that the government would be in a surplus position by 2015.[28] Joe Oliver, the Finance Minister at the time this book was written, expects the 2015 budget will be balanced, yet the falling price of oil, a commodity that generates significant revenue for the federal government, may result in a another budget deficit.[29] Provincial governments also release their own budgets. A province's financial stability affects political decisions and, ultimately, the business environment within the province's boundaries.

✱ Using Monetary Policy to Keep the Economy Growing

Have you ever wondered who lends the federal government money when it spends more than it collects in taxes? One source is the Bank of Canada, a Crown corporation. Its role is to "promote the economic and financial well-being of Canada." The day-to-day administration of monetary policy is the responsibility of the Bank of Canada, in co-operation and in consultation with the federal finance minister. You will learn more about how the Bank of Canada's controls the money supply of the country in Chapter 18.

The federal government passed Bill C-38, referred to as the 'omnibus bill' in 2012. The bill went beyond tax and monetary measures to make major changes to various policy areas, including environment and natural resources.[30] Many Canadians protested the bill, claiming that using such a huge bill prevented debate about key issues unrelated to the budget. Would you participate in a protest about a government budget? What aspects of a federal government budget are important to you?

Monetary policy is the management of the money supply and interest rates. It is controlled by the Bank of Canada. When the economy is booming, the Bank of Canada tends to raise interest rates in an attempt to control inflation. This makes money more expensive to borrow. Businesses thus borrow less, and the economy slows as business people spend less money on everything, including labour and machinery. The opposite is true when the Bank of Canada lowers interest rates. When this happens, businesses tend to borrow more, and the economy improves. Raising and lowering interest rates should therefore help control the business cycles.

monetary policy
The management of the money supply and interest rates.

The Bank of Canada is Canada's central bank. It is not a commercial bank and it does not offer banking services to the public. Rather, it has the responsibilities for Canada's monetary policy, bank notes, financial system, funds management, and retail debt. The Governor of the Bank of Canada is the bank's Chief Executive Officer and has full authority over its business. In the picture above Governor Stephen Poloz speaks at a press conference to update the media about bank activities.

The Bank of Canada also controls the money supply. A simple explanation of how this works is that the more money the Bank of Canada makes available to business people and others, the faster the economy grows. To slow the economy, the Bank of Canada lowers the money supply. (If you are eager to learn more about the money supply, you can turn to Chapter 18 now.) One example of the Canadian government stepping in to stimulate the economy is its reaction to the U.S. subprime mortgage crisis that impacted the global economy. Read about this in the next section.

In summary, the government makes two major efforts to control the economy: fiscal policy (taxes and spending) and monetary policy (control over interest rates and the money supply). The economic goal is to keep the economy growing so that more people can climb up the economic ladder and enjoy a satisfying quality of life.[31]

THE SUBPRIME MORTGAGE CRISIS[32]

Subprime mortgages are loans targeted at people who do not qualify for regular mortgages because their credit records are not good enough or because they do not have a credit history. Some mortgages are interest-only loans that are lower in cost because no principal is paid down. Initially, these loans come with very low rates (thus, subprime).

In the situation that developed in the United States, people holding subprime mortgages found that at the end of the term (e.g., two years), interest rates were much higher and they couldn't afford to make their payments. As housing prices started to fall, they often found that they could no longer afford to sell the homes either. The fallout was decreasing home sales and prices, and rising foreclosures. The resulting crisis contributed to approval of a US$700 billion bank bailout by the U.S. Congress in October 2008 to stabilize the financial sector and reinforce hundreds of financial institutions. Additional bailout funds were approved the following year. Bank bailouts soon followed in England, Germany, France, Italy, and Spain.

While Canadian financial institutions did not face the high default rates experienced in the United States, they were having trouble borrowing money because banks and other lenders in other countries were more cautious. This credit squeeze sent stock markets (to be discussed in Chapter 17) crashing and there were worries of a global meltdown. In response to these conditions, the federal government announced in October 2008 that it would take over $25 billion worth of bank-held mortgages to ease the growing liquidity problems faced by the country's financial institutions. This would provide more money to financial institutions. To further stimulate the economy and encourage banks to continue lending money, the Bank of Canada continued to lower its lending rate.

The government did not agree with critics who characterized this action as a bailout of an industry that generated record profits. "This is not a bailout; this is a market transaction that will cost the government nothing," said Prime Minister Harper. "We are not going in and buying bad assets. What we're doing is simply exchanging assets that we already hold the insurance on and the reason we're doing this is to get out in front. The issue here is not protecting the banks." He believed that the problem Canada's financial institutions faced was not solvency but the availability of credit. This action was expected to make loans and mortgages more available and more affordable for ordinary Canadians and businesses. One month later, another $50 billion allocation was announced.

Fast forward to 2012. A report from the Canadian Centre for Policy Alternatives (CCPA) *<http://www .policyalternatives.ca>* claimed that Canadians were never told the true cost of a $114-billion "secret bailout" for the country's biggest banks during the financial crisis. Study author and CCPA economist David MacDonald wrote "During the worst of the crisis—2008 to 2010—the official line was that Canada's banks did not require the extraordinary bailout measures that were being offered in other countries, particularly in the U.S. . . . At its peak in March 2009, support for Canadian banks reached

$114 billion." Finance Minister Jim Flaherty's spokesperson, Chisholm Pothier, said MacDonald got it wrong and that "There was no 'secret bailout.'" All of the loans provided by the government as part of its relief program for Canadian lenders have been paid back in full, said Pothier.

The Occupy Movement is an international protest movement against economic and social inequality. It was created partially in response to the late-2000s financial crisis and the subprime mortgage crisis. One major concern is the claim that large corporations and the global financial system control the world in a way that disproportionately benefits a minority, undermines democracy, and is unstable. Occupy Vancouver (on a site in front of the Vancouver Art Gallery shown above) was one of over 15 Canadian cities to hold protests. Do you think the Occupy Movement had any impact? Why or why not?

To some extent, the report and the rebuttal to it are a matter of how the facts are interpreted. Where MacDonald says "bailout," a finance ministry official says "liquidity support." Do you agree that this was not a bailout? What would have been the implications for business people and consumers if money had not been made available by financial institutions?

By 2015, the secret bailout issue was replaced with broader concerns about the global financial market. The World Economic Forum ranked Canada's banks as the most sound in the world for the seventh year in a row, at a time when many countries still face banking crisis, including Greece. A 2013 report noted 95 percent of Canadians were proud of how the Canadian banks handled the 2008 global recension, in comparison to banks around the world.

This is an ideal time to pause and to recognize the need and importance for regulatory oversight. The lesson of the subprime mortgage crisis is that not all regulation is bad. That is, the right regulation is in fact necessary to create an environment that encourages entrepreneurship. This being said, the government is expected to be transparent in its actions.

Progress Assessment

- How does the government manage the economy using fiscal policy?
- What is Canada's national debt? What actions can the government take to decrease it?
- Explain the purpose of the federal budget.
- What does the term monetary policy mean? What organization is responsible for Canada's monetary policy?

LO5 Describe how government expenditures benefit consumers and businesses alike.

Government Expenditures

Governments in Canada help disburse tens of billions of dollars annually in old-age pensions, allowances to low-income families or individuals, employment insurance, welfare, workers' compensation, and various other payments to individuals. These transfers give Canadians more purchasing power and, therefore, the creation of a more viable market for businesses.

As people spend their money, large numbers of Canadian companies and their employees benefit as a result of this purchasing power. Increasing or lowering the rates or eligibility for these payments results in further fine-tuning of the economy. Again, government cutbacks have resulted in the reduction of such payments in recent years.

Governments also spend huge sums of money on education, health, roads, ports, waterways, airports, and various other services required by businesses and individuals. They also provide aid through direct and indirect government programs designed to help businesses. The Canadian Subsidy Directory lists more than 3,000 sources of financing and government programs for anyone searching for Canadian grants, loans, and government programs.[33] Governments also intervene on an ad hoc (special or unplanned) basis in important cases. For example, in 2013 the government funding to the National Angel Capital Organization, which provides capital and coaching to early-stage businesses, supported $89 million worth of investment in 199 deals by 29 groups throughout the country.[34]

Financial Aid

All levels of government offer a variety of direct assistance programs to businesses, including grants, loans, loan guarantees, consulting advice, information, and other aids that are designed to achieve certain purposes (see Figure 4.6). For example, the federal government created a program worth up to $7.3 million to foster Aboriginal participation in development, particularly mining projects, in Northern Quebec; the program focused upon the labour market, Aboriginal entrepreneurship, and sustainable revenues.[35]

Some government aid is designed to help industries or companies that are deemed to be very important—at the cutting edge of technology, providing highly skilled jobs, and oriented toward exports. Bombardier Inc. manufactures the C-Series commercial aircraft. In 2013, the Quebec government provided the company $1 billion in financing to help buyers of the plane. The funding and repayment plans for the initiative are overseen by Investissement Quebec.[36] In 2015, the Quebec government announced it was able to provide financial assistance to Bombardier, Inc. because the company was too important to the province's economy.[37]

Spotlight *On* SMALL BUSINESS

Sustainable Development Technology Canada[38]

The federal government invests billions of dollars in grants and programs that stimulate innovation to benefit the Canadian economy. One such program is Sustainable Development Technology Canada (SDTC) <http://www.sdtc.ca> whose mandate is to "fund Canadian cleantech projects and coach the companies that lead them as they move their ground-breaking technologies to market." The cleantech industry represents and estimated value of $4 trillion worldwide. In Canada, the industry consists of over 700 mainly small and medium-sized firms

■ FIGURE 4.6

Rank	Applicant legal name	Total disbursements 2013 $ millions	Number of disbursements	Total disbursements Nominal $ millions	Date of first disbursement	Date of most recent disbursement
	TOP TEN RECIPIENTS, INDUSTRY CANADA FINANCIAL ASSISTANCE PROGRAM, 1961–2013					
1	Pratt & Whitney Canada Corp.	3,306	74	2,038	1970-04-01	2010-12-10
2	Bombardier Inc.	1,145	48	711	1966-03-15	2009-03-23
3	De Havilland Inc.	1,090	34	450	1972-10-16	1996-12-20
4	CAE Inc.	652	44	524	1974-06-12	2009-03-30
5	General Motors of Canada Ltd.	536	7	362	1982-03-31	2005-12-05
6	Bell Helicopter Textron Canada Ltd.	410	9	237	1984-01-05	2005-06-01
7	Groupe Mil Inc. (Le)	394	10	222	1986-02-27	1989-03-28
8	Honeywell ASCa Inc.	321	73	210	1975-03-25	2005-03-29
9	CMC Electronics Inc.	309	82	188	1972-03-02	2009-01-13
10	Litton Systems Canada	307	34	145	1973-01-19	1991-08-20
		8,470	415	5,087		

Source: Mark Milke, "Government Subsidies in Canada: A $684 Billion Price Tag," The Fraser Institute, June 2014, retrieved on April 5, 2015 from http://www.fraserinstitute.org/uploadedFiles/fraser-ca/Content/research-news/research/publications/government-subsidies-in-canada-a-684-billion-price-tag.pdf, p. 15.

involved with oil and gas, mining, power generation, transportation, agriculture, forestry and forest products, and water and energy efficiency. The Canadian cleantech industry generates $11.3 billion in revenues and employs over 41,000 people.

To date the SDTC has supported 269 projects for a total of $684 million in government support. SDTC-funded companies have generated an additional $2.6 billion in follow-up financing dollars from the private sector.

The SDTC impacts many regions of Canada. The Vancouver Economic Council (VEC) ran a SDTC workshop to promote the cleantech industry to entrepreneurs and small businesses in the city. According to Bryan Buggy, VEC's Director, Strategic Initiatives and Sector Development, 33,400 people, or the equivalent of one in twenty jobs in Vancouver, are green jobs, including positions in sustainable building design and development; waste management and recycling; land and water remediation; agriculture management; and sustainability consulting. In Manitoba, a 2004 project involved Prairie Pulp and Paper Inc. <http://stepforwardpaper.com> and the Straw Producers Co-op of Manitoba for a tree-free agriculture-fibre paper mill that created paper products from farm residue.

The salmon aquaculture industry on Vancouver Island also involves cleantech projects; the Middle Bay Sustainable Aquaculture Institute is developing a commercial-scale solid wall containment system to improve salmon production in a way that reduces interference with the marine environment. The Namgis Land-Based Atlantic Salmon Recirculating Aquaculture System (RAS) Pilot Project will reduce the risk of disease for the salmon and treat the solid and liquid waste generated from the salmon rearing. Each of these projects support sustainable business.

Does support to this industry make good business sense? What are some other benefits to supporting cleantech small businesses?

It may help consumers to offer lower-than-cost prices for energy products such as gasoline and electricity, but what are the advantages and disadvantages of such government support? Are fossil fuel subsidies good for the Canadian economy? Do they encourage the development of green energy? Are the subsidies fiscally sustainable for governments to offer?

Fossil fuel subsidies are common in almost every country of the world.[39] They include subsidies for petroleum products, electricity, natural gas, and coal. The International Monetary Fund identified the worldwide cost of fossil fuel subsidies in 2011 as $480 billion for "pre-tax" subsidies and $1.9 trillion for "post tax" subsidies.[40] This represents a range of two to eight percent of government spending. Both "pre" and "post" tax subsidies enable fossil fuel energy to be offered at a lower-than-cost price through support to energy producers (pre) and consumers (post).

In 2011, Canada expended $26 billion to subsidize energy, which reflects 4 percent of government revenues.[41] Based upon Canada's population that year, the subsidies represented $787 for each person. Fossil fuel subsidies include a number of federal and provincial programs. For example, the Alberta government offered Energy Industry Drilling Stimulus, which cost $1.7 billion in 2011, to reduce royalty costs to oil and gas producers in the province. The Ontario government's Fuel Tax Exemption for Coloured Fuel, which cost $285 million in 2011, exempts fuel tax for this type of gas, which is used in forestry, agriculture, and fishing.

However, there is world recognition that fossil fuel subsidies need to adapt to current and future energy needs.[42] Governments provide support to the fossil fuel industry, which has both costs and benefits. On one hand subsidies generate economic growth in the fossil fuel industry, which in turn provide jobs and stimulates further business of other companies that service the industry. On the other hand, the subsidies can have a significant drain on government budgets and intensify climate change through higher energy consumption because energy costs are artificially low. A recent report suggests removal of the subsidies would generate a 13 percent decline in CO_2 emissions and reduce global energy demand.

🏕 Equalization Program[43]

Canada is a very large country with uneven resources, climate, and geography, which has led to uneven economic development. **Transfer payments** are direct payments from governments to other governments or to individuals. Federal transfer payments to individuals include elderly benefits and employment insurance. Such payments provide social security and income support.

> **transfer payments**
> Direct payments from governments to other governments or to individuals.

Equalization is the federal government's transfer program for reducing fiscal disparities among provinces. These payments enable less-prosperous provincial governments to provide their residents with public services that are roughly comparable to those in other provinces, at roughly comparable levels of taxation. While provinces are free to spend the funds on public services according to their own priorities, these payments are intended to fund medicare, post-secondary education, and smaller programs.

> **equalization**
> A federal government program for reducing fiscal disparities among provinces.

In 2015–2016, the federal government will provide $17.3 billion in equalization payments to six provinces (Manitoba, Ontario, Quebec, New Brunswick, Nova Scotia, and Prince Edward Island). Did you notice that this program does not include the territories? The Territorial Formula Financing program provides territorial governments with funding to support public services, in recognition of the higher cost of living in the north.

Progress Assessment

- Explain how governments in Canada spend tax dollars to help Canadians.
- Give two examples of how government has provided financial aid to businesses.
- Who benefits from equalization transfer payments?

LO6   Illustrate how purchasing policies and services assist Canadian businesses.

Purchasing Policies

Most governments are very large purchasers and consumers of goods and services; indeed, in Canada they are the largest buyers. Procurement policies guide how governments buy and sell goods and services for various department and agencies; the intent is to have the best interest of Canadians in mind. The federal and provincial governments use this enormous purchasing power to favour Canadian companies. The provinces favour those companies within their boundaries and have even set up trade barriers between provinces (as discussed earlier). When advanced technology items—civilian or military—must be obtained from foreign companies, our governments usually insist that a certain minimum portion be manufactured in Canada. This enables Canadian companies to acquire advanced technology know-how and to provide employment.

Seeking SUSTAINABILITY

Procurement for the Planet

Governments spend a great deal of money to purchase goods and services. While exact figures are hard to determine, total government programs expenditures totalled $240.4 billion in 2011–2012. By the sheer volume of purchases, governments of all level are able to influence environmental sustainability through policies referred to as "green procurement." These policies ensure environmental considerations are included when governments make purchase decisions.

The objective of the federal government policy on green procurement is to advance the protection of the environment and support sustainable development. At the provincial level, sustainable procurement policies, such as the one for Nova Scotia, integrate environmental, economic, and social considerations in procurement decisions in order to obtain the best value for government and the people it serves. But it is at the municipal level where green procurement is most important since these governments have direct or indirect control over 45 percent of greenhouse gas emissions in Canada.

Municipal governments have developed strategic sustainability plans that include areas such as buildings and facilities, municipal vehicle fleets (including transit), street lighting, and waste management. Dawson Creek, British Columbia, is on its way to becoming a "solar city"; the lighting systems for fire and police stations and City Hall were retrofitted, and solar panels for traffic signs, bus stops, and trail lights were installed throughout the community. The Canadian Urban Transit Association noted there are 14,000 transit buses across Canada, of which nearly 90 percent run on diesel. In an effort to address this significant ecological footprint, several environmental transit fleet initiatives exist in cities across the country to identify the best options for electric and hybrid vehicle purchases.

Does the city or town where you live have an environmental sustainability plan? Does the council follow a green procurement policy? What are the advantages and disadvantages of these initiatives?

Sources: "Federal Expenditures by Year and Item (Total), 1061-1962 to 2011-2012," Government Spending: Canadian Taxpayers Association, January 2013, http://www.taxpayer.com/media/Federal%20Expenditures%20by%20Year%20and%20Item%20 %28Total%29,%201961-1962%20to%202011-2012%281%29.pdf; "Policy on Green Procurement," Public Works and Government Services Canada, 18 February 2015, http://www.tpsgc-pwgsc.gc.ca/ecologisation-greening/achats-procurement/politique-policy-eng. html; "Highlighting best practices – sustainable procurement resources for municipal, academic, schools and health and social service (MASH) organizations," Office of Sustainability, Dalhousie University, 2012; "Environmental technology verification for municipal fleets: a public transit perspective," Canadian Urban Transit Association, 2013, http://www.fcm.ca/Documents/presentations/2013 /SCC2013/Environmental_Technology_Verification_for_Municipal_Fleets_EN.pdf; "Dawson Creek – a near carbon neutral city in the idle of northeastern B.C.'s shale gas boom," Green Energy Futures, 23 June 2012, http://www.greenenergyfutures.ca/episode/08/awesome -dawson-creek-northern-oil-and-gas-town-bets-big-renewable-energy; "Building Canada's green economy: the municipal role," Federation of Canadian Municipalities, 2011, https://fcm.ca/Documents/reports/Building_Canadas_green_economy_the_municipal_role_EN.pdf.

Contracts are often awarded to help Canadian businesses even if they are sometimes more expensive than bids by non-Canadian companies. This is particularly true in the military acquisitions programs. Whatever can be produced or serviced in Canada—ships, electronics, trucks, artillery, ammunition—is acquired from Canadian companies. (See the Seeking Sustainability box for an example of pro-environment government purchasing policies.) These federal and provincial policies are being modified as a result of the general movement to freer trade due to NAFTA.

Be aware that government procurement has some challenges. It is a demanding bidding process that is strictly regulated. In some provinces, government organizations may also include government boards, councils, committees, commissions, and publicly funded academic, health, and social service organizations.[44] It can be demanding to fully understand government procurement and to properly target potential niches. In large cities alone—such as Montreal, Toronto, and Vancouver—there are several hundred public organizations that function differently for their procurement. If a firm is interested in conducting business in the Canadian public sector, MERX Canadian Public Tenders service *<http://www.merx.com>* is an easy, fast, and efficient prospecting tool. New opportunities are listed daily for access to billions of dollars in Canadian public-sector business opportunities. They range from the private sector to all levels of government, and include the MASH (Municipal, Academic, School Boards and Hospitals) sector from across Canada.[45]

Services

The federal government has departments that provide services to businesses and consumers. We will look at two of these important departments: Industry Canada and the Department of Foreign Affairs, Trade and Development. There are corresponding departments in many of the provinces, especially the four largest and most developed ones (British Columbia, Alberta, Ontario, and Quebec).

Industry Canada

For many years, the federal government has implemented a variety of programs to help small businesses get started. These programs are part of a larger one, called Canada Business Network, that involves setting up Canada Business service centres in every province and territory. These centres are operated jointly with provincial governments and certain local organizations. Industry Canada publishes brochures, booklets, and guides informing business people of the help available and how and where to get it. Industry Canada also participates in the production of publications to promote Canadian businesses internationally.

Other programs are designed to encourage businesses to establish themselves or expand in economically depressed areas of the country. These are populated regions that are industrially underdeveloped, have high unemployment, and have lower standards of living. The programs include help for the tourism industry and for Aboriginal residents of remote areas who want to establish businesses.

NATIONAL RESEARCH COUNCIL

The National Research Council (NRC) *<http://www.nrc-cnrc.gc.ca/eng>* is a federal agency that began in 1916. It reports to Parliament through Industry Canada. The NRC plays a significant role in research that helps Canadian industry remain competitive and innovative. Its vision is to be the most effective research and development organization in the world, stimulating sustainable domestic prosperity.[46]

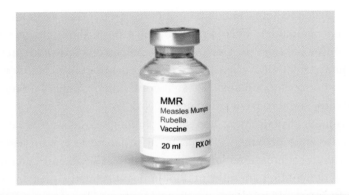

NRC researchers recently signed an agreement with the China National Biotech Group for three collaborative projects related to vaccine development for specific populations. The goal of the NRC is to increase Canada's innovation capacity and translate new science and technology initiatives to profits for businesses and gains for the Canadian economy.

This organization of over 3,500 researchers, technologists, and support staff represents Canada's principal science and technology agency. NRC also benefits from the efforts of guest workers drawn from Canadian and foreign universities, companies, and public- and private-sector organizations. Located in every province, areas of research and industry support include aerospace, biotechnology, engineering and construction, fundamental sciences, information and communications technologies, and manufacturing.

Department of Foreign Affairs, Trade and Development

Because exports are particularly important to Canada's economic well-being, the government has a very large and elaborate system to assist companies in their exporting and foreign-investment activities. The federal government, most provincial governments, and all large municipal governments have various ministries, departments, and agencies that provide a variety of such services. These include information, marketing, financial aid, insurance and guarantees, publications, and contracts. All major trading countries provide similar support to their exporters.

See Figure 4.7 for a list of government sources that are available to assist Canadian businesses. Most of them also provide some support for those that wish to succeed in global markets. We have discussed some of these organizations already in this textbook.

Progress Assessment

- Why do federal and provincial governments tend to favour Canadian companies when contracts are approved?
- How does the NRC contribute to technology advancement in Canada?
- List some organizations that aim to help exporters.

■ FIGURE 4.7

SOME GOVERNMENT RESOURCES AVAILABLE TO ASSIST CANADIAN BUSINESSES		
Government Source	Mission	Website
Business Development Bank of Canada (BDC)	BDC provides small and medium-sized businesses with flexible financing, affordable consulting services, and venture capital. BDC has a particular focus on the emerging and exporting sectors of the economy.	www.bdc.ca
Canada Business Network	Canada Business Network is a government information service for businesses and start-up entrepreneurs in Canada. It serves as a single point of access for federal and provincial/territorial government services, programs, and regulatory requirements for business.	www.canadabusiness.ca
Export Development Canada (EDC)	EDC provides Canadian exporters with financing, insurance, and bonding services as well as foreign market expertise.	www.edc.ca
Industry Canada	The Department's mission is to foster a growing, competitive, knowledge-based Canadian economy. Program areas include developing industry and technology capability, fostering scientific research, and promoting investment and trade.	www.ic.gc.ca
National Research Council (NRC)	NRC helps turn ideas and knowledge into new processes and products. Businesses work with partners from industry, government, and universities.	www.nrc-cnrc.gc.ca

Role of the Canadian Government—Some Final Thoughts

What should be clear is that government always has a critical role to play. This is especially the case during economic downturns or if the Canadian economy is impacted by foreign events such as the financial crisis that started in the late 2000s.

Some people believe that the best way to protect the Canadian economy is for the federal government to reverse its current direction of privatization. Instead of withdrawing from active direction and participation in the economy, it should develop a long-term industrial policy of leadership and take an active role in shaping the future of the economy. An **industrial policy** is a comprehensive, coordinated government plan to guide and revitalize the economy. An industrial policy requires close consultation with business and labour to develop a program for long-term sustainable industrial development.

industrial policy
A comprehensive, coordinated government plan to guide and revitalize the economy.

Others are opposed in principle to such government involvement. As mentioned earlier in this chapter, the 1980s witnessed the start of a movement toward deregulation, privatization, and less government involvement within Canada and other countries. Some believe that these were the right steps for the government to take, and that it should continue with these activities. Interestingly enough, when events such as a mad cow disease crisis for Canadian ranchers or a recession appear, some groups that normally lobby for less government involvement in their industries suddenly believe that government should step in and provide financial assistance. While this is contrary to free-market principles, troubled times are usually followed by calls for more government involvement.

Government intervention with the economy will vary over time but there is one issue that is here to stay: the environment and its impact on the economy.[47] Governments have many policy options available to reduce greenhouse gas emissions. Some are more politically acceptable and easier to implement than others, and not all approaches are likely to be equally effective. Experience in addressing other environmental issues has shown that using a mix of policy measures is more likely to succeed and to spread the responsibility around fairly. It has been a challenge for governments in Canada to come up with effective policy options to address climate change, partly because all three levels of government (federal, provincial, and municipal) have a stake in this issue as well as responsibilities and opportunities. Not all policy options are suitable for all levels of government, so co-operation and collaboration is important to make sure that effective measures are put in place without overlap and duplication.

The National Round Table on the Environment and the Economy has recommended that Canada immediately put in place a hard-cap regime on emissions by 2015, with auctioning of carbon permits to businesses by 2020. To do otherwise would face dire environmental and economic consequences. Round table chairman Bob Page says the United States is moving quickly on capping emissions and will penalize Canadian exports if Canada does not follow suit. "It is the most serious protectionist challenge we've had to face. Now we're going to see in place of the softwood lumber issue, we're going to see the issue that cuts right across manufacturing in Ontario and Quebec, and natural resource products like the oil sands in Alberta and Saskatchewan . . . those products will be subject to a carbon intensity surcharge at the American border unless Canada meets new American standards." Alberta won't like it, but will likely agree, since the oil sands producers are likely concerned about being shut out of the United States and possibly world markets, said Page, a professor of sustainable development at the University of Calgary.

The report says it is imperative that Canada move from the patchwork approach adopted by different provinces and for Ottawa to have a unified policy with identical standards across jurisdictions and industries. And it says it is critical that Canadian policy be compatible with that of its largest trading partners, particularly the United States. The cap-and-trade system is designed to put a price on pollution, but instead of taxing energy use by individuals directly, the cost is borne first by large emitters, who are expected to pass it on to consumers. Emissions permits can be traded on an open market between firms that need extra quota and those who have quota to sell.

While this system will involve a major transformation on the cost, the usage, and even the nature of energy in Canada, it is expected that the Canadian economy will continue to grow through the transformation period and that new industries will be created.

The Constitution Act outlines the powers of all levels of government. Each level of government is focused on creating a competitive environment for businesses of all sizes. As we move forward, the federal government will continue to focus on international trade initiatives to provide opportunities for Canadian businesses. This chapter has highlighted some of the resources that are available to businesses to assist them in their operations.

It is natural for disputes to arise as industries and countries attempt to act in their best interests. These disputes emerge even between established trading partners such as Canada and the United States, as evidenced by the long-running lumber dispute. However, in most instances, trade agreements create opportunities. Did you know, for example, that 95 percent of Canada–U.S. trade due to NAFTA is problem-free?[48] While disputes will not be resolved overnight, they are being addressed in a global arena, and this is at least a step in the right direction. Since Canada is a large exporter of goods and services, it must also be aware how its policies on the environment may impact future trade.

SUMMARY

LO1 **List the six categories of government activities that can affect business.**

There are six categories of government involvement in Canada.

What are the government activities that affect business?

The six categories of government activities are Crown corporations, laws and regulations, taxation and financial policies, government expenditures, purchasing policies, and services. See Figure 4.1 for a brief description of each activity.

What is the relationship between Canada's economic system and government involvement?

As noted in Chapter 2, Canada has a mixed economy, which is an economic system in which some allocation of resources is made by the market and some by the government. As a result of the Constitution Act, the different levels of government have responsibilities and jurisdiction over certain matters of the economy and population.

LO2 **Trace the historical role of government in the Canadian economy and explain why Crown corporations were created.**

The Canadian government played a key role from the beginning of the country in 1867 in protecting young manufacturing industries and getting the railroad built to the west coast, helping to join the country together.

Why did the government have to do what it did?

It had the legal power and responsibility to do so as a result of the Constitution Act. The United States threatened to overwhelm our industries, which were not strong enough by themselves to resist or to build the railway.

Why were Crown corporations necessary?

Companies were not willing or able to assume certain responsibilities or fill some needs in the marketplace. CNR, Air Canada, and Hydro-Québec are some important examples. (CNR and Air Canada are no longer Crown corporations.)

What is the recent trend with Crown corporations?

In recent years, we have seen an increasing trend where governments (both federal and provincial) have been selling Crown corporations. This is called privatization. Some examples include the sale of remaining Petro-Canada shares and the sale of BC Rail Ltd.

LO3 **Demonstrate why understanding laws and regulations at all levels of government is critical to business success.**

Businesses need to understand the laws and regulations that affect them. The Constitution Act defines the powers that can be exercised by the federal government and provincial governments. In the event of a conflict, federal powers prevail.

What are some federal government responsibilities?

The federal government's responsibilities include trade regulations, the incorporation of federal companies, national defence, immigration, and the fisheries.

What are some provincial government responsibilities?

Among other areas, provincial governments oversee natural resources within their boundaries, the administration of justice, municipal affairs, and education.

What are some municipal government responsibilities?

Municipal governments—cities, towns, villages, counties, districts, metropolitan regions—are set up by the provincial legislatures. Municipalities provide services such as water supply, sewage and garbage disposal, roads, sidewalks, street lighting, building codes, parks, playgrounds, libraries, and so forth. They play a role in consumer protection (e.g., inspectors examine restaurants) and the establishment of zoning requirements.

LO4 ### Explain how taxation and financial policies affect the Canadian economy.

Each level of government collects taxes from companies. These taxes allow governments to discharge their legal obligations and to fund social programs.

What is fiscal policy?

Fiscal policy refers to the federal government's effort to keep the economy stable by increasing or decreasing taxes or government spending.

What is the national debt?

The national debt, also known as the federal debt, is the accumulation of past government surpluses and deficits.

How is monetary policy different from fiscal policy?

Controlled by the Bank of Canada, monetary policy is the management of the money supply and interest rates. When the economy is booming, the Bank of Canada tends to raise interest rates in an attempt to control inflation. Since money is more expensive to borrow, businesses borrow less, and the economy slows as business people spend less money on everything. Fiscal policy involves broader government efforts to ensure a stable economy.

LO5 ### Describe how government expenditures benefit consumers and businesses alike.

Government expenditures benefit consumers and businesses alike. Some expenditures specifically target business subsidies, such as research and development initiatives for Canadian manufacturers, or support for agriculture, cleantech, and forestry that enables companies to be competitive in global markets. For consumers, expenditures for a stable income, such as old age security and employment insurance, are important, as is government support for education and job creation, which help people establish a stable income.

How do governments assist consumers with their tax dollars?

Governments disburse tens of millions of dollars annually in social program spending (e.g., old-age pensions, employment insurance, allowances to low-income families, etc.). These transfers give consumers more purchasing power.

How do businesses benefit from government expenditures?

All levels of government provide direct and indirect aid packages as incentives to achieve certain goals. These packages can consist of tax reductions, tariffs and quotas on imports, and subsidies including grants, loans, and loan guarantees.

LO6 **Illustrate how purchasing policies and services assist Canadian businesses**

Purchasing policies and services assist Canadian businesses. The purchasing power of government is very high when considered across the federal, provincial, territorial, and municipal levels. In many instances, Canadian businesses are targeted for opportunities to obtain government contracts or sell goods and services to government departments.

Why is preferential treatment given to Canadian companies when they bid for a government contract?

Contracts are often awarded to help Canadian businesses. This way, companies are employing Canadians and contributing to a strong economy.

What are two government departments that are particularly focused on assisting Canadian businesses?

Industry Canada and the Department of Foreign Affairs, Trade and Development assist businesses domestically and internationally.

KEY TERMS

Crown corporation	fiscal policy	National Policy
deficit	industrial policy	privatization
deregulation	marketing boards	surplus
equalization	monetary policy	transfer payments
federal budget	national debt (federal debt)	

CRITICAL THINKING

1. The issue of how much government should be involved in the economy has been the subject of much debate in Canada. In the United States, ideology has played a major role in influencing Americans to believe that, in principle, government should "butt out." This thinking ignores the significant role that the U.S. government has played and continues to play in the country's economy. (In comparison, the governments in France and Sweden are more socialistic in nature.) In Canada, we are less negative and perhaps more pragmatic: If it works, let's do it. But where do we go from here? Do we need less or more government involvement? Is it a question of the quality of that involvement? Could it be smarter rather than just less? How can the cost of government involvement decrease?

2. What are the implications of a majority federal government to the Canadian political scene? How does this differ from a minority government? (A minority government exists when no one party has a majority of seats in a legislative assembly. To pass legislation and other measures, that government would need the support of at least some members of other parties in the assembly.[49]) Explain.

3. If you represented the federal government, how would you respond to industries that have been seeking government action (e.g., subsidies or changes to policies) but to no avail? For example, take the position of the Canadian forestry industry, which in ten years lost about 114,000 jobs.[50] Keep in mind that other industries (e.g., aircraft manufacturing and automotive) have received such support (i.e., subsidies and bailout money).

DEVELOPING WORKPLACE SKILLS

Key: ● **Team**   ★ **Analytic**   ▲ **Communication**   ▢ **Technology**

▲▢ **1.** Scan your local newspapers, *The Globe and Mail,* the *National Post,* or a Canadian magazine such as *Canadian Business* for references to government programs that help Canadian businesses or have assisted a specific company. Bring these articles to class and discuss.

★▲ **2.** Many foreign governments have developed strong marketing campaigns to attract Canadian
▢ businesses. They also offer many incentives, including financial ones, to lure businesses to move there. Should anything be done about this? Many provincial and municipal governments have similar programs to attract foreign companies to their jurisdictions. Check out your provincial and municipal governments' websites for examples. Bring your information to class to discuss this kind of government expenditure.

●★ **3.** In a group of four, choose an industry (e.g., telecommunications, auto, health care, etc.).
▲▢ Find out if there have been any recent changes in federal and/or provincial legislation that will impact businesses. For example, has the Canadian Radio-television and Telecommunications Commission (CRTC, *<http://www.crtc.gc.ca>*) deregulated the industry? What are advantages and disadvantages of these changes? Have any of the provinces moved closer to a two-tier heath care system? Present your findings in a report or to the class.

★● **4.** Although unemployment remains high, especially among young people, business people complain that they cannot find trained employees to fill existing vacancies. Job candidates lack math and science backgrounds and their written English-language skills are weak. (In Quebec, there are similar complaints, but the language problems are with French.) Further, too many candidates are high-school dropouts. What can be done about this serious problem? Should business or government be working harder on it? What exactly should they be doing? Discuss this in a group of three.

ANALYZING MANAGEMENT DECISIONS

Gambling: A Cash Cow for Provincial Governments

Starting slowly in Quebec in the late 1960s, but catching on quickly across the country, lotteries, casinos, bingo, video lottery terminals (VLTs), and other forms of gambling had become, by the end of the twentieth century, a major source of revenue for many provincial governments.

You can get some idea of how large the gambling business has become by looking at the revenues and profits for the Ontario and Quebec governments for their respective 2014 year ends. The Ontario Lottery and Gaming (OLG) Corporation generated $6.6 billion in economic activity. Total revenue at Loto-Québec *<http://lotoquebec.com>* was approximately $3.5 billion. The OLG and its contracted companies employ 17,000 people. Over the years, both organizations have generated billions of dollars for their respective governments. Both operations also allot millions of dollars to help gamblers whose obsession with gambling has proven destructive to themselves or their families.

Sources: Public Accounts of Ontario – 2013-2014, Volume 2c, Ministry of Finance, Government of Ontario, 2014, pp. 2–83, http://www.fin.gov.on.ca /en/budget/paccts/2014/14vol2cEng.pdf; Loto Quebec 2014 Annual Report, http://lotoquebec.com/cms/dms/Corporatif/en/the-corporation/annual -report/2014_annual_report_pages_C1-C12.pdf, downloaded 5 April 2015.

Discussion Questions

1. Some people and organizations argue that governments should not be in the gambling business, that encouraging gambling is a bad idea. Others argue that private enterprise should run that kind of business, and argue further that companies would generate more profit compared to government run gambling operations, leading to more tax revenues for governments. Governments reply that they want to prevent organized crime from controlling gambling, so they must own and run such operations. What do you think? Is it okay for governments to be in the gambling business?

2. Governments seem to believe that gambling is a great way to raise money because Canadians don't seem to mind creating revenue by having some fun and a chance at big winnings, instead of just paying higher taxes. Besides, they argue, nobody is forced to gamble, so it's a kind of voluntary tax. How do you feel about that? Do you agree with this argument? Explain.

3. Some churches and other institutions concerned with personal and family welfare point to the rising number of family and personal breakdowns caused by people becoming gambling addicts. Also, easy access to video lottery terminals (VLTs) is very bad for young persons. Do you agree with either of these concerns? Why? What can be done to improve the situation?

4. Suppose that you agree with those who are totally opposed to governments encouraging gambling. Wouldn't taxes have to be raised to replace these revenues? Would you mind paying more taxes? Do you think your parents or family members would mind? Do you have any other suggestions for how government can generate this level of revenue?

VIDEO CASE 4

Creating a Buzz: Red Bull

In this chapter, you were introduced to the ways in which government activities can affect businesses. Let us consider how the creation of laws and regulations, one of the six government activities discussed, can create an opportunity for the sale of a product that some believe is dangerous to one's health.

Developed in Austria, Red Bull <http://www.redbull.com> is an energy drink with high caffeine content. It is creating quite a buzz, literally. It is promoted to people who need an energy boost.

Health Canada <http://www.hc-sc.gc.ca> is the federal department responsible for helping Canadians maintain and improve their health while respecting individual choices and circumstances. Health Canada oversees legislation for health products, regulating everything from vitamins to herbal remedies. Under this legislation, Red Bull was approved as a health product, with many warnings. These warnings include the following: Red Bull is not recommended for children, for pregnant women or those who are breastfeeding, or for caffeine-sensitive persons; it is not to be mixed with alcohol; and people should not consume more than 500 mL per day.

Some believe that Red Bull should not have been approved for sale in Canada as a health product. Too much consumption of Red Bull can be dehydrating. Despite allegations to the contrary, there was no evidence at the time of this video supporting the claim that Red Bull negatively affects people's hearts. There was no long-term research on how the combination of ingredients in this product interacts with the body. Regardless, some countries—Norway, Denmark, and France—were so concerned that they banned Red Bull. The governments in Sweden and Iceland have also voiced concerns.

In addition to other marketing activities, Red Bull sponsors extreme sporting events. The product can be purchased in a variety of locations across Canada, including bars and local variety stores. It is a number-one seller in 7-Eleven variety stores, which are easily accessible to children. The video shows how Red Bull representatives are promoting their product throughout Canada and encouraging participants to try it. From the footage shown, it does not appear that they are consistently communicating the warnings on the label, including that Red Bull should not be mixed with alcohol.

Currently, Red Bull has 61 different products (variety is due to numerous can sizes) listed on the Health Canada's Temporary Marketing Authorization Letter list for Caffeinated Energy Drinks (CEDs). The approvals are set to expire at different dates between 2017 and 2019. The ongoing sale of CEDs are considered a food and under the jurisdiction of the Canadian Food Inspection Agency.

Have you tasted Red Bull? If so, did you like it? If not, are you curious to try it?

Discussion Questions

1. What ingredients are found in Red Bull? What is the controversy surrounding these ingredients?

2. Why did Health Canada approve the sale of Red Bull when other countries have banned the sale of this product?

3. Do you agree that people must take responsibility for their own health, including reading labels and following instructions? In your opinion, should Health Canada be doing more? Explain.

4. Does government oversight of this kind infringe upon consumer choice? Explain.

APPENDIX A

*Working Within the Legal Environment of Business**

The Need for Laws

Imagine a society without laws. Just think, no speed limits to control how fast we drive, no age restrictions on the consumption of alcoholic beverages, no limitations on who can practice medicine—a society in which people are free to do whatever they choose, with no interference. Obviously, the more we consider this possibility, the more unrealistic we realize it is. Laws are an essential part of a civilized nation. Over time, though, the direction and scope of the body of laws must change to reflect changes in the needs of society.

In the Canadian system of government, which uses the English model, there are three branches of government. Each has a distinct role in the legal system, though sometimes the lines get blurred. The primary function of the legislative branch, composed of the Parliament of Canada and the legislatures of the provinces and territories, is to make the laws. Municipal councils also make laws, but their legislative power is limited to the scope delegated to them by their provincial legislature. The executive branch (e.g., government departments, administrative boards, and police departments) administers the laws, putting them into practice. The judicial branch (i.e., the courts) applies the law and interprets it when there is a dispute.

One part of the Canada's system of government includes the judiciary, which consists of the Supreme Court of Canada, the Tax Court of Canada, and federal, provincial, and territorial courts. Approximately 750 court locations exist with the Canadian four-tiered court system.[1]

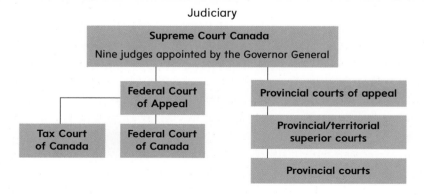

Judiciary

*Original material by Ray Klapstein, Dalhousie University; updated by Rita Cossa and Julie Stevens.

The Canadian court system has both federal and provincial/territorial courts, with jurisdiction that parallels the constitutional division of power between the central and provincial governments. The courts hear cases involving both criminal and civil law. **Criminal law** defines crimes, establishes punishments, and regulates the investigation and prosecution of people accused of committing crimes. **Civil law** involves legal proceedings that do not involve criminal acts; it includes laws regulating marriage, payment for personal injury, and so on. There are also appeal courts that hear appeals of decisions made at the initial trial, brought by the losing party in the case. Appeal courts can review and overturn decisions made by the trial court. The highest level appeal court for all matters is the Supreme Court of Canada.

---

criminal law
Defines crimes, establishes punishments, and regulates the investigation and prosecution of people accused of committing crimes.

civil law
Legal proceedings that do not involve criminal acts.

The law also governs the activities and operations of business in general. In fact, business people often complain that the government is stepping in more and more to govern the behaviour of business. We have laws and regulations regarding sexual harassment on the job, hiring and firing practices, leave for family emergencies, environmental protection, safety, and more. As you may suspect, business people prefer to set their own standards of behaviour. However, the business community has not been perceived as implementing acceptable practices quickly enough. To hasten the process, governments have expanded their control and enforcement procedures. In this appendix we will look at some of the laws and regulations now in place and how they affect business.

Business law refers to rules, statutes, codes, and regulations that are established to provide a legal framework within which business must be conducted and that are enforceable by court action. A business person should be familiar with laws regarding product liability, sales, contracts, fair competition, consumer protection, taxes, and bankruptcy. Let's start at the beginning and discuss the foundations of the law. It's hard to understand the law unless you know what the law entails.

---

business law
Rules, statutes, codes, and regulations that are established to provide a legal framework within which business must be conducted and that are enforceable by court action.

Statutory and Common Law

There are two major kinds of law: statutory law and common law. Both are important for business people.

Statutory law includes the laws that are made by the Parliament of Canada and the provincial legislatures, international treaties, and regulations and bylaws—in short, written law established by or through the legislative branch of government. You can read the statutes that make up this body of law, but they are often written in a language whose meaning must be determined in court. That's one reason why there are so many lawyers in Canada! **Common law** is the body of law that comes from decisions handed down by judges. Common law is often referred to as unwritten law because it does not appear in any legislative enactment, treaty, or other such document. Under common law principles, what judges have decided in previous cases is very important to today's cases. Such decisions are called **precedents**, and they guide judges in the handling of new cases. Common law evolves through decisions made in trial courts, appellate courts, and special courts. Lower courts (trial courts) must abide by the precedents set by higher courts (appeal courts) such as the Supreme Court of Canada. In law classes, therefore, students study case after case to learn about common law as well as statutory law.

> **statutory law**
> Federal and provincial legislative enactments, treaties of the federal government, and bylaws and ordinances—in short, written law.
>
> **common law**
> The body of law that comes from decisions handed down by judges; also referred to as unwritten law.
>
> **precedent**
> Decisions judges have made in earlier cases that guide the handling of new cases.

The Canadian legal system is complicated by the fact that federal law and provincial (including municipal) law in nine provinces operate under the English common law system, while provincial law in the Province of Quebec operates under the French civil law system. The difference lies more in principle than in practice: the common law system recognizes that courts actually make law through their decisions, while the civil law system restricts courts to interpreting the law that is provided by legislation that takes the form of the provincial civil code.

Laws Made Under Delegated Authority: Administrative Agencies

Different organizations within the government issue many rules, regulations, and orders. **Administrative agencies** are federal or provincial institutions and other government organizations created by Parliament or provincial legislatures with delegated power to pass rules and regulations within their mandated area of authority. Legislative bodies can both create administrative agencies and dissolve them. Some administrative agencies hold quasi-legislative, quasi-executive, and quasi-judicial powers. This means that an agency is allowed to pass rules and regulations within its area of authority, conduct investigations in cases of suspected rule violations, and hold hearings to determine whether the rules and regulations have been violated.

> **administrative agencies**
> Federal or provincial institutions and other government organizations created by Parliament or provincial legislatures with delegated power to pass rules and regulations within their mandated area of authority.

Administrative agencies actually issue more rulings affecting business and settle more disputes compared to the courts. There are administrative agencies at the federal, provincial/territorial, and local levels of government. For example, these include:

1. *At the federal level:* The Canadian Radio-television and Telecommunications Commission (CRTC) regulates the use of the airwaves, the Office of the Superintendent of Financial Institutions (OSFI) <*http://www.osfi-bsif.gc.ca*> regulates the operation of banks and other financial institutions, and the Commissioner of Competition is responsible for investigating complaints that the Competition Act has been violated.

2. *At the provincial level:* Public utility commissions and boards regulate prices for services such as electricity, licensing boards set the qualifications required for practising trades and professions (e.g., the practice of medicine or law), and labour relations boards oversee the certification of unions and relations between employers and unionized employees.

3. *At the local level:* Zoning boards and planning commissions control land use and development, and there are school boards and police commissions.

Tort Law

The tort system is an example of common law at work. A **tort** is a wrongful act that causes injury to another person's body, property, or reputation. This area of law comes within provincial jurisdiction, so legislation dealing with the topic comes from the provincial legislatures.

> **tort**
> A wrongful act that causes injury to another person's body, property, or reputation.

Criminal law focuses its attention on punishing and rehabilitating wrongdoers. Tort law, though, focuses on the compensation of victims. There are two kinds of torts. An intentional tort is a wilful act that results in injury. On the other hand, the unintentional tort of **negligence** provides compensation when the wrongdoer should have acted more carefully even though the harm or injury was unintentional. Decisions involving negligence can often lead to huge judgements against businesses. The question of intent was a major factor in the lawsuits against the tobacco industry. Courts had to decide whether tobacco makers intentionally withheld information from the public about the harmful effects of their products. In a highly publicized U.S. case, McDonald's lost a lawsuit to a person severely burned by its hot coffee. The jury felt the company failed to provide an adequate warning on the cup, and awarded a very large amount as compensation. Product liability is another example of tort law that's often very controversial. This is especially true regarding torts related to business actions. Let's look briefly at this issue.

> **negligence**
> Part of tort law where behaviour does not meet the standard of care required and causes unintentional harm or injury.

Product Liability

Few issues in business law raise as much debate as product liability. Critics believe that product liability laws have gone too far and deter product development. Others feel that these laws should be expanded to include products such as software and fast food. **Product liability**, covered under tort law, holds businesses liable for harm that results from the production, design, sale, or use of products they market. At one time, the legal standard for measuring product liability was whether a producer knowingly placed a hazardous product on the market. Today, many provinces have extended product liability to the level of **strict product liability**. Legally, this means without regard to fault. Thus, a company could be held liable for damages caused by placing a defective product on the market even if the company did not know of the defect at the time of sale. In such cases, the company is required to compensate the injured party financially.

> **product liability**
> Part of tort law that holds businesses liable for harm that results from the production, design, sale, or use of products they market.
>
> **strict product liability**
> Legal responsibility for harm or injury caused by a product regardless of fault.

The rule of strict liability has caused serious problems for businesses. For example, companies that produced lead-based paint in the past could be subject to expensive legal liabilities even though lead paint has not been sold for many years. The manufacturers of chemicals and drugs are also often susceptible to lawsuits under strict product liability. A producer may place a drug or chemical on the market that everyone agrees is safe. Years later, a side effect or other health problem could emerge. Under the doctrine of strict liability, the manufacturer could still be held liable.

Numerous examples of product liability cases are available. More than 70 companies have been forced into bankruptcy due to asbestos litigation and the issue is not yet closed.[2] About 2,000 new cases of meso-thelioma (a cancer linked to asbestos exposure) are diagnosed every year according to the Mesothelioma Center, keeping the legal docket busy.[3] Mattel *<http://www.mattel.com>* was forced in the mid-2000s to recall over 9 million toys produced in China due to lead paint concerns. In 2014, Toyota Motors quickly issued stop-sale orders for its Camry and Corolla models after finding seat material did not comply with fire safety standards.[4] The company was forced to recall 8.1 million cars beginning in 2009 due to sudden acceleration incidents, and in 2014 reached a $1.2 billion settlement admitting that it misled consumers by making deceptive statements about safety issues.[5] At the time of this writing, GM is undergoing an investigation of why it took the company years to recall vehicles with known defects linked to 13 deaths.[6]

Businesses and insurance companies have called for legal relief from huge losses awarded in strict product liability suits. They have lobbied to set limits on the amounts of damages for which they are liable should their products harm consumers.

Intellectual Property: Patents, Copyrights, and Trademarks

Many people, perhaps including you, have invented products that may have commercial value. The question that obviously surfaces is what to do next. A first option may be to apply for a patent. A **patent** gives inventors exclusive rights to their inventions for 20 years from the date they file their patent application. The Canadian Intellectual Property Office *<http://www.ic.gc.ca/eic/site/cipointernet-internetopic.nsf /eng/home>* receives the application and grants the patent. In addition to filing forms, the inventor must ensure that the product is truly unique. Most inventors rely on lawyers who specialize in this area to manage the filing process.

> **patent**
> A form of intellectual property that gives inventors exclusive rights to their inventions for 20 years.

Patent owners have the right to sell or license the use of a patent to others. Foreign companies are also eligible to file for Canadian patents. Recent changes in the Patent Act and an international patent co-operation treaty permit any inventor who applies within 12 months of filing in his or her own country to obtain a uniform filing date in all participating countries.

The penalties for violating a patent (patent infringement) can be very severe, but the defence of patent rights is solely the job of the patent holder. In a rather famous U.S. case (where the law regarding patents is much the same as in Canada), the camera and film company Polaroid *<http://www.polaroid .com>* was able to force Kodak *<http://www.kodak.ca>* to recall all of its instant cameras because Polaroid had several patents that Kodak violated. Kodak lost millions of dollars, and Polaroid maintained market leadership in instant cameras for many years. More recently, Dr. Gary Michelson received a settlement of $1.35 billion from Medtronic Inc. *<http://www.medtronic.com>* to end litigation and license patents covering a range of back-surgery products.[7] The possible remedies for patent infringement include compensation in the form of money damages, injunctions prohibiting further infringements, and an accounting for all profits gained from the infringement.

A second option, a **copyright**, protects a creator's rights to materials such as books, articles, photos, paintings, and cartoons (as opposed to a patent that protects an inventor's right to a product or process). Copyright is protected by the Copyright Act, a federal statute. The protection of a copyright extends for the life of the original author plus 50 years after his or her death. Registration of the copyright is not required, but provides the benefit of public notice of its existence and provides proof of the copyright holder's ownership of the work.

> **copyright**
> A form of intellectual property that protects a creator's rights to materials such as books, articles, photos, and cartoons.

Third, a **trademark** is a brand that has been given legal protection for the brand name, symbol, or pictorial design (or combination of these) that identifies the goods or services of one seller and distinguishes them from those of competitors. Trademarks generally belong to the owner forever, as long as they are properly registered and renewed every 15 years. Some well-known trademarks include the Pillsbury Doughboy *<http://www.pillsbury.com>*, the Disney Company's Mickey Mouse, the Nike swoosh, and the golden arches of McDonald's. Like a patent, a trademark is protected from infringement. Companies fight hard to protect trademarks, especially in global markets where pirating can be extensive. Like patents, there are specific requirements imposed by the Trademarks Act, the most difficult one being that the trademark must be "distinctive."

> **trademark**
> A brand that has been given legal protection for the brand name, symbol, or pictorial design (or combination of these).

The fourth and final type of intellectual property protected by federal legislation in Canada is an **industrial design**. Industrial designs differ from things that can be copyrighted by the fact that they are produced by an industrial process. For example, fine china dinnerware would be a product that would fall into this category. As with the other types of intellectual property, the design of the subject matter must be original.

> **industrial design**
> A form of intellectual property that protects the owner's exclusive right to use the visible features of a finished product that identify it.

The Sale of Goods

Each of Canada's provinces has a statute called the Sale of Goods Act. With limited exceptions (i.e., contracts where the price is below the minimum set by the individual province's Act), this Act applies to all contracts for the sale of goods. A sale contract is different from others in that there must be a transfer of ownership of goods in return for money consideration. Except in Ontario and British Columbia, a contract for the sale of goods must be written. There are exceptions, though, where part of the goods has actually been received by the buyer, there has been partial payment of the price, or an "earnest" has been given to demonstrate sincerity. The Sale of Goods Act establishes the rules and requirements associated with the deal, establishing the respective rights and obligations of the parties of the contract.

Warranties

A warranty guarantees that the product sold will be acceptable for the purpose for which the buyer intends to use it. There are two types of warranties. **Express warranties** are specific representations by the seller that buyers rely on regarding the goods they purchase. The warranty you receive in the box with a clock or toaster is an express warranty. **Implied warranties** are legally imposed on the seller. It is implied, for example, that the product will conform to the customary standards of the trade or industry in which it competes. For example, it's expected that a toaster will toast your bread to your desired degree (light, medium, dark) or that food bought for consumption off an establishment's premises is fit to eat.

express warranties
Specific representations by the seller that buyers rely on regarding the goods they purchase.

implied warranties
Guarantees legally imposed on the seller.

Warranties offered by sellers can be either full or limited. A *full warranty* requires a seller to replace or repair a product at no charge if the product is defective, whereas a *limited warranty* typically limits the defects or mechanical problems that are covered. Many of the rights of buyers, including the acceptance and rejection of goods, are spelled out in the Sale of Goods Act, so both buyers and sellers should be familiar with its provisions.

Negotiable Instruments

Negotiable instruments are forms of commercial paper that represent a promise to pay a specific amount and are transferable among businesses and individuals. They come in three types: promissory notes, cheques, and bills of exchange. A *promissory note* is a written contract with a promise to pay a sum of money in the future. A *cheque* is an instruction to a bank to make a payment. A *bill* (or *draft*) is an order to make a payment. All three types are regulated by the federal Bills of Exchange Act. All three types are transferable among businesses and individuals and represent a promise to pay a specified amount. They must be (1) written and signed by the maker or drawer, (2) payable on demand or at a certain time, (3) payable to the bearer (the person holding the instrument) or to a specific order, and (4) contain an unconditional promise to pay a specified amount of money. Negotiable instruments are transferred (negotiated for payment) when the payee signs the back. The payee's signature is referred to as an endorsement.

negotiable instruments
Forms of commercial paper (such as cheques) that are transferable among businesses and individuals and represent a promise to pay a specified amount.

Contract Law

If I offer to sell you my bike for $35 and later change my mind, can you force me to sell the bike, saying we had a contract? If I lose $120 to you in a poker game, can you sue me in court to get your money? If I agree to sing at your wedding for free and back out at the last minute, can you claim that I violated a contract? These are the kinds of questions that contract law answers.

A **contract** is a legally enforceable agreement between two or more parties. **Contract law** specifies what constitutes a legally enforceable agreement. Basically, a contract is legally binding if the following conditions are met:

contract
A legally enforceable agreement between two or more parties.

contract law
Set of laws that specify what constitutes a legally enforceable agreement.

1. *An offer is made.* An offer to do something or sell something can be oral or written. If I agree to sell you my bike for $35, I have made an offer. That offer is not legally binding, however, until other conditions are met.

2. *There is a voluntary acceptance of the offer.* The principle of mutual dependence means that both parties to a contract must voluntarily agree on the terms. If I used duress in getting you to agree to buy my bike, the contract would not create enforceable rights and obligations. Duress occurs if there is coercion through force or threat of force. You couldn't use duress to get me to sell my bike, either. Even if we both agree, though, the contract is still not legally binding without the next four conditions.

3. *Both parties give consideration.* **Consideration** means something of value, and there must be a flow of consideration in both directions. If I agree to sell you my bike for $35, the bike and the $35 are consideration, and we have a legally binding contract. If I agree to sing at your wedding and you do not agree to give me anything in return (consideration), we have no contract.

> **consideration**
> Something of value; consideration is one of the requirements of a legal contract.

4. *Both parties are competent.* A person under the influence of alcohol or drugs, or a person of unsound mind (e.g., one who has been legally declared incompetent), cannot be held to a contract. In many cases, a minor may not be held to a contract either. For example, if a 15-year-old agrees to pay $10,000 for a car, the seller will not be able to enforce the contract due to the buyer's lack of competence.

5. *The contract must be legal.* A contract to do something illegal cannot be enforced. For example, a contract for the sale of illegal drugs or stolen merchandise would not be enforceable, since both types of sales are violations of criminal law.

6. *The contract is in proper form.* Provincial legislation in each province requires that an agreement for the sale of goods for more than a fixed amount (e.g., $200) must be in writing. Contracts that cannot be fulfilled within one year and contracts regarding real property (land and everything attached to it) must be in writing as well.

Breach of Contract

Breach of contract occurs when one party fails to follow the terms of a contract. Both parties may voluntarily agree to end a contract. While in force, however, if one person violates the contract, the following remedies may be available.

> **breach of contract**
> When one party fails to follow the terms of a contract.

1. *Specific performance.* The person who violated the contract may be required to live up to the agreement if money damages would not be adequate. For example, if I legally offered to sell you a rare painting, I may be required to actually sell you that painting.

2. *Payment of damages.* The term **damages** refers to the monetary settlement awarded by the court to a person who is injured by a breach of contract. If I fail to live up to a contract, you can sue me for damages, usually the amount you would lose from my non-performance. If we had a legally binding contract for me to sing at your wedding, for example, and I failed to come, you could sue me for the cost of hiring a new singer of the same quality and reputation.

> **damages**
> The monetary settlement awarded to a person who is injured by a breach of contract.

3. *Discharge of obligation.* If I fail to live up to my end of a contract, you could agree to drop the matter. Generally you would not have to live up to your end of the agreement either.

Lawyers would not be paid so handsomely if the law were always as simple as implied in these rules of contracts. In fact, it is always best to have a contract in writing even if not required under law. The offer and consideration in a contract should be clearly specified, and the contract should be signed and dated. A contract does not have to be complicated as long as it has these elements: it is in writing, mutual consideration is specified, and there is a clear offer and agreement to accept it.

Laws to Promote Fair and Competitive Practices

Competition is a cornerstone of the free-market system (see Chapter 2). One objective of legislators is to pass laws that the courts will enforce to ensure a competitive atmosphere among businesses and to promote fair business practices. In Canada, the Competition Bureau *<http://www.competitionbureau .gc.ca>* and other government agencies serve as watchdogs to ensure that competition among sellers flows freely and that new competitors have open access to the market. The scope of the governments' approach on this is broad and extensive. The Competition Act is a federal law that includes criminal and civil provisions to prevent anti-competitive practices in the marketplace.[8]

Governments have responded to troubling situations and continue to establish new rules to govern how businesses must deal with the new challenges facing them today. For example, the Canadian Anti-Spam Legislation enforcement is not the sole responsibility of one agency but rather includes the Competition Bureau, the Canadian Radio-telecommunications Commission, and the Office of the Privacy Commissioner of Canada *<https://www.priv.gc.ca/index_e.asp>*. The new law came into effect in 2014 and its purpose is address deceptive practices in the electronic marketplace.[9] One of the first changes created by the law was the need for organizations to acquire consent from individuals in order to send email, social media, or instant messaging notifications.[10]

The changing nature of business from manufacturing to knowledge technology has called for new levels of regulation on the part of both federal and provincial agencies. In the early 2000s, Microsoft's competitive practices were the focus of an intense investigation. The charge was that Microsoft hindered competition by refusing to sell its Windows operating system to computer manufacturers that would not sell Windows-based computers exclusively. The case ended with a settlement that expired in 2011. In 2012, Google avoided a long investigation after the company agreed to change some of its business practices[11]. Many advocates believe these cases broadened the definition of anti-competitive behaviour, which helps consumers by holding businesses more accountable for the way they operate.

Laws to Protect Consumers

Consumerism is a social movement that seeks to increase and strengthen the rights and powers of buyers in relation to sellers. Although consumerism is not a new movement, it has taken on new vigour and direction in the early twenty-first century because of the corporate scandals and greed involving companies such as Enron and WorldCom. Consumers have been particularly critical of government for its lack of oversight and action in the securities markets.

> **consumerism**
> A social movement that seeks to increase and strengthen the rights and powers of buyers in relation to sellers.

The protection of consumers has only recently come into vogue as a suitable topic for legislation. In earlier times, legislators deemed it appropriate to leave this to the common law, supplemented by the provisions of the Sale of Goods Act. The modern phenomenon of concentration of economic power in large manufacturing and distributing companies and in financial institutions has dramatically eroded the relative bargaining power of the consumer. The technical sophistication of modern products makes it impossible for consumers to detect product defects in advance. Price, quality, and safety have become matters that are often not negotiable: the consumer's choice is to accept or not accept the product, as is. Because of the inequality of bargaining power held by consumers in comparison to large retailers, manufacturers, and financial institutions, legislators have deemed it appropriate to intervene and readjust the balance in order to better protect the consumer. The topics that have received the most attention are product performance and business practices.

Product Performance

The Parliament of Canada has enacted several major statutes dealing with consumer safety and product performance. The Consumer Packaging and Labelling Act establishes requirements for disclosing ingredients and quantities, and includes provision for some standardization of package sizes. The Textile Labelling Act requires disclosure of the fabrics and fibres in wearing apparel, together with recommended cleaning procedures. The Weights and Measures Act establishes a uniform system for weighing and measuring goods sold to consumers. The Food and Drugs Act provides for inspection and regulation of food and drugs, requires purity and sanitary storage, and restricts the distribution of potentially harmful substances. The Hazardous Products Act establishes a list of dangerous products that it is illegal to manufacture, and regulations governing the manufacture, packaging, and distribution of other products that can be harmful. The Motor Vehicle Safety Act and the Aeronautics Act establish national standards, specifying safety features that must be provided in motor vehicles and aircraft.

This federal legislation is supplemented by provincial legislation in all provinces. Some provinces have been much more active in this regard than others. In most instances, this legislation appears in a provincial Consumer Protection Act, but provisions designed to protect consumers appear in other Acts as well.

Business Practices

With respect to door-to-door sales, most provinces have legislation permitting the consumer to rescind a purchase contract within a specified "cooling off" period. All provinces also have registration and licensing requirements for door-to-door sellers and collection agencies, designed to prevent the use of harassment and pressure. Most also provide that a consumer who receives unsolicited goods through the mail is not liable to pay for them, or even to return them. Most provinces have also established statutory warranties with regard to contracts for the purchase and sale of consumer durables, voiding attempts to negate the warranties implied by the Sale of Goods Act.

Misleading Advertising

One of the major topics addressed by the Competition Act, mentioned earlier in this appendix, is misleading advertising. False or misleading representations about the characteristics of a product are prohibited. These include statements, warranties, and guarantees about the performance, efficacy, or length of life of a product that are not based upon adequate or proper testing, and by placing the onus on anyone making such representations to prove that they are based on testing. Misleading representations about the "ordinary" price of a product are also prohibited, as is the advertising of products for sale at a "bargain" price when the advertiser does not have reasonable quantities available for sale.

Most provinces supplement the federal legislation in this area, in much the same way as they do with regard to product performance requirements. The Ontario Business Practices Act, for example, prohibits false representations about product performance.

Doing Business as a Corporation

A company or corporation is a legal entity, separate from its owners (who are called shareholders or stockholders), in the eyes of the law. The shareholders elect a small group of individuals (called directors) who are given ultimate decision-making authority for the corporation. In turn, the directors appoint the officers (e.g., president), who are placed in charge of the day-to-day management of the corporation. Shareholders do not participate in the normal management processes of the corporation.

The rules for how a corporation is governed and the nature of its rights and obligations are established by statute law (e.g., the Canada Business Corporations Act) and by the principles of common law and equity. The directors and officers of a corporation have obligations to the shareholders, but also have responsibilities to non-shareholder groups, including employees, creditors, customers, and the public at large. Issues in the area of corporate governance have gained much attention in recent years. Notable cases—such as those involving Nortel, Livent, Enron, and WorldCom—have demonstrated clearly the need for corporate officers and directors to act with utmost good faith in discharging their obligations.

Bankruptcy and Insolvency

The **bankruptcy** process recognizes that a debtor can reach a point where he or she will never be able to meet all obligations to creditors. The process is designed to minimize the negative impact of this situation for both debtor and creditor. The Bankruptcy and Insolvency Act, a federal statute, establishes a uniform national system for dealing with the problem. It is designed to achieve a reasonable and fair distribution of the debtor's assets among creditors, and to release the honest debtor in this position from ongoing obligations that cannot possibly be met, allowing him or her to resume productive business activity without them.

> **bankruptcy**
> The legal process by which a person, business, or government entity unable to meet financial obligations is relieved of those obligations by a court that divides debtor assets among creditors, allowing creditors to get at least part of their money and freeing the debtor to begin a new.

The provinces continue to have jurisdiction over an individual's financial affairs until he or she becomes insolvent or bankrupt. Once a person becomes bankrupt, the central government has jurisdiction to enact laws governing the rights and obligations of bankrupts and their creditors.

Bankruptcy can be either voluntary or involuntary. In **voluntary bankruptcy** cases the debtor applies for bankruptcy, whereas in **involuntary bankruptcy** cases the creditors start legal procedures against the debtor. Most bankruptcies today are voluntary because creditors often want to wait in hopes that they will be paid all of the money due them rather than settle for only part of the payment.

> **voluntary bankruptcy**
> Legal procedures initiated by a debtor.
>
> **involuntary bankruptcy**
> Bankruptcy procedures filed by a debtor's creditors.

The Bankruptcy and Insolvency Act establishes the scheme of distribution to be followed by the trustee in settling the claims of a bankrupt person's creditors. There are three basic categories of creditors for these purposes.

The highest priority is given to *secured creditors,* who have a direct claim against a specified asset of the debtor. When a debtor goes through bankruptcy proceedings, secured creditors are entitled to the entire proceeds realized on the sale of the asset in which they hold security, up to the secured amount owed to them by the debtor.

The second class of creditors is *preferred creditors,* and they have priority over general or unsecured creditors. This category includes trustees and lawyers involved in the process, unpaid employees of the bankrupt individual, and unpaid taxes.

The third group is the *unsecured creditors,* who do not have a direct claim against any asset and are not given preferred treatment by the Act. Unsecured claims include amounts owed to secured or preferred creditors that are in excess of the amount secured or preferred. All unsecured claims are treated equally by the Act, with each entitled to receive the same amount per dollar owed from the trustee in settlement of the amount claimed.

The bankruptor's contractual obligations to his or her creditors are discharged once he or she has complied fully with the terms of the arrangement that has been made by the trustee and accepted by the court. Payment of the established proportion of unsecured obligations, rather than payment in full, is sufficient to discharge all obligations. However, the discharge of a bankrupt is not automatic; it is a matter within the court's discretion. Whether a discharge is granted depends on matters like whether the person is a first-time bankrupt. Also, a discharge doesn't cover absolutely all obligations. Some obligations continue anyway. These include fines, child support payments, and amounts gained through fraud.

The Companies' Creditors Arrangement Act

The Companies' Creditors Arrangement Act (CCAA) is a federal statute that provides a second option in the commercial context for insolvent debtors to avoid bankruptcy proceedings. It makes provision for the restructuring of business debt when a company is unable to meet its financial obligations. The CCAA enables a company to submit a proposal to its creditors for an arrangement without bankruptcy proceedings. It permits a company to remain in business even though insolvent, and protects it from proceedings by creditors who might wish to force it into bankruptcy. The benefit to creditors is orderly conduct of the debtor's affairs, by maintaining the status quo while the debtor attempts to gain its creditors' approval of the plan and, if the plan is approved, payment by its terms. The attempts to financially restructure Air Canada and Stelco (now U.S. Steel Canada *<http://www.ussteelcanada.com>*) in the early years of this decade have been made under the CCAA.

The CCAA and the Bankruptcy and Insolvency Act work in concert with each other. The Bankruptcy and Insolvency Act expressly provides that it does not affect the operation of the CCAA, and allows the court to order continuation of a proposal made under the Bankruptcy and Insolvency Act under the CCAA.

Deregulation

Canada now has laws and regulations covering almost every aspect of business. In recent years, public concern that there are too many laws and regulations, and that these laws and regulations cost the public too much money, has developed. Thus began the movement toward deregulation. As you may recall from Chapter 4, deregulation means that the government withdraws certain laws and regulations that seem to hinder competition. Perhaps the most publicized examples of deregulation were those in the airline and telecommunications industries. Government used to severely restrict airlines with regard to where they could land and fly. When such restrictions were lifted, the airlines began competing for different routes and charging lower prices. This has provided a clear benefit to consumers, but puts tremendous pressure on the airlines to be competitive. Airlines such as WestJet have taken advantage of the opportunities, while Air Canada has had difficulty adapting. Similar deregulation in telecommunications has given consumers a flood of options in the telephone, internet, and mobility service markets.

It seems that some regulation of business is necessary to ensure fair and honest dealings with the public. Still, businesses have adapted to the laws and regulations, and have done much toward producing safer, more effective products. However, corporate scandals since the turn of the century have soured what appeared to be better dialogue and co-operation between business and government. Many in government and society called for even more government regulation and control of business operations to protect investors and workers.

During the aftermath of the 2008 global recession, the need for greater regulation in banking and financial markets grew. Much of the reason for Canada's ability to weather the economic storm more effectively than other countries was the fact that Canadian financial institutions were well managed and well regulated. As a result, there was less danger of collapse compared to other banks around the world.[12] The crisis triggered significant changes in the international banking sector. In 2013, the implementation of Basel III, a framework the set regulatory rules generated by the Basel Committee from the Bank for International Settlements <https://www.bis.org>, began in an effort to prevent another global economic crisis like the one in 2008 from happening again.

With global competition increasing and small and medium-sized businesses striving to capture selected markets, business and government need to continue to work together to create a competitive environment that is fair and open. If businesses do not want additional regulation, they must accept their responsibilities to all their stakeholders.

KEY TERMS

administrative agencies	contract law	negotiable instruments
bankruptcy	copyright	patent
breach of contract	criminal law	precedent
business law	damages	product liability
civil law	express warranties	statutory law
common law	implied warranties	strict product liability
consideration	industrial design	tort
consumerism	involuntary bankruptcy	trademark
contract	negligence	voluntary bankruptcy

Ethics and Social Responsibility

LEARNING OBJECTIVES

After you have read and studied this chapter, you should be able to:

LO1 Explain why obeying the law is only the first step in behaving ethically.

LO2 Ask the three questions to answer when faced with a potentially unethical action.

LO3 Describe management's role in setting ethical standards.

LO4 Distinguish between compliance-based and integrity-based ethics codes, and list the six steps that can be considered when setting up a corporate ethics code.

LO5 Define corporate social responsibility and compare corporations' responsibilities to various stakeholders.

LO6 Discuss the importance of ethical behaviour and social responsibility in global markets.

PROFILE

GETTING TO KNOW GEORGE ROTER OF ENGINEERS WITHOUT BORDERS

The global challenges of the twenty-first century mean Canadians and people around the world need to embrace sustainability in their everyday lives. As a 23-year-old engineering graduate, George Roter had a dream—to send young engineering students abroad to help people in rural, sub-Saharan Africa tackle poverty. In 2000, he and Parker Mitchell sat in a coffee shop and brainstormed. The result: the creation of Engineers Without Borders (EWB).

George and Parker's vision was to integrate engineering programs with a social lens that considers global issues. In fact, this way of thinking applies to all post-secondary programs where students can learn

Source: Courtesy of George Roter

their discipline while gaining an appreciation of how they hold potential to positively influence community development at home and abroad. Engineers Without Borders has chapters on campuses across Canada and engages students from all post-secondary programs in a conversation about sustainable social change and about their potential impact.

EWB currently includes 39 Canadian chapters, more than 2,500 volunteers, and 14 ventures. In 2014, 50 percent of its expenses, or just over $2 million, was spent on its social ventures. In Canada, EWB spearheads movements such as social intrapreneurship and establishes a global-engineering curriculum. Its Untie Aid campaign pushed the Canadian government to change the rules surrounding foreign aid, which had required aid recipients to purchase goods and services from Canadian companies.

But it is in Africa where EWB's impact is most significant. For example, its ventures WASH Catalysts and WASH Coordination focus on water point functionality and sanitation in Malawi. The Small and Growing Business Portfolio provides African entrepreneurs with the capital and advice they need to bring their ideas to life.

The organization takes risks that government and business avoid because it believes the bold systemwide change necessary in the twenty-first century can only be achieved through initiatives that empower people. This approach means current government international aid programs need to change because—as George claims, "development is less about infrastructure, more about institutions."

After giving years of leadership to EWB, George Roter stepped away from the CEO position in 2014 and now assumes other volunteer roles in EWB. He believes international development relies upon broad impacts, "If change isn't systemic, it's not change at all." Will EWB inspire you to become a global citizen?

Source: "2014 Annual Report: Leadership and Innovation for Systemic Change," Engineers Without Borders, 2014, http://newsite.ewb.ca/sites/default/files/2014%20EWB%20Annual%20Report_Web_FINAL.pdf; Ashoka, "How to Engineer a Changemaker: George Roter's Engineers Without Borders (Canada) model," *Forbes*, 2 February 2013, http://www.forbes.com/sites/ashoka/2013/02/25/how-to-engineer-a-changemaker-george-roters-engineers-without-borders-canada-model/; George Roter, "Development is less about infrastructure, more about institutions," *The Globe and Mail*, 24 January 2012, http://www.theglobeandmail.com/globe-debate/development-is-less-about-infrastructure-more-about-institutions/article4242209/; Carol Goar, "Canada's best undervalued asset: its social entrepreneurs," *Toronto Star*, 22 May 2012, http://www.thestar.com/opinion/editorialopinion/2012/05/22/canadas_best_undervalued_asset_its_social_entrepreneurs.html.

LO1 Explain why obeying the law is only the first step in behaving ethically.

Ethics Is More Than Legality

It is not uncommon to hear of instances where business people are involved in unethical behaviour. Some examples of Canadian companies that have been caught in such scandals include Livent, CIBC World Markets <*http://www.cibcwm.com*>, Nortel, and WestJet. After two years of denying accusations, WestJet Airlines Ltd. admitted to spying on Air Canada. In a news release, WestJet apologized for accessing a confidential Air Canada website designated for reservations: "This practice was undertaken with the knowledge and direction of the highest management levels of WestJet and was not halted until discovered by Air Canada. This conduct was both unethical and unacceptable and WestJet accepts full responsibility for such misconduct."[1] As part of the settlement, WestJet paid Air Canada's investigation and litigation costs of $5.5 million and it made a $10 million donation in the name of both airlines to children's charities across Canada.[2] The Canadian business environment has also been impacted by notable scandals in other countries such as Enron, Arthur Andersen, Tyco, and Parmalat <*http://www .parmalat.com*>, just to name a few.

It is not just for-profit business people who are accused of unethical behaviour. Government employees have also been implicated. For example, Elections Canada launched an investigation after the 2011 federal election. Voters complained that they had received phone calls on behalf of Elections Canada directing them to the wrong polling stations.[3] A pattern of phone calls was reported in which voters identified as not supporting the Conservatives were targeted with robocalls or live calls directing them to the wrong polling stations.[4] People from seven ridings went to court asking that the election results in their constituency be overturned.[5] A Federal Court Judge found fraud was a factor but no election results were overturned. In 2014, a Conservative Party staffer was found guilty under the Elections Act of willfully preventing a voter form casting a ballot. However, the judge also stated the convicted person did not act alone.[6] Review Figure 5.1 for a brief summary of some of the most-publicized scandals in recent years.

The Ontario government faced 50 land claims in 2015. The largest, The Algonquin Land Claim, covers 32,000 km² in Eastern Ontario that is populated by more than 1.2 million people. A key factor in many land claims across Canada is ownership of natural resources.[7]

■ **FIGURE 5.1**

BRIEF SUMMARY OF SOME CORPORATE SCANDALS[9]

Lottery Corporations: Ontario Ombudsman Andre Marin's Report blasted the Ontario Lottery and Gaming Corporation for not cracking down on retailers who collected tens of millions of dollars in jackpots between 1999 and 2006, some of them fraudulently. As a result, police began probing allegations of fraudulent lottery prize claims by retailers. The Atlantic Lottery Corporation announced it was turning over its files to police over similar concerns of retailers stealing winning tickets from customers. The British Columbia government announced an audit of the province's lottery system following a negative report by its Ombudsman that found it was open to fraud.

Research In Motion (RIM) Stock Option Scandal: An Ontario court approved a settlement between the company and the Ironworkers of Ontario Pension Fund over allegations RIM had backdated stock options to company executives. Under terms of the settlement, RIM's co-founders Jim Balsillie and Mike Lazaridis agreed to pay $2.5 million each (in addition to the $5 million the executives had each agreed to repay earlier). The company has also ceased giving stock options to directors, added more independent directors to the board, and tightened up its executive compensation practices.

Federal Government Sponsorship Scandal: The Auditor General's 2004 Report found that $100 million was paid to a variety of communications agencies in the form of fees and commissions, and said that the program was basically designed to generate commissions for these companies rather than to produce any benefit for Canadians. Implicated in this scandal were high-level officials. Charles Guité, a former senior bureaucrat, was sentenced to 42 months in prison for defrauding the federal government. Other scandal participants who received prison sentences include Jean Brault (30 months) and Paul Coffin (18 months). Gilles-André Gosselin was charged in 2008 with 19 criminal charges, including fraud.

Hollinger International Inc.: Conrad Black, who once headed the Hollinger International Inc. media empire, was convicted of obstruction of justice in 2007. In addition to three other former Hollinger executives, he was found guilty of fraud for funnelling US$6.1 million from the media company. Black was sentenced to 6½ years in federal prison and ordered to pay a six-figure fine plus restitution of $6.1 million. Three former Hollinger executives also received sentences: Jack Boultbee (27 months), Peter Atkinson (24 months), and Mark Kipnis (placed on probation with six months of house arrest). David Radler, one-time CEO of Hollinger International, plead guilty to mail fraud. He received a 29-month sentence and agreed to pay a US$250,000 fine.

Given the ethical lapses that are so prevalent today, what can be done to restore trust in the free-market system and leaders in general? First, those who have broken the law need to be punished accordingly. New laws making accounting records more transparent (easy to read and understand) and more laws making business people and others more accountable may help. But laws do not make people honest, reliable, or truthful. If they did, crime would disappear.

One danger in writing new laws to correct behaviour is that people may begin to think that any behaviour that is within the law is also acceptable. The measure of behaviour, then, becomes: "Is it legal?" A society gets in trouble when people consider only what is illegal and not also what is unethical. Ethics and legality are two very different things. Although following the law is an important first step, ethical behaviour requires more than that. Ethics reflects people's proper relations with one another: How should people treat others? What responsibility should they feel for others? Legality is narrower. It refers to laws we have written to protect ourselves from fraud, theft, and violence. Many immoral and unethical acts fall well within our laws.[8] For example, gossiping about your neighbour or sharing something told to you in confidence is unethical, but not illegal.

Ethical Standards Are Fundamental

We define **ethics** as the standards of moral behaviour; that is, behaviour that is accepted by society as right versus wrong. Many people today have few moral absolutes. Many decide situationally whether it's okay to steal, lie, or text and drive. They seem to think that what is right is whatever works best for the individual, and that each person has to work out for himself or herself the difference between right and wrong. That is the kind of thinking that has led to the recent scandals in government and business. This is not the way it always was. However, in the past decade there has been a rising tide of criticism in Canada (and other countries) of various business practices that many Canadians consider unacceptable.

> **ethics**
> Standards of moral behaviour; that is, behaviour that is accepted by society as right versus wrong.

In a country like Canada, with so many diverse cultures, you might think it would be impossible to identify common standards of ethical behaviour. However, among sources from many different times and places—such as the Bible, Aristotle's *Ethics*, William Shakespeare's *King Lear*, the Quran, and the *Analects* of Confucius—you will find the following basic moral values: integrity, respect for human life, self-control, honesty, courage, and self-sacrifice are right; cheating, cowardice, and cruelty are wrong. Furthermore, all of the world's major religions support a version of the Golden Rule: Do unto others as you would have them do unto you.[10]

LO2 Ask the three questions to answer when faced with a potentially unethical action.

Ethics Begins with Each of Us

It is easy to criticize business and political leaders for their moral and ethical shortcomings, but we must be careful in our criticism to note that ethics begins with each of us. Ethical behaviour should be exhibited in our daily lives, not just in a business environment.

Plagiarizing material from the Internet, including cutting and pasting information from websites without giving credit, is the most common form of cheating in post-secondary institutions today. To fight this problem, many instructors now use services like Turnitin, which scans students' papers against more than 40 billion online sources to provide evidence of copying in seconds.[11] Have you seen students cheat on assignments or exams? How did this make you feel? Students use many reasons to rationalize such behaviour, such as "Everyone else is doing it" or "I ran out of time to prepare, but I will do all my own work next time." What do you think of these reasons?

"I don't know what plagiarizing is, so I'm gonna take the easy way out and just copy something off the internet."

Plagiarizing from the Internet is one of the most common forms of cheating in post-secondary institutions today. Have you ever been tempted to plagiarize a paper or project? What are the possible consequences of copying someone else's material?

In a study, most teens said they were prepared to make ethical decisions in the workforce, but an alarming 51 percent of high school students admit that they have cheated on tests in the last year. Studies have found a strong relationship between academic dishonesty among undergraduates and dishonesty at work.[12] In response, many schools are establishing heavier consequences for cheating and requiring students to perform a certain number of hours of community service to graduate. Do you think such policies make a difference in student behaviour?

It is always healthy when discussing moral and ethical issues to remember that ethical behaviour begins with you and me. We cannot expect society to become more moral and ethical unless we as individuals commit to being moral and ethical ourselves.

The Making Ethical Decisions boxes throughout the text—like the accompanying one on Ponzi schemes—remind you to keep ethics in mind whenever you are making a business decision. The choices are not always easy. Sometimes the obvious solution from an ethical point of view has drawbacks from a personal or professional point of view. For example, imagine that your supervisor at work has asked you to do something you feel is unethical. You have just taken out a mortgage on a new house to make room for your first baby, due in two months. Not carrying out your supervisor's request may get you fired. What would you do? Sometimes there is no easy alternative in such *ethical dilemmas* because you must choose between equally unsatisfactory alternatives.

A new provision under Canada's Copyright Modernization Act, called the "notice and notice" program allows copyright holders, such as a movie studio, to send notices for illegal Internet downloads. The government's intent is to educate people about copyright infringement. Do you think this is an effective way to curtail Internet piracy?

Making ETHICAL DECISIONS

Canadian Ponzi Schemes

News stories of corporate fraud and corruption are all too common. White-collar criminals often assume the complexity of the financial system will hide their crimes, leaving them free to embezzle to their heart's content. But people tend to notice when a few billion dollars suddenly go missing. Eventually, even the most careful corporate criminal gets caught.

(continued)

(continued)

Canadian convictions related to money managers are becoming more prevalent. The managers tell clients they will invest their money in various ventures and pay them back on their returns, minus a commission. With a Ponzi scheme, however, the fraudsters don't invest the money. They simply pass money contributed by new investors on to early investors (minus a healthy sum held back for their own personal use, of course), claiming the money as profits from the existing clients' "investments." The steady income fools the investors into thinking their wealth is growing when in reality it is being siphoned off from other people. Obviously the scheme depends upon being able to continuously attract new "investors."

In 2014, Gary Sorenson and Milowe Brost, owners of a Calgary company, were convicted for what RCMP claim is the largest Ponzi scheme in Canadian history. Their lucrative scam defrauded 3,000 investors from around the world of $300 to $400 million. The money was intended for mining and investment companies but the owners funnelled the cash to themselves. The two men were fined $54 million by the Alberta Securities Commission and prosecutors are seeking the maximum 14 year sentence for the fraudsters.

Do you think the punishment fits the crime in this case?

Sources: Barrie McKenna, "Largest Ponzi scheme in Canadian history exploited boom time Alberta," *The Globe and Mail,* 15 February 2015, http://www.theglobeandmail.com/report-on-business/largest-ponzi-scheme-in-canadian-history-exploited-boom-time-alberta /article23010870/; Annalise Klingbeil, "What's next for Sorenson and Brost? Multi-year sentences common for Canadian Ponzi schemes," *Calgary Herald,* 15 February 2015, http://calgaryherald.com/news/local-news/whats-next-for-sorenson-and-brost-multi-year-sentences-common-for-canadian-ponzi-schemes; Lauren Krugel, "Trial begins into alleged Ponzi scheme called largest in Canadian history," *Macleans,* 8 September 2014, http://www.macleans.ca/news/canada/trial-begins-into-alleged-ponzi-scheme-called-largest-in-canadian-history/.

It can be difficult to balance between ethics and other goals such as pleasing stakeholders or advancing in your career. It is helpful to ask yourself the following questions when facing an ethical dilemma:[13]

1. *Is my proposed action legal?* Am I violating any law or company policy? Whether you're thinking about having a drink and driving home, gathering marketing intelligence, designing a product, hiring or firing employees, getting rid of industrial waste, or using a questionable nickname for an employee, think about the legal implications. This is the most basic question in business ethics, but it is only the first.

2. *Is it balanced?* Am I acting fairly? Would I want to be treated this way? Will I win everything at the expense of another? Win–lose situations often become lose–lose situations and generate retaliation from the loser. Not every situation can be completely balanced, but the health of our relationships requires us to avoid major imbalances over time. An ethical business person has a win–win attitude and tries to make decisions that benefit all.

3. *How will it make me feel about myself?* Would I feel proud if my family learned of my decision? My friends? Could I discuss the proposed situation or action with my supervisor? The company's clients?

Will I have to hide my actions? Has someone warned me not to disclose them? What if my decision was announced on the evening news? Am I feeling unusually nervous? Decisions that go against our sense of right and wrong make us feel bad—they erode our self-esteem. That is why an ethical business person does what is proper as well as what is profitable.

Individuals and companies that develop a strong ethics code and use the three ethics-check questions presented above have a better chance than most of behaving ethically. If you would like to know which style of recognizing and resolving ethical dilemmas you favour, fill out the ethical orientation questionnaire in Figure 5.2.

■ FIGURE 5.2

ETHICAL ORIENTATION QUESTIONNAIRE

Please answer the following questions.

1. Which is worse?
   A. Hurting someone's feelings by telling the truth.
   B. Telling a lie and protecting someone's feelings.
2. Which is the worse mistake?
   A. To make exceptions too freely.
   B. To apply rules too rigidly.
3. Which is it worse to be?
   A. Unmerciful.
   B. Unfair.
4. Which is worse?
   A. Stealing something valuable from someone for no good reason.
   B. Breaking a promise to a friend for no good reason.
5. Which is it better to be?
   A. Just and fair.
   B. Sympathetic and caring.

6. Which is worse?
   A. Not helping someone in trouble.
   B. Being unfair to someone by playing favourites.
7. In making a decision you rely more on
   A. hard facts.
   B. personal feelings and intuition.
8. Your boss orders you to do something that will hurt someone. If you carry out the order, have you actually done anything wrong?
   A. Yes.
   B. No.
9. Which is more important in determining whether an action is right or wrong?
   A. Whether anyone actually gets hurt.
   B. Whether a rule, law, commandment, or moral principle is broken.

To score: The answers fall in one of two categories, J or C. Count your number of J and C answers using this key:
1. A = C, B = J; 2. A = J, B = C; 3. A = C, B = J; 4. A = J, B = C; 5. A = J, B = C; 6. A = C, B = J; 7. A = J, B = C; 8. A = C, B = J; 9. A = C, B = J

What your score means: The higher your J score, the more you rely on an ethic of justice. The higher your C score, the more you prefer an ethic of care. Neither style is better than the other, but they are different. Because they appear so different, they may seem opposed to one another, but they're actually complementary. In fact, your score probably shows you rely on each style to a greater or lesser degree. (Few people end up with a score of 9 to 0.) The more you can appreciate both approaches, the better you'll be able to resolve ethical dilemmas and to understand and communicate with people who prefer the other style.

An ethic of justice is based on principles like justice, fairness, equality, or authority. People who prefer this style see ethical dilemmas as conflicts of rights that can be solved by the impartial application of some general principle. The advantage of this approach is that it looks at a problem logically and impartially. People with this style try to be objective and fair, hoping to make a decision according to some standard that's higher than any specific individual's interests. The disadvantage of this approach is that people who rely on it might lose sight of the immediate interests of particular individuals. They may unintentionally ride roughshod over the people around them in favour of some abstract ideal or policy. This style is more common for men than women.

An ethic of care is based on a sense of responsibility to reduce actual harm or suffering. People who prefer this style see moral dilemmas as conflicts of duties or responsibilities. They believe that solutions must be tailored to the special details of individual circumstances. They tend to feel constrained by policies that are supposed to be enforced without exception. The advantage of this approach is that it is responsive to immediate suffering and harm. The disadvantage is that, when carried to an extreme, this style can produce decisions that seem not simply subjective, but arbitrary. This style is more common for women than men.

To learn more about these styles and how they might relate to gender, go to www.ethicsandbusiness.org/kgl.htm.

Source: Thomas I. White, Discovering Philosophy—Brief Edition, 1e, © Copyright 1996. Adapted by permission of Pearson Education, Inc., Upper Saddle River, NJ.

Progress Assessment

- What is ethics?
- How do ethics differ from legality?
- When faced with ethical dilemmas, what questions can you ask yourself that might help you make ethical decisions?

LO3 Describe management's role in setting ethical standards.

Managing Businesses Ethically and Responsibly

Ethics is caught more than it is taught. That is, people learn their standards and values from observing what others do, not from hearing what they say. This is as true in business as it is at home. Organizational ethics begins at the top, and the leadership and example of strong managers can help instill corporate values in employees.

Trust and co-operation between workers and managers must be based on fairness, honesty, openness, and moral integrity. The same applies to relationships among businesses and among nations. A business should be managed ethically for many reasons: to maintain a good reputation; to keep existing customers and attract new ones; to avoid lawsuits; to reduce employee turnover; to avoid government intervention in the form of new laws and regulations controlling business activities; to please customers, employees, and society; and simply to do the right thing.

Spotlight *On* SMALL BUSINESS

A-Way Express

A-Way Express <http://www.awayexpress.ca> is one of the oldest social enterprises in Canada. Formed in 1987, A-Way is recognized as a progressive enterprise and a model of social responsibility. The social enterprise, which operates a courier service in Toronto, reported nearly $1 million in revenues from government funding and courier operations in 2013. Today A-Way has 70 employees and a base of 1,900 customers.

The organization serves both environmental and social purposes. Its couriers use public transit to provide a low-cost carbon neutral delivery service. At the same time, A-Way employs people living with mental health challenges. These individuals appreciate the opportunity to find a supportive workplace. Many feel the organization and all its members are like a second family and are pleased to find a job where they are treated with respect and kindness.

"Toronto's Social Purpose Transit Courier" may be A-Way's business slogan but its true purpose is to provide "permanent, meaningful, and flexible employment in an environment that can lead to recovery." The organization places a great deal of importance on the health, wellbeing, and recovery of its workforce. "A-Way could hire faster couriers", said former Executive Director Laurie Hall, "but that would not meet its mission. It exists to provide employment to a group that most businesses bypass."

Social enterprises such as A-Way give back to the community in ways that are not found in traditional employee–client business relations. A recent report on social enterprise in Nova Scotia indicated that these types of organizations provide training to 23,000 people and services to over 800,000 people. In many cases the same individual gained multiple benefits from the enterprise through being a member, recipient of services, employee, and volunteer.

The need for social enterprise in Canada is growing. What are other ways social enterprises can tackle major social issues?

Sources: "Nova Scotia Social Enterprise Sector Survey, 2014, Social Enterprise Canada," http://www.sess.ca/english/wp-content /uploads/2015/04/FINAL-REPORT-WEB-Apr-13-SLP-Optimized.pdf, downloaded 23 April 2015; "On the Road to Recovery," A-Way Express 2013 Annual Report, http://www.awaycourier.ca/uploads/2013%20Annual%20Report%2016pg%20master%20copy%20web.pdf, downloaded 25 April 2015; A-Way Express-About Us, http://www.awaycourier.ca/index.php?page=our-promise-goals, downloaded 23 April 2015; Simon Avery, "Canada playing catch-up in social enterprise," *The Globe and Mail*, 23 August 2012, http://www.theglobeandmail .com/report-on-business/small-business/sb-growth/sustainability/canada-playing-catch-up-in-social-enterprise/article1316055/.

Some managers think that ethics is a personal matter—either individuals have ethical principles or they don't. These managers feel that they are not responsible for an individual's misdeeds and that ethics has nothing to do with management. But a growing number of people think that ethics has everything to do with management. Individuals do not usually act alone; they need the implied, if not direct, co-operation of others to behave unethically in a corporation.

For example, there have been reports of cell phone service sales representatives who actually lie to get customers to extend their contracts—or even extend their contracts without the customers' knowledge. Some phone reps intentionally hang up on callers to prevent them from cancelling their contracts. Why do these sales reps sometimes resort to overly aggressive tactics? Because poorly designed incentive programs reward them for meeting certain goals, sometimes doubling or tripling their salaries with incentives. Do their managers say directly, "Deceive the customers"? No, but the message is clear. Overly ambitious goals and incentives can create an environment in which unethical actions like this can occur.

 Distinguish between compliance-based and integrity-based ethics codes, and list the six steps that can be considered when setting up a corporate ethics code.

Setting Corporate Ethical Standards

More and more companies have adopted written codes of conduct. Figure 5.3 offers Johnson & Johnson's code of conduct as a sample. Although ethics codes vary greatly, they can be classified into two categories: compliance-based and integrity-based. **Compliance-based ethics codes** emphasize the prevention of unlawful behaviour by increasing control and penalizing wrongdoers. Where compliance-based ethics codes are based on avoiding legal punishment, **integrity-based ethics codes** define the organization's guiding values, create an environment that supports ethically sound behaviour, and stress shared accountability among employees. See Figure 5.4 for a comparison of compliance-based and integrity-based ethics codes.

compliance-based ethics codes
Ethical standards that emphasize preventing unlawful behaviour by increasing control and by penalizing wrongdoers.

integrity-based ethics codes
Ethical standards that define the organization's guiding values, create an environment that supports ethically sound behaviour, and stress a shared accountability among employees.

■ FIGURE 5.3

OVERVIEW OF JOHNSON & JOHNSON'S CODE OF ETHICS

This is an overview of Johnson & Johnson's code of ethics, which it calls its Credo. To see the company's complete Credo, go to <*www.jnj.com*>, then under the "Our Company" tab click on "Our Credo Values."

Written in 1943 by long-time Chairman General Robert Wood Johnson, the Johnson & Johnson Credo serves as a conscious plan that represents and encourages a unique set of values. Our Credo sums up the responsibilities we have to the four important groups we serve:

- Our customers—We have a responsibility to provide high-quality products they can trust, offered at a fair price.
- Our employees—We have a responsibility to treat them with respect and dignity, pay them fairly, and help them develop and thrive personally and professionally.
- Our communities—We have a responsibility to be good corporate citizens, support good works, encourage better health and protect the environment.
- Our stockholders—We have a responsibility to provide a fair return on their investment.

The deliberate ordering of these groups—customers first, stockholders last—proclaims a bold business philosophy: If we meet our first three responsibilities, the fourth will take care of itself . . . To ensure our adherence to Credo values, we periodically ask every employee to evaluate the company's performance in living up to them. We believe that by monitoring our actions against the ethical framework of our Credo, we will best ensure that we make responsible decisions as a company.

■ FIGURE 5.4

STRATEGIES FOR ETHICS MANAGEMENT

Both codes have a concern for the law and use penalties as enforcement. Integrity-based ethics codes move beyond legal compliance to create a "do-it-right" climate that emphasizes core values such as honesty, fair play, good service to customers, a commitment to diversity, and involvement in the community. These values are ethically desirable, but not necessarily legally mandatory.

FEATURES OF COMPLIANCE-BASED ETHICS CODES		FEATURES OF INTEGRITY-BASED ETHICS CODES	
Ideal	Conform to outside standards (laws and regulations)	Ideal	Conform to outside standards (laws and regulations) and chosen internal standards
Objective	Avoid criminal misconduct	Objective	Enable responsible employee conduct
Leaders	Lawyers	Leaders	Managers with aid of lawyers and others
Methods	Education, reduced employee discretion, controls, and penalties	Methods	Education, leadership, accountability, decision processes, controls, and penalties

The following six-step process can help improve business ethics:[14]

1. Top management must adopt and unconditionally support an explicit corporate code of conduct.

2. Employees must understand that expectations for ethical behaviour begin at the top and that senior management expects all employees to act accordingly.

3. Managers and others must be trained to consider the ethical implications of all business decisions.

4. An ethics office must be set up. Phone lines to the office should be established so that employees who don't necessarily want to be seen with an ethics officer can inquire about ethical matters anonymously. **Whistleblowers** (people who report illegal or unethical behaviour) must feel protected from retaliation as oftentimes this exposure can lead to great career and personal cost.

5. Outsiders such as suppliers, subcontractors, distributors, and customers must be told about the ethics program. Pressure to put aside ethical considerations often comes from the outside, and it helps employees to resist such pressure when everyone knows what the ethical standards are.

6. The ethics code must be enforced. It is important to back any ethics program with timely action if any rules are broken. This is the best way to communicate to all employees that the code is serious.

whistleblowers
People who report illegal or unethical behaviour.

This last step is perhaps the most critical. No matter how well intended, a company's ethics code is worthless if it is not enforced. Engineering and construction firm SNC-Lavalin <*http://www.snclavalin.com*> was in the news after the results of an internal investigation showed that a series of unauthorized payments—to the tune of $56 million—were made in connection to business in Libya.[15] The company CEO, Pierre Duhaime, resigned under the weight of the allegations; Duhaime had not been charged with any crime, but the company said his signing off on payments to undisclosed agents was a breach of the company's code of ethics.[16] Additional fraud and corruption charges were laid in 2015 related to allegations the company paid $47.7 million in bribes for Libyan contracts between 2001 and 2011.[17] In contrast, Maple Leaf Foods' response to a listeria bacteria outbreak in some of its packaged meat products in 2008 shows that enforcing ethics codes can enhance the bottom line. Then CEO, Michael McCain, faced the crisis, admitted the company was at fault, and apologized to victims and their families. He stated, "It's not about money or legal liability; this is about our being accountable for providing consumers with safe food."[18]

An important factor in the success of enforcing an ethics code is selecting an ethics officer. The most competent ethics officers set a positive tone, communicate effectively, and relate well to employees at every level. They are equally comfortable as counsellors and investigators, and can be trusted to maintain confidentiality, conduct objective investigations, and ensure fairness. They can demonstrate to stakeholders that ethics are important in everything the company does.

As more organizations are recognizing the importance of this role, associations are also providing support for those in these roles. One such example is the Ethics Practitioners' Association of Canada (EPAC) <*http://www.epac-apec.ca*>. EPAC's mission is "to enable individuals to work successfully in the field of ethics in organizations by enhancing the quality and availability of ethics advice and services across Canada." This organization supports ethics officers, consultants, educators, students, and others who are interested in the field of ethics as applied to organizations of all kinds.

THE SARBANES-OXLEY ACT OF 2002 (SOX)[19]

The major corporate and accounting scandals in the United States in the early 2000s (e.g., Enron, Tyco, Adelphia, and WorldCom) gave rise to the implementation of U.S. federal legislation known as the Sarbanes-Oxley Act (SOX). The legislation established stronger standards to prevent misconduct and improve corporate governance practices. SOX applies to all publicly traded companies whose shares are listed on the stock exchanges under the jurisdiction of the U.S. Securities and Exchange Commission. The goal of SOX is to ensure the accuracy and reliability of published financial information. Requirements deal with the proper administration routines, procedures, and control activities.

SOX also protects whistleblowers from any company retaliation as it requires that all public corporations provide a system that allows employees to submit concerns regarding accounting and auditing issues both confidentially and anonymously. The purpose is to motivate employees to report any wrongdoing. For example, the legislation provides for reinstatement and back pay to people who were punished by their employers for passing information about frauds to authorities.

In response to SOX, Canada also implemented similar corporate governance legislation.

WHISTLEBLOWER LEGISLATION IN CANADA[20]

One might suggest that for the six steps mentioned earlier to work, there must first be protection in place for whistleblowers. Otherwise, how effective can such a process be? Unfortunately, there is no legislation in place that protects all workers—public sector and private sector—across the country. Regarding public-sector workers, the federal government and some provinces have variations of whistleblower legislation that set up a third-party independent officer, such as the federal integrity commissioner or Saskatchewan's public interest disclosure commissioner, to whom employees can raise concerns. Let us consider one piece of legislation.

The Public Servants Disclosure Protection Act was passed in 2007. The legislation was intended to support "truth telling" by whistleblowers who try to protect the public interest. Critics claim government efforts to impose codes of conduct and nondisclosure agreements place whistleblowers at risk. What do you believe motivates a whistleblower?

The Federal Accountability Act (FAA) applies to approximately 400,000 government employees. It lists a wide range of measures to help make the Canadian federal government more accountable and to increase transparency and oversight in government operations. Among other objectives, it is promoted as protecting federal government employees who come forward, so they need not fear reprisal. This includes direct employee access to the commissioner to report wrongdoing in the workplace. The commissioner has the authority to deal with reprisal complaints, conduct investigations, and attempt to conciliate a settlement between the parties. Democracy Watch <*http://www.dwatch.ca*>, a citizen group advocating democratic reform, government accountability, and corporate responsibility, believes that much more needs to be done to protect whistleblowers. Among some of its criticisms, it maintains that the "FAA established a system that does not provide promised adequate funding for whistleblowers' legal services, and that it requires the whistleblower to prove retaliation has occurred (instead of requiring the government to prove it has not punished the whistleblower)."

While Canadians who work for corporations listed on a U.S. stock exchange may have some protection under the U.S. Sarbanes-Oxley legislation, there is no provision to protect other, private-sector whistleblowers. In a KPMG survey on private corporations' policies on whistleblowers, almost two-thirds of respondents to the business ethics survey stated that they have a written policy requiring employees to report fraud or misconduct in the workplace. However, only 40 percent of respondents reported having formal systems designed to protect whistleblowers from retaliation. One-fifth of respondents lacked any type of protection system. Yet whistleblowers add value to corporations. A PricewaterhouseCoopers study showed that whistleblowers uncovered far more fraud than internal audit and all other management control systems combined. The study, which polled 5,400 senior executives from 40 countries, found that 43 percent of corporate frauds had been initially detected by employee tip-offs.

The Charbonneau Commission examined corruption within the Quebec construction industry. Much of the investigation relied upon whistleblowers who spoke out about collusion that involved connections to organized crime and political parties.

Petro-Canada is a company that has an internal whistleblower policy. An anonymous 1-800 line is in place. A third-party service provider responds and reports all calls to the appropriate members of Petro-Canada's executive or audit committee, depending on the nature of the call. Employees are informed that they will not be discriminated against for stepping forward.

Progress Assessment

- How are compliance-based ethics codes different from integrity-based ethics codes?

- What are the six steps to follow in establishing an effective ethics program in a business?

- What laws are in place to protect whistleblowers?

 LO5 Define corporate social responsibility and compare corporations' responsibilities to various stakeholders.

Corporate Social Responsibility

Just as you and I need to be good citizens, contributing what we can to society, corporations need to be good citizens as well. **Corporate social responsibility (CSR)** is the concern businesses have for the welfare of society, not just for their owners. CSR goes well beyond merely being ethical. It is based on a commitment to integrity, fairness, and respect.[21]

> **corporate social responsibility (CSR)**
> A business's concern for the welfare of society.

There is discussion in this chapter about ethics and CSR. It is important to note that both of these are often judgment calls, depending on which side of the issue you are on. To clarify, one person's unethical behaviour can be considered another person's sound business decision. Also, do not underestimate the impact of cultural values. Differences from country to country also contribute to varying perspectives on the same issue. This can result in decision making that is not in line with one's personal values but is congruent with what is considered ethical in a country.

You may be surprised to know that not everyone thinks that CSR is a good thing. Some critics of CSR believe that a manager's sole role is to compete and win in the marketplace. Economist Milton Friedman made a classic statement when he said that the only social responsibility of business is to make money for shareholders. He thought that doing anything else was moving dangerously toward socialism. Other CSR critics believe that managers who pursue CSR are doing so with other people's money—money they invested to make more money, not to improve society. In this view, spending money on CSR activities is stealing from investors.[22]

CSR defenders, in contrast, believe that businesses owe their existence to the societies they serve and cannot succeed in societies that fail.[23] Firms have access to society's labour pool and its natural resources, in which every member of society has a stake. Even Adam Smith, the father of capitalism, believed that the self-interested pursuit of profit was wrong and that benevolence was the highest virtue. CSR defenders acknowledge that businesses have deep obligations to investors, and that businesses should not attempt government-type social responsibility projects. However, they also argue that CSR makes more money for investors in the long run. Studies show that companies with good ethical reputations attract and retain better employees, draw more customers, and enjoy greater employee loyalty.[24]

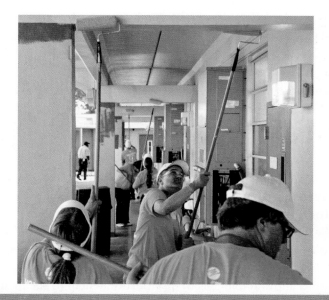

Company employees volunteer in their communities for many causes. Here volunteers work to beautify a school through painting, cleanups, landscaping, and rebuilding a volleyball court. Do companies have responsibilities to the communities in which they operate beyond obeying the laws?

The social performance of a company has several dimensions:

- **Corporate philanthropy** includes charitable donations to non-profit groups of all kinds. Some make long-term commitments to one cause, such as the Canadian Tire Jumpstart Charities, which has helped more than 875,000 kids across Canada since 2005.[25] The charity provides financial support for kids ages four to eight to participate in organized sport and physical activity.

- **Corporate social initiatives** include enhanced forms of corporate philanthropy that are more directly related to the company's competencies.[26] For example, logistics giant TNT keeps a 50-person emergency response team on standby to go anywhere in the world at 48 hours' notice to provide support in aviation, warehousing, transportation, reporting, and communications. Over the years, 225 TNT employees have been involved in 30 emergency response activities.[27]

- **Corporate responsibility** includes everything from hiring minority workers to making safe products, minimizing pollution, using energy wisely, and providing a safe work environment—that is, everything that has to do with acting responsibly within society.

- **Corporate policy** refers to the position a firm takes on social and political issues. For example, Patagonia's <http://www.patagonia.com> corporate policy includes this statement: "A love of wild and beautiful places demands participation in the fight to save them, and to help reverse the steep decline in the overall environmental health of our planet. We donate our time, services and at least 1% of our sales to hundreds of grassroots environmental groups all over the world who work to help reverse the tide."[28]

corporate philanthropy
Dimension of social responsibility that includes charitable donations.

corporate social initiatives
Dimension of social responsibility that includes enhanced forms of corporate philanthropy that are more directly related to the company's competencies.

corporate responsibility
Dimension of social responsibility that includes everything from hiring minority workers to making safe products.

corporate policy
Dimension of social responsibility that refers to the position a firm takes on social and political issues.

So much news coverage has been devoted to the problems caused by corporations that people tend to develop a negative view of the impact that companies have on society. But businesses make positive contributions too. Few people know, for example, that a Xerox <*http://www.xerox.com*> program called Social Service Leave allows employees to take a leave of absence for up to a year to work for a non-profit organization while earning their full Xerox salary and benefits, including job security.[29]

In fact, many companies allow employees to give part-time help to social agencies of all kinds. The recent recession has changed the way that many corporations approach corporate philanthropy. Now they are often likely to give time and goods rather than money. Many companies are now encouraging employees to volunteer more—on company time.[30] For example, Mars Incorporated <*http://www.mars.com*> encourages community involvement by offering paid time off to clean parks, aid medical clinics, and plant gardens. Nearly 10,000 Mars employees volunteer 37,000 hours a year.[31]

The Toronto Dominion Bank demonstrates corporate responsibility through community initiatives that focus upon affordable housing, the environment, and volunteerism.[32] The TD Volunteer Network is an online database that allows charities to post volunteer opportunities to more than 60,000 bank employees. The Volunteer Grants Program donates $500 to a charity where a TD employee volunteered more than 40 hours annually. In 2014, Canada's five biggest banks reported a collective annual profit of $31.7 billion.[33] Given the success of the finance sector in Canada, do you expect Canadian banks to do more for communities?

The Tim Horton Children's Foundation is a national, not-for-profit organization generously supported by Tim Hortons. The Foundation is committed to providing enriching camp experiences that develop lifelong skills for children and youth living in low-income homes.

Two-thirds of the MBA students surveyed by a group called Students for Responsible Business said they would take a reduced salary to work for a socially responsible company.[34] But when the same students were asked to define *socially responsible,* articulating a clear answer was complicated. It appears that even those who want to be socially responsible cannot agree on what it is.

Concepts of Social Corporate Responsibility

What should be the guiding philosophy for business in the twenty-first century? For most of the twentieth century, there was uncertainty regarding the position top managers should take, and this question is still debated today. How a company answers this question depends on its fundamental belief of how stakeholders should be treated and its responsibility to society. There are two different views of corporate responsibility to stakeholders:

1. *The Strategic Approach.* The strategic approach requires that management's primary orientation be toward the economic interests of shareholders. The rationale is this: as owners, shareholders have the right to expect management to work in their best interests; that is, to optimize profits. Furthermore, Adam Smith's notion of the invisible hand suggests that the maximum social gain is realized when managers attend only to their shareholders' interests.

   Friedman and others argue that since (in their view) only people can have social responsibilities, corporations are only responsible to their shareholders and not to society as a whole. Although they accept that corporations should obey the laws of the countries within which they work, they assert that corporations have no other obligation to society.[35] Often, the interests of other stakeholders are considered only when they would adversely affect profits, if ignored.

2. *The Pluralist Approach.* This approach recognizes the special responsibility of management to optimize profits, but not at the expense of employees, suppliers, and members of the community. This approach recognizes the moral responsibilities of management that apply to all human beings. Managers don't have moral immunity when making managerial decisions. This view says that corporations can maintain their economic viability only when they fulfill their moral responsibilities to society as a whole. When shareholders' interests compete with those of the community, as they often do, managers must decide how to act, using ethical and moral principles.

Imperial Tobacco Canada <*http://www.imperialtobaccocanada.com*> promotes itself as a socially responsible company. Among other programs, it supports Operation I.D., a youth smoking prevention program. Overall, what view of corporate responsibility do you believe this company supports?

The guiding philosophy for the twenty-first century will be some version of the pluralist approach. Managerial decision making will not be easy, and new ethical guidelines may have to be drawn. But the process toward such guidelines has been started, and a new era of more responsible and responsive management is under way.

The time when ethics matters the most is when the company is tested. That is, when it is in a crisis. This is when a company can prove that it is staying true to its values and ethics, based on its reaction to the crisis. Moving forward in this chapter, you will be introduced to two examples (highlighted in photos with some details in the captions) of companies that were faced with a crisis. Some would argue that one handled the situation much better than the other. Do some research to discover which was which.

Perhaps it would be easier to understand social responsibility if we looked at the concept through the eyes of the stakeholders to whom businesses are responsible: customers, investors, employees, society in general, and the environment.

Responsibility to Customers

Consumers have four basic rights: (1) the right to safety, (2) the right to be informed, (3) the right to choose, and (4) the right to be heard. These rights will be achieved only if business and consumers recognize them and take action in the marketplace.

A recurring theme of this book is the importance of pleasing customers by offering them real value. Since three of five new businesses fail, we know this responsibility is not as easy to meet as it seems. One sure way of failing to please customers is to be less than honest with them. The payoff for socially conscious behaviour, however, can be new customers who admire the company's social efforts—a powerful competitive edge. Consumer behaviour studies show that, all else being equal, a socially conscious company is likely to be viewed more favourably than others. In fact, a recent Nielsen survey showed that 50 percent of the consumers surveyed were willing to pay more for goods from socially responsible companies.[36]

Given the value customers place on social efforts, how do companies make customers aware of such efforts? One tool many companies use to raise awareness of their social responsibility efforts is social media. The primary value of using social media to communicate CSR efforts is that it allows companies to reach broad and diverse groups, to connect directly with customers in a low-cost, efficient way, and to interact with specific groups more easily compared to more traditional efforts.

It's not enough for companies to brag about their social responsibility efforts; they must live up to the expectations they raise or face the consequences. When herbal tea maker Celestial Seasonings <http://www.celestialseasonings.com> ignored its advertised image of environmental stewardship by poisoning prairie dogs on its property, it incurred customers' wrath.[37] Customers prefer to do business with companies they trust and, even more important, don't want to do business with those they don't trust. Companies earn customers' trust by demonstrating credibility over time; they can lose it at any point.

Responsibility to Investors[38]

Some people believe that before you can do good, you must do well (i.e., make a lot of money); others believe that by doing good, you can also do well. What we do know is that ethical behaviour is good for shareholder wealth. It does not subtract from the bottom line, but rather adds to it. On the other hand, unethical behaviour does cause financial damage. Those cheated by financial wrongdoing are the shareholders themselves. Unethical behaviour may seem to work for the short term, but it guarantees eventual failure. For example, in the early 2000s, accounting irregularities reported at Nortel Networks Corp., once the most-traded stock in Canada, damaged investor trust and subsequently the company's share value. Years later, the company was still being scrutinized amid rumours of bankruptcy when its share price was under $1. In 2009, the company declared bankruptcy.

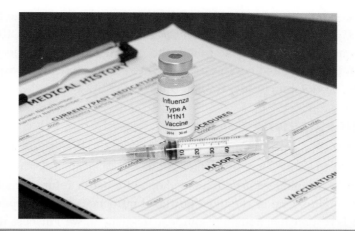

High-risk groups lined up for hours at public clinics when the H1N1 vaccine was released in October 2009, while many non-high-risk Canadians (e.g., some professional athletes and private-clinic members) received the vaccine courtesy of their employers. For weeks following the initial rollout, thousands of those on the priority list did not receive the vaccine due to the shortage. Were the actions of these employers ethical?

Unfortunately, we continue to read of individual business people who abuse the trust that individual investors have placed in them. Some high-profile examples in recent years include financiers Earl Jones and Bernard Madoff. Jones plead guilty to defrauding 158 clients of $50 million in a Ponzi scheme that he operated for more than two decades. He was sentenced to 11 years in prison. Madoff is serving a 150-year sentence after admitting he squandered tens of billions of dollars in investors' money. Madoff's crimes left many investors impoverished and some charities insolvent.

Many investors believe that it makes financial as well as moral sense to invest in companies that plan ahead to create a better environment. By choosing to put their money into companies whose goods and services benefit the community and the environment, investors can improve their own financial health while improving society's health.

INSIDER TRADING[39]

A few investors, known as inside traders, have chosen unethical means to improve their own financial health. **Insider trading** uses private company information to further insiders' own fortunes, or those of their family and friends. For example, Andrew Rankin, a former executive with RBC Dominion Securities *<http://www.rbcds.com>*, was charged by the Ontario Securities Commission (OSC) *<http://www.osc.gov.on.ca>* with 10 counts of tipping his friend, Daniel Duic. Investigators found that Rankin had alerted Duic to upcoming mergers and acquisitions before they were publicly known. The OSC alleges that, based on this information, Duic bought and sold investments in ten companies and saw his investment increase following the release of the merger and acquisition news. Duic agreed to pay just over $3 million in the form of a penalty, taxes, and lawyer's fees and to testify against Rankin. Under the Ontario Securities Act, Rankin was sentenced to six months in jail for Canada's first conviction for illegal stock tipping.

insider trading
An unethical activity in which insiders use private company information to further their own fortunes or those of their family and friends.

The OSC also successfully prosecuted Mitchell Finkelstein, a partner at the law firm Davies Ward Phillips & Vineberg LLP, for feeding insider investor tips to Paul Azeff, a former CIBC investment adviser. While Mr. Finkelstein may appeal the OSC ruling, the case demonstrates one of the rare times the regulator has successfully prosecuted various market gatekeepers including lawyers, bankers, brokers, or investment advisers for violating insider trading rules.

Responsibility to Employees

It's been said that the best social program in the world is a job. Businesses have a responsibility to create jobs if they want to grow. Once they have done so, they must see to it that hard work and talent are fairly rewarded. Employees need realistic hope of a better future, which comes only through a chance for upward mobility. One of the most powerful influences on a company's effectiveness and financial performance is responsible human resource management. We'll discuss this in Chapter 12.

In 2013, over 1,000 people died when the Rana Plaza garment factory in Bangladesh collapsed. Loblaws Cos. Ltd. contracted the business that operated the factory for its Joe Fresh apparel line. In response, the company dropped seven garment makers in Bangladesh due to unsafe working conditions and facilities. It has also contributed $5 million to a long-term compensation package for victims of the tragedy, committed $1 million toward global charity Save the Children and a rehabilitation hospital in Bangladesh, and updated its Supplier Code of Conduct. Do the apparel brands you purchase have similar standards for their suppliers?[40]

If a company treats employees with respect, they usually will respect the company as well. Mutual respect can make a huge difference in a company's bottom line. In their book *Contented Cows Give Better Milk*, Bill Catlette and Richard Hadden compared "contented cow" companies with "common cow" companies. The companies with the contented employees outgrew their counterparts by four to one for more than 10 years. The "contented cow" companies out-earned the "common cow" companies by nearly $40 billion and generated 800,000 more jobs. The authors attribute this difference in performance to the commitment and caring that the companies demonstrate for their employees.[41]

One way a company can demonstrate commitment and caring is to give its employees salaries and benefits that help them reach their personal goals. The wage and benefit packages offered by warehouse retailer Costco are among the best in hourly retail. Even part-time workers are covered by Costco's health plan, and the workers pay less for their coverage than at other retailers such as Walmart. Increased benefits reduce employee turnover, which at Costco is less than a third of the industry average.[42] Estimates show that replacing employees costs between 150 and 250 percent of their annual salaries, so retaining workers is good for business as well as morale.[43]

Costco's approach toward wages and benefits helps the company retain employees. Do you believe these actions reflect Costco's corporate responsibility or is it simply a strategy to improve profits? Why?

When employees feel they have been treated unfairly, they often strike back. Getting even is one of the most powerful incentives for good people to do bad things. Not many disgruntled workers are desperate enough to resort to violence in the workplace, but a great number do relieve their frustrations in more subtle ways, such as blaming mistakes on others, not accepting responsibility for decision making, manipulating budgets and expenses, making commitments they intend to ignore, hoarding resources, doing the minimum needed to get by, making results look better than they are, or even stealing. The loss of employee commitment, confidence, and trust in the company and its management can be very costly indeed. Employee larceny costs Canadian businesses billions of dollars every year. According to a 2014 report by the Association of Certified Fraud Examiners, the average cost of occupational fraud, which includes the misappropriation of assets and financial statement fraud, is approximately $250,000 in Canada.[44] Canadian retailers alone are relieved of approximately $4 billion of merchandise annually, or $10.8 million every day, with employees out-stealing the shoplifters.[45] You will read more about issues that affect employee–management relations in Chapter 13.

Responsibility to Society

One of business's responsibilities to society is to create new wealth, which is disbursed to employees, suppliers, shareholders, and other stakeholders. But if businesses don't create wealth, who will? Non-profit organizations play an important role in distributing the funds they receive from donors, governments, and even their own investments in billions of shares in publicly held companies. As those stock prices increase, more funds are available to benefit society. However, for stock prices to increase, the publicly held company must be successful. For companies to prosper, they need to provide customers with safe products. Businesses today, more than ever before, need to develop long-term profitable relationships with their customers. There is no question that repeat business is based on buying safe and value-laden goods and services, at reasonable prices.

Businesses are also partially responsible for promoting social justice. Many companies believe that business has a role in building a community that goes well beyond giving back. To them, charity is not enough. Their social contributions include a variety of social-oriented activities such as cleaning up the environment, providing computer lessons, caring for the elderly, and supporting children from low-income families.

As concern about global warming increased, the green movement emerged in nearly every aspect of daily life. What makes a product "green"? Some believe that a product's carbon footprint (the amount of carbon released during production, distribution, consumption, and disposal) defines how green it is. Many variables contribute to a product's carbon footprint. The carbon footprint of a package of, say, frozen corn includes not only the carbon released by the fertilizer to grow the corn but also the carbon in the fertilizer itself, the gas used to run the farm equipment and transport the corn to market, the electricity to make the plastic packages and power the freezers, and so on (see the Seeking Sustainability box for a story of companies that reduce their carbon footprint by using recycled clothing to manufacture apparel).

Driving a Prius with a big banana on the roof is an eye-catching way for Mason Arnold of Greenling to attract the attention of potential customers while delivering fresh, nutritious food to local customers. Greenling believes that supporting local organic growers is a good way of supporting sustainable, healthy environments. Similar companies exist in Canada, such as The Organic Box <*https://www.theorganicbox.ca*> in Edmonton, Body Fuel Organics <*http://www.bodyfuelorganics.ca*> in Regina, and Urban Harvest Organic Delivery <*http://www.urbanharvest.ca*> in Kelowna. Do you think a "buy local" approach is an effective way for a business to be socially responsible? Why or why not?

No specific guidelines define the carbon footprints of products, businesses, or individuals or outline how to communicate them to consumers. PepsiCo presents carbon information with a label on bags of cheese-and-onion potato chips, for example, that says "75 grams of CO_2."[46] Simple enough, but what does it mean? (We don't know either.)

The focus of this book is on business; however, one should not forget that government decisions also affect business and society. The Walkerton, Ontario, *E. coli* tragedy that killed seven people and made half of the town's 5,000 residents ill from contaminated water is one such example. After hearing testimony from more than 100 witnesses over nine months, Justice O'Connor concluded that the catastrophe could have been prevented if brothers Stan and Frank Koebel, who ran Walkerton's water system, had properly chlorinated the water and if the Ontario government had heeded warnings that cuts to the provincial environment ministry were resulting in ineffective testing.[47] Clearly, the Koebel brothers were responsible for their individual decisions.

Responsibility to the Environment[48]

Businesses are often criticized for their role in destroying the environment. Such was the case when images of the slow death of 500 ducks on a toxic oil sands tailings pond in northern Alberta flashed around the world. This led to federal and provincial legal action against Syncrude Canada Ltd. *<http://www .syncrude.ca>*, which was charged under the Alberta Environmental Enhancement and Protection Act and the federal Migratory Birds Convention Act. While Syncrude attempted to rescue some of the ducks that landed in the tailings pond, only a handful were taken out of the water for cleaning and none survived. The Analyzing Management Decisions case near the end of this chapter discusses the implications of train spills in various regions of Canada.

We are seeing more efforts to reverse years of neglect to the environment. For example, the Sydney Tar Ponds in Nova Scotia are North America's largest hazardous waste site. More than 80 years of discharges from the steel-producing coke ovens near the harbour filled Muggah Creek with contaminated sediments. By 1983, Environment Canada had pinpointed the coke ovens as the major source of pollution in the Sydney area. Fishing was banned and the Sydney lobster fishery was closed. Statistics show that the area has significantly higher levels of cancers and other debilitating diseases than anywhere else in Canada. Two decades later, there have been several attempts and more than $100 million spent to clean up this toxic site. In May 2004, the governments of Canada and Nova Scotia committed $400 million to the cleanup. Citizens of Sydney are still trying to address contamination issues related to their health and private property through a court trial.[49]

To date, BP Oil has paid $14 billion in restoration and cleanup efforts to help individuals and businesses affected by the 2010 Gulf of Mexico spill. Considered to be the world's biggest accidental oil leak, the explosion killed 11 oil rig workers and unleashed an estimated 3.2 million barrels of oil before the damaged well was capped three months later. There has also been extensive damage to marine and wildlife habitat.[50] How effective do you think the threat of financial punishment is to curbing the damage of business to the environment?

The green movement has provided consumers with many product choices. However, making those choices means sorting through the numerous and confusing claims made by manufacturers. The clutter in the marketplace challenges even the most dedicated green activists, but taking the easy route of buying what's most readily available violates the principles of the green movement. Environmental efforts may increase a company's costs, but they also allow the company to charge higher prices, increase market share, or both. Ciba Specialty Chemicals, a Swiss textile-dye manufacturer, developed dyes that require less salt than traditional dyes. Since used dye solutions must be treated before being released into rivers or streams, less salt means lower water-treatment costs. Patents protect Ciba's low-salt dyes, so the company can charge more for its dyes than other companies can charge for theirs. Ciba's experience illustrates that, just as a new machine enhances labour productivity, reducing environmental costs can add value to a business.

Not all environmental strategies are as financially beneficial as Ciba's, however. In the early 1990s, tuna producer StarKist <*http://starkist.com*> responded to consumer concerns about dolphins in the eastern Pacific dying in nets set out for yellow fin tuna. The company announced it would sell only skip-jack tuna from the western Pacific, which do not swim near dolphins. Unfortunately, customers were unwilling to pay a premium for dolphin-safe tuna and considered the taste of skipjack inferior. Nor was there a clear environmental gain: for every dolphin saved in the eastern Pacific, thousands of immature tuna and dozens of sharks, turtles, and other marine animals died in the western Pacific fishing process.

Seeking SUSTAINABILITY

Green is the New Black

"Green is the New Black" is the translated name of a Dutch newsletter about organic and sustainable clothing brands. But the slogan also signals a new trend in fashion where apparel companies embrace sustainability in a variety of ways.

Vancouver is a hotbed for small boutique stores that design and sell sustainable clothing. Nicole Bridger Design <*http://www.nicolebridger.com*> uses ethically-sourced materials including renewable and biodegradable fabrics from around the world. The owner, Nicole Bridger, intentionally selects fabric suppliers who are Global Organic Textile Standards (GOTS) certified. The business employs over 35 people, including cutters, sewers, and finishers in the local factory, and a management team.

Boardroom Eco© Apparel <*http://www.boardroomecoapparel.com*> is an apparel design and manufacturing company also located in Vancouver. Formed in 1996, Boardroom began to sell low-impact recycled polyester fabrics and closed-loop apparel recycling in 2001 and hasn't looked back. They manufacture 90 percent of their goods in their Vancouver factory and 70 percent of the business is exported to the United States. The company promotes closed-loop by recycling used polyester apparel. "If you don't start setting it up now, where you're starting to take back your own product or other people's products and putting it back into new product," says Boardroom President Mark Trotzuk, "you're not going to be able to do business."

A recent report projects the Canadian apparel market will grow from $30 billion in 2012 to $50 billion in 2025. China's market is expected to increase from $150 billion to $540 billion, and India's market will increase from $45 billion to $200 billion during the same period of time. With growth this size, sustainable apparel manufacturing may be the only option.

Sources: Dixie Gong, "10 Best Canadian Eco-Shops," *Flare,* 28 March 2013, http://www.flare.com/fashion/10-best-canadian-eco-shops/?gallery_page=8#gallery_top; Nicole Bridger: About transparency, 2015, http://www.nicolebridger.com/pages/transparency, downloaded 7 April 2015; Ecofashion World: organizations, 2015, http://www.ecofashionworld.com/Organizations/Green-Is-the-New-Black.html, downloaded 7 April 2015; Betsy Cummings, "Wearables," Advertising Specialty Institute, July 2010, http://www.asicentral.com/asp/open/content/content.aspx?id=4992&green, downloaded 7 April 2015; Apparel market size projections from 2012 to 2025, by region," Statista, http://www.statista.com/statistics/279757/apparel-market-size-projections-by-region/, downloaded April 2015.

The carbon tax, sometimes called a green tax, can refer to any number of measures designed to increase the cost of burning fossil fuels like oil, gas, and coal. A carbon tax would provide an incentive to stop the social harm and move to more positive alternatives. Quebec was the first province to introduce a carbon tax in 2007 but opposition is strong in Alberta where oil and gas production is vital to the economy. What do you think? Could governments, businesses, and consumers be doing more to protect the environment? Do you agree or disagree with a green tax?[51]

Environmental quality is a public good; that is, everyone gets to enjoy it regardless of who pays for it. The challenge for companies is to find the right public good that will appeal to their target markets. Many corporations are publishing reports that document their net social contribution. To do that, a company must measure its positive social contributions and subtract its negative social impacts. We will discuss that process next.

Social Auditing

It is nice to talk about having organizations become more socially responsible. It is also encouraging to see some efforts made toward creating safer products, cleaning up the environment, designing more honest advertising, and treating women and minorities fairly. But is there any way to measure whether organizations are making social responsibility an integral part of top management's decision making? The answer is yes, and the term that represents that measurement is *social auditing*.

A **social audit** is a systematic evaluation of an organization's progress toward implementing programs that are socially responsible and responsive. One of the major problems of conducting a social audit is establishing procedures for measuring a firm's activities and its effects on society. What should a social audit measure? Many social audits consider such things as workplace issues, the environment, product safety, community relations, and respecting the rights of local people. See Figure 5.5 for an outline of business activities that could be considered socially responsible.

> **social audit**
> A systematic evaluation of an organization's progress toward implementing programs that are socially responsible and responsive.

■ FIGURE 5.5

SOCIALLY RESPONSIBLE BUSINESS ACTIVITIES
Community-related activities such as participating in local fundraising campaigns, donating employee time to various non-profit organizations, and participating in urban planning and development
Employee-related activities such as establishing equal opportunity programs, offering flextime and other benefits, promoting job enrichment, ensuring job safety, and conducting employee development programs; you will learn more about such programs in Chapter 12
Political activities such as taking a position on nuclear safety, gun control, pollution control, consumer protection, and other social issues, and working more closely with local, provincial, and federal government officials
Support for higher education, the arts, and other non-profit social agencies
Consumer activities such as ensuring product safety, creating truthful advertising, handling complaints promptly, setting fair prices, and conducting extensive consumer education programs

A commitment to corporate social responsibility implies a commitment to some form of **triple-bottom line (TBL, 3BL, or People, Planet, Profit)** reporting.[52] TBL is used as a framework for measuring and reporting corporate performance against economic, social, and environmental parameters.[53] Corporations that use TBL focus on the economic value they add, but also on the environmental and social value they add and destroy.[54]

> **triple-bottom line (TBL, 3BL, or People, Planet, Profit)**
> A framework for measuring and reporting corporate performance against economic, social, and environmental parameters.

There is some question as to whether positive actions should be added (e.g., charitable donations and pollution control efforts) and negative effects subtracted (e.g., layoffs and overall pollution levels) to get a net social contribution. Or should only positive actions be recorded? In general, social responsibility is becoming one of the aspects of corporate success that business evaluates, measures, and develops.

In addition to the social audits conducted by the companies themselves, there are five types of groups that serve as watchdogs regarding how well companies enforce their ethical and social responsibility policies:

1. *Socially conscious investors* insist that a company extend its own high standards to all its suppliers. Social responsibility investing (SRI) is on the rise. In Canada, investment funds managed

by responsible investing strategies represent more than $1 trillion.[55] Be aware that SRI is highly subjective. Different people have different values, so what is ethically appropriate for one may not be the case for another.

2. *Socially conscious research organizations,* such as Ethisphere *<http://www.ethisphere.com>*, analyze and report on CSR efforts.[56]

3. *Environmentalists* apply pressure by publicly identifying companies that do not abide by the environmentalists' standards.

4. *Union officials* identify violations and force companies to comply to avoid negative publicity.

5. *Customers* make buying decisions based on their social conscience. Many will take their business elsewhere if a company demonstrates unethical or socially irresponsible practices.

What these groups look for constantly changes as the world view changes. One important thing to remember is that it is not enough for a company to be right when it comes to ethics and social responsibility. It also has to *convince* its customers and society that it's right.

SUSTAINABLE DEVELOPMENT[57]

Sustainable development means implementing a process that integrates environmental, economic, and social considerations into decision making. This reinforces the World Commission on Environment and Development's conclusion that development should be sustainable for the benefit of current and future generations. Such a focus has created opportunities for ventures such as Envirotech Office Systems, based in Mississauga, Ontario *<http://www.envirotechoffice.com>*. Corporations that wish to

Ethical Funds *<http://www.ethicalfunds.com>* believes that the best possible returns can be achieved by investing in companies that combine strong financial performance with positive social, environmental, and governance performance. The company does not invest in corporations that derive a significant portion of their income from military weapons, tobacco, or nuclear power. Would you invest in companies on the basis of their environmental, social, and governance performance?

replace aged office furniture can deal with Envirotech. The company provides a cost-effective alternative to updating these items through its re-manufacturing process. For example, one re-manufactured workstation prevents 276 pounds of landfill waste and 800 pounds of raw material consumption.[58] This kind of business activity gives the Earth relief from the pressures of expanding population and waste.

> **sustainable development**
> Implementing a process that integrates environmental, economic, and social considerations into decision making.

The goal of the Rainforest Action Network <http://www.ran.org>, an environmental activist group, is to show companies that it is possible to do well by doing good. It conducts public campaigns designed to put consumer pressure on companies that refuse to adopt responsible environmental policies. For nearly 30 years, RAN has protected millions of acres of forest around the world, including Canada.

Progress Assessment

- What is CSR, and how does it relate to a business's major stakeholders?
- How does the strategic approach differ from the pluralist approach?
- What is a social audit, and what kinds of activities does it monitor?
- Which company—Loblaws Cos. Ltd. or BP Oil—best demonstrated socially responsible behaviour?

LO6 Discuss the importance of ethical behaviour and social responsibility in global markets.

International Ethics and Social Responsibility

Ethical problems and issues of social responsibility are not unique to Canada. Top business and government leaders have been caught in major "influence-peddling" (read bribery) schemes in Japan, South Korea, Brazil, Pakistan, and Zaire. What is new about the moral and ethical standards by which government leaders are being judged? They are much stricter than in previous years.

Government leaders are not the only ones being held to higher standards. Many businesses are demanding socially responsible behaviour from their international suppliers by ensuring that suppliers do not violate domestic human rights and environmental standards. For example, Sears will not import products made by Chinese prison labour. Clothing manufacturer Phillips–Van Heusen <*http://www.pvh.com*> (makers of such brands as Calvin Klein and Tommy Hilfiger) said it would cancel orders from suppliers that violate its ethical, environmental, and human rights code. McDonald's denied rumours that one of its suppliers grazed cattle on cleared rain forest land, but wrote a ban on the practice anyway.

Fairtrade products can include coffee, tea, cocoa, and flowers. The FAIRTRADE Mark has a well-established European and North American base and is becoming recognized in markets such as Brazil, Russia, India, China, and the Middle East. A recent survey found that Fairtrade is the most widely recognized ethical label in the world.[59] Do you ever look for goods with a Fairtrade distinction?

Fair trade is a growing social movement dedicated to making sure that producers in developing countries are paid a fair price for the goods we consume (rather than exploiting desperately poor people), resulting in more money in their pockets.[60] Put another way, it is a strategy for poverty alleviation and sustainable development with the purpose of creating opportunities for producers who have been disadvantaged or marginalized by the traditional economic model.[61] Fairtrade Canada <*http://www.fairtrade.ca*> is responsible for certifying that Canadian products bearing the FAIRTRADE Mark meet international Fairtrade standards. If the product bears the FAIRTRADE Mark on the package, then it means that it has conformed to Fairtrade standards and it has contributed to the development of disadvantaged producers and workers.[62]

In contrast are companies criticized for exploiting workers in less developed countries. Nike, the world's largest athletic shoe company, has been accused by human rights and labour groups of treating its workers poorly while lavishing millions of dollars on star athletes to endorse its products. Cartoonist Garry Trudeau featured an anti-Nike campaign in his popular syndicated series *Doonesbury*.

Nike worked hard to improve its reputation. Nike monitors efforts to improve labour conditions in its 700 contract factories that are subject to local culture and economic conditions. The company released the names and locations of its factories, both as a show of transparency and to encourage its competitors to work on improving conditions as well. The company shared its audit data with a professor at MIT's Sloan School of Management. He concluded that despite "significant efforts and investments by Nike . . . workplace conditions in almost 80% of its suppliers have either remained the same or worsened over time." In 2014, a Nike supplier shut down a factory after four people were shot during a strike over higher wages.[63]

Why has Nike's monitoring program not been as successful as the company hoped? One reason is that in emerging economies, government regulations tend to be weak, which leaves companies to police their suppliers to ensure they comply with laws and regulations. That's a major task for a company like Nike, which produces 98 percent of its shoes in hundreds of factories in many different countries.

Nike has outsourced the manufacture of its products to plants in other countries and has weathered much criticism for operating in low-wage countries where child labour is common. The company has taken many corrective measures, including working with other companies and advocacy groups on a set of common labour standards and factory guidelines. Can a successful firm overcome past ethical errors?

The fairness of requiring international suppliers to adhere to domestic ethical standards is not as clear-cut as you might think. For example, what could be considered a gift in one culture is considered a bribe in another. Is it always ethical for companies to demand compliance with the standards of their own countries? What about countries in which child labour is an accepted part of the society and families depend on the children's salaries for survival? What about foreign companies doing business in Canada? Should these companies have to comply with Canadian ethical standards? What about multinational corporations? Since they span different societies, do they have to conform to all of the societies' standards? None of these questions are easy to answer, but they give you some idea of the complexity of social responsibility issues in international markets (see the Reaching Beyond our Borders box for an example of an ethical culture clash).

Reaching *Beyond* OUR BORDERS

Going by a Different Standard

The extension of corporations' reach into communities across the globe has led to many questions: For which communities are the companies responsible? Are domestic operations more important than foreign ones? Should the interests of employees be put first, or is the company's image the main priority?

Here's an example of how corporate ethics can clash with cultural ethics. Joe, the oldest son of a poor South American cloth peddler, managed to move to the United States, earn an engineering degree, and get a job with a large telecommunications company. After five years, Joe seemed to have bought into the company culture and was happy to be granted a transfer back to his home country. He was told that the company expected him to live there in a safe and presentable home of his choice. To help him afford such a residence, his employer agreed to reimburse him a maximum of $2,000 a month for the cost of his rent and servants. Each month Joe submitted rental receipts for exactly $2,000. The company later found out that Joe was living in what was, by Western standards, a shack in a dangerous area of town. Such a humble home could not have cost more than $200 a month. The company was concerned for Joe's safety as well as for the effect his residence would have on its image. The human resource manager was also worried about Joe's lack of integrity, given he had submitted false receipts for reimbursement.

Joe was upset with what he considered the company's invasion of his privacy. He argued he should receive the full $2,000 monthly reimbursement all employees received. He explained his choice of housing by saying he was making sacrifices so he could send the extra money to his family and put his younger siblings through school. This was especially important since his father had died and his family had no one else to depend on. "Look, my family is poor," Joe said. "So poor that most Westerners wouldn't believe our poverty even if they saw it. This money means the difference between hope and despair for all of us. For me to do anything less for my family would be to defile the honour of my late father. Can't you understand?"

(continued)

(*continued*)

Often it is difficult to understand what others perceive as ethical. Different situations often turn the clear waters of "rightness" downright muddy. Joe was trying to do the honourable thing for his family. Yet the company's wish to have its higher-level people live in safe housing is not unreasonable, given the dangerous conditions of the city in which Joe lived. The policy of housing reimbursement supports the company's intent to make its employees' stay in the country reasonably comfortable and safe, not to increase their salaries. In the United States, where Joe would not receive a housing supplement, it would be unethical for him to falsify expense reports in order to receive more money to send to his family. In South America, though, the issue is not so clear.

Sources: Shirley Engelmeir, "Engage a Diverse Work Force to Capture Foreign Markets," *American Banker,* 13 November 2012; and Meghan M. Biro, "Happy Employees 5 Hefty Profits," *Forbes,* 19 January 2014.

SUMMARY

LO1 **Explain why obeying the law is only the first step in behaving ethically.**

Ethics goes beyond obeying laws. It also involves abiding by the moral standards accepted by society.

How is legality different from ethics?

Ethics reflects people's proper relation with one another. Legality is more limiting; it refers only to laws written to protect people from fraud, theft, and violence.

What influences our ethical decision making?

Ethical behaviour begins with you and me. We are influenced by our society and what it considers to be ethical, the behaviour of others (both socially and in a work setting), and by our own personal values and beliefs.

LO2 **Ask the three questions to answer when faced with a potentially unethical action.**

It can be difficult to maintain a balance between ethics and other goals such as pleasing stakeholders or advancing your career.

How can we tell if our business decisions are ethical?

We can put our business decisions through an ethics check by asking three questions: (1) Is it legal? (2) Is it balanced? and (3) How will it make me feel? Companies (and individuals) that develop strong ethics codes and use these three questions have a better chance than most of behaving ethically.

LO3 **Describe management's role in setting ethical standards.**

Some managers think that ethics is an individual issue that has nothing to do with management, while others believe that ethics has everything to do with management.

What is management's role in setting ethical standards?

Managers often set formal ethical standards, but more important are the messages they send through their actions. Management's tolerance or intolerance of ethical misconduct influences employees more than written ethics codes do.

LO4 **Distinguish between compliance-based and integrity-based ethics codes, and list the six steps that can be considered when setting up a corporate ethics code.**
Business ethics can be improved if companies follow a six-step process.

What is the difference between compliance-based and integrity-based ethics codes?
Whereas compliance-based ethics codes are concerned with avoiding legal punishment, integrity-based ethics codes define the organization's guiding values, create an environment that supports ethically sound behaviour, and stress a shared accountability among employees.

What are the six steps that can improve business ethics?
The six steps are as follows: (1) top management must adopt and support an explicit corporate code of conduct; (2) employees must understand that expectations for ethical behaviour begin at the top and that senior management expects all employees to act accordingly; (3) managers and others must be trained to consider the ethical implications of all business decisions; (4) an ethics office must be set up, and phone lines to the office should be established; (5) outsiders such as suppliers, subcontractors, distributors, and customers must be told about the ethics program; and (6) the ethics code must be enforced.

Which step is the most critical in this six-step process?
The last step is most critical because a company's ethics policy must be enforced to be taken seriously.

LO5 **Define corporate social responsibility and compare corporations' responsibilities to various stakeholders.**
Corporate social responsibility goes beyond merely being ethical.

Define corporate social responsibility.
Corporate social responsibility is the concern businesses have toward stakeholders.

How do businesses demonstrate corporate responsibility toward stakeholders?
Business is responsible to five types of stakeholders: (1) it must satisfy *customers* with goods and services of real value; (2) it must make money for its *investors;* (3) it must create jobs for *employees,* maintain job security, and see that hard work and talent are fairly rewarded; (4) it must create new wealth for *society* and promote social justice, and (5) it must contribute to making its *environment* a better place.

How are a company's social responsibility efforts measured?
A corporate social audit measures an organization's progress toward social responsibility. Some people believe the audit should add together the organization's positive actions and then subtract the negative effects to get a net social benefit.

LO6 **Discuss the importance of ethical behaviour and social responsibility in global markets.**
Social responsibility issues are complex in global markets.

How can companies influence ethical behaviour and social responsibility in global markets?
Many businesses are demanding socially responsible behaviour from their international suppliers by making sure their suppliers do not violate human rights and environmental standards. Companies like Sears and Phillips–Van Heusen will not import products from companies that do not meet their ethical and social responsibility standards.

KEY TERMS

compliance-based ethics codes	corporate social responsibility	social audit
corporate philanthropy	(CSR)	sustainable development
corporate policy	ethics	triple-bottom line (TBL, 3BL, or
corporate responsibility	insider trading	People, Planet, Profit)
corporate social initiatives	integrity-based ethics codes	whistleblowers

CRITICAL THINKING

1. Think of a situation in which you have been involved that tested your ethical behaviour. For example, perhaps your best friend forgot about a term paper due the next day and asked you if he could copy and hand in a paper you wrote for another instructor last semester. What are your alternatives, and what are the consequences of each one? Would it have been easier to resolve the dilemma if you had asked yourself the three questions in the ethics check? Try answering them now and see if you would have made a different choice.

2. Companies appear to act with corporate responsibility but the underlying motive seems to be to increase profits. Does this motive undermine the value of corporate responsibility or is it only the actions that are important? That is, do you think less of a company if you know it is being responsible only to increase its profits?

3. What do you think of the phrase, "It's not personal, it's just business?" Do you agree or disagree with this statement if it were to be used to justify a business decision? Explain.

DEVELOPING WORKPLACE SKILLS

Key: ● **Team** ★ **Analytic** ▲ **Communication** ▢ **Technology**

★▲ 1. What sources have helped shape your personal code of ethics and morality? What influences, if any, have ever pressured you to compromise those standards? Think of an experience you had at work or school that tested your ethical standards. How did you resolve your dilemma? Now that time has passed, are you comfortable with the decision you made? If not, explain what you would do differently.

▢ 2. Newspapers and magazines are full of stories about individuals and businesses that are not socially responsible. What about those individuals and organizations that do take social responsibility seriously? We don't normally read or hear about them. Do a little investigative reporting of your own. Identify a public interest group in your community and identify its officers, objectives, amount of financial support, and size and characteristics of membership. List some examples of its recent actions and/or accomplishments. Consider environmental groups, animal protection groups, political action committees, and so on. (If you don't know where to start, call your local Chamber of Commerce, the Better Business Bureau, or local government agencies for help). Try using one of the Internet search engines to help you find more information.

★ 3. You are the manager of a coffee house called the Morning Cup. One of your best employees wants to be promoted to a managerial position; however, the owner is grooming his son for the promotion your employee seeks. The owner's act of nepotism may hurt a valuable employee's chances for advancement, but complaining may hurt your own chances for promotion. What do you do?

★ ▲ **4.** You are a salesperson at a clothing store. You walk into the storage room to start ticketing some clothes that came in that morning and see a co-worker quickly take some pants from a box and put them into her knapsack. Your colleague does not see you enter the room. What do you do? Do you leave and say nothing to your employer? Do you say something to your colleague? Is your responsibility to your organization, your colleague, or both? What might be the implications of your decision?

▢ ★ **5.** Go to the website of a local corporation and search for its written ethics code. Would you
▲   classify its code as compliance-based or integrity-based? Explain.

★ ▢ **6.** What effects have the new laws protecting whistleblowers had on the business environment? Go online or to the library to research individuals who reported their employers' illegal and/or unethical behaviour. Did the companies change their policies? If so, what effect have these policies had on the companies' stakeholders? What effect did reporting the problems have on the whistleblowers themselves?

ANALYZING MANAGEMENT DECISIONS

CNR's Poor Environmental Track Record

Canadian National Railway (CNR) has a long history of train spills, which have resulted in significant environmental damage. In 2005, CNR was charged by Alberta Environment <*http://www.environment.alberta.ca*> with failing to take all reasonable measures to remedy and confine the spill from a train derailment into a northern Alberta lake. In the incident, 43 cars derailed next to Wabamun Lake, west of Edmonton, spilling almost 800,000 litres of heavy fuel and a potentially cancer-causing wood preservative.

Alberta Environment spokeswoman Kim Hunt said the charges were laid by Alberta Justice after a review. "It's the law in Alberta that the polluter pays," Hunt told the Canadian Press. After the spill, Alberta Environment issued an Environmental Protection Order to CNR. The company was ordered to clean up the spill, begin long-term environmental planning and monitoring of the area, and keep the public informed on its progress. Residents of Wabamun were told in June 2006 that they could use the lake again for swimming and boating, but not for washing dishes, cleaning vegetables, or bathing.

CNR offered nearly $7.5 million on a sliding scale to the area's 1,600 residents. The payments, which ranged from $1,500 to $27,000 for those closest to the spill, were in recognition of loss of property use as a result of the derailment. The Paul First Nation, whose reserve is on the western shore of the lake, also filed a multi-million-dollar lawsuit against CNR, Ottawa, and the province, alleging that the spill destroyed its traditional way of life. In September 2008, CNR reached a $10 million settlement with the band. Earlier in 2008, three charges were laid by Environment Canada and Fisheries and Oceans Canada <*http://www.dfo-mpo.gc.ca*> against CNR: one for allegedly depositing a substance harmful to migratory birds into a lake and the other two for alleged disruption of a fish habitat.

CNR's poor environmental performance continues today. In early 2015, three train spills occurred in Northern Ontario within the span of one month. In one case, crude oil entered the Mattagami River

System. Chief Walter Naveau of the Mattagami First Nation said his community is concerned about smoke inhalation, environmental damage, water safety, and most importantly, the spawning grounds for fish local wildlife habitat upon which the community depends. Environmental activists claim the ecosystem will never be restored to its original health. When asked about CNR's claim that the train spill was cleaned up, Naveau replied, "They may say those things but why should I trust them?" The issue has gained federal government attention as Canadian Transport Minister Lisa Raitt stated CNR should be called to answer questions before a parliamentary committee. "What's going on operationally?" said Raitt. "I can hear from CN, but I think CN should talk to Parliament and should talk to Canadians."

Sources: Raveena Aulakh, "Crude oil spilled in CN derailment will impact ecosystems for long time, activists say," *The Toronto Star*, 9 March 2015, http://www.thestar.com/news/world/2015/03/09/crude-oil-spilled-in-cn-derailment-will-impact-ecosystems-for-long-time-activists-say.html; Adam Miller, "CN crude oil train derailment in Gogama, Ont. 'very concerning', transportation minister says," *The National Post*, 8 March 2015, http://news.nationalpost.com/news/canada/cn-crude-oil-train-derailment-in-gogama-ont-very-concerning-transportation-minister-says; "Canadian National Railway to Pay $10M to Alta. Band in Derailment Along Lake," CANOE Inc., 12 September 2008, http://cnews.canoe.ca /CNEWS/Politics/2008/09/12/6751421-cp.html; "Oil Spill Nets CN Rail Three Charges from Feds," *Canadian Geographic*, 18 March 2008, www.canadiangeographic.ca/cea/archives/news_item.asp?articleid=493; Gordon Kent and Kelly Cryderman, "Wabamun Residents Unhappy with CN Charge," CanWest News Service, 6 June 2006, www.canada.com/topics/news/national/story.html?id=14a77881-cc1b-4ec0-90a7 -fd86af5a9c7c&k=58041; and "CN Rail Charged in Oil Spill at Alta. Lake," The Canadian Press, 6 June 2006, http://sympaticomsn.ctv.ca/servlet /ArticleNews/story/CTVNews/20060605/cn_wabamun_060506.

Discussion Questions

1. What stakeholders were impacted by each of these incidents?
2. Conduct some research into these stories. As a result of the 2008 derailment, what changes were implemented by CNR? How did these changes impact what occurred in 2015?
3. Do you feel that the costs associated with train spills are excessive? Explain.

VIDEO CASE 5

Protect the World You Play In: Ten Tree Apparel

How do you combine a love for nature with a desire to change lives? The answer—create Ten Tree Apparel *<http://www.tentree.com/ca>*. While hiking in Hawaii, Dave Luba and Kalen Emsley reached the top of a mountain looking out over the beautiful forest. The view inspired them to take action—immediately. The pair wanted to create something where consumers could sustain the environment.

Ten Tree Apparel is both a lifestyle apparel company and an environmental advocate. The early phase of the small business was high tempo and soon after being formed on January 1, 2012, the two founders, along with Kalen's brother Derek Emsley, appeared on CBC's *Dragons' Den*. Their pitch was an immediate success and two Dragons agreed to give the social entrepreneurs $100,000 in capital in return for 20 percent of the business. It turned out the company didn't need the funding after all, but they were grateful for the support. It proved their TBL business approach was on the mark. "I think (. . .) it's a shame if business schools aren't teaching 'people, planet, profit' and are just teaching 'profit' because that's not the future of business," said Dragon Arlene Dickson during the telecast.

When you visit the company's website, you are greeted by a wide array of purchase options. Ten Tree's apparel line includes women's and men's hoodies, long-sleeved shirts, t-shirts, tanks, and pants, as well as hats, toques, and bottle accessories. "Our goal is to make our clothes similar to Apple," explains Emsley, referencing the tech giant renowned for designs that are iconic because of their simplicity.

"When you get an Apple package, it's clean; you know exactly what it is. When you get a Ten Tree shirt, we want it to be clean and you know that it's something for the environment, something to get people outdoors and something that plants ten trees." The company's head office follows the same simplicity philosophy—nothing fancy so as much revenue as possible can be directed to its social and environmental goals. Its commitment to stewardship also means the company's production practices, including its suppliers, are socially and environmentally responsible.

Ten Tree's corporate conscience targets more than environmental change in Canada. They reach out to the global community and work with charities throughout the world who believe in the same values. Together, they identify regions with the greatest need for trees to improve social, economic, and environmental sustainability. At the time this textbook was written, Ten Tree had planted almost 5 million tress around the globe, including four-and-a-half million trees in four African countries, nearly 300,000 trees in India, over 50,000 trees in Canada, and approximately 2,500 in Cambodia. Trees are the gift that keeps giving as saplings grow to mature trees and most importantly, propagate seedlings that turn into more trees.

Ten Tree depends on social media to market its products. Each piece of apparel has its own tree code that the consumer registers online. Once your tree code is registered you can track your trees and see where they will be planted. The more codes you register, the more information you are given about your trees and their impact.

Both Luba and Emsley want to encourage other young Canadians to take an interest in nature. In co-operation with the Canadian Wildlife Federation they produced a video series titled *Inspire* that profiles entrepreneurship and environmental stewardship.

The Canadian-born brand continues to grow, and so do the trees!

Discussion Questions

1. Ten Tree Apparel's commitment to TBL, or People, Planet, Profit, is a vital part of the company's success. Do you believe a triple-bottom-line approach will influence the way businesses operate in the future? Explain.

2. A business that espouses social responsibility should be held accountable by its stakeholders to follow through on its commitment. Analyze how Ten Tree Apparel meets these responsibilities for each of its stakeholders: customers, investors, employees, society, and the environment.

3. A key target for Ten Tree is the "young generation" of consumers. Why is CSR so important to this generation compared to other generations? Will Generation Y and Generation Z consumers create enough pressure for small and large companies to adopt sustainable development practices, such as those embraced by Ten Tree Apparel?

Sources: Mary Terea Bitti, "Ten Tree International: Dragons' Den sees seeds of a good company," *Financial Post*, 15 October 2012, http://business .financialpost.com/entrepreneur/dragons-see-the-seeds-of-a-good-company-in-ten-tree-international; Christine Clarke, "How innovative clothing company Ten Tree is helping the environment," SamaritanMag, 31 October 2012, http://www.samaritanmag.com/1418/how-innovative-clothing -company-ten-tree-helping-environment; Sojourn Outdoors—News and Updates, 2012, http://www.sojournoutdoors.com/ten-tree-apparel-is-here-2/, downloaded 25 April 2015; Raquel Fletcher, "Ten Tree sees the forest and the trees," *Degrees*, Fall/Winter 2012, http://www.uregina.ca/business /assets/about-us/news/2012/Degrees-Ten-Tree-Winter2012.pdf; Ten Tree Apparel—About, http://www.tentree.com/ca/, downloaded 25 April 2015.

RUNNING CASE

Ron Foxcroft: The Dream for a Pealess Whistle

For successful Canadian entrepreneur and inventor Ron Foxcroft, it all started in 1982 when he purchased Fluke Transport, a Southern Ontario trucking business. The company slogan—If It's On Time . . . It's A "FLUKE"—was soon recognized throughout North America. Over the years, Foxcroft diversified into new ventures and the Foxcroft Group of Companies now includes Fluke Transportation Group, Fluke Warehousing Inc., Foxcroft Capital Corp., Fox 40 International Inc., and Fox 40 USA Inc.

The formation of Fox 40 International Inc. (Fox 40) is the result of a dream for a pealess whistle. When Foxcroft began developing the whistle, he was motivated by his knowledge and experience as an international basketball referee. Frustrated with faulty pea whistles, he spent three years of development with design consultant Chuck Shepherd, resulting in the creation of the Fox 40 Classic Whistle. (The whistle was named for Foxcroft and that he was 40 when his invention was being developed).

Introduced in 1987, this finely tuned precision instrument doesn't use a pea to generate sound. In fact, there are no moving parts whatsoever. There is nothing to obstruct sound, nothing to stick, freeze, or fail. The patented design moves the air blast through three tuned chambers. Fox 40 whistles are entirely constructed of high-impact ABS plastic so they are impervious to moisture. A quick rinse in disinfectant eliminates bacteria. Every time, they deliver on faultless performance (e.g., loudness), and they never fail.

Fox 40 International Inc., a proudly Canadian company, dominates the global whistle industry. Tens of thousands of Fox 40 whistles are produced monthly for shipment to 140 countries. They are sold to referees, coaches, water safety professionals, search and rescue teams, personal security teams, animal trainers, sport enthusiasts, as well as customers in the outdoor and premium incentive markets. The complete line of Fox 40 products has grown substantially with over 900 active stock-keeping units (SKUs) that include the following: 19 Fox 40 Whistles Styles; Lanyards & Attachments; Fox 40 Gear; SmartCoach Coaching Boards; SICK Self Impression Custom Kit, and Heat Alert Mouthguards; Marine & Outdoor Products; Pink Products; and Logo Imprinted Products.

When you consider the global business environment, the biggest threat is counterfeiters. There are at least five attempts per year to counterfeit the company's products. In response, Fox 40 aggressively polices its patents and trademarks. This includes monitoring offshore websites and catalogue publications for the misuse of Fox 40 intellectual property (IP). It is the company's responsibility to police and look for infringements to protect its IP and distributors worldwide. In addition, when a new product is introduced, an improvement to the new product is already in the vault, ready to be introduced at the first sign of counterfeiters.

Direct exporting is the strategy used to reach global markets. Rather than hiring someone to represent Fox 40 in a foreign country, Fox 40 employees attend global trade shows that service their targeted countries. At these trade shows, they look for three distributors that will deal directly with Fox 40. Orders are then directly exported to these distributors.

Even though offshoring would result in lower overall costs, the company insists on controlling the quality of its products by manufacturing them domestically. International customers especially value Fox 40's "Made in Canada" products as they connote quality. This is reinforced in international business trade shows where Fox 40 employees are often asked to confirm that their products continue to be made in Canada. At an annual ISPO MUNICH trade show, Ron observed that attendance seemed poorer than in the past in the Sourcing section. (ISPO MUNICH is an international leading sports business trade show.

Every year, over 2,000 international exhibitors present their latest products to more than 80,000 visitors from over 100 countries. Exhibitors are categorized by segment: Outdoor, Ski, Action, Sportstyle, Performance Sports, and Sourcing.) This part of the trade show included association members from offshore countries such as China, Taiwan, and India. Ron believes that the lower turnout for some of the offshore exhibitors was in recognition of buyers' concerns with the decreasing quality of offshore-produced products. As a result, buyers are increasingly seeking high standard, quality-made products from manufacturers such as Fox 40.

There has been some discussion in this textbook about the role of government in business. Ron's perspective is as follows: "Government has been a big help to me in business. I simply take what they do and do the exact opposite. They take 12 months to do what I do in 12 minutes. I have learned to have courage, 59-minute stand-up meetings, eliminate large committees, long-winded rhetoric, and keep my company lean and customer focused. If governments practised this, they could be efficient too. However, most politicians are focused on re-election and not customer (citizen) service. Therefore, rather than make correct decisions they make popular decisions. Finally, too many rules in government inhibit innovation."

The company's GREEN PLAN highlights some of the areas where Fox 40 has taken steps to do its part to help to protect the environment. Examples include the following: reusing shipping containers whenever possible; the elimination of all clamshell packaging; bagging whistles and mouthguards in #4 biodegradable packaging; reducing the overall whistle package size by 20 percent to lessen the impact on the environment; and reducing the size of shipping boxes due to package dimension changes, resulting in less boxboard consumed and improved shipping methods. Sustainable packaging solutions include blister packaging made from recycled water and pop bottles, and using print material that contains recyclable and/or recycled post-consumer waste material. Savings over nine months from the use of emission-free electricity in print production includes 93 trees preserved for the future, 128,746 litres of wastewater flow saved, and 15,289 kilograms of air emissions not generated.

Fox 40 is a strong community-conscious company and as a result invests heavily in corporate responsibility initiatives. Over the years, it has helped well over 100 organizations that include non-profits, charities, foundations (e.g., the Foxcroft Family Youth Foundation, which supports disadvantaged youth), hospitals, and educational institutions. Ron also believes that we should support the military and veterans. In recognition of Fox 40's contributions, Ron was appointed as the 2012 Honorary Colonel in The Argyll and Sutherland Highlanders of Canada Reserve Troop.

While Ron has chaired several local high-profile capital campaigns—which include Hillfield Strathallan College, St. Joseph's Hospital, and McMaster University Athletics Capital Campaign—most of the company's contributions are anonymous. These anonymous contributions have often been directed to areas that have been deemed to have the greatest need. The Foxcrofts recognize that there are over 60,000 charities and non-profits in Ontario. By anonymously supporting some of those in need, they do not upset the many worthy ones that are left out.

Ron credits his customers and employees for the improvements to the original whistle. In his words, "When you are the best, you need to be better." This all starts with watching people to understand their needs. It involves developing products and services that customers might want. Making decisions along the way is challenging, but if you are successful, you can make a lot of customers very happy. Throughout this process, you need to have a vision, be focused, adapt to change, and never give up. His advice for future entrepreneurs, in the words of Walt Disney, are to, "Get a good idea and stay with it. Dog it, and work it until it's done and done right."

Sources: Ron Foxcroft, CEO of Fox 40 International Inc. and Chairman and CEO of Fluke Transportation, in-person interview, 25 June 2012, Hamilton; and Dave Foxcroft, President and COO, Fox 40 International Inc., in-person interview, 25 June 2012, Hamilton; "Fox 40 Green Initiatives," Fox 40 International Inc., 1 June 2012, www.fox40world.com/index.cfm?pagepath=ABOUT_US/Green_Initiatives&id=4240; Roy Green, "Roy

Green: A Terrifying Moment Leads to a Canadian Global Success," *The Canadian Business Journal*, 12 May 2012, www.cbj.ca/features/may_12 _features/roy_green_a_terrifying_moment_leads_to_a_canadian_global_success.html; "Visitors," Messe München International, 2012, www.ispo .com/munich/en/All-Sports/Visitors; "Who We Are: The Fox 40 Story," Fox 40 International Inc., 18 December 2011, www.fox40world.com/index .cfm?pagepath=ABOUT_US/Who_We_Are_The_Fox_40_Story&id=4099; "BEDC Inducts Mr. Ron Foxcroft into the Entrepreneur Hall of Fame," Burlington Economic Development Corporation, 10 June 2011, www.bedc.ca/sites/default/files/PDF/businessnews/MediaRelease-BEDCInductsMr .RonFoxcroftintotheEntrepreneurHallofFame.pdf; John Kernaghan, "Fox 40 founder Foxcroft feted," *The Hamilton Spectator*, 18 October 2010, www.thespec.com/sports/local/article/268488-fox-40-founder-foxcroft-feted; REFEREE Staff, "Not An Inadvertent Whistle," *REFEREE Magazine*, July 2007, 45–47; and "Ron Foxcroft, Summit of Life," Global TV, Summer 2005.

Discussion Questions

1. In addition to employees and customers, what other stakeholders does the company consider as part of its business activities?

2. What is the primary reason why the company is unlikely to consider other global market-entry strategies (e.g., licensing)?

3. Visit the company's website at *<http://www.fox40world.com>*. What are some of its newest green initiatives? Can you recommend any new ones?

4. Do you have a dream for a product that has not yet been produced? If yes, how do you plan to develop this idea and turn it into reality?

PART 2

Forms of Business Ownership

LEARNING OBJECTIVES

After you have read and studied this chapter, you should be able to:

LO1 List the advantages and disadvantages of sole proprietorships.

LO2 Describe the advantages and disadvantages of partnerships. Include the differences between general and limited partners.

LO3 Discuss the advantages and disadvantages of corporations.

LO4 Outline the advantages and disadvantages of franchising. Include the challenges of global franchising.

LO5 Describe the role of co-operatives in Canada.

PROFILE

GETTING TO KNOW BRIAN SCUDAMORE, FOUNDER & CEO OF THREE FRANCHISE COMPANIES: 1-800-GOT-JUNK?, WOW 1 DAY PAINTING, AND YOU MOVE ME

In 1989, 18-year-old college student Brian Scudamore could not find a summer job, so he decided to start his own business in Vancouver, British Columbia. Inspired by a junk-hauling truck he saw at a McDonald's, Scudamore bought a used truck for $700 and began a junk removal company called the Rubbish Boys. (He chose the plural name even though he was the owner and sole employee.) His slogan was "We'll Stash Your Trash in a Flash!" Over the following summers Scudamore's business grew, and in 1998 he changed the name to 1-800-GOT-JUNK? <http://www.1800gotjunk.com> and expanded his business through franchising.

With uniformed employees and clean, shiny trucks proudly advertising the company's name and telephone number, Scudamore set his company apart from other independent junk haulers, creating an unlikely

Source: Courtesy of 1-800-GOT-JUNK?. Used with permission.

brand out of hauling people's trash or, as Scudamore sees it, treasure. Servicing both the residential and commercial markets, 1-800-GOT-JUNK? is recognized for outstanding customer service that is based on a simple, yet effective concept: friendly drivers call customers in advance; arrive at the customer site on schedule; and provide a full cleanup after the junk is removed. Whenever possible, items are recycled or donated.

While many companies expand their businesses by transforming into corporations and selling shares on the open market, 1-800-GOT-JUNK? expanded through franchising as a way to achieve rapid market penetration and revenue growth. Today, the company is the world's largest junk removal service through approximately 170 locations across three countries (Canada, the United States, and Australia).

Impressed by entrepreneur Jim Bodden's concept of getting any job done in one day, the two launched WOW 1 DAY Painting *<http://www.wow1day.com>* in 2010. This company leverages several of the strengths of 1-800-GOT-JUNK?, such as a strong brand name, call centre capabilities, established training, and a franchising system to launch franchises across North America. Scudamore expects 1-800-GOT-JUNK? to double its revenues to $200 million by 2016, and sees even more potential in the new painting business.

Scudamore's business interests do not stop here. In 2013, following a poor experience when moving house, Scudamore was inspired to bring his customer service focused business model to the moving industry. He started the franchise, You Move Me *<http://www.youmoveme.com>* and first-year revenues were $14 million.

When asked what the biggest challenge facing his business was, Scudamore responded that it was, "Keeping the right people, keeping them motivated and great. As clichéd as it sounds, having the right people is all a business really is."

Just like Scudamore, all business owners must decide for themselves which form of business is best for them. Whether you dream of starting a business for yourself, going into business with a partner, forming a corporation, or someday being a leading franchisor, it is important to know that each form of ownership has its advantages and disadvantages. You will learn about them all in this chapter.

Sources: "Brian Scudamore," LinkedIn, 24 February 2015, https://www.linkedin.com/in/scudamore; "Brian Scudamore, Founder and CEO," 1-800 GOT JUNK? [2015?], http://www.1800gotjunk.com/ca_en/about/brian_scudamore.aspx; "Meet Brian Scudamore, You Move Me," Small Business BC, 2015, http://smallbusinessbc.ca/success-story/meet-brian-scudamore-you-move-me/; "Start a Franchise," You Move Me, [2015?], http://www.youmoveme.com/ca/franchising/the-opportunity; "Press Kit," 1-800 GOT JUNK? [2013?], http://www.1800gotjunk.com/sites/default/files/PRKIT_2013_NORTHAMERICA.pdf; "Brian Scudamore, Founder and CEO," 1-800 GOT JUNK?, 12 May 2012, www.1800gotjunk.com/us_en/about/brian_scudamore.aspx; Jeff Beer, "Q&A: Brian Scudamore founder/CEO, 1-800-Got-Junk," *Canadian Business*, 7 May 2012, www.canadianbusiness.com/article/81127-q-a-brian-scudamore-founder-ceo-1-800-got-junk; Eric Stites, "Franchise Relations: Different Ideas, Great Solutions," *Franchising World*, 1 May 2008; and "Junk Removal Founder Awarded Entrepreneur of the Year by International Franchise Association," PR Newswire, 11 February 2008.

Starting a Small Business

Like Brian Scudamore, many people start new businesses in Canada every year. Chances are, you have thought of owning your own business or know someone who has. How you set up your business can make a tremendous difference in your long-term success. The three major forms of business ownership are (1) sole proprietorships, (2) partnerships, and (3) corporations. Each has advantages and disadvantages that we will discuss.

It can be easy to get started in your own business. You can begin a lawn mowing service, develop a website, or go about meeting other wants and needs in your community. A business owned, and usually managed, by one person is called a **sole proprietorship**. This is the most common form of business ownership.

sole proprietorship
A business that is owned, and usually managed, by one person.

Many people do not have the money, time, or desire to run a business on their own. When two or more parties legally agree to become co-owners of a business, the organization is called a **partnership**.

partnership
A legal form of business with two or more parties.

With a background in holistic nutrition, Toni Desrosiers, co-owner of Victoria, British Columbia-based Abeego Designs Inc. *<http://www.abeego.com>*, answered the question, "How did we store food before plastic wrap?" She developed an easy-to-use, all natural food wrap made from pure beeswax, jojoba oil, and tree resin that has been infused into hemp and certified organic cotton cloth.[1] Would you try this flexible, plastic-free food covering?

Sole proprietorships and partnerships are relatively easy to form, but there are advantages to creating a business that is separate and distinct from the owners. A legal entity with authority to act and have liability separate from its owners is called a **corporation**.

> **corporation**
> A legal entity with authority to act and have liability separate from its owners.

As you will learn in this chapter, each form of business ownership has advantages and disadvantages. It is important to understand both before attempting to start a business. Keep in mind that just because a business starts in one form of ownership, it does not have to stay in that form. Many companies start out in one form, then add (or drop) a partner or two, and eventually may become corporations or franchisors.[2] The advantages and disadvantages that are highlighted in this chapter may give you an idea of why there may be a change in ownership form as the business grows. Let's begin our discussion by looking at the most basic form of ownership—the sole proprietorship.

LO1   List the advantages and disadvantages of sole proprietorships.

Sole Proprietorships

Advantages of Sole Proprietorships

Sole proprietorships are the easiest kind of businesses for you to explore in your quest for an interesting career. Every city has sole proprietors you can visit. Talk with some of these business people about the joys and frustrations of being on their own. Some advantages they mention may include the following:

1. *Ease of starting and ending the business.* All you have to do to start a sole proprietorship is to buy or lease the needed equipment (e.g., a saw, a word processor, a tractor, a lawn mower, etc.) and put up some announcements saying you are in business. It is just as easy to get out of business; you simply stop. There is no one to consult or to disagree with about such decisions. You may have to get a permit or licence from the local government, but often that is not a problem.

2. *Being your own boss.* Working for others simply does not have the same excitement as working for yourself and setting your own hours. At least, that is the way sole proprietors feel. You can start things quickly and you have the responsibility for all of the key aspects of realizing your vision. You may make mistakes, but they are your mistakes—and so are the many small victories each day.

3. *Pride of ownership.* People who own and manage their own businesses are rightfully proud of their work. They deserve all the credit for taking the risks and providing needed products.

4. *Retention of company profit.* Other than the joy of being your own boss, there is nothing like the pleasure of knowing that you can earn as much as possible and not have to share that money with anyone else (except the government, in taxes).

5. *No special taxes.* All profits of a sole proprietorship are taxed as the personal income of the owner, and the owner pays the normal personal income tax rate on that money. Another tax advantage for sole proprietors is that they can claim any business losses against other earned income. These losses would decrease the personal taxes they would need to pay. Understanding tax planning is an

important factor in choosing the appropriate form of business organization and often requires the advice of professional accountants. Accounting will be discussed in Chapter 16.

6. *Less regulation.* While proprietorships are regulated by the provincial/territorial governments, and the proprietorship may have to be registered, overall they are less regulated than corporations.[3] As well, the administration of a proprietorship is less costly than that of a corporation.

You can federally incorporate your business online for $200. For information on registering your business with the different levels of government, visit Canada Business Network <*http://www.canadabusiness.ca*>.

Disadvantages of Sole Proprietorships

Not everyone is equipped to own and manage a business. Disadvantages of owning your own business may include the following:

1. *Unlimited liability—the risk of personal losses.* When you work for others, it is their problem if the business is not profitable. When you own your own business, you and the business are considered one. You have **unlimited liability**; that is, any debts or damages incurred by the business are your debts and you must pay them, even if it means selling your home, your car, or whatever else you own. This is a serious risk, and one that requires not only thought but also discussion with a lawyer, an insurance agent, an accountant, and others.

> **unlimited liability**
> The responsibility of business owners for all of the debts of the business.

2. *Limited financial resources.* Funds available to the business are limited to the funds that the one (sole) owner can gather. Often it is difficult to save enough money to start a business and keep it going. The costs of inventory, supplies, insurance, advertising, rent, computers, utilities, and so on may be too much to cover alone. Since there are serious limits to how much money one person can raise, partnerships and corporations have a greater probability of obtaining the needed financial backing to start a business and keep it going.

3. *Management difficulties.* All businesses need management; that is, someone must keep inventory records, accounting records, tax records, and so forth. Many people who are skilled at selling things

or providing a service are often not so skilled at keeping records. Sole proprietors often find it difficult to attract good, qualified employees to help run the business because they cannot compete with the salaries and benefits offered by larger companies.

4. *Overwhelming time commitment.* Though sole proprietors may say they set their own hours, it is hard to own a business, manage it, train people, and have time for anything else in life. This is true of any business, but a sole proprietor has no one with whom to share the burden. The owner often must spend long hours working. The owner of a store, for example, may put in 12 hours a day, at least six days a week—almost twice the hours worked by a non-supervisory employee in a large company. Imagine how this time commitment affects the sole proprietor's family life. Many sole proprietors will tell you, "It's not a job, it's not a career, it's a way of life."[4]

5. *Few fringe benefits.* If you are your own boss, you lose the fringe benefits that often come from working for others. You have no paid health insurance, no paid disability insurance, no sick leave, and no vacation pay.

6. *Limited growth.* Expansion is often slow since a sole proprietorship relies on its owner for most of its creativity, business know-how, and funding.

7. *Limited lifespan.* If the sole proprietor dies, the business no longer exists, unless it is sold or taken over by the sole proprietor's heirs.

8. *Possibly pay higher taxes.* If the business is profitable, it may be paying higher taxes than if it was incorporated as a Canadian Controlled Private Corporation (CCPC).[5] (We will discuss private corporations shortly.) That is, tax rates are more advantageous if the business is incorporated. We will expand on this point later on in the chapter under the corporations discussion.

Being the sole proprietor of a company, like a dog-walking service, means making a major time commitment to run the business, including constantly seeking out new customers and looking for reliable employees when the time comes to grow. If you were a sole proprietor, how would you need to prepare at the office if you wanted to take a week's vacation?

Talk with a few local sole proprietors about the challenges they have faced in being on their own. They are likely to have many interesting stories to tell about problems in getting loans from a financial institution, problems with theft, problems simply keeping up with the business, and so on. These drawbacks are also reasons why many sole proprietors choose to find partners to share the load.

Progress Assessment

- What are the three forms of business ownership?
- Most people who start businesses in Canada are sole proprietors. What are the advantages and disadvantages of sole proprietorships?
- Why would unlimited liability be considered a major drawback of sole proprietorships?

LO2 Describe the advantages and disadvantages of partnerships. Include the differences between general and limited partners.

Partnerships

A partnership is a legal form of business with two or more parties. The business can be a partnership of individuals, corporations, trusts, other partnerships, or a combination of these.[6] Two types of partnerships are general partnerships and limited partnerships. A **general partnership** is a partnership in which all owners share in operating the business and in assuming liability for the business's debts. A **limited partnership** is a partnership with one or more general partners and one or more limited partners.

> **general partnership**
> A partnership in which all owners share in operating the business and in assuming liability for the business's debts.
>
> **limited partnership**
> A partnership with one or more general partners and one or more limited partners.

A **general partner** is an owner (partner) who has unlimited liability and is active in managing the firm. Every partnership must have at least one general partner. A **limited partner** is an owner (partner) who invests money in the business but does not have any management responsibility or liability for losses beyond the investment. **Limited liability** means that limited partners are not responsible for the debts of the business beyond the amount of their investment—their liability is limited to the amount they put into the company; therefore, their personal assets are not at risk.

> **general partner**
> An owner (partner) who has unlimited liability and is active in managing the firm.
>
> **limited partner**
> An owner (partner) who invests money in the business but does not have any management responsibility or liability for losses beyond the investment.
>
> **limited liability**
> The responsibility of a business's owners for losses only up to the amount they invest; limited partners and shareholders have limited liability.

Another type of partnership was created to limit the disadvantage of unlimited liability. A **limited liability partnership (LLP)** limits partners' risk of losing their personal assets to the outcomes of only their own acts and omissions and those of people under their supervision. If you are a limited partner in an LLP, you can operate without fear that one of your partners might commit an act of malpractice resulting in a judgment that takes away your house, car, retirement plans, etc. as would be the case in a general partnership. British Columbia has made LLPs available for any kind of business; in other provinces LLPs are usually limited to regulated professions such as lawyers or accountants.[7]

---

limited liability partnership (LLP)
A partnership that limits partners' risk of losing their personal assets to only their own acts and omissions and to the acts and omissions of people under their supervision.

Advantages of Partnerships

Often, it is much easier to own and manage a business with one or more partners. Your partner may be skilled at inventory control and accounting, while you do the selling or servicing. A partner can also provide additional money, support, and expertise as well as cover for you when you are sick or on vacation. Figure 6.1 suggests several questions to ask yourself when choosing a partner.

■ **FIGURE 6.1**

QUESTIONS TO ASK WHEN CHOOSING A BUSINESS PARTNER
There's no such thing as a perfect partner, but you should share some common thoughts on the business. Ask yourself:
Do you share the same goals?
Do you share the same vision for the company's future?
What skills does the person have?
Are those skills the same as yours, or do they complement your skills?
What contacts, resources, or special attributes will the person bring to the business?
What type of decision maker is the person?
Is this someone with whom you could happily share authority for all major business decisions?
Do you trust each other?
How does the person respond to adversity?
Does he or she try to solve the problem or try to defend his or her ego?
Can the person accept constructive criticism without getting defensive?
To what extent can you build fun and excitement into the partnership?

Partnerships usually have the following advantages:

1. *More financial resources.* When two or more people pool their money and credit, it is easier to pay the rent, utilities, and other bills incurred by a business. A limited partnership is specially designed to help raise capital (money). As mentioned earlier, a limited partner invests money in the business but cannot legally have any management responsibility and has limited liability.

2. *Shared management and pooled/complementary skills and knowledge.* It is simply much easier to manage the day-to-day activities of a business with carefully chosen partners. Partners give each other free time from the business and provide different skills and perspectives. Some people find that the best partner is a spouse. That is why you see so many husband-and-wife teams managing restaurants, service shops, and other businesses.

3. *Longer survival.* Partnerships are more likely to succeed than sole proprietorships because being watched by a partner can help a business person become more disciplined.[8]

4. *Shared risk.* A partnership shares the risk among the owners. This includes financial risk in starting the business and ongoing risks as the business grows. Read the Spotlight on Small Business for how taking on a partner *<http://www.profitguide.com/microsite/profitw100>* allowed Inder Bedi to grow his business.

5. *No special taxes.* As with sole proprietorships, all profits of partnerships are taxed as the personal incomes of the owners, and the owners pay the normal income tax rate on that money. Similarly, any business losses can be used to decrease earned income from other sources.

6. *Less regulation.* Like a sole proprietorship, a partnership is less regulated than a corporation.

Lara Murphy and Karen Ryan met on a construction site in Banff, Alberta, while working as project managers. Soon after, they started Ryan Murphy Construction, a construction, renovation, and project management company. Visit the company site *<http://ryanmurphyconstruction.com>* to learn why these women were included in the PROFIT/ Chatelaine W100 ranking *<http://www.profitguide.com/microsite/profitw100>*.

Disadvantages of Partnerships

Any time two people must agree, conflict and tension are possible. Partnerships have caused splits between relatives, friends, and spouses. Let's explore the disadvantages of partnerships next.

1. *Unlimited liability.* Each *general* partner is liable for the debts of the firm, no matter who was responsible for causing those debts. You are liable for your partners' mistakes as well as your own. Like sole proprietors, general partners can lose their homes, cars, and everything else they own if the business loses a lawsuit or goes bankrupt.

2. *Division of profits.* Sharing risk means sharing profits, and that can cause conflicts. There is no set system for dividing profits in a partnership, and they are not always divided evenly. For example, if one partner puts in more money and the other puts in more hours, each may feel justified in asking for a bigger share of the profits.

Spotlight *On* SMALL BUSINESS

Bags That Travel

Inder Bedi started Matt & Nat <*http://mattandnat.com*> in 1995, fresh out of university. "I dreamed of something that no one else in the market was doing: a lifestyle brand that embraces a philosophy of positivity and is environmentally conscious," he says. "Being a vegetarian, I wanted the line to be cruelty-free, using no animal products. But beyond that, I wanted the product to reflect a philosophy, which is why there is a positivity message stamped on all bags, something that has universal appeal."

When he began, Bedi lived with family until he saved enough money to fund the business start-up. During this time, he learned everything he could about design and the trade. "In the first years of the company, the line was produced locally in Montreal," says Bedi. "I got to the point where I wanted to bring the business to the next level. I brought in a business partner and we took production to Asia. This allowed us to make the line more affordable, while maintaining our designer appeal. Due to the attention we give to design and details, we have managed to maintain the perception of a high-end line while taking it to mass market."

Today, the collection remains true to the original philosophy where the products do not use leather or any other animal-based materials. Inspired by MAT(T)erial and NATure, Matt & Nat's line of vegan bags include bags, wallets, backpacks, and accessories for men and women. The company regularly assesses innovative ways to remain sustainable and eco-friendly. This includes experimentation with different recycled nylons, cardboard, rubber, and cork. Have you seen some of the company's products? They can be found in boutiques across Canada, the United States, the United Kingdom, Japan, Germany, and Australia.

Sources: "The Brand," Matt & Nat, 2014, http://mattandnat.com/our-story/; "About Us," Matt & Nat, 14 May 2012, www.mattandnat .com/info/about/; and "Inder Bedi Wins BDC's Young Entrepreneur Award for Québec," Business Development Bank of Canada, 16 October 2007, www.bdc.ca/en/about/mediaroom/news_releases/2007/2007101603.htm.

3. *Disagreements among partners.* Disagreements over money are just one example of potential conflict in a partnership. Who has final authority over employees? Who works what hours? What if one partner wants to buy expensive equipment for the firm and the other partner disagrees? All terms of the partnership should be spelled out in writing to protect all parties and to minimize misunderstandings.[9]

4. *Difficulty of termination.* Once you have committed yourself to a partnership, it is not easy to get out of it. Sure, you can just quit. However, questions about who gets what and what happens next are often very difficult to resolve when the partnership ends. Surprisingly, law firms often have faulty

partnership agreements (legal documents that specify the rights and responsibilities of each partner) and find that breaking up is hard to do. How do you get rid of a partner you do not like? It is best to decide such questions up-front in the partnership agreement. In the absence of an agreement, or if certain provisions are not addressed in the agreement, provincial or territorial laws will determine some or all of the terms of the partnership.[10] Figure 6.2 gives you some ideas about what should be included in a partnership agreement.

partnership agreement
Legal document that specifies the rights and responsibilities of each partner

5. *Possibly pay higher taxes.* Similar to a sole proprietorship, if the partnership is very profitable, it may be paying higher taxes than if it was incorporated as a CCPC.[11]

■ **FIGURE 6.2**

PARTNERSHIP AGREEMENT PROVISIONS

It's not hard to form a partnership, but it's wise for each prospective partner to get the counsel of a lawyer experienced with such agreements. Lawyers' services are usually expensive, so would-be partners should read all about partnerships and reach some basic agreements before calling a lawyer.

For your protection, be sure to put your partnership agreement in writing. The following provisions are usually included in a partnership agreement:

1. The name of the business. All provinces require the firm's name to be registered with the province if the firm's name is different from the name of any of the partners.

2. The names and addresses of all partners.

3. The purpose and nature of the business, the location of the principal office(s), and any other locations where business will be conducted.

4. The date the partnership will start and how long it will last. Will it exist for a specific length of time, or will it stop when one of the partners dies or when the partners agree to discontinue?

5. The contributions made by each partner. Will some partners contribute money, while others provide real estate, personal property, expertise, or labour? When are the contributions due?

6. The management responsibilities. Will all partners have equal voices in management, or will there be senior and junior partners?

7. The duties of each partner.

8. The salaries and drawing accounts of each partner.

9. Provision for sharing of profits or losses.

10. Provision for accounting procedures. Who'll keep the accounts? What bookkeeping and accounting methods will be used? Where will the books be kept?

11. The requirements for taking in new partners.

12. Any special restrictions, rights, or duties of any partner.

13. Provision for a retiring partner.

14. Provision for the purchase of a deceased or retiring partner's share of the business.

15. Provision for how grievances will be handled.

16. Provision for how to dissolve the partnership and distribute the assets to the partners.

The best way to learn about the advantages and disadvantages of partnerships is to interview several people who have experience with such arrangements. They will give you insights and hints on how to avoid problems. The Making Ethical Decisions box leaves you with a dilemma to consider when it comes to making decisions in a partnership.

One fear of owning your own business or having a partner is the fear of losing everything you own if the business loses a lot of money or someone sues the business. Many business people try to avoid this and the other disadvantages of sole proprietorships and partnerships by forming corporations. We discuss this basic form of business ownership in the next section.

Making ETHICAL DECISIONS

Outsourcing or Outsmarting?

Imagine that you and your partner own a construction company. You receive a bid from a subcontractor that you know is 20 percent too low. Such a loss to the subcontractor could put him out of business. Accepting the bid will certainly improve your chances of winning the contract for a big shopping centre project. Your partner wants to take the bid and let the subcontractor suffer the consequences of his bad estimate. What do you think you should do? What will be the consequences of your decision?

Progress Assessment

- What is the difference between a limited partner and a general partner?
- What are some of the advantages and disadvantages of partnerships?
- State four provisions usually included in a partnership agreement.

LO3 Discuss the advantages and disadvantages of corporations.

Corporations

Although the word corporation makes people think of big businesses, such as the Bank of Montreal *<http://www.bmo.com>* or Irving Oil *<http://www.irvingoil.com>*, it is not necessary to be big to incorporate (start a corporation). Obviously, many corporations are big. However, incorporating may be beneficial for small businesses also.

A corporation is a federally or provincially chartered legal entity with authority to act and have liability separate from its owners. The corporation's owners (called shareholders/stockholders, as they hold shares/stock of ownership in the company) are not liable for the debts or any other problems of the corporation beyond the money they invest. Corporate shareholders do not have to worry about losing their homes, cars, and other personal property if the business cannot pay its bills—a very significant benefit. A corporation not only limits the liability of owners, but it also enables many people to share in the ownership (and profits) of a business without working there or having other commitments to it. We will discuss the rights of shareholders in Chapter 17.

Jim Pattison acquired a Pontiac Buick dealership in Vancouver in 1961 and started Jim Pattison Lease. In 1965, he was awarded a licence to operate the Vancouver AM radio station, CJOR. In subsequent years he continued acquisitions across the country until today the Jim Pattison Group *<http://www.jimpattison.com>* is the second-largest private company in Canada. Headquartered in Vancouver, British Columbia, it is comprised of 545 locations worldwide focusing on the automotive, agriculture, media, packaging, food and beverage, magazine distribution, entertainment, export, and financial industries.[12] Do you recognize any of the company's food and beverage brands?

In Canada, corporations are divided into two classes: public and private. A **public corporation** has the right to issue stock (ownership in the company through shares) to the public, which means its shares may be listed on a stock exchange. This offers the possibility of raising large amounts of capital, regardless of the size of the company. That is, public corporations can be small and large companies.

public corporation
Corporation that has the right to issue shares to the public, so its shares may be listed on a stock exchange.

A **private corporation** is usually controlled by a small number of stockholders and its shares are not listed on a stock exchange.[13] (Go to Chapter 18 to learn how a stock exchange works.) This greatly reduces the costs of incorporating. Many small corporations are in the private category. This is the vehicle employed by individuals or partners who do not anticipate the need for substantial financing but want to take advantage of limited liability. Many large corporations are also registered as private corporations. Examples include Apple Canada *<http://www.apple.com/ca/>* (owned by Apple Inc.), and Ford Motor Company of Canada (owned by Ford Motor Company).

private corporation
Corporation that is usually controlled by a small number of shareholders and its shares are not listed on a stock exchange.

Chapman's Ice Cream <*http://www.chapmans.ca*> is a private corporation. Started in 1973 by Penny and David Chapman, it is Canada's largest independent ice cream manufacturer. What do you think is the world's most popular ice cream flavour?

CCPCs have some advantages over public corporations, especially from a taxation perspective. Advantages include the following: a CCPC is eligible for the small-business deduction and as a result, pays a lower rate of federal tax (small-business rate) on the first $500,000 of active business income; CCPCs have an additional month to pay taxes owed; and CCPCs are entitled to enhanced investment tax credits.[14]

Another important advantage for the owner of a private corporation is that he or she can issue stock to a child, or a spouse, making them co-owners of the company. This procedure is not available to a sole proprietor. It is a simple and useful way of recognizing the contribution of these or other family members, or employees, to the company. This procedure may also be a good way for the owner to prepare for retirement by gradually transferring ownership and responsibility to those who will be inheriting the business.

Keep in mind that with any kind of succession planning in private corporations, conflict may arise. In the mid-1990s, brothers Wallace and Harrison McCain of McCain Foods <*http://www.mccain.com*> were bitterly divided over who should be picked to lead the company when they were gone. Wallace wanted his son Michael to take over, while Harrison preferred outside management. The disagreement ultimately wound up in a New Brunswick court, which sided with Harrison. Ousted from the company, Wallace went to Toronto, where he took over Maple Leaf Foods with sons Michael and Scott.[15] The Adapting to Change box discusses some of the challenges associated with family businesses.

There is a formal procedure for forming a corporation that involves applying to the appropriate federal or provincial agency. It is always recommended that company owners seek the services of a competent lawyer and accountant prior to proceeding with any incorporation. The procedure for large or public corporations is much more complex and expensive and definitely requires hiring a legal firm. These costs can easily run into the thousands of dollars. Figure 6.3 describes various types of corporations.

Adapting *to* CHANGE

Challenges of Family Businesses

According to business-heir-turned-author Thomas William Deans, the biggest problem facing family business today is not the business, it is the family. He blames the parents, not the kids in his book, *Every Family's Business.* Mom and Dad's errors include not talking business at the dinner table, not including adult children in the decision-making process, just assuming that their kids want the business, and worst of all, "gifting" the business to their kids, where they do not appreciate it.

Management problems in a family-owned business are somewhat different from similar problems in non-family businesses. When close relatives work together, emotions often interfere with business decisions. When you put up your own money and operate your own business, you prize your independence. "It's my business," you tell yourself. However, "It's our business" in a family company.

Conflicts sometimes abound because relatives look upon the business from different viewpoints. Those relatives who are silent partners, shareholders, and directors may only see dollar signs when judging capital expenditures, growth, and other major matters. Relatives who are engaged in daily operations judge major matters from the viewpoint of the production, sales, and personnel necessary to make the company successful. Obviously, these two viewpoints may conflict in some instances. This natural conflict can be aggravated by family members who have no talent for money or business.

While the majority of family business owners would like to see their businesses transferred to the next generation, few survive the transition to the second generation. According to the Family Business Institute, only about 30 percent of family businesses survive into the second generation, 12 percent are still viable into the third generation, and only about 3 percent of all family businesses operate into the fourth generation or beyond.

Family business failures are primarily due to the lack of family business succession planning. The key to effective governance for a family business is recognizing when the family business is moving from one stage to another, such as from the controlling owner (i.e., the original owner) to a sibling partnership where siblings have an ownership interest and/or some family shareholders are not working in the business. By designing revisions to the governance structure that will meet the needs of the owners for the next stage, expectations and responsibilities are likely to be clearer, contributing to a more successful business venture.

Sources: "Succession Planning," Family Business Institute, [2015?], http://www.familybusinessinstitute.com/index.php /Succession-Planning/; "Succession Planning for Family Business," BDO Canada LLP, [2012?], www.bdo.ca/library/publications /familybusiness/succession/planning1.cfm; "Governance for the Family Business," KPMG in Canada, 2008, www.kpmg.ca /en/services/enterprise/issuesGrowthGovernance.html; "The Parent Trap," *PROFIT,* October 2008, 13; Grant Walsh, "Family Business Succession," KPMG LLP (Canada), 2008, www.kpmg.ca/en/services/enterprise/documents/3468_Succession.pdf; and "Problems in Managing a Family-Owned Business," Canada Business Network, 5 October 2005, www.canadabusiness.ca/servlet/Content Server?cid=1081945276597&pagename=CBSC_FE%2Fdisplay&lang=en&c=GuideFactSheet.

■ **FIGURE 6.3**

SOME CORPORATION TYPES
Corporations can fit in more than one category.
A benefit (B) corporation is certified to meet rigorous standards of social and environmental performance, accountability, and transparency. Review the Seeking Sustainability box for an example.
A Crown corporation is one that can only be registered by the provincial or federal government.
A domestic corporation conducts business in its home country (e.g., Canada only).
A multinational corporation is a firm that operates in several countries.
A non-profit (or not-for-profit) corporation is one that does not seek personal profit for its owners.
A private (closed) corporation is one whose shares are held by a few people and are not available to the general public.
A professional corporation is a private corporation whose owners provide professional services (e.g., accountants and architects).
A public (open) corporation sells shares to the general public.

Seeking SUSTAINABILITY

B Corporations Let Sustainability Set Sail

While vacationing on the small island of Tobago, Michael Dimin and his sons saw a nasty sight as their boat headed to dock after a day of fishing. Tons of rotting fish littered the water, left there by fishermen who caught too much to sell locally. That gave Dimin an idea: what if they sold the surplus fish directly to New York restaurants? After all, demand for fresh seafood would always be high at the city's many upscale eateries. Plus, with an outside market to sell to, fishermen in Tobago wouldn't need to waste so much of their catch.

Dimin knew this venture was likely to be profitable, but more than that he wanted ocean conservation and sustainability to be the driving force of the business. That's why he registered his company, Sea to Table <https://www.sea2table.com>, as a benefit corporation, or B corporation.

(continued)

(continued)

With this business structure, companies are certified to meet rigorous standards of social and environmental performance, accountability, and transparency. They are judged by how well they meet their own set of socially or environmentally beneficial goals. There is a growing community of more than 1,200 Certified B corporations from 38 countries and over 121 industries working together toward one unifying goal: to redefine success in business. In Canada, there are more than 120 B corporations.

For Sea to Table, being a B corporation means developing relationships with sustainable fisheries needing better access to markets, thus creating a direct connection between fishermen and chefs. This allows the company to keep its supply lines transparent while eliminating the costly middlemen. Not only do business models like this help society, but their compassionate goals tend to lure in some of the most talented people in the job market. It just goes to show that profits aren't the only way to measure success in the business world.

Sources: "What are B Corps?" B Lab, 24 February 2015, http://www.bcorporation.net; "Find a B Corp: Canada," B Lab, 24 February 2015, http://www.bcorporation.net/community/find-a-b-corp?search=&=Search1Companies&field_industry=&field_city=&field_state=&field_country=Canada; "Our Story," Sea to Table, 2014, www.sea2table.com; "Sean and Michael Dimin," Future of Fish, www.futureoffish.org, accessed February 2014; and Lindsay Gellman and Rachel Feintzeig, "Social Seal of Approval Lures Talent," *The Wall Street Journal,* 12 November 2013.

Advantages of Corporations

Most people are not willing to risk everything to go into business. Yet for businesses to grow, prosper, and create economic opportunity, many people need to invest money in them. One way to solve this problem is to create an artificial being, an entity that exists only in the eyes of the law—a corporation. This entity is a technique for involving people in business without risking their other personal assets.

A corporation has a separate legal identity from the owners—the shareholders—of the company and files its own tax returns. Let's explore some of the advantages of corporations:

1. *Limited liability.* A major advantage of corporations is the limited liability of owners. Remember, limited liability means that the owners of a business are responsible for losses only up to the amount they invest. Many corporations in Canada have the letters *Ltd.* after their name, which speaks to this limited liability. Others end their names with *Inc.* (for incorporated) or *Corp.* (for corporation) to indicate their status.

   Be aware that you should not incorporate if it is your intention to use this ownership form as a way to avoid your debts. As a sole proprietorship or partnership, the debts the business incurs remain personal liabilities even after they are taken over by a corporation. Legally, it is the status existing at the time the debts were incurred that governs, not what happens subsequently.

2. *Ability to raise more money for investment.* To raise money, a corporation can sell ownership (shares) to anyone who is interested. This way, thousands of people can own part of major companies such as Rogers Communications Inc., TD Bank Group *<http://www.td.com>*, Manulife Financial Corp., EnCana Corp. *<http://www.encana.com>*, Loblaw Companies Ltd. *<http://www.loblaw.ca>*, and smaller companies as well. If a company sold 1 million shares for $50 each, it would have $50 million available to build plants, buy materials, hire people, manufacture products, and so on. Such a large amount of money would be difficult to raise any other way.

   Corporations can also borrow money by obtaining loans from financial institutions like banks. They can also borrow from individual investors by issuing bonds, which involve paying investors interest until the bonds are repaid sometime in the future.[17] You can read about how corporations raise funds through the sale of shares and bonds in Chapter 17.

Companies can change their status over time as outlined in this example. The TDL Group, a private corporation, was the original owner of the Tim Hortons chain. It merged with Wendy's International, Inc. in 1995. In 2006, Wendy's sold 17 percent of the TDL Group to raise approximately $783 million. This money was used to repay debt owed by Wendy's. That same year, Tim Hortons was spun off as a separate company. In 2014, Burger King acquired Tim Hortons to create Restaurant Brands International, the third-largest fast-food chain in the world.[16]

3. *Size.* That one word summarizes many of the advantages of some corporations. Because they can raise large amounts of money to work with, big corporations can build modern factories or software development facilities with the latest equipment. They can hire experts or specialists in all areas of operation. They can buy other corporations in different fields to diversify their business risks. (What this means is that a corporation can be involved in many businesses at once so that if one is not doing well, the negative impact on the total corporation is lessened.) In short, a large corporation with numerous resources can take advantage of opportunities anywhere in the world.

   When one considers size, different criteria can be used. This can include the number of employees, revenues, assets, and profits. Note that corporations do not have to be large to enjoy the benefits of incorporation. Professionals (such as physicians and lawyers) can incorporate. Individuals and partnerships can also incorporate. Figure 6.4 lists some of Canada's largest corporations.

4. *Perpetual life.* Because corporations are separate from those who own them, the death of one or more owners does not terminate the corporation.

5. *Ease of ownership change.* It is easy to change the owners of a corporation. All that is necessary is to sell the shares to someone else.

6. *Ease of attracting talented employees.* Corporations can attract skilled employees by offering benefits such as a pension plan, dental plan, and stock options (the right to purchase shares of the corporation for a fixed price). To be competitive, sole proprietorships and partnerships may offer money or other benefits to compete with such plans. Benefits will be discussed in Chapter 12.

7. *Separation of ownership from management.* **Corporate governance** refers to the process and policies that determine how an organization interacts with its stakeholders. Rules outline how the organization is to be managed by the board of directors and the officers. Corporate governance is necessary because of the evolution of public ownership. In public corporations, unlike sole proprietorships and partnerships, there is a separation between ownership and management.[18] As a result, the board of directors was created.

corporate governance
The process and policies that determine how an organization interacts with its stakeholders, both internal and external.

■ **FIGURE 6.4**

CANADA'S LARGEST CORPORATIONS (2014)			
A. PUBLIC CORPORATIONS BASED ON PROFIT			
Rank	**Company**	**Profit ($ billions)**	**Category**
1	Royal Bank of Canada	8.91	Banks
2	Toronto-Dominion Bank	7.78	Banks
3	Bank of Nova Scotia	7.07	Banks
4	Bank of Montreal	4.28	Banks
5	Canadian Natural Resources	3.93	Oil & Gas Producers
B. PRIVATE CORPORATIONS BASED ON REVENUE			
Rank	**Company**	**Revenue ($ billions)**	**Category**
1	Walmart Canada	23.81	Retailers
2	Costco Wholesale Canada	17.94	Retailers
3	Desjardins Group	17.13	Financial Services
4	Honda Canada	16.62	Automotive
5	Rio Tinto Alcan Inc.	12.12	Mining
C. NON-PROFIT ORGANIZATIONS BASED ON REVENUE			
Rank	**Company**	**Revenue ($ billions)**	**Category**
1	Alberta Health Services	12.52	Health Organizations
2	Vancouver Coastal Health Authority	3.09	Hospitals
3	Toronto District School Board	2.99	Education Institutions
4	Fraser Health Authority	2.96	Health Organizations
5	Governing Council of the University of Toronto	2.68	Education Institutions

Sources: "Top 1000: Exclusive rankings of Canada's most profitable companies," *The Globe and Mail,* 30 June 2015, http://www.theglobeandmail.com /report-on-business/rob-magazine/top-1000/rankings/top-1000-exclusive-rankings-of-canadas-most-profitable-companies/article25010984/; "Canada's 50 biggest private companies," *The Globe and Mail,* 24 June 2015, http://www.theglobeandmail.com/report-on-business/rob-magazine/top-1000/rankings /canadas-50-biggest-private-companies/article25020836/; and "Canada's top 100 non-profit organizations (registered charities)," *The Globe and Mail,* 11 February 2015, http://www.theglobeandmail.com/report-on-business/rob-magazine/top-100-non-profit-organizations-registered-charities/article17298702/.

The board assumes many of the same responsibilities that would typically rest with the sole proprietor, partners, or owners of a private corporation. Board members are often chosen based on their business experience and level of expertise. Those who serve on boards (both for-profit and non-profit) may be held personally liable for the misconduct of the organization. Having directors insurance is one way to try to limit this risk. Risk will be discussed in Appendix C.

The corporate hierarchy in Figure 6.5 shows how the owners/shareholders are separate from the managers and employees. The owners/shareholders elect a board of directors, who in turn hire the officers of the corporation that oversee major policy issues. The owners/shareholders thus have some say in who runs the corporation but have no real control over the daily operations (e.g., setting the price for a product).[19]

■ **FIGURE 6.5**

HOW OWNERS AFFECT MANAGEMENT

Owners have an influence on how business is managed by electing a board of directors. The board hires the top officers (and fires them if necessary). It also sets the pay for those officers. The officers then select other managers and employees with the help of the human resource department.

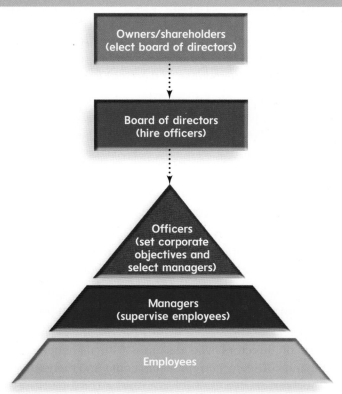

As a result of corporate scandals, board members are under increasing scrutiny to ensure that they are effectively fulfilling their roles and responsibilities to their stakeholders. Consequently, companies continue to review their practices by answering questions such as, "Is the board independent from its officers? Does the company have a statement of corporate governance practices? To truly represent the shareholders, are directors elected every year?"

Disadvantages of Corporations

There are so many sole proprietorships and partnerships in Canada that there must be some disadvantages to incorporation. Otherwise, more people would incorporate their businesses. The following are a few of the disadvantages.

1. *Initial cost.* Incorporation may cost thousands of dollars and involve the services of lawyers and accountants.

2. *Extensive paperwork.* The paperwork filed to start a corporation is just the beginning. A sole proprietor or a partnership may keep rather broad accounting records. A corporation, in contrast, must keep detailed financial records, the minutes of meetings, and more.

3. *Double taxation.* Corporate income is taxed twice. First the corporation pays tax on income before it can distribute any, as *dividends,* to shareholders. Then the shareholders pay tax on the dividends they receive from the corporation. While this is *double* taxation, it is not excessive taxation, as the tax system is designed to provide some offsetting credits such as the dividend tax credit for investors.

4. *Two tax returns.* An individual who incorporates must file both a corporate tax return and an individual tax return. Depending on the size of the corporation, a corporate return can be quite complex and require the assistance of an accountant (e.g., a chartered professional accountant).

5. *Size.* Size may be one advantage of corporations, but it can be a disadvantage as well. Large corporations sometimes become too inflexible and tied down in red tape (i.e., have to follow many regulations) to respond quickly to market changes, and their profitability can suffer.

6. *Difficulty of termination.* Once a corporation has started, it is relatively difficult to end. Legal procedures are costly and more complex than for unincorporated companies.

7. *Possible conflict with shareholders and their board of directors.* Some conflict may brew if the shareholders elect a board of directors who disagree with management.[20] Since the board of directors chooses the company's officers, entrepreneurs could find themselves forced out of the very company they founded. This happened to Tom Freston, one of the founders of MTV.

Some business people are discouraged by the costs, paperwork, and special taxes that corporations must pay. However, many others believe that the advantages of incorporation outweigh the challenges. Figure 6.6 compares the three main types of organizations.

Business Regulations

Companies that wish to operate in Canada must follow federal and provincial/territorial business laws and regulations. Among other things, this applies to registration and to reporting and information.

REGISTRATION

Governments need to know what businesses are in operation to ensure that a wide range of laws and regulations are being followed. Guaranteeing that the names of businesses are not duplicated is important to avoid confusion. Additionally, governments have to be sure that taxes are being paid. To ensure these and other goals, every company must register its business. This is a simple, routine, and inexpensive procedure.

Companies wanting to incorporate must fill out articles of incorporation and file these with the appropriate provincial/territorial or federal authority. **Articles of incorporation** are a legal authorization from the federal or provincial/territorial government for a company to use the corporate format.

■ **FIGURE 6.6**

COMPARISON OF FORMS OF BUSINESS OWNERSHIP					
		PARTNERSHIPS		CORPORATION	
	Sole Proprietorship	General Partnership	Limited* Partnership	Public Corporation	Private Corporation
Documents Needed to Start Business	None, may need permit or licence	Partnership agreement (oral or written)	Written agreement; must file certificate of limited partnership	Articles of incorporation, bylaws	Articles of incorporation, bylaws; must meet criteria
Ease of Termination	Easy to terminate: just pay debts and quit	May be hard to terminate, depending on the partnership agreement	Same as general partnership	Hard and expensive to terminate	Not difficult; pay off debts, sell off assets, withdraw cash, and pay taxes
Length of Life	Terminates on the death of owner, sale, or retirement	Terminates on the death or withdrawal of partner	Same as general partnership	Perpetual life	Perpetual life
Transfer of Ownership	Business can be sold to qualified buyer	Must have agreement of other partner(s)	Same as general partnership	Easy to change owners; just sell shares	Easy—just sell shares†
Financial Resources	Limited to owner's capital and loans	Limited to partners' capital and loans	Same as general partnership	More money to start and operate: sell stock and bonds; loans	Owners' capital and loans; no public stock issue allowed
Risk of Losses	Unlimited liability	Unlimited liability	Limited liability	Limited liability	Limited liability
Taxes	Taxed as personal income	Taxed as personal income	Same as general partnership	Corporate, double taxation	Same as public corporation
Management Responsibilities	Owner manages all areas of the business	Partners share management	Cannot participate in management	Separate management from ownership	Owners usually manage all areas
Employee Benefits	Usually fewer benefits and lower wages	Often fewer benefits and lower wages; promising employee could become a partner	Same as general partnership	Usually better benefits and wages, advancement opportunities	Same as public corporation

* There must be at least one general partner who manages the partnership and has unlimited liability.
† Unless the agreement specifies otherwise.

The main advantage of being a federally incorporated company is that incorporation gives the company name added protection and guarantees its usage across Canada. Depending on the type of business you are considering, you may be required to incorporate federally.

articles of incorporation
A legal authorization from the federal or provincial/territorial government for a company to use the corporate format.

REPORTING AND INFORMATION

Businesses receive many documents from the different levels of government during the course of a year. Some are just information about changes in employment insurance, the Canada or Quebec Pension Plan, or tax legislation as it affects them or their employees. Then there are various forms that all companies must complete so that governments can compile statistical reports that businesses, individuals, research organizations, and governments need to operate effectively. For example, Statistics Canada maintains vast databases and creates useful reports from this information.

All public corporations must file annual reports containing basic data about themselves. An annual report should include the name of the officers, how many shares have been issued, and the head office location. Of course, every corporation must also file an annual tax return containing financial statements and pay the necessary taxes during the year. Review Chapter 16 for examples of financial statements.

Progress Assessment

- What are the major advantages and disadvantages of incorporating a business?
- What is the role of owners (shareholders) in the corporate hierarchy?
- If you buy shares in a corporation and someone is injured by one of the corporation's products, can you be sued? Why or why not?

LO4 Outline the advantages and disadvantages of franchising. Include the challenges of global franchising.

Franchising

In addition to the three basic forms of business ownership, there are two special forms: franchising and co-operatives. Let's look at franchises first. A **franchise agreement** is an arrangement whereby someone with a good idea for a business (the **franchisor**) sells the rights to use the business name and to sell a good or service (the **franchise**) to others (the **franchisee**) in a given territory. As you might suspect, both franchisors and franchisees have a stake in the success of the franchise.

franchise agreement
An arrangement whereby someone with a good idea for a business sells the rights to use the business name and sell its goods and services in a given territory.

franchisor
A company that develops a product concept and sells others the rights to make and sell the products.

franchise
The right to use a specific business's name and sell its goods or services in a given territory.

franchisee
A person who buys a franchise.

Some people, uncomfortable with the idea of starting their own business, would rather join a business with a proven track record through a franchise agreement. A franchise can be formed as a sole proprietorship, a partnership, or a corporation.

Some students mistakenly identify franchising as an industry. It is not a specific industry. Rather, franchising is a business model; it is a method of distributing a good or service, or both, to achieve a maximum market impact with a minimum investment. It is not a separate form of business ownership from those already summarized in Figure 6.6, and it does not replace a form of business. How the franchisee sets up the franchise business (i.e., sole proprietorship, partnership, or corporation) and operates it, however, is dependent on the advantages and disadvantages of each form of business ownership.

Often, what looks like a chain of stores—Home Hardware Stores Ltd. <*http://www.homehardware.ca*>, Quiznos <*http://www.quiznos.com*>, and Great Canadian Dollar Stores <*http://www.dollarstores.com*>—is usually a franchise operation with each unit owned by a different person or company. (There are also corporate locations owned by the franchisor.) Sometimes one person or group may own and operate more than one franchise unit. Regardless of the form of business ownership (e.g., partnership), all units are part of a franchise operation. In the following pages you will see the advantages and disadvantages of this type of business operation, and you will learn what to consider before buying a franchise unit.

Promoted as Canada's premium juice and smoothie chain, Booster Juice <*http://www.boosterjuice.com*> operates over 320 franchised locations in five countries.[21] Would you be interested in purchasing a franchise? If not this one, what type of good or service franchise might appeal to you as a business owner?

According to the Canadian Franchise Association, there are over 78,000 franchise units across Canada and they employ more than one million people. Franchised businesses account for 40 percent of all retail sales and they have been reported to account for one out of every five consumer dollars spent in Canada on goods and services.[22] You may be familiar with food franchises (e.g., Dairy Queen, Swiss Chalet <*http://www.swisschalet.com*>, Kelsey's <*http://www.kelseys.ca*>, and Pizza Pizza <*http://www.pizzapizza.ca*>) and non-food franchises (e.g., Oxford Learning <*http://www.oxfordlearning.com*>, Mr. Lube Canada <*http://www.mrlube.com*>, Molly Maid, and First Choice Haircutters <*http://www.firstchoice.com*>). Have you ever considered owning one of these? Review Figure 6.7 for some tips in evaluating franchises.

Advantages of Franchises

Franchising has penetrated every aspect of Canadian and global business life by offering goods and services that are reliable, convenient, and competitively priced. The worldwide growth of franchising could not have been accomplished by accident. Franchising clearly has some advantages.

1. *Management and marketing assistance.* Compared with someone who starts a new business, a franchisee usually has a much greater chance of succeeding because he or she has an established

■ **FIGURE 6.7**

BUYING A FRANCHISE

Since buying a franchise is a major investment, be sure to check out a company's financial strength before you get involved. A good source of information about evaluating a franchise deal is the handbook "Investigate Before Investing," available from International Franchise Association Publications.

Checklist for Evaluating a Franchise

The Franchise

Did your lawyer approve the franchise contract you're considering after he or she studied it paragraph by paragraph?

Does the franchise give you an exclusive territory for the length of the franchise?

Under what circumstances can you terminate the franchise contract and at what cost to you?

If you sell your franchise, will you be compensated for your goodwill (the value of your business's reputation and other intangibles)?

If the franchisor sells the company, will your investment be protected?

The Franchisor

How many years has the firm offering you a franchise been in operation?

Does it have a reputation for honesty and fair dealing among the local firms holding its franchise?

Has the franchisor shown you any certified figures indicating exact net profits of one or more going firms that you personally checked yourself with the franchisee? Ask for the company's disclosure statement.

Will the firm assist you with:

A management training program? An employee training program?

A public relations program?

Capital?

Credit?

Merchandising ideas?

Will the firm help you find a good location for your new business?

Has the franchisor investigated you carefully enough to assure itself that you can successfully operate one of its franchises at a profit both to itself and to you?

You, the Franchisee

How much capital will you need to purchase the franchise and operate it until your income equals your expenses?

Does the franchisor offer financing for a portion of the franchising fees? On what terms?

Are you prepared to give up some independence of action to secure the advantages offered by the franchise?

Do you have your family's support?

Does the industry appeal to you? Are you ready to spend much or all of the remainder of your business life with this franchisor, offering its product or service to the public?

Your Market

Have you made any study to determine whether the product or service that you propose to sell under the franchise has a market in your territory at the prices you'll have to charge?

Will the population in the territory given to you increase, remain static, or decrease over the next five years?

Will demand for the product or service you're considering be greater, about the same, or less five years from now than it is today?

What competition already exists in your territory for the product or service you contemplate selling?

Source: U.S. Department of Commerce, Franchise Opportunities Handbook; and Steve Adams, "Buying a Brand," Patriot Ledger (Quincy, MA), 1 March 2008.

product to sell, help choosing a location, and assistance in all phases of promotion and operation. It is like having your own store but with full-time consultants when you need them. Franchisors usually provide intensive management training, since they want the franchisees to succeed. For example, franchisor Boston Pizza International Inc. <*http://www.bostonpizza.com*> provides an extensive seven-week training program for new franchisees and their management teams. In-store staff training begins two weeks prior to opening with the arrival of four corporate trainers who teach Boston Pizza's successful systems to staff and management. These trainers stay on to provide support for two weeks post-opening, at which point the restaurant is assigned a Field Services Manager for dedicated operational support.[23]

Some franchisors help their franchisees with local marketing efforts rather than having franchisees depend solely on national advertising. Franchisees also have a network of fellow franchisees facing similar problems who can share their experiences. The goal is to support franchisees however possible. For example, The UPS Store <*http://www.theupsstore.com*> provides its franchisees with a software program that helps them build customer databases along with quick and personal one-on-one phone support and e-mail support.[24]

2. *Personal ownership.* A franchise operation is still your business, and you enjoy many of the incentives and profit of any sole proprietor. You are still your own boss, although you must follow more rules, regulations, and procedures than you would with your own independent business.

3. *Nationally recognized name.* It is one thing to open a gift shop or ice cream store. It is quite another to open a new Hallmark store *<http://www.hallmark.ca>* or a Baskin-Robbins *<http://www.baskin robbins.ca>*. With an established franchise, you get instant recognition and support from an experienced product group with customers around the world.

4. *Financial advice and assistance.* Two major problems for small-business owners are arranging financing and learning to keep good records. Franchisees get valuable assistance and periodic advice from people with expertise in these areas. In fact, some franchisors will even provide financing to potential franchisees they believe will be valuable partners of the franchise system.

5. *Lower failure rate.* Historically, the failure rate for franchises has been lower than that of other business ventures. This is one reason why Canadians find them so attractive. However, franchising has grown so rapidly that many weak franchises have entered the field, so you need to be careful and invest wisely.[25]

To become a Canadian Tire Associate Dealer, successful candidates must be well-rounded individuals who have a positive attitude for success and the passion and dedication necessary to excel. Self-motivation is key. Along with a good mix of experience and personal characteristics, candidates must be willing to make a personal and financial investment—a minimum of $125,000 of accessible capital—to become a Dealer.[26] Does this franchise interest you?

Disadvantages of Franchises

There are some potential pitfalls to franchising. Disadvantages of franchising include the following:

1. *Large start-up costs.* Most franchises will demand a fee for the rights to the franchise. Fees for franchises can vary considerably. Start-up costs for a Kumon Math and Reading Centre *<http://www.kumon.ca>* include $1,000 for the franchise fee and a minimum investment ranging from $62,000 to $158,000.[27] But if you want to own a Keg Steakhouse and Bar *<http://www.kegsteakhouse .com>*, you will need more money. The franchise fee is $50,000 and capital requirements range from $3.0 to $4.5 million.[28]

2. *Shared profit.* The franchisor often demands either a large share of the profits in addition to the start-up fees or a percentage commission based on sales, not profit. This share is called a *royalty*. For example, if a franchisor demands a 10-percent royalty on a franchise's net sales, 10 cents of every dollar the franchisee collects (before taxes and other expenses) must be paid to the franchisor.[29]

3. *Management regulation.* Management "assistance" has a way of becoming managerial orders, directives, and limitations. Franchisees feeling burdened by the company's rules and regulations may lose the spirit and incentive of being their own boss with their own business. Often franchisees will band together to resolve their grievances with franchisors rather than each fighting their battles alone. Tim Hortons franchise owners mounted a $2-billion lawsuit where they accused the franchisor of (1) gouging them under the company's new way of making doughnuts and (2) requiring them to sell new lunch menu items at break-even prices or sometimes at a loss.[30] The judge rejected the lawsuit saying the franchisor was well within its rights to implement new procedures and technologies to its business model.[31]

4. *Coattail effects.* The actions of other franchisees have an impact on your future growth and profitability. Due to this *coattail effect*, you could be forced out of business even if your particular franchise has been profitable. This can be due to the failure of other franchisees and/or their actions. For example, McDonald's and Subway *<http://www.subway.com>* franchisees complain that due to the company's relentless growth, some new stores have taken business away from existing locations, squeezing franchisees' profits per outlet.

5. *Restrictions on selling.* Unlike owners of private businesses, who can sell their companies to whomever they choose on their own terms, many franchisees face restrictions in the reselling of their franchises. To control quality, franchisors often insist on approving the new owners, who must meet their standards.

6. *Fraudulent franchisors.* Contrary to common belief, most franchisors are not large systems like McDonald's or Subway. Most franchisors are honest, but there has been an increase in complaints about franchisors that deliver little or nothing of what they promised. Before you buy a franchise, make certain you check out the facts fully.

E-Commerce in Franchising

The Internet has changed franchising in many ways. Most brick-and-mortar franchises have expanded their businesses online and created virtual storefronts to deliver increased value to customers. Franchisees like Carole Shutts, a Rocky Mountain Chocolate Factory *<http://www.rockychoc.com>* franchisee, increased her sales by setting up her own website. Many franchisors, however, prohibit franchisee-sponsored websites because conflicts can erupt if the franchisor creates its own website. Sometimes franchisors send "reverse royalties" to franchisees who believe their sales were hurt by the franchisor's online sales, but that doesn't always bring about peace. Before buying a franchise, read the small print regarding online sales.

Today potential franchisees can make a choice between starting an online business or a business requiring an office or storefront outside of the home. Quite often the decision comes down to financing. Traditional bricks-and-mortar franchises require finding real estate and often require a high franchise fee. Online franchises, like *Printinginabox.com <http://www.printinginabox.com>*, charge no up-front franchise fee and require little training to start a business. Franchisees pay only a set monthly fee. Online franchises also do not set exclusive territories limiting where the franchisee can compete. An online franchisee can literally compete against the world.

Franchisors often use technology, including social media, to extent their brands, to meet the needs of both their customers and their franchisees, and even to expand their businesses. Formed in Moncton, New Brunswick, PropertyGuys.com *<http://propertyguys.com>* has built on the "For Sale by Owner (FSBO)" Internet concept. The company offers a high tech/high touch service delivered by its expert online PGPros (also known as the local franchise operator), innovative real estate brokers to connect clients to realtor.ca, certified professional appraisers, a unique answering and appointment booking service, and access to real-estate lawyers.[32]

Home-Based Franchises

Home-based businesses offer many obvious advantages, including relief from the stress of commuting, extra time for family activities, and low overhead expenses. One disadvantage is the feeling of isolation; however, home-based franchisees feel less isolated than independent business owners. Experienced franchisors often share their knowledge of building a profitable enterprise with other franchisees. Today you can be a franchisee in areas ranging from cleaning services to tax preparation, child care, pet care, cruise planning, or direct mail services.[33] Before investing in a home-based franchise, it is helpful to ask yourself the following questions: Are you willing to put in long hours? Can you work in a solitary environment? Are you motivated and well organized? Does your home have the space you need for the business? Can your home also be the place you work? It's also important to check out the franchisor carefully.

Franchising in International Markets

Franchising today is truly a global effort. Canadian franchisors are counting their profits in euros, yuan, pesos, won, krona, baht, yen, and many other currencies. What makes franchising successful in international markets is what makes it successful domestically: convenience and a predictable level of service and quality. Because of proximity and language, the United States is by far the most popular target for Canadian-based franchises.

Holiday Inn's InterContinential Amstel hotel in Amsterdam has been celebrated as the Netherlands' most beautiful and luxurious hotel. Holiday Inn franchises try to complement the environment of the area they serve. This hotel is on the crossroads of Amsterdam's financial and exclusive shopping districts. What do you think would have been the reaction if Holiday Inn <http://www.holidayinn.com> built the typical Canadian-style hotel in this area?

Franchisors, though, must be careful and do their homework before entering into global franchise agreements. Three questions to ask before forming a global franchise are: Will your intellectual property be protected? Can you give proper support to global partners? Are you able to adapt to franchise regulations in other countries? If the answer is yes to all three questions, global franchising creates great opportunities. In 1986, brothers Michael and Aaron Serruya, then aged 19 and 20, wanted to buy a franchise, but no one would take a chance on them. So, they started their own frozen yogourt shop, Yogen Früz, in Toronto, Ontario. Today, Yogen Früz has grown to be a world leader in the frozen yogourt category, with over 1,400 locations operating in 46 countries around the world.[34]

LO5 Describe the role of co-operatives in Canada.

Co-Operatives[35]

Some people dislike the notion of having owners, managers, workers, and buyers as separate individuals with separate goals, so they have formed co-operatives, a different kind of organization to meet their needs for child care, housing, food, and financial services. A **co-operative (co-op)** is an organization owned and controlled by people—producers, consumers, or workers—with similar needs who pool their resources for mutual gain. Co-operatives are locally owned and democratically controlled by the members who use their services. They are founded on the common idea that people know what's best for them and can work together to achieve their goals. Boards of directors are elected by members and can be removed if they fail to deliver on the overall vision members have agreed on.

> **co-operative (co-op)**
> An organization owned and controlled by people—producers, consumers, or workers—with similar needs who pool their resources for mutual gain.

Some co-operatives are made up of members who actually make the product being sold, such as Gay Lea Foods <http://www.gaylea.com>, the second-largest dairy co-operative in Canada, which is owned by over 1,200 dairy farmers. Others are worker-owned co-operatives, which are self-managed by employees who directly hire and fire their managers.

One of Canada's best known co-operatives, Mountain Equipment Co-operative (MEC <http://www.mec.ca>), was formed in Vancouver, British Columbia, in 1971. MEC started with $65 in capital and a goal of providing affordable, good-quality climbing gear to an underserved mountaineering community. MEC is now Canada's largest retailer co-operative in terms of membership. Credit unions are another well-known example of the co-operative model. In fact, Canada has the world's largest per-capita credit-union membership in the world.

In their over one-hundred year history in Canada, co-operatives represent a large and diverse heritage of Canadians working together to build better communities based upon co-operative principles. These principles differ from other business principles in several ways:

- *A different purpose.* Co-operatives meet the common needs of their members, whereas most investor-owned businesses exist to maximize profit for their shareholders. Figure 6.8 summarizes some of the philosophical and community benefits of co-operatives.

- *A different control structure.* Co-operatives use a system of one-member/one-vote, not the one-vote-per-share system used by most businesses. This helps the co-operatives serve the common need rather than the individual need.

- *A different allocation of profit.* Co-operatives share profits among their member-owners on the basis of how much they use the organization, not on how many shares they hold. Profits tend to be invested in improving services for the members.

■ **FIGURE 6.8**

SOME CO-OPERATIVE BENEFITS	
Philosophical Benefits	**Community Benefits**
People trump money in terms of priorities	Ability to change things that do not work
Greater community autonomy	Fair market prices
Product and service development by the people for the people	Strong customer/client loyalty
Opportunities to strengthen community bonds by helping one another	Greater employment opportunities
You can define your own needs instead of letting a conglomerate do it for you	Better access to quality products and services
Modest savings for all instead of the excessive accumulation of profits by a few	Economic and social growth in the community

Source: "The Co-Operative Advantage," CoopZone Developers' Network Co-operative, accessed 28 February 2015, http://coopzone.coop.

Since co-operatives distribute their profits to members as a reduction in members' costs, these profits are not subject to income tax. From time to time, various business organizations assert that many co-operatives are now more like large businesses and should be taxed. So far, this viewpoint does not appear to have extensive support.

Canada's 8,500 co-operatives and credit unions have more than 17 million members. Figure 6.9 provides a breakdown of the number of co-operatives by area of activity. Housing co-operatives form the largest category, followed by agricultural co-operatives, and then credit unions and *caisses populaires*. You can infer that co-operatives can be found in many industries. The co-operative model has a long history and a proven track record in social and economic development, having served thousands of groups in both urban and rural areas. They are especially important to many rural and remote communities. In some communities, co-operatives are the only providers of retail and financial services, health and home care services, communications and utility services, tourism facilities, and other basic amenities.

Which Form of Ownership Is Best for You?

You can build your own business in a variety of ways. You can start your own sole proprietorship, partnership, or corporation. Or, you can buy a franchise and be part of a larger corporation. Co-operatives are corporations that usually have a different motivation than traditional for-profit businesses. There are advantages and disadvantages to each. However, there are risks no matter which form you choose. Before you decide which form is best for you, you need to evaluate all of the alternatives carefully.

Progress Assessment

- What are some of the factors to consider before buying a franchise?
- What opportunities are available for starting a global franchise?
- What is a co-operative? How does it differ from a for-profit organization?

■ **FIGURE 6.9**

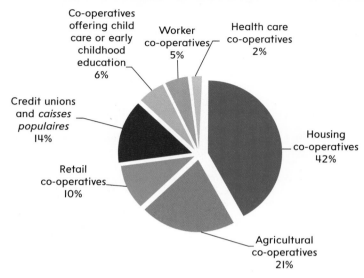

CO-OPERATIVES IN CANADA BY AREA OF ACTIVITY

Co-operatives offering child care or early childhood education 6%

Worker co-operatives 5%

Health care co-operatives 2%

Credit unions and *caisses populaires* 14%

Housing co-operatives 42%

Retail co-operatives 10%

Agricultural co-operatives 21%

Source: Courtesy of Canadian Co-operative Association, The Power of Co-operation: Co-operatives and Credit Unions in Canada, Ottawa. Used with permission.

SUMMARY

LO1 **List the advantages and disadvantages of sole proprietorships.**

A business owned, and usually managed, by one person is called a sole proprietorship.

What are the advantages and disadvantages of sole proprietorships?

The advantages of sole proprietorships include ease of starting and ending the business, being your own boss, pride of ownership, retention of profits, no special taxes, and less regulation than for corporations. The disadvantages include unlimited liability, limited financial resources, difficulty in management, overwhelming time commitment, few fringe benefits, limited growth, limited lifespan, and the possibility of paying higher taxes depending on the level of income.

LO2 **Describe the advantages and disadvantages of partnerships. Include the differences between general and limited partners.**

When two or more parties legally agree to become co-owners of a business, a partnership is formed.

What are the advantages and disadvantages of partnerships?

The advantages include more financial resources, shared management and pooled knowledge, longer survival than sole proprietorships, and less regulation than corporations. The disadvantages include unlimited liability, division of profits, possible disagreements among partners, difficulty of termination, and the possibility of paying higher taxes depending on the level of income.

What are the main differences between general and limited partners?

General partners are owners (partners) who have unlimited liability and are active in managing the company. Limited partners are owners (partners) who have limited liability and are not active in the company.

LO3 **Discuss the advantages and disadvantages of corporations.**

A corporation is a legal entity with authority to act and have liability separate from its owners.

What are the advantages and disadvantages of corporations?

The advantages include more money for investment, limited liability, size, perpetual life, ease of ownership change, ease of drawing talented employees, and separation of ownership from management. The disadvantages include initial costs, paperwork, size, difficulty of termination, double taxation, and possible conflict with a board of directors.

What are some categories of corporations?

Figure 6.3 lists some corporation types. Organization types include benefit, Crown, domestic, multinational, private, professional, and public.

LO4 **Outline the advantages and disadvantages of franchising. Include the challenges of global franchising.**

A franchise agreement is an arrangement whereby the franchisor sells the rights to use the business name and to sell a good or service (the franchise) to others (the franchisee) in a given territory.

What are the benefits and drawbacks of being a franchisee?

The benefits include a nationally recognized name and reputation, a proven management system, promotional assistance, and pride of ownership. Drawbacks include high franchise fees, managerial regulation, shared profits, and transfer of adverse effects if other franchisees fail.

What is the major challenge to global franchises?

It may be difficult to transfer an idea or product that worked well in Canada to another culture. It is essential to adapt to the region.

LO5 **Describe the role of co-operatives in Canada.**

A co-operative is an organization that is owned and controlled by people with similar needs who pool their resources for mutual gain.

What is the role of a co-operative?

Co-operatives are organizations owned by members/customers. Some people form co-operatives to give members more economic power than they would have as individuals. Small businesses often form co-operatives to give them more purchasing, marketing, or product development strength.

How do co-operatives' principles differ from other business principles?

Co-operatives have a different purpose, control structure, and allocation of profit than traditional for-profit businesses. Review Figure 6.8 for a discussion of co-operative benefits.

KEY TERMS

articles of incorporation	franchisor	limited partnership
co-operative (co-op)	general partner	partnership
corporate governance	general partnership	partnership agreement
corporation	limited liability	private corporation
franchise	limited liability partnership	public corporation
franchise agreement	(LLP)	sole proprietorship
franchisee	limited partner	unlimited liability

CRITICAL THINKING

1. Have you ever dreamed of opening your own business? If so, what kind of business? Could you start such a business in your own home? How much would it cost to start? Could you begin the business part-time while you attend school? What satisfaction and profit could you get from owning your own business? What could you lose? (Be aware that you must be careful not to use a name for your business that has already been used or registered by someone else. You may face some local restrictions and licence requirements if you operate from your residence such as requiring to have a certain number of parking spaces for your clients, having a limit on the size and type of vehicle and signage permitted, etc.)

2. Is it accurate to say that franchisees have the true entrepreneurial spirit? Could you see yourself as a franchisee or franchisor? Which one? Do you have an idea that you think could eventually grow into a franchise? Explain.

DEVELOPING WORKPLACE SKILLS

Key: ● **Team**   ★ **Analytic**   ▲ **Communication**   ☐ **Technology**

● ☐ ▲ ★ 1. Research businesses in your area and identify two companies that use the following forms of ownership: sole proprietorship, partnership, and corporation. Arrange interviews with managers from each form of ownership and get their impressions about their businesses. (If you are able to work with a team of fellow students, divide the interviews among team members.) Some questions that you might ask include: How much did it cost to start this business? How many hours do you work? What are some drawbacks that you have encountered with the way your business is set up (i.e., business form), if any? What are the specific benefits of this business form? Share the results with your class.

● ▲ ★ 2. Have you thought about starting your own business? What opportunities seem attractive? Think of a friend or friends whom you might want as a partner or partners in the business. List all of the financial resources and personal skills you will need to launch the business. Then make separate lists of the personal skills and the financial resources that you and your friend(s) might bring to your new venture. How much capital and what personal skills do you need but lack? Develop an action plan to obtain them.

▲ ★ 3. Let's assume you want to open one of the following new businesses. What form of business ownership would you choose for each business? Why?

    a.   Wedding planning service

    b.   Software development firm

    c.   Online bookstore

    d.   Dog grooming service

▢ ★ 4. Find out how much it costs to incorporate a company in your province or territory. Then compare it to the cost of federal incorporation. Is there a significant difference? Why might you choose not to incorporate federally?

▢ ★ 5. Find information online about a business co-operative (e.g., Vancouver City Savings Credit Union, Welch's, etc.). Research how it was formed, who can belong to it, and how it operates.

ANALYZING MANAGEMENT DECISIONS

Going Public

George Zegoyan and Amir Gupta face a difficult decision. Their private auto parts manufacturing company has been a great success—too quickly. They cannot keep up with the demand for their product. They must expand their facilities, but have not had time to accumulate sufficient working capital, nor do they want to acquire long-term debt to finance the expansion. Discussions with their accountants, lawyers, and stockbrokers have confronted them with the necessity of going public to raise the required capital.

Zegoyan and Gupta are concerned about maintaining control if they become a public company. They are also worried about loss of privacy because of the required reporting to various regulatory bodies and to their shareholders. Naturally, they are also pleased that the process will enable them to sell some of their shareholdings to the public and realize a fair profit from their past and expected future successes. They will be able to sell 40 percent of the shares for $500,000, which is ten times their total investment in the company. It will also allow them to raise substantial new capital to meet the needs of their current expansion program.

The proposed new structure will allow them to retain 60 percent of the outstanding voting shares, so they will keep control of the company. Nevertheless, they are somewhat uneasy about taking this step, because it will change the nature of the company and the informal method of operating they are used to. They are concerned about having "partners" in their operations and profits. They are wondering whether they should remain as they are and try to grow more slowly, even if it means giving up profitable orders.

Discussion Questions

1. Do they have any other options besides going public? Is the franchise route a viable option? Explain.

2. Do you think they should try to limit their growth to a manageable size to avoid going public, even if it means forgoing profits now? Why?

3. Would you advise them to sell their business now if they can get a good price and then start a new operation? Explain.

VIDEO CASE 6

Java Nook

Annette Lavigne, mother of six, is starting a business selling coffee with her new life and business partner, John Welter. Apart from a few jobs at minimum wage, Lavigne has spent the last twenty years at home with her children. Armed with a high school "how-to course" in business, Lavigne is becoming a first-time business owner in one of the riskiest service businesses given that as many as 40 percent of new restaurants close within two years.

The partners find a low-rent location for their small café and are hoping for sales of $400 a day to start when they open. We learn of some of the challenges that they face as their opening date keeps getting pushed back. Starting the venture with $20,000 that Lavigne received in an accident settlement, they soon realize that they have underestimated both the amount of money and time needed to commercialize their business. The money is soon gone and the bills keep piling on. Lavigne is approved for $30,000 by putting a second mortgage on her house to continue pursuing this dream of a lifetime.

One week from opening, they still have a lot to do. Among other tasks, they are deciding what food to serve, where to place it, and how to run the espresso machine. With less than twenty hours to go, the carpenter is still putting up walls.

The first week of Java Nook's opening was a great success. So much so, in fact, that the carpenter becomes a full partner. With less than two weeks under their belts, Lavigne and Welter decide to expand. They lease the space next door and plan to sell local art. They're going for broke if they don't go broke. "If it doesn't succeed," says Lavigne, "we know that we will have done our best and at least we will have the Java Nook."

Discussion Questions

1. What are the advantages and disadvantages of starting a partnership?

2. Do Annette and John have the backgrounds needed to succeed in business? Explain.

3. If you were seeking to open a similar business, would you prefer to do it on your own or to purchase a franchise? What are some of the advantages and disadvantages of purchasing a franchise?

Entrepreneurship and Starting a Small Business

LEARNING OBJECTIVES

After you have read and studied this chapter, you should be able to:

LO1 Explain why people are willing to become entrepreneurs, and describe the attributes of successful entrepreneurs.

LO2 Discuss the importance of small business to the Canadian economy.

LO3 Summarize ways to learn how small businesses operate.

LO4 Analyze what it takes to start and run a small business.

LO5 Outline the advantages and disadvantages that small businesses have in entering global markets.

PROFILE

GETTING TO KNOW TONIA JAHSHAN OF STEEPED TEA

On a vacation getaway in 2006 to a bed and breakfast in Mahone Bay, Nova Scotia, Tonia Jahshan and her husband, Hatem, tasted loose-leaf tea for the very first time. They liked it so much that they brought some home to share with friends and family. Before Tonia knew it, she was holding fifteen tea parties a month.

Started in 2006, Steeped Tea <*http://www.steepedtea.com*> sells loose-leaf tea and accessories. The company began with minimal investment. The couple bought their teas in small quantities and stored them in their garage. They grew the business by using a direct-sales model whereby they sold their tea through independent consultants rather than building their own sales force. Mostly women working part-time, these

consultants are independent business owners who run tea parties in people's homes. Some consultants today make up to $21,000 a month in commissions.

A turning point for the company was when the couple appeared on *Dragons' Den.* Their venture-capital pitch resulted in four offers. Dragons David Chilton and Jim Treliving each invested $125,000 for a 10 percent ownership in the company, resulting in an overall $250,000 offer for 20 percent ownership. The owners chose them as Treliving had great connections in the United States—where the Jahshans wanted to establish a presence—and Chilton showed a solid understanding of the company's business model.

When Tonia launched the company in October 2006, it was a one-woman show. Since then, the company has grown exponentially. "We went from a basement to a 1,200-square-foot space, to 6,000 square feet and now to 20,000 in three-and-a-half years," Hatem said. The company now has over 5,000 consultants in Canada and 1,000 in the United States. The vision is to have at least 20,000 representatives in Canada, and 10,000 representatives in the United States, and to keep growing.

Stories about people like Tonia Jahshan, who take on the challenge of starting their own business, are commonplace in this age of the entrepreneur. As you read about more examples in this book, maybe you will become inspired to become an entrepreneur yourself!

Sources: "Our Story," Steeped Tea, 2015, http://www.steepedtea.com/our-story/; "In pictures: Dragons' Den success story feels the summer doldrums," *The Globe and Mail,* 14 August 2014, http://www.theglobeandmail.com/report-on-business/small-business/sb-growth/the-challenge/summer-doldrums-sour-the-milk-for-tea-company /article13736933/; "Stories from the Den: Tonia and Hatem Jahshan, Steeped Tea," YouInc.com, 28 April 2014, https://youinc.com/content/lifestyle/stories-from-the-den -tonia-and-hatem-jahshan-steeped-tea; Julia Chapman, "Steeped in Dragons' Den dollars, Hamilton tea firm grows up," CBC News, 5 October 2013, http://www.cbc.ca/news /canada/hamilton/news/steeped-in-dragons-den-dollars-hamilton-tea-firm-grows-up-1.1913049; Dan Misener, "Dragons' Den success story has caught a cold," *The Globe and Mail,* 14 August 2013, http://www.theglobeandmail.com/report-on-business/small-business/sb-growth/the-challenge/dragons-den-success-story-has-caught-a-summer-cold /article13729083/; and Marjo Johne, "How couple's perfect pitch yielded four offers on Dragons' Den," *The Globe and Mail,* 7 December 2012, http://www.theglobeandmail .com/report-on-business/small-business/starting-out/how-couples-perfect-pitch-yielded-four-offers-on-dragons-den/article6007914/.

The Age of the Entrepreneur[1]

Today, most young people know that it is unlikely they will get a job in a large corporation and work there for 30 years. For those who want more control over their destiny, working in or starting a small business makes sense. **Entrepreneurship** is accepting the challenge of starting and running a business. The word entrepreneur originates from the French word, *entreprendre*, which means "to undertake." In a business context, it means to start a business. You can imagine how the concept of entrepreneurship has a wide variety of meanings. On the one extreme, an entrepreneur is a person of very high aptitude who pioneers change, possessing characteristics found in only a very small fraction of the population. On the other extreme, anyone who wants to work for himself or herself is considered an entrepreneur. It is for this reason that we discuss both entrepreneurship and small business in this chapter.

> **entrepreneurship**
> Accepting the challenge of starting and running a business.

While many people use the terms entrepreneurship and small business interchangeably, there are significant differences. Entrepreneurial ventures differ from small businesses in the following four ways:[2]

1. *Amount of Wealth Creation.* Rather than simply generating an income stream that replaces traditional employment, a successful entrepreneurial venture creates substantial wealth, typically in excess of several million dollars of profit.

2. *Speed of Wealth Creation.* While a successful small business can generate several million dollars of profit over a lifetime, entrepreneurial wealth creation often is rapid. For example, this may occur within five years.

3. *Risk.* The risk of an entrepreneurial venture must be high. Otherwise, with the incentive of sure profits, many people would pursue the idea of entrepreneurship, making business ventures impossibly competitive.

4. *Innovation.* Entrepreneurship often involves substantial innovation beyond what a small business might exhibit. This innovation gives the venture the competitive advantage that results in wealth creation. Innovation may be in new products, new production methods, new markets, and new forms of organizations.

From this list, you can quickly gather that entrepreneurship is not always small and small business is not always entrepreneurial. While most businesses start small, it is the intent to stay small that separates them from entrepreneurship. Explore this chapter and think about the possibilities. That is, the possibility of entrepreneurship and the possibility of starting a small business in your future.

Well-Known Canadian Entrepreneurs[3]

Entrepreneurs have played a major role in developing the Canadian economy. For example, Kenneth Colin Irving opened Bouctouche, New Brunswick's first garage and service station in 1924. That same year, he opened a Ford dealership in Saint John and established Irving Oil. He was 25 years old. Today, Irving Oil operates Canada's largest refinery, eight distribution terminals, a fleet of delivery trucks, and over 900 fuelling locations serving its wholesale, commercial, and retail customers. It sells a range of finished energy products including gasoline, diesel, home heating fuel, jet fuel, and complementary products.

Inspired by their passion for Ontario's Algonquin Park, Michael Budman and Don Green created Roots in 1973. Their goal was to translate their affinity for the Canadian wilderness and sports into a distinctive line of genuine leather products and authentic athletic wear while promoting a healthy, active lifestyle and respect for the environment. The privately held company has more than 120 retail stores in Canada and the United States, and more than 100 stores in Asia. Products include leather goods, natural fibre clothing, accessories, and home furnishings. Next, consider other examples of entrepreneurs who have created companies that are now household names in Canada. Do you recognize these logos?

- Ablan Leon began his career selling clothing from a suitcase door-to-door. When he had enough money, he bought a small building in Welland, Ontario, and in 1909 the A. Leon Company was established. Today, Leon's Furniture Limited *<http://www.leons.ca>* is one of Canada's largest retailers, selling a wide range of merchandise including furniture, major appliances, and home electronics. The company continues to be run by the Leon family.

- In 1922, two brothers, John W. and Alfred J. Billes, purchased the Hamilton Tire and Garage Ltd. store in Toronto, Ontario, with a combined savings of $1,800. In 1923, the brothers sold the shop and moved to the corner of Yonge and Gould streets in Toronto under the name Canadian Tire Corporation. Today, Canadian Tire Corporation, Limited (CTC, *<http://corp.canadiantire.ca>*) is a family of companies. It includes Canadian Tire retail stores, FGL Sports (SportChek, Hockey Experts, Sports Experts, National Sports, Intersport, Pro Hockey Life, and Atmosphere), Mark's, Canadian Tire Financial Services, CT Real Estate Investment Trust, PartSource, Gas+, and Canadian Tire Jumpstart Charities—CTC's affiliated national charity that is dedicated to removing financial barriers so kids across Canada can participate in sports and physical activities.

- In 1907, J. W. Sobey started a meat delivery business in Stellarton, Nova Scotia. With a horse-drawn meat cart, he purchased and collected livestock from local farmers for resale. The first modern Sobeys supermarket opened in 1947. One of Canada's two national grocery retailers with approximately 1,500 stores in all ten provinces, retail banners include Sobeys, Safeway, IGA, Foodland, FreshCo, Price Chopper, Thrifty Foods, and Lawtons Drugs, as well as more than 350 retail fuel locations. Sobeys Inc. *<http://corporate.sobeys.com>* is a wholly-owned subsidiary of Empire Company Limited *<http://www.empireco.ca>*, headquartered in Stellarton.

- In 1957, Wallace and Harrison McCain, supported by brothers Andrew and Robert, founded McCain Foods Limited in Florenceville, New Brunswick. Today, the privately-owned company is an international leader in the frozen food industry. While potatoes are at the heart of its offerings, the company also produces other food products that include pizza, appetizers, oven meals, juice, and desserts that are found in more than 160 countries. McCain also owns the Day & Ross Transportation Group *<http://www.dayross.ca>*, one of the largest transportation companies in Canada.

- In 1969, Jean Coutu and his associate at the time, Louis Michaud, opened a discount pharmacy in Montreal, Quebec. They offered a large array of products, high-quality professional services, and longer store-opening hours. By 1973, there were five branches of Jean Coutu Discount Pharmacies and a franchise system was established. Today, The Jean Coutu Group <*http://www.jeancoutu.com*> is a leading pharmacy franchisor in Canada with 416 stores in Ontario, Quebec, and New Brunswick under the banners of PJC Jean Coutu, PJC Clinique, PJC Santé, and PJC Santé Beauté. The Jean Coutu Group also owns Pro Doc Ltd., a manufacturer of generic drugs.

These stories have much in common. One or a couple of entrepreneurs had a good idea, borrowed some money from friends and family, and started a business. That business now employs thousands of people and helps the country prosper.

LO1   Explain why people are willing to become entrepreneurs, and describe the attributes of successful entrepreneurs.

Why People Take the Entrepreneurial Challenge

Taking the challenge of starting a business can be scary and thrilling at the same time. One entrepreneur described it as almost like bungee jumping. You might be scared, but if you watch six other people do it and they survive, you are then able to do it yourself. There are many triggers to why people become entrepreneurial and some reasons may include the decision to leave corporate life (by choice or after downsizing), a sudden inheritance that allows them to try something different, a change in health that forces a career path adjustment, a change in family responsibility that sparks a search to increase income, or even disliking a supervisor so much that being self-employed is an attractive option. Other reasons why people are willing to take the challenge of starting a business are described in more detail below:

- *New Idea, Process, or Product.* Some entrepreneurs are driven by a firm belief, perhaps even an obsession, that they can produce a better product, or a current product at a lower cost, than anybody else. Perhaps they have gotten hold of a new widget or have conceived of an improvement that they are convinced has a large potential market. That is how Lululemon Athletica Inc. (Lululemon) started. "After 20 years in the surf, skate and snowboard business, founder Chip Wilson took the first commercial yoga class offered in Vancouver and found the result exhilarating. Cotton clothing was being used for sweaty, stretchy power yoga and seemed completely inappropriate to him given his passion in technical athletic fabrics. From this, a design studio was born that became a yoga studio at night to pay the rent. Clothing was offered for sale and an underground yoga clothing movement was born."[4] The Spotlight on Small Business highlights a business that was started by a student while he was still in school.

- *Independence.* Many entrepreneurs simply do not enjoy working for someone else. They like doing things their own way without someone standing over them. This type of person gets a great deal of satisfaction out of what he or she achieves. Melissa Harvey, whose company Will n' Roses LLC <*http://www.willnroses.com*> produces all-natural nut and whole-grain Kizo bars, says one of the best things about being an entrepreneur is the freedom to pursue your passion: "It's about independence. You can take something that motivates you, that inspires you and act on it without roadblocks."[5]

Tops, bottoms, and accessories are produced by Lululemon for women and men. Under what conditions would you prefer to purchase products in the store versus online?

Spotlight *On* SMALL BUSINESS

MyVoice Is My Business

Alexander Levy never planned to start a business. But while working as a student researcher at the University of Toronto, he developed a prototype mobile application. The application allows people with communication disorders—such as those caused by stroke, autism, and amyotrophic lateral sclerosis (ALS)—to make themselves understood audibly at a tiny fraction of the cost of existing hardware systems.

As Levy demonstrated the technology to clinicians and families, he found that an overwhelming number of them wanted to pay to use it. So, the 24-year-old launched MyVoice Inc. *<http://www.myvoiceaac.com>* to distribute the application software of the same name. Thousands of people in 30 countries have downloaded a free version of MyVoice, and many are converting to paid monthly subscriptions that include powerful customization tools. "Our products materially improve the lives of thousands of people with disabilities," says Levy.

For developing a life-changing innovation, creating jobs, and building a company with the potential for explosive growth, Levy was chosen as the FuEL Entrepreneur of the Year. This award celebrates Canada's Future Entrepreneurial Leaders (FuEL). "The winners of the FuEL Awards are eager young Canadians, brimming with innovative ideas and a passion for creating a better future," says Ian Portsmouth, Editor-in-Chief of *PROFIT*, which produces the award in co-operation with Impact Entrepreneurship Group. "They are role models for Canada's youth, and the cornerstone of the country's economic prospects."

Source: Used with permission of Rogers Publishing Limited.

- *Challenge.* Closely related to the previous factors are the excitement and the challenge of doing something new or difficult. Many people thrive on overcoming challenges. These people welcome the opportunity to run their own businesses.

- *Family Pattern.* Some people grow up in an atmosphere in which family members have started their own businesses, perhaps going back several generations. The talk at the dinner table is often about business matters. This background may predispose young men or women to think along the same lines. Sometimes there is a family business, and the next generation grows up expecting to take its place there in due course.

- *Profit.* It is natural for people to benefit monetarily from their ideas and dedication and to be rewarded for the money they risk and their hard work when they run a business. Yet long after a business has produced substantial profits and amassed personal fortunes for its owners, many continue to enjoy the challenge of overcoming the endless problems that every business faces and the satisfaction of continued success.

- *Immigrants.* Some immigrants who come to Canada have no Canadian job experience or weak language skills or both, making it difficult for them to find employment. However, they often have the drive and desire to succeed, and if they can obtain the capital, they can start their own business. As a result, they contribute to the economy and are potential sources of future employment in goods and services-producing businesses. Other immigrants arrive with capital, skills, and strong entrepreneurial backgrounds. British Columbia in general has been a major beneficiary of such immigrants from Hong Kong. Do you know of any businesses started by immigrants?

J.J. and Shannon Wilson, son and wife of Lululemon founder Chip Wilson, have started their own label of athleisure (clothing appropriate for both athletic and leisurely pursuits) called Kit and Ace <*http://kitandace.com*>.[6] The Wilson family is expected to invest as much as $300 million to roll out its stores across the globe with 100 stores projected by 2019.[7] What would these owners need to do to make this business as popular as Lululemon?

What Does It Take to Be an Entrepreneur?

Would you succeed as an entrepreneur? You can learn about the managerial and leadership skills needed to run a firm. However, you may not have the personality to assume the risks, take the initiative, create the vision, and rally others to follow your lead. Those traits are harder to learn or acquire. As you review the following important entrepreneurial attributes, you may ask yourself if you have them:[8]

- *Self-directed.* You should be self-disciplined and thoroughly comfortable being your own boss. You alone will be responsible for your success or failure.

- *Self-nurturing.* You must believe in your idea even when no one else does, and be able to replenish your own enthusiasm. Gary Mauris, President and co-founder of Dominion Lending Centres Inc. *<http://www.dominionlending.ca>*, Canada's top national mortgage company advises, "Prepare yourself for the storm. Everyone, from your family to your competitors, will take a run at you to instill doubt. You have to be passionate and believe in your business model."[9]

- *Action-Oriented.* Great business ideas are not enough. The most important thing is a burning desire to realize, actualize, and build your dream into reality.

- *Highly Energetic.* It is your own business and you must be emotionally, mentally, and physically able to work long and hard. For example, when starting Extreme Pita *<http://www.extremepita.com>*, brothers Mark and Alex Rechichi were so consumed with work that they often slept on cots in the shop's backroom after their evening shift. That way, they could get a few hours of sleep before starting all over again the next morning.

- *Tolerant of Uncertainty.* Successful entrepreneurs take only calculated risks (if they can help it). Still, they must be able to take *some* risks. Remember, entrepreneurship is not for the squeamish or those bent on security. You can't be afraid to fail. The late football coach Vince Lombardi summarized the entrepreneurial philosophy when he said, "We didn't lose any games this season, we just ran out of time twice." New entrepreneurs must be prepared to run out of time a few times before they succeed.

- *Able to Learn Quickly.* Making errors is inevitable. Only those who do nothing make no mistakes. What is important is what you learn from them. Good entrepreneurs are quick to learn such lessons. They adapt and change direction as required instead of letting pride stand in the way of admitting a mistake.

While courage is not considered a skill, it is nevertheless an important element of an entrepreneur. Courage is required to challenge the status quo, to see an opportunity, and then most importantly, to try to do something about it. Entrepreneurs are doers. They do not just think and talk about an idea, they act on it! Also be aware that even if you possess many (or even all) of these attributes, there is no guarantee that you will be successful with every endeavour.

Turning Your Passions and Problems into Opportunities

While many entrepreneurs' business ideas are inspired by their passions, many see business opportunities in their problems. For example, while Celtel's founder Mo Ibrahim saw the opportunity to bring mobile phones to over 1 billion people in Africa who had never even used a phone much less owned one, large telecommunication companies saw only poor peasants and logistical hurdles. Celtel became Africa's largest cell provider.[10]

Most entrepreneurs do not get ideas for products and services from some flash of inspiration. The source of innovation is more like a *flashlight.* Imagine a search party walking in the dark, shining lights, looking around, asking questions, and looking some more. "That's how most creativity happens," says business author Dale Dauten. "Calling around, asking questions, saying 'What if?' till you get blisters on your tongue."

To look at problems or passions and see opportunities in them, ask yourself these questions: What do I want, but can never find? What product or service would improve my life? What really irritates me and what product or service would help?

Four moms started Mabel's Labels <*http://www.mabelslabels.com*> when they got tired of their children losing their belongings or getting them mixed up with those of their friends. Labels go on everything from clothing to containers, for children and adults alike. What items would you label?

Keep in mind, however, that not all ideas are opportunities. If your idea does not meet anyone else's needs, the business will not succeed. You may have a business idea that is a good opportunity if:[11]

- It fills customers' needs;
- You have the skills and resources to start a business;
- You can sell the product or service at a price customers are willing and able to pay—and still make a profit;
- You can get your product or service to customers before your window of opportunity closes or before competitors with similar solutions beat you to the marketplace; and
- You can keep the business going.

If you think you may have the entrepreneurial spirit, complete the Entrepreneurial Readiness Questionnaire that appears in the appendix at the end of this chapter.

Female Entrepreneurs[12]

In the past few decades, more women have gone into business for themselves. Throughout this book, you will see some examples. According to Statistics Canada's *Labour Force Survey* report, there were 950,000 self-employed women in Canada in 2012, accounting for approximately 36 percent of all self-employed persons. Among established businesses (non-startups), the percentage of female entrepreneurs rose from 27 percent in the early 1990s to 33 percent in 2012. A greater concentration of women-run **small and medium-sized enterprises (SMEs)**, which are businesses with fewer than 500 employees, in industries such as professional services, accommodation, and food services. When a woman does decide to start a business, she tends to stay in business longer. In other words, survival rates are higher. Have these numbers changed since this chapter was written?

SMEs (small and medium-sized enterprises)
Refers to all businesses with fewer than 500 employees.

Studies have shown a variety of reasons for the emergence of female entrepreneurs:

- *Financial Need.* Fluctuating employment and drops in average real incomes over the years have encouraged many women to start a business. Steeped Tea, the focus of this chapter's profile, has been successful in attracting consultants who are looking to supplement their incomes.

- *Lack of Promotion Opportunities.* Most positions in higher management are still dominated by men. Although the situation is improving, the pace is extremely slow. Many women who are frustrated by this pace may take the entrepreneurial route.

- *Women Returning to the Workforce.* Many women who return to the job market after raising a family find that their skills are outdated. They also encounter subtle age discrimination. These factors encourage some to try self-employment.

- *Family and Personal Responsibility.* The rate of divorced women and single mothers in recent years has created a situation in which many women find themselves with children and little or no financial support. Some even refuse such support to be more independent. Affordable technology has made it possible for women to start home-based businesses.

- *Public Awareness of Women in Business.* As more publicity highlights the fact that growing numbers of women have started their own ventures, the idea catches on and gives others the confidence to try. Often two or more women will team up to form a partnership.

- *Part-Time Occupations.* Often women with some particular talent—for example, publicity, writing, designing, making clothes, cooking, organizing, or human relations—are encouraged to develop their hobby or skills on a part-time basis to see how far they can go with it. This focus has resulted in many notable success stories.

Christine Magee started Sleep Country Canada <*http://www.sleepcountry.ca*> with partners Steve Gunn and Gord Lownds based on their dream to give customers what they want. Today, the company is Canada's largest mattress retailer. Do you have any colleagues that you would consider partnering up with to start a business?

- *Higher Rate of Success for Women.* Female entrepreneurs seem to have a better success rate than men. Various factors may account for this. Women feel less pressured than men to achieve quick results. They are a little more cautious, so they make fewer mistakes. They also accept advice more readily than men, who may feel that they need to know it all. It will be interesting to follow this process to see if women continue to start ventures at the same rate and maintain their remarkable track record.

There are many resources available to help female entrepreneurs network and get general support. Some examples include the Canadian Women's Business Network *<http://www.cdnbizwomen.com>*, Women's Enterprise Centre *<http://www.wec.ca>*, and the Canadian Association of Women Executives & Entrepreneurs *<http://www.cawee.net>*. Financial institutions also offer small-business products and services aimed at women, which often can be accessed on their websites. In the meantime, if you wish to learn about some of Canada's top female entrepreneurs, review the annual *PROFIT/Chatelaine* W100 rankings *<http://www.profitguide.com/microsite/profitw100>*.

Jennifer Ger and Suzie Chemel met while studying for their business degrees. They set out to build their company, Foxy Originals *<http://www.foxyoriginals.com>*, with a vision: high-style fashion jewellery accessible to young women. Upon graduation, they focused full-time on their business. All pieces are designed and made in Canada and their products are found in hundreds of boutiques throughout Canada, the United States, the United Kingdom, Japan, Australia, and beyond.[13] What are some business challenges unique to students who wish to build a business while still in school?

Entrepreneurial Teams

An **entrepreneurial team** is a group of experienced people from different areas of business who join together to form a managerial team with the skills needed to develop, make, and market a new product. A team may be better than an individual entrepreneur because team members can combine creative skills with production and marketing skills right from the start. Having a team also can ensure more co-operation and coordination among functions.

entrepreneurial team
A group of experienced people from different areas of business who join together to form a managerial team with the skills needed to develop, make, and market a new product.

While Steve Jobs was the charismatic folk hero and visionary of Apple Inc., it was Steve Wozniack who invented the first personal computer model and Mike Markkula who offered the business expertise and access to venture capital. The key to Apple's early success was that the company was built around this "smart team" of entrepreneurs. The team wanted to combine the discipline of a big company with an environment where people could feel they were participating in a successful venture. The trio of entrepreneurs recruited seasoned managers with similar desires. All of the managers worked as a team. Everyone worked together to conceive, develop, and market products.[14]

Progress Assessment

- What are key differences between entrepreneurial ventures and small businesses?
- Why are people willing to become entrepreneurs?
- What are the advantages of entrepreneurial teams?

Micropreneurs and Home-Based Businesses

Not every person who starts a business wants to grow it into a mammoth corporation. Some are interested in maintaining a balanced lifestyle while doing the kind of work they want to do. The smallest of small businesses are called **micro-enterprises**, most often defined as having one to four employees.[15] While other entrepreneurs are committed to the quest for growth, **micropreneurs** (owners of micro-enterprises) know they can be happy even if their companies never appear on a list of top-ranked businesses.

micro-enterprises
A small business defined as having one to four employees.

micropreneurs
Small-business owners with fewer than five employees who are willing to accept the risk of starting and managing the type of business that remains small, lets them do the kind of work they want to do, and offers them a balanced lifestyle.

Jennifer Burnham operates her business, Pure and Simple Organizing <http://pureandsimplecarolinas.com>, from her apartment. Burnham helps people organize their lives, homes, businesses, and more. Can you see why Burnham is considered a micropreneur?

Many micropreneurs are owners of home-based businesses. According to Industry Canada, approximately 55 percent of all employer businesses (610,178 in number) were micro-enterprises, with the highest percentages found in the professional, scientific, and technical services (76 percent).[16] Micropreneurs include writers, consultants, video producers, architects, and bookkeepers.

Many home-based businesses are owned by people who are trying to combine career and family. Do not misunderstand and picture home-based workers as female child-care providers; men also run home-based businesses. In addition to helping business owners balance work and family, other reasons for the growth of home-based businesses include the following:[17]

- *Computer Technology.* Computer technology has levelled the competitive playing field, allowing home-based businesses to look and act as big as their corporate competitors. Broadband Internet connections, smartphones, and other technologies are so affordable that setting up a business takes a much smaller initial investment than it once did.

- *Corporate Downsizing.* Downsizing has led some to venture out on their own. Meanwhile, the work of the downsized employees still needs to be done and corporations are outsourcing much of the work to smaller companies.

- *Change in Social Attitudes.* Whereas home-based entrepreneurs used to be asked when they were going to get a "real" job, they are now likely to be asked instead for how-to-do-it advice.

Working at home has its challenges, of course. In setting up a home-based business, you could expect the following major challenges:[18]

- *Getting New Customers.* Getting the word out can be difficult because you do not have a retail storefront.

- *Managing Time.* You save time by not commuting, but it takes self-discipline to use that time wisely.

- *Keeping Work and Family Tasks Separate.* It is great to be able to throw a load of laundry in the washer in the middle of the workday if you need to, but you have to keep such distractions to a minimum. It also takes self-discipline to leave your work at the office if the office is at home.

- *Abiding by City Ordinances.* Government ordinances restrict the types of businesses that are allowed in certain parts of the community and how much traffic a home-based business can attract to the neighbourhood.

- *Managing Risk.* Home-based entrepreneurs should review their homeowner's insurance policy since not all policies cover business-related claims. Some even void the coverage if there is a business in the home.

Home-based entrepreneurs should focus on finding opportunity instead of accepting security, getting results instead of following routines, earning a profit instead of earning a paycheque, trying new ideas instead of avoiding mistakes, and creating a long-term vision instead of seeking a short-term payoff. Figure 7.1 lists ten ideas for potentially successful home-based businesses. You can find a wealth of online information about starting a home-based business at <*http://sbinfocanada.about.com*> and <*http://www.entrepreneur.com*>.

Web-Based Businesses

The Internet has sprouted a world of small web-based businesses that sell everything from staplers to refrigerator magnets to wedding dresses. These small businesses compete with other small businesses as well as large web-based and bricks-and-mortar businesses. According to a Forrester Research report, online spending will account for 8 percent of overall retail sales in Canada by 2018 and will climb to $33.8 billion.[20]

Food Network host, nutritional activist, and food media producer Michael Smith is one of Canada's best-known chefs and cookbook authors. Seen on Food Network Canada and in more than 100 countries, he hosts *Chef Michael's Kitchen, Chef Abroad,* and *Chef at Home.* He is a judge on *Chopped Canada* and he has travelled the world for his web series, *Lentil Hunter.*[19] Here at home, he is being filmed for one of his shows. Would you follow his Twitter feed to learn more about food?

◼ FIGURE 7.1

POTENTIAL HOME-BASED BUSINESSES	
Many businesses can be started at home. To turn a home business into a success, you need to be prepared to work at it and have the appropriate knowledge and skills that you need to run any business.	
1. Home renovation services	6. Pet products and services
2. Catering services	7. Cleaning services
3. Fall prevention products—sales and service	8. Wedding planner services
4. E-commerce	9. In-home beauty services
5. Sewing and alteration services	10. Business / life coach services

Source: Susan Ward, "The Best Home Business Opportunities Now and Tomorrow," About.com, 2015, http://sbinfocanada.about.com/od/startingahbb /ss/Top-10-Home-Business-Opportunities.htm#step-heading.

Web-based businesses have to offer more than the same merchandise customers can buy at stores—they must offer unique products or services. For example, Marc Resnik started his web-based distribution company after waking up one morning laughing about his business idea. Now *ThrowThings.com <http://www.throwthings.com>* makes money for him as he's shipped products to more than 44 countries. Although the company's offerings seem like a random collection of unrelated items, everything it sells can be thrown. You can buy promotional products in the "Throw Your Name Around!" section, ventriloquist dummies in the "Throw Your Voice!" section, and sporting equipment in the "Things to Throw!" section. About two-thirds of the company's revenue comes from the promotional products section, which allows customers to add a logo to thousands of products. Why is Resnik's business so successful? One frequent customer believes it's because of Resnik's exceptional service and quick turnaround time.[21]

One of the easiest ways to start a web-based business is through affiliate marketing. **Affiliate marketing** is an online marketing strategy in which a business rewards individuals or other businesses (affiliates) for each visitor or customer the affiliate sends to its website. For example, imagine you discovered a backpack online made of an extremely lightweight, amazingly strong fabric that holds everything you need for the day, is easy to carry, and looks great. You want to tell all your friends about it, so you register as an affiliate on the seller's website and post an affiliate link to the product on your Facebook page. Whenever anyone clicks on the widget (an image of the product) and buys a backpack, the seller pays you a commission.[22]

> **affiliate marketing**
> An online marketing strategy in which a business rewards individuals or other businesses (affiliates) for each visitor or customer the affiliate sends to its website.

A web-based business is not always a fast road to success. It can sometimes be a shortcut to failure. Hundreds of high-flying dotcoms crashed after promising to revolutionize the way we shop. That is the bad news. The good news is that you can learn from someone else's failure and spare yourself some pain.

Entrepreneurship Within Firms

Entrepreneurship in a large organization is often reflected in the efforts and achievements of intrapreneurs. **Intrapreneurs** are creative people who work as entrepreneurs within corporations. The idea is to use a company's existing resources—human, financial, and physical—to launch new products and generate new profits.

> **intrapreneurs**
> Creative people who work as entrepreneurs within corporations.

At 3M <*http://www.3m.com*>, which produces a wide array of products from adhesives like Scotch tape to non-woven materials for industrial use, managers are expected to devote 15 percent of their time to thinking up new products or services.[23] You know those brightly coloured Post-it Notes that people use to write messages on just about everything? That product was developed by Art Fry, a 3M employee. He needed to mark the pages of a hymnal in a way that would not damage or fall out of the book. He came up with the idea of the self-stick, repositionable paper. The 3M labs soon produced a sample, but distributors were unimpressed and market surveys were inconclusive. Nonetheless, 3M kept sending samples to secretaries of top executives. Eventually, after a major sales and marketing program, the orders began pouring in, and Post-it Notes became a big winner. The company continues to update the product; making it from recycled paper is just one of many innovations. Post-it Notes have gone international as well—the notepads sent to Japan are long and narrow to accommodate vertical writing. Now you can even use Post-it Notes electronically—the software program Post-it Software Notes allows you to type messages onto brightly coloured notes and store them on memo boards, embed them in documents, or send them through e-mail.

When you come up with a winning idea, stick with it. That has certainly been the motto of the 3M company, the maker of Post-it Notes. 3M encourages intrapreneurship among its employees by requiring them to devote at least 15 percent of their time to thinking about new products. How has this commitment to innovation paid off for the company and its employees?

Encouraging Entrepreneurship: What Government Can Do [24]

The different levels of government provide many services to help entrepreneurs and small businesses succeed. Canada Business Network promotes entrepreneurship and innovation, and it provides assistance through an organized network of service centres across Canada. This collaborative arrangement among federal departments and agencies, provincial and territorial governments, and not-for-profit entities has the goal to provide businesses with the resources they need to grow and prosper, including a wide range of information on government services, programs, and regulations.

Industry Canada's SME Research and Statistics site *<http://www.ic.gc.ca/eic/site/061.nsf/eng/Home>* offers research on small business and entrepreneurship. Recent reports evaluate key small-business statistics, determinants of entrepreneurship in Canada, and financial performance data. Visit this site to learn more about its latest work.

Entrepreneurs and new start-ups can also find assistance from business incubators. **Business incubators** provide space, services, advice, and support to assist new and growing businesses to become established and successful. The business incubator's main goal is to produce successful firms that will leave the program financially viable and freestanding. The other goals of incubation programs are creating jobs, retaining businesses in a community, building or accelerating growth in a local industry, and diversifying local economies.

business incubators
Centres that provide space, services, advice, and support to assist new and growing businesses to become established and successful.

The DMZ at Ryerson University <*https://www.dmz.ryerson.ca*> is a university-affiliated business incubator. It is Canada's largest incubator and multidisciplinary co-working space for young entrepreneurs. The DMZ helps start-ups fast-track product launches, grow their companies, and reach customers in a supportive community by connecting them with customers, advisers, industry professionals, and one another. From 2010 to 2015, the DMZ incubated 184 start-ups that collectively raised $70 million in funding and created more than 1,600 jobs. Does your school have an incubator?

The National Business Incubator Association <*http://www.nbia.org*> estimates that there are about 7,000 business incubators worldwide. Incubator sponsors—organizations or individuals who support an incubation program financially—include academic institutions, economic development organizations, government entities (e.g., the Canada Accelerator and Incubator Program), and for-profit organizations. According to a recent study, 87 percent of incubator graduates remain in business.

Business incubators vary in the way they deliver their services, in their organizational structure, and in the types of clients they serve. Incubators frequently help entrepreneurs prepare plans and proposals, assist them in making contacts to find financing, and assist participants to obtain cheaper insurance. However, most incubators themselves are not investors. The majority of activities are in the form of services and indirect support. The earliest incubation programs focused on technology companies and service firms. In more recent years, they are targeting industries such as food processing, arts and crafts, telecommunications, and software development. Another focus is micro-enterprise creation.

Progress Assessment

- How do micropreneurs differ from other entrepreneurs?
- What are some of the opportunities and risks of web-based businesses?
- List some services for entrepreneurs provided by the federal government.

LO2 Discuss the importance of small business to the Canadian economy.

Getting Started in Small Business

Let's suppose you have a great idea for a new business, you have the attributes of an entrepreneur, and you are ready to take the leap into business for yourself. How do you start a business? How much paperwork is involved? That is what the rest of this chapter is about.

It may be easier to identify with a small neighbourhood business than with a giant global firm, yet the principles of management are similar for each. The management of charities, government agencies, churches, schools, and unions is much the same as the management of small and large businesses. So, as you learn about small-business management, you will make a giant step toward understanding management in general. All organizations demand capital, good ideas, planning, information management, budgets (and financial management in general), accounting, marketing, good employee relations, and good overall managerial know-how. We shall explore these areas as they relate to small businesses and later in the book, apply the concepts to large firms, even to global organizations.

Small Versus Big Business[25]

Industry Canada maintains a count of business establishments. A **business establishment** must meet the following criteria: it must have at least one paid employee, it must have annual sales revenue of $30,000, and it must be incorporated and have filed a federal corporate income tax return at least once in the previous three years. There are over 1.1 million employer businesses in Canada. Figure 7.2 breaks down the number of businesses by sector and number of employees.

> **business establishment**
> Must meet the following minimum criteria: it must have at least one paid employee, it must have annual sales revenue of $30,000, and it must be incorporated and have filed a federal corporate income tax return at least once in the previous three years.

It would be helpful to define what is meant by the term *small business*. A **small business** can be defined as a business that is independently owned and operated, is not dominant in its field, and meets certain standards of size in terms of employees or annual revenues. Many institutions define small business according to their own needs. For example, Industry Canada defines a small business as one that has 1 to 99 paid employees. In Figure 7.2, of the over 1.1 million employer businesses (which exclude those that are self-employed and contract workers) in Canada, .1 percent have more than 500 employees. Businesses employing fewer than 100 employees account for the vast majority (98.2 percent) of all employer businesses.

> **small business**
> A business that is independently owned and operated, is not dominant in its field, and meets certain standards of size in terms of employees or annual revenues.

As you can see, small business is really a big part of the Canadian economy. How big a part? We'll explore that question next.

Small Business Statistics[26]

Small businesses are a dynamic part of the Canadian economy. Nearly all small businesses are Canadian-owned and managed. This is in contrast to large businesses, of which many are foreign-owned and managed. Small businesses thus play a major role in helping to maintain the Canadian identity and Canadian economic independence.

Small businesses also continue to be feeders for future large businesses. As they prosper and develop new goods and services, they are often bought out by large companies, which in turn become more competitive. Alternatively, after small businesses establish a good track record, some of them convert from private to public companies, enabling them to obtain significant financing and become larger companies.

■ FIGURE 7.2

NUMBER OF BUSINESS LOCATIONS BY SECTOR AND FIRM SIZE (NUMBER OF EMPLOYEES), DECEMBER 2012				
Approximately 98 percent of Canadian employers businesses are considered small businesses by Industry Canada.				
		NO. OF BUSINESS LOCATIONS		
	Percentage of Employer Businesses	Total	Goods-Producing Sector	Services-Producing Sector
Small businesses (1–99 employees)	98.2	1,087,803	236,566	851,237
Medium-sized businesses (100–499 employees)	1.7	18,169	4,898	13,271
Large businesses (500 + employees)	0.1	1,568	437	1,131
Total	100.0	1,107,540	241,901	865,639

Source: Statistics Canada, "Number of Business Locations by Sector and Firm Size (Number of Employees), December 2012." Adapted from Statistics Canada, special tabulation, unpublished data, (Business Register Database), December 2011. Reproduced on an "as-is" basis with the permission of Statistics Canada. Accessed on page 7 of https://www.ic.gc.ca/eic/site/061.nsf/vwapj/KSBS-PSRPE_August-Aout2013_eng.pdf/$FILE/KSBS-PSRPE_August-Aout2013_eng.pdf.

According to the most recent *Key Small Business Statistics*, here are some quick facts about small businesses (in this case, defined by Industry Canada as firms that have between 1 to 99 employees):

- 98.2 percent of businesses in Canada have fewer than 100 employees of which 55.1 percent are micro-enterprises;

- Small businesses created a little over 100,000 jobs, on average, between 2002 and 2012;

- Small businesses employed over 7.7 million individuals in Canada in 2012, or 69.7 percent of the total private labour force;

- Depending on various estimates, small businesses contributed between 25 and 41 percent to Canada's gross domestic product;

- In 2011, about 10.4 percent of SMEs exported, which translated into $150 billion or about 41.0 percent of Canada's total value of exports;

- Almost 14 percent of small businesses were solely owned by females while over 18 percent were owned in equal partnerships between male and female owners; and

- 48.4 percent of SME owners were between 50 and 64 years of age, whereas only 1.6 percent were less than 30 years of age.

Importance of Small Businesses

Since most of Canada's jobs are in small businesses, there is a very good chance that you will either work in a small business some day or start one. In addition to providing employment opportunities, small firms believe they offer other advantages over larger companies—more personal customer service and the ability to respond quickly to opportunities.

Bigger is not always better. Picture a hole in the ground. If you fill it with big boulders, there are many empty spaces between them. However, if you fill it with sand, there is no space between the grains. That is how it is in business. Big businesses do not serve all the needs of the market. There is plenty of room for small companies to make a profit filling those niches.

Small-Business Success and Failure

You cannot be naïve about business practices, or you will go broke. There is some debate about how many new small businesses fail each year. There are many false signals about entries and exits. When small-business owners go out of business to start new and different businesses, they may be included in the "failure" category when obviously this is not the case. Similarly, when a business changes its form of ownership from partnership to corporation, it may be counted as a failure. Retirements of sole owners may also be in this category.

Thousands of businesses enter and exit the marketplace throughout the year. *Key Small Business Statistics* discusses survival in the following way:

> Survival is defined as the percentage of new firms that continue to operate when they reach a given age. Geographic location, type of industry, size and age, general economic conditions, and market influences (e.g., the number and size of competitors and new entrants) impact how long a business stays active. Survival reflects their productivity, innovation and resourcefulness, as well as their adaptability to changing market conditions. When considering SMEs, survival rates decline with time. About 80 percent of businesses survive for one year and 72 percent of enterprises that entered the marketplace survived for two years.[27]

Figure 7.3 lists reasons for small-business failure. Managerial incompetence and inadequate financial planning are among them. Keep in mind that when a business fails, it is important that the owners learn from their mistakes. Some who have failed are more realistic than novice business people. Because of the lessons they've learned, they may be more successful in their future ventures.[28]

■ FIGURE 7.3

CAUSES OF SMALL-BUSINESS FAILURE	
Plunging in without first testing the waters on a small scale.	Buying too much on credit.
Underpricing or overpricing goods or services.	Extending credit too freely.
Underestimating how much time it will take to build a market.	Expanding credit too rapidly.
Starting with too little capital.	Failing to keep complete, accurate records so that the owners drift into trouble without realizing it.
Starting with too much capital and being careless in its use.	Carrying habits of personal extravagance into the business.
Going into business with little or no experience and without first learning something about the industry or market.	Not understanding business cycles.
Borrowing money without planning just how and when to pay it back.	Forgetting about taxes, insurance, and other costs of doing business.
Attempting to do too much business with too little capital.	Mistaking the freedom of being in business for oneself for the liberty to work or not, according to whim.
Not allowing for setbacks and unexpected expenses.	

CAUSES OF SMALL-BUSINESS SUCCESS	
The customer requires a lot of personal attention, as in a beauty parlour.	A large business sells a franchise operation to local buyers. (Don't forget franchising as an excellent way to enter the world of small business.)
The product is not easily made by mass-production techniques (e.g., custom-tailored clothes or custom auto-body work).	The owner pays attention to new competitors.
Sales are not large enough to appeal to a large firm (e.g., a novelty shop).	The business is in a growth industry (e.g., computer services or web design).

Choosing the right type of business is critical. Many of the businesses with the lowest failure rates require advanced training to start—veterinary services, dental practices, medical practices, and so on. While training and degrees may buy security, they do not tend to produce much growth—one dentist can fill only so many cavities. If you want to be both independent and rich, you need to go after growth. Often high-growth businesses, such as technology firms, are not easy to start and are even more difficult to keep going.

The easiest businesses to start have the least growth and the greatest failure rates (like restaurants). The easiest to keep alive are difficult to get started (like manufacturing). And the ones that can make you rich are the ones that are both hard to start and hard to keep going (like automobile assembly). See Figure 7.3 to get an idea of the business situations that are most likely to lead to success.

When you decide to start your own business, think carefully. You are unlikely to find everything you want—easy entry, security, and reward—in one business. Choose those characteristics that matter most to you; accept the absence of the others; plan, plan, plan; and then go for it!

Progress Assessment

- What are some quick facts about small businesses?
- Why are small businesses important to Canada?
- What are causes of small-business failure?

LO3   Summarize ways to learn how small businesses operate.

Learning About Small-Business Operations

Hundreds of would-be entrepreneurs of all ages have asked the same question: How can I learn to run my own business? Many of these people had no idea what kind of business they wanted to start; they simply wanted to be in business for themselves. There are several ways to get into your first business venture. They are:

1. Learn from others.
2. Get some experience.
3. Buy an existing business.
4. Buy a franchise.
5. Inherit / take over a family business.

Learn from Others

Investigate your local school for classes on small business and entrepreneurship. There are entrepreneurship programs in post-secondary schools throughout Canada. Some entrepreneurs have started businesses as students—see the Analyzing Management Decisions case near the end of the chapter for an example. One of the best things about such courses is that they bring together entrepreneurs from diverse backgrounds who form helpful support networks. Talk to others who have already done it. They will tell you that location is critical and caution you not to be under-capitalized; that is, to start with enough money. "Everything takes twice as long and costs twice as much as you think it will," shares Rene Goehrum, President and CEO of BioSyent Inc. *<http://www.biosyent.com>*, one of Canada's fastest-growing independent pharmaceutical companies.[29] They will warn you about the problems of finding and retaining good workers. And, most of all, they will tell you to keep good records and hire a good accountant and lawyer before you start. Free advice like this is invaluable.

Get Some Experience

There is no better way to learn small-business management than by becoming an apprentice or working for a successful entrepreneur. Many small-business owners got the idea for their businesses from their prior jobs. An industry standard is to have three years' experience in a comparable business.

About 77 percent of SME owners had ten years of management experience or more.[30] Many new entrepreneurs come from corporate management. They are tired of the big-business life or are being laid off because of corporate downsizing. Such managers bring their managerial expertise and enthusiasm with them. Such was the case with Tom Heintzman and Greg Kiessling, co-founders of Bullfrog Power *<http://www.bullfrogpower.com>*. Prior to starting the company, Heintzman had experience in the private and non-governmental organizations sectors as a consultant and as the director of corporate development for ZENON Environmental. (ZENON has since been acquired by GE Water & Process Technologies.) Kiessling had 18 years of private-sector experience leading high-growth, entrepreneurial organizations.[31]

By running a small business part-time during your off hours or on weekends, you can experience the rewards of working for yourself while still enjoying a regular paycheque at another job. This is what John Stanton, founder of the Running Room *<http://www.runningroom.com>*, did when he first started his company. He kept his full-time job as a vice-president in the grocery business and he opened the Running Room in a house in Edmonton, Alberta. At first, he only sold cotton T-shirts and running shoes. Four years later, he was confident that the company had growth potential. He quit his job and concentrated on building the Running Room chain. Today, the company is North America's largest specialty retailer of sporting goods, apparel, and footwear for runners and walkers, operating 114 corporately-owned stores in Canada and the United States.[32] Learning a business while working for someone else may also save you money because you are less likely to make "rookie mistakes" when you start your own business. The Making Ethical Decisions box presents ethical questions about using the knowledge you have gained as an employee to start your own business.

Buy an Existing Business

Small-business owners work long hours and rarely take vacations. After many years, they may feel stuck in their businesses. They may think they cannot get out because they have too much time and effort invested. Consequently, there are some small-business owners out there eager to get away, at least for a long vacation.

This is where you come in. Find a successful business person who owns a small business. Tell him or her that you are eager to learn the business and would like to serve an apprenticeship—that is, a training period. State that at the end of the training period (one year or so), you would like to help the owner or

Making ETHICAL DECISIONS

Should You Stay or Should You Go?

Suppose you have worked for two years in a company and you see signs that the business is beginning to falter. You and a co-worker have ideas about how to make a company similar to your boss's succeed. Rather than share your ideas with your boss, you and your friend are considering quitting your jobs and starting your own company together. Should you approach other co-workers about working for your new venture? Will you try to lure your boss's customers to your own business? What are your alternatives? What are the consequences of each alternative? What is the most ethical choice?

manager by becoming assistant manager. As assistant manager, you would free the owner to take off weekends and holidays, and to take a long vacation—a good deal for him or her. For another year or so, work very hard to learn all about the business—suppliers, inventory, bookkeeping, customers, promotion, and so on. At the end of two years, make the owner this offer: the owner can retire or work only part-time and you will take over the business. You can establish a profit-sharing plan for yourself plus a salary. Be generous with yourself; you will earn it if you manage the business. You can even ask for 40 percent or more of the profits.

The owner benefits by keeping ownership in the business and making 60 percent of what he or she earned before—without having to work. You benefit by making 40 percent of the profits of a successful firm. This is an excellent deal for an owner about to retire—he or she is able to keep the firm and a healthy profit flow. It is also a clever and successful way to share in the profits of a successful small business without any personal monetary investment. If you think that this is not realistic, be aware that nearly half of Canada's small-business owners plan to retire before 2020.[33]

If profit-sharing does not appeal to the owner, you may want to buy the business outright. How do you determine a fair price for a business? Value is based on (1) what the business owns, (2) what it earns, and (3) what makes it unique. Naturally, your accountant will need to help you determine the business's value.[34]

If your efforts to take over the business through either profit-sharing or buying fail, you can quit and start your own business fully trained.

Buy a Franchise

In Chapter 6, you were introduced to franchising. Many business people first get into business via franchising. Recall that franchising is a method of distributing a good or service, or both, to achieve a maximum market impact with a minimum investment. From your investment perspective, you are not creating a product or service from nothing. Rather, you are benefiting from the experience of the franchisor. Franchising is a way that you can start a business venture, especially if you are more comfortable doing so with an established product and process.

When deciding which method is best for you in terms of getting into your first business venture, be sure to weigh the advantages and disadvantages of each option before proceeding. One example of a successful franchise business is Molly Maid International Inc., a leader in the cleaning industry.

Inherit / Take Over a Family Business[35]

It is not uncommon for the dream of one to evolve into a family business. Some examples highlighted in this textbook include Irving Oil, and Kit and Ace. Husband and wife teams (such as Timothy Snelgrove and Teresa Snelgrove, founders of Timothy's World Coffee *<http://www.timothys.ca>*, and the Jahshans highlighted in the chapter profile) are also quite common when you review the Canadian landscape of family businesses.

There are a number of factors that make family businesses unique. One is ownership. Public companies are typically owned by a large number of shareholders whose primary interest in ownership is generating the best return on investment. However, family businesses are often owned by a much smaller group whose ownership often has elements of personal identity, family legacy, and community responsibility entwined with its economic interests. This "emotional ownership" often results in family businesses having a longer-term view. Another factor that tends to separate successful family firms from their public counterparts is the concept of stewardship. Many family businesses have a clear understanding that the business is something to be preserved and grown for future generations. As Bill Ford, the chairman of Ford Motor Company once said, "I'm working for my children and grandchildren and feel I'm working for our employees' children and grandchildren as well."

The late Israel Asper founded CanWest Global Communications Corp. in 1974. A major media company based in Winnipeg, Manitoba, it held radio, television, broadcasting, and publishing assets in several countries, but primarily in Canada. Do you know of any other family businesses that have not survived the transition to the next generation?

As with any form of business, there are some challenges associated with a family business. According to the Family Business Institute, only about 30 percent of family businesses survive into the second generation, 12 percent are still viable into the third generation, and only about 3 percent of all family businesses operate into the fourth generation or beyond. For example, Israel (Izzy) Asper, founder of CanWest Global Communications Corp., once dreamed of creating a worldwide media empire. When he died in 2003, his son, Leonard, was left in charge as CanWest's CEO. Leonard stepped down as CEO in 2010 when the company was restructured due to bankruptcy.

There are two common reasons why a family does not retain its business. The first reason is straightforward—there is no qualified successor. The second major reason for unsuccessful business transitions is more unfortunate. In many cases, businesses fail or are sold off due to a lack of planning. The Adapting to Change box in Chapter 6 highlights management problems as another factor. Regardless of such challenges, inheriting or taking over a family business is another way that one can learn about small business.

Progress Assessment

- What are ways that one can get into a business venture?
- What are benefits of acquiring an existing business?
- What are challenges associated with family businesses?

LO4   Analyze what it takes to start and run a small business.

Managing a Small Business

One of the major causes of small-business failure is poor management. Keep in mind, though, that the term *poor management* covers a number of faults. It could mean poor planning, record keeping, inventory control, promotion, or employee relations. Most likely it includes poor capitalization. To help you succeed as a business owner, in the following sections we explore the five functions of business in a small-business setting, which are as follows:

1. Planning your business
2. Financing your business (finance)
3. Knowing your customers (marketing)
4. Managing your employees (human resources)
5. Keeping records (accounting)

Although all of the functions are important in both the start-up and management phases of the business, the first two functions—planning and financing—are the primary concerns when you start your business. The remaining functions are the heart of your operations once the business is underway.

Planning

Many people eager to start a small business come up with an idea and begin discussing the idea with professors, friends, and other business people. At this stage, the entrepreneur needs a business plan.

A **business plan** is a detailed written statement that describes the nature of the business, the target market, the advantages the business will have in relation to competition, and the resources and qualifications of the owner(s). A business plan forces potential owners of small businesses to be quite specific about the goods or services they intend to offer. They must analyze the competition, calculate how much money they need to start, and cover other details of operation. A business plan is also mandatory for talking with bankers or other investors. Put another way, a business plan is a tool that is used to transition the entrepreneur from having an idea to actually developing a strategic and operational framework for the business.

> **business plan**
> A detailed written statement that describes the nature of the business, the target market, the advantages the business will have in relation to competition, and the resources and qualifications of the owner(s).

Lenders want to know everything about an aspiring business. First, pick a bank that serves businesses the size of yours. Have a good accountant prepare a complete set of financial statements and a personal balance sheet. Make an appointment before going to the bank, and go to the bank with an accountant and all of the necessary financial information. Demonstrate to the banker that you are a person of good character, civic minded, and respected in business and community circles. Finally, ask for all the money you need, be specific, and be prepared to personally guarantee the loan.

WRITING A BUSINESS PLAN

A good business plan takes a long time to write, but you have got only minutes in the Executive Summary to convince readers not to throw it away. Since bankers receive many business plans every day, the summary has to catch their interest quickly. There's no such thing as a perfect business plan; even the most comprehensive business plan changes as the new business evolves. Figure 7.4 gives you an outline of a comprehensive business plan.

Many software programs can help you get organized. One highly rated business-plan program is Business Plan Pro. You can also review sample business plans and templates on the Canada Business Network.

Getting the completed business plan into the right hands is almost as important as getting the right information into the plan. Finding funding requires research. Next, we discuss sources of money available to new business ventures. All require a comprehensive business plan. The time and effort you invest before starting a business will pay off many times over. The big payoff is survival.

Financing Your Business

When *starting* a business, an entrepreneur can consider different types of financing, as listed in Figure 7.5. Personal savings (79.5 percent) and credit from financial institutions (40.9 percent) represent the most frequently used sources for start-ups.[36] These sources of financing were also used most often to support business acquisitions

Individual investors are also a frequent source of capital for most entrepreneurs. **Angel investors** are private individuals who invest their own money in potentially hot new companies before they go public. A number of websites match people who want money with those willing to lend it. They include Angel One <*http://www.angelonenetwork.ca*>, Canadian Investment Network <*http://www.canadian investmentnetwork.com*>, and Canada Angel Investors <*https://angel.co/canada/investors*>.

> **angel investors**
> Private individuals who invest their own money in potentially hot new companies before they go public.

■ **FIGURE 7.4**

SAMPLE OUTLINE OF A BUSINESS PLAN

LENGTH OF A COMPREHENSIVE BUSINESS PLAN
A good business plan is between 25 and 50 pages long and takes at least six months to write.

Cover Letter
Only one thing is certain when you go hunting for money to start a business: You will not be the only hunter out there. You need to make potential funders want to read your business plan instead of the hundreds of others on their desks. Your cover letter should summarize the most attractive points of your project in as few words as possible. Be sure to address the letter to the potential investor by name. "To Whom It May Concern" or "Dear Sir" is not the best way to win an investor's support.

Section 1—Executive Summary
Begin with a two-page or three-page management summary of the proposed venture. Include a short description of the business, and discuss major goals and objectives.

Section 2—Company Background
Describe company operations to date (if any), potential legal considerations, and areas of risk and opportunity. Summarize the firm's financial condition, and include past and current balance sheets, income and cash-flow statements, and other relevant financial records. (You will learn about these financial statements in Chapter 16.) It is also wise to include a description of insurance coverage. Investors want to be assured that death or other mishaps do not pose major threats to the company.

Section 3—Management Team
Include an organization chart, job descriptions of listed positions, and detailed resumés of the current and proposed executives. A mediocre idea with a proven management team is funded more often than a great idea with an inexperienced team. Managers should have expertise in all disciplines necessary to start and run a business. If not, mention outside consultants who will serve in these roles and describe their qualifications.

Section 4—Financial Plan
Provide five-year projections for income, expenses, and funding sources. Do not assume the business will grow in a straight line. Adjust your planning to allow for funding at various stages of the company's growth. Explain the rationale and assumptions used to determine the estimates. Assumptions should be reasonable and based on industry/historical trends. Make sure all totals add up and are consistent throughout the plan. If necessary, hire a professional accountant or financial analyst to prepare these statements.

Stay clear of excessively ambitious sales projections; rather, offer best-case, expected, and worst-case scenarios. These not only reveal how sensitive the bottom line is to sales fluctuations but also serve as good management guides.

Section 5—Capital Required
Indicate the amount of capital needed to commence or continue operations, and describe how these funds are to be used. Make sure the totals are the same as the ones on the cash-flow statement. This area will receive a great deal of review from potential investors, so it must be clear and concise.

Section 6—Marketing Plan
Do not underestimate the competition. Review industry size, trends, and the target market segment. Discuss strengths and weaknesses of the good or service. The most important things investors want to know are what makes the product more desirable than what is already available and whether the product can be patented. Compare pricing to the competition's. Forecast sales in dollars and units. Outline sales, advertising, promotion, and public relations programs. Make sure the costs agree with those projected in the financial statements.

Section 7—Location Analysis
In retailing and certain other industries, the location of the business is one of the most important factors. Provide a comprehensive demographic analysis of consumers in the area of the proposed business as well as a traffic-pattern analysis and vehicular and pedestrian counts.

Section 8—Manufacturing Plan
Describe minimum plant size, machinery required, production capacity, inventory and inventory-control methods, quality control, plant personnel requirements, and so on. Estimates of product costs should be based on primary research.

Section 9—Appendix
Include all marketing research on the good or service (off-the-shelf reports, article reprints, etc.) and other information about the product concept or market size. Provide a bibliography of all the reference materials you consulted. This section should demonstrate that the proposed company will not be entering a declining industry or market segment.

■ **FIGURE 7.5**

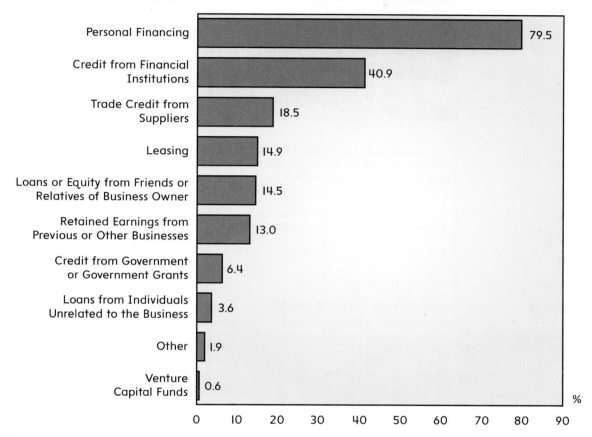

FINANCIAL INSTRUMENTS USED FOR START-UP SMES (2011)

SMEs can use multiple sources of funds when they start up their businesses. Since they often lack both a credit history and the collateral needed to secure a loan, it is not surprising that personal savings represent the largest source (79.5 percent) of funding.

Personal Financing — 79.5
Credit from Financial Institutions — 40.9
Trade Credit from Suppliers — 18.5
Leasing — 14.9
Loans or Equity from Friends or Relatives of Business Owner — 14.5
Retained Earnings from Previous or Other Businesses — 13.0
Credit from Government or Government Grants — 6.4
Loans from Individuals Unrelated to the Business — 3.6
Other — 1.9
Venture Capital Funds — 0.6

*Multiple responses were possible, so estimates will not add up to 100 percent.

Source: Statistics Canada, Survey on Financing and Growth of Small and Medium Enterprises, 2011.

Venture capitalists may finance your project—for a price. **Venture capitalists** may ask for a hefty stake (as much as 60 percent) in your company in exchange for the cash to start your business. If the venture capitalist takes too large a stake, you could lose control of the business. Since the widespread failure of early web start-ups, venture capitalists have been willing to invest less and expect more return on their investment if the new company is sold.[37] Therefore, if you're a very small company, you likely don't have a good chance of getting venture capital. You'd have more success with an angel investor.

venture capitalists
Individuals or companies that invest in new businesses in exchange for partial ownership of those businesses.

Summer Company <*http://www.Ontario.ca/summercompany*> is a Government of Ontario program that gives students between the ages of 15 to 29 years the opportunity to receive hands-on training and mentoring as well as a grant of up to $3,000 to start and operate a summer business. If you do not live in Ontario, is there a similar program in your area?

Dragons' Den is a CBC production where aspiring entrepreneurs pitch their business concepts and products to a panel of Canadian business moguls. If you can convince them to lend you money, they will expect ownership in the business in exchange. Have you seen an episode of this show? Do you think that the Dragons are too harsh? Review this chapter's video case for more information on *Dragons' Den* and see the outcome of the pitch for money.

If your proposed venture does require millions of dollars to start, experts recommend that you talk with at least five investment firms and their clients in order to find the right venture capitalist.[38] You may be able to connect with potential investors through various organizations such as the Canadian Venture Capital & Private Equity Association <http://www.cvca.ca>, and Kensington Capital Partners <http://www.kcpl.ca/index.php>, a federal government–backed venture capital fund.

CROWDFUNDING[39]

Crowdfunding is the raising of funds through the collection of small contributions from the general public (known as the "crowd") using the Internet and social media. Examples of crowdfunding platforms where individuals can ask for or donate money include Kickstarter and Indiegogo. Crowdfunding has its origins in the concept of crowdsourcing. *Crowdsourcing* is the practice of obtaining needed services, ideas, or content by soliciting contributions from a large group of people and especially from the online community rather than from traditional employees or suppliers. The key to crowdfunding is its link to online social networking and its ability to harness the power of online communities in order to extend a project's promotion and financing opportunities.

> **crowdfunding**
> Raising funds through the collection of small contributions from the general public (known as the crowd) using the Internet and social media.

Crowdfunding is becoming an increasingly common form of raising funds in the technology and media industries (including music, film, and video games) as these sites tend to work out best for people whose ideas play to an Internet audience. These artists and video game designers may reward contributors with T-shirts or products. Traditionally, crowdfunding is used to raise money to fund the development of a well-defined, singular project. It offers business people a chance at success by showcasing their businesses and projects to the entire world. It also has a unique dual function of providing both private financing and generating publicity and attention for a project.

ONLINE FINANCING SOURCES

There are many information sources for financing. Examples of government grants and programs include the Scientific Research and Experimental Development program and the National Research Council's Industrial Research Assistance Program.

From the comfort of your desk, you can visit government sites such as the Business Development Bank of Canada <http://www.bdc.ca> or Industry Canada's Small Business Financing Program site <http://www.ic.gc.ca>. The Industry Canada site provides information aimed at helping small and medium-sized businesses, companies, and entrepreneurs in Canada find financing from public- and private-sector sources. You can discover funding programs for your small business through the Centre for Small Business Financing's Grant Finder program <http://www.grants-loans.org/smallbusiness-funding.php>. Another site for federal, provincial, municipal, and private funding is Fundica <http://www.fundica.com>. Financing information can also be found at <http://www.profitguide.com/finances>. While this list is not exhaustive, it serves to highlight that there are many sources.

Obtaining money from financial institutions, investors, and government sources can be a challenge for most small businesses. (You will learn more about financing in Chapter 17.) Those who do survive the planning and financing of their new ventures are eager to get their businesses up and running. Your success in running a business depends on many factors, especially knowing your customers, managing your employees, and keeping good records. These topics will be discussed next.

Knowing Your Customers

One of the most important elements of small-business success is knowing the market. In business, a **market** consists of people with unsatisfied wants and needs who have both the resources and the willingness to buy. Many of our students have the willingness to own a brand-new Maserati sports car. However, few have the resources necessary to satisfy this want. Would you be a good market for a luxury car dealer?

> **market**
> People with unsatisfied wants and needs who have both the resources and the willingness to buy.

Once you have identified your market and its needs, you must set out to fill those needs. The way to meet your customers' needs is to offer top quality at a fair price with great service. Remember, it is not enough to get customers—you have to *keep* them.

One of the greatest advantages that small businesses have over larger ones is the ability to know their customers better and to adapt quickly to their ever-changing needs. The only way to know what your customers' needs are is to listen, listen, listen. Don't let your passion and ego get in the way of changing your products or services to fit what customers really want. The Reaching Beyond Our Borders box discusses how you can use crowdsourcing to let customers and others from around the world help you design your products. You will gain more insights about marketing in Chapters 14 and 15. Now let's consider the importance of effectively managing the employees who help you serve your market.

Mattel founders Ruth and Elliot Handler started their business in their garage—making picture frames. When they found that the dollhouse furniture they made with the wood scraps sold better than the frames, they changed their business. Today, toys like Barbie have helped Mattel grow to be a worldwide leader in the design, manufacture, and marketing of toys and family products.

Reaching *Beyond* OUR BORDERS

Listening to What Your Customers Need

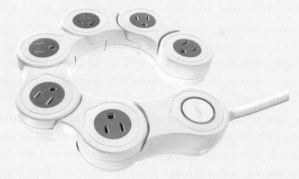

What's better than knowing what your customers need and then designing products to meet those needs? Getting your customers to design the products themselves. That's what Quirky <*http://www.quirky.com*> has done. You may be familiar with Quirky's most successful product, Pivot Power, the pivoting power strip that allows you to bend the strip in order to fit large adapters in every outlet.

Pivot Power's creator, Jake Zien, will be the first Quirky inventor to earn $1 million in royalties a year. When Zien was a college student, he joined the Quirky community and submitted his idea as a simple, basic drawing. A week later, it was selected for development. A year after that, it was on sale at Bed Bath & Beyond <*http://www.bedbathandbeyond.ca*>. Zien just submitted an idea; everything else was done by the Quirky community (i.e., all inventors, influencers, staff, and customers from around the world). Those who contribute their ideas regarding design, style, enhancing, packaging, naming, taglines, or pricing are called influencers. The influencers don't just get a pat on the back for helping out; if their ideas are used, they are paid a portion of the royalty as well. Once a product is ready for production, Quirky decides which of its 21 suppliers and factories (mostly in Asia) will make the product.

Quirky founder and CEO, Ben Kaufman, knew Quirky would work two years ago when he saw a tweet of a Target advertisement for Quirky products. The tweeter wrote, "I made that." Actually, the person hadn't made that. But he was part of the community that helped create it, an experience that gave him a sense of ownership. You can't build a customer relationship stronger than that!

Sources: Stephanie Mlot, "Quirky's Ben Kaufman Gets GE to Share Its Patents," *Bloomberg Businessweek,* 20 March 2014; "Quirky, GE Unveil Aros Smart Air Conditioner," *PC Magazine,* 19 March 2014; and Josh Dean, "Is This the World's Most Creative Manufacturer?" *Inc.,* October 2013.

Managing Your Employees

As a business grows, it becomes impossible for an entrepreneur to oversee every detail, even if he or she is working 60 hours per week. This means that hiring, training, and motivating employees is critical.[40]

It is not easy to find good, qualified help when you offer less money, fewer benefits, and less room for advancement than larger firms do. That is one reason why employee relations is important for small-business management. Employees of small companies are often more satisfied with their jobs than are their counterparts in big businesses. Why? Quite often they find their jobs more challenging, their ideas more accepted, and their bosses more respectful.

Often entrepreneurs reluctantly face the reality that to keep growing, they must delegate authority to others. To whom should you delegate authority, and how much? "The art of management is delegation," says Andrew Faridani, President and CEO of BreezeMaxWeb Ltd. <*http://www.breezemaxweb.*

com>, Canada's leading provider of online solutions. "You've got to be able to relinquish some of the hold or grip that you have on particular departments. And that was the biggest learning curve for me. By nature, I'm fanatic about being in control of the business. You have to realize that when you delegate to people in particular departments, life becomes much easier and everything runs more smoothly. I firmly believe it is the number one thing that makes businesses effective and successful."[41]

This can be a particularly touchy issue in small businesses with long-term employees and in family businesses. As you might expect, entrepreneurs who have built their companies by themselves often feel compelled to promote employees who have been with them from the start—even when they aren't qualified to serve as managers. Common sense probably tells you this could be detrimental to the business.

The same can be true of family-run businesses that are expanding. Attitudes such as "You can't fire family" or "You must promote certain workers because they're family" can hinder growth. Entrepreneurs can best serve themselves and the business if they gradually recruit and groom employees for management positions. By doing this, entrepreneurs can enhance trust and the support of the manager among other employees and themselves. You will learn more about managing employees in Chapters 11 to 13.

Keeping Records

Small-business owners often say that the most important assistance they received in starting and managing the business involved accounting. A business person who sets up an effective accounting system early will save much grief later. Accurate record keeping enables an owner to follow daily sales, expenses, and profits, as well as help owners with inventory control, customer records, and payroll.

Many business failures are caused by poor accounting practices that lead to costly mistakes. A good accountant can help you decide whether to buy or lease equipment and whether to own or rent a building. Help may also be provided for tax planning, financial forecasting, choosing sources of financing, and writing requests for funds.

Other small-business owners may tell you where to find an accountant experienced in small business. It pays to shop around for advice. You will learn more about accounting in Chapter 16.

Looking for Help

Small-business owners have learned, sometimes the hard way, that they need outside consulting advice early in the process. This is especially true of legal, tax, and accounting advice but may also be true of marketing, finance, and other areas. Most small and medium-sized firms cannot afford to hire such experts as employees, so they must turn to outside assistance.

A necessary and invaluable aide is a competent, experienced lawyer who knows and understands small businesses. Lawyers can help with a variety of matters, including leases, contracts (e.g., partnership agreements), and protection against liabilities. They do not have to be expensive. In fact, several prepaid legal plans offer services such as drafting legal documents for a low annual rate.

Make your marketing decisions long before a product is produced or a store is opened. An inexpensive marketing research study may help you determine where to locate, whom to select as your target market, and what would be an effective strategy for reaching those people. Thus, a marketing consultant with small-business experience can be of great help to you, especially one who has had experience with the Internet and social media.

Two other invaluable experts are a commercial account officer and an insurance agent. The commercial account officer can help you design an acceptable business plan and give you valuable financial advice as well as lend you money when you need it. An insurance agent will explain the risks associated with a small business and how to cover them most efficiently with insurance and other means like safety devices and sprinkler systems.

Often, local schools have business professors who will advise small-business owners for a small fee or for free. Some universities have clubs or programs that provide consulting services by master of business administration (MBA) candidates for a nominal fee. Does your school provide such services?

It also is wise to seek the counsel of other small-business owners. Other sources of advice include local chambers of commerce, the Better Business Bureau <*https://www.bbb.org*>, national and local trade associations (such as the Canadian Federation of Independent Business <*http://www.cfib-fcei.ca*>), the business reference section of your library, and small-business–related sites on the Internet. Some have been noted in this chapter.

LO5   Outline the advantages and disadvantages that small businesses have in entering global markets.

Going Global: Small-Business Prospects

As we noted in Chapter 3, the world market is a much larger, much more lucrative market for small businesses than focusing on Canada alone. Despite that potential, most small businesses still do not think internationally, and only a small percentage of small businesses export.

Milt Reimer, founder of FXR Racing <*http://www.fxrracing.com*>, a $45 million-a-year snowmobile and motocross clothing empire, has successfully expanded in the United States, Scandinavia, and Russia.[42] Have you thought of a product that can address an unmet need and would be successful not only in Canada, but globally?

Technological advances have helped increase small-business exporting. For example, PayPal <*http://www.paypal.com*> makes it possible for small businesses to get paid automatically when they conduct global business online. The Internet also helps small businesses find customers without the expense of international travel. As people acquire more wealth, they often demand specialized products that are not mass-produced and are willing to pay more for niche goods that small businesses offer.

Still, many small businesses have difficulty getting started in global business. Why are some companies missing out on the huge global markets? Primarily because getting there involves a few major hurdles: (1) financing is often difficult to find, (2) many would-be exporters do not know how to get started, (3) some do not understand the cultural differences of prospective markets, and (4) the bureaucratic paperwork can threaten to bury a small business.

Besides the fact that most of the world's market lies outside of Canada, there are other good reasons for going global. Exporting can absorb excess inventory, soften downturns in the domestic market, and extend product lives. It can also spice up dull routines.

Small businesses have several advantages over large businesses in international trade, which include the following:

- Overseas buyers enjoy dealing with individuals rather than with large corporate bureaucracies;
- Small companies can usually begin shipping much faster;
- Small companies can support a wide variety of suppliers; and
- Small companies can give customers more personal service and more undivided attention, because each overseas account is a major source of business to them.

The growth potential of small businesses overseas is phenomenal. This is why there are many organizations that offer assistance. Some of these have been cited in this chapter as well as in Chapter 4. web-based business applications are helping small businesses cross boundaries like never before and, in some instances, levelling some of the advantages that large businesses traditionally have had.

Progress Assessment

- What are the five functions of business in a small-business setting?
- There are nine sections in the business plan outline in this chapter. Can you describe at least four of those sections?
- What are some of the advantages and challenges that small businesses have over large businesses in selling in global markets?

SUMMARY

LO1 **Explain why people are willing to become entrepreneurs, and describe the attributes of successful entrepreneurs.**

Entrepreneurship is accepting the challenge of starting and running a business.

What are a few of the reasons people start their own businesses?

Reasons include profit, independence, opportunity, and challenge.

What are the attributes of successful entrepreneurs?

Successful entrepreneurs are self-directed, determined, action-oriented, highly energetic, tolerant of uncertainty, and able to learn quickly.

LO2 **Discuss the importance of small business to the Canadian economy.**

A small business is often defined as a business that is independently owned and operated, is not dominant in its field, and meets certain standards of size in terms of employees or annual revenues.

Why are small businesses important to the Canadian economy?

In Canada, 98.2 percent of businesses have fewer than 100 employees, of which 55.1 percent are micro-enterprises. Depending on various estimates, small businesses contributed between 25 and 41 percent to Canada's gross domestic product. Perhaps more important to tomorrow's graduates, small businesses employ a large portion (69.7 percent) of the total private labour force.

Why do so many small businesses fail?

Many small businesses fail because of managerial incompetence and inadequate financial planning. See Figure 7.3 for a list of causes of small-business failure. Some of these causes include attempting to do too much business with too little capital, underestimating how much time it will take to build a market, and not allowing for setbacks and unexpected expenses.

What factors increase the chances for success?

Figure 7.3 outlines some situations for small-business success. This includes whether the product is not easily made by mass-production techniques, whether sales are not large enough to appeal to a large firm, and whether the owner pays attention to new competitors.

LO3 **Summarize ways to learn how small businesses operate.**

Most people have no idea how to go about starting a small business.

What hints would you give someone who wants to learn about starting a small business?

An entrepreneur can improve the odds by learning from others. First, take courses and talk with some small-business owners. Second, get some experience working for others. Finally, study the latest in small-business management techniques, including the use of programs for things such as payroll, inventory control, and mailing lists.

LO4 **Analyze what it takes to start and run a small business.**

Writing a business plan is the first step in organizing a business.

What goes into a business plan?

See Figure 7.4 to see what goes into a business plan. A business plan includes a section on company background, the financial plan, and the location analysis.

What sources of funds should someone wanting to start a new business consider investigating?

A new entrepreneur has several sources of capital: personal savings, relatives, banks, finance companies, venture-capital organizations, government agencies, angel investors, and more.

What are some of the special problems that small-business owners have in dealing with employees?

Small-business owners often have difficulty finding competent employees. Grooming employees for management responsibilities can be challenging.

Where can potential entrepreneurs find help in starting their businesses?

Help can be found from many sources: accountants, lawyers, marketing researchers, loan officers, insurance agents, the Business Development Bank of Canada, and your instructors.

What online sources are available to assist entrepreneurs?

Entrepreneurs can start by visiting government sources, such as the Industry Canada website. Financial services providers also have sites dedicated to small businesses.

LO5 **Outline the advantages and disadvantages that small businesses have in entering global markets.**

The future growth of some small businesses is in foreign markets.

What are some advantages small businesses have over large businesses in global markets?

Foreign buyers enjoy dealing with individuals rather than large corporations because (1) small companies can support a wide variety of suppliers and can ship products more quickly, and (2) small companies give more personal service.

Why don't more small businesses start trading internationally?

There are several reasons: (1) financing is often difficult to find, (2) many people do not know how to get started, (3) some do not understand the cultural differences in foreign markets, and (4) the bureaucratic red tape is often overwhelming.

KEY TERMS

affiliate marketing	entrepreneurial team	small and medium-sized
angel investors	entrepreneurship	enterprises (SMEs)
business establishment	intrapreneurs	small business
business incubators	market	venture capitalists
business plan	micro-enterprise	
crowdfunding	micropreneurs	

CRITICAL THINKING

1. Small businesses continue to be feeders for future large businesses. As they prosper and develop new goods and services, they are often bought out by large companies. Is this good or bad? Should we do anything about it? If so, what?

2. Are there any similarities between the characteristics demanded of an entrepreneur and those of a professional athlete? Would an athlete be a good prospect for entrepreneurship? Why or why not? Could teamwork be important in an entrepreneurial effort?

3. Imagine yourself starting a small business. What kind of business would it be? How much competition is there? What could you do to make your business more attractive than those of your competitors? Would you be willing to work 60 to 70 hours a week?

DEVELOPING WORKPLACE SKILLS

Key: ● **Team** ★ **Analytic** ▲ **Communication** ▢ **Technology**

▢ ★ 1. Find issues of *Canadian Business, Canadian Business Franchise,* and *PROFIT* magazines in the library, your local bookstore, or on the Internet. Read about the entrepreneurs who are heading today's dynamic new businesses. Write a profile about one entrepreneur.

▲ ★ **2.** Select a small business that looks attractive as a career possibility for you. Talk to at least one person who manages such a business. Ask how he or she started the business. Ask about financing, personnel challenges (e.g., hiring, firing, training, and scheduling), accounting issues, and other managerial matters. Prepare a summary of your findings, including whether the manager found the job to be rewarding, interesting, and challenging—and why.

☐ ★ **3.** Contact a government agency such as Export Development Canada or Business Development Bank of Canada. Write a brief summary of the services that they offer small businesses. (Hint: Each organization has a website: <*http://www.edc.ca*> and <*http://www.bdc.ca*>.)

☐ ★ **4.** Contact a local financial institution (e.g., bank) and make an appointment to speak with a
▲ commercial accounts officer. Ask this person what a small business owner should consider if she or he is looking for financing. (This may include a discussion on the requirements of a business plan and what that institution wishes to see in this document.) Review other sources of financing that might be available. What other resources are available to assist small-business owners. Bring this information to class and share it with your peers.

● ▲ **5.** There has been some discussion in this chapter about entrepreneurship and traits of entrepre-
★ neurs. In a group, highlight the differences between a business person and an entrepreneur.

ANALYZING MANAGEMENT DECISIONS

Starting a Small Business While in School

Brett Sheffield, full-time student at the University of Manitoba and owner of Sheffield Farms and Stay Fit Health Club, was named the 2012 Student Entrepreneur National Champion by the national charitable organization, Advancing Canadian Entrepreneurship (ACE). Sheffield was triumphant after provincial, regional, and national rounds of competition because of his extraordinary achievements operating one flourishing business and launching a second while attending school full-time.

Sheffield Farms is a grain farm located in rural Manitoba that was founded in 2008, and Stay Fit Health Club is a 24-hour fitness centre in its first year of operation. "Sheffield's determination and proven business achievements, such as expanding his farm from 160 to 1,700 acres and pioneering a second business while maintaining his honour roll status at school, are ideal qualities of a Student Entrepreneur champion," said Amy Harder, President, ACE. "ACE is confident that Brett will make Canada proud at the Global Student Entrepreneur Awards in New York City."

Sheffield competed at the national level against five other regional finalists, to a panel of 50 industry leaders and CEOs. In addition to the national title, he received a $10,000 cash prize. "Competitions like the ACE National Exposition allow students from all corners of Canada to showcase our entrepreneurial talent," said Sheffield. "I'm honoured at being named the Student Entrepreneur National Champion and I look forward to continuing to take my business to new heights."

Sources: Sean Stanleigh, "Manitoba student wins national competition," *The Globe and Mail*, 10 May 2012, www.theglobeandmail.com /report-on-business/small business/sb-tools/small-business-briefing/manitoba-student-wins-national-competition/article2428615/#in; "University of Manitoba Student Wins 2012 Student Entrepreneur National Champion Title," Advancing Canadian Entrepreneurship Inc., 9 May 2012, www.acecanada.ca/news/newsItem.cfm?cms_news_id5591; and Martin Cash, "U of M student farmer aces biz award," *Winnipeg Free Press*, 1 May 2012, www.winnipegfreepress.com/business/u-of-m-student-farmer-aces-biz-award-149618705.html.

Discussion Questions

1. What are the advantages and potential problems of starting a business while in school?

2. What kinds of small businesses operate around your school? Talk to the owners and learn from their experiences.

3. What opportunities exist for satisfying student needs at your school? Pick one idea, write a business plan, and discuss it in class (unless it is so good you do not want to share it; in that case, good luck).

4. Search and find what other Canadian competitions exist for student entrepreneurs. Would you enter any of them?

VIDEO CASE 7

Steeped Tea

Dragons' Den <http://www.cbc.ca/dragonsden>, a CBC production, is the highest-rated Canadian unscripted program on during the regular television season with an average weekly audience of more than 1.2 million Canadians. It also boasts an active online community averaging more than 650,000 page views per month. Aspiring entrepreneurs pitch their business concepts and products to a panel of successful Canadian entrepreneurs in exchange for money and ownership in their companies. These aspiring entrepreneurs must get all of the money they are requesting or they will go home with nothing. Let's consider one episode from Season Seven.

On a vacation getaway in 2006 to a bed and breakfast in Mahone Bay, Nova Scotia, Tonia Jahshan and her husband, Hatem, tasted loose-leaf tea for the very first time. They liked it so much that they brought some home to share with friends and family. Before Tonia knew it, she was holding fifteen tea parties a month.

Started in 2006, Steeped Tea sells loose-leaf tea and accessories. The owners have grown the business by using a direct-sales model whereby they sell their tea through independent consultants rather than building their own sales force. Mostly women working part-time, these consultants are independent business owners that run tea parties in people's homes.

A turning point for the company was when the couple appeared on CBC's *Dragons' Den*. Their venture-capital pitch resulted in four offers. Dragons David Chilton and Jim Treliving each invested $125,000 for a 10 percent ownership in the company resulting in an overall $250,000 offer for 20 percent ownership. The owners chose them as Treliving had great connections in the United States—where the Jahshans wanted to establish a presence—and Chilton showed a solid understanding of the company's business model.

I believe in the people first and then the product," Treliving says, who is best known for co-founding Boston Pizza. "They were very well versed in what their company could do...they were passionate and focused, and had everything but some cash." His top three tips for entrepreneurs are (1) make sure you're focused; (2) know your numbers; and (3) be passionate about your business.

Sources: "Our Story," Steeped Tea, 2015, http://www.steepedtea.com/our-story/; "Dragons' Den presents the next gen den, targeting Canadian business start-ups through an online platform," CBC, 21 January 2015, http://www.cbc.ca/mediacentre/dragons-den-presents-the-next-gen-den -targeting-canadian-business-start-ups-through-an-online-platfo.html; "In pictures: Dragons' Den success story feels the summer doldrums," *The Globe and Mail,* 14 August, 2014, http://www.theglobeandmail.com/report-on-business/small-business/sb-growth/the-challenge/summer -doldrums-sour-the-milk-for-tea-company/article13736933/; "Stories from the Den: Tonia and Hatem Jahshan, Steeped Tea," YouInc.com, 28 April 2014, https://youinc.com/content/lifestyle/stories-from-the-den-tonia-and-hatem-jahshan-steeped-tea; Julia Chapman, "Steeped in Dragons' Den dollars, Hamilton tea firm grows up," CBC News, 5 October 2013, http://www.cbc.ca/news/canada/hamilton/news/steeped-in-dragons-den -dollars-hamilton-tea-firm-grows-up-1.1913049; Dan Misener, "Dragons' Den success story has caught a cold," *The Globe and Mail,* 14 August 2013, http://www.theglobeandmail.com/report-on-business/small-business/sb-growth/the-challenge/dragons-den-success-story-has-caught-a-summer-cold /article13729083/; Marjo Johne, "How couple's perfect pitch yielded four offers on Dragons' Den," *The Globe and Mail,* 7 December 2012, http://www .theglobeandmail.com/report-on-business/small-business/starting-out/how-couples-perfect-pitch-yielded-four-offers-on-dragons-den/article6007914/; and "Steeped Tea," CBC - Dragons' Den, 23 September 2012, http://www.cbc.ca/dragonsden/pitches/steeped-tea.

Discussion Questions

1. Describe the direct-sales business model used for Steeped Tea. How many consultants does the company have? How does the company compensate these consultants? How much money can consultants make? In your opinion, is this a good business model?

2. Do some research on Steeped Tea. How has appearing on CBC's *Dragons' Den* impacted the company?

3. Go to *<http://www.cbc.ca/dragonsden/episodes/>* and watch a recent episode. Was the pitch successful? Do you agree with the Dragons' assessments of the business proposal?

RUNNING CASE

Fox 40 International Inc.: A Family Business

For successful Canadian entrepreneur and inventor Ron Foxcroft, it all started in 1982 when he purchased Fluke Transport, a Southern Ontario trucking business. The company slogan—If It's On Time... It's A "FLUKE"—was soon recognized throughout North America. Over the years, Ron diversified into new ventures and the Foxcroft Group of Companies now includes Fluke Transportation Group, Fluke Warehousing Inc., Foxcroft Capital Group, and Fox 40 International Inc. (Fox 40).

All of these companies are private corporations. Although the word corporation makes people think of big businesses, it is not necessary to be big to incorporate. As introduced in this textbook, one of the biggest advantages of incorporation is limited liability. Owners of private corporations can also make decisions more quickly than is typically the case for large, public corporations.

The formation of Fox 40 is the result of a dream for a pealess whistle. When developing his first whistle, Ron was motivated by his knowledge and experience as an international basketball referee. "I always had a problem with whistles," he explains. "They have a cork pea in them and when you blow a pea-whistle really hard, nothing comes out. When they're frozen or wet or get some dirt inside, they lose their efficiency." As a result, Ron, like many other referees, sometimes found himself unable to stop play even though he saw a clear violation take place. In a fast-moving game like basketball, a whistle that fails does not get a second chance to sound. In a really big game, even when the whistle did work, the play occasionally was not stopped because the whistle's sound was drowned out by the noise of the roaring crowds. Frustrated with faulty pea whistles, he spent three years of development with design consultant Chuck Shepherd, resulting in the creation of the Fox 40® Classic Whistle.

Although Ron was convinced a better whistle would sweep the basketball market, he was unable to obtain bank financing for the venture. Very few thought that a pealess whistle would turn out and some believed that it would only be used by a few hundred referee friends. Despite the critics, Ron managed to put together $150,000 from his own private funds and in 1987 he created Fox 40. Ron risked everything as he pursued this dream: his family's financial future (only his wife, Marie, knew how much he was risking), Fluke Transport's reputation, and Fluke Transport's money. While Ron had complete confidence in manufacturing a pealess whistle that would work, he did not know that it would be the commercial success that it is today. Twenty-five years later, Fox 40 remains a proudly Canadian company. It dominates the global whistle industry and tens of thousands of Fox 40® Whistles are produced monthly for shipment to 140 countries.

What about succession planning? Today, Ron plays an active role as Founder and Chief Executive Officer (CEO) of Fox 40, and Chairman and CEO of Fluke Transportation Group. While he has passed the day-to-day running of Fox 40 to his son, Dave, Ron continues to focus on the company's strategic direction. This includes listening to customers and employees (Ron insists that the best ideas still come from them), and concentrating on increasing brand recognition for the Fox 40® brand. While it is up to Ron and Dave to approve a new idea, it is up to Dave and his team to implement it. "Once you have decided on a course of action," says Ron, "failure is not an option."

Dave has listened to whistles all of his life, in addition to the people who use them. As Fox 40's President and Chief Operating Officer, he is responsible for managing Fox 40's global sales, marketing, and operations. This includes overseeing the development of the company's diverse, innovative product base and strategic acquisitions with the company's highly capable team. Outside of the company, he is involved in industry events (e.g., as a delegate for the World Federation of Sporting Goods), he actively supports several charitable associations that support youth, and he works as a professional referee in the Canadian Football League (CFL Referee #30).

To achieve sales and profit growth targets of 10 to 15 percent per year, efforts focus on the development of Fox 40 products. As a take on the "Build a better mousetrap" catchphrase, Dave believes, "You have to build it and then the world will beat a path to your door. . . but you need to still sell it, work it, and be innovative."

While Ron recognizes that very few "seconds in command" (i.e., presidents) are happy, he is quick to point out that these are the individuals that run the show. "Dave is the ideas guy," Ron emphasizes. Examples include new product introductions (e.g., the marine line, the Heat Alert Mouthguard, and the CAUL Fingergrip whistle), and social media initiatives such as Facebook contests. Dave remains modest. "My job is to keep him [Ron] as the face of the company and it will always be the case. . . Maybe it is the referee training. The good one [referee] is never seen."

Ron was motivated to become an entrepreneur for reasons that include, "My fear of working for a dumb boss and fear of being hungry." What is it like for the next generation to work in the family business? "Working for your dad is just like refereeing," says Dave. "The first game you work, they expect you to be perfect. Every game after, they expect you to improve. . . just like working for your dad."

It is evident that there is mutual respect between the Foxcrofts. When asked how they are able to successfully work together, Ron had some answers. "Don't hold grudges," he said. "We do not discuss work outside of the office. When you walk out of the building, it is over until the next morning . . . It cannot be all-consuming in your private life."

Both Ron and Dave are often approached by individuals that seek investment in their ideas or that wish to discuss their ideas. The advice that they routinely give these individuals is: "Don't give away ownership of your business or your product!" Ron adds, "We are not a distributor. We are a manufacturer distributor and we own everything we sell."

Source: Ron Foxcroft, CEO of Fox 40 International Inc. and Chairman and CEO of Fluke Transportation, in-person interview, 25 June 2012, Hamilton.

Discussion Questions

1. What are some advantages of Canadian-owned private corporations over public corporations?

2. What are reasons why people are willing to take the challenge of starting a business?

3. "Immediate family members are given an opportunity to work for the company for a living," says Dave Foxcroft. What are some possible challenges in working with family members? How can these challenges be managed?

Entrepreneur Readiness Questionnaire

Not everyone is cut out to be an entrepreneur. The fact is, though, that all kinds of people with all kinds of personalities have succeeded in starting small and large businesses. There are certain traits, however, that seem to separate those who will be successful as entrepreneurs from those who may not be successful. The following questionnaire will help you determine in which category you fit. Take a couple of minutes to answer the questions and then score yourself at the end. A low score does not mean you will not succeed as an entrepreneur. It does indicate, however, that you might be happier working for someone else.

Each of the following items describes something that you may or may not feel represents your personality or other characteristics about you. Read each item and then circle the response (1, 2, 3, 4, or 5) that most closely reflects the extent to which you agree or disagree that the item seems to fit you. Then return to this scoring key.

SCORING:

Give yourself one point for each 1 or 2 response you circled for questions

1, 2, 6, 8, 10, 11, 16, 17, 21, 22, 23.

Give yourself one point for each 4 or 5 response you circled for questions

3, 4, 5, 7, 9, 12, 13, 14, 15, 18, 19, 20, 24, 25.

Add your points. Find where your score falls within the following ranges to read how you rate.

21–25   Your entrepreneurial potential looks great if you have a suitable opportunity to use it. What are you waiting for?

16–20   This is close to the high entrepreneurial range. You could be quite successful if your other talents and resources are right.

11–15   Your score is in the transitional range. With some serious work you can probably develop the outlook you need for running your own business.

6–10   Things look pretty doubtful for you as an entrepreneur. It would take considerable rearranging of your life philosophy and behaviour to make it.

0–5   Let's face it. Entrepreneurship isn't really for you. Still, learning what it's all about won't hurt anything.

	RESPONSE				
Looking at my overall philosophy of life and typical behaviour, I would say that. . .	Agree Completely (1)	Mostly Agree (2)	Partially Agree (3)	Mostly Disagree (4)	Disagree Completely (5)
1. I am generally optimistic.	1	2	3	4	5
2. I enjoy competing and doing things better than someone else.	1	2	3	4	5
3. When solving a problem, I try to arrive at the best solution first without worrying about other possibilities.	1	2	3	4	5
4. I enjoy associating with co-workers after working hours.	1	2	3	4	5
5. If betting on a horse race, I would prefer to take a chance on a high-payoff "long shot."	1	2	3	4	5
6. I like setting my own goals and working hard to achieve them.	1	2	3	4	5
7. I am generally casual and easy-going with others.	1	2	3	4	5
8. I like to know what is going on and take action to find out.	1	2	3	4	5
9. I work best when someone else is guiding me along the way.	1	2	3	4	5
10. When I am right I can convince others.	1	2	3	4	5
11. I find that other people frequently waste my valuable time.	1	2	3	4	5
12. I enjoy watching football, baseball, and similar sports events.	1	2	3	4	5
13. I tend to communicate about myself very openly with other people.	1	2	3	4	5
14. I don't mind following orders from superiors who have legitimate authority.	1	2	3	4	5
15. I enjoy planning things more than actually carrying out the plans.	1	2	3	4	5
16. I don't think it's much fun to bet on a "sure thing."	1	2	3	4	5
17. If faced with failure, I would shift quickly to something else rather than sticking to my path.	1	2	3	4	5
18. Part of being successful in business is reserving adequate time for family.	1	2	3	4	5
19. Once I have earned something, I feel that keeping it secure is important.	1	2	3	4	5

(continued)

(continued)

Looking at my overall philosophy of life and typical behaviour, I would say that. . .	RESPONSE				
	Agree Completely (1)	Mostly Agree (2)	Partially Agree (3)	Mostly Disagree (4)	Disagree Completely (5)
20. Making a lot of money is largely a matter of getting the right opportunities.	1	2	3	4	5
21. Problem solving is usually more effective when a number of alternatives are considered.	1	2	3	4	5
22. I enjoy impressing others with the things I can do.	1	2	3	4	5
23. I enjoy playing games like tennis and handball with someone who is slightly better than I am.	1	2	3	4	5
24. Sometimes moral ethics must be bent a little in business dealings.	1	2	3	4	5
25. I think that good friends would make the best subordinates in an organization.	1	2	3	4	5

Source: Kenneth R. Van Voorhis, *Entrepreneurship and Small Business Management* (New York: Allyn & Bacon, 1980).

PART 3

Management and Leadership

LEARNING OBJECTIVES

After you have read and studied this chapter, you should be able to:

LO1 Describe the changes occurring today in the management function.

LO2 Describe the four functions of management.

LO3 Relate the planning process and decision making to the accomplishment of company goals.

LO4 Describe the organizing function of management.

LO5 Explain the differences between leaders and managers, and describe the various leadership styles.

LO6 Summarize the five steps of the control function of management.

PROFILE

GETTING TO KNOW SHERYL SANDBERG, COO FACEBOOK

Although women have made great strides in the workplace over the last few decades, in many ways business remains a man's world at the top of the career chain. Women lead only 21 of the Fortune 500 companies.

As Chief Operating Officer of Facebook, Sheryl Sandberg knows more than most about the struggles faced by high-powered women. But her fame isn't just because of her reputation as an all-star corporate manager. Sandberg is also the author of *Lean In: Women, Work and the Will to Lead,* the 2013 bestseller about the ways she thinks women's roles in the workplace should change. While the book's runaway success turned her into a celebrity, people in the business world have known about Sandberg's seemingly superhuman ability to succeed for a long time.

The daughter of an eye doctor dad and PhD-holding mom, Sandberg's first management gig involved looking after her two younger siblings. Even in those early days she displayed an ability to be an assertive leader. In *Lean In* she writes that she taught her brother and sister to "follow me around, listen

to my monologues, and scream the word 'Right!' when I concluded." Sandberg's confident attitude and intelligence set her apart even among the bright minds of her Harvard undergraduate class. Her talents caught the eye of the prominent economist and professor Larry Summers, who became Sandberg's mentor. When she moved on to Harvard Business School to earn an MBA, Summers volunteered to be her thesis adviser. His loyalty didn't stop there. When he received an appointment at the Treasury Department from President Clinton, Summers brought on his protégé as chief-of-staff. Still only in her 20s, Sandberg began to build a reputation in Washington as a tough go-getter who still made time for the people who operated below her.

Once the Clinton presidency ended, though, Sandberg left the capitol to try her hand in Silicon Valley. She joined Google in 2001, years before the search engine became the worldwide force it is today. As an executive in charge of global sales and advertising, Sandberg struck a deal with AOL that set Google on the path to profitability. After playing a key role in the search engine's rise to dominance, Sandberg moved to Facebook in 2008. At the time the social network shared the same problem that Sandberg had faced at Google: the service was popular with millions but profits were hard to come by. To push Facebook into the black, CEO and founder Mark Zuckerberg granted Sandberg total freedom to revitalize the company's earnings structure. Along with her easygoing but dedicated management style, Sandberg also employed her army of high-level business contacts to ink important deals for Facebook. By 2010 the company was profitable. Two years later she helped launch the company's initial public offering, which, after a rocky start, grew into a well-performing stock.

But for all her accomplishments in the business world, Sandberg is still most famous for writing *Lean In.* In it, she argues that women should not have to choose between holding a career and having a family. According to Sandberg, this decision to "pull back" leaves too many women unfulfilled professionally as well as personally. But by "leaning in" to your career with passion and intensity, she claims that women can make the workplace more accessible. Sandberg's message inspired thousands to form their own "Lean In circles" to discuss the book as well as ways to advocate for change. However, others criticized Sandberg for offering advice that was aimed mainly at rich women. But despite how well her strategy works for others, there's certainly no denying that "leaning in" has paid off handsomely for Sheryl Sandberg.

This chapter is all about leadership and management. You will learn that shared leadership is more widespread than you might have imagined. You will also learn about the functions of management and how management differs from leadership. All in all, you should get a better idea of what leaders and managers do and how they do it.

Sources: David de Jong, "Sheryl Sandberg Becomes One of Youngest U.S. Billionaires," Bloomberg, 21 January 2014; Miguel Helft, "Sheryl Sandberg: The Real Story," *Fortune*, 10 October 2013; Paul Harris, "Sheryl Sandberg: The Facebook Boss on a Self-Help Mission," *The Guardian*, 23 February 2013; and Nina Bahaudur, "Lean In Quotes: 11 of the Best Quotations from Sheryl Sandberg's New Book," *The Huffington Post*, 6 March 2013.

LO1   Describe the changes occurring today in the management function.

Managers' Roles Are Evolving

Managers must practice the art of getting things done through organizational resources. **Resources** is a general term that incorporates human resources (e.g., employees), natural resources (e.g., raw materials), and financial resources (e.g., money). Resources include the factors of production, which were introduced in Chapter 1. Every business has scarce resources, and management is about deciding how to effectively use these scarce resources.

resources
A general term that incorporates human resources, natural resources, and financial resources.

At one time, managers were called bosses, and their job consisted of telling people what to do and watching over them to be sure they did it. They were typically more proficient and knew more than

Canada still trails the United States and the rest of the world in developing female leaders. Over 80 percent of organizations don't have a clear strategy for developing female leaders and yet studies have shown that having more senior-level women improves company profit.[1] What should be included in leadership development programs for women?

Rather than telling employees exactly what to do, managers today tend to give their employees enough independence to make their own informed decisions about how best to please customers. How do you think most employees respond to this empowerment on the job?

the employees they supervised. Bosses tended to reprimand those who did not do things correctly, and generally were impersonal. Many managers still behave that way. Perhaps you have witnessed such behaviour; some coaches use this style.

Today, however, most managers tend to be more progressive. For example, they emphasize teams and team building; they create drop-in centres, team spaces, and open work areas. They may change the definition of *work* from a task you do for a specified period in a specific place to something you do anywhere, anytime. They tend to guide, train, support, motivate, and coach employees rather than tell them what to do.[2] Thus most modern managers emphasize teamwork and co-operation rather than discipline and order giving.[3] They may also open their books to employees to share the company's financials.

Managers of high-tech firms, like Google and Apple, realize that many workers often know more about technology than they do. At first, Google tried to get by with no managers. Soon, however, they found that managers were necessary for communicating strategy, helping employees prioritize projects, facilitating co-operation, and ensuring that processes and systems aligned with company goals.[4]

The people entering management today are different from those who entered in the past. Leaders of Fortune 100 companies tend to be younger, more of them are female, and fewer of them were educated at elite universities.[5] Managers in the future are more likely to be working in teams and assuming completely new roles in the firm. For one thing, they'll be doing more expansion overseas.[6] Further, they may be taking a leadership role in adapting to climate change.[7]

Future managers will need to be more globally prepared; that is, they need skills such as adaptability, foreign language skills, and ease in other cultures.[8]

Future changes in the work environment will mean that work will increasingly be completed by teams, and change will come more quickly. Transparency in how managers do their job (in terms of corporate governance, found in Chapter 6) and how they address corporate social responsibility (discussed in Chapter 5) will become increasingly important.

What this means for you and other graduates of tomorrow is that successful management will demand a new kind of person: a skilled communicator and team player as well as a planner, coordinator, organizer, and leader.[9] These trends will be addressed in the next few chapters to help prepare you for your future career in management. In the following sections, management in general and the functions managers perform are discussed.

LO2 Describe the four functions of management.

Functions of Management

Well-known management consultant Peter Drucker says that managers give direction to their organizations, provide leadership, and decide how to use organizational resources to accomplish goals.[10] This description gives you some idea of what managers do. In addition to those tasks, managers today must deal with conflict resolution, create trust in an atmosphere where trust has been badly shaken, and help create balance between work lives and family lives.[11] Managers look at the big picture, and their decisions make a major difference in organizations.[12]

The following definition of management provides the outline of this chapter: **Management** is the process used to accomplish organizational goals through planning, organizing, leading, and controlling people and other organizational resources. (Figure 8.1 provides a comprehensive listing of all the critical tasks in this process.)

> **management**
> The process used to accomplish organizational goals through planning, organizing, leading, and controlling people and other organizational resources.

■ FIGURE 8.1

WHAT MANAGERS DO
Some modern managers perform all of these tasks with the full co-operation and participation of workers. Empowering employees means allowing them to participate more fully in decision making.

Planning

- Setting organizational goals.
- Developing strategies to reach those goals.
- Determining resources needed.
- Setting precise standards.

Leading

- Guiding and motivating employees to work effectively to accomplish organizational goals and objectives.
- Giving assignments.
- Explaining routines.
- Clarifying policies.
- Providing feedback on performance.

Organizing

- Allocating resources, assigning tasks, and establishing procedures for accomplishing goals.
- Preparing a structure (organization chart) showing lines of authority and responsibility.
- Recruiting, selecting, training, and developing employees.
- Placing employees where they will be most effective.

Controlling

- Measuring results against corporate objectives.
- Monitoring performance relative to standards.
- Rewarding outstanding performance.
- Taking corrective action when necessary.

Planning includes anticipating trends and determining the best strategies and tactics to achieve organizational goals and objectives, for example, pleasing customers. The trend today is to have *planning teams* to help monitor the environment, find business opportunities, and watch for challenges. Planning is a key management function because the other management functions depend heavily on having a good plan. Most often this plan is reflected in a set of budgets, which will be talked about more in Chapter 17.

> **planning**
> A management function that includes anticipating trends and determining the best strategies and tactics to achieve organizational goals and objectives.

Organizing includes designing the structure of the organization and creating conditions and systems in which everyone and everything work together to achieve the organization's goals and objectives. Many of today's organizations are being designed to please the customer and in turn, generate a profit. Thus, organizations must remain flexible and adaptable because when customer needs change, organizations must change along with them or risk losing business.[13]

> **organizing**
> A management function that includes designing the structure of the organization and creating conditions and systems in which everyone and everything work together to achieve the organization's goals and objectives.

Whole Foods Market, for example, is known for its high-quality, high-priced food items. But it has introduced many lower-cost items to adjust to the financial losses of its customer base. General Motors lost many customers to manufacturers of more fuel-efficient cars. It hopes to win back market share by offering hydrogen-powered or electric vehicles that cost less to run. This approach has generated some success for the company.[14]

Planning is what helps managers understand the environment in which their businesses must operate. When people's tastes and preferences for restaurant meals change, food service managers must respond with menu alternatives. What changes have occurred in your preferences?

Leading means creating a vision for the organization and communicating, guiding, training, coaching, and motivating others to work effectively to achieve the organization's goals and objectives. Researchers have spent a considerable amount of time studying motivation, given the direct relationship between motivation and output. This subject is explored further in Chapter 11. The trend is to empower employees and give them as much freedom as possible to become self-directed and self-motivated. Empowerment will be further discussed in Chapter 12, Human Resource Management. This function was once known as *directing;* that is, telling employees exactly what to do. In many smaller firms, that is still the role of managers. In most large modern firms, however, managers no longer tell people exactly what to do because knowledge workers and other employees often know how to do their jobs better than the manager.[15] Nonetheless, leadership is necessary to keep employees focused on the right tasks at the right time along with training, coaching, motivating, and the other leadership tasks.[16]

> **leading**
> Creating a vision for the organization and guiding, training, coaching, and motivating others to work effectively to achieve the organization's goals and objectives.

Controlling involves establishing clear standards to determine whether an organization is progressing toward its goals and objectives, reporting the results achieved, rewarding people for doing a good job, and taking corrective action if work is not proceeding according to plan. Basically, it means measuring whether what actually occurs meets the organization's goals.

> **controlling**
> A management function that involves establishing clear standards to determine whether or not an organization is progressing toward its goals and objectives, rewarding people for doing a good job, and taking corrective action if they are not.

The four functions—planning, organizing, leading, and controlling—are the heart of management, so let's explore them in more detail. The process begins with planning; we'll look at that right after the Progress Assessment.

Progress Assessment

- What is the definition of management used in this chapter?
- What are the four functions of management?

LO3   Relate the planning process and decision making to the accomplishment of company goals.

Planning and Decision Making

Planning, the first managerial function, involves setting the organizational vision, values, goals, and objectives. Executives rate planning as the most valuable tool of their workbench. Part of the planning process involves the creation of a vision for the organization. A **vision** is more than a goal; it is a broad explanation of why the organization exists and where it is trying to head.[17] A vision gives the organization a sense of purpose and a set of values that unite workers in a common destiny.[18] **Values** are a set of fundamental beliefs that guide a business in the decisions it makes. Values guide strategic planning through to day-to-day decisions by being mindful of how all stakeholders will be treated. Vision informs values, and together they unite workers in a common purpose. Managing an organization without first establishing a vision can be counterproductive. It is like getting everyone in a rowboat excited about going somewhere, but not telling them exactly where. The boat will just keep changing directions rather than speeding toward an agreed-upon goal.

> **vision**
> An encompassing explanation of why the organization exists and where it is trying to head.
>
> **values**
> A set of fundamental beliefs that guide a business in the decisions it makes.

Top management usually sets the vision for the organization and then works with others in the organization to establish a mission statement. A **mission statement** is an outline of the organization's fundamental purposes and it should address:

- the organization's self-concept;
- the organization's philosophy and goals;
- long-term survival;
- customer needs;
- social responsibility; and
- the nature of the organization's product or service.

> **mission statement**
> An outline of the fundamental purposes of an organization.

Figure 8.2 contains the mission statements for a number of well-known businesses. How well do their mission statements address all of the issues listed above?

■ **FIGURE 8.2**

SAMPLE COMPANY MISSION STATEMENTS
Google's mission: "To organize the world's information and make it universally accessible and useful."
Nike's mission: "To bring inspiration and innovation to every athlete* in the world. *If you have a body, you are an athlete."
Starbuck's mission: "To inspire and nurture the human spirit—one person, one cup and one neighborhood at a time."
Loblaw Companies Ltd.'s mission: "To be Canada's best food, health and home retailer by exceeding customer expectations through innovative products at great prices."
FGL Sports' mission: "To help Canadians live healthy, active lives."

Source: According to the websites of Google *<http://www.google.com>*, Nike, Starbuck's *<http://www.starbucks.ca>*, Loblaw Companies Ltd, and FGL Sports *<https://www.fglsports.com>*.

The mission statement becomes the foundation for setting specific goals and selecting and motivating employees. **Goals** are the broad, long-term accomplishments an organization wishes to attain. Goals need to be mutually agreed on by workers and management. Thus, goal setting is often a team process.

> **goals**
> The broad, long-term accomplishments an organization wishes to attain.

Objectives are specific, short-term statements detailing *how to achieve* the organization's goals. One of your goals for reading this chapter, for example, may be to learn basic concepts of management. An objective you could use to achieve this goal is to answer the chapter's Progress Assessment questions correctly. Objectives must be measurable. For example, you can measure your progress in answering questions by determining what percentage you answer correctly over time.

> **objectives**
> Specific, measurable, short-term statements detailing how to achieve the organization's goals.

Planning is a continuous process. It is unlikely that a plan that worked yesterday would be successful in today's market. Most planning follows a pattern. The procedure you would follow in planning your life and career is basically the same as that used by businesses for their plans. Planning answers two fundamental questions for businesses: What is the gap between where an organization is now and where it wants to be? and then, How can we get there from here?

1. *What is the situation now?* What are the success factors affecting the industry participants and how do we compare? What is the state of the economy and other environments? What opportunities exist for meeting people's needs? What products and customers are most profitable? Who are our major competitors? What threats are there to our business?

   These questions frame the **SWOT analysis.**[19] This is an analysis of an organization's **S**trengths, **W**eaknesses, **O**pportunities, and **T**hreats—how can strengths be used and capitalized on, how can weaknesses be improved, how can opportunities be exploited, and how can threats be mitigated. A company begins such a process by soliciting input from all key stakeholders in order to create a general review of the business situation. Then it identifies its internal strengths and weaknesses, relative to its competitors.

> **SWOT analysis**
> A planning tool used to analyze an organization's strengths, weaknesses, opportunities, and threats.

These strengths and weaknesses are for the most part internal and therefore within the control of the organization. They include elements that are referred to as PRIMO-F: people, resources, innovation and ideas, marketing, operations, and finance. Next, a business environment analysis (you were introduced to some elements, such as the legal environment, in Chapter 1) is conducted. Opportunities and threats in the marketplace are identified—and, while they cannot always be controlled or anticipated, they most definitely affect the organization. Opportunities and threats include concepts referred to as PESTLE: political, economic, social, technological, legal, and environmental.

Figure 8.3 lists some of the potential issues companies consider when conducting a SWOT analysis: What external success factors affect the industry? How does our organization measure up to other organizations? What are our social objectives? What are our personal development objectives? What can we do to survive and prosper during a recession? A SWOT analysis is framed by the vision and when completed may result in the vision being revisited. All of the data are gathered and organized to reflect where a company is today and where a company would like to be. Differences between the two represent gaps. These gaps should then be addressed in the planning described next.

■ **FIGURE 8.3**

SWOT ANALYSIS

This matrix identifies potential strengths, weaknesses, opportunities and threats organizations may consider in a SWOT analysis.

Potential Internal STRENGTHS

- an acknowledged market leader
- core competencies in key areas
- proven and respected management team
- well-conceived functional area strategies
- cost advantages
- better advertising campaigns

Potential Internal WEAKNESSES

- no clear strategic direction
- weak market image
- subpar profitability
- obsolete facilities
- lack of managerial depth and talent
- too narrow a product line

Potential External OPPORTUNITIES

- falling trade barriers in attractive foreign markets
- new government policies (e.g., incentives for R&D, lower taxes, industry deregulation)
- increases in market demand (due to changing buyer needs and tastes, growing incomes)
- ability to transfer skills/technology to new products
- complacency among rival firms

Potential External THREATS

- recession and changing (negative) economic conditions
- introduction of substitute products (by competitors)
- costly regulatory requirements
- entry of low-cost foreign competitors
- changing buyer needs and tastes

2. How can we get there from here? This is the most important part of planning. It takes four forms: strategic, tactical, operational, and contingency planning. See Figure 8.4 for a visual of this. Notice the continuous connection between the four forms. Not only does this illustrate the relationship between them, but also that planning is a continuous process where each of the forms is informed by another of the forms.

■ **FIGURE 8.4**

PLANNING FUNCTIONS

Very few firms bother to make contingency plans. If something changes the market, such companies may be slow to respond. Most organizations do strategic, tactical, and operational planning.

FORMS OF PLANNING

STRATEGIC PLANNING
The setting of broad, long-range goals by top managers

TACTICAL PLANNING
The identification of specific, short-range objectives by lower managers

CONTINGENCY PLANNING
Backup plans in case primary plans fail

OPERATIONAL PLANNING
The setting of work standards and schedules

Strategic planning outlines how the company will meet its objectives and goals. It provides the foundation for the policies, procedures, and strategies for obtaining and using resources to achieve those goals.[20] Policies are broad guides to action, and strategies determine the best way to use resources. At the strategic planning stage, top managers of the company decide which customers to serve, what goods or services to sell, and the geographic areas in which the firm will compete.[21]

> **strategic planning**
> The process of determining the major goals of the organization and the policies and strategies for obtaining and using resources to achieve those goals.

For example, in response to the economic slump that impacted global and North American markets in 2008, Taco Bell <http://www.tacobell.ca> introduced a "value menu" of items like cheese roll-ups and bean burritos with low prices. It also went after the "fourth-meal" (late-night) crowd and introduced several low-calorie, low-fat Fresco items. However, Blockbuster was not as successful in fighting off the introduction of new technology offered by Netflix <https://www.netflix.com/ca> and Hulu <http://www.hulu.com>, making its brick and mortar stores obsolete.

In today's rapidly changing environment, strategic planning is becoming more difficult because changes are occurring so fast that plans—even those set for just months into the future—may soon be obsolete. Think of how the used car dealership had to adjust the price for small fuel-efficient cars when the price of gas went from a dollar per litre to nearly two dollars and then dropped back to the dollar and a half range again.

Clearly, some companies are making shorter-term plans that allow for quick responses to customer needs and requests. The goal is to be flexible and responsive to the market.[22]

Tactical planning is the process of developing detailed, short-term statements about what is to be done, who is to do it, and how it is to be done. Tactical planning is normally the responsibility of managers or teams of managers at *lower* levels of the organization, whereas strategic planning is the responsibility of the *top* managers of the firm (e.g., the president and vice-presidents of the organization). Tactical planning, for example, involves setting annual budgets and deciding on other details and activities necessary to meet the strategic objectives. If the strategic plan of a truck manufacturer, for example, is to sell more trucks in northern Canada, the tactical plan might be to fund more research of northern truck drivers' wants and needs, and to plan advertising to reach those customers.

> **tactical planning**
> The process of developing detailed, short-term statements about what is to be done, who is to do it, and how it is to be done.

Operational planning is the process of setting work standards and schedules necessary to implement the company's tactical objectives. Whereas strategic planning views the organization as a whole, operational planning focuses on the specific responsibilities of supervisors, department managers, and individual employees. Operational plans can include operational budgets. You will read about budgets in more detail in Chapter 17. The operational plan is the department manager's tool for daily and weekly operations. An operational plan could also include, say, the specific dates for certain truck parts to be completed and the quality specifications those parts must meet. You will read about operations management in more detail in Chapter 10.

> **operational planning**
> The process of setting work standards and schedules necessary to implement the company's tactical objectives.

Spotlight *On* SMALL BUSINESS

I'd Rather Be Blue

Some of the best-managed organizations can be found in the most unusual situations. Consider, for example, three entrepreneurs whose product involved shaving their heads, slathering themselves with blue paint, and drumming on homemade instruments such as PVC pipe. Enter the Blue Man Group *<http://www.blueman.com>*. The original Blue Men—Matt Goldman, Phil Stanton, and Chris Wink—manage an organization of over 500 employees, 70 of whom appear nightly as Blue Men in cities around the world. Their Megastar World Tour included a number of shows in central Canada featuring their unique music, comedy, and multimedia theatrics.

Like the founders of any other company, the Blue Man Group creators knew they had to tinker with their product if they wanted to expand and be successful. Planning and organization were critical. The partners locked themselves away for several days to write a detailed 132-page Blue Man operating manual. Writing the manual made the partners realize the vast market potential for their concept, but it also taught them the importance of managing the product's growth and everyday operations. The three leaders also knew they needed to think strategically about how to build their business and maintain audience interest. Today they are set to stage their first tour in Latin America and have branched into other areas including albums, film scores, orchestra performances, and advertising campaigns.

Sources: "Blue Man Group to Launch First Latin American Tour this Summer," BroadwayWorld.com, 1 May 2015, http://www.broadwayworld.com/brazil/article/Blue-Man-Group-to-Launch-First-Latin-American-Tour-This-Summer-20150501#; Liz Welch, "How We Did It: The Blue Man Group," *Inc.,* August 2008; and Blue Man Group, www.blueman.com, downloaded 29 January 2009.

Contingency planning is the process of preparing alternative courses of action that may be used if the primary plans do not achieve the organization's objectives. The economic and competitive environments change so rapidly that it is wise to have alternative plans of action ready in anticipation of such changes. For example, if an organization does not meet its sales goals by a certain date, the contingency plan may call for more advertising or a cut in prices at that time.

contingency planning
The process of preparing alternative courses of action that may be used if the primary plans do not achieve the organization's objectives.

Some companies see opportunities where others see threats. Morneau Shepell Inc. *<http://www .morneaushepell.com>* provides global benefits consulting, administration systems, and outsourcing services. Morneau Shepell believes that most companies view contingency planning solely as a tool to prevent operational shutdowns. A company should be able to mitigate the potential damage and financial loss resulting from an unforeseen emergency or catastrophe, but it encourages companies to re-evaluate their thinking regarding contingency planning and the importance of anticipating health care–related emergencies (HREs). For example, at the time of the widespread SARS epidemic in 2003, a survey to examine how Canadian businesses were managing the health crisis found only 11 percent of the employers had a human resource policy to address HREs. The benefits of an HRE contingency plan include ensuring business continuity, reducing risk to employees and their dependents, maintaining productivity, and minimizing the possibility of litigation.[23]

Crisis planning is a part of contingency planning. **Crisis planning** involves reacting to sudden changes in the environment.[24] For example, many cities and businesses have developed plans to respond to terrorist attacks. You can imagine how important such plans would be to hospitals, airlines, the police, and public transportation authorities. In short, crisis planning is a critical component of contingency planning that requires understanding and acceptance throughout the whole organization. You will read more about risk management in Appendix D.

crisis planning
Involves reacting to sudden changes in the environment.

Organizations of all kinds need contingency plans for unexpected events. Here airport first responders participate in a drill with volunteers who are pretending to be victims in a simulated airplane crash. What contingency plans are you aware of on your campus or at work?

Instead of creating detailed strategic plans, the leaders of market-based companies (companies that respond quickly to changes in competition or to other environmental changes) often simply set direction. They want to stay flexible, listen to customers, and seize opportunities—expected or not. Think of how stores selling to teenagers must adapt to style changes.[25] The opportunities, however, must fit into the company's overall goals and objectives; if not, the company could lose its focus.

Before we consider decision making, let us summarize some of the points in this chapter. A vision ("WHERE we are going . . ."), in combination with values (HOW we will treat our stakeholders . . .), and the mission statement ("Our purpose IS . . ."), provides direction for the company. A company's objectives (WHAT we want to accomplish) are linked to its strategy (HOW we will accomplish the objectives). So, there is a progression from vision and values, to mission, to objectives, and to strategy. Once the strategy has been established, plans must be developed and implemented to ensure that objectives are met. There is never a strategy without there first being an objective. A SWOT analysis alone has little effect unless you match it to the company's strategy and plan.

Clearly, then, much of management and planning requires decision making. The Spotlight on Small Business box (shown earlier in this chapter) illustrates how one unique small business handles planning and decision making.

Decision Making: Finding the Best Alternative

All management functions require decision making. **Decision making** is choosing among two or more alternatives. It sounds easier on paper than it is in practice. In fact, decision making is the heart of all management functions. The *rational decision-making* model is a series of steps that managers often follow to make logical, intelligent, and well-founded decisions.[26] These steps can be thought of as the six Ds of decision making:

1. Define the situation.
2. Describe and collect needed information.
3. Develop alternatives.
4. Decide which alternative is best.
5. Do what is indicated (begin implementation).
6. Determine whether the decision was a good one and follow up.

decision making
Choosing among two or more alternatives.

Managers do not always go through this six-step process. Sometimes decisions have to be made *on the spot*—when little information is available. Managers must make good decisions in all such circumstances.

Problem solving is the process of solving the everyday problems that occur. It is less formal than the decision-making process and usually calls for quicker action to resolve everyday issues. Problem-solving teams are made up of two or more workers who are given an assignment to solve a specific problem (e.g., Why are customers not using our service policies?). Problem-solving techniques that companies use include **brainstorming**, which involves generating as many solutions as possible in a short period of time with no censoring of ideas, and **PMI**, which includes listing all the **P**luses for a solution in one column, all the **M**inuses in another, and the **I**nteresting points for each solution in a third column. PMI is a tool developed by Edward de Bono as part of his work on lateral and creative thinking strategies. You can practice using the PMI system on almost all of your decisions. For example, should you stay home and study tonight? You would list all benefits of your choice (Pluses) in one column: better grades, improved self-esteem, more responsible, and so forth. In the other column, you would put the negatives (Minuses): boredom, less fun, etc. In the third column you would write down the outcomes of taking the action, which often helps to clarify your decision. We hope that the pluses outweigh the minuses most of the time, and that you study often, but sometimes it is best to go out and have fun. In that case, the Interesting would be having fun in a way that would not hurt your grades or job prospects.

> **problem solving**
> The process of solving the everyday problems that occur. Problem solving is less formal than decision making and usually calls for quicker action.
>
> **brainstorming**
> Generating as many solutions to a problem as possible in a short period of time with no censoring of ideas.
>
> **PMI**
> A creative thinking strategy that lists all the pluses, minuses and interesting points for a solution in separate columns.

Progress Assessment

- What is the difference between goals and objectives?
- What does a company analyze when it does a SWOT analysis?
- What is the difference between strategic, tactical, and operational planning?
- What are the six Ds in decision making?

LO4 Describe the organizing function of management.

Organizing: Creating a Unified System

After managers have planned a course of action, they must organize the firm to accomplish their goals. Operationally, organizing means allocating resources (such as funds for various departments), assigning tasks, and establishing procedures for accomplishing the organizational objectives. When organizing, a manager develops a framework that relates all workers, tasks, and resources to each other. That framework is called the organization structure. In Chapter 9, we will look at examples of several organizational structures and will review some of the challenges in developing an organization structure.

Most organizations draw a diagram showing these relationships. This tool is called an organization chart. An **organization chart** is a visual device that shows relationships among people and divides the organization's work; it shows who is accountable for the completion of specific work and who reports to whom. Figure 8.5 shows a simple one. Each rectangle indicates a position (and usually who holds this position) within the organization. The chart plots who reports to whom (as indicated by the lines) and who is responsible for each task. For example, in Figure 8.5, manager C is the finance manager, and this middle manager reports directly to the president. Reporting directly to the finance manager are three first-line supervisors and in turn, three employees report directly to each of these first-line supervisors. The corporate hierarchy illustrated on the organization chart includes top, middle, and first-line managers. The problems involved in developing an organization structure will be discussed later in the text. For now, it is important to know that the corporate hierarchy usually includes three levels of management (see Figure 8.6).

> **organization chart**
> A visual device that shows relationships among people and divides the organization's work; it shows who is accountable for the completion of specific work and who reports to whom.

■ **FIGURE 8.5**

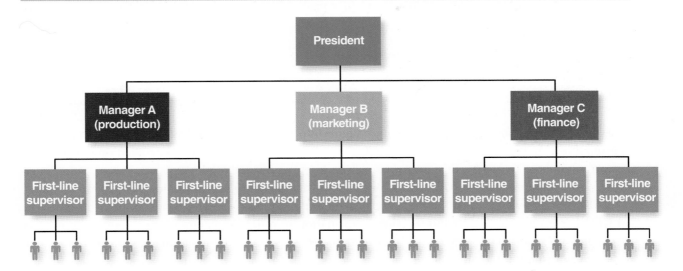

TYPICAL ORGANIZATION CHART

This is a snapshot of a rather standard chart with managers for major functions and supervisors reporting to the managers In this example, each supervisor manages three employees.

President

Manager A (production)

Manager B (marketing)

Manager C (finance)

First-line supervisor | First-line supervisor | First-line supervisor | First-line supervisor | First-line supervisor | First-line supervisor | First-line supervisor | First-line supervisor | First-line supervisor

■ **FIGURE 8.6**

LEVELS OF MANAGEMENT

This figure shows the three levels of management. In many firms, there are several levels within middle management. Many firms have eliminated middle-level managers because fewer staff are needed to oversee self-managed teams and higher skilled employees.

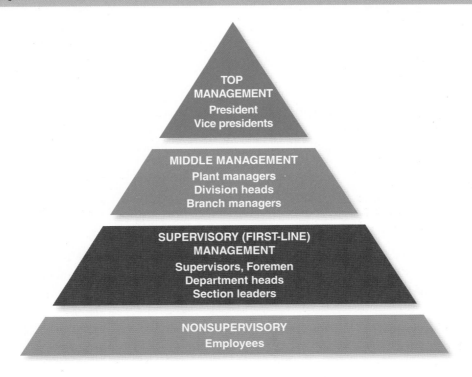

TOP MANAGEMENT
President
Vice presidents

MIDDLE MANAGEMENT
Plant managers
Division heads
Branch managers

SUPERVISORY (FIRST-LINE) MANAGEMENT
Supervisors, Foremen
Department heads
Section leaders

NONSUPERVISORY
Employees

Top management (the highest level of management) consists of the president and other key company executives who develop strategic plans. Terms you are likely to see often are chief executive officer (CEO), chief operating officer (COO), chief financial officer (CFO), and chief information officer (CIO), or in some companies, chief knowledge officer (CKO). The CEO is often the president of the firm and is responsible for all top-level decisions in the firm. The CEO and president are the same person in a majority of large companies, such as United Parcel Services <*http://www.ups.com*>, John Deere <*http://www.deere.ca*>, and General Electric.

> **top management**
> Highest level of management, consisting of the president and other key company executives, who develop strategic plans.

CEOs are responsible for introducing change into an organization. The COO is responsible for putting those changes into effect. His or her tasks include structuring work, controlling operations, and rewarding people to ensure that everyone strives to carry out the leader's vision. Today, many companies are eliminating the COO function as a cost-cutting measure and assigning that role to the CEO. The CFO is responsible for obtaining funds, planning budgets, collecting funds, and so on. The CIO or CKO is responsible for getting the right information to other managers so they can make correct decisions. CIOs are more important than ever to the success of their companies given the crucial role that information technology serves in every aspect of business. Many companies are simplifying their executive committee by combining some of the positions, like COO and CFO, which they believe provides better focus.[27]

Loblaw Companies Limited has been making significant changes in its operations over the past few years. Faced with the growing presence of Walmart and general merchandising distribution problems, which resulted in significant losses for a few years, they are looking to Galen Weston Jr., the executive chairman and president, to implement a series of strategic initiatives to restore their former glory. Loblaws is refocusing on its strong brands, including President's Choice, re-pricing some staple products to provide best-value-for-money, and improving efficiencies in its supply chain. While profits slowly improve the company is still involved in a major overhaul of its infrastructure which included a decrease of top management jobs at its head office and an increase of supervisory management positions at new store openings.[28]

Middle management includes general managers, division managers, and branch and plant managers (in your post-secondary institution, deans and department/area heads) who are responsible for tactical planning and controlling. Many firms have eliminated some middle managers through downsizing, and have given the remaining managers more employees to supervise.

> **middle management**
> The level of management that includes general managers, division managers, and branch and plant managers, who are responsible for tactical planning and controlling.

Supervisory management includes those who are directly responsible for supervising workers and evaluating their daily performance; they are often known as first-line managers (or supervisors) because they are the first level above workers.[29]

> **supervisory management**
> Managers who are directly responsible for supervising workers and evaluating their daily performance.

Tasks and Skills at Different Levels of Management

Few people are trained to be good managers. Usually a person learns how to be a skilled accountant or sales representative or production-line worker, and then—because of his or her technical skills—is selected to be a manager. Once someone becomes a manager she or he spends more time supporting those people they supervise, showing them how to do things, helping them, supervising them, and generally being very active in the operating task. Robert Katz developed a model to explain the types of skills necessary to be a good manager, and the mix of these skills through the various management levels.

The further up the managerial ladder a person moves, the less important his or her original job skills become. At the top of the ladder, the need is for people who are visionaries, planners, organizers, coordinators, communicators, morale builders, and motivators.[30] Figure 8.7 shows that a manager must have three categories of skills:

1. **Technical skills** involve the ability to perform tasks in a specific discipline (such as selling a product or developing software) or department (such as marketing or information systems).

2. **Human relations skills** involve communication and motivation; they enable managers to work through and with people. Such skills also include those associated with leadership, coaching, morale building, delegating, training and development, and help and supportiveness.

3. **Conceptual skills** involve the ability to picture the organization as a whole and the relationships among its various parts. Conceptual skills are needed in planning, organizing, controlling, systems development, problem analysis, decision making, coordinating, and delegating (see the Reaching Beyond our Borders box for more insight about skills training for top managers).

technical skills
Skills that involve the ability to perform tasks in a specific discipline or department.

human relations skills
Skills that involve communication and motivation; they enable managers to work through and with people.

conceptual skills
Skills that involve the ability to picture the organization as a whole and the relationships among its various parts.

■ **FIGURE 8.7**

SKILLS NEEDED AT VARIOUS LEVELS OF MANAGEMENT

All managers need human relations skills. At the top, managers need strong conceptual skills and rely less on technical skills. First-line managers need strong technical skills and rely less on conceptual skills. Middle managers need to have a balance between technical and conceptual skills.

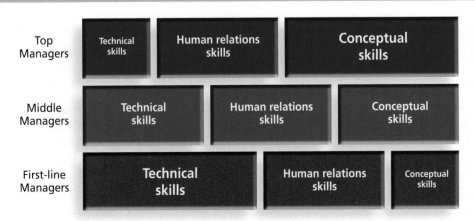

While it is not specifically stated, you can see how time-management skills are a necessary component of each one of these categories of skills. Successful managers effectively handle the daily points of contact that require their attention. This includes a high volume of phone calls, interruptions, meetings, and e-mails.

Reaching *Beyond* OUR BORDERS

Back to School for Top Managers

As the overseer of an organization's "big picture," CEOs need to have strong conceptual skills. In today's global market, the scope of those skills is expanding rapidly as businesses increasingly focus on globalization in their long-term planning.

The shift from a country-focused company to a global-focused company increases the CEO "to-do" list. Business leaders need to study a country's political, legal, and regulatory systems and the impact of each system upon important business functions such as supply chains, capital markets, and the productivity of human resources. It's also critical to thoroughly understand a nation's culture and respect its strengths and challenges.

There isn't a single global market, but rather a complex network of globally connected "local markets." Such "local markets" require their own set of local training, development, and assessment standards. Aligning a company's business applications across such diverse networks is no simple task. However, leaders at companies such as Coca-Cola, Nestlé, and IBM have done a noteworthy job.

Samuel Palmisano, former CEO of IBM, perhaps summed up the global management challenge best in his book *Adapting from Re-Think: A Path to the Future*. In it he states, "The fundamental question for companies is not whether to compete globally, but how to compete globally." That's the challenge CEOs will have to answer company-by-company as they refine their conceptual skills.

Sources: Josh Bersin, "The World Is Not Global, It's Local," *Forbes*, 23 April 2013; Samuel J. Palmisano, "The New Era for Global Enterprise," *Bloomberg Businessweek*, 28 March 2014; and Rana Foroohar, "Globalization in Reverse," *Time*, 7 April 2014.

Looking at Figure 8.7, you will notice that first-line managers need to be skilled in all three areas. However, most of their time is spent on technical and human relations tasks (assisting operating personnel, giving directions, etc.). First-line managers spend little time on conceptual tasks. Top managers, in contrast, need to use few technical skills. Instead, almost all of their time is devoted to human relations and conceptual tasks. A person who is competent at a low level of management may not be competent at higher levels, and vice versa. The skills needed are different at each level of management.

Staffing: Getting and Keeping the Right People

The right kind of incentive is needed to get the right kind of people to staff an organization. For example, Google's gourmet chefs cook up free lunches, dinners, and snacks for employees. Would such an incentive appeal to you? How important to you is pay relative to other incentives?

Staffing is recruiting, hiring, motivating, and retaining the best people available to accomplish the company's objectives. Today, staffing is critical, especially in the Internet and high-tech areas. At most high-tech companies, like Google, Sony, and Microsoft <*https://www.microsoft.com/en-ca/*>, the primary capital equipment is brainpower. A firm with innovative and creative workers can go from start-up to major competitor in just a few years.

> **staffing**
> A management function that includes hiring, motivating, and retaining the best people available to accomplish the company's objectives.

Many people are not willing to work at companies unless they are treated well and get fair pay. They may leave to find a better balance between work and home.[31] Staffing is becoming a large part of each manager's assignment, and all managers need to co-operate with the human resource department of her or his organization in order to attract and maintain effective workers. Chapter 12 is devoted to human resource issues, including staffing.

LO5   Explain the differences between leaders and managers, and describe the various leadership styles.

Leading: Providing Continuous Vision and Values

In business literature there's a trend toward separating the notion of management from that of leadership. One person might be a good manager but not a good leader. Another might be a good leader without being a good manager. One difference between managers and leaders is that managers strive to produce order and stability, whereas leaders embrace and manage change. Leadership is creating a vision for others to follow, establishing corporate values and ethics, and transforming the way the organization does business to improve its effectiveness and efficiency. Good leaders motivate workers and create the environment for workers to motivate themselves. Management is the carrying out of the leadership's vision.[32]

Leaders must therefore:

- *Communicate a vision and rally others around that vision.* The leader should be openly sensitive to the concerns of followers, give them responsibility, and win their trust. A successful leader must influence the actions of others. Ellen Kullman took the reins at DuPont in the middle of a crisis. Nonetheless, she set the tone for growth and prosperity in the future.

- *Establish corporate values.* These values (as discussed earlier in this chapter) include a concern for employees, for customers, for the environment, and for the quality of the company's products. When companies set their business goals, they are defining the values of the company as well. The most important trait that others look for in a leader is honesty, followed by forward looking vision.

- *Promote corporate ethics.* Ethics include an unfailing demand for honesty and an insistence that everyone in the company is treated fairly. That is why we stress ethical decision making through-out this text (as covered in the Making Ethical Decision boxes within each chapter). Many business

Dan Price, CEO of the Seattle-based technology company Gravity Payments <*http://gravitypayments.com*>, wanted to make a difference, so he cut his own salary by 90 percent in order to raise the salary for each of the 120 Gravity employees to $70,000. In an effort to address the issue of inequality, he decided to reduce his nearly $1 million salary and reallocate the funds to help employees earn a wage that keeps pace with today's cost of living. There were many social issues Price considered, but as a business leader he believed "that one [inequality] seemed like a more worthy issue to go after."[33]

people have made the news by giving away huge amounts to charity, thus setting a model of social concern for their employees and others.[34]

- *Embrace transformational change.* A leader's most important job may be to transform the way the company does business so that it is more effective (does things better) and efficient (uses fewer resources to accomplish the same objectives).[35] The Seeking Sustainability box illustrates how management can provide leadership in the area of sustainability.

- *Stress accountability and responsibility.* One thing we have learned from the global recession of 2008–09 is that leaders need to be responsible for their actions and held accountable for their actions. A key word that has emerged from the crisis is transparency. **Transparency** is the presentation of a company's facts and figures in a way that is clear, accessible, and apparent to all stakeholders. Governments are trying to make companies (and themselves) more transparent so that everyone is more aware of what is happening to the economy and to specific businesses and government agencies.[36]

transparency
The presentation of a company's facts and figures in a way that is clear, accessible, and apparent to all stakeholders.

All organizations need leaders, and all employees can help lead. You do not have to be a manager to perform a leadership function. That is, any employee can motivate others to work well, add to a company's ethical environment, and report ethical lapses when they occur.

Over the past 10 years, there has been an increasing trend in compensation packages that involve share ownership for top executives. These packages have been justified as necessary to attract and keep good leaders, but some critics argue that they actually inhibit leadership. McGill University's Henry Mintzberg has been vocal on his disagreement with the increasing CEO compensation packages. In his view, many CEOs focus solely on the short-term increase in the share value of the company and their bonuses. "Find me a chief executive who refuses those bonuses, who takes the long-term view and says his team will share the spoils of their mandate in 10 years' time, and I'll show you a leader," he said.[37] Do you agree that top executives should receive such lucrative packages in today's environment?

Making ETHICAL DECISIONS

To Share or Not to Share

First-line managers assist in the decisions made by their department heads. The department heads retain full responsibility for the decisions—if a plan succeeds, it is their success; if a plan fails, it is their failure. Now picture this: As a first-line manager, you have new information that your department head has not seen yet. The findings in a report indicate that your manager's recent plans are sure to fail. If the plans do fail, the manager will probably be demoted and you're the most likely candidate to fill the vacancy. Will you give your department head the report? What is the ethical thing to do? What will the consequences be of your decision?

Leadership Styles

Nothing has challenged researchers in the area of management more than the search for the "best" leadership traits, behaviours, or styles. Thousands of studies have tried to identify characteristics that distinguish leaders. Intuitively, you would conclude about the same thing they did; leadership styles are hard to pin down. Some leaders are well groomed and tactful, while others are unkempt and abrasive—yet the latter may be just as effective as the former.

Just as no one set of traits describes a leader, no one style of leadership works best in all situations. Even so, we can look at a few of the most commonly recognized leadership styles (see Figure 8.8) and see how they may be effective:

1. **Autocratic leadership** involves making managerial decisions without consulting others. Such a style is effective in emergencies and when absolute "followership" is needed—for example, when fighting fires. Autocratic leadership is also effective sometimes with new, relatively unskilled workers who need clear direction and guidance. Former Los Angeles Lakers Coach Phil Jackson used an autocratic leadership style to take the team to three consecutive National Basketball Association championships in his first three seasons. By following his leadership, a group of highly skilled individuals became a winning team. Today, Jackson is president of the New York Knicks. Do you think he is using the same leadership style as president as he did as coach? What kind of leadership do you

■ FIGURE 8.8

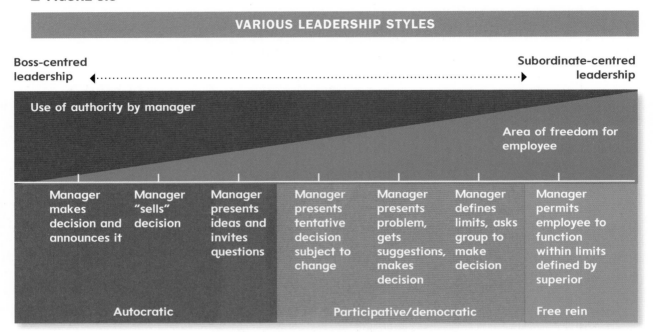

Source: Reprinted by permission of the Harvard Business Review. An exhibit from "How to Choose a Leadership Pattern" by Robert Tannenbaum and Warren Schmidt (May/June 1973). Copyright © 1973 by the Harvard Business School Publishing Corporation. All rights reserved.

see being used most successfully in baseball, football, and other areas? Can you think of a situation where Jackson's leadership style makes sense?

2. **Participative (democratic) leadership** consists of managers and employees working together to make decisions. Research has found that employee participation in decisions may not always increase effectiveness, but it usually increases job satisfaction.[38] Many large organizations like Google, Apple, IBM, Cisco *<http://www.cisco.com>*, and AT&T *<http://www.att.com>*, and most smaller organizations have been highly successful using a democratic style of leadership that values traits such as flexibility, good listening skills, and empathy. Employees meet to discuss and resolve management issues by giving everyone an opportunity to contribute to decisions.

3. **Free-rein leadership** involves managers setting objectives and employees being relatively free to do whatever it takes to accomplish those objectives. Free-rein leadership is often the most successful leadership style in organizations in which managers supervise doctors, professors, engineers, or other professionals. The traits needed by managers in such organizations include warmth, friendliness, and understanding. More and more firms are adopting this style of leadership with at least some of their employees.

autocratic leadership
Leadership style that involves making managerial decisions without consulting others.

participative (democratic) leadership
Leadership style that consists of managers and employees working together to make decisions.

free-rein leadership
Leadership style that involves managers setting objectives and employees being relatively free to do whatever it takes to accomplish those objectives.

Alan Mulally, former CEO of Ford Motors, managed to lead the U.S. auto manufacturer back to profitability after the global economic recession—without a government financial bailout. The reason for this success was the leadership style of the most authoritarian CEO that Ford has seen since its founder, Henry Ford. When an organization is under extreme pressure, why might autocratic leadership be necessary?

Individual leaders rarely fit neatly into just one of these categories. Researchers illustrate leadership as a continuum with varying amounts of employee participation, ranging from purely boss-centred leadership to subordinate-centred leadership

Other research has identified two other styles that can be included in this discussion. **Transformational leadership** occurs when visionary leaders can influence others to follow them in working to achieve a desired outcome or goal. This leadership style works best in situations where dramatic organizational change is required. Can you think of leaders who have been transformational for their organization?

transformational leadership
Leadership style that occurs when leaders can influence others to follow them in working to achieve a desired outcome or goal.

Transactional leadership is associated with employees who are motivated by a system of reward. Here the leader is given power to assign tasks and their successful completion earns rewards and reinforcement. The difference between this style and the autocratic style is that with the former the source of motivation is a reward, while with the latter it is punishment.

transactional leadership
Leadership style where the leader is given the power to assign tasks and their successful completion leads to rewards and reinforcement.

Which leadership style is best? Research suggests that it depends largely on a combination of factors such as organizational goals and values, those being led, and the situation. A manager may be autocratic but friendly with a new trainee, democratic with an experienced employee, and free-rein with a trusted long-term supervisor. No single leadership trait is effective in all situations nor is there one leadership style that will always be effective. A successful leader in one organization may not be successful in another organization.

There's no such thing as a leadership style that always works best. A truly successful leader has the ability to use the leadership style most appropriate to the situation and the employees involved.

Seeking SUSTAINABILITY

Leadership in Sustainability

Sustainability was introduced and defined in Chapters 1 and 5. Sustainability has now become a leadership issue for business. This is due, in part, to the fact that customers make purchase decisions based on the sustainable practices of a business, and companies realizing that through sustainable practices they can also reduce their costs if they implement sustainable practices.

Leadership is shown by making sustainability part and parcel of how a business operates. Leadership opportunities can be found from how a business sources its inputs, to how it produces the goods or services, to how it distributes and services products. Furthermore, standards are emerging that measure sustainability, including measures of energy efficiency, carbon emissions, water usage, and labour practices (examples were discussed in Chapter 5).

As businesses become more mature in their view of sustainability they have moved from initially wanting to protect their value through compliance with regulations to embedding real, measurable, ongoing commitments to sustainability that they believe will differentiate them in the market.

The Network for Business Sustainability *<http://nbs.net>* is a community of managers and researchers who advance the "profits, people, and planet" approach. Leaders from companies with a strong sustainability reputation share their insights with leaders from other organizations.

How might each management function (planning, organizing, leading, controlling) be applied to sustainability?

Source: Tima Bansal, "Sustainability is not a buzzword. It's the future for Canadian business," *The Globe and Mail,* 23 April 2015, http://www.theglobeandmail.com/report-on-business/careers/leadership-lab/sustainability-is-not-a-buzzword-its-the-future-for-canadian-business/article23990341/; PwC, www.pwc.com/ca/en/sustainability/publications.jhtml; Sustainability Advantage, www.sustainabilityadvantage.com/; and Simply Sustain, www.simplysustain.com/a/Sustainability/Ourviews/tabid/57/Default.aspx.

Managing Knowledge

"Knowledge is power." Empowering employees means giving them knowledge—that is, getting them the information they need to do the best job they can. Finding the right information, keeping the information in a readily accessible place, and making the information known to everyone in the firm constitutes **knowledge management.** For example, Canadian Tire was the first major Canadian retailer to use an Internet-based eLearning program. eLearning is an online training and education program that delivers product knowledge and skills training on everything from plumbing to paint mixing. The program is credited with improved customer and employee satisfaction levels. According to Janice Wismer, former vice-president of human resources, "People say the lessons have increased their confidence, that they're happier working here because the company is committing to their growth and development."[39] This is good news for store sales.

---

knowledge management
Finding the right information, keeping the information in a readily accessible place, and making the information known to everyone in the firm.

At fast food chains, the typical approach for managers is to supervise and direct employees rather than empower employees. What do you think are some of the consequences for managers who do not empower their staff with decision-making authority?

The first step to developing a knowledge management system is determining what knowledge is most important. Do you want to know more about your customers? Do you want to know more about competitors? What kind of information would make the company more effective or more efficient or more responsive to the marketplace? Once you have decided what you need to know, you set out to find answers to those questions.

Knowledge management tries to keep people from reinventing the wheel—that is, duplicating the work of gathering information—every time a decision needs to be made. A company really progresses when each person in the firm asks continually, "What do I still not know?" and "Whom should I be asking?" It is just as important to know what is not working as what is working. Employees and managers now have e-mail, text messaging, and other means of keeping in touch with each other, with customers, and with other stakeholders. The key to success is learning how to process that information effectively and turn it into knowledge that everyone can use to improve processes and procedures. That is one way to enable workers to be more effective. (Recall that there is a brief discussion in the Online Supplement about information technology and knowledge management.) See the Adapting to Change box for an example of how GM used social media to manage information customers needed during a time of crisis for the company.

Progress Assessment

- What are some characteristics of leadership today that make leaders different from traditional managers?
- Explain the differences between autocratic and democratic leadership styles.
- What is the first step in developing a knowledge management system?

Adapting *to* CHANGE

Using Social Media During the Worst of Times

When a company struggles with a recall of 1.6 million of their products that are linked to 13 deaths, managers naturally expect a harsh backlash from consumers. This was the situation Mary Barra faced, just a few short weeks after being named CEO of General Motors (GM). GM was forced to recall 2006 Saturn Ions and five other models because of a defective ignition switch that, if bumped or weighed down by a heavy key ring, could turn off, shutting down the engine and disabling the car's air bags.

To make matters worse for the company, investigations indicated that there were employees within the company who knew about the defective switch years ago; yet the problem was not corrected. At the time this textbook was written, over 4,000 claims had been submitted for review to receive funds from the Victim Compensation Fund.

Barra knew it was impossible to undo the damage already done. She decided the best path was to try to redefine GM as an open, transparent, listening organization that customers could trust. One of her first moves was appointing a vehicle-safety czar whose job is to quickly identify and resolve any safety issues facing the company. She also wanted worried owners of recalled vehicles to know that GM was listening and ready to address their concerns. To achieve this, GM's social media group was deployed to reach out to impacted customers to explain their cars were drivable while they waited for repairs so long as extra items were not attached to their key rings. Despite such assurances, GM provided more than 6,000 loaner cars to customers who were skeptical about their car's safety. The company's social media staffers also set up dealership appointments with frustrated owners to have the problem fixed.

CEO Barra's overriding concern was that the recall not permanently tarnish GM's image going forward. The company had made strong financial progress since emerging from bankruptcy and a government bailout. She knew that when it came to social media like Facebook and Twitter, a customer's perception of a brand is influenced by what an organization does and other people's opinion of it. Therefore, GM's social media commitment was to search for complaints, respond quickly, and solve the problems. Professor Roland Rust from the University of Maryland, an expert in managing brand crises, believed GM's responsiveness online was "absolutely the right thing to do." According to Rust, "If they didn't respond to customers, then those customers are going to continue to flame them." Mary Barra certainly hopes he is right and GM's response was on target. For right now, it remains to be seen whether GM can repair its internal quality-control issues and whether consumers will trust its products again.

Sources: James Healey, "GM victims' fund closes with 51 deaths – so far," *USA Today*, 2 February 2015, http://www.usatoday.com /story/money/2015/02/02/gm-ignition-switch-recall-death-victims-compensation/22741027/; "GM ignition-switch victims accepting offers, Feinberg says," *Automotive News*, 30 January 2015, http://www.autonews.com/article/20150130/OEM11/150139985 /gm-ignition-switch-victims-accepting-offers-feinberg-says; Vince Bond Jr., "GM Uses Social Media to Respond to Customer Gripes," *Automotive News*, 8 March2014; Lindsay Gellman, "Companies Turn to Social-Media Coaches," *The Wall Street Journal*, 26 March 2014; and Vindu Goel, "G.M. Uses Social Media to Manage Customers and Its Reputation," *The New York Times*, 23 March 2014.

LO6 Summarize the five steps of the control function of management.

Controlling: Making Sure It Works

The control function involves measuring performance relative to the planned objectives and standards, rewarding people for work well done, and then taking corrective action when necessary. Thus, the control process (see Figure 8.9) is the heart of the management system because it provides the feedback that enables managers and workers to adjust to any deviations from plans and to changes in the environment that have affected performance. Controlling consists of five steps:

1. Establish clear performance standards. This ties the planning function to the control function. Without clear standards, control is impossible.

2. Monitor and record actual performance (results).

3. Compare results against plans and standards.

■ **FIGURE 8.9**

THE CONTROL PROCESS
The control process is based on clear standards. Without such standards, the other steps are difficult, if not impossible. With clear standards, performance measurement is relatively easy and the proper action can be taken.

4. Communicate results and deviations to the employees involved.

5. Take corrective action when needed and provide positive feedback for work well done.

This control process is ongoing throughout the year. Continuous monitoring ensures that if corrective action is required, there is enough time to implement changes. When corrective action is necessary, the decision-making process is a useful tool to apply (recall the six Ds of decision making). Simply, managers are encouraged to review the situation and, based on collected information, develop alternatives with their staff and implement the best alternative. Or, in some circumstances, if significant changes have occurred, management can implement a contingency plan (as discussed earlier in the chapter). The focus is to meet the standards that were initially established during the planning stage or the standards that have since been modified. Since this process is continuous, it may take several attempts before standards are successfully met.

The control system's weakest link tends to be the setting of standards. To measure results against standards, the standards must be specific, attainable, and measurable. Vague goals and standards such as "better quality," "more efficiency," and "improved performance" are not sufficient because they do not describe what you are trying to achieve. For example, let's say you are a runner and you want to improve your distance. When you started your improvement plan last year, you ran 2 kilometres a day. Now you run 2.1 kilometres a day. Did you meet your goal? You did increase your distance, but certainly not by very much. A more appropriate goal statement would be: To increase running distance from 2 kilometres a day to 4 kilometres a day by January 1. It is important to establish a time period for when specific goals are to be met. Here are examples of goals and standards that meet these criteria:

- Cut the number of finished-product rejects from 10 per 1,000 to 5 per 1,000 by March 31.

- Increase the number of times managers praise employees from 3 per week to 12 per week by the end of the quarter.

- Increase sales of product X from $10,000 per month to $12,000 per month by July 31.

One way to make control systems work is to establish clear procedures for monitoring performance. Accounting and finance are often the foundation for control systems because they provide the numbers management needs to evaluate progress. We shall explore both accounting and finance in detail later in the text.

A Key Criterion for Measurement: Customer Satisfaction

Traditional measures of success are usually financial: that is, they define success in terms of profits or return on investment. Certainly these measures are still important, but they are not the whole purpose of a firm. Other purposes may include pleasing customers (including both external and internal customers). **External customers** include dealers, who buy products to sell to others, and ultimate customers (also known as end users) such as you and me, who buy products for their own personal use. **Internal customers** are individuals and units within the firm that receive services from other individuals or units. For example, the field salespeople are the internal customers of the marketing research people who prepare research reports for them.

external customers
Dealers, who buy products to sell to others, and ultimate customers (or end users), who buy products for their own personal use.

internal customers
Individuals and units within the firm that receive services from other individuals or units.

One way colleges and universities measure their performance is to track the number of students who complete their degrees or who graduate within a certain number of years. What are some of the factors that could affect the achievement of this performance standard, and how do post-secondary administrators take corrective action when necessary?

One goal today is to go beyond simply satisfying customers to "delighting" them with unexpectedly good products and services. We'll discuss management in more detail in the next few chapters. Let's pause now, review, and do some exercises. Management is doing, not just reading.

Progress Assessment

- What are the five steps in the control process?
- What is the difference between internal and external customers?

SUMMARY

LO1 **Describe the changes occurring today in the management function.**

Many managers are changing their approach to corporate management.

What reasons can you give to account for these changes in management?

Business people are being challenged to be more ethical and to make their accounting practices more visible to investors and the general public. Change is happening faster than ever, and global competition is just a click away. Managing change is an important element of success, particularly in light of today's emphasis on speed in the global marketplace. National borders mean much less now compared to the past, and co-operation and integration among companies have greatly increased. Within companies, knowledge workers are demanding managerial styles that allow for freedom, and the workforce is becoming increasingly diverse, educated, and self-directed.

How are managers' roles changing?
Leaders of Fortune 100 companies today tend to be younger, more of them are female, and fewer of them are educated at elite universities. They appreciate that many of their employees know more about technology and other practices than they do. Therefore, they tend to put more emphasis on motivation, teamwork, and co-operation. Managers in the future are likely to assume completely new roles in the firm. No matter what, managers will be taking a leadership role in adapting to climate change. Further, they'll be doing more expansion overseas.

LO2 ### Describe the four functions of management.
Managers perform a variety of functions.

What are the four primary functions of management?
The four primary functions are (1) planning, (2) organizing, (3) leading, and (4) controlling.

Describe each of the four functions.
Planning includes anticipating trends and determining the best strategies and tactics to achieve organizational goals and objectives. Organizing includes designing the structure of the organization and creating conditions and systems in which everyone and everything works together to achieve the organization's goals and objectives. Leading involves creating a vision for the organization and guiding, training, coaching, and motivating others to work effectively to achieve the organization's goals and objectives. Controlling involves establishing clear standards to determine whether an organization is progressing toward its goals and objectives, rewarding people for doing a good job, and taking corrective action if they are not.

LO3 ### Relate the planning process and decision making to the accomplishment of company goals.
The planning function involves the process of setting objectives to meet the organizational goals. Goals are broad, long-term achievements that organizations aim to accomplish.

What are the four types of planning, and how are they related to the organization's goals and objectives?
Strategic planning is broad, long-range planning that outlines the goals of the organization. Tactical planning is specific, short-term planning that lists organizational objectives. Operational planning is part of tactical planning and involves setting specific timetables and standards. Contingency planning involves developing an alternative set of plans in case the first set does not work out.

What are the steps involved in decision making?
Decision making is choosing among two or more alternatives and it is the heart of all management functions. The six Ds of decision making are (1) define the situation, (2) describe and collect needed information, (3) develop alternatives, (4) decide which alternative is best, (5) do what is indicated (begin implementation), and (6) determine whether the decision was a good one and follow up.

LO4 ### Describe the organizing function of management.
Organizing means allocating resources (such as funds for various departments), assigning tasks, and establishing procedures for accomplishing the organizational objectives.

What are the three levels of management in the corporate hierarchy?

The three levels of management are (1) top management (highest level consisting of the president and other key company executives who develop strategic plans); (2) middle management (general managers, division managers, and plant managers who are responsible for tactical planning and controlling); and (3) supervisory management (first-line managers/supervisors who evaluate workers' daily performance).

What skills do managers need?

Managers must have three categories of skills: (1) technical skills (ability to perform specific tasks such as selling products or developing software), (2) human relations skills (ability to communicate and motivate), and (3) conceptual skills (ability to see organizations as a whole and how all the parts fit together). Managers at different levels need different skills.

LO5 **Explain the differences between leaders and managers, and describe the various leadership styles.**

Executives today must be more than just managers; they must be leaders as well.

What's the difference between a manager and a leader?

A manager plans, organizes, and controls functions within an organization. A leader has vision and inspires others to grasp that vision, establishes corporate values, emphasizes corporate ethics, and does not fear change.

Which leadership style is most effective?

Figure 8.8 shows a continuum of leadership styles ranging from boss-centred to subordinate-centred leadership. The most effective leadership style depends on the people being led and the situation.

LO6 **Summarize the five steps of the control function of management.**

The control function of management involves measuring employee performance against objectives and standards, rewarding people for a job well done, and taking corrective action if necessary.

What are the five steps of the control function?

Controlling incorporates (1) setting clear standards, (2) monitoring and recording performance, (3) comparing performance with plans and standards, (4) communicating results and deviations to employees, and (5) providing positive feedback for a job well done and taking corrective action if necessary.

What qualities must standards possess to be used to measure performance results?

Standards must be specific, attainable, and measurable.

KEY TERMS

autocratic leadership	controlling	free-rein leadership
brainstorming	crisis planning	goals
conceptual skills	decision making	human relations skills
contingency planning	external customers	internal customers

knowledge management	participative (democratic) leadership	SWOT analysis
leading		tactical planning
management	planning	technical skills
middle management	PMI	top management
mission statement	problem solving	transactional leadership
objectives	resources	transformational leadership
operational planning	staffing	transparency
organization chart	strategic planning	values
organizing	supervisory management	vision

CRITICAL THINKING

Many students say they would like to be a manager someday. Here are some questions to get you thinking like a manager.

1. Would you like to work for a large firm or a small business? Private or public? In an office or out in the field? Give your reasons for each answer.

2. What type of leader would you be? What type of a leader would you most enjoy working with?

3. Do you see any problems with a participative (democratic) leadership style? Can you see a manager getting frustrated when he or she exercises less control over others?

4. Can someone who is trained to give orders (like a military sergeant) be retrained to be a participative leader? How? What problems may emerge?

DEVELOPING WORKPLACE SKILLS

Key: ● **Team**   ★ **Analytic**   ▲ **Communication**   ▢ **Technology**

★▲ 1. Allocate some time to do some career planning by doing a SWOT analysis of your present situation. Choose one career you are interested in and answer the following questions: What does the marketplace for your chosen career(s) look like today? What skills do you have that will make you a winner in that type of career? What weaknesses might you target to improve? What are the threats to that career choice? What are the opportunities? Prepare a two-minute presentation for the class.

●★ 2. Bring several decks of cards to class and have the class break up into teams of four or so mem-
▲ bers. Each team should then elect a leader. Each leader should be assigned a leadership style: autocratic, participative, or free-rein. Have each team try to build a house with a given design. The team that completes the task the quickest wins. Each team member should then report his or her experience under that style of leadership.

★▲ 3. In class, discuss the advantages and disadvantages of becoming a manager. Does the size of the business make a difference? What are the advantages of a career in a profit-seeking business versus a career in a non-profit organization?

★▲ 4. Review Figure 8.8 and discuss managers you have known, worked for, or read about who have practised each style. Students from other countries may have interesting experiences to add. Which management style did you like best? Why? Which were most effective? Why?

★ ▲ **5.** Because of the illegal and unethical behaviour of a few managers, managers in general are under suspicion for being greedy and dishonest. Discuss the fairness of such charges, given the thousands of honest and ethical managers, and what could be done to improve their opinion of managers among the students in your class.

ANALYZING MANAGEMENT DECISIONS

Leading in a Leaderless Company

In an issue of *Business Week* devoted to the future of business, writer John Byrne speculated about the future of leadership. He said that the twenty-first century would be unfriendly to leaders who try to run their companies by sheer force of will, and that success would come instead to companies that are "leaderless"—or companies whose leadership is so widely shared that they resemble ant colonies or beehives. In a world that is becoming more dependent on brainpower, having teams at the top will make more sense than having a single top manager. The Internet enables companies to act more like beehives because information can be shared horizontally rather than sent up to the top manager's office and then back down to lower organizational levels again. Decisions can be made instantly by the best people equipped to make them. One of the best examples of this is Wikipedia *<http://www.wikipedia.org>*.

In the past, uniform thinking from the top could cripple an organization. Today, however, team leadership is ideally suited for the new reality of fast-changing markets. Urgent projects often require the coordinated contribution of many talented people working together. Such thinking does not happen at the top of the organization; it takes place lower down the organization among the workers.

In the future, therefore, managers are more likely to be chosen for their team experience and their ability to delegate rather than to make all key decisions themselves. Companies in the future, it is said, will be led by people who understand that in business, as in nature, no one person can be in control.

Sources: John A. Byrne, "The Global Corporation Becomes a Leaderless Corporation," *Business Week*, 30 August 1999, 88–90; and Etienne C. Wenger and William M. Synder, "Communities of Practice: The Organizational Frontier," *Harvard Business Review*, January–February 2000, 139–145.

Discussion Questions

1. What would you look for on a resumé that would indicate that a job candidate was a self-motivated team player? Are you that type? How do you know?

2. Given your experience with managers in the past, what problems do you see for managers who let employees decide for themselves the best way to do things and give them the power to obtain needed equipment?

3. What would happen if all businesses in your area had their employees interact with customers to hear their comments and complaints? Would that be an effective or ineffective approach? Why?

4. What are the various ways you can think of for companies to pay bonuses to team members? One way is to divide the money equally. What are other ways? Which would you prefer as a team member?

VIDEO CASE 8

Zappos' Team Approach

Located in Las Vegas, Nevada, with its fulfillment centre situated next to the UPS hub, Zappos.com *<http://www.zappos.com>* has $1 billion in annual revenue. In 2010, Zappos. com was ranked #6 by *Fortune* magazine as one of the best places to work in America. The origin of Zappos was an entrepreneurial effort by Nick Swinmurn called ShoeSite.com. Swinmurn launched this company during the dot-com boom. The concept emerged as a result of Swinmurn's inability to locate shoes that he was looking for in malls. Swinmurn took photos of the shoes from various shoe stores and uploaded them onto his website. He would take orders, go to the shoe store and purchase the shoes for the customer, and ship the shoes the next day. At the time, there was no single place online to purchase shoes in that way.

Today, Zappos is owned by Amazon.com *<http://www.amazon.com>*, which purchased the company for US$1.2 billion in 2010. Zappos CEO Tony Hsieh remains at the helm of the company, and the culture of the firm remains intact. In short, Amazon.com has allowed Zappos to continue to operate as it had in the past.

The emphasis on customer satisfaction and employee happiness permeates the culture of Zappos. The name "Zappos" is a derivative of the Spanish word for shoes, "zapatos." Its culture is driven by 10 core values, the first being to "wow" the customer. Two important core values influence the planning, organizing, leading, and controlling functions at the firm. They are (1) to pursue growth and learning; and (2) to have passion and determination. These and the other core values emphasize teams and employee empowerment, so much so that team leaders (management) are required to spend at least 20 percent of their time off the job with their team members.

Relationship building helps drive a management approach that focuses on the primary goal of the company—to provide the best possible experience for the customer. The four functions of management are discussed in the video, and members of the Zappos team indicate how these functions are practised at Zappos.

Thinking It Over

1. What does the vision statement for a company like Zappos include?
2. How does the employee satisfaction and empowerment at Zappos help support the primary goals of the company?
3. Why do you think team leaders at Zappos are required to spend 20 percent of their time with their teams outside the work environment?

Structuring Organizations for Today's Challenges

LEARNING OBJECTIVES

After you have read and studied this chapter, you should be able to:

LO1   Outline the basic principles of organization management.

LO2   Compare the organizational theories of Henri Fayol and Max Weber.

LO3   Evaluate the choices managers make in structuring organizations.

LO4   Contrast the various organizational models.

LO5   Identify the benefits of inter-firm co-operation and coordination.

LO6   Explain how organizational culture can help businesses adapt to change.

PROFILE

GETTING TO KNOW JENNA LYONS, PRESIDENT AND CREATIVE DIRECTOR FOR J CREW

In today's fast-paced business environment, companies need to keep current with trends if they want to succeed. But in the fashion industry, it's not enough for brands to simply know what customers want now. Garment designers and manufacturers must also define the trends that consumers will be following in the years to come. That's what Jenna Lyons does at J. Crew. As president and creative director of the respected fashion label, she must manage the design of clothes that are fashion-forward, but are also likely to sell well.

Striking this balance has been Lyons' top priority since she took over as president in 2010. Her history with J. Crew goes back much further than that. In 1990 she joined the company as a junior designer after graduating with a degree from the Parsons School of Design. In those days, J. Crew was a successful brand with a reputation for making "preppy" clothes that would look appropriate at a country

club or yacht party. While catering to this upscale market proved lucrative at first, both sales and ideas started to decline as the 1990s drew to a close. Despite the drop in sales, executives ordered employees to continue making garments in step with J. Crew's stale branding. According to Lyons, this led to an uninspired atmosphere that stifled creativity. "We were lost soldiers, working away, following orders," said Lyons. "I was shell-shocked . . . fried."

All that changed in 2003 with the arrival of chairman and CEO Mickey Drexler. As the architect of Gap's rise to retail dominance, Drexler was known throughout the industry as a tough boss who could get the most out of an ailing operation. He lived up to this reputation on his first day at J. Crew. "He sat down, pushed his chair back, put his foot up on the table, and he looked around, and he's like, 'You're all interviewing for your jobs,'" said Lyons. At a meeting with staff the next day, he asked Lyons to give her opinion on three different pairs of women's stretch pants that the company sold. "At that point I was like, I have to be honest," said Lyons. "I can't lie to him because this is sort of a do-or-die situation." She told him that only one pair fit the brand. After Drexler threw the other two on the floor, he and Lyons began sorting through the entire women's collection, tossing the items that Lyons deemed unfashionable. He then ordered Lyons to board a plane to Hong Kong and start designing clothes for all the new holes in J. Crew's collection.

Lyons soon proved that she was just as committed to quality as Drexler. While many of her colleagues lost their jobs, she implemented a new company structure that made J. Crew fashionable again. Before Drexler cleaned house, management consultants nitpicked designers' work so that no item strayed too far from the company's established branding. Lyons, on the other hand, employed a compassionate and understanding management style that guided designers to make clothes that were stylish, but still appealing on a wide scale.

Designing fashionable clothing was only the first step in turning J. Crew around. Lyons believed that in order for the company to create a coherent brand that would drive the business forward, every part of the organization had to be unified. She was frustrated that the aesthetic of the products were not reflected in either the stores or catalogue, both run by merchandising. "There were a lot of really talented people, but they were all doing their own thing, and it looked like it." She told her teams that from that point on they should always consider how the brand appears to everyone who comes into contact with it. Lyons started by rehabbing the stores. She then moved on to completely overhauling the catalogue and website, which now look more like fashion magazines than boring catalogues.

When asked how going private in 2011 helped the company, Lyons cited the freedom to invest more in information technology. "It's hard to make those kinds of capital expenditures when you're public," she says.

With sales of J. Crew clothes tripling since 2003, Lyons has shown that she understands all the organization's moving parts and how they connect. This chapter is about changing and adapting organizations to today's markets, as Jenna Lyons did at J. Crew. There are plenty of opportunities in every firm to use the principles of organizing to manage—and benefit from—change.

Sources: David Colman, "Jenna Lyons, The Woman Who Dresses America," *The New York Times,* January 18, 2013; Danielle Sacks, "How Jenna Lyons Turned J. Crew into a Cult Brand," *Fast Company,* May 2013; and Barbara McMahon, "Jenna Lyons: Fashion Queen of America," *The Guardian,* May 25, 2013.

LO1 Outline the basic principles of organization management.

Everyone's Reorganizing

You don't have to look far to find examples of companies reorganizing.[1] A. G Lafley, CEO of legendary Procter & Gamble, transformed the company into one of the most innovative firms in the world. Some entrepreneurial companies are organizing globally from the start, and succeeding. Other organizations have been declining, including some builders within the housing market.[2] Clearly the challenge to reorganize is strong.[3]

Few firms have established as strong an image as Starbucks, but even that company had to restructure to keep its customer base. As the company expanded its menu to include more sandwiches, one of the unexpected results was a change in the smell of the stores (the odour of burning cheese was overwhelming the smell of coffee). The company restored the stores' aroma by cutting back on sandwiches for a while. Many stores had to be closed and other stores were remodelled to recapture the feel of a Milan coffee bar. In the end, Starbucks regained its market image and is prospering again.

Adjusting to changing markets is a normal function in a capitalist economy. There will be big winners, like Amazon, Google and Facebook *<https://www.facebook.com>*, and big losers as well.[4] The key to success is remaining flexible enough to adapt to the changing times.[5] Often that means going back to basic organizational principles and rebuilding the firm on a sound foundation.[6] This chapter will begin by discussing such basic principles.

Building an Organization from the Bottom Up

The principles of management are much the same, no matter the size of the business. Management, as you learned in Chapter 8, begins with planning. Let's say, for example, that you and two of your friends plan to start a lawn-mowing business. One of the first steps is to organize your business. *Organizing,* or structuring, begins with determining what work needs to be done (mowing, edging, trimming, etc.) and then dividing up tasks among the three of you; this is called a *division of labour.*

One of you, for example, might have a special talent for trimming bushes, while another is better at mowing. The success of a firm often depends on management's ability to identify each worker's strengths and assign the right tasks to the right person. Often a job can be done quickly and well when each person specializes. Dividing tasks into smaller jobs is called *job specialization.* For example, you might divide the mowing task into mowing, trimming, and raking.

If your business is successful, you will probably hire more workers to help. You might then organize them into teams or departments to do the various tasks. One team, for example, might mow the lawn while another team uses blowers to clean up the leaves and cut grass. If you are really successful over time, you might hire an accountant to keep records for you, various people to do your marketing (e.g., advertising), and repair people to keep the equipment in good shape.

You can see how your business might evolve into a company with several departments: operations (all tasks related to mowing the lawns), marketing, accounting, and maintenance. The process of setting up individual departments to do specialized tasks is called *departmentalization.* Finally, you would need to assign authority and responsibility to people so that you could control the whole process. If something went wrong in the accounting department, for example, you would know who was responsible.

Structuring an organization, then, consists of devising a division of labour (sometimes resulting in specialization), setting up teams or departments to do specific tasks (e.g., human resources and accounting), and assigning responsibility and authority to people. It also includes allocating resources (such as funds for various departments), assigning specific tasks, and establishing procedures for accomplishing the organizational objectives. Right from the start, you have to make some ethical decisions about how you will treat your workers (see the Making Ethical Decisions box).

Finally, as you learned in Chapter 8, you may develop an *organization chart* that shows relationships among people: it shows who is accountable for the completion of specific work and who reports to whom. Finally, you have to monitor the environment (environmental factors were discussed in Chapter 1) to see what competitors are doing and what customers are demanding. Then, you must adjust to the new realities. For example, a major lawn care company may begin promoting its services in your area. You might have to make some organizational changes to offer even better service at competitive prices. What would be the first thing you would do if you began to lose business to competitors?

The principles of organization apply to businesses of all sizes. Structuring the business, making an appropriate division of labour using job specialization and departmentalization, establishing procedures, and assigning authority are tasks found in most firms. How do these principles operate at your current or most recent job?

LO2 Compare the organizational theories of Henri Fayol and Max Weber.

The Changing Organization

Never before in the history of business has so much change been introduced so quickly—sometimes too quickly, as we saw with the 2011 earthquake and tsunami in Japan. As you learned in earlier chapters, much of that change is due to the dynamic business environment, including heightened global competition, a stagnating economy, faster technological change, and pressure to preserve the natural environment.[7]

Equally important to many businesses is the change in customer expectations. Consumers today expect high-quality products and fast, friendly service—at a reasonable cost. Doug Rauch, former President of Trader Joe's grocery chain <*http://www.traderjoes.com*>, views employees and customers as two wings of a bird: you need both of them to fly. They go together—if you take care of your employees, they'll take care of your customers. When your customers are happier and they enjoy shopping, it also makes your employees' lives happier, so it's a virtuous cycle.[8]

Making ETHICAL DECISIONS

Safety and Environmental Concerns Versus Profit

Imagine that you have begun a successful lawn-mowing service in your neighbourhood. To get some input on what is needed, you observe other lawn-mowing services in the area. Several seem to hire untrained workers, many of them from other countries. The companies pay the workers minimum wage or slightly more, and often provide no safety equipment. Workers do not have ear protection against the loud mowers and blowers, and many do not wear goggles when operating the shredder. Very few workers wear masks when spraying potentially harmful fertilizers.

You are aware that there are many hazards connected with yard work. You also know that safety gear can be expensive and that workers often prefer to work without such protection. You are interested in making as much money as possible, but you also are concerned about the safety and welfare of your workers. Furthermore, you are aware of the noise pollution caused by blowers and other equipment and would like to keep noise levels down, but quiet equipment is expensive.

The corporate culture you create as you begin your service will last for a long time. If you emphasize safety and environmental concern from the start, your workers will adopt your values. On the other hand, you can see the potential for making faster profits by ignoring as many safety rules as you can and by paying little attention to the environment. What are the consequences of each choice? Which will you choose?

Managing change, then, has become a critical managerial function. It may sometimes include redesigning the whole organizational structure. Such change may occur in non-profit and government organizations as well as businesses. Many organizations in the past were designed more to facilitate management than to please the customer. Managers were typically the only members of an organization who had some level of training, and possessed most of the knowledge needed to run the business. Companies designed many rules and regulations to give managers control over employees. As you will learn later, that is called *bureaucracy.* Where did bureaucracy come from? What are the alternatives? To understand where we are, it helps to know where we have been.

The Development of Organizational Design

Until the twentieth century, most businesses were rather small, the processes for producing goods were relatively simple, and organizing workers was fairly easy. Organizing workers is still not too hard in most small firms, such as a lawn-mowing service or a small shop that produces custom-made boats. Not until the 1900s and the introduction of *mass production* (efficiently producing large quantities of goods) did business production processes and organization become complex. Usually, the bigger the plant, the more efficient production became.

Business growth led to what was called **economies of scale**. This term refers to the fact that companies can reduce their production costs if they can purchase raw materials in bulk. The average cost of goods decreases as production levels rise. The cost of building a car, for example, declined sharply when automobile companies adopted mass production and GM and Ford built huge factories.[9] Over time, such innovations became less meaningful as other companies copied their processes. You may have noticed the benefits of mass production in housing and computers.[10]

> **economies of scale**
> The situation in which companies can reduce their production costs if they can purchase raw materials in bulk and develop specialized labour, resulting in the average cost of goods going down as production levels increase.

During the era of mass production, organization theorists emerged. In France, Henri Fayol published his book *Administration industrielle et générale* in 1919. It was popularized in North America in 1949 under the title *General and Industrial Management.*

FAYOL'S PRINCIPLES OF ORGANIZATION

Fayol introduced various management principles, including the following:

- *Unity of command.* Each worker is to report to one, and only one, boss. The benefits of this principle are obvious. What happens if two different bosses give you two different assignments? Which one should you follow? To prevent such confusion, each person should report to one manager. (later we'll discuss an organizational plan that seems to violate this principle.)

- *Hierarchy of authority.* All workers should know to whom they should report. Managers should have the right to give orders and expect others to follow. (In Chapter 12 we will talk about a change to this concept, called empowerment.)

- *Division of labour.* Functions are to be divided into areas of specialization such as production, marketing, and finance. This principle is now being questioned or modified, as you'll read later, and, cross-functional teams are gaining more emphasis.

- *Subordination of individual interests to the general interest.* Workers are to think of themselves as a coordinated team. The goals of the team are more important than the goals of individual workers.

Have you heard this concept applied to hockey and football teams? Did you see this principle at work in the last Stanley Cup?

- *Authority.* Managers have the right to give orders and the power to enforce obedience. Authority and responsibility are related: whenever authority is exercised, responsibility arises. This principle is also being modified as managers are beginning to empower employees.

- *Degree of centralization.* The amount of decision-making power vested in top management should vary by circumstances. In a small organization, it is possible to centralize all decision-making power in the top manager. In a larger organization, however, some decision-making power, for both major and minor issues, should be delegated to lower-level managers and employees.

- *Clear communication channels.* All workers should be able to reach others in the firm quickly and easily.

- *Order.* Materials and people should be placed and maintained in the proper location.

- *Equity.* A manager should treat employees and peers with respect and justice.

- *Esprit de corps.* A spirit of pride and loyalty should be created among people in the firm.

Henri Fayol introduced several management principles still followed today, including the idea that each worker should report to only one manager and that a manager, in turn, should have the right to give orders for others to follow and the power to enforce them. Which of Fayol's principles have you observed?

These principles became synonymous with the concept of management. Organizations were designed so that no person had more than one boss, lines of authority were clear, and everyone knew to whom they were to report. Naturally, these principles tended to be written down as rules, policies, and regulations as organizations grew larger. That process of rulemaking often led to rather rigid organizations that did not always respond quickly to consumer requests. So, where did the idea of bureaucracy come from? We talk about that next.

MAX WEBER AND ORGANIZATIONAL THEORY

Sociologist Max Weber (pronounced "Vay-ber") was writing about organization theory in Germany around the same time Fayol was writing his books in France. Weber's book *The Theory of Social and*

Economic Organizations, like Fayol's, also appeared in North America in the late 1940s. He promoted the pyramid-shaped organization structure that became very popular in large firms. Weber put great trust in managers and felt that the firm would do well if employees simply *did what they were told*. The less decision making employees had to do, the better. Clearly, this is a reasonable way to operate if you are dealing with relatively uneducated and untrained workers. (Where are you likely to find such workers today?) Often, such workers were the only ones available at the time Weber was writing; most employees did not have the kind of educational background and technical skills that today's workers generally have.

Max Weber promoted an organizational structure composed of middle managers who implement the orders of top managers. He believed workers were best managed if managers or supervisors gave them strict rules and regulations to follow and monitored their performance. What industries or businesses today would benefit by using such controls?

Weber's principles of organization were similar to Fayol's. In addition, Weber emphasized:

- Job descriptions;
- Written rules, decision guidelines, and detailed records;
- Consistent procedures, regulations, and policies; and
- Staffing and promotion based on qualifications.

Weber believed that large organizations demanded clearly established rules and guidelines that were to be followed precisely. In other words, he was in favour of *bureaucracy*. Although his principles made a great deal of sense at the time, the practice of establishing rules and procedures was so rigid in some companies that it became counterproductive. However, some organizations today still thrive on Weber's theories[11]. United Parcel Service (UPS), for example, still has written rules and decision guidelines that enable the firm to deliver packages quickly because employees do not have to pause to make decisions—procedures are clearly spelled out for them.

Other organizations are not as effective because they do not allow employees to respond quickly to new challenges. That is clearly the case with disaster relief in many areas, as was the case when Hurricane Katrina hit New Orleans. Later, we shall explore what can be done to make organizations more responsive. First, let's look again at some basic terms and concepts.

Turning Principles into Organizational Design

Following the concepts of theorists like Fayol and Weber, managers in the latter part of the 1900s began designing organizations so that managers could *control* workers. Many organizations are still organized that way, with everything set up in a hierarchy. A **hierarchy** is a system in which one person is at the top of the organization and there is a ranked or sequential ordering from the top down of managers and others who are responsible to that person. Since one person cannot keep track of thousands of workers, the top manager needs many lower-level managers to help. The **chain of command** is the line of authority that moves from the top of the hierarchy to the lowest level.

> **hierarchy**
> A system in which one person is at the top of the organization and there is a ranked or sequential ordering from the top down of managers who are responsible to that person.
>
> **chain of command**
> The line of authority that moves from the top of a hierarchy to the lowest level.

Some organizations have a dozen or more layers of management between the chief executive officer (CEO) and the lowest-level employees. If employees want to introduce work changes, they ask a supervisor (the first level of management), who asks his or her manager, who asks a manager at the next level up, and so on. It can take weeks or months for a decision to be made and passed from manager to manager until it reaches employees. At pharmaceutical company Pfizer *<http://www.pfizer.ca>*, for example, there were once 17 layers in the hierarchy between the chief executive and the lowest employee.

Max Weber used the word *bureaucrat* to describe a middle manager whose function was to implement top management's orders. Thus, **bureaucracy** came to be the term used for an organization with many layers of managers.

> **bureaucracy**
> An organization with many layers of managers who set rules and regulations and oversee all decisions.

When employees in a bureaucracy of any size have to ask managers for permission to make a change, the process may take so long that customers become annoyed. Has this happened to you in a department store or some other organization? Since many customers want efficient service—and they want it *now*—slow service is simply not acceptable in many of today's competitive firms.

Some companies are reorganizing to let employees make decisions on their own to please the customer no matter what. Home Depot *<http://www.homedepot.ca>* has adopted this approach to win more customers from competitors. Nordstrom *<http://shop.nordstrom.com>*, a fashion specialty retailer, empowers employees to accept a return from a customer without managerial approval, even if the item was not originally sold at that store. As you will see in Chapter 12, giving employees such authority and responsibility to make decisions and please customers is called *empowerment*. Remember that empowerment works only when employees are given the proper training and resources to respond. Can you see how much training would help first responders in crisis conditions?

It is important to note that well-run bureaucratic organizations can be extremely effective in certain contexts—when there is little innovation in the marketplace, consistency in demand, low-skilled workers, and adequate time to weigh the consequences of decisions.

Progress Assessment

- What do the terms "division of labour" and "job specialization" mean?
- What are the principles of management outlined by Fayol?
- What did Weber add to Fayol's principles?

LO3 Evaluate the choices managers make in structuring organizations.

Decisions to Make in Structuring Organizations

Henry Mintzberg, an expert on management and business, supports the current view that there is no single structure that will lead to success for all organizations. "Structure should reflect the organization's situation—for example, its age, size, type of production system, and the extent to which its environment is complex and dynamic. Small businesses with up to five employees do not need to spend time on how to structure themselves. However, the effectiveness of larger organizations or those experiencing significant change is impacted by structure. As well, a firm's design decisions (such as span of control, centralization versus decentralization, and matrix structures) need to work within the chosen structure and design."[12] These design decisions will be discussed in this chapter. Mintzberg has also written a book on MBA programs entitled *Managers Not MBAs,*[13] which is an insightful review of the soft practice of managing and management development.

When designing responsive organizations, firms have to make decisions about several organizational issues: (1) centralization versus decentralization, (2) span of control, (3) tall versus flat organization structures, and (4) departmentalization. Their specific choices are based upon a process called change management. This strategic approach begins by preparing for the change, then managing the change, and concludes with re-enforcing the change. Given the risk involved with this type of change, a formal process increases the likelihood of success.

Choosing Centralization Versus Decentralization of Authority

Centralized authority occurs when decision-making authority is maintained at the top level of management at the company's headquarters. The retailing giant Target *<http://www.target.com>*, for example, has a very centralized form of management. *Fortune* magazine commented that Target is so top down that the CEO personally interviews candidates for the top 600 positions. That doesn't mean Target hasn't adapted to different circumstances, however, as you'll see later in this chapter.

> **centralized authority**
> An organization structure in which decision-making authority is maintained at the top level of management at the company's headquarters.

McDonald's believes that purchasing, promotion, and other such decisions are best handled centrally. There's usually little need for each McDonald's restaurant in Canada to carry different items, although, as you have read, the restaurants' menus are often quite different in other countries. The company leans toward centralized authority. Today's rapidly changing markets and global differences in consumer tastes tend to favour some decentralization and thus more delegation of authority, even at McDonald's. Its restaurants in England offer tea, those in France offer a Croque McDo (a hot ham-and-cheese sandwich), those in Japan sell rice, and those in China offer taro and red bean desserts.

Decentralized authority occurs when decision-making authority is delegated to lower-level managers and employees who are more familiar with local conditions compared to headquarters' management.

> **decentralized authority**
> An organization structure in which decision-making authority is delegated to lower-level managers more familiar with local conditions compared to headquarters' management.

Roots customers in Kelowna, for example, are likely to demand clothing styles different from those in Charlottetown or Lethbridge. It makes sense, therefore, to give store managers in various cities the authority to buy, price, and promote merchandise appropriate for each area. Such delegation of authority is an example of decentralized management. Magna International has a decentralized operating structure. Magna's manufacturing divisions operate as independent profit centres aligned by geographic region in each of the company's product areas. This decentralized structure prevents bureaucracy and makes Magna more responsive to customer needs and changes within the global automotive industry as well as within specific regions.[14] Figure 9.1 lists some advantages and disadvantages of centralized versus decentralized authority.

■ **FIGURE 9.1**

ADVANTAGES AND DISADVANTAGES OF CENTRALIZED VERSUS DECENTRALIZED MANAGEMENT

	Centralized	Decentralized
Advantages	• Greater top-management control • More efficiency • Simpler distribution system • Stronger brand/corporate image	• Better adaptation to customer wants • More empowerment of workers • Faster decision making • Higher morale
Disadvantages	• Less responsiveness to customers • Less empowerment • Interorganizational conflict • Lower morale away from headquarters	• Less efficiency • Complex distribution system • Less top-management control • Weakened corporate image

Choosing the Appropriate Span of Control

Span of control refers to the optimum number of subordinates a manager supervises or should supervise. There are many factors to consider when determining span of control. At lower levels, where work is standardized, it is possible to implement a wide span of control (15 to 40 workers). For example, one supervisor can be responsible for 20 or more workers who are assembling computers or cleaning up movie theatres. However, the number gradually narrows at higher levels of the organization because work is less standardized and there's more need for face-to-face communication. Variables in span of control include the following:

- *Capabilities of the manager.* The more experienced and capable the manager, the broader the span of control can be. (A large number of workers can report to that manager.)

- *Capabilities of the subordinates.* The more subordinates need supervision, the narrower the span of control should be. Employee turnover at fast-food restaurants, for example, is often so high that managers must constantly be training new people and thus need a narrow span of control.

- *Geographical closeness.* The more concentrated the work area, the broader the span of control can be.

- *Functional similarity.* The more similar the functions, the broader the span of control can be.

- *Need for coordination.* The greater the need for coordination, the narrower the span of control might be.

- *Planning demands.* The more involved the plan, the narrower the span of control might be.

- *Functional complexity.* The more complex the functions, the narrower the span of control might be.

---

span of control
The optimum number of subordinates a manager supervises or should supervise.

Other factors to consider include the professionalism of superiors and subordinates and the number of new problems that occur in a day.

The trend today is to expand the span of control as organizations adopt empowerment, reduce the number of middle managers, and hire more educated and talented lower-level employees. Information technology makes it possible for managers to handle more information, so the span can be broader still.[15] More companies could expand the span of control if they trained their employees better and were willing to trust them more. Figure 9.2 lists some advantages and disadvantages of a narrow versus a wide span of control.

■ FIGURE 9.2

ADVANTAGES AND DISADVANTAGES OF A NARROW VERSUS A WIDE SPAN OF CONTROL

The flatter the organization the wider the span of control.

	Narrow	Wide
Advantages	• More control by top management • More chances for advancement • Greater specialization • Closer supervision	• Reduced costs • More responsiveness to customers • Faster decision making • More empowerment
Disadvantages	• Less empowerment • Higher costs • Delayed decision making • Less responsiveness to customers	• Fewer chances for advancement • Overworked managers • Loss of control • Less management expertise

Choosing Between Tall and Flat Organization Structures

In the early twentieth century, organizations grew bigger and bigger, adding layer after layer of management to create **tall organization structures**. Some organizations had as many as 17 levels, and the span of control was small (few people reported to each manager).

> **tall organization structure**
> An organization structure in which the pyramidal organization chart would be quite tall because of the various levels of management.

Imagine how a message might be distorted as it moved up through each level of managers, management assistants, secretaries, assistant secretaries, supervisors, trainers, and so on. The cost of all of these managers and support people was quite high, the paperwork they generated was enormous, and the inefficiencies in communication and decision making often became intolerable.

More recently, organizations have adopted **flat organization structures** with fewer layers of management (see Figure 9.3) and a broad span of control (many people reporting to each manager). Flat structures can respond readily to customer demands because lower-level employees have authority

■ **FIGURE 9.3**

NARROW VERSUS WIDE SPAN OF CONTROL

This figure describes two ways to structure an organization with the same number of employees. The tall structure with a narrow span of control has two managers who supervise four employees each. Changing to a flat surface with a wide span of control, the company could eliminate two managers and perhaps replace them with one or two employees, but the top manager would have to supervise ten people instead of two.

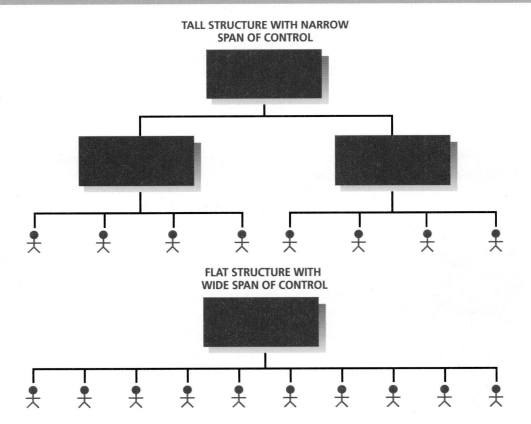

TALL STRUCTURE WITH NARROW SPAN OF CONTROL

FLAT STRUCTURE WITH WIDE SPAN OF CONTROL

and responsibility for making decisions, and managers can be spared certain day-to-day tasks. Chrysler eliminated 6,000 white-collar (middle management) jobs for just that reason.[16]

flat organization structure
An organization structure that has few layers of management and a broad span of control.

Large organizations use flat structures to try to match the friendliness of small firms, whose workers know customers by name. The flatter organizations became, the broader the span of control, which means the elimination of some management positions.

A broad span of control allows one supervisor to be responsible for many workers whose work tasks are predictable and standardized. In addition to assembly lines, can you think of other management situations that might benefit from a broad span of control? What about in a service industry?

Weighing the Advantages and Disadvantages of Departmentalization

Departmentalization divides an organization into separate units. The traditional way to departmentalize organizations is by *function*, such as design, production, marketing, and accounting. Departmentalization groups workers according to their skills, expertise, or resource use so that they can specialize and work together more effectively. It may also save costs and improve efficiency. Other advantages of departmentalization include the following:

1. Employees can develop in-depth skills and progress within a department as they master those skills.

2. The company can achieve economies of scale by centralizing all the resource needs and locating various experts in a specific area.

3. Employees can coordinate work within the function, and top management can easily direct and control various departments' activities.

departmentalization
Dividing an organization into separate units.

Disadvantages of departmentalization by function include the following:

1. Communication across departments may be problematic. For example, the production department may be so isolated from the marketing department and as a result, does not get feedback from customers.

2. Employees may identify with their department's goals rather than the organization's goals. For example, the purchasing department may save money buying a huge volume of goods from one supplier, which is a benefit to the department, but the high cost of storing the goods hurts the overall profitability.

3. The company's response to external changes may be slow.

4. People may not be trained to fulfill multiple managerial responsibilities and as a result they tend to become narrow specialists.

5. Department members may engage in groupthink (they think alike) and may need input from outside the department to become more creative.

Loblaw Companies Limited, Canada's largest food distributor, operates a number of supermarket chains across Canada including Atlantic Cash & Carry, Dominion, Fortinos, Loblaws, Provigo, and Real Canadian Superstore. The company also acquired T&T Supermarket, which has stores based in Vancouver. The company has operated since the 1960s and developed many excellent brands, including the President's Choice line of products. Since 2006 Loblaws has gone through a series of senior management shake-ups as it responds to growing competition from major U.S. merchandizers. Consolidating its distribution centres resulted in serious problems with its supply chain, costing millions of dollars. Loblaws continued to work on this issue over the next five years. How well do you think Loblaws performs today? Has the company's move to a more "responsive organization structure" fostered effective competition with the foreign retail Goliaths?

LOOKING AT ALTERNATIVE WAYS TO DEPARTMENTALIZE

Functional separation is not always the most responsive form of organization. So what are the alternatives? Figure 9.4 shows five ways a firm can departmentalize. One way is by product. A book publisher might have a trade book department (for books sold to the general public), a textbook department, and a technical book department, each with separate development and marketing processes. Such product-focused departmentalization usually results in positive customer relations.

■ **FIGURE 9.4**

WAYS TO DEPARTMENTALIZE

A computer company may want to departmentalize by geographic location, a manufacturing company by function, a pharmaceutical company by customer group, a leather manufacturer by process, and a publisher by product. In each case the structure must fit the firm's goals.

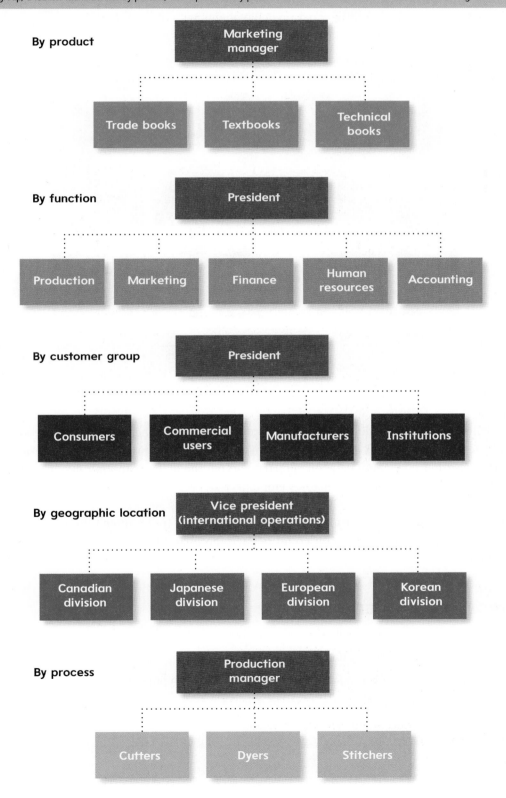

By product

Marketing manager
- Trade books
- Textbooks
- Technical books

By function

President
- Production
- Marketing
- Finance
- Human resources
- Accounting

By customer group

President
- Consumers
- Commercial users
- Manufacturers
- Institutions

By geographic location

Vice president (international operations)
- Canadian division
- Japanese division
- European division
- Korean division

By process

Production manager
- Cutters
- Dyers
- Stitchers

Some organizations departmentalize by customer group. A pharmaceutical company might have one department for the consumer market, another that calls on hospitals (the institutional market), and another that targets doctors. You can see how the customer groups might benefit from having specialists satisfying their needs.

Some firms group their units by geographic location because customers vary so greatly by region. Japan, Europe, and Korea may involve separate departments with obvious benefits.

After the material for footballs has been cut and sewn in the Wilson Sporting Goods factory, it moves on to the lacing department where workers like this one open up the deflated balls and prepare them for lacing. What are the advantages and disadvantages of departmentalizing by process similar to Wilson?

The decision about how to departmentalize depends greatly on the nature of the product and the customers. A few firms find that it is most efficient to separate activities by process. For example, a firm that makes leather coats may have one department cut the leather, another dye it, and a third sew the coat together. Such specialization enables employees to do a better job because they can focus on learning a few critical skills.

Some firms use a combination of departmentalization techniques; they would be called *hybrid forms*. For example, a company could departmentalize by function, by geography, and by customer groups.

Progress Assessment

- What is bureaucracy? What challenges do bureaucratic organizations face in a time of rapid change?
- Why are organizations becoming flatter?
- What are some reasons for having a narrow span of control in an organization?
- What are the advantages and disadvantages of departmentalization?
- What are the various ways a firm can departmentalize?

LO4 Contrast the various organizational models.

Organization Models

Now that we have explored the basic issues of organizational design, let's look in depth at four ways to structure an organization: (1) line organizations, (2) line-and-staff organizations, (3) matrix-style organizations, and (4) cross-functional self-managed teams. You will see that some of these models contradict traditional management principles. The business community is in a period of transition, with some traditional organizational models giving way to new structures. Such transitions can be not only unsettling to employees and managers but also be fraught with problems and errors.

Line Organizations

A **line organization** has direct two-way lines of responsibility, authority, and communication running from the top to the bottom of the organization, with everyone reporting to only one supervisor. The military and many small businesses are organized in this way. For example, the locally owned pizza parlour has a general manager and a shift manager. All general employees report to the shift manager, and he or she reports to the general manager or owner.

> **line organization**
> An organization that has direct two-way lines of responsibility, authority, and communication running from the top to the bottom of the organization, with all people reporting to only one supervisor.

A line organization does not have any specialists who provide managerial support. For example, there would be no legal department, accounting department, human resource department, or information technology (IT) department. Line organizations follow all of Fayol's traditional management rules. Line managers can issue orders, enforce discipline, and adjust the organization as conditions change.

In large businesses, a line organization may have the disadvantages of being too inflexible, of having few specialists or experts to advise people along the line, and of having lengthy lines of communication. Thus a large line organization may be unable to handle complex decisions relating to thousands of products and tons of paperwork. Such organizations usually turn to a line-and-staff form of organization.

Line-and-Staff Organizations

To minimize the disadvantages of simple line organizations, many organizations today have both line and staff personnel. A couple of definitions will help. **Line personnel** are responsible for directly achieving organizational goals and include production workers, distribution people, and marketing personnel. **Staff personnel** advise and assist line personnel in meeting their goals and include those in marketing research, legal advising, information technology, and human resource management.

> **line personnel**
> Employees who are part of the chain of command that is responsible for achieving organizational goals.
>
> **staff personnel**
> Employees who advise and assist line personnel in meeting their goals.

See Figure 9.5 for a diagram of a line-and-staff organization. One important difference between line and staff personnel is authority. Line personnel have formal authority to make policy decisions. Staff personnel have the authority to advise the line personnel and influence those decisions, but they cannot make policy changes themselves. The line manager may choose to seek or to ignore the advice of staff personnel.

■ **FIGURE 9.5**

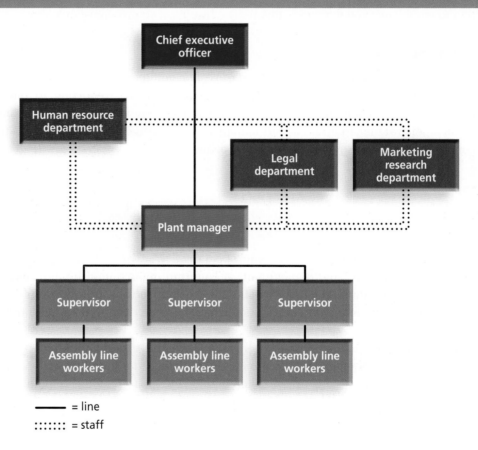

A SAMPLE LINE-AND-STAFF ORGANIZATION

Many organizations have benefitted from the expert staff advice on safety, legal issues, quality control, database management, motivation, and investing. Staff positions strengthen the line positions and are similar to having well-paid consultants on the organization's payroll.

Matrix-Style Organizations

Both line and line-and-staff organization structures suffer from inflexibility. Both allow for established lines of authority and communication, and work well in organizations with stable environments and slow product development (such as firms selling household appliances). In such firms, clear lines of authority and relatively fixed organization structures are assets that ensure efficient operations.

"SEND THIS BACK TO THE LEGAL DEPARTMENT. I THINK THEY COULD MAKE IT MUCH MORE COMPLICATED THAN THIS..."

Members of a legal department are considered staff personnel in a line-and-staff organization. Staff personnel serve an advisory role and can work with colleagues and departments at every level in the firm's hierarchy. What are some of the advantages of this type of organization model?

Today's economy, however, is dominated by high-growth industries like telecommunications, nanotechnology, robotics, and biotechnology, where competition is brisk and the life cycle of new ideas is short. Emphasis is on product development, creativity, special projects, rapid communication, and interdepartmental teamwork. From those changes grew the popularity of the **matrix organization**, in which specialists from different parts of the organization work temporarily on specific projects but still remain part of a line-and-staff structure (see Figure 9.6.). In other words, a project manager can borrow people from different departments to help design and market new product ideas.[17]

matrix organization
An organization in which specialists from different parts of the organization are brought together to work on specific projects but still remain part of a line-and-staff structure.

The matrix structure was developed in the aerospace industry and is now familiar in banking, management consulting firms, accounting firms, advertising agencies, and school systems. Matrix structure advantages include:

- Gives managers flexibility in assigning people to projects.
- Encourages inter-organizational co-operation and teamwork.
- Generates creative solutions for product development problems.
- Makes efficient use of organizational resources.

    Matrix structure disadvantages include:

- Is costly and complex.
- Confuses employees about where their loyalty belongs—with the project manager or their functional unit.

■ **FIGURE 9.6**

A MATRIX ORGANIZATION

In a matrix organization, project managers are in charge of teams comprised of members of several departments. In this case, Project manager 2 supervises Employees A, B, C, and D. These employees are accountable not only to Project manager 2 but also to the head of their individual departments. For example, Employee B, a market researcher, reports to Project manager 2 and to the Vice president of marketing.

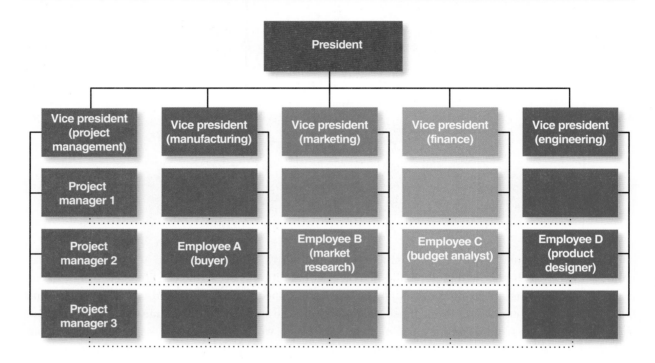

- Requires effective interpersonal skills as well as co-operative employees and managers to avoid communication problems.
- Provides only a temporary solution to a long-term problem.

If you are thinking that matrix organizations violate some traditional managerial principles, you are right. Normally a person cannot work effectively for two bosses. Who has the real authority? Which directive has first priority?

In reality, however, the system functions more effectively than you might imagine. To develop a new product, a project manager may be given temporary authority to "borrow" line personnel from production, marketing, and other line functions. The employees work together to complete the project and then return to their regular positions. Thus, no one really reports to more than one manager at a time.

A potential problem with matrix management, however, is that the project teams are not permanent. They form to solve a problem or develop a new product, and then they disband. There is little chance for cross-functional learning because teams work together for such a short period of time.

In the future, decision making will be distributed throughout the organization so that people can respond rapidly to change, says the *Harvard Business Review*. Global teams will collaborate on the Internet for a single project and then disband. It is likely younger employees who play online games will feel quite comfortable working in such groups.

Matrix organizations are also an effective structure in the world of international sport. The 2015 Pan Am/Parapan Am Games Organizing Committee (TO2015) is an example of a project-based organization. When a major international sporting event is awarded to a city, an organizing committee is formed to serve as the event host. The host committee operations are critical for a successful event that athletes and spectators will enjoy. TO2015 was responsible for the planning, organizing, financing, and staging of the 2015 Pan Am/Parapan Am Games. The organization's overall budget was $1.4 billion and its workforce included 20,000 volunteers. How do you structure this type of massive organization that lasts for such a short time? You design a matrix organization.

TO2015 was structured in a way that managed both the sporting competition and business operations. Departments included marketing, volunteers, ceremonies, logistics (transportation), medical services, and security. Each of these areas were centralized departments but also important aspects for each location, or venue, where a sport competition was held. Given this, project teams of specialists from each department were formed to manage operations at each venue where the competitions were held.

International sport competitions rely upon organizing committees to plan, manage, and stage the event. A matrix structure ensures all the critical areas, such as volunteer, security, and medical services are provided and properly managed at each location where the competition is held.

Cross-Functional Self-Managed Teams

One solution to the disadvantage of the temporary nature of matrix teams is to establish *long-lived teams* and to empower them to work closely with suppliers, customers, and others to quickly and efficiently bring out new, high-quality products while giving great service.

Cross-functional, self-managed teams are groups of employees from different departments who work together on a long-term basis (as opposed to the temporary teams established in matrix-style organizations).[18] Usually the teams are empowered to make decisions without management approval.[19] The barriers among design, engineering, marketing, distribution, and other functions are reduced when interdepartmental teams are created. One Smooth Stone *<http://www.onesmoothstone.com>* is a corporate events company. They put together large, one-time functions for corporate clients. They have a team of highly skilled and trained staff that go from the planning and execution of one corporate function to another. Sometimes the self-managed teams are inter-firm. Toyota, for example, works closely with teams at other firms to produce its cars.

Cross-functional self-managed teams
Groups of employees from different departments who work together on a long-term basis.

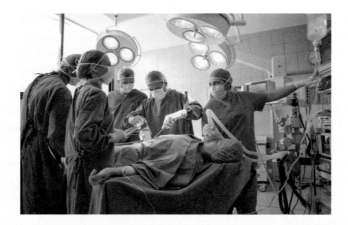

You can think of a team of medical specialists in an operating room as a cross-functional, self-managed team. Doctors, nurses, technicians, and anesthesiologists from different departments and areas in the hospital work together to complete successful operations. What kinds of tasks do cross-functional, self-managed teams complete in an office or retail environment?

Figure 9.7 lists the advantages and disadvantages of these four types of organizations.

■ FIGURE 9.7

TYPES OF ORGANIZATIONS		
Each form of organization has its advantages and disadvantages.		
	👍 Advantages	👎 Disadvantages
Line	• Clarifies responsibility and authority • Simplifies structure and easy understand • Establishes one supervisor for each person	• Is too inflexible • Limits number of specialists to advise workers • Extends lines of communication • Hinders ability to quickly handle complex questions
Line and Staff	• Provides expert advice from staff to line personnel • Establishes lines of authority • Encourages co-operation and better communication at all levels	• Risks overstaffing • Risks overanalyzing • Blurs lines of communication • Increases staff frustrations because of lack of authority
Matrix	• Is flexible • Encourages co-operation among departments • Produces creative solutions to problems • Allows organization to take on new projects without adding to the organizational structure • Provides for more efficient use of organizational resources	• Is costly and complex • Confuses employees • Requires effective interpersonal skills and co-operative managers and employees • Inhibits employee evaluation the and reward systems
Cross-functional Self-Managed Teams	• Enhances interdepartmental coordination and co-operation • Enables quicker response to customers and market conditions • Increases employee motivation and morale	• Confuses responsibility and authority • Generates a perceived loss of control by management • Inhibits employee evaluation and reward systems • Requires self-motivated and highly trained workers

GOING BEYOND ORGANIZATIONAL BOUNDARIES

Cross-functional teams work best when the voice of the customer is prioritized, especially in product development tasks.[20] Suppliers and distributors should be on the team as well. A self-managed team that includes customers, suppliers, and distributors goes beyond organizational boundaries. When suppliers and distributors are in other countries, cross-functional teams may share market information across national boundaries. Government coordinators may assist such projects, letting cross-functional teams break the barriers between government and business. Cross-functional teams are only one way in which businesses can interact with other companies. In the next section we look at other ways that organizations manage their various interactions.

Progress Assessment

- What is the difference between line and staff personnel?
- What management principle does a matrix-style organization challenge?
- What is the main difference between the structure of a matrix-style organization and the use of cross-functional teams?

LO5 Identify the benefits of inter-firm co-operation and coordination.

Managing Interactions Among Firms

Whether it involves customers, suppliers, distributors, or the government, **networking between firms** is using communications technology and other means to link organizations and allow them to work together on common objectives. Let's explore this concept further.

networking between firms
Using communications technology and other means to link organizations and allow them to work together on common objectives.

Seeking SUSTAINABILITY

Ethical Consumerism

Like many companies, Loblaws is working closely with its suppliers to align its values in areas from labour conditions to animal welfare. The year 2014 marked the 25th anniversary of the company's commitment to corporate social responsibility (CSR). Its CSR focuses primarily upon three areas health and wellness, sustainable sourcing, and energy efficiency. The company documents its strategies and achievements in its Corporate Social Responsibility Report. Highlights from the 2014 report include the following:

- It plans to replace all artificial sweeteners with stevia in its President's Choice products by 2015, and has already eliminated artificial colours and flavours.
- It offers Aquaculture Stewardship Council (ASC) certified Atlantic salmon.

(continued)

(continued)

- It is the retail lead on the Canadian Roundtable for Sustainable Beef which, among other things, is working toward a verification process for sustainable beef.
- It follows a Canadian-first buying strategy that supports local and regional suppliers through a *Grown Close to Home* initiative.

To ensure these practices continue, Loblaws now requires all existing and new suppliers to be subject to, at a minimum, an annual Corporate Social Responsibility Audit. Loblaws engages qualified auditors to review all the processes and records of their suppliers. These auditors then report to Loblaws on the results of their investigation. This transparency on the part of Loblaw's suppliers is repeated in many industries so that retailers can demonstrate their social responsibility to consumers. Loblaws' purpose, *Live Life Well,* demonstrates how the company thinks about CSR!

Source: Loblaws "2014 Corporate Social Responsibility Report," http://www.loblaw-reports.ca/responsibility/2014/index.html#4.

Virtual Organizations

Networked organizations are so closely linked by the Internet that each can find out what the others are doing in real time. **Real time** simply means the present moment or the actual time in which something takes place. The Internet has allowed companies to send real-time data to organizational partners as they are developed or collected.[21] The result is transparency. Transparency occurs when a company is so open to other companies working with it that the once-solid barriers between them become see-through and electronic information is shared as if the companies were one. With this integration, two companies can work as closely as two departments once did in traditional firms. As part of the movement to increase corporate social responsibility (as discussed in Chapter 5) many businesses want to ensure that their suppliers are meeting certain standards. The Seeking Sustainability box above describes the approach taken by Loblaw Companies Limited.

> **real time**
> The present moment or the actual time in which something takes place; data sent over the Internet to various organizational partners as they are developed or collected are said to be available in real time.

Can you see the implications for organizational design? Most organizations are no longer self-sufficient or self-contained. Rather, they are part of a vast network of global businesses that work closely together (see the Spotlight on Small Business box below for more discussion). An organization chart showing what people do within any one organization is simply not complete, because the organization is part of a much larger system of firms. A modern chart would show people in different organizations and indicate how they are networked. This is a relatively new concept, however, and very few such charts are yet available.

Spotlight *On* SMALL BUSINESS

Canadian Virtual Assistant Association

As a new graduate looking for work, how can you create the best opportunity to find a job? The answer is to make yourself, and your skills, available to as many employers as possible. That is the goal of a virtual assistant (VA). VA's are typically self-employed and provide professional administrative, technical, and creative services. Their clients need the expertise but want to save the cost of hiring a permanent employee to work "in house."

The Canadian Association of Virtual Assistants (CAVA, *<http://canadianava.org>*) helps people establish and build their personal business. It provides a forum for independent professionals to network and obtain support as they develop their business. CAVA's mission seeks to establish global connection between and among VA's and clients.

Various websites, such as People Per Hour *<http://www.peopleperhour.com>*, help VA's find and bid on contracts but competition is fierce so many VA's gravitate to sites like Time Etc. *<http://web.timeetc.co.uk>*, where the work is found for you. Time Etc. founder Barnaby Lashbrooke believed an online clearinghouse that matched clients with needs to professionals with skills filled an important gap. "The responsibility of having to find new business is what puts some people off. Being a VA requires being proactive, but many VAs find they have excellent contacts who are more than willing to recommend them, or keep them on part time" There are many other VA services that connect companies to highly effective remote professionals.

'The world is your oyster' is a saying often told to new graduates when they finish their education and enter the workforce. With the growth of virtual organizations, this saying has never been so true.

Sources: Alison Coleman, "How to set-up a home-based virtual assistant business," *The Guardian,* 23 April 2015, http://www .theguardian.com/small-business-network/2013/nov/25/virtual-assistant-small-business; "What is CAVA," Canadian Association of Virtual Assistants, http://canadianava.org/what-is-cava/, downloaded 9 May 2015; Sara Angeles, "10 virtual assistant services for your business," Business News daily, 5 February 2014, http://www.businessnewsdaily.com/5878-virtual-assistant-services.html.

Networked organization structures tend to be flexible. A company may work with a design expert from a different company in Italy for a year and then not need that person anymore. It may hire an expert from a company in another country for another project. Such a temporary network, made of replaceable firms that join and leave as needed, is called a **virtual corporation** (see Figure 9.8).

virtual corporation
A temporary networked organization made up of replaceable firms that join and leave as needed.

■ **FIGURE 9.8**

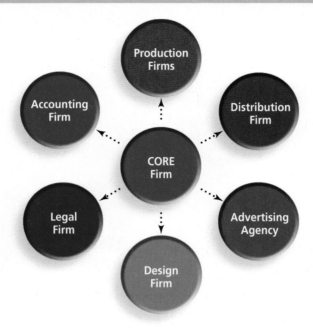

A VIRTUAL CORPORATION

A virtual corporation has no permanent ties to the firms that do its production, distribution, legal, and other work. Such firms are very flexible and can adapt to changes in the market quickly.

People who work within a virtual organization still need to communicate. Many options help ensure co-workers may collaborate and co-operate even though they may be in different physical locations. Simple information sharing platforms such as Dropbox have expanded into virtual private networks to share knowledge. For example, the life sciences industry has a large number of multi-partner virtual organizations who use online collaboration platforms to connect pharmaceutical executives and life sciences researchers.[22] When knowledge sharing reaches a point where face-to-face communication is needed, employees turn to online tools such as Skype and GoToMeeting for business web conferencing. Business leaders are always searching for new virtual team members and these practices help ensure a virtual organization can be successful.

Benchmarking and Core Competencies

Historically, organizations have tried to do all functions themselves. Each had its own department for accounting, finance, marketing, production, and so on. As we have noted, today's organizations look to other organizations to help in areas where they do not generate world-class quality.

Benchmarking compares an organization's practices, processes, and products against the world's best. As one example, K2 Skis <*http://skeeze.k2skis.com*> is a company that makes skis, snowboards, in-line skates, and related products. It studied the compact-disc industry and learned to use ultraviolet inks to print graphics on skis. It went to the aerospace industry to get piezoelectric technology to reduce vibration in its snowboards (the aerospace industry uses the technology for wings on planes). It learned from the cable television industry how to braid layers of fibre-glass and carbon, and adapted that knowledge to make skis. Wyeth, a pharmaceutical company, benchmarked the aerospace industry for project management, the shipping industry for standardization of processes, and computer makers to learn the most efficient way to make prescription drugs. As another example, Suncor <*http://www .suncor.com*>, one of Canada's largest emitters of greenhouse gases, continually benchmarks its environmental and social progress.[23] By doing so, they are able to evaluate their performance in reducing their impact in various areas such as greenhouse gas emissions, water, land and tailings, and improve their impact on biodiversity and renewable energy.

benchmarking
Comparing an organization's practices, processes, and products against the world's best.

Benchmarking also has a direct competitive purpose. In retailing, Sam Walton used to do competitive benchmarking regularly. He would visit the stores of competitors and see what, if anything, the competitor was doing better. When he found something better—say, a pricing program—he would come back to Walmart and make the appropriate changes. Target may compare itself to Walmart to see what, if anything, Walmart does better. Target will then try to improve its practices or processes to become even better than Walmart. How well did this strategy help the company's performance in Canada?

Benchmarking has become a significant activity in Canada. Governments and large and small companies are all involved in procedures to discover and apply the best practices available. Industry Canada and Statistics Canada have accumulated extensive statistics on the use of benchmarking in a variety of industries. Some examples are breweries, flour mixing and cereal production, electronic computing, paperboard manufacturing, musical instruments, and the recording industry. For more information, including a link to a benchmarking tool, go to <*http://www.canadabusiness.ca/eng/blog /entry/3518*>.

If an organization cannot do as well as the best in, say, shipping, it will try to outsource the function to an organization like UPS or FedEx <*http://www.fedex.com*> that specializes in shipping. Remember, outsourcing means assigning one or more functions, such as accounting, production, security, maintenance, and legal work, to outside organizations. Even small firms are getting involved in outsourcing. We have already discussed some problems associated with outsourcing, especially when companies outsource to other countries. Jobs are lost in Canada and this has a negative impact on our economy. Some functions, such as information management and marketing, may be too important to assign to outside firms. In that case, the organization should benchmark the best firms and restructure its departments to try to be equally good. It is important to remember that companies in other countries often outsource their functions to companies in Canada. We call that *insourcing* and it is the basis of many jobs.[24]

When a firm has completed its outsourcing process, the remaining functions are the firm's **core competencies**, those functions that the organization can do as well as or better than any other organization in the world. For example, Nike is great at designing and marketing athletic shoes. Those are its core competencies. It outsources the manufacturing of those shoes, however, to other companies that can make shoes better and less expensively than Nike itself can. Similarly, Dell is best at marketing computers and outsources most other functions, including manufacturing and distribution, to others. Canadian banks, such as the Royal Bank of Canada, have been criticized for outsourcing jobs in areas such as information technology and finance operations.[25]

core competencies
Those functions that an organization can do as well as or better than any other organization in the world.

Nike's core competencies are designing and marketing athletic shoes. The company outsources other functions (i.e., manufacturing) to other businesses that assemble shoes better and cheaper than Nike could do on its own. What are the advantages of focusing on the company's core competencies? What are the disadvantages?

After you have structured an organization, you must keep monitoring the environment (including customers) to learn what changes are needed. Dell, for example, recently reversed its practice of outsourcing customer support and now offers a premium service that enables Canadian customers to access tech support in North America. The following section discusses organizational change in more detail.

Adapting to Change

Once you have structured an organization, you must be prepared to adapt that structure to changes in the market. That is not always easy to do.[26] Over time an organization can get set in its ways. Employees have a tendency to say, "That's the way we've always done things. If it isn't broken, don't fix it." Managers also get complacent. They may say that they have 20 years' experience when the truth is that they have had one year's experience 20 times. Do you think that slow adaptation to change was a factor in the decline of the manufacturing sector in Canada?

Introducing change is one of the hardest challenges facing any manager. Nonetheless, change is what is happening at General Motors (GM), Ford, Facebook, and other companies eager to become more competitive. If you have old facilities that are no longer efficient, you have to unload or update them. That is exactly what GM and other companies are doing. In fact, they have asked the government to lend them billions of dollars to help.[27]

The Internet has created new opportunities, not only to sell to customers directly but also to ask them questions and provide them with any information they want. To win market share, companies must coordinate the efforts of their traditional departments and their Internet staff to create friendly, easy-to-manage interactions. Young people today are called **digital natives** because they grew up with the Internet and cell phones. Using these devices is second nature to them. On the other hand, companies often need to retrain older employees to be more tech-savvy. While the ease and immediacy of communication created by technology may be powerful, there are disadvantages to being constantly connected to work (see Adapting to Change box).

digital natives
Young people who grew up using technology including the Internet and electronic devices such as cell phones.

Adapting *to* CHANGE

When Open Communication Should Not Be So Open

People today use technology to text, tweet, surf the Web, and run apps as they go about their personal lives and, in many cases, their business lives. In fact, many companies provide work-issued smartphones, tablets, and other mobile technology to their employees. The blending of mobile technology and work has been a boon to employees and businesses in many ways, particularly in terms of speed, reach, and efficiency. Unfortunately, it has also encroached on the traditional boundaries between work and home.

According to a survey conducted by Right Management *<http://www.right.com>*, a career and outplacement service, more than one-third of employees receive work-related e-mails after work hours. According to Monika Morrow, senior vice president at Right Management, "The boundaries of the workplace are expanding and now reach deeper into employees' lives. Workers can no longer leave the office at the office." While no one disputes the value of technology, many believe its use has gone overboard and is affecting employees' quality of life. Companies such as Volkswagen *<http://www.vw.ca>*, PricewaterhouseCoopers *<http://www.pwc.com>*, and shipping company PBD *<http://www.pbd.com>* have heard the complaints and created both formal and informal rules regarding e-mail.

The e-mail encroachment problem is not just in Canada. France is considering legislation that would block work e-mails and phone calls, and legally give employees at least 11 hours of daily rest free from mobile technology. What do you think would be the impact upon businesses of imposing a similar law in Canada?

Sources: Cecilia Kang, "Firms Tell Employees: Avoid After-Hours E-Mail," *The Washington Post,* 21 September 2012; Chris Baysden, "Why You're Never Safe from More Work—Even After Hours," *CGMA Magazine,* 4 July 2013; and Scott Sayare, "In France, a Move to Limit Off-the-Clock Work Emails," *The New York Times,* 11 April 2014.

Although Target is a highly centralized organization, the company tries to respond to changes in consumer preferences, in part by keeping in touch with an enormous web of people of all ages, interests and nationalities—its "creative cabinet"—via the Internet. The members of the "cabinet," who never meet so they cannot influence each other, evaluate various new initiatives and recommend new programs to help Target determine out what belongs on store shelves.

But when Target entered the highly competitive Canadian retail market, it faced many challenges that ultimately led to failure. Why didn't the centralization and "cabinet" structure that proved so effective for Target in other markets work for the company in Canada? As soon as Target Canada opened its doors the losses mounted to $1 billion in the first year. In less than two years, the doors closed at 133 stores and 17,000 employees were laid off.[28] It seemed the senior executives didn't know how to communicate with the front-line staff. Even though staff knew all the customer complaints about the lack of product on the shelves and the over-pricing, the centralized structure made it difficult to respond. Management couldn't connect to the staff in the stores, many of whom described the atmosphere as ". . . akin to swimming with smiling sharks."[29] The next section, about restructuring in ways to empower employees, provides insight about the Target Canada story.

Restructuring for Empowerment

To empower employees firms must reorganize dramatically to make front-line workers their most important people. **Restructuring** is redesigning an organization so it can more effectively and efficiently serve its customers. Until recently, department-store clerks, bank tellers, and front-desk staff in hotels were not considered key employees. Instead, managers were considered more important, and they were responsible for directing the work of the front-line people. The organization chart in a typical firm looked much like the pyramid in Figure 9.9.

restructuring
Redesigning an organization so that it can more effectively and efficiently serve its customers.

■ **FIGURE 9.9**

COMPARISON OF A TRADITIONAL ORGANIZATION STRUCTURE AND AN INVERTED ORGANIZATION STRUCTURE

Traditional Organization

Top management
Middle management
Supervisory management
Front-line workers

Inverted Organization

Empowered front-line workers (often in teams)
Support personnel
Top management

A few service-oriented organizations have turned the traditional organization pyramid structure upside down. An **inverted organization** has contact people (like nurses) at the top and the chief executive officer (like the hospital CEO) at the bottom. Management layers are few, and the manager's job is to *assist* and *support* front-line people, not boss them around. Figure 9.9 illustrates the difference between an inverted and a traditional organizational structure.

> **inverted organization**
> An organization that has contact people at the top and the chief executive officer at the bottom of the organization chart.

A good example of an inverted organization is NovaCare *<http://www.novacare.com>*, a diversified health care company.[30] At its top are some 5,000 physical, occupational, and speech therapists. The rest of the organization is structured to serve those therapists. Managers consider the therapists to be their bosses, and the manager's job is to support the therapists by arranging contacts with nursing homes, handling accounting and credit activities, and providing training.

Companies based on this organization structure support front-line personnel with internal and external databases, advanced communication systems, and professional assistance. Naturally, this means that front-line people have to be better educated, better trained, and better paid than in the past. It takes a great deal of trust for top managers to implement such a system—but when they do, the payoff in customer satisfaction and in profits is often well worth the effort.[31]

In the past, managers controlled information—and that gave them power. In more progressive organizations everyone shares information, often through an elaborate database system, *among* firms as well as *within* them. No matter what organizational model you choose or how much you empower your employees, the secret to successful organization change is to focus on customers and give them what they want.

The Restructuring Process

It is not easy to move from an organization dominated by managers to one that relies heavily on self-managed teams. How you restructure an organization depends on the status of the present system. If the system already has a customer focus, but is not working well, a total quality management approach may work.

Total quality management (TQM) is the practice of striving for maximum customer satisfaction by ensuring quality from all departments. TQM calls for *continual improvement of present processes.* Processes are sets of activities joined together for a reason, such as the process for handling a customer's order. The process may consist of receiving the order in the mail, opening it, sending it to someone to fill, putting the order into a package, and sending it out. In Chapter 10 we will review the importance of quality control in operations management.

> **total quality management (TQM)**
> Striving for maximum customer satisfaction by ensuring quality from all departments.

Continuous improvement (CI) means constantly improving the way the organization operates so that customer needs can be satisfied. Many of the companies spotlighted in this book practice CI. No matter what the size of the organization it is possible to innovate. Re-engineering and change is not the sole domain of small, nimble organizations and large companies also demonstrate a propensity for change management.[32] For example, Canadian companies such as HootSuite *<http://signup.hootsuite.com>*

and Shopify *<https://www.shopify.com>* continuously improve products and constantly challenge employees to be creative despite their increase in size.

> **continuous improvement (CI)**
> Constantly improving the way the organization operates so that customer needs can be better satisfied.

It is possible, in an organization with few layers of management and a customer focus, that new computer software and employee training could lead to a team-oriented approach with few problems. However, in bureaucratic organizations with many layers of management, TQM is not useful. Continual improvement does not work when the whole process is incorrect. When an organization needs dramatic changes, only re-engineering will do.

Re-engineering is the fundamental rethinking and radical redesign of organizational processes to achieve dramatic improvements in critical measures of performance. Note the words *radical redesign* and *dramatic improvements*. Stanfield's *<http://www.stanfields.com>*, a Canadian clothing manufacturer based in Nova Scotia, was established in 1856. A "Made in Canada" philosophy is important to the company, both for its brand and its customers. Stanfield's has faced many challenges that prompted it to re-engineer in order to remain competitive.[33] Jon Stanfield, the fifth-generation family member who currently serves as president, recognized the need to adapt: "We have re-engineered the factory as far as making it more efficient and cutting waste to deal with the competitive pressures that occurred during the Free Trade Agreements and then subsequently the North American Free Trade Agreement." Changes have occurred in many areas including revised packaging to develop better supplier relations and energy consumption technology to reduce the company's carbon footprint.

> **re-engineering**
> The fundamental rethinking and radical redesign of organizational processes to achieve dramatic improvements in critical measures of performance.

Can you see how re-engineering is often necessary to change a firm from a managerial orientation to one based on self-managed teams? Re-engineering may also be necessary to adapt an organization to fit into a virtual network. Remember, re-engineering involves radical redesign and dramatic improvements. Not all organizations need such dramatic change. In fact, because of the complexity of the process, many re-engineering efforts fail. In firms where re-engineering is not feasible, restructuring may do. As discussed earlier in this chapter, restructuring involves making relatively minor changes to an organization in response to a changing environment. For example, many firms have added an Internet marketing component to the marketing department. That is a restructuring move, but it is not drastic enough to be called re-engineering.

LO6 Explain how organizational culture can help businesses adapt to change.

Creating a Change-Oriented Organizational Culture

Any organizational change is bound to cause some stress and resistance among members. Firms adapt best when their culture is change-oriented. **Organizational (or corporate) culture** is the widely shared values within an organization that foster unity and co-operation to achieve common goals. Usually the culture of an organization is reflected in its stories, traditions, and myths.

> **organizational (or corporate) culture**
> Widely shared values within an organization that provide coherence and co-operation to achieve common goals.

Each McDonald's restaurant has the same feel, look, and atmosphere; in short, each has a similar organizational culture. It is obvious from visiting almost any McDonald's that the culture emphasizes quality, service, cleanliness, and value.

An organizational culture can also be negative. Have you ever been in an organization where you feel that no one cares about service or quality? The clerks may seem uniformly glum, indifferent, and testy. The mood pervades the atmosphere and patrons become unhappy or upset. It may be hard to believe that an organization, especially a profit-making one, can be run so badly and still survive. Clearly then, when you search for a job, study the organizational culture to see whether you will thrive in it.

Mintzberg notes that culture affects the way in which employees are chosen, developed, nurtured, interrelated, and rewarded. The kinds of people attracted to an organization and the way they can most effectively deal with problems and each other are largely a function of the culture an organization builds and the practices and systems that support the culture.[34]

Empowering employees who deal directly with customers to solve problems without needing a manager's approval makes a higher level of customer service possible and also helps employees develop. What kind of guest issues do you think a front-line hotel employee should be allowed to solve on his or her own?

Some of the best organizations have cultures that emphasize service to others, especially customers. The atmosphere reflects friendly, caring people who enjoy working together to provide a good product at a reasonable price. Companies that have such a culture have less need for close supervision of employees. That usually means fewer policy manuals, organization charts, and formal rules, procedures, and controls. The key to a productive culture is mutual trust. You receive such trust by giving it. The very best companies stress high moral and ethical values such as honesty, reliability, fairness, environmental protection, and social involvement. One such example is TD Bank Group. They have been recognized for multiple years as one of the best workplaces in Canada. The Careers section of their home page provides numerous employee video testimonials on the culture that contributes to this success.[35]

Thus far, we have been talking as if organizational matters were mostly controllable by management. The fact is that the formal organization structure is just one element of the total organizational system. In the creation of organizational culture, the informal organization is of equal or even greater importance. Let's explore this notion next.

The Informal Organization

All organizations have two organizational systems. The **formal organization** details lines of responsibility, authority, and position. It is the structure shown on organization charts. The other is the **informal organization**, the system that develops spontaneously as employees meet and form cliques, relationships, and lines of authority outside the formal organization. It is the human side of the organization that does not show on any organization chart.

> **formal organization**
> The structure that details lines of responsibility, authority, and position; that is, the structure shown on organization charts.
>
> **informal organization**
> The system of relationships and lines of authority that develops spontaneously as employees meet and form power centres; that is, the human side of the organization that does not appear on any organization chart.

The information organization is the system that develops as employees meet and form relationships. The grapevine, or the unofficial flow of information among employees, is the nerve centre of the informal organization. How does the information organization affect the work environment? How might it affect organizational performance?

No organization can operate effectively without both types of organization. The formal system is often too slow and bureaucratic to let the organization adapt quickly although it does provide helpful guides and lines of authority for routine situations.

The informal organization is often too unstructured and emotional to allow careful, reasoned decision making on critical matters. It is extremely effective, however, in generating creative solutions to short-term problems and creating camaraderie and teamwork among employees.[36]

In any organization, it is wise to learn quickly who is important in the informal organization. Following formal rules and procedures can take days. Who in the organization knows how to obtain resources immediately without the normal procedures? Which administrative assistants should you see if you want your work given first priority? Answers to these questions help people work effectively in many organizations.

The informal organization's nerve centre called the *grapevine*, is the system through which unofficial information flows between and among managers and employees. Key people in the grapevine usually have considerable influence.

In the old "us-versus-them" system of organizations, where managers and employees were often at odds, the informal system hindered effective management. Within a more open organization, managers and employees work together to set objectives and design procedures. The informal organization is an invaluable managerial asset that can promote harmony among workers and establish the corporate culture.[37]

As effective as the informal organization may be in creating group co-operation, it can still be equally powerful in resisting management directives. Employees may form unions, go on strike together, and generally disrupt operations. Learning to create the right corporate culture and to work within the informal organization is a key to managerial success.[38]

Progress Assessment

- What is an inverted organization?
- Why do organizations outsource functions?
- What is organizational culture?

SUMMARY

LO1 **Outline the basic principles of organization management.**

The basic principles of organization are much the same regardless of the size of the business.

What is happening today to Canadian businesses?

Canadian businesses are adjusting to changing markets. This is a normal function in a capitalist economy. There will be big winners, like Google and Facebook, and big losers, like Target (in Canada). The key to success is remaining flexible and adapting to the changing times.

What are the principles of organization management?

Structuring an organization means devising a division of labour (sometimes resulting in specialization), setting up teams or departments, and assigning responsibility and authority. It includes allocating resources (such as funds), assigning specific tasks, and establishing procedures for accomplishing the organizational objectives. Managers also have to make ethical decisions about how to treat workers.

LO2 **Compare the organizational theories of Henri Fayol and Max Weber.**

Until the twentieth century, most businesses were rather small, the processes of producing goods were rather simple, and organizing workers was fairly easy. Not until the 1900s and the introduction of mass production did businesses become complex. During this era, business theorists emerged.

What were Fayol's basic principles?

Fayol introduced principles such as unity of command, hierarchy of authority, division of labour, subordination of individual interests to the general interest, authority, clear communication channels, order, and equity.

What principles did Weber add?

Weber added principles of bureaucracy such as job descriptions, written rules and decision guidelines, consistent procedures, and staffing and promotions based on qualifications.

LO3 **Evaluate the choices managers make in structuring organizations.**

What are the four issues in structuring organizations?

Issues involved in structuring and restructuring organizations are (1) centralization versus decentralization, (2) span of control, (3) tall versus flat organization structures, and (4) departmentalization.

What are the latest trends in structuring?

Departments are often replaced or supplemented by matrix organizations and cross-functional self-managed teams that decentralize authority. The span of control becomes larger as employees become self-directed. Another trend is to eliminate managers and flatten organizations.

LO4 **Contrast the various organizational models.**

Organizational design is the coordination of workers so that they can best accomplish the firm's goals. New forms of organization are emerging that enable firms to be more responsive to customers.

What are the two major organizational models?

Two traditional forms of organization are (1) line organizations and (2) line-and-staff organizations. A line organization has clearly defined responsibility and authority, is easy to understand, and provides each worker with only one supervisor. The expert advice of staff assistants in a line-and-staff organization helps in areas such as safety, quality control, computer technology, human resource management, and investing.

What are the key alternative forms to the major organizational models?

Matrix organizations assign people to projects temporarily and encourage inter-organizational co-operation and teamwork. Cross-functional self-managed teams have all the benefits of the matrix style and are long term.

LO5 **Identify the benefits of inter-firm co-operation and coordination.**

Networking is using communications technology and other means to link organizations and allow them to work together on common objectives.

What are the major concepts involved in inter-firm communications?

Communications technology allows firms to work together on common objectives. A virtual corporation is a networked organization of replaceable firms that join and leave as needed. Benchmarking tells firms how their performance measures up to that of their competitors in specific functions. The business may then outsource to companies that perform its weaker functions more effectively and efficiently. The functions that remain within the organization are the firm's core competencies.

What is an inverted organization?

An inverted organization places employees at the top of the hierarchy; managers are at the bottom to train and assist employees.

LO6 **Explain how organizational culture can help businesses adapt to change.**

Organizational (or corporate) culture may be defined as widely shared values that foster unity and co-operation to achieve common goals.

What is the difference between the formal and informal organization of a firm?

The formal organization details lines of responsibility, authority, and position. It is the structure shown on organization charts. The informal organization is the system that develops spontaneously as employees meet and form cliques, relationships, and lines of authority outside the formal organization. It is the human side of the organization. The informal organization is an invaluable managerial asset that often promotes harmony among workers and establishes the corporate culture. As effective as the informal organization may be in creating group co-operation, it can still be equally powerful in resisting management directives.

KEY TERMS

benchmarking
bureaucracy
centralized authority
chain of command
continuous
    improvement (CI)
core competencies
cross-functional self-managed
    teams
decentralized authority
departmentalization

digital natives
economies of scale
flat organization structure
formal organization
hierarchy
informal organization
inverted organization
line organization
line personnel
matrix organization
networking between firms

organizational
    (or corporate) culture
real time
re-engineering
restructuring
span of control
staff personnel
tall organization structure
total quality management(TQM)
virtual corporation

CRITICAL THINKING

Now that you have learned some of the basic principles of organization, pause and think about where you have already applied such concepts yourself or when you have been part of an organization that did.

1. Did you find a division of labour necessary and helpful?

2. Were you assigned specific tasks or left on your own to decide what to do?

3. Were promotions based strictly on qualifications, as Weber suggested? What other factors may have been considered?

4. What problems seem to emerge when an organization expands in size?

5. What organizational changes might you recommend to Canadian manufacturers, such as the auto companies?

DEVELOPING WORKPLACE SKILLS

Key: ● **Team**   ★ **Analytic**   ▲ **Communication**   ▢ **Technology**

●▲ 1. There is no better way to understand the effects of having many layers of management on communication accuracy than to play the game of Message Relay. Choose seven or more members of the class and have them leave the classroom. Then choose one person to read the following paragraph and another student to listen. Call in one of the students from outside and have the "listener" tell him or her the information contained in the paragraph. Then bring in another student and have the new listener repeat the information to him or her. Continue the process with all those who left the room. Do not allow anyone in the class to offer corrections as each listener becomes the storyteller in turn. In this way, all students can hear how the facts become distorted over time. The distortions and mistakes are often quite humorous, but they are not so funny in organizations such as Ford, which once had 22 layers of management.

Here is the paragraph:

Dealers in the Maritimes have received more than 130 complaints about steering on the new Commander and Roadhandler models of our minivans. Apparently, the front suspension system is weak and the ball joints are wearing too fast. This causes slippage in the linkage and results in oversteering. Mr. Berenstein has been notified, but so far only 213 of 4,300 dealers have received repair kits.

★ 2. Describe some informal groups within an organization with which you are familiar (at school, at work, etc.). What have you noticed about how those groups help or hinder progress in the organization?

▲ 3. Imagine that you are working for Kitchen Magic, an appliance manufacturer that produces, among other things, dishwashers for the home. Imagine further that a competitor introduces a new dishwasher that uses sound waves to clean dishes. The result is a dishwasher that cleans even the worst burned-on food and sterilizes the dishes and silverware as well. You need to develop a similar offering fast, or your company will lose the market. Write an e-mail to management outlining the problem, explaining your rationale for recommending the use of a self-managed team to respond quickly, and identifying the type of skills you need.

●★ 4. Divide the class into teams of five. You are a producer of athletic shoes and you have been asked
▲   to join a virtual network. How might you minimize the potential problems of joining? Begin by defining a virtual corporation and listing its advantages and disadvantages. Each team should report its solutions to the class.

●★ 5. A growing number of work groups, including management, are cross-functional and
▲   self-managed. To practice working in such an organization, break into groups of five or so students, preferably with different backgrounds and interests. Each group must work together to prepare a report on the advantages and disadvantages of working in teams. Many of the problems and advantages of cross-functional, self-managed teams should emerge in your group as you try to complete this assignment. Each group should report to the class how it handled the problems and benefitted from the advantages.

ANALYZING MANAGEMENT DECISIONS

IBM Is Both an Outsourcer and a Major Outsource for Others

Few companies are better known for their manufacturing expertise than IBM. Nonetheless, even IBM has to adapt to today's dynamic marketplace. In the area of personal computers, for example, IBM was unable to match the prices or speed of delivery of mail-order firms such as Dell Computer. Dell built machines after receiving orders and then rushed the computers to customers. IBM, in contrast, made machines ahead of time and hoped that the orders would match its inventory.

To compete against firms like Dell, IBM had to custom-make computers for its business customers, but IBM was not particularly suited to do such work. To address this issue IBM entered into a relationship with Lenovo whereby Lenovo became the manufacturer of IBM personal computers and over time replaced IBM in the personal computer market.

IBM's long-range strategy was to move away from hardware toward software development. It acquired PricewaterhouseCoopers to put more emphasis on services rather than hardware. As a result, IBM dominated the IT industry. They offered outsourcing for IT infrastructure, application development, and IT support services. They spent over $6 billion annually on research and development and held the most patents of any U.S. technology company.

While growing this side of their business they outsourced a number of jobs to India in sales, semiconductor, and finance groups, resulting in the layoff of 4600 U.S.-based employees in these positions in 2009.

Today IBM continues to face many challenges. While revenues from cloud computing have helped the company, major competitors such as Amazon, Google, and Microsoft have gained ground in this area. The drop in server hardware sales led IBM to sell this part of its business to Lenovo and focus upon business acquisitions to capitalize on growth within cloud computing. While generating profit for the company, the switch to acquisitions led to a de-emphasis upon innovation.

Despite explicitly stating three strategic areas—clients, innovation, and trust—decision making was driven by a desire to earn more for shareholders. This focus upon investment returns, referred to as "Roadmap 2015," led to massive cost-cutting measures that created high costs for the company and led to further employee layoffs.

Sources: Steve Denning, "Why IBM is in decline," *Forbes*, 30 May 2014, http://www.forbes.com/sites/stevedenning/2014/05/30/why-ibm-is-in-decline/; Julie Bort, "IBM CEO Ginni Rometty is a year away from delivering on a plan that has tied her hands for years," *Business Insider*, 22 May 2014, http://www.businessinsider.com/ibm-ginni-rometty-and-2015-road-map-2014-5; Michael Useem and Joseph Harder, "Leading Laterally in Company Outsourcing," *Sloan Management Review*, Winter 2000, 25–36; Alison Overholt, "In the Hot Seat," *Fast Company*, January 2003, 46; "IBM Outsourcing Thousands of Jobs to India," www.peacerebelgirl.wordpress.com/2009/03/26/ibm-outsourcing-thousands-of-jobs-to-india/, 26 March 2009; and "IBM Outsourcing with Big Blue," www.itouotsourcinghq.com/it-outsourcing-to-ibm, 12 April 2011.

Discussion Questions

1. What does it say about today's competitive environment when leading companies such as IBM give up competing in an area of their business that they dominated for many years and expand significantly into a related area of business they have only been involved in for a relatively short period of time?

2. In what ways does this example demonstrate an organization's ability and/or inability to adapt to change?

VIDEO CASE 9

Whole Foods

Whole Foods Market is a supermarket chain that specializes in fresh, organic produce from local sources. As an international company with locations around the world, employees have a large operation to oversee and a very specific mission to uphold: to sell the highest-quality natural and organic products available.

Sticking to this goal and keeping up with the demands of a rapidly expanding business aren't always easy, though. In order to stay committed to stocking sustainable goods, Whole Foods relies on an organizational structure that combines aspects of a mom-and-pop operation with a traditional corporate hierarchy. Thanks to this unique organizational structure, the company has been able to expand to 360 stores and hire more than 58,000 employees without sacrificing its core principles.

Whole Foods started when John Mackey and Rene Lawson borrowed money from friends and family to open a small natural-food store in Austin, Texas. The pair soon ended up living in the market after they were evicted from their apartment for storing some of their grocery stock there. Fortunately, business began to boom once the pair took on a couple of partners and merged with another store. But they quickly faced another huge setback when the most destructive flood Austin had experienced in 70 years took its toll on the market. Along with incurring damage to their building, the store also lost all of its produce and inventory. Thanks to a massive community cleanup effort, however, the market was soon back in business.

Whole Foods has never forgotten that lesson—that having a local, grass-roots structure sensitive to drastic and sudden changes in the business environment can keep an organization nimble and responsive. In the company's early days, the staff was small enough so that everyone could do every job. While this kept things running smoothly at first, the situation had to change as the company grew and opened more stores. They divided the labour among the four partners, with each specializing in one or more of the tasks critical to the business. After designating the leaders for departments like finance, human resources, and sales, Whole Foods began to look like a big company.

But John Mackey and his partners still wanted their stores to appear like small local markets, not corporate mega-grocers. That meant they had to make tough choices, like whether they should centralize supply in warehouses or depend on separate, local suppliers in each region they had stores. Whole Foods ultimately opted for the latter option. To stay responsive to market changes, each region received its own manager and the autonomy to make certain decisions about supply sources and pricing based on the needs of that region, without being slowed down waiting for responses from the home office. This decentralized structure gives Whole Foods the flexibility to adapt to important changes without involving needless bureaucracy.

Whole Foods Market continues to expand into new markets around the world. Despite that fact, they've managed to keep what's unique about their culture and pure about their mission: focusing on great, natural sources at the local level.

THINKING IT OVER

1. Organizations like Whole Foods need to follow the principles of Henri Fayol, such as the "unity of command." What is unity of command?

2. Whole Foods structures its organization in a decentralized manner. What does that mean for the company's operations?

3. Do you think the corporate culture at Whole Foods is resistant to change or accepting of change? Why?

Producing World-Class Goods and Services

LEARNING OBJECTIVES

After you have read and studied this chapter, you should be able to:

LO1 Describe the current state of Canadian manufacturing and how companies are becoming more competitive.

LO2 Describe the evolution from production to operations management.

LO3 Describe operations management planning issues including facility location, facility layout, materials requirement planning, purchasing, just-in-time inventory control, quality control, and supply chain management.

LO4 Identify various production processes and describe techniques to improve productivity including flexible manufacturing, lean manufacturing, mass customization, and computer-aided design manufacturing.

LO5 Explain the use of PERT and Gantt charts to control manufacturing processes.

PROFILE

GETTING TO KNOW SHAHID KHAN OF FLEX-N-GATE

At the age of 16, Shahid Khan moved to Champaign, Illinois, from his home country Pakistan in order to earn a degree in engineering. Not only was a blizzard bombarding the town upon his arrival, but the dorms at the University of Illinois hadn't opened yet. Reluctantly, Khan paid $3 for a room and a meal at the local YMCA <http://www.ymca.ca>. With precious little money to his name, Khan began to worry about how he would survive for the next four years.

His fears subsided the next morning when he discovered a notice about an opening for a dishwashing job in the YMCA kitchen. With a starting salary of $1.20 per hour, Khan was shocked that he could

recoup his losses from the previous night so quickly. "It's like, wow," said Khan. "If you put the $1.20 per hour in terms of Pakistan, you're making more than 99% of the people over there. I'm breathing oxygen for the first time." The new opportunities fuelled Khan's enthusiasm for his work and after graduating he landed a job overseeing production for a local aftermarket auto parts company called Flex-N-Gate <http://www.flex-n-gate.com>. At first Khan couldn't believe the inefficient manufacturing methods the company used to make its bumpers, which sometimes involved welding together as many as 15 different parts. Using his engineering expertise, Khan refined the process to make it less complicated. His hard work paid off in the form of a revolutionary new product: a bumper stamped from a single piece of steel that managed to slim down the rear end of a truck.

After seven years in the aftermarket business, Khan realized that the value-focused industry didn't provide much room for innovation. If Khan wanted his product to succeed, he knew he had to sell directly to automakers instead of to consumers. So, armed with little more than a post office box and a small business loan, Khan started his own company. Within two years he earned enough money to buy the failing Flex-N-Gate from his old boss, giving him additional revenue streams as well as an established brand name. While business boomed at first, sales eventually ground to a halt when its biggest client, General Motors, simply passed off Khan's bumper design to its large-scale suppliers instead.

Other entrepreneurs would have reacted angrily to such a slight, but Khan remained positive. "It really was the right thing for them," he says. "We had no business going from making 200 bumpers a day to making 40,000." Plus, his dealings with GM put him in contact with executives at Isuzu <http://www.isuzu.com>, one of Japan's biggest auto companies. Khan travelled to Japan in the early 1980s in a last-ditch effort to woo clients. His timing couldn't have been better. Japanese car companies had been preparing to enter the American market, but needed more domestic suppliers to fuel their growth. Not only did Khan's company fill this need, but he also brought his game-changing bumper design to the table. Soon Flex-N-Gate was manufacturing parts for Isuzu, Mazda <http://www.mazda.ca>, and Toyota. As those brands grew into some of the biggest names in the American market, Khan's company grew right along with them. Today Flex-N-Gate auto parts are in two-thirds of the cars and trucks sold in the United States. Flex-N-Gate enjoys over

$3 billion in sales a year. And since Kahn is the sole shareholder, the profit on those sales goes to him, making Kahn one of the richest men in the world.

In 2012 Kahn used some of that immense wealth to purchase the Jacksonville Jaguars, and in the process realized a personal dream to own an NFL franchise. Although the Jaguars aren't exactly Super Bowl contenders now, Khan is confident that the team will become another one of his patented comeback stories.

By setting Flex-N-Gate on the path to productivity, Shahid Khan made a fortune while also creating thousands of jobs. It has also earned him great respect in the auto industry. In this chapter you'll learn about how other company leaders thrive and survive in the production and operations sector. You'll also find out why Canada is generally moving from a production-based economy to a service economy.

Sources: Brian Solomon, "Shahid Khan: I Felt The American Dream in My First 24 Hours Here," *Forbes*, March 27, 2014; Henry Winter, "Fulham Owner Shahid Khan Preaches American Sensibilities, with Respect to English Traditions," *The Telegraph*, October 25, 2013; and Brian Solomon, "Shahid Khan: The New Face of the NFL and the American Dream," *Forbes*, September 5, 2012.

LO1   Describe the current state of Canadian manufacturing and how companies are becoming more competitive.

Canada Today

Canada is a large industrial country with many major industries. We are one of the largest producers of forest products in the world, with plants in nearly all provinces turning out a vast array of wood, furniture, and paper products. There are giant aluminum mills in Quebec and British Columbia, automotive-related manufacturing plants in Ontario and Quebec, and aircraft plants in Ontario, Quebec, and Manitoba. Oil, natural gas, and coal are produced in Alberta, Saskatchewan, Newfoundland and Labrador, Nova Scotia, and British Columbia, and a vast array of metals and minerals come from all parts of Canada.

These are only some of the thousands of components, products, and natural resources produced or processed in Canada. Given that most of our industry is focused on natural resources we can experience significant growth in times when world economies are growing, offset by an equally large retraction when world economies are stagnant or in recession. Such has been the case over the past 7 to 10 years. What happens in the United States, along with world economies including China and India, has a dramatic impact on Canada, as was discussed in Chapter 3.

Canada is facing some serious challenges to its ability to remain a modern, competitive industrial country. Today's business climate is characterized by constant and restless change and dislocation, as ever-newer technologies and increasing global competition force companies to respond quickly to these challenges. Many factors account for our difficulties in the world's competitive race. Among them are inadequate improvement in productivity and unrelenting competition from the United States, Japan, Germany, and more recently from India, China, and other Southeast Asian countries; inadequate education and retraining programs for our workforce; our "branch plant economy," whereby many subsidiaries are owned by foreign parent companies and profits are mostly returned to these foreign-based companies rather than invested in Canada; and a lack of money spent on research and development. Where Canada used to be able to rely on a lower-valued Canadian dollar compared to the U.S. dollar to sustain our exports, an exchange rate closer to parity negates this advantage. Figure 10.1 lists priorities that could improve Canada's competitiveness.

■ **FIGURE 10.1**

MAKING CANADA MORE COMPETITIVE

The Canadian Manufacturing Coalition published a report identifying priorities that would make our country more competitive.[1]

1. Support Investment and Innovation by providing targeted tax credits for specific activities that initiate new investment by manufacturing companies, creating a Manufacturing Innovation Centre of Excellence, and establishing a Strategic Capital Investment Fund for facility upgrades.
2. Strengthen the Labour Market by promoting careers in advanced manufacturing to Canadian youth and expanding the Canada Jobs Grant program.
3. Increase Value-Added Manufacturing Exports by developing policy and regulation to build free trade and expand key trade corridors with other countries.

Source: "Manufacturing our Future 2014: Manufacturing Growth: new frontiers for Canadian manufacturers," Canadian Manufacturing Coalition, 2014, http://www.manufacturingourfuture.ca/_uploads/media/50aoesqq7.pdf, downloaded 29 May 2015.

Despite these challenges, Canada still ranks fairly well in world competitiveness (see the Reaching Beyond our Borders box in this chapter). However, one cannot expect this to continue, as other countries are becoming stronger and more competitive. In response, the federal government's innovation strategy focuses on research and development as a way to improve our competitiveness. Let us look at research and development next.

Research and Development

According to the *Canadian Oxford Dictionary*, **research and development (R&D)** is defined as work directed toward the innovation, introduction, and improvement of products and processes. When evaluating why some companies are more competitive than others, the terms *technology* and *innovation* often come up. What do these terms mean?

research and development (R&D)
Work directed toward the innovation, introduction, and improvement of products and processes.

The Centre for Canadian Studies at Mount Allison University, in co-operation with the Canadian Heritage Canadian Studies Programme, produces the *About Canada* series. Innovation in Canada is the focus of one of these documents.

> *Technology is know-how, knowing how to make and use the tools for the job. It's the combination of technology with markets that creates innovation and gives a competitive edge. An innovation is a new product or process that can be purchased. Put another way, an idea may lead to an invention, but it cannot be called an innovation until it is commercialized. When technological know-how is developed, sold, distributed, and used, then it becomes an innovation.*[1]

In the Survey of Innovation conducted by Statistics Canada, respondents indicated that the three most important objectives of innovation are to improve product quality, to increase production capacity, and to extend product range. Since that time, the Science, Innovation, and Electronic Information Division (SIEID) of Statistics Canada has piloted a greater number of surveys that focus on the importance of innovation. SIEID believes that innovation and the adoption and dissemination of innovative technologies and processes are vital to economic growth and development. It continues to elaborate by stating that, through innovation, new products are introduced in the market, new production processes are developed and introduced, and organizational changes are made. Through the adoption of newer, more advanced technologies and practices, industries can increase their production capabilities, improve their productivity, and expand their lines of new goods and services.[2]

Private industry, Canadian universities, hospitals, and government laboratories spent a combined $30.6 billion on R&D in 2014.[3] The federal government contribution to science and technology funding (considered the principal source of R&D funds in Canada) dropped over 5% to $10.3 billion for 2014–2015.[4] In 2014, Canada dropped out of the world's top-ten list for R&D spending.[5]

Figure 10.2 outlines Canada's top ten corporate R&D spenders. In 2013, corporate spending on R&D rose 4.1% from 2012; however, this increase is not a high as the 12.6% increase the previous year.[6] Two companies with significant decline in R&D spending are IBM Canada Ltd. and Blackberry Ltd. Offsetting the steep declines for these two companies is the significant increase in R&D by Bombardier Inc. and Magna International Inc.

Based on its research, what does RESEARCH Infosource Inc. *<http://www.researchinfosource .com>* forecast? First, the financial crisis in 2008–09 was a logical reason for a decline in R&D spending. However, given the decrease in manufacturing and the increase in the service industry it will be difficult to reverse the trend. Manufacturing typically needs to invest in R&D and has been supported by government, however a similar R&D environment does not traditionally exist in the service sector.

■ FIGURE 10.2

CANADA'S TOP CORPORATE R&D SPENDERS								
Rank			R&D Expenditures			Revenue	Research Intensity	
2013	2012	Company	FY2013 $000	FY2012 $000	% Change 2012–2013	FY2013 $000	R&D as % of Revenue	Industry
1	1	Bombardier Inc.	$ 2,193,719	$1,900,240	15.4	$ 18,693,984	11.7	Aerospace
2	2	Blackberry Limited	$1,324,470	$1,508,396	−12.2	$ 7,016,810	18.9	Communication, Telecom Equipment
3	6	Magna International Inc.	$ 576,752	$ 514,794	12.0	$ 35,877,082	1.6	Automotive
4	3	BCE Inc.	$ 575,400	$ 576,100	−0.1	$20,400,000	2.8	Telecommunication Services
5	5	Pratt & Whitney Canada Corp.	$ 544,782	$ 526,984	3.4	nd		Aerospace
6	4	IBM Canada Ltd.	$ 492,000	$ 540,000	−8.9	nd		Software and Computer Services
7	8	Rogers Communication Inc.	$ 394,000	$ 346,000	13.9	$ 12,706,000	3.1	Telecommunications Services
8	10	Canadian Natural Resources Limited	$ 390,000	$ 270,000	44.4	16,145,000	2.4	Energy/Oil & Gas
9	7	Atomic Energy of Canada	$ 353,600	$ 384,100	−7.9	184,000	192.2	Engineering Services
10	9	Ericsson Canada Inc.	$ 318,000	$ 325,000	2.2	nd		Communication/ Telecom Equipment

Notes: nd = Not disclosed

Source: RE$EARCH Infosource Inc., Canada's Top 100 Corporate R&D Spenders 2014, http://www.researchinfosource.com/top100_corp.php.

Canada's Evolving Manufacturing and Services Base

Over the previous two decades, foreign manufacturers captured huge chunks of the North American market for basic products such as steel, cement, machinery, and farm equipment using the latest in production techniques. That competition forced companies to greatly alter their production techniques and managerial styles. Many firms are now as good as or better than competitors anywhere in the world. What have Canadian manufacturers done to regain a competitive edge? They have emphasized the following:

- Focus on customers;
- Maintain close relationships with suppliers and other companies to satisfy customer needs;
- Practise continuous improvement;
- Focus on quality;
- Save on costs through site selection;
- Rely on the Internet to unite companies; and
- Adopt production techniques such as enterprise resource planning, computer-integrated manufacturing, flexible manufacturing, and lean manufacturing.

As you may recall from Figure 1.8 in Chapter 1, the goods-producing sectors employs 22 percent of Canada's working population. R&D spending by businesses is also critical to our economy, as they contributed $15.4 billion, or 51 percent of total R&D expenditures in 2014.[7] This sector is highly innovative and technology-driven. They continue to invest in facilities increasing their agility, expanding automation capabilities, and facilitating new product introductions.[8]

As we progress through this chapter, you will see that operations management has become a challenging and vital element of Canadian business. The growth of Canada's manufacturing base will likely remain a major business issue in the near future. There will be debates about the merits of moving production facilities to foreign countries. Serious questions will be raised about replacing workers with robots and other machinery. Major political decisions will be made regarding protection of Canadian manufacturers through quotas and other restrictions on free trade. Concerns about the impact of manufacturing on our environment will result in the development of new green technologies (as discussed in the Seeking Sustainability box in this chapter). Regardless of how these issues are decided, however, there will be many opportunities along the way.

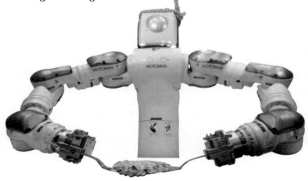

Each year companies discover new ways of automating that eliminate the need for human labour. This robot demonstrates an ability to cook *Okonomiyaki,* a Japanese pancake. The robot can take verbal orders from customers and use standard kitchen utensils. Do you think the robot has a better chance to get your order right compared to a human cook?

The service sector will also continue to get attention as it continues to become a larger part of the overall economy. Service productivity is an important issue, as is the blending of service and manufacturing through the Internet. Since many of tomorrow's graduates will likely find jobs in the service sector, it is important to understand the latest operations management concepts and how they apply to the service sector.

Progress Assessment

- What are some challenges that Canada is facing in its ability to remain a competitive country?
- How is innovation related to research and development?

LO2 Describe the evolution from production to operations management.

From Production to Operations Management

Production is the creation of goods and services using the factors of production: land, labour, capital, entrepreneurship, and knowledge (see Chapter 1). Production has historically meant *manufacturing* and the term **production management** has described the management activities that helped firms create goods. But the nature of business has changed significantly in the last 20 years or so as the service sector, including Internet services, has grown dramatically. As discussed in Chapter 1, Canada is a service economy—that is, one dominated by the service sector. This can be a benefit to future graduates because many of the top-paying jobs are in legal services, medical services, entertainment, broadcasting, and business services such as accounting, finance, and management consulting.

> **production**
> The creation of finished goods and services using the factors of production: land, labour, capital, entrepreneurship, and knowledge.
>
> **production management**
> The term used to describe all of the activities that managers do to help their firms create goods.

   Operations management is a specialized area in management that converts or transforms resources (including human resources) into goods and services. It includes inventory management, quality control, production scheduling, follow-up services, and more. In an automobile plant, operations management transforms raw materials, human resources, parts, supplies, paints, tools, and other resources into automobiles. It does this through the processes of fabrication and assembly.

> **operations management**
> A specialized area in management that converts or transforms resources (including human resources) into goods and services.

   In a college or university, operations management takes inputs—such as information, professors, supplies, buildings, offices, and computer systems—and creates services that transform students into educated people. It does this through a process called education.

Seeking SUSTAINABILITY

Carbon Capture and Storage

One of Canada's primary resources is its fossil fuels. Abundant supplies of oil, natural gas, and coal make this country one of the world's most attractive energy centres for continuing investment and development. However, with this economic opportunity comes a challenge, to mitigate greenhouse gas (GHG) emissions and their impact on climate change. More and more evidence is being gathered by the scientific community that supports the claim that global emissions growth could bring rapid climate change. The challenge is to reduce GHG emissions while continuing economic progress.

Carbon dioxide capture and storage (CCS) is one way to address the carbon challenge. With CCS, carbon dioxide emissions from large industrial facilities are separated from the plant's process or exhaust system, compressed, and injected deep underground.

CCS can be built as an add-on to existing fossil energy infrastructure or incorporated into new and future facilities. The main components of this operation are: capture, transportation, and storage. Once the carbon dioxide is captured at a plant, it needs to be transported to a location with the appropriate geological formation. These stable sedimentary rock formations, that formerly securely held vast oil and gas reserves, can now be used to hold carbon dioxide, which is injected into the underground space.

Both the federal and a number of provincial governments are financially supporting the development of CCS and introducing legislation to reduce GHG emissions. A total of $3 billion in funding for CCS has been provided by all levels of government during the past few years.

Carbon dioxide capture and storage is used by SaskPower <*http://www.saskpower.com*> where a large-scale CCS operation was built for a coal-fired power plant in Estevan, Saskatchewan. The project cost $1.4 billion and officials claim the GHG reduction is equivalent to removing a quarter of a million cars from the road.

While you may initially assume the most important area for CCS is in manufacturing, there are a variety of industries that can benefit from CCS. According to the Integrated CO_2 Network, approximately 24 percent of GHG emissions are generated from personal transportation and residential areas. Do you believe CSC technology will expand beyond large industry to also help Canadians make their everyday living more GHG efficient?

Source: "Carbon capture history made in Saskatchewan, besting once ambitious Alberta," CBC News, 3 October 2014, http://www.cbc.ca/news/canada/calgary/carbon-capture-history-made-in-saskatchewan-besting-once-ambitious-alberta-1.2786478; "A Strategic Investment," 2015, Integrated CO_2 Network, http://www.ico2n.com/, downloaded 10 May 2015; The Canadian CO_2 Capture and Storage Technology Network, Natural Resources Canada, www.CO^{2}network.gc.ca; and Racel Pulfer, "Burying King Coal," *Canadian Business*, 28 April 2008, 21–22.

Some organizations—such as factories, farms, and mines—produce mostly goods. Others—such as hospitals, schools, and government agencies—produce mostly services. Still others produce a combination of goods and services. For example, an automobile manufacturer not only makes cars but also provides services such as repairs, financing, and insurance. Wendy's provides goods such as hamburgers and fries, but customers also receive services such as order taking, order filling, food preparation, and cleanup.

Reaching *Beyond* OUR BORDERS

How Does Canada Shape Up as an International Competitor?

How does Canada rank when compared to other industrialized countries? Canadian businesses have been criticized for not being more productive as productivity contributes to competitiveness. Analysts are concerned that an under-investment in innovation and technology will have a negative impact on the long-term productivity of Canadian businesses. In order to remain competitive with other countries in the world, Canada needs to invest in R&D and higher education.

Assessing international competitiveness is complex and open to varying opinions. There are several indexes that attempt to measure competitiveness, and different criteria and weightings are used by the agencies that produce them. You will notice the importance of economic conditions and the role of government when evaluating a country's attractiveness. Let us consider two popular rankings.

The prestigious World Economic Forum (WEF, *<http://www.weforum.org>*) produces the annual Global Competitiveness Report. The Growth Competitiveness Index is based on estimates of each country's ability to grow over the next five to ten years. Thus, economic conditions and institutions (e.g., government and financial markets) are reviewed. It was determined that Canada's future competitiveness and productive potential would benefit by improving the sophistication and innovative potential of the private sector with greater R&D spending and producing goods and services higher on the value chain.

The International Institute for Management Development (IMD, *<http://www.imd.org>*) produces the World Competitiveness Yearbook, which ranks the ability of a nation to provide an environment that sustains the competitiveness of enterprises. The ranking considers four criteria: economic performance, government efficiency, business efficiency, and infrastructure. In the past it was determined that while Canada ranks well on government policies conducive to competitiveness, Canada would rank higher if it had a more enterprising business community.

There is no single authority on ranking a country's competitiveness. These two examples highlight how different criteria are considered by different organizations. What should be of interest is that the criteria incorporate some of the concepts that are discussed in this textbook (e.g., economic performance). As a business student, be assured that the concepts that you are learning are in fact incorporated in business decision making.

Year	Canada's Rank, WEF's Growth Competitiveness Index	Canada's Rank, IMD's World Competitiveness Ranking
2014	15	7
2013	14	7
2012	14	6
2011	12	7
2010	10	7
2009	10	8
2008	13	8
2007	12	10
2006	14	5
2005	15	3

The business environment is clearly influenced by factors such as economic performance and government policies. Canada's ranking is influenced not only by what happens domestically, but also by what happens internationally. Our fall in the rankings is influenced by our strengths and weaknesses (as assessed by the organizations listed above) and measured against the strengths and weaknesses of other countries. As other countries improve their competitiveness, this will contribute to Canada's fall in the rankings if we do not improve accordingly.

Sources: David Parkinson, "Canada slips a notch in global competitiveness ranking," *The Globe and Mail*, 3 September 2014, http://www.theglobeandmail.com/report-on-business/economy/canada-slips-a-notch-in-global-competitiveness-ranking/article20313100/; "The Global Competitiveness Report 2014-2015 – Canada," World Economic Forum, 2014, http://www3.weforum.org/docs/GCR2014 -15/Canada.pdf, downloaded 10 May 2015; "Canada falls to 15th in global competitiveness ranking," CBC News, 3 September 2014, http://www.cbc.ca/news/business/canada-falls-to-15th-in-global-competitiveness-ranking-1.2754078; "IMD releases its 25th anniversary World Competitiveness Rankings," IMD, 29 May 2013, http://www.imd.org/news/World-Competitiveness-2013.cfm.

Operations management for services is all about enriching the customer experience. Hotels, for instance, have responded to the needs of business travellers with in-room Internet access and other kinds of office-style support, as well as stored information about the preferences of frequent guests. How important do you think guest-recognition programs are to business travellers?

Operations Management in the Service Sector

Operations management in the service industry is all about creating a good experience for those who use the service.[9] For example, in a Four Seasons <*http://www.fourseasons.com*> hotel, operations management includes restaurants that offer the finest in service, elevators that run smoothly, and a front desk that processes people quickly. It may include placing fresh-cut flowers in the lobbies and dishes of fruit in every room. More important, it may mean spending thousands of dollars to provide quality management training for each new employee.

Hotel customers today want in-room Internet access and a help centre with toll-free telephone service. Executives travelling on business may need video equipment and a host of computer hardware and other aids. Foreign visitors would like multilingual customer-support services. Hotel shops need to carry more than souvenirs, newspapers, and some drugstore and food items to serve today's high-tech travellers. The shops may also carry laptop computer supplies, electrical adapters, and the like. At the International House <*http://www.ihhotel.com*>, a hotel in New Orleans, 16 rooms have Apple TV boxes so that mobile device-dependent clients can easily stream live video.[10]

Operations management is responsible for locating and providing such amenities to make customers happy. In short, delighting customers by anticipating their needs has become the quality standard for luxury hotels, as it has for most other service businesses.[11] But knowing customer needs and satisfying them are two different things. That is why operations management is so important: it is the implementation phase of management.

Can you see the need for better operations management in airports, hospitals, government agencies, schools, and non-profit organization such as the Red Cross? The opportunities seem almost unlimited. Although manufacturing still needs innovation, much of the future of Canada's economic growth is in these service areas.

Measuring Quality in the Service Sector

There's strong evidence that productivity in the service sector is rising, but productivity measures do not capture improvements in quality. In an example from health care, positron emission tomography (PET) scans are much better than X-rays, but the quality difference is not reported in productivity figures. The traditional way to measure productivity involves tracking inputs (worker hours) compared to outputs (dollars). Notice that there is no measure for quality improvement. When new information systems are developed to measure the quality improvement of goods and services—including the speed of their delivery and customer satisfaction—productivity in the service sector will go up dramatically.

Using computers is one way in which the service sector is improving productivity, but not the only one. Think about labour-intensive businesses such as fast-food restaurants, where automation plays a big role in controlling costs and improving service. Today, at Burger King <*http://burgerking.ca*>, for example, customers fill their own drink cups from pop machines, which allows workers to concentrate on preparing the food. And because the people working at the drive-up window now wear headsets instead of using stationary mikes, they are no longer glued to one spot and can do four or five tasks while taking an order.

Most of us have been exposed to similar productivity gains in banking. For example, people in most cities no longer have to wait in long lines for tellers to help them deposit and withdraw money. Instead, they use automated teller machines (ATMs), which usually involve little or no waiting and are available 24 hours a day.

Another service that was once very slow was grocery store checkout. The system of marking goods with universal product codes (UPC) enables computerized checkout and allows cashiers to be much more productive than before. Now, many stores have set up automated systems that enable customers to go through the checkout process on their own. Some grocery chains, such as Longo's <*http://www.longos.com*>, are implementing Internet services that allow customers to place orders online and receive home delivery. The potential for productivity gains in this area are enormous.

In short, operations management has led to tremendous productivity increases in the service sector but there is still a long way to go to capture potential improvements. Also, service workers are losing jobs to machines just as manufacturing workers did. The secret to obtaining and holding a good job is to acquire appropriate education and training. Such education and training must go on for a lifetime to keep up with the rapid changes that are happening in all areas of business. That message cannot be repeated too frequently.

Progress Assessment

- Explain the difference between production management and operations management.
- What is the biggest issue with productivity in the service sector?

LO3 Describe operations management planning issues including facility location, facility layout, materials requirement planning, purchasing, just-in-time inventory control, quality control, and supply chain management.

Operations Management Planning

Operations management planning helps solve many of the problems in the service and manufacturing sectors. These include facility location, facility layout, and quality control. The resources used in the two sectors may be different, but the management issues are similar.

Facility Location

Facility location is the process of selecting a geographic location for a company's operations. In keeping with the need to focus on customers, one strategy is to find a site that makes it easy for consumers to use the company's services and to communicate about their needs. For example, German food company Dr. Oetker's <*http://www.oetker.ca*> opened a new pizza plant in London, Ontario, because the location provided skilled workers and a close proximity to consumers in Canada and the United States.[13] Flower shops and banks are putting facilities in supermarkets so that their products are more accessible than they are in freestanding facilities. You can find a McDonalds' inside some Walmart stores and there are Tim Hortons outlets in some gas stations. Customers can buy gas and their meals, all in one location.

> **facility location**
> The process of selecting a geographic location for a company's operations.

The ultimate in convenience is never having to leave home to get services. That is why there is so much interest in Internet banking, Internet shopping, online education, and other services. For brick-and-mortar businesses to beat such competition, they have to choose good locations and offer outstanding service. Study the location of service-sector businesses—such as hotels, banks, athletic clubs, and supermarkets—and you will see that the most successful ones are conveniently located.

FACILITY LOCATION FOR MANUFACTURERS

A major issue of the recent past has been the shift of manufacturing organizations from one city or province to another in Canada, or to other foreign sites. In the past few years several prominent plant closures impacted the Canadian processed food industry. For example, Kellogg Canada closed its cereal

Facility location is a major decision for manufacturing and other companies that must take into account the availability of qualified workers; access to suppliers, customers, transportation, and local regulation including zoning and taxes. How has the growth of Internet commerce affected company location decisions?

plant in London, Ontario, and Heinz closed its tomato processing plant in Leamington, Ontario.[14] Such shifts sometimes result in pockets of unemployment in some geographic areas and lead to tremendous economic growth in others that benefit from these shifts. The Making Ethical Decisions box considers some of the issues surrounding such moves.

Why would companies spend millions of dollars to move their facilities from one location to another? In making these decisions they consider labour costs; availability of resources, including labour; access to transportation that can reduce time-to-market; proximity to suppliers; proximity to customers; crime rates; quality of life for employees; cost of living; and the need to train or retrain the local workforce.

Even though labour is becoming a smaller percentage of total cost in highly automated industries, availability of low-cost labour or the right kind of skilled labour remains a key reason many producers move their plant to Malaysia, China, India, Mexico, and other countries. Some of these firms have been charged with providing substandard working conditions, exploiting children, or both in the countries where some manufacturers have set up factories. Others, such as Grupo M <*http://www.grupom.com.do*>, a textile products and services company in the Dominican Republic, are being used as role models for global manufacturing. Grupo M provides its employees with higher pay relative to local businesses, transportation to and from work, daycare centres, discounted food, and health clinics. Its operations are so efficient that it can compete in world markets and provide world-class services to its employees.

Making ETHICAL DECISIONS

Do We Stay or Do We Go?

Suppose the hypothetical company ChildrenWear Industries has long been the economic foundation for its hometown. Most of the area's small businesses and schools either supply materials the firm needs for production or train its future employees. ChildrenWear has learned that if it were to move its production facilities to Asia it could increase its profits by 15 percent.

Closing operations in the company's hometown would cause many of the town's other businesses, such as restaurants, to fail, which would leave a high percentage of the town's adults unemployed, with no options for re-employment within the local community. As a top manager at ChildrenWear, you must help decide whether the plant should be moved. What alternatives do you have? What are the consequences of each? Which will you choose?

Inexpensive resources are another major reason for moving production facilities. Companies usually need water, electricity, wood, coal, and other basic resources. By moving to areas where natural resources are inexpensive and plentiful, firms can significantly lower not only the cost of buying such resources but also the cost of shipping

(continued)

(continued)

finished products. Often the most important resource is people, so companies tend to cluster in a location where smart and talented people are readily available. Witness the Ottawa area, also known as Silicon Valley North.

Time-to-market is another decision-making factor. As manufacturers attempt to compete globally, they need sites that allow products to move quickly, so that they can offer fast delivery to customers. Thus, access to highways, rail lines, waterways, and airports is critical.[15] Information technology (IT) is also important to quicken response time, so many firms are seeking countries with the most advanced information systems.

Another way to work closely with suppliers in order to satisfy your customers' needs is to locate your production facilities near supplier facilities. This option cuts the cost of distribution and makes communication easier.

Many businesses are building factories in foreign countries to get closer to their international customers. That is a major reason why the U.S. automaker General Motors builds cars in Oshawa, Ontario, and Japanese automaker Toyota builds cars in Cambridge, Ontario. Japanese-based automaker Honda *<http://www.honda.ca>* opened an engine factory plant in Alliston, Ontario, in 2008, close to its two assembly plants. Honda Canada president Hiroshi Kobayashi told a news conference that this site selection "supports Honda's global strategic manufacturing focus of bringing manufacturing and sales operations to the local market."[16] In 2014, Honda announced it will make a $857 million investment to expand the plant in Alliston, Ontario, to upgrade vehicle assembly and engine manufacturing.[17] When firms select foreign sites, they consider whether they are near airports, waterways, and highways so that raw materials and finished goods can be moved quickly and easily.

Businesses also study the quality of life for workers and managers. Are there good schools nearby? Is the weather nice? Is the crime rate low? Does the local community welcome new businesses? Do the chief executive and other key managers want to live there? Sometimes a region with a high quality of life is also an expensive one, which complicates the decision. In short, facility location has become a critical issue in operations management.

A great deal of Germany's economic success is attributed to the strength of its industrial sector, consisting of a longstanding group of small manufacturers, many of which have been in business for centuries. At the core of this manufacturing juggernaut is the Mittelstand, consisting of family-owned, small to midsize companies that account for 52 percent of the country's economic output and supply almost two-thirds of the nation's jobs. The Mittelstand are able to build Germany's economy, especially its exports, without moving facilities to other countries.

OUTSOURCING

The previous chapter noted that many companies now try to divide their production between core competencies, work they do best in-house, and outsourcing, using outside companies with expertise to service specific functional areas. The result is intended to achieve the best-quality products at the lowest possible costs.

Outsourcing goods and services has become a hot practice in North America. Software development, call-centre jobs, and back-office jobs have been moving to developing countries for some time. The range of jobs now shifting to these countries expands beyond manufacturing to also include accounting, financial analysis, medical services, architecture, aircraft maintenance, law, film production, and banking activities.[18]

Based on a survey of its over 120,000 members and affiliates, the International Association of Outsourcing Professionals <*http://www.iaop.org*> has found that increasing business flexibility is the most prominent reason for outsourcing.[19] According to Jerome Thirion with KPMG Canada, consumer-facing companies may renew approximately one-third of a product line on an annual basis in order to remain competitive.[20] In these situations, it makes better economic sense to work with an outsourcer who can adapt to a company's changing production needs.

In the manufacturing sector, employment continues to drop lower and lower through outsourcing. However, outsourcing is expected to also expand in other industries in the future. The survey also found the demand for outsourcing higher-skill activities as opposed to lower-skilled activities rose 6 percent from the previous year. In the past outsourcing was driven by a need for cheap labour but it is now more often that labour expertise is the key reason.[21]

Another industry where significant outsourcing happens is software R&D. For Canadian companies needing software, hourly rates outside of Canada are much lower. Keep in mind that while outsourcing may look good on paper financially, if a company does not do its homework, outsourcing can become a problem due to language and cultural differences, differences in expectations, etc. A Canadian organization, the Centre for Outsourcing Research and Education (CORE, <*http://www.core-outsourcing .org*>), has been formed to provide organizations with the knowledge and skills to manage outsourcing activities.[22] More than just a cost-saving tool, outsourcing is being used as a strategic tool to focus scarce human capital on core business activities.

In 2013, the Canadian Auto Workers (CAW) and Communications, Energy, and Paperworkers Union of Canada (CEP) merged to form a new union called Unifor <*http://www.unifor.org*>. The organization, which represents Canada's biggest private sector union and spans approximately 20 sectors, still represents workers in automotive manufacturing. Many jobs have been lost in this sector due to imports and the global financial crisis. What priorities do you think Unifor should focus upon to help its members who face the challenges of a changing global marketplace?[24]

Future global outsourcing trends are uncertain, but the overall volume of outsourcing by companies around the world is expected to grow. Both private and public sectors need to invest in areas that improve Canada's attraction as a viable and affordable outsourcing destination.[23]

TAKING OPERATIONS MANAGEMENT TO THE INTERNET

Many rapidly growing companies do very little production themselves. Instead, they outsource engineering, design, manufacturing, and other tasks to other companies that specialize in those functions. They create new relationships with suppliers over the Internet, making operations management an *inter-firm* process in which companies work closely together to design, produce, and ship products to customers.

Many manufacturing companies are developing Internet-focused strategies that will enable them and others to compete more effectively in the future. These changes have a dramatic effect on operations managers as they adjust from a one-firm system to an inter-firm environment and from a relatively stable environment to one that is constantly changing and evolving. This linking of firms is called *supply chain management*. We will briefly introduce you to this concept later in the chapter.

FACILITY LOCATION IN THE FUTURE

The use of information technology (IT) such as computers, modems, e-mail, voice mail, text messaging, teleconferencing, etc. gives employees the flexibility to choose where they work while at the same helps keeps the firm in the competitive mainstream (see also the discussion on virtual organizations in Chapter 9). **Telecommuting**, working from home via computer, is a major trend in business. Companies that no longer need to locate near sources of labour will be able to move to areas where land is less expensive and the quality of life may be higher. Furthermore, more salespeople are keeping in touch with the company and its customers through videoconferencing, using computers to talk with and show images to others.[25]

telecommuting
Working from home via computer.

One strong incentive for a business to locate in a particular city, province, or territory is the tax situation. Some provincial and local governments have higher taxes than others, yet many compete fiercely by offering companies tax reductions and other support, such as zoning changes and financial aid, in order to convince the company to locate within its boundaries. The previously mentioned Honda plant expansion in Alliston included a provincial government grant of up to $85.7 million. Have you seen advertisements for entrepreneurs to locate in your hometown?

Facility Layout

Facility layout is the physical arrangement of resources, including people, to most efficiently produce goods and provide services to customers. Facility layout depends greatly on the processes that are to be performed. For services, the layout is usually designed to help the consumer find and buy services, including on the Internet. Some stores have added kiosks that enable customers to search for goods online and place orders or make returns and credit payments in the store. In short, the facilities and Internet capabilities of service organizations are becoming more customer-oriented.

facility layout
The physical arrangement of resources (including people) in the production process.

Many corporations have adopted open office work space, such as RBC and Mastercard Canada. The purpose is to improve productivity through greater collaboration and creativity. However, some researchers have found that a variety of work spaces are needed in order to ensure employees can seek the interaction or the privacy that they need to work effectively. A recent move by Google saw head offices move to open floor concepts in order to foster innovation.[26] What do you think are some of the advantages of such non-traditional office layouts? Are there any disadvantages?

Similar to manufacturers, some service-oriented organizations, such as hospitals, use layouts that improve the efficiency. For manufacturing plants, facilities layout has become critical because the possible cost savings are enormous.

Many companies are moving from an *assembly-line layout,* in which workers do only a few tasks at a time, to a *modular layout,* in which *teams* of workers combine to produce more complex units of the final product.[27] There may have been a dozen or more workstations on an assembly line to complete an automobile engine in the past, but all of that work may be done in one module today.

When working on a major project, such as a bridge or airplane, companies use a *fixed-position layout* that allows workers to congregate around the product to be completed.

A *process layout* is one in which similar equipment and functions are grouped together. The order in which the product visits a function depends on the design of the item. This allows for flexibility. The Igus *<http://www.igus.com>* manufacturing plant in Cologne, Germany, can shrink or expand in a flash. Its flexible design keeps it competitive in a fast-changing market. Because the layout of the plant changes so often, some employees use scooters to more efficiently provide needed skills, supplies, and services to multiple workstations. A fast-changing plant needs a fast-moving employee base to achieve maximum productivity. Figure 10.3 illustrates typical layout designs.

Materials Requirement Planning (MRP)

Materials requirement planning (MRP) is a computer-based operations management system that uses sales forecasts to ensure that needed parts and materials are available at the right time and place. In a diner, for example, employees could enter the sales forecast into the computer, which would specify how many eggs and how much coffee to order, and then print out the proper scheduling and routing sequence. The same can be done with orders for the seats and other parts of an automobile. In the next section, you will read how just-in-time inventory control has a similar objective.

materials requirement planning (MRP)
A computer-based production management system that uses sales forecasts to make sure that needed parts and materials are available at the right time and place.

FIGURE 10.3

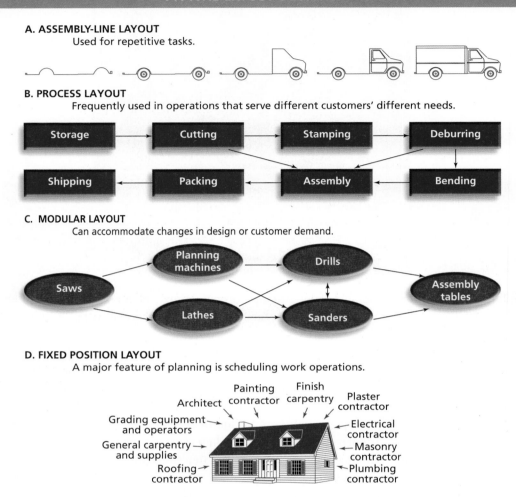

TYPICAL LAYOUT DESIGNS

A. ASSEMBLY-LINE LAYOUT
Used for repetitive tasks.

B. PROCESS LAYOUT
Frequently used in operations that serve different customers' different needs.

Storage → Cutting → Stamping → Deburring

Shipping ← Packing ← Assembly ← Bending

C. MODULAR LAYOUT
Can accommodate changes in design or customer demand.

Saws → Planning machines → Drills → Assembly tables
Lathes → Sanders

D. FIXED POSITION LAYOUT
A major feature of planning is scheduling work operations.

Architect, Painting contractor, Finish carpentry, Plaster contractor
Grading equipment and operators
General carpentry and supplies
Roofing contractor
Electrical contractor
Masonry contractor
Plumbing contractor

Enterprise resource planning (ERP), a newer version of MRP, combines the computerized functions of all the divisions and subsidiaries of the firm—such as finance, human resources, and order fulfillment—into one integrated software program that uses a single database (see Figure 10.4). The result is shorter time between orders and payment, less staff to do ordering and order processing, reduced inventories, and better customer service. For example, the customer can place an order, either through a customer service representative or online, and immediately see when the order will be filled and how much it will cost. The representative can instantly see the customer's credit rating and order history, the company's inventory, and the shipping schedule. Everyone else in the company can see the new order as well; thus when one department finishes its portion of the task, the order is automatically routed via the ERP system to the next department. The customer can see exactly where the order is at any point by logging into the system.

enterprise resource planning (ERP)
A computer application that enables a firm to manage all of its operations (finance, requirements planning, human resources, and order fulfillment) on the basis of a single, integrated set of corporate data.

■ **FIGURE 10.4**

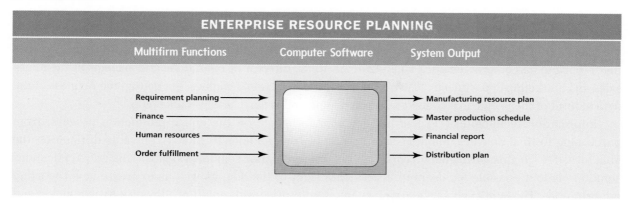

ENTERPRISE RESOURCE PLANNING		
Multifirm Functions	**Computer Software**	**System Output**

Requirement planning → → Manufacturing resource plan
Finance → → Master production schedule
Human resources → → Financial report
Order fulfillment → → Distribution plan

By entering customer and sales information in an ERP system, a manufacturer can generate the next period's demand forecast, which in turn generates orders for raw materials, production scheduling, and financial projections.

ERP software enables the firm to monitor quality and customer satisfaction as it is happening. ERP systems are going global now that the Internet is powerful enough to handle the data flows. At the plant level, dynamic performance monitoring enables plant operators to monitor the use of power, chemicals, and other resources and to make needed adjustments. In short, flows to, through, and from plants have become automated.

Some firms are providing a service called sequential delivery. These firms are suppliers that provide components in an order sequenced to their customers' production process. For example, Ford's seat supplier loads seats onto a truck such that, when off-loaded, the seats are in perfect sequence for the type of vehicle coming down the assembly line.

SAS <*http://www.sas.com*> is the leader in business analytics software and services, and the largest independent vendor in the business intelligence market. SAS Business Analytics helps organizations improve performance and deliver value by making better decisions faster. SAS and the Toronto Maple Leafs recently announced a partnership for hockey analytics that will see the Club use SAS analytics to help analyze aspects of the team's performance; applying a data-driven approach to everything from player performance to on-ice strategy. The analysis will include the use of player performance data to help hockey executives make better decisions at the National Hockey League entry draft and trade deadline.[28]

While ERP can be an effective tool, it also can have its problems. The Royal Canadian Mint *<http://www.mint.ca>* had difficulties extracting and manipulating data from its integrated software system. Departments operated independently, and because it took so long to produce reports for analysis, employees did not trust the reliability of the information once it was in their hands. "Anyone who has used an ERP system knows that reporting can be problematic," says Azfar Ali Khan, director of operations and systems at the Mint's sales and marketing departments. "They're wonderful transactional engines, but getting the richness of the data in front of the people in a context they can understand is particularly challenging."[29]

Information technology (IT) has had a major influence on the entire production process, from purchasing to final delivery. Many IT advances have been add-ons to ERP. To solve its difficulties, the Mint turned to Cognos *<http://www.cognos.com>* for its enterprise solution. Cognos's Analytic Applications solution made it possible for users to access data right to the day, as well as to create new reporting opportunities. The Mint's self-service, web-enabled, enterprise-wide solution allowed it to act quickly and thereby improve customer service. According to Ali Khan, "Buying a prepackaged solution and customizing it to our own unique business requirements has saved us a lot of time and a lot of money."[30]

Purchasing

Purchasing is the function that searches for high-quality material resources, finds the best suppliers, and negotiates the best price for quality goods and services. In the past, manufacturers dealt with many suppliers so that if one could not deliver, the firm could get materials from a different supplier. Today, however, manufacturers rely more heavily on just one or two suppliers, because the relationship between suppliers and manufacturers is much closer than before. Producers share a great deal of information and consequently, they want as few suppliers as possible knowing their business. The Hudson's Bay Company shifted to single merchandise buyers for a growing number of departments at its Bay, Saks Fifth Avenue, and Home Outfitters chains. This move was designed to help improve product selection and save money through less duplication and larger purchase orders.[31]

> **purchasing**
> The functional area in a firm that searches for quality material resources, finds the best suppliers, and negotiates the best price for goods and services.

The Internet has transformed the purchasing function. A business looking for supplies can contact an Internet-based purchasing service and find the best items at the best price. Similarly, a company wishing to sell supplies can use the Internet to find all companies looking for such supplies. Thus, the time and dollar cost of purchasing items has been reduced tremendously.

Just-in-Time Inventory Control

One major cost of production is holding parts and other items in storage for later use. Storage not only subjects such items to obsolescence, pilferage, and damage, but also requires construction and maintenance of costly warehouses. To cut such costs, many companies have implemented a concept called **just-in-time (JIT) inventory control**. JIT systems keep a minimum of inventory on the premises and delivers parts, supplies, and other needs just in time to go on the assembly line. To work effectively, however, the process requires an accurate production schedule (using ERP) and excellent coordination with carefully selected suppliers, who

> **just-in-time (JIT) inventory control**
> A production process in which a minimum of inventory is kept on the premises and parts, supplies, and other needs are delivered just in time for use on the assembly line.

are usually connected electronically so they know what is needed and when. Sometimes the supplier builds new facilities close to the main producer to minimize distribution time. JIT runs into problems when suppliers are farther away. Weather may delay shipments, for example, as happened when weather (earthquakes and the resulting tsunami) disrupted the supply chain of materials from Japan to Canada in 2011.

Delays require that companies adjust their JIT schedules. Today, the longer delays at border crossings due to increased traffic and security measures have forced companies to do just that. Other limitations are that JIT works best with standard products, needs a high and stable demand to justify the cost and savings, and requires extremely reliable suppliers.

JIT systems ensure that the right materials are at the right place at the right time at the cheapest cost in order to meet both customer and production needs. That is a key step in modern production innovation.

Huge warehouses such as the one depicted in the photo would become a thing of the past if all companies implemented just-in-time (JIT) inventory control. What are the advantages and disadvantages of having large amounts of inventory available?

Quality Control

Maintaining **quality** means consistently producing what the customer wants while reducing errors before and after delivery to the customer. In the past, firms often conducted quality control at the end of the production line. Products were completed *and then tested* for quality. This resulted in several problems, including the need to:

1. Utilize extra workers and resources to inspect work.

2. Correct the mistake or scrap the product if an error was found, resulting in higher costs.

3. Risk customer dissatisfaction if she or he found the mistake, and decided to buy from another firm thereafter.

quality
Consistently producing what the customer wants while reducing errors before and after delivery to the customer.

Such problems led to the realization that quality is not an outcome; it is a never-ending process of continually improving what a company produces. Quality control should be part of the operations management planning process rather than simply an end-of-the-line inspection.

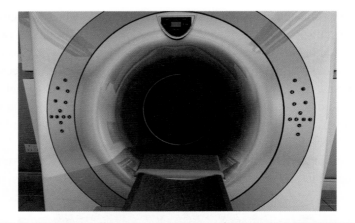

What happens when you combine the zeal of technical innovators with the Six Sigma discipline of a large company like General Electric? You get a medical breakthrough. Janet Burki and her 280-person operations team developed the world's fastest CT scanner. It works ten times faster than other systems and produces clear 3-D images of the beating heart. Can you see how efforts to build in quality lead to better (and faster) products?

Companies have turned to the use of modern quality control standards, such as Six Sigma. **Six Sigma quality**, which sets a benchmark of just 3.4 defects per million opportunities, detects potential problems to prevent their occurrence. That is important to a company that makes 4 million transactions a day, like some banks. The Spotlight on Small Business box explores how small businesses can apply Six Sigma to their operations.

> **Six Sigma quality**
> A quality measure that allows only 3.4 defects per million events.

Statistical quality control (SQC) is the process some managers use to continually monitor all phases of the production process and assure quality is built into the product from the beginning. **Statistical process control (SPC)** is the process of testing statistical samples of product components at each stage of production and plotting the test results on a graph. Managers can thus see and correct any deviation from quality standards. Making sure products meet standards all along the production process reduces the need for a quality-control inspection at the end because mistakes are caught much earlier in the process. Consequently, SQC and SPC save companies much time and money. Some companies use a quality-control approach called the Deming cycle (after the late W. Edwards Deming, the father of the movement toward quality).[32] Its steps are: Plan, Do, Check, Act (PDCA). Again, the idea is to find potential errors *before* they happen. Deming's approach, including implementing standards, was used for many years before the International Organization for Standardization (ISO), which we will talk about shortly, came into being.

> **statistical quality control (SQC)**
> The process some managers use to continually monitor all phases of the production process to assure that quality is being built into the product from the beginning.
>
> **statistical process control (SPC)**
> The process of testing statistical samples of product components at each stage of the production process and plotting those results on a graph. Any variances from quality standards are recognized and can be corrected if beyond the set standards.

Businesses are getting serious about providing top customer service, and many are already doing it. Service organizations find it difficult to provide outstanding service every time because the process is so labour intensive. Physical goods (e.g., a gold ring) can be designed and manufactured to near perfection. However, it is hard to reach such perfection when designing and providing a service experience such as a dance on a cruise ship or a cab drive through Vancouver.

Spotlight *On* SMALL BUSINESS

Meeting the Six Sigma Standard

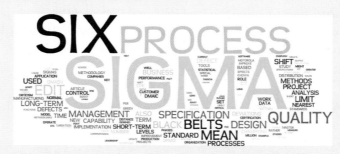

Six Sigma is a quality measure that allows only 3.4 defects per million opportunities. Here is how Six Sigma works: If you can make it to the level of one sigma, two out of three products will meet specifications. If you can reach the two sigma level, then more than 95 percent of products will qualify. But when you meet Six Sigma quality, as we have said, you have only 3.4 defects in a million opportunities (which means that 99.99966 percent of your products will qualify), a quality standard that approaches perfection. Service organizations are also adopting Six Sigma standards through the elimination of any activity involved with the service they provide that does not add value to the customer.

It is one thing for Motorola <*http://www.motorola.com*> (often cited as the driving force behind the development of this standard) or General Electric (GE) to reach for such standards given their vast resources, but what about a small company like Dolan Industries? Dolan is a 41-person manufacturer of fasteners. It spent a few years trying to meet ISO 9000 standards, which are comparable to Six Sigma. Dolan had to do that because its customers were demanding that level of quality.

Small companies can successfully implement Six Sigma if the owner is committed, the company has a routine core of work that can benefit from the standard, and the company's culture is open to change. Any change that is part of a Six Sigma project should not be so significant that any problem would have a major impact on customer relations. While the management buy-in for a Six Sigma initiative may be easier in a small business, resource commitment and employee training are more challenging compared to large companies. As a rule of thumb a small business can begin deploying Six Sigma when one employee can devote one day per week to this work, which represents 0.5 to 1 percent of employee hours (i.e., a minimum of 20 employees is required, which results in combined work hours of 800—based on 8 hour days). They should invest in software and books on the subject, access outside expertise, and pursue each project aggressively—completing most projects in four to six weeks.

While Six Sigma techniques can result in specific improvements, the true value of working toward the standard comes from an organization-wide culture shift. No matter what the size of the organization, there is much to be gained from finding cost-effective methods to deliver quality goods and services.

Sources: Charles Waxer, "Is Six Sigma Just for Large Companies? What about small companies?" ISix Sigma, 2015, http://www.isixsigma.com/new-to-six-sigma/getting-started/six-sigma-just-large-companies-what-about-small-companies/, downloaded 11 May 2015;Virginia Galt, "There's heavy demand in all sectors for 'lean' specialists," *The Globe and Mail,* 15 August 2013, http://www.theglobeandmail.com/report-on-business/careers/career-advice/life-at-work/heavy-demand-for-lean-specialists /article13795394/; Six Sigma Canada Inc – Training, http://www.sixsigmacanada.net/training/, downloaded 15 May 2015.

QUALITY AWARD: THE CANADA AWARDS FOR EXCELLENCE[33]

Excellence Canada <*http://www.excellence.ca*> is the leading authority in Canada on organizational excellence based on quality systems, innovation, and healthy workplace criteria. The *Canada Awards for Excellence (CAE)* are presented annually to private, public, and not-for-profit organizations that have demonstrated continual innovation and sustainable improvement across all business drivers and all departments, including: Leadership and Governance, Corporate Social Responsibility, Planning and Strategy, People Engagement, Psychological and Physical Health & Safety, Customer Experience, Process and Project Management, and relationships with Partners and Suppliers.

The award has honoured hundreds of Canadian organizations, including Ricoh Canada Inc. <*http://www.ricoh.ca*>, ArcelorMittal Dofasco <*http://dofasco.arcelormittal.com*>, Sun Life Financial <*http://www.sunlife.ca*>, and Orono Public School <*http://orono.kprdsb.ca*>. Recent recipients also include Manulife Investment, Toronto East General Hospital <*http://www.tegh.on.ca*>, Hill & Knowlton Strategies Canada <*http://www.hkstrategies.ca*>, and the Peel Regional Police <*http://www.peelpolice.ca*>.

CAE awards categories are: Excellence, Innovation and Wellness; Healthy Workplace; and Mental Health at Work. For more information, visit the Excellence Canada website.

Excellence Canada (formally the National Quality Institute) is an independent, not-for-profit organization founded by Industry Canada. It helps companies understand and apply a focus on excellence through the adoption of the Excellence, Innovation and Wellness Standard. This approach will help companies reduce waste and costs while improving productivity and competitiveness. Do you see how this framework incorporates principles discussed in this textbook?

ISO 9000 AND ISO 14000 STANDARDS

The International Organization for Standardization (ISO) is a worldwide federation of national standards bodies from more than 140 countries that set the global measures for the quality of individual products. ISO is a non-governmental organization established in 1947 to promote the development of world standards to facilitate the international exchange of goods and services. (ISO is not an acronym. It comes from the Greek word *isos,* meaning oneness.) **ISO 9000** is the common name given to quality management and assurance standards. Some of the latest standards include ISO 9004:2008, which primarily targets the strategic and operational management of organizations.

> **ISO 9000**
> The common name given to quality management and assurance standards.

The standards require that a company must determine customer needs, including regulatory and legal requirements, and make communication arrangements to handle issues such as complaints.[34] Other standards involve process control, product testing, storage, and delivery. Improving quality is an investment that can pay off in better customer relations and higher sales.[35]

It is important to know that ISO did not start as a quality certification, the way many people think. In the beginning, it simply meant that your process was under control. In short, it looked to see that companies were consistently producing the same products each time. There is a difference between consistency (flawed products every time) and quality (products free from defects). Today, ISO has developed over 19,500 international standards and includes 163 member countries.[36]

What makes ISO 9000 so important is that the European Union (EU) demands that companies that want to do business with the EU be certified by ISO standards. Some major Canadian companies are also demanding that suppliers meet these standards. Several accreditation agencies in Europe and in North America will certify that a company meets the standards for all phases of its operations, from product development through production and testing to installation. SNC-Lavalin Group Inc., one of the leading groups of engineering and construction companies in the world, has met such standards. It provides engineering, procurement, construction, project management, and project financing services to a variety of industry sectors in more than 120 countries. The Quality Policy at SNC-Lavalin is to "achieve client satisfaction through the careful management of our work processes, with due attention to value creation through scope, schedule, cost control, and with emphasis on safety and the environment." To best serve its various stakeholders, the company has implemented Client Satisfaction and Continual Improvement Programs in every division, business unit, geographic office, and subsidiary. These programs are based on the applicable requirements of ISO 9001 International Standard for Quality Management Systems.[37]

ISO 14000 is a collection of the best practices for managing an organization's impact on the environment. As an environmental management system, it does not prescribe a performance level. Requirements for certification include having an environmental policy, having specific improvement targets, conducting audits of environmental programs, and maintaining top management review of the processes.

> **ISO 14000**
> A collection of the best practices for managing an organization's impact on the environment.

Certification in both ISO 9000 and ISO 14000 would show that a firm has a world-class management system in both quality and environmental standards. In the past, firms assigned employees separately to meet each set of standards. Today, ISO 9000 and ISO 14000 standards have been blended so that an organization can work on both at once. ISO is now working on ISO 26000 standards, which are designed to give guidance on social responsibility.[38]

More recently, consumers have begun to support companies that produce environmentally friendly goods (as discussed earlier in Chapter 5). As a result, businesses have begun to re-examine their operations in order to create sustainable production processes. In 2002, William McDonough and Dr. Michael Braungart published the book *Cradle to Cradle: Remaking the Way We Make Things* which discusses the need to shift from a linear cradle-to-grave production process to an endless, eco-effective production process.[39] The sustainability advocates gifted the licence to provide Cradle to Cradle (C2C) certification to the non-profit organization called the Cradle to Cradle Products Innovation Institute *<http://www .c2ccertified.org>*. The Cradle to Cradle Certified Mark demonstrates a manufacturer's commitment to sustainability.

You know C2C certification has made an impact when you see a major multi-national manufacturer such as Nike take notice. The company responded to the sustainable manufacturing movement through its "Nike Considered" design ethos where the company adopts a sustainable approach to its footwear innovation. Its product redesign included the Nike Trash Talk shoe, which is endorsed by former NBA player Steve Nash, that is manufactured from leather waste and scrap-ground foam, and environmentally-preferred rubber made with fewer toxins.[40] The company continued this trend through its Nike Free footwear line which has reduced waste by nearly 2 million pounds through its Nike Flyknit technology.[41] The company has made a commitment to develop a closed-loop business model that includes reusing, reducing, and composting materials in order to decrease its waste production.[42]

Supply Chain Management

Before we discuss this next topic, it is important to introduce some terms. **Logistics** involves those activities that focus on getting the right amount of the right products or services to the right place at the right time at the lowest possible cost. A **supply chain** is a sequence of firms that perform activities required to create and deliver a good or service to consumers or industrial users. Some companies have been successful in attracting more customers due to their supply chain management efficiencies. **Supply chain management** is the integration and organization of information and logistics activities *across* firms in a supply chain for the purpose of creating and delivering goods and services that provide value to customers.

> **logistics**
> Those activities that focus on getting the right amount of the right products or services to the right place at the right time at the lowest possible cost.
>
> **supply chain**
> The sequence of firms that perform activities required to create and deliver a good or service to consumers or industrial users.
>
> **supply chain management**
> The integration and organization of information and logistics activities across firms in a supply chain for the purpose of creating and delivering goods and services that provide value to customers.

Adapting *to* CHANGE

Your Own Farm in a Box

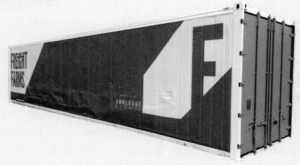

Imagine sitting in your favourite restaurant in Calgary in the middle of winter with a 12-inch snowfall coming your way. You crave some of the fresh, locally grown produce you enjoy so much in the warmer months. Unfortunately, it's winter so it probably won't be on the menu. Well, crave no more. Help is on the way thanks to a couple of entrepreneurs.

Brad McNamara and Jon Friedman could not get the results they wanted growing produce in a rooftop greenhouse. Frustrated, Jon came up with the idea that using a shipping container to grow produce might be more appropriate. Thanks to his insight, Freight Farms' *<http://www.freightfarms.com>* customers can now grow leafy greens, vine crops, and mushrooms hydroponically in insulated, climate-controlled containers. The company uses 320-square-foot shipping containers that are retrofitted and converted into modular, stackable farms that can produce 900 heads of leafy greens per container each week. The entire hydroponic system is simple enough that it can be digitally monitored and controlled from a smartphone. The weekly output from one of Freight Farms containers is approximately equivalent to the annual yield of a one-acre farm.

The immediate goal of Freight Farms is to create an appropriate infrastructure that fosters local food economies. The company targets small and medium-sized food distributors such as wholesalers and restaurants with revenues between $3 million and $75 million. The result is a simpler and shorter supply chain for getting food from "farm to table."

Friedman and McNamara also want to attract non-profit groups involved in food distribution in depressed or disaster-relief areas as buyers for their $60,000 farms-in-a-box. But they don't want to stop here. While attracting enough customers to make local farming a cost-effective option is the key goal of Freight Farms today, the founders have a much broader objective for the future. Predicting a global food shortage in 2050, they believe Freight Farms is the first step in the redesign of the global food system. Bon Appetit!

Sources: Jeremy Quittner, "A One-Acre Farm in a 320-Square-Foot Box," *Inc.*, March 2013; Peter Cohan, "Grow Produce Anywhere in Freight Farms' $60,000 Shipping Container," *Forbes*, 27 June 2013; and Leon Neyfakh, "If Urban Farming Took Off, What Would Boston Look Like?" *The Boston Globe*, 19 January 2014.

■ **FIGURE 10.5**

SUPPLY CHAIN MANAGEMENT

This is an image of supply chain management showing the interrelationships between all of the types of firms involved in the provision of a good or a service to a customer.

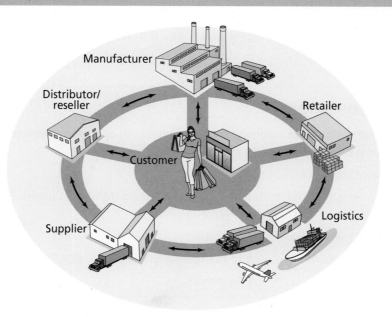

Facilities in supply chain management include factories, processing centres, warehouses, distribution centres, and retail outlets (Figure 10.5). Functions and activities include forecasting, purchasing, inventory management, information management, quality assurance, scheduling, production, delivery, and customer service. Today, the major factors contributing to the importance of supply chain management include: (1) the need for improvement to remain competitive, (2) the increase in outsourcing, (3) shorter product life cycles and increased customization, (4) globalization, (5) the growth of technology and e-commerce, (6) the increase in complexity through JIT inventory, and (7) the need for better management of inventories. When implementing supply chain management, firms try to improve quality, reduce costs, increase flexibility and speed, and improve customer service while at the same time reduce the number of suppliers used. Two examples follow:

• The Coca-Cola Company sought to streamline and simplify its supply chain through a number of measures. Historically, the company has worked with independent bottlers to produce and distribute its products. That changed in 2010 when Coca-Cola purchased its largest bottler and began to reduce its bottling operations. Since 2010, the company's bottling plant network has dropped from 353 ownerships to 73 ownerships with only 100 plants. This change is even more difficult given Coca-Cola's entire line includes 3,500 products. In order to respond to changes the planners are constantly adjusting the supply chain through one guiding principle—DOIP (Demand, Operations, and Inventory Planning). Given Coca-Cola's global reach, operation management is a critical part of the company's success. There mantra—"There is a person at the end of our supply chain"—clearly highlights this priority.[43]

- Source for Sports <*http://www.sourceforsports.com*> is a national brand with over 150 independently owned and operated sport retailers across Canada. Its approach is to enable independents to purchase products at a cheaper price than if stores owners had to buy products on their own. No two stores are alike and therefore operations management is an important part of making this approach a success. In order to build retailer–supplier collaboration, the company adopted a big data analytics platform, called Askuity. The software will help the head office be more responsive to supply needs for each store and better manage the availability of stock as products change from one season to the next. For example, Askuity will identify which types of hockey equipment sold the best at different times of the season, which in turn improves purchase and distribution planning the following year.[44]

Progress Assessment

- Can you name and define three functions that are common to operations management in both the service and the manufacturing sectors?
- What are the major criteria for facility location?
- What is the difference between materials resource planning (MRP) and enterprise resource planning (ERP)?
- What is just-in-time inventory control?
- What is involved in implementing each of the following: Six Sigma, SQC, SPC, ISO 9000, and ISO 14000?

LO4 Identify various production processes and describe techniques to improve productivity including flexible manufacturing, lean manufacturing, mass customization, and computer-aided design and manufacturing

Production Processes

Common sense and some experience have already taught you much of what you need to know about production processes. You know what it takes to write a term paper or prepare a dinner. You need money to buy the materials, you need a place to work, and you need to be organized to get the task done. The same is true of the production process in industry. It uses basic inputs to produce outputs (see Figure 10.6). Production adds value, or utility, to materials or processes.

■ **FIGURE 10.6**

THE PRODUCTION PROCESS

The production process consists of taking the factors of production and using the inputs to produce goods, services, and ideas. Planning, routing, scheduling, and the other activities are the means to accomplish the objective—output.

INPUTS	PRODUCTION CONTROL	OUTPUTS
Land	Planning	Goods
Labour	Routing	Services
Capital	Scheduling	Ideas
Entrepreneurship	Dispatching	
Knowledge	Follow-up	

Form utility is the value producers add to materials in the creation of finished goods and services, such as the transformation of silicon into computer chips or putting services together to create a vacation package. Form utility can exist at the retail level as well. For example, a butcher can produce a specific cut of beef from a whole cow or a baker can make a specific type of cake out of basic ingredients.

form utility
The value added by the creation of finished goods and services.

To be competitive, manufacturers must keep the costs of inputs down. That is, the costs of workers, machinery, and so on must be kept as low as possible. Similarly, the amount of output must be relatively high. The question today is: How does a producer keep costs low and still increase output? This question will dominate thinking in the manufacturing and service sectors for years to come. In the next few sections, we explore production processes and the latest technology used to cut costs.

Manufacturers use several different processes to produce goods. Andrew S. Grove, chairman of computer chip manufacturer Intel, offers a great analogy to explain production:

> Imagine that you're a chef... and that your task is to serve a breakfast consisting of a three-minute soft-boiled egg, buttered toast, and coffee. Your job is to prepare and deliver the three items simultaneously, each of them fresh and hot.

Grove says this task encompasses the three basic requirements of production: (1) to build and deliver products in response to the demands of the customer at a scheduled delivery time, (2) to provide an acceptable quality level, and (3) to provide everything at the lowest possible cost.

Let's use the breakfast example to understand process and assembly. **Process manufacturing** physically or chemically changes materials. For example, boiling physically changes the egg. (Similarly, process manufacturing turns sand into glass or computer chips.) The **assembly process** puts together components (eggs, toast, and coffee) to make a product (breakfast). Cars are made through an assembly process that puts together the frame, engine, and other parts.

process manufacturing
That part of the production process that physically or chemically changes materials.

assembly process
That part of the production process that puts together components.

Production lines allow for the efficient and speedy production of goods that are consistent in size, weight, colour, and other measures of quality. How many products can you think of that are likely made on a production line?

Production processes are either continuous or intermittent. A **continuous process** is one in which long production runs (lots of eggs) turn out finished goods over time. As the chef, you could have a conveyor belt that lowers eggs into boiling water for three minutes and then lifts them out. A three-minute egg would be available whenever you want. A chemical plant, for example, is run on a continuous process.

continuous process
A production process in which long production runs turn out finished goods over time.

It usually makes more sense when responding to specific customer orders to use an **intermittent process**. Here the production run is short (one or two eggs) and the producer adjusts machines frequently to make different products (like the oven in a bakery or the toaster in the diner). Manufacturers of custom-designed furniture would use an intermittent process.

intermittent process
A production process in which the production run is short and the machines are changed frequently to make different products.

An example of a product that uses both long and short production runs is Kodiak boots. In 2006, the company re-established production in Canada after a nine-year absence. "At the end of the day, we're going to service customers a lot better through this core Canadian production," says Kevin Huckle, president of Kodiak Group Holdings Inc. <*http://www.kodiakboots.com*>, which plans to do a third of its production in Canada. Domestic production offers quick, efficient service for Canadian retailers, who may require only small numbers of boots, but need them in a hurry. With Asian production, he has to contract for long production runs—more than 1,200 pairs—and has to carry a high volume of inventory. With domestic manufacturing, the plant keeps enough materials available for relatively short runs. Because of automation and location, it can turn around Canadian production orders in 21 days, compared with 90 days for orders in Asia. While Canadian workers gained jobs from this manufacturing facility re-location, there are also times when a move isn't as beneficial. In 2014, Kodiak announced it would relocate its Terra Nova Shoes plant in Harbour Grace, Newfoundland, to Cambridge, Ontario. The result was a loss of 80 jobs in Harbour Grace.[45]

Today, many new manufacturers use intermittent processes. Computers, robots, and flexible manufacturing processes allow firms to turn out custom-made goods as fast as mass-produced goods were produced. We'll discuss how they do that in more detail in the next few sections as we explore advanced production techniques and technology.

Improving Production Techniques and Cutting Costs

The ultimate goal of operations management is to provide high-quality goods and services instantaneously in response to customer demand. As we stress throughout this textbook, traditional organizations were simply not designed to be so responsive to the customer. Rather, they were designed to make goods efficiently (inexpensively). The idea behind mass production was to make a large number of a limited variety of products at very low cost.

Over the years, low cost often came at the expense of quality and flexibility. Furthermore, suppliers did not always deliver when they said they would, so manufacturers had to carry large inventories of raw materials and components to keep producing. Such inefficiencies made companies vulnerable to foreign competitors that were using more advanced production techniques and less expensive labour.

As a result of global competition, companies have had to make a wide variety of high-quality, custom-designed products at very low cost. Clearly, something had to change on the production floor to make that possible. Several major developments have made companies more competitive: (1) flexible manufacturing, (2) lean manufacturing, (3) mass customization, and (4) computer-aided design and manufacturing.

Bakers, like Duff Goldman of Charm City Cakes, add form utility to materials by transforming basic ingredients into special customized cakes. Can you see how the production of such cakes involves both process manufacturing and assembly processes?

Flexible Manufacturing

Flexible manufacturing means designing machines to do multiple tasks so that they can produce a variety of products. Flexible manufacturing (also known as flex) not only leads to improved productivity, but it may also result in cost savings. Frank Gourneau, plant manager at Ford Motor Company of Canada Ltd., calls the $1-billion Oakville complex "a game changer" and a "jewel" with all the latest advances in auto technology. The first phase of the plant started production in 2006. According to Gourneau, "Undergoing major model changes in traditional plants means weeks of downtime and millions spent on new tooling and equipment. Once a flexible body shop is installed, downtime is reduced dramatically and the equipment changes consist mainly of reprogramming robots. The point is to be able to cease assembly of one model on a Friday and start a new one on a Monday, instead of six, eight or ten weeks later."[46]

> **flexible manufacturing**
> Designing machines to do multiple tasks so that they can produce a variety of products.

At the time, Gourneau estimated productivity would improve at least 20 percent in the new plant and the company expected to achieve $2 billion in production cost savings alone during the next decade.[47] Today, Ford's Oakville facility has the flexibility to produce 11 of its popular mid-sized vehicles on one platform. In turn, Ford will be able to compete and adjust quickly to changes in market conditions. The company's long-term investment to manufacturing and innovation was supported by a federal government $71.6 million repayable contribution from the Automotive Innovation Fund.[48]

Allen-Bradley, part of Rockwell Automation, uses flexible manufacturing to build motor starters. Orders come in daily, and within 24 hours the company's 26 machines and robots manufacture, test, and package the starters—which are untouched by human hands. Allen-Bradley's machines are so flexible that managers can include a special order, even a single item, in the assembly without slowing down the process. Did you notice that these products were made without any labour? One way to compete with cheap labour in other facility locations is to have as few workers as possible.

Lean Manufacturing

Lean manufacturing is the production of goods using less of everything compared to mass production: less human effort, less manufacturing space, less investment in tools, and less engineering time to develop a new product.[49] A company becomes lean by continuously increasing its capacity to produce high-quality goods while decreasing its need for resources.[50] Here are some characteristics of a lean company:

- Takes half the human effort.[51]
- Has half the defects in the finished product or service.
- Requires one-third the engineering effort.
- Uses half the floor space for the same output.
- Carries 90 percent less inventory.

> **lean manufacturing**
> The production of goods using less of everything compared to mass production.

Technological improvements are largely responsible for the increase in productivity and efficiency of Canadian plants. That technology made labour more productive and made it possible to pay higher rates. On the other hand, employees can get frustrated by innovations (e.g., they must learn new processes), and companies must constantly train and retrain employees to stay competitive.[52] The need for additional productivity and efficiency has never been greater. The solution to the economic crisis depends on such innovations. One step in the process is to make products more individualistic. The next section discusses how that happens.

Mass Customization

To *customize* means to make a unique good or provide a specific service to an individual. Although it once may have seemed impossible, **mass customization**, which means tailoring products to meet the needs of a large number of individual customers, is now practised widely. The National Bicycle Industrial Company in Japan made 18 bicycle models in more than 2 million combinations, each designed to fit the needs of a specific customer. The customer chose the model, size, colour, and design. The retailer took various measurements from the buyer and faxed the data to the factory, where robots handled the bulk of the assembly. Thus, flexible manufacturing (discussed earlier) is one of the factors that makes mass customization possible.

> **mass customization**
> Tailoring products to meet the needs of individual customers.

Not only can you customize the colours of your M&Ms, you can also have personal messages and/or images imprinted on them. What other customized products can you think of?

More and more manufacturers are learning to customize their products. For example, General Nutrition Center (GNC, <*http://www.gnc.com*>) stores feature machines that enable shoppers to custom-design their own vitamins, shampoo, and lotions. The Custom Foot <*http://thecustomfoot.com*> stores use infrared scanners to precisely measure each foot so that shoes can be made to fit perfectly. Adidas can make each shoe fit perfectly for each customer.

One unique way of using mass customization can be seen at Moniker Guitars <*https://monikerguitars .com*>.[53] The company follows Nike's model called NikeiD, that allows consumers to customize their shoes. This customer customization is also the basis of Moniker's guitar business. By using online design tools and advanced manufacturing techniques, Moniker can produce top quality, personalized guitars for what a guitar player would pay for a generic model.

Today, Moniker's website guides guitar pickers through a number of steps to customize their instruments using colour and graphics, as well as hardware and pickups. The company uses PPG paint on its guitars—the same paint used for Lamborghini and Ferrari automobiles. If polka dots are your passion, or tiger stripes turn you on, Moniker will deliver. According to founder Kevin Tully, "Every design is different. You never paint the same guitar twice. Every day is a new project. I love it."

Everyday musicians have little money to create a personal signature guitar style. Moniker Guitar makes it easy through mass customization. Despite high production levels, no two guitars made by Moniker are the same.

Mass customization can be used in the service sector as well. Capital Protective Insurance (CPI) uses the latest computer software and hardware to sell customized risk-management plans to companies. Health clubs offer unique fitness programs for individuals, travel agencies provide vacation packages that vary according to individual choices, and some schools allow students to design their own majors. Actually, it is much easier to custom-design service programs than it is to custom-make goods, because there is no fixed tangible good that has to be adapted. Each customer can specify what he or she wants, within the limits of the service organization—limits that seem to be ever widening.

Robotics

Mass customization is easy for industrial robotics where machines can work 24 hours a day, seven days a week, with great precision. While robots replace workers on the assembly line, most of the jobs are dirty or so repetitive that robots are necessary, or at least helpful.[54] No doubt you have heard or seen robots that help doctors perform the most delicate of procedures.[55] Robots are slowly, but surely, either helping workers perform better or are replacing them completely. Soon we may be entering what could be known as the robot economy.[56] Most people think that China is so successful because of cheap labour, but China may soon be the world's largest robot market.[57]

Current studies predict that almost a quarter of automated tasks will be performed by robots in the next decade.[58] This change reflects a 10 percent increase from today and there is no sign of the shift slowing down. The adoption of robotics in manufacturing is strongly influenced by the cost of labour compared to the cost of robotic labour. As the cost of robot technology drops and the cost of employees rises, Canada's manufacturing sectors is poised for some drastic change. How do you think robotics will impact the workplace in the future?

3-D tools allow designers to create cloth prototypes without a pattern's traditional stages (seaming, trying on, alternations, etc.). What advantages might this technology offer to small manufacturing companies?

Computer-Aided Design and Manufacturing

One development that has changed production techniques more than any other is the integration of computers into the design and manufacturing of products. The first impact of computers was in a process called **computer-aided design (CAD)**, or the design of products. Autodesk makes a fully operational computer-aided design software program called 123 Design that's free and allows individuals to do tasks that automakers once required mainframe computers to complete.[59]

computer-aided design (CAD)
The use of computers in the design of products.

The next step was to bring computers directly in the production process with **computer-aided manufacturing (CAM)**. CAD/CAM, the use of both computer-aided design and computer-aided manufacturing made it possible to custom-design products to meet the needs of small markets with very little increase in cost. A manufacturer programs the computer to make a simple design change, and that change is directly incorporated into production. In the clothing industry, a computer program establishes a pattern and cuts the cloth automatically, even adjusting to a specific person's dimensions to create custom-cut clothing at little additional cost. In food service, CAM supports on-site, small-scale, semi-automated, sensor-controlled baking in fresh-baked cookie shops to make consistent quality easy to achieve. The latest CAM technology includes 3D printers that make a product layer by layer until it appears as a finished good.

computer-aided manufacturing (CAM)
The use of computers in the manufacturing of products.

CAD has doubled productivity in many firms. But in the past CAD machines could not talk to CAM machines directly. Today, however, software programs unite CAD with CAM: the result is **computer-integrated manufacturing (CIM)**. The software is expensive, but it cuts as much as 80 percent of the time needed to program machines to make parts. The printing company JohnsByrne used CIM in its Niles, Illinois, plant and noticed a decreased cost in overhead, reduced outlay of resources, and fewer errors. You can consult the *International Journal of Computer-Integrated Manufacturing* for other examples.

> **computer-integrated manufacturing (CIM)**
> The uniting of computer-aided design with computer-aided manufacturing.

Progress Assessment

- What are three basic requirements of production?
- Define and differentiate the following: process manufacturing, assembly process, continuous process, and intermittent process.
- How does flexible manufacturing differ from lean manufacturing?
- What are CAD, CAM, and CIM?

LO5   Explain the use of PERT and Gantt charts to control manufacturing processes.

Control Procedures: PERT and Gantt Charts

Operations managers must ensure products are manufactured and delivered on time, on budget, and to specification. How can managers be sure all will go smoothly and be completed by the required time? One popular technique for monitoring the progress of production was developed in the 1950s for constructing nuclear submarines: the **program evaluation and review technique (PERT)**. PERT users analyze the tasks to complete a given project, estimate the time needed to complete each, and compute the minimum time needed to complete the whole project.

> **program evaluation and review technique (PERT)**
> A method for analyzing the tasks involved in completing a given project, estimating the time needed to complete each task, and identifying the minimum time needed to complete the total project.

The steps used in PERT are (1) analyze and sequence tasks that need to be done, (2) estimate the time needed to complete each task, (3) draw a PERT network illustrating the information from steps 1 and 2, and (4) identify the critical path. The **critical path** is the sequence of tasks that takes the longest time to complete. We use the word *critical* because a delay anywhere along this path will cause the project or production run to be late.

> **critical path**
> In a PERT network, the sequence of tasks that takes the longest time to complete.

Figure 10.7 illustrates a PERT chart for producing a music video. The squares indicate completed tasks, and the arrows indicate the time needed to complete the next task. The path from one completed task to another illustrates the relationships among tasks; the arrow from "set designed" to "set materials purchased" indicates we must design the set before we can purchase the materials. The critical path, indicated by the bold black arrows, indicates producing the set takes more time than auditioning dancers,choreographing dances, or designing and making costumes. The project manager now knows it is critical that set construction remain on schedule if the project is to be completed on time, but short interruptions in dance and costume preparation are unlikely to delay it.

■ **FIGURE 10.7**

PERT CHART FOR A MUSIC VIDEO

The minimum amount of time it will take to produce this video is 15 weeks. To get that number, you add the week it takes to pick a star and a song to the four weeks to design a set, the two weeks to purchase set materials, the six weeks to construct the set, the week before rehearsals, and the final week when the video is made. That is the critical path. Any delay in that process will delay the final video.

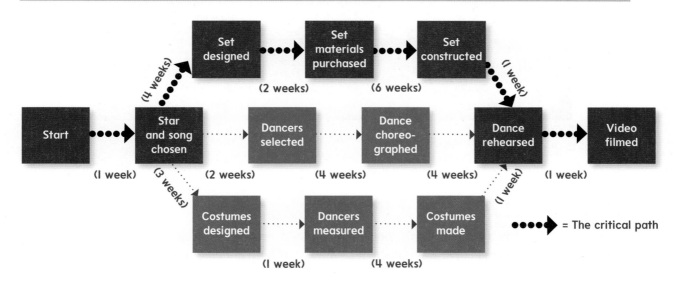

A PERT network can be made up of thousands of events over many months. Today, a computer is utilized to create this complex procedure. Another, more basic strategy manufacturers use for measuring production progress is a Gantt chart. A **Gantt chart** (named for its developer, Henry L. Gantt) is a bar graph, now also prepared by computer, that clearly shows what projects are underway and how much of the project has been completed at any given time. Figure 10.8, a Gantt chart for a doll manufacturer, shows that the dolls' heads and bodies should be completed before the clothing is sewn. It also shows that at the end of week 3, the dolls' bodies are ready, but the heads are about half a week behind. Using a Gantt-like computer program, a manager can trace the production process minute by minute to determine which tasks are on time and which are behind, so that adjustments can be made to allow the company to stay on schedule.

Gantt chart
Bar graph showing production managers what projects are underway and what stage they are in at any given time.

■ **FIGURE 10.8**

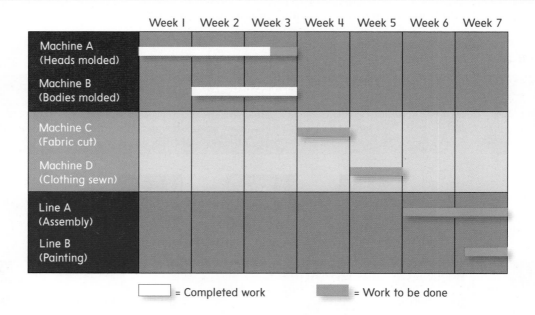

GANTT CHART FOR A DOLL MANUFACTURER

A Gantt chart enables a production manager to see at a glance when projects are scheduled to be completed and what the current status is. For example, the dolls' heads and bodies should be completed before the clothing is sewn, but they could be a little late as long as everything is ready for assembly in week 6. This chart shows that at the end of week 3, the dolls' bodies are ready, but the heads are about half a week behind.

☐ = Completed work   ▩ = Work to be done

Preparing for the Future

Canada is a major industrial country, but competition is growing stronger each year. Tremendous opportunities for careers in operations management exist as both manufacturing and service companies fight to stay competitive. Students who can see future trends and have the skills to own or work in tomorrow's highly automated factories and modern service facilities will benefit.

Progress Assessment

- Draw a PERT chart for making a breakfast of three-minute eggs, buttered toast, and coffee. Define the critical path.

- How could you use a Gantt chart to keep track of production?

SUMMARY

LO1 **Describe the current state of Canadian manufacturing and how companies are becoming more competitive.**

Canada's industrial profile results in significant swings in activity and a number of challenges are faced in an increasingly competitive global environment. Activity in the manufacturing sector has declined which has also led to job loss. Even though manufacturing companies offer fewer jobs, they have become more productive, meaning that they need fewer employees to do the same amount of work.

Where is most of Canada's industry focused?

Most of our industry is focused on natural resources, which results in significant progress when world economies are growing, but is offset by significant retraction when the world economies are stagnant.

What have Canadian manufacturers done to achieve increased output?

Canadian manufacturers have increased output by emphasizing strategies such as close relationships with suppliers and other companies to satisfy customer needs; continuous improvement; quality; site selection; use of the Internet to unite companies, and production techniques such as enterprise resource planning, computer-integrated manufacturing, flexible manufacturing, lean manufacturing, and robotics.

LO2 **Describe the evolution from production to operations management.**

Operations management is a specialized area in management that converts or transforms resources (including human resources) into goods and services.

What kinds of firms use operations managers?

Firms in both the manufacturing and the service sectors use operations managers.

Why is productivity so hard to measure?

The traditional way to measure productivity involves tracking inputs (worker hours) compared to outputs (dollars). Quality improvements are not weighed. New information systems must be developed to measure the quality of goods and services, the speed of their delivery, and customer satisfaction.

LO3 **Describe operations management planning issues including facility location, facility layout, materials requirement planning, purchasing, just-in-time inventory control, quality control, and supply chain management.**

Issues involved in both the manufacturing and the service sectors include facility location, facility layout, materials requirement planning, purchasing, just-in-time inventory control, quality control, and supply chain management.

What is facility location and how does it differ from facility layout?

Facility location is the process of selecting a geographic location for a company's operations. Facility layout is the physical arrangement of resources (including people) to produce goods and services effectively and efficiently.

Why is facility location so important, and what criteria are used to evaluate different sites?

The very survival of manufacturing depends on its ability to remain competitive, and that means either making inputs less costly (reducing costs of labour and land) or increasing outputs from present inputs (increasing productivity). Labour costs and land costs are two major criteria for selecting the right sites. Other criteria include whether (1) resources are plentiful and inexpensive, (2) skilled workers are available or are trainable, (3) taxes are low and the local government offers support, (4) energy and water are available, (5) transportation costs are low, and (6) the quality of life and quality of education are high.

What relationship do materials requirement planning (MRP) and enterprise resource planning (ERP) have with the production process?

MRP is a computer-based operations management system that uses sales forecasts to make sure the needed parts and materials are available at the right time and place. Enterprise resource planning (ERP), a newer version of MRP, combines the computerized functions of all the divisions and subsidiaries of the firm—such as finance, material requirements planning, human resources, and order fulfillment—into an integrated software program that uses a single database. The result is a shorter period of time between orders and payment, less staff to do ordering and order processing, reduced inventories, and better customer service for all the firms involved.

What is just-in-time (JIT) inventory control?

JIT involves having suppliers deliver parts and materials just in time to go on the assembly line so they do not have to be stored in warehouses.

What are the latest quality control concepts?

Six Sigma quality (just 3.4 defects per million products) detects potential problems before they occur. Statistical quality control (SQC) is the process that some managers use to continually monitor all processes in production to ensure that quality is being built into the product from the beginning. Statistical process control (SPC) is the process of taking statistical samples of product components at each stage of the production process and plotting those results on a graph. Any variances from quality standards are recognized and can be corrected.

What quality standards do firms use in Canada?

International standards that Canadian firms strive to meet include ISO 9004:2000 (ISO 9000) and ISO 14000. The first is a European standard for quality and the second is a collection of the best practices for managing an organization's impact on the environment.

LO4 Identify various production processes and describe techniques to improve productivity including flexible manufacturing, lean manufacturing, mass customization, and computer-aided design manufacturing.

There are several different processes that manufacturers use to produce goods along with varying techniques to improve productivity.

What is process manufacturing, and how does it differ from assembly processes?

Process manufacturing physically or chemically changes materials. Assembly processes put together components.

Are there other production processes?

Production processes are either continuous or intermittent. A continuous process is one in which long production runs turn out finished goods over time. An intermittent process is an operation where the production run is short and the machines are changed frequently to manufacture different products.

What is flexible manufacturing?

Flexible manufacturing involves designing machines to produce a variety of products.

What is lean manufacturing?

Lean manufacturing is the production of goods using as little of the needed inputs as possible compared to mass production: less human effort, less manufacturing space, less investment in tools, and less engineering time to develop a new product.

What is mass customization?

Mass customization means making custom-designed goods and services for a large number of individual customers. Flexible manufacturing makes mass customization possible. Given the exact needs of a customer, flexible machines can produce a customized good as fast as mass-produced goods were once made. Mass customization is also important in service industries.

How do CAD/CAM systems work?

Design changes made in computer-aided design (CAD) are instantly incorporated into the computer-aided manufacturing (CAM) process. The linking of the two systems—CAD and CAM—is called computer-integrated manufacturing (CIM).

LO5 **Explain the use of PERT and Gantt charts to control manufacturing processes**

Operations managers must ensure their products or services are provided on time and on budget.

Is there any relationship between a PERT chart and a Gantt chart?

Figure 10.7 shows a PERT chart. Figure 10.8 shows a Gantt chart. Whereas PERT is a tool used for planning, a Gantt chart is a tool used to measure progress.

KEY TERMS

assembly process
computer-aided design (CAD)
computer-aided manufacturing (CAM)
computer-integrated manufacturing (CIM)
continuous process
critical path
enterprise resource planning (ERP)
facility layout
facility location
flexible manufacturing
form utility

Gantt chart
intermittent process
ISO 9000
ISO 14000
just-in-time (JIT) inventory control
lean manufacturing
logistics
mass customization
materials requirement planning (MRP)
operations management
process manufacturing
production

production management
program evaluation review technique (PERT)
purchasing
quality
research and development (R&D)
Six Sigma quality
statistical process control (SPC)
statistical quality control (SQC)
supply chain
supply chain management
telecommuting

CRITICAL THINKING

1. Workers on the manufacturing floor are being replaced by robots and other machines. On the one hand, that is one way in which companies compete with cheap labour from other countries. On the other hand, automation eliminates many jobs. Are you concerned that automation may increase unemployment or under-employment in Canada and around the world? Why or why not?

2. Computer-integrated manufacturing (CIM) has revolutionized the production process. What will such changes mean for the clothing industry, the shoe industry, and other fashion related industries? What will they mean for other consumer and industrial goods industries? How will you benefit as a consumer?

3. One way to create new jobs in Canada is to have more innovation from new graduates of engineering and the sciences. How can Canada motivate more students to study in those areas?

DEVELOPING WORKPLACE SKILLS

Key: ● **Team**   ★ **Analytic**   ▲ **Communication**   ▣ **Technology**

● ★ ▲ 1. Choosing the right location for a manufacturing plant or a service organization is often critical to its success. Form small groups and have each group member pick one manufacturing plant or one service organization in town and list at least three reasons why its location helps or hinders its success. If its location is not ideal, what location would be a better one?

● ★ ▲ 2. In teams of four or five, discuss the need for better operations management in the airline industry. Have the team develop a report listing (1) problems team members have encountered in travelling by air, and (2) suggestions for improving operations so such problems will not occur in the future.

★ ▲ 3. Discuss some of the advantages and disadvantages of producing goods overseas using inexpensive labour. Summarize the moral and ethical issues of this practice.

★ ▲ 4. Think of any retail outlet (e.g., bookstore or food outlet) or service centre (e.g., library, copy centre) at your university or college and redesign the layout (make a pencil sketch) to more effectively serve customers and allow employees to be more effective and efficient.

★ ▲ 5. Think about recent experiences you have had with service organizations and select one in which you had to wait for an unreasonable length of time to get what you wanted. Describe what happens when customers are inconvenienced, and explain how management could make the operation more efficient and customer-oriented.

● ★ ▲ 6. In teams of four or five, have each team build a PERT chart for a business of their choosing. First have each team identify all the tasks involved in producing the good or providing the service and then organize the tasks into a chart. Have teams identify the critical path and identify the minimum amount of time it will take to produce the good or provide the service to customers.

ANALYZING MANAGEMENT DECISIONS

Why Big Companies Fail to Innovate

Matthew Kiernan, based in Unionville, Ontario, is a management consultant whose views command attention. He has a PhD degree in strategic management from the University of London and was a senior partner with an international consulting firm, KPMG <*http://www.kpmg.com*>. Subsequently, he founded his own firm, Innovest Group International, with staff operating out of Geneva, Switzerland; London, United Kingdom; and Toronto, Canada. He was also a director of the Business Council for Sustainable Development based in Geneva.

His book *Get Innovative or Get Dead* took aim at big corporations for their poor record on innovation. Any five-year-old could tell you that companies must innovate to survive, he said, so what's the problem? According to Kiernan, it is one thing to understand something in your head but quite another thing to really feel it in your gut. This is further complicated by the difficulty of getting a big company to shift gears, to turn its culture around so that innovation becomes the norm rather than the special effort. Look back at the discussion on innovation at the beginning of the chapter to re-visit its importance in our increasingly competitive world.

Kiernan called for a company to develop a style and atmosphere that favours individual risk-taking, similar to the intrapreneurial approach discussed in Chapter 7. That means that if a team tries something that does not work, you do not shoot it down. Encouraging innovation, which inevitably involves taking risks with the unknown, means accepting the fact that it may take two or three attempts before something useful is developed. Recently, Matthew has applied this principle to sustainable development, including the topic of carbon finance.

The 3M company is often used as a great example of a company that encourages creativity. Its policy dictates that 30 percent of annual sales come from products less than four years old. However, 3M was not always that progressive. When the now legendary Post-it Notes were first developed by an employee, he had a hard time getting the company to see the potential in his idea. This ultimately triggered a major change in the company's policy. Kiernan pointed out that most companies give lip service to the necessity of innovation but do not act in a credible way as far as their employees are concerned. If you mean business, you must take that "bright guy out of the basement, [the one] everybody knows is a genius, but whose last two enterprise efforts came to grief, and visibly promote him."

Discussion Questions

1. Why do large companies find it difficult to innovate? Is it because they are big or because they are afraid of the unknown?

2. Do smaller companies do better at innovation? Is that because most of them are private companies and not accountable to outside stakeholders?

3. Do some research on 3M and find out how this large company encourages innovation and what it means to them.

VIDEO CASE 10

Keeping Your Eye on the Ball

In recent years it seems like each time we read a newspaper, leaf through a magazine, or listen to a news report the story is the same—Canadian manufacturing is on the decline and many people are losing their jobs in manufacturing plants. It sounds depressing but the question is, "Has Canada really fallen that far behind other countries in manufacturing capability?" The answer is no, and this video is meant to highlight just one example of a successful manufacturing company. There are thousands of others that could be discussed in a similar manner.

There is no doubt that Canadian manufacturers are being challenged by companies in Mexico, China, India, Brazil, Indonesia, and all over the world—but that is nothing new. The question is whether or not

Canada can respond effectively to such challenges today as it has done in the past. Don't forget that many companies—like Honda and Toyota—have built manufacturing plants in Canada.

This video features Ball metal beverage containers. Wherever you see a food, aerosol, or paint can the odds are it was manufactured by Ball Corporation *<http://www.ball.com>*. The company has location in Asia, Europe, South America, and North America, including locations in Whitby, Ontario, and Sherbrooke, Quebec. Ball has been so successful that it expanded operations by buying four manufacturing plants from giant brewer Anheuser-Busch InBev *<http://www.ab-inbev.com>*. But have you given any thought to how those cans came to be?

The text mentions several strategies Canadian manufacturers put into action in order to stay competitive in today's global markets. These practices include focusing on customers; maintaining close relationships with suppliers (e.g., using just-in-time inventory control); practising continuous improvement; focusing on quality; saving on costs through site selection; utilizing the Internet; and adopting new production processes like computer-integrated manufacturing. Speaking of cans, you can see and hear what Ball is doing to stay competitive in the video. Note that Ball is using a continuous process. What other processes might the company use?

Canadian companies are using computer-aided design and computer-aided manufacturing, united in computer-integrated manufacturing. They also do flexible manufacturing, which means they can produce a variety of products using the same machinery. It should not surprise you to learn that Ball located its facilities close to its customers. That makes distribution faster, easier, and cheaper.

Of course, quality is a key consideration in any manufacturing plant. Can you imagine trying to open a can and having the opener break off in your fingers or having a can that leaks all over your car? Manufacturers try for zero defects, but often settle for some slightly lower standard such as Six Sigma (only 3.4 defects per million).

Next time you take a cold drink from a can, think about Ball and the other companies that make Canada a major producer of consumer goods. Think, too, of the opportunities that will present themselves to tomorrow's university and college graduates. Students seem less attracted to manufacturing today, but that means more opportunities tomorrow for those students who see growth in some areas of manufacturing. That includes, of course, companies that produce solar panels, power plants, and more. You only have to look around your home or office to see the many products being made and the many products that will be made using new technology.

Thinking It Over

1. Looking at the future of manufacturing in Canada, do you think companies are adapting to the challenges of foreign manufacturers as well as Ball? What is Ball doing to stay competitive?

2. The video mentions the loss of manufacturing jobs to overseas locations. What is this called? What is the opposite trend that has occurred in Canada with companies like Toyota and Honda?

3. What is meant by Six Sigma?

RUNNING CASE

Leadership, Benchmarking, and Operations Management Planning at Fox 40 International Inc.

For successful Canadian entrepreneur and inventor Ron Foxcroft, it all started in 1982 when he purchased Fluke Transport, a Southern Ontario trucking business. The company slogan—If It's On Time . . . It's A "FLUKE"—was soon recognized throughout North America. Over the years, Ron diversified into new ventures and the Foxcroft Group of Companies now includes Fluke Transportation Group, Fluke Warehousing Inc., Foxcroft Capital Corp., Fox 40 International Inc., and Fox 40 USA Inc.

The formation of Fox 40 International Inc. (Fox 40) is the result of a dream for a pealess whistle. When developing his first whistle, Ron was motivated by his knowledge and experience as an international basketball referee. Frustrated with faulty pea whistles, he spent three years of development with design consultant Chuck Shepherd, resulting in the creation of the Fox 40® Classic Whistle. (The whistle was named for Ron and that he was 40 when he applied for the patent.)

Introduced in 1987, this finely tuned precision instrument does not use a pea to generate sound. In fact, there are no moving parts. The patented design moves the air blast through three tuned chambers. This whistle, and all the subsequent whistles that have been introduced, is 100 percent constructed of high-impact ABS plastic so it is impervious to moisture. Wet or dry, Fox 40 Pealess Whistles cannot be overblown and never fail—the harder you blow, the louder the sound! They can be heard for miles and work in all conditions. They are faultless, reliable, and trusted.

Fox 40, a proudly Canadian company, dominates the global whistle industry. Tens of thousands of Fox 40 Whistles are produced monthly for shipment to 140 countries. A mould may be made offshore due to the cost savings (at least $100,000); however, Fox 40 owns all of its moulds. Approximately 90 percent of the company's products are made in Canada with select components coming from overseas markets. Final assembly occurs in Canada. While the first product was the Fox 40® Classic Whistle, the company now has over 900 active stock-keeping units (SKUs). Its product mix includes 19 Whistles Styles (e.g., Fox 40 electronic whistle); Lanyards & Attachments (e.g., flex coils);additional brands that include Fox 40 Gear; SmartCoach Coaching Boards; SICK Self Impression Custom Kit, and Heat Alert Mouthguards; Marine & Outdoor Products (e.g., Xplorer LED Light); Pink Products; and Logo Imprinted Products.

Leadership at Fox 40 is very much a reflection of the vision of the company's founder and CEO, Ron Foxcroft, along with Dave Foxcroft, President and COO Over the past 25 years of growth, Ron and Dave continue to appreciate that success is very much related to both customers and employees. The importance of satisfying customer needs is central to all they do. As Ron states, "no one (i.e., any employee) needs permission to satisfy a customer." Every employee will do whatever it takes. One of the company's values is to respond to any customer question in 12 seconds, either with an answer or a commitment to, "I don't know but will find out." This vision is also reflected in a firm belief that any employee should be prepared to do any job, except take out the garbage; that is Ron's job.

They also know their vision can only be continually and consistently fulfilled if it is embodied by every employee. So, when hiring staff, Fox 40 knows the importance of hiring the right kind of people; honesty and integrity being key and a very much a reflection of how Ron and Dave behave. Starting in entry-level positions, each employee's strengths and weaknesses are assessed through the assignment of tasks with specific time lines. Performance is monitored not only by management, but by peers. Strengths are channelled to customer satisfaction issues. Weaknesses are discussed and plans for improvement are identified. Senior management are directly accessible to any customer and to any employee. Ron and

Dave embody the importance of front-line interaction. For example, Ron is the first person at work every day and both of them come and leave through the front doors, passing through the main areas of the company's facility to their offices.

Fox 40 embodies benchmarking by comparing itself to the very best. Much of the research and development is focused on "robbing and duplicating" what very successful companies have done. One method is to look to companies that started with a single, simple, product and then have expanded through the addition of complementary products. Gillette *<http://www.gillette.com>* started with a shaving blade, added shaving cream, and then deodorant. Wrigley's *<http://www.wrigley.com>* started with gum. There is also a focus on brand recognition and so they look to market leaders in this area, including Coke. When making decisions on potentially entering a market new to them, the Foxcrofts are guided by a belief that no market is worth considering unless they believe they can become the number one company, in terms of sales, in the new market. They expect to be able to sell to all customers in any market they enter.

When planning facility location, key factors are once more impacted by customers and employees. With sales in 140 countries, both men know the overriding perception of their customers of the importance of "Made in Canada." So, that is an overarching criterion. The large number of global customers supports a focus on logistics. Transportation infrastructure, including highways, shipping, airlines and close proximity to the border, are also important. The majority of employees work in distribution and rely on public transportation to get to work. This is an equally important criterion. For their large customer base in the United States, they have chosen to do customs clearing, so they have a distribution centre in that country, located in Niagara Falls, New York, which is very close to their facilities in Hamilton, Ontario.

The importance of employee input also plays out in terms of layout decisions. The company has recently moved to a new location. Their entire location is very clean and has "hospital operating room" white walls as Dave is a strong proponent of "employees act their environment."

Sources: Ron Foxcroft, CEO of Fox 40 International Inc. and Chairman and CEO of Fluke Transportation, in-person interview, 22 May 2012, Hamilton; and Dave Foxcroft, President and COO, Fox 40 International Inc., in-person interview, 22 May 2012, Hamilton.

Discussion Questions

1. The leadership of Ron and Dave Foxcroft has been influenced by Donald Cooper, former founder and president of Cooper Sporting Goods. Research Donald Cooper's leadership ideas including his concept of "front-line interaction."

2. Access the company's online sites for Fox40, Gillette, and Wrigley. Compare the product offerings of all three companies and comment on how Fox40 has benchmarked itself to the other two companies.

3. Fox 40 has just relocated its business to 340 Grays Road, Hamilton, Ontario. Referring to the above discussion, identify the specifics that supported a move to this location.

PART 4

Motivating Employees

LEARNING OBJECTIVES

After you have read and studied this chapter, you should be able to:

LO1 Explain Taylor's theory of scientific management, and describe the Hawthorne studies and their significance to management.

LO2 Identify the levels of Maslow's hierarchy of needs and apply them to employee motivation. Contrast this with the motivators and hygiene factors identified by Herzberg.

LO3 Differentiate between McGregor's Theory X and Theory Y.

LO4 Explain the key principles of goal setting, expectancy, reinforcement, and equity theories.

LO5 Show how managers put motivation theories into action through such strategies as job enrichment, open communication, and job recognition.

LO6 Show how managers personalize motivation strategies to appeal to employees around the globe and across generations.

PROFILE

GETTING TO KNOW LISA LISSON OF FEDEX EXPRESS CANADA

Lisa Lisson, President of FedEx Express Canada (FedEx), leads a team of 6,000 employees at more than 60 locations coast-to-coast in a growing business of domestic and international express delivery services. The company operates 61 stations, 3 call centres, 1,141 drop-off locations, and 3 hub locations (Vancouver, Toronto, and Montreal). It feeds into the FedEx worldwide network that handles more than 8.5 million daily shipments for Express, Ground, Freight, and expedited delivery services in 228 countries.

Source: THE CANADIAN PRESS/Chris Young.

As a student studying at the University of Guelph for a Bachelor of Commerce degree with a major in marketing, "I knew I wanted to work in the corporate environment," says Lisson. After graduation, she targeted FedEx as a potential employer. "What I loved about what I read is they talked about this thing called PSP. The philosophy is people, service, profit . . . Treat your people well with utmost respect and they in turn will provide service to your customers that's exceptional, which will deliver profit to your shareholders and then you can reinvest back in the people." Lisson joined the company as a junior marketing specialist in 1992. She quickly progressed and in 2003 was appointed Vice-President of Sales, Marketing, and Corporate Communications. In 2006, Lisson gained responsibility for improving the FedEx customer experience in Canada. Four years later, she became the first Canadian to be appointed president of FedEx.

Under her leadership, FedEx has implemented critical improvements to the operation of the sales team, resulting in significant revenue growth for the company. She also drove the introduction of *fedex.ca*, shipping and tracking software, and led initiatives to increase brand awareness and market share for FedEx. Lisson also launched a full range of new domestic and international products reinforced with award-winning advertising and new methods for measuring customer satisfaction. In the annual internal opinion survey, Lisson's own employees have ranked her above the country average in each year that she has been a manager.

In an *Undercover Boss Canada* episode, Lisson wanted to ensure that employees had the tools they needed to succeed—and that FedEx not only delivered to its customers, but also to its valuable employees. Lisson disguised herself as new employee Suzanne, a mother of two re-entering the workforce. The employees she met were all real people, survivors who had come through very difficult life challenges and chosen to move forward with remarkable optimism and hope. And they did so in a corporate culture that supported them—by creating a "second family" for them. It was a powerful lesson for Lisson: if you hire the right people, train them well, engender a strong sense of belonging, listen to their ideas, and expect high standards, you will achieve business success.

Says Lisson, "Going undercover was a life-changing experience for me on so many levels but, more importantly, it reinforced my strong belief in the importance of being a leader who knows the front line. Unless you walk in someone else's shoes and experience what they do, you never actually know. I encourage every FedEx manager—in fact, any manager of any company—to get out on the front line and burn the shoe leather. Go and spend a day doing what your employees do and experience what they experience day in and day out. And do it often. I always say that it's my front-line teams who create my "to-do" list.

As a single mother with a high-stress job, she believes in maintaining a healthy work–life balance. Under her leadership, FedEx employees have ranked FedEx Express Canada one of the best places to work in Canada. She has also helped make the company one of the most respected brands in Canada. On advancing women into leadership: "I mentor many young women who often tell me they can have it all—a family and a great career—just not at the same time. I'm a widow and I'm raising four young children, so I'm living proof that you can have it all at the same time. You can be a devoted mom and a successful, senior leader."

In this chapter, you will learn about the theories and practices managers like Lisa Lisson use in motivating their employees to focus on goals common to them and the organization. This includes being introduced to some motivation theories. As you read through this chapter, consider situations in which you have been involved. Did you witness some of the theories being applied? Looking back, could some of these situations have been handled differently to better motivate the audience?

Sources: "5:30 Club: Lisa Lisson, president of FedEx Express Canada," University of Guelph, 11 February 2015, https://www.uoguelph.ca/business/530-club-lisa-lisson-president -fedex-express-canada; "FedEx Express Facts - Canada," FedEx, 2015, http://www.fedex.com/ca_english/about/overview/fastfacts/expressfactscanada.html; Angus Gillespie, "Lisa Lisson - FEDEX President Triumphs Over Personal Tragedy," *The Canadian Business Journal*, 12 September 2014, http://www.cbj.ca/LISA_LISSON_FEDEX_PRESIDENT _TRIUMPHS_OVER_PERSONAL_TRAGEDY/; "Canada's Most Powerful Women: Top 100 – Current Winners, LISA LISSON PRESIDENT, FEDEX EXPRESS CANADA Bio," WXN, 2014, https://www.wxnetwork.com/TOP-100/TOP-100-WINNERS/; Lisa Lisson, "Uncovering the Heart of FedEx," FedEx Express Canada, 21 May 2012, http://blog.fedex.designcdt .com/blog/uncovering-heart-fedex? page=2; Heather Connelly, "Undercover Analysis: Episode 10; FedEx CEO Lisa Lisson," *Financial Post*, 6 April 2012, http://business .financialpost.com/2012/04/06/undercover-analysis-episode-10-fedex-ceo-lisa-lisson/; "Lisa Lisson," FedEX Express Canada, 2012, http://about.van.fedex.com/executive_bios /lisa_lisson; and "FedEX," Undercover Boss Canada, 2012, www.wnetwork.com/Shows/Undercover-Boss-Canada.aspx.

The Value of Motivation

"If work is such fun, how come the rich don't do it?" quipped comedian Groucho Marx. Well, the rich do work—Bill Gates did not make his billions playing computer games. And workers can have fun—if managers make the effort to motivate them. **Motivation** refers to the overall desire to excel.[1] This is the extent to which persistent effort is directed toward a goal as a motivated person usually works "hard," "keeps at" his or her work, and directs his or her behaviour toward appropriate outcomes.[2] Have you heard the motivation myths listed in Figure 11.1?

motivation
The overall desire to excel.

It is difficult to overstate the importance of workers' job satisfaction as this contributes to motivation. Happy workers lead to happy customers, and happy customers lead to successful businesses. On the opposite side, unhappy workers are likely to leave the company and when this happens, the company usually loses out. The costs associated with losing an employee vary. Studies have shown that it can cost up to 18 months' salary to lose and replace a manager or professional and up to six months' salary to lose and replace an hourly worker.[3] Costs include management time involved in reviewing applications, interviewing candidates, and conducting reference checks; time and resources spent for orientation and training of the new employee; and loss of productivity while the employee is on the learning curve.[4] The "soft" costs of losing employees are even greater: loss of intellectual capital, decreased morale of remaining workers, increased employee stress, and a poor reputation.

While it is costly to recruit and train new workers, it's also expensive to retain those who are disengaged. The word *engagement* is used to describe employees' level of motivation, passion, and commitment. Engaged employees work with passion and feel a connection to their company.[5]

■ **FIGURE 11.1**

MOTIVATION MYTHS

Money is the only effective motivator. In some situations, money is one of the best methods to motivate people. In others, it is entirely ineffective. Most importantly, it is certainly not the only motivator. What will motivate always depends on the people and the situation.

Everyone is motivated by the same things I am. Although many people share common needs and desires, different people in different situations are motivated by an extraordinary range of factors, including financial gain, recognition, esteem, personal achievement, desire for equity, need to belong, fear, freedom, involvement, interesting work, and so on. What motivates one may not motivate another, and the same factor that motivates a person in one situation may not motivate that same person in a different situation.

Punishment does not motivate. Although rarely the first choice to influence behaviour, punishment, or the threat of it, can be an effective motivator. The problem, however, is that this type of motivation tends to be short term and rarely is associated with getting people to do more than the minimum. Its appropriateness will depend on the situation. In some cases, it may be the only or most effective consequence available, and thus it is important to learn how to most fairly administer punishment.

Low performance is always attributable to low motivation. Any performance is a function of motivation, ability, and the opportunity to perform. So, although low motivation is a common cause of low performance, it is certainly not the sole cause. Low performers may well lack the ability or the opportunity to achieve high performance.

Lack of motivation stems largely from lazy and apathetic people. That is sometimes the case, of course, but more often it is the situation that lacks sufficient incentives to energize people. People labelled as unmotivated in one situation (say their job) are sometimes highly engaged and committed in another case (for example, as a Little League coach). The managerial challenge is to discover what brings out the effort in your people and to influence what you can.

Smart people don't need to be motivated. This is a dangerous myth that can have consequences well beyond what a manager may realize. Because smart people have high ability, their motivation is key to obtaining high levels of performance. A smart, but unmotivated person may still perform at an acceptable level, but that person is capable of much more and ultimately will probably become disillusioned with the job and leave it—leaving a hole bigger than will be immediately obvious to most managers.

Source: Timothy T. Baldwin, William H. Bommer, and Robert S. Rubin, *Managing Organizational Behavior, What Great Managers Know and Do,* 2nd ed. (New York: McGraw-Hill Irwin, 2013), 198.

Disengaged workers have essentially checked out; they plod through their day putting in time, but not energy. Not only do they act out their unhappiness at work, but disengaged employees undermine the efforts of engaged employees.

Selected as one of Canada's 100 Best Small and Medium Employers <http://www.canadastop100.com/sme/>, DAC Group <http://www.dacgroup.com> is a digital performance marketing agency that seeks employees with technical skills, industry passion, and the curiosity to learn. New-grad recruiters (above) look to hire 'geeks with personalities.' Would you be motivated if you worked for a company like this whose workspace includes gaming stations, lounge areas, and calming rooms?[6]

Motivating the right people to join the organization and stay with it is a key function of managers. Top-performing managers are usually surrounded by top-performing employees. It is no coincidence that geese fly faster in formation than alone. Although the desire to perform well ultimately comes from within, good managers stimulate people and bring out their natural drive to do a good job. People are willing to work, and work hard, if they feel that their work makes a difference and is appreciated.[7]

People are motivated by a variety of things, such as recognition, accomplishment, and status. An **intrinsic reward** is the personal satisfaction you feel when you perform well and achieve goals. The belief that your work makes a significant contribution to the organization or society is a form of intrinsic reward. An **extrinsic reward** is something given to you by someone else as recognition for good work. Pay increases, praise, and promotions are examples of extrinsic rewards. Although ultimately motivation—the drive to satisfy a need—comes from within an individual, there are ways to stimulate people that bring out their natural drive to do a good job.

intrinsic reward
The good feeling you have when you have done a job well.

extrinsic reward
Something given to you by someone else as recognition for good work; extrinsic rewards include pay increases, praise, and promotions.

Intrinsic (inner) rewards include the personal satisfaction you feel for a job well done. People who respond to such inner promptings often enjoy their work and share their enthusiasm with others. Are you more strongly motivated by your own desire to do well, or by extrinsic (external) rewards like pay and recognition?

This chapter will introduce you to some concepts, theories, and practices of motivation. We begin with a look at some traditional theories of motivation. Why should you bother to know about these theories? Because sometimes "new" approaches are not really new; variations of them have been tried in the past. Knowing what has gone before will help you see what has worked and what has not. We discuss the Hawthorne studies because they created a new interest in worker satisfaction and motivation. Then we'll look at some assumptions about employees that come from the traditional theorists. You will see the names of these theorists over and over in business literature and future courses: Taylor, Mayo, Maslow, Herzberg, and McGregor. Finally, we'll introduce modern motivation theories and show you how managers apply them.

Ultimately, the goal of this chapter is to provide you with information needed to motivate different types of people, to do different types of things, in different circumstances.[8] The question, "How do you motivate people?" should be expanded to "*How do you motivate who, to do what, and under what circumstances?*" as effective motivation strategies always depend on the people involved, their history, and the context.[9]

> **LO1**   Explain Taylor's theory of scientific management, and describe the Hawthorne studies and their significance to management.

Frederick Taylor: The Father of Scientific Management

Several nineteenth-century thinkers presented management principles, but not until the early twentieth century did there appear any significant works with lasting implications. *The Principles of Scientific Management* was written by American efficiency engineer Frederick Taylor and published in 1911, earning Taylor the title "father of scientific management." Taylor's goal was to increase worker productivity to benefit both the firm and the worker. The solution, he thought, was to scientifically study the most efficient ways to do things, determine the one "best way" to perform each task, and then teach people those methods. This became known as **scientific management**. Three elements were basic to Taylor's approach: time, methods, and rules of work. His most important tools were observation and the stopwatch. Taylor's thinking is behind today's measure of how many burgers McDonald's expects its cooks to flip.

> **scientific management**
> Studying workers to find the most efficient ways of doing things and then teaching people those techniques.

A classic Taylor story involves his study of men shovelling rice, coal, and iron ore with the same type of shovel. Believing that different materials called for different shovels, he proceeded to invent a wide variety of sizes and shapes of shovels and, with stopwatch in hand, measured output over time in what were called **time-motion studies**. These were studies of the tasks performed to complete a job and the time needed to do each task. Sure enough, an average person could shovel 25 to 35 tons more per day using the most efficient motions and the proper shovel. This finding led to time-motion studies of virtually every factory job. As the most efficient ways of doing things were determined, efficiency became the standard for setting goals.

> **time-motion studies**
> Studies, begun by Frederick Taylor, of which tasks must be performed to complete a job and the time needed to do each task.

Taylor's scientific management became the dominant strategy for improving productivity in the early 1900s. Hundreds of time-motion specialists developed standards in plants throughout the country. One follower of Taylor was Henry L. Gantt, who developed charts by which managers plotted the work of employees a day in advance down to the smallest detail. Engineers Frank and Lillian Gilbreth used Taylor's ideas in a three-year study of bricklaying. They developed the **principle of motion economy**, which showed that every job could be broken down into a series of elementary motions. They then analyzed each motion to make it more efficient.

> **principle of motion economy**
> Theory developed by Frank and Lillian Gilbreth that every job can be broken down into a series of elementary motions.

Some interpreted scientific management as viewing people largely as machines that needed to be properly programmed. There was little concern for the psychological or human aspects of work. Taylor believed that workers would perform at a high level of effectiveness—that is, be motivated—if they received high enough pay. While Taylor did not use this comparison to machines, he had very precise ideas about how to introduce his system: "It is only through enforced standardization of methods, enforced adoption of the best implements and working conditions, and enforced co-operation that this faster work can be assured. And the duty of enforcing the adoption of standards and enforcing this co-operation rests with management alone."[10] A crusader for better working conditions and pay for the working class, Taylor believed that the resulting improved productivity should then benefit both the workers and the company.

UPS tells drivers how to get out of their trucks, how fast to walk, how many packages to pick up and deliver a day, and even how to hold their keys. Can you see how UPS follows the principles of scientific management by teaching people the one "best way" to perform each task?

Some of Taylor's ideas are still being implemented. Some companies continue to emphasize conformity to work rules rather than creativity, flexibility, and responsiveness. For example, United Parcel Service (UPS) tells drivers how to get out of their trucks (with the right foot first), how fast to walk (three feet per second), how many packages to pick up and deliver a day (an average of 400), and how to hold their keys (teeth up, third finger). Drivers wear ring scanners, which are electronic devices on their index fingers that are wired to a small computer on their wrists. The devices shoot a pattern of photons at a bar code on a package to let a customer check the Internet and know exactly where a package is at any given moment. If a driver is considered inefficient, a supervisor rides along, prodding the driver with stopwatches and clipboards. UPS has a training centre with simulators that teach employees how to properly lift and load boxes, drive their trucks proficiently, and even lessen the risk of slipping and falling when carrying a package.[11]

The benefits of relying on workers to come up with solutions to productivity problems have long been recognized, as we shall discover next.

Elton Mayo and the Hawthorne Studies

One study, inspired by Frederick Taylor's research, began at the Western Electric Company's Hawthorne plant in Cicero, Illinois. The study began in 1927 and ended six years later. Let's see why it was one of the major studies in management literature.

Elton Mayo and his research team forever changed managers' beliefs about employee motivation. Their research at the Western Electric Hawthorne plant (pictured here) gave birth to the concept of human-based motivation by showing that employees behaved differently simply because they were involved in planning and executing the experiments.

Elton Mayo and his colleagues from Harvard University went to the Hawthorne plant to test the degree of lighting associated with optimum productivity. In this respect, their research was a traditional scientific management study. The idea was to keep records of the workers' productivity under different levels of illumination. But the initial experiments revealed what seemed to be a problem. The researchers had expected productivity to fall as the lighting was dimmed. Yet the experimental group's productivity went up regardless of whether the lighting was bright or dim, and even when the lighting was reduced to about the level of moonlight.

In a second series of 13 experiments, a separate test room was set up where researchers could manipulate temperature, humidity, and other environmental factors. Productivity went up each time; in fact, it increased by 50 percent overall. When the experimenters repeated the original condition, they expected productivity to fall to original levels; however, productivity increased yet again. The experiments were considered a total failure at this point. No matter what the experimenters did, productivity went up. What was causing the increase?

In the end, Mayo guessed that some human or psychological factor was at play. He and his colleagues interviewed the workers, asking about their feelings and attitudes toward the experiment. The answers began a profound change in management thinking that has had repercussions today. Here is what the researchers concluded:

- The workers in the test room thought of themselves as a social group. The atmosphere was informal, they could talk freely, and they interacted regularly with their supervisors and the experimenters. They felt special and worked hard to stay in the group. This motivated them.

- The workers were included in the planning of the experiments. For example, they rejected one kind of pay schedule and recommended another, which was adopted. They believed that their ideas were respected and they felt engaged in managerial decision making. This, too, motivated them.

- No matter the physical conditions, the workers enjoyed the atmosphere of their special room and the additional pay for being more productive. Job satisfaction increased dramatically.

Researchers now use the term **Hawthorne effect** to refer to the tendency for people to behave differently when they know they are being studied. The Hawthorne study's results encouraged researchers to study human motivation and the managerial styles that lead to greater productivity. Research emphasis shifted from Taylor's scientific management toward Mayo's new human-based management.

Hawthorne effect
The tendency for people to behave differently when they know they are being studied.

Mayo's findings led to completely new assumptions about employees. One was that pay is not the only motivator. In fact, money was found to be a relatively ineffective motivator. New assumptions led to many theories about the human side of motivation. One of the best-known motivation theorists was Abraham Maslow, whose work we discuss next.

 LO2   Identify the levels of Maslow's hierarchy of needs and apply them to employee motivation. Contrast this with the motivators and hygiene factors identified by Herzberg.

Abraham Maslow's Hierarchy of Needs

Psychologist Abraham Maslow believed that to understand motivation at work, one must understand human motivation in general. It seemed to him that motivation arises from need. That is, people are motivated to satisfy unmet needs. Needs that have been satisfied no longer provide motivation.

He thought that needs could be placed on a hierarchy of importance. Figure 11.2 shows **Maslow's hierarchy of needs**, whose levels—from lower to higher—are as follows:

- *Physiological Needs.* Basic survival needs, such as the need for food, water, and shelter.
- *Safety Needs.* The need to feel secure at work and at home.
- *Social Needs.* The need to feel loved, accepted, and part of the group.
- *Esteem Needs.* The need for recognition and acknowledgement from others, as well as self-respect and a sense of status or importance.
- *Self-Actualization Needs.* The need to develop to one's fullest potential.

Maslow's hierarchy of needs
Theory of motivation that places different types of human needs in order of importance, from basic physiological needs to safety, social, and esteem needs to self-actualization needs.

When one need is satisfied, another higher-level need emerges and motivates us to do something to satisfy it. The satisfied need is no longer a motivator. For example, if you just ate a full-course dinner, hunger would not (at least for several hours) be a motivator, and your attention may turn to your surroundings (safety needs) or family (social needs). Of course, lower-level needs (perhaps thirst) may re-emerge at any time they are not met and take your attention away from higher-level needs (perhaps the need for recognition or status).

■ **FIGURE 11.2**

MASLOW'S HIERARCHY OF NEEDS

Maslow's hierarchy of needs is based on the idea that motivation comes from need. If a need is met, it is no longer a motivator, so a higher-level need becomes the motivator. Higher-level needs demand the support of lower-level needs. This chart shows the various levels of need.

To compete successfully, firms must create a work environment that includes goals such as social contribution, honesty, reliability, service, quality, dependability, and unity—for all levels of employees. Chip Conley of Joie de Vivre *<http://www.jdvhotels.com>*, a chain of boutique hotels, thinks about higher-level needs such as meaning (self-actualization) for all employees, including lower-level workers. Half his employees are housekeepers who clean toilets all day. How does he help them feel they are doing meaningful work? One technique is what he calls the George Bailey exercise, based on the main character in the movie *It's a Wonderful Life.* Conley asks small groups of housekeepers what would happen if they weren't there every day. Trash would pile up, bathrooms would be full of wet towels, and let's not even think about the toilets. Then he asked them to come up with some other name for housekeeping. They offer suggestions like "serenity keepers," "clutter busters," or "the peace-of-mind police." In the end, these employees have a sense of how the customer's experience would not be the same without them. This gives meaning to their work that helps satisfy higher-level needs.[12]

Progress Assessment

- What are the similarities and differences between Taylor's time-motion studies and Mayo's Hawthorne studies?
- How did Mayo's findings influence scientific management?
- Draw a diagram of Maslow's hierarchy of needs. Label and describe the parts.

Frederick Herzberg's Motivating Factors

Another direction in managerial theory is to explore what managers can do with the job itself to motivate employees. (This is a modern-day look at Taylor's research.) In other words, some theorists ask, "Of all the factors controllable by managers, which are most effective in generating an enthusiastic work effort?"

In the mid-1960s, psychologist Frederick Herzberg conducted the most-discussed study in this area. Herzberg asked workers to rank various job-related factors in order of importance relative to motivation. The question was: "What creates enthusiasm for workers and makes them work to full potential?" The most important motivating factors were:

1. Sense of achievement
2. Earned recognition
3. Interest in the work itself
4. Opportunity for growth
5. Opportunity for advancement
6. Importance of responsibility
7. Peer and group relationships
8. Pay
9. Supervisor's fairness
10. Company policies and rules
11. Status
12. Job security
13. Supervisor's friendliness
14. Working conditions

Herzberg believed that motivational factors such as recognition increase worker performance. How do you think Herzberg's motivational factors encourage workers to a higher level of performance on the job?

Factors receiving the most votes all clustered around job content. Workers like to feel that they contribute to the company (sense of achievement was number 1). They want to earn recognition (number 2) and feel that their jobs are important (number 6). They want responsibility (which is why learning is so important) and to earn recognition for that responsibility by having a chance for growth and advancement. Of course, workers also want the job to be interesting. Do you feel the same way about your work?

Workers did not consider factors related to the job environment to be motivators. It was interesting to find that one of those factors was pay. Workers felt that the *absence* of good pay, job security, and friendly supervisors could cause dissatisfaction, but their presence did not motivate employees to work harder; it just provided satisfaction and contentment. Would you work harder if you were paid more?

Herzberg concluded that certain factors, which he called **motivators**, made employees productive and gave them satisfaction. These factors, as mentioned, mostly related to job content. Herzberg called other elements of the job **hygiene factors** (or **maintenance factors**). These related to the job environment and could cause dissatisfaction if missing but would not necessarily motivate employees if increased. See Figure 11.3 for a list of both motivators and hygiene factors.

motivators
In Herzberg's theory of motivating factors, job factors that cause employees to be productive and that give them satisfaction.

hygiene (maintenance) factors
In Herzberg's theory of motivating factors, job factors that can cause dissatisfaction if missing but that do not necessarily motivate employees if increased.

■ **FIGURE 11.3**

HERZBERG'S MOTIVATORS AND HYGIENE FACTORS

There's some controversy over Herzberg's results. For example, sales managers often use money as a motivator. Recent studies have shown that money can be a motivator if used as part of a recognition program.

Motivators	Hygiene (Maintenance) Factors
(These factors can be used to motivate workers.)	(These factors can cause dissatisfaction, but changing them will have little motivational effect.)
Work itself	Company policy and administration
Achievement	Supervision
Recognition	Working conditions
Responsibility	Interpersonal relations (co-workers)
Growth and advancement	Salary, status, and job security

Herzberg's motivating factors led to the following conclusion—the best way to motivate employees is to make their jobs interesting, help them achieve their objectives, and recognize their achievements through advancement and added responsibility.[13] A review of Figure 11.4 shows the similarity between Maslow's hierarchy of needs and Herzberg's motivating factors.

Look at Herzberg's motivating factors, identify those that motivate you, and rank them in order of importance to you. Keep them in mind as you consider jobs and careers. What motivators do your job opportunities offer you? Evaluating your job offers in terms of what is really important to you will help you make a wise career choice. This technique was used by Lisa Lisson, the focus of this chapter's profile.

Applying Herzberg's Theories

Improved working conditions (such as better wages or increased security) are taken for granted after workers get used to them. This is what Herzberg meant by hygiene (maintenance) factors: their absence causes dissatisfaction, but their presence (maintenance) does not motivate. The best motivator for some employees is a simple and sincere "Thanks, I really appreciate what you're doing."

■ **FIGURE 11.4**

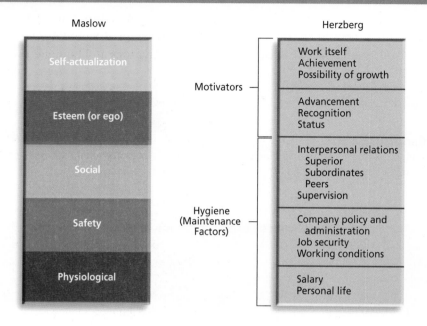

COMPARISON OF MASLOW'S HIERARCHY OF NEEDS AND HERZBERG'S MOTIVATING FACTORS

Maslow

Herzberg

Self-actualization

Esteem (or ego)

Social

Safety

Physiological

Motivators

Work itself
Achievement
Possibility of growth

Advancement
Recognition
Status

Hygiene
(Maintenance
Factors)

Interpersonal relations
   Superior
   Subordinates
   Peers
Supervision

Company policy and
   administration
Job security
Working conditions

Salary
Personal life

Mediacorp Canada Inc. annually publishes a list of Canada's Top 100 Employers *<http://www.canadastop100.com>*. Companies are evaluated on eight key areas: (1) physical workplace; (2) work and social atmosphere; (3) health, financial, and family benefits; (4) vacation and time off; (5) employee communications focused on how employers capture employee feedback; (6) performance management; (7) training and skills development; and (8) community involvement.[14] For example, the unique geographic spread of Canadian Pacific Railway Ltd. *<http://www.cpr.ca>*—from Vancouver to

Canadian Pacific Railway Ltd. has been recognized for its community involvement. Each year, its Holiday Trains make stops in communities raising food and cash donations for local food banks. Free concerts and seasonal festivities are offered from the travelling stage. Can you think of other company examples of community involvement?

Montreal—means employees can literally work in communities across Canada. The company offers tuition subsidies of up to $10,000, a flexible health benefits program that includes retirees, a diverse range of working environments and roles within the firm, and its own training facility for conductors and engineers. Mobility is what the company is all about. "You can start with this company in human resources and end up in operations, finance, public affairs—a career within a career within this railway," says Patti Clarkson, an employment adviser at the company.[15] The Seeking Sustainability box highlights Vancity *<http://www.vancity.com>*, an organization that has been recognized not only as one of Canada's Top 100 Employers, but also as #1 among Canada's Top 50 Socially Responsible Corporations.

Seeking SUSTAINABILITY

Values Drive Vancity's Climate Change Initiatives

Vancouver City Savings Credit Union (Vancity) is Canada's largest community credit union with $18.6 billion in assets, 509,000 member owners, and 58 branches in Metro Vancouver, the Fraser Valley, Victoria, and Squamish. A financial co-operative, Vancity's triple-bottom line business model is driven by its vision to redefine wealth and focus on building healthy communities that are financially, socially, and environmentally sustainable. For example, the company allocates 30 percent of its net earnings to be shared with its members, communities, and employees.

Vancity has a long history of taking action against climate change. It is BC Hydro PowerSmart-certified for its energy-efficiency leadership as it is committed to supporting ways to find positive solutions to climate change. Branches recycle and compost approximately 88 percent of their waste, and head office recycles and composts 81 percent of its waste. Waste audits are performed every two years and head office data is tracked annually. Since 2008, it has been carbon neutral. The goal is to measure and reduce its greenhouse gas emissions, then offset emissions through the purchase of carbon offsets from emission-reducing activities that others have undertaken. As a result of energy-efficiency projects, Vancity has both saved money (over $5 million in energy costs) and avoided greenhouse gas emissions.

The company believes in impact investing and lending. Providing credit is the biggest way to help members and their communities thrive and prosper. Deposits are invested in local businesses, organizations, and initiatives that create positive impacts in the community, such as creating jobs, reducing greenhouse gases, and fighting homelessness. "If you're a business, not-for-profit, First Nation government, social enterprise, co-operative, or strata," asserts the website, "and you're looking to finance a green building project, energy-efficiency upgrade, or innovative environmental or clean technology initiative, then we want to talk to you." The Green Business program provides support in the forms of financing (eco-efficiency and micro-loans for green business start-up and expansion), grants, partnerships, and learning, networking, resources, and events.

(continued)

(continued)

You have learned a little about Vancity and its value-driven business model. Visit its site to read stories of impact investing in the energy and environment fields. Would you like to work for an organization that is so committed to addressing climate change?

Sources: "Values-based banking helps Vancity post strong 2014 results," Vancouver City Savings Credit Union, 5 March 2015, https://www.vancity.com/AboutVancity/News/MediaReleases/Financials_March5_2015/; "Vancity is carbon neutral," Vancouver City Savings Credit Union, 2015, https://www.vancity.com/AboutVancity/VisionAndValues/ValuesBasedBanking/EnvironmentalSustainability /VancityIsCarbonNeutral/; "Impact lending and investing," Vancouver City Savings Credit Union, 2015, https://www.vancity.com /AboutVancity/InvestingInCommunities/ImpactLending/?xcid=about_megamenu_implendinv; "Organizations in B.C. receive funding for green building initiatives that reduce environmental impact," Vancouver City Savings Credit Union, 22 May 2012, https://www.vancity .com/AboutUs/OurNews/MediaReleases/May22/; and "Climate Change Solutions," Vancouver City Savings Credit Union, 2012, https://www.vancity.com/AboutUs/OurValues/CorporateSocialResponsibility/ClimateChangeSolutions/.

LO3   Differentiate between McGregor's Theory X and Theory Y.

Douglas McGregor's Theory X and Theory Y

The way managers go about motivating people at work depends greatly on their attitudes toward workers. Management theorist Douglas McGregor observed that managers' attitudes generally fall into one of two entirely different sets of managerial assumptions, which he called Theory X and Theory Y.

Theory X

The assumptions of Theory X management are:

- The average person dislikes work and will avoid it if possible.
- Because of this dislike, workers must be forced, controlled, directed, or threatened with punishment to make them put forth the effort to achieve the organization's goals.
- The average worker prefers to be directed, wishes to avoid responsibility, has relatively little ambition, and wants security.
- Primary motivators are fear and money.

The natural consequence of such attitudes, beliefs, and assumptions is a manager who is very busy and who watches people closely, telling them what to do and how to do it. Motivation is more likely to take the form of punishment for poor work rather than reward for good work. Theory X managers give workers little responsibility, authority, or flexibility. Taylor and other theorists who preceded him would have agreed with Theory X. Time-motion studies calculated the one best way to perform a task and the optimal time to devote to it. Researchers assumed workers needed to be trained and carefully watched to see that they conformed to standards.

Some managers and entrepreneurs still suspect that employees cannot be fully trusted and need to be closely supervised.[16] No doubt you have seen such managers in action. How did this make you feel? Were these managers' assumptions accurate regarding the workers' attitudes?

Theory Y

Theory Y makes entirely different assumptions about people:

- Most people like work; it is as natural as play or rest.
- Most people naturally work toward goals to which they are committed.

Theory X managers come in all sizes and shapes. Such managers may have an in-your-face style. Would you prefer to work for a Theory X or a Theory Y manager?

- The depth of a person's commitment to goals depends on the perceived rewards for achieving them.
- Under certain conditions, most people not only accept responsibility, but also seek it.
- People are capable of using a relatively high degree of imagination, creativity, and cleverness to solve problems.
- People are motivated by a variety of rewards. Each worker is stimulated by a reward unique to that worker (e.g., time off, money, recognition, etc.).

Rather than authority, direction, and close supervision, Theory Y managers emphasize a relaxed managerial atmosphere in which workers are free to set objectives, be creative, be flexible, and go beyond the goals set by management. (Figure 11.5 compares both Theories X and Y.) A key technique in meeting these objectives is *empowerment*, which includes giving employees the authority to make

■ FIGURE 11.5

A COMPARISON OF THEORIES X AND Y	
Theory X	**Theory Y**
1. Employees dislike work and will try to avoid it.	1. Employees view work as a natural part of life.
2. Employees prefer to be controlled and directed.	2. Employees prefer limited control and direction.
3. Employees seek security, not responsibility.	3. Employees will seek responsibility under proper work conditions.
4. Employees must be intimidated by managers to perform.	4. Employees perform better in work environments that are non-intimidating.
5. Employees are motivated by financial rewards.	5. Employees are motivated by many different needs.

decisions and the tools to implement the decisions they make. For empowerment to be a real motivator, management should follow these three steps:

1. Find out what people think the problems in the organization are.
2. Let them design the solutions.
3. Get out of the way and let them put those solutions into action.

Often employees complain that although they are asked to engage in company decision making, their managers fail to actually empower them to make decisions. Have you ever worked in such an atmosphere? How did that make you feel?

Progress Assessment

- Explain the distinction between what Herzberg called motivators and hygiene factors.
- Briefly describe the managerial attitudes behind Theories X and Y.
- Which of the theories introduced so far resonates the most with you? Explain.

LO4   Explain the key principles of goal setting, expectancy, reinforcement, and equity theories.

Goal-Setting Theory and Management by Objectives

Goal-setting theory says setting ambitious but attainable goals can motivate workers and improve performance if the goals are accepted, accompanied by feedback, and if conditions in the organization pave the way for achievement. All organization members should have some basic agreement about both overall goals and specific objectives for each department and individual. Thus, there should be a system to engage everyone in the organization in goal setting and implementation.

> **goal-setting theory**
> The idea that setting ambitious but attainable goals can motivate workers and improve performance if the goals are accepted, accompanied by feedback, and facilitated by organizational conditions.

The late management expert Peter Drucker developed such a system in the 1960s. "Managers cannot motivate people; they can only thwart people's motivation because people motivate themselves," he said. Managers, he believed, can only create the proper environment for the seed to grow. Called **management by objectives (MBO)**, Drucker's system of goal setting and implementation involves a cycle of discussion, review, and evaluation of objectives among top- and middle-level managers, supervisors, and employees. It calls on managers to formulate goals in co-operation with everyone in the organization, to commit employees to those goals, and then to monitor results and reward accomplishments.

> **management by objectives (MBO)**
> A system of goal setting and implementation that involves a cycle of discussion, review, and evaluation of objectives among top- and middle-level managers, supervisors, and employees.

MBO is most effective in relatively stable situations when managers can make long-range goals and implement them with few changes. Managers must also understand the difference between helping and coaching subordinates. *Helping* means working with the subordinate and doing part of the work, if necessary. *Coaching* means acting as a resource—teaching, guiding, and recommending—but not participating actively or doing the task. The central idea of MBO is that employees need to motivate themselves.

Employee input and expectations are important.[17] Problems can arise when management uses MBO as a strategy for forcing managers and workers to commit to goals that are not agreed on together but are instead set by top management.[18]

Victor Vroom identified the importance of employee expectations and developed a process called expectancy theory. Let's examine this concept next.

Meeting Employee Expectations: Victor Vroom's Expectancy Theory

According to Victor Vroom's **expectancy theory**, employee expectations can affect motivation. That is, the amount of effort employees exert on a specific task depends on their expectations of the outcome. Vroom contends that employees ask three questions before committing their maximum effort to a task: (1) Can I accomplish the task? (2) If I do accomplish it, what is my reward? (3) Is the reward worth the effort? (See Figure 11.6 for a summary of this process.)

> **expectancy theory**
> Victor Vroom's theory that the amount of effort employees exert on a specific task depends on their expectations of the outcome.

■ FIGURE 11.6

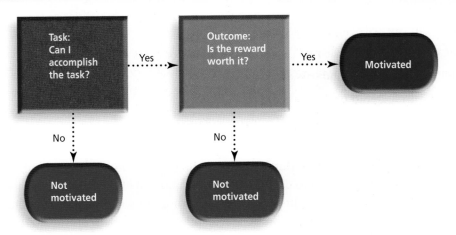

EXPECTANCY THEORY

The amount of effort employees exert on a task depends on their expectations of the outcome.

Performance feedback is crucial for the motivation of employees. The feedback session is also ideal for setting goals.

Recall the start of the chapter, when it was stated that motivation comes from within, when you consider this next example. Think of the effort you might exert in your class under the following conditions. Suppose your instructor says that to earn an A in the course you must achieve an average of 90 percent on coursework plus jump two metres high. Would you exert maximum effort toward earning an A if you knew you could not possibly jump two metres high? Or what if your instructor said that any student can earn an A in the course but you know that this instructor has not awarded an A in 25 years of teaching? If the reward of an A seems unattainable, would you exert significant effort in the course? Better yet, let's say that you read online that businesses prefer hiring C-minus students to hiring A-plus students. Does the reward of an A seem worth it? Now think of similar situations that may occur on the job.

Expectancy theory does note that expectation varies from individual to individual. Employees establish their own views in terms of task difficulty and the value of the reward.[19] Researchers David Nadler and Edward Lawler modified Vroom's theory and suggested that managers follow five steps to improve employee performance:[20]

1. Determine what rewards employees value.

2. Determine each employee's desired performance standard.

3. Ensure that performance standards are attainable.

4. Guarantee rewards tied to performance.

5. Be certain that employees consider the rewards adequate.

Now that we have covered several theories, you may have realized that they try to explain all behaviour, by all people, all of the time. But this is impossible given the complexity of human behaviour. The value of being briefly introduced to different theories (you will discuss these theories in more detail in an Organizational Behaviour course) is that each theory offers some piece of the puzzle. No theory is complete, as people are very complex and our attempts to theorize about behaviour will never be complete. Successful leaders are sensitive to the differences between their employees and what motivates them. A starting point is understanding these theories.

Reinforcing Employee Performance: Reinforcement Theory

According to **reinforcement theory**, positive reinforcers, negative reinforcers, and punishers motivate a person to behave in certain ways. In other words, motivation is the result of the carrot-and-stick approach whereby individuals act to receive rewards (i.e., the carrot) and avoid punishment (i.e., the stick). Positive reinforcements are rewards such as praise, recognition, and a pay raise. Punishment includes reprimands, reduced pay, and layoffs or firing. Negative reinforcement occurs when people work to escape the punishers (i.e., the punishment). Escaping the punishment reinforces or rewards the positive behaviour. A manager might also try to stop undesirable behaviour by not responding to it. This response is called *extinction* because managers hope the unwanted behaviour will become extinct. Figure 11.7 illustrates how a manager can use reinforcement theory to motivate workers.

> **reinforcement theory**
> Theory that positive and negative reinforcers motivate a person to behave in certain ways.

■ **FIGURE 11.7**

REINFORCEMENT THEORY		
Managers can either add or subtract stimuli (positive reinforcement, negative reinforcement, or punishers) to increase desired behaviour or decrease undesired behaviour.		
	ADD STIMULI	**SUBTRACT STIMULI**
Increase Behaviour	Positive Reinforcement: Jill gets praise (the reinforcement added) for turning in her reports on time (target behaviour to increase).	Negative Reinforcement: Jack is on probation (punishment that will be removed) until such time as he can turn in three reports on time (target behaviour to increase).
Decrease Behaviour	Punishment: Jack gets written up (the punisher) for turning in his reports late (target behaviour to decrease).	Extinction: Jill does not get praise (reinforcement is removed) when her reports are turned in late (target behaviour to decrease), no matter how well done they are.

Source: Casey Limmer, MSW, LCSW, Washington University.

Treating Employees Fairly: Equity Theory

Equity theory looks at how employees' perceptions of fairness affect their willingness to perform. It assumes employees ask, "If I do a good job, will it be worth it?" and "What's fair?" Employees try to maintain equity between what they put into the job and what they get out of it, comparing those inputs and outputs to those of others in similar positions. Workers find comparative information through personal relationships, professional organizations, and other sources.

> **equity theory**
> The idea that employees try to maintain equity between inputs and outputs compared to others in similar positions.

When workers perceive inequity, they will try to re-establish fairness in a number of ways. For example, suppose that you compare the grade you earned on a term paper with your classmates' grades. If you think you received a lower grade compared to the students who put out the same effort as you,

you may (1) reduce your effort on future class projects, or (2) rationalize the difference by saying, "Grades are overvalued anyway!" If you think that your paper received a higher grade than comparable papers, you will probably (1) increase your effort to justify the higher reward in the future, or (2) rationalize by saying, "I'm worth it!"

In the workplace, inequity may lead to lower productivity, reduced quality, increased absenteeism, and voluntary resignation.

If you attend class regularly but do not do well on your first mid-term exam, how do you react? Do you stop going to class regularly as you do not think that it is worthwhile? Or, do you go and speak with your instructor to find out how to improve for the next exam?

Remember that equity judgments are based on perception and are therefore subject to error. When workers overestimate their own contributions—as happens often—they feel *any* rewards given out for performance are inequitable.[21] Sometimes organizations try to deal with this by keeping employee salaries secret, but secrecy may make things worse. Employees are likely to overestimate the salaries of others, in addition to overestimating their own contributions. The best remedy is generally clear and frequent communication. Managers must communicate as clearly as possible both the results they expect and the outcomes that will occur.[22]

Progress Assessment

- Explain goal-setting theory.
- Evaluate expectancy theory. When could expectancy theory apply to your efforts or lack of effort?
- Describe reinforcement theory. What are examples of positive and negative reinforcers?
- Explain the principles of equity theory.

Show how managers put motivation theories into action through such strategies as job enrichment, open communication, and job recognition.

Putting Theory into Action

Now that you know what a few theorists have to say about motivation, you might be asking yourself "So what? What do all of these theories have to do with what really goes on in the workplace today?" Let's look at how companies put the theories into action through job enrichment, open communication, and job recognition.

Motivating Through Job Enrichment

Managers have extended both Maslow's and Herzberg's theories through **job enrichment**, a strategy that motivates workers through the job itself. Work is assigned so that individuals can complete an identifiable task from beginning to end and are held responsible for successful achievement. Job enrichment is based on Herzberg's higher motivators, such as responsibility, achievement, and recognition.[23] It stands in contrast to *job simplification,* which produces task efficiency by breaking a job into simple steps and assigning people to each. Review Maslow's and Herzberg's work to see how job enrichment grew from those theories.

> **job enrichment**
> A motivational strategy that emphasizes motivating the worker through the job itself.

J. Richard Hackman and Greg R. Oldham proposed the Job Characteristics Model, which defines core job characteristics that have a certain psychological impact on workers. In turn, the psychological states induced by the nature of the job lead to certain outcomes that are relevant to the worker and the organization.[24] Put another way, when people are matched to a job that really "fits" them, most of the problems associated with "unmotivated" or "lazy" people disappear.[25] The five characteristics of work that are important in affecting individual motivation and performance are as follows:[26]

1. *Skill Variety.* The extent to which a job demands different skills.
2. *Task Identity.* The degree to which the job requires doing a task with a visible outcome from beginning to end.
3. *Task Significance.* The degree to which the job has a substantial impact on the lives or work of others in the company.
4. *Autonomy.* The degree of freedom, independence, and discretion in scheduling work and determining procedures.
5. *Feedback.* The amount of direct and clear information that is received about job performance.

Variety, identity, and significance contribute to the meaningfulness of the job. Autonomy gives people a feeling of responsibility, and feedback contributes to a feeling of achievement and recognition.

One type of job enrichment is **job enlargement,** which combines a series of tasks into one challenging and interesting assignment. Maytag, the home appliance manufacturer, redesigned its washing machine production process so that employees could assemble an entire water pump instead of just adding one part. Another example is **job rotation**, which makes work more interesting and motivating by moving employees from one job to another. One problem is the need to train employees to do several different jobs. However, the resulting increase in employee motivation and the value of having flexible, cross-trained employees offsets the costs.

job enlargement
A job-enrichment strategy that involves combining a series of tasks into one challenging and interesting assignment.

job rotation
A job-enrichment strategy that involves moving employees from one job to another.

Here a worker in Baccarat's factory puts the finishing touches on a crystal vase. One of the hallmarks of job enrichment is the worker's ability to perform a complete task from beginning to end. Why do you think this might be more motivating than simply adding a few parts to a product on an assembly line?

Figure 11.8 summarizes the theories discussed throughout this chapter. Review the motivation myths in Figure 11.1. Is it clearer now why these are myths?

Motivating Through Open Communication

Communication and information must flow freely throughout the organization when employees are empowered to make decisions—they can't make these decisions in a vacuum. It is crucial for people to be able to access the knowledge they need when they need it. The entire organization must be structured so that managers and employees can talk to one another. Procedures for encouraging open communication include the following:[27]

● *Create an organizational culture that rewards listening.* Top managers must create places to talk, and they must show employees that talking with superiors counts—by providing feedback, adopting employee suggestions, and rewarding upward communication—even if the discussion is negative. Employees must feel free to say anything they deem appropriate and believe their opinions are valued. Vancouver, British Columbia-based Great Little Box Company Ltd. (GLBC, *<http://www.greatlittlebox.com>*) is a private company that manufactures custom and stock corrugated boxes, point-of-purchase displays, folding cartons, labels, and flexible and protective packaging. To keep employees up-to-date, GLBC opens its books for all employees every month and splits 15 percent of its profits and splits it evenly among all employees regardless of seniority, position, or salary.[28] GLBC

■ FIGURE 11.8

SUMMARY OF MOTIVATION THEORIES	
Theory Name	**Description**
Scientific Management	Studying workers to find the most efficient ways of doing things and then teaching workers those techniques.
The Hawthorne Effect	The tendency for people to behave differently when they know they are being studied.
Hierarchy of Needs	People are motivated to satisfy unmet needs. Needs are placed in order of importance, from basic physiological needs to safety, social, and esteem needs to self-actualization needs.
Theory of Motivating Factors	Motivators are job factors that cause employees to be productive and that give them satisfaction. Hygiene (maintenance) factors are job factors that can cause dissatisfaction if missing but that do not necessarily motivate employees if increased.
Theory X and Theory Y	Theory X managers believe workers dislike work and will avoid it. Theory Y managers believe people like working and will accept responsibility.
Goal-Setting Theory	Setting ambitious but attainable goals can motivate workers and improve performance if the goals are accepted, accompanied by feedback, and if conditions in the organization pave the way for achievement.
Management by Objectives	A system of goal setting and implementation that involves a cycle of discussion, review, and evaluation of objectives among top- and middle-level managers, supervisors, and employees.
Expectancy Theory	The amount of effort employees exert on a specific task depends on expectations of the outcome.
Reinforcement Theory	Positive and negative reinforcers motivate a person to behave in certain ways.
Equity Theory	Employees try to maintain equity between inputs and outputs compared to others in similar positions.
Job Enrichment	Emphasizes motivating the worker through the job itself by considering five characteristics (skill variety, task identity, task significance, autonomy, and feedback). Examples of job enrichment include job enlargement and job rotation.

president and CEO, Robert Meggy, states that "Communication skills are becoming more important all the time. CEOs must build relationships with their staff, listen to their staff, and communicate to their staff. I think that communication skills are No. 1 for the twenty-first century CEOs."[29]

● *Train supervisors and managers to listen.* Most people receive no training in how to listen, in school or anywhere else, so organizations must do such training themselves or hire someone to do it.

● *Use effective questioning techniques.* We get information through questioning. Different kinds of questions yield different kinds of information. Closed questions that generate yes/no answers do not encourage the longer, more thoughtful responses that open questions do. Appropriate personal questions can create a sense of camaraderie between employees and managers.

● *Remove barriers to open communication.* Separate offices, parking areas, bathrooms, and dining rooms for managers only set up barriers. Other barriers are different dress codes and different ways of addressing one another (like calling workers by their first names and managers by their last). Removing such barriers will require willingness on the part of managers to give up their special privileges.

● *Avoid vague and ambiguous communication.* Passive voice appears weak and tentative. Statements such as "Mistakes were made" leave you wondering who made the mistakes. Hedging is another way managers send garbled messages. Terms like *possibly* and *perhaps* sound wishy-washy to employees who need more definitive direction.

- *Make it easy to communicate.* Encouraging employees to eat together at large lunch tables, allowing employees to gather in conference rooms, having organizational picnics and athletic teams, and so on can help workers at all levels mix with one another.

- *Ask employees what is important to them.* Managers should not wait until the exit interview to ask an employee, "What can I do to keep you?" At that point it is too late. Instead they should have frequent *stay interviews* to find out what matters to employees and what they can do to keep them on the job.[31]

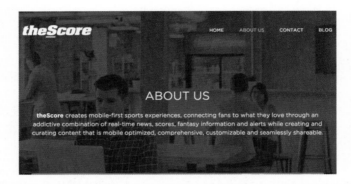

At theScore Inc. *<http://www.thescore.com>*, you can find employees in social workspaces. Employees can enjoy an outdoor terrace or lounge, complete with comfortable seating, television, video games, foosball, and table tennis.[30] Would you want to work for this digital sports media company?

Applying Open Communication in Self-Managed Teams

At Ford Motor Company, a group known as Team Mustang set the guidelines for how production teams should be formed. Given the challenge to create a car that would make people dust off their old "Mustang Sally" records and dance into showrooms, the 400-member team was also given the freedom to make decisions without waiting for approval from headquarters. Everyone worked under one roof in an old warehouse where drafting experts sat next to accountants, and engineers next to stylists. Budgetary walls between departments were knocked down as department managers were persuaded to surrender some control over their subordinates on the team.

When the resulting Mustang convertible displayed shaking problems, engineers were so motivated to finish on time and under budget that they worked late into the night, sleeping on the floor when necessary. Senior Ford executives were tempted to intervene, but they stuck with their promise not to meddle. Working with suppliers, the team solved the shaking problem and still came in under budget and a couple of months early. The new car was a hit with drivers, and sales soared.[32]

To implement such teams, managers at most companies must reinvent work. This means respecting workers, providing interesting work, developing workers' skills, allowing autonomy, decentralizing authority, and rewarding good work. In the process of reinventing work, it is essential that managers behave ethically toward all employees. The Making Ethical Decisions box illustrates a problem managers may face when filling temporary positions.

In the car business nothing works like the "wow" factor. At Ford, the 400-member Team Mustang group was empowered to create the "wow" response for the company's sleek Mustang convertible. The work team, suppliers, company managers, and even customers worked together to make the Mustang a winner in the very competitive automobile market.

Making ETHICAL DECISIONS

Motivating Temporary Employees

Say that you work as a manager for Highbrow's, a rather prestigious department store. Each year, to handle the large number of holiday shoppers, you must hire temporary employees. Because of store policy and budget constraints, all temporaries must be discharged on January 10. As you interview prospective employees, however, you give the impression that the store will hire at least two new full-time retail salespeople for the coming year. You hope that this will serve to motivate the temporary workers and even foster some competition among them. You also instruct your permanent salespeople to reinforce the falsehood that good work during the holiday season is the path to full-time employment. Is this an ethical way to try to motivate your employees? What are the dangers of using a tactic such as this?

Job Recognition: Recognizing a Job Well Done

A recent survey indicated that 79 percent of employees who voluntarily left their jobs did so because of lack of appreciation.[33] Letting people know you appreciate their work is usually more powerful than giving a raise or bonus alone.[34] When 8,000 recent graduates were asked what was most important to them as they were deciding where to work, salary was not the ultimate motivator. Yes, they needed enough money to cover their basic needs; however, the majority of participants rated career advancement opportunities as well as interesting and challenging work to be the most important things.[35] Clearly, providing advancement opportunities is important in attracting and retaining valuable employees.

Promotions are not the only way to celebrate a job well done. Recognition can be as simple as noticing positive actions out loud, making employees feel their efforts are worthwhile and valued enough to be noticed. For example: "Sarina, you didn't say much in the meeting today. Your ideas are usually so valuable; I missed hearing them." This comment lets Sarina know her ideas are appreciated, and she will be more likely to participate fully in the next meeting.

Travelocity's Gnomie Award, based on the company's mascot, the travelling gnome, is given to employees nominated by their peers for outstanding performance. Winners receive a $750 travel voucher, a paid day off, recognition at the company's quarterly meeting, and a golden gnome. What part do you think these awards play in motivating the winners to continue their outstanding performance?

Here are just a few examples of ways managers have raised employee spirits without raising paycheques:

- FedEx Office <*http://www.fedexoffice.ca*> sent high-achieving employees to Disneyland *and* put the company's top executives in those employees' places while they were gone.

- Give More Media <*http://www.givemoremedia.com*> offers perks like Netflix and XM Satellite Radio memberships. It also encourages participation in its Smile and Give program, which gives employees three paid days off to work for non-profit organizations of their choice.

- Hewlett-Packard (HP) bestows its Golden Banana Award for a job well done. The award started when an engineer burst into his manager's office saying he had found the solution to a long-standing problem. In his haste to find something to give the employee to show his appreciation, the manager grabbed a banana from his lunch and said, "Well done! Congratulations!" The Golden Banana is now one of the most prestigious honours awarded to an inventive HP employee.

Giving valued employees prime parking spots, more vacation days, or more flexible schedules may help them feel their work is appreciated, but sometimes nothing inspires workers like the prospect of a payout down the road. Companies that offer a small equity stake or stock options often have a good chance of developing loyal employees. The Spotlight on Small Business offers examples of what a number of small businesses have done to motivate employees.

The same things do not motivate all employees. Next we'll explore how employees from different cultures and generations are motivated.

Spotlight *On* SMALL BUSINESS

Motivators for Small Businesses

The competition to attract and retain top notch workers is "job one" for all businesses big or small. But how can small companies compete against the likes of Apple and Amazon? Wouldn't any talented person choose to work for one of these big name employers that offer such perks as onsite gourmet meals, putting greens, gymnasiums, and massages?

It's true small businesses cannot offer the money, benefits, or glory of working for one of the corporate heavyweights. But they can offer more intangible benefits such as collaborative management, less bureaucracy, more work–life balance, a sense of independence, and sometimes even potential ownership. Many small businesses strive to create an upbeat, relaxed company culture that encourages employees to bond with one another rather than compete against each other for the next promotion. By instilling the idea that the business's culture belongs to the employees, culture can equal perks, fun, and happiness. Small businesses also can take advantage of motivating employees with open communication and broad responsibility on the job. Individual workers can have more say in the company and not feel like just another drone in a giant corporate beehive.

This doesn't mean small businesses can't also try their hand at the innovative perks department. Vigilant Global <*http://www.vigilantglobal.com/*> provides free breakfast and lunch to its staff, "smoothie stations," and two games rooms. At Sparta Systems <*http://www.spartasystems.com*> employees are invited to step away from their desks and engage in video and board games. Bigcommerce <*https://www.bigcommerce.com*> offers employees a weekly boot camp with a certified trainer. Zoosk <*https://www.zoosk.com*> invites employees to bring their dogs to work. Not only do businesses hope these methods help employees bond with their colleagues, they also hope they become productive workers. Do you think such workplaces might appeal to you? Why?

Sources: "Canada's 100 Best Small & Medium Employers - Eat well: Vigilant Global goes all-out on perks," *The Globe and Mail* and Mediacorp Canada Inc., March 2015, 61; Michael Fertik, "How to Cultivate the Culture That Makes Your Company Succeed," *Inc.,* February 2014; Laura Garnett, "3 Questions That Will Motivate Your Employees," *Inc.,* February 2014; and Gene Marks, "Startup Perks WalMart and Amazon Can Never Offer," *Entrepreneur,* 22 October 2013.

Progress Assessment

- Explain job-enrichment theory.

- What procedures can firms implement to encourage open communication?

- List examples of ways managers can improve motivation without raising paycheques.

Show how managers personalize motivation strategies to appeal to employees around the globe and across generations.

Personalizing Motivation

Managers cannot use one motivational formula for all employees. They have to get to know each worker personally and tailor the motivational effort to the individual. This is further complicated by the increase in global business and the fact that managers now work with employees from a variety of cultural backgrounds. Cultural differences also exist between generational cohorts raised in the same country. Let's look at how managers personalize their strategies to appeal to employees around the globe and across generations.

There's no magic formula to successfully motivating every worker. Each generation of employees has different attitudes about what is important to them in seeking a balance between a successful career and happy private life. What expectations do you have of your potential supervisor and company?

Motivating Employees Around the Globe

Different cultures experience motivational approaches differently; therefore, managers study and understand these cultural factors in designing a reward system. In a *high-context culture*, workers build personal relationships and develop group trust before focusing on tasks. In a *low-context culture*, workers often view relationship building as a waste of time that diverts attention from the task. Koreans, Thais, and Saudis tend to be high-context workers who may view their North American colleagues as insincere due to their need for data and quick decision making (low-context culture).

Dow Chemical <*http://www.dow.com*> solved a cross-cultural problem with a recognition program for its 54,000 employees in over 36 countries who use a wide variety of languages and currencies. Globo-force Ltd. <*http://www.globoforce.com*> created a web-based program for Dow called Recognition@Dow that automatically adjusts for differences created by cultural preferences, tax laws, and even local standards of living. Thus a Canadian employee might receive a gift certificate for Canadian Tire, whereas a Chinese employee receives one for online retailer Dangdang.com. The system even allows employees to nominate colleagues for recognition using an "award wizard" to help determine the appropriate award.[36]

Understanding motivation in global organizations and building effective global teams is still a new task for most companies. Developing group leaders who are culturally astute, flexible, and able to deal with ambiguity is a challenge businesses face in the twenty-first century. See the Reaching Beyond Our Borders box for more about managing culturally diverse employees.

Reaching *Beyond* OUR BORDERS

Beyond Just Knowing Cross-Cultural Differences

As companies today become more global and employees more diverse than ever before, managers are well aware of their need to develop cross-cultural competencies. This means not only understanding different languages, but also understanding different food choices, customs, how people want to be addressed, how much space should be between people, and particularly, how employees expect to be managed.

Many companies do a respectable job in developing cultural intelligence in managers before they move to different global assignments. For example, IBM works closely with leaders in business, government, academia, and community organizations before entering a new market. Why then do seasoned managers, who appreciate diversity and are schooled in cross-cultural differences, often have problems motivating employees in their new global environment?

According to Professor Andrew Molinsky of Brandeis University's International Business School, the problems occur because of what he refers to as "cultural code-switching." This problem appears when managers are aware of how they should approach and deal with global employees, but deep down they lack the ability to adapt their behaviour to the situation. When this happens, their behaviour seems unauthentic to global employees, and therefore not effective. An example would be an American executive giving feedback to Japanese employees. The American's natural style is to "tell-it-like-it-is," but Japanese workers expect a much more indirect approach. That may be difficult for the American to do. What managers need to develop is "global dexterity," the ability to shift one's own cultural behaviour in a way that's effective and appropriate in the global setting. It always helps to know what to do, but it's even more important to know how to do it.

Sources: Samuel J. Palmisano, "The Former CEO of IBM on Working at a Global Scale," *Fast Company*, 10 April 2014; Dan Schawbel, "Andy Molinsky: How to Adapt to Cultural Changes in Foreign Countries," *Forbes*, 10 April 2013; and Andrew Molinsky, Thomas H. Davenport, Bala Iyer, and Cathy Davidson, "Three Skills Every 21st-Century Manager Needs," *Harvard Business Review*, February 2012.

Motivating Employees Across Generations[37]

Age is among the most frequently used demographic characteristic to determine the size and lifestyles of groups of individuals. The terms "cohort" and "generation" are often used interchangeably to refer to such groups. Determining the size of these groups is challenging as the year spans are widely debated. Figure 11.9, for example, contrasts two Canadian sources. Environics Research Group *<http://www.environics.ca>*, co-founded by Michael Adams, is a leading public opinion and market research firm. David Foot, Professor Emeritus of Economics at the University of Toronto, and founder of Footwork Consulting Inc. *<http://www.footwork.com>*, is a demographics expert. Foot explores how changing demographics is redefining society's needs. While Adams and Foot are best-selling authors, each has a different perspective on the impact of demographics. "Demography is not destiny," writes Adams. Contrast this with "Demographics explains about two-thirds of everything," according to Foot. For the purposes of this discussion, the Environics terms will be used.

■ **FIGURE 11.9**

	TWO EXAMPLES OF GENERATIONAL COHORT TERMS	
Year Born (Environics Research Group)	**Term**	**Year Born (Footwork Consulting Inc.)**
1946 to 1964	Baby Boomers	
	Baby Boomers	1947 to 1966
1965 to 1976	Generation X	
	Generation X (subset of Baby Boomers)	1961 to 1966
	Baby Bust	1967 to 1979
1977 to 1994	Generation Y / Millennials / Echo Boomers	
	The Baby-Boom Echo	1980 to 1995
1995 to Present	Generation Z	
	The Millennium Busters	1996 to 2010

Sources: Based on "Generations Variables - 2013," Environics Analytics, 2012, http://www.environicsanalytics.ca/docs/default-source/2014-variables/generations-variables—2013.pdf; and Colonel James C. Taylor, "Whither march the cohorts: The validity of generation theory as a determinant of the sociocultural values of Canadian Forces personnel," Canadian Forces College, June 2008, http://www.cfc.forces.gc.ca/259/281/280/taylor.pdf, 6.

Members in each generation are linked through shared life experiences in their formative years—usually the first 10 years of life. The beliefs that you accept as a child affect how you view risk and challenge, authority, technology, relationships, and economics. Companies need to understand each generational cohort because they have unique workplace expectations, needs, and goals and as a result, the management styles and recruiting techniques required to successfully engage with them will vary.[38]

Some generalities apply to these different groups. Baby Boomers were raised in families that experienced unprecedented economic prosperity, secure jobs, and optimism about the future. Gen Xers were raised in dual-career families with parents who focused on work. As children, some attended day care or became latchkey kids. (Latchkey kids are school-aged children of working parents who must spend part of the day unsupervised at home.[39]) Their parents' layoffs added to their insecurity about a lifelong job.

Across Canada, there are 10 million Millennials (also known as Gen Y), and they are forecasted to represent 75 percent of the Canadian workforce by the year 2028.[40] Millennials were raised by indulgent parents, and most do not remember a time without cell phones, computers, and electronic entertainment. Gen Z is also a big group; there are 2 billion worldwide, 7 million in Canada and 20 million in the United States.[41] They are growing up in an era of global economic turmoil and climate change. According to social researcher Mark McCrindle, "They are the most connected, educated, and sophisticated generation in history. They don't just represent the future, they are creating it."[42]

A constant in the lives of Gen Xers, Millennials, and Gen Zers is inconstancy. Consider the unprecedented change in the past 20 years in every area (e.g., economic, technological, scientific, social, and political). These groups expect change. It is the absence of change they find questionable.

Generational differences among these groups affect motivation in the workplace. Boomer managers need to be flexible with their Gen X and Millennial employees, or they will lose them. Gen X employees need to use their enthusiasm for change and streamlining to their advantage. Although many are unwilling to pay the same price for success their parents and grandparents did, their concern about undue stress and long hours does not mean they lack ambition. They want economic security as much as older workers, but they have a different approach to achieving it. Rather than focusing on job security, Gen Xers tend to focus on career security instead and are willing to change jobs to find it.

Future managers are influenced by their experiences as a child. When in a management position, these experiences can even affect who they hire, fire, or promote.

Many Gen Xers are now managers themselves, responsible for motivating other employees. In general, they are well equipped to motivate people. They usually understand that there is more to life than work, and they think a big part of motivating is letting people know you recognize that fact. Gen X managers tend to focus more on results than on hours in the workplace. They tend to be flexible and good at collaboration and consensus building. They often think in broader terms than their predecessors because the media has exposed them to problems around the world. They also have a big impact on their team members. They are more likely to give them the goals and outlines of the project and leave them alone to do their work.

Perhaps the best asset of Gen X managers is their ability to give employees feedback, especially positive feedback. One reason might be that they expect more of it themselves. One new employee was frustrated because he had not received feedback from his boss since he was hired—two weeks earlier. In short, managers need to realize that young workers demand performance reviews and other forms of feedback more than the traditional one or two times a year.

As a group, Millennials tend to share a number of characteristics: they're often impatient, skeptical, blunt, expressive, and image-driven. Like any other generation, they can transform their characteristics into unique skills. For example, Millennials tend to be adaptable, tech-savvy, able to grasp new concepts, practised at multitasking, efficient, and tolerant.[43] They tend to place a higher value on work–life balance, expect their employers to adapt to them (not the other way around), and are more likely to rank fun and stimulation in their top-five ideal job requirements.[44]

Many Millennials are not rushing to find lifetime careers after graduation. They tend to "job surf" and aren't opposed to living with their parents while they test out jobs. Some of this career postponement isn't by choice as much as a result of the state of the economy. The recession hurt younger workers more deeply than other workers. Today, Millennials are less likely to be employed than Gen Xers or Boomers were at the same age. Downturns in the economy have increased competition for jobs as younger workers struggle to enter the job market, Boomers try to make up lost retirement savings, and Gen Xers fight to pay mortgages and raise families. *The Gen Z and Gen Y Workplace Expectations Study,* counter to previous research, found that Millennials now prioritize money over meaningful work because the economy and student loans have forced them to do so.[45]

As Millennials assume more responsibility in the workplace, they sometimes must manage and lead others far older than themselves. How can young managers lead others who may have more experience than they do? Perhaps the three most important things to keep in mind are to be confident, to be open-minded, and to solicit feedback regularly.[46] Just remember that asking for input and advice is different from asking for permission or guidance.

Each generation is motivated by different things. Companies need to provide mentoring, feedback, and meaningful projects if they want to reach Gen Z and retain them.[47] What does effective mentoring and feedback look like to you?

As Gen Zers begin to enter the workplace, they are likely to be more cautious and security-minded, but inspired to improve the world. Since they've seen the effects of an economic downturn first-hand, they are more aware of troubling times. Given the young nature of this cohort (between 0 to 20 years of age when this chapter was written), research is not conclusive as Gen Zers are still developing. A study titled, *Meet Generation Z: Forget everything you learned about Millennials,* reported that 60 percent of Gen Zers want jobs that have a social impact, compared with 31 percent of Millennials. It called Gen Zers entrepreneurial (72 percent want to start their own businesses), community-oriented (26 percent already volunteer), and prudent (56 percent said they were savers, not spenders). Gen Z is also seen to be more tolerant than Millennials of racial, sexual, and generational diversity, and less likely to subscribe to traditional gender roles.[48]

The Gen Z and Gen Y Workplace Expectations Study found that Gen Z appears to be more entrepreneurial, loyal, open-minded, and less motivated by money than Millennials. (The latter could be that Gen Z has not experienced workforce challenges to the extent of the earlier cohort.) The study confirms that Canadian Gen Zers want their managers to engage them to do their best work by assigning meaningful projects, while secondly serving as mentors and providing regular feedback so that they have a better transition into the work force. Gen Z can also be defined by its potential loyalty to future employers. While Millennials expect to work for five companies in their lifetime, Gen Zers expect to work for fewer than four. In response, companies should stress the benefits of loyalty and longevity and reward those who serve longer and accomplish more.[49]

Gen Z may be more entrepreneurial than Millennials due to the amount of information and people accessible at a younger age. Is there more pressure on this generation to succeed? What might success mean for Gen Z?

It is important for managers of all ages to be aware that employees of different generations communicate differently. The Traditionalists, the generation that lived through the Great Depression and World War II, prefer to communicate face-to-face. Their second choice is by phone, but recordings often frustrate them. Boomers generally prefer to communicate in meetings or conference calls. Gen Xers generally prefer e-mail and will choose meetings only if there are no other options. Millennials most often use technology to communicate, particularly through social media.[50] How do you think Gen Z prefers to communicate?

In every generational shift, the older generation tends to say the same thing about the new: "They break the rules." The Traditionalists said it of the Baby Boomers. Boomers look at Gen Xers and say, "Why are they breaking the rules?" And now Gen Xers are looking at Millennials and Gen Zers and saying, "What's wrong with these kids?" And you know that this will be the same for the next generation someday.

One thing in business is likely to remain constant: much motivation will come from the job itself rather than from external punishments or rewards. Managers need to give workers what they require to do a good job: the right tools, the right information, and the right amount of co-operation. Motivation does not have to be difficult. It begins with acknowledging a job well done—and especially doing so in front of others. After all, as we said earlier, the best motivator is frequently a sincere "Thanks, I really appreciate what you're doing."

Progress Assessment

- What is the difference between a high-context culture and a low-context culture?

- Compare how motivation strategies may differ for Millennials versus Gen Zers.

- Why is it important to adjust motivational styles to individual employees? Are there any general principles of motivation that today's managers should follow?

SUMMARY

LO1 **Explain Taylor's theory of scientific management, and describe the Hawthorne studies and their significance to management.**

Human efficiency engineer Frederick Taylor was one of the first people to study management and has been called the father of scientific management. He conducted time-motion studies to learn the most efficient way of doing a job and then trained workers in those procedures.

What led to the more human-based managerial styles?

The greatest impact on motivation theory was generated by the Hawthorne studies in the late 1920s and early 1930s. In these studies, Elton Mayo found that human factors such as feelings of involvement and participation led to greater productivity gains than did physical changes in the workplace.

LO2 **Identify the levels of Maslow's hierarchy of needs and apply them to employee motivation. Contrast this with the motivators and hygiene factors identified by Herzberg.**

Abraham Maslow studied basic human motivation and found that motivation was based on needs. He said that a person with an unfilled need would be motivated to satisfy it and that a satisfied need no longer served as motivation.

What levels of need did Maslow identify?

Starting at the bottom of Maslow's hierarchy of needs and going to the top, the levels of need are physiological, safety, social, esteem, and self-actualization.

How can managers use Maslow's theory?

Managers can recognize what unmet needs a person has and design work so that it satisfies those needs.

What is the difference between Frederick Herzberg's motivators and hygiene factors?

Herzberg found that while some factors motivate workers (motivators), others cause job dissatisfaction if missing but are not motivators if present (hygiene or maintenance factors).

What are the factors called motivators?

The work itself, achievement, recognition, responsibility, growth, and advancement are motivators.

What are the hygiene (maintenance) factors?

Company policies, supervision, working conditions, interpersonal relations, and salary are examples of hygiene factors.

LO3 **Differentiate between McGregor's Theory X and Theory Y.**

Douglas McGregor held that managers will have one of two opposing attitudes toward employees. They are called Theory X and Theory Y.

What is Theory X?

Theory X assumes that the average person dislikes work and will avoid it if possible. Therefore, people must be forced, controlled, and threatened with punishment to accomplish organizational goals.

What is Theory Y?

Theory Y makes entirely different assumptions about people. It assumes that people like working and will accept responsibility for achieving goals if rewarded for doing so.

LO4 Explain the key principles of goal setting, expectancy, reinforcement, and equity theories.

More modern motivation theories include goal setting, expectancy, reinforcement, and equity theories.

What is goal setting theory?

Goal-setting theory is based on the notion that setting ambitious but attainable goals will lead to high levels of motivation and performance if the goals are accepted, accompanied by feedback, and facilitated by organizational conditions. Management by objectives (MBO) is a system of goal setting and implementation. It includes a cycle of discussion, review, and evaluation by objectives among top and middle-level managers, supervisors, and employees.

What are the key elements involved in expectancy theory?

According to Victor Vroom's expectancy theory, employee expectations can affect an individual's motivation. Expectancy theory centres on three questions employees often ask about performance on the job: (1) Can I accomplish the task? (2) If I do accomplish it, what is my reward? and (3) Is the reward worth the effort?

What are the variables in reinforcement theory?

Positive reinforcers are rewards like praise, recognition, or pay raises that a worker might strive to receive after performing well. Negative reinforcers are punishments such as reprimands, pay cuts, layoffs, or firing that a worker might be expected to try to avoid.

According to equity theory, employees try to maintain equity between inputs and outputs compared to other employees in similar positions. What happens when employees perceive that their rewards are not equitable?

If employees perceive that they are under-rewarded, they will either reduce their effort or rationalize that it is not important. If they perceive that they are over-rewarded, they will either increase their effort to justify the higher reward in the future or rationalize by saying, "I'm worth it!" Inequity leads to lower productivity, reduced quality, increased absenteeism, and voluntary resignation.

LO5 Show how managers put motivation theories into action through such strategies as job enrichment, open communication, and job recognition.

Job enrichment describes efforts to make jobs more interesting.

What characteristics of work affect motivation and performance?

The job characteristics that influence motivation are skill variety, task identity, task significance, autonomy, and feedback.

Name two forms of job enrichment that increase motivation.

Job-enrichment strategies include job enlargement and job rotation.

How does open communication improve employee motivation?

Open communication helps both managers and employees understand the objectives and work together to achieve them.

How can managers encourage open communication?

Top managers can create an organizational culture that rewards listening, train supervisors and managers to listen, use effective questioning techniques, remove barriers to open communication, avoid vague and ambiguous communication, and actively make it easier for all to communicate.

What are some job recognition techniques that managers can consider?

Letting people know you appreciate their work is usually more powerful than giving a raise or bonus alone. Job recognition techniques can include noticing positive actions out loud, offering perks like Netflix memberships, and bestowing awards.

LO6 **Show how managers personalize motivation strategies to appeal to employees around the globe and across generations.**

Managers cannot use one motivational formula for all employees.

What is the difference between high-context and low-context cultures?

In high-context cultures people build personal relationships and develop group trust before focusing on tasks. In low-context cultures, people often view relationship building as a waste of time that diverts attention from the task.

How are Generation X managers likely to be different from their Baby Boomer predecessors?

Baby Boomers tend to be willing to work long hours to build their careers and often expect their subordinates to do likewise. Gen Xers may strive for a more balanced lifestyle and are likely to focus on results rather than on how many hours their teams work. Gen Xers tend to be better than previous generations at working in teams and providing frequent feedback. They are not bound by traditions that may constrain those who have been with an organization for a long time and are willing to try new approaches to solving problems.

What are some common characteristics of Millennials?

Millennials tend to be adaptable, tech-savvy, able to grasp new concepts, practised at multi-tasking, efficient, and tolerant. They often place a higher value on work–life balance, expect their employers to adapt to them, and are more likely to rank fun and stimulation in their top five ideal job requirements.

What will employers need to do to hire or engage with Gen Z?

Employers will need to emphasize incentives for loyalty and training and development over money. Companies need to provide mentoring, feedback, and meaningful projects if they want to reach Gen Z and retain these employees.

KEY TERMS

equity theory	job enlargement	motivators
expectancy theory	job enrichment	principle of motion economy
extrinsic reward	job rotation	reinforcement theory
goal-setting theory	management by objectives	scientific management
Hawthorne effect	(MBO)	time-motion studies
hygiene (maintenance) factors	Maslow's hierarchy of needs	
intrinsic reward	motivation	

CRITICAL THINKING

1. The textbook introduced you to the theory of scientific management. What do you think are problems that would arise as a result of breaking jobs into a series of discrete steps and treating people as cogs in a wheel? How can you motivate employees if this is how they are managed?

2. Look over Maslow's hierarchy of needs and try to determine where you are right now on the hierarchy. What needs of yours are not being met? How could a company go about meeting those needs and thus motivate you to work better and harder?

DEVELOPING WORKPLACE SKILLS

Key: ● **Team** ★ **Analytic** ▲ **Communication** ▢ **Technology**

★▲ 1. Talk with several of your friends about the subject of motivation. What motivates them to work hard or not work hard on projects in teams? How important is self-motivation to them?

★▲ 2. Speak to a manager in the workplace. Find out what this manager does to motivate his or her direct reports.

★▲ 3. Think of all of the groups with which you have been associated over the years—sports groups, friendship groups, and so on—and try to recall how the leaders of those groups motivated the group to action. What motivational tools were used and to what effect? Discuss your answers in class.

●★ 4. Partner with two of your classmates and discuss motivation. Herzberg concluded that pay was
▲ not a motivator. If you were paid to get better grades, would you be motivated to study harder? In your employment experiences, have you ever worked harder to obtain a raise or as a result of receiving a raise? Do you agree with Herzberg?

●★ 5. Partner with two of your classmates and discuss the recent managerial idea to let employees
▲ work in self-managed teams. There is no reason why such teams could not be formed in schools as well as businesses. Discuss the benefits and drawbacks of dividing your class into self-managed teams for the purpose of studying, completing assignments, and so forth.

ANALYZING MANAGEMENT DECISIONS

Motivation Tips for Tough Times

With company cutbacks, layoffs, and economic uncertainty weighing heavily on everybody, it is no wonder some employees are dragging their feet into work. But according to Steven Stein, Toronto-based psychologist and entrepreneur, there are ways to lift and maintain motivation, even in tough times. In *Make Your Workplace Great: The 7 Keys to an Emotionally Intelligent Organization,* he offers these valuable tips for motivating employees.

- *What motivates your workers.* You may be surprised to discover how small changes, such as those in job design or reporting systems, can motivate certain people. It might not take much, but the only way to discover what your employees want, and how they react to change, is to ask them.

- *Offer ongoing feedback.* No time is better than now to open up lines of communication with your employees, if you have not already. Whether you offer feedback formally or informally, it is important to regularly let your staff know how they are doing, where they are performing well, and where there is room for improvement.

- *Emphasize personal accountability.* Self-management can be highly motivating, and if you are short-staffed, it can make a lot of sense, too. Most people will work much harder for their own sense of accomplishment than they will because they were told to do something.

- *Involve everyone in decision making.* By involving workers in certain company decisions, especially those that involve them directly, you are much more likely to get support for your initiatives. And you may even get some creative input along the way as your front-line staff might have knowledge about the impact of certain decisions that you may not be aware of.

- *Be flexible.* Time is an important commodity for people today, especially if they are taking on more work than usual. By giving your employees the opportunity to juggle their time around critical personal or family events and responsibilities, you will increase their motivation.

- *Celebrate employee and company success.* It is important to stop and recognize successes, whether individual, team, or organizational. Let everybody see that hard work is recognized and worth carrying out.

Source: "Great Ideas: Motivation Tips for Tough Times," *PROFIT*, 4 June 2009, www.canadianbusiness.com/entrepreneur/human_resources/article .jsp?content=20090603_115416_7820; "Business Owners Try to Motivate Employees," and *The Wall Street Journal*, 14 January 2012, http://online.wsj .com/article/SB10001424052748704362004575000911063526360.html.

Discussion Questions

1. What other suggestions might you add to this list?

2. If you are employed now (or have been in the past), how has your supervisor motivated you? If you have never been employed before, how might a supervisor motivate you?

3. Apply each one of these tips to group work. How might you implement these suggestions so that group members, including yourself, are motivated to do well in the assigned work?

VIDEO CASE 11

Appletree Answers

Service industries strive to relieve their customers' anxieties, but often those stresses are transferred to the service employees. For example, help desk call-centre workers face so much tension that turnover rates can reach as high as 125 percent per year. That amounts to a loss of every employee plus a quarter of their replacements in a single year. Since finding new people to fill all those positions can be expensive, the savviest companies look for ways to motivate their employees to be productive and happy so that they choose to stick around for a while.

John Ratliff of Appletree Answers *<http://www.appletreeanswers.com>*, a company that provides call-centre and receptionist services for other businesses, was able to expand his company from a one-man operation to a thriving business with 650 employees at more than 20 locations. Appletree supports clients ranging from sole proprietors to Fortune 500 companies in every industry imaginable.

Early in its growth, however, Appletree suffered the same high turnover rate that is common in the call-centre industry. Ratliff decided to restructure the business to focus on employee satisfaction and wellness. First, he developed a new set of company principles that encouraged staffers to "think like a customer" and "take care of each other." In order to accommodate his largely Generation Y employees, Ratliff instituted flexible schedules and arranged for additional training programs. Ratliff also encourages employees to submit ideas regarding the company's projects. A desktop app called Idea Flash lets staffers send their suggestions to executives, further enriching the job experience.

In his quest to turn his company around, Ratliff discovered that some of his employees struggled with problems such as serious illnesses, financial hardships, and even homelessness. To combat these crises, he created the Dream On program to provide personalized motivation that doesn't come in a standard paycheque. Similar to the Make a Wish Foundation, Dream On strives to help make selected employees' "dreams" come true, whether it is a trip to the Walt Disney World Resort for a sick child or a luxury honeymoon for a loyal worker.

Working in this newly fulfilling environment had a profound effect on Appletree's staff. No longer just seat fillers, their personal commitment to the company became an integral part of its goals and culture. Because of all this positive reinforcement, Appletree staffers are not only more willing to stay at their jobs, but they also perform their tasks with more energy and effort. John Ratliff's unique approach gives his company a leg up on the industry while still caring deeply for his employees. That's known as a "win–win."

Discussion Questions

1. Why is employee turnover so costly for companies?

2. How did John Ratliff increase employee motivation by understanding and adapting the motivational theories discussed in the chapter? Which theory do you think is most appropriate?

3. How did the Dream On program motivate workers and help build stability within the organization?

Human Resource Management: Finding and Keeping the Best Employees

LEARNING OBJECTIVES

After you have read and studied this chapter, you should be able to:

LO1 Explain the importance of human resource management as a strategic contributor to organizational success, and summarize the five steps in human resource planning.

LO2 Describe methods that companies use to recruit new employees, and explain some of the issues that make recruitment challenging.

LO3 Outline the five steps in selecting employees, and illustrate the use of various types of employee training and development methods.

LO4 Trace the six steps in appraising employee performance, and summarize the objectives of employee compensation programs.

LO5 Describe the ways in which employees can move through a company: promotion, reassignment, termination, and retirement.

LO6 Illustrate the effects of legislation on human resource management.

PROFILE

GETTING TO KNOW LINDA HASENFRATZ, CHIEF EXECUTIVE OFFICER OF LINAMAR CORPORATION

In today's business world the prospect of lifetime employment at a single company is becoming increasingly unlikely. Thanks to a sluggish economy and never-ending technological innovation, workers no longer have much of a chance to stay in one place until their retirement. As staff sizes rise and fall with the global marketplace, many companies continue to require a skilled and flexible workforce of people. Workers in turn may require specialized training and flexible schedules to help balance work and life.

Source: Courtesy Linamar Corporation.
Used with permission.

Linamar Corporation *<http://www.linamar.com>*, Canada's second-largest auto-parts maker, is a worldwide leader in the design, development, and production of highly engineered products. This includes precision metallic products for powertrain systems (such as engines, transmissions, gears, and camshafts) and the Skyjack brand aerial work platforms that supply the construction industry. The company has more than 19,500 employees in 14 countries in North and South America, Europe, and Asia. Linamar generated sales of $4.2 billion in 2014 with a goal to grow to $10 billion by 2024.

Founded by Frank Hasenfratz in the 1960s, daughter Linda Hasenfratz became the CEO in 2002 after rotating through various positions throughout the company. She started on the shop floor running a machine and learning the business from the bottom up. Linda then worked in different plants, and in different areas such as engineering, accounting, estimating, quality assurance, and factory management. This was followed by five years as an executive. Under her leadership, she has quadrupled the company's size, which is the result of double-digit annual growth. This is all during a decade that has been described as both the best and the worst in the automotive industry. Such growth requires skilled workers to run the company's 48 manufacturing locations, 5 R&D centres, and 15 sales offices around the world. Let's consider some of Linamar's human resource practices.

Former Guelph Chamber of Commerce president, Lloyd Longfield, reacted with some concern to the company's expansion announcement that 1,200 new jobs would be created in Guelph by 2024. The city has the second-lowest unemployment rate in Ontario and a skills gap in the area. Work to narrow the skills gap problem includes promoting a skills matching program with the Ontario Chamber of Commerce and Ryerson University to help match businesses to the right potential employees. Hasenfratz 's response to such concerns is that Linamar will likely fill most of these positions internally as the company does a lot of work to train current employees. After this, it will consider local opportunities. While Linamar has "occasionally used the temporary foreign worker program to find skilled people abroad when we weren't able to fill our needs internally or elsewhere in Canada," she believes that it is "unlikely" that the company will use the temporary foreign worker program to fill the new positions.

A five-year management-training program develops promising employees to become plant general managers. After a rigorous screening process, trainees spend two years rotating in different departments, then another three years in mid-level management positions that expose them to materials, accounting, and quality management. The program aims to mirror an entrepreneur's experience. Says Hasenfratz, "As an entrepreneur, you initially have to do everything: You are the salesperson, the person running the machine, the delivery person. As a consequence, you become very familiar with the company."

Hasenfratz's focus on innovation, financial performance, and her ability to find opportunities during a recession contributed to her recognition as the first female EY Entrepreneur of the Year. "I'm a big believer in the competitiveness of our manufacturers," says Hasenfratz. "I think we have an incredible employee base in Canada—skilled trades, engineers, machinists, metallurgists, technologists, quality assurance— great technical people who have the ability to innovate, which is the key to competitiveness."

In this chapter, you will learn how businesses of all sizes recruit, manage, and make the most of their employees. Training and development programs like the ones at Linamar are just one important area of human resource management.

Sources: "Linamar Delivers Record 2014 Sales & Earnings on Nearly 50% Earnings Growth," Linamar Inc., 4 March 2015, http://www.linamar.com/sites/default/files/q4_2014 _press_release.pdf; May Warren, "Who will get Linamar's 1,200 new Guelph jobs?" *The Hamilton Spectator*, 18 January 2015, http://www.thespec.com/news-story/5263902-who -will-get-linamar-s-1-200-new-guelph-jobs-/; Joanna Pachner, "A Second-Generation Success Story: Linda Hasenfratz at Linamar," PROFITguide.com, 15 January 2015, http:// www.profitguide.com/manage-grow/leadership/a-second-generation-success-story-linda-hasenfratz-at-linamar-73054/3; "About," Linamar Inc., 2015, http://www.linamar .com/about-linamar; Mary Teresa Bitti, "Linamar chief Linda Hasenfratz continues to prove she belongs at the top," *Financial Post*, 15 December 2014, http://business .financialpost.com/2014/12/15/linamar-chief-linda-hasenfratz-continues-to-prove-she-belongs-at-the-top/; and Joanna Pachner, "Linda Hasenfratz's bet on auto manufacturing is paying off—big time," *Canadian Business*, 27 November 2014, http://www.canadianbusiness.com/lists-and-rankings/richest-people/linda-hasenfratz-linamar-ceo/.

LO1 Explain the importance of human resource management as a strategic contributor to organizational success, and summarize the five steps in human resource planning.

Working with People Is Just the Beginning

Students often say they want to go into human resource management because they want to "work with people." Human resource managers do work with people, but they are also deeply involved in planning, record keeping, and other administrative duties. To begin a career in human resource management, you need to develop a better reason than "I want to work with people." This chapter will discuss what else human resource management is all about.

Human resource management is the process of determining human resource needs and then recruiting, selecting, developing, motivating, evaluating, compensating, and scheduling employees to achieve organizational goals (see Figure 12.1). For many years, human resource management was called "personnel" and involved clerical functions such as screening applications, keeping records, processing the payroll, and finding new employees when necessary. The roles and responsibilities of human resource management have evolved primarily because of two key factors: (1) organizations' recognition of employees as their ultimate resource and (2) changes in laws that rewrote many traditional practices. We will explore the first key factor next and end the chapter considering how laws affect human resource management.

> **human resource management**
> The process of determining human resource needs and then recruiting, selecting, developing, motivating, evaluating, compensating, and scheduling employees to achieve organizational goals.

■ **FIGURE 12.1**

HUMAN RESOURCE MANAGEMENT

As this figure shows, human resource management is more than hiring and firing personnel. All activities are designed to achieve organizational goals within the laws that affect human resource management. (Note that human resource management includes motivation, as discussed in Chapter 11, and employee–management relations, which will be discussed in Chapter 13.)

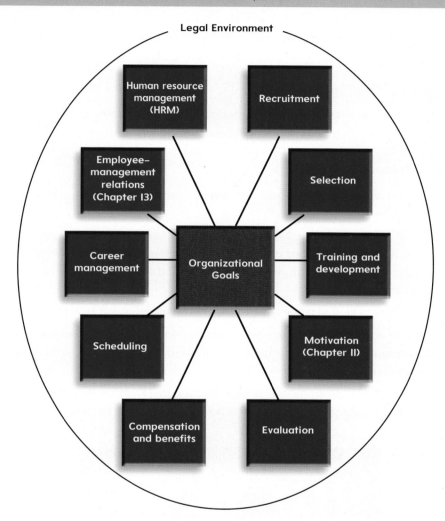

Developing the Ultimate Resource

One reason human resource management is receiving increased attention is the major shift from traditional manufacturing industries to service and high-tech manufacturing industries that require highly technical job skills. This shift means that many workers must be retrained for new, more challenging jobs. They truly are the ultimate resource. People develop the ideas that eventually become the products that satisfy consumers' wants and needs. Take away their creative minds and leading firms such as Cirque du Soleil, Linamar, Apple, and Disney would be nothing.

In the past, human resources were plentiful, so there was little need to nurture and develop them. If you needed qualified people, you simply hired them. If they did not work out, you fired them and found others. Most firms assigned the job of recruiting, selecting, training, evaluating, compensating, motivating, and, yes, firing people to the functional departments that employed them, such as accounting and marketing. Today, the job of human resource management has taken on an increased role in the firm since *qualified* employees are scarcer, which makes recruiting and retaining people more important and more difficult.[1]

In the future, human resource management may become the firm's most critical function, responsible for dealing with all aspects of a business's most critical resource—people. In fact, the human resource function has become so important that it is no longer the responsibility of just one department; it is a responsibility of *all* managers. What are some human resource challenges all managers face? We'll outline a few next.

Human Resource Challenges

Many of the changes that have had the most dramatic impact on business are the changes in the labour force. The ability to compete in global markets depends on new ideas, new products and services, and new levels of productivity. In other words, on people with good ideas. These are some of the challenges and opportunities in human resources (HR):

- Shortages of trained workers in growth areas, such as computer technology, biotechnology, robotics, green technology, and the sciences.

- Large numbers of skilled and unskilled workers from declining industries, such as steel and automobiles, who are unemployed or underemployed and need retraining. *Underemployed workers* are those who have more skills or knowledge than their current jobs require or those with part-time jobs who want to work full-time.

- A shortage of workers in skilled trades due to the retirement of aging Baby Boomers.[2]

- An increasing number of Baby Boomers who, due to downturns in the economy, delay retirement (preventing the promotion of younger workers) or move to lower-level jobs (increasing the supply of workers for such jobs).

- An increasing number of both single-parent and two-income families, resulting in a demand for job sharing, parental leave, and special career advancement programs for women.

Firms face a shortage of workers skilled in areas like science, robotics, and the development of clean energy sources like these solar panels. What other job markets do you think will grow as companies focus more on environmentally friendly policies? Which ones appeal to you?

- A shift in employee attitudes toward work. Leisure time has become a much higher priority, as have flextime and a shorter workweek.

- A declining economy that is taking a toll on employee morale as well as increasing the demand for temporary and part-time workers.[3]

- A challenge from overseas labour pools whose members work for lower wages and are subject to fewer laws and regulations than Canadian workers. This results in jobs being outsourced overseas.

- An increased demand for benefits tailored to the individual, yet still cost-effective to the company.

- Growing concerns over health care, elder care, child care, and opportunities for people with disabilities.

- A decreased sense of employee loyalty, which raises employee turnover and consequently the cost of replacing lost workers.

Given the issues mentioned, and others that are sure to develop, you can see why human resource management has taken a more central position in management thinking than ever before. While the HR challenges are greater than ever before, so too are the opportunities for companies to excel through their HR strategies.

Determining Your Human Resource Needs

All management, including human resource management, begins with planning. The five steps in the human resource planning process are:

1. *Preparing a human resource inventory of the organization's employees.* This inventory should include ages, names, education, capabilities, training, specialized skills, and other relevant information (e.g., languages spoken). It reveals whether the labour force is technically up to date and thoroughly trained.[4]

2. *Preparing a job analysis.* A **job analysis** is a study of what is done by employees who hold various job titles. It is necessary to recruit and train employees with the necessary skills to do the job. The results of job analysis are two written statements: job descriptions and job specifications. A **job description** specifies the objectives of the job, the type of work to be done, the responsibilities and duties, the working conditions, and the relationship of the job to other functions. **Job specifications** are a written summary of the minimum qualifications (e.g., education and skills) required of workers to do a particular job. In short, job descriptions are statements about the job, whereas job specifications are statements about the person who does the job. See Figure 12.2 for hypothetical examples of a job description and job specifications.

job analysis
A study of what is done by employees who hold various job titles.

job description
A summary of the objectives of a job, the type of work to be done, the responsibilities and duties, the working conditions, and the relationship of the job to other functions.

job specifications
A written summary of the minimum qualifications required of workers to do a particular job.

3. *Assessing future human resource demand.* Because technology changes rapidly, effective human resource managers are proactive; that is, they forecast the organization's requirements and train people ahead of time or ensure trained people are available when needed.

■ **FIGURE 12.2**

JOB ANALYSIS
A job analysis yields two important statements: job descriptions and job specifications. Here you have a job description and job specifications for a sales representative position.

Job Analysis
Observe current sales representatives doing the job. Discuss job with sales managers. Have current sales resentatives keep a diary of their activities.

Job Description	Job Specifications
Primary objective is to sell the company's products to stores in Territory D. Duties include servicing accounts and maintaining positive relationships with clients. Responsibilities include: • introducing the new products to store managers in the area • helping the store managers estimate the volume to order • negotiating prime shelf space • explaining sales promotion activities to store managers • stocking and maintaining shelves in stores that wish such service	Characteristics of the ideal person qualifying for this job include: • bilingual • self-motivated • positive attitude • strong written and communication skills • have a valid driver's licence • two years of sales experience • a diploma or degree in Business

4. *Assessing future human resource supply.* The labour force is constantly shifting: getting older, becoming more technically oriented, and attracting more women and immigrants. Some workers will be scarcer in the future, like biomedical engineers and robotic repair workers, and others will be oversupplied, like assembly-line workers.

5. *Establishing a strategic plan.* The plan must address recruiting, selecting, training, developing, appraising, compensating, and scheduling the labour force. Because the first four steps lead up to this one, we'll focus on them in the rest of the chapter.

Some companies use advanced technology to perform the human resource planning process more efficiently. For example, IBM manages its global workforce of about 100,000 employees and 100,000 subcontractors with a database that matches employee skills, experiences, schedules, and references with jobs available. The company also created a cloud-hosted software suite that's designed for automating and improving human resource tasks.[5] If a client in Nova Scotia has a month-long project requiring a consultant who can speak English and French, has an advanced degree in engineering, and has experience with Linux programming, IBM's database can find the best-suited consultant available and put him or her in touch with the client.

 Describe methods that companies use to recruit new employees, and explain some of the issues that make recruitment challenging.

Recruiting Employees from a Diverse Population

Recruitment is the set of activities for obtaining the right number of qualified people at the right time. Its purpose is to select those who best meet the needs of the organization. You might think a continuous flow of new people into the workforce makes recruiting easy. On the contrary, recruiting has become very difficult, for several reasons:

- Some organizations have policies that demand promotions from within, operate under collective labour agreements (to be discussed in Chapter 13), or offer low wages, which makes recruiting and keeping employees difficult or subject to outside influence and restrictions.

- There are legal guidelines that surround hiring practices. The Canadian Human Rights Act requires that employers provide equal employment opportunities. For example, a human rights complaint could be made if an employer said that he would not hire a woman or a visible minority for a particular job, regardless of that person's competency. The Canadian Human Rights Act protects those that work for federally regulated organizations or service providers (e.g., chartered banks and airlines). Other employees are protected by provincial or territorial jurisdiction.

- An emphasis on corporate culture, teamwork, and participative management makes it important to hire people who not only are skilled but also fit in with the culture and leadership style of the organization.

- Sometimes people with the necessary skills are not available; consequently, workers must be hired and then trained internally.[6] An example was shared in the profile.

recruitment
The set of activities used to obtain a sufficient number of the right people at the right time.

Had the proposed Quebec Charter of Values become law, public workers would have been banned from wearing conspicuous symbols that indicate religious affiliation such as turbans, kippahs, hijabs (shown above), and niqabs. Why do you think this proposal was so controversial? Does it infringe on the Canadian Charter of Rights and Freedoms which encourages Canadians to maintain their mother tongue, traditions, and culture?

Human resource managers turn to many sources for assistance (see Figure 12.3). *Internal sources* include employees who are already within the firm (and may be transferred or promoted) and employees who can recommend others to hire. For example, Montreal, Quebec-based accounting firm Richter LLP *<http://www.richter.ca>* offers referral bonuses up to $4,000 to employees when they successfully recruit a new candidate.[7] Using internal sources is less expensive than recruiting outside the company. The greatest advantage of hiring from within is that it helps maintain employee morale. Review the Making Ethical Decisions box for a dilemma that can apply to hiring from within.

■ **FIGURE 12.3**

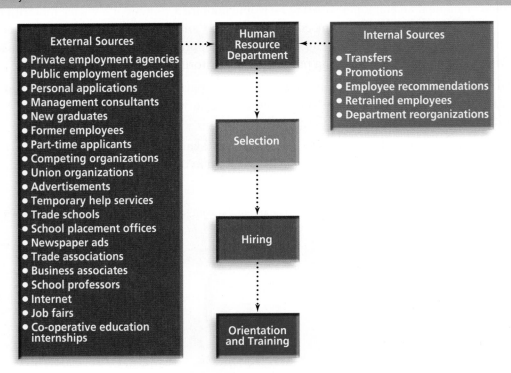

EMPLOYEE SOURCES

Internal sources are often given first consideration. So it is useful to get a recommendation from a current employee of the firm for which you want to work. School placement offices are also an important source. Be sure to learn about these services early so that you can plan an employment strategy throughout your academic career.

External Sources
- Private employment agencies
- Public employment agencies
- Personal applications
- Management consultants
- New graduates
- Former employees
- Part-time applicants
- Competing organizations
- Union organizations
- Advertisements
- Temporary help services
- Trade schools
- School placement offices
- Newspaper ads
- Trade associations
- Business associates
- School professors
- Internet
- Job fairs
- Co-operative education internships

Human Resource Department

Selection

Hiring

Orientation and Training

Internal Sources
- Transfers
- Promotions
- Employee recommendations
- Retrained employees
- Department reorganizations

It is not always possible to find qualified workers within the company, however, so human resource managers must use *external sources* such as advertisements, public and private employment agencies, school placement offices, management consultants, professional organizations, referrals, and online and walk-in applications. Management consulting firm McKinsey & Company *<http://www.mckinsey.com>* uses a database of 27,000 former consultants who left the firm in good standing as brand ambassadors and recruiters for the firm.[8]

Making ETHICAL DECISIONS

Recruiting Employees from Competitors

As the human resource director for Technocrat, Inc., it is your job to recruit the best employees. Your most recent human resource inventory indicates that Technocrat currently has an abundance of qualified designers and that several lower-level workers will soon be eligible for promotions to designer positions. Despite the surplus of qualified designers within the firm, you are considering recruiting a designer who is now with a major competitor. Your thinking is that the new employee will be a source of information about the competition's new products. What are your ethical considerations in this case? Will you lure the employee away from the competition even though you have no need for a designer? What will be the consequences of your decision?

Spotlight *On* SMALL BUSINESS

Competing for the Cream of the Crop

Most small business owners would agree that attracting top-quality employees is one of their major challenges. Unfortunately, competing for the cream of the crop is difficult when you can't afford expensive recruiters or pay gold-plated benefits to lure qualified workers. Despite these hurdles, small businesses can compete if they follow certain recruiting recommendations. Here are a few helpful tips:

- *Define who you are as a company.* Instead of describing what skills and experience are required of a prospective employee, start off by explaining what your company does and what its vision is all about. Quite often top-quality candidates will not agree to an interview until they know what the job is all about.
- *Build a strong staff referral program.* The more your current staff is engaged in the search and interview process, the better the chance to find recruits with the right personality and skills. Remember, no recruiter or website knows the organization's culture better than its employees.
- *Have future employees audition for the job.* Hiring workers first on a temporary basis or an internship allows you to test candidates before deciding whether to make an offer of permanent employment.
- *Look at your customers.* Loyal and informed customers can often be a source of potential employees. Build-A-Bear Workshop, for example, often hires customers who come into its stores and exhibit a real interest in the company and its products.
- *Become involved with community organizations.* Many community organizations have top-notch volunteers or employees who may be looking for a new opportunity. Also, don't forget non-profit organizations or agencies that welcome immigrants new to a region or people in need of a job who may be excellent candidates you can train.
- *Actively seek publicity and word-of-mouth to create a "buzz" for your company.* Publicity is more believable than advertising. Word-of-mouth is also a very effective recruiting tool. Building an image of a dynamic workplace with eager and energetic workers will attract others.
- *Make use of Internet services, social media, and local government agencies.* Recruiting on an online service like Monster.ca is cost efficient. Government employment services are free and social media creates opportunities to target key employee groups. While not as potent as staff referrals, all provide a source of reaching potential prize employees.

Sources: Marc Wayshak, "5 Things You Should Not Do When Hiring for Your Organization," *Entrepreneur*, 1 April 2014; Ritika Puri, "Four Ways Small Businesses Can Recruit Top Talent," *Forbes*, 18 February 2014; and Raj Sheth, "Small Business Advice: How to Establish a Recruiting Process and Develop a Culture," *The Washington Post*, 29 January 2014.

Rohit Gupta, president of Edmonton, Alberta based Rohit Group of Companies *<http://www .rohitgroup.com>* says the key to the company's success is the talented people it has managed to attract by utilizing a wide range of recruitment sources that include post-secondary institutions, industry associations, and online tools. "We know talented people like to be around other talented people," he says. "So retention is quite easy when you make sure you are bringing in the best people."[9]

At L'Oréal Canada, social media has been particularly successful when it comes to attracting students. "Everyone is digital nowadays," says VP Catherine Bédard, "but at L'Oréal we're going much further than just using LinkedIn—many of our employees are attracted from YouTube or Instagram. When we're at job fairs on campus, you have so many students coming to you with a C.V. and asking you to employ them. Instead of taking their résumé, we ask them to go on YouTube and post a clip explaining why they're such a good fit for L'Oréal and why they're interested in working for us." It's a win–win strategy—not only do the videos let the L'Oréal team see the creativity and eligibility of a student in a short clip, but as more videos make it online, the company's employer branding improves.[10]

Recruiting qualified workers may be particularly difficult for small businesses with few staff members and less-than-competitive compensation to attract external sources.[11] The Spotlight on Small Business box outlines some ways in which small businesses can recruit.

Some popular recruiting Internet sites include Workopolis.com, Monster.ca, CareerBuilder.ca, and Indeed.ca. Passion Inc. *<http://www.passioninc.ca>* was founded by brothers Mark and Nathan Laurie from their student residence with $500 in savings and the dream of graduating from Dalhousie University debt free. You may be familiar with Jobpostings.ca, one of Passion's divisions. It is promoted as Canada's premiere job-hunting resource for students and fresh grads. Online job boards advertise entry-level jobs, student jobs, internships, summer jobs, seasonal work, and co-op placements. You can also find specialty titles that include the Grad School Planning Guide, Career Planning Guide, DisAbility (a career magazine for students with disabilities), and Canada's Top Employers for Young People.[12]

Progress Assessment

- What is human resource management?
- What are the five steps in human resource planning?
- What factors make it difficult to recruit qualified employees?

LO3 Outline the five steps in selecting employees, and illustrate the use of various types of employee training and development methods.

Selecting Employees Who Will Be Productive

Selection is the process of gathering information and deciding who should be hired, under legal guidelines, to serve the best interests of the individual and the organization. Selecting and training employees are extremely expensive processes in some firms. Think of what is involved: interview time, medical exams in some instances, training costs, unproductive time spent learning the job, possible travel and moving expenses, and more. Calculating the cost-per-hire can get complicated and numbers vary, depending on the source. It can cost one and a half times the employee's annual salary to recruit, process, and train even an entry-level worker, and over six figures for a top manager.[13]

selection
The process of gathering information and deciding who should be hired, under legal guidelines, to serve the best interests of the individual and the organization.

A typical selection process involves five steps:

1. *Obtaining complete application forms.* Although employment laws limit the kinds of questions that may appear on an application form, applications help reveal the applicant's educational background, work experience, career objectives, and other qualifications directly related to the requirements of the job. Canada's Wonderland *<http://www.canadaswonderland.com>* receives over 28,000 applications for seasonal employment each year. With 4,000 positions to fill, a stringent screening process has been developed to select and hire candidates. All applications are individually screened and only those qualified will be granted an opportunity to move on to the interview stage of the process. Candidates who submit applications online receive automated e-mail responses that confirm that their applications have been successfully transmitted.[14]

2. *Conducting initial and follow-up interviews.* A staff member from the human resource department often screens applicants in a first interview. If the interviewer considers the applicant a potential employee, the manager who will supervise the new employee may interview the applicant as well. It is important that managers prepare adequately for the interview to avoid selection decisions they may regret.[15] No matter how innocent the intention, missteps such as asking about pregnancy or child care could later be evidence if that applicant files discrimination charges. In the past, an employer might have asked if the applicant had children to determine whether the applicant could work shift work or on weekends. Today, the applicant would be asked if working shift work or on weekends would be a problem (without asking about children), as this is a relevant job-related question.

3. *Giving employment tests.* Organizations often use tests to measure basic competency in specific job skills like welding or firefighting, and to help evaluate applicants' personalities and interests. The tests should always be directly related to the job. Many companies test potential employees in assessment centres, where applicants perform actual job tasks. Such testing can make the selection process more efficient and will generally satisfy legal requirements.

4. *Conducting background investigations.* Most organizations now investigate a candidate's work record, school record, credit history, and references more carefully than in the past to help identify

Depending on the job, it is not uncommon to be involved in several interviews, one of which might include a panel interview. How would you prepare differently if this was the case?

those most likely to succeed. It is simply too costly to hire, train, and motivate people only to lose them and have to start the process over. Services such as LexisNexis allow prospective employers to not only conduct speedy background checks of criminal records, driving records, and credit histories, but also to verify work experience and professional and educational credentials.[16] The Adapting to Change box discusses how companies use social media to screen job applicants and weed out those with undesirable traits.

5. *Establishing trial (probationary) periods.* Often, an organization will hire an employee conditionally to let the person prove his or her value on the job. After a specified probationary period (perhaps three months or a year), the firm can either permanently hire or discharge that employee on the basis of supervisors' evaluations. Although such systems make it easier to fire inefficient or problem employees, they do not eliminate the high cost of turnover.

Adapting *to* CHANGE

Keeping the Right Face on Social Media

Today, the Internet offers companies a gold mine of information concerning potential employees. Estimates are that three out of five organizations use social networking sites such as LinkedIn, Twitter, and Facebook to screen prospective hires and evaluate a person's fit with a company's culture. What this means to you is that your social-media footprint could be a selling tool in your job search—or could end up costing you a job.

What you do online goes into the virtual world and stays there. The online personality you project reflects to employers who you really are. The growing use of social-media background checks has created a new set of candidate disqualifiers. Some of the most flagrant violations that will put you in a company's reject pile include:

- Posting provocative or inappropriate photos
- Information about excessive drinking or using drugs
- Bad mouthing a previous employer
- Discriminatory comments related to race, gender, religion, etc.

It's best to use social media to your advantage. Many companies in fact admit to hiring a candidate because of the professional image he or she conveyed on social media. If you have reservations about posting something on a social-media site, the best advice is, don't.

Sources: Ed Zitron, "Social Media Habits of Highly Annoying People," *Inc.,* 7 February 2014; Kerry Hannon, "Social Media Can Cost You a Job: 6 Solutions," *Forbes,* 30 June 2013; and Leslie Kwoh, "Beware: Potential Employers Are Watching You," *The Wall Street Journal,* 29 October 2012.

The selection process is often long and difficult, but it is worth the effort to select new employees carefully because of the high cost of replacing them.[17] Care helps ensure that new employees meet all requirements, including communication skills, education, technical skills, experience, and personality. Finally, where a company has a collective labour agreement (a union contract with its employees) the selection process must also follow the provisions of that agreement. This is discussed in more detail in the next chapter.

Hiring Contingent Workers

A company with employment needs that vary—from hour to hour, day to day, week to week, and season to season—may find it cost-effective to hire contingent workers. **Contingent workers** are defined as workers who do not have regular, full-time employment. Such workers include part-time workers (according to Statistics Canada, this includes "employed persons who usually work less than 30 hours per week, at their main or only job"), temporary workers (workers paid by temporary employment agencies), seasonal workers, independent contractors, interns, and co-op students.

> **contingent workers**
> Workers who do not have regular, full-time employment.

Clear Stream Energy Services *<http://www.clearstreamenergy.ca>* in Sherwood Park, Alberta, relies heavily on contract workers, who make up 35 percent of the workforce, due to the nature of its project-based work, said JoAnne Mather, Vice-President of HR, Health and Safety and Environment. The 2,000-employee oilfields services company doesn't know what projects it will be awarded from year to year, so it has many contractors in its database it can call upon. "Some of the work is 20 days, some can be two months . . . and the only way to get those folks is to engage them in a contract because you can't offer them the traditional, long-term employment relationship," she said. "The work is so variable so a contract situation is what works."[18]

Companies may also hire contingent workers when full-time employees are on some type of leave (such as maternity leave), when there is a peak demand for labour or products (like the holiday shopping

Seasonal businesses depend on hiring contingent workers to help them through the limited time they are operational. What are the advantages and disadvantages of hiring contingent workers for employers? For employees?

season), or when quick service to customers is a priority. Companies tend to hire more contingent workers in an uncertain economy, particularly when they are available and qualified, and when the jobs require minimal training. According to *Workforce 2020*, a global study conducted by Oxford Economics and sponsored by SAP, however, 83 percent of executives indicate they're increasingly using contingent workers at any time, on an ongoing basis even if the global economy is improving.[19]

Contingent workers receive few benefits; they are rarely offered health insurance, vacation time, or company pensions. They also tend to earn less than permanent workers do. On the positive side, some on temporary assignments may be offered full-time employment. Managers see using temporary workers as a way of weeding out poor workers and finding good hires. Experts say temps are filling openings in an increasingly broad range of jobs, from unskilled manufacturing and distribution positions to middle management. Increasing numbers of contingent workers are educated professionals such as accountants, attorneys, and engineers. Because temporary workers are often told that they may, at some point, be hired as permanent workers, they are often more productive than those on the permanent payroll.

Many companies include college and university students in their contingent workforce plan. Working with temporary staffing agencies, companies have easier access to workers who have already been screened. Of course, temp agencies benefit students as well. Once the agencies have assessed the workers, their information is entered into their databases. Then when students are coming back in town for vacations or whatever, they can call the agency and ask them to put their names into the system for work assignments. There is no need to spend time searching for openings or running around town for interviews. In an era of rapid change and economic uncertainty, some contingent workers have even found that temping can be more secure than full-time employment.

Traditionally, unpaid internships have been a great way for young people to gain work experience. What are the advantages and disadvantages for both employees and employers? Under what conditions are unpaid internships illegal in Canada?

Training and Developing Employees for Optimum Performance

As technology and other innovations change the workplace, companies must offer training programs that often are quite sophisticated. The term **training and development** includes all attempts to improve productivity by increasing an employee's ability to perform. A well-designed training program often leads to higher retention rates, increased productivity, and greater job satisfaction. Employers find that spending money on training is usually money well spent. Training focuses on *short-term* skills, whereas development focuses on *long-term* abilities. Both include three steps: (1) assessing organization needs and employee skills to determine training needs; (2) designing training activities to meet identified needs; and (3) evaluating the training's effectiveness. Some common training activities are employee orientation, on-the-job training, apprenticeships, off-the-job training, online training, vestibule training, and job simulation. Management development will be discussed in a separate section.

training and development
All attempts to improve productivity by increasing an employee's ability to perform. Training focuses on short-term skills, whereas development focuses on long-term abilities.

It is important to engage a new employee right from the start so employees don't experience disappointment in their decision to join the organization.[20] **Orientation** is the activity that initiates new employees to the organization, to fellow employees, to their immediate supervisors, and to the policies, practices, values, and objectives of the firm. Orientation programs range from informal talks to formal activities that last a day or more and often include scheduled activities to various departments and required reading of handbooks. At Zappos, every new employee in the online retailer's headquarters must spend two weeks answering customer calls, two weeks learning in a classroom, and a week shipping boxes in the company's fulfillment centre.[21]

orientation
The activity that introduces new employees to the organization; to fellow employees; to their immediate supervisors; and to the policies, practices, values, and objectives of the firm.

On-the-job training lets the employee learn by doing, or by watching others for a while and then imitating them, right at the workplace. For example, salespeople are often trained by watching experienced salespeople perform (often called *shadowing*). Naturally, this can be either quite effective or disastrous, depending on the skills and habits of the person being watched. On-the-job training is obviously the easiest kind of training to implement when the job is relatively simple (such as clerking in a store) or repetitive (such as collecting refuse, cleaning carpets, or mowing lawns). More demanding or intricate jobs require a more intense training effort. Intranets and other forms of technology make cost-effective, on-the-job training programs available 24 hours a day. Computer systems can monitor workers' input and give them instructions if they become confused about what to do next.

on-the-job training
Training at the workplace that lets the employee learn by doing or by watching others for a while and then imitating them.

In **apprentice programs**, a trainee works alongside an experienced employee to master the skills and procedures of a craft. Some apprentice programs also involve classroom training. Labour unions in skilled crafts, such as bricklaying and plumbing, require a new worker to serve as an apprentice for several years to ensure excellence among their members as well as to limit entry to the union. Workers who successfully complete an apprenticeship earn the classification *journeyman.* Currently 30 percent of the skilled trade workers in Canada are Baby Boomers and shortages in skilled workers are expected in certain areas that include the construction, mining, and petroleum industries.[22] Skills Canada, a group that promotes careers in skilled trades and technologies to Canadian youth, has estimated that one million skilled trade workers will be needed by 2020.[23] Apprentice programs may be shortened to prepare people for skilled jobs in changing industries, such as auto repair and aircraft maintenance, that require increased knowledge of computer technology.

apprentice programs
Training programs during which a learner works alongside an experienced employee to master the skills and procedures of a craft.

The Labourers' International Union of North America (LiUNA) is the most progressive, aggressive, and fastest growing union of construction workers, waste management workers, show service workers, and health-care workers in Canada. Here at the LiUNA Local 183 Training Centre, Asphalt Program, the class is building additional parking spaces at the Vaughan, Ontario training site. Have you considered an apprentice program?

Off-the-job training occurs away from the workplace and consists of internal or external programs to develop any of a variety of skills or to foster personal development. Training is becoming more sophisticated as jobs become more sophisticated. Furthermore, training is expanding to include education (e.g., an MBA) and personal development. Subjects may include time management, stress management, health and wellness, physical education, nutrition, and even art and languages.

off-the-job training
Internal or external training programs away from the workplace that develop any of a variety of skills or foster personal development.

Online training offers an example of how technology is improving the efficiency of many off-the-job training programs. Most colleges and universities now offer a wide variety of online classes, sometimes called *distance learning,* including introductory business courses. Technology giants like EMC

<*http://www.emc.com*> and large manufacturers like Timken <*http://www.timken.com*> use the online training tool GlobeSmart to teach employees how to operate in different cultures.[24] Online training's key advantage is the ability to provide a large number of employees with consistent content tailored to specific training needs at convenient times.

> **online training**
> Training programs in which employees complete classes via the Internet.

Vestibule training (near-the-job training) is done in classrooms with equipment similar to that used on the job so employees learn proper methods and safety procedures before assuming a specific job assignment. Computer and robotics training is often completed in a vestibule classroom.

> **vestibule training**
> Training done in schools where employees are taught on equipment similar to that used on the job.

Job simulation is the use of equipment that duplicates job conditions and tasks so that trainees can learn skills before attempting them on the job. It differs from vestibule training in that it duplicates the *exact* combination of conditions that occur on the job. This is the kind of training given to astronauts, airline pilots, operators, ship captains, and others who must learn difficult procedures off the job.

> **job simulation**
> The use of equipment that duplicates job conditions and tasks so that trainees can learn skills before attempting them on the job.

Management Development

Managers often need special training. To be good communicators, they especially need to learn listening skills and empathy. They also need time management, planning, and human relations skills.

Management development can include on-the-job and off-the-job training. The activities will vary depending on the person being developed and the purpose of the program.

Management development, then, is the process of training and educating employees to become good managers and then monitoring the progress of their managerial skills over time. Management development programs are widespread, especially at colleges, universities, and private management development firms. Managers participate in role-playing exercises, solve various management cases, and attend films and lectures to improve their skills.

> **management development**
> The process of training and educating employees to become good managers, and then monitoring the progress of their managerial skills over time.

Management development is increasingly being used as a tool to accomplish business objectives. Most management training programs include several of the following:

- *On-the-job coaching.* A senior manager assists a lower-level manager by teaching needed skills and providing direction, advice, and helpful feedback. E-coaching is being developed to coach managers electronically, though it will take time and experimentation before firms figure out how to make coaches come to life online.

- *Understudy positions.* Job titles such as "undersecretary" and "assistant" are part of a relatively successful way of developing managers. Selected employees work as assistants to higher-level managers and participate in planning and other managerial functions until they are ready to assume such positions themselves.

- *Job rotation.* Managers are often given assignments in a variety of departments so that they can learn about different functions of the organization. Such job rotation gives them a broad picture of the organization that can contribute to their effectiveness. The chapter profile highlights Linamar's program. Job rotation is also valuable when starting out. For example, Loblaw Companies Limited created Grad@Loblaw, a rotational program for new graduates that covers multiple streams including store management, supply chain, merchandising, marketing, IT, finance, and HR.[25]

- *Off-the-job courses and training.* Managers periodically go to classes or seminars off-site to hone technical and human relations skills. McDonald's Corporation has its own Hamburger University. Managers and potential franchisees attend six days of classes and complete a course of study equivalent to 36 hours of business-school credit.[26]

EMPOWERING WORKERS

Historically, many managers gave explicit instructions to workers, telling them what to do to meet the goals and objectives of the organization. The term for such an approach is *directing*. In traditional organizations, directing involves giving assignments, explaining routines, clarifying policies, and providing feedback on performance. Many organizations still follow this model, especially in firms such as fast-food restaurants and small retail establishments where the employees do not have the skills and experience needed to work on their own, at least at first.

Progressive managers, such as those in many high-tech firms and Internet companies, are less likely than traditional managers to give specific instructions to employees. Rather, they are more likely to empower employees to make decisions on their own. Empowerment means giving employees the *authority* (the right to make a decision without consulting the manager) and *responsibility* (the requirement to accept the consequences of one's actions) to respond quickly to customer requests. Managers are often reluctant to give up the power they have to make such decisions; thus, empowerment is often resisted. In those firms that are able to implement the concept, the manager's role is becoming less that of a boss and director and more that of a coach, assistant, counsellor, or team member.

Cisco Canada has been listed on Aon Hewitt's *Best Employers in Canada* study. "Cisco has a culture of improvement," says David Clarkson, Director of Human Resources. He attributes the company's success to employee engagement, where hiring those with the right approach to life is essential. "We're looking for candidates with enthusiasm—they need to be passionate about something in their lives," says Clarkson. "We find that same passion often carries over into their work." Willa Black, Cisco Canada's Vice-President, states that employees are self-starters who don't need to be micromanaged: "We communicate from the top down—as well as from the bottom up and the middle out. But employees control their own destiny. They know what they need to do to succeed as individuals as well as how to help the company succeed."[27]

Networking

Networking is the process of establishing and maintaining contacts with key managers in your own organization and other organizations, and using those contacts to weave strong relationships that serve as informal development systems. Of equal or greater importance is a **mentor**, a corporate manager who supervises, coaches, and guides selected lower-level employees by introducing them to the right people and generally acting as their organizational sponsor.[28] In most organizations, informal mentoring occurs as experienced employees assist less experienced workers. However, many organizations formally assign mentors to employees considered to have strong potential.[29] Sodexo Canada <*http:// ca.sodexo.com*> also thinks globally; it organizes an international mentorship program that pairs new graduates with overseas mentors for a week in that country.[30]

networking
The process of establishing and maintaining contacts with key managers in and outside the organization and using those contacts to weave strong relationships that serve as informal development systems.

mentor
An experienced employee who supervises, coaches, and guides lower-level employees by introducing them to the right people and generally being their organizational sponsor.

Networking provides you with an array of personal contacts on whom you can call for career advice and help. Have you begun creating your network yet? Are you part of someone else's network?

It's also important to remember that networking and mentoring go beyond the business environment. For example, school is a perfect place to begin networking. Associations you nurture with instructors, with local business people through internships, and especially with your classmates might provide you with a valuable network you can turn to for the rest of your career.

Randstad Canada's survey, *From Y to Z – A Guide to the Next Generation of Employees*, reports that Gen Y (also known as Millennials) and Gen Z welcome a mentoring approach to support their advancement, one of their highest priorities.[31] To do so, managers should keep the communication lines open so employees can ask questions and receive constructive advice. As well, employees should be encouraged to attend webinars, take part in industry networking activities, and do some job shadowing. Finally, managers should show these younger generations how their work fits into the big picture and brings value to the team and to the organization.[32] As discussed in Chapter 11, each generation is motivated by different approaches. A targeted training and development program is one way to communicate that these employees are valuable resources.

Diversity in Management Development

As women moved into management, they also learned the importance of networking and of having mentors. Unfortunately, women often have more difficulty than men in networking or finding mentors, since most senior managers are male. More women are now entering established networking systems or, in some instances, creating their own. Some examples of organizations include the Canadian Women's Business Network, Women's Enterprise Centre, and Canadian Association of Women Executives & Entrepreneurs.

Selected as one of Canada's Best Diversity Employers *<http://www.canadastop100.com/diversity/>*, TD Bank has a formal diversity strategy targeted to women, those with disabilities, visible minorities, Aboriginal people, and the lesbian, gay, bisexual and transgender (LGBT) peoples. Specific initiatives include the following:[33]

- creating a formal diversity leadership council that meets bi-monthly to establish priorities and monitor progress in all areas of diversity and inclusion, such as increasing the diversity of the candidate pool for executive roles and ways to address unconscious bias;

- working with Lime Connect to provide summer internship and scholarship opportunities for third-year university students with disabilities, and in partnership with the Job Opportunity Information Network, offer mentoring to select candidates;

One of Canada's Best Diversity Employers, CIBC *<http://www.cibc.com>* has a diversity and inclusion program with a focus on attracting, motivating, and retaining a qualified workforce that represents the diversity of its clients and communities. Would you seek out a company that has been recognized for its diversity initiatives?

- encouraging the career development of visible minority employees by hosting annual, enterprise-wide Visible Minority High Potential speed mentoring events; and

- maintaining 11 regional LGBT employee resource groups across Canada and the enterprise-wide LGBTA Pride Network, with nearly 3,000 members.

Companies that take the initiative to develop female and minority managers understand three crucial principles: (1) grooming women and minorities for management positions is not about legality, morality, or even morale but rather about bringing more talent in the door—the key to long-term profitability; (2) the best women and minorities will become harder to attract and retain, so the companies that commit to development early have an edge; and (3) having more women and minorities at all levels lets businesses serve their female and minority customers better. If you do not have a diversity of people working in the back room, how are you going to satisfy the diversity of people coming in the front door?

Progress Assessment

- What are the five steps in the selection process?

- What are contingent workers? Why do companies hire such workers?

- Can you name and describe four training and four development techniques?

LO4 Trace the six steps in appraising employee performance, and summarize the objectives of employee compensation programs.

Appraising Employee Performance to Get Optimum Results

If an organization is to achieve its goals, managers must be able to determine whether their workers are doing an effective and efficient job, with a minimum of errors and disruptions. They do this by using a **performance appraisal**, an evaluation that measures employee performance against established standards in order to make decisions about promotions, compensation, training, or termination. Performance appraisals have six steps:

> **performance appraisal**
> An evaluation that measures employee performance against established standards in order to make decisions about promotions, compensation, training, or termination.

1. *Establishing performance standards.* This is a crucial step. Standards must be understandable, subject to measurement, and reasonable. Both managers and subordinates must accept them.

2. *Communicating standards.* It's dangerous to assume that employees know what is expected of them. They must be told clearly and precisely what the standards and expectations are and how to meet them.

3. *Evaluating performance.* If the first two steps are done correctly, performance evaluation is relatively easy. It is a matter of evaluating the employee's behaviour to see whether it matches standards.

4. *Discussing results.* Employees often make mistakes and fail to meet expectations at first. It takes time to learn a job and do it well. Discussing an employee's successes and areas that need improvement can provide managers an opportunity to be understanding and helpful and guide the employee to better performance. The performance appraisal can also allow employees to suggest how a task could be done better.

5. *Taking corrective action.* As part of the performance appraisal, a manager can take corrective action or provide corrective feedback to help the employee perform better. The key word is *perform.* The primary purpose of an appraisal is to improve employee performance, if possible.[34]

6. *Using the results to make decisions.* Decisions about promotions, compensation, training, or termination are all based on performance evaluations. (Be aware that sometimes new hires and promotions are also influenced by other factors such as a family connection or whether the employee is particularly liked by his or her supervisor. Make sure that decisions are based on the performance evaluation.) An effective performance-appraisal system is also a way of satisfying legal requirements about such decisions.

Managing effectively means getting results through top performance. That's what performance appraisals are for at all levels of the organization, including at the top, where managers benefit from performance reviews by their subordinates and peers. In the *360-degree review,* for example, management gathers opinions from those around the employee, including those under, above, and on the same level, to get an accurate, comprehensive idea of the worker's abilities. Figure 12.4 illustrates how managers can make performance appraisals more meaningful.

■ **FIGURE 12.4**

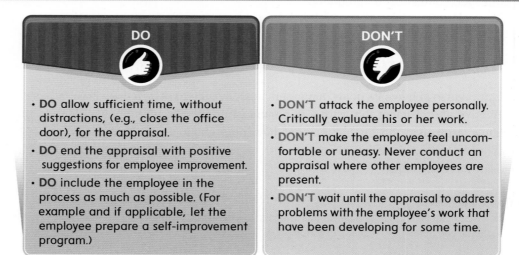

CONDUCTING EFFECTIVE APPRAISALS AND REVIEWS

DO

- **DO** allow sufficient time, without distractions, (e.g., close the office door), for the appraisal.
- **DO** end the appraisal with positive suggestions for employee improvement.
- **DO** include the employee in the process as much as possible. (For example and if applicable, let the employee prepare a self-improvement program.)

DON'T

- **DON'T** attack the employee personally. Critically evaluate his or her work.
- **DON'T** make the employee feel uncomfortable or uneasy. Never conduct an appraisal where other employees are present.
- **DON'T** wait until the appraisal to address problems with the employee's work that have been developing for some time.

Progress Assessment

- What is the primary purpose of a performance appraisal?
- What are the six steps in a performance appraisal?
- Why do employers and employees find the appraisal process so difficult?

Compensating Employees: Attracting and Keeping the Best

Companies do not just compete for customers; they also compete for employees. Compensation is one of the main tools that companies use to attract (and retain) qualified employees, and one of their largest operating costs. The long-term success of a firm—perhaps even its survival—may depend on how well it can control employee costs and optimize employee efficiency. Service organizations like hospitals, hotels, and airlines struggle with high employee costs since these firms are *labour intensive* (the primary cost of operations is the cost of labour). Manufacturing firms in the auto and steel industries have asked employees to take reductions in wages (called givebacks) to make the firms more competitive. (We discuss this in Chapter 13.) Those are just a few reasons compensation and benefit packages require special attention.[35] In fact, some experts believe that determining how best to compensate employees is today's greatest human resource challenge.

A carefully managed and competitive compensation and benefits program can accomplish several objectives:

- Attract the kinds of people the organization needs, and in sufficient numbers.
- Provide employees with the incentive to work efficiently and productively.
- Keep valued employees from going to competitors, or starting competing firms.
- Maintain a competitive position in the marketplace by keeping costs low through high productivity from a satisfied workforce.
- Provide employees with some sense of financial security through fringe benefits (to be discussed soon) such as insurance and retirement benefits.

Pay Systems

The way an organization chooses to pay its employees can have a dramatic effect on efficiency and productivity. Managers thus look for a system that compensates employees fairly.

Many companies still use the pay system known as the Hay system, devised by Edward Hay. This compensation plan is based on job tiers, each of which has a strict pay range. The system is set up on a point basis with three key factors considered: know-how, problem solving, and accountability.

John Whitney, author of *The Trust Factor,* believes that companies should set pay at the market level or better and then award all employees the same percentage merit raise. Doing so, he says, sends out the message that everyone in the company is important. Fairness remains the issue. Figure 12.5 outlines some of the most common pay systems. Which do you think is the fairest?

Compensating Teams

Thus far we have talked about compensating individuals. What about teams? Since you want your teams to be more than simply a group of individuals, would you compensate them like individuals? If you can't answer that question immediately, you are not alone. Most managers believe in using teams, but fewer are sure how to pay them. Team-based pay programs are not as effective or as fully developed as managers would hope. Measuring and rewarding individual performance on teams, while at the same time rewarding team performance, is tricky—but it can be done. Football players are rewarded as a team when they go to the playoffs and to the Super Bowl, but they are paid individually as well. Companies are now experimenting with and developing similar incentive systems.

■ **FIGURE 12.5**

PAY SYSTEMS

Salary

Fixed compensation computed on weekly, bi-weekly, or monthly pay periods (e.g., $400 per week or $1,500 per month). Salaried employees do not receive additional pay for any extra hours worked.

Hourly wage or daywork

Wage based on number of hours or days worked. Used for most blue-collar and clerical workers. Often employees must punch a time clock when they arrive at work and when they leave. Hourly wages vary greatly. This does not include benefits such as retirement systems, which may add 30 percent or more to the total package.

Piecework system

Wage based on the number of items produced rather than by the hour or day. This type of system creates powerful incentives to work efficiently and productively.

Commission plans

Pay based on some percentage of sales. Often used to compensate salespeople, commission plans resemble piecework systems.

Bonus plans

Extra pay for accomplishing or surpassing certain objectives. There are two types of bonuses: monetary and cashless. Money is always a welcome bonus. Cashless rewards include written thank-you notes, appreciation notes sent to the employee's family, movie tickets, flowers, time off, gift certificates, shopping sprees, and other types of recognition.

Profit-sharing plans

Annual bonuses paid to employees based on the company's profits. The amount paid to each employee is based on a predetermined percentage. Profit-sharing is one of the most common forms of performance-based pay.

Gain-sharing plans

Annual bonuses paid to employees based on achieving specific goals such as quality measures, customer satisfaction measures, and production targets.

Cost-of-living allowances (COLAs)

Annual increases in wages based on increases in the Consumer Price Index. This is usually found in union contracts.

Stock options

Right to purchase stock in the company at a specific price over a specific period of time. Often this gives employees the right to buy stock cheaply despite huge increases in the price of the stock. For example, if over the course of his employment a worker received options to buy 10,000 shares of the company stock at $10 each and the price of the stock eventually grows to $100, he can use those options to buy the 10,000 shares (now worth $1 million) for $100,000.

Jim Fox, founder and senior partner of compensation and human resource specialist firm Fox Lawson & Associates *<http://www.foxlawson.com>*, insists that setting up the team right in the first place is the key element to designing an appropriate team compensation plan. He believes the pay model to enhance performance will be a natural outcome of the team's development process. Jay Schuster, co-author of a study of team pay, found that when pay is based strictly on individual performance, it erodes team cohesiveness and makes it less likely that the team will meet its goals as a collaborative effort. Workplace studies indicate over 50 percent of team compensation plans are based on team goals. Skill-based pay and gain-sharing are the two most common compensation methods for teams.

Skill-based pay rewards the growth of both the individual and the team. Base pay is raised when team members learn and apply new skills. Eastman Chemical Company *<http://www.eastman.com>* rewards its teams for proficiency in technical, social, and business knowledge skills. A cross-functional compensation policy team defines the skills. The drawbacks of the skill-based pay system are twofold: the system is complex, and it is difficult to relate the acquisition of skills to profit gains.

Most *gain-sharing* systems base bonuses on improvements over previous performance.[36] For example, steel producer Nucor Steel *<http://www.nucor.com>* calculates bonuses on quality—tonnes of steel that go out the door with no defects. There are no limits on bonuses a team can earn; they usually average $20,000 per employee each year.[37]

It is important to reward individual team players also. Outstanding team players—who go beyond what is required and make an outstanding individual contribution to the firm—should be separately recognized, with cash or non-cash rewards. A good way to compensate for uneven team participation is to let the team decide which members get what type of individual award. After all, if you really support the team process, you need to give teams the freedom to reward themselves.

Fringe Benefits

Fringe benefits include sick-leave pay, vacation pay, pension plans, and health plans that represent additional compensation to employees beyond base wages. They may be divided into three categories.

According to a Randstad Canada study on Gen Y and Gen Z, one in three (32 percent) say health insurance is the most important employee benefit they expect. Other benefits include work flexibility (29 percent), training and development (17 percent), individual performance bonuses (10 percent), a stock purchase plan and profit-sharing program (4 percent), and tuition reimbursement (4 percent).[38] Do you agree with this order? What are ways that companies can highlight their benefit plans when recruiting?

Federal and provincial legislation (which varies somewhat from province to province) and requires compulsory deductions from employees' pay cheques, employer contributions, or both. These *statutory benefits* include the Canada/Quebec Pension Plan, employment insurance, and workers' compensation. You have probably seen some of these deductions on your pay stub. The second category consists of *legally required benefits,* including vacation pay, holiday pay, overtime pay, and unpaid maternity leave with job protection. The third category includes *all other benefits* and stems from voluntary employer programs and from collective labour agreements. Some are paid by the employer alone and others are jointly paid by the employer and employee. Among the most common are bonuses, company pension plans, and group insurance.

---

fringe benefits
Benefits such as sick-leave pay, vacation pay, pension plans, and health plans that represent additional compensation to employees beyond base wages.

Benefits in recent years have grown faster than wages and can't really be considered fringe anymore. Farrah Press, VP of Sales and Marketing at Executive Link, states that companies can be widely different in the scope of the plans they can offer. "A large, publicly traded company can offer a more competitive plan than a small private company because the former can afford to and because it has a larger base of employees."[39] According to the Conference Board of Canada, employer-sponsored benefits programs cost Canadian organizations an average of 10 percent of payroll. Across all organizations, the average annual cost of benefits per full-time equivalent employee is $7,061.[40] Review Figure 12.6 for a breakdown.

Benefits policies can have a significant impact on attracting and retaining high-performing employees.[41] Benefits will not replace performance incentives as motivators, but especially for older generations, health and pension benefits can make a great difference in corporate loyalty.[42] Health-care costs—particularly drug and dental-care costs—are expected to continue to rise as people spend more on health care as they age. The government, which already spends a large percentage of its revenue on health care, will likely continue to shift costs to private plans by limiting and eliminating health services.

Published annually, *Canada's Top 100 Employers* <http://www.canadastop100.com> highlights employers that lead their industries in providing the best benefits and working conditions. You can also read about Canada's top employers for young people <http://www.canadastop100.com/young_people/>. Would you consider these resources when looking for a job?

■ **FIGURE 12.6**

ANNUAL COST OF BENEFITS PER FULL-TIME EMPLOYEE ($7,061)	
Legally required components comprise more than half of all spending on employer-sponsored benefits programs. This excludes the cost of wellness programs, paid time off (e.g., vacation, statutory holidays, maternity leave, etc.), and pension or retirement plans.	
Component	**Cost for Active Full-Time Employee**
Legally Required Payments	
CPP/QPP	2,120
Employment Insurance (EI) Premiums	929
Workers' Compensation	448
Extended Health-Care Plans	**1,433**
Dental Plans	**800**
Life and Accident Insurance Plans	
Group Life Insurance	234
Accidental Death and Dismemberment Insurance	30
Critical Illness Insurance	8
Disability and Casual Absence Plans	
Paid Sick Leave	379
Short-term Disability	232
Long-term Disability	471
Total Annual Benefit Costs	**$7,061**

Note: Due to incomplete data, the percentage of payroll for total annual benefits costs is not the sum of all benefits listed.

Source: Courtesy of The Conference Board of Canada. Used with permission.

As a result, employers are trying to control costs in various ways and are making cuts where possible. For example, the Ontario provincial government will continue to pay 100 percent of the premiums for those retiring prior to 2017; however, Ontario public-sector employees retiring in 2017 and later will have to pay half of their benefits premiums for life, health, dental, and vision care.[43]

Understanding that it takes many incentives to attract and retain the best employees, companies offer soft benefits. *Soft benefits* help workers maintain the balance between work and family life that is often as important to hardworking employees as the nature of the job itself. These perks include things such as on-site haircuts, shoe repair, and concierge services. Freeing employees from errands and chores gives them more time for family—and work. For example, Montreal, Quebec-based Vigilant Global offers its employees free breakfast and lunch, while biotechnology firm Genetech <*http://www.gene.com*> offers doggie day care.[44] Varafin Inc. <*http://verafin.com*>, based in St. John's, Newfoundland, offers employees a flexible "no limit" vacation policy.[45] Would you value such benefits?

Reaching *Beyond* OUR BORDERS

Cultural Challenges Working Worldwide

Human resource management of a global workforce begins with understanding the customs, laws, and local business needs of every country in which the organization operates. Country-specific cultural and legal standards can affect a variety of human resource functions:

- *Compensation.* Salaries must be converted to and from foreign currencies. Often employees with international assignments receive special allowances for relocation, children's education, housing, travel, or other business-related expenses.
- *Health and pension standards.* There are different social contexts for benefits in other countries. In the Netherlands, for example, the government provides retirement income and health care.
- *Paid time off.* Four weeks of paid vacation is the standard of many European employers. But many other countries lack the short-term and long-term absence policies offered in Canada, including sick leave, personal leave, family leave, and medical leave. Global companies need a standard definition of *time off.*
- *Taxation.* Each country has different taxation rules, and the payroll department must work within each country's regulations.
- *Communication.* When employees leave to work in another country, they often feel disconnected from their home country. Wise companies use their intranet and the Internet to help these faraway employees keep in direct contact.

Human resource policies at home are influenced more and more by conditions and practices in other countries and cultures. Human resource managers need to sensitize themselves and their organizations to the cultural and business practices of other nations.

Sources: Roy Mauer, "SHRM Identifies Global HR Trends for 2014," *Society for Human Resource Management,* 3 February 2014; and Will Yakowicz, "The Fine Art of Negotiating in Different Cultures," *Inc.,* 6 December 2013.

At one time, most employees sought benefits that were similar. Today, however, some may seek child-care benefits while others prefer attractive pension plans.[46] To address such growing demands, over half of all firms offer **cafeteria-style benefits (flexible benefits) plans**, in which employees can choose the benefits they want up to a certain dollar amount. Such plans let human resource managers equitably and cost-effectively meet employees' individual needs by allowing them choice.

cafeteria-style benefits (flexible benefits) plans
Benefit plans that allow employees to choose which benefits they want up to a certain dollar amount.

As the cost of administering benefits programs has accelerated, many companies have chosen to outsource this function. Managing benefits can be especially complicated when employees are located in other countries. The Reaching Beyond Our Borders box discusses the human resource challenges faced by global businesses. To put it simply, benefits are often as important to recruiting top talent as salary and may even become more important in the future.

Scheduling Employees to Meet Organizational and Employee Needs

Workplace trends and the increasing costs of transportation have led employees to look for scheduling flexibility. Flextime, telecommuting, and job sharing are important benefits employees seek. Choice will be influenced by the type of job, employers' needs, and each individual's needs.

Flextime Plans

A **flextime plan** gives employees some freedom to choose which hours to work, as long as they work the required number of hours or complete their assigned tasks. The most popular plans allow employees to come to work between 7:00 and 9:00 a.m. and leave between 4:00 and 6:00 p.m. Flextime plans generally incorporate core time. **Core time** refers to the period when all employees are expected to be at their job stations. For example, an organization may designate core time as 9:00 and 11:00 a.m. and 2:00 and 4:00 p.m. During these hours, all employees are required to be at work, as highlighted in Figure 12.7. Flextime allows employees to adjust to work–life demands. Two-income families find them especially helpful. Companies that use flextime say it boosts employee productivity and morale.[47]

> **flextime plan**
> Work schedule that gives employees some freedom to choose when to work, as long as they work the required number of hours.
>
> **core time**
> In a flextime plan, the period when all employees are expected to be at their job stations.

■ **FIGURE 12.7**

A FLEXTIME CHART

At this company, employees can start work anytime between 6:30 and 9:30 a.m. They take a half hour for lunch anytime between 11:00 a.m. and 2:00 p.m., and can leave between 3:00 and 6:30 p.m. Everyone works an eight-hour day. The blue arrows show a typical employee's flextime day.

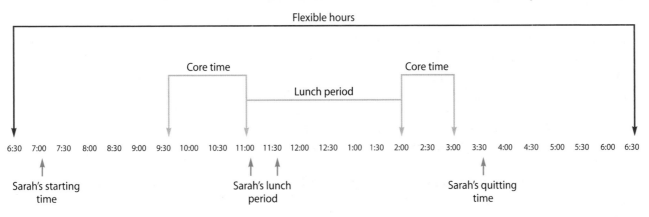

Flextime is not for all organizations, however. It doesn't suit shift work, like fast-food or assembly-line processes in manufacturing, where everyone on a given shift must be at work at the same time. Another disadvantage is that managers often have to work longer days to assist and supervise in organizations that may operate from 6:00 a.m. to 6:00 p.m. Flextime also makes communication more difficult since certain employees may not be there when others need to talk to them. Furthermore, if not carefully supervised, some employees could abuse the system, causing resentment among others.

Some companies encourage employees to take short naps during the workday so that they replenish their energy and creativity. These EnergyPods block noise and light and are in use at some firms including Google and Procter & Gamble <http://www.pg.com>. Is napping a job benefit that appeals to you?

Another option is a **compressed workweek**. An employee works a full number of hours, but fewer than the standard number of days. For example, an employee may work four 10-hour days and then enjoy a long weekend instead of working five 8-hour days with a traditional, two-day weekend. There are obvious advantages of compressed workweeks, but some employees get tired working such long hours, and productivity can decline. Others find the system of great benefit, however, and are enthusiastic about it.[48] Nurses often work compressed weeks.

compressed workweek
Work schedule that allows an employee to work a full number of hours per week but in fewer days.

Telecommuting

Providing employees with the ability to choose their work location is another opportunity for organizations to demonstrate flexibility.[49] Using computers linked to the company's network, mobile employees can transmit their work to the office from anywhere. This can include home-based work or working from a client's site. Introduced in Chapter 10, telecommuting (also known as telework), decreases travel time and overall costs and often increases productivity. Having fewer employees in the office also means that a company can get by with smaller, and therefore less expensive, office space than before.

Telecommuting enables men and women to work while staying home with small children or elders. It has also been a tremendous boon for workers with disabilities. Employees who can work after hours on their home computers, rather than staying late at the office, report lowered stress and improved morale. Telecommuting is most successful among people who are self-starters, who don't have home distractions, and whose work doesn't require face-to-face interaction with co-workers.

Rising gas prices, technology, and the push for work–life flexibility have all contributed to an increase in telecommuting. What do you think would be your biggest challenge if you worked from home?

Electronic communication can never replace face-to-face communication for creating enthusiasm and team spirit, however. Even as telecommuting has grown in popularity, some telecommuters report that a consistent diet of long-distance work leaves them feeling dislocated or left out of the loop. Some miss the energy of social interaction or dislike the intrusion of work into what is normally a personal setting. Often people working from home don't know when to turn the work off. Some companies are therefore using telecommuting only as a part-time alternative. Others offer "hotelling" (being assigned to a desk through a reservation system) or "hot-desking" (sharing a desk with other employees who work at different times) as alternatives. American Express Canada <*https://www.americanexpress.com*> has moved to a hotelling-style environment where employees are assigned one of four work styles: Hub,

Some young new moms, whose careers are not as established, are choosing to stay home because day care is expensive. (More dads are also choosing to stay home.) If more companies offered alternative work arrangements, do you think that this might change?

Club, Home, or Roam. The majority (80 percent) are Club workers who reserve desks online or work at one of the building's many informal work spaces.[50] Figure 12.8 outlines the benefits and challenges of home-based work to organizations, individuals, and society.

■ FIGURE 12.8

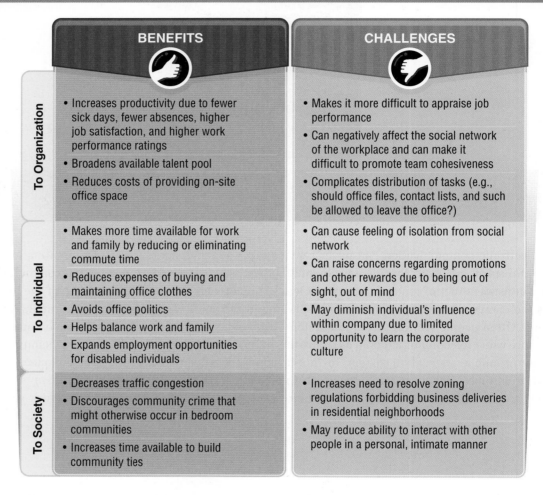

BENEFITS AND CHALLENGES OF TELECOMMUTING

BENEFITS	CHALLENGES
To Organization • Increases productivity due to fewer sick days, fewer absences, higher job satisfaction, and higher work performance ratings • Broadens available talent pool • Reduces costs of providing on-site office space	• Makes it more difficult to appraise job performance • Can negatively affect the social network of the workplace and can make it difficult to promote team cohesiveness • Complicates distribution of tasks (e.g., should office files, contact lists, and such be allowed to leave the office?)
To Individual • Makes more time available for work and family by reducing or eliminating commute time • Reduces expenses of buying and maintaining office clothes • Avoids office politics • Helps balance work and family • Expands employment opportunities for disabled individuals	• Can cause feeling of isolation from social network • Can raise concerns regarding promotions and other rewards due to being out of sight, out of mind • May diminish individual's influence within company due to limited opportunity to learn the corporate culture
To Society • Decreases traffic congestion • Discourages community crime that might otherwise occur in bedroom communities • Increases time available to build community ties	• Increases need to resolve zoning regulations forbidding business deliveries in residential neighborhoods • May reduce ability to interact with other people in a personal, intimate manner

Job-Sharing Plans

Job sharing lets two or more part-time employees share one full-time job. For instance, students may work only after school hours and parents with small children may work only during school hours, and older workers can work part-time before fully retiring or after retiring. Benefits of job sharing include:

- Employment opportunities for those who cannot or prefer not to work full-time.
- An enthusiastic and productive workforce.
- Reduced absenteeism and tardiness.
- The ability to schedule part-time workers into peak demand periods (e.g., banks on payday).
- Retention of experienced employees who might otherwise leave.

job sharing
An arrangement whereby two part-time employees share one full-time job.

Seeking SUSTAINABILITY

How Employers Can Support Work–Life Balance

Do you find it difficult to balance the different roles in your life? If so, you're not alone as 58 percent of Canadians report "overload" as a result of the pressures associated with work, home and family, friends, physical health, and volunteer and community service. Kevin O'Leary, Chairman of O'Leary Financial Group, agrees that finding the right balance between work and living a life outside of work can be difficult, especially for entrepreneurs. "Unfortunately, this is one of the great sacrifices entrepreneurs have to make because if you're not spending 25 hours a day on your business, your competitor is. And it's not just the Canadian competitor, it's a global competitor," said O'Leary. He says that finding the right partner in life who is willing to ride the journey with you is also important.

Not all employees will have the same work–life balance issues. Baby Boomers will most likely have different issues than Millennials. Age, culture, gender, family and marital status, care giver demands, socio-economic status, and other factors affect an employee's work–life balance. Those same factors can also influence how individuals are affected by demands. Everyone responds differently to stress. What creates a serious problem for one employee may not be felt in the same way by colleagues.

To help employees achieve/maintain a sense of work–life balance, Health Canada suggests that employers:

- Identify ways of reducing employee workloads. Special attention needs to be given to reducing the workloads of managers and professionals in all sectors. Employees should be asked for suggestions as they often are in the best position to identify ways of streamlining work.
- Reduce reliance on both paid and unpaid overtime by employees.
- Recognize and reward overtime work.
- Reduce job-related travel time for employees.
- Make alternative work arrangements more widely available within the organization. These might include flextime or the opportunity to work at home for part of the work week.
- Give employees the opportunity to say "no" when asked to work overtime. Saying "no" should not be a career-limiting move. Employees should not have to choose between having a family and career advancement.

More organizations are creating health and welfare committees that are responsible for recognizing health and safety concerns and identifying solutions. Wellness program options include flexible work arrangements such as those discussed in this chapter, leaves of absence and vacation, education and training opportunities, encouraging fitness and healthy living, providing supportive managers, and incorporating other management approaches.

There are many benefits for companies that invest in work–life balance initiatives. These include a reduction in absenteeism, an increase in productivity, decreased stress, and stronger working relationships. In addition, such initiatives help to attract new employees and retain current ones as employees are drawn to organizations that help them find balance and personal satisfaction.

Sources: William Kee, "For entrepreneurs there is no work–life balance: Kevin O'Leary," BNN.ca, 27 March 2015, http://www.bnn.ca /News/2015/3/27/Life-is-very-Darwinian-OLeary.aspx; "Work-Life Balance," Workplace Mental Health Promotion, 15 February 2015, http://wmhp.cmhaontario.ca/workplace-mental-health-core-concepts-issues/issues-in-the-workplace-that-affect-employee-mental-health /work-life-balance; Canadian Mental Health Association, 2015, http://www.cmha.ca/mental-health/your-mental-health/worklife-balance/; and "Workplaces that Work," HRCouncil.ca, [n.d.], http://hrcouncil.ca/hr-toolkit/workplaces-health-safety.cfm.

Disadvantages include having to hire, train, motivate, and supervise twice as many people (or more) and perhaps having to prorate some fringe benefits. But firms are finding that the benefits outweigh the disadvantages.

Implementing workplace alternative work arrangements such as flextime plans, telecommuting, and job sharing more widely available, when appropriate, would contribute to a better work–life balance. The Seeking Sustainability box offers additional suggestions for employers.

Progress Assessment

- Can you name and describe four alternative compensation systems?
- What advantages do compensation plans such as profit-sharing offer an organization?
- What are the benefits and challenges of flextime? Telecommuting? Job sharing?

LO5 Describe the ways in which employees can move through a company: promotion, reassignment, termination, and retirement.

Career Management: Up, Over, and Out

Employees do not always stay in the position they were hired to fill. They may excel and move up the corporate ladder or fail and move out the front door. Employees can also be reassigned or retire. Of course, some choose to move themselves by going to another company.

Promoting and Reassigning Employees

Many companies find that promotion from within the company improves employee morale. It is also cost-effective in that the promoted employees are already familiar with the corporate culture and procedures and don't need to spend valuable time on basic orientation.

In the new, flatter corporate structures identified in Chapter 9, there are fewer levels for employees to reach than in the past. Thus they often move *over* to a new position rather than *up* to a new one. Such lateral transfers allow employees to develop and display new skills and to learn more about the company overall. Reassignment is one way of motivating experienced employees to remain in a company that offers limited upward advancement opportunities.

Terminating Employees

The relentless pressure of global competition, shifts in technology, increasing customer demands for greater value, and uncertain economic conditions have human resource managers struggling to manage layoffs and firings. Even if the economy is booming, many companies are hesitant to hire or rehire workers full-time. Why is that the case? One reason is that the cost of terminating employees is prohibitively high in terms of severance packages, lost training costs, and possible damages and legal fees for wrongful discharge suits. (This is why is it critical to have a good system of verbal and written notices and record keeping to deal with poorly-performing employees.) To save money, many companies are either using temporary employees or outsourcing certain functions.

Some companies set up in-house outplacement facilities so that terminated employees can get counselling on how to obtain a new job. For senior managers, companies usually pay for private-agency career counselling.

When there is a downturn in the economy, managers sometimes terminate employees. Do you think they will rehire full-time employees when the economy recovers? Why or why not? What alternatives do they have?

Retiring Employees

Companies looking to downsize sometimes offer early retirement benefits to entice older (and more expensive) workers to retire. Such benefits can include one-time cash payments, known in some companies as *golden handshakes*. The advantage early retirement benefits have over layoffs or firing is the increased morale of remaining employees. Retiring senior workers earlier also increases promotion opportunities for younger employees.

Losing Valued Employees

In spite of a company's efforts to retain them, some talented employees will choose to pursue opportunities elsewhere. Knowing their reasons for leaving can be invaluable in preventing the loss of other good people in the future. One way to learn the reasons is to have an outside expert conduct an *exit interview.* Outsiders can provide confidentiality and anonymity that earns more honest feedback than employees are comfortable giving in face-to-face interviews with their supervisors. Web-based systems can capture, track, and statistically analyze employee exit interview data to generate reports that identify trouble areas. Such programs can also coordinate exit interview data with employee satisfaction surveys to predict which departments should expect turnover to occur.

Attracting and retaining the best employees is the key to success in the competitive global business environment. Changes in laws have also had a major influence. Let's look at this next.

LO6　Illustrate the effects of legislation on human resource management.

Laws Affecting Human Resource Management[51]

The Charter of Rights and Freedoms, which is part of the Constitution of Canada, guarantees equality before the law for every Canadian. The Human Rights Act seeks to provide equal employment opportunities without regard to race and colour, national or ethnic origin, religion, age, sex, sexual orientation, marital status, family status, disability, or pardoned convictions. Human rights legislation requires that every employer ensure equal opportunities and that there is no discrimination. This legislation affects nearly every human resource function (which includes planning, recruiting, selection, training, and compensation) and it has made managing these activities more complicated. This is true in both a non-union environment, which is governed by these laws and regulations, and a union environment, which must also reflect the conditions outlined in the labour contract (to be discussed in Chapter 13).

Since Canada is a confederation of provinces and territories, jurisdiction over many aspects of our lives is divided between the federal and provincial governments. The federal government legislates on national issues (e.g., employment insurance) and it has jurisdiction over certain types of businesses that are deemed to be of a national nature. Federally regulated businesses and industries are defined by the Canada Labour Code. The Canada Labour Code applies to approximately 12,000 enterprises with 820,000 employees, accounting for 6 percent of all Canadian workers. These firms are involved in banking; marine shipping, ferry, and port services; air transportation; railway and road transportation that involves crossing provincial or international borders; canals, pipelines, tunnels, and bridges (crossing provincial borders); telephone, telegraph, and cable systems; radio and television broadcasting; many First Nation activities; and most federal Crown corporations.

Provincial or territorial labour laws outline employment standards that apply to the majority (94 percent) of employees. This includes employment standards in areas such as minimum wage, hours of work, overtime, statutory holidays, parental leave, employment of people under 18 years of age, and discrimination in the workplace.

Employees are guaranteed protection against age discrimination in the workplace. Coupled with the elimination of a mandatory retirement age, these employees have more opportunities to retire later. What are workplace benefits in keeping these workers?

What all of this means is that there are hundreds of laws and regulations at different levels of government that apply to all aspects of human resource management. Furthermore, these laws are constantly being revised because of the changing social and political environments, as well as rulings by human rights commissions and courts. One of the most regulated areas involves discrimination.

Pay Equity[52]

Pay equity refers to equal pay for work of equal value. It compares the value of male and female jobs by objectively evaluating the jobs in terms of four neutral factors: skill, effort, responsibility, and working conditions. If a female job is approximately equal in value to a higher-paying job done mainly by men, the female job gets the same wages as the male job.

---

pay equity
Equal pay for work of equal value.

The **gender wage gap** is the difference between wages earned by men and wages earned by women. On average, Canadian women earn less than men. The persistent wage gap that women face, combined with fewer hours of work (twice as many women work part-time as men), make for a significant earnings gap. Women continue to earn on average 73 cents for every dollar men earn, with the same level of education. Historical factors that have contributed to the gender wage gap include the following:

- Women choosing or needing to leave and re-enter the workforce to meet family care giving responsibilities, resulting in a loss of seniority, advancement opportunities, and wages.

- Occupational segregation in historically undervalued and low-paying jobs, such as child care and clerical work.

- Traditionally lower levels of education (although this is becoming less of a factor as more and more women graduate from all levels of education).

- Less unionization among female workers.

- Discrimination in hiring, promotion, and compensation practices in the workplace, which is estimated to represent as much as 10 to 15 percent of the gender wage gap.

---

gender wage gap
The difference between wages earned by men and wages earned by women.

Studies have shown that women's jobs with the same value as men's work are underpaid. What actions can you take once you are in the workforce to close this gap?

Today, women are more educated, they are working in greater numbers and for longer hours, they are having fewer children, and they are taking less time away from work. Despite these changes, women's hourly wages continue to fall below men's wages at all levels of education. Generally speaking, the wage gap between men and women has been narrowing as education level rises.

Canada has a variety of pay equity laws and policies that differ depending on where one works. In a federally regulated industry (e.g., banking, telecommunications, transportation, or the federal government), one is covered by federal labour and human rights laws. Ontario and Quebec have proactive pay equity laws that cover both the public and private sectors. Other provinces enacted pay equity legislation that covered only the public sector. Still other jurisdictions, including the Territories, have provisions in their human rights laws that depend on an individual filing an official complaint against the employer.

For some organizations, legislation has been difficult to implement. First, how do you define equal (or comparable) value? For example, which job has more value, that of a nurse or that of a trash collector? As well, officials cite budget cutbacks and the huge costs of making up for past inequitable compensation to female employees as the reasons for delaying the implementation of this legislation. After 14 years in court and millions of dollars in lawyers' fees, BCE Inc. agreed in 2006 to pay up to $100 million to almost 5,000 mostly female employees who worked for the company during the 1990s. As you can imagine, this is not an issue that can easily be resolved.

Employment Equity[53]

A well-known 1980s case of discrimination highlights a major problem and how it was solved. A group of women accused the Canadian National Railway (CNR) of not hiring them because they were women. The CNR, like many other companies, did not hire women for jobs that were thought to be traditional men's jobs, those for which heavy physical labour was required. In this case, the jobs involved maintenance and repairs of the tracks. The Canadian Human Rights Commission ruled in favour of the women. The CNR appealed and the courts ruled against it all the way to the Supreme Court of Canada.

Employment equity refers to employment activities designed to increase employment opportunities for four groups given past discrimination toward the designated groups. These four groups are (1) women; (2) Aboriginal people (people who are Indian, Inuit, or Métis); (3) persons with disabilities; and (4) members of visible minorities (people, other than Aboriginal peoples, who are non-Caucasian in race or non-white in colour). Employment equity programs are developed by employers to remedy past discrimination or to prevent discrimination in the future. Employment equity "encourages the establishment of working conditions that are free of barriers, corrects the conditions of disadvantage in employment, and promotes the principle that employment equity requires special measures and the accommodation of differences for the four designated groups in Canada." Introduced in 1986, the Employment Equity Act applies to federally regulated industries, Crown corporations, and other federal organizations with 100 employees or more, as well as portions of the federal public administration. At the provincial level, these programs are implemented almost exclusively on a voluntary basis.

employment equity
Employment activities designed to increase employment opportunities for four groups (women, Aboriginal people, persons with disabilities, and members of visible minorities) given past discrimination.

How did this apply in the CNR example? The Canadian Human Rights Commission ordered CNR to develop a plan that would result in more women than men being hired for such jobs until the balance was more even. Specifically, women had to be hired for one in four non-traditional or blue-collar jobs in its St. Lawrence region until women held 13 percent of such jobs. When a man and a woman were equally qualified, the woman was expected to be selected until the balance was achieved.

The Employment Equity Act promotes equitable representation for women, Aboriginal peoples, persons with disabilities, and visible minorities who work in federally regulated workplaces. If you belong to one of these groups, would you consider employment in these workplaces? If you do not belong to one of these groups, would employment equity programs discourage you from applying to these workplaces?

Interpretation of the employment equity law eventually led employers to actively recruit and give preference to women and minority group members. Employment equity, for many employers, has become mostly a reporting function. They keep track of the numbers of employees that belong to these groups, and they try to remove any discrimination from hiring procedures, including trying to advertise positions more widely. As you might expect, interpretation of the law is often controversial and enforcement is difficult. Questions persist about the effect the program could have in creating a sort of reverse discrimination in the workplace.

Reverse discrimination has been defined as discriminating against members of a dominant or majority group (say, whites or males) usually as a result of policies designed to correct previous discrimination against minorities or disadvantaged groups. Charges of reverse discrimination have occurred when companies have been perceived as unfairly giving preference to women or minority group members, for example, in hiring and promoting. The Canadian Charter of Rights and Freedoms specifically allows for employment equity as a method to overcome long-standing discrimination against specific groups. Although preferential treatment will always raise questions of fairness, the Canadian Human Rights Act declares employment equity programs non-discriminatory if they fulfill the spirit of the law. This continues to be a controversial issue today.

reverse discrimination
Discriminating against members of a dominant or majority group (say, whites or males) usually as a result of policies designed to correct previous discrimination against minority or disadvantaged groups.

LAWS THAT PROTECT THE DISABLED

Legislation protects people with disabilities. Businesses cannot discriminate against people on the basis of any physical or mental disability. Employers are required to give disabled applicants the same consideration for employment as people without disabilities. Employers used to think that being fair meant treating everyone the same, but *accommodation* means treating people *according to their specific needs*. That can include putting up barriers to isolate people readily distracted by noise, reassigning workers to new tasks, and making changes to supervisors' management styles. Accommodations are not always expensive; for example, an inexpensive headset can allow someone with cerebral palsy to talk on the phone.

Progress Assessment

- Name three areas of human resource management responsibility that are affected by government legislation.
- Explain what employment equity is and give one example of it.
- What are ways employers can accommodate people with disabilities?

Effects of Legislation

Clearly, laws and regulations affect all areas of human resource management. It should be apparent that a career in this field offers a challenge to anyone willing to put forth the effort. Figure 12.9 lists some sites that you may consult to learn about some of the topics discussed in this chapter. In summary:

- Employers must know and act in accordance with the legal rights of their employees or risk costly court cases.
- Legislation affects all areas of human resource management, from hiring and training to compensation.

■ **FIGURE 12.9**

HUMAN RESOURCE INFORMATION SITES	
Human Resource Sites	**URL**
Benefits Canada	www.benefitscanada.com
Canadian Council of Human Resources Associations	www.chrp.ca
Canadian HR Reporter	www.hrreporter.com
Canadian Human Rights Reporter	www.cdn-hr-reporter.ca
The Conference Board of Canada	www.conferenceboard.ca
Society for Human Resource Management	www.shrm.org
Government Sites	**URL**
Canadian Human Rights Commission	www.chrc-ccdp.ca
Employment Equity	www.labour.gc.ca/eng/standards_equity/eq/emp/index.shtml
Government of Canada	www.canada.gc.ca
Statistics Canada	www.statcan.gc.ca

- Managers must be sensitive not only to legal requirements, but also to union contracts and social standards and expectations, which can be even more demanding.

- Court cases demonstrate that it is sometimes legal to implement special employment policies (e.g., employment equity) and training to correct past discrimination.

- New court cases and legislation change human resource management almost daily. The only way to keep current is to read business literature and stay familiar with emerging issues.

SUMMARY

LO1 **Explain the importance of human resource management as a strategic contributor to organizational success, and summarize the five steps in human resource planning.**

Human resource management is the process of evaluating human resource needs, finding people to fill those needs, and getting the best work from each employee by providing the right incentives and job environment, all with the goal of meeting organizational objectives.

What are current challenges and opportunities in human resource management?

Many current challenges and opportunities arise from changing demographics: more women, minorities, immigrants, and older workers in the workforce. Others include a shortage of trained workers and an abundance of unskilled workers, skilled workers in declining industries requiring retraining, changing employee work attitudes, and complex laws and regulations.

What are the five steps in human resource planning?

The five steps are (1) preparing a human resource inventory of the organization's employees; (2) preparing a job analysis; (3) assessing future demand; (4) assessing future supply; and (5) establishing a strategic plan.

LO2 **Describe methods that companies use to recruit new employees, and explain some of the issues that make recruitment challenging.**

Recruitment is the set of activities used to obtain a sufficient number of the right people at the right time.

What methods do companies use to recruit new employees?

Recruiting sources are classified as either internal or external. Internal sources include hiring from within the firm (e.g., transfers and promotions) and employees who recommend others to hire. External recruitment sources include advertisements, public and private employment agencies, school placement offices, management consultants, professional organizations, referrals, walk-in applications, and the Internet.

Why has recruitment become more challenging?

Legal restrictions complicate hiring practices. Finding suitable employees can also be made more difficult if companies are considered unattractive workplaces.

LO3 **Outline the five steps in selecting employees, and illustrate the use of various types of employee training and development methods.**

Selection is the process of gathering and interpreting information to decide which applicants should be hired.

What are the five steps in the selection process?

The steps are (1) obtaining complete application forms; (2) conducting initial and follow-up interviews; (3) giving employment tests; (4) conducting background investigations; and (5) establishing a trial period of employment.

What are some employee training methods?

After assessing the needs of the organization and the skills of the employees, training programs are designed that may include the following activities: orientation, on-the-job training, apprentice programs, off-the-job training, online training, vestibule training, and job simulation.

What methods are used to develop managerial skills?

Management development methods include on-the-job coaching, understudy positions, job rotation, and off-the-job courses and training.

How does networking fit in this process?

Networking is the process of establishing contacts with key managers within and outside the organization to get additional development assistance.

LO4 **Trace the six steps in appraising employee performance, and summarize the objectives of employee compensation programs.**

A performance appraisal is an evaluation of the performance level of employees against established standards to make decisions about promotions, compensation, training, or termination.

What are the six steps in appraising employee performance?

The six steps are (1) establish performance standards; (2) communicate those standards; (3) evaluate performance; (4) discuss results; (5) take corrective action when needed; and (6) use the results for decisions about promotions, compensation, training, or termination.

What are examples of compensation systems?

Compensation systems include salary systems, hourly wages, piecework, commission plans, bonus plans, profit-sharing plans, and stock options. The most common compensation systems appropriate for teams are skill-based and gain-sharing compensation programs. Managers also reward outstanding individual performance within teams.

What are objectives of employee compensation programs?

Compensation is one of the main tools that companies use to attract and retain qualified employees. These programs can attract the right kinds of people the organization needs and in sufficient numbers. They provide employees with the incentive to work efficiently and productively. They also provide employees with some sense of financial security through fringe benefits.

What are fringe benefits?

Fringe benefits include such items as sick leave, vacation pay, pension plans, and health plans that provide additional compensation to employees beyond base wages. Cafeteria-style fringe benefits plans let employees choose the benefits they want, up to a certain dollar amount.

LO5 **Describe the ways in which employees can move through a company: promotion, reassignment, termination, and retirement.**

Employees do not always stay in the position they were hired to fill.

How can employees move within a company?

Employees can be moved up (promotion), over (reassignment), or out (termination or retirement) of a company. Employees can also choose to leave a company to pursue opportunities elsewhere.

LO6 **Illustrate the effects of legislation on human resource management.**

There are many laws that affect human resource management.

What do the Charter of Rights and Freedoms and the Human Rights Act guarantee?

The Charter of Rights and Freedoms guarantees equality before the law for all Canadians. The Human Rights Act seeks to provide equal employment opportunities without regard to race and colour, national or ethnic origin, religion, age, sex, sexual orientation, marital status, family status, disability, or pardoned convictions.

What areas does the federal government legislate?

The federal government legislates on national issues and it has jurisdiction over certain types of businesses that are deemed to be of a national nature (e.g., banking, air transportation, and many First Nation activities). Provincial or territorial labour laws apply to the majority (94 percent) of all employees.

What are some examples of employment laws?

Pay equity, employment equity, and laws that protect the disabled are highlighted in this chapter.

KEY TERMS

apprentice programs	human resource management	online training
cafeteria-style benefits	(HRM)	on-the-job training
(flexible benefits)	job analysis	orientation
plans	job description	pay equity
compressed workweek	job sharing	performance appraisal
contingent workers	job simulation	recruitment
core time	job specifications	reverse discrimination
employment equity	management development	selection
flextime plan	mentor	training and development
fringe benefits	networking	vestibule training
gender wage gap	off-the-job training	

CRITICAL THINKING

1. Does human resource management interest you as a career? What are your experiences working with human resource professionals?

2. Why should you be interested in the subject matter of human resource management, even if you are not majoring in this field?

3. What effects have dual-career families had on the human resource function? How about single-parent families? Are there any similarities?

4. Do you think that most vacancies in firms are filled through a competitive process? Explain.

5. Performance appraisals are often done poorly for different reasons. For example, people may not like to complete them or have them completed for them. The company's perspective also affects the effectiveness of this process. Is the appraisal conducted so employees can be assessed and corrected (some might say punished) or so that the collective can do better? What can a company do to ensure that appraisals are effectively conducted?

6. Imagine that you must delete a position due to budgetary (not performance) reasons. What effect might the dismissal have on remaining employees? Explain how you would tell the affected employee and your remaining subordinates.

DEVELOPING WORKPLACE SKILLS

Key: ● **Team**   ★ **Analytic**   ▲ **Communication**   ▣ **Technology**

▣ ★ 1. Look for job listings online or in your local newspaper and find at least two positions that you might like to have when you graduate. List the qualifications specified in each of the ads and identify methods the companies might use to determine how well applicants meet each of those qualifications.

▣ ★ 2. Secure a blank performance-appraisal form from any company for any category of entry-level employment. State specifically what dimensions of work performance are being measured and how the dimensions are measured.

★ ● 3. Consider the following occupations: doctor, car salesperson, computer software developer, teacher, and assembly worker. Identify in a team of three students the method of compensation you think is appropriate for each. Explain your answer.

★ ▲ 4. Recall any on-the-job and off-the-job training sessions you've experienced. Write a brief critique of each. How would you improve each? Share your ideas with the class.

● ▣ 5. The federal government's Temporary Foreign Worker Program touches on both immigration
★ ▲   and employment as it permits Canadian employers to hire foreign nationals to fill temporary labour and skill shortages when qualified Canadian citizens or permanent residents are not available.[54] In a group, investigate program advantages and disadvantages to the Canadian economy. Which industries employ these temporary foreign workers? Where in Canada do they work? What are some recent program changes as a result of abuse allegations? Share your information with the class.

ANALYZING MANAGEMENT DECISIONS

Dual-Career Planning

Carey Moler is a 32-year-old account executive for a communications company. She is married to Mitchell Moler, a lawyer. Carey and Mitchell did not make any definite plans about how to juggle their careers and family life until Carey reached age 30. Then they decided to have a baby, and career planning took on a whole new dimension. A company named Catalyst talked to 815 dual-career couples and found that most of them, like the Molers, had not made any long-range career decisions regarding family lifestyle.

From the business perspective, such dual-career families create real concerns. There are problems with relocation, with child care, and so on that affect recruiting, productivity, morale, and promotion policies.

For a couple such as the Molers, having both career and family responsibilities is exhausting. But that is just one problem. If Carey is moving up in her firm, what happens if Mitchell gets a terrific job offer a thousand kilometres away? What if Carey gets such an offer? Who is going to care for the baby? What happens if the baby becomes ill? How do they plan their vacations when there are three schedules to balance? Who will do the housework? Dual careers require careful planning and discussion, and those plans need to be reviewed over time. A couple that decides at age 22 to do certain things may change their minds at age 30. Whether or not to have children, where to locate, how to manage the household— all such issues and more can become major problems if not carefully planned.

The same is true for corporations. They too must plan for dual-career families as well as single-parent families. They must give attention to job sharing, flextime, parental leave policies, transfer policies, nepotism rules (i.e., rules about hiring family members), and more.

Discussion Questions

1. In addition to the examples stated above, what other issues can you see developing because of dual-career families? How is this affecting children in such families?

2. What kind of corporate policies need changing to adapt to these new realities?

3. What are the advantages of dual careers? What are the disadvantages? What can couples do to minimize the problems of dual careers? How can a couple reap the rewards?

VIDEO CASE 12

Recruiting on Social Media

Social-media recruitment expert, Shahid Wazed, shares that traditionally recruiters have been heavily using job boards in Canada to attract potential candidates. Talent leaders are now finding that people are not going to their career sites. So what is an alternate method to reach out to people? His advice is that recruiters need to consider unconventional methods to reach new talent. That is, search for future opportunities that are social, mobile, and inbound.

According to Manpower data, 72 percent of job seekers are looking to Facebook for company information or job openings versus LinkedIn. While LinkedIn remains the best platform for talent hunting, Facebook is best for passive recruitment where companies can build a relationship with candidates before ever actually making contact with them.

On average, people are spending more time on Facebook (40 minutes a day) than on LinkedIn (17 minutes a month). If employers are not on social media such as Facebook building their brands and recruiting passive talent, then these employers are missing out on opportunities for top talent.

Discussion Questions

1. How can employers build a relationship with candidates through Facebook?

2. How does Canada rank to other countries when it comes to passive recruitment? What are the risks to employers if this does not improve?

3. What is your online job search approach? Do you visit the company's job board? Do you agree with Shahid Wazed that social media should be used more effectively by employers when recruiting talent? Explain.

Dealing with Employee–Management Issues and Relations

LEARNING OBJECTIVES

After you have read and studied this chapter, you should be able to:

LO1	Trace the history of organized labour in Canada.
LO2	Discuss the major legislation affecting labour unions.
LO3	Describe the collective bargaining process.
LO4	Outline the objectives of labour unions.
LO5	Describe the negotiation tactics used by labour and management during conflicts.
LO6	Explain some of today's employee–management issues.

PROFILE

GETTING TO KNOW GERALD (GERRY) VARRICCHIO, REGIONAL ORGANIZING DIRECTOR FOR CENTRAL AND EASTERN CANADA, LABORERS' INTERNATIONAL UNION OF NORTH AMERICA (LIUNA)

The Laborers' International Union of North America (LiUNA, <http://www.LiUNA.ca>) is the most progressive, aggressive, and fastest growing union of construction workers, waste management workers, show service workers, and health-care workers in Canada. Although LiUNA began in 1903 as a construction union, its members now work in many types of factories and processing plants. They also work in stores, hotels, restaurants, and offices. An international union with members both in Canada and the United States, LiUNA has over half a million members. In Canada it represents 100,000 members and retirees with affiliates from coast to coast, and the Canadian arm of LiUNA is proud to be a part of one of North America's oldest and most powerful unions.

Source: Courtesy of LiUNA. Used with permission.

Gerry Varricchio is an International Representative with LiUNA and a labour organizer. He specializes in the construction industry in the province of Ontario, though he regularly runs campaigns in the industrial sector. As the Regional Organizing Director for the LiUNA Central and Eastern Canada Region, Varricchio works with LiUNA's District Councils and Local Unions across Ontario and the Atlantic Provinces. Together, they develop and implement LiUNA's regional and local union organizing plans. This includes training and hiring union organizers as required to meet the needs of each of the organizing plans across the region.

As Regional Organizing Director for CECOF (the Central and Eastern Canada Organizing Fund), Varricchio has over 70 regional organizers reporting to him. Contrast this to 1993 when he was the sole regional organizer employed. LiUNA is a highly motivated and powerful unit dedicated to organizing the unorganized and to preserving work for its members, while keeping management competitive. To achieve this goal, Varricchio's vision encompasses a joint, co-operative effort between labour and management. As a result of LiUNA's organizing initiatives through CECOF, and the efforts of Varricchio and the affiliates, LiUNA has the distinct honour of being the most prolific union organizer in Canada.

Varricchio started his working life on the tools, first as a carpenter, and then as a member of LiUNA Local 1089 in his hometown of Sarnia, Ontario, working in "Chemical Valley." He was elected to the LiUNA Local 1089 executive board and as a delegate to the LiUNA Ontario Provincial District Council in 1985, and re-elected every four years subsequently. Experiencing his own health issues as a result of chemical spills in the workplace, Varricchio was personally aware of the difficulties faced in the work environment, including health and safety issues. He recognized early on that some of the major protections for workers are accessible only thorough unionization. Consequently, when offered a job in 1987 by the LiUNA Ontario Provincial District Council as an organizer, Varricchio jumped at the chance.

In addition to his organizing duties on behalf of LiUNA, Varricchio also serves as a Trustee on the Local 1089 Training and Rehabilitation Trust Fund and on the Benefits Trust Fund. One accomplishment is that he pioneered the first union benefit plan that integrates a registered educational scholarship plan for members and their children into a union benefit trust plan as part of the standard benefit package.

Throughout the past 28 years, Varricchio has adapted to the demands of the workplace. He was at the forefront in introducing the process of "top-down" organizing, a system of engaging the employer in the initial stages of organizing, with the intent of levelling the playing field for all of the employers in the industry. This reassures individual employers who believe that the presence of a union in the workplace will lead to inequalities in terms of bid power and limit their access to future contracts. Varricchio has expressed this as follows: "Unions have a dual responsibility—to ensure that their members are getting the best wage and benefit packages and working conditions available in the marketplace, and equally as important, to ensure that their contractual employers not only remain competitive, but have a labour partner that can assist them in expanding their business and market share."

Managers in both profit-seeking and non-profit organizations address labour-relations challenges every day. This chapter discusses some of these employee–management relations and issues. When asked what his thoughts are for the future of labour–management relations, Varricchio points out that the labour–management community is at the mercy of the political climate, both federally and provincially. It is important for labour and management to partner together to achieve common goals and look out for each other's interests. "Perhaps in spite of the adversarial beginnings between unions and employers and the prejudices that evolved over time," says Varricchio, "the true business value of unions will be recognized and utilized when it is most needed."

Sources: Gerry Varricchio, Regional Organizing Director for Central and Eastern Canada, The Labourers' International Union of North America, interview, 25 March 2015, Hamilton; and "About LiUNA," accessed 25 March 2015, LiUNA Canada, http://www.LiUNA.ca/aboutLiUNA.php.

Employee–Management Issues

A good starting point in discussing employee–management relations in Canada is a discussion of labour unions. A **labour union** is an employee organization whose main goal is representing its members in employee–management negotiations of job-related issues. Private-sector labour unions include those who work as employees of a private firm or business.[1] Unionized public sector employees work in public administration at the federal, provincial, territorial, municipal, First Nations, and other Aboriginal levels as well as in Crown corporations, liquor control boards, and other government institutions such as schools (including colleges and universities), hospitals, and public libraries.[2] Recently labour unions have been in the news more than they have been for years. For example, a major issue involves dealing with public-sector labour unions. With provinces facing serious debt problems, government officials are trying to cut public sector costs, particularly labour costs. There will be challenges for both governments and unions moving forward due to increasing labour and pension costs. Before we get into such issues, however, let's explore the nature of unions in general and what the issues have been over time.

labour union
An employee organization whose main goal is representing its members in employee–management negotiation of job-related issues.

The relationship between management (representing owners or shareholders) and employees is not always smooth. Management's responsibility to produce a profit by maximizing productivity sometimes necessitates hard decisions, which limits a manager's chance to win popularity contests with workers. Labour (the collective term for non-management workers) is interested in fair and competent management, human dignity, decent working conditions, and a reasonable share in the wealth that its work generates. (One could argue that management is also interested in these same ideals.) Like other managerial challenges, employee–management issues require open discussion, goodwill, and compromise.

Workers originally formed unions to protect themselves from intolerable work conditions and unfair treatment, and also to secure some say in the operation of their jobs. As the number of private-sector union members grew, workers gained more negotiating power with managers and more political power as well. For example, labour unions were largely responsible for the establishment of minimum-wage laws, overtime rules, workers' compensation, severance pay, child-labour laws, job safety regulations, and more.[3]

The United Food and Commercial Workers (UFCW) union <*http://ufcw.ca*> offers a national youth internship program open to young members interested in organizing, labour history, globalization, anti-racism/anti-oppression, and other topics.[4] Would you consider applying for this program? How could the knowledge gained help you during your working career?

Union strength among private workers, however, has waned as private labour unions have lost the economic and political power they once had, and memberships has declined. Economists suggest that increased global competition, shifts from manufacturing to service and high-tech industries that are less heavily unionized, growth in part-time work, and changes in management philosophies are some of the reasons for labour's decline.[5] Others contend the decline is the result of labour's success in seeing the issues it championed become law.

Some labour analysts forecast that unions will regain strength as companies engage in more unpopular practices such as outsourcing; others insist that unions have seen their brightest days. Few doubt that the role and influence of unions—particularly in selected regions—will continue to arouse emotions and opinions that contrast considerably. Let's briefly look at labour unions and then analyze other key issues affecting employee–management relations.

Labour Unions Yesterday and Today

Are labour unions essential today? This is a very political subject with strongly-held opposing positions. An electrician carrying a picket sign in Sudbury, Ontario, would say yes and elaborate on the dangers to a free society if employers continue to try to bust, or break apart unions. A small manufacturer would disagree, and complain about being restricted by union wage and benefit obligations in an increasingly competitive global economy.

Historians generally agree that today's unions are an outgrowth of the economic transition caused by the Industrial Revolution of the nineteenth and early twentieth centuries. Workers who once toiled in the fields, dependent on the mercies of nature for survival, found themselves relying on the continuous roll of factory presses and assembly lines for their living. Making the transition from an agricultural economy to an industrial economy was quite difficult. Over time, workers in business learned that strength through unity (unions) could lead to improved job conditions, better wages, and job security. These improvements did not come easily or quickly. Even today, while both sides have a vested interest in seeing their organizations thrive, the needs and desires of both sides can sometimes be wholly different.

While the technological achievements of the Industrial Revolution brought countless new products to market and reduced the need for physical labour in many industries, they also put pressure on workers to achieve higher productivity in factory jobs that called for long hours and low pay. Can you see how these conditions made it possible for labour unions to become relevant by the turn of the twentieth century?

Today's critics of organized labour maintain that few of the inhumane conditions once dominant in Canadian history exist in the modern workplace. They argue that labour is an industry in itself, and protecting workers has become secondary.[6] Some workplace analysts maintain that the current legal system and changing management philosophies minimize the possibility that sweatshops (industrial revolution workplaces with unsatisfactory, unsafe, or oppressive labour conditions) could reappear in Canada.

"In a perfect world," states Gerry Varricchio, Regional Organizing Director for Central and Eastern Canada for the Laborers' International Union of North America (LiUNA), "labour and management partner together to achieve common goals and look out for each other's interests. Unfortunately, human nature being what it is, greed, incompetence, and self-serving interests of players from one side or the other, or both, can supersede the common good thereby creating conflict and negative perceptions about unions. In any market, competing on a level playing field is extremely important to the success and future growth of a business. The most effective vehicle for competing businesses to utilize in creating and sustaining a level playing field, in their respective markets, is a union.[7]

LO1   Trace the history of organized labour in Canada.

The Early History of Organized Labour

The presence of formal labour organizations in Canada dates back to the 1800s. Early unions on the wharves of Halifax, St. John's, and Quebec during the War of 1812 existed to profit from labour scarcity. Others, such as the Montreal shoemakers or the Toronto printers of the 1830s, were craft unions. A **craft union** is an organization of skilled specialists in a particular craft or trade, typically local or regional. These unions were formed to address fundamental work issues of pay, hours, conditions, and job security—many of the same issues that dominate labour negotiations today. By forming a union, these skilled workers hoped to protect their craft and status from being undermined.

> **craft union**
> An organization of skilled specialists in a particular craft or trade; typically local or regional.

Many of the early labour organizations were local or regional in membership. Also, most were established to achieve some short-range goal (e.g., a pay increase) and disbanded after attaining a specific objective. This situation changed dramatically in the late nineteenth century with the expansion of the Industrial Revolution and the emergence of modern industrial capitalism. The system of producing the necessities of society in small, home-based workplaces gave way to production in large factories driven by steam and later electricity. Enormous productivity increases were gained through mass production and job specialization. However, this brought problems for workers in terms of productivity expectations, long hours of work, low wages, and unemployment.

A legal holiday since 1894, Labour Day is a celebration of workers and their families. (Here you see workers participating in a Labour Day parade.) It was inspired by the first significant workers' demonstration in 1872 where, accompanied by four bands, unionists marched through the streets of Toronto. Leaders demanded better conditions for all workers, as well as the release of 24 union members who were imprisoned for going on strike. About 10,000 Torontonians turned out that day to see the parade and listen to the speeches.

Workers were faced with the reality that production was vital. Those who failed to produce, or stayed home because they were ill or had family problems, lost their jobs. Over time, the increased emphasis on production led firms to expand the hours of work. The length of the average workweek in 1900 was 60 hours, compared to 40 hours today, but an 80-hour workweek was not uncommon for some industries.[8] Wages were low and child labour was widespread. Minimum-wage laws and unemployment benefits were non-existent, which meant that periods of unemployment were hard on families who earned subsistence wages. As you can imagine, these were not short-term issues that would easily go away. The workplace was ripe for the emergence of labour organizations.

The struggle for more humane working conditions and wages was not an easy one because before 1872, it was illegal to attempt to form a union in Canada. The pioneers in the early struggles were treated as common criminals. They were arrested, beaten, and often shot. The Winnipeg General Strike of 1919 is Canada's best known general strike, where almost 30,000 workers left their jobs. A charge by police into a crowd of protesters resulted in 30 casualties, including one death.[9]

As the years progressed, more unions were formed and more employees joined them. Other types of unions—such as industrial unions—were created to represent certain workers. An **industrial union** is one that consists of unskilled and semi-skilled workers in mass-production industries such as automobile manufacturing and mining.

> **industrial union**
> Consists of unskilled and semi-skilled workers in mass-production industries such as automobile manufacturing and mining.

Long after it was no longer illegal, the idea of workers forming unions to protect their interests was still regarded with suspicion by employers and governments in Canada. Democratic rights for all was still a weak concept, and the idea of people getting together to fight for their rights was not accepted as it is today. The union movement was greatly influenced by immigrants from Europe (especially Britain), who brought with them the ideas and experiences of a more advanced and often more radical background. The growing union movement in the United States also influenced Canada. Many Canadian unions started as locals of American unions, and this relationship continues today. As democracy gradually gained strength, the union movement grew with it. Its participation, in turn, helped democracy sink deeper, wider roots in Canada.

The Structure of Labour Unions in Canada[10]

The organizational structure of unions in Canada is quite complex. Unions in Canada can be divided into four types of labour organizations: independent local, directly chartered, national, and international. According to the Workplace Information and Research Division of the Labour Program, the vast majority of covered workers (94.5 percent) are represented by national (69.5 percent) and international (25.0 percent) unions. Of the remainder, 3.8 percent are represented by independent local unions and 1.6 percent by directly chartered unions. Let's consider these four types next.

The most basic unit is an **independent local organization** (also called the *union local*, *local*, or *local union*) which is a union that is not formally connected or affiliated with any other labour organization. One local usually represents one school, government office, or a specific factory or office of a company. However, that local can also cover several small companies or other work units. Contrast this with a **directly chartered union**, which is a union that is directly affiliated to a labour congress. It pays per capita dues directly to the congress and receives services from the congress.

independent local organization
A union that is not formally connected or affiliated with any other labour organization; also called the union local, local, or local union.

directly chartered union
A union that is directly affiliated to a labour congress to whom it pays per capita dues and receives services.

While a local can be an independent organization within a specific geographic area, it is usually part of a larger structure, namely one that is provincial or regional in focus, or a **national union**, which is a union that only represents workers in Canada. Two examples that will be discussed shortly include the Canadian Union of Public Employees (CUPE) and Unifor. An **international union** represents workers in Canada and the United States. Examples include the United Steelworkers (USW) and the International Brotherhood of Teamsters (IBT).

national union
A union that only represents workers in Canada.

international union
A union that represents workers in Canada and the United States.

Consider Local 1089, based in Sarnia, Ontario. It is affiliated with LiUNA's Canadian national union as well as LiUNA's international union. You can read more about LiUNA in the chapter profile and throughout this chapter.

In addition, unions affiliate with labour congresses, also known as *union centrals,* for assistance at national and international levels. The main functions of these union centrals has been to coordinate the activities of member unions when representing the interests of labour to local, provincial, and federal governments as well as to organized labour on the world scene. The Canadian Labour Congress (CLC, *<http://canadianlabour.ca>*) represents the largest share of workers covered by a collective agreement (69.2 percent). It is followed by Quebec-based Confédération des Syndicats Nationaux/ Confederation of National Trade Unions (CSN/CNTU, *<http://www.csn.qc.ca>*), which represents 7 percent of workers.[11]

The CLC and its affiliated unions have been promoting the creation of green jobs for decades. This includes reducing the distance between producer and consumer and encouraging the production of everything from green vehicles to windmill blades in Canada. How might this contribute to more jobs?

The CLC represents the interests of more than 3 million affiliated workers in every imaginable occupation from coast to coast. It is the umbrella organization for dozens of affiliated Canadian and international unions, as well as provincial federations of labour and regional labour councils. The CLC lobbies the different levels of government on social and economic issues, human rights and equality, workplace issues, international issues, and environmental issues.

Figure 13.1 charts the structure of the international union of LiUNA. Based in the United States, it is structured under a governing constitution, which is reviewed and amended every five years at a constitutional convention. This convention brings together elected delegates from every local union and district council in North America. Along with constitutional resolutions, the convention also elects the General Executive Board, which is composed of the general president, general secretary treasurer, and ten regional vice-presidents. The international union issues and holds the charters of all local unions

■ **FIGURE 13.1**

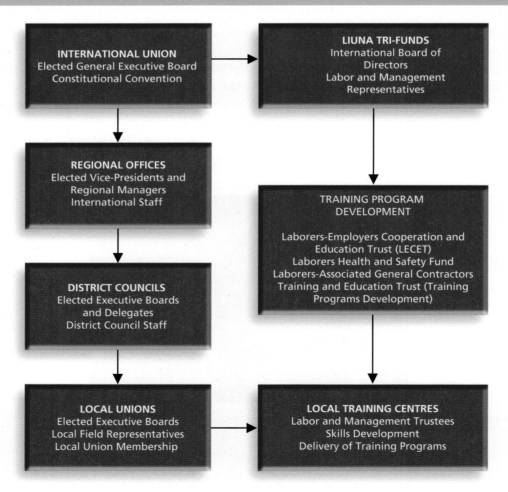

THE STRUCTURE OF THE LABORERS' INTERNATIONAL UNION OF NORTH AMERICA (LIUNA)

Elections are democratic at LiUNA as members vote for representation at each level of the union's structure. Members at the union local elect their local's executive board and officers. Each local then elects a district council delegate. These delegates elect the district council's executive board. Local union members also elect the international vice-president and regional managers for their regional office. At the international union, each local member elects the general president of the union (the equivalent of a CEO) and the general secretary treasurer (the equivalent of a CFO).

and district councils that operate under the rule of the LiUNA Constitution. District councils are composed of elected delegates from local unions within a state, states, province, or provinces. These councils are responsible for collective bargaining and are the holders of "bargaining rights" on behalf of their members. LiUNA also has established national labour–management funds that are directed toward training, health and safety, and the promotion of unionized construction. The funds are referred to as the Tri-Funds. These unique funds, which are supported by joint contributions, provide a broad range of services to both labour and management.

Union Coverage

The **unionization rate**, also known as **union density**, refers to the percentage of employed individuals who are union members. The **coverage rate** refers to the percentage of employed individuals (including both union and non-unionized members) who are covered by a collective agreement.[12] The Canadian coverage rate is approximately 30 percent (4.6 million) of all employed individuals.[13] While union membership has been increasing (i.e., the number of workers that belong to a union), this has not been reflected in an increase in the unionization rate (i.e., the percentage of workers that belong to a union). [14]

unionization rate (union density)
A measure of the percentage of employed individuals who are union members.

coverage rate
A measure of the percentage of employed individuals (including both union and non-unionized members) who are covered by a collective agreement.

Full-time work, longer job tenure, large firms, higher educational attainment, and better wages are associated with higher unionization rates. Figure 13.2 summarizes union coverage by selected characteristics.

■ **FIGURE 13.2**

UNION COVERAGE BY SELECTED CHARACTERISTICS, 2014

Coverage represents union members and persons who are not union members but are covered by collective agreements. For example, full-time workers (31.9 percent) are more likely to be covered than part-time workers (23.7 percent)

Characteristic	Percentage	Characteristics	Percentage
Public sector	74.8	No degree, certificate, or diploma	20.1
Private sector	16.8	University degree	35.3
Aged 15 to 24	15.3	Workplace size: under 20 employees	14.2
Aged 45 to 54	36.1	Workplace size: over 500 employees	55.3
Men	28.9	Least unionized industry—agriculture	4.7
Women	31.9	Most unionized industry—public administration	72.4
Goods-producing industries	27.9	Most unionized province—Newfoundland and Labrador	37.8
Services-producing industries	31.1	Least unionized province—Alberta	22.1

Source: Compiled from CANSIM tables 282-0220 to 282-0225, Statistics Canada, 30 January 2015.

Before we discuss labour legislation, let us consider two unions that are often in the news.

Canada's Largest Unions

Canada's largest union is the Canadian Union of Public Employees (CUPE). Unifor is Canada's largest private-sector union. Let's briefly look at each next.

CUPE[15]

Formed in 1963, CUPE has over 628,000 members and more than 70 offices across Canada. It represents workers in health care, emergency services, education, early learning and child care, municipalities, social services, libraries, utilities, transportation, airlines, and more. Collectively, the payroll for CUPE members is over $21.8 billion. CUPE has more than 2,623 locals and chartered organizations across the country ranging in size from 20 to 20,000 members. More than 70 percent of CUPE's 3,946 collective agreements are with locals of 100 members or less.

UNIFOR[16]

Unifor represents more than 305,000 workers. It was formed during the 2013 Labour Day weekend when the Canadian Auto Workers (CAW) and the Communications, Energy, and Paperworkers (CEP) unions merged. Like its name, it is a union for everyone—workers, the unemployed, and those that are self-employed. Its diverse membership includes workers in nearly every industry including communications, resources, manufacturing, and services. There are 750 local unions operating under the Unifor banner, of all different sizes.

Progress Assessment

- Why were unions originally formed?
- What are the four types of labour organizations? Describe each one.
- Name Canada's two largest unions.

LO2 Discuss the major legislation affecting labour unions.

Labour Legislation

The growth and influence of organized labour in Canada have depended primarily on two major factors: the law and public opinion. As with other movements that promoted greater fairness and equity in our society—such as women's right to vote, equal rights for minorities and women, and protection for children—when support for employees' rights became widespread in Canada, laws were passed to enforce them. Today we have laws establishing minimum wage, paid minimum holidays and vacation, maximum hours, overtime pay, health and safety conditions, workers' compensation, employment insurance, the Canada/Quebec Pension Plan, and a host of other rights. It is strange to realize that at one time or another, these were all on the agenda of unions and were opposed by employers and governments for many years. They often denounced these demands as radical notions.

The effect of unions goes far beyond their numbers. Companies that want to keep unions out often provide compensation, benefits, and working conditions that match or exceed those found in union plants or offices. Thus, the levels established by unions spill over to non-union companies.

Unions are regulated by federal and provincial legislation, and they are required by law to be democratic and financially accountable to their members. In addition, all unions have constitutions that must be registered with government labour boards.

The federal government has control over specified fields of activity that are national in nature. As stated in Chapter 12, such activities apply to approximately 6 percent of Canadian workers.[17] These employees work for banks, railways, airlines, telephone and cable companies, and radio and broadcasting companies. The federal government also has jurisdiction over many First Nations activities. Federal legislation applies to unions and labour–management relations in these businesses as well as to all federal Crown corporations and federal civil servants. The major legislation that governs labour–management relations for these employees is the Canada Labour Code, which is administered by Employment and Social Development Canada. It is also responsible for the Employment Equity Act as well as other legislation on wages and working conditions.

Provincial or territorial laws apply to the rest of the Canadian workforce. As you can imagine, these laws vary and it is the responsibility of businesses to know the rights of their workers and vice versa. Keep in mind, the Supreme Court of Canada can still intervene in these jurisdictions as highlighted in this next example:[18]

> Saying it was unconstitutional, the Supreme Court of Canada struck down a controversial Saskatchewan law that prevented public sector employees from striking. In the absence of employer and union agreements, the law had permitted the provincial government to decide which workers were considered essential and therefore could not strike. The Supreme Court affirmed the principle that any labour-relations scheme that gives management a final authoritative say over the conditions of its workers was not appropriate. The ruling will affect public service unions in provinces across the country, such as British Columbia, Nova Scotia, and Newfoundland, which have essential services laws for health-care workers.

The Supreme Court of Canada struck down a federal law that forbade the Royal Mounted Police from unionizing, saying it violated the Canadian Charter of Rights and Freedom. The court suggested forming a traditional union as one option that would restore the employees' collective bargaining rights.[19] Do you think that all workers should have the right to unionize?

Workplace Laws[20]

As mentioned already, most workers in Canada (approximately 94 percent) are protected by the employment laws of their province or territory. The remainder are in jobs covered by federal laws. All workers in Canada have the right to work in a safe and healthy environment. Legislation protects workers against health and safety hazards in the workplace.

One workplace law is the *right to know about workplace hazards*. By knowing about workplace hazards, workers can ensure that employers make work safer, provide protection to workers, and give training so that workers can work with the smallest possibility of injury or illness. Unfortunately, and in spite of some of the best workplace health and safety laws in the world, over 1,000 Canadian workers die each year due to an unsafe workplace. Close to one million workers are injured at work every year.

New and young employees are particularly vulnerable in the workplace. They are three times more likely to be hurt in their first month on the job than any other time in their career. "One thing we know is that if workers—particularly young and new workers—know their rights and know how to work safely, we can continue to reduce the number of injuries across the province," says Ontario Labour Minister Kevin Flynn.

Another example is the *right to refuse unsafe work*, which entitles a worker to step away from work that he or she believes is unsafe. This right allows the worker to have the refused work investigated, and repaired if it is dangerous. During this time, the worker receives pay and is protected from an employer's possible reprisal, since it is illegal for an employer to fire or discipline a worker who refuses work that she or he believes is unsafe.

All provinces and territories provide for workers compensation benefits that are paid if a worker *gets hurt at work*. This includes if someone becomes sick on the job. If a worker has an accident at work, the supervisor must be notified right away. A health-care professional should be contacted and a claim filed with the workers compensation board.

Labour Relations Boards[21]

To enforce labour legislation, the federal and provincial governments have created their own **labour relations boards (LRBs)**. An LRB functions more informally than a court but it has the full authority of the law. In all jurisdictions, the LRB's decision is final and binding and cannot be appealed except for procedural matters.

> **labour relations board (LRB)**
> An organization created by the federal or provincial government to enforce labour legislation.

For example, the federal government created the Canada Industrial Relations Board (CIRB, <http://www.cirb-ccri.gc.ca>). Its mandate includes supporting constructive labour–management relations in the sectors regulated by Part I of the Canada Labour Code. With this in mind, the CIRB provides a variety of dispute resolution services, it adjudicates matters where necessary, and it also provides mediation assistance with a goal to seek a resolution of matters that best meets the needs of the parties. Specific activities include dealing with the following: applications and complaints involving the acquisition and termination of bargaining rights; unfair labour practices; the determination of the levels of services required to be maintained during a work stoppage; unlawful strikes or lockouts; the labour relations implications of corporate mergers and acquisitions; and other matters brought forward by employees, trade unions or employers in federal jurisdiction.

The Spotlight on Small Business shares suggestions on what employers can do to limit potential liability in the areas of workplace harassment and violence.

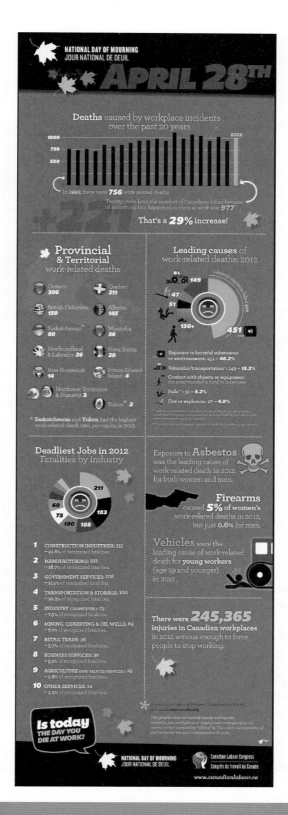

What can employees do to protect themselves from injuries? What are ways that employers can do more to protect their workers? Do you think that enough attention is being focused on enforcement?

Spotlight *On* SMALL BUSINESS

Helping Reduce Harassment and Violence in the Workplace

Robinson Heeney LLP <*http://www.robinsonheeney.com*>, a Toronto- based employment law firm, was founded in 2011 by lawyers Kevin Robinson and James Heeney. The firm provides advice to both employers and employees on all aspects of employment law. The firm also provides third-party workplace investigations and training services.

Partner James Heeney has been named by *Canadian HR Reporter* as a leading employment lawyer in Toronto. His employer-side practice focuses on providing strategic advice and litigation support in the areas of employment agreements, policy manuals, terminations, and human rights issues. On the employee side of his practice, Heeney routinely advises clients on both unionized and non-unionized issues relating to executive compensation, employment contracts, terminations, and human rights.

Why take on the challenge of starting your own business? Heeney was motivated to create a firm focused on integrity and exceptional legal advice, while still ensuring it was provided in a manner that was cost effective, timely, and practical. He wanted to influence an organization that ranked a good work environment as one of its top priorities. While he admits that running a business is not easy, there is certainly more satisfaction out of its successes. "No one wants to work long hours, but it is easier when it happens and you know it's to build your own business," says Heeney. "Many of my clients are long standing and I am so proud to be able to say that."

One area in which Heeney advises his clients is anti-harassment legislation. The courts provide anti-harassment protections throughout Canada for both complainants and respondents. Whether a province has harassment legislation or not, the courts will find employers liable where an inappropriate workplace investigation occurs or where harassment isn't addressed. An employee found to have been terminated for requesting that an employer comply with the harassment and violence provisions, for example, may be entitled to back wages and to being reinstated in his or her job. These are significant remedies which can be costly to businesses.

In Ontario, Bill 168 is part of the Occupational Health and Safety Act. It provides new protections to employees regarding workplace violence and harassment. (Similar legislation exists in Quebec, Manitoba, and Saskatchewan.) All employers, regardless of size, are required to actively adopt policies and training designed to prevent workplace harassment and violence. Employees who feel there has been a breach of the harassment and violence provisions in their workplace can file a complaint with the Ontario Labour Relations Board, and the Board has extraordinary powers when it feels a breach has occurred.

Heeney recommends the following tips on what businesses can do to limit an employer's potential liability:

1. *Take complaints seriously.* When complaints are filed by an employee, ensure that they are given serious consideration.
2. *Acknowledge receipt of the complaint.* Make sure that when complaints are filed you acknowledge to the employee that the complaint has been received and will be investigated.
3. *Perform an unbiased investigation.* Advise the employee alleged to have committed wrongdoing that there is a complaint. Conduct an unbiased investigation and then make the decision.

4. *Report back with your findings.* Advise both sides of the findings, and in writing.

5. *Avoid retaliation.* Always advise all parties that they will not be subjected to retaliation for participating in the investigation.

"Preparing for changes in legislation can be a lengthy and detailed process for employers," counsels Heeney, "particularly for smaller businesses with limited resources. However, the changes to the legislation are an essential step in ensuring that employers are doing their part in reducing the risk of violence and harassment in their workplaces and to avoiding possible fines and liability."

Sources: James Heeney, Partner, Robinson Heeney LLP, interview, 17 March 2015, 416-646-5169; "James Heeney, Partner," Robinson Heeney LLP, 2015, http://www.robinsonheeney.com/toronto-employment-lawyers/lawyers_jheeney/; James Heeney, "Don't get blindsided by workplace harassment, violence laws," CBC News, 30 September 2011, www.cbc.ca/news/business/smallbusiness/story/2011/09/30/f-smallbiz-james-heeney.html; and James Heeney, "Is your business ready for new harassment and violence legislation?," CBC News, 28 May 2010, www.cbc.ca/money/smallbusiness/story/2010/05/28/f-james-heeney-workplace-harassment.html.

LO3 Describe the collective bargaining process.

The Collective Bargaining Process

The LRB oversees **collective bargaining**, which is the entire process whereby union and management representatives negotiate a contract for workers. Collective bargaining includes more than the contract itself. Collective bargaining determines how unions are selected, actions that are allowed during the period prior to certification, certification, and ongoing contract negotiations. Collective bargaining also determines behaviour while a contract is in force and during a breakdown in negotiations for a contract renewal, as well as decertification. **Certification** is a formal process whereby a union is recognized by the LRB as the bargaining agent for a group of employees. **Decertification** is the process by which workers can take away a union's right to represent them.

> **collective bargaining**
> The process whereby union and management representatives negotiate a contract for workers.
>
> **certification**
> Formal process whereby a union is recognized by the Labour Relations Board (LRB) as the bargaining agent for a group of employees.
>
> **decertification**
> Process by which workers can take away a union's right to represent them.

The whole bargaining process and the important certification procedure are shown in Figure 13.3. As you can see, the process is regulated. This process is also democratic and, as in any election, the minority has to accept the majority's decision. All parties involved have to follow a strict procedure to ensure that everybody is playing by the rules. For example, did you know that it is illegal for employers to fire employees for union activities?

LO4 Outline the objectives of labour unions.

Objectives of Organized Labour

The objectives of labour unions shift with social and economic trends. For example, in the 1970s the primary objective of unions was to obtain additional pay and benefits for their members. Throughout the 1980s, objectives shifted toward issues related to job security and union recognition. In the 1990s

■ FIGURE 13.3

STEPS IN COLLECTIVE BARGAINING

Employees interested in joining a union contact a union representative.

The union campaigns for employees to sign union membership cards.

When enough cards are signed (each province/territory and the federal government has laws outlining the exact percentage of workers who must sign), an application to represent the employees is made by the union to the LRB.

The LRB reviews the application and will either order a vote or certify the union automatically, depending on the province/territory.

If the majority votes against the union, it is not certified and workers cannot reapply for another vote for six months or a year.

If employees vote for the union (each province/territory and the federal government has laws outlining the exact percentage of workers who must accept), it becomes the sole bargaining agent for that group of employees. This is known as certification.

A large company may have several locations and the union local may be part of a larger unit that bargains with the employer on behalf of all employees, negotiating a master contract.

A union local is established and members elect officers who appoint a negotiating committee to negotiate a contract with the employer.

If rejected, the negotiating committee must try to renegotiate and come up with a contract that a majority of members will accept.

Members vote to accept or reject the negotiated contract.

If an acceptable contract is not negotiated and the LRB conciliation procedures fail, then a strike or lockout may take place.

If accepted by the majority, the contract governs all of the working conditions during the contract. Strikes or lockouts are illegal while the contract is in force.

A grievance committee is set up with members from both sides to handle any contract violation complaints.

If a new contract is not negotiated before existing one expires, it still remains in force until various LRB conciliation procedures have been followed.

If disagreement persists, a strike or lockout is then legal; should either occur, the contract then lapses.

and 2000s, unions again focused on job security, but the issue of global competition and its effects often took centre stage. Unions were a major opponent of NAFTA, passed by Parliament in 1994. They feared that their members would lose their jobs to low-wage workers in other countries. Today, we are seeing increasing emphasis on skills upgrading as the basis of job security. In some industries, union jobs have been declining due to outsourcing and offshoring. Unions recognize that they must work closely with management if jobs are going to be kept within Canada. Having a skilled and productive workforce is one major way to do this.

"Unions have a dual responsibility—to ensure that their members are getting the best wage and benefit packages and working conditions available in the marketplace, and equally as important, to ensure that their contractual employers not only remain competitive, but have a labour partner that can assist them in expanding their businesses and market share," says Varricchio. Through the union structure and the collective bargaining process, employers can level off labour costs across entire markets and create optimum standards in training and health and safety practices that can be properly enforced through their collective agreements."[22]

The **negotiated labour–management agreement**, informally referred to as the **labour contract**, sets the tone and clarifies the terms and conditions under which management and the union will function over a specific period. "Common sense and good business practice dictates the importance of having a binding written contract between parties engaged in a business transaction, thereby protecting the interests of all parties involved," says Varricchio. "Such a contract spells out the responsibilities and obligations of both parties, itemizes the compensation package agreed to for services rendered or products purchased, and identifies a mechanism to be employed to settle differences in the event either party violates the terms of the mutually agreed-to contract. How much more important is it then to have such a contract between an employer and his/her employees that protects the interests of everyone, especially in an environment where the interaction between personalities could negatively impact the productivity of the workforce and the business?"[23]

negotiated labour–management agreement (labour contract)
Agreement that sets the tone and clarifies the terms and conditions under which management and labour agree to function over a period of time.

According to the Ontario Ministry of Labour, collective bargaining may be triggered by either side. "Notice to bargain is given within the 90 days before the agreement is due to expire or during any other period set out in the agreement."[24]

Unions attempt to address their most pressing concerns in the labour contract, such as job security and outsourcing. Negotiations can cover a wide range of work topics, and it can take a long time to reach an agreement. Figure 13.4 lists topics commonly negotiated by management and labour.

Labour unions generally insist that contracts contain a **union security clause** stipulating that employees who benefit from a union must either officially join or at least pay dues to the union. There are basically four types of agreements:

union security clause
Provision in a negotiated labour–management agreement that stipulates that employees who benefit from a union must either officially join or at least pay dues to the union.

1. A **closed shop agreement** specifies that workers have to be members of a union before being hired for a job. In effect, hiring is done through the union.

closed shop agreement
Clause in a negotiated labour–management agreement that specifies workers need to be members of a union before being hired.

■ **FIGURE 13.4**

ISSUES IN A NEGOTIATED LABOUR–MANAGEMENT AGREEMENT

Labour and management often meet to discuss and clarify the terms that specify employees' functions within the company. The topics listed in this figure are typically discussed during these meetings.

1. Management rights
2. Union recognition
3. Union security clause
4. Strikes and lockouts
5. Union activities and responsibilities
   a. Dues checkoff
   b. Union notices
   c. Shop stewards on the floor
6. Wages
   a. Wage structure
   b. Shift differentials
   c. Wage incentives
   d. Bonuses
   e. Piecework conditions
   f. Tiered wage structures
7. Hours of work and time-off policies
   a. Regular hours of work
   b. Holidays
   c. Vacation policies
   d. Overtime regulations
   e. Leaves of absence
   f. Break periods
   g. Flextime
   h. Mealtime allotments

8. Job rights and seniority principles
   a. Seniority regulations
   b. Transfer policies and bumping
   c. Promotions
   d. Layoffs and recall procedures
   e. Job bidding and posting
9. Discharge and discipline
   a. Suspension
   b. Conditions for discharge
10. Grievance procedures
    a. Arbitration agreement
    b. Mediation procedures
11. Employee benefits, health, and welfare

2. In a **union shop agreement**, the employer is free to hire anybody but the recruit must then join the union within a prescribed period (usually 30, 60, or 90 days).

union shop agreement
Clause in a negotiated labour–management agreement that says workers do not have to be members of a union to be hired, but must agree to join the union within a prescribed period.

3. The **agency shop agreement** states that employers may hire workers who are not required to join the union but the workers must pay a special union fee or regular union dues. Based on the **Rand formula** devised by Supreme Court Justice Rand in 1946, employees in a unionized environment have to fund the bargaining and administration of the collective agreement.[25] Labour leaders believe that such fees or dues are justified because the union represents all workers in collective bargaining, not just its members. Workers who benefit from a labour contract should help pay for the costs of maintaining that union—its officers, union expenses, negotiating committee, shop stewards, and so forth.

agency shop (Rand formula) agreement
Clause in a negotiated labour–management agreement that says employers may hire non-union workers; employees are not required to join the union but must pay union dues.

4. An **open shop agreement** gives workers the option to join or not join the union if one exists. A worker who does not join cannot be forced to pay a fee or dues.[26]

> **open shop agreement**
> Clause in a negotiated labour–management agreement that says employees are free to join or not join the union and to pay or not pay union dues.

Regardless of which hiring condition prevails, the labour contract usually contains **checkoff** as a standard clause. Checkoff requires the employer to deduct union dues from employees and to pay and remit them to the union (except for non-members in an open shop). Otherwise, it would be harder to collect union dues individually.

> **checkoff**
> A contract clause requiring the employer to deduct union dues from employees' pay and remit them to a union.

Future contract negotiations will likely focus on evolving workplace issues such as child and elder care, worker retraining, two-tiered wage plans, outsourcing, and other such work-related issues. Job security will remain a top union priority due to the threat of job losses from outsourcing and offshoring and free trade agreements.

"A collective agreement provides protection if an employer wishes to discharge an employee," states employment lawyer, Aaron Rousseau, founder of Rousseau Law. "In the absence of a collective agreement, employers can fire non-union employees for almost any reason so long as the employees are given reasonable notice, or payment in lieu of notice. In a union environment, the employer needs to prove misconduct on the part of the employee before he or she can be fired."[27] Review Figure 13.5 for some additional advantages of joining a union. Note the disadvantages as well.

■ **FIGURE 13.5**

SOME ADVANTAGED AND DISADVANTAGES OF JOINING A UNION	
Union Advantages	**Union Disadvantages**
Members are generally better protected when disputes arise	Promotion and pay may be determined by seniority
Usually receive higher wages* and better benefit coverage (e.g., pension plan, supplemental health care, and dental plan)	Negotiated compensation usually leads to higher production costs
Better negotiating power as a group rather than as an individual	You may not be agree with all of the union's decisions (e.g., to go on strike)

*Unionized workers across Canada earn $5.17/hour more than non-union workers. Women earn on average $6.89/hour more, and young workers (aged 14 to 24) earn on average $3.16/hour more.

Sources: "Union Advantage 2014," Canadian Labour Congress, http://www.canadianlabour.ca/about-clc/union-advantage-2014, downloaded 1 April 2015; and "Joining a union in Canada," Working in Canada, [n.d.], www.workingin-canada.com/jobs/job-tools/joining-a-union.

Resolving Labour–Management Disputes

The negotiated labour–management agreement becomes a guide to work relations between management and the union. However, it does not necessarily end negotiations between them because sometimes there are differences concerning interpretations of the agreement. For example, managers may interpret a certain clause in the agreement to mean that they are free to select who works overtime. Union members may interpret the same clause to mean that managers must select employees for overtime on the basis of employee seniority. If the parties can't resolve such disagreements, employees may file a grievance.

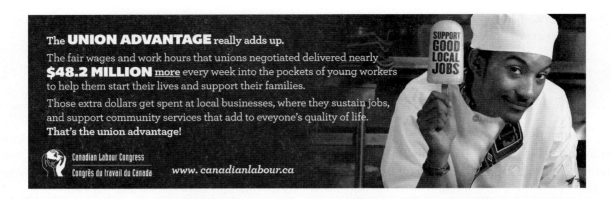

A CLC study confirms there were 361,300 union members between 15 and 24 years of age working in Canada in 2013, representing about 15 percent of the workforce in this age group.[28] What do unions need to do to engage young workers and increase the coverage rate with this age group?

A **grievance** is a charge by employees that management is not abiding by or fulfilling the terms of a negotiated labour–management agreement as they perceive it. Overtime rules, promotions, layoffs, transfers, and job assignments are generally sources of employee grievances. Handling grievances demands a good deal of contact between union officials and managers. Grievances, however, do not imply that the company has broken the law or the labour agreement. In fact, the vast majority of grievances are negotiated and resolved by **shop stewards** (union officials who work permanently in an organization and represent employee interests on a daily basis) and supervisory-level managers. However, if a grievance is not settled at this level, formal grievance procedures will begin.

> **grievance**
> A charge by employees that management is not abiding by or fulfilling the terms of the negotiated labour–management agreement.
>
> **shop stewards**
> Union officials who work permanently in an organization and represent employee interests on a daily basis.

Figure 13.6 illustrates the steps a formal grievance could follow. If the grievance cannot be settled at one level, it moves up to the next level. The number of steps in the grievance procedure and the staff involved at each step will vary from organization to organization but most grievance procedures have between three to five steps.[29]

Conciliation, Mediation, and Arbitration

During the contract negotiation process, there is generally a **bargaining zone**, which is the range of options between the initial and final offers that each party will consider before negotiations dissolve or reach an impasse. If labour and management negotiators aren't able to agree on alternatives within this bargaining zone, conciliation is the next necessary step. In their legislation, all jurisdictions provide for conciliation and mediation services.[30]

> **bargaining zone**
> Range of options between the initial and final offer that each party will consider before negotiations dissolve or reach an impasse.

■ FIGURE 13.6

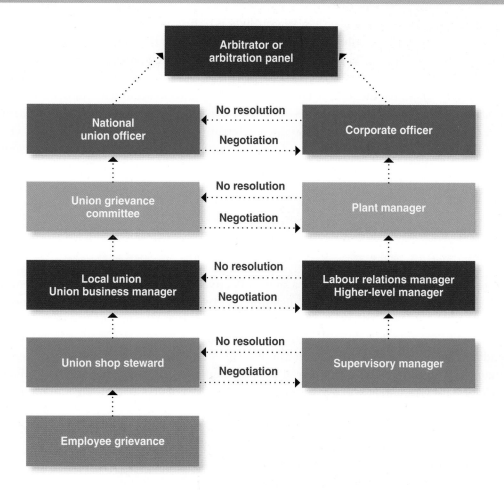

GRIEVANCE RESOLUTION PROCESS

The grievance process may move through several steps before the issue is resolved. At each step, the issue is negotiated between union officials and managers. If no resolution is achieved, an outside arbitrator may be mutually agreed on. If so, the decision by the arbitrator is binding (legally enforceable).

Conciliation is the use of a government-appointed third party (usually through the Ministry of Labour) to explore solutions to a labour–management dispute.[31] If conciliation fails, the union is then in a legal position to strike and the employer is also in a legal position to declare a lockout.

conciliation
The use of a government-appointed third part to explore solutions to a labour–management dispute.

Mediation is the use of a third party, called a *mediator*, who encourages both sides in a dispute to consider negotiating and often makes suggestions for resolving the matter. Keep in mind that mediators evaluate facts in the dispute and then make suggestions, not decisions. Elected officials (current and past), attorneys, and professors often serve as mediators in labour disputes. In 2011, the National Football League and the Players Association asked for the assistance of a federal mediator in their attempt to forge a new contract. The National Hockey League made the same request during the labour dispute in 2012.[32]

mediation
The use of a third party, called a mediator, who encourages both sides in a dispute to continue negotiating and often makes suggestions for resolving the dispute.

A more extreme approach used to resolve conflicts is **arbitration**, which is an agreement to bring in an impartial third party (a single arbitrator or arbitration panel) to render a binding decision in a labour dispute. Arbitration may be *voluntary;* in this case both sides decide to submit their case to an arbitrator. Arbitration may also be *compulsory,* where a decision is imposed by the government (e.g., by Parliament or a provincial legislature). Compulsory arbitration usually occurs in a major or prolonged strike with serious consequences for the public. Usually, non-grievance arbitration (say, for contract disputes) is voluntary and grievance arbitration is compulsory. Employees who are designated as having essential positions (e.g., police, firefighters, and hospital employees) usually do not have the right to strike as stated in their collective agreements, and their disputes must be settled through binding arbitration.[33]

arbitration
An agreement to bring in an impartial third party (a single arbitrator or a panel of arbitrators) to render a binding decision in a labour dispute.

While binding arbitration may result in a new collective agreement, it can leave contentious issues unresolved. Under threat of back-to-work legislation and two unwarranted referrals to the CIRB by the Federal Labour Minister, CUPE agreed to binding arbitration with Air Canada. "Awarding flight attendants an agreement they rejected a month ago does not in any way address serious workplace issues and flight attendants are rightfully disappointed and angry," said Paul Moist, National President of CUPE. "If Air Canada is truly interested in running a professional and efficient company they must invest in their workforce. This agreement will leave flight attendants exhausted, frustrated, and underpaid."[34]

With changes to collective bargaining laws, the federal government now has the right to decide whether labour disputes are solved by conciliation, arbitration, or strike. Smaller unions that have picked arbitration in the past could be forced to go on strike in the event of an impasse.[35] What can these smaller unions do to strengthen their positions in such negotiations?

Both mediation and arbitration can be difficult, lengthy, and costly procedures, especially when both sides are locked into rigid positions. That is why negotiators from both sides usually try to settle their differences before resorting to these steps.

Progress Assessment

- How do labour relations boards regulate labour–management relations?
- In the collective bargaining process, what happens after certification?
- What are the differences between conciliation, mediation, and arbitration?

LO5 Describe the negotiation tactics used by labour and management during conflicts.

Negotiation Tactics

If labour and management cannot reach an agreement through collective bargaining and negotiations break down, either side, or both, may use specific tactics to enhance their negotiating position and perhaps sway public opinion. Be aware that the great majority of labour negotiations end successfully without the disruption of a strike or lockout. Remember that mediation and arbitration are always available to the parties in dispute. They may take advantage of these procedures before, during, or after any of these tactics are exercised. Let us look at some examples next.

Union Tactics

Unions primarily use strikes and boycotts to get desired changes. A **strike** occurs when workers collectively refuse to go to work. Strikes have been the most potent union tactic. They attract public attention to a labour dispute and can cause operations in a company to slow down or totally cease. Besides refusing to work, strikers may also *picket* the company, walking around carrying signs and talking with the public and the media about the issues in the dispute. Unions also use picketing as an informational tool before going on strike. One purpose of picketing is to alert the public to an issue stirring labour unrest, even though a strike has not yet been approved by the union's membership. Strikes sometimes lead to the resolution of a labour dispute; however, they also have generated violence and extended bitterness. Often after a strike is finally settled, labour and management remain openly hostile toward each other and mutual complaints of violations of the negotiated labour–management agreement continue

strike
A union strategy in which workers refuse to go to work.

Prior to the actual strike, union leaders call for a *strike vote*, which is a secret ballot authorizing the union leadership to call a strike. This democratic vote is necessary if a potential strike is to be considered legal. If the union gets a strong mandate—say, more than 80 percent in favour of a strike—it can use this as a lever to convince management to accept its demands without actually going on strike.

Union tactics include rotating strikes—on and off or alternating among different plants or cities—rather than a full-fledged strike in which all employees are off the job for the duration. With rotating strikes, employees still get some pay, which is not the case in an all-out strike. Many unions build up a strike fund from union dues and use it to give their members strike pay, but that is usually a fraction of their normal wages. Sometimes, in important or long-lasting strikes, other unions will give moral or financial aid.

Do you recall the recent strikes at two of Canada's largest universities, York University and the University of Toronto? Here you see CUPE 3903 members made up of contract faculty and teaching assistants at York University setting up picket lines outside the main entrance. What were the issues? How long did the strikes last? What were conditions of the new labour-management agreements? Would news of a strike impact your decision to apply to that school?

Both labour and management seek to avoid strikes. However, as technological change, outsourcing, wage disparities, and reductions in work benefits continue, it's unlikely that strikes will disappear.[36] Strikes in entertainment, health care, transportation, fast food, professional sports, and other industries prove the strike is not dead as a labour tactic.

Unions can use boycotts as a means to obtain their objectives in a labour dispute. A **primary boycott** occurs when organized labour encourages both its members and the general public not to buy the products or services of a firm engaged in a labour dispute. A **secondary boycott** is an attempt by labour to convince others to stop doing business with a firm that is the subject of a primary boycott. For example, a union can initiate a secondary boycott against a supermarket chain because the chain carries goods produced by a company that is the target of a primary boycott.

> **primary boycott**
> When a union encourages both its members and the general public not to buy the products of a firm involved in a labour dispute.
>
> **secondary boycott**
> An attempt by labour to convince others to stop doing business with a firm that is the subject of a primary boycott.

Sabotage (where workers damage their machines), *sit-ins* (where they occupy the workplace and refuse to move), or *work-to-rule* (where they follow the operating rules of the workplace in every detail to slow down the work) are other tactics that have been used by unions. Why might unions prefer these tactics to going on strike?

Management Tactics

Like labour, management also uses specific tactics to achieve its workplace goals. A **lockout** is an attempt by management to put pressure on union workers by temporarily closing the business. It may seem less costly to close down and cease paying wages than to put up with slowdowns, rotating strikes, or work-to-rule union tactics, all of which can be very disruptive. When workers don't work, they don't get paid. However, without products and services, there are no profits.

> **lockout**
> An attempt by management to put pressure on unions by temporarily closing the business.

Were you impacted by the 2012–2013 National Hockey League (NHL) lockout that lasted almost four months? Here you see fans protesting the lockout outside of the NHL offices. What were the starting and ending positions of the NHL and the NHL Players Association?

An **injunction** is a court order directing someone to do something or to refrain from doing something. Management has sought injunctions to order striking workers back to work, limit the number of pickets that can be used during a strike, or otherwise deal with actions that could be detrimental to the public welfare. For a court to issue an injunction, management must show a "just cause," such as the possibility of violence or the destruction of property.

> **injunction**
> A court order directing someone to do something or to refrain from doing something.

Sometimes, a company may try to bring in replacement workers. Known as **strikebreakers** (called *scabs* by unions), they are workers who are hired to do the jobs of striking employees until the labour dispute is resolved. Why do you think strikebreakers have been a particular source of hostility and violence in labour relations? Read the Making Ethical Decisions box on this issue for further insight.

> **strikebreakers**
> Replacement workers hired to do the jobs of striking employees until the labour dispute is resolved.

The battle for public support is a tactic that is used by both management and the union. In major cases where the public is affected—postal service, health care, education, transportation, telecommunication, and civil service—each side plays a propaganda game to win the public to its side. It can be difficult for those not directly involved to sort out the issues. Sometimes management, if it thinks that the public is on its side and the union is perhaps not well organized or lacks strong support, will provoke the union into an unsuccessful strike, weakening the union's bargaining position.

Making ETHICAL DECISIONS

Crossing the Line or Double-Crossing?

Your wallet is almost empty and bills for school, food, and other expenses keep going up. You read on the weekend that your local grocery store, More-4-Less, is looking for workers to replace striking members of the United Food and Commercial Workers (UFCW union). The workers are striking because of a reduction in health benefits and employer contributions to their pensions.

Some of the students at your school are employed at More-4-Less and are supporting the strike. The store also employs people from your neighbourhood whose families depend on the income and benefits. More-4-Less argues that its management has made a fair offer to the union, but with the increasing cost of health care and other benefits, the workers' demands are excessive and could force the company into bankruptcy.

More-4-Less is offering replacement workers an attractive wage rate and flexible schedules to cross the picket line and work during the strike. As a struggling student, you could use the job and the money for tuition and expenses. Will you cross the picket line and apply for the job? What could be the consequences of your decision? Is your choice ethical? What are the ethical dilemmas faced by unions? Give some examples. How do these differ from those faced by management?

Legislation[37]

Under the Labour Relations Code, essential services legislation restricts the right to strike for various levels of civil servants and quasi-government employees such as hospital workers and electric and telephone utility workers. The provinces and the federal government forbid some employees under their jurisdiction from striking. In other cases, certain minimum levels of service must be provided. For example, the Ontario government designated the Toronto Transit Commission (TTC) as an essential service based on the argument that the city could not afford another transit strike or lockout. The last one cost Toronto's economy an estimated $50 million a day. Essential service designation means that in the event that a new agreement cannot be reached, unresolved issues will go to arbitration unless the government imposes a new contract unilaterally.

Federal or provincial governments have the power to end a particular strike or lockout by passing back-to-work legislation. **Back-to-work legislation** is a special law passed by the federal or provincial government that orders an end to a labour–management dispute in an industry the government decides is essential to the operation of the economy. Such legislation has been used to end strikes by teachers, nurses, postal workers, bus drivers, and others. Typically, back-to-work legislation is imposed only after some time has passed, further efforts at reaching a settlement have failed, there is considerable public pressure to end the dispute, or the service provided by striking workers is deemed essential to the economy or public safety. On some occasions, it has been introduced as a pressure tactic to get negotiations to move faster.

> **back-to-work legislation**
> A special law passed by the federal or provincial government that orders an end to a labour–management dispute in an industry the government decides is essential to the operation of the economy.

Union supporters believe that back-to-work legislation is a denial of the legal right to strike; therefore, to a certain extent it is a restriction of the democratic rights of individuals. Consequently, there is often much controversy about such legislation. It is rarely used to deal with strikes against private businesses. If union members remain on strike after they have been legislated back to work, they are engaging in an illegal strike and are subject to punishment (e.g., substantial fines), as are all lawbreakers.

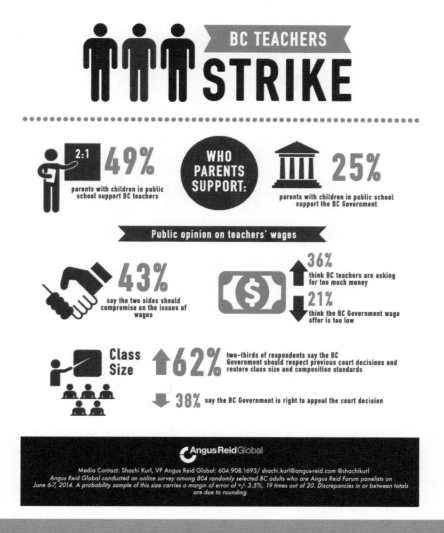

Half a million public school students lost five weeks of classes (two in June and three in September) when more than 40,000 of British Columbia's public school teachers went on strike in 2014.[38] These survey results consider public opinion early in the strike. The BC Teachers' Federation's tactics included rotating strikes and a full strike. The provincial government locked out high school teachers and refused binding arbitration. What were the issues? Why did the government refuse arbitration? What were the terms of the new contract?

The Future of Unions and Labour–Management Relations

To save jobs, some unions have granted management concessions, or **givebacks**, of previous gains. (Review the Analyzing Management Decisions discussion near the end of the chapter for more on this topic.) Both public and private-sector unions face challenges as they try to maintain remaining wage and fringe benefits achieved in past negotiations.

givebacks
Concessions made by union members to management; gains from previous labour negotiations are given back to management to help employers remain competitive and thereby save jobs.

After months of negotiations, Air Canada flight attendants rejected a tentative agreement and voted overwhelmingly for a strike mandate. After a decade of givebacks, flight attendants were negotiating for a better contract.[39] CUPE developed this ad as support for its members during this dispute. Do you support the right to strike? Are you less sympathetic of striking workers if you are impacted by the strike?

Unions in the future will be quite different from those in the past. To grow, unions will have to include more white-collar and foreign-born workers than they have traditionally included. The labour movement must find a way to make strides in organizing some industries that have remained elusive such as the service, agriculture, and financial sectors.[40] Unifor plans to grow to about double its current membership by devoting 10 percent of its revenue to groups that include students, retirees, and the unemployed. These goals demonstrate its commitment to move beyond the limits of the traditional union model.[41]

Many unions have taken on a new role in assisting management in training workers, redesigning jobs, and assimilating the changing workforce. They help recruit and train foreign workers, unskilled workers, and others who need special help in adapting to the job requirements of the new service and knowledge-work economy.

Unions seek improved job security, profit sharing, and sometimes increased wages. Management looks for a productive, dedicated workforce capable of handling the challenges of global competition. Joseph S. Mancinelli, LiUNA International Vice-President and Regional Manager for Central and Eastern Canada, understands these challenges and opportunities. According to Mancinelli, "Pensions, level of skills, quality of work, productivity, and safety in the workplace have become our new challenges. These challenges cannot be met through adversarial conflict, but in a new era of unionism, through good relations with our employer partners. Good relations are paramount in ensuring such progress and evolution. Working closely with our employer partners can produce more benefits for our members, our employers, and the entire construction industry. In recognition of this fact, LiUNA has established a labour–employer co-operation trust specifically set up for both parties to work together, outside of the bargaining table, every day of the year to find creative and innovative solutions and initiatives that result in an ongoing win–win scenario for both labour and management. Concurrently, LiUNA has actively pursued public–private partnerships. Through the successful Labourers' Pension Fund of Central and Eastern Canada—a plan whose value is in excess of $5 billion, and is the fifth largest growing pension fund in Canada—sound, financially viable partnerships have evolved resulting in a doubly viable result: excellent returns on pension fund dollars and employment opportunities for our members across the country. An example of this relationship is LiUNA joining numerous construction companies to build several hospitals throughout the province of Ontario."[42]

How organized labour and management handle such challenges may well define the future of labour unions. After the Progress Assessment, we will look at other issues facing employees and managers in the twenty-first century.

Progress Assessment

- How have union objectives changed over time?
- What are the major tactics used by unions and by management to assert their power in contract negotiations?
- When is back-to-work legislation used?

LO6 Explain some of today's employee–management issues.

Controversial Employee–Management Topics

This is an interesting time in the history of employee–management relations. Organizations are active in global expansion, outsourcing, and technology changes. The government has eliminated some social benefits to workers. In other instances the government is taking a more active role in mandating what benefits businesses must provide to workers. The implementation of a compassionate care program in 2004 is just one instance.

Employees continue to raise questions about fairness and workplace benefits. They look increasingly at company policies as they apply to workplace discrimination (e.g., wages and sexual orientation), sexual harassment, and mandatory testing (e.g., drug testing). Three other areas that are in the news include executive compensation, child care, and elder care. Let us briefly look at each of these areas.

Executive Compensation

Is it out of line for some of Canada's top executives to make millions of dollars in annual compensation (e.g., salary, bonuses, and incentives)? Chapter 2 explained that the free-market system is built on incentives that allow top executives to make large amounts of money. Today, however, the government, boards of directors, shareholders, unions, and employees are challenging this principle and arguing that executive compensation has gotten out of line. In fact, way out of line. Reaching Beyond Our Borders explores the disparity between what U.S. college head coaches earn (millions) and what the athletes earn (nothing).

In theory, CEO compensation and bonuses are determined by the firm's profitability or an increase in its stock price. The logic of this assumption was that as the fortunes of a company and its shareholders grew, so would the rewards of the CEO. Today, however, executives generally receive *stock options* (the ability to buy company stock at a set price at a later date) and *restricted stock* (stock issued directly to the CEO that cannot be sold for usually three or four years) as part of their compensation.

What is even more frustrating to those who question how much chief executives are paid is that the CEOs are often rewarded richly if their company does not meet expectations, or they leave under pressure.[43] Target Canada's failed expansion into Canada, in addition to the company's credit card data breach, contributed to Gregg Steinhafel's exit as Target Corporation's CEO. Estimated by *Fortune Magazine* to be $61 million, his overall severance package included severance pay of $15.9 million, stock options, and pension and deferred compensation. Contrast this to the $70 million Target made available for designated employee trust funds offered to the 17,600 workers that were laid off due to the closure of its 133 Canadian stores.[44] Some CEOs are also awarded fat retainers, consulting contracts, and lavish perks when they retire. What do you think of such decisions? Do you agree?

The late management consultant Peter Drucker criticized executive pay levels and he suggested that CEOs should not earn more than 20 times the salary of the company's lowest-paid employee. Noted economist Thomas Piketty believes this income inequality is harmful and unnecessary by stating, "When you pay $10 million instead of $1 [million], you don't have necessarily better performance or much higher productivity. . . . So I think there is really very little evidence that we need to pay people 100 times or 200 times the average wage to get them to work. I think you have people who would accept the work for only 10 or 20 times the average wage."[45] Whole Foods is one company that follows the suggestions of Piketty. There, executive pay is capped at 19 times the average employee's salary. Unfortunately, not many companies have placed such limits on executive compensation.

According to *PayScale.com*, the average CEO in Canada makes 206 times as much as the average worker, while the average U.S. CEO makes 354 times as much.[46] The Canadian Centre for Policy Alternatives (CCPA) reports that the top 100 highest-paid CEOs in Canada on average make $9.2 million, which is more than 190 times the average Canadian income of $47,358. This list was topped by Onex CEO Gerry Schwartz, who had a total pay package of $87.9 million.[47] Another area that concerns the CCPA is Canada's low-wage problem. Read the Seeking Sustainability box for a discussion on the living wage.

Conversely, many executives are responsible for multi-billion-dollar corporations, work 70-plus hours a week, and often travel. Many have made decisions that turned potential problems into successes and reaped huge compensation for employees and shareholders as well as themselves. Furthermore, there are few seasoned, skilled professionals who can manage large companies, especially troubled companies looking for the right CEO to accomplish a turnaround. There's no easy answer to the question of what is fair compensation for executives, but it is a safe bet that the controversy will not go away.

Reaching *Beyond* OUR BORDERS

U.S. College Athletes: What Are They Worth?

Few would argue that football is a booming profit centre for many colleges in the National Collegiate Athletic Association (NCAA) Division I, the highest level of NCAA sports. NCAA basketball is no slacker either. The 2014 NCAA Men's Championship drew a sellout crowd at the AT&T Stadium in Dallas while more than 23 million watched on television. Broadcasting rights for the entire tournament cost CBS $771 million. Regional economies in college towns like Columbia, Missouri, College Station, Texas, and South Bend, Indiana, generate huge revenues on sports weekends. For example, the University of Texas enjoyed revenues of $163 million from athletics in 2014. Coaches are given contracts worth millions. All is good for everyone.

Well, not everyone. There's one group of stakeholders noticeably absent from this payday: the players. College athletes are not allowed to draw a salary or receive any gifts or other compensation for their extracurricular efforts. Of course, some college athletes do receive scholarships that cover part or all of their tuition and room and board. However, the amount of revenue generated by competitions like basketball's March Madness or football's National Championship have led many to demand that student athletes receive a cut of the action. After all, they believe they invest just as much time with practice and travel as their coaches do.

Northwestern University's football players won a ruling from the National Labor Relations Board (NLRB) that gave them the right to unionize. The players argued they deserved collective bargaining rights, financial coverage for sports-related injuries, an educational trust to help players graduate, and a team of concussion experts to be placed on the sidelines at games. With football workweeks stretching out to as long as 60 hours, the players believed they deserved compensation to justify the sport's dominance over their lives.

Northwestern is appealing this ruling, claiming the players have an educational relationship with the school rather than an economic one. The school also sees Title IX requirements as an obstacle. For instance, if the college began paying its men's football and basketball team, it would need to do the same for its unprofitable athletic programs, regardless of sport or gender. This is a pay issue that could be a game changer.

What do you think? Are athletes employees of the school or are they students? Should players be paid for their participation or should they be treated like participants in any other voluntary extracurricular activity? Was Northwestern's appeal successful? What are the implications of the most recent ruling on this issue?

Sources: Brian Bennett, "Northwestern Players Get Union Vote," ESPN, 26 March 2014; Ken Badenhausen, "NCAA Tournament 2014: By the Numbers," *Forbes*, 20 March 2014; and Alejandra Cancino, "Northwestern, Football Players Cap Off Arguments in Union Effort," *Chicago Tribune*, 18 March 2014.

Seeking SUSTAINABILITY

The Living Wage: Why Minimum Wage Is Not Enough

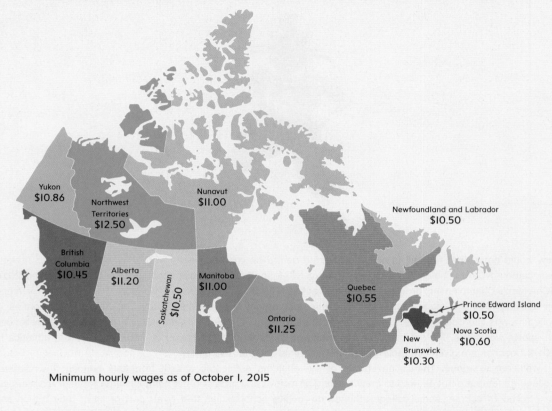

Minimum hourly wages as of October 1, 2015

Source: Data based on: "Payroll Legislation," Payworks Inc., accessed 22 October 2015, http://www.payworks.ca/payroll-legislation/MinimumWage.asp.

The minimum (hourly) wage refers to the legal minimum all employers must pay their workers. It varies across Canada and even within some provinces, depending on the job. For example, in Quebec, the minimum wage is $10.55 but if gratuities apply to the role, the wage is $9.05. In recent years, there has been a rise in the living wage movement due to a recognition of Canada's low-wage problem. A significant proportion of full-time workers earn significantly less than a middle-class wage, and struggle to make ends meet.

With a higher standard than the minimum wage, a living wage is calculated as the hourly rate at which a household can meet its basic needs, once government transfers (such as the Universal Child Care Benefit) have been added to the family's income and deductions have been subtracted (such as income taxes and employment insurance premiums). The basic idea of a living wage is that persons and families working full time should earn enough to secure a decent standard of living, one that goes beyond a bare bones poverty line to include modest spending on items like recreation.

The living wage varies across communities and sometimes varies markedly from the provincial minimum wage. For example, in 2014 the living wage in metro Vancouver was $20.10, in contrast to British Columbia's minimum wage of $10.25 at the time. The Community Social Planning Council of British Columbia believes that the difference between the minimum and the living wage is the result of public policy failure to provide inputs such as universal affordable child care, affordable rental and social housing, affordable enrolment in health care, and affordable transportation. If there were adequate universal supports for low-income families in these areas, their struggles to make ends meet would be significantly reduced, which would be reflected in a lower living wage. Do you agree with this assessment?

According to a Canadian Centre for Policy Alternatives (CCPA) report, many workers do not earn a living wage because of discrimination. Female workers and those who are not Caucasian, immigrants, Aboriginal people, those living with disabilities, or similarly disadvantaged people are all segregated into low-wage job ghettos—their work systemically devalued. The CCPA calls on governments and employers to deliver more equitable compensation incomes for vulnerable workers so that the right to work and to earn wages free of discrimination is realized for Canada's low-paid workers.

Living wages are adopted voluntarily by employers rather than applied by law. Living wage employers include Vancity, the Canadian Cancer Society <http://www.cancer.ca>, the Calgary Chamber of Commerce <https://www.calgarychamber.com>, and the Hamilton-Wentworth District School Board <http://www.hwdsb.on.ca>. Visit Living Wage Canada <http://www.livingwagecanada.ca> for a list of additional employers.

What are employer reservations for a living wage policy? How can employees influence a living wage policy in their place of employment? What is the government's role, if any, in influencing living wage policies?

Sources: "Canadian Living Wage Framework," Living Wage Canada, http://livingwagecanada.ca/files/3913/8382/4524/Living_Wage _Full_Document_Nov.pdf, downloaded 3 April 2015; "Minimum Wage by Province," Retail Council of Canada, http://www.retailcouncil.org /quickfacts/minimum-wage, downloaded 3 April 2015; "Payroll Legislation," Payworks Inc., http://www.payworks.ca/payroll-legislation /MinimumWage.asp, downloaded 3 April 2015; "2014 Living Wage for Greater Victoria is $18.93/hour," Community Social Planning Council, 29 April 2014, http://www.communitycouncil.ca/initiatives/livingwage; Mary Cornish, "A Living Wage As a Human Right," Canadian Centre for Policy Alternatives, 5 October 2012, https://www.policyalternatives.ca/publications/reports/living-wage-human-right; and Andrew Jackson, "Why paying a living wage makes good business sense," *The Globe and Mail,* 9 November 2012, http://www .theglobeandmail.com/report-on-business/economy/economy-lab/why-paying-a-living-wage-makes-good-business-sense/article5152175/.

Child Care

Child care became an increasingly important workplace issue as questions involving responsibilities for child-care subsidies, child-care programs, and even parental leave spurred debate in the private and public sectors of the economy. Employee child care also raises the controversial workplace question of who should pay for child-care services; many workers strongly question workplace benefits for parents, and argue that single workers and single-income families should not subsidize child care for dual-income families. Although men are increasingly shouldering child-care responsibility, most of that responsibility still falls on women. This often leads to greater stress and absenteeism in the workplace. Employers are increasingly concerned as businesses lose millions annually in lost productivity.

On-site day care is not a common employee benefit. Although it is often expensive to operate, it can contribute to greater employee satisfaction and productivity. Who should pay for employee benefits like child care and elder care? Should it be the employee or the company or both?

Some large firms, such as IBM and Johnson & Johnson, offer child care as an employee benefit. Some additional child-care benefits provided by employers include:

- Discount arrangements with national child-care chains.
- Vouchers that offer payments toward child care the employee selects.
- Referral services that help identify high-quality child-care facilities to employees.
- On-site child-care centres where parents can visit children at lunch or during lag times throughout the workday.
- Sick-child centres to care for moderately ill children.

Increasing numbers of single-parent and two-income households ensure that child care will remain a key employee–management issue even as businesses face the growing challenge of elder care.[48]

Elder Care

The workforce in Canada is aging. While Baby Boomers will not have to concern themselves with finding child care for their children, they will confront another problem: how to care for older parents and other relatives. In the future, more workers are expected to be involved in the time-consuming and stressful task of caring for an aging relative. Companies are seeing reduced productivity, and increased absenteeism and turnover from employees who are responsible for aging relatives.[49]

Employees with elder-care responsibilities need information on medical, legal, and insurance issues, as well as the full support of their supervisors and company.[50] This issue may require some employees to switch to flextime, telecommuting, part-time employment, or job sharing. Some firms offer employee assistance programs. Such elder-care management services can include a needs assessment program for the employee, and health-spending accounts in which employees can put aside pre-tax income for elder-care expenses.

As more experienced and high-ranking employees begin caring for older parents and relatives, the costs to companies will rise even higher. This argument makes sense, since older workers often hold jobs more critical to the company than those held by younger workers (who are most affected by child-care

Canadians are living longer which means that they will likely require elder care in addition to providing elder care for older parents or relatives. Do you have a relative that requires elder care? What support is available for the person receiving care as well as for the care provider? Is this level of care sustainable?

problems). Firms now face the fact that transfers and promotions are often out of the question for employees whose elderly parents need ongoing care. Unfortunately, as Canadians age, the elder-care situation will grow considerably worse, meaning this employee–management issue will persist well into the future.

You and Unions

Do you think that unions are still necessary? We are fortunate to be living in a democratic country where free and private enterprise is the vital feature of our economic system. We believe that all citizens have the right to do what they can, within legal and ethical limits, to better themselves. Improving your financial situation is an admired goal, and those who do so are usually seen as good examples.

If you select the entrepreneurial route, you will try to build a successful company by providing a necessary service or product in a manner that your customers appreciate. If you are successful, you will ultimately accumulate profits, personal wealth, and financial security for yourself and your family. One of the costs of doing business that you will be keeping an eye on is wages, salaries, and benefits paid to employees. Will you consider unions nothing but a hindrance?

Suppose that you do not see yourself as an entrepreneur and instead go the employee route. Imagine yourself ten years down the road: you have a partner and two children and are now working for a large company in a non-managerial role. Will you seek the best salary you can possibly get? How about working hours? Your partner also works and you need flexible arrangements to be able to spend time with your children and deliver them to school and various other activities. How about overtime demands on the job that cut into time with your children? Will you have adequate, affordable child care?

These are just ideas to consider. Firms that have healthy employee–management relations have a better chance to prosper than those that do not. As managers, taking a proactive approach is the best way to ensure workable employee–management environments. The proactive manager anticipates potential problems and works toward resolving those issues before they get out of hand—a good lesson to remember.

Progress Assessment

- How does top-executive pay in Canada compare with the pay of average workers?
- How does the living wage compare to the minimum wage?
- What are some of the issues related to child care and elder care, and how are companies addressing these issues?

SUMMARY

LO1 **Trace the history of organized labour in Canada.**

Organized labour in Canada dates back to the 1800s. Early unions on the wharves of Halifax, St. John's, and Quebec existed during the War of 1812 to profit from labour scarcity. Craft unions represented shoemakers and printers. Many of the early labour organizations were local or regional in nature.

Describe some of the main objectives of labour and whether they were achieved.

Unions hoped to improve workers' poor conditions and wages by forming unions that would fight for workers' rights. This has largely been achieved, and many early demands are now entrenched in law.

Describe some of the unions in existence today.

CUPE and Unifor are two of the largest unions in Canada. They represent workers from different industries in the economy. Many unions in Canada are national in nature. Many also belong to international organizations. The Canadian Labour Congress, which represents over 3 million unionized workers, is the largest labour congress in Canada.

LO2 Discuss the major legislation affecting labour unions.

Much labour legislation has been passed by federal and provincial governments.

What is the major piece of labour legislation?

The Canada Labour Code outlines labour legislation as it applies to federal government employees, who represent approximately 6 percent of all workers in Canada. Each provincial jurisdiction in Canada has its own labour legislation and employment standards that apply to workers within its borders.

What are workplace rights?

All workers in Canada have the right to work in a safe and healthy environment. Workplace laws include the right to know about workplace hazards and the right to refuse unsafe work.

LO3 Describe the collective bargaining process.

Collective bargaining is the process by which a union represents employees in relations with their employer.

What is included in collective bargaining?

Collective bargaining includes how unions are selected, the period prior to a vote, certification, ongoing contract negotiations, and behaviour while a contract is in force.

What are the steps in the collective bargaining process?

Refer to Figure 13.3 for the steps in the collective bargaining process.

LO4 Outline the objectives of labour unions.

The objectives of labour unions shift in response to changes in social and economic trends.

What is the purpose of the negotiated labour–management agreement?

Informally referred to as the labour contract, the labour–management agreement sets the tone and clarifies the terms and conditions under which management and the union will function over a specific period.

What topics typically appear in labour–management agreements?

Labour–management agreements may include issues such as management rights, union security clauses, hours of work, vacation policies, job rights and seniority principles, and employee benefits. See Figure 13.4 for a more detailed list.

LO5 Describe the negotiation tactics used by labour and management during conflicts.

If negotiations between labour and management break down, either or both sides may use certain tactics to enhance their positions or sway public opinion.

What are the tactics used by unions in conflicts?
Unions can use strikes, boycotts, and picketing.

What are the tactics used by management in conflicts?
Management can use lockouts, injunctions, and strikebreakers.

LO6 **Explain some of today's employee-management issues.**
Some employee-management issues are executive compensation, child care, and elder care.

What is a fair wage for executives?
The market and the businesses in it set executives' salaries. What is fair is open to debate.

How are some companies addressing the child-care issue?
Responsive companies are providing child care on their premises, discounts with child-care chains, vouchers to be used at the employee's chosen care centre, and referral services.

What problems do companies face with regard to elder care?
Companies are seeing reduced productivity and increased absenteeism and turnover from employees who are responsible for aging relatives. As more experienced and high-ranking employees begin caring for elders, the costs to companies will rise even higher since older workers often hold jobs more critical to the company than those held by younger workers.

KEY TERMS

agency shop (Rand formula) agreement	decertification	national union
arbitration	directly chartered union	negotiated labour–management agreement (labour contract)
back-to-work legislation	givebacks	open shop agreement
bargaining zone	grievance	primary boycott
certification	independent local organization	secondary boycott
checkoff	industrial union	shop stewards
closed shop agreement	injunction	strike
collective bargaining	international union	strikebreakers
conciliation	labour relations board	union security clause
coverage rate	labour union	union shop agreement
craft union	lockout	unionization rate (union density)
	mediation	

CRITICAL THINKING

1. In the last few years, thousands of government employees have lost their jobs due to budget cuts. What are the political and economic implications of such actions?

2. Why are unionization rates much higher in the public sector than in the private sector? Are you more or less attracted to the public sector as a result of this coverage?

3. Do you agree that back-to-work legislation is a denial of the legal right to strike; therefore, to a certain extent it is a restriction of the democratic rights of individuals? Factor in the rights of employers in your answer.

DEVELOPING WORKPLACE SKILLS

Key: ● **Team** ★ **Analytic** ▲ **Communication** ☐ **Technology**

● ☐ ★ ▲ 1. With several classmates, investigate the emerging role of employee associations and professional associations as replacements for labour unions. What are the advantages and disadvantages of each of these three models? Which model provides the greatest legal protection in case of a disagreement between labour and management? Share your findings with the class.

★ ▲ 2. Do businesses and government agencies have a duty to provide additional benefits to employees beyond fair pay and good working conditions? Propose a benefits system that you consider fair and workable for both employees and employers.

● ★ ▲ 3. Debate the following statement with several classmates: Non-union firms are better managed (or perform better) than unionized firms. To get a better feeling for the other side's point of view, take the opposite side of this issue from the one you normally would. Consider such questions as: Do unions serve a purpose in some industries? Do unions make Canada less competitive in global markets?

★ ● ▲ 4. Compile a list of two employee–management issues not covered in the chapter. Compare your list with those of several classmates and see which issues you selected in common and which are unique to each individual. Pick an issue you all agree will be important in the future and discuss its likely effects and outcomes.

● ☐ ★ ▲ 5. With a classmate, investigate which unions have been in the news over the past six months. What were the issues? Were these issues resolved? Share this information with the class. (Hint: For a list of labour organizations with 30,000 or more workers, visit the Labour Program <*http://www.labour.gc.ca/eng/resources/info/publications/union_coverage/union_coverage.shtml#fnb2>*.)

ANALYZING MANAGEMENT DECISIONS

Plant Closings, Unions, and Concessions

Over the past decade, the Canadian economy has witnessed a series of plant closing or lockout actions taken by foreign companies against employees in Canada. As well, Canada has experienced a fragile recovery from the recession, the decreasing value of the Canadian dollar, and a perception that workers are in a weak position. Plants and offices have laid off thousands of people or closed because of bankruptcy, consolidation, or transfer of operations to other lower-wage countries. In some cases, management advised unions that the only way that they could avoid closing would be substantial concessions in wages and other changes in existing contracts.

American-based heavy equipment maker Caterpillar Inc. <*http://www.cat.com>* ended a one-month standoff with locked-out workers by closing its 62-year-old Electro-Motive plant in London, Ontario, eliminating about 450 manufacturing jobs that mostly paid twice the rate of a U.S. counterpart. Caterpillar spokesman Rusty Dunn summed up the reasoning as follows: "All facilities must achieve competitive costs, quality, and operating flexibility to remain viable in the global marketplace. Expectations at the London plant were no different." These jobs are expected to be transferred to Muncie, Indiana, where Caterpillar had opened a locomotive plant and was trying to fill positions at about half the pay of the workers in Ontario.

The closing angered former CAW president Ken Lewenza. Caterpillar had demanded pay cuts of 50 percent in many job categories, elimination of a defined-benefit pension plan, reductions in dental and other benefits, and the end of a cost-of-living adjustment. "I've never had a situation where I've dealt with such an unethical, immoral, disrespectful, highly profitable company like Caterpillar," said Lewenza. He said that during bargaining he told the company's negotiators: "If it's in your business plan to close us, don't punish us, let's work out a closure agreement. They said, 'We have no intention of closing the facility.'"

The situation was different in another industry, but the concessions were hard ones. Workers at international mining giant Vale *<http://www.vale.com>* in Ontario approved a new labour agreement, ending a year-long strike in 2010. Vale said it needed to cut labour costs to keep its operations competitive, but workers argued the Brazilian company made billions of dollars a year and did not need concessions from workers. The strike was bitter at times, with the union accusing Vale of bad faith bargaining and the company taking the union to court over a variety of alleged incidents on the picket lines. The output from the Canadian operations—which account for more than 10 percent of the world's nickel supply—was significantly decreased during the strike. The agreement resulted in more than 3,000 workers receiving a raise and a big signing bonus. However, it also saw new employees placed on a defined-contribution pension plan, as opposed to the existing defined-benefit plan. Defined-contribution plans depend on market returns and do not guarantee a steady income, unlike defined-benefit plans.

Givebacks are not being asked just by foreign-owned companies. For example, since Air Canada came out of bankruptcy protection in 2004, it has received concessions from its unions as part of its restructuring conditions. This has included concessions in the area of wages, jobs (e.g., since the end of 2000, Air Canada has reduced its total full-time equivalent staff by 47 percent, resulting in a loss of over 20,000 jobs), and pensions. Eight years later, in 2012, union members grew tired of givebacks and voted to go on strike. The federal government stepped in and threatened the unions with back-to-work legislation before imposing binding arbitration in some instances.

Keep in mind that non-unionized employees also saw tens of thousands of jobs eliminated. At the start of 2001, Nortel Networks Corporation had more than 90,000 employees worldwide. By 2006, the company had cut its workforce by two-thirds as it restructured several times in an attempt to regain profitability. In the first two months of 2009, an additional 5,000 jobs were eliminated as the company filed for bankruptcy protection. In late November of that year, Nortel's union and former employees failed to persuade an Ontario appeals court they were entitled to retirement and severance payments. On July 1, 2011, Nortel reached a deal to sell the last of its assets. No employees are safe as companies try to remain competitive in the marketplace.

Union leaders and their members are in a quandary when faced with such decisions. Sometimes they think management is bluffing. Sometimes they are reluctant to give up contract conditions they fought long and hard for.

Accepting wage cuts or benefit reductions when the cost of living continues to rise is not easy. Agreeing to staff reductions to save other jobs is also a tough decision. Unions worry about where these concessions will end. Will there be another round of layoffs or even worse in a few months?

These examples highlight some of the dilemmas facing unions and employers. The business environment demands that companies become more efficient and productive. However, this will not happen unless there is mutual respect between management and labour.

Sources: James R. Hagerty, "Caterpillar Closes Plant in Canada After Lockout," *The Wall Street Journal*, 4 February 2012, http://online.wsj.com /article/SB10001424052970203889904577200953014575964.html; Greg Keenan, "Caterpillar pulls plug on London plant," *The Globe and Mail*, 3 February 2012, www.theglobeandmail.com/globe-investor/caterpillar-pulls-plug-on-london-plant/article544321/; "Timeline: Nortel—The rise and fall of a telecom giant," Global News, 18 January 2012, www.globalnews.ca/timeline+nortel+-+the+rise-+and+fall+of+a+telecom+giant/6442560329 /story.html; "Ont. Vale workers vote to approve new contract," The Canadian Press, 13 January 2010, www.ctvnews.ca/ont-vale-workers-vote-to -approve-new-contract-1.530694; Brent Jang, "Air Canada, Union at Odds Over Proposed Moratorium on Pension Payments," *The Globe and Mail*,

5 May 2009, www.theglobeandmail.com/servlet/story/LAC.20090505.RAIR CANADA05ART1908/TPStory/Business; "Study: The Year in Review in Manufacturing," Statistics Canada, 29 April 2009, www.statcan.gc.ca/daily-quotidien/090429/dq090429b-eng.htm; Paul Kunert, "Nortel Networks Lays off 3,200 Staff," *Computer Weekly*, 26 February 2009, www.computerweekly.com/Articles/2009/02/26/235029/nortel-networks-lays-off-3200-staff.htm; "Air Canada: Fly it Right!," Canadian Auto Workers Union, 2009, www.caw.ca/en/7423.htm; and "Nortel Rebuilding and Hiring Again: CEO," CBC News, 29 September 2006, www.cbc.ca/money/story/2006/09/29/zafirovski-nortel.html.

Discussion Questions

1. What would you recommend to union workers whose employer is threatening to close down unless they agree to wage decreases or other concessions?

2. Is there some alternative to cutting wages or closing down? What is it?

3. Union workers often feel that the company is bluffing when it threatens to close. How can such doubts be settled so that more open negotiations can take place?

4. Does government have a right to interfere with organizations (i.e., union and employer) that have already negotiated a collective agreement and force them to renegotiate? Explain.

VIDEO CASE 13

HR Is Key to Positive Labour Relations

Basil (Buzz) Hargrove served as national president of the Canadian Auto Workers Union from 1992 until his retirement in September 2008. One of the most recognized labour leaders in Canada, Hargrove has been a figurehead in the fight for workplace and social justice. Hargrove is co-director of the Centre for Labour Management Relations *<http://www.ryerson.ca/clmr>* at the Ted Rogers School of Management, Ryerson University. The Centre promotes collaborative, ethical, proactive, and sustainable best-practice labour–management relations by sponsoring ground-breaking academic research and transferring knowledge to receptor communities.

A positive labour–management relationship benefits companies in many ways. HR plays a vital role in making this happen. HR professionals are the ones that deal with and communicate with unions on a daily basis. Positive relationships are an investment in the workforce that lead to cost savings.

To build a strong relationship, HR should start by spending the appropriate amount of time building a relationship with the union representative. The bargaining agent represents the workers and through him or her, information should be shared. Hargrove states that HR best practices include having open and honest communication, knowing the people you are dealing with, knowing the important issues, having a good sense of humour, and having integrity.

Sources: "Buzz Hargrove," Ryerson University, 2015, http://www.ryerson.ca/tedrogersschool/facultystaff/faculty/buzz-hargrove.html; and "HR Key to Positive Labour Relations," *Canadian HR Reporter*, 10 March 2015, http://www.hrreporter.com/videodisplay/376-hr-key-to-positive-labour-relations.

Discussion Questions

1. In Buzz Hargrove's opinion, what is the driver of productivity, quality, and delivery for companies?

2. What are drawbacks of dealing directly with the workers rather than the bargaining agent?

3. What is the general attitude in your class toward labour unions? Are there many union workers in your city? Where do you see labour unions gaining strength in the future?

RUNNING CASE

Human Resources at Fox 40 International Inc.

For successful Canadian entrepreneur and inventor Ron Foxcroft, it all started in 1982 when he purchased Fluke Transport, a Southern Ontario trucking business. The company slogan—If It's On Time . . . It's A "FLUKE"—was soon recognized throughout North America. Over the years, Foxcroft diversified into new ventures and the Foxcroft Group of Companies now includes Fluke Transportation Group, Fluke Warehousing Inc., Foxcroft Capital Group, Fox 40 International Inc., and Fox 40 USA Inc.

The formation of Fox 40 International Inc. (Fox 40) is the result of a dream for a pealess whistle. When developing his first whistle, Ron was motivated by his knowledge and experience as an international basketball referee. Frustrated with faulty pea whistles, he spent three years of development with design consultant Chuck Shepherd, resulting in the creation of the Fox 40® Classic Whistle. Fast forward 25 years and Fox 40 dominates the global whistle industry.

Fox 40 is a privately held, family-run organization with Ron as the Chief Executive Officer and son, Dave, as the President and Chief Operating Officer. The company employs 35 individuals, and as many as 45 during peak seasons. You may be surprised to learn that there is no formal human resource department in this company. In fact, there are no layers of management. Among other reasons, this is to empower employees, regardless of position, to develop solutions to problems, with the goal of satisfying customers.

It is important to create a good working environment. Open communication is encouraged throughout the organization. There is an open-door policy within the three teams—Corporate, Product and Marketing, and Sales and Customer Service—and across the teams. Senior management is directly accessible by both employees and customers. The lack of internal titles is another signal that the owners do not stand on ceremony. Outside of the organization, however, employees have titles as this is expected by external stakeholders.

Hiring the right people is critical. According to Ron, "Managers hire people that are dumber than them, but owners hire people that are smarter than them." With this in mind, new hires are expected to contribute to the organization. There is a focus on hiring self-starters who require minimum supervision. Chemistry with current employees (i.e., organizational fit), strong communication skills, a customer-focus, enthusiasm, and honesty are required qualities. Initiative is expected and employees should have the courage to go to Ron or Dave with suggestions on how to make the company better. Examples can include improving processes, developing new products, or improving the customer experience.

For example, Dave and his team approached Ron with the idea to develop a new variation of the Fox 40 Classic. Ron struggled with this as the Fox 40 Classic was his first whistle and he was not convinced that this was the right direction. The team believed that there were some untapped opportunities. One advantage would be that a new whistle could be registered for an 18-year patent and trademark. Ron agreed and the Fox 40 Classic Eclipse was created. This whistle was re-engineered for maximum performance and style. The Fox 40 Classic Eclipse was also the first whistle to be developed using exclusive SpectraBurst™ glow-in-the dark colours that would last up to ten hours. Since its introduction in the marketplace, feedback has been tremendous.

At Fox 40, new hires start in entry-level positions. They should be prepared to do any job (except take out the garbage; this is the CEO's job). Orientation includes on-the-job training. As Dave says, "The best way to learn is by doing." Employees are assigned tasks with a timeline and their performance is monitored. During a performance review, discussions centre on finding opportunities that will tap into each employee's strengths while also discussing how to improve on any weaknesses.

Fox 40 is a non-unionized work environment. "We pay our employees fairly," says Ron. For the production staff, manufacturing output is tracked. Those that exceed their targets are also compensated with money and gift certificates that can be redeemed at local retailers.

Sources: Ron Foxcroft, CEO of Fox 40 International Inc. and Chairman and CEO of Fluke Transportation, in-person interview, 25 June 2012, Hamilton; and Dave Foxcroft, President and COO, Fox 40 International Inc., in-person interview, 25 June 2012, Hamilton.

Discussion Questions

1. Considering Douglas McGregor's research on managers' attitudes toward their workers. How would you categorize the management style described at Fox 40?

2. What pay systems does Fox 40 use for its production staff? (Hint: Review Figure 12.5 for some examples.)

3. What are some company advantages in not having a unionized workforce? What are some employee advantages in not belonging to a labour union?

PART 5

Marketing: Helping Buyers Buy

LEARNING OBJECTIVES

After you have read and studied this chapter, you should be able to:

LO1	Define marketing and explain how the marketing concept applies to both for-profit and non-profit organizations.
LO2	Describe the four Ps of marketing.
LO3	Identify the steps in the marketing research process, and explain how marketers use environmental scanning to learn about the changing marketing environment.
LO4	Compare the consumer market to the business-to-business market.
LO5	Describe the market segmentation process, and the role of relationship marketing.
LO6	Explain how marketers meet the needs of the consumer market through the study of consumer behaviour.

PROFILE

GETTING TO KNOW SOFIA COLUCCI, MARKETING DIRECTOR—QUAKER FOODS AND SNACKS, PEPSICO AMERICA

Celestica. Maple Leaf Foods. PepsiCo Beverages Canada. What do these seemingly different companies have in common? They were all stepping stones to Sofia Colucci's current role as the Marketing Director of Quaker Foods and Snacks for PepsiCo America. PepsiCo products are offered in over 200 countries and territories and generate more than $66 billion in net revenue. Its food and beverage portfolio includes 22 brands that generate more than $1 billion each in estimated annual retail sales. You may recognize some of its brands—Quaker, Tropicana, Gatorade, Frito-Lay, and Pepsi-Cola.

Colucci's career at PepsiCo began in her role as a Marketing Manager for Aquafina & O.N.E. Coconut Water at PepsiCo Beverages Canada. In 2012, she transferred to Chicago to begin her role as a Senior Marketing Manager of Quaker Foods and Snacks for the PepsiCo America division. As a Senior Marketing Manager, she was responsible for growing the top-line sales of her brands, which required the development and execution of a marketing plan. No two days were the same as she worked with different cross-functional partners to achieve targets. Examples include partnering with Sales to launch successful products to customers, collaborating with the Consumer Insights team to develop creative concepts, and analyzing the numbers with Finance.

Today, Colucci is a Marketing Director of Quaker Granola Bars. She is responsible for the entire granola bar portfolio, including brands like Chewy and Real Medley Bars. Colucci continues to focus on driving breakthrough innovation, delivering hard-hitting communication, and achieving strong business results through portfolio management. However as her scope of responsibility has grown, it has become imperative for her to achieve results through others, and therefore she invests a lot of time coaching and developing her team.

"Get as involved as much as possible in extra-curricular activities to get more exposure," Colucci advises students. "Competition is so strong that you need to do more than just go to class. Businesses want to see that you have demonstrated leadership outside of the classroom." While a student at the DeGroote School of Business, McMaster University, she participated in a six-month international student exchange to Mexico, a sixteen-month internship as a Supply Chain Analyst at Celestica, and she held a teaching assistant role in the Marketing area.

Colucci credits these undergraduate experiences with landing her first post-graduation job in the Maple Leaf Foods Management Trainee Program. This three-year rotational program gave her exposure to three different functional roles in product management, finance, and marketing. In subsequent years she held two marketing manager roles (one in Innovation and the second in the Bacon Category) at Maple Leaf Foods before moving to PepsiCo Beverages Canada.

Colucci links much of her success at PepsiCo to the invaluable general business management training she gained at Maple Leaf Foods. As business increasingly becomes more global and competitive, it is critical to not only think as a marketer, but also as a business manager, collaborating with partners across all functions. The other key success factor that Colucci stresses is the desire to make a difference. "Get visibly passionate about your work—know your business cold, be curious about the world around you, and come to the table with creative solutions."

In this chapter, you will be introduced to the importance of marketing. All companies must conduct an environmental scan to discover opportunities and threats in their industries. Customers demand a four-P marketing mix (product, price, place, and promotion) that will meet their expectations. With a greater customer-relationship management focus today, marketers need to reach their customers wherever they may be.

Sources: Sofia Colucci, Marketing Director, Quaker Foods and Snacks, PepsiCo America, interview, 31 March 2015; and "The Pepsi Challenge: Epic. Music. Sports. Tech. Design. Purpose." PepsiCo Inc., 11 March 2015, http://www.pepsico.com/live/pressrelease/the-pepsi-challenge-epic-music-sports-tech-design-purpose.

LO1   Define marketing and explain how the marketing concept applies to both for-profit and non-profit organizations.

What Is Marketing?

The term marketing means different things to different people. Many think of marketing as simply "selling" or "advertising." Yes, selling and advertising are part of marketing, but it is much more. The Canadian Marketing Association defines **marketing** as a set of business practices designed to plan for and present an organization's products or services in ways that build effective customer relationships.[1] We can also think of marketing, more simply, as the activities buyers and sellers perform to facilitate mutually satisfying exchanges. A market (note that this is the core word in *marketing*) is defined as a group of people with unsatisfied wants and needs who have the resources and the willingness to buy. A market is, therefore, created as a result of this demand for goods and services. What marketers do at any particular time will depend on what needs to be done to fill customers' needs. This "find a need and fill it" concept is core to marketing.

> **marketing**
> A set of business practices designed to plan for and present an organization's products or services in ways that build effective customer relationships.

In the past marketing focused almost entirely on helping the seller sell. That is why many people still think of it as mostly selling, advertising, and distribution *from the seller to the buyer*. Today, much of marketing is instead about *helping the buyer buy*.[2] Let's examine a couple of examples.

Today, when people want to buy a new or used car, they often go online first. They go to a website like Cars.ca to search for the vehicle they want. At other websites they compare prices and features. By the time they go to the dealer, they may know exactly which car they want and the best prices available. The websites have *helped the buyer buy*. Not only are customers spared searching one dealership after another to find the best price, but manufacturers and dealers are eager to participate so that they do not lose customers. The future of marketing is doing everything you can to help the buyer buy. The easier a marketer makes the purchase decision process, the more that marketer will sell.[3]

Let's look at another example. In the past, one of the few ways students and parents could find the school with the right "fit" was to travel from campus to campus, a gruelling and expensive process. Today, schools use podcasts, virtual tours, live chats, and other interactive technologies to make on-campus visits less necessary. Such virtual tours help students and their parents buy.

Shoppers around the world look for bargains as these consumers in Austria are doing. How many different ways can marketers appeal to shoppers' desires to find the lowest prices? Do online retailers have a pricing advantage over traditional bricks-and-mortar retailers?

Of course, helping the buyer buy also helps the seller sell. Think about that for a minute. In the vacation market, many people find the trip they want themselves. They go online to find the right spot, and then make choices, sometimes questioning potential sellers. In industries like this, the role of marketers is to make sure that a company's products or services are easily found online, and that the company responds effectively to potential customers. Websites like Expedia *<http://www.expedia.ca>*, Travelocity *<http://www.travelocity.ca>*, and Priceline *<http://www.priceline.com>* allow customers to find the best prices or set their own prices.

These are only a few examples of the marketing trend toward helping buyers buy. Consumers today spend hours searching the Internet for good deals. Wise marketers provide a wealth of information online and even cultivate customer relationships using blogs and social networking sites such as Facebook and Twitter.

Online communities provide an opportunity to observe people (customers and others) interacting with one another, expressing their own opinions, forming relationships, and commenting on various goods and services. It is important for marketers to track what relevant bloggers are writing by doing blog searches using key terms that define their market. Vendors who have text-mining tools can help companies measure conversations about their products and their personnel. Much of the future of marketing lies in mining such online conversations and responding appropriately. For example, marketers are learning why people shop online, put the goods into a shopping cart, but then end the sale before they give their credit card information.[4] Retailers and other marketers who rely solely on traditional advertising and selling are losing out to the new ways of marketing.[5] Review the Spotlight on Small Business to learn about a company that incorporates some of the activities just mentioned.

Spotlight *On* SMALL BUSINESS

Making the Right Cut

Floral Dress from ModCloth's
Private Label "Myrtlewood"

The fashion industry is a complicated combination of designers, buyers, brands, and media taste-makers who work hard to make fashion exclusive and unpredictable. Started out of high school, ModCloth <*http://www .modcloth.com*> was founded by then-sweethearts, but now husband and wife, Eric and Susan Gregg Koger. For them, fashion is a more democratic endeavour than fashion gurus at *Vogue* let on. The company's website sells the work of more than 600 independent designers. The vintage-style outfits on ModCloth appeal to shoppers looking for funky clothes that don't normally find their way into women's shops or department stores.

For the Kogers, stocking unique merchandise is the key to their success. After all, the Internet is home to thousands of apparel sites, from big name retailers to small independent vendors. The most successful online operations have a defining characteristic that separates them from the rest of the pack. Customers keep coming back to ModCloth because of the interactivity of the brand.

The company is able to retain customer loyalty by continuously trying to engage their customers. For example, the company's clothing design contest, "Make the Cut," invites customers to submit their own dress sketches. Contest winners have a chance to have their designs produced and sold on the company's website. In the most recent contest, more than 1,900 designs were sent in during the two-week submission period. With the company's "Be the Buyer" program, ModCloth accepts a sample from a designer, puts the photos online, then asks customers if they should produce the item. As another example, any customers who would like the help of a fashion adviser can get help from Modstylists, who are available 24/7. Customers can chat, call, or e-mail an in-house stylist to get advice dealing with questions about fit, sizing, or styling. The company's marketing objective is to be "the fashion company you are friends with."

Both Kogers have been listed together on *Forbes'* "30 Under 30" list. They continue to look for even more ways to engage customers. In addition to visiting the company site, you can take a virtual tour of Susan's closet, read her blog posts, and follow her on Instagram, Twitter, and Pinterest. As she comments, "ModCloth is not just another retailer, but a social-shopping community with our customer at the center of everything we do."

Sources: "Susan's Story," ModCloth, http://www.modcloth.com/about_us/susans-story, downloaded 6 April 2015; Alice Truong, "ModCloth Wraps Up a Very Social Year," *Fast Company,* 17 January 2014; Barbara Thau, "Retailers Wake Up to Plus-Size Market with Trendier, Tonier Fare," *Forbes,* 10 January 2014; and Marisa Meltzer, "Modcloth Is Selling an Era They Missed Out On," *New York Times,* 11 September 2013.

The Evolution of Marketing

What marketers do at any particular time depends on what they need to do to fill customers' needs and wants, which continually change. Let's take a brief look at how those changes have influenced the evolution of marketing. The evolution of marketing includes five eras, also known as orientations: (1) production, (2) sales, (3) marketing concept, (4) market orientation, and (5) social media marketing. Figure 14.1 highlights the timeline for these eras.

■ **FIGURE 14.1**

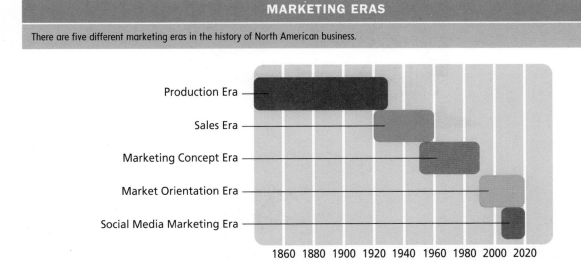

MARKETING ERAS

There are five different marketing eras in the history of North American business.

THE PRODUCTION ERA

From the time the first European settlers arrived in Canada until the start of the 1900s, the general philosophy of business was, "Produce as much as you can because there is a limitless market for it." Given the limited production capability and the vast demand for products in those days, that production philosophy was both logical and profitable, as demand exceeded supply. Business owners were mostly farmers, carpenters, and trade workers. They needed to produce more and more, so their goals centred on *production*.

THE SALES ERA

By the 1920s, businesses had developed mass production techniques (such as automobile assembly lines), and production capacity often exceeded the immediate market demand. Therefore, the business philosophy turned from producing to *selling*. Most companies emphasized selling and advertising in an effort to persuade customers to buy existing products. Few offered extensive service after the sale.

THE MARKETING CONCEPT ERA

After World War II ended in 1945, returning soldiers started new careers and began families, sparking a tremendous demand for goods and services. The postwar years launched the sudden increase in the birth rate that we now call the baby boom, and also a boom in consumer spending. Competition for the customer's dollar was fierce. Businesses recognized that they needed to be responsive to customers if they wanted to get their business, and a philosophy called the marketing concept emerged in the 1950s.

During the Sales Era, the focus of marketing was on selling, with little service afterward and less customization. What economic and social factors made this approach appropriate for the time?

The **marketing concept** had three parts:

1. *A customer orientation.* Find out what consumers want and provide it for them.[6] That is exactly what Cassandra Rush, founder of Sassy Cassy's Boots Inc. did when she started her company, which specialized in boots with varying calf sizes; "Every other boot company only does standard sizing for calves, which is about 15 inches around the calf of the leg," she said. "The market calls for bigger sizes because a lot of women can't zip up regular boots. My product is different because I offer different calf sizing so the boots are better customized to the woman's leg."[7] (Note the emphasis on meeting customer needs rather than on promotion or sales.)

2. *A service orientation.* Make sure that everyone in the organization has the same objective: customer satisfaction. This should be a total and integrated organizational effort. That is, everyone from the president of the firm to the delivery people should be customer oriented. Does that seem to be the norm today?

3. *A profit orientation.* Focus on those goods and services that will earn the most profit and enable the organization to survive and expand to serve more customers' wants and needs.

marketing concept
A three-part business philosophy: (1) a customer orientation, (2) a service orientation, and (3) a profit orientation.

It took a while for businesses to implement the marketing concept. That process went slowly during the 1960s and 1970s. During the 1980s, businesses began to apply the marketing concept more aggressively than they had done over the preceding 30 years.

THE MARKET ORIENTATION ERA[8]

Many organizations transitioned from the marketing concept era to the market orientation era. Firms with a **market orientation** focus their efforts on (1) continuously collecting information about customers' needs and competitors' capabilities, (2) sharing this information throughout the organization, and (3) using the information to create value, ensure customer satisfaction, and develop customer relationships.

> **market orientation**
> Focusing efforts on (1) continuously collecting information about customers' needs and competitors' capabilities, (2) sharing this information throughout the organization, and (3) using the information to create value, ensure customer satisfaction, and develop customer relationships.

It is not surprising that organizations with a market orientation actually engage in **customer-relationship management (CRM)**—the process of building long-term relationships with customers by delivering customer value and satisfaction. Retaining customers over time, or managing the entire customer life cycle, is a cost-effective way for firms to grow in competitive markets. The idea is to enhance customer satisfaction and stimulate long-term customer loyalty. For example, most airlines offer frequent-flyer programs that reward loyal customers with free flights.

> **customer-relationship management (CRM)**
> The process of building long-term relationships with customers by delivering customer value and satisfaction.

WildPlay Element Parks <http://www.wildplay.com> is an aerial adventure company w[...] and Alberta—and upcoming expansion across Canada and into the United States. Th[...] gives people wacky ways to have fun and challenge their self-perceived boundaries. W[...] for adults, teens, and kids include Canada's original bridge-based Bungy Jump, giant P[...] Aerial Adventure courses, What's To Fear Jumps, and long Zip Line rides. Would you b[...] How would you share it with your friends via social media?

THE SOCIAL MEDIA MARKETING ERA[9]

Social media is the term commonly given to websites and online tools that allow users to interact with each other in some way—by sharing information, opinions, knowledge, and interests. As the name implies, social media involves the building of communities or networks, encouraging participation and engagement. There are two distinct dimensions to the **social media marketing** era:

1. Social media marketing is about consumer-generated online-marketing efforts to promote brands and companies for which they are fans (or conversely, negatively promoting brands and companies for which they are non-fans).

2. Social media marketing is the use by marketers of online tools and platforms to promote their brands or organizations. The most common tools or platforms used by both consumers and organizations are social networking sites (e.g., Facebook, LinkedIn, and Twitter), blogs, wikis, podcasts, and other shared media sites such as YouTube.

> **social media**
> The term commonly given to websites and online tools that allow users to interact with each other in some way—by sharing information, opinions, knowledge, and interests.
>
> **social media marketing**
> Consumer-generated online-marketing efforts to promote brands and companies for which they are fans (or conversely, negatively promoting brands and companies for which they are non-fans), and the use by marketers of online tools and platforms to promote their brands or organizations.

It is the former dimension of social media marketing that is changing the rules of marketing and ushering in a new era of business. Social media creates a platform that empowers customers and provides them with an opportunity to communicate with an organization and with other customers. In fact, one author, Erik Qualman, suggests social media marketing is creating a new form of economy called *socialnomics,* where consumers will no longer search for products or services, but rather will find them via social media. He suggests that social media is transforming the way we live and the way organizations do business. He argues that social media platforms such as Facebook connect hundreds of millions of people to each other via instant communication and that this is creating a socio-economic shift where online communities can build or destroy brands and can make traditional marketing obsolete.

To survive in this new social media world, Qualman suggests that organizations must understand, navigate, and adapt to this new landscape. Others, however, suggest that social media marketing is not necessarily a major structural shift in the marketing era. They believe that organizations must be capable of taking advantage of social media to increase sales, cut marketing costs, and communicate more directly with their customers.

Some organizations are heeding this advice. As was mentioned in Chapter 1, a report from BMO Financial Group found that 57 percent of small businesses in Canada now use social media, and Facebook and LinkedIn are the most common tools.[10] Business owners are now using social networks to track sentiment about their company and their competitors, to recruit top employees, and to sell their products and services.[11] Lindsay Goertzen and her brother started Kelowna, British Columbia–based Aura Beauty, a company that offers a "mobile spa" for groups such as bachelorette parties, corporate events, and home parties. "We wouldn't be here if it wasn't for social media," says Goertzen. "Our events and promotions are run 100 percent through social media and it works for us." Do not think, however, that social media is being leveraged only by small businesses; the Ford Explorer launch on Facebook received more traffic than a Super Bowl advertisement.

Non-Profit Organizations Prosper from Marketing

Even though the marketing concept emphasizes a profit orientation, marketing is a critical part of all organizations, including non-profits.[12] Charities use marketing to raise funds to combat world hunger, for instance, or to obtain other resources. Canadian Blood Services uses promotion to encourage people to donate blood when local or national supplies run low. Greenpeace *<http://www.greenpeace.org>* uses marketing to promote ecologically safe technologies. Environmental groups use marketing to try to cut carbon emissions. Churches use marketing to attract new members and to raise funds. Politicians use marketing to get votes.

Advertising Standards Canada (ASC, *<http://www.adstandards.com>*), a non-profit organization, is committed to ensuring the integrity and viability of advertising in Canada through responsible industry self-regulation. Would you complain to ASC if you saw an ad that you thought was untrue?

Provinces and territories use marketing to attract new businesses and tourists. Some provinces, for example, have competed to get automobile companies from other countries to locate plants in their areas. Schools use marketing to attract new students. Other organizations, such as arts groups, unions, and social groups, also use marketing. Organizations use marketing, in fact, to promote everything from environmentalism and crime prevention ("Take A Bite Out of Crime") to social issues ("Don't Drink and Drive").

LO2 Describe the four Ps of marketing.

The Marketing Mix

We can divide much of what marketers do into four factors called the four Ps to make them easy to remember and implement. They are:

1. Product
2. Price
3. Place
4. Promotion

Managing the controllable parts of the marketing process, then, involves (1) designing a want-satisfying *product*, (2) setting a *price* for the product, (3) getting the product in a *place* where people will buy it, and (4) *promoting* the product. These four factors, highlighted in Figure 14.2, are called the **marketing mix** because businesses blend them in a well-designed marketing program.

> **marketing mix**
> The ingredients that go into a marketing program: product, price, place, and promotion.

■ **FIGURE 14.2**

MARKETING MANAGERS AND THE MARKETING MIX

Marketing managers must choose how to implement the four Ps of the marketing mix: product, price, place, and promotion. The goals are to please customers and make a profit.

Marketing Manager

Marketing mix

Product   Price   Place   Promotion

The customer drives the marketing mix. The features and benefits of the product should meet, if not exceed, customer expectations. The price, place, and promotion is also driven by a desire to communicate with the customer in such a meaningful way that he or she seeks out the product (i.e., place) and is willing to purchase the product at the set price. These marketing decisions also need to achieve the organization's goals and objectives.

Applying the Marketing Process

The four Ps are a convenient way to remember the basics of marketing, but they do not include everything that goes into the marketing process for all products. One of the best ways to understand the entire marketing process is to take a product and follow the process that led to its development and sale. Figure 14.3 outlines some of these steps.

Imagine, for example, that you and your friends want to start a money-making business near your school. You noticed a lot of vegetarians among your friends. You do a quick survey in a couple of dorms and other campus clubs and find many vegetarians—and other students who like to eat vegetarian meals once in a while. Your preliminary research indicates some demand for a vegetarian restaurant nearby.

■ **FIGURE 14.3**

THE MARKETING PROCESS WITH THE FOUR PS

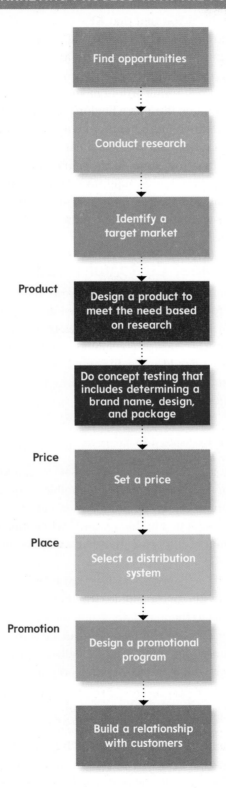

Find opportunities

Conduct research

Identify a
target market

Product

Design a product to
meet the need based
on research

Do concept testing that
includes determining a
brand name, design,
and package

Price

Set a price

Place

Select a distribution
system

Promotion

Design a promotional
program

Build a relationship
with customers

You check the fast-food stores in the area and find none offer more than one or two vegetarian meals. In fact, most do not have any, except salads and some soups.

You note that haute-vegetarian menus are big in Europe.[13] Why not in Canada? You also note that McDonald's went vegetarian in India.[14] You find that KFC Canada offers a vegan version of its chicken sandwich and KFC offers vegetarian burgers in India.[15] Further research indicates that there are a number of different kinds of vegetarians. For example, fruitarians eat mostly raw fruits, grains, and nuts. Vegans eat neither eggs nor dairy products.

You conclude that a vegetarian restaurant would have to appeal to all kinds of vegetarians to be a success. Your research identifies organic farmers who don't use any synthetic chemical fertilizers, pesticides, herbicides, or genetically modified ingredients. You also find that there is a company that is making an egg-like product from vegetables. That would appeal to those vegetarians who don't eat eggs.[16]

You have just performed the first few steps in the marketing process. You noticed an opportunity (a need for vegetarian food, perhaps near campus). You conducted some preliminary research to see whether your idea had any merit. And then you identified groups of people who might be interested in your product. They will be your *target market* (the people you will try to persuade to come to your restaurant).

Designing a Product to Meet Customer Needs

Once you have researched customer needs and found a target market (which we will discuss in more detail later) for your product, the four Ps of marketing come into play. You start by developing a product or products. A **product** is any physical good, service, or idea that satisfies a want or need plus anything that would enhance the product in the eyes of consumers, such as the brand name. In this case, your proposed product is a restaurant that would serve different kinds of vegetarian meals. You continue with your research, and find that a restaurant called Freshii is bringing quinoa and kale to the masses.[17] You are getting a better idea of what your products should be.

> **product**
> Any physical good, service, or idea that satisfies a want or need.

Many products today are not pure goods or pure services. Figure 14.4 illustrates the service continuum, which is a range from the tangible to the intangible or good-dominant to service-dominant offerings.[18] The service sector employs approximately 78 percent of all working Canadians so there is a strong possibility that you will be employed in this sector.[19] While this text briefly introduces you to the concepts of marketing, services marketing is an area that warrants more attention as you pursue your studies in this discipline.

It is a good idea at this point to do *concept testing*. That is, you develop an accurate description of your restaurant and ask people, in person or online, whether the idea of the restaurant and the kind of meals you intend to offer appeals to them. If it does, you might go to a supplier that offers vegetarian products to get the ingredients to prepare samples you can take to customers to test their reactions. The process of testing products among potential users is called **test marketing**. For example, you can test market your vegetarian burgers and learn how best to prepare them.[20]

> **test marketing**
> The process of testing products among potential users.

If customers like the product and agree that they would buy it, you have the information you need to find investors and a convenient location to open a restaurant. You will have to think of a catchy name for the restaurant. (For practice, stop for a minute and try to think of one.) We'll use Very Vegetarian in this text.

■ **FIGURE 14.4**

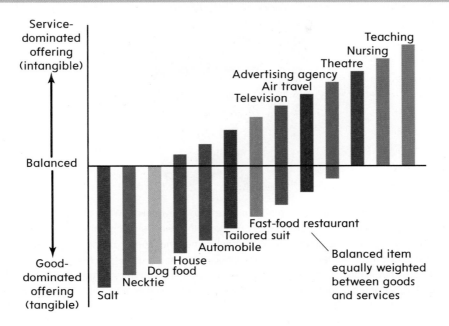

THE SERVICE CONTINUUM

Products and services range from the tangible to the intangible.

You may want to offer some well-known brand names to attract people right away. A **brand name** is a word, letter, or group of words or letters that differentiates one seller's goods or services from those of competitors. Brand names of vegetarian meals include Tofurky, Mori-Nu, and Yves Veggie Cuisine. We will discuss the product development process in detail in Chapter 15, in addition to the other Ps. You will follow the Very Vegetarian case to show you how all marketing and other business decisions tie together. For now, we are simply sketching the marketing process to give you an idea of the overall picture. So far, we have covered the first P of the marketing mix: product. After your read the Reaching Beyond Our Borders box that discusses product names in more depth, consider price next.

> **brand name**
> A word, letter, or group of words or letters that differentiates one seller's goods or services from those of competitors.

Setting an Appropriate Price

After you have decided what products and services you want to offer, you have to set appropriate prices. From a marketing viewpoint, **price** is the money or other consideration (including other goods and services) exchanged for the ownership or use of a good or service.[21] The price depends on a number of factors. In the restaurant business, the price could be close to what other restaurants charge to stay competitive. Or you might charge less to attract business, especially at the beginning. Or, you may offer high-quality products for which customers are willing to pay a little more (as Starbucks does). You also have to consider the costs of producing, distributing, and promoting the product, which all influence your price.

> **price**
> The money or other consideration (including other goods and services) exchanged for the ownership or use of a good or service.

Reaching *Beyond* OUR BORDERS

Playing the Name Game

So, you've developed a product and you're ready to take it to the market. What should you call it? America's favourite cookie, Oreo, is said to be a great name because the two Os nicely mirror the shape of the cookie itself. Could the name be part of the charm? Think of other names that come to mind when you think of American products: Coke, Nike, and Häagen-Dazs <*http://www.haagendazs.us*>.

Are you surprised that Häagen-Dazs is an American product? Häagen-Dazs was founded in 1961. Company founder Reuben Mattas wanted a name that projected high quality. Being enamoured with Dutch/Swedish modern architecture and impressed with the quality of Duncan Hines products, Mattas played around with words until he came up with the name Häagen-Dazs. The name means absolutely nothing but it seemed to project old-world quality for his premium ice cream. Today, the Häagen-Dazs name resonates around the globe, including nations like Japan where they have just introduced innovative veggie flavours like tomato cherry and carrot orange.

At one time, finding a name like Häagen-Dazs was relatively simple. Now, with a couple hundred countries on the cyber-platform, choosing the right name is a global issue. For example, when Russian gas company Gazprom formed a joint venture with Nigeria's NNPC, the company was called NiGaz. Not a great name, we'd say. On the other hand, a web development company in New Zealand chose the name hairyLemon. It has been estimated that at least a third of hairyLemon's business was because of its name.

Every once in a while, a successful name is created by accident. Google is a good example. The global search engine was supposed to be called Googol (a scientific name for 1 followed by one hundred zeros). However, the founders made a typo when registering the domain name. The error resulted in a warm, catchy, human-sounding name. Some mistakes turn out to be luckier than others.

Sources: Greg Emerson, "Häagen-Dazs Vegetable Ice Cream Flavors to Debut in Japan," *Newsday*, 20 April 2014; Gwen Moran, "5 Strategies to Build a Global Brand," *Entrepreneur*, 7 May 2013; and Interbrand, www.interbrand.com, downloaded April 2014.

Getting the Product to the Right Place

There are several ways you can serve the market for vegetarian meals. You can have people come in, sit down, and eat at the restaurant, but that is not the only alternative. Think of pizza. You could deliver the food to customers' dorms, apartments, and student unions. You may want to sell your products in supermarkets or health-food stores, or through organizations that specialize in distributing food products. Such *intermediaries* are the middle links in a series of organizations that distribute goods from producers to consumers. (The more traditional word for them is *middlemen*.) Getting the product to customers when and where they want it is critical to market success. Do not forget to consider the Internet as a way to reach customers.

A vegetarian restaurant might fill a popular need in the neighbourhood of many school campuses today. Is there one near your school? What can you tell about its application of the four Ps of marketing—product, price, place, and promotion?

Developing an Effective Promotional Strategy

The last of the four Ps of marketing is promotion. **Promotion** consists of all of the techniques sellers use to inform people and motivate them to buy their goods or services. They include advertising, personal selling, public relations, direct marketing, and sales promotion (such as coupons, rebates, and samples).

promotion
All of the techniques sellers use to motivate customers to buy their products.

Promotion often includes relationship building with customers. Among other activities, that means responding to suggestions customers make to improve the products or their marketing, such as price and packaging. For Very Vegetarian, postpurchase (or after-sale) service may include refusing payment for meals that were not satisfactory and stocking additional vegetarian products customers say they would like. Listening to customers and responding to their needs is the key to the ongoing process that is marketing.

Progress Assessment

- What does it mean to "help the buyer buy"?
- State each marketing era and the emphasis for each.
- What are the three parts of the marketing concept?
- Describe each of the four Ps of the marketing mix.

LO3 Identify the steps in the marketing research process, and explain how marketers use environmental scanning to learn about the changing marketing environment.

Providing Marketers with Information

Every decision in the marketing process depends on information. When they conduct **marketing research**, marketers analyze markets to determine opportunities and challenges, and to find information they need to make good decisions.

> **marketing research**
> The analysis of markets to determine opportunities and challenges, and to find the information needed to make good decisions.

Marketing research helps identify what products customers have purchased in the past, and what changes have occurred to alter what they want now and what they are likely to want in the future. Marketers also conduct research on business trends, the ecological impact of their decisions, global trends, and more. Businesses need information to compete effectively, and marketing research is the activity that gathers it. Besides listening to customers, marketing researchers also pay attention to what employees, shareholders, dealers, consumer advocates, media representatives, and other stakeholders have to say. As noted earlier, some of that research is now being gathered online through social media. Despite all that research, however, marketers still have difficulty understanding their customers as well as they should.[22]

The Marketing Research Process

A simplified marketing research process consists of at least four key steps:

1. Defining the question (the problem or opportunity) and determining the present situation;
2. Collecting research data;
3. Analyzing the research data; and
4. Choosing the best solution and implementing it.

The following sections look at each of these steps.

STEP 1: DEFINING THE QUESTION AND DETERMINING THE PRESENT SITUATION

Marketing researchers need the freedom to discover what the present situation is, what the problems or opportunities are, what the alternatives are, what information they need, and how to go about gathering and analyzing data.

STEP 2: COLLECTING DATA

Usable information is vital to the marketing research process. Research can become quite expensive, however, so marketers must often make a trade-off between the need for information and the cost

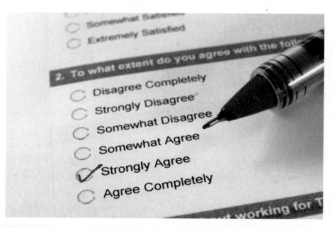

Primary research can be used to collect information about customers' needs, wants, and buying habits. Which primary data source do you prefer when asked to answer questions about a product or product category you use?

of obtaining it. Normally the least expensive method is to gather information that has already been compiled by others and published in journals and books or made available online.

Such existing data are called **secondary data** since you are not the first one to gather them. Figure 14.5 lists the principal sources of secondary marketing research information. Despite its name, *secondary* data is what marketers should gather *first* to avoid incurring unnecessary expense. To start your secondary data search about vegetarians, go to the website for *Vegetarian Times <http://www.vegetariantimes.com>* or search other websites on vegetarianism.

> **secondary data**
> Information that has already been compiled by others and published in journals and books or made available online.

■ **FIGURE 14.5**

SELECTED SOURCES OF PRIMARY AND SECONDARY INFORMATION	
Primary Sources	
Survey (e.g., phone, online, and mail) Personal interview	Focus group Observation
Secondary Sources	
Newspapers *The Globe and Mail* *The National Post* Local newspapers (e.g., *The Chronicle Herald*) **Internal Sources** Company records Balance sheets Income statements Prior research reports **Company Directories and Information** Canadian Business Database Mergent Online Business Source Complete Hoovers Infomart SEDAR Passport **General Internet Sites** Industry Canada—www.ic.gc.ca Statistics Canada—www.statcan.gc.ca Market news, company sites, etc.	**Trade Sources** Nielsen Canada Conference Board of Canada Dun & Bradstreet Canada Canadian Marketing Association Retail Council of Canada Advertising Standards Canada **Periodicals** *Journal of Marketing* *Journal of Consumer Research* *Journal of Small Business Management* *Marketing Magazine* *Advertising Age* *Maclean's* *Canadian Business* *PROFIT* **Databases** CANSIM (Statistics Canada) Canadian Business and Current Affairs Factiva LexisNexis Academic

Often, secondary data do not provide all of the information managers need to make important decisions. To gather additional, in-depth information, marketers must do their own research. The results of such *new* studies are called primary data. **Primary data** are facts, figures, and opinions that you have gathered yourself (not from secondary sources such as books, journals, and newspapers). Four sources of primary data are surveys (also known as questionnaires), personal interviews, focus groups, and observation.

> **primary data**
> Data that you gather yourself (not from secondary sources such as books, journals, and newspapers).

Primary data can be gathered by developing a list of questions and conducting a survey. Surveys (telephone, online, and mail) and personal interviews are the most common forms of primary data collection. Surveys are best carried out by independent third parties so that the information gathered and the results reported can be as objective as possible. You can use the information to understand behaviours, perceptions, preferences, and opinions. While the information gathered is useful, there are some disadvantages to this method. Not everyone who is approached may be willing to answer your questions, respondents may not be truthful, and (for written surveys) not everyone can read and write. What do you think would be the best way to survey students about your potential new restaurant? Would you conduct a different kind of survey after you have been open a few months? How could you help vegetarians find your restaurant? That is, how could you help your buyers buy? One question that researchers pay close attention to is this: "Would you recommend this product to a friend?"

To increase the response and accuracy rate, marketers use personal interviews. *Personal interviews* are a face-to-face opportunity to ask individuals prepared questions. While this research method can be more expensive than surveys, the interviewer has the opportunity to observe reactions and to dig a little deeper with the questions if the respondent wishes to add more information.

A **focus group** is a group of people who meet under the direction of a discussion leader to communicate their opinions about an organization, its products, or other given issues. These questions should be free of bias and participants should be encouraged to answer questions honestly without being influenced by the responses of others in the focus group.

focus group
A small group of people who meet under the direction of a discussion leader to communicate their opinions about an organization, its products, or other issues.

Marketers gather both secondary and primary data online. The authors of this text, for example, do much research online as well as gather data from books, articles, databases, and other sources. Through focus groups, faculty and students tell us how to improve this book and its support materials. We listen carefully and make as many changes as we can in response. Suggestions have included adding more descriptive captions to the photos and making the text as user-friendly as possible. How are we doing so far?

Observation involves watching how people behave, either mechanically (e.g., Nielsen Media Research's *people meter*, which is a box attached to television sets, cable boxes, and satellite dishes in selected households in Canada and the United States in order to determine the size of audiences watching television programs delivered by the networks) or in person.[23] Observation may provide insight into behaviours that consumers do not even know they exhibit while shopping by watching them in person or by videotaping them. For example, companies follow customers into supermarkets to record their purchasing behaviours for products such as meat, bread, and laundry detergent. These marketers may observe that consumers do not bend to look at products, that they compare prices, and that they handle products to assess their weight. In some circumstances, the speed of events or the number of events being observed make mechanical or electronic observation more appropriate than personal observation; retailers, for example, can use electronic cameras to count the number of customers entering or leaving a store.[24]

---

observation
Involves watching, either mechanically or in person, how people behave.

Another creative approach to obtaining observational data is the hiring of *mystery shoppers*, who are people hired to pose as real customers that go through an exchange process and then record their observations in detailed reports. For example, a mystery shopper might be paid to travel to a vacation resort, eat at restaurants, play golf, open bank accounts, test drive new cars at auto dealers, or shop for groceries or clothes. The information they provide based on their observations often gives marketers unique insight that cannot be obtained any other way. More and more often this information is being collected via mobile technology and passed along in real time.[25]

Social media is playing an important role in data mining as there is a lot of free and available information on Facebook, Twitter, blogs, and other social platforms.[26] It is now common for marketers such as Coca-Cola and WestJet Airlines to scan the Web for posts that offer positive and negative comments on the companies and their products.[27] What are the advantages and disadvantages of this research? Do you agree that social media should complement traditional marketing research methods?

STEP 3: ANALYZING THE RESEARCH DATA

Marketers must turn the data collected in the research process into useful information. Careful, honest interpretation of the data collected can help a company find useful alternatives to specific marketing challenges. For example, by conducting primary research, Fresh Italy, a small Italian pizzeria, found that its pizza's taste was rated superior to that of the larger pizza chains. However, the company's sales lagged behind the competition. Secondary research on the industry revealed that free delivery (which Fresh Italy did not offer) was more important to customers than taste. Fresh Italy now delivers—and has increased its market share.

STEP 4: CHOOSING THE BEST SOLUTION AND IMPLEMENTING IT

After collecting and analyzing the data, marketing researchers determine alternative strategies and make recommendations about which strategy may be best and why. This final step in a research effort also includes following up on the actions taken to see if the results were what was expected. If not, the company can take corrective action and conduct new studies in its ongoing attempt to provide customer satisfaction at the lowest cost. You can see, then, that marketing research is a continuous process of responding to changes in the marketplace and in customer preferences.

In today's customer-driven market, ethics is important in every aspect of marketing. Ideally, companies should therefore do what is right as well as what is profitable. This step could add greatly to the social benefits of marketing decisions. See the Making Ethical Decisions box for such an example.

Making ETHICAL DECISIONS

No Kidding

Marketers have long recognized that children can be an important influence on their parents' buying decisions. In fact, many direct appeals for products are focused on children. Let's say that you have experienced a great response to a new high-fibre, high-protein cereal among health-conscious consumers. The one important group you have not been able to attract is children. Therefore, the product development team is considering introducing a child-oriented brand to expand the product line.

The new children's cereal may have strong market potential if you follow two recommendations of the research department. First, coat the flakes generously with sugar (significantly changing the cereal's nutritional benefits). Second, promote the product exclusively on children's TV programs. Such a promotional strategy should create a strong demand for the product, especially if you offer a premium (a toy or other "surprise") in each box. The consensus among the research department is that kids will love the new taste and parents will agree to buy the product because of their positive impression of your best-selling brand. The research director commented, "The chance of a parent actually reading our label and noting the addition of sugar is nil."

Would you introduce the children's cereal following the recommendations of your research department? What are the benefits of doing so? What are the risks involved in following these recommendations? What would you do if you were the marketing manager for this product?

The Marketing Environment

Marketing managers must be aware of the surrounding environment when making marketing mix decisions. **Environmental scanning** is the process of identifying the factors that can affect marketing success. Figure 14.6 should look familiar; it is a duplication of Figure 1.5. As introduced in Chapter 1, the business environment consists of six elements—global, technological, social, competitive, economic, and legal—that either help or hinder the development of businesses. It is helpful to review them strictly from a marketing perspective.

> **environmental scanning**
> The process of identifying the factors that can affect marketing success.

GLOBAL ENVIRONMENT

Using the Internet, businesses can reach many of the world's customers relatively easily and carry on a dialogue with them about the goods and services they want. See the Adapting to Change box for an example. The globalization process puts more pressure on those whose responsibility it is to deliver products to these global customers.

■ **FIGURE 14.6**

ENVIRONMENTAL SCANNING OF THE DYNAMIC BUSINESS ENVIRONMENT

TECHNOLOGICAL ENVIRONMENT

The most important technological changes also relate to the Internet. Using customer databases, blogs, social networking and the like, firms can develop products and services that closely match customers' needs. Firms can now produce customized goods and services for about the same price as mass-produced goods. Thus, flexible manufacturing and mass customization are also major influences on marketers. You can imagine, for example, using databases to help you devise custom-made fruit mixes and various salads for your customers at Very Vegetarian.

SOCIAL ENVIRONMENT

Marketers must monitor social trends to maintain their close relationship with customers since population growth and changing demographics can have an effect on sales. The fastest-growing segment of the Canadian population is the Baby Boomers who are approaching retirement. Looking ahead, the increase in the number of older adults creates growing demand for retirement communities, health care, prescription drugs, recreation, and more. Do you see any evidence that older people would enjoy having more vegetarian meals?

COMPETITIVE ENVIRONMENT

Of course, marketers must pay attention to the dynamic competitive environment. Many bricks-and-mortar companies must be aware of new competition on the Internet, including companies that sell

Adapting *to* CHANGE

Two Is Better Than One

After more than 35 years of a strict one-child policy, China agreed to change the infamous regulation. The new law allows married couples to have two children if one of the spouses is an only child. Besides affecting countless families, the new reform promises to have a big impact on businesses as the policy switch could mean 9.5 million additional babies coming into the Chinese market in the next five years. Producers of everything from baby formula and diapers, to violins and guzhengs (a Chinese string instrument) predict a future sales windfall with the new policy.

While many businesses can expect added growth due to the policy shift, one the greatest long-term beneficiaries of the change may be Lego <http://www.lego.com>, the world's second largest toymaker. Since the company has little room to grow in the United States (where Lego controls 85 percent of the construction toy market), China is now one of its key target markets. In 2013, Lego enjoyed sales growth in China of 70 percent as parents sought educational toys for their children. Chinese parents are particularly attracted to Lego because they feel the toy helps develop their children's creativity.

Lego, however, faces a price obstacle in China because its sets cost twice as much as they do in the United States due to import and distribution costs. To reduce the high cost of Legos in China, the company has committed to build a factory in Jiaxing, an industrial town near Shanghai. The cost of building a factory may be a relatively small price to pay since the Asia-Pacific region is predicted to overtake North America as the largest regional toy market sometime in the next few years. With the number of Chinese children expected to grow significantly, Lego feels this is a market they can clearly "build on."

Sources: Susan Scutti, "One-Child Policy Is One Big Problem for China," *Newsweek*, 23 January 2014; Isabella Steger and Laurie Burkitt, "Chinese Couples—and Investors—Are Pregnant with Anticipation," *The Wall Street Journal*, 19 November 2013; and Ted Trautman, "The Year of the Lego," *The New Yorker*, 11 November 2013.

automobiles, insurance, music, and clothes. In the book business, Chapters.indigo.ca is competing with Amazon.ca's huge selection of books at good prices in Canada as well as its U.S. counterpart, Amazon .com. Amazon also offers the largest selection of electronic books, comics, and newspapers in the world that are accessible through a number of avenues, such as computers, Blackberry, iOS, Android, Windows Phone smartphones, or tablets using a dedicated Kindle app.[28] What challenges might traditional booksellers continue to face from Kindle and other eReaders? Now that consumers can literally search the world for the best buys through the Internet, marketers must adjust their pricing policies accordingly. Similarly, they have to adjust to competitors who can deliver products quickly or provide excellent service. Do you see any opportunities to sell vegetarian food over the Internet?

Shifts in the Canadian population are creating new opportunities for marketers as they adjust their products to meet the tastes and preferences of growing ethnic groups. To appeal to diverse groups, marketers must listen better and be more responsive to unique needs. What might you do to appeal to specific ethnic groups with Very Vegetarian?

ECONOMIC ENVIRONMENT

When Canada experiences unparalleled growth, customers are eager to buy expensive automobiles, watches, and vacations. But when the economy slows, marketers have to adapt by offering products that are less expensive and more tailored to customers with modest incomes. You can see, therefore, that environmental scanning is critical to a company's success during rapidly changing economic times. What economic changes are occurring around your school that might affect a new restaurant?

LEGAL ENVIRONMENT

Governments enact laws to protect consumers and businesses. Businesses must be aware of how these laws may impact their practices. For example, the Canadian Radio-television and Telecommunications Commission (CRTC) ruled that telecommunications provider, Northwestel *<http://www.nwtel.ca>*, must lower its rates for certain residential Internet services in the Yukon and the Northwest Territories. "Although we recognize the exceptional situation that exists in Northwestel's territory, we must not let these challenges hinder the development and affordability of telecommunications services in the North," said Jean-Pierre Blais, the CRTC's chairman. As part of this decision, Northwestel will not be able to increase residential Internet rates until the end of 2017 at the earliest, and will have to have the CRTC's permission before any price hikes.[29]

A change in one environment can have an impact on another environment, or more. This is why marketers *continuously* scan the business environment to understand the impact of changes on their businesses. For example, a change in legislation that decreases barriers to entry will contribute to a more competitive marketplace as reflected in the increased number of competitors. Due to increased competition, prices could be lowered, and this could then be reflected in lower expenses as reflected in economic indicators.

Progress Assessment

- What are the four steps in the marketing research process?
- What is environmental scanning? How often do marketers scan the business environment?
- What factors do you consider in environmental scanning?

LO4   Compare the consumer market to the business-to-business market.

Two Different Markets: Consumer and Business-to-Business

Marketers must know as much as possible about the market they wish to serve. There are two major markets in business: the consumer market and the business-to-business market.

The Consumer Market

The **consumer market** consists of all individuals or households that want goods and services for personal consumption or use and have the resources to buy them. The total potential global consumer market consists of the billions of people in global markets. Because consumer groups differ greatly in age, education level, income, and taste, a business usually cannot fill the needs of every group. It must decide which groups to serve, and then develop products and services specially tailored to their needs.

> **consumer market**
> All individuals or households that want goods and services for personal consumption or use.

Take the Campbell Soup Company *<http://www.campbellsoup.ca>*, for example. Here we have a company that has had some success studying the consumer market, breaking it down into categories, and developing products for separate groups.

Created to help address the growing issue of hunger in Canada and abroad, Nourish is a complete meal that delivers vegetables, fibre, and 18 grams of protein thanks to a uniquely Canadian grain innovation. Nourish is a first-of-its kind product designed to be a reliable and appealing food source for those who prosper, those in need at food banks, and those impacted by disaster situations abroad.[32] Would you buy this product?

You likely know Campbell for its traditional soups such as chicken noodle and tomato. Campbell has expanded its product line to appeal to a number of different tastes. In Texas and California, for example, where people like their food with a bit of kick, Campbell makes its nacho cheese soup spicier than in other markets. With a goal to fight hunger, Nourish was created in partnership with Food Banks Canada. This nutritionally-dense meal-in-a-can is an example of **cause marketing**, which occurs when the charitable contributions of a firm are tied directly to the customer revenues produced through the promotion of one of its products.[30] Nourish is the first Canadian private-sector, not-for-profit product tailored to address the growing problem of world hunger.[31]

> **cause marketing**
> Occurs when the charitable contributions of a firm are tied directly to the customer revenues produced through the promotion of one of its products.

The Business-to-Business (B2B) Market

The **business-to-business (B2B) market** consists of all individuals and organizations that want goods and services to use in producing other goods and services or to sell, rent, or supply goods to others.[33] So, businesses selling to other businesses. Oil-drilling bits, cash registers, display cases, office desks, public accounting audits, and business software are B2B goods and services. Traditionally, they have been known as *industrial* goods and services because they are used in industry.

> **business-to-business (B2B) market**
> All individuals and organizations that want goods and services to use in producing other goods and services or to sell, rent, or supply goods to others.

B2B marketers include manufacturers; intermediaries such as wholesalers; institutions like hospitals, schools, and charities; and the government. The B2B market is larger than the consumer market because items are often sold and resold several times in the B2B process before they are sold to the final consumer. B2B marketing strategies also differ from consumer marketing because business buyers have their own decision-making process. Consider factors that make B2B marketing different from consumer marketing:

1. *Customers in the B2B market are relatively few.* There are far fewer B2B firms (e.g., construction or mining operations) compared to the more than 35 million potential customers in the Canadian consumer market.

Business customers, such as Ford Motor Company of Canada, are relatively large compared to consumer purchasers. Just think of the number of tires that are purchased by the company compared to your consumer tire purchase order. There are many job opportunities in the B2B market. Have you considered a career in this area of marketing?

2. *Business customers are relatively large.* Big organizations account for most of the employment, production of various goods and services, and purchases. Nonetheless, there are many small to medium-sized firms in Canada that together make an attractive market.

3. *B2B markets tend to be geographically concentrated.* Companies tend to locate close to their suppliers and customers. For example, diamond mines tend to be concentrated in Canada's Northwest Territories. Consequently, firms selling mining equipment may be concentrated close to these customers (or at least, within a reasonable distance).

4. *Business buyers are generally more rational and less emotional than ultimate consumers.* They use product specifications to guide buying choices and often more carefully weigh the total product offer, including quality, price, and service.

5. *B2B sales tend to be direct, but not always.* Tire manufacturers sell directly to auto manufacturers but use intermediaries, such as retailers, to sell to ultimate consumers.

6. *There is much more emphasis on personal selling in B2B markets.* Whereas consumer promotions are based on *advertising*, B2B sales are based on *selling*. There are fewer customers and they usually demand more personal service. As well, the quantities being purchased justify the expense of a sales force.

Figure 14.7 shows some of the differences between buying behaviour in the B2B market and the consumer market. B2B buyers also use the Internet to make purchases. You'll learn more about the business market in advanced marketing courses.

■ **FIGURE 14.7**

COMPARING BUSINESS-TO-BUSINESS AND CONSUMER BUYING BEHAVIOUR		
	Business-to-Business Market	**Consumer Market**
Market structure	Relatively few potential customers Larger purchases Geographically concentrated	Many potential customers Smaller purchases Geographically dispersed
Products	Require technical, complex products Frequently require customization Frequently require technical advice, delivery, and after-sale service	Require fewer technical products Sometimes require customization Sometimes require technical advice, delivery, and after-sale service
Buying procedures	Buyers are trained Negotiate details of most purchases Follow objective standards Formal process involving specific employees Closer relationships between marketers and buyers Buy from pre-approved suppliers	No special training Accept standard terms for most purchases Use personal judgment Informal process involving household members Impersonal relationships between marketers and consumers Buy from multiple sources

The important thing to remember is that the buyer's reason for buying—that is, the end use of the product—determines whether a product is considered a consumer product or a B2B product. A cup of yogourt that a student buys for breakfast is a consumer product. However, when Very Vegetarian purchases a cup of yogourt to sell to its breakfast customers, this transaction between the manufacturer and the restaurant is considered a B2B transaction.

Many goods could be classified as consumer goods or business-to-business (B2B) goods, based on their uses. For example, a computer that a person uses at home for personal use would be a consumer good. But that same computer used in a business setting, such as a manufacturing plant or an accounting firm, would be classified as a B2B good.

Progress Assessment

- Define the terms consumer market and business-to-business (B2B) market?
- What are examples of B2B marketers?
- How does B2B marketing differ from consumer marketing?

LO5 Describe the market segmentation process, and the role of relationship marketing.

Defining Your Market

Before marketers develop a 4P marketing mix for each product, they need to know the details of their customers and how the product being sold will meet these customers' needs.

Market Segmentation: Segmenting the Consumer Market

You can appreciate the challenge a marketer may have in creating a product that will appeal to every Canadian. The starting point is **market segmentation**, which means dividing the total market into groups with similar characteristics. There are several ways a firm can segment the consumer market, as outlined in Figure 14.8. For example, rather than trying to sell a product throughout Canada, you might try to focus on just one or two regions of the country where you might be most successful. Dividing the market by geographic area (i.e., cities, counties, provinces, etc.) is called **geographic segmentation**.

> **market segmentation**
> The process of dividing the total market into groups with similar characteristics.
>
> **geographic segmentation**
> Dividing the market by geographic area.

■ **FIGURE 14.8**

CONSUMER MARKET SEGMENTATION

This table shows some of the consumer dimensions and variables that marketers use to select their markets. The aim of segmentation is to divide the market into smaller units.

Segmentation Base	Sample Variables	Possible Segments
Geographic Segmentation	Region	British Columbia, Prairies, Nunavut, Eastern Quebec, Prince Edward Island; Sydney, St. John's
	City or Area Size	Under 5,000; 5,000–20,000; 20,001–50,000; 50,001–100,000; 100,001–250,000; 250,001–500,000; 500,001–1,000,000; 1,000,000+
	Density	Urban; suburban; rural
Demographic Segmentation	Age	Under 6; 6–11; 12–17; 18–24; 25–34; 35–49; 50–64; 65+
	Gender	Male; female
	Generational Cohort	Baby Boomer (1946 to 1964); Generation X (1965 to 1976); Generation Y/Millennials/Echo Boomers (1977 to 1994); Generation Z (1995 to present)
	Marital Status	Never married; married; separated; divorced; widowed
	Family Size	1–2; 3–4; 5+
	Education Attainment	0 to 8 years; some high school; high school graduate; some post-secondary; post-secondary certificate or diploma; bachelor's degree; above bachelor's degree
	Ethnic Origin	Canadian; English; French; Scottish; Irish; German; Italian; Chinese; First Nations; South Asian; Ukrainian; East Indian; Dutch; Polish; Jewish; Russian; Vietnamese
	Occupation	Professional; managerial; technical; clerical; labourer; sales; farmer; homemaker; self-employed; student; unemployed; retired; other
	Religion	Christianity; Muslim; Hindu; Sikh; Buddhist; Jewish; no affiliation
Psychographic Segmentation	Personality	Gregarious; compulsive; extroverted; ambitious
	Social Class	Upper class; middle class; working class
	Lifestyle	Actualizers; Fulfillers; Achievers; Experiencers; Believers; Strivers; Makers; Survivors
Behavioural Segmentation	Benefits Sought	Convenience; quality; service; economy; luxury; safety; prestige; environmental impact
	Usage Rate	Light user; medium user; heavy user
	User Status	Non-user; ex-user; prospect; first-time user; regular user
	Loyalty Status	None; medium; strong

Alternatively, you could aim your product's promotions toward people aged 25 to 45 who have some post-secondary training and have above-average incomes. Automobiles such as Lexus are often targeted to this audience. Segmentation by age, income, and education level are criteria for **demographic segmentation**. So are religion, ethnic origin, and profession. Demographics are the most widely used segmentation variable.

demographic segmentation
Dividing the market by age, income, and education level.

You may want your ads to portray a target group's lifestyle. To do that, you would study the group's values, attitudes, and interests in a strategy called **psychographic segmentation**. If you decide to target Generation Z, you would do an in-depth study of their values and interests, like which TV shows they watch and which personalities they like the best. With that information you would develop advertisements for those TV shows using those stars.

psychographic segmentation
Dividing the market using the group's values, attitudes, and interests.

When marketers use a consumer's behaviour with or toward a product to segment the market, they are using **behavioural segmentation**.[34] Let us examine questions that you might ask while considering different variables of this segmentation strategy as it applies to Very Vegetarian:

behavioural segmentation
Dividing the market based on behaviour with or toward a product.

- *Benefits Sought*—What benefits of vegetarianism and your food might you discuss? Should you emphasize freshness, heart-healthiness, taste, or something else?

- *Usage Rate*—In marketing, the *80/20* rule says that 80 percent of your business is likely to come from just 20 percent of your customers. Determine who the heavy users are of vegetarian food. Does your restaurant attract more men or more women? More students or more faculty and staff members?

- *User Status*—Are your repeat customers from the local community or are they commuters? Once you know who your customer base is, you can design your promotions to better appeal to that specific group.

The best segmentation strategy is to use all the variables to come up with a consumer profile that represents a sizable, reachable, *and* profitable target market. That may mean not segmenting the market at all and instead going after the total market (everyone). Or it may mean going after ever-smaller segments. We'll discuss that strategy next.

On W Network <*http://www.wnetwork.com*>, you can watch Hilary Farr (interior designer) and David Visentin (real estate agent) compete on *Love It or List It*. She renovates the home so homeowners will 'love it' and stay, while he tries to find homeowners a new home they love more than their renovated home. If he is successful, he will hear "list it" from them. On *Property Brothers*, twins Jonathan and Drew Scott help couples find fixer-uppers and transform them into dream homes. Each brother has a role: Drew is the real estate agent and Jonathan is the contractor. (The brothers also have other shows.) When considering viewers for each show, what segmentation variables can you apply?

Target Marketing and Reaching Smaller Market Segments

Once one applies the consumer market segmentation bases to the total market, a marketer may end up with a number of potential market segments to consider. Due to limited resources, it is not feasible to consider all of them. As a result, **target marketing** is the next step as it allows marketers to select which segment(s) an organization can serve profitably. For example, a shoe store may choose to sell only women's shoes, only children's shoes, or only athletic shoes. The issue is finding the right *target market*—the most profitable segment—to serve.

> **target marketing**
> Marketing directed toward those groups (market segments) an organization decides it can serve profitably.

In the world of mass production following the Industrial Revolution, marketers responded by practising mass marketing. **Mass marketing** means developing products and promotions to please large groups of people resulting in little market segmentation. The mass marketer tries to sell products to as many people as possible, using mass media, such as TV, radio, and newspapers to reach them. Although mass marketing led many firms to success, marketing managers often got so caught up with their products and competition that they became less responsive to the market. Historically, Canadian Tire tried to sell everything to everybody (mass marketing). As part of a three-year growth plan, Canadian Tire will more closely target 30- to 49-year-olds with a focus on young families and products that appeal to them. For example, instead of ads featuring dad painting the deck, you will see a father and his young son building a tree house.[35]

> **mass marketing**
> Developing products and promotions to please large groups of people.

Niche marketing is identifying small but profitable market segments and designing or finding products for them. Because it so easily offers an unlimited choice of goods, the Internet is transforming a consumer culture once based on big hits and bestsellers into one that supports more specialized niche products. The *long tail* is a phrase coined by Chris Anderson, editor-in-chief of *Wired* magazine, in an article explaining how companies selling more products with lower demand can easily compete with (or even surpass) those solely dependent on big sellers.[36] Just how small such a segment can be is illustrated by FridgeDoor.com <*http://www.fridgedoor.com*>. This company sells refrigerator magnets on the Internet. It keeps some 1,500 different magnets in stock and sells as many as 400 a week.

> **niche marketing**
> The process of finding small but profitable market segments and designing or finding products for them.

One-to-one marketing (also known as **micromarketing**) means developing a unique mix of goods and services for each *individual* customer. Travel agencies often develop such packages for individual customers, including airline reservations, hotel reservations, rental cars, restaurants, and admission to museums and other attractions. Dell and Apple can produce a unique computer system for each customer.

> **one-to-one marketing (micromarketing)**
> Developing a unique mix of goods and services for each individual customer.

Can you envision designing special Very Vegetarian menu items for individual customers? Consider what competitors are offering their customers. McDonald's is introducing a concept called "Create Your

Taste" to offer customers the ability to customize their meals.[37] In response to changing tastes, Pizza Hut re-launched its products by offering 11 new signature pizzas, six new sauces, 10 new crust flavours, and four drizzles, resulting in enough options to allow for 2 billion unique pizza combinations.[38]

As you have learned when reading the running case at the end of each text part, Fox 40 International Inc. produces an array of product lines in addition to Whistles. Is this ad an example of mass marketing, niche marketing, or one-to-one marketing?

Positioning[39]

Next, **product positioning**, which refers to the place an offering occupies in customers' minds on important attributes relative to competitive products, is applied for each product. A **positioning statement**, which expresses how a company wants to be perceived by customers, can be useful with establishing a product's position relative to that of its competitors. For example, a positioning statement for 7-Up is as follows: "for non-cola consumers, 7-Up is a non-caffeinated soft drink that is light, refreshing, lemon-lime flavoured and, unlike colas, it has a crisp, bubbly, and clean taste."

product positioning
The place an offering occupies in customers' minds on important attributes relative to competitive products.

positioning statement
Expresses how a company wants to be perceived by customers.

The topics of market segmentation, target marketing, and positioning will be discussed in greater detail when you take a Marketing course. In the meantime, recognize that a product cannot usually be all things to all people. As a result, this process of (1) applying market segmentation bases to arrive at potential market segments, (2) selecting the most profitable target market(s), and (3) developing the product positioning for each target market, is necessary before marketers can create a 4P marketing mix that will meet the wants and needs of each target market.

Building Marketing Relationships

Relationship marketing tends to lead away from mass production and toward custom-made goods and services. The goal is to keep individual customers over time by offering them new products that exactly meet their requirements. Technology enables sellers to work with individual buyers to determine their wants and needs and to develop goods and services specifically designed for them, like hand-tailored shirts and unique vacations.

> **relationship marketing**
> Marketing strategy with the goal of keeping individual customers over time by offering them products that exactly meet their requirements.

To build strong relationships, many firms undertake active CRM programs that identify and focus on building loyalty with the firm's most valued customers. CRM systems include a customer database or data warehouse where customer information (e.g., transaction, contact, preferences, and market segment) is input. Data is then analyzed and CRM programs are developed.[40] For example, a customer can deal with a salesperson in a store, online, or in a call centre. A customer's information can be quickly accessed via the CRM system that provides the information needed to address the purpose of the point of contact.

Firms sometimes reward dedicated customers with loyalty or CRM programs, such as points that customers can redeem for extra discounts or free services, advance notice of sale items, and invitations to special events sponsored by the company.[41] Loyalty programs include Shoppers Optimum

G Adventures offers small-group experiences. As the world's largest independent adventure travel company, it offers tours, safaris, and expeditions all over the world. Start with your travel style—classic, comfort, active, yolo, marine, family, or local living—and then take it from there when targeting a location. Would you consider booking through this company?

Rewards Program <*https://www1.shoppersdrugmart.ca/en/optimum*> and the popular SCENE Card Rewards Program <*https://www.scene.ca*>, which is a partnership between Scotiabank and Cineplex Entertainment. What loyalty program cards do you have in your wallet?

CRM systems are of value to firms of all sizes. As Canada's fastest-growing mobile tire franchise, GoTire <*http://gotire.com*> trains its franchisees for three weeks in the areas of technical skills, product knowledge, sales and marketing, social media training on Facebook and Twitter, and they learn GoTire's proprietary CRM system.[42] Social media is a way that businesses can engage with their customers. G Adventures <*http://www.gadventures.com*>, a leading small-group adventure tour operator, has been chosen as Canada's favourite adventure tour operator for several years in Baxter Travel Media's Agents' Choice Awards.[43] "Twitter has revolutionized our business," says founder Bruce Poon Tip. "Facebook has done the same thing. We have the ability to deliver our culture anywhere in the world now."[44]

Understanding consumers is so important to marketing that a whole area of marketing emerged called consumer behaviour. We explore that area next.

Progress Assessment

- Define market segmentation, target marketing, and positioning.
- Name and describe four ways to segment the consumer market.
- What are different target marketing approaches?
- What might be the product positioning for your favourite pair of shoes? What about one of your electronic items (e.g., computer, tablet, or phone)?

 Explain how marketers meet the needs of the consumer market through the study of consumer behaviour.

Consumer Behaviour

Marketing researchers investigate consumer-thought processes and behaviour at each stage in a purchase to determine the best way to help the buyer buy. This area of study in marketing is called **consumer behaviour**.

> **consumer behaviour**
> When marketing researchers investigate consumer thought processes and behaviour at each stage in a purchase to determine the best way to help the buyer buy.

Central to studying consumer behaviour is understanding the five steps of the decision-making process. The first step is *problem recognition*, which may occur when your washing machine breaks down and you realize you need a new one or it needs to be repaired. Let's assume you decide that you will purchase a new one. This leads to an *information search*—you look for ads and brochures about washing machines. You may consult a secondary data source such as *Consumer Reports* or other information online. And you will likely seek advice from other people who have purchased washing machines. After compiling all this information, you *evaluate alternatives* and make a *purchase decision*. But your buying process doesn't end there. After the purchase, you may be asked to complete a *postpurchase evaluation* where you are asked to assess your satisfaction (or dissatisfaction) with your purchase. *Cognitive dissonance* is a type of psychological conflict that can occur after a purchase. Consumers who make a major purchase (e.g., washing machines) may have doubts (i.e., cognitive dissonance) about whether they got the best product at the best price. Marketers must reassure such consumers after the sale that they made a good decision. An auto dealer, for example, may send positive press articles about the particular car purchased, offer product guarantees, and provide certain free services.

Consumer behaviour researchers also study the various influences that affect consumer behaviour. Figure 14.9 shows several such influences: marketing mix variables (the four Ps); psychological influences, such as perception and attitudes; situational influences, such as the type of purchase and the physical surroundings; and sociocultural influences, such as reference groups and culture.

■ **FIGURE 14.9**

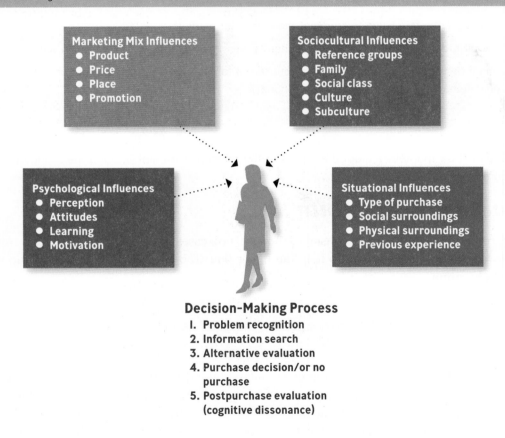

THE CONSUMER DECISION-MAKING PROCESS AND OUTSIDE INFLUENCES

There are many influences on consumers as they decide which goods and services to buy. Marketers have some influence, but it is not usually as strong as sociocultural influences. Helping consumers in their information search and their evaluation of alternatives is a major function of marketing.

Marketing Mix Influences
- Product
- Price
- Place
- Promotion

Sociocultural Influences
- Reference groups
- Family
- Social class
- Culture
- Subculture

Psychological Influences
- Perception
- Attitudes
- Learning
- Motivation

Situational Influences
- Type of purchase
- Social surroundings
- Physical surroundings
- Previous experience

Decision-Making Process
1. Problem recognition
2. Information search
3. Alternative evaluation
4. Purchase decision/or no purchase
5. Postpurchase evaluation (cognitive dissonance)

Consider some of these factors:[45]

- *Learning* creates changes in an individual's behaviour resulting from previous experiences and information. If you have tried a particular brand of shampoo and you do not like it, you have learned not to buy it again.

- *Reference group* is the group an individual uses as a reference point in forming beliefs, attitudes, values, or behaviour. A student who carries a briefcase instead of a backpack may see business people as his or her reference group.

- *Culture* is the set of values, attitudes, and ways of doing things transmitted from one generation to another in a given society. Attitudes toward work, lifestyles, and consumption are evolving and examples include the following: more women are working outside the home, contributing to *time poverty* (the increasing need for convenient products due to having less time); Canadians are changing their attitudes toward health and as a result, fitness activity and sports participation are on the rise; there is a trend toward *value-consciousness* (the concern for obtaining the best quality, features, and performance of a product or service for a given price); and another emerging trend is *eco-consciousness* or *going green*. Let's look at two of these examples.

Health-conscious Canadians are buying more health supplements and medical self-diagnostic kits. As a result, sales of multivitamins and calcium supplements are soaring, and brands such as Centrum *<http://www.centrum.com>*, Shoppers Drug Mart's *<http://www1.shoppersdrugmart.ca>* Life brand, and Roots Canada's vitamin lines are enjoying growth. Similarly, LifeScan Canada is doing well with its self-testing kits that can monitor cholesterol or test for colorectal cancer. When you consider these trends, do you see how Very Vegetarian could profit from healthy takeout food that is quickly prepared?

Canadians are more sensitive about the impact their consumption has on their natural environment, and they make their buying decisions accordingly. This may mean buying more environmentally safe or more environmentally friendly products, buying products that can be reused or recycled, or actually reducing consumption altogether. The Hotel Association of Canada, for instance, says six in ten Canadians look for an environmentally friendly hotel as part of their travel plans. The Seeking Sustainability

Canadians are becoming increasingly health-conscious, creating opportunities for marketers that can develop products to address this change in buying behaviour. Do you think that Baby Boomers are driving this demand, or is it being driven by people of all ages?

box highlights some concerns that consumers have raised about "green" advertising claims. You will be introduced to the terms **green marketing**—the process of selling products and/or services based on their environmental benefits, and **greenwashing**—when businesses try to make themselves or their products or services look green or socially responsible without the action to back it up.

> **green marketing**
> The process of selling products and/or services based on their environmental benefits.
>
> **greenwashing**
> When businesses try to make themselves or their products or services look green or socially responsible without the action to back it up.

- *Subculture* is the set of values, attitudes, and ways of doing things that results from belonging to a certain ethnic group, religious group, or other group with which one closely identifies (e.g., teenagers). Ethnic groups, for example, spend more than $42 billion on retail goods and services, which translates into attractive target marketing opportunities. Consider that one out of every five Canadians was not born here. More than 100 different ethnic groups are represented in Canada with visible minorities projected to represent almost 30 percent of the Canadian population by 2031. The two largest groups will be the Chinese (from Hong Kong, mainland China, and Taiwan) and South Asians (from India, Pakistan, Sri Lanka, and Bangladesh).

  Canadian companies engage in **ethnic marketing**—combinations of the marketing mix that reflect the unique attitudes, race or ancestry, communication preferences, and lifestyles of ethnic Canadians. Walmart runs ads targeted specifically to ethnic markets using ethnic television and speaking to these customers in native languages such as Chinese, Italian, Portuguese, and Spanish. Through its new store concept, FreshCo, Sobeys has targeted the unique needs of the ethnic consumer. FreshCo is a value-driven concept with low prices, like No Frills or Food Basics, but with a focus on fresh produce, halal meats, and freshly baked breads. The international food aisles highlight Asian, West Indian, Middle Eastern, and Eastern European food products.

> **ethnic marketing**
> Combinations of the marketing mix that reflect the unique attitudes, race or ancestry, communication preferences, and lifestyles of ethnic Canadians.

Subculture also considers generational cohorts. Generation Y (Millennials) represent over 25 percent of the Canadian population, making them a very important consumer group. In response, Toyota Canada created a new brand of vehicles called Scion to appeal to the Generation Y group, while still marketing its traditional brands, such as the Toyota Camry, to the Baby Boomers.

Similar to courses in business marketing, consumer behaviour is a long-standing part of a marketing curriculum. Do you think you will take this course in the future?

Progress Assessment

- List the five steps in the decision-making process.
- Describe each of the four major influencers on the decision-making process.
- How is green marketing different from greenwashing?
- Why is ethnic marketing an important focus for companies?

Seeking SUSTAINABILITY

When Green Is Not Really Green

Companies are responding to concerns about the environment and global warming through a variety of ways. Green marketing refers to the process of selling products and/or services based on their environmental benefits. Such a product or service may be environmentally friendly in itself or produced and/or packaged in an environmentally friendly way. Green advertising is a useful way to communicate important information to consumers who want to make responsible and environmentally conscious choices between competing products that claim to respect the environment. The green marketing assumption is that potential consumers will view a product or service's "greenness" as a benefit and base their buying decisions accordingly. The not-so-obvious assumption of green marketing is that consumers will be willing to pay more for green products than they would for a less-green comparable alternatives.

Businesses are sometimes accused of greenwashing when they try to make themselves or their products or services look green or socially responsible without the action to back it up. An example of this is when a company spends more resources on advertising its sustainability attributes than resources spent on its sustainability programs. Other examples include vague and meaningless product claims like "environmentally friendly" that are not explained, or claims that are not backed up, such as shampoos and conditioners advertised as not having been tested on animals while offering no evidence or certification of such claims.

There are no laws specifically governing green claims. Federally, the Competition Bureau and the Canadian Standards Association (now CSA Group, <http://www.csagroup.org/global/en/home>) developed green guidelines in a document titled, *Environmental Claims: A Guide for Industry and Advertisers*. While the guidelines are ultimately helpful, compliance is voluntary. This document addresses a number of commonly used green claims and provides examples of best practices on how businesses can comply with provisions of the laws enforced by the Competition Bureau concerning false or misleading claims. Among other practices, the Guide states that:

- The use of vague claims implying general environmental improvement are insufficient and should be avoided.
- Environmental claims should be clear, specific, accurate, and not misleading.
- Environmental claims should be verified and substantiated prior to being made.

Studies confirm that job seekers are attracted to organizations with sustainable practices. Other studies show the same in relation to social practices more generally (e.g., community involvement and ethical governance). Not only may greenwashing hurt the company's image and bottom line, but if new employees find that the messages about sustainable practices that initially attracted them are really just a green veneer, many will become resentful and some will leave. Messages about sustainability need to match the reality that new hires will experience. Have you been attracted to companies with sustainable practices? Would you be turned off by companies that have been accused of greenwashing?

Sources: Susan Ward, "Green Marketing," About.com, http://sbinfocanada.about.com/od/marketing/g/greenmarketing, downloaded 5 April 2015; "Three Reasons Job Seekers Prefer Sustainable Companies," Network for Business Sustainability, 7 June 2013, http://nbs .net/knowledge/three-reasons-job-seekers-prefer-sustainable-companies/; Rebecca Harris, "Greenwashing: Cleaning Up By 'Saving the World'," *Marketing*, 25 April 2013, http://www.marketingmag.ca/brands/greenwashing-cleaning-up-by-saving-the-world-77259; and "SME Sustainability Roadmap," Industry Canada, 30 September 2011, https://www.ic.gc.ca/eic/site/csr-rse.nsf/eng/rs00182.html.

Your Prospects in Marketing

There is a wider variety of careers in marketing than in most business disciplines. If you major in marketing, an array of career options will be available to you. You could conduct marketing research or get involved in product management. You could become a manager in a retail store. You could work in transportation, storage, or international distribution. You could go into selling, advertising, sales promotion, or public relations. You could design interactive websites. These are just a few of the possibilities. As you read further into this topic in Chapter 15, consider whether a marketing career would interest you.

SUMMARY

LO1 **Define marketing and explain how the marketing concept applies to both for-profit and non-profit organizations.**

Marketing is the process of determining customer wants and needs and then providing customers with goods and services that meet or exceed these expectations.

How has marketing changed over time?

What marketers do at any particular time depends on what they need to do to fill customers' needs and wants, which continually change. The evolution of marketing includes five eras, also known as orientations: (1) production, (2) sales, (3) marketing concept, (4) market orientation, and (5) social media marketing.

What are the three parts of the marketing concept?

The three parts of the marketing concept are (1) a customer orientation, (2) a service orientation, and (3) a profit orientation (that is, market goods and services that will earn the firm a profit and enable it to survive and expand to serve more customers' wants and needs).

What kinds of organizations are involved in marketing?

All kinds of organizations use marketing, both for-profit and non-profit organizations. Examples of non-profit organizations include the provinces and other government agencies, charities (e.g., churches), politicians, and schools.

LO2 **Describe the four Ps of marketing.**

The marketing mix consists of the four Ps of marketing: product, price, place, and promotion.

What is required before marketers develop a product?

Once marketers have researched customer needs and found a target market, the four Ps come into play, starting with the development of a product. Recall that a product is any physical good, service, or idea which falls somewhere on the service continuum which is highlighted in Figure 14.4.

How do marketers implement the four Ps?

The idea is to design a product that people want, price it competitively, get it in a location where customers can find it easily, and promote it—considering advertising, personal selling, public relations, direct marketing, and sales promotion—so that customers know it exists. While this chapter briefly outlined these four Ps, they will be discussed in more detail in Chapter 15.

LO3 **Identify the steps in the marketing research process, and explain how marketers use environmental scanning to learn about the changing marketing environment.**

Marketing research is the analysis of markets to determine opportunities and challenges and to find the information needed to make good decisions.

What are the steps to follow when conducting marketing research?

The four steps are (1) define the problem or opportunity and determine the present situation, (2) collect data, (3) analyze the research data, and (4) choose the best solution and implement it.

What are different methods used to gather research?

Research can be gathered through secondary data (information that has already be compiled by others) and published in sources such as journals, newspapers, directories, databases, and internal sources. Primary data (data that you gather yourself) includes observation, surveys, interviews, and focus groups.

What is environmental scanning?

Environmental scanning is the process of identifying the trends that can affect marketing success. Marketers pay attention to all environmental trends that create opportunities and threats. Figure 14.6 shares the six environments - global, technological, social, competitive, economic, and legal - that are considered in environmental scanning.

What are some of the more important environmental trends in marketing?

The most important global and technological change is probably the Internet. Another is the growth of customer databases, with which companies can develop products and services that closely match the needs of customers. Marketers must also monitor social trends like population growth and shifts to maintain their close relationship with customers. Of course, marketers must also monitor the dynamic competitive environment and pay attention to the economic environment. Changes in laws can create opportunities and threats for business activities; thus, this is another important environment to scan.

LO4 **Compare the consumer market to the business-to-business market.**

The consumer market consists of all individuals or households that want goods and services for personal consumption or use and have the resources to buy them. The total potential global consumer market consists of the billions of people in global markets.

What types of businesses operate in the business-to-business (B2B) market?

The B2B market consists of manufacturers, intermediaries such as wholesalers, institutions (e.g., hospitals, schools, and charities), and the government.

What makes the business-to-business market different from the consumer market?

The number of customers in the B2B market is relatively small, and the size of business customers is relatively large. B2B markets tend to be geographically concentrated, and industrial buyers generally are more rational than ultimate consumers in their selection of goods and services. B2B sales tend to be direct, and there is much more emphasis on personal selling in B2B markets than in consumer markets.

LO5 **Describe the market segmentation process, and the role of relationship marketing.**

The process of dividing the total market into several groups whose members have similar characteristics is called market segmentation.

What are some of the ways that marketers segment the consumer market?

See Figure 14.8 for a summary of consumer segmentation variables. *Geographic* segmentation means dividing the market into different regions. Segmentation by age, income, and education level are methods of *demographic* segmentation. We study a group's values, attitudes, and interests using *psychographic* segmentation. *Behavioural* segmentation divides the market based on behaviour with or toward a product. Different variables of behavioural segmentation include benefits sought, usage rate, and user status. The best segmentation strategy is to use as many of these segmentation bases as possible to come up with a target market that is sizable, reachable, and profitable.

What is the relationship between target marketing and product positioning?

Following market segmentation, marketers need to select the segment(s) that is (are) the most profitable. This is known as target marketing. Product positioning, which refers to the place an offering occupies in customers' minds on important attributes relative to competitive products, is then applied for each product. Market segmentation, target marketing, and positioning are necessary before marketers can create a 4P marketing mix for each target market that will meet their wants and needs.

What is the difference between mass marketing and relationship marketing?

Mass marketing means developing products and promotions to please large groups of people. Relationship marketing tends to lead away from mass production and toward custom-made goods and services. Its goal is to keep individual customers over time by offering them goods or services that meet their needs.

LO6 **Explain how marketers meet the needs of the consumer market through the study of consumer behaviour.**

Marketing researchers investigate consumer-thought processes and behaviour at each stage in a purchase to determine the best way to help the buyer buy. This area of study is called consumer behaviour.

What are the five steps of the decision-making process?

As listed on Figure 14.9, the five steps of the decision-making process are (1) problem recognition, (2) information search, (3) evaluate alternatives, (4) purchase decision, and (5) postpurchase evaluation.

What is cognitive dissonance?

Cognitive dissonance may occur in the postpurchase evaluation step. It is a type of psychological conflict that can occur after a purchase. If customers are satisfied with their purchases, they will not regret their purchases (i.e., experience cognitive dissonance).

What are some of the factors that influence the consumer decision-making process?

See Figure 14.9 for the four major influences on consumer decision making. Some specific factors include learning, reference group, culture, and subculture.

KEY TERMS

behavioural segmentation	business-to-business (B2B)	cause marketing
brand name	market	consumer behaviour

consumer market

customer-relationship
   management (CRM)

demographic segmentation

environmental scanning

ethnic marketing

focus group

geographic segmentation

green marketing

greenwashing

market orientation

market segmentation

marketing

marketing concept

marketing mix

marketing research

mass marketing

niche marketing

observation

one-to-one marketing
   (micromarketing)

positioning statement

price

primary data

product

product positioning

promotion

psychographic segmentation

relationship marketing

secondary data

social media

social media marketing

target marketing

test marketing

CRITICAL THINKING

1. Do you agree that individual consumers are not rational decision makers? Are you aware of marketers' efforts, and in some cases successes, in targeting you for goods and services?

2. When businesses buy goods and services from other businesses, they usually buy in large volumes. Salespeople in the B2B area usually are paid on a commission basis. Do you agree that it is more professionally rewarding for employees to be engaged in B2B marketing/sales?

3. Retailers such as the Hudson's Bay Company (HBC Rewards) and Shoppers Drug Mart (Shoppers Optimum) offer loyalty programs. Are you encouraged to visit these retailers more often as a result of such programs? Do you buy more products as a result of such programs? Retailers also offer incentives to use their credit cards. For example, you may get 10 percent off your purchase if you open an HBC credit card account. Do you feel that companies are trying to bribe you to support their businesses, or do you think that these are good business practices? How effective is social networking in building loyalty? Explain.

4. Marketers must adapt as new technologies emerge. For example, younger consumers now watch programs on the Internet and/or PVR, rather than during the scheduled television slots. Services such as Netflix, Crave TV *<http://www.cravetv.ca>*, and Shomi *<http://discover.shomi .com>* also offer another programming alternative. What does this mean for traditional television advertisements (i.e., commercials)? How should marketers evaluate and plan a move to marketing through these newer alternatives as compared to scheduled television programming?

DEVELOPING WORKPLACE SKILLS

Key: ● **Team** ★ **Analytic** ▲ **Communication** ☐ **Technology**

★ ▲ 1. Think of an effective marketing mix for a new electric car or a brushless car wash for your neighbourhood. Be prepared to discuss your ideas in class.

● ★ 2. Working in teams of three, think of a product your friends want but cannot get on or near
▲   campus. You might ask your friends at other schools what is available there. What kind of product would fill that need? Discuss your results in class and determine how you might go about marketing that new product.

★ ▲ 3. Relationship marketing efforts include frequent-flyer programs at airlines, special discounts for members at certain supermarkets (e.g., Sobeys), and websites that remember your name and what you have purchased in the past and recommend new products that you may like (e.g., Amazon.ca). Evaluate any one of these programs. (If you have no personal experience with them, look up such programs on the Internet.) What might these companies do to increase your satisfaction and loyalty? Be prepared to discuss these programs in class.

● ★ 4. Working in teams of four or five, list as many brand names of pizza as you can from pizza
▲ shops, restaurants, supermarkets, and so on. Merge your list with the lists from other groups or classmates. Then try to identify the target market for each brand. Do they all seem to be after the same market, or are there different brands for different markets? What are the separate appeals?

★ ▲ 5. Take a little time to review the concepts in this chapter as they apply to Very Vegetarian, the restaurant we used as an example throughout. Have an open discussion in class about (a) a different name for the restaurant, (b) a location for the restaurant, (c) a promotional program, and (d) a way to establish a long-term relationship with customers.

ANALYZING MANAGEMENT DECISIONS

Applying Customer-Oriented Marketing Concepts at Thermos

Thermos <http://www.thermos.com> is the company made famous by its Thermos bottles and lunch boxes. Thermos also manufactures cookout grills. Its competitors include Sunbeam <http://www.sunbeam.com> and Weber <http://www.weber.com>. To become a world-class competitor, Thermos completely reinvented the way it conducted its marketing operations. By reviewing what Thermos did, you can see how new marketing concepts affect organizations.

First, Thermos modified its corporate culture. It had become a bureaucratic firm organized by function: design, engineering, manufacturing, marketing, and so on. That organizational structure was replaced by flexible, cross-functional, self-managed teams. The idea was to focus on a customer group—for example, buyers of outdoor grills—and build a product development team to create a product for that market.

The product development team for grills consisted of six middle managers from various disciplines, including engineering, manufacturing, finance, and marketing. They called themselves the Lifestyle Team because their job was to study grill users to see how they lived and what they were looking for in an outdoor grill. To get a fresh perspective, the company hired Fitch, Inc. <http://www.fitch.com>, an outside consulting firm, to help with design and marketing research. Team leadership was rotated based on needs of the moment. For example, the marketing person took the lead in doing field research, but the R&D person took over when technical developments became the issue.

The team's first step was to analyze the market. Together, team members spent about a month on the road talking with people, videotaping barbecues, conducting focus groups, and learning what people wanted in an outdoor grill. The company found that people wanted a nice-looking grill that did not pollute the air and was easy to use. It also had to be safe enough for apartment dwellers, which meant that it had to be electric.

As the research results came in, engineering began playing with ways to improve electric grills. Manufacturing kept in touch to ensure that any new ideas could be produced economically. Design people were already building models of the new product. R&D people relied heavily on Thermos's strengths. The company's core strength was the vacuum technology it had developed to keep hot things hot and cold things cold in Thermos bottles. Drawing on that strength, the engineers developed a domed lid that contained the heat inside the grill.

Once a prototype was developed, the company showed the model to potential customers, who suggested several changes. Employees also took sample grills home and tried to find weaknesses. Using the input from potential customers and employees, the company used continuous improvement to manufacture what became a world-class outdoor grill.

No product can become a success without communicating with the market. The team took the grill on the road, showing it at trade shows and in retail stores. The product was such a success that Thermos is now using self-managed customer-oriented teams to develop all of its product lines.

Discussion Questions

1. How could the growth of self-managed cross-functional teams affect marketing departments in other companies? Do you believe that would be a good change or not? Explain.

2. How can Thermos now build a closer relationship with its customers using the Internet?

3. What other products might Thermos develop that would appeal to the same market segment that uses outdoor grills?

VIDEO CASE 14

Using the 4Ps at Energizer

The Energizer Bunny is a marketing icon. How many people are not familiar with this marketing campaign? The precursor to the company known today as Energizer was founded by two inventors: the inventor of the battery and the inventor of the flashlight. The synergy should be obvious. This partnership grew into the leading manufacturer and seller of batteries in the world today.

Energizer has developed and implemented an outstanding marketing approach to its product lines. In fact, Energizer demonstrates the full range of marketing concepts, including the use of social media and marketing research in successfully promoting and sustaining a brand.

Advertising Age magazine ranks the Energizer Bunny as the number five brand icon of the twentieth century. This supports Energizer's competitive advantage in many of its markets. The company is continually involved in new-product development through the identification and understanding of consumer needs, including how a person intends to use a battery, in what devices, and the types of users for various products where Energizer batteries can be used.

Energizer has a well-developed and highly effective marketing division that is responsible for helping to ensure the success of current and new products. The video walks the viewer through the four Ps of marketing—product, price, place, and promotion—and shows how Energizer utilizes marketing concepts effectively.

The company views its approach to marketing and selling its product lines as one that is focused on developing, cultivating, and expanding customer relationships. Energizer is a company that has been significantly impacted by the growth of technology and uses this and the growth of the Internet as parts of its overall marketing communications approach to develop strong and lasting relationships with its customers.

You will learn about the importance of relationship marketing as a key to Energizer's success. The complexities involved in the marketing mix, marketing research, and new-product development are highlighted through specific examples, such as the new product introduced by the company each summer. We see how the company uses qualitative data such as focus groups and secondary data to test market its product, elicit customer feedback, collect demographic and other data, and match its marketing strategy to be consistent with the appropriate segmentation factors.

Discussion Questions

1. Identify the elements that must be considered in the marketing environment.

2. Briefly discuss the evolution of marketing at Energizer as described in the video.

3. The Energizer Bunny is considered a marketing icon. What does this mean?

Managing the Marketing Mix: Product, Price, Place, and Promotion

LEARNING OBJECTIVES

After you have read and studied this chapter, you should be able to:

LO1 Explain the concept of a total product offer, and summarize the functions of packaging.

LO2 Describe the product life cycle.

LO3 Identify various pricing objectives and strategies, and explain why non-pricing strategies are growing in importance.

LO4 Explain the concept of marketing channels, and the importance of retailing.

LO5 Define promotion, and list the five traditional tools that make up the promotion mix.

PROFILE

GETTING TO KNOW HEATHER REISMAN OF INDIGO BOOKS & MUSIC INC.

Heather Reisman is the founder and CEO of Indigo Books & Music Inc. (Indigo, <*http://www.chapters.indigo.ca*>), Canada's largest book and specialty retailer. She was born in Montreal and educated at McGill University. For the first 16 years of her career, she was Managing Director of Paradigm Consulting, the strategy and change management firm she co-founded in 1979. Paradigm was the world's first strategic change consultancy and pioneered many organizational change strategies still in use today.

Reisman left Paradigm in 1992 to become President of Cott Corporation <*http://www.cott.com*>. During her tenure as President, Cott grew from a Canadian-based regional bottler to the world's largest retailer-branded beverage supplier. Harvard Business School wrote two case studies focusing on the company's growth and development under her leadership.

In 1996, Reisman launched Indigo. She wanted to create a book-lover's cultural department store. With big box stores booming, Indigo became the go-to place for literary goods, eventually acquiring rival Chapters in 2001 to form the largest book retailer in Canada.

Indigo operates in all ten provinces and one territory under different banners including 91 superstores under the banners Indigo and Chapters, and 130 small-format stores under the banners Coles, Indigo, IndigoSpirit, SmithBooks, and The Book Company. It also operates *indigo.ca*, a popular online destination offering millions of products including books, eBooks, toys, stationery, home décor, gourmet confections, and more. Indigo's membership rewards programs include the Plum Rewards and irewards programs. Plum Rewards is a free program offering points on almost everything purchased in store and preferred pricing online at *indigo.ca*. The Plum Rewards program was created to provide Indigo customers with personalized and inspirational book and product recommendations, promotional offers, and VIP experiences. Indigo's irewards program—for an annual fee of $35—offers a 10 percent discount on books and a 5 percent discount on most non-book products.

Indigo is committed to reading, regardless of the format. It created and launched the global eReading service, Kobo. With one of the largest eReading catalogues in the world, Kobo grew its membership to over 6 million readers in 100 countries. In November 2011, Indigo agreed to the sale of Kobo to Rakuten Inc., one of the world's leading Internet service companies, for US$315 million. Indigo received US$146 million from the sale.

Reisman's goal is to build the organization into the most valued retailer in the world for booklovers and their friends. Connecting with customers is important to Indigo and its Facebook fan base has grown to more than 419,000.

Reisman clearly recognizes that there will continue to be hurdles moving forward. "Starting Indigo was the single most challenging thing I've ever done," says Reisman. "I am at an equally challenging moment now. While sustaining the book business for all people who care about it, we also have to transform it to deal with the reality that 30 or 40 percent of books will be bought digitally. That means 30 percent of my business that needs to be replaced. That's a big transformation." Adapting her bookstores to the current consumer need has Reisman reinstalling inviting armchairs, working on an expanded role for Starbucks, enhancing Indigo's housewares offerings, and embracing the new demand for digital books.

Marketing begins with watching people to understand their needs. It then involves developing products and services that customers might want. Those products and services need to be perfected and tested in the marketplace. Then one must decide how to distribute and sell those products. Should they be sold through retailers, on the Internet, or a combination of these options? This profile has briefly introduced you to some of the retailing options that Indigo offers its customers. One must develop a marketing mix that will resonate with the target market. Making such decisions is challenging, but if you are successful, you can make a lot of customers very happy. This is what marketing is all about.

Sources: "Our Company," Indigo Books & Music Inc., *http://www.chapters.indigo.ca/en-ca/our-company/fast-facts,* downloaded 1 September 2015; Dawn Calleja, "Legends of the Small," *Report on Business—The Globe and Mail,* June 2012, 12; and Carolyn Patricia Grisold, "Founder & CEO, Indigo Books & Music Inc.," Women of Influence, 1 October 2011, *www.womenofinfluence.ca/heather-reisman-2/.*

LO1   Explain the concept of a total product offer, and summarize the functions of packaging.

Product Development and the Total Product Offer

Global managers continue to challenge Canadian managers with new products at low prices.[1] The best way to compete is to design and promote better products, meaning products that customers perceive to have the best **value**—good quality at a fair price. When customers calculate the value of a product, they look at the benefits and then subtract the cost (price) to see whether the benefits exceed the cost, including the cost of driving to the store (or shipping fees if they buy the product online). You may have noticed that some restaurants offer "value meals" as a way to attract customers.

value
Good quality at a fair price.

How would you like a beer or glass of wine with your Big Mac? You can get both at this McDonald's in Paris (shown left). Around the world, McDonald's adapts its architectural scheme, menus, and interior design to fit the tastes and cultural demands of each country. On the right, you see a McDonald's in Indonesia.

Whether customers perceive a product as the best value depends on many factors, including the benefits they seek and the service they receive. To satisfy customers, marketers must learn to listen better and constantly adapt to changing market demands.[2] See the Spotlight on Small Business box for an example of how one bar uses social media to grow its business.

Mixing Social Media with Beer

Social media is in a constant state of change. Do businesses have to keep up with it? Absolutely. At least that's how Chris Dilla, owner of Bocktown Beer and Grill <*http://www.bocktown.com*>, sees it. As she puts it, "The minute I met Twitter, I realized how valuable it would be." Without having the money for advertising, she turned to social media to help make the gastro pub a staple on the city's craft beer scene. In addition to making maximum use of Twitter and Facebook, Bocktown also optimized its mobile website, making it easier for customers to engage with the brand when they are on the go.

But Dilla's relationship with social media isn't limited to giants like Twitter and Facebook. A few years back, the pub introduced Tabbedout <*http://www.tabbedout.com*>, a mobile payment app that allows customers to pay straight from their smartphones. Customers can get started with the service by entering their credit card information on the app. The data is stored on their devices and remains encrypted, ensuring that it's even safer than dropping off their credit cards with a server. Bar patrons can use Tabbedout to immediately open a tab through the app. They can also create a unique five-digit code that tallies their total bill. When they are ready to call it a day or night, all customers need to do to settle their tabs is to press a button on the app and then walk out the door.

Dilla has no intention of slowing down Bocktown Beer and Grill's social media presence. The bar recently added a new app called NoWait <*http://nowaitapp.com*>, which allows customers to see the restaurant's wait time, add their name to a wait list, check their place in line, and receive a text when their table is ready. It's places like Bocktown that are fuelling the tremendous growth of the craft beer industry. Who knows when Bocktown Beer and Grill's relationship with social media will come to a head.

Sources: Bocktown Beer & Grill, www.bocktown.com, downloaded April 2014; Kim Lyons, "Passionate Owner of Two Suburban Pittsburgh Restaurants Attuned to Social Media," *Pittsburgh Post-Gazette*, 5 March 2014; and Brad Tuttle, "7 Signs that the Craft Beer Craze Has Gone Totally Mainstream," *Time*, 22 September 2013.

Marketers have learned that adapting products to new competition and new markets is an ongoing process. We are sure that you have noticed menu changes at your local fast-food restaurant over time. An organization cannot do a one-time survey of customer wants and needs, design a group of products to meet those needs, put them in the stores, and then just relax. It must constantly monitor changing customer wants and needs, and adapt products, services, and policies accordingly. For example, customers are looking for healthier food choices today than in the past. Did you know that McDonald's now sells as much chicken as beef? It has added smoothies and oatmeal with fruit. It also offers a choice of side salad, fruit, or vegetables in the place of fries with its value meals. It is also trying an all-day breakfast menu.[3]

Product development, then, is a key activity in any modern business, anywhere in the world. There's a lot more to new-product development than merely introducing goods and services, however. What marketers do to create excitement for those products is as important as the products themselves.

Developing a Total Product Offer

From a strategic marketing viewpoint, a total product offer is more than just the physical good or service. A **total product offer**, also called a **value package**, consists of everything that customers evaluate when deciding whether to buy something. Thus, the basic good or service may be a washing machine, an insurance policy, or a beer, but the total product offer includes some or all of the *value enhancers* in Figure 15.1. You may hear some people call the basic product the "core product" and the total product offer the "augmented product." Can you see how sustainability can be part of the augmented product?[4]

> **total product offer (value package)**
> Everything that customers evaluate when deciding whether to buy something; also called a value package.

When people buy a product, they may evaluate and compare total product offers on many dimensions. Some are tangible (the product itself and its package); others are intangible (the producer's reputation and the image created by advertising). A successful marketer must think like a customer and evaluate the total product offer as a collection of impressions created by all of the factors listed in Figure 15.1. It is wise to talk with customers to learn which features and benefits are most important to them and which value enhancers they want or don't want in the final offering.[5] Frito-Lay, for example, had to drop biodegradable bags because they were too noisy. Who would think of such a thing when developing a product?

What questions might you ask customers when developing the total product offer for your Very Vegetarian restaurant? (Recall the business idea introduced in Chapter 14.) Remember, store surroundings are important in the restaurant business, as are the parking lot and the condition of the bathrooms.

Sometimes an organization can use low prices to create an attractive total product offer.[6] For example, outlet stores offer brand-name goods for less. Shoppers like getting high-quality goods at low prices, but they must be careful. Outlets also carry lower-quality products with similar but not exactly the same features as goods carried in regular stores. Different customers may want different total product offers, so a company must develop a variety of offerings.

Product Lines and the Product Mix

Companies usually do not sell just one product. A **product line** is a group of products that are physically similar or are intended for a similar market. They usually face similar competition. Procter & Gamble's (P&G) product lines include hair care, oral care, and household cleaners. In one product line, there may be several competing brands. For example, P&G has many brands in its laundry detergent product line, including Tide, Era, Downy, and Bold. All of P&G's product lines make up its **product mix**, the combination of product lines offered by an organization.

■ **FIGURE 15.1**

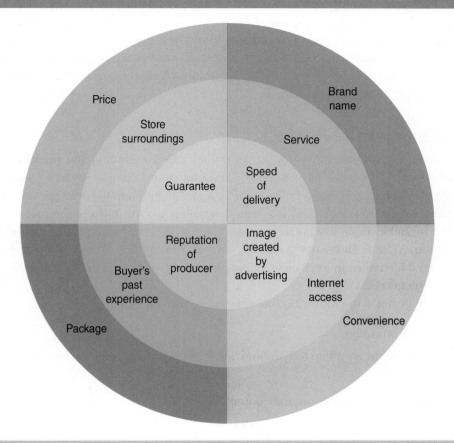

POTENTIAL COMPONENTS OF A TOTAL PRODUCT OFFER

product line
A group of products that are physically similar or are intended for a similar market.

product mix
The combination of product lines offered by an organization.

Service providers have product lines and product mixes as well. Financial services firms such as banks and credit unions may offer a variety of services, such as savings products (including chequing accounts and term deposits), credit products (including loans, mortgages, and credit cards), and a variety of other services (such as safety deposit boxes).

Product Differentiation

Product differentiation is the creation of real or perceived product differences. Actual product differences are sometimes quite small, so marketers must use a creative mix of branding, pricing, advertising, and packaging (value enhancers) to create a unique, attractive image. Various bottled water companies, for example, have successfully achieved product differentiation. These companies made their bottled waters so attractive through pricing and promotion that some restaurant customers order water by brand name (e.g., Perrier).

product differentiation
The creation of real or perceived product differences.

There's no reason why you couldn't create a similar attractive image for Very Vegetarian, your vegetarian restaurant. Small businesses can often win market share with creative product differentiation. One yearbook entrepreneur competes by offering multiple clothing changes, backgrounds, and poses along with special allowances, discounts, and guarantees. His small business has the advantage of being more flexible in adapting to customer needs and wants, and he is able to offer attractive product options. He has been so successful that companies use him as a speaker at photography conventions. How would you respond creatively to the consumer wants of vegetarians? Note the success that companies have had using the term "organic" in their promotions.[7]

Packaging Changes the Product

Customers evaluate many aspects of the total product offer, including the package. It is surprising how important packaging can be in such evaluations. Many companies have used packaging to change and improve their basic products. We have squeezable ketchup bottles that stand upside down; square paint cans with screw tops and integrated handles; plastic bottles for motor oil that eliminate the need for funnels; single-use packets of spices; and so forth. Another interesting innovation is aromatic packaging. Arizona Beverage Company <*https://www.drinkarizona.com*> now has aromatic caps on its flavoured iced teas. In each case, the package changed the product in the minds of customers and opened large markets.

Packaging must perform the following functions:

1. Attract the buyer's attention.
2. Protect the goods inside, stand up to handling and storage, be tamperproof, and deter theft.
3. Be easy to open and use.
4. Describe and give information about the contents.
5. Explain the benefits of the core product inside.
6. Provide information on warranties, warnings, and other customer matters.
7. Give some indication of price, value, and uses.

Packaging can also make a product more attractive to retailers. The Universal Product Codes (UPCs) on many packages help stores control inventory. They combine a bar code (black and white lines) and a preset number that gives the retailer information about the product's price, size, colour, and other attributes. In short, packaging changes the product by changing its visibility, usefulness, or attractiveness.

One relatively new packaging technology for tracking products is the radio frequency identification (RFID) chip, especially the ones made with nanoparticle powder. When attached to a product, the chip sends out signals telling a company where the product is at all times. RFID chips carry more information than bar codes, do not have to be read one at a time (whole pallets can be read in an instant), and can be read at a distance. Walmart has been a leader in using RFID technology.

THE GROWING IMPORTANCE OF PACKAGING

Today, packaging carries more of the promotional burden than in the past. Many products once sold by salespeople are now being sold in self-service outlets, and the package has acquired more sales responsibility.

The Heinz Dip & Squeeze® ketchup package allows restaurant owners to offer their customers a choice of peeing off the lid for dipping or tearing off the top for squeezing. The package contains three times as much ketchup as traditional sachets and uses less packaging. Shaped like the iconic Heinz tomato ketchup glass bottles, the packets reinforce the Heinz Ketchup brand.

Packaging may make use of a strategy called **bundling**, which combines goods and/or services for a single price. Virgin <*http://www.virgin.com*> has bundled door-to-door limousine service and in-flight massages in its total product offer. Financial institutions are offering everything from financial advice to help in purchasing insurance, stocks, bonds, mutual funds, and more. When combining goods or services into one package, marketers must not include so much that the price gets too high. It's best to work with customers to develop value enhancers that meet their individual needs.

bundling
Grouping two or more products together and pricing them as a unit.

Progress Assessment

- What are some examples of value enhancers in a value package?
- What's the difference between a product line and a product mix?
- What functions does packaging perform?

Branding

A **brand** is a name, symbol, or design (or combination thereof) that identifies the goods or services of one seller or group of sellers, and distinguishes them from the goods and services of competitors. The word brand includes practically all means of identifying a product. Brand names you may be familiar with include Air Canada, Roots, President's Choice, Red Bull, and Campbell Soup.

brand
A name, symbol, or design (or combination thereof) that identifies the goods or services of one seller or group of sellers, and distinguishes them from the goods and services of competitors.

Brand names give products a distinction that tends to make them attractive to customers. For the buyer, a brand name assures quality, reduces search time, and adds prestige to purchases. For the seller, brand names facilitate new-product introductions, support promotional efforts, add to repeat purchases, and differentiate products so that prices can be set higher. Companies sue other companies for too closely matching brand names.

MARS Apprentice is an annual undergraduate experiential learning program at the DeGroote School of Business, McMaster University. It is centred around six weekly case challenges in the fields of Marketing, Advertising, Retail, and Sales (MARS). Through program partners like PepsiCo, Microsoft, Canadian Tire Bank, and others, the teams are introduced to real life business situations and challenges. Each challenge week culminates in a boardroom assessment by senior industry professionals. Top-performing Apprentices are rewarded with career starts and internships besides cash prizes that recognize effort and results. In this boardroom, the teams had to design an incentive and rewards program to engage the field marketing representatives for Canadian Tire Bank. Do you see branding examples?

Generating Brand Equity and Loyalty

Brand equity is the value of the brand name and associated symbols. Usually the company cannot know the value of its brand until it sells it to another company. In the past, companies tried to boost their short-term performance by offering coupons and price discounts to move goods quickly. This eroded customers' commitment to brand names, especially of grocery products. Now companies realize the value of brand equity, and are trying harder to measure the earning power of strong brand names.[8]

> **brand equity**
> The value of the brand name and associated symbols.

The core of brand equity is brand loyalty. **Brand loyalty** is the degree to which customers are satisfied, enjoy the brand, and are committed to further purchases. A loyal group of customers represents substantial value to a firm, and that value can be calculated. Canadian brand names with the highest brand values—that is, how much profit the brands are likely to generate for their owners—and their corresponding brand values are as follows: the Royal Bank of Canada (US$12.5 billion), the Toronto-Dominion Bank (US$11.1 billion), Bell (US$7.6 billion), Scotiabank (US$7.0 billion), and Bank of Montreal (US$6.9 billion).[9] One way manufacturers are trying to create more brand loyalty is by lowering the carbon footprints of their products.

> **brand loyalty**
> The degree to which customers are satisfied, enjoy the brand, and are committed to further purchase.

By creating the Canadian Tire Drivers Academy <*https://driversacademy.canadiantire.ca*>, Canadian Tire Corp., Ltd. hopes to strengthen its presence in the automotive market by fighting off competition and improving customer loyalty.[10] Courses include beginner driver education, a G1 and G2 road-test package, a pre-test package for seniors, a driving skills assessment for new Canadians, and a two-hour car maintenance program. Would this service influence your loyalty? If one was available in your area, would you register for a course?

Brand Management

A **brand manager** (known as a *product manager* in some firms) has direct responsibility for one brand or product line. This individual also manages all the elements of the marketing mix—product, price, place, and promotion—throughout the life cycle of each product and service. Thus, you might think of the brand manager as the president of a one-product firm.

> **brand manager**
> A manager who has direct responsibility for one brand or one product line; called a product manager in some firms.

One reason many large consumer product companies created this position was to have greater control over new-product development and product promotion. Some companies have brand management teams to bolster the overall effort. In B2B companies, brand managers are often known as product managers.

Greenpeace's report, *Dirty Laundry*, alleged that clothing from top brands such as Calvin Klein, H&M, Abercrombie & Fitch, Converse, and Ralph Lauren are tainted with various hazardous chemicals.[11] As part of Greenpeace's Detox Campaign, Puma was the first to promise a toxin-free product and also to eliminate toxins from its entire supply chain and life cycle by 2020; Nike and Adidas followed with their own initiatives.[12] What role do brand managers have in developing such programs? Do you seek out products that are sold by companies that support corporate social responsibility?

LO2   Describe the product life cycle.

The Product Life Cycle

Once a product has been developed and tested, it goes to market. There it may pass through a **product life cycle** of four stages: introduction, growth, maturity, and decline as noted in Figure 15.2. This cycle is a *theoretical* model of what happens to sales and profits for a *product class* over time. However, not all individual products follow this life-cycle shape, and particular brands may act differently. For example, while frozen foods as a product class may go through the entire cycle, one brand may never get beyond the introduction stage. Some product classes, such as microwave ovens, stay in the introductory stage for years. Other products, like ketchup, become classics and never experience decline. Fad products (think Beanie Babies and mood rings) may go through the entire cycle in a few months. Still others may be withdrawn from the market altogether. Nonetheless, the product life cycle may provide some basis for anticipating future market developments and for planning marketing strategies.

> **product life cycle**
> A theoretical model of what happens to sales and profits for a product class over time; the four stages of the cycle are introduction, growth, maturity, and decline.

Example of the Product Life Cycle

The product life cycle can give marketers valuable clues to successfully promoting a product over time. Some products, like crayons and sidewalk chalk, have very long product life cycles, change very little, and never seem to go into decline. Crayola's *<http://www.crayola.com>* crayons have been popular for 100 years! How long do you think the new virtual video games will last?

You can see how the theory works by looking at the product life cycle of instant coffee. When it was introduced, most people did not like it as well as "regular" coffee, and it took several years for instant coffee to gain general acceptance (introduction stage). At one point, though, instant coffee grew rapidly in popularity, and many brands were introduced (growth stage). After a while, people became attached to one brand and sales levelled off (maturity stage). Sales then went into a slight decline when freeze-dried coffees were introduced (decline stage). Now freeze-dried coffee is, in turn, in the decline stage as consumers are buying fresh specialty beans from companies such as Second Cup and Starbucks and brewing them at home. It is extremely important for marketers to recognize what stage a product is in so that they can make intelligent and efficient marketing decisions about it.

Using the Product Life Cycle

Different stages in the product life cycle call for different marketing strategies. Figure 15.2 outlines some marketing mix decisions you might make. As you go through the figure, you will see that each stage calls for multiple marketing mix changes. These concepts are largely theoretical and you should use them only as guidelines. (We'll discuss the price strategies mentioned in the figure later in this chapter.)

Note that at the maturity stage, the product may reach the top in sales growth while profit is decreasing. At that stage, a marketing manager may decide to create a new image for the product to start a new growth cycle. You may have noticed how Arm & Hammer baking soda gets a new image every few years to generate new sales. One year it is positioned as a deodorant for refrigerators and then, as a substitute for harsh chemicals in swimming pools. Knowing what stage in the cycle a product has reached helps marketing managers decide when such strategic changes in the marketing mix are needed.

■ **FIGURE 15.2**

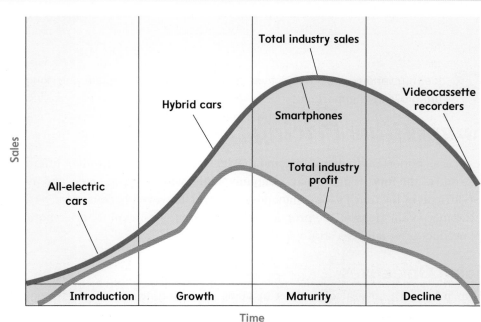

STAGES OF THE PRODUCT LIFE CYCLE

Profit levels start to fall *before* sales reach their peak. This is due to increasing price competition. When profits and sales start to decline, it is time to come out with a new product or to remodel the old one to maintain interest and profits. Note how stages of the product life cycle relate to a firm's marketing objectives and marketing mix actions.

MARKETING OBJECTIVE	GAIN AWARENESS	STRESS DIFFERENTIATION	MAINTAIN BRAND LOYALTY	HARVESTING, DELETION
Competition	Few	More	Many	Reduced
Product	One	More versions	Full product line	Best sellers
Price	Skimming or penetration	Gain market share, deal	Defend market share, profit	Stay profitable
Place (distribution)	Limited	More outlets	Maximum outlets	Fewer outlets
Promotion	Inform, educate	Stress points of difference	Reminder-oriented	Minimal promotion

Progress Assessment

- What is a brand? What are the benefits of branding?
- What are the key components of brand equity?
- Explain the role of brand managers.
- What is the theory of the product life cycle?

LO3   Identify various pricing objectives and strategies, and explain why non-pricing strategies are growing in importance.

Competitive Pricing

Pricing is so important to marketing and the development of total product offers that it has been singled out as one of the four Ps in the marketing mix, along with product, place, and promotion. It is one of the most difficult of the four Ps for a manager to control, however, because price is such a critical ingredient in customer evaluations of the product. In this section, we'll explore price both as an ingredient of the total product offer and as a strategic marketing tool.

Pricing Objectives

A firm may have several objectives in mind when setting a pricing strategy. When pricing a new vegetarian offering, we may want to promote the product's image. If we price it *high* and use the right promotion, maybe we can make it the BMW of vegetarian meals. We also might price it high to achieve a certain profit objective or return on investment. We could also price our product *lower* than its competitors, because we want low-income people to afford this healthy meal. That is, we could have some social or ethical goal in mind. Low pricing may also discourage competition because it reduces the profit potential, but it may also help us capture a larger share of the market.

A firm may have several pricing objectives over time, and it must formulate these objectives clearly before developing an overall pricing strategy. Popular objectives include the following:

1. *Achieving a target return on investment or profit.* Ultimately, the goal of marketing for profit-oriented firms is to make a profit by providing goods and services to others. Naturally, one long-run pricing objective of almost all firms is to optimize profit.

2. *Building traffic.* Supermarkets often advertise certain products at or below cost to attract people to the store. These products are called *loss leaders.* The long-run objective is to make profits by following the short-run objective of building a customer base. By offering free access to extensive music videos, all completely shareable, and almost all assembled in smart playlists, YouTube is the world's biggest music streaming service.[13] In an effort to increase revenue, customers have the option to pay for an "ads-free" version of YouTube for a monthly fee.[14] Do you agree that mobile users may find this option particularly attractive? Would you pay the fee?

3. *Achieving greater market share.* One way to capture a larger part of the market is to offer lower prices, low finance rates (like 0 percent financing), low lease rates, or rebates.

4. *Creating an image.* Certain watches (e.g., Rolex), perfumes, and other socially visible products are priced high to give them an image of exclusivity and status.

One way companies have tried to increase profit is by reducing the amount provided to customers. Thus, cereal companies have cut the amount of cereal in a box, toilet paper companies are making their products smaller, and so on. Have you noticed this happening to products you buy?

5. *Furthering social objectives.* A firm may want to price a product low so that people with little money can afford it. The government often subsidizes the price of farm products to keep basic necessities, like milk, affordable.

A firm may have short-run objectives that differ greatly from its long-run objectives. Managers should understand both types at the beginning and put both into their strategic marketing plan. They should also set pricing objectives in the context of other marketing decisions about product design, packaging, branding, distribution, and promotion. All these marketing decisions are interrelated.

Intuition tells us the price charged for a product must bear some relationship to the cost of producing it. Prices usually *are* set somewhere above cost. But as we'll see, price and cost are not always related. In fact, there are three major approaches to pricing strategy: cost-based, demand-based (target costing), and competition-based.

COST-BASED PRICING

Producers often use cost as a primary basis for setting the price. They develop elaborate cost accounting systems to measure production costs (including materials, labour, and overhead), add in a margin of profit, and come up with a price. Picture the process in terms of producing a car. You add up all the various components—engine parts, body, tires, radio, door locks, windows, paint, and labour—add a profit margin, and come up with a price. The question is whether the price will be satisfactory to the market as well. In the long run the market—not the producer—determines what the price will be (see Chapter 2). Pricing should take into account costs, but it should also include the expected costs of product updates, the marketing objectives for each product, and competitors' prices.

DEMAND-BASED PRICING

Unlike cost-based pricing, **target costing** is demand-based. That means we design a product so it not only satisfies customers but also meets profit margins we've set. Target costing makes the final price an *input* to the product development process, not an outcome of it. You first estimate the selling price people would be willing to pay for a product and then subtract your desired profit margin. The result is your target cost of production, or what you can spend to profitably produce the item.

> **target costing**
> Designing a product so that it satisfies customers and meets the profit margins desired by the firm.

Imagine how demand-based pricing is used for custom-made jewellery. Can you think of any other products where this approach is used?

COMPETITION-BASED PRICING

Competition-based pricing is a strategy based on what all the other competitors are doing. The price can be at, above, or below competitors' prices. Pricing depends on customer loyalty, perceived differences, and the competitive climate.[15] **Price leadership** is the strategy by which one or more dominant firms set pricing practices that all competitors in an industry then follow. You may have noticed this practice among oil and gas companies and some fast-food companies.[16]

> **competition-based pricing**
> A pricing strategy based on what all the other competitors are doing. The price can be set at, above, or below competitors' prices.
>
> **price leadership**
> The strategy by which one or more dominant firms set the pricing practices that all competitors in an industry then follow.

Break-Even Analysis

Before you begin selling a new vegetarian sandwich, it may be wise to determine how many sandwiches you would have to sell before making a profit. You would then determine whether you could reach such a sales goal. **Break-even analysis** is the process used to determine profitability at various levels of sales. The break-even point is the point where revenue from sales equals all costs. The formula for calculating the break-even point is as follows:

$$\text{Break-even point (BEP)} = \frac{\text{Total fixed cost (FC)}}{\text{Price of one unit (P)} - \text{Variable cost (VC) of one unit}}$$

> **break-even analysis**
> The process used to determine profitability at various levels of sales.

Total fixed costs are all expenses that remain the same no matter how many products are made or sold. Among the expenses that make up fixed costs are the amount paid to own or rent a factory or warehouse and the amount paid for business insurance. **Variable costs** change according to the level of production. Included are the expenses for the materials used in making products and the direct costs of labour used to make those products.

> **total fixed costs**
> All expenses that remain the same no matter how many products are made or sold.
>
> **variable costs**
> Costs that change according to the level of production.

To produce a specific product, let's say you have a fixed cost of $200,000 (for mortgage interest, real estate taxes, equipment, and so on). Your variable cost (e.g., labour and materials) per item is $2. If you sold each product for $4, the break-even point would be 100,000 items. In other words, you would not make any money selling this product unless you sold more than 100,000 of them:

$$\text{BEP} = \frac{\text{FC}}{(\text{P} - \text{VC})} = \frac{\$200{,}000}{(\$4.00 - \$2.00)} = \frac{\$200{,}000}{(\$2.00)} = 100{,}000 \text{ items}$$

Pricing Strategies for New Products

Let's say that a firm has just developed a new line of products, such as 3D printers. The firm has to decide how to price these units at the introductory stage of the product life cycle. A **skimming price strategy** prices a new product high, to recover research and development costs and to make as much profit as possible while there's little competition. Of course, those large profits will eventually attract competitors.

> **skimming price strategy**
> A strategy in which a new product is priced high to make optimum profit while there's little competition.

A second strategy would be to price the new printers low. Low prices will attract more buyers and discourage other companies from making these printers because profits are slim. This **penetration price strategy** enables the firm to penetrate or capture a large share of the market quickly.[17]

> **penetration price strategy**
> A strategy in which the product is priced low to attract many customers and discourage competitors.

Retailer Pricing Strategies

Retailers use several pricing strategies. **Everyday low pricing (EDLP)** is the choice of Walmart, for example. It sets prices lower than competitors and does not usually have special sales. The idea is to bring customers to the store whenever they want a bargain rather than waiting until there is a sale.

> **everyday low pricing (EDLP)**
> Setting prices lower than competitors and then not having any special sales.

Department stores and some other retailers most often use a **high–low pricing strategy**. Regular prices are higher than at stores using EDLP, but during special sales they are lower. The problem with such pricing is that it encourages customers to wait for sales, thus cutting into profits. As online shopping continues to grow, you may see fewer stores with a high–low strategy because customers will be able to find better prices on the Internet.

> **high–low pricing strategy**
> Set prices that are higher than EDLP stores, but have many special sales where the prices are lower than competitors.

> With hundreds of locations across the country, Dollarama is the leading dollar store operator in Canada. In each location, you will find products that are sold in individual or multiple units at select fixed price points up to $3.00.[18] What is this company's pricing strategy?

Retailers can use price as a major determinant of the goods they carry. Some promote goods that sell for only $1 (e.g., Dollarama), or another amount (e.g., $10). Dollar stores have raised some of their prices to over one dollar because of rising costs.

Psychological pricing means pricing goods and services at price points that make the product appear less expensive than it is. A house might be priced at $299,000 because that sounds like a lot less than $300,000. Gas stations almost always use psychological pricing.

> **psychological pricing**
> Pricing goods and services at price points that make the product appear less expensive than it is.

How Market Forces Affect Pricing

Recognizing that different customers may be willing to pay different prices, marketers sometimes price on the basis of customer demand rather than cost or some other calculation. That is called *demand-oriented pricing* and it is reflected by movie theatres (such as Cineplex Odeon <*http://www.cineplex.com*>) that charge lower prices on Tuesdays, and by retailers (such as Shoppers Drug Mart) that offer discounts to senior citizens if they shop on certain days (e.g., Thursdays).

Today, marketers are facing a new pricing problem: customers comparing prices of goods and services online. Priceline.com introduced customers to a "demand collection system," in which buyers post the price they are willing to pay and invite sellers to either accept or decline the price. Customers can get great prices on airlines, hotels, and other products by naming their price. They can also buy used goods online at sites such as eBay <*http://www.ebay.ca*>, Kijiji, or Craigslist. Clearly, price competition is going to heat up as customers have more access to price information from around the world. As a result, non-price competition is likely to increase.

Non-Price Competition

Marketers often compete on product attributes other than price. You may have noted that price differences are small with products such as gasoline, candy bars, and even major products such as compact cars. You will not typically see price as a major promotional appeal on television. Instead, marketers tend to stress product images and customer benefits such as comfort, style, convenience, and durability.

Often marketers emphasize non-price differences because prices are so easy to match. In order to compete with bigger firms, many small organizations promote the services that accompany basic products rather than prices. Good service will enhance a relatively homogeneous product. However, few competitors can match the image of a friendly, responsive, customer-oriented company. Other strategies to avoid price wars include adding value (e.g., home delivery from a drugstore), educating customers on how to use the product, and establishing relationships. Customers will pay extra for goods and services when they have a friendly relationship with the seller. The services are not always less expensive, but they offer more value.

Progress Assessment

- Can you list four pricing objectives?
- What's a disadvantage of using a cost-based pricing strategy?
- How do you calculate a product's break-even point?
- Why is increasing focus being placed on non-price competition?

LO4 Explain the concept of marketing channels, and the importance of retailing.

The Importance of Channels of Distribution

Managing the flow of goods has become one of the most important managerial functions for many organizations. **Marketing intermediaries** (once called *middlemen*) are organizations that assist in moving goods and services from producers to businesses (B2B) and from businesses to consumers (B2C). They are called intermediaries because they are in the middle of a series of organizations that join together to push products through the channel of distribution. A **channel of distribution** consists of a whole set of marketing intermediaries (such as agents, brokers, wholesalers, and retailers) that join together to transport and store goods in their path (or channel) from producers to consumers.

marketing intermediaries
Organizations that assist in moving goods and services from producers to business and consumer users.

channel of distribution
A set of marketing intermediaries, such as agents, brokers, wholesalers, and retailers, that join together to transport and store goods in their path (or channel) from producers to consumers.

Distribution warehouses, such as Amazon's distribution centre, store goods until they are needed. Have you ever thought about the benefits of having food, furniture, clothing, and other needed goods close at hand?

Agents/brokers are marketing intermediaries who bring buyers and sellers together and assist in negotiating an exchange, but do not take title to the goods. That is, at no point do they own the goods. Think of real estate agents as an example.

agents/brokers
Marketing intermediaries that bring buyers and sellers together and assist in negotiating an exchange but do not take title to the goods.

A **wholesaler** is a marketing intermediary that sells to other organizations, such as retailers, manufacturers, and institutions (e.g., hospitals).[19] Wholesalers are part of the B2B system. Because of high distribution costs, Walmart has been trying to eliminate independent wholesalers from its system and do the job itself. That is, Walmart provides its own warehouses and has its own trucks. It has over 120 distributions centres and 53,000 trailers to distribute goods to its stores.

wholesaler
A marketing intermediary that sells to other organizations.

A **retailer** is an organization that sells to ultimate consumers (that is, people like you and me) who buy for their own use. For consumers to receive the maximum benefit from marketing intermediaries, the various organizations must work together to ensure a smooth flow of goods and services to the customer.

retailer
An organization that sells to ultimate consumers.

Channels of distribution help ensure communication flows *and* the flow of money and title to goods. They also help ensure that the right quantity and assortment of goods will be available when and where needed. Figure 15.3 shows selected channels of distribution for both consumer and industrial goods.

■ **FIGURE 15.3**

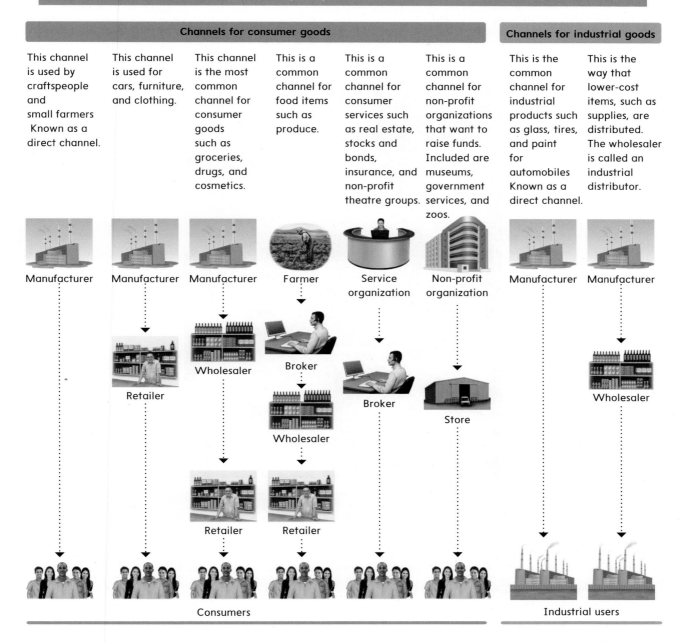

SELECTED CHANNELS OF DISTRIBUTION FOR CONSUMER AND INDUSTRIAL (B2B) GOODS AND SERVICES

| Channels for consumer goods | | | | | | Channels for industrial goods | |

This channel is used by craftspeople and small farmers Known as a direct channel.

This channel is used for cars, furniture, and clothing.

This channel is the most common channel for consumer goods such as groceries, drugs, and cosmetics.

This is a common channel for food items such as produce.

This is a common channel for consumer services such as real estate, stocks and bonds, insurance, and non-profit theatre groups.

This is a common channel for non-profit organizations that want to raise funds. Included are museums, government services, and zoos.

This is the common channel for industrial products such as glass, tires, and paint for automobiles Known as a direct channel.

This is the way that lower-cost items, such as supplies, are distributed. The wholesaler is called an industrial distributor.

Manufacturer Manufacturer Manufacturer Farmer Service organization Non-profit organization Manufacturer Manufacturer

Retailer Wholesaler Broker Broker Wholesaler

Wholesaler Store

Retailer Retailer

Consumers

Industrial users

How Intermediaries Create Exchange Efficiency

When you consider that some manufacturers sell directly to customers, known as a *direct channel,* you may wonder why have intermediaries at all? The answer is that intermediaries perform certain marketing tasks—such as transporting, storing, selling, advertising, and relationship building—faster and more cheaply than most manufacturers could. A simple analogy is this: You could deliver packages in person to people anywhere in the world, but usually you do not. Why not? Because it is usually more efficient to have them delivered by Canada Post or a private firm such as Purolator. While marketing intermediaries can be eliminated, their activities cannot if customers are to have access to products and services. Intermediary organizations have survived because they have performed marketing functions faster and cheaper than others could.

Are food trucks a direct channel or an indirect channel? Some vendors use Twitter and other social media to reveal their current locations and build customer relationships. You might find cuisine such as specialty crepes, kimchi pork fries, osso bucco, banh mi, and Gruyère grilled cheese. Would a Very Vegetarian truck make sense? Watch the Chapter 16 video to learn about Dougie Luv (middle) and his pitch on the *Dragons' Den*.

Here is a way to see the benefits of using marketing intermediaries, known as an *indirect channel*. Suppose five manufacturers of various food products each tried to sell directly to five retailers. The number of exchange relationships that would have to be established is 5 times 5, or 25. But picture what happens when a wholesaler enters the system. The five manufacturers would contact one wholesaler to establish five exchange relationships. The wholesaler would have to establish contact with the five retailers. That would also mean five exchange relationships. Note that the number of exchanges is reduced from 25 to only 10 by the addition of a wholesaler. Figure 15.4 shows this exchange.

■ FIGURE 15.4

HOW INTERMEDIARIES CREATE EXCHANGE EFFICIENCY

Adding a wholesaler to the channel of distribution cuts the number of contacts from 25 to 10. This improves the efficiency of distribution.

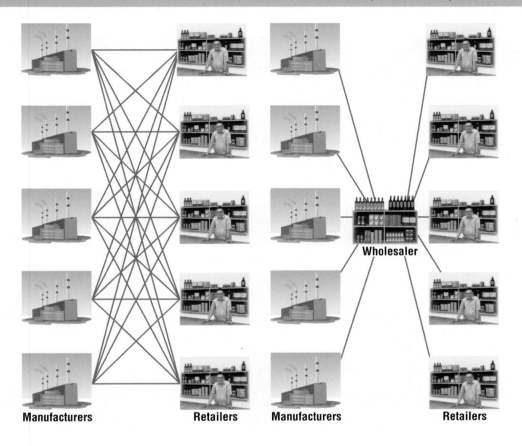

| Manufacturers | Retailers | Manufacturers | Wholesaler | Retailers |

Progress Assessment

- What is a channel of distribution, and what intermediaries are involved?
- Why do we need intermediaries? What are some examples?
- Compare a direct and indirect channel of distribution.

Retail Intermediaries

Perhaps the most useful marketing intermediaries, as far as you are concerned, are retailers. Remember that retailers sell to ultimate consumers. They are the ones who bring goods and services to your neighbourhood and make them available day and night. Retailing is important to our economy. In 2014, retail trade generated over $505 billion and employed more than 1.9 million Canadians.[20] These numbers do not include online sales.

Figure 15.5 lists, describes, and gives examples of various kinds of retailers. What seems to be the advantage of each? For example, some retailers compete mostly on price while others, such as specialty stores, use variety as a competitive tool.

■ FIGURE 15.5

TYPES OF RETAIL STORES		
Type	Description	Example
Department store	Sells a wide variety of products (clothes, furniture, and housewares) in separate departments	Sears, Hudson's Bay, Ogilvy
Discount store	Sells many different products at prices generally below those of department stores	Giant Tiger, Great Canadian Dollar Store
Supermarket	Sells mostly food with other non-food products such as detergent and paper products	Metro, Sobeys, Provigo
Warehouse club	Sells food and general merchandise in facilities that are usually larger than supermarkets and offers discount prices; membership may be required	Costco Wholesale, Wholesale Club
Convenience store	Sells food and other often-needed items at convenient locations; may stay open all night	Mac's, Daisy Mart, Provi-Soir
Category killer	Sells a huge variety of one type of product to dominate that category of goods	Indigo Books & Music, Sleep Country Canada, Staples
Outlet store	Sells general merchandise directly from the manufacturer at a discount; items may be discontinued or have flaws ("seconds")	Nike, Rockport, Liz Claiborne
Specialty store	Sells a wide selection of goods in one category	Jewellery stores, shoe stores, bicycle stores
Supercentre	Sells food and general merchandise at discount prices; no membership required	Loblaws (some locations), Walmart (some locations)

Retail Distribution Strategy

A major decision that marketers must make is selecting the right retailers to sell their products. Different products call for different retail distribution strategies.

Intensive distribution puts products into as many retail outlets as possible, including vending machines. Products that need intensive distribution include candy, gum, and popular magazines.

intensive distribution
Distribution that puts products into as many retail outlets as possible.

Selective distribution uses only a preferred group of the available retailers in an area. Such selection helps assure producers of quality sales and service. Manufacturers of appliances, furniture, and clothing use selective distribution.

selective distribution
Distribution that sends products to only a preferred group of retailers in an area.

Exclusive distribution is the use of only one retail outlet in a given geographic area. The retailer has exclusive rights to sell the product and is therefore likely to carry a large inventory, give exceptional service, and pay more attention to this brand than to others. Auto manufacturers usually use exclusive distribution, as do producers of specialty goods such as skydiving equipment.

exclusive distribution
Distribution that sends products to only one retail outlet in a given geographic area.

Non-Store Retailing

Non-store retailing includes electronic retailing; telemarketing; vending machines, kiosks and carts; and direct selling. Small businesses can use non-store retailing to open up new channels of distribution for their products.

ELECTRONIC RETAILING

Electronic retailing consists of selling products to ultimate consumers online. **Social commerce** is a form of electronic commerce that involves using social media and user contributions to assist in the online buying and selling of products and services. Figure 15.6 shares a list of different types of social commerce. Social commerce is relevant as 74% of consumers rely on social networks to guide their purchases.[21]

electronic retailing
Selling goods and services to ultimate customers (e.g., you and me) over the Internet.

social commerce
A form of electronic commerce that involves using social media and user contributions to assist in the online buying and selling of products and services.

Thanks to website improvements and discounting, online retail sales have risen dramatically over the last few years.[22] But getting customers is only half the battle. The other half is delivering the goods, providing helpful service, and keeping your customers. When electronic retailers fail to have sufficient inventory or fail to deliver goods on time (especially during holidays and other busy periods), customers give up and go back to bricks-and-mortar stores.

■ **FIGURE 15.6**

TYPES OF SOCIAL MEDIA COMMERCE

Social commerce denotes a wide range of shopping, recommending, and selling behaviours. As these models are tested and proven to increase sales and customer satisfaction, more will be introduced.

1. **Peer-to-peer sales platforms** (eBay, Etsy, Amazon Marketplace): Community-based marketplaces, or bazaars, where individuals communicate and sell directly to other individuals
2. **Social network-driven sales** (Facebook, Pinterest, Twitter): Sales driven by referrals from established social networks
3. **Group buying** (Groupon, LivingSocial): Products and services offered at a reduced rate
4. **Peer recommendations** (Amazon, Yelp, JustBoughtIt): Sites that aggregate product or service reviews, recommend products based on others' purchasing history
5. **User-curated shopping** (The Fancy, Lyst, Svpply): Shopping-focused sites where users create and share lists of products and services where others can shop
6. **Participatory commerce** (Threadless, Kickstarter, CutOnYourBias): Consumers become involved directly in the production process through voting, funding, and collaboratively designing products
7. **Social shopping** (Motilo, Fashism, GoTryItOn): Sites that attempt to replicate shopping offline with friends by including chat and forum features for exchanging advice and opinions

Source: Lauren Indvik, "The 7 Species of Social Commerce," Mashable, *http://mashable.com*, downloaded 13 April 2015.

Most Internet retailers now offer e-mail confirmation. But sometimes electronic retailers are not as strong at handling complaints, accepting returns, and providing personal help. Some are improving customer service by adding help buttons that lead customers to real-time assistance from a human employee. The Adapting to Change box discusses how online reviews influence consumer decision making, a topic introduced in Chapter 14.

Bricks and mortar are stores that have a physical presence. If they add an online presence, they are called *bricks and clicks* (or *clicks and bricks*). Bricks and clicks allow customers to choose which shopping technique suits them best. Most companies that want to compete in the future will probably need both a physical store and an online presence to provide customers with all the options they want.

Adapting *to* CHANGE

Turning a Negative to a Positive

When Amazon invited customers to start posting reviews of products 20 years ago, many thought the online retailer had lost its good sense. Today, market researchers admit that Amazon's move created a monumental change in the consumer decision-making process. A Nielsen research report helped confirm this shift. The company surveyed 28,000 Internet users in 56 countries and found that online reviews from sites like Amazon are the second most trusted source of a brand's reliability (second only to the recommendations of friends and family). It's no wonder then that in this digital age, we are overwhelmed with the opinions of others about products, opinions we tend to treat as trustworthy and factual. But exactly how reliable are the ratings assigned by reviewers? Is the trust we place in these ratings misplaced? The best answer might be "maybe."

As human beings we have a "herding" tendency that often causes us to think and act in the same way as people around us. Therefore, if reviewers read other product reviews that lean positively toward a product, there's a good chance they may rate the product favourably even if that was not their original impression. Such behaviour may be a major reason why extremely high ratings easily outnumber negative ratings on Amazon. Researchers also believe that online reviewers are more positively predisposed to a product because they voluntarily bought the product and are less likely to criticize it. This is generally referred to as selection bias.

Another problem with the validity of online reviews is that reviewers will sometimes rate products negatively when there are shipping or other ordering problems that have nothing to do with the quality of the products themselves. Amazon has tried to correct these inherent challenges through the creation of Amazon Vine, an invitation-only program that involves the site's top reviewers. These elite reviewers are sent free merchandise to review. Amazon believes working with the site's most trusted reviewers provides more useful reviews for customers to consider. Still, critics contend that giving products for free might create a bias toward a positive rather than a negative rating. However, research has shown that the Vine reviewers actually bestow fewer stars than regular reviewers. Strangely, research has also shown that even a product with only negative reviews sells better than a product with no reviews at all. Go figure.

Sources: Sinan Aral, "The Problem with Online Ratings," *MIT Sloan Management Review*, Winter 2014; Joe Queenan, "Why I'm Hating All That Online Rating," *The Wall Street Journal*, 21 February 2014; and Lisa Chow, "Top Reviewers on Amazon Get Tons of Free Stuff," NPR, 30 October 2013.

TELEMARKETING

Telemarketing is the sale of goods and services by telephone. Companies use it to supplement or replace in-store selling and to complement online selling. Many telemarketers send catalogues to customers and let them order by calling a toll-free number. Many electronic retailers provide a help feature online that serves the same function.

telemarketing
The sale of goods and services by telephone.

To reduce telemarketing calls, register your telephone number(s) on the National Do Not Call List <*http://www.lnnte-dncl .gc.ca*>. Exemptions from this list include calls on behalf of Canadian registered charities, political parties, and calls from companies with whom you have an existing business relationship.[23] Do you dislike such calls?

VENDING MACHINES, KIOSKS, AND CARTS

Vending machines dispense convenience goods when customers deposit sufficient money in the machine. These machines carry the benefit of location—they are found in airports, schools, office buildings, service stations, and other areas where people want convenience items. In Japan, they sell everything from bandages and face cloths to salads and spiced seafood. North American vending machines sell food, iPods, headphones, sneakers, digital cameras, and DVD movies. An ATM in Abu Dhabi dispenses gold.

Kiosks and carts have lower overhead costs than stores do, so they can offer lower prices on items such as T-shirts, purses, watches, and cell phones. You often see vending carts outside stores on the sidewalk or along walkways in malls. Some mall owners love them because they are colourful and create a marketplace atmosphere. Kiosk workers often dispense coupons and provide all kinds of helpful product information. You may have noticed airlines using kiosks to speed the process of getting on the plane. Most provide a boarding pass and allow you to change your seat. Many kiosks serve as a gateway to the Internet, so in one place customers can shop at a store and still have access to all of the products available on the Internet.

DIRECT SELLING

Direct selling reaches customers in their homes or workplaces. Many businesses use this technique to sell products such as cosmetics, household goods, lingerie, artwork, and candles. Because so many men and women work outside the home and are not in during the day, companies that use direct selling sponsor parties at workplaces or at homes on evenings and weekends. Other companies, however, such as those in encyclopedia sales, have dropped most of their direct selling efforts in favour of online selling.

> **direct selling**
> Selling to customers in their homes or where they work.

Choosing the Right Distribution Mode

As discussed in Chapter 10, a supply chain is a sequence of firms that perform activities required to create and deliver a good or service to consumers or industrial users. The supply chain is *longer* than a channel of distribution because it includes links from suppliers that provide raw materials to manufacturers, whereas the channel of distribution begins with manufacturers. Included in the supply chain are farmers, miners, suppliers of all kinds (e.g., parts, equipment, and supplies), manufacturers, wholesalers, and retailers.

As shown in Figure 15.7, channels of distribution are part of the overall supply chain. A key issue today is making the supply chain sustainable because so much of what affects the environment is caused by distribution.[24]

■ **FIGURE 15.7**

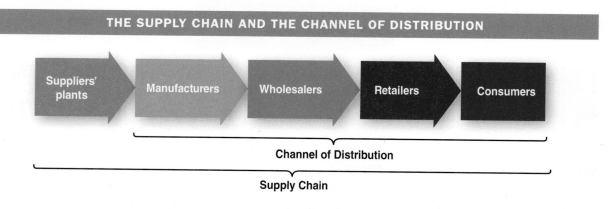

THE SUPPLY CHAIN AND THE CHANNEL OF DISTRIBUTION

A primary concern of supply-chain managers is selecting a transportation mode that will minimize costs and ensure a certain level of service. (*Modes*, in the language of distribution, are the various means used to transport goods, such as by truck, train, plane, ship, and pipeline.) Generally speaking, the faster the mode of transportation, the higher the cost. The job of the supply-chain manager is to find the most efficient combination of these forms of transportation. Figure 15.8 shows the advantages and disadvantages of each mode.

Today, supply chains involve more than simply moving products from place to place; they involve all kinds of activities such as processing orders and taking inventory of products. In other words, logistics systems involve whatever it takes to see that the right products are sent to the right place quickly and efficiently.

■ **FIGURE 15.8**

COMPARING TRANSPORTATION MODES						
Combining trucks with railroads lowers cost and increases the number of locations reached. The same is true when combining trucks with ships. Combining trucks with airlines speeds goods long distances and gets them to almost any location.						
Mode	Cost	Speed	On-Time Dependability	Flexibility Handling Products	Frequency of Shipments	Reach
Railroad	Medium	Slow	Medium	High	Low	High
Trucks	High	Fast	High	Medium	High	Highest
Pipeline	Low	Medium	Highest	Lowest	Highest	Lowest
Ships (water)	Lowest	Slowest	Lowest	Highest	Lowest	Low
Airplane	Highest	Fastest	Low	Low	Medium	Medium

Progress Assessment

- What are some of the ways in which retailers compete?

- What kinds of products would call for each of the different distribution strategies: intensive, selective, and exclusive?

- Give examples of non-store retailing and describe each.

- Which transportation mode is fastest, which is cheapest, and which is most flexible?

LO5 Define promotion, and list the five traditional tools that make up the promotion mix.

Promotion and the Promotion Mix

Recall from Chapter 14 that promotion consists of all techniques that sellers use to motivate customers to buy their products. Marketers use many different tools to promote their products and services. Traditionally, as shown in Figure 15.9, those tools include advertising, personal selling, public relations, sales promotion, and direct marketing. Today they also include e-mail promotions, mobile promotions, social networking, blogging, podcasting, tweets, and more.[25] The combination of promotional tools an organization uses is called its **promotion mix**. The product is shown in the middle of Figure 15.9 to illustrate that the product itself can also be a promotional tool, such as when marketers give away free samples.

promotion mix
The combination of promotional tools an organization uses.

Each target group calls for a separate promotion mix. For example, large homogeneous groups of customers (i.e., groups whose members share specific similar traits) are usually most efficiently reached through advertising. Large organizations are best reached through personal selling.

■ **FIGURE 15.9**

THE TRADITIONAL PROMOTION MIX

Integrated marketing communication (IMC) combines all of the promotional tools into one comprehensive and unified promotional strategy.[26] With IMC, marketers can create a positive brand image, meet the needs of customers, and meet the strategic marketing and promotional goals of the firm. Emphasis today is on integrating traditional media like TV with social media, or integrating print media with online sites.[27] Let us briefly explore each of the promotional tools.

integrated marketing communication (IMC)
A technique that combines all of the promotional tools into one comprehensive and unified promotional strategy.

Advertising: Informing, Persuading, and Reminding

Advertising is paid, non-personal communication through various media by organizations and individuals who are in some way *identified in the message*. Ads are informative. Direct mail is full of information about products, prices, features, store policies, and more. So is newspaper advertising. Not only does advertising inform us, but the money advertisers spend for commercial time pays the production costs of TV and radio programs. Advertising also covers the major costs of producing newspapers and magazines. Subscription and newsstand revenues cover only mailing and promotional costs. Figure 15.10 discusses the advantages and disadvantages of various advertising media to the advertiser. Notice that newspapers, radio, and directories are especially attractive to local advertisers.

advertising
Paid, non-personal communication through various media by organizations and individuals who are in some way identified in the advertising message.

The number of people who don't have a TV subscription with a cable, satellite, or telecommunications company is growing in Canada; they account for one-fifth of all Canadian households (approximately 3.1 million homes).[28] More Canadians are opting to consume content through online-streaming platforms such as Netflix or even from illegal downloads.[29] Marketers must choose which media can best be used

■ **FIGURE 15.10**

ADVANTAGES AND DISADVANTAGES OF VARIOUS ADVERTISING MEDIA		
The most effective media are often very expensive. The inexpensive media may not reach your target market. The goal is to use the media that can reach your desired target market most efficiently.		
Medium	**Advantages**	**Disadvantages**
Newspapers	Good coverage of local markets; ads can be placed quickly; high customer acceptance; ads can be clipped and saved	Ads compete with other features in paper; poor colour; ads get thrown away with paper (short lifespan)
Television	Uses sight, sound, and motion; reaches all audiences; high attention with no competition from other material	High cost; short exposure time; takes time to prepare ads; digital video recorders skip over ads
Radio	Low cost; can target specific audiences; very flexible; good for local marketing	People may not listen to ad; depends on one sense (hearing); short exposure time; audience can't keep ad
Magazines	Can target specific audiences; good use of colour; long life of ad; ads can be clipped and saved	Inflexible; ads often must be placed weeks before publication; cost is relatively high
Outdoor	High visibility and repeat exposures; low cost; local market focus	Limited message; low selectivity of audience
Direct mail	Best for targeting specific markets; very flexible; ad can be saved	High cost; customers may reject ad as junk mail; must conform to post office regulations
Directories (Yellow Pages-type print and online advertising)	Great coverage of local markets; widely used by customers	Competition with other ads; cost may be too high for very small businesses
Internet	Inexpensive global coverage; available at any time; interactive	Customers may leave the site before buying
Mobile advertising	Great reach among younger shoppers	Easy to ignore and avoid
Social media	Wonderful communication tools	Time drain

to reach the audience they desire. Radio advertising, for example, is less expensive than TV advertising and often reaches people when they have few other distractions, such as while they are driving. Radio is especially effective at selling services people do not usually read about in print media—services such as banking, mortgages, continuing education, and brokerage services, to name a few. On the other hand, radio has become so commercial-ridden that some people are switching to commercial-free satellite radio. Marketers also search for other places to put advertising, such as on video screens mounted in elevators. Have you noticed ads on park benches and grocery carts?[30] You have certainly seen them on websites you visit.

Mobile marketing via cell phones started out mostly as text messages, but messages are now more sophisticated. For example, Starbucks can send signals to your phone as you approach the store, reminding you to stop in for a latte. The Kraft Heinz Company *<http://www.kraftheinzcompany.com>* developed the iPhone Assistant, an iPhone application that serves up recipes for users—recipes made with Kraft products. Other retailers use e-mail advertisements to build brand awareness and drive people to their stores or websites. Social media in general is growing so fast that some marketers can hardly keep up.

Another way to get more impact from advertising is to appeal to the interest in green marketing among consumers and businesses. A brief glance through magazines and the business press reveals all kinds of appeals that refer to sustainability and carbon-cutting. Review the Seeking Sustainability box for one such example.

GLOBAL ADVERTISING

Global advertising involves developing a product and promotional strategy that can be implemented worldwide. Global advertising that is the same everywhere can save companies money in research and design. In some cases, however, promotions tailored to specific countries or regions may be much more successful since each country or region has its own culture, language, and buying habits.

Problems can arise when marketers use one campaign in all countries. When a Japanese company named a popular drink, it came up with Pocari Sweat, not a good image for most English-speaking people. Canadians may have difficulty with Krapp toilet paper from Sweden. Clairol introduced its curling iron, the Mist Stick, to the German market, not realizing that mist in German can mean "manure." Getting the words right in international advertising is tricky and critical, which calls for researching each country, designing appropriate ads, and testing them. The Reaching Beyond Our Borders box discusses how a well-known company promotes products in foreign markets.

Reaching *Beyond* OUR BORDERS

What's in Your Oreo?

For more than 100 years, an Oreo was just an Oreo: two layers of crunchy cookie sandwiching a creamy vanilla centre. For many years, Kraft, the Oreo maker, followed the old adage "If it ain't broke, don't fix it." Today, however, if you visit the cookie aisle in your local supermarket, you may find variations of Oreo such as cookie dough, marshmallow crispy, and even birthday cake. Kraft knew that to keep the brand vibrant and to reach different segments, expanding its flavours was a good option.

It was a good decision to expand the Oreo brand into global markets. Today, you can find Oreos in more than 100 countries across the globe. However, Kraft understands that globally consumer tastes vary just like in North America. What some people consider mouth-watering in one country will be frowned upon somewhere else. So with Oreo spanning the globe, additional variations of the original cookie-and-cream formula became even more extreme. China, for instance, prefers green tea–flavoured Oreos. In Indonesia, consumers prefer Blueberry Ice Cream and Orange Ice Cream–flavoured Oreos. Argentines like their Oreos stuffed with banana and dulce de leche, a type of candied milk. What is your favourite flavour?

Sources: Gina Pace, "Oreo to Launch Two New Cookie Flavors," *The New York Daily News*, 24 January 2014; and Samantha Grossman, "Oreo Launches Two New Flavors, and They're Both Delicious," *Time*, 23 January 2014.

Seeking SUSTAINABILITY

Corporate Knights and Sustainability

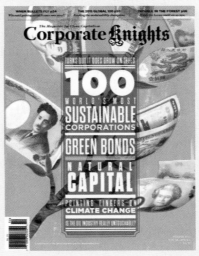

Corporate Knights Inc. (CK, <http://www.corporateknights.com>) has two subsidiaries: CK Media, which includes the award-winning business and society magazine, *Corporate Knights,* and CK Capital, which produces corporate rankings, research reports, and financial products based on corporate sustainability performance. CK's rankings include the Best 50 Corporate Citizens in Canada and the Global 100 Most Sustainable Corporations.

Founded in 2002 by Toby A. Heaps and Paul Fengler, *Corporate Knights* magazine is distributed quarterly as an insert in *The Globe and Mail* and the *Washington Post* newspapers. Individual copies can be purchased at magazine newsstands across North America or via CK's online newsstand. Print and digital subscriptions are also available.

As one of the world's largest circulation (125K+) magazines focused on the intersection of business and society, *Corporate Knights* is the most prominent brand in the clean capitalism media space. "Clean capitalism" is defined as an economic system in which prices incorporate social, economic, and ecological benefits and costs, and companies know the full impacts of their actions. The vision is to provide information empowering markets to foster a better world.

Determining which companies are sustainable and which are not is a challenging enterprise. Not only is there no single, universally accepted definition of corporate sustainability, but publicly traded companies are exceedingly complex institutions, often spanning multiple geographies and industries. As a result, corporate sustainability is unpackaged into component parts. Global 100 companies are scored on a percent rank basis against their global industry peers on a list of 12 quantitative key performance indicators that include energy and water use, to employee compensation, and corporate tax strategy. The top three global companies in the 2015 ranking include Bogen Idec (United States—73.5 percent), Allergan (United States—72.8 percent), and Adidas (Germany—72.6 percent). In eleventh place, the top Canadian company was Tim Hortons with a ranking of 68.2 percent.

The Top 30 under 30 Sustainability Leaders ranking is a collection of young entrepreneurs, activists, corporate professionals, and students eager to make the world a better place. The Millennial generation makes up roughly 25 percent of the North American population and an estimated 2.5 billion global citizens. The economic and political influence of Millennials is growing as they enter or move through the workforce toward their peak spending years. Following closely is Generation Z. For both, the Internet is an appendage, climate change is a nagging reality, mobility is just the way things are, and the weight of the future is on their shoulders. It's for this reason the United Nations says youth from around the world must be an active part of all levels of decision making related to sustainable development. "It affects their lives today and has implications for their futures," the global agency says. Take a few minutes to visit the CK website. Do any of their initiatives interest you? Are you inspired by the actions of these individuals? What can you do to make a difference, small or big?

Sources: "About Us," Corporate Knights Inc., accessed 13 April 2015, *http://www.corporateknights.com/us/about-us/*; CK Staff, "2015 Global 100 Methodology," Corporate Knights Inc., 21 January 2015, *http://www.corporateknights.com/reports/2015-global-100 /methodology/*; and CK Staff, "2015 Global 100 Results," Corporate Knights Inc., 21 January 2015, *http://www.corporateknights.com /magazines/2015-global-100-issue/2015-global-100-results-14218559/.*

Even in Canada we have regional differences that are important enough to constitute separate market segments. Each province has its own history and culture. The large metropolitan areas such as Vancouver, Toronto, and Montreal are different from the rest of the provinces in which they are located. All require their own promotions and advertising.

Many marketers today are moving from *globalism* (one ad for everyone in the world) to *regionalism* (specific ads for each country or for specific groups within a country). In the future, marketers will prepare more custom-designed promotions to reach smaller audiences—audiences as small as one person.

Personal Selling: Providing Personal Attention

Personal selling is the face-to-face presentation and promotion of goods and services. It also involves the search for new prospects and follow-up service after the sale. Effective selling is not simply a matter of persuading others to buy. In fact, it is more accurately described today as helping others satisfy their wants and needs (again, helping the buyer buy).

> **personal selling**
> The face-to-face presentation and promotion of goods and services.

With this focus, salespeople use smartphones, tablets, laptops, and other technology to help customers search for information, design custom-made products, look over prices, and generally do everything it takes to complete the order. With personal selling, there is a person to help you complete a transaction. The salesperson should listen to your needs, help you reach a solution, and do everything possible to make accomplishing it smoother and easier.

It is costly for firms to provide customers with personal attention, so those companies that retain salespeople must train them to be especially effective, efficient, and helpful. To attract new salespeople, companies are paying them quite well. The average cost of a single sales call to a potential business-to-business (B2B) buyer is about $500.[31] To get the most value from the sales call, companies need to have skillful and highly trained professional salespeople and consultants.

THE BUSINESS-TO-CONSUMER (B2C) SALES PROCESS

Most sales to consumers take place in retail stores where knowing the product comes first. It is also important to understand as much as possible about the type of people who shop at a given store. One thing is certain, though: a salesperson needs to focus on the customer and refrain from talking to fellow salespeople—or, worse, talking on the phone to friends—while customers are around.

The first formal step in the B2C sales process, then, is the *approach*. Sometimes, the second step of *ask questions* is also added to this first step. For example, many salespeople approach customers with an opening line like "May I help you?" but the answer too often is "No." A better approach is "How may I help you?" or simply "Welcome to our store." The idea is to show the customer that you are there to help and that you are friendly and knowledgeable.[32]

Discover what the customer wants first, and then make a *presentation*. Show customers how your products meet their needs and answer questions that help them choose the right products for them.

Next comes the *trial close*. "Would you like me to put that on hold?" or "Will you be paying for that with your store credit card?" are two such efforts. Selling is an art, and a salesperson must learn how to walk the fine line between being helpful and being pushy. Often individual buyers need some time alone to think about the purchase. The salesperson must respect that need but still be clearly available when needed.

You're familiar with all kinds of situations in which people apply personal selling. They sell all kinds of goods and services like food, clothing, automobiles, insurance, and real estate. What could they do to be more helpful to you, the customer?

After-sale *follow up* is an important but often neglected step. If the product is to be delivered, the salesperson should follow up to be sure it is delivered on time. The same is true if the product has to be installed. There is often a chance to sell more merchandise when a salesperson follows up on a sale. Figure 15.11 shows the B2C selling process.

■ **FIGURE 15.11**

STEPS IN THE BUSINESS-TO-CONSUMER (B2C) SELLING PROCESS

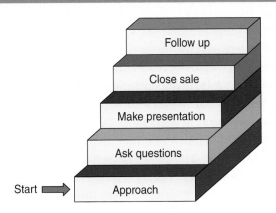

Progress Assessment

- What are the five traditional elements of the promotion mix?
- Define integrated marking communication and explain why it is important.
- Explain why advertising is moving from globalism to regionalism.
- What are the five steps in the B2C selling process?

Public Relations: Building Relationships

Public relations (PR) is the function that evaluates public attitudes, changes policies and procedures in response to the public's requests, and executes a program of action and information to earn public understanding and acceptance. The PR department maintains close ties with company stakeholders (e.g., customers, media, community leaders, and government officials). Public relations is a good alternative to advertising. As newspapers cut back on their reporting staff, they are looking for other sources of news information, including publicity releases. Linking up with bloggers has become an important way to keep company names in the news.

> **public relations (PR)**
> The function that evaluates public attitudes, changes policies and procedures in response to the public's requests, and executes a program of action and information to earn public understanding and acceptance.

PUBLICITY: THE TALKING ARM OF PR

Publicity is the talking arm of PR and one of the major functions of almost all organizations. Suppose you want to introduce your restaurant, Very Vegetarian, but you have little money to promote it. One effective way to reach the public is through publicity.

> **publicity**
> Any information about an individual, product, or organization that is distributed to the public through the media and that is not paid for or controlled by the seller.

Publicity is any information about an individual, product, or organization that is distributed to the public through the media and that is not paid for, or controlled, by the seller. It takes skill to write interesting or newsworthy press releases that the media will want to publish. You may need to write different stories for different media.[33] One may introduce the new owners. Another may talk about the unusual product offerings. If the stories are published, news about your restaurant will reach many potential customers (and investors, distributors, and dealers), and you may be on your way to becoming a successful marketer. Publicity works only if the media find the material interesting or newsworthy. The idea, then, is to write publicity that meets those criteria.

Besides being free, publicity has several further advantages over other promotional tools, such as advertising. It may reach people who would not read an ad. It may appear on the front page of a newspaper or in some other prominent position, or be given air time on a television news show. Perhaps the greatest advantage of publicity is its believability. When a newspaper or magazine publishes a story as news, the reader treats that story as news—and news is more believable than advertising. Review the Making Ethical Decisions box for a dilemma that you might face as a marketer when you consider publicity.

Publicity has several disadvantages. Marketers have no control over whether, how, and when the media will use the story. The media are not obligated to use a publicity release, and most are ignored. Furthermore, the story may be altered so that it is not so positive. Also, once a story has run, it is not likely to be repeated, unlike advertising. To see that publicity is handled well by the media, establish a friendly relationship with media representatives and be responsive when they seek information. Then, when you want their support, they are more likely to co-operate.

Progress Assessment

- What is the responsibility of the public relations department?
- What are the advantages and disadvantages of publicity versus advertising?

Making ETHICAL DECISIONS

Is the Ad as Honest as the Product?

You are producing a high-fibre, nutritious cereal called Fiberrific and are having a modest degree of success. Research shows that your number of customers, or market segment, is growing but is still a relatively small percentage of breakfast cereal buyers. Generally, Fiberrific appeals mostly to health-conscious people aged 25 to 60. You are trying to broaden the appeal of your cereal to the under-25 and over-60 age groups. You know that Fiberrific is a tasty and healthy product that is good for customers. Joan, one of your managers, suggests that you stretch the truth a bit in your advertising and publicity material so that it will attract more consumers in the age groups you are targeting. After all, your product can't hurt anybody and is actually good for them.

Joan's idea is to develop two ads, each with two segments. The first segment of one ad would show two senior citizens. She is on a tennis court holding a racquet and talking across the net to a man. She is complaining that she seems to tire easily. The next segment would show the same two people, with the woman looking lively and saying that she tried this new breakfast cereal, Fiberrific, for two weeks and feels so energized, like a new person. A similar ad would be used to show two young men walking uphill and talking. The first segment would show the man wondering why he tires so easily and the second one would show the same scene, with one man now a little ahead of the other, looking lively and stating that he is amazed at the improvement in his energy and endurance after eating Fiberrific for only two weeks. Would you go along with Joan's suggestion? What is your decision based on? Explain.

Sales Promotion: Giving Buyers Incentives

Sales promotion is the promotional tool that stimulates consumer purchasing and dealer interest by means of short-term activities See Figure 15.12 for business-to-consumer sales promotion examples, as well as advantages and disadvantages of each. You can stimulate sales at Very Vegetarian by putting half-off coupons in the school paper and home mailers. Business-to-business sales promotion techniques include trade shows, portfolios for salespeople, deals (e.g., price reductions), catalogues, and conventions.

> **sales promotion**
> The promotional tool that stimulates consumer purchasing and dealer interest by means of short-term activities.

Sales promotion programs are designed to supplement personal selling, advertising, PR, and other promotional efforts by creating enthusiasm for the overall promotional program. Sales promotion can take place both within and outside the company. The most important internal sales promotion efforts are directed at salespeople and other customer-contact people, such as customer-service representatives

■ **FIGURE 15.12**

BUSINESS-TO-CONSUMER SALES PROMOTION TECHNIQUES

KIND OF SALES PROMOTION	OBJECTIVES	ADVANTAGES	DISADVANTAGES
Coupons	Stimulate demand	Encourage retailer support	Consumers delay purchases
Deals	Increase trial; retaliate against competitor's actions	Reduce consumer risk	Consumers delay purchases; reduce perceived product value
Premiums	Build goodwill	Consumers like free or reduced-price merchandise	Consumers buy for premium, not product
Contests	Increase consumer purchases; build business inventory	Encourage consumer involvement with product	Require creative or analytical thinking
Sweepstakes	Encourage present customers to buy more; minimize brand switching	Get customer to use product and store more often	Sales drop after sweepstakes
Samples	Encourage new product trial	Low risk for consumer	High cost for company
Loyalty programs	Encourage repeat purchases	Help create loyalty	High cost for company
Point-of-purchase displays	Increase product trial; provide in-store support for other promotions	Provide good product visibility	Hard to get retailer to allocate high-traffic space
Rebates	Encourage customers to purchase; stop sales decline	Effective at stimulating demand	Easily copied; steal sales from future; reduce perceived product value
Product placements	Introduce new products; demonstrate product use	Positive message in a non-commercial setting	Little control over presentation of product

and clerks. Internal sales promotion efforts include (1) sales training; (2) the development of sales aids such as flip charts, portable audiovisual displays, and videos; and (3) participation in trade shows where salespeople can get leads. Other employees who deal with the public may also receive special training to improve their awareness of the company's offerings and make them an integral part of the total promotional effort.

After generating enthusiasm internally, marketers may want to make distributors and dealers eager to help promote the product. Trade shows allow marketing intermediaries to see products from many different sellers and make comparisons among them. Today, virtual trade shows on the Internet, called *webinars,* enable buyers to see many products without leaving the office. Such promotions are usually interactive, so buyers can ask questions, and the information is available 24/7.

After the company's employees and intermediaries have been motivated with sales promotion efforts, the next step is to promote to final consumers using samples, coupons, store demonstrations, rebates, displays, and so on. Sales promotion is an ongoing effort to maintain enthusiasm, so sellers use different strategies over time to keep the ideas fresh. You could put food displays in your Very Vegetarian restaurant to show customers how attractive the products look. You could also sponsor in-store cooking demonstrations to attract new vegetarians.

Sampling lets people try a new product for no charge. Grocery stores have people handing out small portions of food and beverage products to encourage new-product trial and hopefully, purchase. What are some advantages of sampling food products that advertising can't duplicate? Would you recommend standing outside Very Vegetarian and giving out samples as a way to attract attention and generate sales?

Direct Marketing

Direct marketing includes any activity that directly links manufacturers or intermediaries with the ultimate customer. It includes direct mail, catalogue sales, and telemarketing. It uses direct communication with customers to generate a response in the form of an order, a request for further information, or a visit to a retail outlet.

direct marketing
Any activity that directly links manufacturers or intermediaries with the ultimate customer.

Direct marketing has become popular because shopping from home or work is more convenient for consumers than going to stores. Instead of driving to a mall, people can shop online. Or they can browse catalogues and advertising supplements in the newspaper and magazines and then buy by phone, mail, or online. For example, clothing company L.L. Bean *<http://www.llbean.com>* put pressure on rivals by eliminating shipping charges. That made the company even more attractive for people who like to shop by catalogue or online.

Direct marketing took on a new dimension with interactive video. Companies that use interactive video have become major competitors to those who market through static paper catalogues. For example, customers watching a video of a model moving and turning around in a dress get a much better idea of the look and feel than simply seeing it in a printed photo.

Progress Assessment

- What are the sales promotion techniques used to reach consumers?
- What are the sales promotion techniques used to reach businesses?
- Why has direct marketing become popular?

Word of Mouth and Other Promotional Tools

Although word of mouth was not traditionally listed as one of the major promotional efforts (it was not considered to be manageable), it is now one of the most effective, especially on the Internet.[34] In **word-of-mouth promotion**, people tell other people about products they have purchased. We've already discussed the role of social media in spreading word of mouth. Beyond word of mouth is customer participation. That is, getting customers to provide constructive suggestions and share their ideas on how to shape product and service offerings.[35]

> **word-of-mouth promotion**
> A promotional tool that involves people telling other people about products they have purchased.

Anything that encourages people to talk favourably about an organization can be effective word of mouth.[36] For example, stores use clowns, banners, music, fairs, and other attention-getting devices to create word of mouth. Clever commercials can also generate word of mouth. The more that people talk about your products and your brand name, the more easily customers remember them when they shop.

One especially effective strategy for spreading positive word of mouth is to send testimonials to current customers. Most companies use these only in promoting to new customers, but testimonials are also effective in confirming customers' beliefs that they chose the right company. Some companies make it a habit to ask their satisfied customers for referrals.

Word of mouth is so powerful that negative word of mouth can hurt a firm badly. Criticism of a product or company can spread through online forums, social media, and websites. Addressing customer complaints quickly and effectively is one of the best ways to reduce the effects of negative word of mouth.

What are some strategies for creating positive word of mouth about Very Vegetarian? If your efforts are successful, your message may "go viral" and be seen by millions of consumers.[37] **Viral marketing** includes any strategy that encourages people to pass on a marketing message to others, creating exponential growth in the message's influence as the message can reach thousands to millions of potential customers.[38] Many viral marketing programs give away free products or services, often in exchange for valuable e-mail addresses. Free attracts attention: once you have their attention, customers can see other products or services you offer and buy those.

viral marketing
Any strategy that encourages people to pass on a marketing message to others, creating exponential growth in the message's influence as the message reaches thousands to millions of potential customers.

Blogging

A **blog**—short for web log—is an online diary that looks like a web page but is easier to create and update by posting text, photos, or links to other sites. There are hundreds of millions of blogs online. How do blogs affect marketing? Creating a blog is a great way to interact with customers. Businesses can attract new customers when they coordinate their social media profiles with their blogs. As people click through the social media profile, it helps to improve the company's website ranking. People love to share content they find relevant.

blog
An online diary (web log) that looks like a web page but is easier to create and update by posting text, photos, or links to other sites.

In order for a blog to succeed, a business must take time to post and respond to the customers that leave comments. They can use some of the comments to help create new posts. They have to keep customers coming back to the blog for new information. If the blog isn't kept updated, it will lose traffic and as a result, its power as a promotional tool.

Mobile marketing allows marketers to reach customers through text messaging. Have you received such promotional messages? For which products are they most effective? Would this be a good strategy for Very Vegetarian?

Podcasting

Podcasting is a means of distributing multimedia digital files on the Internet for downloading to a portable media player. Podcasts are important because they are a great way to capture your existing and prospective customers' attention for an extended period of time by giving them something of value that is easy for them to understand.[39] Many companies have also found success in creating videos for YouTube.

> **podcasting**
> A means of distributing multimedia digital files on the Internet for downloading to a portable media player.

Mobile Marketing

Most marketers make sure their media are viewable on mobile devices like tablets and smartphones. One key to success, therefore, is to keep the message brief because mobile users do not want to read through too much text. With mobile media, marketers can use text messaging to promote sweepstakes, send customers news or sports alerts, and give them company information. Companies can determine where you are and send you messages about restaurants and other services in your vicinity.

Managing the Promotion Mix: Putting It All Together

Each target group calls for a separate promotion mix. Advertising is most efficient for reaching large groups of customers whose members share similar traits. Personal selling is best for selling to organizations. To motivate people to buy now rather than later, marketers use sales promotions like sampling, coupons, discounts, special displays, and premiums. Publicity supports other efforts and can create a good impression among all customers. Word of mouth is often the most powerful promotional tool. Generate it by listening, being responsive, and creating an impression worth passing on to others that you spread through blogging, podcasting, and tweeting.

Push and Pull Strategies

How do producers move products to consumers? In a **push strategy**, the producer uses advertising, personal selling, sales promotion, and all other promotional tools to convince *channel members* (e.g., wholesalers and retailers) to stock and sell merchandise, *pushing* products through the distribution system to the stores. If the push strategy works, consumers will walk into a store, see the product, and buy it.

> **push strategy**
> Promotional strategy in which the producer uses advertising, personal selling, sales promotion, and all other promotional tools to convince wholesalers and retailers to stock and sell merchandise.

A **pull strategy** directs heavy advertising and sales promotion efforts toward *consumers*. If the pull strategy works, consumers will go to the store and ask for the products. The store owner will order them from the wholesaler, who in turn will order them from the producer. Products are thus *pulled* through

Ads in bus shelters are nothing new, but Kraft pumped hot air into 10 bus stops to promote its Stove Top stuffing mix. The idea was to remind consumers of the warm feeling they got when eating the product. Do you think giving consumers experiences (like warmth on a cold day) is an effective way to remind them of a product?

the distribution system. Of course, a company could use both strategies in a major promotional effort. The latest pull and push strategies are being conducted online with companies sending messages to both consumers and businesses.

pull strategy
Promotional strategy in which heavy advertising and sales promotion efforts are directed toward consumers so that they will request the products from retailers.

It is important to make promotion part of a total systems approach to marketing. That is, promotion is part of supply-chain management. Retailers work with producers and distributors to make the supply chain as efficient as possible. Then a promotional plan could be developed for the *whole* system. The idea is to develop a total product offer that would appeal to everyone: manufacturers, distributors, retailers, and customers.

Progress Assessment

- What is viral marketing?
- Describe word-of-mouth promotion and list three other promotional tools.
- How does a push strategy differ from a pull strategy?

SUMMARY

LO1 **Explain the concept of a total product offer, and summarize the functions of packaging.**
A total product offer consists of everything that customers evaluate when deciding whether to buy something.

What's included in a total product offer?
A total product offer includes price, brand name, satisfaction in use, and more.

What are the functions of packaging?
The functions of packaging include the following: (1) attract the buyer's attention; (2) protect the goods inside, stand up under handling and storage, be tamperproof, and deter theft; (3) be easy to open and use; (4) describe the contents; (5) explain the benefits of the core product inside; (6) provide information about warranties, warnings, and other customer matters; and (7) indicate price, value, and uses.

LO2 **Describe the product life cycle.**
The product life cycle is a theoretical model of what happens to sales and profits for a product class over time.

What are the four stages in the product life cycle?
The four product life cycle stages are introduction, growth, maturity, and decline. Review Figure 15.2 for a discussion on how the stages of the product life cycle relate to a firm's marketing objectives and marketing mix actions.

LO3 **List the various pricing objectives and strategies, and explain why non-pricing strategies are growing in importance.**
Pricing is one of the four Ps of marketing.

What are pricing objectives?
Pricing objectives include achieving a target profit, building traffic, increasing market share, creating an image, and meeting social goals.

What's the break-even point?
At the break-even point, total cost equals total revenue. Sales beyond that point are profitable.

What strategies can marketers use to determine a product's price?
For new products, a skimming price or a penetration price strategy is considered. Other strategies include cost-oriented pricing, demand-oriented pricing, and competition-oriented pricing.

Why do companies use non-price strategies?
Pricing is one of the easiest marketing strategies to copy. Therefore, often it is not a good long-run competitive tool. Instead, marketers may compete using non-price strategies that are harder to copy, including offering great service, educating customers, and establishing long-term relationships with customers.

LO4 **Explain the concept of marketing channels, and the importance of retailing.**
A channel of distribution consists of a set of marketing intermediaries, such as agents, brokers, wholesalers, and retailers, that join together to transport and store goods in their path (or channel) from producers to customers.

How do marketing intermediaries add value?

Intermediaries perform certain marketing tasks—such as transporting, storing, selling, advertising, and relationship building—faster and cheaper than most manufacturers could. Channels of distribution ensure communication flows and the flow of money and title to goods. They also help ensure that the right quantity and assortment of goods will be available when and where needed.

Why is retailing important?

A retailer is an organization that sells to ultimate consumers. Retailing is important to our economy. In 2014, retail trade generated over $505 billion and employed more than 1.9 million Canadians.

What is non-store retailing?

Non-store retailing is retailing done outside a traditional store. Non-store retailing includes electronic retailing; telemarketing; vending machines, kiosks, and carts; and direct selling. Telemarketing can also be used as part of direct marketing, which is a promotional tool.

LO5 **Define promotion, and list the five traditional tools that make up the promotion mix.**
Promotion is an effort by marketers to inform and remind people in the target market about products and to persuade them to participate in an exchange.

What are the five traditional promotional tools that make up the promotional mix?

The five traditional promotional tools are advertising, personal selling, public relations, sales promotion, and direct marketing. The product can also be a promotional tool which is why it's shown in the middle of Figure 15.9.

What are examples of other promotional tools?

In word-of-mouth promotion, people tell other people about products they have purchased. Other promotional tools include blogging, podcasting, and mobile marketing.

KEY TERMS

advertising	exclusive distribution	psychological pricing
agents/brokers	high–low pricing strategy	public relations (PR)
blog	integrated marketing	publicity
brand	communication (IMC)	pull strategy
brand equity	intensive distribution	push strategy
brand loyalty	marketing intermediaries	retailer
brand manager	penetration price strategy	sales promotion
break-even analysis	personal selling	selective distribution
bundling	podcasting	skimming price strategy
channel of distribution	price leadership	social commerce
competition-based pricing	product differentiation	target costing
direct marketing	product life cycle	telemarketing
direct selling	product line	total fixed costs
electronic retailing	product mix	total product offer (value
everyday low pricing (EDLP)	promotion mix	package)

value   viral marketing   word-of-mouth promotion
variable costs   wholesaler

CRITICAL THINKING

1. What value enhancers affected your choice of school to attend? Did you consider size, location, price, reputation, library and research services, sports, courses offered, job placement opportunities (e.g., internship), and exchange opportunities? What factors were most important? Why? What schools were your alternatives? Why didn't you choose them?

2. Which intermediary do you think is most important and why? What changes are happening to companies in that area?

3. What kinds of problems can emerge if a firm doesn't communicate with environmentalists, the news media, and the local community? Do you know of any firms that aren't responsive to your community? What are the consequences?

4. As interactive communications between companies and customers grow, do you think traditional advertising will grow or decline? What will be the effect of this growth or decline on the price we pay for TV programs, newspapers, and magazines?

5. How have blogging, podcasting, and social media affected other media you use, like newspapers or television? Do you read print newspapers now or do you get your news some other way? Do you watch programs on TV or on other devices? How has the move away from print and network television affected advertising?

DEVELOPING WORKPLACE SKILLS

Key: ● **Team**   ★ **Analytic**   ▲ **Communication**   ◻ **Technology**

★▲ 1. Look around your classroom and notice the different types of shoes students are wearing. What product qualities do you think they considered when they chose their shoes? Then, ask them this question: How important were price, style, brand name, and colour? Describe the product offerings you would feature in a new shoe store designed to appeal to students.

●★ 2. In small groups, discuss the importance of price when buying the following products: clothes,
▲   milk, computers, haircuts, and rental cars. What non-price factors, if any, are more important than price? How much time did you and your peers spend evaluating factors other than price when making such purchases?

▲★ 3. In class, discuss the differences between wholesaling and retailing and why retailing has more appeal for students considering jobs. Since fewer students seek jobs in wholesaling than in retailing, do you think wholesaling jobs may be easier to get?

▲★ 4. Scan your local newspaper or search online for examples of publicity, such as stories of new products and sales promotion (e.g., coupons, contests, and sweepstakes). Share your examples and discuss the effectiveness of such promotional efforts with the class.

●★ 5. In small groups, list six goods and services most students own or use and discuss promotional
▲   techniques—advertising, personal selling, PR, sales promotions, direct marketing, social media, or word of mouth—that prompt them to buy. Which technique(s) seems most effective for your group? Why?

ANALYZING MANAGEMENT DECISIONS

Measuring Marketing Effectiveness

One of the major issues facing marketers today is measuring the effectiveness of various marketing campaigns. In the past, marketers set a budget for advertising, personal selling, and the like based on past sales or the need to push future sales. Measuring results has always been difficult and was given less attention. Now, however, marketers are demanding more accountability from their advertising agencies, their sales forces, and their website activities. They want to know who is receiving their messages and what the results are.

Many companies do not know how to establish such *metrics*, or measures of effectiveness. Digital media have more accurate metrics, and these are forcing marketers to find more reliable statistics for traditional marketing methods like TV advertising. Some companies have turned to the finance department to help develop metrics. The question often comes down to whether the measure should be of sales or of customer attitudes. Some 60 percent of marketers measure customer attitudes as a result of marketing campaigns, but fewer than 40 percent use the data for preparing their marketing budgets, preferring instead to rely on their own instincts.

Discussion Questions

1. You are planning a marketing campaign for Very Vegetarian. How might you go about measuring the effectiveness of your advertising?

2. What would your reaction be if you found potential customers had heard about your restaurant but had not yet acted on that information and come in to buy?

3. Using your own reactions, discuss what marketing tools are most effective in reaching students and others. Talk with fellow students from different ethnic and age groups to determine whether their answers are different from yours and how.

VIDEO CASE 15

AWAKE Chocolate

Dragons' Den, a CBC production, is the highest-rated Canadian unscripted program on during the regular television season with an average weekly audience of more than 1.2 million Canadians. It also boasts an active online community averaging more than 650,000 page views per month. Aspiring entrepreneurs pitch their business concepts and products to a panel of successful Canadian entrepreneurs in exchange for money and ownership in their companies. These aspiring entrepreneurs must get all of the money they are requesting or they will go home with nothing.

Based on their experience at Kraft Canada and PepsiCo, friends Dan Tzotzis, Matt Schnarr, and Adam Deremo decided to start a business. They knew that products with functional benefits were the single biggest driver of growth over the past decade in consumer packaged goods. Their company is AWAKE Chocolate <*http://www.awakechocolate.com*>, and the product, AWAKE, is a caffeinated chocolate bar that delivers 140 milligrams of caffeine. This is equivalent to a cup of coffee. Priced at $2.50, it is also one dollar less than an energy drink.

Armed with commitments to list the chocolate bar in 3,000 stores, including Shell, Shoppers Drug Mart, and Husky, the partners entered *Dragons' Den* with a venture capital pitch of $200,000 in exchange for 20 percent of the company. The company valuation of $1 million was based on 50 percent of Year 1 sales forecasts. The result was two offers with Dragons David Chilton and Kevin O'Leary in a deal that included a 7.5 percent return of capital royalty.

"The taste of the chocolate brought me in," states Chilton. "I expected it to have a caffeine aftertaste and be an inferior chocolate and neither was the case. I also thought they were very credible—they answered all the questions well, the math was right, they had the right backgrounds. It was an unusual pitch in that I liked everything about it," Chilton said.

Sources: "Who is AWAKE?" AWAKE Chocolate, *http://www.awakechocolate.com/*, downloaded 13 April 2015; "Dragons' Den Presents The Next Gen Den, Targeting Canadian Business Start-Ups Through An Online Platform," CBC, 21 January 2015, *http://www.cbc.ca/mediacentre/dragons-den-presents-the-next-gen-den-targeting-canadian-business-start-ups-through-an-online-platfo.html*; "Dragons' Den Canada—AWAKE Chocolate," *Dragons' Den*, YouTube video, 28 August 2013, *https://www.youtube.com/watch?v=dkKt4N-8RBg*; and Mary Teresa Bitti, "Dragons eat up Awake chocolate's pitch," *The Financial* Post, 11 February 2013, *http://business.financialpost.com/entrepreneur/dragons-eat-up-awake-chocolates-pitch*.

Discussion Questions

1. Who is the target market for this chocolate bar? What promotional recommendations do you have that would attract this target market?

2. Do some research on AWAKE Chocolate. How has appearing on CBC's *Dragons' Den* impacted the company?

3. As more competitors enter the marketplace, what can the company do to protect its sales?

RUNNING CASE

Marketing: The Fox 40® Sonik Blast Whistle: Breaking the Sound Barrier!

For successful Canadian entrepreneur and inventor Ron Foxcroft, it all started in 1982 when he purchased Fluke Transport, a Southern Ontario trucking business. The company slogan—If It's On Time . . . It's A "FLUKE"—was soon recognized throughout North America. Over the years, Foxcroft diversified into new ventures and the Foxcroft Group of Companies now includes Fluke Transportation Group, Fluke Warehousing Inc., Foxcroft Capital Corp., Fox 40 International Inc., and Fox 40 USA Inc.

The formation of Fox 40 International Inc. (Fox 40) is the result of a dream for a pealess whistle. When developing his first whistle, Ron was motivated by his knowledge and experience as an international basketball referee. Frustrated with faulty pea whistles, he spent three years of development with design consultant Chuck Shepherd. They had about 25 prototypes but narrowed them down after two years to 14 prototypes, and then down to 2 prototype whistles that worked. This resulted in the Fox 40® Classic Whistle. (The Whistle was named for Ron and that he was 40 when he applied for the patent.)

Introduced in 1987, this finely tuned precision instrument does not use a pea to generate sound. In fact, there are no moving parts. The patented design moves the air blast through three tuned chambers. This whistle, and all the subsequent whistles that have been introduced, is 100 percent constructed of high-impact ABS plastic so it is impervious to moisture. Wet or dry, Fox 40 Pealess Whistles cannot be overblown and never fail—the harder you blow, the louder the sound! They can be heard for miles and work in all conditions. They are faultless, reliable, and trusted.

Fox 40, a proudly Canadian company, dominates the global whistle industry. Tens of thousands of Fox 40 Whistles are produced monthly for shipment to 140 countries. A mould may be made offshore due to the cost savings (at least $100,000); however, Fox 40 owns all of its moulds. Approximately 90 percent of the company's products are made in Canada with select components coming from overseas markets. Final assembly occurs in Canada. While the first product was the Fox 40® Classic Whistle, the company now has over 900 active stock-keeping units (SKUs). Its product mix includes 19 Fox 40 Whistles styles (e.g., Fox 40 electronic whistle); Lanyards & Attachments (e.g., flex coils); additional brands that include Fox 40 Gear; SmartCoach Coaching Boards; SICK Self Impression Custom Kit, and Heat Alert Mouthguards; Marine & Outdoor Products (e.g., Xplorer LED Light); Pink Products; and Logo Imprinted Products.

How did Ron tackle the $150,000 debt that he had incurred in developing the Fox 40® Classic Whistle? The answer is marketing. "I took the two whistles to the Pan Am Games in August 1987. I went upstairs in the dorm where the referees were living, and at 2 a.m., I blew the Whistle. Hundreds of referees opened the doors, standing there in their underwear, wondering what kind of whistle they heard. The next day, I got orders for 20,000 Whistles at $6.00 each in U.S. funds. That was $8.00 per Whistle in Canadian funds. My $150,000 debt was covered."

Over the years, Fox 40® has continued to introduce new whistles in its whistle product line. One example is the Fox 40® Sonik Blast. This whistle was in response to referee requests for a louder whistle in large stadiums. Let us consider how the four Ps of marketing were applied to this product.

Product: Introduced in 2010, the Fox 40® Sonik Blast is a two-chamber whistle that exceeds 120 decibels of sound. (This is louder than the Fox 40® Classic Whistle's 115 decibels of power.) It also has no down side, which means that it does not matter which side you put in your mouth as both sides are up. As a result, a referee (or anyone else that uses the whistle) does not have to think about which side of the whistle needs to go "up" before blowing it. To slow down counterfeiters, the cushioned mouth guard

(CMG) feature became available at the same time. The CMG is a cushioned mouthgrip for better grip, better control, and a softer feel on one's teeth.

In support of its GREEN PLAN the company has changed its packaging. The packaging is made from recycled water and pop bottles that use virgin polyethylene terephthalate (PET). The switch to PET plastic for the blister is more environmentally friendly. There has also been a movement away from clam packaging. This has been replaced with a packaging system that uses radio frequency (RF) and heat, known as RF/heat packaging, to seal the blister within two cards. The blister and cards can be separated and added to Blue Box recycling. An added benefit is that the packaging is tamper proof. Included in each package is print material that contains recyclable and/or recycled post-consumer waste material. This colourful cardboard communicates the product's brand name and benefits, head office location, and contact information.

According to Dave Foxcroft, President and COO, one advantage that the company has in manufacturing the whistles in Canada is that they can build to order products and different packages, given the market. Since different markets require different packages, the actual package will vary depending on the marketing channel. For example, the package and label for a Fox 40® Whistle sold in a Canadian Tire store may be different for a whistle that is targeted to referees in the sports aisle versus a whistle that is placed in the marine area. Lately, Dave has noticed that more distributors are moving away from these private labels (whereby Fox 40® manufactures the product with the distributor's name on it) and requesting that the whistles focus on the Fox 40® brand. These distributors were noticing that they were losing sales as customers were looking specifically for the Fox 40 brand and did not realize that the private labels were also Fox 40® Whistles.

The total product offer also includes the high level of service that employees provide to customers. "We stand out," states Ron. "When you call the company, you get a live person. You don't need to go through layers of management to get an answer. The employee can answer a question or find someone right away to answer the question. Customers will not get unanswered questions."

Price: Similar to the other whistles, the Fox 40® Sonik Blast is a premium-priced whistle. This is justified by the product's features, benefits, and high quality. When the Whistle was first introduced, an introductory promotional price was offered to the company's distributors, including trade show specials. The price Fox 40® charges to its distributors varies depending on several factors: the target market (e.g., sports or marine); the geographic market; and the volume purchased. For example, some global markets are driven by price versus quality. While the suggested retail price is $8.95, it is the distributors that ultimately set the price in their markets. According to Dave, "These distributors own their markets and they know the best price to charge in their specific area. Fox 40® provides its customers with the best products and the goal is that all of the channel members in the distribution channel are financially successful along the way."

Pricing decisions are influenced by many factors that impact costs. For example, Dave cites the ever-changing government regulations around the world in reference to colour, plastics, chemicals, etc. As a result, the Whistle is not the same today as it was 20 years ago due to product restrictions. According to Juliana Child, Manager, Marketing & Events, the company also considers the cost of new imprinting techniques that produce better quality logos. Given such changes, the costs and price are revised annually for imprinted products.

Place: The majority of sales are generated through an indirect channel of distribution. Fox 40® follows a B2B marketing channel structure that incorporates distributors between the company and its ultimate users. These distributors perform a variety of marketing channel functions including selling, stocking, and delivering the Fox 40® products.

Customers interested in buying Fox 40® products can do so directly from established distributors and retail partners or through electronic marketing channels such as <http://www.fox40shop.com>. If a customer chooses to purchase a product through this direct online site, a commission is paid to the local distributor or retail partner. The commission can be used toward future purchases. This unique arrangement is in recognition of the importance of this business-to-business relationship and the company's commitment to support its channel members. For those channel members that choose to join the site, Fox 40 communicates their information (e.g., name and location) in the package that includes the ordered product. This way, customers are made aware of local channel members for future purchases. Information is also sent to channel members about products that are being ordered by customers in their local area so that they can review products that they carry.

Promotion: The overall promotion budget is 12 percent of the previous year's sales. Money is directed primarily in the areas of advertising and sales. This budget is broken down as follows:

- 65 percent is allocated to direct sales (45 percent is for awareness and 25 percent includes online social media activities, support of the *www.fox40shop.com* site, etc.)
- 9 percent is allocated to research and development
- 6 percent is allocated to public relations (which includes community social responsibility initiatives)
- 20 percent is allocated to trade shows and customer visits

When the Fox 40® Sonik Blast was introduced, *public relations* activities included media releases that highlighted the features and benefits of the new product. Web blasts were sent to channel members in the different segments (i.e., marine, safety, etc.) via e-mail marketing tool, Constant Contact. Fox 40 also has a B2B online site where channel members can access information such as catalogues, product images, etc. While the paper catalogue continues to be available as it remains the company's best sales tool, the online site supports channel members.

Advertising is a large part of the promotional budget. While on occasion there may be ads that highlight only one whistle, the majority of ads highlight the family of Fox 40® Whistles. Advertising in trade magazines that target the company's different markets, such as *REFEREE Magazine,* occurred to promote the Fox 40® Sonik Blast. Social media initiatives were also created to introduce the new product. This included banner ads and Facebook advertising.

Product seeding was a *trade sales promotion* strategy that was targeted to channel members. This form of sampling meant getting the product into the hands of those that would actually use the whistle. For example, free Fox 40® Sonik Blast Whistles, with the distributor's contact information printed on them, were sent to approved distributors. These distributors were then encouraged to hand out the free whistles to users in their markets.

When you consider *personal selling* efforts, company representatives attend approximately 20 trade shows per year. The product was promoted at trade shows that target the sport, safety, outdoor, pet, and marine markets. Occasionally, a show promotion was offered but it was primarily the distributor that would offer the promotion. Distributor site visits around the world are also an ongoing aspect of the personal selling element of the promotion mix. These efforts are used to maintain and build long-term and profitable relationships with global distributors.

Increasingly, company attention is focusing on *direct marketing.* Information from current customers and prospects that is generated at trade shows is updated in the company's database. Personalized communications (i.e., e-blasts, letters, etc.) are created and sent out. This is followed by personal communication to confirm if a sale could be generated. There is a particular focus on current customers. As Ron states, "The best increase in sales is from within the company."

Fox 40 also runs a promotional products division. Approximately 65 percent of all whistles sold have another organization's logo on them. According to Juliana, since the Fox 40® brand is so well established, it can effectively be directed to promotional sales. This co-branding is another opportunity to link the Fox 40® brand with a company brand that is meaningful to the receiver of the whistle. Given the different package and imprint capabilities, the company can quickly fill personalized orders. Dave believes that this number will increase to 70 percent by mid-2013 as safety awareness is growing. "Organizations recognize the increasing importance of safety," says Dave. "These organizations want to associate themselves with a superior performing safety brand like Fox 40®."

Sources: Ron Foxcroft, CEO of Fox 40 International Inc. and Chairman and CEO of Fluke Transportation, in-person interview, 25 June 2012, Hamilton; and Dave Foxcroft, President and COO, Fox 40 International Inc., in-person interview, 25 June 2012, Hamilton; "The Fox 40 pea-less whistle story," *Canada.com*, 4 April 2012, *www.canada.com/sports/football/less+whistle+story/6410154/story.html*; Kelley Horton, Vice President Sales, Fox 40 International Inc., interview, 24 June 2008; Juliana Child, Manager, Marketing & Events, Fox 40 International Inc., interview, 24 June 2008; and "Not An Inadvertent Whistle," *REFEREE*, July 2007, 45–47

Discussion Questions

1. What new-product pricing strategy did Fox 40 International Inc. use for the Fox 40® Sonik Blast?

2. What retail distribution strategy do you think is used for the Fox 40® Sonik Blast? Justify your answer.

3. Which promotional strategy is the most effective when selling the Fox 40® Sonik Blast? Explain.

PART 6

CHAPTER 16

Understanding Accounting and Financial Information

LEARNING OBJECTIVES

After you have read and studied this chapter, you should be able to:

LO1 Describe the role that accounting and financial information play for a business and for its stakeholders.

LO2 Identify the different disciplines within the accounting profession.

LO3 List the steps in the accounting cycle, distinguish between accounting and bookkeeping, and explain how computers are used in accounting.

LO4 Explain how the major financial statements differ.

LO5 Demonstrate the application of ratio analysis in reporting financial information.

PROFILE

GETTING TO KNOW DEBORAH WATT OF LOCKHEED MARTIN CANADA INC.

Headquartered in Bethesda, Maryland, in the United States, Lockheed Martin Corporation is a global security and aerospace company that employs about 112,000 people worldwide. It is principally engaged in the research, design, development, manufacture, integration, and sustainment of advanced technology systems, products, and services. Lockheed Martin Canada <*http://www.lockheedmartin.ca*>, a wholly-owned subsidiary of Lockheed Martin Corporation, has been a valued partner to the Canadian military since 1937 when it first established a business presence. Today, more than 500 professionals work in locations across the country in support of all branches of the Canadian Forces.

Lockheed Martin Canada is the prime contractor for the modernization of the combat systems on board the Halifax-class frigates. Awarded the contract in 2008, the company works in partnership with the

Source: Alan Dean Photography

navy and shipyards on both West and East Coasts to replace major critical sensors and command and control systems, modernize operations rooms, and deliver a suite of related simulation/training systems.

Additionally, Lockheed Martin Canada is a key provider of information management/information technology systems for both military and civil government departments, including the Canadian Forces Health Information System, the Canadian Forces Command System, the Air Force Command Information System, and the Defence Information Services Broker.

The company delivered mission-critical software to Statistics Canada for the past two censuses that allowed the country to be the first in the world to conduct an online census.

Lockheed Martin Canada has a rich history in providing electronic products and systems to all branches of the Forces. In-service support is a critical element of the company's business and it currently supports various elements of Canada's fleet of CP-140, CF-18, and CC-130J aircraft as well as coastal radar systems located on Vancouver Island and Newfoundland.

Taking into account its historic relationship with the Canadian forces and future plans and commitments, the company has over a century of commitment to Canada and the development of a North American defence industrial base. Beyond its defence partnerships, it stands ready to continue and grow its support to Canada's Census, health care management, information technology, as well as infrastructure and border security to ensure the safe, secure, and efficient transit of people, goods, and services between Canada and the United States.

Debbie Watt is the Controller at Lockheed Martin Canada in Ottawa, Ontario. With over 25 years' experience in accounting and auditing, she manages the accounting operations, internal controls, financial reporting, and cash management for this defence and security company that operates in six provinces across Canada. Watt enjoys working in a large company that focuses on leadership development and is committed to the highest standards of ethical conduct in all aspects of the business.

Prior to joining Lockheed Martin Canada, Watt worked closely with the owners of Trillium Converting Corporation, a paper converting company servicing Domtar *<http://www.domtar.com>*, to obtain financing to purchase several large paper converting machines to triple production at the Ottawa production facility and expand business into Montreal. Within her first five years as Controller, she developed and implemented a profit-sharing plan to motivate employees.

Watt worked her way up from a Waterloo, Ontario, co-op position to Audit Manager at Ginsberg, Gluzman, Fage & Levitz, Chartered Accountants *<http://www.ggfl.ca>* in Ottawa. She obtained her Chartered Accountant designation and her Certified Financial Planner designation after graduating from the University of Waterloo with a Bachelor of Mathematics, CA Option.

In addition to her busy family life with her supportive husband and two energetic teenage daughters, Watt is actively involved in her community. She prepares financial statements and charity returns as a board member for three charities: Suzart Productions Inc., Diamond United Cemetery, and the Arnprior and District Breast Cancer Support Group. She is also involved as the Scenic Artist at Suzart Productions Inc. where she explores her creative side painting sets for musical theatre productions.

Controlling costs, managing cash flows, understanding profit margins and taxes, and reporting financial results accurately are keys to survival for both profit-seeking and not-for-profit organizations. This chapter will introduce you to the accounting fundamentals and financial information critical to business success. The chapter also briefly explores the financial ratios that are essential in measuring business performance in a large or small business.

Sources: "Who We Are," Lockheed Martin Corporation, http://www.lockheedmartin.ca/us/who-we-are.html, downloaded 8 September 2015; and information provided by Lockheed Martin Canada Communications Department, June 2012.

 Describe the role that accounting and financial information play for a business and for its stakeholders.

The Role of Accounting Information

Small and large businesses often survive or fail according to how well they handle financial procedures. Financial management is the heartbeat of competitive businesses, and accounting information helps keep the heartbeat stable.

Accounting reports and financial statements reveal as much about a business's health as pulse and blood pressure readings tell us about a person's health. Thus, you have to know something about accounting if you want to succeed in business. It's almost impossible to understand business operations without being able to read, understand, and analyze accounting reports and financial statements.

By the end of this chapter, you should have a good idea of what accounting is, how it works, and the value it offers businesses. You should also know some accounting terms and understand the purpose of accounting statements. Your new understanding will pay off as you become more active in business, or will help you in simply understanding what is going on in the world of business and finance.

What Is Accounting?

Accounting is the recording, classifying, summarizing, and interpreting of financial events and transactions in an organization to provide management and other interested parties the financial information they need to make good decisions about its operation. Financial transactions include buying and selling goods and services, acquiring insurance, paying employees, and using supplies. Once the business's transactions have been recorded, they are usually classified into groups that have common characteristics. For example, all purchases are grouped together, as are all sales transactions. The method used to record and summarize accounting data into reports is an *accounting system* (see Figure 16.1).

accounting
The recording, classifying, summarizing, and interpreting of financial events and transactions to provide management and other interested parties the information they need to make good decisions.

■ **FIGURE 16.1**

THE ACCOUNTING SYSTEM

The inputs to an accounting system include sales documents and other records. The data are recorded, classified, and summarized. They are then put into summary financial statements, such as the income statement and balance sheet.

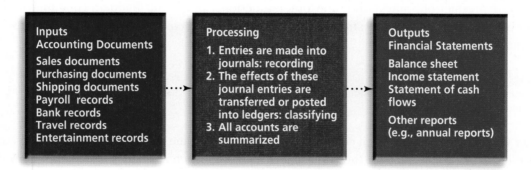

Inputs
Accounting Documents
Sales documents
Purchasing documents
Shipping documents
Payroll records
Bank records
Travel records
Entertainment records

Processing
1. Entries are made into journals: recording
2. The effects of these journal entries are transferred or posted into ledgers: classifying
3. All accounts are summarized

Outputs
Financial Statements
Balance sheet
Income statement
Statement of cash flows

Other reports
(e.g., annual reports)

A major purpose of accounting is to help managers make well-informed decisions. Another is to report financial information about the firm to interested stakeholders, such as employees, owners, creditors, suppliers, unions, community activists, investors, and the government (for tax purposes). Review Figure 16.2 for an overview. Accounting is divided into five key areas. Let's look at those areas next.

■ **FIGURE 16.2**

USERS OF ACCOUNTING INFORMATION AND THE REQUIRED REPORTS

Many types of organizations use accounting information to make business decisions. The reports needed vary according to the information each user requires. An accountant must prepare the appropriate forms.

Users	Type of Report
Government taxing authorities (e.g., Canada Revenue Agency)	Tax returns
Government regulatory agencies	Required reports
People interested in the organization's income and financial position (e.g., owners, creditors, financial analysts, and suppliers)	Financial statements found in annual reports (e.g., income statement, balance sheet, and statement of cash flows)
Managers of the firm	Financial statements and various internally distributed financial reports

LO2 Identify the different disciplines within the accounting profession.

Accounting Disciplines

You may think that accounting is only for profit-seeking firms. Nothing could be further from the truth. Accounting, often called the language of business, allows us to report financial information about not-for-profit organizations, such as churches, schools, hospitals, and government agencies.[1] The accounting profession is divided into five key working areas: (1) managerial accounting, (2) financial accounting, (3) auditing, (4) tax accounting, and (5) government and not-for-profit accounting. All five areas are important, and all create career opportunities.[2] Let's explore each in the following pages.

Managerial Accounting

Managerial accounting provides information and analyses to managers *inside* the organization to assist them in decision making. Managerial accounting is concerned with measuring and reporting costs of production, marketing, and other functions; preparing budgets (planning); checking whether or not business units are staying within their budgets (controlling); and designing strategies to minimize taxes.

> **managerial accounting**
> Accounting used to provide information and analyses to managers inside the organization to assist them in decision making.

Data within a company is often compared over a period of time to identify trends, or it is compared to other companies operating in the same industry when benchmarking a company's performance. For example, analysis of the accounts receivable (money that is owed to the company) will help in evaluating the credit policies of a company. Monitoring profit margins, unit sales, travel expenses, cash flow, inventory turnover, and other such data is critical to the success of a firm. Management decision making is based on such data.

Assembling an aircraft engine requires many tools, parts, raw materials, and other components as well as labour costs. Keeping these costs at a minimum and setting realistic production schedules is critical to a business's survival. What other internal departments must management accountants team with to ensure the company's competitiveness?

Some of the questions that managerial accounting reports are designed to answer include:

- What goods and services are selling the most and what promotional tools are working best?
- How quickly is the firm selling what it buys?
- What is the appropriate allocation of expenses between products?
- Which expenses change with changes in revenue?
- How much tax is the firm paying and how can it minimize that amount?
- Will the firm have enough cash to pay its bills? If not, has it made arrangements to borrow that money?

Another aspect of managerial accounting concerns sustainability practices employed by business organizations. At the age of 23, CEO Anshula Chowdhury founded Social Asset Measurements Inc. <*http://www.socialassets.org*>. The company uses a methodology called "social return on investment" to broadly assess the dollar value of a social or environmental action.[3] Social metrics focus on drivers of success, not just indicators, so that social organizations can make smarter decisions about where to put their limited resources.[4] See the Seeking Sustainability box for a discussion on what one company includes in its annual accountability report. With growing emphasis on global competition, outsourcing, and organizational cost-cutting, managerial accounting is an area of importance in terms of anyone's career.

Financial Accounting

Financial accounting differs from managerial accounting in that the information and analyses it generates are for people primarily *outside* the organization. The information goes not only to company owners, managers, and employees but also to creditors and lenders, unions, customers, suppliers, government agencies, and the general public. External users are interested in questions like:

- Is the organization profitable? Should we invest in this company?
- Is it able to pay its bills?
- How much debt does it owe?
- If we lend money to this company, will it be able to pay it back?

financial accounting
Accounting information and analyses prepared for people outside the organization.

These questions and others are often answered in the company's **annual report**, a yearly statement of the financial condition, progress, and expectations of an organization. As pressure from stakeholders for detailed financial information has grown, companies have poured more information than ever into their annual reports. Companies are seeking to reduce costs, as well as to be more environmentally responsible, by posting their annual reports on their websites.[5]

annual report
A yearly statement of the financial condition, progress, and expectations of an organization.

The annual reports of publicly traded companies are significantly more elaborate than for privately held companies for several reasons. First of all, securities commissions impose additional reporting requirements on publicly traded companies than for privately held companies. For publicly traded

Seeking SUSTAINABILITY

Annual Accountability Report: MEC

A sustainability report is a report published by a company or organization about the economic, environmental, and social impacts caused by its everyday activities. It also presents the organization's values and governance model, and demonstrates the link between its strategy and its commitment to a sustainable global economy. An increasing number of companies and organizations want to make their operations sustainable (i.e., last for a long time or indefinitely) and contribute to sustainable development. Sustainability reporting can help organizations to measure, understand, and communicate their economic, environmental, social, and governance performance.

More companies are committing to reporting their "green" initiatives via sustainability reports. Mountain Equipment Co-op's (MEC) most recent sustainability report highlights its performance in 13 areas: Bluesign®-approved materials, environmentally preferred materials, improving factory conditions, MEC carbon footprint, waste diversion, employee engagement, active members, member satisfaction, in-stock rating, community contributions, funding by area, annual sales, and inventory turnover. The results are subject to independent assurance or external review. Let's consider some examples.

MEC sources or requires organically grown cotton in the clothing it sells along with the growing use of recycled content. There has been a reduction in packaging materials. All factories that work with MEC must sign a Supplier Code of Conduct related to worker health and safety. More importantly, the company follows up with rotational audits, categorizing non-compliance issues up to a level of zero tolerance (e.g., in terms of child labour). It then works on reducing these issues.

Operationally, the company is working toward a goal of zero carbon emissions, which means diverting all material waste from landfills. It is currently at 91 percent. When tracking its carbon footprint, the key performance indicator (KPI) measures total greenhouse gas emissions from product transportation, facilities, business flights, and employee commuting in tonnes of carbon dioxide equivalent emissions. The goal is to reduce the footprint from the year before. Employee KPIs include training and support, hourly compensation rates, health and safety, turnover rates, and employee diversity (including numbers of female and visible minorities employed). Employee surveys are used to obtain some of the data.

Members are surveyed on issues such as product quality, functionality, and form; satisfaction; and product availability and advice provided. MEC reports on its promotion of recreation and leisure activity in Canada and its multi-million dollar contributions supporting community-based conservation. There is also some comment on its own economic viability using accounting data, which we will talk about in this chapter.

MEC takes issues surrounding sustainability very seriously. Why do you think companies like MEC are committing significant time and resources to these types of activities?

Source: Courtesy of Mountain Equipment Co-op and "About Sustainability Reporting," Global Reporting Initiative, https://www.globalreporting.org /information/sustainability-reporting/Pages/default.aspx, downloaded 20 April 2015.

Every public company is required to provide financial information. Users can access this information either from the company's website (e.g., Investor Relations tab) or from sites like SEDAR <*http://www.sedar.com*>. This information varies from a quarterly set of financial statements with accompanying notes to annual reports with a breadth of financial information. Have you analyzed a company's annual report for a project?

companies, many use their annual reports as public relations tools to communicate non-accounting information to stakeholders, such as shareholders, customers, the press, and others.[6] See Figure 16.3 for what can be found in an annual report.

It's critical for firms to keep accurate financial information. Some organizations employ a **private accountant** who works for a single firm, government agency, or not-for-profit organization. For those firms that do not need a full-time accountant, independent accounting firms provide the services needed,

■ **FIGURE 16.3**

ANNUAL REPORT INFORMATION

The annual reports of public companies are normally split into two sections. You may see photos of products, facilities, and personnel in the first section.

Section 1 (Non-Financial)	Section 2 (Financial)
A letter to shareholders from the chairperson and CEO	Summarized financial data
Descriptions of the company's management philosophy	Management's discussion and analysis, covering financial condition and results of operations
Products, successes, and occasionally failures	The basic financial statements
Exciting prospects and challenges for the future	Notes to the financial statements
	Report of independent accountants (auditor's opinion) and the management report

Source: Robert Libby et al., *Financial Accounting,* 5th Canadian ed. (Canada: McGraw-Hill Ryerson Ltd., 2014), 301.

for a fee. These **public accountants** provide accounting services to individuals or businesses, such as designing an accounting system and analyzing the financial strength of an organization. Large accounting and auditing firms operate internationally to serve large transnational companies.

> **private accountant**
> An accountant who works for a single firm, government agency, or not-for-profit organization.
>
> **public accountant**
> An accountant who provides his or her accounting services to individuals or businesses on a fee basis.

Accountants know it's vital for users of a firm's accounting information to be assured the information is accurate. The independent Accounting Standards Board (AcSB) has the authority to develop and establish accounting standards for use by all Canadian entities outside the public sector.[7] The AcSB adheres to a Statement of Best Practice, which is a memorandum of understanding between the International Accounting Standards Board (IASB) and other accounting standard setters.[8] For example, it develops and maintains Canadian accounting standards to support the **international financial reporting standards (IFRS)**, which are the common set of accounting principles, standards and procedures that accountants and companies use to compile financial statements.[9] Publicly traded companies are required to follow IFRS, while private companies can follow IFRS or another set of standards called ASPE (accounting standard for private enterprises). If accounting reports are prepared in accordance with IFRS or ASPE, users can expect the information to meet standards upon which accounting professionals have agreed.

> **international financial reporting standards (IFRS)**
> The common set of accounting principles, standards, and procedures that accountants and companies use to compile financial statements.

Unfortunately, the accounting profession suffered a dark period in the early 2000s when accounting scandals involving high-profile companies, such as Enron, WorldCom, and Tyco, raised public suspicions about the profession and of corporate integrity in general. Arthur Anderson, one of the world's leading accounting firms, was forced out of business after being convicted of obstruction of justice for shredding records in the Enron case. (The conviction was later overturned by the U.S. Supreme Court.) Canadian companies are not immune either; Nortel (no longer in business) was investigated for its accounting practices related to large bonuses paid to senior management.

Scrutiny of the accounting industry intensified and culminated with the U.S. Congress's passage of the Sarbanes-Oxley Act (called Sarbox).[10] Figure 16.4 lists some of the major provisions of Sarbox. This legislation created new government reporting standards for publicly traded companies. This Act also applies to any Canadian public company wishing to have its shares traded on an American stock

■ **FIGURE 16.4**

KEY PROVISIONS OF THE SARBANES-OXLEY ACT

- Prohibits accounting firms from providing certain non-auditing work (such as consulting services) to companies they audit
- Strengthens protection for whistleblowers who report wrongful actions of company officers
- Requires company CEOs and CFOs to certify the accuracy of financial reports and imparts strict penalties for any violation of securities reporting (e.g., earnings misstatements)
- Prohibits corporate loans to directors and executives of the company
- Establishes the five-member Public Company Accounting Oversight Board under the Securities and Exchange Commission (SEC) to oversee the accounting industry
- Stipulates that altering or destroying key audit documents will result in felony charges and significant criminal penalties

Reaching *Beyond* OUR BORDERS

Speaking a Universal Accounting Language

Throughout this text you've read about the tremendous impact the global market has on business. Companies like Coca-Cola, for example, earn the majority of their revenue from global markets, which helps their profitability. However, this also creates considerable accounting headaches. Since no global accounting system exists, multinationals like Coca-Cola must adapt their accounting procedures to different countries' rules. Each set of rules could result in differing amounts appearing in a set of financial statements based on the same set of transactions.

To eliminate this issue, over 100 countries are agreeing to use one set of rules, the international financial reporting standards (IFRS). This shift to global standards for accounting is supported by many accountants. For example, James Quigley, former chief executive officer of Deloitte Touche Tohmatsu <*http://www2.deloitte.com*>, one of the Big Four accounting firms, believes that since we have global capital markets, we need global standards for accounting.

In Canada, the AcSB has adopted the mandatory use of IFRS by all publicly accountable enterprises (PAEs). IFRS replaces previous Canadian generally accepted accounting principles as the acceptable set of accounting standards for PAEs. Canada Revenue Agency (CRA, <*http://www.cra-arc.gc.ca*>) does not specify that financial statements must be prepared following any particular type of accounting principles or standards; however, the AcSB requires PAEs to use IFRS in the preparation of all interim and annual financial statements. Most private companies also have the option to adopt IFRS for financial statement preparation.

Sources: "International Financial Reporting Standards (IFRS)," Canada Revenue Agency, 3 March 2015, http://www.cra-arc.gc.ca/tx/bsnss/tpcs/frs/menu-eng.html; Emily Chasan, "SEC's New Strategic Plan Backs Away from IFRS," *The Wall Street Journal*, 4 February 2014; Michael Cohn, "NASBA Questions FAF Funding of IFRS Foundation," *Accounting Today*, 20 February 2014; and Securities and Exchange Commission, www.sec.gov, accessed March 2014.

exchange. In Canada, the Ontario Securities Commission introduced Bill 198. CEOs and CFOs of public companies are now required to certify reports. Auditors are now also required to be part of the Canadian Public Accountability Board Oversight Program, which reviews the audited financial statements of public companies. In addition, standards for the independence and education experience of Audit Committees were defined.

Like other business disciplines, accounting is subject to change. The accounting profession is feeling the impact of the global market. The Reaching Beyond Our Borders box discusses a movement to globalize accounting procedures.

Auditing

Reviewing and evaluating the records used to prepare a company's financial statements is referred to as **auditing**. Private accountants within the organization often perform internal audits to guarantee that

Adapting *to* CHANGE

Elementary, Mr. Auditor, Elementary

Fraud damages businesses both large and small. According to the Association of Certified Fraud Examiners, many large corporations lose almost 5 percent of their revenue each year due to fraud, and nearly half of all small businesses deal with financial fraud at some time in their business lives. Mary Jo White, Chairman of the Securities and Exchange Commission (SEC, <*http://www.sec.gov*>), has made it clear that the SEC is committed to fighting financial fraud. As a result, the SEC has increased efforts to investigate and punish accounting wrongdoers.

Unfortunately, that may be a problem. Company auditors and chartered professional accountants (CPA) are not specifically trained in uncovering financial fraud. They are trained to make sure accounting standards are being applied correctly and management's estimates are fairly stated. In fact, less than 1 percent of the CPA exam focuses on fraud. So, if auditors and CPAs are not prepared to search for and identify signs of financial fraud, "Who you gonna call?"

The answer is elementary. Meet the Sherlock Holmes of the accounting industry—a forensic accountant. Forensic accountants sift through mountains of company information, trying to put together a paper trail to identify any rogues responsible for fraud. Jack Damico, founding partner of MDD Forensic Accountants, described such people as "investigative accountants who look below the surface and read between the lines." Many schools now offer advanced degrees and specialties in forensic accounting. With companies coming under closer scrutiny from the SEC, the Sarbanes-Oxley Act, and provincial exchanges, expect forensic accountants to stay busy.

Sources: Ben DiPietro, "Accountants Should Focus on Detecting Fraud, Experts Say," *The Wall Street Journal*, 9 October 2013; Brian Fox, "Accounting for Fraud," *Financial Times*, 5 December 2013; and Janet Novack, "How SEC's New RoboCop Profiles Companies for Accounting Fraud," *Forbes*, 9 August 2013.

the organization is carrying out proper accounting procedures and financial reporting. Public accountants also conduct independent audits of accounting information and related records. An **independent audit** is an evaluation and unbiased opinion about the accuracy of a company's financial statements. You may recall from Figure 16.3 that annual reports often include an auditor's unbiased written opinion.[11]

auditing
The job of reviewing and evaluating the records used to prepare a company's financial statements.

independent audit
An evaluation and unbiased opinion about the accuracy of a company's financial statements.

All stakeholders, including the public, governments, financial institutions, and shareholders (owners) are interested in the results of these audits. Audits are required for all public corporations in Canada whose shares are traded in a public stock exchange.

After the accounting scandals of the early 2000s, questions surfaced about the ethics of allowing an accounting firm to do both auditing and consulting work for the same company. In response, the Sarbanes-Oxley Act put in place new rules about auditing and consulting to ensure the integrity of the auditing process.[12] Auditing procedures, however, again came under fire in 2011, causing many to call for stricter controls over auditing procedures after analyzing the failure of Lehman Brothers in 2008 and the financial crisis that followed.

In doing their job, auditors not only examine the financial health of an organization but also its operational efficiencies and effectiveness.[13] A relatively new area of accounting that focuses its attention on fraudulent activity is **forensic accounting**. This field of accounting gathers evidence for presentation in a court of law. This evidence comes from a review of financial and other records. Review Adapting to Change for a further discussion.

> **forensic accounting**
> A relatively new area of accounting that focuses its attention on fraudulent activity.

Tax Accounting

Taxes enable governments to fund roads, parks, schools, social services, police protection, and other functions. Federal and provincial governments require individuals and organizations to file tax returns at specific times and in precise formats. A **tax accountant** is trained in tax law and is responsible for preparing tax returns or developing tax strategies. Since governments often change tax policies according to specific needs or objectives, the job of the tax accountant is certainly challenging.[14] As the burden of taxes grows in the economy, the role of the tax accountant becomes increasingly valuable to the organization, individual, or entrepreneur.

> **tax accountant**
> An accountant trained in tax law and responsible for preparing tax returns or developing tax strategies.

Government and Not-for-Profit Accounting

Government and not-for-profit (non-profit) accounting supports organizations whose purpose is not generating a profit but rather serving ratepayers, taxpayers, and others according to a duly approved budget. The different levels of government require an accounting system that helps taxpayers, special interest groups, legislative bodies, and creditors ensure that each level of government is fulfilling its obligations and making proper use of the funding with which it has been provided. Canada's auditor general regularly audits the federal government. CRA administers tax laws for the Government of Canada and for most provinces and territories, and it also administers various social and economic benefit and incentive programs delivered through the tax system.[15]

> **government and not-for-profit (non-profit) accounting**
> Accounting system for organizations whose purpose is not generating a profit but rather serving ratepayers, taxpayers, and others according to a duly approved budget.

Not-for-profit organizations often require accounting professionals. Charities like the Canadian Cancer Society and the United Way of Canada *<http://www.unitedway.ca>*, museums, universities and colleges, and hospitals all hire accountants to show contributors how their money is spent. During the recent recession, many businesses and individuals cut back on donations, making it more important than ever to account for every dollar contributed.[16]

Government organizations employ accountants, auditors, and financial managers. For example, the Department of Tourism and Culture for Prince Edward Island supports initiatives to encourage visitors to visit the island. Have you considered working for a government organization?

As you can see, managerial and financial accounting, compliance, tax accounting, and governmental and not-for-profit accounting each require specific training and skills. Before we leave this section, let's look at Canada's accounting designations.

The Chartered Professional Accountant (CPA) Designation[17]

Canada has three legacy professional accounting designations. Accountants with any of these designations work in all areas of business. Each designation is as follows:

1. A *chartered accountant (CA)* has met the examination, education, and experience requirements of the Canadian Institute of Chartered Accountants (CICA). This includes passing the Uniform Final Evaluation (UFE), widely recognized as one of the most rigorous professional examinations in the world. Debbie Watt, the focus of the chapter profile, has her CA designation.

2. A *certified management accountant (CMA)* has met certain educational and experience requirements, passed a qualifying exam in the field, participated in a two-year professional development program, and was certified by the Management Accountants of Canada (CMA Canada).

3. *Certified general accountants (CGAs)* have met the examination, education, and experience requirements of the Certified General Accountants Association of Canada (CGA-Canada).

Chartered Professional Accountants of Canada (CPA Canada, *<http://www.cpacanada.ca>*) was formed by the integration of the three organizations mentioned above, namely CICA, CMA Canada, and CGA-Canada. CPA Canada was created to unify Canadian provincial accounting bodies at the national level. All 40 of the accounting bodies in Canada have now either unified or are participating in discussions to unite under the CPA banner. The timing for integration and use of the CPA designation will vary from province to province because the profession is provincially regulated and mergers will occur at different times. As such, some of the provinces and regions will be represented by a merged CPA body, while others will be represented by the legacy bodies until an integrated CPA organization is in place. Once unification is completed the profession will move to 14 governing bodies and represent more than 190,000 members.

The **Chartered Professional Accountant (CPA) designation** is the internationally recognized Canadian accounting designation. One needs to have both an undergraduate degree and specific subject area coverage to be admitted to the new CPA Professional Education Program (CPA PEP). There is a different path for those who do not have an undergraduate degree.

chartered professional accountant (CPA) designation
The internationally recognized Canadian accounting designation.

This designation emerged from the belief that Canada needed a single, unified accounting profession. A combined Canadian accounting profession built on the strengths of the three legacy designations would be better positioned to represent its interests in Canada and abroad. "With unification, operations and governance will be simplified, efficiencies found, and the profession will speak with a stronger voice," explains Kevin Dancey, president and CEO of CPA Canada. A unified profession will best serve the public interest by establishing common codes of professional conduct, disciplinary systems, and licensing regimes. Dancey adds that with unification will come a nationally consistent regulatory framework that will facilitate labour mobility and the integration of foreign-trained professionals. "Unification will ease confusion about the legacy designations for employers," notes Dancey. "Soon, everyone will be operating under the CPA banner."

What role can accountants play to help organizations adapt to climate change? A new strategic initiative—sponsored by CPA Canada and Natural Resources Canada <http://www.nrcan.gc.ca>, and managed by the Network for Business Sustainability—says accountants are ideally positioned to be key contributors. As creators, enablers, preservers, and reporters of sustainable value, accountants can make their organizations' adaptation efforts more effective. Would working in this area of accounting interest you?

Progress Assessment

- What are the five key working areas of the accounting profession?
- What is the key difference between managerial and financial accounting?
- How is the job of a private accountant different from that of a public accountant?
- What ideas contributed to the creation of the CPA designation?

List the steps in the accounting cycle, distinguish between accounting and bookkeeping, and explain how computers are used in accounting.

The Accounting Cycle

The **accounting cycle** is a six-step procedure (see Figure 16.5) that results in the preparation and analysis of the major financial statements. It relies on the work of both the bookkeeper and an accountant. **Bookkeeping**, the recording of business transactions, is a basic part of financial reporting. Accounting, however, goes far beyond the mere recording of financial information. Accountants classify and summarize financial data provided by bookkeepers, interpret the data, and then report the information to management. They also suggest strategies for improving the financial condition and prepare financial analysis and income tax returns.

---

accounting cycle
A six-step procedure that results in the preparation and analysis of the major financial statements.

bookkeeping
The recording of business transactions.

■ **FIGURE 16.5**

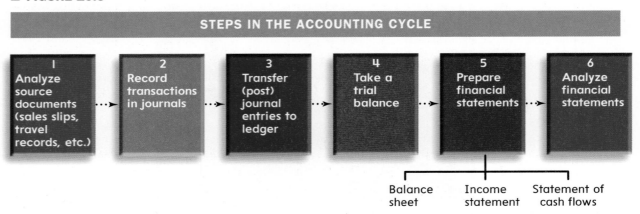

A bookkeeper's first task is to divide all of the firm's transactions into meaningful categories, such as sales documents, purchasing receipts, and shipping documents, being very careful to keep the information organized and manageable. Bookkeepers then record financial data from the original transaction documents (sales slips and so forth) into a record book or computer program called a **journal**. The word *journal* comes from the French word *jour*, which means "day." Therefore, a journal is where the day's transactions are kept.

---

journal
The record book where accounting data are first entered.

It's quite possible to make a mistake when recording financial transactions, like entering $10.98 as $10.89. That's why bookkeepers record all transactions in two places, so they can check one list of transactions against the other to make sure both add up to the same amount. If the amounts are not equal, the bookkeeper knows there is a mistake. The practice of writing every transaction in two places is called **double-entry bookkeeping**. It requires two entries in the journal and in the ledgers (discussed next) for each transaction.

> **double-entry bookkeeping**
> The concept of every business transaction affecting at least two accounts.

Suppose a business wanted to determine how much it paid for office supplies in the first quarter of the year. Without a specific bookkeeping tool, that would be difficult—even with accurate accounting journals. Therefore, bookkeepers use a specialized accounting book or computer program called a **ledger**. In the ledger, they transfer (or post) information from accounting journals into specific categories so managers can find all the information about a single account, like office supplies or cash, in one place.

> **ledger**
> A specialized accounting book in which information from accounting journals is accumulated into accounts and posted so that managers can find all of the information about a specific account in one place.

The next step in the accounting cycle is to prepare **a trial balance**, a summary of all the financial data in the account ledgers that ensures the figures are correct and balanced. If the information in the account ledgers is not accurate, the accountant must correct it before preparing the firm's financial statements. Using the correct information, the accountant then prepares the firm's financial statements—including a balance sheet, an income statement, and a statement of cash flows—according to IFRS.

> **trial balance**
> A summary of all of the data in the account ledgers to show whether the figures are correct and balanced.

Using Technology in Accounting

A long while ago, accountants and bookkeepers needed to enter all of a firm's financial information by hand. The advent of adding machines and calculators made the job a bit simpler, but still generally required a paper entry. Toward the end of the twentieth century, technology simplified the accounting process. Today, computerized accounting programs can post information from journals instantaneously, from remote locations to encrypted laptops or cell phones, making financial information available whenever the organization needs it. The company's sensitive financial information is safe and secure, but is in the accountant's hands when needed. Such assistance frees accountants' time for more important tasks such as financial analysis and financial forecasting.

Computerized accounting programs are also particularly helpful to small-business owners, who don't often have the variety of accounting personnel within their companies that larger firms enjoy. Accounting software—such as Sage 50, Quicken, and QuickBooks—addresses the specific needs of small businesses that are often significantly different from the needs of a major corporation.[18] Small-business owners, however, need to understand exactly which programs are best suited for their particular company needs. That is one reason why entrepreneurs planning to start a company should hire or consult with an accountant to identify the particular needs of the firm.[19] They can then develop a specific accounting system that works with the accounting software they have chosen.

Cloud computing is becoming more affordable for small and mid-sized companies as lower prices make data storage and other online services affordable.[20] Over one third of Microsoft Canada's annual

$2.2 billion revenue is generated from small and medium-sized businesses, and that revenue is growing much faster than the rest of the business, said Janet Kennedy, president of Microsoft Canada.[21] According to a Boston Consulting Group study, smaller companies that embrace tools such as social media and cloud computing grow their revenues 15 percent faster and hire more workers than companies with lower levels of technology adoption.[22]

With sophisticated accounting software available and technology capabilities growing, you might wonder why you need to study and understand accounting. Without question, technology has greatly assisted business people and certainly eased the monotony of bookkeeping and accounting work. Unfortunately the work of an accountant requires training and very specific competencies that computers are not programmed to handle. It's the partnership of technology and an accountant's knowledge that helps a firm make the right financial decisions. After the Progress Assessment, we'll explore the balance sheet, income statement, and statement of cash flows. It's from the information contained in these financial statements that the accountant analyzes and evaluates the financial condition of the firm.

Progress Assessment

- How is the job of the bookkeeper different from that of an accountant?
- What is the purpose of accounting journals and ledgers?
- Why does a bookkeeper prepare a trial balance?
- How has computer software helped businesses maintain and compile accounting information?

LO4 Explain how the major financial statements differ.

Understanding Key Financial Statements

An accounting year is either a calendar or fiscal year. A calendar year begins January 1 and ends December 31. A fiscal year can begin at any date designated by the business. A **financial statement** is a summary of all the transactions that have occurred over a particular period. Financial statements indicate a firm's financial health and stability and are key factors in management decision making.[23] That is why shareholders, bondholders and financial services providers (people and institutions that lend money to the firm), unions, employees, and the CRA are all interested in a firm's financial statements. There are three key business financial statements:

1. The *balance sheet* reports the firm's financial position *on a specific date,* normally at the end of a period.

2. The *income statement* summarizes revenues, cost of goods, and expenses (including taxes) for a specific period of time, and it highlights the total profit or loss the firm experienced *during that period.*

3. The *statement of cash flows* provides a summary of money coming into and going out of the firm *during a period.* It tracks a company's cash receipts and cash payments.

> **financial statement**
> A summary of all of the transactions that have occurred over a particular period.

The differences among the financial statements can best be summarized this way: The balance sheet details what the company owns and owes on a certain day; the income statement shows the revenue a firm earned selling its products compared to its selling costs (profit or loss) over a specific period of time; and the statement of cash flows highlights the difference between cash coming in and cash going out of a business over a specific period of time. To fully understand this important financial information, you need to know the purpose of an organization's financial statements. To help you with this task, we'll explain each statement in more detail. Before this, consider the fundamental accounting equation.

The Fundamental Accounting Equation

Imagine you don't owe anybody any money. That is, you have no liabilities (debts). In this case, your assets (cash and so forth) are equal to what you *own* (your equity). However, if you borrow some money from a friend, you have incurred a liability. Your assets are now equal to what you *owe* plus what you own. Translated into business terms, Assets = Liabilities + Owners' equity, which is the **fundamental accounting equation**. Different types of assets, liabilities, and owners' equity (which will be discussed later), are **accounts**.

> **fundamental accounting equation**
> Assets are equal to liabilities plus owners' equity; this is the basis for the balance sheet.
>
> **accounts**
> Different types of assets, liabilities, and owners' equity.

In accounting, this equation must always be balanced. For example, suppose that you have $50,000 in cash and decide to use that money to open a small coffee shop. Your business has assets of $50,000 and no debts. The accounting equation would look like this:

$$\text{Assets} = \text{Liabilities} + \text{Owners' equity}$$
$$\$50,000 = \quad \$0 \quad + \quad \$50,000$$

Each business transaction impacts at least two accounts. Each entry has at least one debit and one credit. Debits or credits on their own are neither good nor bad, simply a mechanism for maintaining the balance of the accounting equation.

Referring back to our example, your business has $50,000 cash and $50,000 owners' equity (the amount of your investment in the business—sometimes referred to as net worth). However, before opening the business, you borrow $30,000 from a local bank. As a result, the accounting equation now changes. You have $30,000 of additional cash, but you also have a debt (liability) of $30,000. (Remember, in double-entry bookkeeping we record each business transaction in two places.)

Your financial position within the business has changed. The equation is still balanced but is changed to reflect the borrowing transaction:

$$\text{Assets} = \text{Liabilities} + \text{Owners' equity}$$
$$\$80,000 = \quad \$30,000 \quad + \quad \$50,000$$

This fundamental accounting equation is the basis for the balance sheet.

The Balance Sheet

A **balance sheet** (also known as the **statement of financial position**) is the financial statement that reports a firm's financial condition at a specific time. As highlighted in the sample balance sheet in Figure 16.6 (for our hypothetical vegetarian restaurant, Very Vegetarian, introduced in Chapter 14), assets are listed first in a separate column, followed by liabilities and owners' (or shareholders' or stockholders') equity. The assets are equal to or *balanced* with the liabilities and owners' equity. The balance is that simple.

balance sheet (statement of financial position)
The financial statement that reports a firm's financial condition at a specific time and is composed of three major types of accounts: assets, liabilities, and owners' (shareholders' or stockholders') equity.

■ **FIGURE 16.6**

SAMPLE VERY VEGETARIAN BALANCE SHEET

① Current assets: Items that can be converted to cash within one year.
② Fixed assets: Items such as land, buildings, and equipment that are relatively permanent.
③ Intangible assets: Items of value, such as patents and copyrights, that do not have a physical form.
④ Current liabilities: Payments that are due in one year or less.
⑤ Long-term liabilities (also called non-current liabilities): Payments due in over one year.
⑥ Owners' equity (also called shareholders' or stockholders' equity): The value of what shareholders own in a firm.

Some information is bolded for learning purposes. Note how Total assets = Total liabilities + Owners' equity.

VERY VEGETARIAN
Balance Sheet
December 31, 2015

Assets			
① Current assets			
Cash		$15,000	
Accounts receivable		200,000	
Notes receivable		50,000	
Inventory		335,000	
Total current assets			$600,000
② Fixed assets			
Land		$40,000	
Building and improvements	$200,000		
Less: Accumulated amortization	−90,000		
		110,000	
Equipment and vehicles	$120,000		
Less: Accumulated amortization	−80,000		
		40,000	
Furniture and fixtures	$26,000		
Less: Accumulated amortization	−10,000		
		16,000	
Total fixed assets			206,000
③ Intangible assets			
Goodwill		$20,000	
Total intangible assets			20,000
Total assets			**$826,000**

VERY VEGETARIAN Balance Sheet December 31, 2015		
Liabilities and Owners' or Shareholders' Equity		
④ **Current liabilities**		
Accounts payable	$40,000	
Notes payable (due June 2016)	8,000	
Accrued taxes	150,000	
Accrued salaries	90,000	
Total current liabilities		$288,000
⑤ **Long-term liabilities**		
Notes payable (due Mar. 2020)	$35,000	
Bonds payable (due Dec. 2025)	290,000	
Total long-term liabilities		325,000
Total liabilities		$613,000
⑥ **Owners' equity**		
Common stock (1,000,000 shares)	$100,000	
Retained earnings	113,000	
Total owners' equity		213,000
Total liabilities & Owners' equity		$826,000

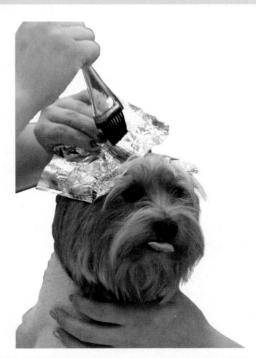

Service businesses, like dog groomers, rely on the same sets of financial statements as manufacturers like Ford and retail sales firms such as Best Buy <http://www.bestbuy.ca> do. What are some of the assets and liabilities a typical service business like a dog groomer would carry on its balance sheet?

Let's say that you want to know what your financial condition is at a given time. Maybe you want to buy a house or car and therefore need to calculate your available resources. One of the best measuring sticks is your balance sheet. First, add up everything you own—cash, property, and money owed you. These are your assets. Subtract from that the money you owe others—credit card debt, IOUs, car loan, student loans, and the like. These are your liabilities. The resulting figure is your net worth, or equity. This is fundamentally what companies do in preparing a balance sheet: they follow the procedures set in the fundamental accounting equation. In that preparation, any company that is publicly traded is required to follow IFRS.[24]

Since it is critical that you understand the financial information on the balance sheet, let's take a closer look at what is in a business's asset account and what is in its liabilities and owners' equity accounts.

ASSETS

Assets are economic resources (things of value) owned by a firm. Assets include productive, tangible items, such as equipment, buildings, land, furniture, and motor vehicles, that help generate income, as well as intangible items with value, like patents, trademarks, copyrights, or goodwill. Goodwill is included on the balance sheet when one firm acquires another firm and pays more for it than the value of its tangible assets. Think of the value of brand names such as Roots, WestJet, and Canadian Tire. Not all companies, however, list intangible assets on their balance sheets.

> **assets**
> Economic resources (things of value) owned by a firm.

Accountants list assets on the firm's balance sheet in order of their **liquidity**, or ease with which they can convert them to cash. Speedier conversion means higher liquidity. For example, an *account receivable* is an amount of money owed to the firm that it expects to receive within one year. It is considered a liquid asset because it can be quickly converted to cash. Land, however, is not considered a liquid asset because it takes time, effort, and paperwork to sell. It is considered a fixed or long-term asset. Assets are thus divided into three categories according to how quickly they can be turned into cash:

1. **Current assets** are items that can or will be converted into cash within one year. Current assets include cash, accounts receivable, and inventory.

2. **Fixed assets** are long-term assets that are relatively permanent, such as land, buildings, and equipment. They are acquired to produce products for a business. They are not bought to be sold but to generate revenue. (On a balance sheet they are also referred to as capital assets or property, plant, and equipment.)

3. **Intangible assets** are long-term assets that have no physical form but do have value. Patents, trademarks, and copyrights (recall Appendix A), as well as goodwill are intangible assets.

> **liquidity**
> The ease with which an asset can be converted into cash.
>
> **current assets**
> Items that can or will be converted into cash within one year.
>
> **fixed assets**
> Assets that are relatively permanent, such as land, buildings, and equipment.
>
> **intangible assets**
> Long-term assets (e.g., patents, trademarks, and copyrights) that have no physical form but do have value.

LIABILITIES AND OWNERS' EQUITY ACCOUNTS

Liabilities are what the business owes to others—its debts. *Current liabilities* are debts due in one year or less. *Long-term liabilities* (also called non-current liabilities) are debts due in over one year. The following are common liability accounts recorded on a balance sheet. Look at Figure 16.6 again for these accounts:

1. **Accounts payable** are current liabilities or bills a company owes others for merchandise or services it purchased on credit but have not yet paid for. The longer you take to pay, the greater the risk that a supplier will no longer grant you credit.

2. **Notes payable** can be short-term or long-term liabilities (like loans from banks) that a business promises to repay by a certain date.

3. **Bonds payable** are long-term liabilities. This is money lent to the firm that must be paid back. (We will discuss bonds in Chapters 17.)

liabilities
What the business owes to others (debts).

accounts payable
Current liabilities or bills a company owes others for merchandise or services purchased on credit but not yet paid for.

notes payable
Short-term or long-term liabilities that a business promises to repay by a certain date.

bonds payable
Long-term liabilities that represent money lent to a firm that must be paid back.

As you saw in the fundamental accounting equation, the value of things you own (assets) minus the amount of money you owe others (liabilities) is called *equity*. The value of what shareholders own in a firm, minus liabilities, is called *shareholders' equity* (or *stockholders' equity*). Because shareholders are the owners of a firm, we call shareholders' equity **owners' equity**, or that amount of the business that belongs to the owners, minus any liabilities the business owes. This consists of all that the owners have invested in the company plus all profits that have accumulated since the business commenced but that have not yet been paid out to them. This figure always equals the book value of the assets minus the liabilities of the company.

owners' equity
The amount of the business that belongs to the owners minus any liabilities owed by the business.

The owners' equity account will differ according to the type of organization. For sole proprietors and partners, owners' equity means the value of everything owned by the business minus any liabilities of the owner(s), such as bank loans. Owners' equity in these firms is called the *capital* account. In a sole proprietorship, it is called *owner's* or *proprietor's equity* or *capital*. In a partnership, owners' equity is called *partners' equity* or *capital*.

For corporations, it is called shareholders' equity and is divided in two separate accounts. The amount the owners (shareholders) invest is shown in one account, called common stock. The second account is **retained earnings**, which are accumulated earnings from the firm's profitable operations that remain in the business and are not paid out to shareholders as dividends. (Dividends, which are distributions of profits, will be discussed in Chapter 17). Take a few moments to review Figure 16.6 and see what facts you can determine about Very Vegetarian from its balance sheet. After the Progress Assessment, have some fun and estimate your own personal net worth, following the directions in Figure 16.7.

retained earnings
The accumulated earnings from a firm's profitable operations that remains in the business and are not paid out to shareholders as dividends.

■ FIGURE 16.7

YOU INCORPORATED				
How does You Inc. stack up financially? Take a little time to find out. You may be pleasantly surprised, or you may realize that you need to think hard about planning your financial future. Remember, your net worth is nothing more than the difference between what you own (assets) and what you owe (liabilities). Be honest, and do your best to give a fair evaluation of your private property's value.				

ASSETS			LIABILITIES	
Cash	$ _____		Instalment loans & interest	$ _____
Savings account	_____		Other loans & interest	_____
Chequing account	_____		Credit card accounts	_____
Home	_____		Mortgage	_____
Stocks & bonds	_____		Taxes	_____
Automobile	_____		Cell phone service	_____
TFSA & RRSP	_____		Other liabilities	_____
Personal property	_____			
Other assets	_____			
Total assets	$ _____		Total liabilities	$ _____
Determine your net worth:				
Total assets	$ _____			
Total liabilities	_____			
Net worth	$ _____			

Progress Assessment

- What is the formula for the balance sheet? What do we call this formula?
- What does it mean to list various assets according to liquidity?
- What is included in the liabilities section in the balance sheet?
- What is owners' equity and how is it determined?

The Income Statement

The financial statement that shows a firm's bottom line—that is, its profit after costs, expenses, and taxes—is the **income statement** (also known as the **statement of earnings**). The income statement summarizes all of the resources, called *revenue*, that have come into the firm from operating activities, money resources the firm used up, expenses it incurred in doing business, and resources it has left after paying all costs and expenses, including taxes. See Figure 16.8 for an example. The resources (revenue) left over or depleted are referred to as **net income** or **net loss**.

> **income statement (statement of earnings)**
> The financial statement that shows a firm's profit after costs, expenses, and taxes.
>
> **net income (or net loss)**
> Revenue left over (or depleted if a net loss) after all costs and expenses, including taxes, are paid.

FIGURE 16.8

SAMPLE VERY VEGETARIAN INCOME STATEMENT

① Revenues: Value of what is received from goods sold, services rendered, and other financial sources.
② Cost of goods sold: Cost of merchandise sold or cost of raw materials or parts used for producing items for resale.
③ Gross profit: How much the firm earned by buying or selling merchandise.
④ Operating expenses: Cost incurred in operating a business.
⑤ Net income after taxes: Profit or loss over a specific period after subtracting all costs and expenses including taxes.

Some of the information is bolded for learning purposes.

VERY VEGETARIAN
Income Statement
For the Year Ended December 31, 2015

① **Revenues**			
Gross sales		$720,000	
Less: Sales returns and allowances	$12,000		
Sales discounts	8,000	−20,000	
Net sales			$700,000
② **Cost of goods sold**			
Beginning inventory, Jan. 1		$200,000	
Merchandise purchases	$400,000		
Freight	40,000		
Net purchases		440,000	
Cost of goods available for sale		$640,000	
Less ending inventory, Dec. 31		−230,000	
Cost of goods sold			−410,000
③ **Gross profit**			$290,000
④ **Operating expenses**			
Selling expenses			
Salaries for salespeople	$90,000		
Advertising	18,000		
Supplies	2,000		
Total selling expenses		$110,000	
General expenses			
Office salaries	$67,000		
Amortization	1,500		
Insurance	1,500		
Rent	28,000		
Light, heat, and power	12,000		
Miscellaneous	2,000		
		112,000	
Total operating expenses			222,000
Net income before taxes			$68,000
Less: Income tax expense			19,000
⑤ **Net income after taxes**			$ 49,000

The income statement reports the firm's financial operations over a particular period of time, usually a year, a quarter of a year, or a month. It is the financial statement that reveals whether the business is actually earning a profit or losing money. The income statement includes valuable financial information for shareholders, lenders, potential investors, employees, and the government. Let's take a quick look at how to compile the income statement. Then we will discuss what each element in it means.

> Revenue
> − Cost of goods sold
> ───────────────────
> = Gross profit (gross margin)
> − Operating expenses
> ───────────────────
> = Net income before taxes
> − Taxes
> ───────────────────
> = Net income or loss

REVENUE

Revenue is the monetary value of what a firm received for goods sold, services rendered, and other payments (such as rents received, money paid to the firm for use of its patents, interest earned, etc.). Be sure not to confuse the terms *revenue* and *sales;* they are not the same thing. True, most revenue the firm earns does come from sales, but companies can also have other sources of revenue. Also, a quick glance at the income statement shows you that *gross sales* refers to the total of all sales the firm completed. *Net sales* are gross sales minus returns, discounts, and allowances.

Jennifer Behar runs a small bakery that sells products like chocolate biscotti and rosemary flatbread to high-end retailers like Whole Foods Market <*http://www.wholefoodsmarket.com*>. Behar began her business with borrowed funds and doubled revenues in one year. What is the difference between revenue and sales?

COST OF GOODS SOLD

The **cost of goods sold** (also known as **cost of goods manufactured**) measures the cost of merchandise the firm sold or the cost of raw materials and supplies it used in producing items for resale. It makes sense to compare how much a business earned by selling merchandise over the period being evaluated, compared to how much it spent to buy or produce the merchandise. The cost of goods sold includes the purchase price plus any freight charges paid to transport goods, plus any costs associated with storing the goods.

cost of goods sold (cost of goods manufactured)
A measure of the cost of merchandise sold or cost of raw materials and supplies used for producing items for resale.

In financial reporting, it does not matter when a firm places a particular item in its inventory, but it does matter how an accountant records the cost of the item when the firm sells it. To find out why, read the Spotlight on Small Business about two different inventory valuation methods.

Spotlight *On* SMALL BUSINESS

The Ins and Outs of Valuing Inventory

IFRS sometimes permit an accountant to use different methods of accounting for a firm's inventory. Two of the most popular methods are first in, first out (FIFO) and last in, first out (LIFO).

Let's look at a simple example. Say your bookstore buys 100 copies of a particular textbook in July at $100 a copy. When classes begin in September, the bookstore sells 50 copies of the text to students at $120 each. Since the same book will be used again next term, the bookstore places the 50 copies it did not sell in its inventory until then.

In late December, the bookstore orders 50 additional copies of the text to sell for the next term. However, the publisher's price has increased from $100 to $120 a copy due to inflation and other increased production and distribution costs. The bookstore now has in its inventory 100 copies of the same textbook, purchased during different buying cycles. If it sells 50 copies to students at $140 each at the beginning of the new term in January, what's the bookstore's cost of the book for accounting purposes? Actually, it depends.

The books sold are identical, but the accounting treatment could be different. If the bookstore uses FIFO, the cost of goods sold is $100 for each textbook, because the textbook the store bought first—the first in—cost $100. The bookstore could use another method, however. Under LIFO, its last purchase of the textbooks, at $120 each, determines the cost of each of the 50 textbooks sold.

If the book sells for $140, what is the difference in gross profit (margin) between using FIFO and using LIFO? Eventually, when all 100 copies are sold the cumulative net income will be the same regardless of whether FIFO or LIFO is used. The choice between the two methods solely affects the timing of when the net income is realized.

When we subtract the cost of goods sold from net sales, we get gross profit or gross margin. **Gross profit** (or **gross margin**) is how much a firm earned by buying (or making) and selling merchandise. In a service firm, there may be no cost of goods sold; therefore, gross profit *could* equal net sales. Gross profit does not tell you everything you need to know about the firm's financial performance. To get that, you must subtract the business's expenses.

> **gross profit (gross margin)**
> How much a firm earned by buying (or making) and selling merchandise.

OPERATING EXPENSES

In selling goods or services, a business incurs certain **operating expenses**, such as rent, salaries, supplies, utilities, and insurance. Other operating expenses that appear on an income statement, like depreciation, are a bit more complex. For example, have you ever heard that a new car depreciates in market value as soon as you drive it off the dealer's lot? The same principle holds true for assets such as equipment and machinery. **Depreciation** is the systematic write-off of the cost of a tangible asset over its estimated useful life. Under accounting rules set by IFRS and CRA (which are beyond the scope of this chapter), companies are permitted to recapture the cost of these assets over time by using depreciation as an operating expense.

> **operating expenses**
> Costs involved in operating a business, such as rent, utilities, and salaries.
>
> **depreciation**
> The systematic write-off of the cost of a tangible asset over its estimated useful life.

Operating expenses can generally be classified into two categories: selling expenses and general expenses. *Selling expenses* are expenses related to the marketing and distribution of the firm's goods or services (such as salaries for salespeople, advertising, and supplies). *General expenses* are administrative expenses of the firm (such as office salaries, amortization, insurance, and rent). Accountants are trained to help you record all applicable expenses and find other relevant expenses you need to deduct as part of doing business.

NET PROFIT OR NET LOSS

After deducting all expenses, we can determine the firm's net income before taxes, also referred to as net earnings or net profit (refer to Figure 16.8). After deducting taxes, we get to the *bottom line*, which is the net income (or perhaps net loss) the firm incurred from revenue minus sales returns, costs, expenses, and taxes over a period of time. We can now answer the question "Did the business earn or lose money in the specific reporting period?"

The basic principles of the balance sheet and income statement are familiar to you. You know how to keep track of costs and expenses when you prepare your own budget. If your rent and utilities exceed your earnings, you know you are in trouble. If you need more money, you may need to sell some of the things you own to pay your expenses. The same is true in business. Companies need to keep track of how much money they earn and spend and how much cash they have on hand. The only difference is that companies tend to have more complex problems and a good deal more information to record than you do.

Users of financial statements are interested in how a firm handles the flow of cash coming into a business and the cash flowing out of the business. Cash flow problems can plague both businesses and individuals. Keep this in mind as we look at the statement of cash flows next.

Most businesses incur operating expenses, including rent, salaries, utilities, supplies, and insurance. What are some of the likely operating expenses for companies like Starbucks?

The Statement of Cash Flows

The **statement of cash flows** (also known as the **cash flow statement**) reports cash receipts and cash disbursements related to the three major activities of a firm:

- *Operations* are cash transactions associated with running the business.
- *Investments* are cash used in or provided by the firm's investment activities.
- *Financing* is cash raised from taking on new debt or equity capital, or cash used to pay business expenses, past debts, or company dividends. We will discuss equity capital and dividends in Chapter 17.

> **statement of cash flows (cash flow statement)**
> A financial statement that reports cash receipts and cash disbursements related to a firm's three major activities: operations, investing, and financing.

Accountants analyze all changes in the firm's cash that have occurred from operating, investing, and financing in order to determine the firm's net cash position. The statement of cash flows also gives the firm some insight into how to handle cash better so that no cash flow problems occur—such as having no cash on hand for immediate expenses.[25]

Figure 16.9 shows a sample statement of cash flows, again using the example of Very Vegetarian. As you can see, the statement of cash flows answers such questions as: How much cash came into the business from current operations, such as buying and selling goods and services? Did the firm use cash to buy stocks, bonds, or other investments, such as capital assets? Did it sell some investments that brought in cash? How much money did the firm take in from issuing shares?

We analyze these and other financial transactions to see their effect on the firm's cash position. Managing cash flow can mean the success or failure of any business, which is why we analyze it in more depth in the next section.

■ **FIGURE 16.9**

SAMPLE VERY VEGETARIAN STATEMENT OF CASH FLOWS

① Operating activities: Cash receipts from sales, commissions, fees, interest, and dividends. Cash payments for salaries, inventories, operating expenses, interest, and taxes.
② Investing activities: Includes cash flows that are generated through a company's purchase or sale of long-term operational assets, investments in other companies, and lending activities.
③ Financing activities: Cash inflows and outflows associated with the company's own equity transactions or its borrowing activities.

Some information is bolded for learning purposes.

VERY VEGETARIAN
Statement of Cash Flows
For the Year Ended December 31, 2015

① **Cash flows from operating activities**		
Cash received from customers	$150,000	
Cash paid to suppliers and employees	(90,000)	
Interest paid	(5,000)	
Income tax paid	(4,500)	
Interest and dividends received	1,500	
Net cash provided by operating activities		$52,000
② **Cash flows from investing activities**		
Proceeds from sale of plant assets	$4,000	
Payments for purchase of equipment	(10,000)	
Net cash provided by investing activities		(6,000)
③ **Cash flows from financing activities**		
Proceeds from issuance of short-term debt	$3,000	
Payment of long-term debt	(7,000)	
Payment of dividends	(15,000)	
Net cash inflow from financing activities		(19,000)
Net change in cash and equivalents		$27,000
Cash balance (beginning of year)		(2,000)
Cash balance (end of year)		$25,000

THE NEED FOR CASH FLOW ANALYSIS

Cash flow, if not properly managed, can cause a business much concern.[26] Understanding cash flow analysis is important and not difficult to understand. Let's say that you borrow $100 from a friend to buy a used bike and agree to pay her back at the end of the week. You then sell the bike for $150 to someone else, who also agrees to pay you by the end of the week. Unfortunately, by the weekend, your buyer does not have the money as promised and says he will have to pay you next month. Meanwhile, your friend wants the $100 you agreed to pay her by the end of the week!

Cash flow is the difference between money coming into and going out of a business. Careful cash flow management is a must for a business of any size, but it's particularly important for small businesses and for seasonal businesses like ski resorts. Have you read of any firms that were forced into bankruptcy because of cash flow problems?

What seemed a great opportunity to make an easy $50 profit is now a cause for concern. You owe $100 and have no cash. What do you do? If you were a business, you might default on the loan and possibly go bankrupt, even though you had the potential for profits.

It is possible for a business to increase its sales and profits yet still suffer cash flow problems. **Cash flow** is simply the difference between cash coming in and cash going out of a business. Poor cash flow constitutes a major operating problem for many companies, and is particularly difficult for small and seasonal businesses.[27] Accountants sometimes face tough ethical challenges in reporting the flow of funds into a business. Read the Making Ethical Decisions box to see how such an ethical dilemma can arise.

cash flow
The difference between cash coming in and cash going out of a business.

How do cash flow problems start? Often in order to meet the growing demands of customers, a business buys goods on credit (using no cash). If it then sells a large number of goods on credit (getting no cash), the company needs more credit from a lender (usually a bank) to pay its immediate bills. If a firm has reached its credit limit and can borrow no more, it has a severe cash flow problem. It has cash coming in at a later date, but no cash to pay current expenses. That problem could, unfortunately, force the firm into bankruptcy, even though sales may be strong. This is all because no cash was available when it was most needed. Cash flow analysis shows that a business's relationship with its lenders is critical to prevent cash flow problems. Accountants provide valuable insight and advice to businesses in managing cash flow, suggesting whether or not they need cash and how much.

Progress Assessment

- What are the key steps in preparing an income statement?
- What is the difference between revenue and income on the income statement?
- What is the connection between the income statement and the balance sheet?
- Why is the statement of cash flows important in evaluating a firm's operations?

Making ETHICAL DECISIONS

Would You Cook the Books?

The recent recession hit small manufacturers very hard. Many did not survive the downturn. You are the lone accountant employed by Keegan's Feast, a small producer of premium dog food that sells directly online. Many of the company's customers became cost-conscious during the downturn and purchased lower-cost brands. Fortunately, with the economy recovering, many of the firm's former customers are returning and things are looking up.

The problem is the company's cash flow suffered during this time and the firm needs immediate funding to continue to pay its bills. You know the CEO has prepared a proposal to a local bank asking for short-term financing. Unfortunately, financial statements for the past year will not show good results. Your expectation is that the bank will not approve the loan on the basis of the financial information, even though the firm seems to be doing better.

Before you close the books for the end of the year, the CEO suggests you might "improve" the company's financial statements by treating the sales that were made at the beginning of January of the current year as if they were made in December of the past year. He is confident the company auditors will not discover this discrepancy.

You know that this is against the rules of the Accounting Standards Board, and you refuse to alter the information. The CEO warns you that without the bank loan, the business is likely to close, meaning you and everyone else will be out of a job. You know he's probably right, and also know that with the current economic downturn, finding a job will be tough for you and for others in the company. What are your alternatives? What are the likely consequences of each alternative? What would you do?

LO5 Demonstrate the application of ratio analysis in reporting financial information.

Analyzing Financial Performance Using Ratios

The firm's financial statements—its balance sheet, income statement, and statement of cash flows—form the basis for financial analyses performed by accountants inside and outside the firm. **Ratio analysis** is the assessment of a firm's financial condition, using calculations and financial ratios developed from the firm's financial statements. Financial ratios are especially useful in comparing the company's performance to its financial objectives and to the performance of other firms in its industry. You probably are already familiar with the use of ratios. For example, in basketball, we express the number of shots made from the foul line with a ratio: shots made to shots attempted. A player who shoots 85 percent from the foul line is considered an outstanding foul shooter; you do not want to foul this player in a close game.

ratio analysis
The assessment of a firm's financial condition using calculations and interpretations of financial ratios developed from the firm's financial statements.

Whether ratios measure an athlete's performance or the financial health of a business, they provide valuable information. Financial ratios provide key insights into how a firm compares to other firms in its industry on liquidity, amount of debt, profitability, and overall business activity. Understanding and interpreting business ratios is important to sound financial analysis. Let's look briefly at four key types of ratios businesses use to measure financial performance.

Liquidity Ratios

As discussed earlier, liquidity refers to how fast an asset can be converted to cash. Liquidity ratios measure a company's ability to turn some assets into cash to pay its short-term debts (liabilities that must be repaid within one year). These short-term debts are of particular importance to the firm's lenders who expect to be paid on time. Two key liquidity ratios are the current ratio and the acid-test ratio.

The *current ratio* is the ratio of a firm's current assets to its current liabilities. This information can be found on the firm's balance sheet. Look back at Figure 16.6, Very Vegetarian's balance sheet. The company lists current assets of $600,000 and current liabilities of $288,000. The firm therefore has a current ratio of 2.08, which means Very Vegetarian has $2.08 of current assets for every $1 of current liabilities. See the following calculation:

$$\text{Current ratio} = \frac{\text{Current assets}}{\text{Current liabilities}} = \frac{\$600,000}{\$288,000} = \$2.08$$

The question the current ratio attempts to answer is: "Is Very Vegetarian financially secure for the short term (less than one year)?" It depends! Usually a company with a current ratio of 2 or better is considered a safe risk for lenders granting short-term credit, since it appears to be performing in line with market expectations. However, lenders will also compare Very Vegetarian's current ratio to that of competing firms in its industry and to its current ratio from the previous year or so to note any significant changes.

Another key liquidity ratio, called the *acid-test* or *quick ratio*, measures the cash, marketable securities (such as stocks and bonds), and receivables of a firm, compared to its current liabilities. Again, this information is on a firm's balance sheet. See the following calculation:

$$\text{Acid-test ratio} = \frac{\text{Cash} + \text{Receivables} + \text{Marketable securities}}{\text{Current liabilities}}$$
$$= \frac{\$265,000}{\$288,000} = 0.92$$

This ratio is particularly important to firms with relatively large inventory, which can take longer than other current assets to convert into cash. It helps answer such questions as: "What if sales drop off and we cannot sell our inventory? Can we still pay our short-term debt?" Though ratios vary among industries, an acid-test ratio between .5 and 1.0 is usually considered satisfactory, but bordering on cash flow problems. Therefore, Very Vegetarian's acid-test ratio of .92 could raise concerns that perhaps the firm may not meet its short-term debt obligations and may have to go to a high-cost lender for financial assistance.

Leverage (Debt) Ratios

Leverage (debt) ratios measure the degree to which a firm relies on borrowed funds in its operations. A firm that takes on too much debt could experience problems repaying lenders or meeting promises made to shareholders. The *debt to owners' equity ratio* measures the degree to which the company is financed by borrowed funds that it must repay. Again, we can use data from Figure 16.6 to measure Very Vegetarian's level of debt:

$$\text{Debt to owners' equity ratio} = \frac{\text{Total liabilities}}{\text{Owners' equity}} = \frac{\$613,000}{\$213,000} = 288\%$$

Anything above 100 percent shows that a firm has more debt than equity. With a ratio of 288 percent, Very Vegetarian has a rather high degree of debt compared to its equity, which implies that lenders and investors may perceive the firm to be quite risky. However, it is *important to compare a firm's debt ratios to those of other firms in its industry*, because higher levels of debt financing are more acceptable in some industries than in others. Comparisons with the same firm's past debt ratios can also identify trends within the firm or industry.

Building luxury hotels, like the Cosmopolitan and Vdara hotels in Las Vegas, Nevada, generally requires taking on a high degree of debt before the hotel ever earns its first dollar. Once opened, the companies incur high daily expenses just to keep the business functioning efficiently. Would monitoring the four key accounting ratios be a major part of the accountants' jobs at the new hotels?

Profitability (Performance) Ratios

Profitability (performance) ratios measure how effectively a firm's managers are using its resources to achieve profits. Three of the more important ratios are earnings per share (EPS), return on sales, and return on equity.

EPS is a revealing ratio because earnings help stimulate the firm's growth and provide for shareholder dividends. Companies report their quarterly EPS in two ways: basic and diluted. The *basic earnings per share (basic EPS) ratio* helps determine the amount of profit a company earned for each share of outstanding common stock. The *diluted earnings per share (diluted EPS) ratio* measures the amount of profit earned for each share of outstanding common stock, but also considers stock options, warrants, preferred stock, and convertible debt securities the firm can convert into common stock. For simplicity's sake, we will compute only the basic EPS for Very Vegetarian:

$$\text{Basic earnings per share} = \frac{\text{Net income after taxes}}{\text{Number of common stock shares outstanding}}$$

$$= \frac{\$49,000}{\$1,000,000 \text{ shares}} = \$0.049 \text{ per share}$$

Another reliable indicator of performance is *return on sales*, which tells us whether the firm is doing as well as its competitors in generating income from sales. We calculate it by comparing net income to total sales. Very Vegetarian's return on sales is 7 percent, a figure we must measure against similar numbers for competing firms to judge Very Vegetarian's performance.

$$\text{Return on sales} = \frac{\text{Net income after tax}}{\text{Net sales}} = \frac{\$49,000}{\$700,000} = 7\%$$

The higher the risk of failure or loss in an industry, the higher the return investors expect on their investment as they expect to be well compensated for shouldering such odds. *Return on equity* indirectly measures risk by telling us how much a firm earned for each dollar invested by its owners. We calculate it by comparing a company's net income to its total owners' equity. Very Vegetarian's return on equity looks reasonably sound given that some believe anything over 15 percent is considered a reasonable return:

$$\text{Return on equity} = \frac{\text{Net income after tax}}{\text{Total owners' equity}} = \frac{\$49,000}{\$213,000} = 23\%$$

Remember that profits help companies like Very Vegetarian grow. That is why profitability ratios are such closely watched measurements of company growth and management performance.

Inventory turnover is critical to just about any business, particularly restaurants that serve perishable items and that must turn over tables to keep the flow of food moving and profits up. (They are limited in their earnings potential by the number of seats they have.) Can you think of other businesses that need to watch their inventory turnover closely?

Activity Ratios

Converting the firm's inventory to profits is a key function of management. Activity ratios tell us how effectively management is turning over inventory.

The *inventory turnover ratio* measures the speed with which inventory moves through a firm and gets converted into sales. Idle inventory sitting in a warehouse earns nothing and costs money. The more efficiently a firm sells or turns inventory, the higher its revenue. Very Vegetarian's inventory turnover ratio is:

$$\text{Inventory turnover} = \frac{\text{Costs of goods sold}}{\text{Average inventory}} = \frac{\$410,000}{\$215,000} = 1.9 \text{ times}$$

The average inventory is calculated by adding the beginning and ending inventories and dividing by two.

A lower-than-average inventory turnover ratio often indicates obsolete merchandise on hand or poor buying practices. A higher-than-average ratio may signal lost sales because of inadequate stock. Of course, like other ratios, rates of inventory turnover vary from industry to industry.

Managers need to be aware of proper inventory control and anticipate inventory turnover to ensure proper performance. For example, have you ever worked as a food server in a restaurant? How many times did your employer expect you to *turn over* a table (keep changing customers at the table) in an evening? The more times a table turns, the higher the return to the owner.

Accountants and other finance professionals consider other ratios in addition to the ones we have discussed to learn more about a firm's financial condition. (To review where the accounting information in ratio analysis comes from, see Figure 16.10 for a quick reference of the ratios we have discussed.) Remember, financial analysis begins where the accounting statements end.

We hope that you can see from this chapter that there is more to accounting than meets the eye. It can be fascinating and it is critical to the firm's operations. It is worth saying once more that, as the language of business, accounting is a worthwhile language to learn.

■ **FIGURE 16.10**

ACCOUNTS IN THE BALANCE SHEET AND INCOME STATEMENT						
BALANCE SHEET ACCOUNTS			INCOME STATEMENT ACCOUNTS			
Assets	Owners' Liabilities	Owners' Equity	Revenues	Cost of Goods Sold	Expenses	
Cash	Accounts payable	Capital stock	Sales revenue	Cost of buying goods	Wages	Interest
Accounts receivable	Notes payable	Retained earnings	Rental revenue	Cost of storing goods	Rent	Donations
Inventory	Bonds payable	Common stock	Commissions revenue		Repairs	Licences
Investments	Taxes payable		Royalty revenue		Travel	Fees
Equipment						
Land					Insurance	Supplies
Buildings					Utilities	Advertising
Motor vehicles					Entertainment	Taxes
Goodwill					Storage	

Progress Assessment

- What is the primary purpose of performing ratio analysis using a firm's financial statements?
- Describe the four main categories of financial ratios.
- Why is EPS a revealing ratio?

SUMMARY

LO1 **Describe the role that accounting and financial information play for a business and for its stakeholders.**

Financial information is critical to the growth and development of an organization.

What is accounting?

Accounting is the recording, classifying, summarizing, and interpreting of financial events that affect an organization. The methods used to record and summarize accounting data into reports are called an accounting system.

What role does accounting play?

Accounting provides the information to measure a firm's financial condition in support of managing a business.

LO2 **Identify the different disciplines within the accounting profession.**

The accounting profession covers five major areas: managerial accounting, financial accounting, auditing, tax accounting, and governmental and not-for-profit accounting.

How does managerial accounting differ from financial accounting?

Managerial accounting provides information (often of segments of a business) for planning and control purposes to managers within the firm to assist them in decision making. Financial accounting provides information in the form of the three basic financial statements to managers and external users of data such as creditors and lenders.

What is the difference between a private accountant and a public accountant?

A public accountant provides services for a fee to a variety of companies, whereas a private accountant works for a single company. Private and public accountants do essentially the same things, with the exception of independent audits. Private accountants do perform internal audits, but only public accountants supply independent audits.

What has happened to the nature of rules used to record business transactions?

For many years each country had its own set of rules. Each set of rules could result in differing amounts appearing in a set of financial statements based on the same set of transactions. To eliminate this issue, more and more countries are agreeing to use one set of rules, IFRS.

LO3 **List the steps in the accounting cycle, distinguish between accounting and bookkeeping, and explain how computers are used in accounting.**

Many people confuse bookkeeping and accounting.

What are the six steps of the accounting cycle?

The six steps of the accounting cycle are (1) analyzing documents, (2) recording information into journals, (3) posting that information into ledgers, (4) developing a trial balance, (5) preparing financial statements (the balance sheet, income statement, and statement of cash flows), and (6) analyzing financial statements.

What is the difference between bookkeeping and accounting?

Bookkeeping is part of accounting and includes the mechanical part of recording data. Accounting also includes classifying, summarizing, interpreting, and reporting data to management.

How can computers help accountants?

Computers can record and analyze data and provide financial reports. Software can continuously analyze and test accounting systems to be sure they are functioning properly (e.g., the accounting equation is always in balance when recording each transaction). Computers can help decision making by providing appropriate information, but they cannot themselves make good financial decisions independently. Accounting applications and creativity are still human traits.

LO4 Explain how the major financial statements differ.

Financial statements are a critical part of the firm's financial results/position.

What is a balance sheet?

A balance sheet reports the financial position of a firm on a particular day. The fundamental accounting equation used to prepare the balance sheet is Assets = Liabilities + Owners' equity.

What is an income statement?

An income statement reports revenues, costs, and expenses for a specific period of time (e.g., for the year ended December 31, 2016). The formulas used in preparing the income statement are:

Revenue − Cost of goods sold = Gross margin

Gross margin − Operating expenses = Net income before taxes

Net income before taxes − Taxes = Net income (or Net loss)

What is a statement of cash flows?

Cash flow is the difference between cash receipts (money coming in) and cash disbursements (money going out). The statement of cash flows reports cash receipts and disbursements related to the firm's major activities: operations, investing, and financing.

What are LIFO and FIFO?

LIFO and FIFO are methods of transferring a cost of inventory sold to the income statement. FIFO means first in, first out; LIFO means last in, first out. The method an accountant uses to value the transfer, FIFO or LIFO, can affect a firm's net income.

LO5 Demonstrate the application of ratio analysis in financial information.

Financial ratios are a key part of analyzing financial information.

What are the four key categories of ratios?

There are four key categories of ratios: liquidity ratios, leverage (debt) ratios, profitability (performance) ratios, and activity ratios.

What is the major value of ratio analysis to the firm?

Ratio analysis provides the firm with information about its financial position in key areas for comparison to similar firms in its industry and to its own past performance.

KEY TERMS

accounting	double-entry bookkeeping	liabilities
accounting cycle	financial accounting	liquidity
accounts	financial statement	managerial accounting
accounts payable	fixed assets	net income or net loss
annual report	forensic accounting	notes payable
assets	fundamental accounting	operating expenses
auditing	equation	owners' equity (shareholders' or
balance sheet (statement of	government and not-for-profit	stockholders' equity)
financial position)	(non-profit) accounting	private accountant
bonds payable	gross profit (gross margin)	public accountant
bookkeeping	income statement (statement of	ratio analysis
cash flow	earnings)	retained earnings
chartered professional	independent audit	statement of cash flows (cash
accountant (CPA) designation	intangible assets	flow statement)
cost of goods sold (cost of	international financial reporting	tax accountant
goods manufactured)	standards (IFRS)	trial balance
current assets	journal	
depreciation	ledger	

CRITICAL THINKING

1. In business, hundreds of documents are received or created every day, so you can appreciate the valuable role an accountant plays. Can you see why most businesses hire people to do this work? Would it be worth the owner's time to do all the paperwork? Can you understand why most accountants find it easier to do this work on a computer?

2. As a potential investor in a firm or perhaps the buyer of a business, would it be advisable for you to evaluate the company's financial statements? Why or why not? What key information would you seek from a firm's financial statements?

3. Why must accounting reports be prepared according to specific procedures (e.g., IFRS)? Should we allow businesses some flexibility or creativity in preparing financial statements? Why or why not?

4. What value do financial ratios offer investors in reviewing the financial performance of a company? Why is it important to remember financial ratios can differ from industry to industry?

DEVELOPING WORKPLACE SKILLS

Key: ● **Team**   ★ **Analytic**   ▲ **Communication**   ▣ **Technology**

▲ ★ 1. Contact an accountant at a firm in your area, or talk with one in your school's accounting department. Ask what challenges, changes, and opportunities he or she foresees in the accounting profession in the next five years. List the forecasts on a sheet of paper and then compare them with the information gathered by your classmates.

★ ▲ **2.** Place yourself in the role of a small-business consultant. One of your clients, Be Pretty Fashions, is considering opening two new stores. The fashion industry experiences continuous style changes. Prepare a formal draft memo to Be Pretty Fashions explaining the difficulties a firm experiences when it encounters the cash flow problems that typically occur in this industry. Think of a business option that Be Pretty Fashions could try to avoid cash flow problems.

★ ▲ **3.** You are a new board member for an emerging not-for-profit organization hoping to attract new donors. Contributors want to know how efficiently not-for-profit organizations use their donations. Unfortunately, your fellow board members see little value in financial reporting and analysis and believe the good works of the organization speak for themselves. Prepare a fact sheet convincing the board of the need for effective financial reporting with arguments about why it would help the organization's fund-raising goals.

▣ ★ **4.** Obtain the most recent annual report for a publicly traded Canadian company of your choice. (Hint: You can visit the company's website or SEDAR.) Using data from the annual report, try your hand at computing financial ratios, such as the current ratio, debt to owners' equity ratio, and return on sales for the firm. Next, obtain an annual report of one of the company's competitors and compute the same ratios for that company. What did you find?

▣ ★ **5.** Obtain the most recent annual report for a publicly traded Canadian company of your choice. (Hints: You can visit the company's website or SEDAR.) Look over the firm's financial statements and see how they match the information in this chapter. Read the auditor's opinion (usually at the end of the report) and evaluate what you think are the most important conclusions of the auditors.

ANALYZING MANAGEMENT DECISIONS

Getting Through the Hard Times at Hard Rock

In the mid-1990s, the theme-dining business seemed like a path lined with gold. With regularity, celebrity stargazers, enthusiastic press from around the globe, and hungry customers gathered at the openings of theme restaurants such as Planet Hollywood and Motown Cafe. Unfortunately, the situation changed. In the late 1990s and early 2000s, Planet Hollywood filed for bankruptcy protection and Motown Cafe closed units across the country. Consumer boredom, a slowing economy, and a saturated market were blamed.

The changing "entertainment" market raised eyebrows at the granddaddy of theme restaurants, the Hard Rock Cafe (HRC, <*http://www.hardrock.com*>). HRC knew that its market position was shaky due to increased competition and shifting consumer attitudes. The company also felt growing financial pressures and speculated that a change in financial management might be needed. HRC had operated with a traditional, competent accounting department that ensured that the company paid its bills, had money left at the end of the day, and could state how much it was earning. The problem was that HRC lacked the ability to analyze its financial information fully and use it to improve operations. To address these concerns, the company recruited a new CFO and dedicated itself to changing the financial reporting and information structure at the company.

Management believed that it had a tremendous undervalued asset—a premium global brand. The company dedicated itself to protecting and expanding that asset. However, it was evident that without revenue, brand loyalty did not matter. The company's CFO was astonished to find that HRC sold $180 million per year in merchandise (primarily its well-known T-shirts) in addition to food. Yet, there was no exact explanation how individual items contributed to the firm's profit. As a result, the decision was made to change the company's accounting and financial management systems.

To begin, the company piloted a food and beverage management system to track usage and item profitability. This system included information such as daily and seasonal buying patterns, profitability of one menu versus another, average weekly guest counts per restaurant, and specific cost of sales and profit margins per item. The company then shifted the responsibility of the firm's accountants. Instead of being responsible for profit-and-loss statements for a certain number of restaurants, company accountants now were responsible for one major financial category only, such as cost of goods sold, for all of the company's operations. The objective was to compile companywide information for sound financial decision making.

Hard Rock Cafe also broke down the barriers that existed between the finance and accounting departments as well as operations, merchandising, and marketing. Today, financial information is shared directly with managers who can execute the recommendations at the restaurant level. There are now over 192 locations, which include restaurants, hotels, casinos, and live music venues, in 60 countries around the world. It's hard to believe that it all started with the search for a good burger.

Sources: "Hard Rock History," Hard Rock Cafe International, Inc., accessed 15 April 2015, http://www.hardrock.com/corporate/history.aspx; "Rank Is Betting on Another Good Year," *Birmingham (UK) Post*, 1 March 2003, 15; Jon Griffin, "Rank Is Backing a Winner," *Evening Mail (UK)*, 28 February 2003, 26; and Larry Bleiberg, "Cafe Quest Has Retiree on a Roll," *Dallas Morning News*, 15 March 2000, 12G.

Discussion Questions

1. Why is it important for Hard Rock Cafe to know how different products contribute financially to overall company profits?

2. Do you think that Hard Rock Cafe's focus on improved financial reporting helped its company planning capabilities? How?

3. In terms of accounting principles, what would you need to remember when analyzing the financial performance of the Hard Rock Cafe, a U.S. business, to the Keg Steakhouse and Bar, a Canadian business?

VIDEO CASE 16

dougieDOG

Dragons' Den, a CBC production, is the highest-rated Canadian unscripted program on during the regular television season with an average weekly audience of more than 1.2 million Canadians. It also boasts an active online community averaging more than 650,000 page views per month. Aspiring entrepreneurs pitch their business concepts and products to a panel of successful Canadian entrepreneurs in exchange for money and ownership in their companies. These aspiring entrepreneurs must get all of the money they are requesting or they will go home with nothing.

In this segment, we meet Dougie Luv, a Vancouver entrepreneur with a gourmet take on a campfire classic. President of dougieDOG Hot Dogs <*http://dougiedog.com*>, he is seeking $200,000 for 25 percent of his company. Two and a half years ago, Luv decided to research the hot dog, a comfort food. He drove to Los Angeles and spent eight weeks on the road, eating hot dogs. Returning to Vancouver, he opened British Columbia's first hot dog restaurant.

The hot dogs are all natural, free of hormones, preservatives, and chemical additives. His restaurant serves more than 26 varieties of this all-natural hot dog. Costing $7 each, the price is more than double the price of a hot dog that is purchased from a street vendor (also known as "street meat").

The operation is 650 square feet with monthly sales between $25,000 to $30,000. While the operation lost $10,000 in its first year, Luv has since adjusted the food costs and wages. It is in a great location, Vancouver's entertainment district. A lot of his business occurs after 10:00 p.m. when people leave the bars and clubs in the area.

Luv is passionate about his company, and he is convinced that it is going to make money on this exclusive brand of hot dog. In fact, he is legally ready to franchise his business. "This is what being an entrepreneur is about," says Luv. "Believing in your product, doing it, and making it work."

Unfortunately, Luv is not successful in convincing the Dragons to give him the money. Watch the video to learn why believing in your product and making it work is not always enough.

Sources: "Dragons' Den Presents the Next Gen Den, Targeting Canadian Business Start-Ups through an Online Platform," CBC, 21 January 2015, http://www.cbc.ca/mediacentre/dragons-den-presents-the-next-gen-den-targeting-canadian-business-start-ups-through-an-online-platfo.html; and "DougieDOG," CBC, accessed 15 April 2015, http://www.cbc.ca/dragonsden/pitches/dougiedog.

Discussion Questions

1. According to Dragon Jim Treliving, how much does a business between 600 to 800 square feet have to make to break even in a year? How close is this business, as it now stands, to this point?

2. Conduct some research on this company. Was Dougie Luv successful in his pitch the second time on the *Den?* (Hint: Visit *<http://www.cbc.ca/dragonsden/pitches/dougiedog>* for this episode.) How has appearing on CBC's *Dragons' Den* impacted the company?

3. Would you invest in a dougieDOG franchise based on what you learned in this video? Explain.

Financial Management

LEARNING OBJECTIVES

After you have read and studied this chapter, you should be able to:

LO1   Explain the role and responsibilities of financial managers.

LO2   Outline the financial planning process, and explain the three key budgets in the financial plan.

LO3   Explain why firms need operating funds.

LO4   Identify and describe different sources of short-term financing.

LO5   Identify and describe different sources of long-term financing.

PROFILE

GETTING TO KNOW SABRINA SIMMONS, EXECUTIVE VICE PRESIDENT AND CHIEF FINANCIAL OFFICER OF GAP INC.

As Executive Vice President (EVP) and Chief Financial Officer (CFO) of Gap Inc. (Gap, <http://www.gapinc.com>), Sabrina Simmons knows a thing or two about keeping current with trends. Fashion is a volatile industry that can shift suddenly on the whims of consumers. Companies that lose their "cool" factor can quickly disappear from the market if they fail to rebuild their brand. Gap was in the middle of a crisis of this scale when Simmons joined as treasurer in 2001. Besides being stuck in a creative rut, a series of poor capital market investments had hurt the company's finances. In her first act on the job, Simmons balanced the books and made executives swear that the company would never rely on risky investments to drive revenue again. It's an accomplishment that she remains proud of to this day.

Before making a splash at Gap, Simmons earned her bachelor's degree in finance from the University of California, Berkeley, and her MBA from UCLA. A certified public accountant, Simmons spent her post-grad

years in various bookkeeping jobs at companies like Hewlett-Packard and Ford subsidiary, USL Capital. She took her first foray into fashion as an assistant treasurer at Levi Strauss <*http://www.levistrauss.com*>. Her performance at the iconic blue jean maker caught the eye of British genetics firm, Sygen International, which hired Simmons as its CFO in the late 1990s. However, the slow world of science made Simmons miss the apparel business. When a treasurer position at Gap opened up, she seized the opportunity to get back into fashion.

While her handling of the company's early-2000s identity crisis put her in the spotlight, Simmons didn't have time to celebrate. Soon Gap began investing millions in an offshoot store called Forth & Towne. Unlike the company's collection of youthful brands, like Old Navy and Banana Republic, Forth & Towne was meant to appeal to older shoppers who had lost touch with Gap over the years. Unfortunately, the retailer's heavily hyped launch did little to generate interest among its target market. "After investing tens of millions of dollars, we made the difficult decision to cut our losses and shut it down after two years," said Simmons. "The silver lining is we learned many tough lessons. And this failure, though very public, didn't stop us from taking those lessons learned and investing in other good ideas."

In recognition of her accomplishments with the company, Gap appointed Simmons CFO in 2008. She's had to put out a number of fires since then, including the closing of hundreds of stores in 2012. In 2015, nine-year old online boutique, Piperlime, an accessories brand, was also closed so the company could focus on its larger brands. Simmons remains steadfast in her commitment to never accept defeat. "Take intelligent risks and accept sensible failures," said Simmons. "Tenacity and persistence are great traits. And don't be afraid to fail. It's a great way to learn."

Risk and uncertainty clearly define the role of financial management. In this chapter, you'll explore the role of finance in business. We'll discuss the challenges and the tools top managers like Sabrina Simmons use to attain financial stability and growth.

Sources: Kim Bhasin, "The End of Piperlime: Gap Wants Only Extra-Large Brands," BloombergBusiness, 27 January 2015, http://www.bloomberg.com/news/articles/2015-01-27/the-end-of-piperlime-gap-wants-only-extra-large-brands; Paul Quintaro, "Gap Offers Details on Advances in Omni-Channel Retailing, Global Growth," Benzinga, 16 April 2014; Susan Berfield, "Can Rebekka Bay Fix the Gap?" *Bloomberg BusinessWeek*, 20 March 2014; "Gap CFO Sabrina Simmons, BS 85, to Give Undergrad Commencement Speech," *Haas Now*, 29 March 2010; and Sabrina Simmons, "Commencement Address 2010: Berkeley-Haas Undergraduate Program," University of California, Berkeley: Haas School of Business, 19 May 2010, www.haas.berkeley.edu.

LO1 Explain the role and responsibilities of financial managers.

The Role of Finance and Financial Managers

The goal of this chapter is to answer two major questions: "What is finance?" and "What do financial managers do?" **Finance** is the function in a business that acquires funds for the firm and manages them within the firm. Finance activities include preparing budgets; completing cash flow analysis; and planning for the expenditure of funds on assets such as plant, equipment, and machinery. **Financial management** is the job of managing a firm's resources to meet its goals and objectives. Without a carefully calculated financial plan and sound financial management, a firm has little chance for survival, regardless of its products or marketing effectiveness. Let's briefly review the roles of accountants and financial managers.

> **finance**
> The function in a business that acquires funds for the firm and manages them within the firm.
>
> **financial management**
> The job of managing a firm's resources to meet its goals and objectives.

We can compare an accountant to a skilled laboratory technician who takes blood samples and other measures of a person's health and writes the findings on a health report (in business, this process is the preparation of financial statements). A financial manager is like the doctor who interprets the report and makes recommendations that will improve the patient's health. In short, **financial managers** examine the financial data prepared by accountants and recommend strategies for improving the financial performance of the firm.

> **financial managers**
> Managers who examine the financial data prepared by accountants and recommend strategies for improving the financial performance of the firm.

Clearly, financial managers can make sound financial decisions only if they understand accounting information. That is why we examined accounting in Chapter 16. Similarly, a good accountant needs to understand finance. Accounting and finance go together like peanut butter and jelly. In large and medium-sized organizations, both the accounting and the finance functions are generally under the control of a chief financial officer (CFO). A CFO is generally the second-highest paid person in an organization and CFOs often advance to the top job of CEO.[1] However, financial management could also be in the hands of a person who serves as company treasurer or vice president of finance. A comptroller is the chief *accounting* officer.

Figure 17.1 highlights a financial manager's tasks. As you can see, two key responsibilities are to obtain funds and to effectively control the use of those funds. Finance is a critical activity in both profit-seeking and not-for-profit organizations.[2] The role of advising top management on financial matters has become even more important in recent years as risk has increased. Appendix C, immediately following this chapter, is devoted to the subject of financial risk.

Finance is important no matter what the firm's size. Financing a small business is essential if a firm expects to survive its important first five years. But the need for careful financial management remains a challenge that a business, large or small, must face throughout its existence. For example, the Canadian divisions of General Motors and Chrysler required significant loans from both the federal and Ontario governments because of severe financial problems.[3]

■ **FIGURE 17.1**

WHAT FINANCIAL MANAGERS DO

- Auditing
- Planning
- Managing taxes
- Budgeting
- Advising top management on financial matters
- Obtaining funds
- Collecting funds (credit management)
- Controlling funds (funds management)

Cash

The Value of Understanding Finance

Three of the most common reasons a firm fails financially are:

1. Undercapitalization (insufficient funds to run a business)
2. Poor control over cash flow
3. Inadequate expense control

You can see all three in the following story:

Two friends, Elizabeth Bertani and Pat Sherwood, started a company called Parsley Patch on what can best be described as a shoestring budget. It began when Bertani prepared salt-free seasonings for

Michael Miller overhauled the underperforming Goodwill Industries <*http://goodwillindustries.ca*> operation in his area by treating the not-for-profit like a for-profit business. He trimmed operating expenses; compared sales by store, closing weak outlets and opening new ones in better locations; and cut distribution costs. Sales soared from $4 million to over $135 million, eliminating the need for outside funding.

her husband, who was on a no-salt diet. Her friend Sherwood thought the seasonings were good enough to sell. Bertani agreed, and Parsley Patch Inc. was born. The business began with an investment of $5,000 that was rapidly depleted on a logo and label design. Bertani and Sherwood quickly learned the need for capital in getting a business going. Eventually, they invested more than $100,000 of their own money to keep the business from being undercapitalized.

Everything started well, and hundreds of gourmet shops adopted the product line. But when sales failed to meet expectations, the women decided the health-food market offered more potential because salt-free seasonings were a natural for people with restricted diets. The choice was a good one. Sales soared, approaching $30,000 a month. Still, the company earned no profits.

Bertani and Sherwood were not trained in monitoring cash flow or in controlling expenses. In fact, they had been told not to worry about costs, and they hadn't. They eventually hired a certified public accountant (CPA) and an experienced financial manager, who taught them how to compute the costs of their products, and how to control expenses as well as cash moving in and out of the company (cash flow). The business was still not making a profit and Bertani sold her share to Jon Gage. Parsley Patch introduced more blends and before long, Parsley Patch was earning a comfortable margin on operations that ran close to $1 million a year. Luckily, the owners—now also husband and wife—were able to turn things around before it was too late. Eventually, they sold the firm to spice and seasonings giant McCormick.[4]

If Bertani and Sherwood had understood finance before starting their business, they may have been able to avoid the problems they encountered. The key word here is *understood*. You do not have to pursue finance as a career to understand it. Understanding finance is important to anyone who wants to start a small business, invest in stocks and bonds, or plan a retirement fund. In short, finance and accounting are two areas everyone involved in business should study. Since we discussed accounting in Chapter 16, let's look more closely at what financial management is all about.

What Is Financial Management?

Financial managers are responsible for paying a company's bills at the appropriate time and for collecting overdue payments to make sure the company does not lose too much money to bad debts (people or firms that do not pay their bills). Therefore, finance functions, such as buying merchandise on credit

Most businesses have predictable day-to-day needs, like the need to buy supplies, pay for fuel and utilities, and pay employees. Financial management is the function that helps ensure firms have the funds they need when they need them. What would happen to the company providing the work in this photo if it couldn't buy fuel for its trucks?

(accounts payable) and collecting payments from customers (accounts receivable), are key components of the financial manager's job (see Figure 17.1). While these functions are vital to all types of businesses, they are particularly critical to small and medium-sized businesses, which typically have smaller cash or credit cushions than large corporations.[5]

It is essential that financial managers stay abreast of changes or opportunities in finance, such as changes in tax laws, since taxes represent an outflow of cash from a business.[6] Financial managers must also analyze the tax implications of managerial decisions to minimize the taxes the business must pay. Usually a member of a firm's finance department, the internal auditor, also checks the journals, ledgers, and financial statements the accounting department prepares, to make sure all transactions are in accordance with the international financial reporting standards (IFRS). (Recall the brief discussion on IFRS in Chapter 16.). Without such audits, accounting statements would be less reliable.[7] Therefore, it is important that internal auditors be objective and critical of any improprieties or deficiencies noted in their evaluations.[8] Thorough internal audits assist the firm in financial planning, which we'll look at next.

LO2 Outline the financial planning process, and explain the three key budgets in the financial plan.

Financial Planning

Financial planning means analyzing short-term and long-term money flows to and from a firm. Its overall objective is to optimize the firm's profitability and make the best use of its money. It has three steps: (1) forecasting a firm's short-term and long-term financial needs, (2) developing budgets to meet those needs, and (3) establishing financial control to see whether the company is achieving its goals (see Figure 17.2). Let's look at each step and the role it plays in improving the organization's financial health.

Forecasting Short-Term and Long-Term Financial Needs

Forecasting is an important part of any firm's financial plan. A **short-term forecast** predicts revenues, costs, and expenses for a period of one year or less. Part of the short-term forecast may be a **cash flow forecast**, which predicts the cash inflows and outflows in future periods, usually months or quarters. The inflows and outflows of cash recorded in the cash flow forecast are based on expected sales revenues and on various costs and expenses incurred, as well as when they are due for payment. The company's sales forecast estimates the firm's projected sales for a particular period. A business often uses its past financial statements as a basis for projecting expected sales and various costs and expenses.

> **short-term forecast**
> Forecast that predicts revenues, costs, and expenses for a period of one year or less.
>
> **cash flow forecast**
> Forecast that predicts the cash inflows and outflows in future periods, usually months or quarters.

A **long-term forecast** predicts revenues, costs, and expenses for a period longer than one year, and sometimes as long as five or ten years. This forecast plays a crucial part in the company's long-term strategic plan, which asks questions such as these: "What business are we in? Should we be in it five years

■ **FIGURE 17.2**

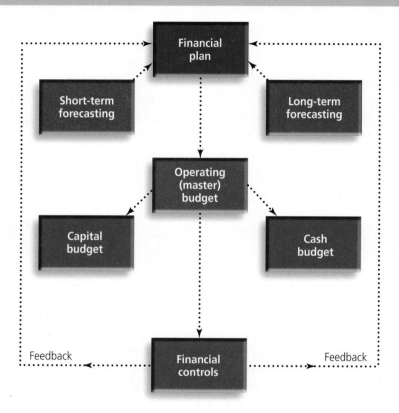

FINANCIAL PLANNING

Note the close link between financial planning and budgeting.

from now? How much money should we invest in technology and new plant and equipment over the next decade? Will we have cash available to meet long-term obligations?" Web-based software helps financial managers address these long-term forecasting questions.

long-term forecast
Forecast that predicts revenues, costs, and expenses for a period longer than one year, and sometimes as far as five or ten years into the future.

The long-term financial forecast gives top management, as well as operations managers, some sense of the income or profit of different strategic plans.[9] It also helps in preparing company budgets.

Working with the Budget Process

A **budget** sets forth management's expectations for revenues and, on the basis of those expectations, allocates the use of specific resources throughout the firm. As a financial plan, it depends heavily on the accuracy of a firm's balance sheet, income statement, statement of cash flows, and short-term and long-term financial forecasts, all of which need to be as accurate as possible. To effectively prepare budgets, financial managers must therefore take their forecasting responsibilities seriously.[10] A budget becomes the primary guide for the firm's financial operations and expected financial needs.

> **budget**
> A financial plan that sets forth management's expectations, and, on the basis of those expectations, allocates the use of specific resources throughout the firm.

There are usually several types of budgets established in a firm's financial plan:

- Capital budget;
- Cash budget; and
- Operating (master) budget.

A **capital budget** highlights a firm's spending plans for major asset purchases that often require large sums of money, like property, buildings, and equipment.

> **capital budget**
> A budget that highlights a firm's spending plans for major asset purchases that often require large sums of money, like property, buildings, and equipment.

Special processing equipment turns an average potato into the chips and fries we consume. The firm's capital budget is the financial tool that controls business spending for expensive assets such as this processing equipment. Such major assets are referred to as capital assets or property, plant, and equipment. What items would be in your school's capital budget?

A **cash budget** estimates cash inflows and outflows during a particular period, like a month or a quarter. It helps managers anticipate borrowing needs, debt repayment, operating expenses, and short-term investments. It is often the last budget prepared. A sample cash budget for our company, Very Vegetarian, is provided in Figure 17.3.

> **cash budget**
> A budget that estimates a firm's cash inflows and outflows during a particular period (e.g. monthly or quarterly).

The **operating (master) budget** ties together the firm's other budgets and summarizes the business's proposed financial activities. More formally it estimates costs and expenses needed to run a business, given projected revenues. The firm's spending on supplies, travel, rent, technology, advertising, and salaries is determined in the operating budget. This budget is generally the most detailed a

■ FIGURE 17.3

A SAMPLE CASH BUDGET FOR VERY VEGETARIAN			
VERY VEGETARIAN Monthly Cash Budget for December 31, 2016			
	January	February	March
Sales forecast	$50,000	$45,000	$40,000
Collections			
Cash sales (20%)		$9,000	$8,000
Credit sales (80% of past month)		$40,000	$36,000
Monthly cash collection		$49,000	$44,000
Payments schedule			
Supplies and material		$11,000	$10,000
Salaries		12,000	12,000
Direct labour		9,000	9,000
Taxes		3,000	3,000
Other expenses		7,000	6,000
Monthly cash payments		$42,000	$40,000
Cash budget			
Cash flow		$7,000	$5,000
Beginning cash		21,000	6,000
Total cash		$6,000	$11,000
Less minimum cash balance		−6,000	−6,000
Excess cash to market securities		$0	$5,000
Loans needed for minimum balance		0	0

firm prepares. Most firms will prepare 12 monthly operating budgets for the next year. Typically, those responsible for the activities reflected within the operating budget(s) are involved in its preparation. Ultimately the firm's board of directors is responsible for approving all budgets. Often the entire budget process can take months and involve a significant amount of time.

operating (master) budget
The budget that ties together all of a firm's other budgets and summarizes the business's proposed financial activities.

Financial planning obviously plays an important role in the firm's operations and often determines what long-term investments it makes, when it will need specific funds, and how it will generate them. Once a company forecasts its short-term and long-term financial needs (Step 1) and compiles budgets to show how it will allocate funds (Step 2), the final step in financial planning is to establish financial controls (Step 3). Before we talk about those, however, Figure 17.4 challenges you to check your personal financial planning skill by developing a monthly budget for You Incorporated.

■ **FIGURE 17.4**

YOU INCORPORATED MONTHLY BUDGET

In Chapter 16 you compiled a sample balance sheet for You Inc. Now, let's develop a monthly budget for You Inc. Be honest and think of everything that needs to be included for an accurate monthly budget for You! Much like a small business, when putting the monthly budget together, remember that the norm is to overestimate income and underestimate expenses. Often you need to revisit the budget a number of times before finalizing the numbers as you try to balance the income with the expenses to hopefully eliminate cash deficits.

	Expected	Actual	Difference
Monthly income			
Wages (net pay after taxes)			
Savings account withdrawal			
Family support			
Other sources			
Total monthly income			
Monthly expenses			
Fixed expenses			
Rent or mortgage			
Car payment			
Life insurance			
Tuition or fees			
Other fixed expenses			
Subtotal of fixed expenses			
Variable expenses			
Food			
Clothing			
Entertainment			
Transportation			
Phone			
Utilities			
Publications			
Internet connection			
Cable television			
Other expenses			
Subtotal of variable expenses			
Total expenses			
Total monthly income − Total expenses = Cash on hand or Cash deficit			

Establishing Financial Controls

Financial control is a process in which a firm periodically compares its actual revenues, costs, and expenses with its budget. Most companies hold at least monthly financial reviews as a way to ensure financial control. Such control procedures help managers identify variances to the financial plan and allow them to take corrective action if necessary. Financial controls also provide feedback to help reveal which accounts, which departments, and which people are varying from the financial plan. Finance managers can judge if these variances may or may not be justified, allowing them to make some financial adjustments to the plan when needed.

> **financial control**
> A process in which a firm periodically compares its actual revenues, costs, and expenses with its projected ones.

Decreasing oil prices have caused some companies to adjust their financial plans. For example, oil sands producer MEG Energy Corp. <*http://www.megenergy.com*> slashed its capital program by 75 percent from $1.2 billion to $305 million.[11] "The revision of our 2015 capital investment plan is in response to the continuing deterioration of global crude oil markets," Bill McCaffrey, president and CEO, said in a statement. "While our projects remain economic at current strip pricing, we believe it is prudent to reduce capital spending until we see a sustained improvement."[12] The Making Ethical Decisions box details a management situation related to financial control.

Making ETHICAL DECISIONS

Sail Smoothly or Rock the Boat?

Assume you have recently taken a new job as financial manager at a mid-sized pharmaceutical company. After working there just a few months, you sense the attitude of most employees at the company is, "Who cares?" Salespeople do not turn in detailed expense reports for their travel, nor do they provide receipts to receive reimbursement for meals and other expenses, through the company operations manual say such documentation is required. You also notice employees readily help themselves to office supplies, like pens, paper, and staplers, with no questions asked. What actions will you take, if any?

FINANCIAL MANAGEMENT IN TRYING TIMES

The collapse of financial markets in 2008 put the spotlight directly on the failure of financial managers to do their jobs effectively. Poor investment decisions and risky financial dealings (especially in areas such as real estate, although financial dealings in Canada were far less risky than the United States) caused financial markets to suffer their worst fall since the 1920s and 1930s. As the requirements of financial institutions became more stringent following the financial crisis, the job of the financial manager has become more challenging. Investors who watched long-standing financial firms, such as Lehman Brothers, close their doors not only saw respected businesses disappear, but they also saw their invested funds disappear with them. Without a doubt, financial managers have a long road back to earning the trust of the public.

Progress Assessment

- Name three finance functions important to the firm's overall operations and performance.
- What are the three primary financial problems that cause firms to fail?
- How do short-term and long-term financial forecasts differ?
- What is the purpose of preparing budgets in an organization? Can you identify three different types of budgets?

LO3 Explain why firms need operating funds.

The Need for Operating Funds

In business, the need for funds never seems to cease. That is why sound financial management is essential to all businesses. And like our personal financial needs, the capital needs of a business change over time. Remember the example of Parsley Patch to see why a small business's financial requirements can shift considerably. The same is true for large corporations, such as integrated oil major Husky Energy Inc. *<http://www.huskyenergy.ca>*. With operations in Western Canada, the East Coast offshore, the United States, and Asia, whenever it ventures into new product areas or markets, the company's funding needs change.[13] Virtually all organizations have needs for which funds must be available. Key areas include:

- Managing day-to-day needs of the business;
- Controlling credit operations;
- Acquiring needed inventory; and
- Making capital expenditures.

Let's look carefully at the financial needs of these key areas, which affect both the smallest and the largest of businesses.

Managing Day-to-Day Needs of a Business

If workers expect to be paid on Friday, they do not want to wait until Monday for their paycheques. If tax payments are due on the 15th of the month, the government expects the money on time. If the payment on a business loan is due on the 30th of this month, the lender does not mean the 1st of the next month. As you can see, funds have to be available to meet the daily operational costs of a business.

Financial managers must ensure that funds are available to meet daily cash needs without compromising the firm's opportunities to invest money for its future. Money has *time value*.[14] In other words, if someone offered to give you $200 today or one year from today, you would benefit by taking the $200 today. Why? It is very simple. You could invest the $200 you receive today, start collecting interest, and over a year's time it would grow. The same thing is true in business; the interest a firm gains on its investments is important in maximizing the profit it will gain. That is why financial managers often try to minimize cash expenditures to free up funds for investment in interest-bearing accounts. They suggest the company pay its bills as late as possible (unless a cash discount is available for early payment). They also advise companies to try to collect what is owed to them as fast as possible in order to maximize the investment potential of the firm's funds. Unfortunately, collecting funds as fast as possible can be particularly challenging. Efficient cash management is particularly important to small firms since their access to capital is much more limited than that of larger businesses.[15]

It's difficult to think of a business that doesn't make credit available to its customers. However, collecting accounts receivable from some customers can be time-consuming and costly. Accepting credit cards, such as Visa, MasterCard, and American Express, can simplify transactions for sellers and guarantee payment. What types of products do you regularly purchase with a credit card?

Controlling Credit Operations

Financial managers know that in today's highly competitive business environment, making credit available helps keep current customers happy and attracts new ones. Credit for customers can be especially important during tough financial times, like a recession, as lenders are more hesitant to approve loans.

The problem with selling on credit is that a large percentage of a non-retailer's business assets could be tied up in its credit accounts (accounts receivable). This forces the firm to use its own funds to pay for goods or services sold to customers who bought on credit. Financial managers in such firms often develop efficient collection procedures like offering cash or quantity discounts to buyers who pay their accounts by a certain (usually earlier) date. They also scrutinize old and new credit customers to see whether they have a history of meeting their credit obligations on time.

One convenient way to decrease the time and expense of collecting accounts receivable is to accept bank credit cards such as MasterCard or Visa. The banks that issue these cards have already established the customer's creditworthiness, which reduces the business's risk. Businesses must pay a fee to accept credit cards, but the fees are usually offset by the benefits.[16] In an effort to reduce those credit card costs as well as speed up the transaction process, many businesses today accept mobile payments through services like Square and Level Up.[17] For example, Chipotle <*https://www.chipotle.com*>, Starbucks, and Dunkin Donuts <*https://www.dunkindonuts.com*> have invested in mobile payment systems.[18] Mobile payment systems not only make transactions quick and simple, the processors usually charge lower fees than traditional credit card companies.[19]

Acquiring Needed Inventory

As you read in Chapter 14, effective marketing requires focusing on the customer and providing high-quality service and readily available goods. A carefully constructed inventory policy helps manage the firm's available funds and maximize profitability. For example, Dozzle's, an ice cream parlour, deliberately ties up fewer funds in its inventory of ice cream in the winter. It is obvious why; demand for ice cream is lower in the winter.

Just-in-time inventory control (discussed in Chapter 10) and other such methods can reduce the funds a firm must tie up in inventory. Carefully evaluating its inventory turnover ratio (discussed in Chapter 16), can also help a firm control the outflow of cash for inventory. A business of any size must understand that poorly managed inventory can seriously affect cash flow and drain its finances.

Making Capital Expenditures

Capital expenditures are major investments in either tangible long-term assets, such as land, buildings, and equipment, or intangible assets, such as patents, trademarks, and copyrights. In many organizations the purchase of major assets—such as land for future expansion, manufacturing plants to increase production capabilities, research to develop new product ideas, and equipment to maintain or exceed current levels of output—is essential. Expanding into new markets can be expensive with no guarantee of success. Therefore, it is critical that companies weigh all possible options before committing a large portion of available resources.

> **capital expenditures**
> Major investments in either tangible long-term assets, such as land, buildings, and equipment, or intangible assets, such as patents, trademarks, and copyrights.

Consider a firm that needs to expand its production capabilities due to increased customer demand. It could buy land and build a new plant, purchase an existing plant, or rent space. Can you think of financial and accounting considerations at play in this decision?

The need for operating funds raises several questions for financial managers: "How does the firm obtain funds to finance operations and other business needs? Will it require specific funds in the long or the short term? How much will it cost (i.e., interest) to obtain these funds? Will they come from internal or external sources?" We address these questions next.

Alternative Sources of Funds

We described finance earlier as the function in a business responsible for acquiring and managing funds. Sound financial management determines the amount of money needed and the most appropriate sources from which to obtain it. A firm can raise needed capital by borrowing money (debt), selling ownership (equity), or earning profits (retained earnings).

Debt financing refers to funds raised through various forms of borrowing that must be repaid. **Equity financing** is money raised from operations within the firm or through the sale of ownership in the firm (shares). Firms can borrow funds either for the short-term or the long-term. **Short-term**

financing refers to funds needed for one year or less. **Long-term financing** refers to funds needed for more than one year (usually two to ten years). Figure 17.5 highlights why firms may need short-term and long-term funds.

debt financing
Funds raised through various forms of borrowing that must be repaid.

equity financing
Funds raised from operations within the firm or through the sale of ownership in the firm.

short-term financing
Borrowed funds that are needed for one year or less.

long-term financing
Borrowed funds that are needed for a period more than one year.

We'll explore the different sources of short-term and long-term financing next. Let's first pause to check your understanding by completing the Progress Assessment.

■ **FIGURE 17.5**

WHY FIRMS NEED FUNDS	
Short-Term Funds	Long-Term Funds
Monthly expenses	New-product development
Unanticipated emergencies	Replacement of capital equipment
Cash flow problems	Mergers or acquisitions
Expansion of current inventory	Expansion into new markets (domestic or global)
Temporary promotional programs	New facilities

Progress Assessment

- Money has time value. What does this mean?
- Why is accounts receivable a financial concern to a firm?
- What's the primary reason an organization spends a good deal of its available funds on inventory and capital expenditures?
- What is the difference between debt and equity financing?

LO4 Identify and describe different sources of short-term financing

Obtaining Short-Term Financing

The bulk of a finance manager's job does not relate to obtaining long-term funds. In small businesses, for example, long-term financing is often out of the question.[20] Instead, day-to-day operations call for the careful management of *short-term* financial needs. Firms may need to borrow short-term funds to purchase additional inventory or to pay unexpected bills. Like an individual, a business, especially a small business, sometimes needs to secure short-term funds when its cash reserves are low. Let's consider how it does so.

Trade Credit

Trade credit is the practice of buying goods or services now and paying for them later. It is the most widely used source of short-term funding, the least expensive, and the most convenient. Small businesses rely heavily on trade credit from firms such as Purolator *<http://www.purolator.com>*, just as do large firms such as the Hudson's Bay Company. When a firm buys merchandise, it receives an invoice (a bill) much like the one you receive when you buy something with a credit card. As you will learn, however, the terms businesses receive are often different than those on your monthly statement.

> **trade credit**
> The practice of buying goods and services now and paying for them later.

Business invoices usually contain terms such as *2/10, net 30*. This means the buyer can take a 2 percent discount for paying the invoice within 10 days. Otherwise the total bill (net) is due in 30 days. Financial managers pay close attention to such discounts because they create opportunities to reduce the firm's costs. Think about it for a moment: If terms are 2/10, net 30, the customer will pay 2 percent more by waiting an extra 20 days to pay the invoice. If the firm *can* pay its bill within 10 days, it is needlessly increasing its costs by not doing so.

Some suppliers hesitate to give trade credit to an organization with a poor credit rating, no credit history, or a history of late payments. They may insist the customer sign a **promissory note**, a written

One thing you can never have too much of is cash. Financial managers must make certain there is enough cash available to meet daily financial needs and still have funds to invest in its future. What does it mean when we say cash has a time value?

contract with a promise to pay a supplier a specific sum of money at a definite time. Promissory notes are negotiable. The supplier can sell them to a bank at a discount (the amount of the note less a fee for the bank's services in collecting the amount due), and the business is then responsible for paying the bank.

promissory note
A written contract with a promise to pay.

Family and Friends

Firms often have several bills coming due at the same time with no source of funds to pay them. Many small firms obtain short-term funds by borrowing money from family and friends. Such loans can create problems, however, if both the lender and borrower do not understand cash flow. That's why it is

Spotlight *On* SMALL BUSINESS

Threading the Financial Needle

Coming up with a great idea is only the first step in starting a business. Entrepreneurs need money to turn their ideas into reality. Luckily, a number of potential investors are willing to open their wallets for what they think is going to be the next big thing. But to attract these angel investors, entrepreneurs must be sure their business concepts have been carefully planned. James Reinhart, CEO of the clothing exchange website, thredUP <https://www.thredup.com>, knows this as well as anyone.

While attending college, Reinhart and his roommate realized that they owned too many clothes. After gathering start-up funds of $70,000 from family, friends, and personal savings, Reinhart and his partners launched thredUP, a website where people could buy and sell used clothing cheaply. Within three months, the site drew in more than 10,000 members.

Reinhart soon discovered that the market for used children's clothes was much larger than the adult market since children grow out of their clothes every three to six months. So the site changed its focus to targeting parents looking to "trade up" their kids' wardrobes. Parents send in clothes that are assessed by professional buyers who judge quality and the firm's ability to resell them. The higher the quality, the more money the company pays the sender. The company then resells the clothing on its website.

Reinhart was able to improve the site thanks to a $250,000 angel investor that loved thredUP's new strategy. Soon thredUP attracted $1.4 million more in investment. The money was used to phase out the site's original service entirely due to its new focus on solely children's clothing. The next year, the company secured a round of venture capital funding, this time topping out at $50 million. With the new investment, Reinhart could have expanded thredUP into other areas. Instead he focused on spending the money improving the current business model. "As an entrepreneur, you're always thinking about the adjacent things to do, but we have the opportunity to build a really big, important business in the market," Reinhart said. "That's what we're going to do."

Sources: thredUP, www.thredUP.com, accessed April 2014; Philip Levinson, "thredUP's HBS Founders Master the Art of the Pivot," *The Harbus,* 7 March 2012; and "*thredUP.com* Releases Second Annual Clothing Resale Report," *The Providence Journal,* 26 February 2014.

sometimes better to go to a commercial bank that fully understands the business's risk and can help analyze its future financial needs rather than to borrow from friends or relatives.[21]

Entrepreneurs appear to be listening to this advice. According to the National Federation of Independent Business, entrepreneurs today are relying less on family and friends as a source of borrowed funds than they have in the past.[22] If an entrepreneur decides to ask family or friends for financial assistance, it is important that both parties (1) agree to specific loan terms, (2) put the agreement in writing, and (3) arrange for repayment in the same way they would for a bank loan. Such actions help keep family relationships and friendships intact. The Spotlight on Small Business highlights a company that was first financed through family and friends before it had to consider other sources of financing to fund its growth.

Commercial Banks

Banks, being sensitive to risk, generally prefer to lend short-term funds to larger, established businesses. Imagine the different types of business people who go to banks for a loan, and you will get a better idea of the requests bankers evaluate. Picture, for example, a farmer going to the bank in the spring to borrow funds for seed, fertilizer, supplies, and other needs that will be repaid after the fall harvest. Or consider a local toy store buying merchandise for holiday sales. The store borrows the money for such purchases in the summer and plans to pay it back after the holidays. Restaurants often borrow funds at the beginning of the month and then repay the funds at the end of the month.

How much a business borrows and for how long depends on the kind of business it is and how quickly it can resell the merchandise it purchases with a bank loan or use the funds to generate funds. In a large business, specialists in a company's finance and accounting departments create a cash flow forecast. Small-business owners generally lack such specialists and monitor cash flow themselves.

What is important for a small firm to remember is if it gets a bank loan, the owner or person in charge of finance should keep in close touch with the bank and send regular financial statements to keep the bank up-to-date on its operations. The bank may spot cash flow problems early or be more willing to lend money in a crisis if a business has established a strong relationship built on trust and sound management.

Did you ever wonder how retailers get the money to buy all of the items available during the holiday season? Department stores and other large retailers make extensive use of commercial banks and other lenders to borrow the money needed to buy merchandise to stock their shelves. How do stores benefit from using this type of financing?

Forms of Short-Term Loans

Banks and other financial institutions offer different forms of short-term loans. A **secured loan** is backed by *collateral,* something valuable such as property. If the borrower fails to pay the loan, the lender may take possession of the collateral. An automobile loan is a secured loan. If the borrower does not repay it, the lender will repossess the car. Inventory of raw materials, like coal, copper, and steel, often serve as collateral for business loans. Collateral removes some of the bank's risk in lending the money.

> **secured loan**
> A loan backed by collateral, something valuable such as property.

A secured loan is backed by collateral, a tangible item of value. A car loan, for instance, is a secured loan in which the car itself is the collateral. What is the collateral in a mortgage loan?

Accounts receivable are company assets often used as collateral for a loan; the process is called *pledging* and works as follows: A percentage of the value of a firm's accounts receivable pledged (usually about 75 percent) is advanced to the borrowing firm. As customers pay off their accounts, the funds received are forwarded to the lender in repayment of the funds that were advanced.

An **unsecured loan** is more difficult to obtain because it does not require any collateral. Normally, lenders give unsecured loans only to highly regarded customers—long-standing businesses considered financially stable.

> **unsecured loan**
> A loan that does not require any collateral.

If a business develops a good relationship with a bank, the bank may open a **line of credit** for the firm. This is a given amount of unsecured short-term funds a bank will lend to a business, provided the funds are readily available. A line of credit is *not* guaranteed to a business. However it speeds up the borrowing process since a firm does not have to apply for a new loan every time it needs funds.[23] As a business matures and becomes more financially secure, banks will often increase the line of credit. Some even offer a **revolving credit agreement**, a line of credit that is guaranteed but usually comes with a fee. Both lines of credit and revolving credit agreements are particularly good sources of funds for unexpected cash needs.

> **line of credit**
> A given amount of unsecured funds a bank will lend to a business.
>
> **revolving credit agreement**
> A line of credit that is guaranteed but usually comes with a fee.

If a business is unable to secure a short-term loan from a bank, the financial manager may seek short-term funds from **commercial finance companies**. These non-deposit-type organizations make short-term loans to borrowers who offer tangible assets (e.g., property, plant, and equipment) as collateral. Commercial finance companies will often make loans to individuals and businesses that cannot get funds elsewhere. Since commercial finance companies assume higher degrees of risk than banks, they usually charge higher interest rates.

> **commercial finance companies**
> Organizations that make short-term loans to borrowers who offer tangible assets as collateral.

EVALUATING CREDITWORTHINESS[24]

Whether you are a business or a consumer, each time you apply to borrow money, you build a credit history. When you apply for credit, lenders consider your financial track record, along with information about your employment and other debts and assets you have. This information is captured in your **credit profile**, which is your financial reputation. It reflects your financial track record based on your borrowing history (e.g., applications for credit and credit repayment).

> **credit profile**
> A borrower's financial track record in the form of borrowing history.

When considering a credit application (e.g., a loan or revolving credit agreement), a lender will consider creditworthiness. Creditworthiness is determined by the **4 Cs of credit**—character, capacity, capital, and conditions. (These 4Cs can also apply to you.) Let's briefly consider each next.

> **4 Cs of credit**
> A business's creditworthiness is determined by its character, capacity, capital, and conditions.

Character includes factors such as business size, location, number of years in business, business structure, number of employees, history of principals, appetite for sharing information about itself, media coverage, liens, judgments or pending lawsuits, stock performance, and comments from references.

Capacity considers the ability of the business to pay its bills (i.e., its cash flow). It also includes the structure of the company's debt—whether secured or unsecured—and the existence of any unused lines of credit. Any defaults must also be identified.

Capital assesses whether a company has the financial resources to repay its creditors. This information is obtained from financial records. In general, this portion of the credit report is the one most closely reviewed by the credit analyst. Heavy weighting is given to such balance sheet items as working capital, net worth, and cash flow.

Conditions includes the external factors surrounding the business under consideration, including influences such as market fluctuations, industry growth rate, legal factors (e.g., political and legislative), and currency rates.

To build a positive credit history, consider these dos and don'ts. Do pay your bills on time, pay at least the minimum amount, and check your credit profile for errors. Don't use credit you don't understand, wait to report problems, pay bills late, or exceed your credit limit. Request a free copy of your credit profile from a credit bureau agency, such as TransUnion <*http://www.transunion.ca/ca*> or Equifax <*http://www.consumer.equifax.ca*>. Were you surprised by what was captured in your profile?

A credit bureau agency takes several elements of your credit profile and identifies a score that rates your creditworthiness on a scale. Your *credit score* may influence the interest rate that you pay and help determine whether lenders approve you for credit (e.g., a credit card or a car loan).

The 4Cs are also taken into consideration by other service providers, such as insurance companies, to set premiums. More than ever, lenders input scores and ratings that summarize the 4 Cs into a financial model to determine the risk of doing business with organizations and consumers. To learn more about risk, review Appendix C.

Factoring Accounts Receivable

One relatively expensive source of short-term funds for a firm is **factoring**, the process of selling accounts receivable for cash. Factoring dates as far back as 4,000 years to the days of ancient Babylon. Here is how it works: Let's say a firm sells many of its products on credit to consumers and other businesses, creating a number of accounts receivable. Some buyers may be slow in paying their bills, so a large amount of money is due the firm. A *factor* is a market intermediary (usually a financial institution such as a commercial bank) that agrees to buy the firm's accounts receivable, at a discount, for cash. The discount depends on the age of the accounts receivable, the nature of the business, and the condition of the economy. When it collects the accounts receivable that were originally owed to the firm, the factor keeps them.

factoring
The process of selling accounts receivable for cash.

While factors charge more than banks' loan rates, remember many small businesses cannot qualify for a loan. So even though factoring is an expensive way of raising short-term funds, it is popular among small businesses. A company can often reduce its factoring cost if it agrees to reimburse the factor for slow-paying accounts, or to assume the risk for customers who do not pay at all. Remember factoring is not a loan; it is the sale of a firm's asset (accounts receivable). Factoring is common in the clothing and furniture businesses, and in growing numbers of global trade ventures.

Commercial Paper

Often a corporation needs funds for just a few months and prefers not to have to negotiate with a commercial bank. One strategy available to larger firms is to sell commercial paper. **Commercial paper** consists of *unsecured* promissory notes, in amounts of $100,000 and up, that mature (come due) in 270 days or less.[25] Commercial paper states a fixed amount of money the business agrees to repay to the lender (investor), on a specific date, and at a specific rate of interest.

> **commercial paper**
> Unsecured promissory notes of $100,000 and up that mature (come due) in 270 days or less.

Because commercial paper is unsecured, only financially stable firms (mainly large corporations with excellent credit reputations) are able to sell it. Commercial paper can be a quick path to short-term funds at a lower interest than the interest charged by commercial banks. Since most commercial paper matures in 30 to 90 days, it is an investment opportunity for buyers who can afford to put up cash for short periods to earn some interest on their money.[26]

Credit Cards

Credit cards provide a business with ready access to money that can save time and the likely embarrassment of being rejected for a bank loan. Of course, in contrast to the convenience that credit cards offer, they are extremely risky and costly. Interest rates can be exorbitant, and there can be penalties if users fail to make their payments on time.

When credit grew tight in the recent economic downturn, John Mickey, who makes promotional items with corporate logos, tapped his retirement funds to obtain start-up money for his new venture. Why is this financing strategy considered risky?

Savvy business people study the perks that are offered with many cards and determine which might be the most beneficial to their companies. Joe Speiser, of pet-food distributor *Petflow.com*, found a cash-back card that helped put additional dollars back into his business.[27] Still, when dealing with credit cards, remember it's an expensive way to borrow money and credit cards are probably best used as a last resort.

After checking your progress, we'll look into long-term financing.

Progress Assessment

- What does an invoice containing the terms "2/10, net 30" mean?

- What's the difference between trade credit and a line of credit?

- What's the key difference between a secured loan and an unsecured loan?

- What is factoring? What are some of the considerations involved in establishing the discount rate?

LO5   Identify and describe different sources of long-term financing.

Obtaining Long-Term Financing

In a financial plan, forecasting determines the amount of funding the firm will need over various periods and the most appropriate sources for obtaining those funds. In setting long-term financing objectives, financial managers generally ask three questions:

1. What are the organization's long-term goals and objectives?

2. What funds do we need to achieve the firm's long-term goals and objectives?

3. What sources of long-term funding (capital) are available, and which will best fit our needs?

Firms need long-term capital to purchase expensive assets such as plant and equipment, to develop new products, and perhaps finance their expansion. In major corporations, the board of directors and top management usually make decisions about long-term financing, along with finance and accounting executives. Pfizer, one of the world's largest research-based biomedical and pharmaceutical companies, spends over $6 billion a year researching and developing new products.[28] The development of a single new drug could take 10 years and cost the firm over $1 billion before it brings in any profit. Plus, the company loses its patent protection on a drug after 20 years.[29] It is easy to see why high-level managers make the long-term financing decisions at Pfizer. Owners of small and medium-sized businesses are almost always actively engaged in analyzing long-term financing decisions.

As we noted earlier, long-term funding comes from two major sources: debt financing and equity financing. Before we consider these two sources, read the Reaching Beyond Our Borders box to learn why a source of long-term funding is raising some eyebrows.

Debt Financing

Debt financing is borrowing money a company has a legal obligation to repay. Firms can borrow either by getting a loan from a lending institution or by issuing bonds.

Reaching *Beyond* OUR BORDERS

Sovereign Wealth Funds (SWFs)

Sovereign wealth funds (SWFs) are large investment companies that are owned by governments. These funds are used by federal governments to set aside revenues from oil and gas, mining, and other commodities. The savings are then invested in financial assets, such as stocks and bonds, with the potential to create wealth for future generations. They have been a part of global financial markets for decades and today are valued at over $6 trillion. The largest SWFs are operated by Norway, United Arab Emirates, Saudi Arabia, China, Kuwait, and Singapore.

Canada's federal government does not have a national fund. In her report on SWFs, Madelaine Drohan, the Canada correspondent for *The Economist* and author of *The Nine Habits of Highly Effective Resource Economies: Lessons for Canada,* does not recommend a national fund for Canada. This is because of the way Canada's Constitution is set up whereby the resources belong to the provinces. If there was any attempt by the federal government to set up a national fund, she thinks that would probably lead to 30 years of debate and in-fighting and a national SWF might still never happen.

Canada has two provincial funds. The first is the Alberta Heritage Savings Trust Fund, which was established in 1976. (You were briefly introduced to this fund in Chapter 4.) The Alberta SWF is used as an example of what not to do as it was not structured well or managed wisely. As a result, the provincial assembly passed a law in 2012 requiring the government to deposit a certain share of the revenues from oil, gas, and mining into it. The fund also has clear mandates about what it should be investing in, and explicit benchmarks for its manager to meet.

The second provincial fund, established in 2006, is the Quebec government's Generations Fund. The government deposits mining royalties to the fund in addition to those from hydropower concessions and profits from Hydro-Québec, a utility owned by the province.

The Northwest Territories is setting up an SWF, and both Saskatchewan and British Columbia are considering SWFs of their own.

During the recent financial crisis, SWFs were hailed as heroes and saviours in the U.S. financial community because of the billions of dollars they invested in U.S. companies that were struggling to survive. Although SWFs provide distressed companies with much-needed capital when it is needed, the presence of foreign governments in the U.S. business world makes some people nervous. Such activity has caused some politicians and business executives to question the motives and intentions of these government-operated investment funds. This was especially true with SWFs controlled by nations with which the United States sometimes has shaky relationships in global affairs. To date, the facts don't seem to support the suspicions about SWFs.

Sources: "The year of the ant," *The Economist*, 25 January 2014, http://www.economist.com/news/finance-and-economics/21595052-resource-rich-provinces-canada-are -becoming-more-parsimonious-year; Eliot Brown, "Time Warner Nears Deal to Sell Headquarters," *The Wall Street Journal,* 15 January 2014; Ashley Stahl, "The Promise and Perils of Sovereign Wealth Funds," *Forbes,* 19 December 2013; John Aziz, "Does the United States Need a Sovereign Wealth Fund?" *The Week,* 20 January 2014; and Madhavi Acharya-Tom Yew, "The case for sovereign wealth funds in Canada," The Star.com, 8 January 2013, http://www.thestar.com/business/2013/01/08/the_case_for_sovereign_wealth_funds_in_canada.html.

DEBT FINANCING BY BORROWING MONEY FROM LENDING INSTITUTIONS

Long-term loans are usually due within 3 to 7 years but may extend to 15 or 20 years. A **term-loan agreement** is a promissory note that requires the borrower to repay the loan, with interest, in specified monthly or annual instalments. A major advantage is that the loan interest is tax deductible.

> **term-loan agreement**
> A promissory note that requires the borrower to repay the loan in specified instalments.

Long-term loans are both larger and more expensive to the firm than short-term loans. Since the repayment period can be quite long, lenders assume more risk and usually require collateral, which may be real estate, machinery, equipment, company shares, or other items of value. Lenders may also require certain restrictions to force the firm to act responsibly. The interest rate is based on the adequacy of collateral, the firm's credit rating, and the general level of market interest rates. The greater the risk a lender takes in making a loan, the higher the rate of interest. This principle is known as the **risk/return trade-off**.

> **risk/return trade-off**
> The principle that the greater the risk a lender takes in making a loan, the higher the interest rate required.

DEBT FINANCING BY ISSUING BONDS

If an organization is unable to obtain its long-term financing needs by getting a loan from a lending institution, such as a bank, it may try to issue bonds. A **bond** is a corporate certificate indicating that an investor has lent money to a firm or a government. An organization that issues bonds, such as different levels of governments and corporations, has the legal obligation to make regular interest payments during the term of the bond and to repay the entire bond principal amount at a prescribed time.

> **bond**
> A corporate certificate indicating that an investor has lent money to a firm or a government.

Bonds are usually issued in units of $1,000. The *principal* is the face value (dollar value) of a bond, which the issuing company is legally bound to repay in full to the bondholder on the **maturity date**. **Interest** is the payment the bond issuer makes to the bondholders to compensate them for the use of their money. If Very Vegetarian issues a $1,000 bond with an interest rate of 5 percent and a maturity date of 2025, the company is agreeing to pay a bondholder a total of $50 in interest each year until a specified date in 2025, when the full $1,000 must be repaid. Maturity dates for bonds can vary. For example, in 2014 the federal government raised $2.5 billion worth of 50-year bonds in two rounds. The second round of bonds, with an interest rate of 2.76 percent, mature on December 1, 2064.[30] Firms such as Disney, IBM, and Coca-Cola have issued century bonds with 100-year maturity dates.[31]

> **maturity date**
> The exact date the issuer of a bond must pay the principal to the bondholder.
>
> **interest**
> The payment the bond issuer makes to the bondholders for use of the borrowed money.

You may already be familiar with bonds. You may own investments like Canada Savings Bonds *<http://www.csb.gc.ca>*. As the first government in Canada to issue green bonds, the Ontario provincial government will use proceeds from its green bond program to help Ontario finance transit and other environmentally-friendly infrastructure projects across the province.[32] Maybe your community is building a new stadium or cultural centre and is selling bonds to finance the project. Businesses and governments compete when issuing bonds. Potential investors (individuals and institutions) measure the risk of purchasing a bond against the return the bond promises to pay—the interest—and the issuer's ability to repay when promised.

Bond interest is sometimes called the *coupon rate*, a term that dates back to when bonds were issued as *bearer* bonds. The holder, or bearer, was considered the bond's owner. Back then, the company issuing the bond kept no record of changes in ownership. Bond interest was paid to whoever clipped the coupons attached to the bond and sent them to the issuing company for payment. Today, bonds are registered to specific owners and changes in ownership are recorded electronically.

Like other forms of long-term debt, the interest rate paid on a bond varies according to factors such as the general level of market rates, the reputation of the company issuing the bond, and the going interest rate for government bonds or bonds of similar companies. Once an interest rate is set for a corporate bond issue (except in the case of what is called a floating-rate bond), it cannot be changed. Though bond interest is quoted for an entire year, it is usually paid in two instalments.

Bond-rating organizations assess the creditworthiness of a corporation's bond issue. Independent rating firms, such as Dominion Bond Rating Service *<http://www.dbrs.com>* and Standard & Poor's Rating Services *<http://www.standardandpoors.com>*, rate bonds according to their degree of risk. Bond ratings can range from the highest quality to junk bonds. Naturally, the higher the risk associated with the bond issue, the higher the interest rate the organization must offer investors. Investors should not assume high levels of risk if they do not feel that the potential return is worth it. Due to the European debt crisis, many European governments are facing significant interest costs on the debt they are issuing because lenders believe the risk is high.

Major League Baseball is a big business, and building a new stadium requires big dollars. When the St. Louis Cardinals needed financing to replace its old stadium with a new state-of-the-art facility, St. Louis County issued bonds that helped finance the construction of the Cardinals' new home. What organizations in your community have issued bonds, and for what purposes?

Advantages and Disadvantages of Issuing Bonds Bonds offer long-term financing advantages to an organization:

- Bondholders are creditors of the firm, not owners. They seldom vote on corporate matters; thus, management maintains control over the firm's operations.

- Bond interest is a business expense and as a result, it is a tax deduction for the firm.

- Bonds are a temporary source of funding. They are eventually repaid and the debt obligation is eliminated.

- Bonds can be repaid before the maturity date if they are *callable*. Some bonds may also be converted to common shares. Both of these bond features will be discussed soon.

Bonds also have financing drawbacks:

- Bonds increase debt (long-term liabilities) and may adversely affect the market's perception of the firm.

- Paying interest on bonds is a legal obligation. If interest is not paid, bondholders can take legal action to force payment.

- The face value (denomination) of bonds must be repaid on the maturity date. Without careful planning, this obligation can cause cash flow problems when the repayment comes due.

Different Classes of Bonds Corporations can issue two different classes of corporate bonds. **Unsecured bonds**, usually called **debenture bonds**, are not backed by any specific collateral (such as land or equipment). Only firms with excellent reputations and credit ratings can issue **debenture bonds**, due to the lack of security they provide investors. **Secured bonds**, sometimes called **mortgage bonds**, are backed by collateral, such as land or buildings, that is pledged to bondholders if interest or principal is not paid when promised. A corporate bond issuer can choose to include different bond features. Let's look at some special features.

> **debenture bonds (unsecured bonds)**
> Bonds that are unsecured (i.e., not backed by any collateral such as equipment).
>
> **mortgage bonds (secured bonds)**
> Bonds that are secured (i.e., backed by collateral such as land).

Special Bond Features Now you understand that bonds are issued with an interest rate, are unsecured or secured by some type of collateral, and must be repaid at their maturity dates. This repayment requirement often leads companies (or governments) to establish a reserve account called a **sinking fund**. Its primary purpose is to ensure that enough money will be available to repay bondholders on the bond's maturity date. Firms issuing sinking-fund bonds periodically *retire* (set aside) some part of the principal prior to maturity so that enough funds will accumulate by the maturity date to pay off the bond. Sinking funds are generally attractive to both issuing firms and investors for several reasons:

- They provide for an orderly retirement (repayment) of a bond issue.

- They reduce the risk the bond will not be repaid.

- They support the market price of the bond because they reduce the risk the bond will not be repaid.

> **sinking fund**
> A reserve account in which the issuer of a bond periodically retires some part of the bond principal prior to maturity so that enough capital will be accumulated by the maturity date to pay off the bond.

To make bonds more attractive, decisions are made on the best combination of features before new bonds are issued. After all, new bonds will be competing against not only other new bond issues, but also against current bonds in the marketplace, both domestically and internationally. What special bond features would make a bond more attractive to a potential investor?

A *callable bond* permits the bond issuer to pay off the bond's principal before its maturity date. This gives companies some discretion in their long-term forecasting. Suppose Very Vegetarian issued $10 million in 20-year bonds at 5 percent interest. Its yearly interest expense is $500,000 ($10 million times 5 percent). If market conditions change and new bonds issued of the same quality now pay only 3 percent, Very Vegetarian will be paying 2 percent, or $200,000 ($10 million times 2 percent) in excess interest yearly. The company could benefit by calling in (paying off) the old bonds and issuing new bonds at the lower rate. If a company calls a bond before maturity, it often pays investors a price above the bond's face value.

Investors can convert *convertible bonds* into common shares in the issuing company. This can be an incentive for an investor because common share values tend to grow faster than a bond. Therefore, if the value of the firm's common share grows sizably over time, bondholders can compare the value of the bond interest earned with the potential profit of a specified number of common shares into which the bonds can be converted.[33] When we discuss common shares in the next section, this advantage will become more evident to you.

Progress Assessment

- What are the major forms of debt financing available to a firm?
- What does it mean when a firm states that it is issuing a 9 percent debenture bond due in 2025?
- What are advantages and disadvantages of bonds?
- Why do companies like callable bonds? Why might investors dislike them?

Equity Financing

Rather than obtaining a long-term loan from a lending institution or selling bonds to investors, a firm may look at equity financing. Equity financing makes funds available when the owners of the firm sell shares of ownership (including selling shares to venture capitalists) or when they reinvest earnings. Let's look more closely at each of these options.

EQUITY FINANCING BY SELLING STOCK (SHARES)

Stock (shares) represent ownership in a company. Both common and preferred shares (to be discussed soon) form the company's capital stock, also known as equity capital. The key thing to remember about stocks is that stockholders (also known as shareholders) become owners in the organization. Generally, the corporation's board of directors decides the number of shares of stock that will be offered to investors for purchase.

> **stocks (shares)**
> Shares of ownership in a company.

An **initial public offering (IPO)** occurs the first time a corporation offers to sell new stock to the general public. After this initial sale, the *secondary market* handles the trading of these securities between investors, with the proceeds of the sale going to the investor selling the stock, not to the corporation whose stock is sold. For example, Cara Operations Ltd. *<http://www.cara.com>* is Canada's third-largest single restaurant owner (after Tim Hortons and McDonald's) with 837 restaurants across Canada and brands including Milestones, Kelsey's, Bier Markt, and East Side Mario's.[34] While its IPO share price of $23 raised $200.1 million for the company, the share price did not stop there; the share price was as high as $33 in its first day of trading on the Toronto Stock Exchange (secondary market), benefitting investors who may have chosen to sell their shares for a profit.[35] What did the company plan to do with this money? What is the share price now?

> **initial public offering (IPO)**
> The first public offering of a corporation's stock.

A **stock certificate** represents stock ownership. It specifies the name of the company, the number of shares owned, and the type of stock it represents. Companies, however, are not required to issue paper stock certificates to owners since stock is generally held electronically.

> **stock certificate**
> Evidence of stock ownership that specifies the name of the company, the number of shares it represents, and the type of stock being issued.

Stock certificates sometimes indicate a stock's *par value*, which is a dollar amount assigned to each share of stock by the corporation's charter. Today, since par values do not reflect the market value of the stock (what the stock is actually worth), most companies issue stock with a very low par value or no par value.

Dividends are part of a firm's profits that may be (but is not required to) distributed to shareholders as either cash payments or additional shares of stock.[36] Dividends are declared by a corporation's board of directors and are generally paid quarterly. As a result of almost tripling its profit in the fourth quarter, Canadian Natural Resources Ltd. *<http://www.cnrl.com>* announced it would raise its quarterly dividend by half a cent to 23¢ per share.[37] Increasing profits also contributed to the decision to raise BCE Inc.'s annual common share dividend by 5.3 percent, to $2.60 per common share.[38]

> **dividends**
> Part of a firm's profits that may be distributed to shareholders as either cash payments or additional shares of stock.

When Twitter issued its IPO, the company raised more than US$2.1 billion from the sale. Can you see why issuing stock can be an appealing option for financing a company's growth?

Advantages and Disadvantages of Issuing Stock   Some advantages to a firm of issuing stock include:

- As owners of the business, shareholders never have to be repaid.

- There is usually no legal obligation to pay dividends to stockholders; therefore, the firm can reinvest income (retained earnings) to finance future needs.

- Selling stock can improve the condition of a firm's balance sheet since issuing stock creates no debt. (A corporation may also buy back its stock to improve its balance sheet and make the company appear stronger financially.[39])

Disadvantages of issuing stock include:

- As owners, stockholders (usually only common shareholders) have the right to vote for the company's board of directors. (Typically one vote is granted for each share of stock.) Issuing new shares of stock can thus alter the control of the firm.

- Dividends are paid from profit after taxes and thus are not tax deductible.

- The need to keep stockholders happy can affect managers' decisions.

Companies can issue two classes of stock: common and preferred. Let's see how these two forms of equity financing differ.

Issuing Shares of Common Stock   **Common stock** is the most basic form of ownership in a firm. In fact, if a company issues only one type of stock, by law it must be common stock. Holders of common stock have the right to (1) elect members of the company's board directors, and vote on important issues affecting the company, and (2) share in the firm's profits through dividends, if approved by the firm's board of directors. Having voting rights in a corporation allows common stockholders to influence corporate policy because the board members they elect both choose the firm's top management as well as make major policy decisions. Common stockholders also have a *pre-emptive right* to purchase new shares of common stock that may be issued via an IPO before anyone else. This allows common stockholders to maintain their proportional share of ownership in the company.

> **common stock**
> The most basic form of ownership in a firm; it confers voting rights and the right to share in the firm's profits through dividends, if offered by the firm's board of directors.

Issuing Shares of Preferred Stock   Owners of **preferred stock** enjoy a preference in the payment of company dividends and must be paid their dividends in full before any common stock dividends can be distributed; hence, the term *preferred.* They also have a prior claim on company assets—before common shareholders—if the firm is forced out of business and its assets sold. Normally, however, preferred shareholders do not get voting rights in the firm.

> **preferred stock**
> Stock that gives its owners preference in the payment of dividends and an earlier claim on assets than common shareholders if the company is forced out of business and its assets are sold.

Preferred stock may be issued with a par value that becomes the base for a fixed dividend the firm is willing to pay. For example, if a preferred share's par value is $50 a share and its dividend rate is 4 percent, the dividend is $2 a share ($50 times 4 percent = $2). An owner of 100 shares would receive a fixed yearly dividend of $200 if dividends are declared by the board of directors.

Preferred stock are therefore quite similar to bonds; both have a face (or par) value and both have a fixed rate of return. Also, like bonds, rating services assess preferred shares according to risk. So how do bonds and preferred shares differ? Remember that companies are legally bound to pay bond interest and to repay the face value (denomination) of the bond on its maturity date. In contrast, even though preferred share dividends are generally fixed, they do not legally have to be paid. Also, shares (preferred or common) never have to be repurchased by the issuing company. Though both bonds and stock can increase in market value, the price of stock generally increases at a higher percentage than bonds. Of course, the market value of both could also go down. Figure 17.6 compares features of bonds and stock.

Optional Preferred Stock Features   Preferred shares can have special features that do not apply to common shares. For example, like bonds, preferred shares can be *callable,* which means that preferred shareholders could be required to sell back their shares to the corporation. Preferred shares can also be converted to common shares (but not the other way around). They can also be *cumulative.* That is, if one or more dividends are not paid when promised, they accumulate and the corporation must pay them in full at a later date before it can distribute any common stock dividends.[40] Figure 17.7 lists optional features of preferred shares.

EQUITY FINANCING FROM VENTURE CAPITAL

The hardest time for a business to raise money is when it is just starting up or just beginning to expand.[41] A start-up business typically has few assets and no market track record, so the chances of borrowing significant amounts of money from a bank are slim. Recall from Chapter 7 that venture capitalists are a potential source of funds. **Venture capital** is money that is invested in new or emerging companies that some investors—venture capitalists—believe have great profit potential. Venture capitalists invest in a

■ **FIGURE 17.6**

COMPARISON OF BONDS AND STOCK OF PUBLIC COMPANIES

The different features help both the issuer and the investor decide which vehicle is right for each of them at a particular time.

	Bonds	Common Stock	Preferred Stock
Interest (Bonds) or Dividends (Stock)			
Must be paid	Yes	No	Depends
Pays a fixed rate	Yes	No	Usually
Deductible from issuer's income tax	Yes	No	No
Canadian investor pays reduced tax rate	No	(if issuing company is Canadian) Yes	Yes
Bond or Stock			
Has voting rights	No	Yes	Not normally
May be traded on the stock exchange	Yes	Yes	Yes
Can be held indefinitely	No	Yes	Depends
Is convertible to common shares	Maybe	No	Maybe

■ **FIGURE 17.7**

OPTIONAL PREFERRED STOCK FEATURES

Each feature holds some attraction for potential investors.

Preferred Share Feature	Description
Convertible	The shares may be exchanged after a stated number of years for common shares at a pre-set rate, at the option of the shareholder.
Cumulative	If the dividend is not paid in full in any year, the balance is carried forward (accumulates). The cumulative unpaid balance must be paid before any dividends are paid to common shareholders.
Callable	The company that issued the shares has the right after a stated number of years to call them back by repaying the shareholders their original investment.*
Redeemable	After a stated number of years, the investor may return the stock and ask for repayment of his or her investment.*

*If the shares are also cumulative, all dividend arrears must be paid as well.

business in return for part ownership of the business. They expect higher-than-average returns and competent management performance for their investing. Venture capital has helped firms like Intel *<http://www.intel.com>*, Apple, and Cisco Systems get started and let Facebook and Google expand and grow.

venture capital
Money that is invested in new or emerging companies that are perceived as having great profit potential

EQUITY FINANCING FROM RETAINED EARNINGS

You probably remember from Chapter 16 that the profits the company keeps and reinvests in the firm are called *retained earnings*. Retained earnings are often a major source of long-term funds, especially for small businesses since they often have fewer financing alternatives, such as selling bonds or stock, than large businesses do. However, large corporations also depend on retained earnings for long-term funding. In fact, retained earnings are usually the most favoured source of meeting long-term capital needs. A company that uses them saves interest payments, dividends (payments for investing in stock), and any possible underwriting fees for issuing bonds or stock. Retained earnings also create no new ownership in the firm, as stock does.

Suppose you want to buy an expensive personal asset such as a new car. Ideally you would go to your personal savings account and take out the necessary cash. No hassle! No interest! Unfortunately, few people have such large amounts of cash available. Most businesses are no different. Even though they would like to finance long-term needs from operations (retained earnings), few have the resources available to accomplish this.

Comparing Debt and Equity Financing

Figure 17.8 compares debt and equity financing options. Raising funds through borrowing to increase the firm's rate of return is referred to as **leverage**. Though debt increases risk because it creates a financial obligation that must be repaid, it also enhances a firm's ability to increase profits. Recall that two key jobs of the financial manager or CFO are forecasting the firm's need for borrowed funds and planning how to manage these funds once they are obtained.

leverage
Raising needed funds through borrowing to increase a firm's rate of return.

■ FIGURE 17.8

DIFFERENCES BETWEEN DEBT AND EQUITY FINANCING		
TYPE OF FINANCING		
	Debt	**Equity**
Management influence	There's usually none unless special conditions have been agreed on	Common shareholders have voting rights
Repayment	Debt has a maturity date	Stock has no maturity date
	Principal must be repaid	The company is never required to repay equity
Yearly obligations	Payment of interest is a contractual obligation	The firm is not usually legally liable to pay dividends
Tax benefits	Interest is tax deductible	Dividends are paid from after-tax income and are not deductible

Firms are concerned with the cost of capital. **Cost of capital** is the rate of return a company must earn in order to meet the demands of its lenders and expectations of its equity holders (shareholders or venture capitalists). If the firm's earning are greater than the interest payments on borrowed funds, business owners can realize a higher rate of return than if they had used equity financing. Figure 17.9 shows

■ **FIGURE 17.9**

USING LEVERAGE (DEBT) VERSUS EQUITY FINANCING			
Very Vegetarian wants to raise $200,000 in new capital. Compare the firm's debt and equity options. Return on equity is calculated by dividing operating profit by total shareholders' equity.			
Additional Debt		**Additional Equity**	
Shareholders' equity	$500,000	Shareholders' equity	$500,000
Additional equity	—	Additional equity	$200,000
Total equity	$500,000	Total equity	$700,000
Bond @ 8% interest	$200,000	Bond interest	—
Total shareholders' equity	$500,000	Total shareholders' equity	$700,000
Year-End Earnings			
Gross Profit	$100,000	Gross Profit	$100,000
Less bond interest ($200,000 times 8%)	−$16,000	Less interest	—
Operating Profit	$84,000	Operating Profit	$100,000
Return on equity ($84,000 × $500,000)	16.8%	Return on equity ($100,000 × $700,000)	14.3%

an example, again involving our vegetarian restaurant, Very Vegetarian (introduced in Chapter 14). If Very Vegetarian needed $200,000 in new financing, it could consider debt by selling bonds or equity through offering stock. Comparing the two options in this situation, you can see that Very Vegetarian would benefit by selling bonds since the company's earnings are greater than the interest paid on borrowed funds (bonds). However, if the firm's earnings were less than the interest paid on borrowed funds (bonds), Very Vegetarian could lose money. It is also important to remember that bonds, like all debt, have to be repaid at a specific date.

> **cost of capital**
> The rate of return a company must earn in order to meet the demands of its lenders and expectations of its equity holders.

Individual firms must determine exactly how to balance debt and equity financing by comparing the costs and benefits of each. Leverage ratios (discussed in Chapter 16) can also give companies an industry standard for this balance, to which they can compare themselves. Still, debt varies considerably among major companies and industries. Tech leader Apple, for example, has long-term debt of almost $29 billion even though it has almost $14 billion in cash and cash equivalents available.[42] Compare this to automaker Ford Motor Company, which has over $119 billion in long-term debt and not quite $11 billion in cash and cash equivalents on its balance sheet.[43] According to Standard & Poor's and Moody's Investors Service *<http://www.moodys.com>* (firms that provide corporate and financial research as well as the bond rating services mentioned earlier), the debt of large industrial corporations and utilities typically range between 30 and 35 percent of total assets. The amount of small-business debt obviously varies considerably from firm to firm.

Your Prospects in Finance[44]

A career in finance can include analyst positions (e.g., research and corporate finance), management positions (e.g., relationship, portfolio, and risk), financial consultants, investment bankers, chief information officer (CIO) positions, and more. Are any of these of interest to you?

In Chapter 16, you were introduced to the chartered professional accountant (CPA) designation. Another well-known finance designation is the chartered financial analyst (CFA) designation. Administered through the CFA Institute *<http://www.cfainstitute.org>*, it has become the most respected and recognized investment designation in the world.[45] Graduation requires successful completion of three levels. Level I focuses on a basic knowledge of the topic areas and simple analysis using investment tools. Level II emphasizes the application of investment tools and concepts with a focus on the valuation of all types of assets. Level III focuses on synthesizing all of the concepts and analytical methods in a variety of applications for effective portfolio management and wealth planning. Would you consider this designation as a way to round out your studies and experience? Regardless of your career choice, an understanding of finance will support sound decision making.

CFA candidates report dedicating in excess of 300 hours of study to prepare for each exam. What are some of the advantages and disadvantages of completing this designation while you are working full time?

Progress Assessment

- What are the major forms of equity financing available to a firm?
- Name at least two advantages and two disadvantages of issuing stock as a form of equity financing.
- What are the major differences between common shares and preferred shares?
- In what ways are preferred shares similar to bonds? How are they different?

SUMMARY

LO1 **Explain the role and responsibilities of financial managers.**

Finance comprises those functions in a business responsible for acquiring funds for the firm, managing funds within the firm (e.g., preparing budgets and doing cash flow analysis), and planning for the expenditure of funds on various assets.

What are the most common ways in which firms fail financially?

The most common financial problems are (1) undercapitalization, (2) poor control over cash flow, and (3) inadequate expense control.

What do financial managers do?

Financial managers plan, budget, control funds, obtain funds, collect funds, conduct audits, manage taxes, and advise top management on financial matters.

LO2 **Outline the financial planning process, and explain the three key budgets in the financial plan.**

Financial planning involves forecasting short-term and long-term needs, budgeting, and establishing financial controls.

What are the three budgets in a financial plan?

The capital budget is the spending plan for expensive assets, such as property, plant, and equipment. The cash budget is the projected cash inflows and outflows for a period and the balance at the end of a given period. The operating (master) budget summarizes the information in the other two budgets. It projects dollar allocations to various costs and expenses given various revenues.

LO3 **Explain why firms need operating funds.**

During the course of a business's life, its financial needs shift considerably.

What are firms' major financial needs?

Businesses need financing for four major tasks: (1) managing day-to-day needs of the business, (2) controlling credit operations, (3) acquiring needed inventory, and (4) making capital expenditures.

How can a firm access operating funds?

A firm can raise needed capital by borrowing money (debt), selling ownership (equity), or earning profits (retained earnings).

LO4 **Identify and describe different sources of short-term financing.**

Short-term financing raises funds to be repaid in less than one year.

What are major forms of short-term financing?

Sources of short-term financing include trade credit, family and friends, commercial banks and other financial institutions, short-term loans, factoring accounts receivable, commercial paper, and credit cards.

Why should businesses use trade credit?

Trade credit is the least expensive and most convenient form of short-term financing. Businesses can buy goods today and pay for them sometime in the future.

What is a line of credit and a revolving credit agreement?

A line of credit is an agreement by a bank to lend a specified amount of money to the business at any time, as long as certain conditions are met. A revolving credit agreement is a line of credit that guarantees a loan will be available—for a fee.

What is the difference between a secured loan and an unsecured loan?

An unsecured loan has no collateral backing it. Secured loans have collateral backed by assets, such as accounts receivable, inventory, or other property of value.

Is factoring a form of secured loan?

No, it is not. Factoring means selling accounts receivable at a discounted rate to a factor (an intermediary that pays cash for those accounts and keeps the funds it collects on them).

What is commercial paper?

Commercial paper is a corporation's unsecured promissory note maturing in 270 days or less.

LO5 **Identify and describe different sources of long-term financing.**

Long-term financing raises funds that will be repaid over a period greater than one year.

What are the major sources of long-term financing?

Debt financing involves borrowing from lending institutions, and the issuance of bonds to investors. Equity financing is obtained through the sale of company stock, which includes selling to venture capitalists, and taking funds from the firm's retained earnings.

What is leverage and how do firms use it?

Leverage is borrowing funds to invest in expansion, major asset purchases, or research and development. Firms measure the risk of borrowing against the potential for higher profits.

KEY TERMS

4 Cs of credit	equity financing	preferred stock
bond	factoring	promissory note
budget	finance	revolving credit agreement
capital budget	financial control	risk/return trade-off
capital expenditures	financial management	secured loan
cash budget	financial managers	short-term financing
cash flow forecast	initial public offering (IPO)	short-term forecast
commercial finance companies	interest	sinking fund
commercial paper	leverage	stock certificate
common stock	line of credit	stocks (shares)
cost of capital	long-term financing	term-loan agreement
credit profile	long-term forecast	trade credit
debenture bonds (unsecured bonds)	maturity date	unsecured loan
debt financing	mortgage bonds (secured bonds)	venture capital
dividends	operating (master) budget	

CRITICAL THINKING

1. Budgets are designed to keep decision makers informed of progress compared to company plans. An important theme of this book is the need for managers to be flexible so that they can adapt quickly to rapidly changing conditions. This often means modifying previous plans. How

do managers stay within the confines of budgets when they must shift gears to accommodate a rapidly changing world?

2. What are the primary sources of short-term funds for new business owners? What are the major sources of long-term funds?

3. Why does a financial manager need to understand the accounting information if the firm has a trained accountant on its staff?

4. Considering the advantages and disadvantages of different forms of raising funds, which method would you adopt if you had to make that decision for your company? How would your decision be impacted if interest rates are relatively high in relation to the past?

DEVELOPING WORKPLACE SKILLS

Key: ● **Team** ★ **Analytic** ▲ **Communication** ▢ **Technology**

▲★ 1. Contact a lending officer at a local bank in your community or visit the bank's website to review the bank's policies on providing a business line of credit and a revolving line of credit. Under what circumstances would a business qualify for either form of short-term financing?

●★ 2. One of the most difficult concepts to get across to small-business owners is the need to take
▲ all the trade credit they can get. For example, the credit terms 2/10, net 30 can save businesses money if they pay their bills in the first 10 days. Work with a group of classmates to build a convincing financial argument for using trade credit.

▢★ 3. Go online and check the capitalization required to open a franchise of your choice, like Subway or McDonald's. Does the franchisor offer financial assistance to prospective franchisees? Evaluate the cost of the franchise versus its business potential using the risk/return trade-off discussed in this chapter.

▢★ 4. Factoring accounts receivable is a form of financing used since the days of Babylonian King
▲ Hammurabi approximately 4,000 years ago. Today it is still a source of short-term funds used by small businesses. Visit <http://www.21stfinancialsolutions.com> to get more in-depth information about factoring and be prepared to discuss the pros and cons of factoring to the class.

▢★ 5. Go to your school's website and see whether its operating budget is online. If not, go to the campus library and see if the reference librarian can help you access this information. Try to identify major capital expenditures your school has planned for the future.

ANALYZING MANAGEMENT DECISIONS

Making Dreams Come True

Carlos Galendez had big dreams but very little money. He worked more than 10 years washing dishes and then as a cook for two major restaurants, all the while saving enough money to start his own Mexican restaurant. Finally, his dream came true. Galendez opened his restaurant, Casa de Carlos, with a guaranteed loan. His old family recipes and appealing Hispanic decor helped the business gain immediate success. He repaid his small-business loan within 14 months and immediately opened a second location, and then a third. Casa de Carlos became one of the largest Mexican restaurant chains in the area.

Galendez decided that the company needed to go public to help finance expansion. He believed that continued growth was beneficial to the company, and that offering ownership was the way to bring in loyal investors. Nevertheless, he wanted to make certain that his family maintained a controlling interest in the firm's stock. Therefore, in its IPO, Casa de Carlos offered to sell only 40 percent of the company's available shares to investors. The Galendez family kept control of the remaining 60 percent.

As the public's craving for Mexican food grew, so did the fortunes of Casa de Carlos. By early 2007, the company enjoyed the enviable position of being light on debt and heavy on cash. But the firm's debt position changed dramatically when it bought out Captain Ahab's Seafood Restaurants. Two years later, it expanded into the full-service wholesale distribution of seafood products with the purchase of Ancient Mariner Wholesalers.

The firm's debt increased, but the price of its stock was up and all of its business operations were booming. Then tragedy struck the firm when Carlos Galendez died suddenly from a heart attack. His oldest child, Maria, was selected to take control as CEO. Maria Galendez had learned the business from her father, who had taught her to keep an eye out for opportunities that seemed fiscally responsible. Even so, the fortunes of the firm began to shift. Two major competitors were taking market share from Casa de Carlos, and the seafood venture began to flounder (pun intended). Also, consumer shifts in eating habits and the recession encouraged consumers to spend less, causing the company some severe cash flow problems. It was up to Maria Galendez as CEO to decide how to get the funds the firm needed for improvements and other expenses. Unfortunately, several local banks would not expand the firm's credit line, so she considered the possibility of a bond or stock offering to raise capital for the business. Her decision could be crucial to the future of the firm.

Discussion Questions

1. What advantages do bonds offer a company such as Casa de Carlos? What disadvantages do bonds impose?

2. What would be the advantages and disadvantages if the company sold new stock to investors?

3. Are any other options available to Maria Galendez?

4. What choice would you make and why?

VIDEO CASE 17

Tom and Eddie's

This video features the start-up company called Tom and Eddie's, an upscale hamburger restaurant. Started in 2009 at the height of the recession, partners Tom Dentice and Ed Rensi had a difficult time securing bank financing. As a result, they financed the operation themselves with the help of a third partner, Vince Nocarando. The partners both had long and successful careers as executives with McDonald's. Dentice was Executive Vice President for New Locations and Rensi was the President and CEO of North American operations.

Both partners, as a result of their experience at McDonald's, are well suited for the restaurant business. One of the most challenging and important elements of a successful start-up, like Tom and Eddie's, is a talented financial manager. Recognizing the importance of the finance function, they hired another former McDonald's executive, Brian Gordon, as CFO. Gordon explains that cash flow is the most important element in starting up a restaurant. In fact, cash flow is more important than profits in the first and perhaps second year of operation. Second to cash flow in terms of importance for sustainability is the management and control of inventory.

Cash flow is important, according to the CFO, because of the "known" costs, such as rent, payroll, inventory, taxes, and utilities. These are known costs because they are recurring and the relative costs are known on a weekly or monthly basis. Gordon explains that cash flow is important in managing these known costs because of the significant "unknown" factor, which is sales.

Tom and Eddie's uses a technology-intensive inventory management and control system because of the perishable nature of foodstuffs associated with the restaurant business. According to Gordon, the restaurant has "net 14" terms with its food vendors. This means that the invoice is paid 14 days after the receipt of the goods. This is a form of financing, according to the CFO, that allows the company to turn that inventory once or twice during the 14-day period.

At the time of the video, Tom and Eddie's was in its fifteenth month of operation with three restaurants. The goal is to grow to 10 restaurants and then look at franchising the operation. When considering where to open a new operation, Rensi indicates that careful consideration is given to the demographics of the area, including the average income level of those working and living in the area to be served, the age of the population, the square footage of the surrounding commercial space, and ease of access to the location. Equipment is purchased rather than financed by the partners.

According to the partners, entrepreneurs think in terms of opportunities, not in terms of potential failure. With 15 months of successful operation, capital will be easier to raise from traditional sources of financing, such as banks, to expand the operation. Who knows, maybe a franchised Tom and Eddie's will be opening soon in a location near you.

Discussion Questions

1. What are the three factors associated with operating funds?
2. What is meant by the term "front of the house"?
3. Why, according to the video, was bank financing unavailable for this start-up?

Managing Risk

APPENDIX

C

Understanding Business Risks

Managing risk is a challenge for businesses throughout the world. Almost every day you hear about a tornado, hurricane, earthquake, flood, fire, airplane crash, terrorism threat, or car accident that destroyed property or injured or killed someone. The Insurance Institute for Business & Home Safety *<https://www.disastersafety.org>* says that one out of four small businesses is forced to permanently close after a disaster.[1]

Hackers and viruses are an increasing threat to computers, and identity theft is commonplace. Theft and fraud can destroy a small business. Business lawsuits in recent years have covered everything from job-related accidents to product liability.

Such reports are so much a part of the news that we tend to accept these events as part of everyday life. But the losses of property, equipment, transportation, communications, security, energy, and other resources mean a great deal to the people and organizations injured by them. In some areas, insurance is not available or is too expensive for high-risk businesses. New legislation has been passed in some areas to lessen some of these risks so that companies can obtain insurance coverage at a reasonable price.

Real financial risk relates to the variability of costs and revenue resulting in the inability to cover off all obligations. The future cannot be predicted, but the financial risk that arises from uncertainty can be managed. Business needs to identify, measure, and appreciate the consequences of financial risk, and then take action to transfer or mitigate it. Financial risk management and risk taking are two sides of the same coin. **Risk management** is the process of understanding, costing, and efficiently managing unexpected levels of variability in the financial outcomes for a business. Risk management is about firms actively selecting the type and level of risk that is appropriate for them to assume. It is all about minimizing the losses from unexpected events.

> **risk management**
> The process of understanding, costing, and efficiently managing unexpected levels of variability in the financial outcomes for a business.

A recent report found that 80 percent of organizations either have or are in the process of developing an Enterprise Risk Management (ERM) program.[2] An ERM program usually has a few well-defined goals, such as defining (1) which risks the program will manage; (2) what risk management processes, technologies, and investments will be required; and (3) how risk management efforts will be coordinated across the firm.[3]

How Rapid Change Affects Risk Management

Risk goes beyond the obvious dangers of fire, theft, or accident. It is inherent in every decision a manager makes, and the prudent company assesses its exposure in all of them. Risk managers are expanding their expertise into human resources, information technology, security, legal, site construction, and more. Change is occurring so fast that it is difficult to identify new risks until they are upon us. Who can evaluate the risks of buying or selling products online? How will currencies fluctuate in the next financial crisis, and how will their daily ups and downs affect the profits of global trade?[4] How will climate change affect farms, raising cattle, and the price of food?[5] What would happen to the economy if there were a new terrorist attack or a flu epidemic? What can we do to manage the risks of financial failure at home and social unrest abroad?[6] Let's explore how companies go about managing risk. We'll begin by going over a few key terms.

Managing Risk

The concept of risk was introduced in Chapter 1. Risk is the chance of loss, the degree of probability of loss, and the amount of possible loss. There are two kinds of risk:

- **Speculative risk** can result in *either* profit or loss. A firm takes on speculative risk by buying new machinery, acquiring more inventory, and making other potentially profitable decisions in which the probability of loss may be relatively low and the amount of loss known. An entrepreneur's chance to make a profit is a speculative risk. Banks that bought mortgage-backed securities were taking a speculative risk.

- **Pure risk** is the threat of loss with *no* chance for profit, such as the threat of fire, accident, or theft. If such events occur, a company loses money. But, if such events do not occur, the company gains nothing.

speculative risk
A chance of either profit or loss.

pure risk
The threat of loss with no chance for profit.

The risk that most concerns business people is pure risk. It threatens the very existence of some firms. Once they identify pure risks, firms have several options:

1. Reduce the risk.
2. Avoid the risk.
3. Self-insure against the risk.
4. Buy insurance to cover the risk.

We'll discuss the option of buying insurance in detail later. First, we will discuss each of the other alternatives for managing risk, which reduces the need for outside insurance.

Reducing Risk

A firm can reduce risk by establishing loss-prevention programs, such as fire drills, health education, safety inspections, equipment maintenance, accident prevention programs, and so on. Many retail stores use mirrors, video cameras, and other devices to prevent shoplifting. Water sprinklers and smoke detectors minimize fire loss. Most industrial machines have safety devices to protect workers' fingers, eyes, and so on.

Employees as well as managers can reduce risk. Truck drivers can wear seat belts to minimize injuries from accidents, operators of loud machinery can wear earplugs to reduce the chance of hearing loss, and those who lift heavy objects can wear back braces. The beginning of an effective risk management strategy is a good loss-prevention program.[7] However, high insurance rates have forced some firms to go beyond merely preventing risks to avoiding them. In extreme cases, they have done this by going out of business. Avoiding accidents is critical to the survival of the firm and its workers.[8]

Avoiding Risk

We cannot avoid every risk. There is always the chance of fire, theft, accident, or injury. But some companies are avoiding risk by not accepting hazardous jobs and by outsourcing shipping and other functions. The threat of lawsuits has driven some drug companies to stop manufacturing vaccines, and some consulting engineers refuse to work on hazardous sites. Some companies are losing outside members of their boards of directors who do not have liability coverage protecting them from legal action against the firms they represent. Many companies have cut back on their investments to avoid the risk of financial losses.

Self-Insurance Against the Risk

Self-insurance is the practice of setting aside money to cover routine claims and buying only "catastrophe" insurance policies to cover big losses. It is most appropriate when a firm has several widely distributed facilities. Firms with a single huge facility, in which a major fire or earthquake could destroy the entire operation, usually turn to insurance companies to cover the risk of loss.

> **self-insurance**
> The practice of setting aside money to cover routine claims and buying only "catastrophe" policies to cover big losses.

One of the riskier self-insurance strategies is for a company to "go bare," paying claims from its operating budget instead of from a special fund. The whole firm could go bankrupt over one claim if the damages are high enough. A less risky alternative is to form group-insurance pools that share similar risks.

Buying Insurance to Cover the Risk

Although well-designed and enforced risk-prevention programs reduce the probability of claims, accidents do happen. Insurance is the armour individuals, businesses, and not-for profit organizations use to protect themselves from various financial risks. Together they spend about 10 percent of gross domestic product on insurance premiums. Some insurance protection is provided by governments (see Figure C.1), but individuals and businesses must cover most on their own.

To reduce the cost of insurance, some companies buy a business ownership policy (BOP), an insurance package that includes property and liability insurance. We will continue our discussion of insurance by identifying the types of risks that are uninsurable and insurable.

■ **FIGURE C.1**

PUBLIC INSURANCE	
Provincial or federal government agencies that provide insurance protection for qualified Canadians.	
Type of Insurance	**What It Does**
Canadian Public Health Care	Provides Canadians with free basic health care, free doctor visits, free hospital ward care, free surgery, and free drugs and medicine while in hospital.
Employment Insurance	Provides financial benefits, job counselling, and placement services for unemployed workers.
Old Age Security/Canada Pension Plan/Quebec Pension Plan	Provides retirement benefits and life insurance.
Canada Mortgage Housing Corporation (CMHC)	Provides mortgage insurance to lenders to protect against default by home buyers.
Canada Deposit Insurance Corporation (CDIC)	Provides re-imbursement of up to $100,000 for funds held in banks, trust companies, and loan companies that fail.
Provincial Auto Insurance (British Columbia, Saskatchewan, Manitoba, and Quebec)	Government-run insurance companies sell the basic/required minimum auto insurance (e.g., collision, liability, and accident benefits).[9] Auto insurance is also sold by private companies in all ten provinces and the three territories.[10]

What Risks Are Uninsurable?

Not all risks are insurable. An **uninsurable risk** is one that no insurance company will cover. Examples of things that you cannot insure include market risks (e.g., losses that occur because of price changes, style changes, or new products that make your product obsolete); political risks (e.g., losses from war or government restrictions on trade); some personal risks (e.g., loss of a job); and some risks of operation (e.g., strikes or inefficient machinery).

uninsurable risk
A risk that no insurance company will cover.

What Risks Are Insurable?

An **insurable risk** is one that the typical insurance company will cover, using the following guidelines:

1. The policyholder must have an **insurable interest,** which means that the policyholder is the one at risk to suffer a loss. You cannot, for example, buy fire insurance on your neighbour's house and collect if it burns down.
2. The loss must be measurable.
3. The chance of loss must be measurable.
4. The loss must be accidental.

5. The insurance company's risk should be dispersed; that is, spread among different geographical areas so that a flood or other natural disaster in one area will not bankrupt the insurance company.

6. The insurance company must be able to set standards for accepting the risk.

> **insurable risk**
> A risk that the typical insurance company will cover.
>
> **insurable interest**
> The possibility of the policyholder to suffer a loss.

Understanding Insurance Policies

An **insurance policy** is a written contract between the insured—whether an individual or organization—and an insurance company that promises to pay for all or part of a loss by the insured. A **premium** is the fee the insurance company charges, and it represents the cost of the policy to the insured. A **claim** is a statement of loss that the insured sends to the insurance company to request payment.

> **insurance policy**
> A written contract between the insured and an insurance company that promises to pay for all or part of a loss.
>
> **premium**
> The fee charged by an insurance company for an insurance policy.
>
> **claim**
> A statement of a loss that the insured sends to the insurance company to request payment.

Like all private businesses, insurance companies are designed to make a profit. They therefore gather data to determine the extent of various risks. What makes it possible for insurance companies to accept risk is the law of large numbers.

The **law of large numbers** says that if a large number of people or organizations are exposed to the same risk, a predictable number of losses will occur during a given period of time. (For example, over the course of a 30-year mortgage, a home has a 9 percent chance of catching fire and a 26 percent chance of flooding.) Once the insurance company predicts the number of losses likely to occur, it can determine the appropriate premiums for each policy it issues against the loss. The premium will be high enough to cover expected losses and yet earn a profit for the firm and its shareholders. Today, many insurance companies are charging high premiums not for expected losses but for the costs they anticipate from the increasing number of court cases and high damage awards.

> **law of large numbers**
> Principle that if a large number of people are exposed to the same risk, a predictable number of losses will occur during a given period of time.

Insurance companies can also earn revenue from investing the premiums they collect. Premiums are usually collected at the beginning of a policy period. Until policy claims need to be paid out, premiums can be placed in secure, interest-paying investments.

Rule of Indemnity

The **rule of indemnity** says that an insured person or organization cannot collect more than the actual loss from an insurable risk. Nor can you buy two insurance policies, even from two insurance companies, and collect from both for the same loss. You cannot gain from risk management; you can only minimize losses.

> **rule of indemnity**
> Rule saying that an insured person or organization cannot collect more than the actual loss from an insurable risk.

Types of Insurance Companies

There are two major types of insurance companies. A **stock insurance company** is owned by shareholders, just like any other investor-owned company. A **mutual insurance company** is owned by its policyholders. It is a not-for-profit organization where any excess funds (over losses, expenses, and growth costs) go to the policyholders in the form of dividends or premium reductions. Equitable Life of Canada *<http://www.equitable.ca>* is an example of a mutual insurance company.

> **stock insurance company**
> A type of insurance company owned by shareholders.
>
> **mutual insurance company**
> A type of insurance company owned by its policyholders.

Insurance Coverage for Various Kinds of Risk

There are many types of insurance that cover various losses: property and liability insurance, health insurance, and life insurance. Property losses result from fires, accidents, theft, or other perils. Liability losses result from property damage or injuries suffered by others for which the policyholder is held responsible. Figure C.2 lists the types of insurance available. Let's consider a few of these in more detail.

Property and Liability Insurance

Property and liability insurance includes liability insurance, insurance coverage for home-based businesses, and protection from cyber attacks.

LIABILITY INSURANCE

Professional liability insurance covers people who are found liable for professional negligence. If a lawyer gives advice carelessly and the client loses money, the client may sue the lawyer for an amount equal to that loss, and liability insurance would cover the lawyer's loss. Professional liability insurance is also known as *malpractice insurance*. That term may bring doctors and dentists to mind, but many other professionals, including accountants, mortgage brokers, and real estate appraisers are buying professional liability insurance because of large lawsuits their colleagues have faced.

Product liability insurance covers liability arising out of products sold. (You may recall the product liability discussion in Appendix A.) A person who is injured by, say, a ladder or some other household good may sue the manufacturer for damages. Insurance usually covers such losses.

Personal liability insurance covers liability of any individual through a negligent act either at work or at home.

Premises liability insurance would cover claims resulting from an accident occurring either at a place of work or personal residence.

■ FIGURE C.2

PRIVATE INSURANCE	
Types of Insurance	What Insurance Does
Property and Liability Insurance	
Fire	Covers losses to buildings and their contents from fire
Automobile	Covers property damage, bodily injury, collision, fire, theft, vandalism, and other related vehicle losses
Homeowner's	Covers the home, other structures on the premises, home contents, expenses if forced from the home because of an insured peril, third-party liability, and medical payments to others
Computer coverage	Covers loss of equipment from fire, theft, and sometimes spills, power surges, and accidents
Professional liability	Protects from suits stemming from mistakes made or bad advice given in a professional context
Business interruption	Provides compensation for loss due to fire, theft, or similar disasters that close a business. Covers lost income, continuing expenses, and utility expenses
Non-performance loss protection	Protects from failure of a contractor, supplier, or other person to fulfill an obligation
Criminal loss protection	Protects from loss due to theft, burglary, or robbery
Commercial credit insurance	Protects manufacturers and wholesalers from credit losses due to insolvency or default
Public liability insurance	Provides protection for businesses and individuals against losses resulting from personal injuries or damage to the property of others for which the insured is responsible
Extended product liability insurance	Covers potentially toxic substances in products, environmental liability, as well as for corporations, director, and officer liability
Fidelity bond	Protects employers from employee dishonesty
Surety bond	Covers losses resulting from a second party's failure to fulfill a contract
Title insurance	Protects buyers from losses resulting from a defect in title to property
Cyber attack insurance	Helps protect companies from hackers
Health Insurance	
Workplace safety	Pays wages, medical care, and rehabilitation services for employees injured on the job
Extended health care	Pays a percentage of prescription drug costs, dental care, vision care, and paramedical services
Disability income insurance	Pays income while the insured is disabled as a result of accident or illness
Life Insurance	
Group life insurance	Covers all the employees of a firm or members of a group
Owner or key executive insurance	Enables businesses of sole proprietors or partnerships to pay bills and continue operating, saving jobs if the owner or a key executive dies. Enables corporations to hire and train or relocate another manager with no loss to the firm.
Retirement and pension plans	Provides employees with supplemental retirement and pension plans incomes
Credit life insurance	Pays the amount due on outstanding credit (e.g., loan, line of credit, etc.) if the debtor dies

INSURANCE COVERAGE FOR HOME-BASED BUSINESSES

Homeowners policies usually do not have adequate protection for a home-based business.[11] For example, they may have a limit for business equipment. For more coverage, you may need to add an *endorsement,* sometimes called a *rider,* to your homeowners policy. If clients visit your office or if you receive deliveries regularly, you may need home-office insurance. It protects you from slip-and-fall lawsuits and other risks associated with visitors. For more elaborate businesses, such as custom cabinetry shops and other types of manufacturing or inventory-keeping businesses, you may need a business-owner policy. Unless you are an expert on insurance, you will need to consult an insurance agent about the best insurance for your home-business needs.

PROTECTION FROM CYBER ATTACKS

Often you will see articles in newspapers about a company being hacked by some outside (or inside) individuals or groups that steal your private information, such as social insurance numbers, credit card information, address, etc. Cyber risk insurance can help a business prepare for the worst. For example, it will cover companies should their employees or customers decide to file against them in the event that their information is leaked.[12]

Health Insurance

Health insurance coverage includes workplace safety, extended health care, and disability insurance.

WORKPLACE SAFETY

Provincial workplace safety and insurance boards guarantee payment of wages, medical care, and rehabilitation services (e.g., retraining) for employees who are injured on the job. Employers in all provinces and territories are required to provide this insurance. It also pays benefits to the survivors of those who die as a result of work-related injuries. The cost of insurance varies in relation to the company's safety record, the size of its payroll, and the types of hazards its workers face. For example, it usually costs more to insure a steelworker than an accountant because the risk of injury is greater for a steelworker.

EXTENDED HEALTH CARE

Canada provides universal health care for every citizen. (The description of the coverage provided is found in Figure C.1.) Above and beyond this insurance, individuals can be covered by benefit plans usually provided through their employer or a group the individual is affiliated with. Coverage typically includes dental, extended health care, worldwide travel benefits, survivors' benefits, and income continuance.

Dental coverage can vary from basic preventive care through to major procedures (e.g., dentures). Extended health care can cover prescription drugs, a number of paramedical services (e.g., massage and physiotherapy), vision care, and upgraded hospital accommodation, normally up to a semi-private room. Worldwide travel benefits cover expenses that are the result of an accident or unexpected illness incurred while on business or vacation in a foreign country. Eligible expenses may include hospital accommodation and private duty nursing. Survivors' benefits can include a death benefit (lump sum payment) for a spouse and dependent children, as well as a pension. Income continuance provides for both short- and long-term disability.

DISABILITY INSURANCE

Disability insurance replaces part of your income—usually 50 to 70 percent—if you become disabled and unable to work. You must usually be disabled for a certain period, such as 60 days, before you can begin collecting. Insurance experts recommend getting disability insurance if your employer does not offer it, because the chances of becoming disabled by a disease or accident when young are much higher than the chance of dying. The premiums for disability insurance vary according to age, occupation, and income.

Over the past few years, the cost of benefit plans has increased significantly. As a result, coverage limits have been reduced, and a greater share of the cost has become the responsibility of the insured.

Life Insurance

As listed in Figure C.2, life insurance includes group life insurance, owner or key executive insurance, retirement and pension plans, and credit life insurance.

OWNER OR KEY EXECUTIVE INSURANCE

Regardless of how careful we are, we all face the prospect of death. To ensure that those left behind will be able to continue the business, entrepreneurs often buy life insurance that will pay partners and others what they need to keep the firm going.[13] The same risk for businesses relates to the loss of a key employee. The best kind of insurance to cover executives in the firm is term insurance, but dozens of new policies with interesting features are now available.[14]

The Risk of Damaging the Environment

Risk management now goes far beyond the protection of individuals, businesses, and not-for-profit organizations from known risks. It means the evaluation of worldwide risks, with many unknowns, such as climate change.[15] It also means prioritizing these risks so that international funds can be spent where they can do the most good. No insurance company can protect humanity from all such risks. These risks are the concern of businesses and governments throughout the world, with the assistance of the international scientific community. They should also be your concern as you study risk management in all its dimensions. For example, think of the risks that accompany the search for natural gas using fracking. Now that such a search has gone global, companies throughout the world are examining the risks involved.[16] That means more jobs and more interest in risk management in general.

KEY TERMS

claim	mutual insurance company	self-insurance
insurable interest	premium	speculative risk
insurable risk	pure risk	stock insurance company
insurance policy	risk management	uninsurable risk
law of large numbers	rule of indemnity	

Money, the Bank of Canada, and the Canadian Financial System

LEARNING OBJECTIVES

After you have read and studied this chapter, you should be able to:

LO1   Explain what money is and what makes it useful.

LO2   Describe how the Bank of Canada controls the money supply.

LO3   List the three components of the Canadian financial system, and explain how it is regulated.

LO4   Discuss the role that financial institutions play in providing services.

LO5   Describe the role of the financial markets.

LO6   Outline the role of the clearing and settlement systems.

PROFILE

GETTING TO KNOW ANISH CHOPRA, MANAGING DIRECTOR OF TD ASSET MANAGEMENT INC.

Anish Chopra graduated from the University of Waterloo with a Master's Degree in Accounting (Gold Medalist). He has focused his career in the financial services industry where his academic training and designations—Chartered Accountant, Chartered Financial Analyst, Chartered Alternative Investment Analyst, and Chartered Business Valuator (Canadian Gold Medalist)—have all contributed to his professional success. One of his numerous awards has included being the inaugural recipient of the Top Chartered Business Valuator Under 40 Award given by the Canadian Institute of Chartered Business Valuators (CICBV).

    After working as a member of TD Securities' mergers and acquisitions group, Chopra joined TD Asset Management Inc. (TDAM, <https://www.tdassetmanagement.com>) in 1998. Today, he has overall supervisory responsibility for TDAM's Canadian Value, Core Canadian Equity, and Target Return teams. Chopra also has lead management responsibilities on the TD Canadian Value Fund for TD Mutual Funds and the Target

Return strategies for both TD Mutual Funds and TD Private Investment Counsel. He is also a member of the TD Pension Plan managing team and Wealth Asset Allocation Committee.

TDAM operates in the United States as TDAM USA Inc. and in Canada as TD Asset Management Inc. Both firms are wholly-owned subsidiaries of the Toronto-Dominion Bank. TDAM is a North American investment manager offering investment solutions to both institutional (e.g., pension plan sponsors, corporations, endowments, and foundations) and individual investors. The key areas of portfolio management include active, enhanced, and passive pooled fund strategies; segregated account management; alternative investment strategies; and customized investment solutions. Assets under management at TDAM were over $333 billion as of June 30, 2015.

Chopra has over 11 years' experience managing proprietary funds within TDAM, with knowledge in Canadian, U.S., and global equities as well as numerous absolute return strategies. As a result of his expertise, he appears regularly on television as well as in print media discussing business and investment issues. He has presented at numerous investment industry conferences across North America. For over a decade, Chopra has also served as a Course Leader and Course Co-Author for several finance courses with the CICBV. He has served as an instructor for the Institute of Chartered Accountants of Ontario. In addition, he has been a guest lecturer at Canadian business schools.

Chopra is also involved in the community. At the University of Waterloo, he held roles as the Chair for the School of Accounting and Finance Student Investment Fund, and was an Honouree in the Student Fellowship Program. He is also the Vice Chair of the User Advisory Council of the CICA, serves as a member of the Ontario Judicial Council, and is a Chapter Executive with the Chartered Alternative Investment Analyst (CAIA) Association of Toronto. He also held numerous positions on the Board of Directors of the Canadian Cancer Society (Central Toronto Unit) where, as Chairperson of the Fundraising Committee, he led the unit in receiving the Toronto Regional Fundraising Award.

The Canadian financial system includes financial institutions, the financial markets, and clearing and settlement systems. Professionals like Anish Chopra have played a key role in the dollar value growth of investments in the financial markets. It's through the financial system that most commercial activity (e.g., saving; borrowing; investing; and buying and selling by means of debit and credit cards, cheques, and e-money) is carried out. Read further to learn how governments, corporations, and individuals benefit from the stability of the Canadian financial system.

Sources: "About Us," TD Asset Management Inc., 12 September 2015, https://www.tdassetmanagement.com/aboutUs.form?lang=en; : "About TDAM," TD Asset Management, 3 May 2015, http://www.tdaminstitutional.com/tmi/content/AU_AboutUs?language=en_CA; "Wealth Asset Allocation Committee - Anish Chopra, CA, CFA," TD Asset Management, https://www.tdassetmanagement.com/getManagerDetails.form?id=16028&teamTitle=Wealth%20Asset%20Allocation%20Committee&teamTitleFrench=Comit%C3%A9%20de%20r%C3%A9partition%20de%20l'actif%20de%20Gestion%20de%20patrimoine&lang=en, downloaded 2 May 2015; Diana Cawfield, "Anish Chopra - TD Asset Management," Morningstar Research Inc., 26 April 2013, http://www.morningstar.ca/globalhome/industry/managermonitor.asp?changeprtl=y&reportid=593949; Anish Chopra's profile provided by the School of Accounting and Finance of the University of Waterloo, June 2012; and "The Canadian Financial System," Bank of Canada, April 2012, http://www.bankofcanada.ca/wp-content/uploads/2010/11/canadian_financial_system.pdf.

LO1   Explain what money is and what makes it useful.

Why Money Is Important

Two of the most critical issues in Canada today—economic growth and the creation of jobs—depend on the ready availability of money. Money is so important to the economy that many institutions have evolved to manage it and make it available when it is needed. Today, you can get cash from an automated teller machine (ATM) almost anywhere in the world, and most organizations will accept a cheque, credit card, debit card, or smart card for purchases.

Behind the scenes is a complex system of banking that makes the free flow of money possible. Each day, about $4 trillion is exchanged in the world's currency markets. Therefore, what happens to any major country's economy has an effect on the Canadian economy and vice versa.

Let's start at the beginning by discussing exactly what the word *money* means. Soon after, you will learn how the supply of money affects the prices you pay for goods and services.

What Is Money?

Money is anything that people generally accept as payment for goods and services. In the past, objects as diverse as salt, feathers, fur pelts, stones, rare shells, tea, and horses have been used as money. In fact, until the 1880s, cowrie shells were one of the world's most popular currencies.

> **money**
> Anything that people generally accept as payment for goods and services.

Barter is the direct trading of goods or services for other goods and services.[1] Though barter may sound like something from the past, many people have discovered the benefits of bartering online.[2] One entrepreneur describes his bartering experience as follows: "Last year we bartered the creation of a full-color graphic novel in exchange for a new website design. . . . The value of the trade was $50,000. We provided three months of writing services to provide the graphic novel story line . . . and then five months of illustration. In exchange, they helped us to define, design, and then program our new website."[3]

Some people barter goods and services the old-fashioned way. In Siberia, for example, people have bought movie tickets with two eggs, and in Ukraine people have paid their energy bills with sausages and milk. Today you can go to a *barter exchange* where you can put goods or services into the system and get trade credits for other goods and services that you need. The barter exchange makes it easier to barter because you do not have to find people with whom to barter. The exchange does that for you.

Although people have long used barter to exchange goods without money, one problem is that objects like chickens and eggs are harder to carry around than a ten-dollar bill. What other drawbacks does bartering have?

barter
The direct trading of goods and services for other goods and services.

The problem with traditional barter is that eggs and milk are difficult to carry around. Most people need some object that is portable, divisible, stable, and durable so that they can trade goods and services without carrying the actual goods around with them. One solution is coins and paper bills. Five standards for a useful form of money are:

- *Portability.* Coins are a lot easier to take to market than are pigs or other heavy products.

- *Divisibility.* Different-sized coins and bills can represent different values. Because silver is now too expensive, today's coins are made of other metals, but the accepted face values remain.

- *Stability.* When everybody agrees on the value of coins, the value of money is relatively stable. Due to its stability, much of the world has used the U.S. dollar as the measure of value. If the value of the dollar fluctuates too rapidly, the world may turn to some other form of money, such as the euro, for the measure of value. You may recall that the Royal Canadian Mint stopped producing and distributing pennies due to rising costs relative to the face value and the significant handling costs of the penny for retailers, financial institutions, and the economy in general.[4] Despite this, pennies are still legal tender in Canada.

- *Durability.* Coins last for thousands of years, even when they have sunk to the bottom of the ocean, as you have seen when divers find old coins in sunken ships.

- *Uniqueness.* It is hard to counterfeit, or copy, elaborately designed and minted coins. With the latest colour copiers, people are able to duplicate the look of paper money relatively easily. Thus, the government has gone to extra lengths to ensure that Canadian dollars are readily identifiable. Security features include raised ink, transparent text, metallic portraits, a transparent window, the display of small numbers, use of hidden numbers, and a maple leaf border.[5] How can you tell if you have a counterfeit note?

Canada's new banknotes are printed on polymer, which lasts at least 2.5 times longer than paper notes, reducing processing, replacement costs, and environmental impact.[6] How do these notes reflect the five standards of money?

Adapting *to* CHANGE

The Bitcoin Is in the Mail

It's difficult to imagine a currency being called cool or trendy. But these terms are often used when describing bitcoin, a form of digital currency created in 2008. Bitcoin *<https://bitcoin.org/en>* is accepted at online operations ranging from tech-savvy retailers and pizza parlours to some gambling sites.

Bitcoin is attractive to many users because there's no central authority that regulates the currency. (The Bank of Canada regulates currency in Canada.) Transactions involve two people anywhere in the world with no middlemen (e.g., a commercial bank), government regulations, or transaction fees involved. In fact you do not even have to give your name. Bitcoins are stored in a digital wallet that serves as a virtual bank account or on a user's computer. Several marketplaces, called "bitcoin exchanges," are available for consumers to buy bitcoins using different currencies. MtGox was once the largest bitcoin exchange. (Claiming it had been hacked, MtGox lost around $412.5 million belonging to customers and over $55 million of its own money. The company filed for bankruptcy in 2014.)

So just how much is a bitcoin worth? That's a very good question. Bitcoin's volatility stems from its decentralized valuation system. Value is based on demand, as transactions run across a peer-to-peer network of personal computers. Since bitcoins are not managed from a central bank like typical currencies, an arsenal of algorithms constantly recalculates the currency's value. This system has caused the value of bitcoins to spike wildly—then fall in value almost as fast. The value of bitcoins has fluctuated from $13 in 2012 to $1,200 in December 2013. This unpredictability has given skeptics plenty of reasons to question bitcoin's practicality. Governments are concerned about illegal activities being conducted through bitcoin transactions. They are also considering taxation issues.

Bitcoin is just one of many digital currencies that have hit the market. Whether these currencies achieve a level of stability or just become interesting financial case studies for the digital age remains to be seen.

Sources: Sunny Freeman, "What Is Bitcoin? 11 Things You Need to Know About the Digital Currency," *Huffington Post,* 26 January 2014; Jose Pagliary, "New IRS Rules Make Using Bitcoins a Fiasco," CNN Money, 31 March 2014; Ashley Vance and Brad Stone, "The Bitcoin-Mining Arms Race Heats Up," *Bloomberg Businessweek,* 9 January 2014; and Ryan Derousseau, "Boom in Virtual Money Mints Real Gains and Losses," *Money,* January–February 2014.

Coins and paper money simplify exchanges. Most countries have their own currencies, and they are all about equally portable, divisible, and durable. However, they are not always equally stable.

Electronic cash (e-cash) is one of the newest forms of money. You can make online payments using Quicken or Microsoft Money or send e-cash using PayPal. Recipients can choose automatic deposit to their financial institutions, e-dollars for spending online, or a traditional cheque in the mail. Bitcoin is a digital version of money that is tougher to forge, cuts across national boundaries, and can be stored on your hard drive instead of in a bank; however, the bitcoin is not generally accepted.[7] Nonetheless, efforts will be made in the future to create a cashless society using some other form of currency than the bills and coins we now use. Cryptocurrencies, like bitcoin, are too new to know their value, but many competitors have arisen in recent years. They include Litecoin, Peercoin, NXT, and Dogcoin.[8] Do you know that Bitcoin has its own online store? See the Adapting to Change box for more about Bitcoin.

LO2   Describe how the Bank of Canada controls the money supply.

The Bank of Canada

As introduced in Chapter 4, the Bank of Canada's role is to promote the economic and financial welfare of Canada. It is responsible for Canada's monetary policy, bank notes, financial system, funds management, and retail debt.[9] Recall how the U.S. subprime mortgage crisis translated into a global financial crisis due to the global interconnectivity of banking systems. This resulted in a widespread liquidity crisis, which led to major government interventions through banking actions. To understand the Canadian economy, one needs to understand global money exchanges and the institutions involved in the creation and management of money.

The Global Exchange of Money

A *falling dollar value* means that the amount of goods and services you can buy with a dollar decreases. A *rising dollar value* means that the amount of goods and services you can buy with a dollar goes up. Thus, the price in U.S. dollars you pay for a cool pair of jeans you buy at an outlet mall in the United States will be lower if the Canadian dollar rises relative to the U.S. dollar, and vice versa.

What makes the dollar weak (falling dollar value) or strong (rising dollar value) is the position of the Canadian economy relative to other economies. When the economy is strong, the demand for dollars is high, and the value of the dollar rises. When the economy is perceived as weakening, however, the demand for dollars declines, and the value of the dollar falls. The value of the dollar thus depends on a relatively strong economy. (Review Chapter 3 for a discussion on exchange rates.) Let's consider the money supply next.

What Is the Money Supply?

The **money supply** is the amount of money the Bank of Canada (the Bank) makes available for people to buy goods and services. You may wonder why the Bank of Canada can't directly increase or decrease the money supply at will since it regulates the supply of paper currency in circulation.[10] The answer is that the bank notes issued by the Bank represent only a small portion of all the money circulating in the economy at any one time; the bulk of the money supply consists of deposits that the public holds at financial institutions.[11] The amount of money in circulation, called *monetary aggregates*, can be measured in a number of ways as described in Figure 18.1.

> **money supply**
> The amount of money the Bank of Canada makes available for people to buy goods and services.

■ FIGURE 18.1

CANADA'S MONEY SUPPLY	
MI+ and MI++ are narrow measures of money. They represent money that can be accessed quickly and easily. Broader measures of money include M2, M3, M2+, and M2++.	
Monetary Aggregates	**Description**
MI+	Currency outside banks plus all chequable deposits held at chartered banks, trust and mortgage loan companies, credit unions, and *caisses populaires* (excluding deposits of these institutions) plus continuity adjustments
MI++	The currency (bank notes and coins) in circulation plus chequable and non-chequable deposits (other than fixed-term deposits) at banks, trust and mortgage loan companies, credit unions, and *caisses populaires*
M2	MI++ plus bank personal deposits, bank non-personal demand, and notice deposits
M3	M2 plus bank non-personal term deposits and foreign-currency deposits of residents
M2+	M2 plus deposits at trust and mortgage loan companies and at government savings institutions, deposits and shares at credit union and *caisses populaires*, life insurance company individual annuities, and money market mutual funds
M2++	M2+ plus Canada Savings bonds and other retail debt instruments, plus non-money market mutual funds

Source: "Canada's Money Supply," Bank of Canada, October 2011, www.bankofcanada.ca/wp-content/uploads/2010/11/canada_money_supply.pdf.

Before we consider how the Bank of Canada influences the money supply, let us first consider why the money supply needs to be controlled.

Managing Inflation and the Money Supply

Imagine what would happen if governments or non-governmental organizations were to generate twice as much money as exists now. There would be twice as much money available, but still the same amount of products. What would happen to prices? (Hint: Remember the laws of supply and demand from Chapter 2.) Prices would go *up*, because more people would try to buy goods and services with their money and bid up the price to get what they wanted. This rise in price is called *inflation*, which some people call "too much money chasing too few goods."

Now think about the opposite: What would happen if the Bank of Canada took money out of the economy, or put less money in? Prices would go *down* because there would be an oversupply of goods and services compared to the money available to buy them; this decrease in prices is called *deflation*. If too much money is taken out of the economy, a recession might occur. That is, people would lose jobs and the economy would stop growing.

Now we come to a second question about the money supply: Why does it need to be controlled? The reason is that doing so allows us to manage, somewhat, the prices of goods and services. The size of the money supply also affects employment and economic growth or decline. The global money supply is controlled by *central banks* like the Bank of Canada, the U.S. Federal Reserve Bank, and the European Central Bank. Decisions made by central banks affect the economies of the world.

Control of the Money Supply[12]

The Bank of Canada is in charge of monetary policy, and the country's money supply influences monetary policy. The objective of the Bank of Canada's monetary policy is to support a level of spending by Canadians that is consistent with the Bank's goal of price stability. With this in mind, the Bank will conduct monetary policy aimed at keeping inflation within the inflation-control target range of 1 to 3 percent. By influencing the rate at which the supply of money and credit is growing, total spending on goods and services in the economy can be stabilized. Referring back to Figure 18.1, the growth of the broader monetary aggregates is a leading indicator of the rate of inflation. For example, changes in M1++ provide useful information about changes that are occurring in the economy. The availability of money and credit must expand over time, and the Bank of Canada is responsible for ensuring that the rate at which more money is introduced into the economy is consistent with long-term stable growth.

Some of the Bank of Canada's specialized duties here at the Bank's headquarters include $15 billion in payments processed daily, and the management of more than $600 billion in federal government debt and $68 billion in foreign reserves. Visit <http://www.bankofcanada.ca/multimedia/bank-of-canada-count-on-us> to learn more how its activities benefit us all.

The Bank of Canada carries out monetary policy by influencing short-term interest rates. It does this by raising and lowering the target for the overnight rate, also called the Bank's *policy interest rate*. The **overnight rate** is the interest rate at which major financial institutions borrow and lend one-day (or overnight) funds among themselves. Changes in the target rate for the overnight rate then influence the **prime rate** which is the interest rate that banks charge their most creditworthy customers. The prime rate serves as a benchmark for other interest rates, such as those for consumer loans and mortgages, and interest paid on bank accounts, term deposits, and other savings.

> **overnight rate**
> The interest rate at which major financial institutions borrow and lend one-day (or overnight) funds among themselves.
>
> **prime rate**
> The interest rate that banks charge their most creditworthy customers.

There is a common misconception that the cost of credit provided by banks to their customers is driven by the Bank of Canada's overnight rate. While the Bank of Canada's overnight rate does influence the pricing of very short-term credit, this is less than 1 percent of funding that banks use for lending. Banks obtain funding from a wide variety of short- and long-term funding sources, certificates of deposit (to be discussed later), and bonds.

Transmission of Monetary Policy[13]

The transmission of monetary policy is the process by which changes in the Bank of Canada's policy interest rate work their way through the economy, ultimately to affect the rate of inflation. Changes in this interest rate affect various kinds of economic activity (and over time, inflation) through four main channels, as shown in Figure 18.2. Let's consider these three additional channels as the fourth channel, exchange rates, was discussed earlier.

■ **FIGURE 18.2**

THE TRANSMISSION OF MONETARY POLICY

It can take six to eight quarters for a change in the policy interest rate to have its full effect on inflation. While changes can affect commercial interest rates, asset prices, and the exchange rate quite quickly, there can be a significant lag before interest rate changes influence expectations (i.e., spending and saving decisions).

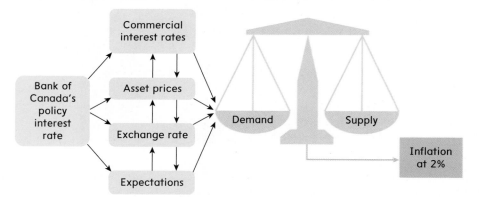

Source: "How Monetary Policy Works: The Transmission of Monetary Policy," Bank of Canada, April 2012, http://www.bankofcanada.ca/wp-content/uploads/2010/11/how_monetary_policy_works.pdf.

When interest rates go down, people and businesses are encouraged to borrow more from commercial banks (the first channel), and thus spend more. This behaviour then boosts the economy as the demand for goods and services increases. But if the economy grows too fast, it can lead to inflation. The Bank may then raise the overnight rate (which then increases the prime rate and other interest rates) to slow down borrowing and spending by putting a brake on inflation. When interest rates rise, consumers and businesses tend to hold less money, to borrow less, and to pay back existing loans.

The second channel for the transmission of monetary policy is the effect that changes in interest rates have on the prices of various assets such as bonds, stocks, and houses. An increase in interest rates can put a damper on the prices of these assets, thus decreasing household wealth, which in turn may discourage borrowing and spending.

The fourth channel is the effect of changes in interest rates on people's expectations of future interest rates, growth, and inflation. These expectations often affect decisions of firms and households about current saving and investment choices, and they affect wages, the prices of goods and services, and asset prices.

In choosing a target for the overnight rate, the Bank of Canada picks a level that it feels will keep future inflation low, stable, and predictable. Keeping inflation low and stable helps provide a good climate for sustainable economic growth, investment, and job creation.

Progress Assessment

- What are the five characteristics of useful money?
- What is the money supply and why is it important?
- How does the Bank of Canada control the money supply?

LO3   List the three components of the Canadian financial system, and explain how it is regulated.

The Canadian Financial System[14]

The financial system makes a vital contribution to the welfare of Canadians. The system includes (1) financial institutions, (2) the financial markets, and (3) clearing and settlement systems. It is through the financial system that most commercial activity (e.g., saving, borrowing, investing, and buying and selling by means of debit and credit cards, cheques, and e-money) is carried out.

With a focus on promoting a stable and efficient financial system in Canada, the Bank of Canada provides liquidity to the financial system, gives policy advice to the federal government on the design and development of the system, oversees major clearing and settlement systems, and provides banking services to these systems and their participants. The Bank also contributes to international discussions on important financial system issues.

The International Monetary Fund has concluded that the system "is mature, sophisticated, and well-managed," that "financial stability is underpinned by sound macroeconomic policies and strong prudential regulation and supervision," and that "deposit insurance and arrangements for crisis management and failure resolution are well-designed." Let's consider how the financial system is regulated.

Regulating the Financial System[15]

The 2007–09 global financial crisis underscored the importance of financial regulation and surveillance to ensure a stable financial system. In Canada, this systemwide approach is the shared responsibility of the Department of Finance and other federal financial regulatory authorities, including the Bank of Canada, the Office of the Superintendent of Financial Institutions (OSFI), and the Canada Deposit

Insurance Corporation (CDIC, <*http://www.cdic.ca*>). Ultimately, it is the Minister of Finance who is responsible for the financial system.

Due to its important role in the economy, the financial system is heavily regulated. Regulation is designed to ensure the integrity, safety, and soundness of financial institutions and markets. Legislative, self-regulatory, and other initiatives help minimize crises and company failures. In addition, they protect investors, depositors, and policyholders. Keep in mind, though, that these compliance requirements require a lot of time and money for companies in this industry to complete.

In Canada, there is no single body that regulates the financial system. It is a responsibility shared among different organizations and levels of government. To start with, financial institutions may be regulated at either the federal or the provincial level, or jointly. For example, banks are federally regulated. Securities commissions, which regulate and administer the issuance and trade in securities, such as stocks and bonds, are provincially regulated. Likewise, credit unions, and *caisses populaires*, a form of credit unions, are provincially regulated. Insurance providers, trust and loan companies, and cooperative credit associations may be federally and/or provincially regulated, depending on the jurisdiction under which the company is incorporated or registered. For a summary, review Figure 18.3.

■ **FIGURE 18.3**

REGULATORY RESPONSIBILITY FOR FINANCIAL INSTITUTIONS			
Financial Institution	Federal	Provincial	Depends on Jurisdiction
Banks	X		
Securities Commissions		X	
Credit Unions		X	
Caisses Populaires		X	
Insurance Providers			X
Trust and Loan Companies			X
Cooperative Credit Associations			X

Source: "Regulation of the Canadian Financial System," Bank of Canada, April 2012, http://www.bankofcanada.ca/wp-content/uploads/2010/11/regulation_canadian_financial.pdf.

For institutions under provincial jurisdiction, the province(s) in which a company is incorporated or registered is (are) responsible for regulating the company's overall powers. As at the federal level, provinces are supported by agencies and organizations that supervise the ongoing operations of these institutions.

For institutions under federal responsibility, the Department of Finance is charged with overseeing their overall powers—in other words, what they can and cannot do. The Department of Finance relies on three federal agencies to supervise the ongoing operations of these institutions and their compliance with legislation:

● OSFI monitors the day-to-day operations of financial institutions with respect to their financial soundness. It regulates and supervises all banks in Canada, and all federally incorporated or registered trust and loan companies, insurance companies, co-operative credit associations, and private pension plans. OSFI's mandate does not include consumer-related issues or the securities industry.

- CDIC oversees the deposit insurance system, which protects deposits that Canadians have in their federal financial institutions. CDIC insures eligible deposits at member institutions (e.g., banks and trust companies) against these institutions' failure or collapse. CDIC guarantees deposits up to $100,000 (principal and interest), in Canadian dollars, in each member institution. It is funded primarily by premiums paid by banks and trust companies that belong to this program.

- The Financial Consumer Agency of Canada (FCAC, *<http://www.fcac-acfc.gc.ca>*) monitors financial institutions to ensure that they comply with federal consumer protection measures, which range from disclosure requirements to complaint-handling procedures. FCAC also provides information, and in some cases online tools, on the following topics: banking; budgeting and debt management; credit cards; mortgages; credit report and score; savings and investments; insurance; and fraud.

After the Progress Assessment, let's consider financial institutions, one area of Canada's financial system. This will be followed by a discussion on the financial markets, and then the clearing and settlement systems.

CDIC does not cover all deposits. Foreign-currency accounts, certificates of deposit with terms greater than five years, stocks, bonds, and mutual funds are not covered. Some CDIC members have subsidiaries that are CDIC members in their own right. As a result, depending on how deposits are registered, you can be protected for more than $100,000. This sign will confirm the parent company is a CDIC member as well as its subsidiaries. Have you seen this sign in your financial institution's branch? Visit www.cdic.ca for more information.

Progress Assessment

- What areas does the Canadian financial system oversee?
- Give three examples of financial institutions. Include which level of government regulates each example.
- Describe the roles of three federal agencies: OSFI, CDIC, and FCAC.

LO4   Discuss the role that financial institutions play in providing services.

The Canadian Financial System: Financial Institutions

Until the middle of the 1980s, Canada had a "four-pillar system" that included (1) banks, (2) trust companies, (3) insurance companies, and (4) securities dealers. Regulation was designed to foster competition within each pillar, but not among them. When the government permitted commercial banks to acquire securities firms in the late 1980s, this segregation of functions began to erode.

Since that time, changes in regulations have eliminated many of the old barriers that prohibited financial institutions from competing in each other's business, and consequently, the four pillars. As a result of legislative changes in 1992, the banks were allowed to own insurance, trust, and securities subsidiaries. Today, most of Canada's large banks have subsidiaries in these areas. For example, Scotiabank further diversified its Canadian operations through major acquisitions that included investment dealer McLeod Young Weir (1988), and trust companies Montreal Trust (1994) and National Trust (1997).[16]

Financial institutions include commercial banks, credit unions, trust and loan companies, insurance companies, and non-banks.[17] The financial services sector in Canada includes financial institutions that support businesses and consumers. Today, it is increasingly difficult to distinguish firms by type of function, as financial institutions have become highly competitive. For example, a life insurance company can now own a bank, and vice versa. As a result of Bill C-8 (in force since October 2001), important changes were made to federal financial institutions legislation and how the financial services sector is regulated. This included relaxing ownership and organization rules for banks. Consequently, we see non-traditional financial services providers—such as Walmart Canada Bank and Canadian Tire Bank—taking advantage of changes in the regulatory environment to offer financial services to their customer base. Next, consider some of the competitors in this business.

Commercial Banks

A **commercial bank** is a profit-seeking organization that receives deposits from individuals and corporations in the form of chequing and savings accounts and then uses some of these funds to make loans. A bank makes a profit by efficiently using customer deposits as inputs (on which it pays interest) to invest in interest-bearing loans to other customers. If the revenue generated by loans exceeds the interest paid to depositors plus all other operating expenses, the bank makes a profit.

> **commercial bank**
> A profit-seeking organization that receives deposits from individuals and corporations in the form of chequing and savings accounts and then uses some of these funds to make loans.

As major players in Canada's financial system, banks serve millions of customers. They include individuals, small- and medium-sized businesses, large corporations, governments, institutional investors, and non-profit organizations. The banking industry includes 29 domestic banks, 24 foreign bank subsidiaries, 27 full-service foreign bank branches, and 3 foreign bank lending branches operating in Canada.[18] Did you know that the Canadian banking system was ranked the soundest in the world by the World Economic Forum for seven years in a row?[19]

The Canadian Bankers Association (CBA, <http://www.cba.ca>) provides a summary of the scope of banks. The major domestic banks offer a full range of banking, investment, and financial services. They have extensive, nationwide distribution networks and also are active in the United States, Latin America, the Caribbean, Asia, and other parts of the world. Many large international banks have a presence here—through a subsidiary, representative office, or branch of the parent bank; most specialize in corporate and investment banking (e.g., niche financing) and have only one or two offices/branches. A notable exception is HSBC Bank Canada, which has a strong retail presence with branches across Canada.[20]

Review Figure 18.4 for a list of Canada's big six banks. Based on assets, the five largest banks represent upwards of 80 percent of the national financial institution market.[21]

■ FIGURE 18.4

Ranking	Bank Name	Total Assets (C$ billions)
CANADA'S BIG SIX BANKS		
1	Royal Bank of Canada (RBC)	1,086.7
2	Toronto-Dominion Bank (TD)	1,080.2
3	Bank of Nova Scotia (Scotiabank)	851.9
4	Bank of Montreal (BMO)	672.4
5	Canadian Imperial Bank of Commerce (CIBC)	445.2
6	National Bank of Canada	214.5

Source: "Banks in Canada," *Banks around the World*, 2015, http://www.relbanks.com/north-america/canada.

SOME SERVICES PROVIDED BY COMMERCIAL BANKS

Individuals and corporations that deposit money in a chequing account can write personal cheques to pay for almost any purchase or transaction. The technical name for a chequing account is a **demand deposit** because the money is available on demand from the depositor. Some banks impose a service charge for cheque-writing privileges or demand a minimum deposit. They might also charge a small handling fee for each cheque written.[22] For business depositors, the service charge depends on the average daily balance in the chequing account, the number of cheques written, and the firm's credit rating and credit history.

demand deposit
The technical name for a chequing account; the money in a demand deposit can be withdrawn anytime on demand from the depositor.

In the past, chequing accounts paid no interest to depositors, but interest-bearing chequing accounts have experienced phenomenal growth in recent years. Commercial banks also offer a variety of savings account options. A savings account is technically a **time deposit** because the bank can require notice before you make a withdrawal.

time deposit
The technical name for a savings account; the bank can require prior notice before the owner withdraws money from a time deposit.

A **certificate of deposit** is a time-deposit (savings) account that earns interest, to be delivered on the certificate's maturity date. The depositor agrees not to withdraw any of the funds in the account until then. The longer the term deposit is to be held by the bank, the higher the interest rate. The interest rates also depend on economic conditions. Some financial institutions refer to certificates of deposit as *Guaranteed Investment Certificates (GICs)*.

certificate of deposit
A time-deposit (savings) account that earns interest to be delivered at the end of the certificate's maturity date; also called a Guaranteed Investment Certificate (GIC).

Banks also offer a variety of products and services. Examples include credit cards and loans for creditworthy customers, life insurance policies, inexpensive brokerage services, financial counselling, automatic bill payments, safe-deposit boxes, registered retirement savings accounts, traveller's cheques, ATMs, and overdraft protection. The latter means preferred customers can automatically get loans when they've written cheques exceeding their account balance. The Making Ethical Decisions box explores a more minor issue that could occur in your banking efforts.

Making ETHICAL DECISIONS

Would You Tell the Teller?

You are at the teller window of your bank making a withdrawal. The teller counts out your money and says, "OK, here's your $300." You count the money and see that the teller has given you $320 by mistake. When you point this out, the teller replies indignantly, "I don't think so. I counted the money in front of you." You are upset by her quick denial of a mistake and her attitude. You have to decide whether or not to give her back the overpayment of $20. What are your alternatives? What would you do? Is that the ethical thing to do?

MANAGING YOUR PERSONAL FINANCES

A major reason for studying business is that it prepares you for finding and keeping a good job. You already know that one of the secrets to finding a well-paying job is to have a good education. With your earnings, you can take vacations, raise a family, make investments, buy the products you want, and give generously to others.

Money management, however, is not easy. You have to earn the money in the first place. Then you have to learn how to save money, spend money wisely, and insure yourself against any financial and health risks. Review Appendix D for a discussion on managing your personal finances.

Credit Unions and Trust Companies

A **credit union** is a non-profit, member-owned financial co-operative that offers a full variety of banking services to its members. They include interest-bearing chequing accounts at relatively high rates, short-term loans at relatively low rates, financial counselling, life insurance policies, and a limited number of home mortgage loans. (Recall some of the key differences between co-operatives and for-profit organizations from our Chapter 6 discussion.) They are organized by government agencies, corporations, unions, and professional associations. *Caisses populaires* are located predominantly in Quebec. Today, credit unions are growing in popularity.[23]

credit union
A non-profit, member-owned financial co-operative that offers a full variety of banking services to its members.

You might want to visit a local credit union to see whether you are eligible to belong, and then compare the rates to those at local banks. Credit unions often have fewer branches than banks and less access to ATMs. It is best to determine what services you need and then compare those services to the same services offered by banks.

Credit unions are member-owned financial co-operatives that offer their members a wide range of banking services. If you do not belong to a credit union, what would a credit union need to offer you to get you to switch?

A **trust company** is a financial institution that over the years conducted activities similar to those of banks. How they differ is that trust companies have a fiduciary role. Due to this role, trust companies can administer estates, pension plans, and agency contracts, which banks cannot do as it was originally considered a conflict of interest for banks. Changes in regulations over the years have seen trust companies expand their quasi-banking operations—designed originally to attract savings and term deposits to fund mortgage lending—into complete banking facilities for both individuals and businesses.[24] After a series of acquisitions due to the elimination of the four pillars, there are 56 remaining trust companies: 10 are now bank subsidiaries, 8 are life insurance company subsidiaries, 11 are credit union subsidiaries, and 27 are owned or controlled by corporations.[25]

trust company
A financial institution that can administer estates, pension plans, and agency contracts, in addition to other activities conducted by banks.

Other Financial Institutions: Non-Banks

There are also a variety of other institutions called non-banks. **Non-banks** are financial organizations that accept no deposits but offer many services provided by regular banks. Examples include brokerage firms, pension funds, life insurance companies, and commercial and consumer finance companies.

> **non-banks**
> Financial organizations that accept no deposits but offer many services provided by regular banks.

As competition between banks and non-banks has increased, the differences between them have become less apparent. The diversity of financial services and investment alternatives non-banks offer has led banks to expand their own services. Some banks acquired *brokerage firms* to offer full-service financial assistance, such as when CIBC acquired Merrill Lynch Canada's retail brokerage firm in 2001. In addition, CIBC also bought Merrill's Canadian mutual fund and securities services businesses, beating out rivals reported to have included TD, Scotiabank, National Bank, and a group of Merrill insiders backed by the Caisse de dépôt et placement du Québec.[26]

Pension funds are amounts of money put aside by corporations, non-profit organizations, or unions to help fund their members' financial needs when they retire. Contributions to pension funds are made by employees, employers, or both. To generate additional income, pension funds typically invest in low-return, but safe, corporate stocks or other conservative investments, such as government securities and corporate bonds.

> **pension funds**
> Amounts of money put aside by corporations, non-profit organizations, or unions to cover part of the financial needs of their members when they retire.

Recall from Appendix C that *life insurance companies* provide financial protection for policyholders, who periodically pay premiums. In addition, insurers invest the funds they receive from policyholders in corporate and government bonds. More insurance companies have begun to provide long-term financing for real estate development projects. Do you think that was a wise decision?

Commercial and consumer finance companies offer short-term loans to businesses or individuals who cannot meet the credit requirements of regular banks, such as new businesses, or those who have exceeded their credit limit and need more funds. Be careful when borrowing from such institutions as their interest rates can be high. Corporate financial systems established at major corporations, such as Sears, General Motors, and American Express, offer considerable financial services to customers. The Spotlight on Small Business offers an example of a newer type of non-bank that offers a way for small business owners to raise the funds they need.

Using Technology to Improve Efficiency

Imagine the cost to a financial institution of approving a written cheque, physically processing it, and mailing it back to you. Such transactions are processed by the third component of the financial system, the clearing and settlement systems. They can be expensive, so it should not be a surprise that financial institutions continue to consider ways to make the system more efficient.

In an **electronic funds transfer (EFT) system**, messages about a transaction are sent from one computer to another. Thus, organizations can transfer funds more quickly and economically than with paper cheques. EFT tools include electronic cheque conversion, debit cards, smart cards, direct deposits, and direct payments.

Spotlight *On* SMALL BUSINESS

Taking a Bite Out of the Sharks

Ivan Rincon was convinced his online swimwear shop could float if he could just get needed capital. Unfortunately, banks rejected him because he didn't have collateral. This caused him to do what many small businesses have to do; he turned to a non-bank lender called a merchant cash advance provider. He obtained a cash advance of $200,000, but soon realized he was paying an annual interest rate of more than 50 percent. Fortunately, he was able to pay back the loan before things got desperate. He then heard about Dealstruck <http://www.dealstruck.com>.

Dealstruck is an example of a new type of alternative, non-bank lender. The company provides a middle ground between banks that only lend to very creditworthy small businesses, and merchant cash advance lenders that have lower criteria for lending, but much higher interest rates. Dealstruck, like competitors Funding Circle <https://www.fundingcircle.com> and Fundation <http://www.fundation.com>, uses a peer-to-peer model where wealthy investors provide the capital for the loans. The loans are secured by the owner's personal guarantees or business assets. Dealstruck's interest rates range from 8 to 24 percent for loans up to $250,000, and can stretch over a period of three years. Ethan Senturia, CEO of Dealstruck, promises, "Our loans are not always cheap, but we tell you what we are charging and why."

The peer-to-peer lending model has played an active role in individual lending for a while, with Lending Club <https://www.lendingclub.com> a pioneer in this area. As Dealstruck and its competitors grow and heat up the market for peer-to-peer small business lending, Lending Club has decided to become one of the newest competitors in small business lending and offer peer-to-peer loans to small businesses too.

Sources: Patrick Clark, "A U.K. Peer-to-Peer Lender Wants U.S. Businesses to Forget Banks," *Bloomberg Businessweek,* 24 October 2013; and Amy Cortese, "Can't Get a Bank Loan? The Alternatives Are Expanding," *The New York Times,* 5 March 2014.

---

electronic funds transfer (EFT) system
A computerized system that electronically performs financial transactions such as making purchases, paying bills, and receiving paycheques.

A **debit card** serves the same function as a cheque—it withdraws funds from a chequing account. When the sale is recorded, the debit card sends an electronic signal to the bank, automatically transferring funds from your account to the seller's. A record immediately appears online. Debit transactions surpassed cheques years ago and continue to grow.

---

debit card
An electronic funds transfer tool that serves the same function as cheques: it withdraws funds from a chequing account.

Payroll debit cards are an efficient way for some firms to pay their workers, and are an alternative to cash for those who don't qualify for a credit or debit card—the so-called unbanked.[27] Employees can access funds in their accounts immediately after they are posted to withdraw, pay bills online, or transfer funds to another cardholder. The system is much cheaper for companies than issuing cheques, and it is more convenient for employees. On the other hand, debit cards don't offer the same protection as credit cards. If someone steals your credit card, you may be liable for a certain amount. This is not necessarily the case for your debit card if someone steals it.[28]

A **smart card** is an electronic funds transfer tool that combines a credit card, debit card, phone card, driver's licence card, and more. Smart cards replace the typical magnetic strip on a credit or debit card with a microprocessor. The card can then store a variety of information, including the holder's bank balance. Merchants can use this information to verify the card's validity and spending limits, and they can then engage in transactions up to the amount on the card.

> **smart card**
> An electronic funds transfer tool that is a combination credit card, debit card, phone card, driver's licence card, and more.

Some smart cards have embedded radio frequency identification (RFID) chips that make it possible to enter buildings and secure areas and to buy gas and other items with a swipe of the card. Students use smart cards to open locked doors to dorms and identify themselves to retailers near campus and online. The cards also serve as ATM cards.

For many, the ultimate convenience in banking is automatic transactions, such as direct deposit and direct payments. A *direct deposit* is a credit made directly to a chequing or savings account in place of a paycheque. The employer contacts the bank and orders it to transfer funds from the employer's account to the worker's account. Individuals can use direct deposits to transfer funds between accounts.

A *direct payment* is a preauthorized electronic payment. Customers authorize a company, whose bill they would like to automatically pay, to take money from their chequing or savings account on a specified date. The customer's bank completes each transaction and records it on the customer's monthly statement.

Smartphone apps, such as PayPal's, allow users to pay for purchases with their phones. What problems could there be with such capabilities?

Financial institutions allow customers to access their accounts online, and most have bill-paying capacity. You can complete your financial transactions from home by using your telephone, computer, or mobile device to transfer funds from one account to another, pay your bills, and review the balance in each of your accounts. You can apply for a car loan or mortgage and get a response while you wait. Buying and selling stocks and bonds is also easy.

Key trends released from CBA support that Canadians are embracing new technologies in their daily lives, and value innovative ways to make their banking more accessible and convenient. Examples include the increasing use of online and mobile banking, with payments quickly evolving as mobile wallets and "tap and go" contactless payments become more widely available.[29] Do you agree with the 23 percent of Canadians who don't think they will be carrying cash in 10 years and the 54 percent who don't anticipate using cheques?[30]

Financial institutions face new threats from digital players like Apple, which has introduced a mobile payment system, and Snapchat *<https://www.snapchat.com>*, which has developed a way to send money to friends called Snapcash.[31] Not to be left behind, the Bank of Nova Scotia has developed an app for the Samsung smartwatch, while the Royal Bank paired up with technology developer, Nymi (pronounced Nim-ee), to test a wristband that identifies owners through their unique heartbeats and then lets them charge purchases to their credit cards.[32] Since then, Nymi launched the world's first biometrically authenticated payment using one's heartbeat.[33]

Internet banks, such as Tangerine *<http://www.tangerine.ca>*, have been created to offer branchless banking. They can offer customers slightly higher interest rates and lower fees because they do not have the overhead costs being incurred by traditional financial institutions such as commercial banks. Even branchless banks can't risk being caught off guard by technological change; Tangerine has announced plans to add fingerprint recognition and voice control to its banking apps.[34] While many consumers are pleased with the savings and convenience, not all are happy with such technological advancements. Why? Some are nervous about security. People fear putting their financial information into cyberspace, where others may see it despite all the assurances of privacy.

After the Progress Assessment, let's learn about financial markets, another area of Canada's financial system.

Progress Assessment

- What components of the financial services industry were known as the four pillars?
- Describe some changes to the industry as a result of Bill C-8.
- Contrast credit unions and *caisses populaires,* and list some non-bank competitors.
- How does a debit card differ from a smart card?

LO5   Describe the role of the financial markets.

The Canadian Financial System: Financial Markets[35]

Financial markets consist of markets for money, bonds, equities, derivatives, and foreign exchange. It is mainly through the financial markets that the Bank of Canada's key policy rate influences interest rates and the exchange rate. This, in turn, helps the Bank achieve its monetary policy objectives.

The Bank is also involved in financial markets through auctions of government securities. On rare occasions, the Bank may also intervene in the foreign exchange market on behalf of the government to promote orderly markets for the Canadian dollar.

A **security** is a negotiable financial instrument that represents some type of financial value. It represents an ownership position in a publicly-traded corporation (stock), a creditor relationship with a government body or a corporation (bond), or rights to ownership as represented by an option. A **securities dealer** (also known as an investment dealer or brokerage house) is a firm that trades securities for its clients and offers investment services. Financial markets are involved with the following services: providing financial advice to investors and executing trades on their behalf, raising all forms of capital for new and expanding businesses, underwriting and acting as the primary distributor for government debt, and creating markets by trading on their own accounts.

> **security**
> A negotiable financial instrument that represents some type of financial value.
>
> **securities dealer**
> A firm that trades securities for its clients and offers investment services; also known as an investment dealer or brokerage house.

Let's consider the important role of stock exchanges next.

The Function of Stock Exchanges

A **stock exchange** is an organization whose members can buy and sell (exchange) securities for companies and investors. The Toronto Stock Exchange (TSX, <*http://www.tmx.com*>) and the Montréal Exchange (MX, <*http://www.m-x.ca*>) are just two examples of securities markets in Canada. Financial markets include securities markets. *Securities markets*—financial marketplaces for stocks, bonds, and other investments—serve two major functions. First, they assist businesses in finding long-term funding to finance capital needs, such as expanding operations, developing new products, or buying major goods and services. (Recall this discussion in Chapter 17.) Second, they provide private investors a place to buy and sell securities, such as stocks and bonds, that can help them build their financial future.

> **stock exchange**
> An organization whose members can buy and sell (exchange) securities for companies and investors.

Securities markets are divided into primary and secondary markets. *Primary markets* handle the sale of new securities. This is an important point to understand. Corporations make money on the sale of their securities (stock) only once—when they sell it on the primary market. As introduced in Chapter 17, the first public offering of a corporation's stock is called an initial public offering (IPO). After the IPO, the *secondary market* handles the trading of these securities between investors, with the proceeds of the sale going to the investor selling the stock, not to the corporation whose stock is sold.

For example, imagine your vegetarian restaurant, Very Vegetarian, has grown into a chain and your products are available in many retail stores throughout the country. You want to raise additional funds to expand further. If you offer 1 million shares of stock in your company at $10 a share, you can raise $10 million at this initial offering. However, after the initial sale, if Shareholder Jones decides to sell 100 shares of her Very Vegetarian stock to Investor Liu, Very Vegetarian collects nothing from that transaction. Liu buys the stock from Jones, not from Very Vegetarian. It is possible, however, for companies like Very Vegetarian to offer (new) additional shares of stock for sale to raise additional capital.

Two main groups of products—equities (stock) and debt (fixed-income securities such as bonds, and money market instruments such as treasury bills, commercial paper, and bankers' acceptances)—are heavily traded. Equities are traded on stock exchanges while fixed-income products are traded over the dealing desks of investment dealer firms. Mutual funds are also offered by these firms. Firms themselves trade more sophisticated instruments, such as options, futures, or other risk-management products. These examples will be discussed in an advanced financial management course.

There has been an increase in invested funds as more Canadians are turning to the financial markets to ensure their financial security. Companies and government agencies are also investing more and more in securities. In all cases, investors want to increase their returns, but this also comes with increased risks.

The TSX and the TSX Venture Exchange are not the only fish in the stock exchange sea. Exchanges like the NYSE Euronext (pictured here) are located throughout the world, even in former communist-bloc countries like Poland and Hungary. Today, stocks are bought and sold primarily through electronic networks.

Securities Regulations

As mentioned earlier in the textbook, one of the reasons why private corporations become public corporations is to raise capital to expand their existing operations. Companies seeking public financing must issue a prospectus. A **prospectus** is a condensed version of economic and financial information that a company must make available to investors before they purchase the security. The prospectus must be approved by the securities commission in the province where the public funding is being sought.

> **prospectus**
> A condensed version of economic and financial information that a company must make available to investors before they purchase a security.

A **securities commission** is a government agency that administers provincial securities legislation.[36] The mandate for the Alberta Securities Commission <*http://www.albertasecurities.com*>, for example, is to "foster a fair and efficient capital market in Alberta and to protect investors."[37] Canada's ten provinces and three territories are responsible for the securities regulations within their respective borders. The Canadian Securities Administrators (CSA, <*http://www.securities-administrators.ca*>) is an umbrella organization of Canada's provincial and territorial securities regulators whose objective is to improve, coordinate, and harmonize regulation of the Canadian capital markets. It aims to achieve consensus on policy decisions that affect capital markets and their participants. It also aims to work collaboratively in the delivery of regulatory programs across Canada, such as the review of continuous disclosure and prospectus filings.[38]

> **securities commission**
> A government agency that administers provincial securities legislation.

For years, the federal government has been working toward the creation of a national securities regulator. Citing that Canada is the only industrialized country without a national regulator, the government believes that "by pooling provincial, territorial and federal jurisdiction and expertise, Canada could have a world-leading securities regulatory regime that contributes to a stronger national economy and allows Canada to better compete in global capital markets. Canadian businesses would be able to raise funds throughout Canada more quickly and at lower cost, which would stimulate investment. Businesses would also benefit from more expedited regulatory decisions."[39] Not all of the provinces and territories agree, however. Recent federal efforts have focused on the establishment of a co-operative capital markets regulatory system and all provinces and territories were invited to participate.[40] Six governments—Yukon, British Columbia, Saskatchewan, Ontario, New Brunswick, and Prince Edward Island—have agreed to join the federal government in the Cooperative System, with the offer remaining open to the other governments. Have more provinces and territories joined since this textbook was published?

Progress Assessment

- Describe the financial markets in Canada.
- What are two main functions of securities markets?
- What is the primary purpose of a stock exchange? Can you name a stock exchange in Canada?
- Describe the role of securities commissions.

How Investors Buy Securities

Investing in bonds, stocks, or other securities is not difficult. First, you decide what bond or stock you want to buy. After that, you find a registered brokerage firm authorized to trade securities to execute your order. A **stockbroker** is a registered representative who works as a market intermediary to buy and sell securities for clients. Stockbrokers place an order and negotiate a price. After the transaction is completed, the trade is reported to your broker, who notifies you. Today, large brokerage firms maintain automated order systems that allow brokers to enter your order the instant you make it. The order can be confirmed in seconds.

> **stockbroker**
> A registered representative who works as a market intermediary to buy and sell securities for clients.

A broker can also be a source of information about what stocks or bonds would best meet your financial objectives, but it is still important to learn about stocks and bonds on your own.[41] Investment analysts' advice may not always meet your specific expectations and needs.[42]

Investing Through Online Brokers

Investors can also choose from multiple online trading services to buy and sell stocks and bonds. BMO InvestorLine *<http://www.bmo.com/self-directed>*, TD Waterhouse *<http://www.tdwaterhouse.ca>*, and iTrade Canada *<http://www.scotiabank.com/itrade>* are among the leaders. Investors who trade online are willing to do their own research and make investment decisions without the direct assistance of a broker. This allows online brokers to charge much lower trading fees than traditional stockbrokers. The leading online services do provide important market information, such as company financial data, price histories of a stock, and analysts' reports. Often the level of information services you can get depends on the size of your account and your level of trading.

Whether you decide to use an online broker or to invest through a traditional stockbroker, remember that investing means committing your money with the hope of making a profit. The dot-com bubble in the early 2000s and the financial crisis that began in 2008 proved again that investing is a risky business.[43] Therefore, the first step in any investment program is to determine your level of risk tolerance. Other factors to consider include your desired income, cash requirements, the need to hedge against inflation, and the investment's growth prospects.

You are never too young or too old to invest, but you should first ask questions and consider investment alternatives. Let's take a look at several strategies.

David and Tom Gardner, the Motley Fools *<http://www.fool.ca>*, are passionate about spreading the message that securities markets can provide opportunities for all. The brothers have built their careers on providing high-quality financial information to investors regardless of education or income.

Choosing the Right Investment Strategy and Diversification

Investment objectives change over the course of a person's life. A young person can better afford to invest in high-risk investment options such as stocks than can a person nearing retirement. Younger investors generally look for significant growth in the value of their investments over time. If stocks go into a tailspin and decrease in value, a younger person has time to wait for stocks to rise again. Older people, perhaps on a fixed income, lack the luxury of waiting, and may be more inclined to invest in bonds that offer a steady return as a protection against inflation.

Consider five key criteria when selecting investment options:

1. *Investment risk.* The chance that an investment will be worth less at some future time than it is worth now.

2. *Yield.* The expected rate of return on an investment, such as interest or dividends, usually over a period of one year.

3. *Duration.* The length of time your money is committed to an investment.

4. *Liquidity.* How quickly you can get back your invested funds in cash if you want them.

5. *Tax consequences.* How the investment will affect your tax situation.

Reaching *Beyond* OUR BORDERS

Global Stocks: Love Them or Leave Them

Concerns about the ups and downs of Canadian stocks may keep you from even thinking about investing in global stocks. If you also read the news about conflicts in Eastern Europe and the Middle East and natural disasters in Japan and Indonesia, the thought of investing globally may grow even less attractive. Your inclination may be to forget about global stocks and play it safe with what may seem to be relatively secure Canadian securities. However, financial analysts generally recommend investing in some global stocks in order to diversify your investments.

Let's consider a few market facts that support their recommendation. If you research respected blue-chip stocks, like Scotiabank and Coca Cola, you will find they earn a large portion of their revenue from global markets. Economists also project developing economies in areas such as Asia and Africa will grow at a much faster pace than Canada.

Given the potential return, you would be remiss to not at least explore the opportunities that exist in global markets. However, like any investments, set your long-term financial goals and stay abreast of the daily news. Keep the following suggestions in mind as you consider global investments:

- Invest in familiar global companies with a solid reputation and record of performance. Companies like Honda (Japan), Nestlé (Switzerland), Samsung (South Korea), and Siemens *<http://www.siemens.com>* (Germany) come to mind.
- Invest in only global stocks listed on Canadian or U.S. exchanges. These companies must comply with Canadian and U.S. accounting standards, and rules of the securities exchanges such as the TSX and the U.S. Securities Exchange Commission (SEC).

- Investing in mutual and exchange-traded funds (ETFs) offers a wide range of global opportunities. Many funds and ETFs have a mix of Canadian and foreign stocks. Others may focus strictly on specific countries, such as China, on entire regions, such as Africa, Asia, Europe, or Latin America, or on the entire world. Mutual funds and ETFs will be discussed shortly.
- Investing in stocks from countries with a history of currency problems or political instability might be investments you want to avoid.

Sources: Selena Maranjian, "Foreign Stocks with Dividends," The Motley Fool, 2 January 2014; Robert Schmansky, "How Much Should You Invest in International Stock Mutual Funds?" *Forbes,* 8 August 2013; and John Waggoner, "Investing: Simplify Life, Go Global, with Funds," *USA Today,* 14 March 2013.

What is important in any investment strategy is the risk/return trade-off. Setting investment objectives such as *growth* (choosing stocks you believe will increase in price) or *income* (choosing stocks that pay consistent dividends) should set the tone for your investment strategy.

Diversification involves buying several different types of investments to spread the risk of investing. An investor may put 25 percent of his or her money into Canadian stocks that have relatively high risk but strong growth potential, another 25 percent in conservative government bonds, 25 percent in dividend-paying stocks that provide income, 10 percent in an international mutual fund (mutual funds will be discussed later), and the rest in the bank for emergencies and other possible investment opportunities. By diversifying with such a *portfolio strategy* or *allocation model,* investors decrease the chance of losing everything they have invested.[44]

diversification
Buying several different investment alternatives to spread the risk of investing.

Both stockbrokers and certified financial planners (CFPs) are trained to give advice about the investment portfolio that would best fit each client's financial objectives. However, the more investors themselves read and study the market, the higher their potential for gain. A short course in investments can also be useful. Stocks and bonds are investment opportunities individuals can use to enhance their financial future. The Reaching Beyond Our Borders box discusses growing opportunities investors can find in global stocks. After the Progress Assessment, we will look at stocks and bonds in depth.

Progress Assessment

- What is a key advantage and disadvantage of investing through a stock broker?
- What is a key advantage and disadvantage of investing through an online broker?
- List the five key criteria when selecting investment options.
- What is the benefit of diversifying investments?

Investing in Stocks

Buying stocks makes investors part owners of a company who participate in its success. Shareholders can also lose money if a company does not do well or if the overall stock price declines.

Stock investors are often called bulls or bears according to their perceptions of the market. *Bulls* believe that stock prices are going to rise; they buy stock in anticipation of the increase. A bull market is when overall stock prices are rising. *Bears* expect stock prices to decline and sell their stocks in anticipation of falling prices. That's why when stock prices are declining, the market is called a bear market.

Investing in the stock market has never been for the faint of heart. The market seems to have continuous steep climbs and sharp falls. Do you have the risk tolerance to survive the market swings?

The market price and growth potential of most stocks depends heavily on how well the corporation is meeting its business objectives. A company that achieves its objectives offers great potential for **capital gains**, the positive difference between the price at which you bought a stock and what you sell it for. For example, an investment of $2,250 in 100 shares of McDonald's when it first went public in 1965 would have grown to 74,360 shares (after the company's 12 stock splits) worth approximately $7.0 million as of December 31, 2014.[45] That's a lot of Big Macs!

capital gains
The positive difference between the purchase price of a stock and its sale price.

Investors often select stocks depending on their investment strategy. Stocks issued by higher-quality companies, such as BCE Inc. and the Canadian National Railway Company, are referred to as *blue-chip stocks* (a term derived from poker where the highest-value chip is the blue chip). These stocks generally pay regular dividends and experience consistent stock price appreciation.

Stocks in corporations in emerging fields, such as technology, biotechnology, or Internet-related firms, whose earnings are expected to grow at a faster rate than other stocks, are referred to as *growth stocks*. While riskier, growth stocks may offer the potential for high returns. Stocks of public utilities are considered *income stocks* because they usually offer investors a higher dividend yield that generally keeps pace with inflation. There are even *penny stocks*, representing ownership in companies that compete in high-risk industries like oil exploration. Penny stocks sell for less that $2 (some analysts say less than $5) and are considered risky investments.[46]

When purchasing stock, investors have choices when placing buy orders. A *market order* tells a broker to buy or to sell a stock immediately at the best price available. A *limit order* tells the broker to buy or sell a stock at a specific price, if that price becomes available. Let's say a stock is selling for $40 a share. You believe the price will eventually go higher but could drop to $36 first. You can place a limit order at $36 so your broker will buy the stock at $36 if it drops to that price. If the stock never falls to $36, the broker will not purchase it for you.

Stock Splits

Brokers prefer to make stock purchases in *round lots* of 100 shares at a time. Investors, however, usually cannot afford to buy 100 shares, and therefore often buy in *odd lots,* or fewer than 100 shares at a time. High per-share prices often induce companies to declare **stock splits**, in which they issue two or more shares for every one that is outstanding. If Very Vegetarian stock were selling for $100 a share, the firm could declare a two-for-one stock split. Investors who owned one share of Very Vegetarian would now own two shares, each worth only $50 (half as much as before the split).

> **stock splits**
> An action by a company that gives shareholders two or more shares of stock for each one they own.

Stock splits cause no change in the firm's ownership structure and no immediate change in the investment's value. Investors generally approve of stock splits, however, because they believe demand for a stock may be greater at $50 than at $100, and the price may then go up in the near future. A company cannot be forced to split its stock, and today stock splits are becoming less common.[47] Legendary investor Warren Buffett's firm, Berkshire Hathaway, has never split its Class A stock even when its per-share price surpassed $150,000. Google, however, decided to split its stock two-for-one after the stock price exceeded $1,000 per share, and credit card giant MasterCard split its stock ten-for-one as its stock price neared $900 per share.[48]

Stock Indexes

Stock indexes measure the trend of different stock exchanges. Every country with a stock exchange has such indexes. In Canada, there are several thousand companies listed, and the prices of their shares fluctuate constantly. Some may be rising over a certain period and others may be falling. Various indexes have been developed to give interested parties useful information about significant trends, and more indexes are being developed. Another use of an index is as an investment vehicle. Investors who do not have the time or expertise to actively manage their investments are choosing to be passive investors by investing in index funds.

The largest Canadian index is the S&P/TSX Composite Index. Reviewed quarterly, the index (which contains stocks of the largest companies on the TSX) is calculated by Standard and Poor's, and it includes both common stock and income trust units.[49]

Staying abreast of what is happening in the market will help you decide what investments seem most appropriate to your needs and objectives. Remember two key investment realities: your personal financial objectives will change over time, and markets can be volatile.

Buying Stock on Margin

Buying stock on margin means borrowing some of the stock's purchase cost from the brokerage firm. The margin is the portion of the stock's purchase price that the investor must pay with his or her own money. Provincial regulatory agencies, such as the Ontario Securities Commission, set *margin* rates. If the margin rate is 50 percent, an investor who qualifies for a margin account may borrow up to 50 percent of the stock's price from the broker.

> **buying stock on margin**
> Purchasing securities by borrowing some of the cost from the broker.

Although buying on margin sounds like an easy way to buy more stocks, the downside is that investors must repay the credit extended by the broker, plus interest. If the investor's account goes down in value, the broker may issue a *margin call*, requiring the investor to come up with funds to cover the losses the account has suffered.[50] If the investor in unable to fulfill the margin call, the broker can legally sell off shares of the investor's stock to reduce the broker's chance of loss. Margin calls can force an investor to repay a significant portion of his or her account's loss within days or even hours. Buying on margin is thus a risky way to invest in stocks.

Understanding Stock Quotations

Publications like the *Globe and Mail*, the *Financial Post*, and possibly your local newspaper carry information concerning stocks and other investments. Financial websites like Yahoo! Finance Canada *<https://ca.finance.yahoo.com>* carry up-to-the-minute information about companies that is much more detailed and only a click away. Look at Figure 18.5 to see an example of a stock quote from MSN Money for Microsoft Corporation, which trades under the symbol MSFT.

■ **FIGURE 18.5**

UNDERSTANDING STOCK QUOTATIONS

Microsoft Corporation (MSFT) - NasdaqGS ⭐ Follow

45.22 ↑0.27 (0.60%) 4:00PM EDT

After Hours : **45.20** ↓0.02 (0.04%) 5:59PM EDT

Prev Close:	44.95	Day's Range:	44.83 - 45.25
Open:	44.88	52wk Range:	30.95 - 45.71
Bid:	45.18 x 600	Volume:	22,272,025
Ask:	45.20 x 100	Avg Vol (3m):	28,677,000
1y Target Est:	47.00	Market Cap:	372.61B
Beta:	0.68	P/E (ttm):	16.94
Earnings Date:	Oct 22 - Oct 27 (Est.)	EPS (ttm):	2.67
		Div & Yield:	1.12 (2.70%)

Information provided in the quote includes the highest and lowest price the stock traded for that day, the stock's high and low over the past 52 weeks, the dividend paid (if any), the stock's dividend yield (annual dividend as a percentage of the price per share), and important ratios like the price/earnings (P/E) ratio which is the price of the stock divided by the firm's per share earnings. Investors can also see the total market capitalization of the firm. More technical features, such as the stock's beta (which measures degree of risk), may also appear. Figure 18.5 illustrates the stock's intraday trading (trading throughout the current day), but you can also click to see charts for different time periods. Similar information about bonds, mutual funds, and other investments is available online.

Progress Assessment

- What is a bull market? What is a bear market?
- Compare blue-chip stocks to penny stocks.
- What is a stock split? Why do companies sometimes split their stock?
- What is meant by buying stock on margin?

Investing in Bonds

Investors looking for guaranteed income and limited risk often turn to government bonds for a secure investment as these bonds have the financial backing of the government. In recent history no government in Canada has defaulted on a bond issue. Corporate bonds are a bit more risky and challenging. Taxes are another consideration when evaluating bonds and stocks. Bond interest is fully taxable in the hands of the bond holder, while dividend income qualifies for tax credits.

First-time corporate bond investors often ask two questions. The first is, "If I purchase a corporate bond, do I have to hold it until the maturity date?" No, you do not. Bonds are bought and sold daily on major securities exchanges (the secondary market we discussed earlier). However, if you decide to sell your bond to another investor before its maturity date, you may not get its face value. If your bond does not have features that make it attractive to other investors, like a high interest rate or early maturity, you may have to sell at a *discount,* which is a price less than the bond's face value. But if other investors value it, you may be able to sell your bond at a *premium,* which is a price above its face value. Bond prices generally fluctuate inversely with current market interest rates. This means *as interest rates go up, bond prices fall, and vice versa.* Like all investments, bonds have a degree of risk.

The second question is, "How can I assess the investment risk of a particular bond issue?" Standard & Poor's and Moody's Investors Service rate the risk of many corporate and government bonds. In evaluating the ratings, recall the risk/return trade-off: The higher the risk of a bond, the higher the interest rate the issuer must offer. Investors will consider a bond that is considered risky only if the potential return (interest) is high enough. Remember that investors have many investment options besides stocks and bonds. Let's consider mutual funds next.

Investing in Mutual Funds

A **mutual fund** buys stocks, bonds, and other investments, and then sells shares in those pooled securities to the public. A mutual fund is like an investment company that pools investors' money and then buys stocks or bonds, for example, in many companies in accordance with the fund's specific purpose. Mutual fund managers pick what they consider to be the best securities available and help investors diversify their investments. Mutual fund companies (e.g., Investors Group *<http://www.investorsgroup.com>*, Mackenzie Financial *<http://www.mackenziefinancial.com>*, and TDAM) are regulated by provincial securities commissions. According to the Investment Funds Institute of Canada *<http://www.ific.ca>*, total assets under administration are $1.24 trillion.[51]

---

mutual fund
A organization that buys stocks and bonds and other investments, then sells shares in those pooled securities to the public.

For a fee, mutual funds provide professional investment management and help investors diversify their investments. Funds range from conservative funds that invest only in government securities or secure corporate bonds, to others that specialize in emerging biotechnology firms, online companies, foreign companies, precious metals, and other higher risk investments. The asset mix may include stocks and bonds while others may focus on *index funds* (stock indexes). Others may be interested in socially responsible investing, as discussed in the Seeking Sustainability box.

With mutual funds it is simple to change your investment focus if your financial objectives change. For example, moving your money from a bond fund to a stock fund is no more difficult than making a phone call, clicking a mouse, or tapping your cell phone. Another advantage of mutual funds is that you can generally buy directly from the fund and avoid broker fees or commissions. However, check for fees and charges of the mutual fund because they can differ significantly. A *load fund,* for example, charges investors a commission to buy or sell its shares; a *no-load fund* charges no commission.[52]

Seeking SUSTAINABILITY

Social Responsible Investing (SRI)

As introduced in Chapter 5, socially responsible investing (SRI) incorporates social and environmental values into the traditional investment process. Socially responsible investments consider factors relating to environmental sustainability, social responsibility, and corporate governance (ESG factors) with traditional financial analysis. This approach enables buyers to choose investments that are consistent with both their financial goals and personal values. Common themes for socially responsible investments include avoiding investment in companies that produce or sell addictive substances (like alcohol, gambling, and tobacco), and seeking out companies engaged in environmental sustainability and alternative energy/clean technology efforts.

Consider that Canadian assets in SRI now represent $1 out of every $5 of assets under management. Socially responsible investments can be made in individual companies or through a socially conscious mutual fund or ETF (e.g., iShares Jantzi Social Index ETF). Resources and investment products that cater to SRI for Canadian investors include:

- Sustainalytics <http://www.sustainalytics.com> is an independent ESG research and analysis firm supporting investors around the world with the development and implementation of responsible investment strategies.
- *Corporate Knights* covers the best and worst ideas in SRI, and it produces special reports on corporate citizens.
- Some mutual fund companies (e.g., Ethical Funds and IA Clarington) offer specific products that might work for you. Some of these products are available for purchase through a discount broker or a financial adviser.

Sources: "Socially Responsible Investing," RBC Global Asset Management, 2015, http://funds.rbcgam.com/investment-solutions /socially-responsible-investments/; "Socially Responsible Investment - SRI," Investopedia, 2015, http://www.investopedia.com/terms/s /sri.asp; "What we do," Sustainalytics, 2015, http://www.sustainalytics.com/what-we-do; and Bruce Sellery, "Guide to socially responsible investing," *MoneySense,* 27 August 2012, http://www.moneysense.ca/columns/guide-to-socially-responsible-investing.

Investing in Exchange-Traded Funds

Exchange-traded funds (ETFs) resemble both stocks and mutual funds. They are collections of stocks, bonds, and other investments that are traded on securities exchanges, but are traded more like individual stocks than like mutual funds. Mutual funds, for example, permit investors to buy and sell shares only at the close of the trading day. ETFs can be purchased or sold at any time during the trading day just like individual stocks.

exchange-traded funds (ETFs)
Collections of stocks that are traded on exchanges but are traded more like individual stocks than like mutual funds.

The key points to remember about mutual funds and ETFs is that they offer small investors a way to spread the risk of stock and bond ownership while having their investments managed by a financial specialist for a fee. Financial advisers put mutual funds and ETFs high on the list of recommended investments, particularly for small or first-time investors.[53] Consider Figure 18.6 as it evaluates bonds, stocks, mutual funds, and ETFs according to risk, income, and possible investment growth (capital gain).

■ **FIGURE 18.6**

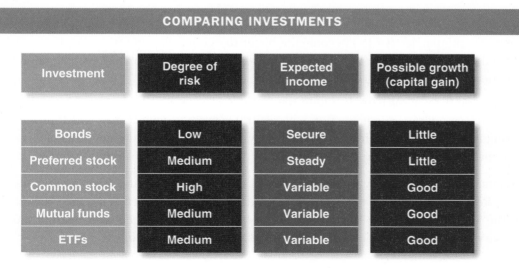

COMPARING INVESTMENTS			
Investment	Degree of risk	Expected income	Possible growth (capital gain)
Bonds	Low	Secure	Little
Preferred stock	Medium	Steady	Little
Common stock	High	Variable	Good
Mutual funds	Medium	Variable	Good
ETFs	Medium	Variable	Good

After the Progress Assessment, consider the third component of Canada's financial system, the clearing and settlement systems.

Progress Assessment

- Explain what is meant that bond prices generally fluctuate inversely with current market interest rates.

- What are advantages and disadvantages of mutual funds?

- What are ETFs? How do they differ from mutual funds?

LO6 Outline the role of the clearing and settlement systems.

The Canadian Financial System: Clearing and Settlement Systems[54]

A **financial market infrastructure (FMI)** is a system that facilitates the clearing, settling, or recording of payments, securities, derivatives, or other financial transactions among participating entities. It is also called a "clearing and settlement system." FMIs play an important role in enhancing financial stability by enabling consumers and firms to safely and efficiently purchase goods and services, make financial investments, and transfer funds.

> **financial market infrastructure (FMI)**
> A system that facilitates the clearing, settling, or recording of payments, securities, derivatives, or other financial transactions among participating entities; also called a clearing and settlement system.

Under the Payment Clearing and Settlement Act, the Bank of Canada is responsible for the oversight of FMIs that have the potential to pose systemic or payments system risk. It is therefore essential that FMIs incorporate appropriate risk-control mechanisms so that systemic risk is adequately controlled. There are three types of FMIs:

1. Payment systems facilitate the transfer of funds.

2. Central counterparties (CCPs) become the buyer to every seller and the seller to every buyer of a financial contract to ensure that, even if a buyer or a seller fails to meet its obligation to the CCP, obligations will be met on all contracts.

3. Securities settlement systems facilitate the transfer of securities and other financial assets. These systems often operate in conjunction with central securities depositories which provide securities accounts, central safekeeping, and asset services. Securities settlement systems may provide additional securities clearing and settlement services, such as CCP clearing services.

In summary, economic growth and the creation of jobs depend on the ready availability of money. Given this importance, the Bank of Canada plays a pivotal role in overseeing the Canadian financial system. The three components—financial institutions, the financial markets, and clearing and settlement systems—are connected and they work together to support the welfare of Canadians.

Progress Assessment

- What is the third component to the Canadian financial system?
- What is the Bank of Canada's responsibility under the Payment Clearing and Settlement Act?
- List three types of FMIs.

SUMMARY

LO1 **Explain what money is and what makes it useful.**

Money is anything that people generally accept as payment for goods and services.

What are the five standards for a useful form of money?

The five standards are portability, divisibility, stability, durability, and uniqueness.

What are "Bitcoins" and can you buy things online with them?

Bitcoins are a form of online money. Bitcoin has an online store that accepts the currency.

LO2 **Describe how the Bank of Canada controls the money supply.**

The money supply is the amount of money the Bank of Canada makes available to buy goods and services.

Why does the money supply need to be controlled?

The value of money depends on the money supply; that is, how much money is available to buy goods and services. Too much money in circulation causes inflation. Too little money causes deflation, recession, and unemployment. Controlling the money supply allows us to manage, somewhat, the prices of goods and services. The size of the money supply also affects employment and economic growth or decline.

How is the money supply controlled?

The Bank of Canada is in charge of monetary policy, and the country's money supply influences monetary policy. The Bank of Canada carries out monetary policy by influencing short-term interest rates. It does this by raising and lowering the target for the overnight rate.

LO3 **List the three components of the Canadian financial system, and explain how it is regulated.**

The financial system makes a vital contribution to the welfare of Canadians.

What are the three components of the Canadian financial system?

The financial system includes financial institutions, the financial markets, and clearing and settlement systems. It is through the financial system that most commercial activity is carried out.

How is the financial system regulated?

Due to its important role in the economy, the financial system is heavily regulated by different organizations and levels of government. Organizations include the Bank of Canada, OSFI, and CDIC. Ultimately, it is the Minister of Finance who is responsible for the financial system. Review Figure 18.3 for some examples of regulatory responsibility.

LO4 **Discuss the role that financial institutions play in providing financial services.**

Financial institutions include commercial banks, credit unions, trust and loan companies, insurance companies, and non-banks.

How are commercial banks important players in the financial system?

Commercial banks serve millions of customers that include individuals, small and medium-sized businesses, large corporations, governments, institutional investors, and non-profit organizations. Based on assets, the five largest Canadian banks represent upwards of 80 percent of the national financial institution market.

How do credit unions differ from commercial banks?

A credit union is a non-profit, member-owned financial co-operative that offers a full variety of banking services to its members. Credit unions often have fewer branches than banks and less access to ATMs.

What are some non-banks?

Non-banks include life insurance companies that lend out their funds, pension funds that invest in stocks and bonds and make loans, brokerage firms that offer investment services, and commercial finance companies that offer short-term loans to those who do not meet the credit requirements of banks.

LO5 **Describe the role of the financial markets.**

Financial markets consist of markets for money, bonds, equities, derivatives, and foreign exchange.

What is the link between the Bank of Canada and financial markets?

It is mainly through the financial markets that the Bank's key policy rate influences interest rates and the exchange rate. This, in turn, helps the Bank achieve its monetary policy objectives. The Bank is also involved in financial markets through auctions of government securities. The Bank may also intervene in the foreign exchange market on behalf of the government to promote orderly markets for the Canadian dollar.

Explain the different options discussed in this chapter for investing in securities.

The options include stocks, bonds, mutual funds, and ETFs. Review Figure 18.6 as it evaluates these options according to risk, income, and possible investment growth (capital gain).

LO6 **Outline the role of the clearing and settlement systems.**

A clearing and settlement system, also called a financial market infrastructure (FMI), plays an important role in enhancing financial stability by enabling consumers and firms to safely and efficiently purchase goods and services, make financial investments, and transfer funds.

Who is responsible for FMIs?

The Bank of Canada is responsible for the oversight of FMIs that have the potential to pose systemic or payments system risk.

List three examples of FMIs.

Three examples of FMIs are payment systems, central counterparties, and securities settlement systems.

KEY TERMS

barter

buying stock on margin

capital gains

certificate of deposit

commercial bank

credit union

debit card

demand deposit

diversification

electronic funds transfer (EFT)
   system

exchange-traded funds (ETFs)

financial market infrastructure
   (FMI)

money

money supply

mutual fund

non-banks

overnight rate

pension funds

prime rate

prospectus

securities commission

securities dealer

security

smart card

stock exchange

stock splits

stockbroker

time deposit

trust company

CRITICAL THINKING

1. Imagine that you have just inherited $100,000 and you want to invest it to meet two financial goals: (a) to save for your wedding, which you plan to have in two years, and (b) to save for your retirement, 30 to 35 years from now. How would you invest the money? Explain your answer.

2. The overnight bank rate, set by the Bank of Canada, is currently very low. What circumstance(s) would cause the Governor of the Bank of Canada to raise this rate? What impact would this increase have on individuals and businesses with debt?

3. Do you keep your savings in a bank, a credit union, a *caisse populaire,* or some combination? Have you compared the benefits you could receive from each? Where would you expect to find the best loan rates?

4. If you were thinking of investing in the securities market, would you prefer individual stocks, mutual funds, or ETFs? Explain your choice by comparing the advantages and disadvantages of each.

DEVELOPING WORKPLACE SKILLS

Key: ● **Team** ★ **Analytic** ▲ **Communication** ▣ **Technology**

● ★ 1. In a small group, discuss the following: What services do you use from financial institutions?
▣ ▲   Does anyone use online or mobile banking? What seem to be the pros and cons of online banking? What about mobile banking? Use this opportunity to compare the rates and services of various local banks and credit unions.

★ ▲ 2. Poll the class to see who uses a bank, a credit union, a *caisse populaire,* or a combination of these. Have class members compare the services at each (e.g., interest rates on savings accounts, the services available, and loan rates). If anyone uses an online service, see how those rates compare. If no one uses a credit union, a *caisse populaire,* or an online bank, discuss the reasons.

● ★ 3. In small groups discuss when and where you use cheques, credit cards, debit cards, and cash.
▲   Do you often write cheques for small amounts? Would you stop if you calculated how much it

costs to process each cheque? Have you switched to using your debit card as a result? Discuss your findings with the class.

● ▣ **4.** See whether others in the class are interested in forming an investment group. If so, each
★ ▲   member should choose one stock and one mutual fund or ETF. Record each student's selections and the corresponding prices. In two weeks, measure the percentage of change in the investments and discuss the results.

★ ▲ **5.** Write a one-page paper on the role of the World Bank and the International Monetary Fund in providing loans to countries. Is it important for Canadian citizens to lend money to people in other countries through such organizations? Why or why not? Be prepared to debate the value of these organizations in class.

ANALYZING MANAGEMENT DECISIONS

Financial Crisis—Banking Disaster

2011 was characterized as a year with a sluggish economy and high unemployment, when millions of Americans lost their homes and businesses closed. How did this happen? Back in 2008, there was a global banking crisis that was the worst since the Great Depression of the 1930s. Several major American investment banks went bankrupt, markets plummeted around the world, and there was a global recession. The causes of the crisis included failures in financial regulations in some countries, such as the United States, reckless behaviour by financial firms, excessive borrowing by households and investment banks, and a lack of accountability and ethics at many levels.

Back even further, in 2000, the tech bubble burst. Share prices in high-tech companies fell dramatically and major financial frauds were discovered, including Worldcom, Enron, and Global Crossings. Governments wanted to keep consumers spending to head off an economic slowdown, so they chose to dramatically cut interest rates by over 5 percent, down to near 1 percent. Given this historic low cost of credit, consumers borrowed money, lots of it. By far the most significant borrowing related to home loans, that is, mortgages. By 2007, household debt rose to 127 percent of disposable income in the United States and Canadian household debt was climbing also. Home mortgages resulting from the housing boom became the biggest financial bubble in history. As more and more homes were purchased, housing costs rose rapidly.

While everyone wants a home, the reality is that not everyone can afford the cost of buying one. But with relatively cheap mortgage interest, many were buying homes, from first-time homeowners to long-time homeowners who wanted bigger and fancier houses. And banks were writing up mortgages for people who would not normally qualify. Banks typically look at the income of the borrower and assess the ability of the borrower to make the mortgage payments. But this criterion was overlooked more and more because the banks and everyone else believed that the prices of houses would continue to rise. These mortgages were called subprime mortgages. In 2004, subprime mortgages made up 10 percent of all mortgages. By 2006, this percentage doubled.

These riskier mortgages became an international problem. After mortgages were written, the banks sold them to investment banks. The investment banks in turn bundled these mortgages into securities, selling them in the open market to investors. They were called mortgage-backed securities, or MBSs.

MBSs have been traded since the 1980s as a safe investment, as only low-risk conventional mortgages were bundled. With the rapid increase in mortgages being written, more and more MBSs appeared.

Investors liked the increasing return that was promised given the higher and higher percentage of sub-prime mortgages that made up the newer MBSs. And bank lenders wrote riskier and riskier mortgages because investment banks demanded them and the banks were passing on the risk to investment banks and investors. Given the involvement of banks, investment banks, and investors, it was very difficult to know where the risk was. Investors relied on ratings agencies, specifically Moody's and Standard and Poor's, for advice on safe investments. And these agencies were more than willing to oblige. Between 2000 and 2006 the number of AAA ratings exploded. MBSs were rated as AAA even though they consisted of a higher percentage of subprime mortgages.

The potential return from MBSs convinced the investment banks to request that the limits on the amount of money they could borrow to buy these securities be raised. In 2004, the SEC relaxed limits on leverage and these banks were allowed to take on as much risk as they liked. By 2007, the five largest investment banks increased their leverage significantly; they believed that housing prices would continue to go up and that MBSs were a good source of income.

In 2007, the real estate bubble burst and the growing recession left many homeowners unable to pay their mortgages, especially subprime mortgages. The number of foreclosures jumped 79 percent. As housing prices fell, many homeowners found themselves "underwater," with mortgages higher than the value of their homes. The financial incentive to pay their mortgages was gone, so they defaulted. The value of MBSs plummeted, leaving both investment banks and investors with hundreds of billions of dollars of defaulted mortgages with little chance of recouping the value of the mortgages. All the major investment banks were impacted; some consolidated, while others failed.

Many countries and international companies, including Canadian banks and investors, had invested in the U.S. housing market through MBSs. They were all affected. Foreign markets collapsed, and the crisis went global.

As we look back on this time period, we realize that this financial crisis was the largest the world had ever experienced. Not since the Great Depression of the 1930s have we seen, on a global scale, rising unemployment, many failed businesses, plummeting consumer wealth, declining international trade, and the near-collapse of foreign governments, especially in Europe. At the writing of this book we still do not fully comprehend the long-term impact of this crisis.

Discussion Questions

1. What does "household debt increasing to 127 percent of disposable income" mean and what is the implication for homeowners?

2. How is a subprime mortgage different from a conventional mortgage, and why were banks so willing to approve this type of mortgage?

3. Why did the returns from MBSs continue to rise?

4. Why did the housing bubble burst?

VIDEO CASE 18

Morningstar Research Inc.

We all hear about the importance of investing, but how do you know what the best investments are? Is there an objective source you can use to get investment advice? The answer is, yes. You can get helpful and unbiased information from a company called Morningstar Research Inc. *<http://www2.morningstar.ca>*.

Many people consider stocks and bonds. When you buy stocks, you buy part ownership of a firm. You can choose from large firms, like Thomson Reuters Corp. *<http://thomsonreuters.com>* and Manulife Financial, or smaller firms. Morningstar can help you choose from the thousands of firms available.

One way to spread the risk of investing in stock is to diversify. That is, you can buy stock in a variety of firms in a variety of industries. For example, you can buy stock in firms from other countries, in service firms, manufacturing firms, health-care firms, and so on. One easy way to diversify is to buy mutual funds. Such funds buy a whole range of stocks and then sell you a portion of that fund. ETFs, or exchange-traded funds, are much like mutual funds, but you buy and sell them through stock exchanges much like you would buy individual shares of stock.

In the long run, most investment advisers recommend investing in stock. Yes, the stock market goes up and down, but they say, in the long run, stocks usually go up. Since young people can wait for years to sell their stock, investment advisers like Morningstar would usually recommend stock (or mutual funds) to them.

Would Morningstar also be likely to recommend bonds? Sure. When you buy a bond, you are actually lending a company, the government, or some government agency money. The company (or the government) promises to return the money to you, plus interest. If the interest is high enough, such an investment makes sense. Of course, some companies are riskier than others, so the interest paid on bonds varies. Morningstar will help you choose bonds that are appropriate for you and your situation.

Almost everyone needs some investment advice. This video is meant to reveal the benefits and drawbacks of investing. But stocks and bonds can earn you a nice return on your investment if you know what you are doing. If you don't know what you are doing, you can lose your savings rather quickly. Morningstar is just one source of information, but you should explore as many sources as possible to learn about investing. Examples include your textbook, a national newspaper, magazines such as *MoneySense* and *Personal Finance,* and TV shows featuring financial news (e.g., BNN—Business News Network).

Everyone should have some money set aside in a financial institution for emergencies. It is also a good practice to diversify investments among stocks, bonds, real estate, and other areas, depending on one's income and willingness to assume risk. Real estate, stocks, bonds, gold, oil, and other investments involve risk, and expert advice is often wrong; but in any case, it pays to have the best, unbiased advice you can get. It also helps to have several other sources of advice, including your own knowledge, gathered carefully over time.

Discussion Questions

1. What is the core difference between stocks and bonds?
2. What is the key differentiator for Morningstar as an investment information service provider?
3. What are mutual funds?

RUNNING CASE

Accounting, Financial Management, and Risk Management at Fox 40 International Inc.

For successful Canadian entrepreneur and inventor Ron Foxcroft, it all started in 1982 when he purchased Fluke Transport, a Southern Ontario trucking business. The company slogan—If It's On Time . . . It's A "FLUKE"—was soon recognized throughout North America. Over the years, Foxcroft diversified into new ventures and the Foxcroft Group of Companies now includes Fluke Transportation Group, Fluke Warehousing Inc., Foxcroft Capital Corp., Fox 40 International Inc., and Fox 40 USA Inc.

The formation of Fox 40 International Inc. (Fox 40) is the result of a dream for a pealess whistle. When developing his first whistle, Ron was motivated by his knowledge and experience as an international basketball referee. Frustrated with faulty pea whistles, he spent three years of development with design consultant Chuck Shepherd. They had about 25 prototypes but narrowed them down after two years to 14 prototypes, and then down to two prototype whistles that worked. This resulted in the Fox 40® Classic Whistle. (The whistle was named for Ron and that he was 40 when he applied for the patent.)

Introduced in 1987, this finely tuned precision instrument does not use a pea to generate sound. In fact, there are no moving parts. The patented design moves the air blast through three tuned chambers. This whistle, and all the subsequent whistles that have been introduced, is 100 percent constructed of high-impact ABS plastic so it is impervious to moisture. Wet or dry, Fox 40 Pealess Whistles cannot be overblown and never fail—the harder you blow, the louder the sound! They can be heard for miles and work in all conditions. They are faultless, reliable, and trusted.

Fox 40, a proudly Canadian company, dominates the global whistle industry. Tens of thousands of Fox 40 Whistles are produced monthly for shipment to 140 countries. A mould may be made offshore due to the cost savings (at least $100,000); however, Fox 40 owns all of its moulds. Approximately 90 percent of the company's products are made in Canada with select components coming from overseas markets. Final assembly occurs in Canada. While the first product was the Fox 40® Classic Whistle, the company now has over 900 active stock-keeping units (SKUs). Its product mix includes 19 whistles styles (e.g., Fox 40 electronic whistle); lanyards & attachments (e.g., flex coils); additional brands that include Fox 40 Gear; SmartCoach Coaching Boards; SICK Self Impression Custom Kit, and Heat Alert Mouthguards; marine and outdoor products (e.g., Xplorer LED Light); Pink products; and logo imprinted products.

Let's consider the nature of Fox 40's financial statements and the scope of the business. The company has close to 200 accounts in its general ledger, of which 70 are expense accounts. There are over 3,000 products grouped into 12 product lines. The product lines are then grouped in the income statement into three markets: Domestic, Export USA, and Export International. Expenses are grouped into three departments: sales and marketing, production and distribution, and general management administration. When comparing these statistics to the financial statements of Very Vegetarian you should appreciate the increased complexity of Fox 40's operations. Even with this level of complexity, Fox 40 prepares monthly financial statements by the 12th to the 15th of the following month. For CEO Ron Foxcroft, with all the financial data available, he first looks at the bottom line—the net profit as reflected in the income statement.

Foxcroft is also concerned with profitability by product, which is reflected in a product's gross margin. There is an expected range in gross margins between 40 percent to 60 percent. He is also focused on how well receivables and inventory are managed. The expectation is that the accounts receivable turnover is 8, which translates into average days credit sales in receivables of 45. Meanwhile, inventory turnover will range from 1 to 12 depending on the product. This translates into average inventory by product being sold between 30 days to 1 year.

The company's lenders closely monitor the debt-to-equity ratio and debt-service coverage ratio. The latter ratio compares the cash flow to the principal and interest payments on bank loans. Bank balances are managed daily, and transfers can be made between any of the associated company bank accounts to ensure that sufficient funds are available to cover operating requirements and to properly manage the various operating lines.

Financial planning is managed through a set of monthly budgeted financial statements for their fiscal year, which starts July 1. When comparing actual to budgeted performance, any variance of more than 3 percent on a product line and any negative variance on expense items is investigated. Sales meetings are held every other week and current monthly sales are always discussed.

The majority of Fox 40's approximately 200 credit customers are Canadian businesses. Their terms range from 15 to 90 days. New international customers are required to pay in advance for their purchases until Fox 40 has experience in dealing with a particular customer. After a good relationship has been established, about 25 percent of these customers are given credit. Export Development Corporation (EDC), introduced in Chapter 4, insures these credit sales.

Operating lines are in place and inventory and receivables are pledged as collateral. These lines are set up with the bank, which the company has been with for 20 years. In fact, it has been the same bank manager during this time. Long-term financing is arranged through the same bank for certain capital assets, such as moulds and dies used to manufacture many of the company's products, and leasehold improvements for office and assembly space in the buildings. In addition, there is a relatively small amount of long-term leasing arrangement. In addition, the company's financing needs are met in part through investments by the shareholders.

Risks are twofold in nature. One risk relates to major receivables defaulting, which occurs when a credit customer goes bankrupt. The second risk relates to the economy in general, when a downturn occurs. The former is managed through the rigour employed from the decision to first grant a customer credit, to regularly reviewing each credit customer's account. According to Foxcroft, since this last happened in 2008 and 2009, "our company has to be able to 'turn-on-a-dime'." In terms of the second risk, Fox 40 frequently monitors sales and quickly makes decisions on controlling costs when they see sales contracting.

Source: Ron Foxcroft, CEO of Fox 40 International Inc. and Chairman and CEO of Fluke Transportation, in-person interview, 22 May 2012, Hamilton.

Discussion Questions

1. A ratio mentioned above is the debt-service coverage, which is not covered in Chapter 16. Based on the definition provided, why would a lender be interested in this ratio? Would the lender be looking for the cash flow to be more than, equal to, or less than interest payments?

2. Why are the financial controls for expenses so tight that every negative dollar variance needs to be investigated while on sales there is a leeway of 3 percent?

3. When compared to domestic credit customers, why are international credit customers less creditworthy? Consider that there are a limited number of international credit customers and the fact that EDC insures credit sales to international customers.

4. What does it mean for Fox40 to be able to "turn-on-a-dime" if the economy experiences a downturn? What would be an example of a decision that could be made in such a situation?

Managing Personal Finances

The Need for Personal Financial Planning

The secret to success is to have capital, or money. With capital, you can pay off loans, take nice vacations, raise a family, invest in stocks and bonds, buy the goods and services you want, give generously to others, and retire with enough money to see you through. Money management, however, is not easy. You have to earn the money in the first place. Your chances of becoming wealthy are much greater if you choose to become an entrepreneur. That is one of the reasons why we have put so much emphasis on entrepreneurship throughout the text, including a chapter on the subject. Of course, there are risks in starting a business, but the best time to take risks is when you are young.

After you earn money, you have to learn how to spend it wisely, save some, and insure yourself against the risks of serious accidents, illness, or death. We shall discuss each of these issues in this appendix so that you can begin making financial plans for the rest of your life.

You'll likely need some help. **Financial literacy** is defined as having the knowledge, skills, and confidence to make responsible financial decisions. Canada is developing a national strategy for financial literacy that will set out goals and priorities in working to strengthen the financial literacy of Canadians at different stages of their lives.[1] The Financial Consumer Agency of Canada (FCAC) has launched the Canadian Financial Literacy Database, a collaborative tool that contains comprehensive information on financial literacy resources and events offered by public, private, and non-profit providers of financial education.[2] Take some time to review this tool as it can help you better understand financial matters and improve your money management skills. Since financial literacy is important to your fiscal health, you may even enjoy taking an entire class on it.[3] Check your school to see what is available.

financial literacy
Having the knowledge, skills, and confidence to make responsible financial decisions.

Financial Planning Begins with Making Money

You already know that one of the secrets to finding a good-paying job is having a good education. This is still true, although what you major in does matter.[4] Throughout history, an investment in business education has paid off regardless of the state of the economy or political ups and downs. Education has become even more important since we entered the information age.

Making money is one thing; saving, investing, and spending it wisely is something else. Following the advice in the next section will help you become one of those with enough to live in comfort throughout your life.[5]

Six Steps to Controlling Your Assets

The only way to save enough money to do all of the things you want to do in life is to spend less than you make. Although you may find it difficult to save today, it not only possible but also imperative if you want to accumulate enough to be financially secure. The following are six steps you can take today to get control of your finances.

STEP 1: TAKE AN INVENTORY OF YOUR FINANCIAL ASSETS

To take inventory, you need to develop a balance sheet for yourself, like the one in Chapter 16. Remember, a balance sheet starts with the fundamental accounting equation: Assets = Liabilities + Owners' Equity. List your tangible assets (such as an iPad, TV, DVR player, computer, cell phone, car, jewellery, clothes, and savings account) on one side, and your liabilities (including rent or mortgage, credit card debt, and auto and education debt) on the other.

Assign a dollar value to each of your assets, based on its current value, not what you originally paid for it. If you have debts (liabilities), subtract them from your assets to get your net worth. If you have no debts, your assets equal your net worth. If your liabilities exceed the value of your assets, you are *not* on the path to financial security. You may need more financial discipline in your life.

Let's also create an income statement for you. At the top of the statement is revenue (all the money you take in from your job, investments, and so on). Subtract all your costs and expenses to get net income or profit. Software programs like Quicken *<http://www.quicken.com>* and websites like Dinkytown *<http://www.dinkytown.net/java/ca.html>* offer a variety of tools that can easily help you with these calculations.

Now is an excellent time to think about how much money you will need to accomplish all your goals. The more clearly you can visualize your goals, the easier it is to begin saving for them.

STEP 2: KEEP TRACK OF ALL YOUR EXPENSES

Do you occasionally find yourself running out of cash? If you experience a cash flow problem, the only way to trace where the money is going is to keep track of every cent you spend. Keeping records of your expenses can be tedious, but it's a necessary step if you want to learn discipline. Actually, it could turn out to be enjoyable because it gives you such a feeling of control.

Here's what to do: List everything you spend as you go through the day. That list is your journal. At the end of the week, transfer your journal entries into a record book or computerized accounting program.

The Royal Bank of Canada has developed the Spend-o-meter tool *<http://www.rbcroyalbank.com /savingsspot/spend-o-meter.html>* as a way to highlight how some expenses can add up monthly and yearly. For example, if you buy two magazines a week, it is estimated that you will spend $624 per year. A tip to save money is to subscribe to your favourite magazine since it is less expensive than buying off the shelf each month. Alternatively, share a subscription with a friend to save even more. Going to two movies per month will cost you $360 per year. To cut down on this cost, you can stream directly to your device. To estimate some of your expenses, visit this site. Were you surprised by some of the calculations?

Develop spending categories (accounts) to make your task easier and more informative. You can have a category called "Food" for all of the food you buy from the grocery store and the convenience store during the week. You might want a separate account for meals eaten away from home because you can dramatically cut these costs if you make your meals at home. Other accounts could include rent, insurance, automobile repairs, gasoline, clothing, utilities, toiletries, entertainment, and donations to charity. Most people also like to have a category called "Miscellaneous" for impulse items like candy and lattes. You won't believe how much you fritter away on miscellaneous items unless you keep a *detailed* record for at least a couple of months.

Develop your accounts on the basis of what's most important to you or where you spend the most money. Once you have recorded all of your expenses for a few months, you'll easily see where you are spending too much and what you have to do to save more. For examples of expense categories to track your spending, visit *<http://frugalliving.about.com/library/pdfs/BudgetWorksheet.pdf>*.

STEP 3: PREPARE A BUDGET

Once you know your financial situation and your sources of revenue and expenses, you're prepared to make a personal budget. Remember, budgets are financial plans. A household budget includes rent or mortgage, utilities, food, clothing, furniture, insurance, and taxes.

You will need to choose how much to allow for expenses such as eating out, entertainment, cell phone use, and so on. Keep in mind that what you spend now reduces what you can save later. For example, deciding not to spend $5 a day for coffee or cigarettes adds up to about $35 a week, $140 a month, and $1,700 a year. Keep this up during four years of school and you'll have about $7,000 by graduation. And that's before adding any interest your money will earn. If you invest the savings in a mutual fund earning 6 percent compounded annually, you would double your money every 12 years. The Rule of 72 says that your money doubles every 12 years at 6 percent. You do that calculation by dividing the percentage earned into 72 (72 divided by 6 = 12).

Running a household is similar to running a small business. It takes the same careful record keeping, the same budget processes and forecasting, and the same control procedures. Sometimes it also creates the same need to borrow funds or rely on a credit card and become familiar with interest rates. The time you spend practising budgeting techniques will benefit you throughout your life.

Gail Vaz-Oxlade, financial expert and TV host of *Til Debt Do Us Part* and *Princess*, recommends the money jar system as a way to manage money. That is, you stop spending when there is no more money in the jar. This is especially helpful for those who need to see their money in order to understand how much they have to spend. Visit *<http://www.money-saving-ideas.net/money-jar.html#a0>* to learn more about this system.

STEP 4: PAY OFF YOUR DEBTS

The first thing to do with the money remaining after you pay your monthly bills is to pay off your debts, starting with those carrying the highest interest rates. Credit card debt, for example, may be costing you 18 percent or more a year. A survey of 100 campuses found that over one-fourth of students said they had been charged a fee for a late payment. It is better to pay off debt that costs 18 percent than to put the money in a bank account that earns, say, 2 percent or less.[6] Check credit card statements and other mailings carefully to make certain the charges are accurate.

STEP 5: START A SAVINGS PLAN

It is important to save some money each month in a separate account for large purchases you're likely to make, such as a trip, computer, car, or house. Then, when it comes time to make that purchase, you'll have the needed cash. Save at least enough for a significant down payment so that you can reduce the finance charges you'll pay to borrow the rest.

The best way to save money is to pay yourself first. David Chilton, Canadian author of *The Wealthy Barber*, has sold over 2 million copies in Canada (and close to another million in the United States) of his self-published book reinforcing this advice. His key advice is to invest 10 percent of what you earn for long-term growth by paying yourself first and live within your means.[7] "It's crucial to understand that wealth flows from savings, not from income," says Chilton. So when you get an unexpected windfall or a raise at work, or you take on a part-time job to generate more income, it's important to put away at least 10 to 15 percent of your income. Life happens, and money might not come as easily down the road. A divorce, a bad investment return, or an illness can leave you financially crippled if you haven't planned ahead.[8]

You can arrange with your financial institution to deduct a certain amount every two weeks or once a month. You will be pleasantly surprised when the money starts accumulating and earning interest over time. With some discipline, you can eventually reach your goal of financial security. It is not as difficult as you may think. Figure D.1 illustrates how $5,000 grows over various periods, and at different rates of return. If you start at age 40, you'll have 25 years in by the time you reach 65.

■ **FIGURE D.1**

ANNUAL RATE OF RETURN				
How Money Grows: This chart illustrates how the $5,000 would grow at various rates of return. Recent savings account interest rates were very low (less than 2 percent), but in earlier years, they've been over 5 percent.				
Time	2%	5%	8%	11%
5 years	$5,520	$ 6,381	$ 7,347	$ 8,425
10 years	6,095	8,144	10,795	14,197
15 years	6,729	10,395	15,861	23,923
20 years	7,430	13,266	23,305	40,312
25 years	8,203	16,932	34,242	67,927

STEP 6: BORROW ONLY TO BUY ASSETS THAT INCREASE IN VALUE OR GENERATE INCOME

Don't borrow money for ordinary expenses; you'll only get into more debt that way. If you have budgeted for emergencies, such as car repairs, you should be able to stay financially secure. Financial experts advise saving anywhere from three months (if you are single with no dependents) to six months (if you are married with dependents) of earnings for contingencies (i.e., basic living expenses). Keep this money in highly liquid accounts, such as a bank account or a term deposit.

Only the most unexpected of expenses should cause you to borrow. It is hard to wait until you have enough money to buy what you want, but learning to wait is a critical part of self-discipline. Of course, you can always try to produce more income by working overtime or by taking on other jobs for extra income.

If you follow these six steps, not only will you have money for investment, but you'll have developed most of the financial techniques needed to become financially secure. If you find it hard to live within a budget at first, remember the payoff is well worth the effort.

Building Your Financial Base

The path to financial success is to have capital (money) to invest, yet many students today graduate with debt. As you've read, accumulating capital takes discipline and careful planning. With the money you save, however, you can become an entrepreneur, one of the fastest ways to wealth.

Living frugally is extremely difficult for the average person. Most people are eager to spend their money on a new car, furniture, electronics, clothes, entertainment, and the like. They look for a fancy apartment with all the amenities. A capital-generating strategy may require foregoing most (though not all) of these purchases to accumulate investment money. It might mean living like a frugal student in a relatively inexpensive apartment furnished in hand-me-downs from parents, friends, resale shops, etc .

For five or six years, you can manage with the old sound system, a used car, and a few nice clothes. The strategy is sacrifice, not luxury. It is important not to feel burdened by this plan; instead, feel happy knowing your financial future will be more secure. That is the way the majority of millionaires got their money. If living frugally seems too restrictive for you, you can still save at least a little. It is better to save a smaller amount than none at all.

It is wise to plan your financial future with the same excitement and dedication you bring to other aspects of your life. If you get married, for example, it is important to discuss financial issues with your spouse. Conflicts over money are a major cause of divorce, so agreeing on a financial strategy before marriage is very important.

A great strategy for couples is to try to live on one income and to save the other. The longer you wait before marriage, the more likely it will be that one or the other of you can be earning enough to do that, as a college or university graduate. If the second spouse makes $35,000 a year after taxes, saving that income for five years quickly adds up to $175,000 (plus interest).

Tax-Free Savings Account (TFSA)[9]

What do you do with the money you accumulate? Where do you invest this money? In Chapter 18, some options discussed included depositing money into a savings account or a term deposit (also known as a certificate of deposit). Also consider a **Tax-Free Savings Account (TFSA),** where Canadian residents who are 18 years of age or older and who have a valid social insurance number are eligible to contribute up to $5,500 annually. The initial amount contributed as well as the income earned in the account (e.g., interest income) is tax free, even when it is withdrawn. Generally, the types of investments that will be permitted in a TFSA include cash, mutual funds, securities listed on a designated stock exchange, term deposits, bonds, and certain shares of small business corporations.

> **Tax-Free Savings Account (TFSA)**
> An investment option into which Canadian residents 18 years of age or older who have a valid social insurance number can contribute up to $5,500 annually; the amount contributed as well as the income earned in the account is tax free, even when it is withdrawn.

One strategy is to save your money in a TFSA and when you accumulate enough to make a large purchase (e.g., home or a trip) you withdraw the money and pay for the purchase. Let us look at real estate next as an investment option.

Real Estate

Your first major investment might be a low-priced home. The purpose of this investment is to lock in payments for your shelter at a fixed amount. This is possible by owning a home, but not by renting. Through the years, home ownership has been a wise investment, unlike renting, but that may be changing.[10] Many people take huge risks by buying too much home for their income. Another uncertain strategy is to take out interest-only loans (e.g., a secured line of credit where the minimum monthly payment is the interest) or other loans that are very risky.

Real estate is likely to provide several investment benefits. First, a home is the one investment that you can live in. Second, once you buy a home, the payments are relatively fixed (though taxes and utilities may go up). As your income rises, mortgage payments get easier to make, but renters often find that rents go up at least as fast as income. On the other hand, the changes in home prices have made it more important than ever for you to check whether it is better to own or rent.[11] Paying for a home has historically been a good way of forcing yourself to save. You must make the payments every month. Those payments are an investment that can prove to be very rewarding over time for most people. A home is also a good asset to use when applying for a business loan.

Some couples have used the seed money accumulated from saving one income (in the strategy outlined earlier) to buy two attached homes so that they can live in one part and rent out the other. The rent they earn covers a good part of the payments for both homes, so the couple can live comfortably, yet inexpensively, while their investment in a home appreciates. In this way, they accumulate capital, and, as they grow older, they pull ahead of their peers in terms of financial security. As capital accumulates and values rise, they can sell, and then buy an even larger apartment building or a single-family home. Many have made fortunes in real estate this way.

Many people are making an income by renting unused space on Airbnb <*http://www.airbnb.ca*>.[12] Of course, it all depends on how valuable your space is. An apartment in Toronto may bring in some real income if you rent it while away. Such rentals may be part of a "shared economy" that is emerging. That is, people are learning to share cars, homes, bicycles, driveways, and tools as a way of saving some money.[13]

Once you understand the benefits of home ownership versus renting, you can decide whether those same principles apply to owning the premises where you set up your own business—or owning your own equipment, vehicles, and the like. Furthermore, you may start thinking of real estate as a way to earn a living. You could, for example, buy older homes, fix them up, and sell them—a path many have taken to attain financial security. To calculate the cost differences between renting and buying a house, complete the Rent or Buy calculator found at <*genworth.ca/en/homebuyers/rent-or-buy.aspx*>.

The Stock Market

You have learned that one place to invest the money you have saved is in a home. What are some other good places to save your money? For a young person, it is generally not recommended to keep *long-term* investments in a savings account or term deposit. (This is different for your contingency funds.) One of the best places to invest over time has been the stock market. The stock market does tend to go up and down, but over a longer period of time it has proven to be one of the best investments.

The future always looks gloomy during a financial crisis, but that does not mean you shouldn't take risks. Remember the greater the risk, usually the greater the return. When stock prices are low, that's the time to *buy*. When stocks collapse, it is an opportunity to get into the stock market—not avoid it. The average investor buys when the stock market is high and sells when it is low. Clearly, that is not a good idea. It takes courage to buy when everyone else is selling. In the long run, however, this **contrarian approach** to investing is the way the rich get richer.[14]

> **contrarian approach**
> Buying stock when everyone else is selling or vice versa.

Chapter 17 introduced you to stocks and bonds. There are tools that track the performance of such investments over time. For example, the Andex Chart summarizes the performance of some key indices such as the S&P/TSX Composite (the Canadian stock market), the S&P 500, U.S. small stocks, Canadian bonds, fixed-term investments, Canadian Treasury bills, and the cost of living.[15] As you can see in Figure D.2, this chart captures historical performances that have been impacted by trends in the business environment. No one knows what will happen in the future and this is where doing your homework and knowing your risk tolerance is very important when making financial investments. Bonds, as another alternative, have traditionally lagged behind stocks as a long-term investment.

FIGURE D.2

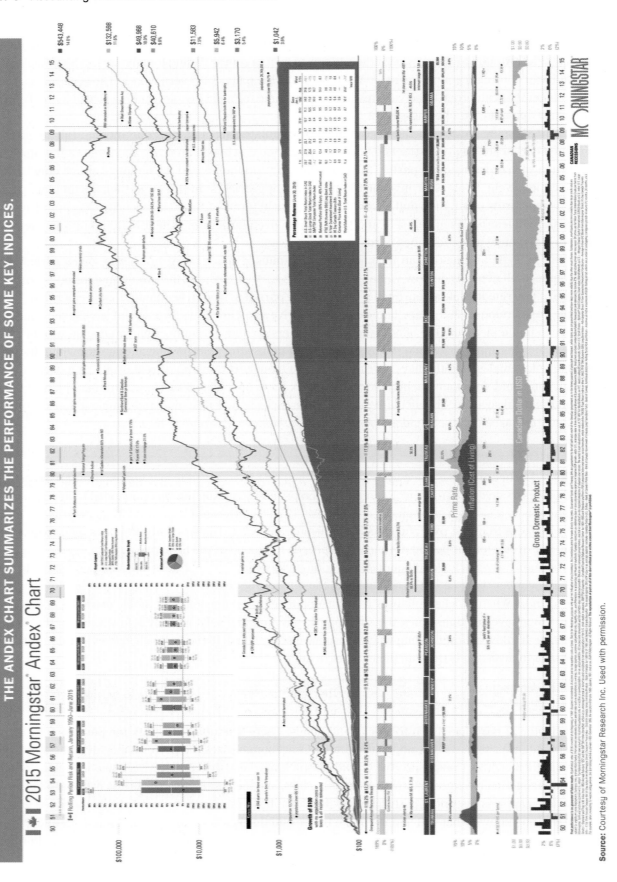

THE ANDEX CHART SUMMARIZES THE PERFORMANCE OF SOME KEY INDICES.

Source: Courtesy of Morningstar Research Inc. Used with permission.

Learning to Manage Credit

Credit cards are an important element in a personal financial system, even if you rarely use them. First, you may have to own a credit card to buy certain goods or even rent, because some businesses require one for identification and to ensure payment. Second, you can use a credit card to keep track of purchases. A gasoline credit card, for example, gives you records of purchases over time for your income tax returns (if you drive for work) and financial planning purposes. Third, a credit card is more convenient than cash or cheques. You can carry less cash and easily cancel a stolen card to protect your account. The most secure cards will be PIN and chip cards since such cards are much less prone to identity theft.[16]

If you do use a credit card, you should pay the balance in full during the period when no interest is charged. Not having to pay 18 percent interest, as an example of the interest charged, is as good as earning 18 percent tax free. You may want to choose a card that pays you back in cash (e.g., *Scotia Momentum*® no-fee VISA credit card) or offers pay-backs like credits toward the purchase of gas (e.g., Canadian Tire Financial Service's *Gas Advantage*™ *MasterCard*®), or frequent-flier air miles. The value of these givebacks can vary. Some cards have no annual fees while others offer lower interest rates. To learn more about credit cards that will best suit your needs, visit the Financial Consumer Agency of Canada's website.

The danger of a credit card is the flip side of its convenience. It's too easy to buy things you wouldn't buy if you had to pay cash, or to pile up debts you can't repay. If you aren't the type who can stick to a financial plan or household budget, it may be better not to have a credit card at all. Imagine a customer who has a $10,000 balance on his or her credit card with a 16 percent interest rate and pays the minimum monthly payment established by the credit card company (e.g., 4 percent). How long will it take to pay off the debt, and what would the cost for interest be? The answers are 14 years and nearly $5,000—and that's without using the card again to purchase so much as a candy bar.

Another danger of credit cards is the issue of hacking. Stores like Target and Michaels <*http://www.michaels.com*> have had credit card numbers stolen.[17] This identity theft results in people getting access to customers' e-mail addresses, names, and account numbers. As mentioned earlier, the newer credit cards use both a chip embedded in the card and a customer PIN. Time will tell if these cards will cut down on the losses due to stolen credit card numbers.[18]

Some people would be better off with a debit card only. Debit cards don't allow you to spend more than what you have in your financial institution, which is a great benefit for those who are not as careful with their spending as they should be.[19] Furthermore, there are no interest payments or annual fees, other than account-specific fees, if applicable.

Protecting Your Financial Base: Buying Insurance

One of the last things people think about is the idea that they may become sick, get injured, or die. It is not a pleasant thought, but the unexpected happens every day. To protect your loved ones from the loss of your income, you should buy life insurance (recall the discussion on risk in Appendix C).[20]

The simplest and least expensive form of life insurance is **term insurance.** It is pure insurance protection for a given number of years that typically costs less the younger you are when you buy it. When your term expires, you would need to renew the policy, and the premium could then rise. Compare prices through a service like Insurance-Canada <*http://www.insurance-canada.ca/index.php*>.

term insurance
Pure insurance protection for a given number of years.

How much insurance do you need? The answer depends on the objectives that you have. For an idea, complete a life insurance needs calculator (e.g., *<http://www.kanetix.ca/life_cov_calc>*). Figure D.3 summarizes why you should buy term insurance.

■ FIGURE D.3

WHY BUY TERM INSURANCE?	
Insurance Needs in Early Years Are High	**Insurance Needs Decline as You Grow Older**
1. Children are young and need money for education	1. Children are grown
2. Mortgage is high relative to income	2. Mortgage is low or completely paid off
3. Often there are auto payments and other bills to pay	3. Debts are paid off
4. Loss of income would be disastrous	4. Insurance needs are few
	5. Retirement income is needed

Multi-year level-premium insurance guarantees that you'll pay the same premium for the life of the policy. Recently, 40 percent of new term policies guaranteed a set rate for 20 years. Some companies allow you to switch your term policy for a more expensive whole or universal life policy.

Whole life insurance combines pure insurance and savings, so you are buying both insurance and a savings plan. This may be a good idea for those people who have trouble saving money. A universal life policy lets you choose how much of your payment should go to insurance and how much to investments. The investments traditionally are very conservative but pay a steady interest rate.

> **whole life insurance**
> Life insurance that combines pure insurance and savings.

Variable Life Insurance

Variable life insurance is a form of whole life insurance that invests the cash value of the policy in stocks or other high-yielding securities. Death benefits may thus vary, reflecting the performance of the investments.

> **variable life insurance**
> A form of whole life insurance that invests the cash value of the policy in stocks or other high-yielding securities.

Life insurance companies recognized the desire that people had for higher returns on their insurance (and to protect themselves against running out of money before they die) and began selling annuities. An **annuity** is a contract to make regular payments to a person for life or a fixed period. With an annuity, you are guaranteed to have an income until you die or for the agreed upon time.

> **annuity**
> A contract to make regular payments to a person for life or a fixed period.

There are two kinds of annuities: fixed and variable. *Fixed annuities* are investments that pay the policyholder a specified interest rate. They are not as popular as *variable annuities*, which provide investment choices identical to mutual funds. Such annuities are becoming more popular than term or whole life insurance. But buyers must be careful in selecting an insurance company and the investments made with their money.

Before buying any insurance, it is wise to consult with both an insurance agent and a financial adviser. They can help you make the wisest decision about insurance based on your overall needs.

Disability Insurance

Your chances of becoming disabled at an early age are much higher than your chances of dying from an accident. It is a good idea to supplement Canada's public health coverage with **disability insurance** that pays part of the cost of a long-term illness or an accident. Disability insurance replaces part of your lost income, and, in some cases, pays disability-related expenses not covered by health insurance. Call an insurance agent or check online for possible quotes for such insurance. The cost is relatively low to protect yourself from losing your income for an extended period of time.

> **disability insurance**
> Insurance that pays part of the cost of a long-term illness or an accident.

Homeowners or Renters Insurance

You may be surprised to see how much it would cost to replace all the things you own. As you begin to accumulate possessions, you may want to have apartment or homeowner's insurance that covers any losses. Specify that you want *guaranteed replacement cost*. That means that the insurance company will give you whatever it costs to buy all of those things new. It costs a little bit more than a policy without guaranteed replacement, but you will get a lot more if you have a loss.[21]

The other option is insurance that covers the *depreciated cost* of the items. For example, a sofa you bought five years ago for $600 may only be worth $150 now. That current value is what you would get from insurance, not the $700 or more you may need to buy a brand-new sofa. If your computer is stolen, you might only get a few hundred dollars for it rather than its replacement cost.

Most policies don't cover expensive items like engagement and wedding rings. You can buy a *rider* to your insurance policy that will cover such items at a reasonable cost.

Other Insurance: Car and Liability Insurance

You should buy insurance for your car. Consider selecting a large deductible of $1,000 or so to keep the premiums low, and pay for small damages on your own. Be sure to include insurance against losses from uninsured motorists. You will also need liability insurance to protect yourself against being sued by someone you accidentally injure.

Often you can get a discount by buying all your insurance (e.g., life, disability, homeowners, automobile, etc.) with one company. This is called an **umbrella policy**. Look for other discounts such as for safe driving, good grades, using snow tires, and more.

> **umbrella policy**
> A broadly based insurance policy that saves you money because you buy all your insurance from one company.

Planning Your Retirement

It may seem a bit early to be planning your retirement; however, not doing so would be a big mistake. Successful financial planning means long-range planning, and retirement is a critical phase of life. What you do now could make a world of difference in your quality of life when you retire. If you think that it is too early, as a minimum you can start to gather information.

How much do you need for retirement? The answer is that it depends on factors such as your age, your spending patterns, your health, etc. For example, retirement length has a big impact on when you can retire; the average Canadian retires at age 62 according to Statistics Canada, and the average life expectancy is age 84.[22] This suggests an average of 22 years of retirement to fund, but not every Canadian is an average Canadian as some will have much shorter or longer retirements.[23]

Retirement income may come from what is commonly referred to as the *three pillars approach*. Pillar 1 consists of the federal Old Age Security (OAS) program. Retirement income from Pillar 2 consists of income from the Canada Pension Plan (CPP) and the Québec Pension Plan (QPP). Government pensions were designed to replace only 40 percent of pre-retirement income for individuals who were earning the average national wage. Pillar 1 represents 15 percent and Pillar 2 represents 25 percent of pre-retirement income. You can see how Pillar 3—at 60 percent, or more if one does not quality for OAS or CPP/QPP—has some heavy lifting to do. It consists of income generated from private savings and retirement savings plans, with the most common being employer-sponsored pension plans (EPPs) and Registered Retirement Savings Plans (RRSPs).[24]

The retirement income system in Canada is based on both public (Pillars 1 and 2) and private (Pillar 3) retirement savings plans. Almost all of today's seniors receive income from Canada's public pensions.

Pillar I: OAS Program[25]

The OAS program is one of the cornerstones of Canada's retirement income system. Benefits include the basic OAS pension, the Guaranteed Income Supplement (for low-income seniors), the Allowance (a benefit available to the spouses of Guaranteed Income Supplement recipients), and the Allowance for the Survivor. OAS generates a pension at age 65 if one has lived in Canada for at least 10 years since the age of 18. The age of eligibility for the OAS pension will gradually increase between the years 2023 and 2029, from 65 to 67.

This program is financed from general tax revenues collected by the Government of Canada. All benefits payable under the Old Age Security Act are adjusted four times a year if there are increases in the cost of living, as measured by the consumer price index (CPI). Between October to December 2015, the maximum monthly benefit was $569.95 per recipient. For updated benefit information, visit Service Canada <*http://www.servicecanada.gc.ca*>.

Pillar 2: CPP and QPP[26]

Established in 1966, the CPP provides basic benefits when a contributor to the Plan becomes disabled or retires. At the contributor's death, the Plan provides benefits to his or her survivors. The CPP is a "contributory" plan. This means that all its costs are covered by the financial contributions paid by employees, employers, and self-employed workers, and from revenue earned on CPP investments. The CPP may provide monthly benefits starting as early as 60 years of age. As a point of reference, the maximum CPP or QPP monthly benefit per retired recipient (at age 65) for 2015 was $1,065. For updated benefit information, visit Service Canada.

The QPP is the equivalent of the CPP but it is provided to residents of Quebec. It is a compulsory public insurance plan whose purpose is to provide persons who work in Quebec (or have worked in Quebec) and their families with basic financial protection in the event of retirement, death, or disability. The Plan is financed by contributions from Quebec workers and employers. These contributions are collected by Revenu Québec and are managed by the Caisse de dépôt et placement du Québec. As with the CPP, the QPP may provide monthly benefits starting as early as 60 years of age.

Pillar 3: EPPs and RRSPs

Based on the values noted earlier, between OAS and the CPP/QPP, the government(s) will pay out a maximum of approximately $1,635 a month to an eligible 65-year-old. Clearly, this is not a lot of money, which is why you need to take charge of saving for retirement. Financial experts recommend that we need 70 percent of our pre-retirement income in order to have a comfortable retirement. As a result, the third pillar must make up what is not covered by the public pensions. EPPs can be one element of Pillar 3.

EPPS[27]

Private pension plans are employer-specific and, if applicable, are introduced during an employee's orientation period at the new place of employment. EPPs include registered pension plans (RPPs) and deferred profit sharing plans (DPSPs). In Canada, employer pension plans cover just over 6.2 million workers, which is 38.4 percent of all employees.

With RPPs, both the employer and employee typically contribute to the plan. A DPSP is an employer-sponsored savings plan in which an employer makes contributions for the employees (who cannot contribute) based on profits. The amount accumulated in these plans can be paid out as a lump sum at retirement or termination of employment, transferred to an RRSP, received in instalments over a period not to exceed ten years, or used to purchase an annuity.

RRSPS[28]

As you read above, a minority of working Canadians have access to an EPP. Consequently, the majority of Canadians need to proactively consider other personal investment strategies such as RRSPs. A **registered retirement savings plan (RRSP)** is a federally-regulated, tax-sheltered savings plan designed to encourage Canadians to save for their retirement. Any earnings from cash or investments held within an RRSP are not taxed until they are withdrawn. An RRSP lets you save for retirement and save taxes at the same time. Not only do you avoid paying income tax on the money you contribute, but you postpone paying tax on your investment earnings until you take the money out of your plan later on. And because you'll earn interest on the interest, the tax-free compounding will make a huge difference in the amount of money you'll be able to save for retirement. You, your spouse, or a common-law partner can establish and contribute to an RRSP.

> **registered retirement savings plan (RRSP)**
> A federally-regulated, tax-sheltered savings plan designed to encourage Canadians to save for their retirement.

The exact amount you're entitled to contribute for the tax year is shown in a separate section of the Notice of Assessment you receive from Canada Revenue Agency after you file last year's tax return. The amount you're allowed to deduct for tax purposes is referred to as your *contribution room* or *deduction room*. The dollar limit (or maximum) that you can contribute for any tax year is 18 percent of your earned income from the previous year (up to a certain limit), minus any "pension adjustment" (if applicable, this refers to the amount of a work pension that you may have built up in the pension plan during the year), plus any unused contributions from previous years.

You may deduct the entire amount from your taxable income when you make the contribution. The amount of tax you save will depend on your marginal tax rate. For tax planning purposes, the **marginal tax rate** is defined as the rate of tax payable on the last dollar earned. The marginal tax rate varies from province to province. Your tax rate tells you how much money you get to keep if you make an extra dollar, or how much you save in taxes by reducing your taxable income by a dollar. The higher your income, the more tax you will save by contributing to your RRSP.

marginal tax rate
The rate of tax payable on the last dollar earned.

Consider Figure D.4, which lists the marginal tax rate (combined provincial and federal tax rates) for our example. Your friend has earned $25,000 and you have earned $75,000. A $1,000 investment into an RRSP would save your friend $260 and would save you $360 in tax. Despite investing the same $1,000, everyone derives different tax benefits depending on each person's marginal tax rate.

■ **FIGURE D.3**

MARGINAL TAX RATE AND PERSONAL INCOME EXAMPLE	
Marginal Tax Rate	Personal Income Range
26%	$8,169 to $32,625
32%	$32,626 to $65,254
36%	$65,255 to $106,090
39%	$106,091 and up

The RRSP contribution deadline is 60 days after the end of the year (i.e., March 1). You can buy an RRSP at any financial institution or through a broker or financial adviser.

When you start contributing to your RRSP earlier in life, you'll allow more time for the income earned in your RRSP to compound. You may also find that you can make a smaller total investment in your RRSP, and still be further ahead. While this sounds straightforward, be aware that over 40 percent of Canadians contribute nothing at all to their RRSPs.[29] Like any savings program, this requires discipline.

There are other uses for this money, other than for retirement. Two plans allow you to withdraw money from your RRSP without penalty, assuming that you pay back these funds within a certain period of time. For example, the Home Buyers' Plan allows you to withdraw up to $25,000 from your RRSP to buy or build a home for yourself or for a related person with a disability. The Lifelong Learning Plan allows you to withdraw up to $20,000 from your RRSP to finance training or education for you, your spouse, or common-law partner.

Contributing to an RRSP is one of several strategies that Canadians can pursue when planning for retirement. There are free online programs that will help you determine how much you need to save in your RRSP to achieve your retirement goals. One such example is Toronto-Dominion Bank's RRSP Contribution Calculator at *<http://www.tdcanadatrust.com/planning/life-events/rrsp-planning-calc.jsp>*. Visit the site to find out more information.

Financial Planners

If the idea of developing a comprehensive financial plan seems overwhelming, relax. Help is available from financial planners. Financial planners assist in developing a comprehensive program that covers investments, taxes, insurance, and other financial matters. Be careful, though. Since financial planning is not regulated in most Canadian provinces, anyone can claim to be a "financial planner" but not everyone is qualified.[30] It's often best to find a person who has earned the distinction of being a certified financial planner (CFP) or a similar designation. For a list and description of financial designations, as well as advice on finding an adviser, visit Financial Advisors Association of Canada *<http://www.advocis.ca>*.

It pays to shop around for financial advice. Ask your friends and family. Find someone who understands your situation and is willing to spend some time with you. Financial planning covers all aspects of investing, all the way to retirement and death. Financial planners can advise you on the proper mix of investments, insurance, and retirement planning.

Estate Planning

It is never too early to begin thinking about estate planning, although this may be decades away. You may need to contact a lawyer or a financial planner, or both, to help you prepare the paperwork and do the planning necessary to preserve and protect your investments for your beneficiaries. Two important documents are a will and a power of attorney.

A **will** is a document that states how you want your assets distributed, it names the executor for your estate, and it names the guardian(s) for your children (if applicable). An **executor** assembles and values your estate, files income and other taxes, and distributes assets. This document takes effect when you pass away.

> **will**
> A document that states how you want your assets distributed, names the executor for your estate, and names the guardian(s) for your children (if applicable) when you die.
>
> **executor**
> An individual who assembles and values your estate, files income and other taxes, and distributes assets when you pass away.

A **power of attorney,** which can take effect when you are alive, is a written document in which you appoint someone else to act on your behalf on matters that you specify. This can be made to start immediately, or upon mental incapacity.[31] Be aware that the rules regulating powers of attorney tend to vary significantly from province to province.[32]

> **power of attorney**
> A written document in which you appoint someone else to act on your behalf on matters that you specify; this can be made to start immediately, or upon mental incapacity.

There are hundreds of books on estate planning, so we can only give you a hint as to what is involved. It all begins with a strong financial base.

KEY TERMS

annuity	power of attorney	umbrella policy
contrarian approach	registered retirement savings	variable life insurance
disability insurance	plan (RRSP)	whole life insurance
executor	Tax-Free Savings Account	will
financial literacy	(TFSA)	
marginal tax rate	term insurance	

Endnotes

Chapter 1

1. Yuri Ostrovsky and Marc Frenette. "The Cumulative Earnings of Postsecondary Graduate Over 20 Years: Results by Field of Study. Statistics Canada. 2014, October. Catalogue no. 11-626-X. Retrieved from http://www.statcan.gc.ca/pub/11-626-x/11-626-x2014040-eng.htm on March 15, 2015.
2. Marc Frenette. An Investment of a lifetime: The Long Term Labour Market Premiums Associated with a Postsecondary Education. 2014, February. Statistics Canada. Catalogue no. 11F0019M. Retrieved from http://www.statcan.gc.ca/pub/11f0019m/11f0019m2014354-eng.htm on March 15, 2015.
3. U.S. Census Bureau, www.census.gov, accessed May 2014.
4. Tennile M. Robinson, "Borrowing Trouble," *Black Enterprise*, January 2009.
5. Jim McElhatton, "Community Colleges Seen as Essential," *The Washington Times*, 14 April 2008.
6. Heron Marquez Estrada, "EdCampus Aims to Transform Higher Education," *The Washington Times*, 31 March 2008.
7. "Key Small Business Statistics," Industry Canada, July 2010, www.ic.gc.ca/eic/site/sbrp-rppe.nsf/vwapj/KSBS-PSRPE_July-Juillet2010_eng.pdf/$FILE/KSBS-PSRPE_July-Juillet2010_eng.pdf.
8. Small Business Quarterly, "Business Insolvencies," Industry Canada, May 2008, www.ic.gc.ca/epic/site/sbrp-rppe.nsf/vwapj/SBQ_May2008_Eng.pdf/$FILE/SBQ_May2008_Eng.pdf.
9. Fareed Zakaria, "Switched-On Highways," *Newsweek*, 19 January 2009.
10. Tesla Motors Ends 2014 with a Loss, After Building 35,000 Cars. CBC News, February 12, 2015. http://www.cbc.ca/news/business/tesla-motors-ends-2014-with-a-loss-after-building-35-000-electric-cars-1.2954866.
11. "Cost of Living Comparison Between Canada and Japan," Numbeo.com, July 26, 2015, www.numbeo.com/cost-of-living/compare_countries_result.jsp?country1=Canada&country2=Japan.
12. Jonathan Clements, "Down the Tube: The Sad Stats on Happiness, Money and TV," *The Wall Street Journal*, 2 April 2008.
13. Pete Engardio, "The Future of Outsourcing," *BusinessWeek*, 30 January 2006, 50–58.
14. John R. Baldwin and Wulong Gu, "Outsourcing and Offshoring in Canada," Statistics Canada, May 2008, www.statcan.ca/english/research/ 11F0027MIE/11F0027MIE2008055.pdf.
15. Erin White, "Smaller Companies Join the Outsourcing Trend," *The Wall Street Journal*, 8 May 2006, B3.
16. Baldwin and Gu, "Outsourcing and Offshoring in Canada,"
17. Pete Engardio and Bruce Einhorn, "Outsourcing Innovation," *BusinessWeek*, 21 March 2005, 84–94.
18. Ibid.
19. 2014 Global Outsourcing and Insourcing Survey Results: Executive Summary. Deloitte Consulting LLP, May 2014. http://www2.deloitte.com/us/en/pages/strategy/articles/2014-global-outsourcing-and-insourcing-survey.html.
20. Ford to Pay Full Wages to Some New Hires Under Two-Tier Wage Deal, The Associate Press, February 4, 2015. http://www.cbc.ca/news/business/ford-to-pay-full-wages-to-some-newer-hires-under-two-tier-pay-deal-1.2945228.
21. Jeff Beer, "The Real Reason Rogers and Bell Bought MLSE," *Canadian Business*, January 2012, http://www.canadianbusiness.com /business-strategy/the-real-reason-rogers-and-bell-bought-mlse/; Sean Fitz-Gerald, "MLSE Deal: What the Rogers and Bell Buyout Means for Fans," *National Post*, December 2011, http://news.nationalpost.com/2011/12/09/rogers-bell-buy-majority-stake-in-mlse/; "Rogers, Bell Finalize MLSE Purchase,"

Toronto Star, August 2012, http://www.thestar.com/sports/leafs/2012/08/22/rogers_bell_finalize_mlse_purchase.html.
22. Canada's Top 100 Nonprofit Organization (registered charities), *The Globe and Mail*, February 5, 2015, http://www.theglobeandmail.com/report-on-business/rob-magazine/top-100-non-profit-organizations-registered-charities/article17298702/
23. Steve Hamm, "When the Bottom Line Is Ending Poverty," *BusinessWeek*, 10 March 2008.
24. Key Facts about Canada's Charities, Imagine Canada, http://www.imaginecanada.ca/resources-and-tools/research-and-facts/key-facts-about-canada%E2%80%99s-charities
25. "2013 Corporate Profile," Tim Hortons, http://www.timhortons.com/ca/en/corporate/profile.php.
26. Jamie Sturgeon, "It's Official, Tim Hortons, Burger King become one," *Global News*, 12 December 2014, http://globalnews.ca/news/1724238/its-official-tim-hortons-burger-king-become-one/.
27. Frederick G. Crane et al., *Marketing*, 8th Canadian ed., (Canada: McGraw-Hill Ryerson, 2011), 92.
28. Ibid.
29. Amir Efrati, "Scope of Alleged Fraud Is Still Being Assessed," *The Wall Street Journal*, 18 December 2008.
30. Annys Shin, "Economic Picture Bleak in Fed Report," *The Washington Post*, 15 January 2009.
31. "The Origins of the Financial Crisis: Crash Course," *The Economist*, September 7, 2013, http://www.economist.com/news/schoolsbrief/21584534-effects-financial-crisis-are-still-being-felt-five-years-article.
32. "'Sense of Urgency,' as Premiers Meet with Central Banker," CBC News, 18 July 2008, www.cbc.ca/canada/saskatchewan/story/2008/07/18/premiers-economy.html.
33. Brenda Bouw, "New Anti-Spam Law a 'Big Deal' for Small Business," *The Globe and Mail*, March 2014, http://www.theglobeandmail.com/report-on-business/small-business/sb-digital/biz-categories-technology/businesses-rush-to-comply-with-tough-new-anti-spam-law/article17609044/.
34. Frederick G. Crane et al., *Marketing*, 8th Canadian ed. (Toronto: McGraw-Hill Ryerson Ltd., 2011), 86.
35. Richard Stengel, "Made in America, Again," *Time*, 22 April 2013.
36. Sharaz Kahn, "Wearable Intelligence Coming to a workplace near you," *The Globe and Mail*, February 2013, http://www.theglobeandmail.com/report-on-business/small-business/sb-tools/sb-how-to/wearable-intelligence-coming-to-a-workplace-near-you/article22746277/; www.vivametrica.com; Start-up of the Week – Vivametrica, Calgary.
37. Digital Technology and Internet Use, 2013" Statistics Canada, 11 June 2014, http://www.statcan.gc.ca/daily-quotidien/140611/dq140611a-eng.pdf.
38. "How to Get the Most from Kijiji and Craigslist," *Toronto Star*, 18 January 2012, http://www.thestar.com/business/personal_finance/spending_saving/2012/01/18/how_to_get_the_most_from_kijiji_and_craigslist.html.
39. "Wanted: Stand-out Sellers for EBay Canada's 10th Annual Entrepreneur of the Year Awards," *The Globe and Mail*, 21 July 2014, http://www.theglobeandmail.com/globe-investor/news-sources/?mid=cnw.20140721.C2300.
40. "Numbers," *Time*, 5 May 2008.
41. "E-BUSINESS," Webster's Online Dictionary, 2009, www.websters-online-dictionary.org/definition/e-business.
42. "Introduction to e-Business," Kioskea.net, 16 October 2008, http://en.kioskea.net/contents/entreprise/e-business.php3.

43. Jena McGregor, "Customer Service Champs," *Businessweek,* 3 March 2008.

44. Jack Neff, "Marketers Become Big Data Hoarders," *Advertising Age,* 13 March 2013.

45. Maggie McGrath, "Target Profit Falls 46% on Credit Card Breach and the Hits Could Keep on Coming," *Forbes,* 26 February 2014.

46. "Privacy Legislation in Canada," Office of the Privacy Commissioner of Canada, 5 December 2008, www.priv.gc.ca /fs-fi/02_05_d_15_e.cfm.

47. Lisa Gerstner, "What You Need to Know about Identity Theft," Kiplinger's Personal Finance, June 2013.

48. Crane et al., *Marketing,* 18.

49. "Use of Social Media Among Canada's Small Business Owners Up 42 Percent from 2012," BMO Financial Group, 25 October 2013, http://newsroom.bmo.com/press-releases /bmo-report-use-of-social-media-among-canada-s-sma-tsx -bmo-201310250906689001.

50. Crowdsourcing to Stand Out from the Masses. Canada Business Network, 9 March 2015, http://www.canadabusiness.ca/eng /blog/entry/5012/.

51. Ivor Tossel, "Don Tapscott: Let's Crowdsource Canada," *The Globe and Mail,* 20 February 2013, http://www.theglobeandmail.com/ report-on-business/economy/canada-competes/don-tapscott -lets-crowdsource-canada/article8897102/.

52. Crane et al., *Marketing,* 90.

53. Adapted from "Population Projections for Canada, Provinces and Territories 2009–2036," Cat. No. 91-520-X, June 2010.

54. *Boom, Bust & Echo, Profiting from the Demographic Shift in the 21st Century,* Footwork Consulting Inc., 2008, www.footwork .com/21c.asp.

55. "Population projections," *The Daily,* Statistics Canada, 15 December 2015, http://www.statcan.gc.ca/daily-quotidien /051215/dq051215b-eng.htm.

56. World Economic Forum, 2011, "Global Talent Risks – Seven Responses" http://www.bcg.com/documents/file69643.pdf. accessed 6 Marcy 2015, http://www.bcg.com/media /PressReleaseDetails.aspx?id=tcm:12-69648.

57. Facts and Figures 2010 – Immigration overview: Permanent and Temporary residents," Citizenship and Immigration Canada, 30 August 2011, www.cic.gc/english/resources/statistics /facts2010/permanent/01.asp; "Census Snapshot – Immigration in Canada: A portrait of the foreign-born population, 2006 Census," Statistics Canada, 21 November 2008, www.statcan.gc.ca/pub/11-008-x/2008001/article/10556-eng. htm#1.

58. Backgrounder – 2014 Immigration Levels Planning: Public and Stakeholder Consultations, Statistics Canada, http://www.cic .gc.ca/english/department/media /backgrounders/2013/2013-06-21.asp#role.

59. Andrea Cooper, "The Influencers," *Entrepreneur,* March 2008.

60. Charrnchai Athitchitskul, "Towards a Sustainable Society," *Global Management Review,* 5, no. 4, August 2011, 1–28.

61. Gross domestic product at basic prices, manufacturing and construction industries," Statistics Canada, 23 December 2011, www40.statcan.gc.ca/l01/cst01/manuf10-eng.htm.

62. *Manufacturing Our Future: A manufacturing action plan for Canada,* Canadian Manufacturers and Exporters Association, March 2012, http://www.cme-mec.ca/download .php?file=h8q5gph6.pdf.

63. Ibid.

64. "Canadian Manufacturing Today: Cautiously Optimistic: BDOs perspective on CMEs 2014 Management Issues Survey," BDO Canada LLP, http://www.cme-mec.ca/_uploads/_media /51wjbzblm.pdf.

65. Ibid.

66. Deborah Aarts. "Canada's Fastest Growing Company is Built for Growth," ProfitGuide.com, 12 June 2014, http://www.profitguide.com/small-business /canadas-fastest-growing-company-is-built-for-growth-66142.

Chapter 2

1. Jeff Gray, "Canadian Documentary Warns Tax Havens Threaten Democracy," *The Globe and Mail,* 11 March 2015, http://www.theglobeandmail.com/report -on-business/industry-news/the-law-page/canadian -documentary-warns-tax-havens-threaten-democracy /article23409274/.

2. Romain Hatchuel, "The Coming Global Wealth Tax," *The Wall Street Journal,* 15 January 2014.

3. Richard Blackwell, "Green energy sector jobs surpass total oil sands employment," *The Globe and Mail,* 2 December 2014, http://www.theglobeandmail.com /report-on-business/industry-news/energy-and-resources /green-energy-sector-jobs-surpass-oil-sand-employment-total /article21859169/.

4. "Ballard Closes Technology Solutions Transaction with Volkswagen Group," Burnaby: Ballard Power Systems, 23 February 2015, http://www.ballard.com/about-ballard /newsroom/news-releases/news02231502.aspx.

5. Roger Lowenstein, "Macro Master," *The Wall Street Journal,* 4 December 2013.

6. Nidaa Bakhsh, "Shale Goes Global," *Bloomberg Businessweek,* 18 November 2013–2 January 2014.

7. Canadian Aquaculture Industry Alliance, "The Canadian Aquaculture Industry – A success story," http://www.aquaculture .ca/files/CanAquacultureFacts-08.pdf.

8. Ed Feulner, "The Slow Fade of Economic Freedom," *The Washington Times,* 14 January 2014.

9. Gordan Harris and Glen Miller, "How Aging Boomers will Disrupt Canada's Demographic 'Crisis'," *The Globe and Mail,* 4 February 2015, http://www.theglobeandmail.com/globe-debate /how-aging-boomers-will-disrupt-canadas-demographic-crisis /article22780291/.

10. Randall Stephenson, "A Business Shortlist for Growth," *The Wall Street Journal,* 15 January 2015.

11. Ed Feulner, "The Slow Fade of Economic Freedom," *The Washington Times,* 14 January 2014.

12. Sara Mojtehedzadeh, "Toronto now Canada's inequality capital, United Way study shows," *The Toronto Star,* 27 February 2015, http://www.thestar.com/news/gta/2015/02/27/toronto-now -canadas-inequality-capital-united-way-study-shows.html.

13. Charles Lane, "The Politics of Inequality," *The Washington Post,* 10 December 2013.

14. "The Philanthropic," *Forbes,* 2 December 2013.

15. John Mackey and Raj Sisodia, *Conscious Capitalism,* (Boston, MA: Harvard Business review press, 2013).

16. Ibid., p. 11.

17. Romano Prodi, "To Avoid a Food Disaster," *The Washington Times,* 27 April 2008.

18. Peter Coy, "The Sting of Long-Term Unemployment," *Bloomberg Businessweek,* 11 February 2013.

19. "Bill Gates No Longer Tops World's-Richest List," *The Chronicle of Philanthropy,* 6 March 2008, http://philanthropy. com/news/philanthropytoday/4105/bill-gates-no-longer-tops -worlds-richest-list.

20. "Global Citizenship," Cirque du Soleil, [2015?], www.cirquedusoleil .com/en/about/global-citizenship/community.aspx.

21. Marjory Abrams, "The Economy in a Nutshell," *Bottom Line Personal,* 1 May 2008.

22. Brian M. Carney, "Europe Hasn't Outgrown 'That '70s Show,'" *The Wall Street Journal,* 9 May 2005, A23.

23. Laura D'Andrea Tyson, "How Europe Is Revving Its Engine," *BusinessWeek,* 21 February 2005, 24.

24. "Latest Indicators, Population Estimate (April 2012)," Statistics Canada, 31 August 2012, www.statcan.gc.ca /start-debut-eng.html.

25. Matthew Coutts, "Complacency Hurts Nation: Think-Tank; Quality of Life Declining, Report Warns," *National Post,* 30 June 2008, A4.

26. Ibid.

27. "Economic Concepts—Unemployment Rate," Government of Canada, 4 May 2007, http://canadianeconomy.gc.ca/english /economy/unemployment2.html.

28. Ibid.

29. Ibid.

30. "Classification of Labour Status," Statistics Canada, 21 July 2011, http://www.statcan.gc.ca/pub/71-543-g/2014001/part -partie2-eng.htm.

31. David Pilling, "Japan Still in Grip of Deflation as Prices Fall," *Financial Times,* 27 April 2005, 7.

32. Carol Goar, "Worried Economists Tell Flaherty to Stop Starving the Economy," *The Toronto Star,* 11 February 2014, http:// www.thestar.com/opinion/commentary/2014/02/11/worried _economists_tell_flaherty_to_stop_starving_the_economy_goar .html.

33. Consumer Price Index, Statistics Canada, CANSIM, table 326-0020 and Catalogue nos. 62-001-X and 62-010-X.

34. The 2014 Human Development Report : Sustaining Human Progress: Reducing Vulnerabilities and Building Resilience, United Nations, 2014, http://hdr.undp.org/en/content /human-development-index-hdi.

35. Victor Zarnowitz and Dara Lee, "Can U.S. Business Cycles Still Be Dated by Monthly Coincident Indicators Alone?" *Business Cycle Indicator,* March 2005, 3–4.

36. "Business Cycle," Wikimedia Foundation Inc., 18 August 2008, http://en.wikipedia.org/wiki/Business_cycle.

Chapter 3

1. Robert J. Thomas, Joshua Bellin, Claudy Jules, and Nandani Lynton, "Developing Tomorrow's Global Leaders," *Sloan Management Review,* Fall 2013; and Gregory C. Unruh and Angel Cabera, "Join the Global Elite," *Harvard Business Review,* May 2013.

2. "World Population Clock," U.S. Census Bureau, http://www .census.gov/popclock/, April 2014; and WorldAtlas.com, April 2014; "Canada's Population Estimates: Fourth Quarter, 2014," Statistics Canada, 15 March 2015, http://www.statcan.gc.ca /daily-quotidien/150318/dq150318c-eng.pdf.

3. Russell Flannery, "What Can Be Done about the Big U.S. Trade Deficit with China?" *Forbes,* 3 August 2013; and Paul Davidson, "U.S. Trade Deficit Drops to 4-Year Low," *USA Today,* 7 January 2014.

4. Pascal Tremblay, "Canadian Trade and Investment Activity: Canada-China," Trade and Investment Series 2013, 14 July 2014, Library of Parliament Research Publications, http://www.parl.gc.ca/Content/LOP/ResearchPublications /2014-54-e.html.

5. "TSN shut out as Rogers signs 12-year $5.2B NHL deal, CBC job cuts loom after losing editorial control of HNIC," *National Post,* 26 November 2013, http://news.nationalpost.com/2013/11/26 /nhl-rogers-reach-12-year-5-2-billion-broadcast-deal-that-would -see-cbc-keep-hockey-night-in-canada/.

6. "Premiere League rights in Canada won by Sportsnet and TSN," News and Features, 29 October 2012, http://www .premierleague.com/en-gb/news/news/2012-13/oct/premier -league-rights-in-canada-won-by-sportsnet-and-tsn.html.

7. Ian Thomas, "NHL, union link World Cup, European appeal," *Street and Smith's SportBusiness Journal,* 2–8 March 2015, page 5; Chris Johnston, "NHL calls off next season's European premiere games," *The Globe and Mail,* 14 March 2012, http://www.theglobeandmail.com/sports/hockey/nhl-calls-off -next -seasons-european-premiere-games/article533801/.

8. "Profile," Bombardier Inc., 2015, http://ir.bombardier.com/en /profile.

9. Ibid.

10. "Hargrove calls for help from feds after another round of Chrysler cuts," CBC News, 24 July 2008, www.cbc.ca/canada /story/ 2008/07/24/chrysler-caw.html; Nicolas Van Praet, "Polywheels grinds to halt in Oakville," *Financial Post,* 10 July 2008, http://network.nationalpost.com/np/blogs/fpposted /archive/2008/07/10/polywheels-grinds-to-halt-in-oakville.aspx; "2,000 jobs lost as auto-parts plants close," The Canadian Press, 3 July 2008, www.cbc.ca/canada/toronto/story/2008/07/03 /plant-closure.html.

11. Kristine Owrami, "'We're fighting an uphill battle': When automakers' promises end, Canada may have to say goodbye," *Financial Post,* 23 August 2014, http://business.financialpost .com/2014/08/23/were-fighting-an-uphill-battle-when -automakers-promises-end-canada-may-have-to-say-goodbye/.

12. Matthew J. Slaughter, "Exports Sagging? Try Some Free Trade," *The Wall Street Journal,* 23 January 2013.

13. Robert Skidelsky, "In a World Based on Free Trade, Love Will Cost You," *Global Times,* 23 January 2014.

14. David Parkinson, "Canada's Trade Surplus Narrows to $99 million in October," *The Globe and Mail,* 5 December 2014, http://www .theglobeandmail.com/report-on-business/canadas-trade-surplus -narrows-to-99-million-in-october/article21966651/.

15. Michael McCrae, "Canada will double diamond production in four years," Mining.com, 13 October 2014, http://www.mining.com /chart-of-the-day-canada-on-track-to-double-diamond-production -over-the-next-four-years-97740/.

16. "Key Small Business Statistics," Industry Canada, August 2013, https://www.ic.gc.ca/eic/site/061.nsf/vwapj/KSBS -PSRPE_August-Aout2013_eng.pdf/$FILE/KSBS-PSRPE_August -Aout2013_eng.pdf.

17. "Canada's State of Trade 2011," Foreign Affairs and International Trade Canada, 2011, www.international.gc.ca/economist -economiste/assets/pdfs/SoT_2011_e.pdf; "Importing into Canada," Foreign Affairs and International Trade Canada, 26 May 2010, www.international.gc.ca/controls-controles /about-a_propos/impor/canada.aspx?menu_id=1&view=d; "Canada's Merchandise and Service Trade, 2007," adapted from Statistics Canada website "Exports of Goods on a Balance-of -Payments Basis, by Product," Statistics Canada, 13 August 2008, www40.statcan.ca/l01/cst01/gblec04.htm; "Imports of Goods on a Balance-of-Payments Basis, by Product," Statistics Canada, 13 August 2008, www40.statcan.ca/l01 /cst01/gblec05.htm; and "Canada's Balance of International Payments," Statistics Canada, 29 May 2008, www40. statcan.ca.libaccess.lib.mcmaster.ca/l01/cst01/econ01a. htm?sdi=services.

18. Canada's State of Trade: Trade and Investment Update 2012 - Table 2-1 World Merchandise Trade by Region and Selected Countries (US$ billions and %)," Foreign Affairs and International Trade Canada, 13 September 2012, http://www.international. gc.ca/economist-economiste/assets/pdfs/performance/ SoT_2012/SoT_2012_Eng.pdf, 16 and 23; and "Canada's State of Trade 2011," 35.

19. World Trade Organization, "International Trade Statistics, 2014," accessed 25 March 2015, https://www.wto.org/english /res_e/statis_e/its2014_e/its14_world_trade_dev_e.pdf.

20. "Canada's State of Trade: Trade and Investment Update 2014," Foreign Affairs, Trade, and Development Canada, accessed 27 March 2015, http://www.international.gc.ca/economist -economiste/performance/state-point/state_2014_point/index. aspx?lang=eng#2.0.

21. World Trade Organizations, "International Trade Statistics, 2014," accessed 25 March 2015, https://www.wto.org/english/res_e /statis_e/its2014_e/its14_world_trade_dev_e.pdf.

22. "Less dependent on Uncle Sam," *The Globe and Mail,* 6 February 2012, B10.

23. "Canada's State of Trade: Trade and Investment Update—2009," Foreign Affairs and International Trade Canada, 2009, www .international.gc.ca/economist-economiste/assets/pdfs /DFAIT_SoT_2009_en.pdf; "Seizing Global Advantage: A Global Commerce Strategy for Securing Canada's Growth & Prosperity," Foreign Affairs and International Trade Canada, 2008, www.international.gc.ca/commerce/assets/pdfs/GCS-en.pdf; "A Global Commerce Strategy for Securing Canada's Growth and Prosperity, A Message from the Minister," Foreign Affairs and

International Trade Canada, 12 August 2008, www.international
.gc.ca/commerce/strategy-strategie/minister-ministre.aspx; Jim
Middlemiss, "Canada Readying to Ride the Tiger," *Financial Post*,
28 May 2008, www.financialpost.com/reports/legal
/story.html?id=546037; "International Science and Technology
Partnerships Program—ISTPP," Foreign Affairs and International
Trade Canada, 5 June 2007, www.infoexport.gc.ca/science
/istpp-en.htm.

24. *Global Markets Action Plan*, Foreign Affairs, Trade and
Development Canada, accessed 27 March 2015 from http://
international.gc.ca/global-markets-marches-mondiaux/plan
.aspx?lang=eng#message.

25. www.goldmarks.com, accessed April 2014.

26. "About Us," Yogen Fruz, 2015, www.yogenfruz.com/home/en
/about-us.

27. "History and Company Facts," BeaverTails Pastry, 2015, www
.beavertailsinc.com.

28. "'YumBrands' world hunger relief efforts result in record breaking
$37 million in cash and food donations," *The Wall Street Journal*,
9 January 2014.

29. AnnaLisa Kraft, "Crazy Food you can't get here," *The Motley Fool*,
4 January 2014.

30. Flextronics, www.flextronics.com, accessed May 2012.

31. "FouFou Dog," *PROFIT*, 2009, http://list.canadianbusiness.com
/rankings/hot50/2008/DisplayProfile.aspx?profile=32; Jerry
Langton, "Canine Couture," *Toronto Star*, 17 November 2008,
www.thestar.com/Business/SmallBusiness/article/538014;
"About Us," FouFou Dog, 2009, www.foufoudog.com/about.html.

32. Zhou Wenting, "Full steam ahead for Shanghai Disney in 2015,"
China Daily USA, 24 January 2014.

33. Alby Gallum, "European hotel chain coming to River North,"
Crane Chicago Business, 24 January 2014.

34. "Pepsi announces plans for $5billion investment in Mexico,"
The Wall Street Journal, 24 January 2014.

35. CNNMoney, www.cnnmoney.com, accessed April 2014, and
Nestlé, wwwmestle.com, accessed 2014.

36. Mark Srite, "Levels of Culture and Individual Behavior:
An Integrative Perspective," *Journal of Global Information
Management*, 1 April 2005.

37. Susan Bergfield, "4 Countries Walmart Can't Conquer," *MSN
Money*, 15 October 2013; Walter Loeb, "Walmart: What
Happened in India?" *Forbes*, 16 October 2013; and Agustino
Fontevecchia, "IBM Falls Off Cliff as Q3 Sales Fall on Services
and Hardware Weakness," *Forbes*, 16 October 2013.

38. Nikhul Gulati and Rumman Ahmed, "India Has 1.2 Billion People
but Not Enough Drink Coke," *The Wall Street Journal*, 13 July
2012; Coca Cola, www.cocacola.com, accessed April 2014.

39. "In Dollars They Trust," *The Economist*, 27 April 2013.

40. Michelle Higgins, "The Greenback Is Losing Universal Appeal,"
The New York Times, 10 February 2008.

41. Simon Kennedy, "Developed Economies Seen Fighting Off
Emerging Market Contagion," *Bloomberg Businessweek*, 27
January 2014.

42. Taos Turner, Ken Parks, and Juan Foreno, "Crisis Squeeze Two
Latin Leaders," *The Wall Street Journal*, 26 January 2014; and
Jonathan Gilbert, Simon Romero, and William Neuman, "Erosian
of Argentine Peso Sends a Shudder Through Latin America," *The
New York Times*, 24 January 2014.

43. Christina LeBeau, "Rules of the Trade," *Entrepreneur*, February
2014.

44. www.wto.com, accessed April 2014.

45. Alexandra Wrage, "What Companies Can't Do about Corruption,"
Forbes, 24 January 2014.

46. United States Department of Commerce, International Trade
Administration – Fact Sheet, accessed 27 March 2015 http://
enforcement.trade.gov/download/factsheets/factsheet
-multiple-certain-crystalline-silicon-photovoltaic-products-ad-cvd
-final-121614.pdf.

47. Richard Blackwell, "Tariffs on Chinese solar panels may hurt
Canadian renewables industry," *The Globe and Mail*, 8 March 2015.

48. John Cotter, "Agriculture Minister Gerry Ritz threatens tariffs
on U.S. goods over meat labeling laws," *Huffington Post*, 29
December 2014, http://www.huffingtonpost.ca/2014/12/29
/country-of-origin-laws-gerry-ritz_n_6389276.html.

49. "Controlled Products," Foreign Affairs, Trade and Development
Canada, 2 February 2012, www.international.gc.ca/controls
-controles/prod/index.aspx?menu_id=1&view=d.

50. "Exporting," Foreign Affairs, Trade and Development Canada,
2 February 2012, www.international.gc.ca/controls-controles
/about-a_propos/expor/before-avant.aspx?lang=eng&view=d.

51. "Canadian Sanctions Related to North Korea," Foreign Affairs,
Trade and Development Canada, 13 November 2013, http://
www.international.gc.ca/sanctions/certificates_permits
-certificats_permis.aspx?lang=eng.

52. "The Hidden Persuaders: Protectionism Can Take Many Forms,
Not All of Them Obvious," *The Economist*, 12 October 2013.

53. "Canadian beef banned in Peru, Taiwan, and Belarus over mad
cow case," CBC.ca, 23 February 2015, http://www.cbc.ca/news
/canada/calgary/canadian-beef-banned-in-peru-taiwan-and
-belarus-over-mad-cow-case-1.2968050.

54. David Nicklaus, "WTO Talks Could Boost Trade by $1 Trillion," *St.
Louis Post Dispatch*, 8 December 2013.

55. "Life After Doha," *The Economist*, 14 December 2013.

56. "North American Free Trade Agreement (NAFTA), Foreign Affairs,
Trade and Development Canada, 24 December 2014, http://
www.international.gc.ca/trade-agreements-accords-commerciaux
/agr-acc/nafta-alena/info.aspx?lang=eng.

57. The World Bank, "Data: European Union," accessed 8 July 2015,
http://data.worldbank.org/region/EUU.

58. Emma Ross Thomas, "EU Says Spain Should Improve Bank
Monitoring as Bailout Ends," *Bloomberg Businessweek*, 29
January 2014; and Juergen Baetz, "EU Seeks to Make Mega-
Banks Less Risky," *Bloomberg Businessweek*, 29 January 2014.

59. "Canadian-European Union: Comprehensive Economic and Trade
Agreement," Foreign Affairs, Trade and Development Canada,
accessed 27 March 2015, http://international.gc.ca
/trade-agreements-accords-commerciaux/agr-acc/ceta-aecg
/understanding-comprendre/overview-apercu.aspx?lang=eng.

60. Ibid.

61. Canada's Free Trade Agreements, Foreign Affairs, Trade and
Development Canada, 18 December 2013, http://www
.international.gc.ca/trade-agreements-accords-commerciaux
/agr-acc/fta-ale.aspx?lang=eng; "Canada–India Joint Study
Group Report: Exploring the Feasibility of a Comprehensive
Economic Partnership Agreement," 14 February 2013, http://www
.international.gc.ca/trade-agreements-accords-commerciaux
/agr-acc/india-inde/summary-resume-1.aspx?lang=eng.

62. Jamil Anderlini and Lucy Hornby, "China Overtakes U.S. as
World's Largest Goods Trader," *Financial Times*, 10 January 2014.

63. Liyan Qi and Grace Zhu, "China's Capital Inflows, Foreign Direct
Investment Rose in 2013," *The Wall Street Journal*, 16 January
2014.

64. www.goldmansachs.com, accessed April 2014; and Morris
Beschloss, "Will China Overtake U.S. GDP World Leadership by
2028?" *The Desert Sun (Gannett)*, 23 January 2014.

65. Samuel Shen and Norihiko Shirozu, "China Auto Market Seen
Cruising to Another Strong Year," Reuters, January 12, 2014.

66. Yvonne Lee and Prudence Ho, "IMAX Bets on China
with $300 Million Hong Kong IPO," *The Wall Street
Journal*, 16 June 2014, http://www.wsj.com/articles
/imax-bets-on-china-with-300-million-hong-kong-ipo-1434433944.

67. Profile, Strategy and Market, Bombardier Inc., February 2015,
http://ir.bombardier.com.

68. "Can India Become a Great Power?" *The Economist*, 30 March
2013; and Philip Stephens, "India Still a Contender in the Asian
Race," *Financial Times*, 30 January 2014.

69. Paul Hannon, "EBRD Reduces Investment in Russia," *The Wall
Street Journal*, 15 January 2014; Mark Adomanis, "Russia's
Economic Performance Is Actually Very Similar to Other East
European Countries," *Forbes*, 20 January 2014.

Chapter 4

1. Ongoing Free Trade Negotiations, Canada's Free Trade Agreements, Foreign Affairs, Trade and Development Canada, 2013, http://www.international.gc.ca/trade-agreements-accords -commerciaux/agr-acc/fta-ale.aspx?lang=eng downloaded 29 March 2015.
2. Corporate Profiles-Crown Corporations, Treasury Board of Canada Secretariat, 2015, http://www.tbs-sct.gc.ca/reports-rapports /cc-se/corporate-societe/ccp-pse-eng.asp' downloaded 29 March 2015.
3. Crown Corporations, Government of Saskatchewan, 2015, https://www.saskatchewan.ca/government/government -structure/crown-corporations; downloaded 29 March 2015.
4. "Alberta Heritage Savings Trust Fund 2014-15 Third Quarter Update," 24 February 2015, http://www.finance.alberta.ca /business/ahstf/quarterly-reports/2014-3rdq/Heritage -Fund-2014-15-3rd-Quarter-Report.pdf.
5. Nicholas Van Preet, "Quebec turns to pension giant Caisse to help fund transit projects," The Globe and Mail, 12 January 2015, http://www.theglobeandmail.com/report-on-business /quebec-turns-to-pension-giant-caisse-to-help-fund-transit-projects /article22421827/.
6. Adrian Morrow, Jacqueline Nelson, and Sean Silcoff, "The long road to privatization of Hydro One," The Globe and Mail, 13 March 2015, http://www.theglobeandmail.com/report-on -business/wynnes-quest-for-full-valuethe-long-road-to-privatization /article23461789/.
7. "Where Our Legal System Comes From," Department of Justice Canada, 11 March 2015, http://www.justice.gc.ca/eng/csj-sjc /just/03.html.
8. Forsey, How Canadians Govern Themselves, 6th ed., Government of Canada, 2005, www.parl.gc.ca/information/library/idb /forsey/index-e.asp; "Canada Health Transfer," Department of Finance Canada, 19 December 2011, www.fin.gc.ca/fedprov /cht-eng.asp.
9. "Federal Support to Provinces and Territories," Department of Finance, 15 December 2014, http://www.fin.gc.ca/fedprov/mtp -eng.asp; "Future Cost of health Care in Canada, 2000–2020," Conference Board of Canada, 2011, http://www.teamgrant .ca/M-THAC%20Greatest%20Hits/Bonus%20Tracks/FutureHealth .pdf; downloaded 4 April 2015.
10. Jamie Sturgeon, "5 ways trade barriers are harming Canada's economy," Globalnews, 19 August 2014.
11. Jeff Gray, "Hershey, Cadbury lose bid to keep documents secret," 11 February 2015, The Globe and Mail, http://www .theglobeandmail.com/report-on-business/industry-news /the-law-page/hershey-cadbury-lose-bid-to-keep-documents -secret/article22925825/; Peter Taylor, "How Canada's Competition Bureau makes products more expensive," MoneySense, 25 March 2015, http://www.moneysense .ca/spend/price-fixing-of-consumer-products; "Chocolate price fixing coasts candy makers $23M," CBCNews, 17 September 2013, http://www.cbc.ca/news/business /chocolate-price-fixing-costs-candy-makers-23m-1.1857642.
12. "In Focus – EU-Canada Comprehensive Economic and Trade Agreement," Trade, European Commission, 19 December 2014, http://ec.europa.eu/trade/policy/in-focus/ceta/.
13. Paul Waldie, "Judge weights Wheat Board bid for injunction against Tories," The Globe and Mail, 17 January 2012, www .theglobeandmail.com/news/politics/judge-weighs-wheat-board -bid-for-injunction-against-tories/article2305555/; "About Us," Canadian Wheat Board, 29 June 2009 and 7 September 2008, www.cwb.ca; "Canadian Wheat Board Gag Order Unconstitutional, Court Rules," CBC.ca, 20 June 2008, www.cbc.ca/canada /saskatchewan/story/2008/06/20/cwb-ruling.html; and "Strahl Must Defend Canadian Wheat Board and Supply Management," Liberal Party of Canada, 15 March 2006, www.liberal.ca/news_e .aspx? id=11502.
14. Eric Atkins, "Canadian Wheat Board deal with U.S., Saudi group ends an era," The Globe and Mail, 15 April 2015, http://www.theglobeandmail.com/report-on-business /us-saudi-firms-to-buy-former-canadian-wheat-board /article23966156/.
15. Janyce McGregor, "Canadian Wheat Board prepares for takeover," CBCNews, 1 December 2014, http://www.cbc.ca/news /politics/canadian-wheat-board-prepares-for-corporate-takeover-1.2853874.
16. Forsey, How Canadians Govern Themselves; "What the world can learn from Canada's P3 record," Canadian Council for Public-Private Partnerships, February 2015, http://www.pppcouncil.ca /news/551-report-what-the-world-can-learn-from-canadas-p3-record .html; "The P3 Pulse: National and Community Opinions on Public-Private Partnerships in Canada," Canadian Council for Public-Private Partnerships, 10 April 2014, http://www.pppcouncil.ca /resources/issues/public-opinion-and-communications.html.
17. "Canada's evolving internal market: an agenda for a more cohesive economic union," Canada's Public Policy Forum, October 2013, http://www.ppforum.ca/sites/default/files/PPF%20 AIT%20final%20report.pdf; Patrick Grady and Lathleen Macmillan, "Inter-provincial barriers to labour mobility in Canada: policy, knowledge gaps and research issues," Working Paper Series, Industry Canada, 2007, https://www.ic.gc.ca/eic/site/eas-aes .nsf/vwapj/wp200710.pdf/$file/wp200710.pdf, downloaded 5 April 2015; "Improving Internal Trade: A Bold Approach," Certified General Accountants Association of Canada, 2008, www.cga -canada.org/en-ca/DiscussionPapers/ca_rep_internal_trade _position-paper2008.pdf; "Overview of the Agreement on Internal Trade, 2009."
18. Forsey, How Canadians Govern Themselves.
19. "Government subsidies in Canada: a $684 billion price tag," Fraser Institute, 13 May 2014, https://www.fraserinstitute.org /research-news/display.aspx?id=21186.
20. "Pratt & Whitney jet engine plants get $300M in investment," CBCNews, 8 December 2014, http://www.cbc.ca/news /business/pratt-whitney-jet-engine-plants-get-300m-in-federal -investment-1.2864129.
21. Milagros Palacios and Niels Veldhuis, "Taxes versus the Necessities of Life: The Canadian Consumer Tax Index 2012 Edition," The Fraser Institute, April 2012, www.fraserinstitute. org/uploadedFiles/fraser-ca/Content/research-news/research/ publications/canadian-consumer-tax-index-2012.pdf.
22. Palacios and Lamman, "Taxes versus the Necessities of Life,"
23. Elliot Ferguson, "Report distracts from problematic tax system: Pro," The Whig-Standard, 27 April 2012, www.thewhig.com /ArticleDisplay.aspx?e=3545447.
24. Madhavi Yes, "Does cutting business tax stimulate the economy?" The Toronto Star, 15 May 2014, http://www.thestar .com/business/2014/05/15/does_cutting_business_tax _stimulate_the_economy.html.
25. Milagros Palacio, Hugh MacIntyre, and Charles Lamman, "Canadian Government Debt 2014," Fraser Institute, April 2014, https://www.fraserinstitute.org/uploadedFiles/fraser-ca /Content/research-news/research/publications/canadian-government-debt-2014.pdf.
26. Vito Pilieci, "Quebec made most of $2B Economic Action Plan infrastructure fund," Ottawa Citizen, 3 March 2015, http:// ottawacitizen.com/news/national/majority-of-loans-from-key -canada-economic-action-plan-fund-went-to-quebec-shining-a -spotlight-on-government-loan-programs-during-recession.
27. "Budget Deficit in 2009–10, Flaherty Confirms," CBC News, 17 December 2008, www.cbc.ca/canada/story/2008/12/17 /finance-meeting.html; "Top TD Economist Sees Lingering Canadian Deficits," Reuters, 2 June 2009, http://finance .sympatico.msn.ca/investing/news/breakingnews/article .aspx?cp-documentid=20169426.
28. "Key numbers in Canada's provincial budgets – Federal," CBCNews, 24 April 2012, www.cbc.ca/news/interactives /budgets/provinces.
29. Lee Whittington, "Joe Oliver postpones federal budget as oil price plummets," The Toronto Star, 15 January 2015, http://www .thestar.com/news/canada/2015/01/15/joe-oliver-postpones -federal-budget-as-oil-price-plummets.html.

30. Meaghan Fitzpatrick, "15 ways to use a 450-page federal budget bill," CBCNews, 23 May 2012, http://www.cbc.ca/news/politics/15-ways-to-use-a-450-page-federal-budget-bill-1.1131127; Robin Grant, "Everything you need to know about budget Bill C_38," *Vancouver Observer,* 27 June 2012, http://www.vancouverobserver.com/politics/bill-c-38-explainer.

31. Tavia Grant, "Study finds Canadians aren't feeling economic growth in their daily lives," *The Globe and Mail,* 23 October 2012, http://www.theglobeandmail.com/news/national/study-finds-canadians-arent-feeling-economic-growth-in-their-daily-lives/article4630393/.

32. "Global Banking Regulations and Banks in Canada," Canadian Bankers Association, 13 March 2015, http://www.cba.ca/en/media-room/50-backgrounders-on-banking-issues/667-global-banking-regulations-and-banks-in-canada; "Research Findings: What Canadians think about their banks," Canadian Bankers Association, December 2013, http://www.cba.ca/contents/files/submissions/msc_2013cba-poll_en.pdf; "Glossary: Vocabulary for a Financial Crisis," CBC News, 24 March 2009, www.cbc.ca/money/story/2008/10/24/f-econoglossary.html; "Canada's Banks: Admired Worldwide for their Management—and Cash," CBC News, 3 March 2009, www.cbc.ca/money/story/2009/03/03/f-canada-banks.html; "$25B Credit Backstop for Banks 'Not a Bailout': Harper," CBC News, 10 October 2008, www.cbc.ca/canada/story/2008/10/10/flaherty-banks.html; Michel Chossudovsky, "Canada's 75 Billion Dollar Bank Bailout," Global Research, 25 January 2009, www.globalresearch.ca/index.php?context=va&aid=12007; Stefan Theil, "Europe's Bank Bailout: Is It Enough?" *Newsweek,* 13 October 2008, http://blog.newsweek.com/blogs/ov/archive/2008/10/13/europe-bank-bailout-is-it-enough.aspx; Kimberly Amadeo, "Understanding the Subprime Mortgage Crisis," About.com, 2008, http://useconomy.about.com/od/economicindicators/tp/Subprime-Mortgage-Primer.htm; Joel Schlesinger, "Why the Bank of Canada Is Doing What It's Doing," *Winnipeg Free Press,* 31 May 2009, www.winnipegfreepress.com/business/making-the-money-move-46566862.html?viewAllComments=y; Peter Henderson, "Canadians not told about 'secret bailout' for banks: study," *The Gazette,* 30 April 2012, www.montrealgazette.com/business/Canadians+told+about+secret+bailout+banks+study/6543481/story.html; "Occupy movement," Wikimedia Foundation, Inc., 5 May 2012, http://en.wikipedia.org/wiki/Occupy_movement.

33. "Canadian Subsidy Directory," Canadian Publications, 2015, http://grantscanada.org/grants-and-loans.htm#CSD.

34. "FedDev Ontario invests in Angel Organizations across Southern Ontario," Government of Canada, 20 November 2014, http://news.gc.ca/web/article-en.do?nid=906429.

35. "Harper Government supports Aboriginal participation in the development of Northern Quebec," Government of Canada, 19 November 2014, http://news.gc.ca/web/article-en.do?nid=906169.

36. "Quebec pledges $1-billion to Bombardier CSeries buyers," *Financial Post,* 3 April 2013, http://business.financialpost.com/news/transportation/quebec-pledges-1-billion-bombardier-cseries-buyers.

37. Nicholas Van Praet, "Quebec prepares to bailout Bombardier, minister says," *The Globe and Mail,* 18 February 2015, http://www.theglobeandmail.com/report-on-business/quebec-prepared-to-bail-out-bombardier-minister-says/article23051005/.

38. Sustainable Development Technology Canada-About Us, 2015, https://www.sdtc.ca/en/about/about-us, downloaded 5 April 2015; "Canada's Economic Action Plan," Sustainable Development Technology Canada, http://actionplan.gc.ca/en/initiative/sustainable-development-technology-canada, downloaded 5 April 2015; Sustainable Development Technology Canada-Projects, 2015, https://www.sdtc.ca/en/about-sdtc/about-us, downloaded 5 April 2015; "Green entrepreneurs attend Sustainable Development Technology Canada Workshop," PR Associates, 29 September 2014, http://www.prassociates.com/blog/2014/green-entrepreneurs-attend-sustainable-development-technology-canada-workshop.

39. Phillipe Karam, "Energy Subsidy Reform Lessons and Implications," International Monetary Fund, November 2013, http://www.oecd.org/gov/budgeting/Doha%202013%20-%208%20presentations%20in%20ENGLISH.pdf.

40. "Energy Subsidy Reform: Lessons and Implications," International Monetary Fund, 28 January 2013, http://www.imf.org/external/np/pp/eng/2013/012813.pdf.

41. Derek Wong, "Fossil fuel subsidies nearly $800 per Canadian, says the IMF," Toronto Sustainability Speaker Series, 17 April 2013, http://ecoopportunity.net/2013/04/fossil-fuel-subsidies-nearly-800-per-canadian-says-the-imf/.

42. Jehan Sauvage, "Through the looking glass: transparency and fossil-fuel subsidies," OECD, Trade and Agriculture Directorate, November 2013, http://www.oecd.org/gov/budgeting/Doha%202013%20-%208%20presentations%20in%20ENGLISH.pdf.

43. "Federal support to provinces and territories," Department of Finance Canada, 15 December 2014, http://www.fin.gc.ca/fedprov/mtp-eng.asp.

44. "Preparing to sell to the Government," Government of Canada, 5 May 2012, www.canadabusiness.ca/eng/page/2757/.

45. "Overview," MERX, 2012, www.merx.com/English/NonMember.asp?WCE=Show&TAB=1&PORTAL=MERX&State=6&hcode=G4neZSoJOB3Ef%2bl2%2bfWuBQ%3d%3d.

46. "About NRC," National Research Council Canada, 15 January 2015, http://www.nrc-cnrc.gc.ca/eng/about/index.html.

47. Control Greenhouse Emissions or Face Trade Sanctions, Panel Tells Governments," The Canadian Press, 16 April 2009, www.cbc.ca/news/story/2009/04/16/tech-090416-cap-and-trade-greenhouse-gas.html; "Government Policy Options," The Pembina Foundation, 2009, www.greenlearning.ca/climate/policy/canadian-policy-directions/2.

48. "Trade and Investment at 10," Foreign Affairs and International Trade Canada, 10 July 2007, www.dfait-maeci.gc.ca/canada-magazine/issue24/06-title-en.asp.

49. "Glossary of Key Terms: Minority Government," British Columbia Referendum Office, 2009, www.gov.bc.ca/referendum_info/first_past_the_post_bc_stv/glossary.html.

50. "Paper trail: the decline of Canada's forestry industry," *The Globe and Mail,* 5 December 2014, http://www.theglobeandmail.com/report-on-business/economy/paper-trail-the-fall-of-forestry/article21967746/.

Chapter 5

1. Brent Jang, "WestJet Admits Spying," globeandmail.com, 29 May 2006, www.theglobeandmail.com/servlet/story/RTGAM.20060529.waircanada0529/BNStory/Business.

2. Ibid.

3. Laura Payton, "Conservatives deny party focus of robocalls probe," CBC News, 17 April 2012, www.cbc.ca/news/politics/story/2012/04/17/pol-robocalls-guelph-investigation-extends.html.

4. Ibid.

5. "Key facts in Canada's robocalls controversy," CBCNews, 14 August 2014, http://www.cbc.ca/news/politics/key-facts-in-canada-s-robocalls-controversy-1.2736659.

6. Ottawa Citizen Editorial Board, "Editorial: Elections Canada should re-open robocalls investigation," *Ottawa Citizen,* 15 August 2014, http://ottawacitizen.com/news/national/editorial-elections-canada-should-re-open-robocalls-investigation.

7. Government of Ontario, *Land Claims in Ontario, 2012–2015,* https://www.ontario.ca/aboriginal/land-claims-ontario, downloaded 20 April 2015; Brian Hutchison, "Supreme Court B.C. land-claim ruling has staggering implications for Canadian resource projects," *The National Post,* 26 June 2014, http://news.nationalpost.com/news/canada/supreme-court-b-c-land-claim-ruling-has-staggering-implications-for-canadian-energy-projects.

8. Pallavi Guniganti, "Ethics' Place in Education," *University Wire,* 16 April 2002.

9. Mark Steyn, "Conrad Black Trial," *Maclean's,* 24 December 2008, http://forums.macleans.ca/advansis/?mod=for&act=dis&eid=52&so=1&sb=1&ps=5; "Former Sponsorship Ad Exec Facing Criminal Charges," CBC News, 17 December 2008, www.cbc.ca/canada/story/2008/12/17/gosselin-charges.html; "Chicago Judges Reject Request to Reconsider Conrad Black's Appeal," CBC News, 21 August 2008, www.cbc.ca/money/story/2008/08/21/black.html; "Police Probe in Lottery Scandal not Over Yet," CBC News, 20 December 2007, www.cbc.ca/canada/toronto/story/2007/12/20/lottery-investigation.html; "Forgive and (Maybe) Forget," Canadian Business Online, 6 November 2007, www.canadianbusiness.com/columnists/john_gray/article.jsp?content=20071106_153800_5340; "Lotto 6/49 Bonus Rounds Coincided with Lottery Scandals," CBC News, 30 May 2007, www.cbc.ca/canada/toronto/story/2007/05/30/lotto649-bonus-rounds.html; "U.S. Judge Decides not to Revoke Black's Bond," CTV.ca, 26 June 2006, www.ctv.ca/servlet/ArticleNews/story/CTVNews/20060626/black_bond_060626/20060626/; Ross Marowits, "Guite Sentenced to 3 1/2 Years in Prison," Canoe Inc., 19 June 2006, http://CNRews.canoe.ca/CNREWS/Law/2006/03/29/1511209-cp.html; and "Federal Sponsorship Scandal," CBC News Online, 19 June 2006, www.cbc.ca/news/background/groupaction/.

10. Jahnabi Barooah, "The Golden Rule in World Religions (Quotes)," *Huffington Post,* www.huffingtonpost.com, downloaded April 2014.

11. Turnitin, www.turnitin.com, downloaded April 2014; and "Turnitin for iPad Surpasses 100,000 Downloads," *The Sacramento Bee,* 14 January 2014.

12. Thomas Ehrlich and Ernestine Fu, "Cheating in Schools and Colleges," *Forbes,* 22 August 2013.

13. Kenneth Blanchard and Norman Vincent Peale, *The Power of Ethical Management* (New York: William Morrow, 1996).

14. Will Yakowicz, "A New Website That Helps CEOs Lead More Ethically," *Inc.,* 22 January 2014; "Integrity in the Boardroom," www.wsj.com, downloaded April 2014; Donna Boehme, "5 New Year's Compliance Resolutions for Boards in 2014," *Connecticut Law Tribune,* 2 January 2014; Victor Lipman, "New Study Shows Transparency Isn't Just Good Ethics—It's Good Business," *Forbes,* 11 December 2013; Rachel Louis Ensign, "Whistleblowers Coming from Compliance Departments," *The Wall Street Journal,* 6 November 2013; Venessa Wong, "So You Want to Be a Whistle-Blower . . .," *Bloomberg Businessweek,* 11 June 2013; and Paul J. H. Schoemaker, "How to Defuse an Ethical Time-Bomb in Your Company," *Inc.,* 10 June 2014.

15. "A brief history of SNC-Lavalin," CBC News, 30 April 2012, www.cbc.ca/news/business/story/2012/04/30/snc-lavalin-faq.html.

16. Ibid.

17. Graeme Hamilton, "RCMP charges SNC-Lavalin with fraud and corruption linked to Libyan projects," *The Financial Post,* 19 February 2015, http://business.financialpost.com/news/rcmp-charges-snc-lavalin-with-fraud-and-corruption-linked-to-libyan-projects.

18. Tony Wilson, "The Best Legal Advice is Often an Apology," *The Globe and Mail,* 1 February 2011, http://www.theglobeandmail.com/report-on-business/small-business/sb-growth/day-to-day/the-best-legal-advice-is-often-an-apology/article626797/.

19. Stephen Spector, "SOX and SOX North, Part 3 The Impact of SOX," Professional Development Network, www.cga-pdnet.org/Non_VerifiableProducts/ArticlePublication/SOX_E/SOX_part_3.pdf; "What is SOX?" Metso Corporation, 10 March 2006, www.metso.com/corporation/home_eng.nsf/FR?ReadForm&ATL=/corporation/articles_eng.nsf/WebWID/WTB-050704-2256F-A1200; Curtis Verschoor, "Is This the Age of Whistleblowers?" *Strategic Finance,* 1 February 2005; Guillermo Contreras, "San Antonio Whistleblower Doubly Rewarded in Exposing HealthSouth Fraud," *San Antonio Express News,* 14 January 2005; and Paul K. Mcmasters, "Inside the First Amendment: Blowing the Whistle Can Also Blow a Career," *Gannett News Service,* 16 January 2006.

20. Rob Ferguson, "ORNGE: Proposed bill would block ombudsman oversight," Queen's Park Bureau, 27 April 2012, www.thestar.com/news/canada/politics/article/1169002–ornge-proposed-bill-would-block-ombudsman-oversight; James Wood, "Alberta's lack of whistleblower law criticized," FAIR, 19 March 2012, http://fairwhistleblower.ca/content/albertas-lack-whistleblower-law-criticized; Kevin Donovan, "$25M in ORNGE money unaccounted for," *The Toronto Star,* 24 February 2012, www.thestar.com/news/canada/politics/article/1136628–25m-in-ornge-money-unaccounted-for; Kevin Donovan, "Whistleblower warned Ministry about ORNGE in 2008, "Federal Accountability Initiative for Reform, 3 February 2012, http://fairwhistleblower.ca/content/ministry-was-warned-about-ornge-spending-four-years-ago-whistleblower-says; "Federal Conservatives broke their whistleblower protection and open government election promises, as the Afghan prisoner scandal makes clear," Democracy Watch, 2010, www.dwatch.ca/camp/OpEdNov2509.html; David Hutton and Gerard Seijts, "Canada needs whistleblowers to protect stimulus package," *The Hill Times,* 16 February 2009, http://fairwhistleblower.ca/news/articles/2009-02-16_Canada_needs_whistleblowers_to_protect_stimulus_package.html; "Ontario passes whistleblower law," Canadian Press, 13 December 2006, www.thestar.com/news/article/148456—ontario-passes-whistleblower-law; and "Providing real protection for whistleblowers," Treasury Board of Canada Secretariat, 11 April 2006, www.tbs-sct.gc.ca/faa-lfi/fs-fi/16/09fs-fi-eng.asp.

21. John S. McClenahen, "Defining Social Responsibility," *Industry Week,* 1 March 2005.

22. Doug Guthrie, "A Conversation on Corporate Social Responsibility," *Forbes,* 9 January 2014.

23. Aoltan J. Acs, "A Buffett Rule Worth Following," *The Wall Street Journal,* 28 March 2013.

24. Michael Cohn, "Investors Swayed by Corporate Social Responsibility Reputation," *Accounting Today,* 10 January 2014.

25. Canadian Tire Jumpstart: How we can help, http://jumpstart.canadiantire.ca/en/how-we-help/how-jumpstart-helps, downloaded 22 April 2015.

26. Annie Gasparro, "A New Test for Panera's Pay-What-You-Can," *The Wall Street Journal,* 5 June 2013.

27. TNT, www.tnt.com, downloaded April 2014.

28. Patagonia, www.patagonia.com, downloaded April 2014.

29. Xerox, www.xerox.com, downloaded April 2014.

30. Sarah Halzack, "Paid Time Off for Volunteering Gains Traction as Way to Retain Employees," *The Washington Post,* 11 August 2013.

31. David A. Kaplan, "Inside Mars," *Fortune,* 4 February 2013.

32. Toronto Dominion Bank-Corporate Responsibility Communities, http://www.td.com/corporate-responsibility/community/index.jsp, downloaded 22 April 2015.

33. "Canada's big banks saw profits up in 2014, warn challenges ahead," CTVNews, 5 December 2015, http://www.ctvnews.ca/business/canada-s-big-banks-saw-profits-up-in-2014-warn-challenges-ahead-1.2135107.

34. Debbie Haski-Leventhal, *MBA Students Around the World and Their Attitudes Towards Responsible Management,* Second Annual Study (Macquarie Graduate School of Management, 2013).

35. "Corporate Social Responsibility," Wikimedia Foundation, Inc., 5 June 2009, http://en.wikipedia.org/wiki/Corporate_social_responsibility.

36. "50 Percent of Global Consumers Surveyed Willing to Pay More for Goods, Services from Socially Responsible Companies, Up From 2011," Nielsen, www.nielsen.com, downloaded March 2014.

37. Kris Hudson, "Oh, Give Me a Home Where the Prairie Dogs Roam—in Boulder," *The Wall Street Journal,* 20 May 2006, http://www.wsj.com/articles/SB114808815360858621.

38. Eric Gneckow, "'Socially Responsible Investing Steps Toward Mainstream," *North Bay Business Journal,* 6 January 2014; "Earl Jones gets 11 years for $50M Ponzi scheme," *The Gazette,* 16 February 2010, www.montrealgazette.com/news/Earl+Jones+gets+years+swindling/2567329/story.html;

Sidhartha Banerjee, "Disgraced Financier Lived Lavishly," The Canadian Press, 30 July 2009, www.thestar.com/news/canada/article/673888; "Trustee Sues Madoff's Wife for $45M," CBS News, 29 July 2009, www.cbsnews.com/stories/2009/07/29/business/main5196249.shtml?source=related_story&tag=related; "Nortel May Lose NYSE Listing," CBC News, 11 December 2008, www.cbc.ca/mobile/text/story_news-technology.html?/ept/html/story/2008/12/11/nortellisting.html; Steven Skurka, "Black vs. Drabinsky: Two Trials, Two Very Different Systems," National Post, 4 June 2009, http://network.nationalpost.com/np/blogs/fullcomment/archive/2009/06/04/steven-skurka-on-black-vs-drabinsky-two-trials-two-very-different-systems.aspx; "Livent Sentencing Hearing Postponed," The Canadian Press, 3 June 2009, www.thestar.com/article/644834; Joe Schneider, "Livent Founders Convicted of C$500 Million Fraud (Update3)," Bloomber.com, 25 March 2009, www.bloomberg.com/apps/news?pid=20601082&sid=aBkY_Qtnf9y8&refer=Canada; Stephen Payne, "Investors Oppose SEC Proposal on Shareholder Rights," Oil & Gas Investor, 1 January 2008; and Robert Kuttner, "Dishonest Capitalism Won't Go Unpunished," Businessweek, 23 May 2005, 32.

39. Jeff Gray and Jacquie McNish, "Mitchell Finkelstein passed deal tips to fraternity friend, OSC rules," The Globe and Mail, 25 March 2015, http://www.theglobeandmail.com/report-on-business/industry-news/the-law-page/osc-rules-finkelstein-fed-tips-to-friend-on-corporate-deals/article23610690/; Tara Perkins, "Andrew Rankin Gets 6 Months in Canada's 1st Stock-Tipping Conviction," CBC News, 10 April 2005, www.cbc.ca/cp/business/051027/b1027100.html; "Former RBC Dominion Securities Exec Faces Insider Trading Charges," CBC News, 5 February 2004, www.cbc.ca/stories/2004/02/04/rankin040204; Nancy Carr, "Daniel Duic to Pay $1.9M, Stop Trading in Ont., Testify at Rankin Trial: OSC," Canoe Money, 3 March 2004, http://money.canoe.ca/News/Other/2004/03/03/369029-cp.html.

40. Marina Strauss, "Foot-dragging in garment factory reform draws ire of Loblaw's Weston," The Globe and Mail, 18 September 2013, http://www.theglobeandmail.com/report-on-business/international-business/asian-pacific-business/foot-dragging-in-garment-factory-reform-draws-ire-of-loblaws-weston/article14403359/; "Loblaw Companies Limited updated statement on Bangladesh," Loblaw Companies limited: Company Statements, http://www.loblaw.ca/English/Media-Centre/announcements/default.aspx, downloaded 23 April 2014.

41. Bill Catlette and Richard Hadden, Contented Cows Still Give Better Milk, Contented Cow Partners, www.contentedcows.com, downloaded March 2014.

42. Costco, www.costco.com, downloaded March 2014.

43. Heather Boushey and Sarah Jane Glenn, "There Are Significant Business Costs to Replacing Employees," Center for American Progress, www.centerforamericanprogress.org, downloaded March 2014; and Suzanne Lucas, "How Much Employee Turnover Really Costs You," Inc., August 13. 2013.

44. "2014 Global Fraud Study," Association of Certified Fraud Examiners, http://www.acfe.com/rttn/docs/2014-report-to-nations.pdf, downloaded 25 April 2015.

45. Canadian Retail Security Survey, 2012, PricewaterhouseCoopers LLP, http://www.pwc.com/ca/retailsecuritysurvey, downloaded 24 April 2015.

46. Heather Green and Kerry Capell, "Carbon Confusion," Businessweek, 6 March 2008.

47. Colin Perkel, "Harris Apologizes for Government's Role in Tragedy," 18 January 2002, Canoe C-Health, www.canoe.ca/EcoliTragedy/020118_report-cp.html.

48. Eric Pfeiffer, "BP oil spill two-year anniversary marked by somber statistics," The Sideshow, 20 April 2012, http://news.yahoo.com/blogs/sideshow/bp-oil-spill-two-anniversary-marked-somber-statistics-185242840.html; "BP oil disaster largely blamed on cement failure," The Associated Press, 14 September 2011, www.cbc.ca/news/world/story/2011/09/14/bp-offshore-oil-spill-report.html; Sylvia Pfeifer and Sheila McNulty,

"BP oil spill confirmed as 'world's worst," The Financial Times, 3 August 2010, www.ft.com/cms/s/0/3e40d4ac-9e5d-11df-a5a4-00144feab49a.html#axzz1uZlfDvgn; Jim MacDonald, "Syncrude Charged after 500 Ducks Perished on Oilsands Pond," The Canadian Press, 9 February 2009, www.thestar.com/article/584719; "About Imagine—Who We Are," Imagine Canada, 2008, www.imagine.ca/content/about_imagine/who_we_are.asp?section=about; "Home," Jantzi Research, 2005, www.jantziresearch.com; "Our Site Overview," Province of Nova Scotia: Sydney Tar Ponds Agency, 2004, www.gov.ns.ca/stpa; Chris Sebastian, "Canada Getting Tough on Spills," Times Herald, 12 May 2004, www.thetimesherald.com/news/stories/20040512/localnews/403633.html; Pat Currie, "All's Not Well in This Valley," Lake Ontario Waterkeeper, 3 April 2004, www.waterkeeper.ca/lok; "The Great Lakes Atlas," The United States Environmental Protection Agency, 2003, www.epa.gov/glnpo/atlas; "Tar Ponds in Sydney, Nova Scotia," PageWise Inc., 2002, http://tntn.essortment.com/tarpondssydney_rhxq.htm; and "Sydney Nova Scotia Tar Ponds Move Closer to Cleanup" Ellicott, www.dredge.com/casestudies/enviro8.htm.

49. Erin Pottie, "Sydney tar ponds lawsuit quashed by Supreme Court," Herald News, 16 January 2015, http://thechronicleherald.ca/novascotia/1263229-sydney-tar-ponds-lawsuit-quashed-by-supreme-court.

50. Associated Press, "Judge's decision could cost BP $13bn for Deepwater Horizon oil spill," The Guardian, 15 January 2015, http://www.theguardian.com/business/2015/jan/15/bp-13bn-cost-deepwater-horizon-oil-spill.

51. "Just What Is a Carbon Tax?" CBC News, 29 September 2008, www.cbc.ca/news/canadavotes/story/2008/09/19/f-carbontaxprimer.html; "Carbon Taxes: Cash Grab or Climate Saviour?" CBC News, 19 June 2008, www.cbc.ca/canada/story/2008/06/18/f-carbon-tax.html; and "B.C. Carbon Tax Kicks in on Canada Day," CBC News, 1 July 2008, www.cbc.ca/canada/british-columbia/story/2008/06/30/bc-carbon-tax-effective.html.

52. Timothy Slaper and Tanya Hall, "The triple bottom line: what is it and how does it work?" Indiana Business Research Centre, Indiana University Kelley School of Business, http://www.ibrc.indiana.edu/ibr/2011/spring/pdfs/article2.pdf, downloaded 25 April 2015.

53. Ibid.

54. Ibid.

55. "Canadian RI assets surpass $1 trillion: 2015 Canadian RI trends report," Responsible Investment Association, http://riacanada.ca/trendsreport/, downloaded 24 April 2015.

56. Ethisphere, www.ethisphere.com, downloaded March 2014.

57. "Defining Sustainability," Sustainability Reporting Program, 2000, www.sustreport.org/background/definitions.html; "Introducing Revive," Green Solutions North American, Inc., 2009, http://revive-d.com/revive_overview.cfm; and "Loblaws, Sobeys put a wrap on plastic bags," The Canadian Press, 27 November 2008, www.cbc.ca/consumer/story/2008/11/27/loblaw-sobeys-bags.html.

58. "Envirotech Savings Calculator," Envirotech Office Systems, http://www.envirotechoffice.com/why-envirotech/remanufactured-products, downloaded 27 July 2015.

59. "Socially Conscious Consumer Trends: Fair Trade," Market Analysis Report, Agriculture and Agri-Food Canada, April 2012, http://www5.agr.gc.ca/resources/prod/Internet-Internet/MISB-DGSIM/ATS-SEA/PDF/6153-eng.pdf.

60. "Fair trade – An alternative economic model," CBC News, 23 April 2007, www.cbc.ca/news/background/fair-trade/.

61. Ibid.

62. "Fairtrade Canada – What is Fair Trade," Fairtrade Canada, http://fairtrade.ca/en/about-fairtrade/what-fair-trade, downloaded 25 April 2015.

63. Russell Flannery, "Cambodia Factory Shootings Underscore Shifts, Openings in the Global Apparel Business," Forbes, 16 January 2014.

Appendix A

1. "The Canadian Judicial System," Supreme Court of Canada, 2015, http://www.scc-csc.gc.ca/court-cour/sys-eng.aspx, downloaded 17 May 2015.
2. Henry C. Jackson, "House Votes to Increase Asbestos Claim Disclosure," *Bloomberg Businessweek,* 13 November 2013; and "W.R. Grace Emerges from Bankruptcy," *Bloomberg Businessweek,* 3 February 2014.
3. Mesothelioma Center, www.asbestos.com, downloaded May 2014.
4. Joann Muller, "Toyota Halts Sales of Popular Models to Fix Seat Heaters," *Forbes,* 30 January 2014; and Ben Klayman, "Toyota Tells U.S. Agency Seat Issue Could Lead to Recall," *Chicago Tribune,* 30 January 2014.
5. Shaya Tayefe Mohajir, "Toyota Settlement: Orange County to Receive $16 Million over Acceleration, Braking Issues," *Huffington Post,* 5 April 2013; Jerry Hirsch, "NHTSA Opens Probe into Brake Failures of Toyota Camry Hybrid Sedan," *Los Angeles Times,* 27 January 2014; and Chris Woodward and Kevin Johnson, "Toyota to Pay $1.2 Billion to Settle Criminal Probe," *USA Today,* 20 March 2014.
6. Jeff Plungis, "GM Investigated over Ignition Recall Linked to 13 Deaths," *Bloomberg Businessweek,* 27 February 2014.
7. Larry Gordon, "Surgeon and Inventor Gives $50 Million for USC Building," *Los Angeles Times,* 13 January 2014.
8. "Competition Bureau – Our Legislation," 2015, Competition Bureau, http://www.competitionbureau.gc.ca/eic/site/cb-bc.nsf/eng/h_00148.html; downloaded 17 May 2015.
9. "Competition Bureau – Canada's Anti-Spam Law," 2015, Competition Bureau, http://www.competitionbureau.gc.ca/eic/site/cb-bc.nsf/eng/03390.html; downloaded 17 May 2015.
10. "Software updates, installations now require consent," CBC News, 15 January 2015, http://www.cbc.ca/news/technology/software-updates-installations-now-require-consent-1.2901868.
11. Sharon Gaudin, "Antitrust Deal Leaves Google Unscathed," *Computerworld,* 6 February 2014.
12. "Global Banking Regulations and Banks in Canada," Canadian Bankers Association, 13 March 2015, http://www.cba.ca/en/media-room/50-backgrounders-on-banking-issues/667-global-banking-regulations-and-banks-in-canada.

Chapter 6

1. Media Kit, Abeego, http://abeego.com/pages/media-kit, downloaded 19 March 2015.
2. *My Own Business,* www.myownbusiness.org, downloaded March 2014.
3. "Proprietorship," Canadian Tax and Financial Information, Taxtips.ca, 25 May 2013, www.taxtips.ca/smallbusiness/incorporate.htm.
4. Elaine Pofeldt, "Going It Alone," *Inc.,* February 2014.
5. "Proprietorship," World Wide Web.
6. "SR&ED Claims for Partnerships Policy," Canada Revenue Agency, 18 December 2014, http://www.cra-arc.gc.ca/txcrdt/sred-rsde/clmng/clmsfrprtnrshpsplcy-eng.html#s3_1.
7. "Partnership Structures," INC Business Lawyers, 2015, http://www.incorporate.ca/partnership-structures.
8. Bureau of Labor Statistics, www.bis.gov, downloaded March 2014.
9. Paula Andruss, "Divide & Conquer," *Entrepreneur,* April 2013.
10. "Partnership," Canadian Tax and Financial Information, Taxtips.ca, 25 May 2013, www.taxtips.ca/smallbusiness/incorporate.htm.
11. Ibid.
12. About, The Jim Pattison Group, 2015, http://www.jimpattison.com/about/our-story/.
13. "Differences Between Private and Public Corporation," LawDepot.com, 2015, http://wiki.lawdepot.ca/wiki/Differences_Between_Private_and_Public_Corporations.
14. Susan Ward, "Corporate Tax Advantages of the Canadian-Controlled Private Corporation," About.com, 2015, http://sbinfocanada.about.com/od/corporatetax/a/ccpcadvantages.htm.
15. "McCain Business Empire has Deep Roots," CBC.ca, 19 March 2004, http://www.cbc.ca/stories/2004/03/19/mccainbiz_040319.
16. Jamie Sturgeon, "It's official, Tim Hortons, Burger King become one," Global News, 12 December 2014, http://globalnews.ca/news/1724238/its-official-tim-hortons-burger-king-become-one/; "The Story of Tim Hortons," Tim Hortons, 2012, www.timhortons.com/ca/en/about/index.html; and Josh Fineman and David Scanlan, "Tim Hortons Shares May Rise After Raising $671 Million in IPO," Bloomberg, 24 March 2006, www.bloomberg.com/apps/news?pid=newsarchive&sid=aq7mLjay_GVs&refer=us.
17. "Nellie Akalp, "Top Reasons to Incorporate Your Business," *Small Business* Trends, 3 February 2014.
18. "The Basics of Corporate Structure," Investopedia.com, 2008, www.investopedia.com/articles/basics/03/022803.asp.
19. "Carol Hymowitz, "Not Going Anywhere," *Bloomberg BusinessWeek,* May 27–June 2, 2013.
20. "Geoff Colvin, "Inside the Boardroom," *Fortune,* 29 May 2013.
21. "Booster Juice," Canadian Franchise Association, 2015, http://lookforafranchise.ca/browse-franchises/food-quick-service-restaurants/booster-juice/.
22. "Fast Franchise Facts," Canadian Franchise Association, 2015, http://www.cfa.ca/tools_resources/franchise-research-facts/.
23. Company Information, Boston Pizza International, 2015, http://bostonpizza.com/en/franchising/why-boston-pizza.
24. United Parcel Service, www.theupsstore.com, downloaded 14 March 2014.
25. Jason Daly, "What Is the Real Survival Rate of a Franchised Business?" *Entrepreneur,* 13 September 2013.
26. "The Selection Process," Canadian Tire Corporation, Ltd., http://corp.canadiantire.ca/EN/JOINOURTEAM/RETAILOWNERSHIP/Pages/TheSelectionProcess.aspx, downloaded 28 February 2015.
27. "Kumon Math and Reading Centres," Canadian Franchise Association, 2015, http://lookforafranchise.ca/browse-franchises/educational-products-services/kumon-math-and-reading-centres/.
28. "Keg Restaurants Ltd.," Canadian Franchise Association, 2015, http://lookforafranchise.ca/browse-franchises/food-restaurants-dining-rooms/keg-restaurants-ltd/.
29. Leslie Patton, "McDonald's Aiming for Better Bottom Line, Shifts More of the Burden to Its Franchisees," *St. Louis Post-Dispatch,* 11 August 2013.
30. "$2B Tim Hortons franchisee lawsuit deemed half-baked," CBC News, 28 February 2012, www.cbc.ca/news/business/story/2012/02/28/tim-hortons-class-action.html.
31. Ibid.
32. "We're Not Your Parent's Real Estate Company," PropertyGuys.com, 2015, http://propertyguys.com/site/about/.
33. Arlene Satchell, "Cruise Planners Expect Growth in 2014," *Sun Sentinel,* 23 January 2014.
34. "About Us," Yogen Früz, 2015 and 2012, www.yogenfruz.com/home/en/about-us.
35. "What is a Co-operative?" CoopZone Developers' Network Co-operative, http://coopzone.coop/en/what, downloaded 28 February 2015; "The Co-Operative Advantage," CoopZone Developers' Network Co-operative, http://coopzone.coop/en/coop_advantage, downloaded 28 February 2015; Blake Richards, "STATUS OF CO-OPERATIVES IN CANADA - Report of the Special Committee on Co-operatives," House of Commons, September 2012, http://www.parl.gc.ca/content/hoc/Committee/411/COOP/Reports/RP5706528/cooprp01/cooprp01-e.pdf?s1=pub&page=intro#ann; "FAQs About MEC and Co-ops," Mountain Equipment Co-Operative, 2015, http://www.mec.ca/AST/ContentPrimary/AboutMEC/AboutOurCoOp/CoOpFaqs.jsp; "The Gay Lea Story," Gay Lea Foods Co-operative Ltd., 2015, http://www.gaylea.com/gay-lea-story/gay-lea-story/the-gay-lea-story; and Sara Mojtehedzadeh, "Ontario co-op movement could use a legislative leg-up," *The Toronto Star,* 1 December 2014, http://www.thestar.com/business/2014/12/01/ontario_coop_movement_could_use_a_legislative_legup.html#.

Chapter 7

1. "A Definition of Entrepreneurship," Internet Center for Management and Business Administration, Inc., www.quickmba .com/entre/definition/, downloaded 6 March 2015.

2. Ibid.

3. Downloaded 4 March 2015 from the following company Web sites: http://www.leons.ca/shared/customerservice /aboutus.aspx; http://www.jimpattison.com/ and http://www .jimpattison.com/food/default.aspx; http://corp.canadiantire.ca /EN/AboutUs/Pages/default.aspx; http://www.mccain.com /GoodBusiness/Pages/History.aspx, http://www.mccain.com /GoodBusiness/business/Pages/default.aspx, and http://www .mccain.com/GoodBusiness/business/Documents /McCain%20Foods%20Fast%20Facts.pdf; http://www.irvingoil .com/who_we_are/our_leadership/ and http://www.irvingoil .com/who_we_are/; http://corporate.sobeys.com/at-a-glance/; http://www.jeancoutu.com/en/corpo/our-company/profile/; and http://rootsinformation.com/about/.

4. "lululemon athletica: our company history," lululemon athletica, 2015, http://www.lululemon.com/about /history?mnid=ftr;company_history.

5. Will n' Rose's, www.willnroses.com, downloaded March 2014.

6. Lauren Watson, "Introducing Kit and Ace: The new luxury tech wear brand from the family that brought you Lululemon," FASHION, 12 November 2014, http://www.fashionmagazine .com/fashion/2014/11/12/kit-and-ace/.

7. Solarina Ho, "Lululemon-backed clothing line Kit and Ace goes global," Toronto Sun, 5 March 2015, http://www.torontosun .com/2015/03/05 /lululemon-backed-clothing-line-kit-and-ace-goes-global.

8. Thomas Duening, "Nature vs. Nurture: Are Entrepreneurs Made, or Are They Born?" Phoenix Business Journal, 18 January 2009; "Lessons from the Leaders," PROFIT, June 2008, p. 31; Michelle Simms, "Are Entrepreneurial Characteristics Inherited or Learned?" Bellingham Business Journal, 1 June 2008; Sarah Pierce, "Spirit of the Entrepreneur," Entrepreneur.com, 28 February 2008; and Karen E. Klein, "Starting a Startup," Businessweek, 11 June 2008.

9. "Dominion Lending Centres Chief Economist Comments on Bank of Canada Rate Hold," Dominion Lending Centres Inc., 4 March 2015, http://www.dominionlending.ca /about-dominion#mediakit; and "Startup Advice from Successful Entrepreneurs," PROFITguide.com, 3 June 2013, http://www .profitguide.com/startup/best-practices /startup-advice-from-successful-entrepreneurs-53046.

10. "Crazy Diamonds," The Economist, 20 July 2014.

11. Chuck Green, "When Entrepreneurs Don't Take No for an Answer," The Wall Street Journal, 29 April 2013; Lizette Chapman "Extreme Sports Get a Camera," The Wall Street Journal, 20 Jane 2013; Lisa Quast, "Turning Your Passion into Business," Forbes, 2 September 2013; and Gautam Gupta, "How to Transform Your Passion into a Successful Business," Entrepreneur, 20 November 2013.

12. Josie L. Mousseau and Zoe Hawa, "Facts and Figures on Canadian Women Entrepreneurs," The Canadian Trade Commissioner Service, March 2014, http://www.owit-ottawa .ca/wp-content/uploads/2014/03/Facts-and-figures-on-women -entrepreneurs.pdf.

13. "Designer Profile," Foxy Originals, http://www.foxyoriginals.com /Designer-Profile.html, downloaded 7 March 2015; and "Young Entrepreneur: Jennifer Ger," Entrepreneurs, 12 June 2011, http://notable.ca/nationwide/entrepreneurs /Young-Entrepreneur-Jennifer-Ger/.

14. Cadie Thompson, "Is Apple Still the King of Consumer Design?" Entrepreneur, 17 July 2013.

15. "Key Small Business Statistics," Industry Canada, August 2013, https://www.ic.gc.ca/eic/site/061.nsf/vwapj/KSBS -PSRPE_August-Aout2013_eng.pdf/$FILE/KSBS-PSRPE _August-Aout2013_eng.pdf, p. 5.

16. Ibid., p. 7.

17. Lauren Folino, "Recession Feeds Increase of Home-based Businesses," Inc., www.inc.com, downloaded March 2014; and Rebecca Reeve, "Snapchat, Radio, and Other Unlikely Workplace Engagement-Boosting Tools," Fast Company, 28 October 2013.

18. Paul Tassi, "11 Ways to Stay Motivated While Working from Home," Forbes, 22 January 2014; Jacquelyn Smith, "How to Succeed at Working from Home," Forbes, 12 August 2013; and Ruth Blatt, "What Musicians Teach Us about the Challenges of Being Your Own Boss," Forbes, 17 January 2014.

19. "About Chef Michael Smith," Chef Michael Smith, 2015, http:// chefmichaelsmith.com/michael/.

20. Hollie Shaw, "Online retail sales to hit $34-billion in Canada by 2018," Financial Post, 23 July 2013, http://business .financialpost.com/2013/07/23 /online-retail-sales-to-hit-40-billion-in-canada-by-2018/.

21. Throw Things, www.throwthings.com, downloaded March 2014.

22. Mark Cohen, "Surviving the Dark Side of Affiliate Marketing," The New York Times, 4 December 2014; Francine Hardaway, "10 Tips for Small Business Marketing from Infusioncon," Fast Company, 29 March 2013; and HBS Working Knowledge, "The Tricky Business of Managing Web Advertising Affiliates," Forbes, 2 February 2014.

23. 3M, www.3mc.om, downloaded March 2014.

24. "About Canada Business Network," Government of Canada, 6 March 2015, http://www.canadabusiness.ca/eng /page/3711/; Humaira Irshad, "Business Incubation in Canada," Alberta Agriculture and Rural Development, 14 June 2014, http://www1.agric.gov.ab.ca/$Department/deptdocs.nsf/all /csi14921/$FILE/business-%20incubators%20.pdf; "Business Incubator FAQs," National Business Incubation Association, 2014, https://www.nbia.org/resource_library/faq/index.php#; National Business Association, downloaded March 2014, www.nbia.org; "Give It the Old College Try," Inc., June 2013; Kristen Heredia, "DMZ Ranked Fifth Globally and First in Canada in University Business Incubator's Global Ranking, Digital Media Zone, 24 June 2014, http://digitalmediazone.ryerson.ca/dmznews/digital -media-zone-ryerson-university-ranked-fifth-globally-first-canada -university-business-incubators-global-ranking/; Alan Shepard, "University-based startup incubators to play a critical role in renaissance of Canadian city-states, Financial Post, 13 November 2013, http://business.financialpost.com/2013/11/13 /university-based-startup-incubators-play-a-critical-role-in -renaissance-of-canadian-city-states/.

25. "Key Small Business Statistics," Industry Canada, August 2013, https://www.ic.gc.ca/eic/site/061.nsf/vwapj/KSBS -PSRPE_August-Aout2013_eng.pdf/$FILE/KSBS-PSRPE_August -Aout2013_eng.pdf.

26. Ibid.; and "Financing Statistics," Industry Canada, November 2013, https://www.ic.gc.ca/eic/site/061.nsf/vwapj /FinancingKSBS-FinancementPSRPE_2013_eng.pdf/$FILE /FinancingKSBS-FinancementPSRPE_2013_eng.pdf.

27. "Key Small Business Statistics," Industry Canada, August 2013, https://www.ic.gc.ca/eic/site/061.nsf/vwapj/KSBS -PSRPE_August-Aout2013_eng.pdf/$FILE/KSBS-PSRPE_August -Aout2013_eng.pdf.

28. Kathy Caprino, "The 7 Worst Marketing Blunders Small Businesses Make," Forbes, 24 January 2014; Eric T. Wagner, "Five Reasons 8 out of 10 Businesses Fail," Forbes, 12 September 2013; Steve Tobak, "It's a Marathon, Not a Sprint: The Real Reason Start-ups Fail," Inc., 6 March 2013; and Norm Brodsky, "Everyone Fails. What's Key Is to Learn the Right Lessons," Inc., July/August 2013.

29. "Corporate Profile," BioSyent, 2015, http://www.biosyent.com /rx/corporate_profile/#.VPyukGBOwek; and "The PROFIT 500 Reveal Their Best Business Lessons," PROFITguide.com, 12 June 2014, http://www.profitguide.com/manage-grow/leadership /the-profit-500-reveal-their-best-business-lessons-66171.

30. Industry, Canada, "Financing Statistics," https://www.ic.gc.ca /eic/site/061.nsf/vwapj/FinancingKSBS -FinancementPSRPE

Endnotes

_2013_eng.pdf/$FILE/FinancingKSBS-FinancementPSRPE_2013 _eng.pdf.

31. "About Bullfrog Power," Bullfrog Power, http://www.bullfrogpower .com/about/team.cfm, downloaded 8 March 2015; and www .bullfrogpower.com/about/about/cfm, downloaded 22 September 2008.

32. "Company Profile," Running Room, 2015, http://www .runningroom.com/hm/inside.php?lang=1&id=3652; and "History," Running Room, 2012, www.runningroom.com/hm /inside.php?lang=1&id=3036.

33. Andy Holloway, "Fill Your Shoes: Small-Business Succession," *Canadian Business,* March 27–April 9, 2006, www.canadianbusiness.com/managing/strategy/article. jsp?content=20060327_75741_75741.

34. Steve Blank, "Takeover University," *Forbes,* 28 October 2013.

35. "Succession Planning," Family Business Institute, [2015?], http://www.familybusinessinstitute.com/index.php/Succession -Planning/; Dana Flavelle and Rita Trichur, "CanWest's newspaper empire for sale," *Toronto Star,* 9 January 2010, www.thestar .com/news/canada/article/748513-canwest-s-newspaper -empire-for-sale; "Leonard Asper stepping down from Canwest," *Financial Post,* 4 March 2010, www.financialpost.com /Leonard+Asper+stepping+down+from+Canwest/2640633 /story.html; "Governance for the Family Business," KPMG in Canada, 2008, www.kpmg.ca/en/services/enterprise /issuesGrowthGovernance.html; and "Succession Planning for Family Business," BDO Canada LLP, [2012?], www.bdo.ca /library/publications/familybusiness/succession/planning1.cfm.

36. Industry, Canada, "Financing Statistics," https://www.ic.gc.ca /eic/site/061.nsf/vwapj/FinancingKSBS-FinancementPSRPE _2013_eng.pdf/$FILE/FinancingKSBS-FinancementPSRPE_2013 _eng.pdf.

37. Mahendra Ramsinghani, "Venture Capital 2013 Recap—Oh What a Year It Was," *Forbes,* 26 December 2013.

38. Deepak Malhotra, "How to Negotiate with VCs," *Harvard Business Review,* May 2013.

39. "Definition of CROWDSOURCING," Merriam-Webster, Inc., 2015, http://www.merriam-webster.com/dictionary/crowdsourcing; "Crowdfunding," National Crowdfunding Association of Canada, 2015, http://ncfacanada.org/crowdfunding/; Tanya Prive, "What Is Crowdfunding And How Does It Benefit The Economy?" *Forbes,* 27 November 2012, http://www.forbes.com/sites /tanyaprive/2012/11/27/what-is-crowdfunding-and-how-does-it -benefit-the-economy/; Mark Quinlan, "The pros and cons of crowd funding," CBC News, 22 June 2012, http://www.cbc.ca /news/canada/the-pros-and-cons-of-crowd-funding-1.1136449; Ruth Simon and Angus Loten, "Crowdfunding Gets State-Level Test Run," *The Wall Street Journal,* 4 December 2013; J. Craig Andersen, "Maine 'Crowd Investing' Bill Becomes Law," *Portland Press Herald,* 6 March 2014; and Nicole Fallon, "Equity Crowdfunding: 3 Facts Entrepreneurs Should Know," *Business News Daily,* 21 March 2014.

40. "Not Open for Business," *The Economist,* 12 October 2013; and Eric Paley, "Go Beyond Visionary; Be a Leader," *Inc.,* February 2014.

41. "The PROFIT 500 Reveal Their Best Business Lessons," PROFITguide.com, 12 June 2014, http://www.profitguide.com /manage-grow/leadership/the-profit-500-reveal-their-best -business -lessons-66171.

42. John Lorinc, "A Global Business Built on Lateral Thinking," PROFITguide.com, 5 August 2014, http://www.profitguide.com /manage-grow/international-trade/a-global-business-built-on -lateral-thinking-68047.

Chapter 8

1. Katherine Duncan, "Command Performance," *Entrepreneur,* March 2013.

2. Christian Stadler and Davis Dyer, "Why Good Leaders Don't Need Charisma," *Sloan Management Review,* Spring 2013.

3. David A. Garvin, "How Google Sold Its Engineers on Management," *Harvard Business Review,* December 2013.

4. "The 23 Female CEOs Running Fortune 500 Companies," *San Jose Mercury News,* 10 December 2013.

5. David Malpass, "Five Big Steps Toward Global Growth," *Forbes,* 10 February 2014.

6. Steven Overly, "Going Green, Bit by Bit," *The Washington Post,* 22 April 2013.

7. Stephanie Marton, "The mysterious success of female-led firms," 20 February 2013, *Forbes,* http:// www.forbes.com/sites/85broads/2013/02/20 /the-mysterious-success-of-female-led-firms/.

8. Daniel Goleman, "The Focused Leader," *Harvard Business Review,* December 2013.

9. Alan Bird and James Root, "Making Star Teams Out of Star Players," *Harvard Business Review,* January–February 2013.

10. Marcus Buckingham, "What Great Managers Do," *Harvard Business Review,* March 2005, 70–79.

11. Elizabeth Fenner, "Happiness," *Fortune,* 21 February 2005, 36.

12. Kenneth R. Brousseau, Michael J. Driver, Gary Hourihon, and Rikard Larsson, "The Seasoned Executive's Decision-Making Style," *Harvard Business Review,* February 2006, 111–121.

13. Leigh Buchanan, "The Essential Management Book You're Not Reading," *Inc.,* December 2013–January 2014.

14. Jeff Bennett and John Kell, "GM Restores Annual Dividend as Sales Shine," *The Wall Street Journal,* 15 January 2014.

15. Roger L. Martin, "Rethinking the Decision Factory," *Harvard Business Review,* October 2013.

16. "What Is the Difference Between Management and Leadership?" *The Wall Street Journal,* downloaded March 2014.

17. Interesting contrasts among purpose, mission, and vision can be found in: John Mackey and Raj Sisodia, *Conscious Capitalism* (Boston, MA: Harvard Business Review Press, 2013).

18. Eric Paley, "Go Beyond Visionary; Be a Leader," *Inc.,* February 2014.

19. "SWOT Analysis," www.MindTools.com, downloaded January 2014.

20. Roger L. Martin, "The Big Lie of Strategic Planning," *Harvard Business Review,* February 2014.

21. Giovanni Gavetti and Jan W. Rivkin, "How Strategists Really Think," *Harvard Business Review,* April 2005, 54–63.

22. Greg Bensinger, "Amazon Plans to Compete with Paypal and Square in Retail Stores," *The Wall Street Journal,* 30 January 2014.

23. Anne Nicoll, "Beyond SARS: Developing Health Related Emergency Policies," Benefits and Pensions Online, June 2003, http://www.bpmmagazine.com/02_archives/2003/june /beyond_sars.html; "The New Contingency Plan—Health-Related Emergencies," 27 May 2003, www.morneausobeco.com/PDF /SARSCommuniqué_E.pdf.

24. Gregory J. Millman and Samuel Rubenfeld, "For Corporate America, Risk Is Big Business," *The Wall Street Journal,* 16 January 2014.

25. Miriam Gottfried, "This Eagle Must Hunt Elsewhere," *The Wall Street Journal,* 24 January 2014.

26. Paul Rogers and Marcia Blenko, "Who Has the D?" *Harvard Business Review,* January 2006, 53–61.

27. "Trends in Airline Governance, Management Structures and Mandates," 14 June 2011, www.iaaia.com/PDF/ent_trends_in _airline_governance_at_14-06-11.pdf.

28. Julia Hunter, "Loblaw Announces Leaner Head Office Structure," Loblaw Companies Limited, http://www.loblaw.ca/English/Media -Centre/news-releases/news-release-details/2012/Loblaw -Announces-Leaner-Head-Office-Structure1131481/default.aspx, downloaded 3 May 2015; Sunny Freeman, "Loblaw Profits Jump 20 Per Cent But Still Hit by Infrastructure Overhaul, 16 November 2011, www.canadianbusiness.com/article/57306-loblaw-profits -jump-20-per-cent-but-still-hit-by-infrastructure-overhaul.

29. Andreas Priestland and Robert Hanig, "Developing First-Level Leaders," *Harvard Business Review,* June 2005, 113–120.

30. Robert Kutz, "Skills of an Effective Administrator," *Harvard Business Review,* Sept–Oct 1974, 90–101.

31. "The 10 Best Companies to Work For in 2014," www.forbes.com, downloaded March 2014.

32. Amy C. Cooper, "Unite and Conquer," *Entrepreneur*, March 2013.

33. Patricia Cohen, "One company's new minimum wage: $70,000 a year," *The New York Times*, 13 April 2015, http://www.nytimes.com/2015/04/14/business/owner-of-gravity-payments-a-credit-card-processor-is-setting-a-new-minimum-wage-70000-a-year.html?_r=0; Adam Witnall, "Dan Price: Seattle CEO cuts own salary by 90% to pay every worker at least $70,000," *The Independent*, 15 April 2015, http://www.independent.co.uk/news/world/americas/seattle-ceo-dan-price-cuts-own-salary-by-90-to-pay-every-worker-at-least-70000-10177261.html; All Points West, "Gravity Payments CEO Dan Price of Seattle cuts his salary to boost company's minimum wage to $70K," CBCNews, 15 April 2015, http://www.cbc.ca/news/canada/british-columbia/gravity-payments-ceo-dan-price-cuts-his-salary-to-boost-company-s-minimum-wage-to-70k-1.3035051.

34. Kerry Dolan, "Billionaires, Led by Zuckerberg, Dig a Bit Deeper with 10 Biggest Charitable Gifts of 2013," www.forbes.com, 1 January 2014.

35. Dorrie Clark, "How the Best Leaders Embrace Change," www.forbes.com, 5 November 2013.

36. Barry Glassman, "In Business, Transparency Wins," *Forbes*, 15 January 2014.

37. Bertrand Marotte, "Management Guru Assails Excessive CEO Salaries," *The Globe and Mail*, 8 May 2003, B7.

38. Jim Pawlak, "Treating Employees as Assets, Not Expenses Boosts Profits," *Hartford Business Journal*, February 24, 2014.

39. Laura Bogomolny, "Most Innovative Exec/Canadian Tire—Janice Wismer," *Canadian Business*, 2004, www.canadianbusiness.com/allstars/best_innovative_exec.html.

Chapter 9

1. John Jullens, "How Emerging Giants Can Take On the World," *Harvard Business Review*, December 2013.

2. Jonathan House and Kathleen Madigan, "U.S. Factories Bounce Back in February," *The Wall Street Journal*, 2 March 2014.

3. Ann Hadley, "What Not to Do," *Entrepreneur*, September 2013.

4. Amol Sharma, Shalini Ramachandran, and Don Clark, "Amazon Joins the TV Crush," *The Wall Street Journal*, 22 January 2014.

5. Natalie Kaddas, "Being Flexible," www.huffingtonpost.com, 23 November 2013.

6. Mary Jordan, "The Promise of a 'Made in America' Era," *The Washington Post*, 1 May 2013.

7. Fredrik Eliasson, "Emphasizing the Management in 'Change Management,'" *The Wall Street Journal*, 24 January 2014.

8. John Mackey and Raj Sisodia, *Conscious Capitalism* (Boston, MA: Harvard Business Review Press, 2013).

9. Jeff Bennett and John Kell, "GM Restores Annual Dividend as Sales Shine," *The Wall Street Journal*, 15 January 2014.

10. Rashik Parmar, Ian Mackenzie, David Cohn, and David Gann, "The New Patterns of Innovation," *Harvard Business Review*, January–February 2014.

11. Raymond Fisman and Tim Sullivan, "The Unsung Beauty of Bureaucracy," *The Wall Street Journal*, 16–17 May 2014.

12. Henry Mintzberg and James Brian Quinn, *The Strategy Process: Concepts and Contexts* (New Jersey: Prentice Hall Inc., 1992).

13. Henry Mintzberg, *Managers not MBAs* (San Francisco: Berrett-Koehler Publishers, 2004).

14. Magna International, "2014 Annual Report to Shareholders," 2014, http://www.magna.com/investors/financial-reports-public-filings.

15. Gary L. Neilson and Julie Wulf, "How Many Direct Reports?" *Harvard Business Review*, April 2012.

16. Harry Maurer, "News You Need to Know," *BusinessWeek*, 6 February 2006, 32.

17. David Gann, Ammon Salter, Mark Dodgson and Nelson Phillips, "Inside the World of the Project Baron," *Sloan Management Review*, Spring 2012.

18. Jeff Weiss and Jonathan Hughes, "Want Collaboration?" *Harvard Business Review*, March 2005, 93–101.

19. Bill Fischer and Andy Boynton, "Virtuoso Teams," *Harvard Business Review*, July–August 2005, 117–21.

20. Braden Kowitz, "Why You Should Listen to the Customer," *The Wall Street Journal*, 19 February 2014.

21. Mary C. Lacity and Leslie P. Willcocks, "Outsourcing Business Processes for Innovation," *Sloan Management Review*, Spring 2013.

22. David Raths, "KM infrastructure for the life sciences virtual organization," KKM World, 1 March 2015, http://www.kmworld.com/Articles/Editorial/Features/KM-infrastructure-for-the-life-sciences-virtual-organization-102166.aspx.

23. Suncor 2014 Report on Sustainability, Suncor, http://sustainability.suncor.com/2014/en/goals/environment-and-social-progress-reports.aspx, downloaded 9 May 2015.

24. Kasia Klimasinska, "Obama Budget Predicts Strongest U.S. Growth since 2005," *Bloomberg BusinessWeek*, 4 March 2014.

25. "Outsourcing bank jobs is common practice, say employees," CBCNews, 9 April 2013, http://www.cbc.ca/news/canada/outsourcing-bank-jobs-is-common-practice-say-employees-1.1333814.

26. Robert I. Sutton and Huggy Rao, "Before You Make Any Changes, Ask These Questions," *Bloomberg BusinessWeek*, 4 March 2014.

27. "Ottawa doesn't regret GM bailout," 21 April 2010, www.cbc.ca/news/canada/windsor/story/2010/04/21/wdr-detroit-gm-government-loans-100421.html.

28. Why did Target fail in Canada? It wasn't the U.S. Target," CBCNews, 15 January 2015, http://www.cbc.ca/news/canada/manitoba/why-did-target-fail-in-canada-it-wasn-t-the-u-s-target-1.2901676.

29. Darah Hansen, "How to fix Target Canada's problems in six easy steps," *Canadian Business*, 28 July 2014, http://www.canadianbusiness.com/companies-and-industries/how-to-fix-target-canada/.

30. Novocare Rehabilitation – About, 2015, Novocare, http://www.novacare.com/about/, downloaded 9 May 2015; David Ernst and James Bamford, "Your Alliances Are Too Stable," *Harvard Business Review*, June 2005, 133–141.

31. Michael E. Raynor and Mumtaz Ahmed, "Three Rules for Making a Company Truly Great," *Harvard Business Review*, April 2013.

32. Deborah Aarts, "Innovate at any size: we fetishize tiny startups, but lots of companies get big and keep their disruptive streak intact," *Canadian Business*, October 2014, 38.

33. Tracey Hilderley, "Keeping things comfortable for over 100 years," *Business in Focus*, 9 May 2014, http://www.businessinfocusmagazine.com/2012/11/keeping-things-comfortable-for-over-100-years/.

34. Henry Mintzberg and James Brian Quinn, *The Strategy Process: Concepts and Contexts* (New Jersey: Prentice Hall Inc., 1992).

35. www.td.com/careers

36. Alex (Sandy) Pentland, "The New Science of Building Great Teams," *Harvard Business Review*, April 2012.

37. Jay Rao and Joseph Weintraub, "How Innovative Is Your Company's Culture?" *Sloan Management Review*, Spring 2013.

38. Christopher Hann, "Good Vibes," *Entrepreneur*, February 2014.

Chapter 10

1. "*Innovation in Canada*," Sackville: Centre for Canadian Studies at Mount Allison University, www.mta.ca/faculty/arts/canadian_studies/english/about/innovation/.

2. Innovation Analysis Bulletin, Vol. 6, No. 1, March 2004, www.statcan.gc.ca/pub/88-003-x/88-003-x2004001-eng.pdf.

3. "Spending on research and development, 2014 (intentions)," 17 October 2014, http://www.statcan.gc.ca/daily-quotidien/141017/dq141017c-eng.htm.

4. "Federal government spending on science and technology, 2014–2015," *The Daily*, 28 May 2014, http://www.statcan.gc.ca/daily-quotidien/140528/dq140528g-eng.htm.

5. Barrie McKenna, "Canada falling behind global leaders in R&D," *The Globe and Mail,* 16 November 2014, http://www.theglobeandmail.com/report-on-business/economy/canada-falling-behind-in-research-and-development/article21605656/.

6. "Canada's Top 100 Corporate Spenders List 2014 Analysis," Research Infosource Inc., http://www.researchinfosource.com/pdf/2014Top100Corporate%20-%20Article.pdf, downloaded 10 May 2015.

7. "Spending intentions on industrial research and development, 2014," 19 August 2014, http://www.statcan.gc.ca/daily-quotidien/140819/dq140819a-eng.htm.

8. Canadian Manufacturers & Exporters, "Canadian Manufacturing Today: Cautiously Optimistic," 2014, http://www.cme-mec.ca/_uploads/_media/51wjbzblm.pdf.

9. Andrea Petersen, "Checking In? Hidden Ways Hotels Court Guests Faster," *The Wall Street Journal,* 12 April 2012.

10. Alina Dizik, "Why All the Locals Are Lounging in the Hotel Lobby," *The Wall Street Journal,* 19 April 2012.

11. H. David Sherman and Joe Zhu, "Analyzing Performance in Service Organizations," *Sloan Management Review,* Summer 2013.

12. "The Method – before and after examples," 2014, Information Mapping Canada, http://www.informationmapping.com/ca/the-method-ca/before-a-after-examples, downloaded 10 May 2015.

13. Eric Atkins, "Dr. Oetker's new pizza plant gives Ontario manufacturing a boost," *The Globe and Mail,* 20 May 2014, http://www.theglobeandmail.com/report-on-business/dr-oetker-builds-ontario-plant/article18748722/.

14. Dave Hall, "Kellogg, Heinz plant closures part of trend," *The Windsor Star,* 10 December 2013, http://blogs.windsorstar.com/business/kellogg-heinz-plant-closures-part-of-a-trend.

15. David Simchi-Levi, James Paul Peruvankal, Narenda Mulani, Bill Read, and John Ferreira, "Is It Time to Rethink Your Manufacturing Strategy?" *MIT Sloan Management Review,* Winter 2012.

16. Gary Norris, "Honda Putting New Assembly Plant in U.S.; Ontario Gets $154M Engine Factory," Canadian Business Online, 17 May 2006, http://www.canadianbusiness.com/markets/headline_news/article.jsp?content=b051777A.

17. Canadian Press, "Honda to invest $857M in Ontario plant to build next generation of Civic car," *Financial Post,* 6 November 2014, http://business.financialpost.com/news/transportation/honda-to-invest-857-million-in-alliston-operations-ontario-kicks-in-10.

18. Dave Coles, "Sending jobs offshore hurts Canadian workers," *Times Colonist,* 11 April 2013, http://www.timescolonist.com/opinion/op-ed/comment-sending-jobs-offshore-hurts-canadian-workers-1.108110.

19. International Association of Outsourcing Professionals, "Key Findings for the State of the Industry Survey 2014," www.iaop.org.

20. Diane Peters, "When does it pay to outsource your production?" *The Globe and Mail,* 22 January 2015, http://www.theglobeandmail.com/report-on-business/small-business/sb-growth/going-global/when-does-it-pay-to-outsource-your-production/article22565115/.

21. Amanda Lang, "Let's worry about skills, not outsourcing," *The Globe and Mail,* 12 April 2013, http://www.theglobeandmail.com/globe-debate/lets-worry-about-skills-not-outsourcing/article11084876/.

22. CORE Centre for Outsourcing Research and Education, www.core-outsourcing.org.

23. Danielle Goldfarb, "How Canada wins from global services outsourcing," C.D. Howe Institute, November 2004, http://www.cdhowe.org/pdf/commentary_206.pdf, downloaded 12 May 2015.

24. Tony Van Alphen, "CAW head Ken Lewenza resigns before historic union merger," *Toronto Star,* 7 July 2013, http://www.thestar.com/news/canada/2013/07/07/caw_head_ken_lewenza_resigns_before_historic_union_merger.html.

25. Brad Feld, "The Simple Change That's Completely Transformed How I Get Things Done," *Inc.,* December/January 2014.

26. .James Stewart, "Looking for Lesson in Goggle's Perks," *New York Times,* 15 March 2013, http://www.nytimes.com/2013/03/16/business/at-google-a-place-to-work-and-play.html?_r=1.

27. Janet Bealer Rodie, "Brückner, M-Tec Partner to Provide Carpet Solutions," *Textile World,* 1 May 2005.

28. James Mirtle, "Maple Leafs bet big on Big Data with analytics partnership," *The Globe and Mail,* 15 October 2014, http://www.theglobeandmail.com/sports/hockey/maple-leafs-bet-big-on-big-data-with-analytics-partnership/article21119849/.

29. "Royal Canadian Mint," September 2003, Cognos, www.cognos.com/products/applications/success.html.

30. Ibid.

31. Daren Fonda, "Why the Most Profitable Cars Made in the U.S.A. are Japanese and German," *Time,* June 2003, A9–A13.

32. Davis Balestracci, "When Processes Moonlight as Trends," *Quality Digest,* June 2005, 18.

33. "More about NQI" and "Canada Awards for Excellence," Toronto: National Quality Institute, www.nqi.ca.

34. John E. West, "Making Products Better," *Quality Digest,* February 2008.

35. Scott M. Paton, "The Cost of Quality," *Quality Digest,* January 2006, 128.

36. "ISO Standards," International Organization for Standardization, www.iso.org/iso/iso_catalogue.htm.

37. SNC-Lavalin Group Inc., "Quality Policy," www.snclavalin.com/en/6_0/6_10.aspx.

38. "Extensive debate improves consensus on future ISO 26000 standard on social responsibility," International Organization for Standardization, 4 June 2009, www.iso.org/iso/pressrelease.htm?refid=Ref1229.

39. William McDonough and Michael Baungart, *Cradle to Cradle: remaking the way we make things,* 2012, Douglas & McIntyre Limited.

40. Matthew Wheeland, "Design and performance reconsidered," *GreenBiz,* 11 June 2008, http://www.greenbiz.com/news/2008/06/11/design-and-performance-reconsidered.

41. "2015 Nike Free Collection: Five reasons less is more," Nike, http://news.nike.com/news/2015-nike-free-collection, downloaded 23 March 2015.

42. "The future: closed-loop business model," FY2007-FY2009 Nike Inc. Corporate Responsibility Report, http://www.nikebiz.com/crreport/content/strategy/2-1-1-corporate-responsibility-strategy-overview.php?cat=cr-strategy, downloaded 17 May 2015.

43. Robert Bowman, "The sign in the elevator banks at Coca-Cola Refreshments reads: 'There is a person at the end of our supply chain.' Well, that's a start," Supply Chain Brain, 2 March 2015, http://www.supplychainbrain.com/content/nc/general-scm/business-strategy-alignment/single-article-page/article/demand-planning-at-coca-cola-whats-the-secret-formula/.

44. Alicia Fiorletta, "Source for Sports streamlines supply chain with Askuity," Retail Touch Points, 25 June 2014, http://www.retailtouchpoints.com/features/retail-success-stories/source-for-sports-streamlines-supply-chain-with-askuity; "Source for Sports – We Know Our Stuff," 2015, Source for Sports, accessed 12 May 2015 from http://www.sourceforsports.com/AboutUs.aspx.

45. "Kodiak to close Terra Nova Shoes, move jobs to Ontario," CBC News, 8 July 2014, http://www.cbc.ca/news/canada/newfoundland-labrador/kodiak-to-close-terra-nova-shoes-move-jobs-to-ontario-1.2699713; Gordon Pitts, "Kodiak Comes Home," *The Globe and Mail,* 15 May 2006, www.theglobeandmail.com/servlet/story/LAC.20060515.RKODIAK15/TPStory/?query=kodiak.

46. Greg Keenan, "Ford's New Maxim: Flex Manufacturing; New Oakville Plant Should Be Able to Switch Models in Days, not Weeks," *The Globe and Mail,* 10 May 2006, B3.

47. Ibid.

48. Brad Fougere, "Harper government celebrates completion of Ford Oakville assembly plant transformation," Canadian Manufacturers and Exporters, 26 February 2015, http://www.cme-mec.ca/?lid=JCKNC-E742G-1W6JA&comaction=show&cid=HBDPT-FYRU4-FTN9D.

49. Ann C. Logue, "Trimming the Fat," *Entrepreneur,* February 2014.
50. Steve Blank, "'Lean' Is Shaking Up the Entrepreneurial Landscape," *Harvard Business Review,* July–August 2013.
51. Dennis Sowards, "Lean Construction," *Quality Digest,* November 2007.
52. Thomas R. Cutler, "Bored by Lean," *Quality Digest,* May 2008.
53. Sandra Zaragoza, "Boston Duo Starts Customized Guitar Shop in Austin," *Austin Business Journal,* 23 July 2012; and Chris Raymond, "Design Your Own Guitar—This Startup Will Build It," *Popular Mechanics,* 7 February 2014.
54. Kevin Kelly, "Better than Human," *Wired,* January 2013.
55. Bill Alpert, "Robots in Search of Added Employment," *Barron's,* 28 January 2013.
56. David Von Drehle, "The Robot Economy," *Time,* 9 September 2013.
57. Dexter Roberts, "The March of Robots into Chinese Factories," *Bloomberg Businessweek,* 29 November 2012.
58. Tavia Grant, "Rise of machines: robots poised to transform global manufacturing," *The Globe and Mail,* 10 February 2015, http://www.theglobeandmail.com/report-on-business/rise-of-the-machines-robots-poised-to-transform-global-manufacturing/article22884032/.
59. John Koten, "What's Hot in Manufacturing Technology," *The Wall Street Journal,* 11 June 2013.

Chapter 11

1. Gary J. Bissonette, *Business,* 1st ed. (Toronto: McGraw-Hill Ryerson, 2012), 441.
2. Gary Johns and Alan M. Saks, *Organizational Behaviour,* 8th ed. (Toronto: Pearson Canada, 2011), 146
3. "Employee Turnover—How Much Is It Costing You?" go2HR, 2015, https://www.go2hr.ca/articles/employee-turnover-how-much-it-costing-you.
4. Ibid.
5. Victor Lipman, "Why Are So Many Employees Disengaged?" *Forbes,* 18 January 2014.
6. "Canada's 100 Best Small & Medium Employers - DAC Group values 'geeks with personalities'," *The Globe and Mail* and Mediacorp Canada Inc., March 2015, p. 24.
7. Jacquelyn Smith, "The Best Companies to Work for in 2014," *Forbes,* 11 December 2013; and "100 Best Companies to Work For," www.fortune.com, accessed March 2014.
8. Timothy T. Baldwin, William H. Bommer, and Robert S. Rubin, *Managing Organizational Behavior, What Great Managers Know and Do,* 2nd ed. (New York: McGraw-Hill Irwin, 2013), 198.
9. Ibid., 197.
10. Jay Velury, "Empowerment to the People," *Industrial Engineer,* 1 May 2005.
11. Devin Leonard, "He'll Make Your Dreams Come True," *Bloomberg Business News,* 5 January 2014.
12. Joie de Vivre Hotels, www.jdvhotels.com, accessed March 2014; Tomio Geron, "Airbnb Hires Joie de Vivre's Chip Conley as Head of Hospitality," *Forbes,* 17 February 2013; and Mike Hofman, "The Idea That Saved My Company," *Inc.,* October 2007.
13. Nadia Goodman, "Methods for Building Employee Loyalty," *Entrepreneur,* 9 January 2013.
14. Diane Jermyn, "Canada Top 100 Employers make their workplaces exceptional," *The Globe and Mail,* 4 November 2014, http://www.theglobeandmail.com/report-on-business/careers/top-employers/canadas-top-100-employers-make-their-workplaces-exceptional/article21427767/.
15. Derek Sankey, "CP Railway Offers Best Overall Package," *Financial Post,* 22 October 2008, www.financialpost.com/working/story.html?id=899342.
16. Caleb Hannan, "Management Secrets from the Meanest Company in America," *Bloomberg Businessweek,* 2 January 2013.
17. Steve Denning, "The Golden Age of Management Is Now," *Forbes,* 5 August 2013.
18. Victor Lipman, "Without This Quality, Management Doesn't Work," *Forbes,* 1 October 2013.
19. "The Best Ways to Reward Employees," www.entrepreneur.com, accessed March 2014; Kevin Kruse, "25 Low Cost Ways to Reward Employees," *Forbes,* 1 March 2013; and Peter Economy, "5 Secrets for Rewarding Employees," *Inc.,* 3 December 2013.
20. David Nadler and Edward Lawler, "Motivation—A Diagnostic Approach," in *Perspectives on Behavior in Organizations* (New York: McGraw-Hill, 1977).
21. David Nicklaus, "What Price Awards?" *St. Louis Post-Dispatch,* 19 April 2013.
22. Jason Daley, "In It for the Long Haul," *Entrepreneur,* February 2013.
23. "What Makes Employees Unhappy," *Inc.,* February 2013.
24. Gary Johns and Alan M. Saks, *Organizational Behaviour,* 8th edition (Toronto: Pearson Canada, 2011), 194.
25. Baldwin, Bommer, and Rubin, *Managing Organizational Behavior, What Great Managers Know and Do,* 212.
26. Rob Gofee, "Creating the Best Workplace on Earth," *Harvard Business Review,* May 2013.
27. Glenn Llopis, "6 Ways Effective Listening Can Make You a Better Leader," *Forbes,* 20 May 2013; Josh Patrick, "Do You Listen to Your Employees," *The New York Times,* 7 March 2013; Shirley Engelmeier, "As Employees 'Lean In,' Companies Must 'Listen In,'" *Fast Company,* 10 May 2013; and Rajat Paharia, "Your Employees Are Telling You What Motivates Them. Why Aren't You Listening?" *Wired,* 12 September 2013.
28. "2014 BC CEO Awards—Manufacturer puts people first," *Business Vancouver,* November 4–10, 2014, B8–B9, http://glbc.com/wp-content/uploads/2014/11/CEO-Awards-2014.pdf.
29. Ibid., B8.
30. "Canada's 100 Best Small & Medium Employers - theScore Inc.," *The Globe and Mail* and Mediacorp Canada Inc., March 2015, p. 8.
31. Paula Ketter, "What's the Big Deal about Employee Engagement?" *Training and Development,* 1 January 2008.
32. Alisa Priddle and Chris Woodyard, "Ford improves the Convertible in New Mustang," *USA Today,* 27 February 2014; and Patrick Rall, "Late Run Rush Pushes Ford Mustang Past Chevrolet Camaro in February Sales," *Torque News,* 3 February 2014.
33. Maria Elena Duran, "How to Boost Morale at Your Business," *U.S. News & World Report,* 6 March 2014.
34. Megan M. Biro, "5 Best Ways Leaders Rock Employee Recognition," *Forbes,* 13 January 2013.
35. Jacquelyn Smith, "What Employers Need to Know about the Class of 2012," *Forbes,* 3 April 2012; and Tim Logan, "What Makes for a Good Workplace?" *St. Louis Post-Dispatch,* 27 June 2013.
36. Dow Chemical Company, www.dow.com, accessed March 2014.
37. "Michael Adams," Environics Research Group, 2015, http://www.environics.ca/michael-adams; "Profile - David K. Foot," Footwork Consulting Inc., [n.d.], http://www.footwork.com/profile.asp; Colonel James C. Taylor, "Whither march the cohorts: The validity of generation theory as a determinant of the sociocultural values of Canadian Forces personnel," Canadian Forces College, June 2008, http://www.cfc.forces.gc.ca/259/281/280/taylor.pdf; John Markert, "Demographics of Age: Generational and Cohort Confusion," *Journal of Current Issues and Research in Advertising,* 26, no. 2 (Fall 2004), 1; and Dan Schawbel, "Employers, prepare to meet Gen Z," *The Globe and Mail,* 2 September 2014, http://www.theglobeandmail.com/report-on-business/careers/leadership-lab/employers-prepare-to-meet-gen-z/article20280755/.
38. Dan Schawbel, "Employers, prepare to meet Gen Z," *The Globe and Mail,* 2 September 2014.
39. "Latchkey child," Merriam-Webster, Inc., 2015, http://www.merriam-webster.com/dictionary/latchkey%20child.
40. Lisa Rochon, "Why the cities of the future belong to the millennial generation," *The Globe and Mail,* 15 April 2015, http://www.theglobeandmail.com/arts/why-the-cities-of-the-future-belong-to-the-millennial-generation/article11154532/; and Ray Williams, "Like it or not, Millennials will change the workplace," *Financial Post,* 16 September 2013,

Endnotes

http://business.financialpost.com/2013/09/16/like-it-or-not -millennials -will-change-the-workplace/.

41. Anne Kingston, "Get ready for Generation Z," *Maclean's*, 15 July 2014, http://www.macleans.ca/society/life /get-ready-for-generation-z/.

42. Ibid.

43. Vineer Nayar, "Handing the Keys to Gen Y," *Harvard Business Review*, May 2013.

44. Christopher Hann, "We're All in This Together," *Entrepreneur*, March 2013.

45. Dan Schawbel, "Employers, prepare to meet Gen Z,"

46. Ryan Inzana, "Your New Office BFFs," *Money*, May 2013.

47. Dan Schawbel, "Employers, prepare to meet Gen Z,"

48. Anne Kingston, "Get ready for Generation Z,"

49. Dan Schawbel, "Employers, prepare to meet Gen Z,"

50. Marina Khidekel, "The Misery of Mentoring Millennials," *Bloomberg Businessweek*, 18–24 March 2013.

Chapter 12

1. "Coming to an Office Near You," *The Economist*, 18 January 2014; and "The Onrushing Wave," *The Economist*, 18 January 2014.

2. Joshua Wright, "America's Skilled Trades Dilemma: Shortages Loom as Most-in-Demand Group of Workers Age," *Forbes*, 7 March 2013.

3. Brad Plumer, "CBO: Expect Slower Growth This Decade—And as a Result Higher Deficits," *The Washington Post*, 4 February 2014.

4. Julian L. Alssid, "A New Gallup Survey Says Colleges and Employers Disagree about How Workforce-Ready Graduates Are. Who's Right?" *Huffington Post*, 27 February 2014.

5. Juan Carlos Perez, "IBM Preps Talent Suite for Human Resources Tasks," *PC World*, 27 January 2014.

6. Patricia Stilwell, "Report : Economy Will Face Shortage of 20 Million Workers in 2020," *US News & World Report*, 8 July 2013.

7. "Canada's 100 Best Small & Medium Employers—Richter LLP," *The Globe and Mail* and Mediacorp Canada Inc., March 2015, 7.

8. "Gone But Not Forgotten," *The Economist*, 1 March 2014.

9. "Canada's 100 Best Small & Medium Employers - Rohit Group's winning ways: challenge and teamwork," *The Globe and Mail* and Mediacorp Canada Inc., March 2015, 54.

10. Nicola Middlemiss, "Leveraging technology: because it's worth it," HRM Online, 23 March 2015, http://www.hrmonline.ca /hr-news/leveraging-technology-because-its-worth-it-189482.aspx.

11. Mark Cohen, "Online Hiring Tools Are Changing Recruiting Techniques," *The New York Times*, 15 May 2013; and Raj Sheth, "How to Establish a Recruiting Process and Develop a Culture," *The Washington Post*, 29 January 2014.

12. "About Us," Jobpostings, accessed 25 March 2015, http://www .jobpostings.ca/about-us.

13. John Brandon, "The Real Cost of Hiring the Wrong Employee," *Inc.*, September 2013.

14. "IMPORTANT THINGS TO KNOW: Our Hiring Process," Cedar Fair Parks, 2015, https://www.canadaswonderland.com/jobs /important-things-to-know.

15. Brandon, "The Real Cost of Hiring the Wrong Employee,"

16. LexisNexis, www.lexisnexis.com, accessed March 2014; and Dave Larsen, "LexisNexis Wins Software Industry Award," *Dayton Daily News*, 11 February 2014.

17. Suzanne Lucas, "How Much Employee Turnover Really Costs You," *Inc.*, August 2013; and Jena MacGregor, "What It Costs to Replace a Twenty-Something," *The Washington Post*, 6 August 2013.

18. Amanda Silliker, "More firms hiring contract workers," *Canadian HR Reporter*, 7 May 2012, http://www.hrreporter.com /articleview/13016-more-firms-hiring-contract-workers.

19. Mike Ittling, "The Rise of the Contingent Worker," *Forbes*, 19 December 2014, http://www.forbes.com/sites /sap/2014/12/19/the-rise-of-the-contingent-worker/.

20. Hermann Schwind et al., *Canadian Human Resource Management: A Strategic Approach*, 10th ed. (Toronto: McGraw-Hill Ryerson, 2013), 261.

21. Scott Levy, "Why Stellar Customer Service is Key to Building Your Online Brand," *Entrepreneur*, 23 December 2013.

22. Susana Mas, "Shortage of skilled workers could jeopardize the economy," CBC News, 25 June 2014, http://www.cbc.ca /news/politics/shortage-of-skilled-workers-could-jeopardize-the -economy-1.2687365.

23. Ibid.

24. GlobeSmart, www.globesmart.com, accessed March 2014.

25. "Canada's Top Employer for Young People," Mediacorp Canada Inc., 2015, http://www.eluta.ca /jobs-at-loblaws#young:young-more.

26. McDonald's, www.mcdonalds.com, accessed March 2014.

27. "Best Employers in Canada," Aon Hewitt, 2015, http://www .aon.com/canada/products-services/human-capital-consulting /consulting/best_employers/documents/casestudy_cisco.pdf.

28. Ross McCammon, "Guiding Lights," *Entrepreneur*, March 2013.

29. Jeffrey Dauksevich, "How to Be an Effective Mentor," *Entrepreneur*, 27 December 2013; and John Brandon, "How to Maximize the Benefits of Mentoring," *Inc.*, January 2014.

30. "Creating Opportunity for Generation Next: This Year's 'Canada's Top Employers for Young People' are Announced," CNW Group Inc., 24 April 2014, http://www.newswire.ca/en /story/1345087/creating-opportunity-for-generation-next-this -year-s-canada-s-top-employers-for-young-people-are-announced.

31. "From Y to Z a guide to the next generation of employees," Randstad, 2015, http://w.randstad.ca/y2z/.

32. Ibid.

33. Kristina Leung and Richard Yerema, "TD Bank Group," Mediacorp Canada Inc., 30 March 2015, http://www.eluta.ca /jobs-at-td-bank#diversity:diversity-more.

34. Daniel Bortz, "Ace Your Annual Review," *Money*, March 2014.

35. Sharon Wienbar, "Making Sense Out of Cents: Determining Employee Compensation," *Entrepreneur*, 13 February 2014.

36. Ronald J. Recardo and Diane Pricones, "Is Gainsharing for You?" www.qualidtydigest.com, accessed March 2014.

37. Motley Fool Staff, "Q-and-A with Nucor CEO Dan MiMicco," *The Motley Fool*, www.foolcom, 10 January 2011.

38. "Younger Generations Expect Companies to Stimulate Economy and Close Gender Gap—But Don't Expect Their Loyalty," PRNewswire, 26 February 2015, http://www.prnewswire .com/news-releases/younger-generations-expect-companies -to-stimulate-economy-and-close-gender-gap—but-dont-expect -their-loyalty-294174141.html.

39. Amanda Frank, "Do You Know How Much You're Paying for Health Benefits?" Monster.ca, accessed 31 March 2015, http://career -advice.monster.ca/salary-benefits/benefits-information/how -much-are-health-benefits-canada/article.aspx.

40. Karla Thorpe, Heidi Martin, and Elyse Lamontagne, "Benefits Benchmarking 2012," The Conference Board of Canada, October 2012, http://www.conferenceboard.ca/temp/0a77bd89-28c1 -4484-b58c-4ca1c91113b8/13-119_benefitsbenchmarking2012 .pdf, 44–47.

41. Schwind et al., *Canadian Human Resource Management — A Strategic Approach*, 366.

42. Ibid.

43. "Ontario public servants to pay more for retirement benefits," The Canadian Press, 18 February 2014, http://globalnews.ca/news/1157468/ ontario-public-servants-to-pay-more-for-retirement-benefits/.

44. "Canada's 100 Best Small & Medium Employers—Eat well: Vigilant Global goes all-out-on-perks," 61; and Patrick Schober, "10 incredible benefits employees like—and you can afford," HRBenefitsAlert.com, 12 June 2013, http://www.hrbenefitsalert .com/incredible-low-cost-benefits/.

45. "Canada's 100 Best Small & Medium Employers - Verafin Inc.," 8.

46. Scott Liebs, "You Can Buy Employee Happiness. (But Should You?) Companies That Offer Lavish Benefits Believe There Is a Return on their Investment. The Challenge: Figuring Out How to Calculate It," *Inc.*, January 2014.

47. Gwen Moran, "Surviving the Open-Floor Plan," *Entrepreneur*, 13 February 2014.

48. Scott Benson, "Why Compressed Workweeks Can Be Great for Employers and Employees," *Huffington Post,* 5 March 2014.

49. Schwind et al., *Canadian Human Resource Management,* 110.

50. Kristen Quan, "Amex Canada's Howard Grosfield," *Canadian Business,* April 2015, 18.

51. Schwind et al., *Canadian Human Resource Management,* 136–141; "Federal Labour Standards," Government of Canada, 16 March 2015, http://www.labour.gc.ca/eng/standards _equity/st/; and "Federally Regulated Businesses and Industries," Government of Canada, 10 February 2015, http://www.labour .gc.ca/eng/regulated.shtml.

52. "Budget 2012—What Does it Mean for Women's Economic Equality?" Canadian Labour Congress, May 2012, www .canadianlabour.ca/news-room/publications/budget-2012 -what-does-it-mean-women-s-economic-equality; "The Gender Wage Gap," Pay Equity Commission, 7 February 2012, www .payequity.gov.on.ca/en/about/pubs/genderwage/wagegap .php; "Women's Economic Equality Campaign," Canadian Labour Congress, 2009, www.canadianlabour.ca/en/womens_economic _equa; "Labour Force and Participation Rates by Sex and Age Group," Statistics Canada, 8 January 2009, http://www40 .statcan.gc.ca/l01/cst01/labor05-eng.htm; "Status Report on Pay Equity Laws in Canada," Canadian Labour Congress, 10 November 2008, http://canadianlabour.ca/en/status-report -pay-equity-laws-canada;"Working Women: Still a Long Way from Equality," Canadian Labour Congress, 3 March 2008, http:// canadianlabour.ca/sites/clc/files/updir/WorkingWomenEn.txt; "Pay Equity and Women in Canada," Canadian Feminist Alliance for International Action, 1 January 2007, www.fafia-afai.org /en/pay_equity_and_women_in_canada; and Colin Freeze, "Bell Settles Pay Equity Dispute," *The Globe and Mail,* 16 May 2006, A5.

53. "Employment Equity," Government of Canada, 5 December 2014, http://www.labour.gc.ca/eng/standards_equity/eq/emp/; and Schwind et al., *Canadian Human Resource Management,* 147–151.

54. "Fact Sheet—Temporary Foreign Worker Program," Government of Canada, 19 February 2015, http://www.cic.gc.ca/english /resources/publications/employers/temp-foreign-worker -program.asp; and Bill Curry, "Everything you need to know about temporary foreign workers," *The Globe and Mail,* 24 June 2014, http://www.theglobeandmail.com/news /politics/temporary-foreign-workers-everything-you-need-to -know/article18363279/.

Chapter 13

1. Statistics Canada, "Table 282-0089" Labour force survey estimates (LFS), employment by class of worker and sex, seasonally adjusted and unadjusted monthly (persons x 1,000)," Statistics Canada, 13 March 2015, http://www5.statcan.gc.ca /cansim/pick-choisir?lang=eng&p2=33&id=2820089#F3.

2. Statistics Canada, "Table 282-0223: Labour Force Survey estimates (LFS), employees by union status, North American Industry Classification System (NAICS) and sex," Statistics Canada, 30 January 2015, http://www5.statcan.gc.ca/cansim /pick-choisir?lang=eng&p2=33&id=2820223.

3. Tom Watson, "Jobs with Justice: New Campaign Takes Aim at Low Wages, Working Poor, Falling Middle Class," *Forbes,* 30 December 2013.

4. "Youth," UFCW Canada, 2015, http://ufcw.ca/index .php?option=com_content&view=article&id=2000:youth-homepa ge&catid=57:youth&Itemid=189&lang=en.

5. Kevin O'Marah, "The Real Threat to U.S. Manufacturing," *Forbes,* 23 April 2008; and Steven Greenhouse, "Union Membership Up Sharply in 2008, Report Says," *New York Times,* 29 January 2009.

6. Luke Rosiak, "Union Bosses' Salaries Put 'Big' in Big Labor," *Washington Times,* 11 January 2013; and Andrew Doughman, "Union Leaders Salaries Stay High Even in Hard Times," *Las Vegas Sun,* 19 August 2013.

7. Gerry Varricchio, Regional Organizing Director for Central and Eastern Canada, The Labourers' International Union of North America, interview, 25 March 2015, Hamilton.

8. Morgan Housal, "50 Reasons Why This is the Greatest Time Ever," *USA Today,* 2 February 2014.

9. "Winnipeg General Strike," *The Canadian Encyclopedia,* accessed 30 March 2015, http://www.thecanadianencyclopedia.ca/en /article/winnipeg-general-strike/.

10. "Union Coverage in Canada, 2013," Government of Canada - Labour Program, 12 June 2014, http:// www.labour.gc.ca/eng/resources/info/publications /union_coverage/union_coverage.shtml#fnb2; "National Union Centrals," *The Canadian Encyclopedia,* accessed 30 March 2015, www.thecanadianencyclopedia.com/index. cfm?PgNm=TCE&Params=A1ARTA0008214; "About the CLC," Canadian Labour Congress, accessed 31 March 2015, http:// www.canadianlabour.ca/about-clc; and "Green Jobs," Canadian Labour Congress, accessed 31 March 2015, http://www .canadianlabour.ca/issues/green-jobs.

11. "Union Coverage in Canada, 2013," World Wide Web.

12. Diane Galarneau and Thao Sohn, "Long-term trends in unionization," Statistics Canada, November 2013, http://www .statcan.gc.ca/pub/75-006-x/2013001/article/11878-eng.pdf, 5.

13. "Table 282-0220: Labour Force Survey estimates (LFS), employees by union status, sex and age group, Canada and provinces annual (persons)," Statistics Canada, 30 January 2015, http://www5.statcan.gc.ca/cansim/pick-choisir.

14. Galarneau and Sohn, "Long-term trends in unionization," 4.

15. "CUPE at a glance," Canadian Union of Public Employees, accessed 31 March 2015, http://cupe.ca/cupe-glance.

16. "About Unifor," Unifor, accessed 31 March 2015, http://www .unifor.org/en/about-unifor; "Sectors," Unifor, accessed 31 March 2015, http://www.unifor.org/en/member-services/sectors; and "FAQs," Unifor, accessed 31 March 2015, http://www.unifor.org /en/why-unifor/faq.

17. "Federally Regulated Businesses and Industries," Government of Canada, 10 February 2015, http://www.labour.gc.ca/eng /regulated.shtml.

18. Mike Blanchfield, "Public Sector Workers' Right To Strike Protected By Constitution: Top Court," The Canadian Press, 30 January 2015, http://www.huffingtonpost.ca/2015/01/30 /public-sector-workers-strike-supreme-court_n_6577280.html; and Mike Blanchfield, "Supreme Court strikes down law that prevents public sector strikes," *The Toronto Star,* 30 January 2015, http://www.thestar.com/news/canada/2015/01/30/supreme -court-strikes-down-law-that-prevents-public-sector-strikes.html.

19. James Fiz-Morris, "Ruling says union is one option, as federal government given a year to amend law," CBC News, 16 January 2015, http://www.cbc.ca/news/politics/rcmp-officers-have-right -to-collective-bargaining-supreme-court-rules-1.2912340.

20. "Day of mourning for workers killed or injured on the job," Public Service Alliance of Canada, 27 April 2015, http://psacunion.ca /national-day-mourning; "Workers' Rights in Canada," Government of Canada, 5 March 2014, http://www .servicecanada.gc.ca/eng/about/publication/workers_rights. shtml; "Federally Regulated Businesses and Industries," World Wide Web; "Think Workplace Fatalities are a Thing of the Past? Together, we have made progress but we must keep fighting for safer workplaces," Canadian Labour Congress, 24 April 2014, http://www.canadianlabour.ca/news-room/statements /think-workplace-fatalities-are-thing-past-together-we-have-made -progress-we-mus; "Day of Mourning," Canadian Labour Congress, [n.d.], http://www.canadianlabour.ca/issues/day-mourning; Sara Mojtehedzadeh, "Ministry of Labour inspection uncovers thousands of youth safety violations," TheStar.com, 14 January 2014, http://www.thestar.com/news/gta/2015/01/14 /ministry-of-labour-inspection-uncovers-thousands-of-youth -safety-violations.html; "Safe Workplaces: The Right to a Safe and Healthy Workplace," Workrights.ca, www.workrights.ca /Health+and+Safety/Safe+Workplaces.htm; "Workplace Dangers

(Right to Know About Workplace Dangers)," Workrights.ca, www
.workrights.ca/Health+and+Safety/Workplace+dangers.htm.

21. Hermann Schwind et al., *Canadian Human Resource Management:
A Strategic Approach,* 10th ed. (Toronto: McGraw-Hill Ryerson,
2013), 473; "Labour Relations—Canada Labour Code Part I,"
Government of Canada, 3 April 2013, http://www.cirb-ccri.gc.ca
/eic/site/047.nsf/eng/h_00008.html; and "Canada Industrial
Relations Board: Welcome to the CIRB," Canada Industrial
Relations Board, 5 January 2015, http://www.cirb-ccri.gc.ca/eic
/site/047.nsf/eng/home.

22. Varricchio, interview, 25 March 2015.

23. Ibid.

24. Pierre Poilievre, "Unions ignore the Rand formula," *Financial Post,*
5 January 2013, http://business.financialpost.com/fp-comment
/unions-ignore-the-rand-formula.

25. www.carpenters.org, accessed April 2014; and Austin Smith,
"What Right-to-Work Would Do for New York," *New York Post,*
12 December 2012.

26. Aaron Rousseau, Founder and Lawyer, Rousseau Law, interview,
17 March 2015.

27. "Union Advantage 2014," Canadian Labour Congress, http://
www.canadianlabour.ca/about-clc/union-advantage-2014,
downloaded 1 April 2015.

28. Schwind et al., *Canadian Human Resource Management:
A Strategic Approach,* 481.

29. Ibid., 480.

30. Ibid.

31. Ira Podell, "NHL Lockout 2012: Mediator Gets League, Union
Back Together," Associated Press, 5 January 2013; and Mike
Brehm and Kevin Allen, "NHL Lockout Ends at 113 Days: A Daily
Look Back," *USA Today,* 6 January 2013.

32. "Arbitration award for flight attendants profoundly disappointing:
Moist," Canadian Union of Public Employees, 7 November 2011,
http://cupe.ca/airlines/arbitration-award-flight-attendants.

33. "Essential Services," CBC News, 6 May 2008, www.cbc.ca
/news/background/strike/.

34. Kathryn May, "Head of smaller union proposes sharing
strike fund with PSAC, PIPSC," *Ottawa Citizen,* 29 March 2015,
http://ottawacitizen.com/news/national/head-of-smaller-union
-proposes-sharing-strike-fund-with-psac-pipsc.

35. Steve Greenhouse, "Wage Strike Planned at Fast Food Outlets,"
New York Times, 1 December 2013.

36. "FAQ: Back-to-work legislation," CBC News,
15 June 2011, http://www.cbc.ca/news/canada
/faq-back-to-work-legislation-1.1000525.

37. Yuliya Talmazan, "Nearly half of B.C. parents with children in
school support teachers: poll," Global News, 9 June 2014,
http://globalnews.ca/news/1383769/nearly-half-of-b-c-parents
-with-children-in-school-support-teachers-poll/; and Steven Chua,
"B.C. Teachers Return To School As Public Classes Finally
Start," The Canadian Press, 21 September 2014, http://
www.huffingtonpost.ca/2014/09/21/bc-teachers-school-
starts_n_5858208.html.

38. "New ads ask Air Canada to offer a fair deal and avoid a strike,"
Canadian Union of Public Employees, 17 September 2011,
http://cupe.ca/air-canada/ads-air-canada-offer-fair-deal-avoid.

39. Karla Thorpe, "The State of Canadian Unions—Down but Not
Out," The Conference Board of Canada, 31 January 2013, http://
www.conferenceboard.ca/topics/humanresource
/commentaries/13-01-31/the_state_of_canadian_unions
—down_but_not_out.aspx.

40. Ibid.

41. Joseph S. Mancinelli, International Vice-President for Central and
Eastern Canada for the Labourers' International Union of North
America, interview, 25 March 2015.

42. Jeff Green, "Golden Hellos," *Bloomberg Businessweek,*
8 December 2013.

43. Jonathan R. Costa, "Target CEO's severance pay-
out causes online outrage," *The Toronto Observer,*
4 February 2015, http://torontoobserver.ca/2015/02/04
/target-ceos-severance-pay-out-causes-online-outrage/.

44. Damian Paletta, "5 Takeaways on Wealth and Inequality from
Picketty," *The Wall Street Journal,* 14 April 2014.

45. Costa," "Target CEO's severance pay-out causes online outrage,"
World Wide Web.

46. Graham F. Scott, "Canada's Top 100 highest-paid CEOs,
Canadian Business, 20 January 2015, http://www
.canadianbusiness.com/lists-and-rankings/richest-people
/top-100-highest-paid-ceos-2015/.

47. www.censusbureau.gov, downloaded April 2014.

48. www.caregiving.org, downloaded April 2014.

49. Julie Landry Laviolette, "Tips in Caring for Your Aging Parents,"
Miami Herald, 4 February 2014.

Chapter 14

1. "Code of Ethics and Standards of Practice," Canadian Marketing
Association, www.the-cma.org/regulatory/code-of-ethics,
downloaded 6 April 2015.

2. Brent Adamson, Matthew Dixon, and Nicholas Toman, "A New
Guide to Selling," *Harvard Business Review,* August 2012.

3. Patrick Spenner and Karen Freemen, "To Keep Your Customers,
Keep It Simple," *Harvard Business Review,* May 2012.

4. Kasey Wehrum, "Their Carts Are Full, So Why Won't They Buy?"
Inc., December 2013.

5. J.J. Martin, "The Shopping Social Networks," *The Wall Street
Journal,* 27–28 October 2012.

6. A. G. Lafley and Ram Charan, "The Consumer Is Boss," *Fortune,*
17 March 2008.

7. Ryan Charkow, "5 young Canadian entrepreneurs reveal secrets
to success," CBC News, 6 October 2011, www.cbc.ca/news
/business/smallbusiness/story/2011/09/28/f-smallbiz-young
-entrepreneurs.html.

8. Frederick G. Crane et al., *Marketing,* 9th Canadian ed. (Toronto:
McGraw-Hill Ryerson, 2014), 15–16.

9. Ibid., 18; "Social Media Marketing Quick-Start Guide," Canadian
Marketing Association, 19 July 2011, www.the-cma.org
/Media/Default/Downloads/Library/2011/SocialMediaQSG
.pdf; "blogYOUR TAKE/Mobile spa relies 100% on social
media," CBC News, 17 October 2011, www.cbc.ca/news
/business/smallbusiness/story/2011/10/17/small-business
-your-take-blog-goertzen.html; "Social Media Revolution 2015
#Socialnomics," YouTube.com, 26 January 2015, https://
www.youtube.com/watch?v=jottDMuLesU; and Erik Qualman,
Socialnomics (New York: Wiley, 2009).

10. "Use of Social Media Among Canada's Small Business
Owners Up 42 Percent from 2012," BMO Financial Group,
25 October 2013, http://newsroom.bmo.com/press-releases
/bmo-report-use-of-social-media-among-canada-s-sma-tsx-
bmo-201310250906689001.

11. Ibid.

12. Vanessa Small, "LinkedIn Connects Members with Volunteer
Options," *The Washington Post,* 21 January 2014.

13. Alexander Lobrano, "La Nouvelle Veg," *The Wall Street Journal,*
20–21 April 2013.

14. Annie Gasparro and Juoie Jargon, "McDonald's to Go Vegetarian
in India," *The Wall Street Journal,* 5 September 2012.

15. Jolinda Hackett, "Quick update about KFC's vegetarian chicken
in Canada," About.com, 28 June 2013, http://vegetarian.about.
com/b/2013/06/28/quick-update-about-kfcs-vegetarian-chicken
-in-canada.htm; and Rachit Vats, "KFC goes curry, vegetarian
to bounce back in India," *Hindustan Times,* 6 January 2013,
http://www.hindustantimes.com/business-news/CorporateNews
/KFC-goes-curry-vegetarian-to-bounce-back-in-India
/Article1-985900.aspx.

16. Terence Chea, "San Francisco Startup Seeks Egg Alternatives,"
The Washington Times, 9 December 2013.

17. Dinah Eng, "A Fresh Take on Food," *Fortune,* 29 April 2013.

18. Crane et al., *Marketing,* 316.

19. "Employment by industry," Statistics Canada, 28 January 2015,
http://www.statcan.gc.ca/tables-tableaux/sum-som/l01/cst01
/econ40-eng.htm.

20. Tim Kraft, "The Trick to Getting NoBull on More Grills," *The Washington Post,* 20 January 2013.

21. Crane et al., *Marketing,* 337.

22. Susan Dumenco, "Data, Data Everywhere, and Not an Insight in Sight," *Advertising Age,* 18 March 2013.

23. Crane et al., *Marketing,* 219.

24. Ibid., 220.

25. Ibid.

26. Ibid., 205.

27. Ibid.

28. Seamus Bellamy, "A good e-reader gets better: Amazon Kindle Paperwhite," *The Globe and Mail,* 10 January 2014, http://www.theglobeandmail.com/technology/gadgets-and-gear/gadgets/a-good-e-reader-gets-better-amazon-kindle-paperwhite/article16283359/.

29. "CRTC decision reduces some Northwestel internet rates for NWT, Yukon," *Nunatsiq News,* 5 March 2015, http://www.nunatsiaqonline.ca/stories/article/65674crtc_decision_to_lower_internet_rates_in_some_northern_communities/.

30. Crane et al., *Marketing,* 114.

31. Jessica Leeder, "Campbell's Nourish brand tackles hunger through Canada's food banks," *The Globe and Mail,* 23 August 2012, http://www.theglobeandmail.com/news/national/campbells-nourish-brand-tackles-hunger-through-canadas-food-banks/article568486/; "The Story of Nourish from Campbell Canada," Campbell Soup Company, YouTube video, 29 January 2012, https://www.youtube.com/watch?v=KUUqJIjObwY; and "Campbell Canada launches Nourish in response to growing hunger issue here and abroad," CNW Group, 28 February 2011, http://smr.newswire.ca/en/campbell-company-of-canada/campbell-canada-launches-nourish.

32. "Campbell Canada launches Nourish in response to growing hunger issue here and abroad," World Wide Web.

33. Mark Henricks, "B2B," *Inc.,* February 2-14.

34. Crane et al., *Marketing,* 241.

35. Francine Kopun, " Canadian Tire announces 'generational shift' in new billion-dollar strategy," *The Toronto Star,* 9 October 2014, http://www.thestar.com/business/2014/10/09/canadian_tire_announces_generational_shift_billiondollar_digital_and_expansion.html.

36. Susan Greco, "A World without Bestsellers: Creating a 'Long Tail' Product Mix," *Inc.,* September 2007.

37. Susan Krashinsky, "Healthy food trend sees McDonald's, Coca-Cola's profits slim down, "*The Globe and Mail,* 21 October 2014, http://www.theglobeandmail.com/report-on-business/healthy-food-trend-sees-mcdonalds-coco-colas-profits-slim-down/article21209076/.

38. Josh Sanburn, "What Pizza Hut's Radical New Menu Actually Tastes Like," *Time,* 10 November 2014, http://time.com/3576913/pizza-hut-menu-new/.

39. Crane et al, *Marketing,* 248; and Dhruv Grewal et al., *Marketing,* 3rd Canadian ed. (Toronto: McGraw-Hill Ryerson, 2014), 189.

40. Grewal et al., *Marketing,* 490.

41. Ibid., 288.

42. Ibid., 306.

43. "G adventures named Canada's favourite adventure travel tour operator," G Adventures, 28 Jun 2012, www.gadventures.com/press-releases/2012/Jun/28/g-adventures-named-canadas-favourite-adventure-travel-tour-operator/.

44. "LEGENDS OF THE SMALL," Report on Small Business, *The Globe and Mail,* June 2012, p. 17.

45. Crane et al., *Marketing,* 83-86; and Grewal et al., *Marketing,* 91–92.

Chapter 15

1. Timothy Appel, "A Crib for Baby: Made in China or Made in U.S.A.," *The Wall Street Journal,* 22 May 2012.

2. Dana Mattioli and Miguel Bustillo, "Can Texting Save Stores?" *The Wall Street Journal,* 9 May 2012.

3. Annie Gasparro and Melodie Warner, "New Menu Boosts McDonalds," *The Wall Street Journal,* 11 June 2013; Maureen Morrison, "The Breakfast Club: Restaurant Marketers Wake Up to $50 Billion Opportunity," *Advertising Age,* 13 May 2013; Julie Jargon, "McDonald's Pledges to Offer Veggies," *The Wall Street Journal,* 27 September 2013; and editorial in Nutrition Action Newsletter, January/February 2014.

4. Kurt Haanaes, David Michael, Jeremy Jurgens, and Subramanian Ragan, "Making Sustainability Profitable," *Harvard Business Review,* March 2013.

5. Emma K. Macdonald, Hugh N. Wilson, and Umut Konus, "Better Customer Insight—In Real Time," *Harvard Business Review,* March 2013.

6. Serena Ng, "At P&G, New Tide Comes In, Old Price Goes Up," *The Wall Street Journal,* 11 February 2014.

7. Sarah Nassauer, "Organic Tries to Grow Up," *The Wall Street Journal,"* 23 January 2014.

8. Keith Goldberg, "How You Can Stay in Control of Your Brand's Reputation," *Advertising Age,* 9 February 2009.

9. Linda Nguyen, "The country's most valuable brands? Banks," The Canadian Press, 27 February 2015, http://www.thestar.com/business/2015/02/27/the-countrys-most-valuable-brands-banks.html.

10. Akhila Vijayaraghavan, "Puma, Nike and Adidas Run Towards Toxin-Free Products With Greenpeace," Triple Pundit.com, 7 September 2011, www.triplepundit.com/2011/09/puma-nike-adidas-greenpeace/.

11. Ibid.

12. Paul Resnikoff, "15 Reasons Why You Should Never, Ever Buy a Streaming Service . . .," Digital Music News, 30 January 2015, http://www.digitalmusicnews.com/permalink/2015/01/30/15-reasons-never-ever-buy-streaming-service.

13. Sarah Perez, "YouTube Confirms Plans For An Ad-Free, Subscription-BasedService," TechCrunch, 8 April 2015, http://techcrunch.com/2015/04/08/youtube-confirms-plans-for-an-ad-free-subscription-based-service/.

14. Geoffrey A. Fowler, "Price Check: Do Online Grocers Beat Supermarkets?" *The Wall Street Journal,* 8 January 2014.

15. Anne Gasparro, "McDonald's, Wendy's in Price Fight," *The Wall Street Journal,* 9 May 2013.

16. Judith Ohikuare, "New Year, No Excuses," *Inc.,* February 2013.

17. "About Dollarama," Dollarama Inc., 2015, http://www.dollarama.com/about_us/.

18. Norm Brodsky, "The Wholesalers Dilemma," *Inc.,* October 2012.

19. "Retail sales, by industry (unadjusted)," Statistics Canada, 21 August 2015, www.statcan.gc.ca/tables-tableaux/sum-som/l01/cst01/trad15a-eng.htm; and "Employment, payroll employment, by industry (Retail Trade)," Statistics Canada, 31 March 2015, www.statcan.gc.ca/tables-tableaux/sum-som/l01/cst01/labr71a-eng.htm.

20. Lauren Indvik, "The 7 Species of Social Commerce," Mashable, http://mashable.com/2013/05/10/social-commerce-definition/, downloaded 13 April 2015.

21. James K. Glassman, "Top Dogs in E-tailing," *Kiplinger's Personal Finance,* June 2012.

22. "Who Can Still Call You?" Canadian Radio-television and Telecommunications Commission, 12 March 2015, https://www.lnnte-dncl.gc.ca/cofi-fico-eng.

23. David Beederman, "Charting Sustainability," *The Journal of Commerce,* 2 September 2013.

24. Julie Liesse, "15 on 15: Council Founders Share Industry Highlights," *Advertising Age,* Special Advertising Section, 11 November 2013.

25. "Coke: Buzz Doesn't Work, but Social Is Crucial," *Advertising Age,* editorial, 25 March 2013.

26. Wes Nichols," The Future of Advertising," *Harvard Business Review,* March 2013.

27. Christina Pellegrini, "Number of TV cable cord-cutters growing faster than expected," *Financial Post,* 14 April 2014, http://business.financialpost.com/fp-tech-desk/number-of-tv-cable-cord-cutters-growing-faster-than-expected?__lsa=3196-70e9.

28. Ibid.
29. Lena H. Sun, "Captivating an Audience," *The Washington Post*, 6 April 2008.
30. Russ Hill, "What Is the Cost of a B2B Sales Call?" *CRM Highlights*, 4 November 2013, http://www.crm-insights.com.
31. Katrina Pugh and Laurance Prusak, "Designing Effective Knowledge Networks," *Sloan Management Review*, Fall 2013.
32. Lisa Ward, "What to Do after Your 15 Minutes of Fame," *The Wall Street Journal*, 2 December 2013.
33. Rakesh Niraj, "Just How Much Is Word of Mouth Worth?" *Weatherhead Collection*, Fall 2013.
34. Michael McCarthy, "Tesla Generates Small Sales, Huge Buzz Without Paid Ads," *Advertising Age*, 10 June 2013; and Omar Merlo, Andreas B. Eisingerich and Seigyoung Auh, "Why Customer Participation Matters," *Sloan Management Review*, Winter 2014.
35. "Get 'Em Talking," *Entrepreneur*, editorial, August 2012.
36. Michael Fitzgerald, "The Myth about Viral Marketing," *Sloan Management Review*, Spring 2013.
37. Ralph F. Wilson, "The Six Simple Principles of Viral Marketing," *Web Marketing Today*, 12 May 2012, http://www.webmarketingtoday.com.
38. Kim Garst, "Social Media Marketing World 2014," *Huffington Post*, 9 April 2014, http://www.huffingtonpost.com.

Chapter 16

1. Eric Sobota, "Doing Business with the Government: Administrative Challenges Faced by Nonprofits," *Nonprofit Quarterly*, 14 June 2014; and John A. Byrne, "The GMAT: An Exam with Greater Profit Margins Than Apple," *Fortune Magazine*, 17 February 2014.
2. Evan Taylor, "Best Jobs: Accountant," *U.S. News and World Report*, 22 January 2014.
3. "Anshula Chowdhury," *Canadian Business*, April 2015, p. 7.
4. "About Us," Social Asset Measurements Inc., http://www.socialassets.org/about-us/history/, downloaded 20 April 2015.
5. Nellie S. Huang, "Make the Most of an Annual Report," *Kiplinger's Personal Finance*, March 2014.
6. Robert Libby et al., *Financial Accounting*, 5th Canadian ed. (Canada: McGraw-Hill Ryerson Ltd.), 301.
7. "About the AcSB," Financial Reporting & Assurance Standards Canada, http://www.frascanada.ca/accounting-standards-board/what-we-do/about-the-acsb/index.aspx, downloaded 18 April 2015.
8. Ibid.
9. Mariella Segarra, "FASB Issues New Private Company Accounting Alternatives," *CFO*, 20 January 2014; and "Generally Accepted Accounting Principles-GAAP," Investopedia, LLC, 2015, http://www.investopedia.com/terms/g/gaap.asp.
10. "Shining a Light on the Auditors," *The Economist*, 7 December 2013.
11. Michael Rapoport, "Audit Reports Add Beef," *The Wall Street Journal*, 13 August 2013; and Nellie Huang, "7 Clues for Investors to Look for Within Annual Reports," *Kiplinger's Personal Finance*, March 2014.
12. Michael Rapport, "KPMG to Pay $8.2 Million to Settle SEC Charges," *The Wall Street Journal*, 24 January 2014.
13. Kathy Hoffelder, "To Audit Deficiency: Evidence Collection," *CFO*, 10 May 2013.
14. Amrick Randhawa, "Don't Have a Tax Pro Yet? Time to Get Moving," *Entrepreneur*, 12 February 2014; and Pamela Yip, "Be Picky When Choosing a Tax Preparer," *Dallas Morning News*, 26 January 2014.
15. "About the Canada Revenue Agency (CRA)," Government of Canada, 22 October 2014, http://www.cra-arc.gc.ca/gncy/menu-eng.html.
16. Colleen O'Connor, "More Than Half of Nonprofits Haven't Recovered Recession Losses," *The Denver Post*, 10 December 2013.
17. "Adapting to a changing climate: Getting more accountants engaged," CPA Canada, 20 February 2015, https://www.cpacanada.ca/en/connecting-and-news/news/professional-news/2015/February/adapting-to-climate-change-engaging-accountants;

"CPA provincial and regional accounting bodies," CPA Canada, 2015, https://www.cpacanada.ca/en/the-cpa-profession/cpa-provincial-and-regional-accounting-bodies; "Uniting the Canadian accounting profession," CPA Canada, 2015, https://www.cpacanada.ca/en/the-cpa-profession/uniting-the-canadian-accounting-profession; "The new Canadian CPA Bringing together three legacy accounting designations," Hays Canada, *Connected*, issue 6, October 2014, https://www.cpapro.ca/pdfs/hays_1242697.pdf; and "Become a CPA," CPA Canada, 2015, https://www.cpapro.ca/become-a-cpa.
18. Michael Cohn, "Wave Adds Bank Reconciliation to Online Accounting Software," *Accounting Today*, 11 February 2014; and Pedro Hernandez, "Plan for Small Business Success," *Small Business Computing*, 14 February 2014.
19. Tom Taulli, "Xero: Taking Aim at the Intuit Goliath," *Forbes*, 26 January 2014.
20. Barrie McKenna, "As Microsoft targets small business, cloud computing costs fall," *The Globe and Mail*, 3 June 2014, http://www.theglobeandmail.com/report-on-business/international-business/microsoft-grows-cloud-computing-clients/article18977153/.
21. Ibid.
22. Ibid.
23. Mary Ellen Biery, "What Are Your Financial Statements Telling You?" *Forbes*, 22 December 2013.
24. Catherine Clifford," New Accounting Framework to Ease Burdens for Small Business," *Entrepreneur*, 10 June 2013.
25. Jonathan Lack, "How to Manage Your Cash Flow Better in 2014," *Houston Business Journal*, 23 January 2014.
26. Jill Hamburg-Conlon, "Don't Run Out of Cash: 3 Growth Company Case Studies," *Inc.*, January 2014.
27. Joe Worth, "How Much Cash On Hand Is Too Much? And What Should I Do with It?" *Entrepreneur*, January 2014.

Chapter 17

1. Karen Weise, "Big Paydays for CFOs," *Bloomberg Businessweek*, 19 May 2013; and Emily Coyle, "Meet the Five Highest Paid CFOs in the S&P 500," *The Week*, 8 July 2013.
2. Mariella Segarra and David M. Katz, "What's It Like to be a Nonprofit CFO?" CFO.com, 27 November 2013.
3. "Targeted Assistance for the Automotive Sector (Budget 2009 and Budget 2010), www.actionplan.gc.ca/initiatives/eng/index.asp?initiativeID=179&mode=3.
4. McCormick, www.mccormick.com, accessed February 2014.
5. Amy Haimerl, "15 Costly Mistakes Startups Make," *Crain's Detroit Business*, 10 February 2014.
6. Glenn Kessler, "Senator Scott's Claim That the Medical Device Tax Will Cost Small Business $29 Billion," *The Washington Post*, 4 February 2014.
7. Kathy Hoffelder, "Poor Internal Control Tests Hurt Financial Statement Audits," *CFO*, 13 October 2013.
8. Kathy Hoffelder, "Internal Audit Shines Brighter with Boards," *CFO*, 22 March 2013.
9. Bill Conerly, "Long-Term Economic Forecast: Key Issues and Business Strategy Implications," *Forbes*, 12 January 2014.
10. Russ Banham, "May the Field Be with You," *CFO*, 9 October 2013.
11. Claudia Cattaneo, "Canadian oil producers brace for long downturn as Husky, MEG Energy, Penn West axe budgets," *Financial Post*, 17 December 2014, http://business.financialpost.com/news/energy/canadian-oil-producers-brace-for-long-downturn-as-husky-meg-energy-penn-west-axe-budgets?__lsa=e9ed-cd75.
12. Ibid.
13. Ibid.
14. Khan Academy, www.khanacademy.org, accessed February 2014.
15. Scott Liebs, "4 Money Mistakes That Entrepreneurs Must Avoid," *Inc.*, February 2014.
16. T. J. McCue, "Why Don't More Small Businesses Accept Credit Cards?" *Forbes*, 8 August 2013; and "What You May Not Know

about Your Credit Card Processor," *Milwaukee Journal Sentinel,* 3 February 2014.

17. Scott Kirsner, "Startups Offer Tech to Change the Way You Pay," *The Boston Globe,* 9 February 2014.

18. Venessa Wong, "Chipotle Wants to Speed Up with Mobile Payments," *Bloomberg Businessweek,* 3 February 2014.

19. J.J. Colao, "Interchange Fees Are for Suckers: LevelUp Hints at the Future of Mobile Payments," *Forbes,* 21 March 2013.

20. Ty Kisel, "Small Business Financing Is Available, Just Not Where You're Looking," *Forbes,* 24 September 2013.

21. Karen Haywood Queen, "Borrowing from Friends and Family," *MSN Money,* 3 September 2013.

22. National Federation of Independent Businesses, www.nfib.com, accessed February 2014.

23. Stephen D. Simpson, CFA, "The Basics of Lines of Credit," Forbes.com, 6 August 2013.

24. "Your Credit Profile," Canadian Bankers Association, 2015, http://yourmoney.cba.ca/students/inside/your_credit_profile/; "Understanding the Basics of Business Credit," Dun & Bradstreet, Inc., 2015, https://iupdate.dnb.com/iUpdate/whatAre4Cs.htm.

25. "Commercial Paper," Investopedia, LLC, accessed 21 April 2015, http://www.investopedia.com/terms/c/commercialpaper.asp.

26. John Parry, "U.S. Commercial Paper Contracts to Lowest Level Since September," *Bloomberg Businessweek,* 23 January 2014.

27. Annamaria Andriotis, "The Return of Small-Business Credit Cards," *The Wall Street Journal,* 16 January 2012; "American Express OPEN Revamps Simple Cash® Business Credit Card by Giving Small Business Owners the Ability to Customize Their Cash Back Rewards," *The Wall Street Journal,* 28 January 2014; and "Petflow.com Continues Dominant Rise to Become Highest-Trafficked Online Pet Property in North America," Business Wire, 13 February 2014.

28. Jonathan D. Rockoff and Tess Stynes, "Pfizer is Upbeat about Breast Cancer Drug, Pneumonia Vaccine," *The Wall Street Journal,* 28 January 2014.

29. Dan Carroll, "Pfizer Beats Falling Profit as the Dow Bounces Back from Recent Lows," *The Motley Fool,* 28 January 2014; and Johanna Bennett, "Pfizer's Finally a Buy," *Barron's,* 12 February 2014.

30. "Canada sells more 50-year bonds," CBC News, 11 July 2014, http://www.cbc.ca/news/business /canada-sells-more-50-year-bonds-1.2703972.

31. Katy Burne, "Bankers Pitch 100-Year Bonds," *The Wall Street Journal,* 23 August 2010; Vivianne Sander, Michael Mackenzie, and Henny Sander, "Verizon Eyes Maturities of 100 Years for Bonds," *Financial Times,* 7 September 2013; and Katie Linsell, "EDF's Borrowing Exceeds $12 Billion This Week with 100-Year Bond," *Bloomberg News,* 17 January 2014.

32. "Strong Demand for Ontario's First Green Bond Nearly $2.4 Billion in Orders for the $500 Million Offering," Ontario Ministry of Finance, 9 October 2014, http://news.ontario.ca/mof/en/2014 /10/strong-demand-for-ontarios-first-green-bond.html.

33. William Baldwin, "Six Ways to Inflation-Proof Your Bonds," *Forbes,* 2 March 2011; and "4 Ways Your Bonds Can Fit into Your Portfolio," *Forbes,* 9 February 2012.

34. "Cara to raise $200M in IPO as early as April," CBC News, 23 March 2015, http://www.cbc.ca/news/business /cara-to-raise-200m-in-ipo-as-early-as-april-1.3005465.

35. "Cara shares jump 40% as parent of Harvey's and Swiss Chalet returns to TSX," *Financial Post,* 10 April 2015, http:// business.financialpost.com/investing/cara-shares -jump-40-as-parent-of-harveys-and-swiss-chalet-returns-to-tsx; and Eric Lam, "Cara's a Beautiful Thing in Best IPO Debut Since 2007," Bloomberg L.P., 10 April 2015, http://www.bloomberg .com/news/articles/2015-04-10 /cara-s-a-beautiful-thing-in-best-ipo-debut-since-2007.

36. Shirley A. Lazo, "Global Payouts Hit $1 Trillion," *Barron's,* 1 March 2014.

37. "Canadian Natural Resources raises dividend as profit almost triples," The Canadian Press, 5 March 2014, http://www.cbc.ca /news/business/canadian-natural-resources-raises-dividend-as -profit-almost-triples-1.2982571.

38. "BCE hikes dividend 5% as Bell sees profit rise 10%," The Canadian Press, 5 February 2015, http://www.cbc .ca/news/business/bce-hikes-dividend-5-as-bell-sees -profit-rise-10-1.2945982.

39. "Common and Preferred Stock: What's the Difference," *The Motley Fool,* 23 February 2014.

40. Tom Konrad, "Power REIT's Preferred Stock Offering: A Hedge that Pays 7.75%," *Forbes,* 7 February 2014.

41. Sam Hogg, "Why So Many Startups Never Reach Their Second Funding Round," *Entrepreneur,* 8 February 2014.

42. "Apple Inc.," YAHOO Finance, http://finance.yahoo.com/q /bs?s=AAPL+Balance+Sheet&annual, downloaded 22 April 2015.

43. "Ford Motor Company," YAHOO Finance, http://finance.yahoo .com/q/bs;_ylt=AwrBTvyb3TdV1wIAaRPrFAx.;_ ylu=X3oDMTByMG04Z2o2BHNIYwNzcgRwb3MDMQRjb2xvA2Jm MQR2dGlkAw—?s=F&annual, downloaded 22 April 2015.

44. "Information on CFA," Knowledge Academy, http:// knowledgeacademy.in/cfa.php; "CFA Program," CFA Institute, 2015, http://www.cfainstitute.org/programs/cfaprogram/Pages /index.aspx; and "CFA Program Course of Study," CFA Institute, 2015, http://www.cfainstitute.org/programs/cfaprogram /courseofstudy/Pages/index.aspx, downloaded 22 April 2015.

45. "CFA Program," World Wide Web.

Chapter 18

1. Christina Le Beau, "Rules of the Trade," *Entrepreneur,* February 2014.

2. Norm Brodsky, "Don't Worry: Grow Happy," *Inc.,* May 2013.

3. J.D. Harrison, "When Cashflow Is Tight, Some Businesses Barter," *The Washington Post,* 17 March 2013.

4. "Phasing Out the Penny in Canada," Canadian Bankers Association, 4 February 2013, http://www.cba.ca/en/consumer -information/40-banking-basics/658-phasing-out-the-penny-in -canada.

5. "Security," Bank of Canada, http://www.bankofcanada.ca /banknotes/bank-note-series/polymer/security/, downloaded 7 May 2015.

6. "Benefits for You," Bank of Canada, http://www.bankofcanada.ca /banknotes/bank-note-series/polymer/, downloaded 7 May 2015.

7. Mohana Ravidranath, "In D.C, Bitcoin Starting to Gain Currency," *The Washington Post,* 23 December 2013.

8. Tomorrow in Review, tomorrowinreview@Agorafinancial.com, 16 January 2014.

9. "Canada's Money Supply," Bank of Canada, October 2011, www.bankofcanada.ca/wp-content/uploads/2010/11/canada _money_supply.pdf.

10. Ibid.

11. "Canada's Money Supply," World Wide Web; "The Bank's Headquarters," Bank of Canada, http://www.bankofcanada.ca /about/bank-headquarters/, downloaded 4 May 2015; "Renewal of the Inflation-Control Target," Bank of Canada, November 2011, http://www.bankofcanada.ca/wp-content/uploads/2011/1 /background_nov11.pdf ; "How Monetary Policy Works: The Transmission of Monetary Policy," Bank of Canada, April 2012, http://www.bankofcanada.ca/wp-content/uploads/2010/11 /how_monetary_policy_works.pdf; "Key Interest Rates," Bank of Canada, 25 August 2010, http://www.bankofcanada.ca /core-functions/monetary-policy/key-interest-rate/; and "Banks and Interest Rates," Canadian Bankers Association, 28 January 2015, http://www.cba.ca/en/media-room/50-backgrounders-on- banking-issues/126-banks-and-interest-rates.

12. "How Monetary Policy Works: The Transmission of Monetary Policy," World Wide Web.

13. "The Canadian Financial System," Bank of Canada, April 2012, http://www.bankofcanada.ca/wp-content/uploads/2010/11 /canadian_financial_system.pdf; and "Financial System," Bank of Canada, accessed 5 May 2015, http://www.bankofcanada.ca /core-functions/financial-system/.

14. "Regulation of the Canadian Financial System," Bank of Canada, April 2012, http://www.bankofcanada.ca/wp-content /uploads/2010/11/regulation_canadian_financial.pdf; "Laws,

regulations and other obligations," Financial Consumer Agency of Canada, 15 January 2015, http://www.fcac-acfc.gc.ca/Eng /forIndustry/publications/lawsReg/Pages/home-accueil.aspx; "Regulated entities," Financial Consumer Agency of Canada, 17 December 2013, http://www.fcac-acfc.gc.ca/Eng/forIndustry /regulatedEntities/Pages/home-accueil.aspx; "For the industry," Financial Consumer Agency of Canada, 1 October 2013, http:// www.fcac-acfc.gc.ca/Eng/forIndustry/Pages/home-accueil.aspx; "Tools and calculators," Financial Consumer Agency of Canada, 20 March 2015, http://www.fcac-acfc.gc.ca/Eng/Pages /home-accueil.aspx; "About Us," Office of the Superintendent of Financial Institutions, 1 May 2015, http://www.osfi-bsif. gc.ca/Eng/osfi-bsif/Pages/default.aspx; and "The CDIC Quick Reference Guide," Canada Deposit Insurance Corporation, http:// www.cdic.ca/Coverage/QuickRefGuide/Documents /quickRefGuide.pdf, downloaded 8 May 2015.

15. "The Scotiabank Story," Scotiabank, 2015, http:// www.scotiabank.com/ca/en/0,,476,00.html.

16. "Financial Institutions and Markets," Department of Finance Canada, 14 November 2014, http://www.fin.gc.ca/access /fininst-eng.asp.

17. "Banks Operating in Canada," Canadian Bankers Association, 6 May 2014, http://www.cba.ca/en/component/content /category/61-banks-operating-in-canada.

18. "Invest in Canada - Financial Services Sector," Government of Canada, 2014, http://www.international.gc.ca/investors -investisseurs/assets/pdfs/download/canada-financial _services-2014.pdf.

19. "Banks Operating in Canada," World Wide Web.

20. Phil Moore, "Credit Union System Structure: A look at where we are today and some of our challenges for the future," Credit Union Central of Canada, 31 July 2014, http://www.cucentral. ca/Documents/Credit%20Union%20System%20Structure.pdf.

21. Anna Maria Andriotis and Saabira Chaudhuri, "Free Checks Go Way of Free Lunch," The Wall Street Journal, 6 February 2014.

22. Lisa Brown, "Credit Unions Promote, Gain Share," St. Louis-Dispatch, 30 August 2013.

23. "Trust Companies," The Canadian Encyclopedia, 16 December 2013, http://www.thecanadianencyclopedia.ca/en/article /trust-company/.

24. Ibid.

25. "CIBC buys Merrill Lynch Canada's retail brokerage," CBC News, 22 November 2001, http://www.cbc.ca/news/business /cibc-buys-merrill-lynch-canada-s-retail-brokerage-1.256343.

26. Danielle Douglas, "Rise in Prepaid Credit Cards Entices Banks to Sponsor Them," The Washington Post, 24 January 2014.

27. Danielle Douglas, "When It Comes to Plastic, Credit and Debit Not Created Equally," The Washington Post, 7 February 2014.

28. "Canadians embrace value and convenience from new banking and payment technologies - CBA research," Canadian Bankers Association, 15 October 2014, http://www.cba.ca/en /media-room/65-news-releases/718-canadians-embrace-value -and-convenience-from-new-banking-and-payment-technologies-cba -research.

29. Ibid.

30. Joe Castaldo, "Help banks act more like Apple," Canadian Business, February 2015, 34.

31. Ibid.; and "Royal Bank to test out Toronto company's Nymi technology," The Canadian Press, 9 November 2014, http:// www.cbc.ca/news/canada/toronto/royal-bank-to-test-out-toronto -company-s-nymi-technology-1.2829259.

32. "The Official Launch of Our Wearable Payment Pilot," Nymi, accessed 12 September 2015, https://www.nymi.com/news /official-launch-wearable-payment-pilot/.

33. Castaldo, "Help banks act more like Apple," 34; and "Tangerine Brings The Future of Banking to Canadians with New Biometrics Offerings," Tangerine, 1 October 2014, https://www.tangerine .ca/en/about-us/press-releases/PR-2014-10-01.html.

34. "About Financial Markets," Bank of Canada, http://www .bankofcanada.ca/markets/about-financial-markets/, downloaded 8 May 2015; and "Security," Investopedia, 2015, http://www .investopedia.com/terms/s/security.asp.

35. "Glossary - Securities Commission," Financial Consumer Agency of Canada, 30 April 2015, http://www.fcac-acfc.gc.ca/Eng /resources/Pages/Glossary-Glossair.aspx#S.

36. "Who We Are," Alberta Securities Commission, 2015, http:// www.albertasecurities.com/about/Pages/default.aspx.

37. "Overview," Canadian Securities Administrators, https://www .securities-administrators.ca/aboutcsa.aspx?id=45, downloaded 8 May 2015.

38. "Regulation of Capital Markets," Government of Canada, accessed 8 May 2015, http://actionplan.gc.ca/en/initiative /regulation-capital-markets.

39. "The Canadian Securities Transition Office," Government of Canada, http://csto-btcvm.ca/home.aspx, downloaded 8 May 2015.

40. Kevin Harlan, "The Changing Broker Scene Offers Options for Traders," Investor's Business Daily, 25 April 2011; and Eve Kaplan, "The Difference between a Stockbroker, Financial Advisor, and Planner Explained," Forbes, 15 March 2012.

41. Ben White and Kathleen Day, "SEC Approves Wall Street Settlement; Conflict of Interest Targeted," Washington Post, 29 April 2003, A1.

42. Carolyn Bigda, "Happy Fifth Birthday, Mr. Bull," Kiplinger's Personal Finance, March 2014.

43. Ryan Caldeck, "Successful Venture Investing: The Importance of Understanding Risks, and Diversification," Forbes, 19 February 2014.

44. "Stock Split," McDonald's, http://www.aboutmcdonalds.com /mcd/investors/stock_information/stock_split.html, downloaded 8 May 2015.

45. Andrew Tangel, "Massive Trading Suspensions' Highlight Threat of Penny Stock Fraud," Los Angeles Times, 3 February 2014.

46. Ben Levisohn, "Splits Dive: Cheap Stocks Thrive," Barron's, 6 January 2014.

47. Dakin Campbell and Elizabeth Dexheimer, "MasterCard Boosts Dividend 83%, Announces 10 for 1 Stock Split," Bloomberg Personal Finance, 10 December 2013; and Alistar Barr, "Google Hits Record on Revenue Gain, Stock Split," USA Today, 30 January 2014.

48. "S&P/TSX Composite Index," Investopedia, 2015, http://www .investopedia.com/terms/s/sp-tsx-composite-index.asp.

49. "Motley Fool - Buying on Margin Is a Tightrope Deal," The Columbus Dispatch, 2 February 2014.

50. "Stats and Facts," The Investment Funds Institute of Canada, 2015, https://www.ific.ca/en/info/stats-and-facts/. This value is as of July 31, 2015.

51. Jeff Sommer, "Give Fees an Inch and They'll Take a Mile," The New York Times, 1 March 2014.

52. Patrick Graham, "Wealth Advisor: Embracing ETFs Over Index Mutual Funds," The Wall Street Journal, 21 February 2014; and David Ning, "Signs Index Funds Aren't for You," U.S. News & World Report, 26 February 2014.

53. "Regulatory Oversight of Designated Clearing and Settlement Systems," The Bank of Canada, 31 March 2015, http://www .bankofcanada.ca/core-functions/financial-system /oversight-designated-clearing-settlement-systems/.

Appendix C

1. Jeffrey McKinney, "Before Disaster Strikes," Black Enterprise, May 2013.

2. David Gould, "The Root of Risk," Bloomberg Businessweek, October 7–October 13, 2013.

3. A special advertisement in Bloomberg Businessweek, 10 March 2013.

4. Rachel Ensign and Ari I. Weinberg, "Now Let's All Raise Our Glasses to Risk-Modeling and Optimization," The Wall Street Journal, 4 March 2013.

5. Evan Rothman, "Strategic Security," Bloomberg Businessweek, 4 February 2013.

6. A special advertisement in Bloomberg Businessweek, 4 March–10 March 2013.

7. Ensign and Weinberg, "Now Let's All Raise Our Glasses to Risk Modeling and Optimization,"

8. Gregory J. Millman and Samuel Rubenfeld, "For Corporate America, Risk Is Big Business," *The Wall Street Journal,* 16 January 2014.

9. "Auto Insurance," Government of Canada-Consumer Information, 8 July 2013, http://www.consumerinformation.ca/eic/site/032.nsf/eng/01246.html.

10. Ibid.

11. Lisa Gibbs, "Covered? Don't Be So Sure," *Money,* April 2013.

12. Lisa Gerstner, "Why Chip Cards Are a Safer Bet," *Kiplinger's Personal Finance,* April 2014.

13. Bill Harris, "Irreplaceable You," *Inc.,* February 2013.

14. Charles Passy, "Outliving Expectations," *Smart Money,* March 2012; and Russ Banham, "Protecting the Corporate Executive," *The Wall Street Journal,* 21 May 2013.

15. David Deming, "Another Year of Global Cooling," *The Washington Times,* 17 January 2014.

16. Brian Swint, "Shale Goes Global," *Bloomberg Businessweek,* 18 November 2013–2 January 2014.

Appendix D

1. "Toward a National Strategy for Financial Literacy," Financial Consumer Agency of Canada, 1 August 2014, http://www.fcac-acfc.gc.ca/Eng/financialLiteracy/financialLiteracyCanada/Pages/home-accueil.aspx.

2. "Minister Sorenson and Financial Literacy Leader participate in financial education fair for children," Financial Consumer Agency of Canada, 15 April 2015, http://news.gc.ca/web/article-en.do?mthd=tp&crtr.page=1&nid=963809&crtr.tp1D=1.

3. Veronica Dagher, "Wanted: Ideas to Teach Teenagers about Money," *The Wall Street Journal,* 4 February 2014.

4. Alexandra Wolfe, "Drew Faust," (President of Harvard), *The Wall Street Journal,* 1–2 February 2014.

5. Anne Tergesen, "Seven Resolutions to Get Your Nest Egg in Shape," *The Wall Street Journal,* 14 January 2013.

6. Elizabeth Dwoskin and Frank Bass, "Who's Complaining About Your Bank," *Bloomberg Businessweek,* 8 April–14 April 2013.

7. Iris Winston, "David Chilton Returns with a Wealthier Barber," *Fifty-Five Plus Magazine,* 2012, http://www.fifty-five-plus.com/david_chilton_returns_with_a_wealthier_barber; and Lori Chalmers Morrison, "Dollars & Sense," *Laurier Campus,* Winter 2010, 25.

8. Krystal Yee, "5 essential money lessons from The Wealthy Barber Returns," *Canadian Living,* 2015, http://www.canadianliving.com/life/money/5_essential_money_lessons_from_the_wealthy_barber_returns.php.

9. "The Tax-Free Savings Account," Canada Revenue Agency, 24 April 2015; and Garry Marr, "Bump-up for TFSA in 2015 doesn't have to wait for the budget to be passed," *The Globe and Mail,* 23 April 2015, http://business.financialpost.com/personal-finance/tfsa/after-some-confusion-banks-now-letting-canadians-top-up-tfsa-for-2015?__lsa=e9ed-cd75.

10. "Signs You Should Keep Renting," *The Week,* 9 May 2014.

11. Carol Hymowitz, "The Buy/Rent Balance Shifts," *Bloomberg Businessweek,* January 6–January 12, 2014.

12. Emily Belz, "A Room of One's Own," *World,* 14 December 2013.

13. Tomio Geron, "The Share Economy," *Forbes,* 11 February 2013.

14. Anne Kates Smith, "Where to Put Your Money Now," *Kiplinger's Personal Finance,* July 2014.

15. "Detailed. Historical. Precise. Client conversation starters," Morningstar Canada, 2015, http://corporate.morningstar.com/ca/asp/subject.aspx?xmlfile=6775.xml.

16. Anne Kates Smith, "Where to Put Your Money Now," *Kiplinger's Personal Finance,* July 2014.

17. Charles Levinson and Danny Yadron, "Card-Theft Code Grew in the Net's Dark Alleys," *The Wall Street Journal,* 22 January 2014.

18. Bill Saporito, "Plastic Surgery," *Time,* 10 February 2014.

19. Lisa Gerstner, "Credit or Debit: Pick Your Plastic," *Kiplinger's Personal Finance,* August 2013.

20. Peter Katt, "Life Insurance Cash Value: A Practical Discussion," *AAII Journal,* January 2014.

21. An editorial in *AAA World,* November/December 2013.

22. Jason Heath, "How much money is enough to retire? Only you can figure that out," *Financial Post,* 22 April 2014, http://business.financialpost.com/personal-finance/retirement/how-much-money-is-enough-to-retire-only-you-can-figure-that-out.

23. Ibid.

24. Karim Moussally, "Participation in Private Retirement Savings Plans, 1997 to 2008," Statistics Canada, March 2010, http://www.statcan.gc.ca/pub/13f0026m/13f0026m2010001-eng.pdf.

25. "Old Age Security pension," Service Canada, 9 April 2015, http://www.servicecanada.gc.ca/eng/services/pensions/oas/pension/index.shtml; and "Old Age Security payment amounts," Service Canada, 25 March 2015, http://www.servicecanada.gc.ca/eng/services/pensions/oas/payments/index.shtml.

26. "Canada Pension Plan payment amounts," Service Canada, 24 March 2015, http://www.servicecanada.gc.ca/eng/services/pensions/cpp/payments/; "Canada Pension Plan Retirement Pension," Service Canada, 31 March 2015, http://www.servicecanada.gc.ca/eng/services/pensions/cpp/retirement/; "The Québec Pension Plan," Régie des rentes Québec, 2015, http://www.rrq.gouv.qc.ca/en/programmes/regime_rentes/Pages/regime_rentes.aspx; and "Quebec Pension Plan Figures," Régie des rentes Québec, 2015, http://www.rrq.gouv.qc.ca/en/programmes/regime_rentes/regime_chiffres/Pages/regime_chiffres.aspx.

27. "Employer Pension Plan (trusteed pension funds), third quarter 2014," Statistics Canada, 10 March 2015, http://www.statcan.gc.ca/daily-quotidien/150310/dq150310b-eng.pdf; Moussally, "Participation in Private Retirement Savings Plans, 1997 to 2008," World Wide Web; and "Percentage of Labour force and employees covered by a registered pension plan (RPP)," Statistics Canada, 29 April 2014, http://www.statcan.gc.ca/tables-tableaux/sum-som/l01/cst01/labor26a-eng.htm.

28. "Registered Retirement Savings Plan (RRSP)," Canada Revenue Agency, 23 January 2015, http://www.cra-arc.gc.ca/tx/ndvdls/tpcs/rrsp-reer/rrsps-eng.html; "Home Buyers' Plan (HBP)," Canada Revenue Agency, 20 March 2015, http://www.cra-arc.gc.ca/tx/ndvdls/tpcs/rrsp-reer/hbp-rap/menu-eng.html; "Lifelong Learning Plan (LLP)," Canada Revenue Agency, 2 February 2015, http://www.cra-arc.gc.ca/tx/ndvdls/tpcs/rrsp-reer/llp-reep/menu-eng.html; and Sarah Efron and Rob Gerlsbeck, "RRSP: Your top 20 questions answered," Breakfast Television, 19 February 2015, http://www.bttoronto.ca/2015/02/19/rrsp-your-top-20-questions-answered/.

29. Lisa Wright, "Fewer Canadians contribute to RRSPs this year," *Toronto Star,* 4 March 2015, http://www.thestar.com/business/personal_finance/investing/2015/03/04/fewer-canadians-contribute-to-rrsps-this-year.html.

30. "Why CFP Certification?" Financial Planning Standards Council, 2012, https://www.fpsc.ca/about-fpsc.

31. "Free Power of Attorney," LawDepot.com, 2015, http://www.lawdepot.com/contracts/powerattny/?a=t&loc=CA&%20pid=google-pwratt_camain_d-s-ggkey_power%20of%20attorney&&s_kwcid=power%20of%20attorney|3522121665.

32. Lloyd Duhaime, "An Introduction to Powers of Attorney in Canada," Duhaime.org, http://www.duhaime.org/legalresources/elderlawwillstrustsestates/lawarticle-25/introduction-to-powers-of-attorney-in-canada.aspx, downloaded 24 April 2015.

Online Supplement

1. John Naughton, "We're All Being Mined for Data—But Who Are the Real Winners?" *The Guardian,* 7 June 2014.

2. Ryan Mulcahy, "Business Intelligence Definition and Solutions," CIO, www.cio.com, accessed June 2014.

3. Ernest von Simson, "The New Role of the CIO," *Bloomberg Businessweek,* May 22, 2013; and Shane O'Neill, "Digital Business Skills: Most Wanted List," *InformationWeek,* 1 May 2014.

4. Meridith Levinson, "The Brain Behind the Big, Bad Burger," *CIO,* 15 March 2005, 49–58; and Meridith Levinson, "Business Intelligence: Not Just for Bosses Anymore," *CIO,* 15 January 2006.

5. "Kodak Files for Bankruptcy, No More Kodak Moments," *Business Today,* www.businesstoday.com, accessed June 2014.

6. Glover Ferguson, Sanjay Mathur, and Baiju Shah, "Evolving from Information to Insight," *MIT Sloan Management Review,* Winter 2005, 51–58.

Endnotes

7. "Are any Canadian companies using RFID?", 20 November 2013, *RFID Journal,* http://www.rfidjournal.com/blogs/experts/entry?10828.
8. Ibid.
9. Scott Young, "Bringing Eye-Tracking to the Stores," Perception Research Services, www.prservices.com, accessed June 2014.
10. Jilly Duffy, "Get Organized: How to Clean Out Your Inbox," *PCMagazine,* 23 September 2013; and Jennifer Forker, "Tips to Organize Your Email and Other Digital Clutter," *Huffington Post,* 5 March 2013.
11. Brady Dale, "In Brooklyn, a Grasp at Giving 'Big Data' Meaning," *CNN Money,* 28 April 2014; Irving Wladawsky-Berger, "Data-Driven Decision Making: Promises and Limits," *The Wall Street Journal,* 27 September 2013; and Katherine Noyes, "IBM Stakes Its Claim in 'Scale-Out' Storage for Big Data," *CNN Money,* 14 May 2014.
12. Joshua Klein, "When Big Data Goes Bad," *CNN Money,* 5 November 2013.
13. Roland Waddilove, "How to Set Up a VPN Service to Surf the Web Anonymously," *PC World,* 19 May 2014.
14. "Canadian Internet Use Survey, 2012" Statistics Canada, 26 November 2013, http://www.statcan.gc.ca/daily-quotidien/131126/dq131126d-eng.htm.
15. Ibid.
16. Peter Nowak, "Why internet upload speed in Canada lags behind world average," 20 March 2014, CBC News, http://www.cbc.ca/news/technology/why-internet-upload-speed-in-canada-lags-behind-world-average-1.2578682.
17. Ookla Net Index, accessed 15 May 2015, http://www.netindex.com/download/2,7/Canada/.
18. Kazi Statsna, "Net neutrality changes in U.S. could impact Canada," 12 November 2015, CBC News, http://www.cbc.ca/news/technology/net-neutrality-changes-in-u-s-could-impact-canada-1.2831423.
19. Daniel Tencer, "A win for net neutrality: CRTC shuts down 'unlawful' Bell, Videotron practice," 29 January 2015, *Huffington Post,* http://www.huffingtonpost.ca/2015/01/29/crtc-net-neutrality-bell-videotron_n_6571944.html.
20. Betsy Issacson, "Web 3.0: What the Web Could Look Like without Net Neutrality," *Huffington Post,* 25 January. 2014.
21. Fiber Google, www.fiber.google.com, accessed June 2014.
22. Jim Clayman, "Internet2 CIO to Discuss the Emerging Higher Education Community Cloud at Three Rivers Systems' Annual Global Users Conference," *St. Louis Post-Dispatch,* 8 June 2014.
23. Internet2, www.internet2.edu, accessed June 2014.
24. 4food, www.4food.com, accessed June 2014.
25. Randy Hlavac, "Because We're Happy: Using Social Media to Turn Audiences Around," *Forbes,* 3 June 2014.
26. Amol Sharma and Jessica E. Vascellaro, "Companies Eye Location-Services Market," *The Wall Street Journal,* 28 November 2009.
27. Oxera Consulting Ltd, "What Is the Economic Impact of Geo Services?" January 2013, http://www.oxera.com/oxera/media/oxera/downloads/reports/what-is-the-economic-impact-of-geo-services_1.pdf.
28. Trish Winters, "Web 3.0," *Bitcoin Magazine,* 25 April 2014 www.bitcoinmagazine.com, and Harry Siegel, "Humanity, We Had a Good Run," *The New York Daily News,* 9 June 2014.
29. Anthony Wing Cosner, "Famo.us Part I: New Concepts Will Increase the Flow of Highly Dynamic Web 3.0 Apps," *Forbes,* 27 May 2014.
30. World Wide Web Consortium, www.w3c.org, accessed June 2014.
31. PR Newswire, "Amdocs Announces Self-Optimizing Networks Solution for Customer Experience-Driven Network Automation," *Web 2.0 Journal,* web2.sys-con.com, 10 February 2014.
32. George Glover, "Why Responsive Web Design Is the Cornerstone to Any Mobile Strategy," *Business 2 Community,* www.business2community.com, 2 June 2014.
33. "Intel Brings Immersive, Human Interaction to Devices in 2014," *The Wall Street Journal,* 6 January 2014; Bob Tita, "How 3-D Printing Works," *The Wall Street Journal,* 11 June 2013; and Mark Jenkins, "3-D Printing Can Make Everyone a Designer," *Washington Post,* 15 March 2013.
34. Lori Kozlowski, "Everything Is Connected: What the 'Internet of Things' Means Now," *Forbes,* 23 April 2014; and Stuart Dredge, "10 Things We Learned from Pew Research's Internet of Things Report," *The Guardian,* 14 May 2014.
35. "An Uncommon Thread," *The Economist,* "8 March. 2014.
36. Chris Murphy, "Internet of Things: What's Holding Us Back," *InformationWeek,* www.informationweek.com, 5 May 2014.
37. Network Virtualization, Webopedia, www.webopedia.com, accessed June 2014; and Kurt Marko, "Network Virtualization: The Final Piece of the Private Cloud," *Forbes,* 25 March 2014.
38. Quentin Hardy, "Cloud Computing, in Translation," *New York Times,* 11 June 2014.
39. David Kramer, "A Layman's Guide to Cloud Computing," *Huffington Post,* 12 June 2014.
40. Quentin Hardy, "The Era of Cloud Computing," *New York Times,* 11 June 2014; and "Migration: A Planned, Structured Cloud Approach," *CIO.* www.cio.com, 11 June 2014.
41. Joe McKendrick, "5 Benefits of Cloud Computing You Aren't Likely to See in a Sales Brochure," *Forbes,* 12 July 2013; Ian Stone, "Cloud Computing Enables Businesses to Discover Their Entrepreneurial Spirit," *The Guardian,* 15 April 2014; and "Cloud Computing Industry Analysis and Infographic: Companies Overspend on Infrastructure by 30% or More," PRWeb, www.prweb.com, 3 June 2014.
42. Archana Venkatraman, "Advantages and Disadvantages of Cloud Computing," *ComputerWeekly,* www.computerweekly.com, accessed June 2014; and Mikal E. Belicove, "Will the Cloud Rain on My Parade?" *Entrepreneur,* August 2013.
43. Zack Whittaker, "Dropbox Hit by Outage; File Sync Busted," ZDNet, www.zdnet.com, 14 March 2014.
44. Warwick Ashford, "Dropbox Can Be Hacked, Say Security Researchers," Computer Weekly, www.computerweekly.com, 29 August 2014.
45. Minda Zetlin, "Would Your Network Survive a Targeted Attack?" www.technology.inc.com, accessed 9 February 2009.
46. C.J. Ariottta, "Top Emerging Managed Security Service Providers," MSPMentor, www.mspmentor.com, 14 January 2013.
47. "Starbucks app used to hack into bank accounts, credit cards," 14 May 2015, CBC News, http://www.cbc.ca/news/business/starbucks-app-used-to-hack-into-bank-accounts-credit-cards-1.3074242.
48. "Firewalls and Firefights," *The Economist,* 10 August 2013.
49. "Cybercrime: an overview of incidents and issues in Canada," 2014, Royal Canadian Mounted Police, accessed 17 May 2015, http://www.rcmp-grc.gc.ca/pubs/cc-report-rapport-cc-eng.pdf.
50. Armina Ligaya, "'Grasping in the Dark': how Canada's 'undercounting' of cybercrime costs may be leaving us vulnerable," 9 June 2014, *The Financial Post,* http://business.financialpost.com/fp-tech-desk/grasping-in-the-dark-how-canadas-undercounting-of-cybercrime-costs-may-be-leaving-us-vulnerable?__lsa=89cc-2e21.
51. Ibid.
52. Treena Hein, "Barbarians Inside the Gates," *tq Magazine,* Summer 2006, 28.
53. Ibid.
54. Shan Li, "Target Hires New Security Chief from General Motors after Security Breach," *Los Angeles Times,* 11 June 2014.
55. Daniel Terdiman, "The Most Anticipated SXSW Talk in Years, Snowden Fires Up Austin," CNet, www.cnet.com, 10 March 2014.
56. Platform for Privacy Preferences, www.w3.org/P3P, accessed June 2014.
57. Donovan Vincent, "Ontario's welfare computer glitches are not the first," 25 January 2015, *Toronto Star,* http://www.thestar.com/news/canada/2015/01/25/ontarios-welfare-computer-glitches-are-not-the-first.html.

Glossary

4 Cs of credit A business's creditworthiness is determined by its character, capacity, capital, and conditions.

Absolute advantage The advantage that exists when a country has a monopoly on producing a specific product or is able to produce it more efficiently than all other countries.

Accounting The recording, classifying, summarizing, and interpreting of financial events to provide management and other interested parties the financial information they need to make good decisions.

Accounting cycle A six-step procedure that results in the preparation and analysis of the major financial statements.

Accounts Different types of assets, liabilities, and owners' equity.

Accounts payable Current liabilities or bills a company owes to others for merchandise or services purchased on credit but not yet paid for.

Administrative agencies Federal or provincial institutions and other government organizations created by Parliament or provincial legislatures with delegated power to pass rules and regulations within their mandated area of authority.

Advertising Paid, non-personal communication through various media by organizations and individuals who are in some way identified in the advertising message.

Affiliate marketing An online marketing strategy in which a business rewards individuals or other businesses (affiliates) for each visitor or customer the affiliate sends to its website.

Agency shop (Rand formula) agreement Clause in a negotiated labour–management agreement that says employers may hire non-union workers; employees are not required to join the union but must pay union dues.

Agents/brokers Marketing intermediaries that bring buyers and sellers together and assist in negotiating an exchange but don't take title to the goods.

Angel investors Private individuals who invest their own money in potentially hot new companies before they go public.

Annual report A yearly statement of the financial condition, progress, and expectations of an organization.

Annuity A contract to make regular payments to a person for life or a fixed period.

Apprentice programs Training programs during which a learner works alongside an experienced employee to master the skills and procedures of a craft.

Arbitration An agreement to bring in an impartial third party (a single arbitrator or a panel of arbitrators) to render a binding decision in a labour dispute.

Articles of incorporation A legal authorization from the federal or provincial/territorial government for a company to use the corporate format.

Assembly process That part of the production process that puts together components.

Assets Economic resources (things of value) owned by a firm.

Auditing The job of reviewing and evaluating the records used to prepare a company's financial statements.

Autocratic leadership Leadership style that involves making managerial decisions without consulting others.

Baby boomers A demographic group of Canadians that were born in the period from 1947 to 1966.

Back-to-work legislation A special law passed by the federal or provincial government that orders an end to a labour–management dispute in an industry the government decides is essential to the operation of the economy.

Balance of payments The difference between money coming into a country (from exports) and money leaving the country (for imports) plus money flows from other factors such as tourism, foreign aid, military expenditures, and foreign investment.

Balance of trade A nation's ratio of exports to imports.

Balance sheet (statement of financial position) The financial statement that reports a firm's financial condition at a specific time and is composed of three major types of accounts: assets, liabilities, and owners' equity.

Bankruptcy The legal process by which a person, business, or government entity unable to meet financial obligations is relieved of those obligations by a court that divides debtor assets among creditors, allowing creditors to get at least part of their money and freeing the debtor to begin anew.

Bargaining zone Range of options between the initial and final offer that each party will consider before negotiations dissolve or reach an impasse.

Barter The trading of goods and services for other goods and services directly.

Behavioural segmentation Dividing the market based on behaviour with or toward a product.

Benchmarking Comparing an organization's practices, processes, and products against the world's best.

Blog An online diary (web log) that looks like a web page but is easier to create and update by posting text, photos, or links to other sites.

Bond A corporate certificate indicating that an investor has lent money to a firm or a government.

Bonds payable Long-term liabilities that represent money lent to a firm that must be paid back.

Bookkeeping The recording of business transactions.

Boom A period that brings jobs, growth, and economic prosperity.

Brain drain The loss of educated people to other countries.

Brainstorming Generating as many solutions to a problem as possible in a short period of time with no censoring of ideas.

Brand A name, symbol, or design (or combination thereof) that identifies the goods or services of one seller or group of sellers and distinguishes them from the goods and services of competitors.

Brand equity The value of the brand name and associated symbols.

Brand loyalty The degree to which customers are satisfied, enjoy the brand, and are committed to further purchase.

Brand manager A manager who has direct responsibility for one brand or one product line; called a product manager in some firms.

Brand name A word, letter, or group of words or letters that differentiates one seller's goods or services from those of competitors.

Breach of contract When one party fails to follow the terms of a contract.

Break-even analysis The process used to determine profitability at various levels of sales.

Broadband technology Technology that offers users a continuous connection to the Internet and allows users to send and receive mammoth files that include voice, video, and data much faster than ever before.

Budget A financial plan that sets forth management's expectations, and, on the basis of those expectations, allocates the use of specific resources throughout the firm.

Bundling Grouping two or more products together and pricing them as a unit.

Bureaucracy An organization with many layers of managers who set rules and regulations and oversee all decisions.

Business Any activity that seeks to provide goods and services to others while operating at a profit.

Business cycles (economic cycles) The periodic rises and falls that occur in economies over time.

Business environment The surrounding factors that either help or hinder the development of businesses.

Business establishment Must meet the following minimum criteria: it must have at least one paid employee, it must have annual sales revenue of $30,000, and it must be incorporated and have filed a federal corporate income tax return at least once in the previous three years.

Business incubators Centres that provide space, services, advice, and support to assist new and growing businesses to become established and successful.

Business intelligence (BI) The use of data analytic tools to analyze an organization's raw data and derive useful insights.

Business law Rules, statutes, codes, and regulations that are established to provide a legal framework within which business must be conducted and that are enforceable by court action.

Business plan A detailed written statement that describes the nature of the business, the target market, the advantages the business will have in relation to competition, and the resources and qualifications of the owner(s).

Business-to-business (B2B) market All individuals and organizations that want goods and services to use in producing other goods and services or to sell, rent, or supply goods to others.

Buying stock on margin Purchasing securities by borrowing some of the cost from the broker.

Cafeteria-style benefits (flexible benefits) plans Benefit plans that allow employees to choose which benefits they want up to a certain dollar amount.

Capital budget A budget that highlights a firm's spending plans for major asset purchases that often require large sums of money, like property, buildings, and equipment.

Capital expenditures Major investments in either tangible long-term assets such as land, buildings, and equipment, or intangible assets such as patents, trademarks, and copyrights.

Capital gains The positive difference between the purchase price of a stock and its sale price.

Capitalism An economic system in which all or most of the factors of production and distribution are privately owned and operated for profit.

Cash budget A budget that estimates a firm's cash inflows and outflows during a particular period (e.g., monthly, quarterly).

Cash flow The difference between cash coming in and cash going out of a business.

Cash flow forecast Forecast that predicts the cash inflows and outflows in future periods, usually months or quarters.

Cause marketing Occurs when the charitable contributions of a firm are tied directly to the customer revenues produced through the promotion of one of its products.

Centralized authority An organization structure in which decision-making authority is maintained at the top level of management at the company's headquarters.

Certificate of deposit A time-deposit (savings) account that earns interest to be delivered at the end of the certificate's maturity date; also called a Guaranteed Investment Certificate (GIC).

Certification Formal process whereby a union is recognized by the Labour Relations Board (LRB) as the bargaining agent for a group of employees.

Chain of command The line of authority that moves from the top of a hierarchy to the lowest level.

Channel of distribution A set of marketing intermediaries, such as agents, brokers, wholesalers, and retailers, that join together to transport and store goods in their path (or channel) from producers to consumers.

Chartered professional accountant (CPA) designation The internationally recognized Canadian accounting designation.

Checkoff A contract clause requiring the employer to deduct union dues from employees' pay and remit them to a union.

Civil law Legal proceedings that do not involve criminal acts.

Claim A statement of a loss that the insured sends to the insurance company to request payment.

Climate change The movement of the temperature of the planet up or down over time.

Closed shop agreement Clause in a negotiated labour–management agreement that specifies workers need to be members of a union before being hired.

Cloud computing A form of virtualization in which a company's data and applications are stored at offsite data centres that are accessed over the Internet (the cloud).

Collective bargaining The process whereby union and management representatives negotiate a contract for workers.

Command economy An economy in which the government largely decides what goods and services are produced, who gets them, and how the economy will grow.

Commercial bank A profit-seeking organization that receives deposits from individuals and corporations in the form of chequing and savings accounts and then uses some of these funds to make loans.

Commercial finance companies Organizations that make short-term loans to borrowers who offer tangible assets as collateral.

Commercial paper Unsecured promissory notes of $100,000 and up that mature (come due) in 365 days or less.

Common law The body of law that comes from decisions handed down by judges; also referred to as unwritten law.

Common market (trading bloc) A regional group of countries that have a common external tariff, no internal tariffs, and a coordination of laws to facilitate exchange; also called a trading bloc. An example is the European Union.

Common stock The most basic form of ownership in a firm; it confers voting rights and the right to share in the firm's profits through dividends, if offered by the firm's board of directors.

Communism An economic and political system in which the state (the government) makes all economic decisions and owns almost all of the major factors of production.

Comparative advantage theory A theory that states that a country should sell to other countries those products that it produces most effectively and efficiently, and buy from other countries those products that it cannot produce as effectively or efficiently.

Competition-based pricing A pricing strategy based on what all the other competitors are doing. The price can be set at, above, or below competitors' prices.

Compliance-based ethics codes Ethical standards that emphasize preventing unlawful behaviour by increasing control and by penalizing wrongdoers.

Compressed workweek Work schedule that allows an employee to work a full number of hours per week but in fewer days.

Computer-aided design (CAD) The use of computers in the design of products.

Computer-aided manufacturing (CAM) The use of computers in the manufacturing of products.

Computer-integrated manufacturing (CIM) The uniting of computer-aided design with computer-aided manufacturing.

Conceptual skills Skills that involve the ability to picture the organization as a whole and the relationships among its various parts.

Conciliation The use of a government-appointed third party to explore solutions to a labour–management dispute.

Consideration Something of value; consideration is one of the requirements of a legal contract.

Consumer behaviour When marketing researchers investigate consumer thought processes and behaviour at each stage in a purchase to determine the best way to help the buyer buy.

Consumer market All individuals or households that want goods and services for personal consumption or use.

Consumer Price Index (CPI) A monthly statistic that measures the pace of inflation or deflation.

Consumerism A social movement that seeks to increase and strengthen the rights and powers of buyers in relation to sellers.

Contingency planning The process of preparing alternative courses of action that may be used if the primary plans do not achieve the organization's objectives.

Contingent workers Workers who do not have regular, full-time employment.

Continuous improvement (CI) Constantly improving the way the organization operates so that customer needs can be better satisfied.

Continuous process A production process in which long production runs turn out finished goods over time.

Contract A legally enforceable agreement between two or more parties.

Contract law Set of laws that specify what constitutes a legally enforceable agreement.

Contract manufacturing A foreign country's production of private-label goods to which a domestic company then attaches its brand name or trademark; also called outsourcing.

Contrarian approach Buying stock when everyone else is selling or vice versa.

Controlling A management function that involves establishing clear standards to determine whether or not an organization is progressing toward its goals and objectives, rewarding people for doing a good job, and taking corrective action if they are not.

Cookies Pieces of information, such as registration data or user preferences, sent by a website over the Internet to a web browser that the browser software is expected to save and send back to the server whenever the user returns to that website.

Co-operative (co-op) An organization owned and controlled by people—producers, consumers, or workers—with similar needs who pool their resources for mutual gain.

Copyright A form of intellectual property that protects a creator's rights to materials such as books, articles, photos, and cartoons.

Core competencies Those functions that an organization can do as well as or better than any other organization in the world.

Core time In a flextime plan, the period when all employees are expected to be at their job stations.

Corporate governance The process and policies that determine how an organization interacts with its stakeholders, both internal and external.

Corporate philanthropy Dimension of social responsibility that includes charitable donations.

Corporate policy Dimension of social responsibility that refers to the position a firm takes on social and political issues.

Corporate responsibility Dimension of social responsibility that includes everything from hiring minority workers to making safe products.

Corporate social initiatives Dimension of social responsibility that includes enhanced forms of corporate philanthropy that are more directly related to the company's competencies.

Corporate social responsibility (CSR) A business's concern for the welfare of society.

Corporation A legal entity with authority to act and have liability separate from its owners.

Cost of capital The rate of return a company must earn in order to meet the demands of its lenders and expectations of its equity holders.

Cost of goods sold (cost of goods manufactured) A measure of the cost of merchandise sold or cost of raw materials and supplies used for producing items for resale.

Countertrading A complex form of bartering in which several countries may be involved, each trading goods for goods or services for services.

Coverage rate A measure of the percentage of employed individuals (including both union and non-unionized members) who are covered by a collective agreement.

Craft union An organization of skilled specialists in a particular craft or trade; typically local or regional.

Credit profile A borrower's financial track record in the form of borrowing history.

Credit union A non-profit, member-owned financial co-operative that offers a full variety of banking services to its members.

Criminal law Defines crimes, establishes punishments, and regulates the investigation and prosecution of people accused of committing crimes.

Crisis planning Involves reacting to sudden changes in the environment.

Critical path In a PERT network, the sequence of tasks that takes the longest time to complete.

Cross-functional, self-managed teams Groups of employees from different departments who work together on a long-term basis.

Crowdfunding Raising funds through the collection of small contributions from the general public (known as the crowd) using the Internet and social media.

Crowdsourcing Using the expertise of a large group of people to solve a business problem.

Crown corporations Companies that are owned by the federal or provincial government.

Culture The set of values, beliefs, rules, and institutions held by a specific group of people.

Current assets Items that can or will be converted into cash within one year.

Customer relationship management (CRM) The process of building long-term relationships with customers by delivering customer value and satisfaction.

Damages The monetary settlement awarded to a person who is injured by a breach of contract.

Data analytics The process of collecting, organizing, storing, and analyzing large sets of data ("big data") in order to identify patterns and other information that is most useful to the business now and for making future decisions

Data processing Name for business technology in the 1970s; included technology that supported an existing business and was primarily used to improve the flow of financial information.

Database An electronic storage file for information.

Debenture bonds (unsecured bonds) Bonds that are unsecured (i.e., not backed by any collateral such as equipment).

Debit card An electronic funds transfer tool that serves the same function as cheques: it withdraws funds from a chequing account.

Debt financing Funds raised through various forms of borrowing that must be repaid.

Decentralized authority An organization structure in which decision-making authority is delegated to lower-level managers more familiar with local conditions compared to headquarters management.

Decertification Process by which workers can take away a union's right to represent them.

Decision making Choosing among two or more alternatives.

Deficit Occurs when a government spends over and above the amount it gathers in taxes for a specific period of time (namely, a fiscal year).

Deflation A situation in which prices are declining.

Demand The quantity of products that people are willing to buy at different prices at a specific time.

Demand deposit The technical name for a chequing account; the money in a demand deposit can be withdrawn anytime on demand from the depositor.

Demographic segmentation Dividing the market by age, income, and education level.

Demography The statistical study of the human population with regard to its size, density, and other characteristics such as age, race, gender, and income.

Departmentalization Dividing an organization into separate units.

Depreciation The systematic write-off of the cost of a tangible asset over its estimated useful life.

Depression A severe recession.

Deregulation Government withdrawal of certain laws and regulations that seem to hinder competition

Devaluation Lowering the value of a nation's currency relative to other currencies.

Digital natives Young people who grew up using technology including the Internet and electronic devices such as cell phones.

Direct marketing Any activity that directly links manufacturers or intermediaries with the ultimate customer

Direct selling Selling to customers in their homes or where they work.

Directly chartered union A union that is directly affiliated to a labour congress to whom it pays per capita dues and receives services.

Disability insurance Insurance that pays part of the cost of a long-term illness or an accident.

Disinflation A situation in which price increases are slowing (the inflation rate is declining).

Diversification Buying several different investment alternatives to spread the risk of investing.

Dividends Part of a firm's profits that may be distributed to shareholders as either cash payments or additional shares of stock.

Double-entry bookkeeping The concept of every business transaction affecting at least two accounts.

Dumping Selling products in a foreign country at lower prices than those charged in the producing country.

E-business Any information system or application that empowers business processes.

E-commerce The buying and selling of goods and services over the Internet.

Economics The study of how society chooses to employ resources to produce goods and services and distribute them for consumption among various competing groups and individuals.

Economies of scale The situation in which companies can reduce their production costs if they can purchase raw materials in bulk and develop specialized labour; resulting in the average cost of goods going down as production levels increase.

Electronic funds transfer (EFT) system A computerized system that electronically performs financial transactions such as making purchases, paying bills, and receiving paycheques.

Electronic retailing Selling goods and services to ultimate customers (e.g., you and me) over the Internet.

Embargo A complete ban on the import or export of a certain product or the stopping of all trade with a particular country.

Employment equity Employment activities designed to increase employment opportunities for four groups (women, Aboriginal people, persons with disabilities, and members of visible minorities) given past discrimination.

Empowerment Giving front-line workers the responsibility, authority, and freedom to respond quickly to customer requests.

Enterprise portal A centralized and secure online network for information and transactions.

Enterprise resource planning (ERP) A computer application that enables a firm to manage all of its operations (finance, requirements planning, human resources, and order fulfillment) on the basis of a single, integrated set of corporate data.

Entrepreneur A person who risks time and money to start and manage a business.

Entrepreneurial team A group of experienced people from different areas of business who join together to form a managerial team with the skills needed to develop, make, and market a new product.

Entrepreneurship Accepting the challenge of starting and running a business.

Environmental scanning The process of identifying the factors that can affect marketing success.

Equalization A federal government program for reducing fiscal disparities among provinces.

Equity financing Funds raised from operations within the firm or through the sale of ownership in the firm.

Equity theory The idea that employees try to maintain equity between inputs and outputs compared to others in similar positions.

Ethics Standards of moral behaviour; that is, behaviour that is accepted by society as right versus wrong.

Ethnic marketing Combinations of the marketing mix that reflect the unique attitudes, race or ancestry, communication preferences, and lifestyles of ethnic Canadians.

Ethnocentricity An attitude that one's own culture is superior to all others.

Everyday low pricing (EDLP) Setting prices lower than competitors and then not having any special sales.

Exchange rate The value of one nation's currency relative to the currencies of other countries.

Exchange-traded funds (ETFs) Collections of stocks that are traded on exchanges but are traded more like individual stocks than like mutual funds.

Exclusive distribution Distribution that sends products to only one retail outlet in a given geographic area.

Executor An individual who assembles and values your estate, files income and other taxes, and distributes assets when you pass away.

Expectancy theory Victor Vroom's theory that the amount of effort employees exert on a specific task depends on their expectations of the outcome.

Exporting Selling products to another country.

Express warranties Specific representations by the seller that buyers rely on regarding the goods they purchase.

External customers Dealers, who buy products to sell to others, and ultimate customers (or end users), who buy products for their own personal use.

Extranet A semi-private network that uses Internet technology and allows more than one company to access the same information or allows people on different servers to collaborate.

Extrinsic reward Something given to you by someone else as recognition for good work; extrinsic rewards include pay increases, praise, and promotions.

Facility layout The physical arrangement of resources (including people) in the production process.

Facility location The process of selecting a geographic location for a company's operations.

Factoring The process of selling accounts receivable for cash.

Factors of production The resources used to create wealth: land, labour, capital goods, entrepreneurship, and knowledge.

Federal budget A comprehensive report that reveals government financial policies for the coming year.

Finance The function in a business that acquires funds for the firm and manages them within the firm.

Financial accounting Accounting information and analyses prepared for people outside the organization.

Financial control A process in which a firm periodically compares its actual revenues, costs, and expenses with its projected ones.

Financial literacy Having the knowledge, skills, and confidence to make responsible financial decisions.

Financial management The job of managing a firm's resources to meet its goals and objectives.

Financial managers Managers who examine the financial data prepared by accountants and recommend strategies for improving the financial performance of the firm.

Financial market infrastructure (FMI) A system that facilitates the clearing, settling, or recording of payments, securities, derivatives, or other financial transactions among participating entities; also called a clearing and settlement system.

Financial statement A summary of all of the transactions that have occurred over a particular period.

Fiscal policy The federal government's effort to keep the economy stable by increasing or decreasing taxes or government spending.

Fixed assets Assets that are relatively permanent, such as land, buildings, and equipment.

Flat organization structure An organization structure that has few layers of management and a broad span of control.

Flexible manufacturing Designing machines to do multiple tasks so that they can produce a variety of products.

Flextime plan Work schedule that gives employees some freedom to choose when to work, as long as they work the required number of hours.

Focus group A small group of people who meet under the direction of a discussion leader to communicate their opinions about an organization, its products, or other issues.

Foreign direct investment (FDI) The buying of permanent property and businesses in foreign nations.

Foreign subsidiary A company owned in a foreign country by the parent company.

Forensic accounting A relatively new area of accounting that focuses its attention on fraudulent activity.

Form utility The value added by the creation of finished goods and services.

Formal organization The structure that details lines of responsibility, authority, and position; that is, the structure shown on organization charts.

Franchise The right to use a specific business's name and sell its goods or services in a given territory.

Franchise agreement An arrangement whereby someone with a good idea for a business sells the rights to use the business name and sell its goods and services in a given territory.

Franchisee A person who buys a franchise.

Franchisor A company that develops a product concept and sells others the rights to make and sell the products.

Free trade The movement of goods and services among nations without political or economic barriers.

Free-market economy An economy in which the market largely determines what goods and services are produced, who gets them, and how the economy grows.

Free-rein leadership Leadership style that involves managers setting objectives and employees being relatively free to do whatever it takes to accomplish those objectives.

Fringe benefits Benefits such as sick-leave pay, vacation pay, pension plans, and health plans that represent additional compensation to employees beyond base wages.

Fundamental accounting equation Assets are equal to liabilities plus owners' equity; this is the basis for the balance sheet.

Gantt chart Bar graph showing production managers what projects are underway and what stage they are in at any given time.

Gender wage gap The difference between wages earned by men and wages earned by women

General Agreement on Tariffs and Trade (GATT) A 1948 agreement that established an international forum for negotiating mutual reductions in trade restrictions.

General partner An owner (partner) who has unlimited liability and is active in managing the firm.

General partnership A partnership in which all owners share in operating the business and in assuming liability for the business's debts.

Generation Y (Millennials) A demographic group of Canadians that were born in the period from 1980 to 1995; the children of the baby boomers.

Generation Z A demographic group of Canadians that were born in the period from 1995 to 2009.

Geographic segmentation Dividing the market by geographic area.

Givebacks Concessions made by union members to management; previous gains from labour negotiations are given up to help employers remain competitive and thereby save jobs.

Goals The broad, long-term accomplishments an organization wishes to attain.

Goal-setting theory The idea that setting ambitious but attainable goals can motivate workers and improve performance if the goals are accepted, accompanied by feedback, and facilitated by organizational conditions.

Goods Tangible products such as computers, food, clothing, cars, and appliances.

Government and not-for-profit (non-profit) accounting Accounting system for organizations whose purpose is not generating a profit but rather serving ratepayers, taxpayers, and others according to a duly approved budget.

Green marketing The process of selling products and/or services based on their environmental benefits.

Greening The trend toward saving energy and producing products that cause less harm to the environment.

Greenwashing When businesses try to make themselves or their products or services look green or socially responsible without the action to back it up.

Grievance A charge by employees that management is not abiding by or fulfilling the terms of the negotiated labour–management agreement.

Gross Domestic Product (GDP) The total value of goods and services produced in a country in a given year.

Gross profit (gross margin) How much a firm earned by buying (or making) and selling merchandise.

Hacker Someone who illegally accesses online information.

Hawthorne effect The tendency for people to behave differently when they know they are being studied.

Hierarchy A system in which one person is at the top of the organization and there is a ranked or sequential ordering from the top down of managers who are responsible to that person.

High–low pricing strategy Set prices that are higher than EDLP stores, but have many special sales where the prices are lower than competitors.

Human development index A measure of a country's progress that includes wealth, health, and education.

Human relations skills Skills that involve communication and motivation; they enable managers to work through and with people.

Human resource management (HRM) The process of determining human resource needs and then recruiting, selecting, developing, motivating, evaluating, compensating, and scheduling employees to achieve organizational goals.

Hygiene (maintenance) factors In Herzberg's theory of motivating factors, job factors that can cause dissatisfaction if missing but that do not necessarily motivate employees if increased.

Identity theft Obtaining an individuals' personal information, such as Social Insurance Number and credit card numbers, for illegal purposes.

Implied warranties Guarantees legally imposed on the seller.

Import quota A limit on the number of products in certain categories that a nation can import.

Importing Buying products from another country.

Income statement (statement of earnings) The financial statement that shows a firm's profit after costs, expenses, and taxes.

Independent audit An evaluation and unbiased opinion about the accuracy of a company's financial statements.

Independent local organization A union that is not formally connected or affiliated with any other labour organization; also called the union local, local, or local union.

Industrial design A form of intellectual property that protects the owner's exclusive right to use the visible features of a finished product that identify it.

Industrial policy A comprehensive, coordinated government plan to guide and revitalize the economy.

Industrial union Consists of unskilled and semi-skilled workers in mass-production industries such as automobile manufacturing and mining.

Inflation A general rise in the prices of goods and services over time.

Informal organization The system of relationships and lines of authority that develops spontaneously as employees meet and form power centres; that is, the human side of the organization that does not appear on any organization chart.

Information systems (IS) Technology that helps companies do business; includes such tools as automated teller machines (ATMs) and voice mail.

information technology (IT) Technology that helps companies change business by allowing them to use new methods.

Initial public offering (IPO) The first public offering of a corporation's stock.

Injunction A court order directing someone to do something or to refrain from doing something.

Insider trading An unethical activity in which insiders use private company information to further their own fortunes or those of their family and friends.

Insourcing Assigning various functions that could go to an outside organization to employees in the company.

Insurable interest The possibility of the policyholder to suffer a loss.

Insurable risk A risk that the typical insurance company will cover.

Insurance policy A written contract between the insured and an insurance company that promises to pay for all or part of a loss.

Intangible assets Long-term assets (e.g., patents, trademarks, copyrights) that have no real physical form but do have value.

Integrated marketing communication (IMC) A technique that combines all of the promotional tools into one comprehensive and unified promotional strategy.

Integrity-based ethics codes Ethical standards that define the organization's guiding values, create an environment that supports ethically sound behaviour, and stress a shared accountability among employees.

Intensive distribution Distribution that puts products into as many retail outlets as possible.

Interest The payment the bond issuer makes to the bondholders for use of the borrowed money.

Intermittent process A production process in which the production run is short and the machines are changed frequently to make different products.

Internal customers Individuals and units within the firm that receive services from other individuals or units.

International financial reporting standards (IFRS) The common set of accounting principles, standards, and procedures that accountants and companies use to compile financial statements.

International Monetary Fund (IMF) An international bank that makes short-term loans to countries experiencing problems with their balance of trade.

International union A union that represents workers in Canada and the United States.

Internet2 The private Internet system that links government supercomputer centres and a select group of universities; it runs more than 22,000 times faster than today's public infrastructure and supports heavy-duty applications.

Intranet A companywide network, closed to public access, that uses Internet-type technology.

Intrapreneurs Creative people who work as entrepreneurs within corporations.

Intrinsic reward The good feeling you have when you have done a job well.

Inverted organization An organization that has contact people at the top and the chief executive officer at the bottom of the organization chart.

Invisible hand A phrase coined by Adam Smith to describe the process that turns self-directed gain into social and economic benefits for all.

Involuntary bankruptcy Bankruptcy procedures filed by a debtor's creditors.

ISO 14000 A collection of the best practices for managing an organization's impact on the environment.

ISO 9000 The common name given to quality management and assurance standards.

Job analysis A study of what is done by employees who hold various job titles.

Job description A summary of the objectives of a job, the type of work to be done, the responsibilities and duties, the working conditions, and the relationship of the job to other functions.

Job enlargement A job-enrichment strategy that involves combining a series of tasks into one challenging and interesting assignment.

Job enrichment A motivational strategy that emphasizes motivating the worker through the job itself.

Job rotation A job-enrichment strategy that involves moving employees from one job to another.

Job sharing An arrangement whereby two part-time employees share one full-time job.

Job simulation The use of equipment that duplicates job conditions and tasks so that trainees can learn skills before attempting them on the job.

Job specifications A written summary of the minimum qualifications required of workers to do a particular job.

Joint venture A partnership in which two or more companies (often from different countries) join to undertake a major project.

Journal The record book where accounting data are first entered.

Just-in-time (JIT) inventory control A production process in which a minimum of inventory is kept on the premises and parts, supplies, and other needs are delivered just in time for use on the assembly line.

Knowledge management Finding the right information, keeping the information in a readily accessible place, and making the information known to everyone in the firm.

Labour relations board (LRB) An organization created by the federal or provincial government to enforce labour legislation.

Labour union An employee organization whose main goal is representing its members in employee–management negotiation of job-related issues.

Law of large numbers Principle that if a large number of people are exposed to the same risk, a predictable number of losses will occur during a given period of time.

Leading Creating a vision for the organization and guiding, training, coaching, and motivating others to work effectively to achieve the organization's goals and objectives.

Lean manufacturing The production of goods using less of everything compared to mass production.

Ledger A specialized accounting book in which information from accounting journals is accumulated into accounts and posted so that managers can find all of the information about a specific account in one place.

Leverage Raising needed funds through borrowing to increase a firm's rate of return.

Liabilities What the business owes to others (debts).

Licensing A global strategy in which a firm (the licensor) allows a foreign company (the licensee) to produce its product in exchange for a fee (a royalty).

Limited liability The responsibility of a business's owners for losses only up to the amount they invest; limited partners and shareholders have limited liability.

Limited liability partnership (LLP) A partnership that limits partners' risk of losing their personal assets to only their own acts and omissions and to the acts and omissions of people under their supervision.

Limited partner An owner (partner) who invests money in the business but does not have any management responsibility or liability for losses beyond the investment.

Limited partnership A partnership with one or more general partners and one or more limited partners.

Line of credit A given amount of unsecured funds a bank will lend to a business.

Line organization An organization that has direct two-way lines of responsibility, authority, and communication running from the top to the bottom of the organization, with all people reporting to only one supervisor.

Line personnel Employees who are part of the chain of command that is responsible for achieving organizational goals.

Liquidity The ease with which an asset can be converted into cash.

Lockout An attempt by management to put pressure on unions by temporarily closing the business.

Logistics Those activities that focus on getting the right amount of the right products or services to the right place at the right time at the lowest possible cost.

Long-term financing Borrowed funds that are needed for a period more than one year.

Long-term forecast Forecast that predicts revenues, costs, and expenses for a period longer than one year, and sometimes as far as five or ten years into the future.

Loss When a business's expenses are more than its revenues.

Macroeconomics The part of economic study that looks at the operation of a nation's economy as a whole.

Management The process used to accomplish organizational goals through planning, organizing, leading, and controlling people and other organizational resources.

Management by objectives (MBO) A system of goal setting and implementation that involves a cycle of discussion, review, and evaluation of objectives among top- and middle-level managers, supervisors, and employees.

Management development The process of training and educating employees to become good managers and then monitoring the progress of their managerial skills over time.

Managerial accounting Accounting used to provide information and analyses to managers inside the organization to assist them in decision making.

Marginal tax rate The rate of tax payable on the last dollar earned.

Market People with unsatisfied wants and needs who have both the resources and the willingness to buy.

Market orientation Focusing efforts on (1) continuously collecting information about customers' needs and competitors' capabilities, (2) sharing this information throughout the organization, and (3) using the information to create value, ensure customer satisfaction, and develop customer relationships.

Market price The price determined by supply and demand.

Market segmentation The process of dividing the total market into groups with similar characteristics.

Marketing A set of business practices designed to plan for and present an organization's products or services in ways that build effective customer relationships.

Marketing boards Organizations that control the supply or pricing of certain agricultural products in Canada.

Marketing concept A three-part business philosophy: (1) a customer orientation, (2) a service orientation, and (3) a profit orientation.

Marketing intermediaries Organizations that assist in moving goods and services from producers to business and consumer users.

Marketing mix The ingredients that go into a marketing program: product, price, place, and promotion.

Marketing research The analysis of markets to determine opportunities and challenges, and to find the information needed to make good decisions.

Maslow's hierarchy of needs Theory of motivation that places different types of human needs in order of importance, from basic physiological needs to safety, social, and esteem needs to self-actualization needs.

Mass customization Tailoring products to meet the needs of individual customers.

Mass marketing Developing products and promotions to please large groups of people.

Materials requirement planning (MRP) A computer-based production management system that uses sales forecasts to make sure that needed parts and materials are available at the right time and place.

Matrix organization An organization in which specialists from different parts of the organization are brought together to work on specific projects but still remain part of a line-and-staff structure.

Maturity date The exact date the issuer of a bond must pay the principal to the bondholder.

Mediation The use of a third party, called a mediator, who encourages both sides in a dispute to continue negotiating and often makes suggestions for resolving the dispute.

Mentor An experienced employee who supervises, coaches, and guides lower-level employees by introducing them to the right people and generally being their organizational sponsor.

Microeconomics The part of economic study that looks at the behaviour of people and organizations in particular markets.

Micro-enterprise A small business defined as having one to four employees.

Micropreneurs Small-business owners with fewer than five employees who are willing to accept the risk of starting and managing the type of business that remains small, lets them do the kind of work they want to do, and offers them a balanced lifestyle.

Middle management The level of management that includes general managers, division managers, and branch and plant managers, who are responsible for tactical planning and controlling.

Mission statement An outline of the fundamental purposes of an organization.

Mixed economies Economic systems in which some allocation of resources is made by the market and some by the government.

Monetary policy The management of the money supply and interest rates.

Money Anything that people generally accept as payment for goods and services.

Money supply The amount of money the Bank of Canada makes available for people to buy goods and services.

Monopolistic competition The market situation in which a large number of sellers produce products that are very similar but that are perceived by buyers as different.

Monopoly A market in which there is only one seller for a product or service.

Mortgage bonds (secured bonds) Bonds that are secured (i.e., backed by collateral such as land).

Motivation The overall desire to excel.

Motivators In Herzberg's theory of motivating factors, job factors that cause employees to be productive and that give them satisfaction.

Multinational corporation An organization that manufactures and markets products in many different countries and has multinational stock ownership and multinational management.

Mutual fund A fund that buys stocks and bonds and then sells shares in those securities to the public.

Mutual insurance company A type of insurance company owned by its policyholders.

National debt (federal debt) The accumulation of government surpluses and deficits over time.

National policy Government directive that placed high tariffs on imports from the United States to protect Canadian manufacturing, which had higher costs.

National union A union that only represents workers in Canada.

Negligence Part of tort law where behaviour does not meet the standard of care required and causes unintentional harm or injury.

Negotiable instruments Forms of commercial paper (such as cheques) that are transferable among businesses and individuals and represent a promise to pay a specified amount.

Negotiated labour–management agreement (labour contract) Agreement that sets the tone and clarifies the terms and conditions under which management and labour agree to function over a period of time.

Net income or net loss Revenue left over or depleted after all costs and expenses, including taxes, are paid.

Networking The process of establishing and maintaining contacts with key managers in and outside the organization and using those contacts to weave strong relationships that serve as informal development systems.

Networking between firms Using communications technology and other means to link organizations and allow them to work together on common objectives.

Niche marketing The process of finding small but profitable market segments and designing or finding products for them.

Non-banks Financial organizations that accept no deposits but offer many services provided by regular banks.

Non-profit organization An organization whose goals do not include making a personal profit for its owners or organizers.

North American Free Trade Agreement (NAFTA) Agreement that created a free-trade area among Canada, the United States, and Mexico.

Notes payable Short-term or long-term liabilities that a business promises to repay by a certain date.

Objectives Specific, measurable, short-term statements detailing how to achieve the organization's goals.

Observation Involves watching, either mechanically or in person, how people behave.

Offshoring Sourcing part of the purchased inputs outside of the country.

Off-the-job training Internal or external training programs away from the workplace that develop any of a variety of skills or foster personal development.

Oligopoly A form of competition in which just a few sellers dominate the market.

One-to-one marketing (micromarketing) Developing a unique mix of goods and services for each individual customer.

Online training Training programs in which employees "attend" classes via the Internet.

On-the-job training Training at the workplace that lets the employee learn by doing or by watching others for a while and then imitating them.

Open shop agreement Clause in a negotiated labour–management agreement that says employees are free to join or not join the union and to pay or not pay union dues.

Operating (master) budget The budget that ties together all of a firm's other budgets and summarizes the business's proposed financial activities.

Operating expenses Costs involved in operating a business, such as rent, utilities, and salaries.

Operational planning The process of setting work standards and schedules necessary to implement the company's tactical objectives.

Operations management A specialized area in management that converts or transforms resources (including human resources) into goods and services.

Organization chart A visual device that shows relationships among people and divides the organization's work; it shows who is accountable for the completion of specific work and who reports to whom.

Organizational (or corporate) culture Widely shared values within an organization that provide coherence and co-operation to achieve common goals.

Organizing A management function that includes designing the structure of the organization and creating conditions and systems in which everyone and everything work together to achieve the organization's goals and objectives.

Orientation The activity that introduces new employees to the organization; to fellow employees; to their immediate supervisors; and to the policies, practices, values, and objectives of the firm.

Outsourcing Assigning various functions, such as accounting, production, security, maintenance, and legal work to outside organizations.

Overnight rate The interest rate at which major financial institutions borrow and lend one-day (or overnight) funds among themselves.

Owners' equity (shareholders' or stockholders' equity) The amount of the business that belongs to the owners minus any liabilities owed by the business.

Participative (democratic) leadership Leadership style that consists of managers and employees working together to make decisions.

Partnership A legal form of business with two or more parties.

Partnership agreement Legal document that specifies the rights and responsibilities of each partner

Patent A form of intellectual property that gives inventors exclusive rights to their inventions for 20 years.

Pay equity Equal pay for work of equal value.

Penetration price strategy A strategy in which the product is priced low to attract many customers and discourage competitors.

Pension funds Amounts of money put aside by corporations, non-profit organizations, or unions to cover part of the financial needs of their members when they retire.

Perfect competition The market situation in which there are many sellers in a market and no seller is large enough to dictate the price of a product.

Performance appraisal An evaluation that measures employee performance against established standards in order to make decisions about promotions, compensation, training, or termination.

Personal selling The face-to-face presentation and promotion of goods and services.

phishing E-mails embellished with a stolen logo for a well-known enterprise (often from financial institutions) that make the messages look authentic, but which are used to collect personal data and use it to commit fraud.

Planning A management function that includes anticipating trends and determining the best strategies and tactics to achieve organizational goals and objectives.

PMI A creative thinking strategy that lists all the pluses, minuses, and interesting points for a solution in separate columns.

Podcasting A means of distributing multimedia digital files on the Internet for downloading to a portable media player.

Positioning statement Expresses how a company wants to be perceived by customers.

Power of attorney A written document in which you appoint someone else to act on your behalf on matters that you specify; this can be made to start immediately, or upon mental incapacity.

Precedent Decisions judges have made in earlier cases that guide the handling of new cases.

Preferred stock Stock that gives its owners preference in the payment of dividends and an earlier claim on assets than common shareholders if the company is forced out of business and its assets are sold.

Premium The fee charged by an insurance company for an insurance policy.

Price The money or other consideration (including other goods and services) exchanged for the ownership or use of a good or service.

Price leadership The procedure by which one or more dominant firms set the pricing practices that all competitors in an industry then follow.

Primary boycott When a union encourages both its members and the general public not to buy the products of a firm involved in a labour dispute.

Primary data Data that you gather yourself (not from secondary sources such as books, journals, and newspapers).

Prime rate The interest rate that banks charge their most creditworthy customers.

Principle of motion economy Theory developed by Frank and Lillian Gilbreth that every job can be broken down into a series of elementary motions.

Private accountant An accountant who works for a single firm, government agency, or non-profit organization.

Private corporation Corporation that is usually controlled by a small number of shareholders and its shares are not listed on a stock exchange.

Privatization The process of governments selling Crown corporations.

Problem solving The process of solving the everyday problems that occur. Problem solving is less formal than decision making and usually calls for quicker action.

Process manufacturing That part of the production process that physically or chemically changes materials.

Producers' cartels Organizations of commodity-producing countries that are formed to stabilize or increase prices to optimize overall profits in the long run.

Product Any physical good, service, or idea that satisfies a want or need.

Product differentiation The creation of real or perceived product differences.

Product liability Part of tort law that holds businesses liable for harm that results from the production, design, sale, or use of products they market.

Product life cycle A theoretical model of what happens to sales and profits for a product class over time; the four stages of the cycle are introduction, growth, maturity, and decline.

Product line A group of products that are physically similar or are intended for a similar market.

Product mix The combination of product lines offered by an organization.

Product positioning The place an offering occupies in customers' minds on important attributes relative to competitive products.

Production The creation of finished goods and services using the factors of production: land, labour, capital, entrepreneurship, and knowledge.

Production management The term used to describe all of the activities that managers do to help their firms create goods.

Productivity The amount of output that is generated given the amount of input (e.g., hours worked).

Profit The amount a business earns above and beyond what it spends for salaries and other expenses.

Program evaluation and review technique (PERT) A method for analyzing the tasks involved in completing a given project, estimating the time needed to complete each task, and identifying the minimum time needed to complete the total project.

Promissory note A written contract with a promise to pay.

Promotion All of the techniques sellers use to motivate customers to buy their products.

Promotion mix The combination of promotional tools an organization uses.

Prospectus A condensed version of economic and financial information that a company must make available to investors before they purchase a security.

Psychographic segmentation Dividing the market using the group's values, attitudes, and interests.

Psychological pricing Pricing goods and services at price points that make the product appear less expensive than it is.

Public accountant An accountant who provides his or her accounting services to individuals or businesses on a fee basis.

Public corporation Corporation that has the right to issue shares to the public, so its shares may be listed on a stock exchange.

Public relations (PR) The function that evaluates public attitudes, changes policies and procedures in response to the public's requests, and executes a program of action and information to earn public understanding and acceptance.

Publicity Any information about an individual, product, or organization that is distributed to the public through the media and that is not paid for or controlled by the seller.

Pull strategy Promotional strategy in which heavy advertising and sales promotion efforts are directed toward consumers so that they will request the products from retailers.

Purchasing The functional area in a firm that searches for quality material resources, finds the best suppliers, and negotiates the best price for goods and services.

Pure risk The threat of loss with no chance for profit.

Push strategy Promotional strategy in which the producer uses advertising, personal selling, sales promotion, and all other promotional tools to convince wholesalers and retailers to stock and sell merchandise.

Quality Consistently producing what the customer wants while reducing errors before and after delivery to the customer.

Quality of life The general well-being of a society in terms of its political freedom, natural environment, education, health care, safety, amount of leisure, and rewards that add to the satisfaction and joy that other goods and services provide.

Ratio analysis The assessment of a firm's financial condition and performance through calculations and interpretations of financial ratios developed from the firm's financial statements.

Real time The present moment or the actual time in which something takes place; data sent over the Internet to various organizational partners as they are developed or collected are said to be available in real time.

Recession Two or more consecutive quarters of decline in the GDP.

Recovery When the economy stabilizes and starts to grow.

Recruitment The set of activities used to obtain a sufficient number of the right people at the right time.

Re-engineering The fundamental rethinking and radical redesign of organizational processes to achieve dramatic improvements in critical measures of performance.

Registered retirement savings plan (RRSP) A federally-regulated, tax-sheltered savings plan designed to encourage Canadians to save for their retirement.

Regulations Restrictions that provincial and federal laws place on businesses with respect to the conduct of their activities.

Reinforcement theory Theory that positive and negative reinforcers motivate a person to behave in certain ways.

Relationship marketing Marketing strategy with the goal of keeping individual customers over time by offering them products that exactly meet their requirements.

Research and development (R8D) Work directed toward the innovation, introduction, and improvement of products and processes.

Resource development The study of how to increase resources and the creation of the conditions that will make better use of those resources (e.g., recycling).

Resources A general term that incorporates human resources, natural resources, and financial resources.

Restructuring Redesigning an organization so that it can more effectively and efficiently serve its customers.

Retailer An organization that sells to ultimate consumers.

Retained earnings The accumulated earnings from a firm's profitable operations that remains in the business and not paid out to shareholders as dividends.

Revenue The total amount of money received during a given period for goods sold and services rendered, and from other financial sources.

Reverse discrimination Discriminating against members of a dominant or majority group (say, whites or males) usually as a result of policies designed to correct previous discrimination against minority or disadvantaged groups.

Revolving credit agreement A line of credit that is guaranteed but usually comes with a fee.

Risk The chance of loss, the degree of probability of loss, and the amount of possible loss (i.e., time and money).

Risk management The process of understanding, costing, and efficiently managing unexpected levels of variability in the financial outcomes for a business.

Risk/return trade-off The principle that the greater the risk a lender takes in making a loan, the higher the interest rate required.

Rule of indemnity Rule saying that an insured person or organization cannot collect more than the actual loss from an insurable risk.

Sales promotion The promotional tool that stimulates consumer purchasing and dealer interest by means of short-term activities.

Scientific management Studying workers to find the most efficient ways of doing things and then teaching people those techniques.

Secondary boycott An attempt by labour to convince others to stop doing business with a firm that is the subject of a primary boycott.

Secondary data Information that has already been compiled by others and published in journals and books or made available online.

Secured loan A loan backed by collateral, something valuable such as property.

Securities commission A government agency that administers provincial securities legislation.

Securities dealer A firm that trades securities for its clients and offers investment services; also known as an investment dealer or brokerage house.

Security A negotiable financial instrument that represents some type of financial value.

Selection The process of gathering information and deciding who should be hired, under legal guidelines, to serve the best interests of the individual and the organization.

Selective distribution Distribution that sends products to only a preferred group of retailers in an area.

Self-insurance The practice of setting aside money to cover routine claims and buying only "catastrophe" policies to cover big losses.

Services Intangible products (i.e., products that can't be held in your hand) such as education, health care, insurance, recreation, and travel and tourism.

Shop stewards Union officials who work permanently in an organization and represent employee interests on a daily basis.

Short-term financing Borrowed funds that are needed for one year or less.

Short-term forecast Forecast that predicts revenues, costs, and expenses for a period of one year or less.

Sinking fund A reserve account in which the issuer of a bond periodically sets aside some part of the bond principal prior to maturity so that enough capital will be accumulated by the maturity date to pay off the bond.

Six Sigma quality A quality measure that allows only 3.4 defects per million events.

Skimming price strategy A strategy in which a new product is priced high to make optimum profit while there's little competition.

Small and medium-sized enterprises (SMEs) Refers to all businesses with fewer than 500 employees.

Small business A business that is independently owned and operated, is not dominant in its field, and meets certain standards of size in terms of employees or annual revenues.

Smart card An electronic funds transfer tool that is a combination credit card, debit card, phone card, driver's licence card, and more.

Social audit A systematic evaluation of an organization's progress toward implementing programs that are socially responsible and responsive.

Social commerce A form of electronic commerce that involves using social media and user contributions to assist in the online buying and selling of products and services.

Social media The term commonly given to websites and online tools that allow users to interact with each other in some way—by sharing information, opinions, knowledge, and interests.

Social media marketing Consumer-generated online-marketing efforts to promote brands and companies for which they are fans (or conversely, negatively promoting brands and companies for which they are non-fans), and the use by marketers of online tools and platforms to promote their brands or organizations.

Socialism An economic system based on the premise that some, if not most, basic businesses should be owned by the government so that profits can be evenly distributed among the people.

Sole proprietorship A business that is owned, and usually managed, by one person.

Span of control The optimum number of subordinates a manager supervises or should supervise.

Speculative risk A chance of either profit or loss.

Staff personnel Employees who advise and assist line personnel in meeting their goals.

Staffing A management function that includes hiring, motivating, and retaining the best people available to accomplish the company's objectives.

Stagflation A situation in which the economy is slowing but prices are going up regardless.

Stakeholders All the people who stand to gain or lose by the policies and activities of a business.

Standard of living The amount of goods and services people can buy with the money they have.

Statement of cash flows (cash flow statement) A financial statement that reports cash receipts and cash disbursements related to a firm's three major activities: operations, investing, and financing.

Statistical process control (SPC) The process of taking statistical samples of product components at each stage of the production process and plotting those results on a graph. Any variances from quality standards are recognized and can be corrected if beyond the set standards.

Statistical quality control (SQC) The process that some managers use to continually monitor all phases of the production process to ensure that quality is being built into the product from the beginning.

Statutory law Federal and provincial legislative enactments, treaties of the federal government, and bylaws and ordinances—in short, written law.

Stock certificate Evidence of stock ownership that specifies the name of the company, the number of shares it represents, and the type of stock being issued.

Stock exchange An organization whose members can buy and sell (exchange) securities for companies and investors.

Stock insurance company A type of insurance company owned by shareholders.

Stock split An action by a company that gives shareholders two or more shares of stock for each one they own.

Stockbroker A registered representative who works as a market intermediary to buy and sell securities for clients.

Stocks (shares) Shares of ownership in a company.

Strategic alliance A long-term partnership between two or more companies established to help each company build competitive market advantages.

Strategic planning The process of determining the major goals of the organization and the policies and strategies for obtaining and using resources to achieve those goals.

Strict product liability Legal responsibility for harm or injury caused by a product regardless of fault.

Strike A union strategy in which workers refuse to go to work.

Strikebreakers Replacement workers hired to do the jobs of striking employees until the labour dispute is resolved.

Supervisory management Managers who are directly responsible for supervising workers and evaluating their daily performance.

Supply The quantity of products that manufacturers or owners are willing to sell at different prices at a specific time.

Supply chain The sequence of firms that perform activities required to create and deliver a good or service to consumers or industrial users.

Supply chain management The integration and organization of information and logistics activities across firms in a supply chain for the purpose of creating and delivering goods and services that provide value to customers.

Surplus An excess of revenues over expenditures.

Sustainability Development that meets the needs of present and future generations.

Sustainable development Implementing a process that integrates environmental, economic, and social considerations into decision making.

SWOT analysis A planning tool used to analyze an organization's strengths, weaknesses, opportunities, and threats.

Tactical planning The process of developing detailed, short-term statements about what is to be done, who is to do it, and how it is to be done.

Tall organization structure An organization structure in which the pyramidal organization chart would be quite tall because of the various levels of management.

Target costing Designing a product so that it satisfies customers and meets the profit margins desired by the firm.

Target marketing Marketing directed toward those groups (market segments) an organization decides it can serve profitably.

Tariff A tax imposed on imports.

Tax accountant An accountant trained in tax law and responsible for preparing tax returns or developing tax strategies.

Tax-Free Savings Account (TFSA) An investment option into which Canadian residents 18 years of age or older who have a valid social insurance number can contribute up to $10,000 annually; the amount contributed as well as the income earned in the account is tax free, even when it is withdrawn.

Technical skills Skills that involve the ability to perform tasks in a specific discipline or department.

Technology Everything from phones and copiers to computers, mobile devices, medical imaging machines, and the various software programs and apps that make business processes more effective, efficient, and productive.

Telecommuting Working from home via computer.

Telemarketing The sale of goods and services by telephone.

Term insurance Pure insurance protection for a given number of years.

Term-loan agreement A promissory note that requires the borrower to repay the loan in specified instalments.

Test marketing The process of testing products among potential users.

Time deposit The technical name for a savings account; the bank can require prior notice before the owner withdraws money from a time deposit.

Time-motion studies Studies, begun by Frederick Taylor, of which tasks must be performed to complete a job and the time needed to do each task.

Top management Highest level of management, consisting of the president and other key company executives, who develop strategic plans.

Tort A wrongful act that causes injury to another person's body, property, or reputation.

Total fixed costs All expenses that remain the same no matter how many products are made or sold.

Total product offer (value package) Everything that customers evaluate when deciding whether to buy something; also called a value package.

Total quality management (TQM) Striving for maximum customer satisfaction by ensuring quality from all departments.

Trade credit The practice of buying goods and services now and paying for them later.

Trade deficit An unfavourable balance of trade; occurs when the value of a country's imports exceeds that of its exports.

Trade protectionism The use of government regulations to limit the import of goods and services.

Trade surplus A favourable balance of trade; occurs when the value of a country's exports exceeds that of its imports.

Trademark A brand that has been given exclusive legal protection for the brand name, symbol, or pictorial design (or combination of these).

Training and development All attempts to improve productivity by increasing an employee's ability to perform. Training focuses on short-term skills, whereas development focuses on long-term abilities.

Transactional leadership Leadership style where the leader is given the power to assign tasks and their successful completion leads to rewards and reinforcement.

Transfer payments Direct payments from governments to other governments or to individuals.

Transformational leadership Leadership style that occurs when leaders can influence others to follow them in working to achieve a desired outcome or goal.

Transparency The presentation of a company's facts and figures in a way that is clear, accessible, and apparent to all stakeholders.

Trial balance A summary of all of the data in the account ledgers to show whether the figures are correct and balanced.

Triple-bottom line (TBL, 3BL, or People, Planet, Profit) A framework for measuring and reporting corporate performance against economic, social, and environmental parameters.

Trust company A financial institution that can administer estates, pension plans, and agency contracts, in addition to other activities conducted by banks.

Umbrella policy A broadly based insurance policy that saves you money because you buy all your insurance from one company.

Unemployment rate The percentage of the labour force that actively seeks work but is unable to find work at a given time.

Uninsurable risk A risk that no insurance company will cover.

Union security clause Provision in a negotiated labour–management agreement that stipulates that employees who benefit from a union must either officially join or at least pay dues to the union.

Union shop agreement Clause in a negotiated labour–management agreement that says workers do not have to be members of a union to be hired, but must agree to join the union within a prescribed period.

Unionization rate (union density) A measure of the percentage of employed individuals who are union members; also known as union density.

Unlimited liability The responsibility of business owners for all of the debts of the business.

Unsecured loan A loan that does not require any collateral.

Value Good quality at a fair price.

Values A set of fundamental beliefs that guide a business in the decisions it makes.

Variable costs Costs that change according to the level of production.

Variable life insurance A form of whole life insurance that invests the cash value of the policy in stocks or other high-yielding securities.

Venture capital Money that is invested in new or emerging companies that are perceived as having great profit potential

Venture capitalists Individuals or companies that invest in new businesses in exchange for partial ownership of those businesses.

Vestibule training Training done in schools where employees are taught on equipment similar to that used on the job.

Viral marketing Any strategy that encourages people to pass on a marketing message to others, creating exponential growth in the message's influence as the message reaches thousands to millions of potential customers.

Virtual corporation A temporary networked organization made up of replaceable firms that join and leave as needed.

Virtual networking A process that allows software-based networked computers to run multiple operating systems and pro-grams, and share storage.

Virtual private network (VPN) A private data network that creates secure connections, or "tunnels," over regular Internet lines.

Virus A piece of programming code inserted into other programming to cause some unexpected and, for the victim, usually undesirable event.

Vision An encompassing explanation of why the organization exists and where it is trying to head.

Voluntary bankruptcy Legal procedures initiated by a debtor.

Web 2.0 The set of tools that allow people to build social and business connections, share information, and collaborate on projects online (including blogs, wikis, social networking sites and other online communities, and virtual worlds).

Web 3.0 A combination of technologies that adds intelligence and changes how people interact with the Web, and vice versa (consists of the semantic web, mobile web, and immersive Internet).

Whistleblowers People who report illegal or unethical behaviour.

Whole life insurance Life insurance that combines pure insurance and savings.

Wholesaler A marketing intermediary that sells to other organizations.

Will A document that states how you want your assets distributed, names the executor for your estate, and names the guardian(s) for your children (if applicable) when you die.

Word-of-mouth promotion A promotional tool that involves people telling other people about products they have purchased.

World Bank An autonomous United Nations agency that borrows money from the more prosperous countries and lends it to less-developed countries to develop their infrastructure.

World Trade Organization (WTO) The international organization that replaced the General Agreement on Tariffs and Trade, and was assigned the duty to mediate trade disputes among nations.

Photo Credits

Chapter 1

p. 3, Courtesy of Fox 40 International Inc. Used with permission; p. 5, dynamicgraphics/Jupiterimages; p. 7, © Sam Edwards/age fotostock; p. 10, © Skip Brown/National Geographic/Getty Images; p. 12, ValeStock/Thinkstock; p. 13, Courtesy of Canadian Blood Services; p. 14, Zurainy Zain/Shutterstock; p. 15, AndreyPopov/iStock/Thinkstock; p. 18, © Rosemarie Gearhart/E+/Getty Images RF; p. 20, © Partha Pal/The Image Bank/Getty Images; p. 21, shironosov/iStock/Thinkstock; p. 23, danlefeb/Getty Images; p. 28, Courtesy of GTAA. Used with permission; p. 30, © Monkey Business Images Ltd./photolibrary RF; p. 34, ©Erik Isakson/Blend Images LLC.

Chapter 2

p. 43, Photos by @jibees for LeWeb11 Conference @ Les Docks -Paris /https://www.flickr.com/photos/leweb3/6491865213/07/23/14; p. 46, © Jeff Gilbert/Alamy; p. 45 (top), © Lucas Vallecillos/age fotostock; p. 45 (bottom), © Ng Han Guan/AP Images; p. 47, © Stephen Shaver/UPI/Landov; p. 48, Courtesy of the Pan Am/Parapan Am Games TO2015 Organizing Committee. Used with permission; p. 50 (top), © Kim Karpeles/Alamy; p. 50 (bottom), Design Pics/Kristy-Anne Glubish; p. 52 (top), MHHE004174; p. 52 (bottom), © John Minchillo/AP Images; p. 53, Courtesy of FINCA. Used with permission; p. 54, © Frank Gunn/CP Images; p. 57, rmnoa357/Shutterstock.com; p. 59, © Kathy deWitt/Alamy; p. 61, © Dmitry Rogulin/ITAR-TASS/Newscom; p. 65, Spotmatik Ltd/Shutterstock; p. 68, Paul Sancya/CP Images; p. 70, © Paul Sakuma/ AP Images.

Chapter 3

p. 79, https://www.flickr.com/photos/postcodelotterygreen challenge/8202992042/06/18/2014; p. 81, Paul Gilham/Getty Images; p. 83, FRED LUM/THE GLOBE AND MAIL DIGITAL IMAGE/CP Images; p. 84, © Top Photo Corporation /Alamy; p. 85, Antonio Scorza /Shutterstock.com; p. 87, https://www.flickr .com/photos/riverap1/3258668503/06/18/2014; p. 88, Lorenzo Rossi/Hemera/Thinkstock; p. 90, Andrew Milligan/CP Images; p. 92, © Rex Features/AP Images; p. 93, Courtesy of Domino's Pizza; p. 94, © Andrey Rudakov/Bloomberg/Getty Images; p. 95, FRED LUM/THE GLOBE AND MAIL DIGITAL IMAGE/CP Images; p. 97, THE CANADIAN PRESS IMAGES/Stephen C. Host; p. 99, © Johann Brandstatter/Alamy; p. 102, SkyF/iStock/Thinkstock; p. 105 (top), Elenathewise/Getty Images; p. 105 (bottom), REUTERS/Paul Darrow /Landov; p. 107 (top), Jonathan Hayward/TCPI/The Canadian Press; p. 107 (bottom), © Sam Panthaky/AFP/Getty Images; p. 109, Reuters /LARRY DOWNING /LANDOV; p. 111, TODD KOROL/Reuters /Landov; p. 113, MIKE CASSESE/Reuters /Landov; p. 114, © Imaginechina/Corbis; p. 115, filitova/Shutterstock.

Chapter 4

p. 123, © National Post/BEN NELMS; p. 125, Reproduced with the permission of the Public Service Commission of Canada, 2012; p. 127, Ian Willms/Getty/Thinkstock; p. 128, rmnoa357/Shutterstock .com; p. 129, Courtesy of the Supreme Court of Canada. Used with permission; p. 130, © All rights reserved. How Canadians Govern Themselves, latest edition published by the Library ofParliament in consultation with the author's family. Reproduced with the permission of the Minister of PublicWorks and Government Services Canada, April 2015; p. 132, Radu Bercan/Shutterstock. com; p. 134, © Francis Vachon/Alamy; p. 136, PATRICK FULGENCIO/CP Images; p. 138, ZOU ZHENG/Xinhua /Landov; p. 141, Lightspring/Shutterstock; p. 142, Curioso/Shutterstock;

p. 143 (top), THE CANADIAN PRESS/Adrian Wyld; p. 143 (bottom), CHRIS WATTIE/Reuters /Landov; p. 145, © JSMimages/Alamy; p. 150, © Radharc Images/Alamy; p. 148, The Canadian Press Images/Larry MacDougal; p. 152, dina2001/iStock/Thinkstock.

Chapter 5

p. 177, Courtesy of George Roter; p. 178, THE CANADIAN PRESS/Fred Chartrand; p. 180, © Marty Bucella, www.cartoonstock .com; p. 181, Daisuke Morita/Getty Images; p. 182, Devonyu/iStock/Thinkstock; p. 184, Courtesy A-Way Express. Used with permission; p. 188, wildpixel/iStock/Thinkstock; p. 189, OLIVIER JEAN/Reuters /Landov; p. 191, © Lannis Waters/Zuma Press/Newscom; p. 192, Courtesy of Tim Hortons; p. 193, Janis Christie/Getty Images; p. 195, Sherry Yates Young/Shutterstock; p. 196, Tupungato/Shutterstock.com; p. 197, © Steve Marcus/Reuters/Corbis; p. 198, © Jody Horton; p. 199, Katherine Welles/Shutterstock.com; p. 200, stevanovicigor/iStock/Thinkstock; p. 201, paintings/Shutterstock.com; p. 203, MartinLisner/iStock/Thinkstock; p. 204, Courtesy of Rainforest Action Network; p. 205, © Fairtrade Canada. This Mark appears on products which have been independently audited and adhere to international standards of Fairtrade; p. 206, © Richard Vogel/AP Images; p. 207, © David R. Frazier/Alamy.

Chapter 6

p. 219, Courtesy of 1-800-GOT-JUNK?. Used with permission; p. 220, Courtesy of Abeego Designs Inc. Used with permission; p. 222, Jmiks/Shutterstock; p. 223, GoGo Images/photolibrary; p. 226, Courtesy of Ryan Murphy Construction. Used with permission; p. 227, Peter McCabe/The Gazette; p. 230, Courtesy of The Jim Pattison Group. Used with permission; p. 231, Image courtesy of Chapman's Ice Cream Ltd. Used with permission; p. 232, Westend61/SuperStock; p. 233, Daniel Acker/Bloomberg via Getty Images; p. 235, © Robert Wagenhoffer/Corbis; p. 237, © Anderson Ross/Blend Images LLC; p. 241, Courtesy of Booster Juice. Used with permission; p. 243, Trademarks of CTC Corporation, Limited use under licence; p. 245 (top), Courtesy of PropertyGuys.com. Used with permission; p. 245 (bottom), © InterContinental Hotels Groups.

Chapter 7

p. 255, Courtesy of Steeped Tea. Used with permission; p. 257 (top), Courtesy of Leon's. Used with permission; p. 257 (upper middle), Trademarks of CTC Corporation, Limited use under licence; p. 257 (lower middle), Courtesy of Sobeys Inc. Used with permission; p. 257 (bottom), McCain Foods Limited; p. 258, Courtesy of The Jean Coutu Group (PJC) Inc. Used with permission; p. 259 (top), Stuart C. Wilson/Getty Images for Lululemon Athletica; p. 259 (bottom), ©JGI/Tom Grill/Blend Images LLC; p. 260, BEN NELMS/Reuters /Landov; p. 262, Courtesy of Mabel's Labels. Photo by Bryn Gladding Photography. Used with permission; p. 263, Courtesy of Sleep Country Canada. Used with permission; p. 264, Courtesy of Foxy Originals. Used with permission; p. 265, © Abbi O'Leary/MCT/Newscom; p. 267, Courtesty of Culinart Ltd. Used with permission; p. 269, © Lucidio Studio, Inc./Moment/Getty Images RF; p. 270, Photo by Mariane Bulger. Used with permission; p. 277, CP PHOTO/Kevin Frayer; p. 282 (top), Postcard for Summer Company, the Government of Ontario's flagship youth entrepreneurship program © Queen's Printer for Ontario, 2014. Reproduced with permission; p. 282 (bottom), © CBC; p. 284, © Zuma Press, Inc./Alamy; p. 285, Courtesy of Quirky; p. 287, Courtesy of Milt Reimer, FXR Racing. Used with permission; p. 275, abluecup/iStock/Thinkstock.

Chapter 8

p. 301, © D Dipasupil/FilmMagic/GettyImages; p. 303, © Jason Plotkin/York Daily Record/AP Images; p. 305, © Creatas/ photolibrary RF; p. 311, 360b/Shutterstock.com; p. 312, © Jonathan Ernst/Reuters/Corbis; p. 318, Rawpixel/Shutterstock; p. 320, Courtesy of Gravity Payments. Photo by Jose Mandojana. Used with permission; p. 321, Feng Yu/Shutterstock; p. 323, © Jeff Kowalsky/Bloomberg/Getty Images; p. 324, patpitchaya/ Shutterstock; p. 325, © Richard Graulich/ZUMA Press/Corbis; p. 326, © Michael Spooneybarger/Reuters/Corbis; p. 302, © Robert Nicholas/age fotostock; p. 329, © Andrew Burton/Getty Images.

Chapter 9

p. 337, © D Dipasupil/FilmMagic/GettyImages; p. 339, © Huntstock, Inc./age fotostock RF; p. 340, Yuriy Vlasenko/ Shutterstock; p. 342, Public Domain; p. 343, © Interfoto/Alamy Images; p. 349, © Jens Wolf/dpa/Corbis; p. 350, mikecphoto/ Shutterstock.com; p. 352, © Amy Sancetta/AP Images; p. 355, © Dave Carpenter, www.cartoonstock.com; p. 357, © PCN Photography/Alamy; p. 358, © Wavebreak Media LTD/age fotostock RF; p. 360, © Image Source/age fotostock; p. 361, Maciej Frolow/Getty Images; p. 364, © Lucy Nicholson/Reuters/Corbis; p. 365, ©almagami/ Alamy RF; p. 369, © Mark Edward Atkinson/ Blend Images/Alamy; p. 370, © SuperStock.

Chapter 10

p. 379, © Catherine Ivill/AMA/Matthew Ashton/AMA Sports Photo/AMA/Corbis; p. 383, © Kim Kyung-Hoon/Reuters/Landov; p. 385, wloven/iStock/Thinkstock; p. 386, Royalty-Free/CORBIS; p. 387, © PBNJ Productions/Blend Images/Getty Images RF; p. 389, vasabii/iStock/Thinkstock; p. 390, © euroluftbild.de/ age fotostock; p. 391, Christopher Penler/iStock/Thinkstock; p. 392, © Caro/Alamy; p. 393, © Lee Brown/Alamy; p. 395, © VIEW Pictures Ltd/Alamy; p. 397, Courtesy of SAS Institute; p. 399, Alistair Berg/Getty Images; p. 400, MedicalRF.com/Getty Images; p. 401, MacXever/iStock/Thinkstock; p. 402, Courtesy of Excellence Canada; p. 404, Courtesy of Freight Farms; p. 408, ChameleonsEye/Shutterstock.com; p. 409, © Vince Lupo; p. 411, © PRNewsFoto/MY M&M'S Chocolate Candies/AP Images; p. 412, Courtesy of Moniker Guitars; p. 413, © Benoit Decout/REA/Redux.

Chapter 11

p. 427, THE CANADIAN PRESS/Chris Young; p. 429, Image courtesy of DAC Group. Used with permission; p. 430, © RF/ Corbis; p. 432, © Dennis MacDonald/Alamy; p. 433, Courtesy of AT&T Archives and History Center; p. 436, © Wavebreakmedia Ltd | Dreamstime.com; p. 438, Courtesy of Canadian Pacific. Used with permission; p. 439, Courtesy of VanCity. Used with permission; p. 441, Wavebreakmedia Ltd/Thinkstock; p. 444, Purestock; p. 446, © Stockbyte/Getty Images; p. 448, © Sipa/AP Images; p. 450, Courtesy of the Score Inc. Used with permission; p. 451, © Bryan Smith/Zuma Press/Corbis; p. 452, Courtesy of Travelocity; p. 453, © walik/E+/Getty Images RF; p. 454, Nasi Sakura/Purestock/Superstock; p. 455, © Wavebreakmedia Ltd | Dreamstime.com; p. 457, Pressmaster/Shutterstock; p. 458, © Marcel Weber/Getty Images RF; p. 459, © Beau Lark/Corbis.

Chapter 12

p. 467, Courtesy Linamar Corporation. Used with permission; p. 470, © Tim Boyle/Bloomberg/Getty Images; p. 473, ©Hill Street Studios/Blend Images LLC; p. 475, © Iqoncept | Dreamstime .com; p. 477, Wavebreakmedia Ltd/Thinkstock; p. 478, Bloomua/ Shutterstock.com; p. 479, © Vignes81 | Dreamstime.com; p. 480, © AVAVA/iStock/360/Getty Images RF; p. 482, Courtesy of LiUNA. Used with permission; p. 483, Wavebreakmedia Ltd/Thinkstock; p. 485, © Skip Brown/National Geographic/Getty Images; p. 486, Courtesy of CIBC. Used with permission; p. 491, © Fredrick Kippe/Alamy; p. 492, © 2010 Mediacorp Canada Inc. Canada's Top 100 Employers logo, used with permission; p. 494, © Guy

Bubb/Gallo Images/Getty Images RF; p. 496, © Stan Honda/ AFP/Getty Images; p. 497 (top), Mark Adams/Media Bakery; p. 497 (bottom), Monkey Business Images/Shutterstock; p. 499, © Sirikul Thirasuntrakul | Dreamstime.com; p. 501, © Steve Cole/Getty Images; p. 502, Khakimullin Aleksandr/Shutterstock; p. 503, © Monalyn Gracia/Fancy/age fotostock RF; p. 505, michaeljung/Shutterstock.

Chapter 13

p. 513, Courtesy of LiUNA. Used with permission; p. 515, Courtesy of UFCW. Used with permission; p. 516, © Lewis W. Hine/ Buyenlarge/Getty Images; p. 517, Tibor Kolley/CP Images; p. 519, Comstock Images/Jupiterimages; p. 523, © Finnbarr Webster/ Alamy; p. 525, Courtesy of Canadian Labour Congress (2014). Used with permission; p. 526, Comstock/Jupiterimages; p. 532, Courtesy of Canadian Labour Congress (2014). Used with permission; p. 534, TeerawatWinyarat/iStock/Thinkstock; p. 536, Bernard Weil/Getty Images; p. 537, Allison Joyce/Getty Images; p. 538, © Ian Lishman/ Juice Images/Corbis; p. 539, Courtesy of Angus Reid Global. Used with permission; p. 540, Courtesy of CUPE National. Used with permission; p. 542, © Wesley Hitt/Getty Images; p. 545, © Michael Hall Photography Pty Ltd/Corbis; p. 546, © Radius Images/Alamy.

Chapter 14

p. 557, Courtesy of Sofia Colucci. Used with permission; p. 559, © Hug Threlfall/Alamy; p. 560, Courtesy of Modcloth, www .modcloth.com; p. 562, © Bettmann/Corbis; p. 563, Courtesy of WildPlay Element Parks. Used with permission; p. 565, © Advertising Standards of Canada. Used with permission; p. 570, © Mbr/MCRT/Newscom; p. 571, © Burke/Triolo/Brand X Pictures; p. 572, zimmytws/Shutterstock; p. 574, © David Sacks/Getty Images RF; p. 576, © Dynamic Graphics/PunchStock; p. 578, © NI QIN/E+/ Getty Images RF; p. 579, Rawpixel Ltd/iStock/Thinkstock; p. 580, Keith Beaty/GetStock; p. 581, © Torsten Silz/AFP/Getty Images; p. 583 (left), © Image Source, all rights reserved; p. 583 (right), ©Jetta Productions LLC; p. 585 (left), Courtesy of Corus Entertainment. Photo by Brandon Barré. Used with permission; p. 585 (right), Photo proviced courtesy of HGTV; p. 587, Courtesy of Fox 40 International Inc. Used with permission; p. 588, Courtesy of G Adventures. Used with permission; p. 591, Noel Hendrickson/Getty Images; p. 593, Jakub Jirsák/iStock/Thinkstock.

Chapter 15

p. 603, Courtesy of Indigo. Used with permission; p. 604 (left), © Jeff Greenberg 2 of 6/Alamy; p. 604 (right), The McGraw-Hill Companies, Inc./Christopher Kerrigan, photographer; p. 605, Courtesy of Bocktown Beer and Grill; p. 609, Courtesy of H. J. Heinz Company; p. 610, MARS Apprentice; p. 611 (top), Trademarks of CTC Corporation, Limited use under licence; p. 611 (bottom), Courtesy of Greenpeace. Used with permission; p. 615, © Joshua Rainey | Dreamstime.com; p. 616, Sunil Kumar/ Hemera/Thinkstock; p. 618, © Helen Sessions/Alamy; p. 620, © Ralph D. Freso/Reuters/Corbis; p. 622, Courtesy of Dougie Dog Diner Truck. Used with permission; p. 627, Image Source/ Getty Images; p. 632, Courtesy of Corporate Knights Magazine. Used with permission; p. 633, © Jonathan Ellgen; p. 635, Digital Vision/Photodisc/Thinkstock; p. 637, ©Plush Studios/Blend Images LLC; p. 639, © Jeff Greenberg/Alamy Images; p. 641, © monkeybusinessimages/iStock; p. 643, © Kevin Zolkiewicz.

Chapter 16

p. 655, Photo: Alan Dean Photograpy; p. 658, © Balint Porneczi/ Bloomberg/Getty Images; p. 659, bubaone/iStock/Thinkstock; p. 661, ©Hill Street Studios/Blend Images LLC; p. 663, Jon Feingersh/Getty Images; p. 664, © Pixattitude | Dreamstime. com; p. 666, Design Pics/Bilderbuch/Getty Images; p. 667, MOF/ Getty Images; p. 673, © Saxon Reed/AP Images; p. 678, © Chip Litherland/Redux; p. 679, © Photodisc/Getty Images RF; p. 681, © Imaginechina/Corbis; p. 683, © ImageShop/Corbis RF; p. 684, Photographer's Choice/Getty Images; p. 686, © Texas StockPhoto/ Alamy; p. 687, © Franck Guiziou/Hemis/Corbis.

Photo Credits

Chapter 17

p. 697, © Kim White/Bloomberg/Getty Images; p. 699, © Jim Thompson/Albuquerque Journal/Zumapress.com/Alamy; p. 670, © Justin Kase/Alamy RF; p. 703, AndrisTkachenko/iStock/Thinkstock; p. 706, © Cornelius20 | Dreamstime.com; p. 708, © ICP/age fotostock; p. 711, © Piet Mall/Getty Images; p. 712, Courtesy of thredUP; p. 713, bibiphoto/Shutterstock.com; p. 714, © benedek/iStock/360/Getty Images RF; p. 716, The McGraw-Hill Companies, Inc./John Flournoy, photographer; p. 717, © Steve Kagan/Redux; p. 719, Androsov/iStock/Thinkstock; p. 721, © James A. Finley/AP Images; p. 723, Stockbyte/Getty Images; p. 725, © Scott Eells/Bloomberg/Getty Images; p. 730, Digital Vision/Getty Images.

Chapter 18

p. 747, Courtesy of Anish Chopra; p. 749, © Photodisc/Getty Images RF; p. 750 (top), With permission of the © Bank of Canada;

p. 750 (bottom), © pagadesign/iStock/360/Getty Images RF; p. 753, © Susan Mcarthur-letellier | Dreamstime; p. 758, Courtesy of CDIC. Used with permission; p. 760, Ryan McVay/Getty Images; p. 761, © Lee Brown/Alamy Stock Photo; p. 763, © YAY Media AS/Alamy RF; p. 764, © George Ruhe/Redux; p. 767, © Scott Eells/Bloomberg/Getty Images; p. 769, © Deborah Feingold/Corbis; p. 770, Rtbilder | Dreamstime.com; p. 772, © Shenval/Alamy RF; p. 776, © Vaeenma | Dreamstime.com; p. 794.

Online Supplement

p. OS-6, © Ted S. Warren/AP Images; p. OS-6, © Anthony Lee/caia image/Alamy RF; p. OS-12, © Martin McCarthy/iStock/360/Getty Images RF; p. OS-16, © epa european pressphoto agency b.v./Alamy; p. OS-18, © liewy/iStock/360/Getty Images RF; p. OS-21, © The Detroit Free Press/MCT/Getty Images; p. OS-22, © Design Pics Inc./Alamy RF.

Index